Y0-BDO-169

WINNING THE WHITE HOUSE 2008

THE GALLUP POLL, PUBLIC OPINION, AND THE PRESIDENCY

WINNING THE WHITE HOUSE 2008

THE GALLUP POLL, PUBLIC OPINION, AND THE PRESIDENCY

BY
FRANK NEWPORT
JEFFREY M. JONES
LYDIA SAAD
ALEC M. GALLUP
FRED L. ISRAEL

Montante Family Library
D'Youville College

MAR 1 0 2010

Facts On File
An imprint of Infobase Publishing

Winning the White House 2008: The Gallup Poll, Public Opinion, and the Presidency

Copyright © 2009 by Infobase Publishing

All rights reserved. No part of this book may be reproduced or utilized in any form or by any means, electronic or mechanical, including photocopying, recording, or by any information storage or retrieval systems, without permission in writing from the publisher. For information contact:

Facts On File, Inc.
An imprint of Infobase Publishing
132 West 31st Street
New York NY 10001

Library of Congress Cataloging-in-Publication Data
Winning the White House 2008: the Gallup poll, public opinion, and the presidency/by Frank Newport...[et al.].
    p. cm.
    Includes index.
    ISBN 978-0-8160-7566-9
    1. Presidents—United States—Election—2008. 2. Political campaigns—United States. 3. Election forecasting—United States.
I. Newport, Frank.
    JK5262008.W56 2009
    324.973'0931—dc22

                            2008043415

Facts On File books are available at special discounts when purchased in bulk quantities for businesses, associations, institutions, or sales promotions. Please call our Special Sales Department in New York at (212) 967-8800 or (800) 322-8755.

You can find Facts On File on the World Wide Web at http://www.factsonfile.com

Text design and illustrations by Mary Susan Ryan-Flynn
Cover design by Takeshi Takahashi
Printed in the United States of America
Sheridan MSRF 10 9 8 7 6 5 4 3 2 1
This book is printed on acid-free paper.

Montante Family Library
D'Youville College

JK526
2008
.W56
2009

CONTENTS

CONTRIBUTORS

Frank Newport, Ph.D., has been the Editor-in-Chief of the Gallup Poll since 1991. He holds a doctorate in sociology from the University of Michigan. Newport is Vice President of the National Council on Public Polls, is on the Executive Council of the American Association of Public Opinion Research, and serves on the Board of Directors of the Roper Center for Public Opinion Research. He reports regularly for *USA Today*, NPR, CNBC, and other media organizations. Among his several publications is *Polling Matters: Why Leaders Must Listen to the Wisdom of the People.*

Jeffrey M. Jones, Ph.D., is Managing Editor of the Gallup Poll. He has written numerous public opinion analyses for Gallup, including an extensive study of Hispanic American voting patterns. He holds a doctorate in political science from the State University of New York.

Lydia Saad is the Senior Editor of the Gallup Poll. She has been associated with Gallup since 1992. Saad has written dozens of essays on polling, public opinion, and politics. She holds an M.A. degree in political science from the University of Connecticut.

Alec M. Gallup is Chairman of the Gallup Poll and Vice Chair of the George H. Gallup International Institute. He has been responsible for many of Gallup's most ambitious research projects, including *Human Needs and Satisfaction*, the first global survey ever conducted. This study covered more than 70 nations and two-thirds of the world's population.

Fred L. Israel, Ph.D., is Professor Emeritus of American History, City College of New York. He holds the Scribe's Award from the American Bar Association for his joint editorship of *The Justices of the United States Supreme Court* (4 vols.). For 25 years, Professor Israel compiled and edited the Gallup Poll into annual reference volumes.

PREFACE

This volume is an analysis of public opinion and the 2008 presidential election—the candidates and the issues. It is the most comprehensive public opinion record of any presidential election in American history.

It has been my privilege to edit for book publication this outstanding study written by Frank Newport, Jeffrey Jones, and Lydia Saad. They—and the Gallup Organization—have earned a debt of gratitude from presidential historians, from political scientists, and from all Americans who share George Gallup's commitment "to learn and report the will of the people—the pulse of democracy."

George Gallup (1901–84) founded the American Institute of Public Opinion, the precursor of the Gallup Poll, in 1935. To ensure his independence and objectivity, Dr.

Gallup resolved that he would undertake no polling paid for or sponsored in any way by special-interest groups such as the Republican and Democratic parties. Adhering to this principle, the Gallup Organization has refused thousands of requests for surveys from organizations representing every shade of the political spectrum and with every kind of special agenda. The organization that Dr. Gallup founded has become a world leader in public opinion and market research. His legacy of political independence has made the Gallup name famous and among the most trusted brand names in the world, synonymous with integrity and the democratic process.

—Fred L. Israel

INTRODUCTION

Of the 56 presidential elections in American history, the 2008 contest ranks among the most exciting, compelling, and important. When the campaign began in late 2006, no one could have predicted the remarkable, pathbreaking events and turnarounds that followed, concluding with the historic election of Barack Obama on November 4, 2008.

This campaign marked many firsts. A biracial man, Barack Obama, and a white woman, Hillary Rodham Clinton, competed against each other for the Democratic nomination. Also, Sarah Palin was the first woman to run for vice president on the Republican Party ticket. Obama, 47 years old, became the first African American to win the nomination of a major political party. In contrast, his Republican opponent, John McCain, at age 72, was the oldest person ever to run for president on a major party ticket. The 25-year age difference was the widest in American history between two presidential nominees. The 2008 election also was the first in which two sitting U.S. senators ran against each other, and the first in which neither candidate was born in the continental United States. (Obama was born in Hawaii and McCain in the Panama Canal Zone, on a U.S. naval base.)

The 2008 election marked the first time since 1952 that neither an incumbent president nor a former vice president was on the ticket. In both the Democratic and Republican primaries, voters had a wide choice over whom to select to represent their party and ultimately lead the nation. Voter turnout broke records in both the primary and general elections. And throughout this entire process, the Gallup Poll tracked the views, attitudes, and preferences of Americans with respect to dozens of issues relating to the presidential campaign. This book represents an extraordinary compilation of public opinion polls and political analysis of the 2008 presidential campaign.

A pioneer in polling and public opinion, Gallup has studied human nature and behavior for more than 70 years. Gallup's reputation for relevant, impartial, and timely research into what people think—in America and around the world—is the cornerstone of the organization. Under the leadership of Alec Gallup, chairman of the Gallup Poll, and Jim Clifton, CEO of the Gallup Organization since 1988, Gallup has evolved the innovative Gallup World Poll, designed to give the world's 6 billion citizens a voice on key global issues. The Gallup World Poll continually surveys citizens in more than 140 countries, representing 95% of the world's adult population. General and region-specific questions, developed in collaboration with the world's leading behavioral economists, are organized into indexes and topic areas that correlate with real-world concerns. Jim Clifton has written that global innovation in economics, social well-being, national leadership, food and shelter, and dozens of other areas depends on an accurate understanding of the world's citizens. To achieve this end, Clifton has pledged the Gallup Organization to continue this effort to collect citizens' opinions, thoughts, and behaviors for at least 100 years.

Winning the White House 2008 is based on several thousand polls that Gallup conducted over the course of the presidential campaign. It also includes data from past polls and public opinion surveys, enabling the reader to compare the 2008 campaign with earlier presidential elections. The book follows the campaign on a month-by-month basis, revealing voters' shifting attitudes toward each candidate and Americans' evolving views on key issues, from the economy and the Iraq War to energy and immigration. Many polls are broken down by subgroups, such as age, race, religion, sex, and party identification, to give a more nuanced sense of the campaign's dynamics. The commentary analyzes this vast amount of information, providing a lively, thorough, and original account of the 2008 election. We believe this is the most definitive record of public opinion regarding any presidential election. When historians, political scientists, and general readers assess the significance and meaning of the 2008 presidential election, we believe that this study will be of inestimable assistance.

FOREWORD

The United States was the first country to have an elected president—and a president with a stated term of office. Every four years since the ratification of the Constitution in 1788, the nation has held a presidential election. Elections have been held even during major economic downturns and war. And except for the tragic Civil War, which followed the 1860 election of Abraham Lincoln, the electorate always has accepted the peaceful transfer of power.

The Founding Fathers did their work well. Representative government has endured. "We the People" have prevailed. The electorate expresses itself through its quadrennial elections, the best measurement of public opinion. In November 2008, a record number of Americans—including record numbers of new, young, and black voters—cast their votes for president, a vivid testimonial, indeed, to our country's democratic heritage.

Polls and Public Opinion

Although public opinion surveys remain controversial, they have increasingly become an accepted part of American life and politics. For more than 70 years, we have been able to measure public opinion. Intellect and technology have combined to perfect the sampling procedure: the public opinion poll. Polls are but a statistical snapshot of a moment in time. They reflect the process, but are not part of it. Dr. George Gallup conducted his first public opinion poll in September 1935. He asked: "Do you think expenditures by the [federal] government for relief and recovery are too little, too great, or just about right?" 60% of the general public and 89% of registered Republicans responded that "government spending was too great."

George Gallup believed that scientific polling overcame what British historian James Bryce described in the 1880s as a major obstacle to democracy: the absence of a way to measure public opinion accurately and continuously. Dr. Gallup considered polls as an ongoing referendum on the issues of the day, and certainly not as a spectator sport as to who wins and who loses. He fervently agreed with Thomas Jefferson, who wrote more than 200 years ago: "The basis of our government [is] the opinion of the people."

Since 1935, the Gallup Poll has asked more than 100,000 questions of approximately 10 million people. For the past 74 years, Gallup interviewers have polled Americans on virtually every conceivable topic, from political issues to such social problems as healthcare and AIDS treatment. These records are a superb source for understanding American public opinion since the New Deal. The bulk of the questions, however, have dealt with government—its policies and problems—and with electoral politics—that is, our leaders and their challengers. The very first question dealing with government's war powers appeared in November 1935. "In order to declare war," George Gallup asked, "should Congress be required to obtain the approval of the people by means of a national vote?" Seventy-five percent replied in the affirmative.

Since the first Gallup Poll appeared almost three-quarters of a century ago, dramatic changes in the attitude and behavior of Americans have occurred. The most profound change is in the growth of tolerance. The number of those who say they would vote for a black, a Jew, or a Catholic for president or a member of Congress has risen dramatically since the 1930s. So, too, has the expressed willingness to vote for a woman. In 1937, only 37% said they would vote for a woman for president, compared with 88% in 2008. (In 1969, the year Hillary Rodham Clinton graduated from Wellesley College, just 53% said they would support a well-qualified female presidential candidate.)

Today, a vast majority of Americans tell pollsters they are willing to vote for a qualified African-American candidate for president. This was not always the case. In 1958, when Gallup first asked a version of this question, over a majority—53%—said they would not vote for a black candidate. In 1984, 16% told Gallup they would not do so, and in 2008, only 6% said they would not do so. An overwhelming 92% said they would vote for a qualified black candidate for president. Racial attitudes in the United States have clearly become more tolerant over the past five decades, and African-American candidates have won high office in many states (although very few have been elected as state governors or U.S. senators). It is also true, however, that the expression of racist attitudes is less socially acceptable now than in the past. This may lead some people to tell pollsters that they are more tolerant than they actually are. Problems with pre-election polls in several high-profile elections featuring biracial candidates in the 1980s and early 1990s raised the question whether covert racism remained an impediment to black candidates. White candidates in most of these races did better on Election Day than they had been doing in the polls—though their black opponents tended to end up with about the same level of support as had been indicated in pre-election polls. Nevertheless, a review of exit polls and electoral outcomes in the 2008 primary elections suggests that fewer people are making judgments about candidates based solely, or even mostly, on race. The high standing of Barack Obama in presidential polling represents a significant change in American politics.

The 2008 presidential election was notable for many reasons, foremost among them Barack Obama's and Hillary Clinton's breaking race and gender barriers in their quests for their party's nomination. It was also the first

Gallup Poll Accuracy Record in Presidential Elections, 1936-2004

Year	Candidates	Final Gallup Survey %	Election Result %	Gallup Deviation %
2004	Bush	49.0	51.0	-2.0
	Kerry	49.0	48.0	+1.0
2000	Bush	48.0	47.9	+0.1
	Gore	46.0	48.4	-2.4
	Nader	4.0	2.7	+1.3
1996	Clinton	52.0	49.2	+2.8
	Dole	41.0	40.9	+0.1
	Perot	7.0	8.5	-1.5
1992	Clinton	49.0	43.0	+6.0
	Bush	37.0	37.5	-0.5
	Perot	14.0	18.9	-4.9
1988	Bush	56.0	53.4	+2.6
	Dukakis	44.0	45.7	-1.7
1984	Reagan	59.0	58.8	+0.2
	Mondale	41.0	40.6	+0.4
1980	Reagan	47.0	50.8	-3.8
	Carter	44.0	41.0	+3.0
	Anderson	8.0	6.6	+1.4
	Other	1.0	1.6	-0.6
1976	Carter	48.0	50.1	-2.1
	Ford	49.0	48.1	+0.9
	McCarthy	2.0	0.9	+1.1
	Other	1.0	0.9	+0.1

election since 1976 in which the incumbent vice president was not a candidate for either the presidency or vice presidency. The election also coincided with senatorial contests in 33 states, House of Representatives elections in all states, and gubernatorial elections in 11 states, along with a variety of state referenda and numerous local elections. As in the 2004 presidential election, the allocation of electoral votes to each state was based on the 2000 census, with the winning candidate needing a majority of 270 electoral votes out of a total of 538.

Presidential Characteristics

All 42 individuals who served as president from 1789 to 2009 were white and male. Beyond these two characteristics,

Gallup Poll Accuracy Record, by Era

Elections	Average Error
1936-1948	3.6%
1952-1964	2.4%
1968-2004	1.5%
Cumulative	
1936-2004	2.1%

Year	Candidates	Final Gallup Survey %	Election Result %	Gallup Deviation %
1972	Nixon	62.0	60.7	+1.3
	McGovern	38.0	37.6	+0.4
1968	Nixon	43.0	43.4	-0.4
	Humphrey	42.0	42.7	-0.7
	Wallace	15.0	13.5	+1.5
1964	Johnson	64.0	61.3	+2.7
	Goldwater	36.0	38.7	-2.7
1960	Kennedy	51.0	50.1	+0.9
	Nixon	49.0	49.9	-0.9
1956	Eisenhower	59.5	57.8	+1.7
	Stevenson	40.5	42.2	-1.7
1952	Eisenhower	51.0	55.4	-4.4
	Stevenson	49.0	44.6	+4.4
1948	Truman	44.5	49.5	-5.0
	Dewey	49.5	45.1	+4.4
	Wallace	4.0	2.4	+1.6
	Other	2.0	3.0	-1.0
1944	Roosevelt	51.5	53.8	-2.3
	Dewey	48.5	46.2	+2.3
1940	Roosevelt	52.0	55.0	-3.0
	Willkie	48.0	45.0	+3.0
1936	Roosevelt	55.7	62.5	-6.8
	Landon	44.3	37.5	+6.8

however, they seem to have had very little else in common. Five were never elected president. John Tyler, Millard Fillmore, Andrew Johnson, Chester Arthur, and Gerald Ford entered the presidency through the death or resignation of their predecessor. Each failed to win election on his own, either through personal decision not to run or political fate. Some of these 42 were surprisingly strong-willed, while others were simply miscast. Although Abraham Lincoln prevented the permanent breakup of the Union and Woodrow Wilson and Franklin D. Roosevelt each confronted a world war, most presidents were average men, doing the best they could in a complicated job.

Likewise, there does not seem to be a pattern in the kind of person whom the voters have chosen to be their leader. American presidents have been as young as John F. Kennedy (43 when elected, although Teddy Roosevelt was 42 when be became president upon William McKinley's assassination) and as old as Ronald Reagan (69 when first elected). They have been intellectuals like Thomas Jefferson, James Madison, James Garfield, William Howard Taft, and Woodrow Wilson, or plain thinkers like the imposing Andrew Jackson and the failed Warren Harding. Personality types have run the gamut, from the ebullient spirits of the two Roosevelts and Harry Truman to the taciturn Calvin Coolidge and dour Richard Nixon. The Adamses, John and John Quincy, were father and son, as were the Bushes, George H. W. and George W. Benjamin Harrison's grandfather was William Henry Harrison of "Old Tippecanoe" fame. Theodore Roosevelt was Franklin's admired cousin.

American presidents have come from states across the country, from Vermont to Hawaii. Mostly they have come to the White House from Congress and from governors' mansions. Eight generals—Washington, Jackson, William Henry Harrison, Zachary Taylor, Grant, Hayes, Garfield, and Eisenhower—have been elected to the presidency. Most of these 43 men sought the responsibilities of the presidency; others landed there by accident. Regardless, each man occupied a position of power and did his best to exercise leadership as he understood it. Each had the opportunity to make major decisions, in both foreign and domestic matters, that affected the direction of the nation.

As with other presidential comparisons, no clear pattern emerges from the presidents' varied educations. However,

most presidents from Washington through Wilson had some form of classical education that included Bible study. Of the 25 pre-1900 presidents, 16 experienced some formal higher education. Lincoln was self-educated, as were Andrew Jackson, Martin Van Buren, Zachary Taylor, Millard Fillmore, Andrew Johnson, and Grover Cleveland. William Henry Harrison attended medical school; Garfield studied for the ministry. All 17 presidents since 1900 except for Harry Truman attended college—the colleges varying from Harding's Ohio Central, with its three instructors, to the prestigious schools of Harvard, Yale, and Princeton. Herbert Hoover majored in geology at Stanford; Lyndon Johnson trained as an elementary school teacher at rural Southwest Texas State Teachers College. Dwight Eisenhower graduated from West Point and Jimmy Carter from Annapolis. Wilson was the only president to earn a doctoral degree, and George W. Bush the only one to receive a graduate degree in business administration. Barack Obama is an alumnus of Columbia University and Harvard Law School and John McCain is an Annapolis graduate—as were his father and paternal grandfather, both four-star United States Navy admirals.

The aim of this study is to analyze public opinion and discern how it coalesced behind the winning candidate, the 44th president of the United States. In 2008, Gallup began a daily tracking survey, interviewing no fewer than 1,000 adults nationwide each day. The resulting extraordinary array of incoming information enabled Gallup to probe the political thinking of subgroups, such as Hispanics and Jews, and to examine regional voting patterns in depth. This tracking also provided 24-hour updates on specific questions regarding the election. In 1936, Gallup asked approximately 50 questions about that year's presidential election; by 1960 the number had jumped to about 150. In the 2008 presidential election cycle, because of a continued commitment to better measure public opinion and electoral politics combined with the availability of the latest electronic technology, Gallup asked more questions than were asked in all 1936–2004 presidential election surveys combined. This volume stands as a living testament to George Gallup's original vision and commitment to learning and reporting "the will of the people."

—Fred L. Israel

PROLOGUE

In February 2007, at the inception of this 2008 Gallup presidential election project, Frank Newport, editor in chief of the Gallup Poll, wrote:

> The 2008 presidential election will be the first election since 1928 in which neither party has an incumbent president or vice president attempting to get his party's nomination. We are thus facing a rare election year with a wide-open field in both parties. This will fuel interest in the primary process in 2007 and in early 2008 and in the general election in November. Political furor over the Iraq War may also increase voter interest in this election. All in all, this promises to be an election in which voters are as "invested" as any in recent history.

In nonincumbent years, Republican front-runners have often emerged early and made it through the primary process fairly easily: George W. Bush in 2000, Bob Dole in 1996, Ronald Reagan in 1980, and Richard Nixon in 1968. On the Democratic side in nonincumbent years, there has been much more uncertainty leading into the primaries, as exemplified by John Kerry in 2004, Bill Clinton in 1992, Michael Dukakis in 1988, Jimmy Carter in 1976, and George McGovern in 1972. However, in many of those elections, the party lacked a clear front-runner at the beginning of the campaign, either because there was none or because the presumptive dominant candidate (Edward Kennedy in 1976, Mario Cuomo in 1992, and Hillary Rodham Clinton in 2004) decided not to run.

So far, as of early 2007, there are early indications that a front-runner is developing in each party, even though all candidates have yet to announce and much appears fluid within both parties. On the Democratic side, New York senator Hillary Clinton is the clear front-runner, well ahead of Illinois senator Barack Obama. On the Republican side, former New York City mayor Rudolph Giuliani has emerged as the front-runner, well ahead of Arizona senator John McCain.

Overall, it is reasonable to anticipate high voter turnout in 2008—perhaps approaching the 55% of the general adult public that turned out in the 1992 election, which was energized by the third party candidacy of Ross Perot. Some of the causes of a possible high-turnout election in 2008 include the following:

- The disputed 2000 election result promoted a more energized electorate, and that appears to have carried over to more recent elections.
- Voter turnout was up in 2004.
- There was relatively high voter interest in the 2006 midterm elections as compared with previous midterm elections.
- The Bush years (2001–9) have refocused the public's attention on the power of the presidency, and thus increased the public's perception that voting in presidential elections is important.
- The public is more politically polarized than in the past, and thus Americans may perceive a greater stake in their side's winning.
- The war in Iraq has provided a galvanizing issue that may motivate voters on both sides.
- Candidates are campaigning earlier in the process, which may work to generate a more interested electorate.

The Hillary Clinton factor may further heighten public interest in the election, particularly if she gains her party's nomination in the summer of 2008 and is in a realistic position to be the first female president in U.S. history. In addition, Barack Obama may be the strongest black contender to ever seek his party's nomination. That a prominent Hispanic (Bill Richardson) and a Mormon (Mitt Romney) are likely to be candidates may also increase voter interest. Finally, it is possible that there will be a significant third-party presence in the election.

At this point in early 2007, it appears that the two most important issues in the 2008 election will be terrorism/Iraq and the economy. The economy is usually, but not always, a fundamental factor in presidential elections:

- A perceived bad economy was instrumental in the outcomes of the elections in 1980 and 1992.
- A rebounding economy helped incumbents Reagan in 1984 and Clinton in 1996.
- The "dot-com" boom economy of the late 1990s did not, however, propel Al Gore to victory in 2000, nor did a less-than-stellar economy cripple Bush in 2004.

Voters now define economic problems broadly. Voters are worried about a broad range of consumer expenses—healthcare costs, college costs, the price of gasoline—rather than just unemployment and the stock market. Gallup analysis suggests that the jobs situation is the single most important component of the economy for Americans.

No one can predict the state of the economy in 2008. As of early 2007, Americans' views of the economy are more positive than they have been for the previous several years. One key to the effect the economy will have in 2008 will be the degree to which Iraq or terrorism overwhelms it as an issue.

The effects of the Iraq War and terrorism on the 2008 election are unknown at this time, pending real-world events. The war in Iraq was the most important issue in the 2006 midterm congressional elections and continues to be voters' top concern as of early 2007. Concern about terrorism will most probably continue to be a strong latent issue. If voters want a change after eight years of George W. Bush, then candidates who emphasize a different approach to international relations (for example, more multinational cooperation), more direct government involvement with domestic issues (rather than the "personal responsibility"/business focus), and a more bipartisan attitude (in contrast to the extreme partisanship of recent years) could be well positioned.

From a historical perspective, it is reasonable to project that the odds are at least slightly in the Democrats' favor in 2008.

- It is relatively rare for the same party to hold the presidency for more than two successive terms. The Republican run from 1981 to 1993 was the first such for either party since the New Deal era (1935–53).

- The Republican presidential victory was razor-thin in 2000, of course, and it was not much larger in 2004.
- The Democrats were able to gain control of both the House of Representatives and the Senate in the 2006 midterm congressional elections, after being out of power in the House since 1994 and the Senate since 2001.

Much Can Change

It is still early in the process. History shows that poll results at this phase—approximately one year before the first primaries and roughly 22 months before the general election—do not necessarily bear a strong relationship to the reality that unfolds in the election year itself.

There is an important distinction here by party:

- On the Democratic side, Carter in 1976, Dukakis in 1988, Clinton in 1992, and Kerry in 2004 were dark horses who emerged as front-runners only during the primary process.
- In 1975, just one year ahead of the 1976 election, Gallup found that Democrats' preference list was Edward Kennedy, 36%; George Wallace, 15%; Hubert Humphrey, 9%; Henry Jackson, 6%; Edmund Muskie, 4%; and George McGovern, 2%—with Jimmy Carter receiving less than 1%. Carter went on to get the nomination.
- In February 1991, Mario Cuomo was the leader of the Democratic field at 18%, followed by Jesse Jackson at 12%, George McGovern at 9%, and Richard Gephardt at 8%. None of these possible candidates ultimately ran, leaving an opening for Bill Clinton (then at 2%) to emerge as the winner.
- A January 2003 Gallup Poll on Democratic candidates for the party's 2004 nomination showed Joe Lieberman at 19%; John Kerry (who eventually won the nomination) with 16%; Richard Gephardt, 13%; John Edwards, 12%; and Howard Dean, 4%.
- The Republican Party, in recent elections, has been more certain with its choices. The early front-runner has gone on to win the nomination in most recent elections: Nixon in 1960 and 1968, Reagan in 1980, George H. W. Bush in 1988, Dole in 1996, and George W. Bush in 2000. The only exception was Nixon, who was the front-runner in early 1964 but did not actively seek the nomination. Barry Goldwater, an early front-runner, ultimately won a closely contested nomination.

The Current Democratic Landscape

In every available public opinion poll in early 2007, Hillary Clinton leads as the Democrats' choice for their party's nomination. She is getting 40% of the vote among Democrats in Gallup's February 9–11 poll, while the next closest competitor, Barack Obama, registers only 21% of the vote. Candidates such as Christopher Dodd, Tom Vilsack, Joe Biden, and Bill Richardson—who have already filed to run for president or who have formed exploratory committees—are not well known across the country at this time. But neither were Carter, Dukakis, and Clinton a year before they won their party's nomination. Obama, who formally announced his candidacy in early February, is, at this point, in second place among Democrats behind Clinton. Obama is well liked among those who know him, but his image is still developing.

Al Gore and John Edwards form a third tier of potential contenders behind Clinton and Obama. Edwards has announced that he is running for president; Gore has said he has no plans to run. Gore and Edwards have both previously sought the presidential nomination; both have been nominated as Democratic presidential or vice presidential candidates (Gore has been both); and both have relatively high name identification. However, it has been unusual for the Democrats, as opposed to the Republicans, to nominate a candidate who has previously sought the nomination and lost (Gore's 2000 nomination being an obvious exception). Gore's visibility as a spokesperson for global warming issues has given him a strong issue identification and prominence that could have a significant effect on the race if he eventually makes a decision to run again. Bottom line: Hillary Clinton is the front-runner at this point, but much can change before the first caucus and primary.

The Current Republican Landscape

Two well-known Republicans, Rudolph Giuliani and John McCain, have led the Republican list in most polls in recent months, but in Gallup's latest measure, Giuliani has jumped ahead of McCain, 40% to 24%. A key question is the ability of a candidate to make it through the gauntlet of the Republican primaries, where the conservative vote can be very powerful.

Republicans' general opinion of McCain is not overwhelmingly positive, but he is rated more favorably among Democrats and independents than are most other Republican politicians. The degree to which McCain's support for sending more troops to Iraq will affect his bid for the presidency is unknown at this time (early 2007) and to a large degree will depend on events in Iraq leading up to the first primaries.

Giuliani has high favorable ratings and scores much better than McCain in terms of being likable and able to handle issues such as crime and terrorism. But his image appears to be based to a substantial degree on his performance as New York City mayor after the terrorist attacks of September 11, 2001. His more liberal positions on abortion and gay rights are not widely known to Republicans. As is the case with Obama, much will depend on how Giuliani's image develops over the course of 2007.

As of early 2007, Republicans nationwide believe that Giuliani and McCain are roughly tied in terms of their ability to win the Republican nomination, but that Giuliani would be better positioned to win the general election in November 2008. Many Republicans who have indicated a strong interest in becoming a presidential candidate— Sam Brownback, Chuck Hagel, Mike Huckabee, Duncan Hunter, George Pataki, and Mitt Romney (who officially entered the race in February)—have little national name identification at this point. History on the Republican side suggests that dark horse candidates do not tend to emerge to capture their party's nomination. In sum, the two high–name identification candidates—Giuliani and McCain—are one and two on the Republican list at this point, but there are significant issues attached to both that will affect their candidacies.

The Clinton Factor

Hillary Clinton is extremely well known, having been at the center of national attention since 1992. Like her husband, she can be a polarizing political figure, with a substantial segment of Americans rating her negatively. An in-depth analysis by Gallup shows that Clinton's gender may be a significant positive for her candidacy. She scores better among Republican women and independent women than do other Democratic candidates. It is possible that women may disproportionately swing to her in hopes of supporting the first female president. Her negatives are, in essence, already established. Although McCain and Giuliani are well known, it can be assumed that they have not come under the harsh national scrutiny that Clinton has faced (although McCain certainly came under scrutiny when he ran in Republican primaries in 2000). Clinton's image is strong on issues and leadership dimensions, but she performs less well compared with her opponents in terms of being likable and being in touch with ordinary people.

Conclusion

As a result of all these factors, the 2008 presidential nomination battles for both parties and the election in

November are more wide open than at any time in the nation's history. Voters' shifting views and unexpected events will likely make this the most unpredictable political contest in recent memory, and certainly one of the most remarkable and historic campaigns Americans have ever witnessed.

—Fred L. Israel

DECEMBER 2006

Public opinion polls throughout 2006 indicated that the issue of greatest concern among Americans was the ongoing war in Iraq. Spiraling Sunni-Shia violence diminished hope that at least some of the roughly 140,000 U.S. troops would be withdrawn before the year's end. Also, as winter approached, Americans became increasingly aware of the sweeping counterterrorism measures that the Bush administration had implemented with little congressional oversight or legal scrutiny. These events led to diminishing approval ratings for President Bush and his policies.

The Democratic strategy of running against the war, which was encouraged by poll after poll, proved effective, and the November midterm elections resulted in a dramatic change in national politics. For the first time since 1994, the Democrats gained control of both the House of Representatives and the Senate. The chaotic Iraq War, with its images of battlefield violence and regular reports of American casualties; Bush's low approval ratings; and a number of Republican corruption scandals were responsible for the Democratic congressional victory. On the Friday before Election Day, Vice President Dick Cheney had stated that the White House would push "full speed ahead" with its Iraq policy, no matter what the election outcome. But five days later, on the day after the election, President Bush acknowledged that Republicans "took a thumpin'" and that Secretary of Defense Donald Rumsfeld would resign, both possible indicators of a change in direction.

Attention soon shifted to the much-anticipated release of the report by the Iraq Study Group (ISG), a bipartisan commission authorized by Congress to assess the war and suggest strategies. Chaired by former secretary of state James Baker, a Republican, and former congressman Lee Hamilton, a Democrat, the ISG released its findings on December 6. The 142-page report stated that "the situation in Iraq is grave and deteriorating" and urged stepped-up diplomatic and political efforts to stabilize Iraq so as to allow American combat forces to be removed responsibly. Whether Bush would endorse these aims remained the central political question as the year ended and the 2008 presidential campaign began.

DECEMBER 5
"Don't Know" Leads for President in 2008

Many Americans cannot spontaneously think of the name of a person they would like to see elected president in 2008. While this lack of firm conviction about presidential candidates over a year before the first 2008 primaries is not necessarily unusual, it underscores the certainty of change as various politicians announce their candidacies and jockey for position in the months ahead.

Beyond the "don't know" category, eight men and women are mentioned spontaneously as desired candidates by 2% or more of Americans as their choice for president in 2008. Two candidates top the list: New York senator Hillary Clinton, with 15% of spontaneous mentions, and Arizona senator John McCain, with 11%. The other six mentioned by between 2% and 6% of respondents are Illinois senator Barack Obama, former New York City mayor Rudolph Giuliani, former North Carolina senator John Edwards, Secretary of State Condoleezza Rice, former speaker of the House Newt Gingrich, and former vice president Al Gore. Five other individuals are named by 1%: Massachusetts governor Mitt Romney, Delaware senator Joe Biden, Massachusetts senator John Kerry, Tennessee senator Bill Frist (who has formally said he won't run), and former secretary of state Colin Powell.

When people are asked in a separate question if they would like to see any on a given list of candidates run for president, McCain and Giuliani are the only two candidates

CHRONOLOGY

NOVEMBER/ DECEMBER 2006

November 7 The Democrats regain control of the House of Representatives and win an effective majority in the Senate.

November 7 Sarah Palin becomes the first woman and, at age 42, the youngest person to be elected governor of Alaska.

November 8 Secretary of Defense Donald Rumsfeld resigns. He is replaced by former CIA director Robert Gates.

November 16 Nancy Pelosi is unanimously chosen as the Democratic candidate for Speaker of the House of Representatives.

November 17 British prime minister Tony Blair says the Iraq War "is pretty much a disaster."

November 30 Governor Tom Vilsack of Iowa announces his candidacy for the Democratic presidential nomination.

December 3 The *New York Times* reports on a leaked November 6 memo by then Secretary of Defense Donald Rumsfeld that stated that America's Iraq policy "is not working well enough or fast enough."

December 6 The Iraq Study Group, a bipartisan panel led by former defense secretary James Baker and former representative Lee Hamilton, issues its final report, which criticizes the progress of the Iraq War, noting that "the situation in Iraq is grave and deteriorating."

December 11 Representative Dennis Kucinich of Ohio announces his candidacy for the Democratic presidential nomination.

December 18 Robert Gates is sworn in as secretary of defense, replacing Donald Rumsfeld, who resigned in November.

December 19 Open gun battles rage between Palestinian factions Fatah and Hamas in the Gaza Strip.

December 28 John Edwards, former senator from North Carolina and 2004 vice presidential candidate, announces his candidacy for the Democratic presidential nomination.

December 28 The total of American soldiers killed in the Iraq War reaches the 3,000 mark.

December 30 Saddam Hussein, former dictator of Iraq, is executed by hanging.

---

who get a "yes" answer from more than half of Americans. Clinton tops the list among Democrats, over three-quarters of whom would like to see her run, but the majority of independents and Republicans say they would not like to see her run.

According to Gallup's first post-election survey on November 27–29, asked what issues they want the president and Congress to make their top priorities, Americans mention the Iraq War more than at any time since Gallup began polling this measure in April 2006. Over two-thirds of Americans say Iraq should be the government's highest priority. The next most frequently named issues—the economy, healthcare, and immigration—are each mentioned by fewer than one in five Americans. The traditional way of measuring a candidate's standing a year or more before an election is to read a list of names and ask Americans which person they would support if they had to vote for one that day. Another measurement technique involves asking Americans to react to each in a list of names, indicating if

they have ever heard of the person and, if so, whether their opinion of that person is favorable or unfavorable.

The November 27–29, 2006, Gallup Poll study approached the issue of the 2008 presidential race in a somewhat different way. The poll asked a representative sample of Americans to respond to this question: "Thinking about the election for president in 2008, who would you most like to see elected president?" This technique allows us to get a sense of the strength of each candidate at this juncture, over a year before the first primaries and caucuses in January 2008. The fact that many Americans cannot name anyone in response to the question shows that a significant number of voters are simply not focused at this point on the coming election, have not begun to sort out the various candidates, or have not yet settled on a favorite.

Among Democrats, there are no major surprises. Clinton leads the way, with 31% mentions among Democrats as the person they would like to see elected president, more

Carrying his own luggage, Senator Barack Obama arrives in New Hampshire on December 9, 2006, more than a year before the state's first-in-the-nation presidential primary. *(Jim Cole/AP images)*

gets 5% among independents but not enough mentions among Republicans to round up to 1%.

A slightly different way of measuring the strength of individuals who might potentially run for president at this point was also included in the November 27–29 poll: "Now I am going to read a list of people who may run for president in 2008. For each, please say whether you, personally, would or would not like to see this person run for president in the next election." The most significant difference here is that only 44% of Americans say they would like to see Clinton run for president, putting her in fourth place on the list, in contrast to her first-place showing in the open-ended format. The primary reason for her not being number one on this list is the tepid response of independents and Republicans. Clinton is tops on the list among Democrats, 77% of whom would like to see her run. But only 11% of Republicans and 44% of independents would like to see her run.

The man at the top of the list—McCain—has a much broader base of support. His candidacy is favored by 62% of Republicans, but also by a very healthy 58% of independents and 48% of Democrats. Giuliani does better than McCain among Republicans (74%), but less well among independents and Democrats. Edwards does less well among Democrats than Clinton, but does as well among independents and better among Republicans, giving him an overall total that puts him one point higher than Clinton among all Americans. All in all, this measure shows that Clinton and Edwards are at the top of the list of Democrats' preferences regarding whom they would like to see run in 2008, while Giuliani, McCain, and Rice are at the top

than twice as many "votes" as received by any other candidate. Obama is in second place at 14% among Democrats, followed by the generic "a Democrat" at 6%, Edwards at 4%, and McCain at 3%. Among Republicans, there is no dominant leader as is the case among Democrats. McCain gets 15% of the vote, followed by Giuliani with 10%. Other Republicans with measurable support include Rice at 4%, Gingrich and "a Republican" at 4%, and Romney with 3%. Among the crucial group of Americans who describe themselves as independents, McCain leads, followed by Clinton.

McCain does well in the overall results because of his strong appeal—at least based on this measure—among independents in addition to his strength within his Republican base. McCain is first among independents with 16% mentions (and is fifth among Democrats, with 3% mentions). Hillary Clinton comes in second to McCain among independents, with 11% of their vote. Like McCain, she gets only a minimal number of mentions from those who identify with the opposite party. Giuliani gets only 3% among independents and 1% among Democrats. Obama

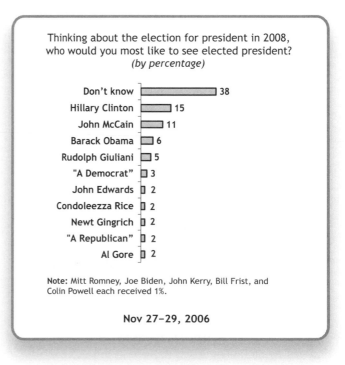

Thinking about the election for president in 2008, who would you most like to see elected president?
(by percentage)

Don't know	38
Hillary Clinton	15
John McCain	11
Barack Obama	6
Rudolph Giuliani	5
"A Democrat"	3
John Edwards	2
Condoleezza Rice	2
Newt Gingrich	2
"A Republican"	2
Al Gore	2

Note: Mitt Romney, Joe Biden, John Kerry, Bill Frist, and Colin Powell each received 1%.

Nov 27–29, 2006

of the list among Republicans. Importantly, independents would most like to see two Republicans run: McCain and Giuliani. Clinton has low crossover appeal to voters who are not Democrats, while McCain and Giuliani are much better positioned at this point among voters who are independents and Democrats.

DECEMBER 7

Credentials and Personality Both Factor in Defining 2008 Democratic Hopefuls

"What first comes to mind when you think about some of the top Democrats considering a run for president in 2008?" Gallup asked just that question in a recent national survey, focusing on four potential candidates: Hillary Rodham Clinton, Barack Obama, John Kerry, and Al Gore.

Personality and political leadership credentials are closely matched as the top factors people have in mind when reflecting on these political figures. Issues barely register, except in the case of Gore, whose name conjures up the environment for many people. According to respondents' verbatim answers to the November 27–29 Gallup survey, each Democrat triggers a wide array of public reactions. Gallup categorized the responses as positive, negative, or neutral. Clinton and Obama enjoy the greatest extent of laudatory comments—significantly more than Gore and twice as many as Kerry. Americans have little negative to say about Obama (mostly just "young and inexperienced"), in part because more than a third can't think of anything at all to say about him. By contrast, few Americans are at a loss for words when asked to give their impressions of Clinton, Kerry, or Gore. The remaining distribution is more negative than positive for each of these three, but is particularly negative for Kerry.

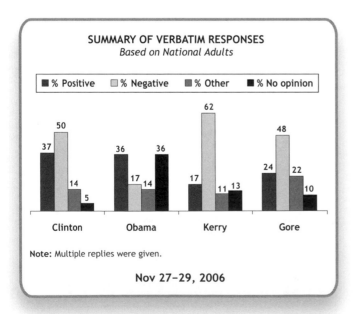

SUMMARY OF VERBATIM RESPONSES
Based on National Adults

■ % Positive   □ % Negative   ■ % Other   ■ % No opinion

Clinton: 37, 50, 14, 5
Obama: 36, 17, 14, 36
Kerry: 17, 62, 11, 13
Gore: 24, 48, 22, 10

Note: Multiple replies were given.

Nov 27–29, 2006

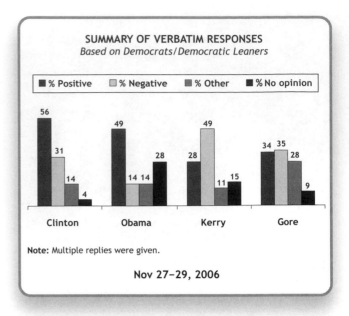

SUMMARY OF VERBATIM RESPONSES
Based on Democrats/Democratic Leaners

■ % Positive   □ % Negative   ■ % Other   ■ % No opinion

Clinton: 56, 31, 14, 4
Obama: 49, 14, 14, 28
Kerry: 28, 49, 11, 15
Gore: 34, 35, 28, 9

Note: Multiple replies were given.

Nov 27–29, 2006

The first test of whether any of these figures is true presidential timber will come from Democrats during the nomination process that is already beginning. Commentary about each is more positive among the Democrats surveyed than among the general population. However, Kerry's image among Democrats is still highly problematic for someone hoping to get a second chance at the nomination. Gore is viewed more positively than Kerry, but about as many Democrats say something negative about him as say something positive.

The overall positive/negative ratios for these individuals among national adults closely mirror the support each received in the same poll on a question asking whether he or she should run for president in 2008. The general-public results were 44% saying Clinton should run, 38% for Obama, 31% for Gore, and 23% for Kerry. The main association that people have with each candidate puts some flesh on these ratings. In the coming months, these individuals would, as candidates, presumably want to emphasize and develop the positive associations people have with them, while they would want to manage or downplay the negatives.

Accentuate the Positive

So what are the positives that spring to people's minds about Clinton? It's nearly a tie between her political credentials (she is "capable of being president," "a good politician," poised to be the first woman president, and "experienced") and her personality ("intelligent," "strong," and "honest"). An additional 1% of national adults (including 2% of Democrats) say they "like her views." The positive attributes associated with Obama are also closely divided between leadership credentials—particularly the sense that he is new on the block, bringing some fresh energy to Washington—and personal traits. On the personal side, people like him for a variety of reasons, such as for being "intelligent," "charismatic," "honest," "articulate," and "interesting."

DECEMBER 12

Public Trusts Iraq Study Group More Than Bush on Iraq

The majority of Americans have not been closely following news of the newly released report from the Iraq Study Group and do not have a specific opinion about whether or not the Bush administration should adopt the group's recommendations regarding U.S. policy and troop levels in Iraq. Among those Americans who do have an opinion, however, there is a very strong sentiment that the Bush administration should follow the group's recommendations.

Regardless of their familiarity with the Iraq Study Group, more than 7 in 10 Americans support three of the group's key recommendations in principle: withdrawing most combat troops from Iraq by 2008, negotiating directly with the Iranians and Syrians about regional security, and jump-starting peace talks between the Israelis and the Palestinians. A significantly higher percentage of Americans say they trust the Iraq Study Group to make recommendations about Iraq than say they trust President George W. Bush. Americans have the most trust in the military when it comes to decisions about doing what is right in Iraq.

Iraq Study Group Report

Only 18% of Americans have followed news about the Iraq Study Group report released on December 6 very closely,

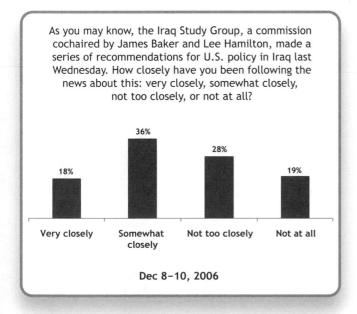

As you may know, the Iraq Study Group, a commission cochaired by James Baker and Lee Hamilton, made a series of recommendations for U.S. policy in Iraq last Wednesday. How closely have you been following the news about this: very closely, somewhat closely, not too closely, or not at all?

Dec 8–10, 2006

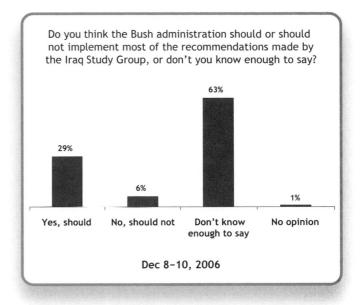

Do you think the Bush administration should or should not implement most of the recommendations made by the Iraq Study Group, or don't you know enough to say?

Dec 8–10, 2006

and another 36% have followed news about the report somewhat closely.

This level of attention being paid to the Iraq Study Group report is well below average by Gallup's historic measures of reaction to news events over the past decade and a half. Of about 170 news events included in Gallup's database, the average percentage of Americans saying they were following particular news events very closely was 28%, while 71% were following the events very or somewhat closely.

Perhaps because of the low level of attention paid to the group's report, nearly two in three Americans say they do not know enough about the report to have an opinion about whether or not the Bush administration should follow its recommendations. But among those who do have an opinion, sentiment is clear. By almost a five-to-one margin, 29% to 6%, this group says that President Bush should implement the group's recommendations.

The relatively small group of those who claim to have followed the report very closely say by a 64% to 13% margin that Bush should implement the Iraq Study Group's recommendations.

Whom Do You Trust About Iraq?

Americans were asked to rate their perceived trust in a list of six individuals and organizations in terms of recommending the "right thing for the United States to do in Iraq." The list comprised Bush, the Iraq Study Group, the U.S. military and Defense Department, Arizona Senator John McCain, the U.S. State Department, and Democratic leaders in Congress. The results show that Americans at this point have the least amount of trust in President Bush to do the right thing in Iraq (46% say they have a great or fair degree of trust), and the most trust in the U.S. military and the Defense Department (81%). Americans have a good deal more trust in the Iraq Study Group to recommend the right thing to do in Iraq than they do in Bush, by a 66% (fair or great degree of trust) to 46% margin.

Specific Recommendations

The poll included a question asking Americans whether or not the Bush administration should follow each of three key recommendations from the Iraq Study Group. Gallup asked respondents about withdrawing most U.S. combat troops by 2008, negotiating directly with the Iranians and Syrians to promote regional security, and jump-starting peace talks between the Israelis and the Palestinians. In each case, about three-quarters of Americans say that the Bush administration should follow the group's recommendation. There are some partisan differences, but a majority of Republicans also favor each of these three recommendations.

Overall, the poll results suggest that while Americans are not all that familiar with the specifics of the initial Iraq Study Group report, they appear to be strongly sympathetic to its recommendations. In particular, Americans favor removing most combat troops from Iraq by 2008, negotiating with Iran and Syria, and jump-starting the Israeli-Palestinian peace process.

The data suggest that President Bush is in a generally weak position in relation to the American public in terms of making decisions about the Iraq situation going forward. Fewer than half of Americans are willing to say that they have a great deal or a fair amount of trust in Bush to recom-

mend the right actions for Iraq, some 20 percentage points lower than the percentage of Americans who trust the Iraq Study Group.

DECEMBER 13
Majority Predict History Will Judge Bush Harshly

That ticking sound in the Oval Office may seem louder to President George W. Bush now that there are only two years left in his presidency. Focusing on his legacy may be more satisfying than dealing with the newly elected Democratic Congress, but a new USA Today/Gallup Poll suggests it won't be any easier. According to the December 8–10, 2006 survey, more than half of Americans predict Bush will go down in history as a "below average" or "poor" president. Only 19% think history will judge him as either "outstanding" or "above average."

The poll also asked about the six most recent presidents: George W. Bush, Bill Clinton, George H. W. Bush, Ronald Reagan, Jimmy Carter, and Gerald Ford. Fifty-four percent of Americans believe history will consider Bush a below average or poor president. The closest any of the previous five presidents comes to that level is Bill Clinton, with 25% of Americans expecting history to judge him harshly.

Few Americans predict that either Gerald Ford or George H. W. Bush will be remembered as stellar presidents; their respective 23% and 32% outstanding/above average scores are not that much better than the current president's 19%. But rather than predicting that history will be critical of Ford and the elder Bush as they do with respect to the current Bush, half or more of Americans believe Gerald Ford and George H. W. Bush will be remembered as "average."

George W. Bush's ratings are nearly the inverse of the most lauded of recent presidents: Ronald Reagan. Nearly

SUPPORT FOR IRAQ STUDY GROUP RECOMMENDATIONS

□ % Yes, should   ■ % No, should not

	Jump-start peace talks aimed at resolving the Israeli-Palestinian conflict	Withdraw most U.S. combat troops from Iraq by March 2008, leaving only a limited number to help train and advise the Iraqis	Negotiate directly with neighboring countries like Iran and Syria on regional security
% Yes, should	76	74	72
% No, should not	18	22	23

Dec 8–10, 2006

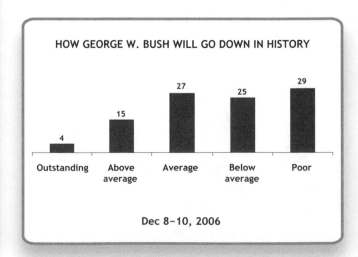

HOW GEORGE W. BUSH WILL GO DOWN IN HISTORY

Outstanding	Above average	Average	Below average	Poor
4	15	27	25	29

Dec 8–10, 2006

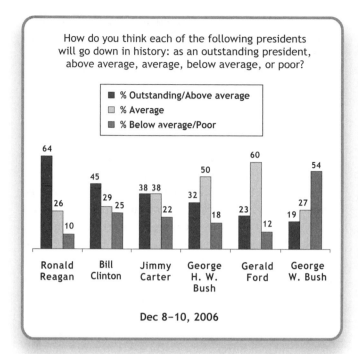

How do you think each of the following presidents will go down in history: as an outstanding president, above average, average, below average, or poor?

- ■ % Outstanding/Above average
- ▨ % Average
- ▧ % Below average/Poor

Dec 8–10, 2006

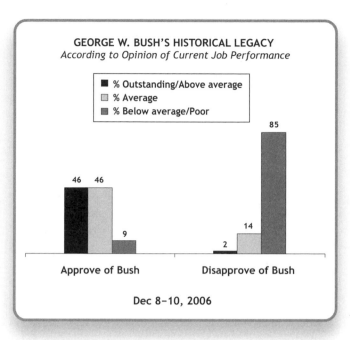

GEORGE W. BUSH'S HISTORICAL LEGACY
According to Opinion of Current Job Performance

- ■ % Outstanding/Above average
- ▨ % Average
- ▧ % Below average/Poor

Dec 8–10, 2006

two-thirds of Americans believe Reagan will go down in history as an outstanding or above-average president; only 10% believe he will be judged harshly.

Legacy vs. Job Approval

According to the new poll, 38% of Americans approve of the job Bush is doing as president while 59% disapprove. Thus, there is nearly a one-to-one correspondence between the percentage disapproving of Bush and the percentage saying he will be remembered as a subpar president (59% vs. 54%, respectively). Two years ago, there was a bigger gap between these figures (49% disapproval vs. 38% subpar rating). What has happened is that people who disapprove of the job Bush is doing have grown more intense in their feelings. In June 2004, only 62% of those disapproving of his job performance said he would go down in history as subpar. Today that figure is 85%. Bush's supporters are much less extreme in their predictions about Bush's legacy than his opponents are in theirs. Only 46% of those who approve of Bush's job performance say he will be remembered as a superior president. The rest of his supporters mostly believe he will be remembered as just average.

This indication of the intensity of anti-Bush sentiment is different from the pattern with most respect to other recent presidents. With presidents Ford, Reagan, and the elder Bush, the percentages saying each would be remembered as below average or poor were generally much lower than the percentages disapproving of their job performance when the two dimensions of opinion were measured. How-

ever, as with Bush, Clinton's job disapproval and negative legacy ratings were also very similar.

A Troublesome Comparison

Bush's current image ratings appear to be similar to those of former president Richard Nixon, who resigned in disgrace in 1974 over his role in the Watergate affair. Gallup last measured public opinion about Nixon's legacy in June 2004, at which time 14% of Americans thought he would be considered an outstanding or above average president, 34% said he would be considered average, and 51% predicted he would be remembered as below average or poor.

Whether Bush's current legacy ratings would be similar to Nixon's if the two were rated in the same poll is, however,

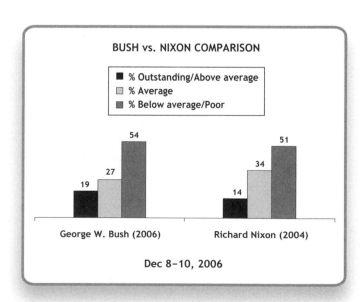

BUSH vs. NIXON COMPARISON

- ■ % Outstanding/Above average
- ▨ % Average
- ▧ % Below average/Poor

Dec 8–10, 2006

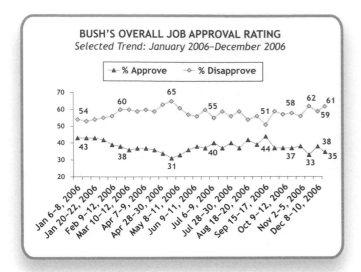

BUSH'S OVERALL JOB APPROVAL RATING
Selected Trend: January 2006–December 2006

unclear. It is possible that each president's ratings are affected by the context of other presidents included in the same poll, thus making the evaluations more relative in nature, rather than absolute.

DECEMBER 20
Bush Approval Holds Steady in Mid-30s

President George W. Bush's latest job approval rating from the American people remains where it has generally been for the last three months—in the mid-30s. According to the December 11–14 Gallup Poll, 35% of Americans now approve of the job Bush is doing while 61% disapprove. Bush's approval rating has seesawed within a fairly narrow range during 2006. It averaged 40% in the first three months of the year, dipped to 35% from April through June, recovered to 40% over the summer, and has been down again to 36% since October.

Demographic Patterns Hold Steady

Bush's current levels of support from various demographic and political subgroups are generally consistent with where these subgroup ratings have been for the past three months. Bush continues to earn higher approval from men than from women: 43% vs. 28% in the latest poll. Since October, Bush has averaged 40% approval from men and 33% from women. This gender gap reflects the more fun-

damental political difference between the genders, which is that women tend to be more Democratic in their political affiliation than are men. Also, whites are more positive about Bush than is the much more Democratic-oriented nonwhite population (39% vs. 22%). Current approval of Bush by age is similar to the October–December average by age. The December 11–14 poll shows Bush receiving the most support from middle-aged adults (39% from those age 30 to 49) and somewhat lower support from those age 18 to 29 (29%) and 50+ (33%).

Throughout his presidency, Bush has typically received higher ratings in the South and Midwest than in the East and West. That pattern is maintained in the current poll, in which his approval score is about 40% in the Midwest and South but below 30% in the West and East. Roughly 8 in 10 Republicans approve of the job Bush is doing, compared with only 3 in 10 independents and fewer than 1 in 10 Democrats. Bush's latest approval scores by party are nearly identical to his averages among these groups over the past three months.

The Coming Year: 2007

Between December 18 and December 20, Gallup asked a representative sample of Americans to predict whether each of 15 possible events would happen in 2007. The list spanned politics, the economy, public policy, national disasters, and even sports. Among the items listed, Americans are most likely to believe that Hillary Clinton will announce her intention to run for president, and are least likely to believe the Supreme Court will overturn the 1973 *Roe v. Wade* decision that legalized a woman's right to abortion in the first trimester of pregnancy. However, 38% of Americans cannot think of the name of a person they would like to see elected president in 2008.

Aside from the forthcoming presidential election, the Iraq War is clearly the dominant issue facing the United States at this time. The perceived lack of progress there is forcing many military and political leaders to re-evaluate U.S. policy toward Iraq. While some Americans call for a drawdown in the number of American troops there, others are now calling for an increase. In any case, Americans are dubious that the United States will significantly reduce the number of troops in Iraq during 2007; 63% believe this will not happen. As the year comes to a close, the Iraq War seems likely to remain the dominant issue of the presidential campaign.

JANUARY 2007

Throughout January 2007, Gallup surveys showed President George W. Bush's approval rating hovering around 30%. In the last 35 years, only presidents Richard Nixon and Jimmy Carter have had lower approval ratings. On January 23, President Bush appealed to Congress in his State of the Union address to give his plan to stabilize Iraq by sending 20,000 additional troops "a chance to work." The president mentioned Iraq 34 times, the most ever in his seven annual addresses to the nation. Bush first cited Iraq in his 2002 State of the Union message, when he referred to it twice and included it as part of an "axis of evil," along with North Korea and Iran. At that time 85% of Americans approved of his job performance. In 2003, the United States invaded Iraq.

Iraq—and only Iraq—stood out as a significant concern for Americans in Gallup's January 2007 monthly reading of the "most important problem" facing the country. From the start of the Iraq War in March 2003 until January 1, 2007, American deaths exceeded 3,000, with another 20,000 suffering combat wounds. For their part, Iraqi authorities reported that in 2006 alone, more than 16,000 Iraqis died violent deaths.

With Inauguration Day 2009 still two years away, the presidential election kicked into full gear as prominent Republicans and Democrats officially announced their candidacies or the establishment of exploratory committees. Democrats included Delaware senator Joe Biden, New York senator Hillary Clinton, Connecticut senator Christopher Dodd, former North Carolina senator John Edwards, former Alaska senator Mike Gravel, Ohio representative Dennis Kucinich, Illinois senator Barack Obama, and New Mexico governor Bill Richardson; two others, former vice president Al Gore and former general Wesley Clark, were mentioned as possible candidates. Also by the end of January, eight Republicans had declared their intention to seek the party's 2008 presidential nomination: Kansas senator

Sam Brownback, former New York City mayor Rudolph Giuliani, former Arkansas governor Mike Huckabee, California representative Duncan Hunter, Arizona senator John McCain, Texas representative Ron Paul, former Massachusetts governor Mitt Romney, and Colorado representative Tom Tancredo. Two others, former Tennessee senator Fred Thompson and former House speaker Newt Gingrich of Georgia, were prominently mentioned as possible nominees.

While Iraq dominated the news throughout January 2007, Gallup's annual "Mood of the Nation" poll, conducted between January 15 and January 18, included two consumer sentiment trends established three decades ago. The first asks respondents whether they are financially better or worse off than they were a year ago. The second asks whether they expect to be financially better or worse off a year in the future. Exactly half of Americans believe they are financially better off today than they were a year ago. This is up from only 37% saying this last February, and from an average of 39% across the last six years, going back to January 2001.

Americans are typically upbeat when asked to forecast their finances over the next year. Except for the 1970s and early 1980s, Gallup has found that the percentage of Americans predicting year-to-year improvement in their financial situation has rarely dipped below 50%. But this measure, too, is a bit more positive today than it has been for the last few years. According to the new poll, nearly two-thirds of Americans (65%) expect to be financially better off in a year than they are today. This is up from 59% in 2005, and from an average of 60% over the past three years.

The positive shift in Americans' views of their present financial situation closely parallels improved public ratings of the U.S. economy over the same period. At the same time that Gallup has seen a 13-percentage-point increase (from 37% to 50%) in those saying their personal finances

CHRONOLOGY

JANUARY 2007

January 4 A newly Democratic-controlled Congress, the first in 12 years, takes office in Washington. In the House of Representatives, the Democrats have a 233–202 edge over the Republicans, and Nancy Pelosi becomes the first ever female Speaker of the House. In the Senate, the Democrats number 49, but two independents agree to caucus with the party, giving them a slim two-vote majority.

January 4 General David Petraeus is appointed commanding general, Multi-National Force–Iraq.

January 8 U.S. planes bomb what it claims are al-Qaeda targets in Somalia, thereby supporting anti-Islamist Somali forces, who are also being supported by Ethiopian planes and troops.

January 10 President Bush announces that 20,000 more troops will be deployed to Iraq in a "surge" designed to reduce sectarian violence.

January 11 Senator Christopher Dodd of Connecticut announces his candidacy for the Democratic presidential nomination.

January 16 The perjury trial of Lewis "Scooter" Libby begins in Washington, D.C. Libby, the former chief of staff to Vice President Dick Cheney, is accused of leaking the identity of CIA operative Valerie Plame for political reasons.

January 16 Bombs at a Baghdad university kill at least 70, mostly Shiite students and professors.

January 16 The United Nations reports that over 34,000 Iraqi civilians died during 2006 as a direct result of violent conflict.

January 20 In a videotaped message posted on her Web site, Hillary Clinton announces her plans for a presidential exploratory committee, saying, "I'm in, and I'm in to win."

January 20 Senator Sam Brownback of Kansas announces his candidacy for the Republican presidential nomination.

January 22 Two car bombs kill more than 80 at a Baghdad market.

January 23 President Bush delivers the annual State of the Union address. While generally positive, it admits that the Iraq War is not going completely as planned: "This is not the fight we entered in Iraq, but it is the fight we are in."

January 25 Representative Duncan Hunter of California announces his candidacy for the Republican presidential nomination.

January 27 Tens of thousands of protesters gather in the National Mall in Washington, D.C., to oppose President Bush's plans to increase the number of American troops in Iraq.

January 28 Heavy fighting in Najaf kills at least 250 Shiite militants in Iraq; two American soldiers die when their helicopter is shot down.

January 31 Senator Joe Biden of Delaware announces his candidacy for the Democratic presidential nomination.

---

have improved over the past year, there has been a 14-point increase (from 38% to 52%) in the percentage describing current economic conditions in the country as "excellent" or "good."

JANUARY 4

Americans' Biggest Concern About Iraq: Lives and Safety of Those Fighting There

President George W. Bush will address the nation on January 10 with a major speech on the situation in Iraq, announcing—after weeks of study and consultation—his plans for "the way forward" in that difficult situation. Given that the Iraq War is overwhelmingly considered by Americans to be the most important problem facing the country today, such a speech will no doubt be listened to with very receptive ears.

But how well the thrust and content of the speech will go over with the average American is not clear at this point. Addressing the public's concerns, White House press secretary Tony Snow recently said: "The president believes that in putting together a way forward he will be able to address a lot of the concerns that the American public has, the most important of which is, 'What is your plan for winning?'"

Is the development of a plan for winning in Iraq really Americans' most important concern regarding that country? To answer that question, a late December 2006 Gallup Poll survey asked Americans: "What is your biggest concern about the war in Iraq?" It does not appear that the most important concern of the American public about the war in Iraq is developing a plan for winning, as Snow asserts. Instead, the largest category of responses focuses on the costs of the war or the lack of a rationale for being in the war to begin with. About one-third of Americans answer the question probing for their biggest concern about Iraq by saying that it is a concern for the lives and safety of the troops being asked to serve in Iraq. An additional 10 percent say their biggest concern is the lack of a rationale for being in Iraq.

The second most frequently occurring category of responses to the question focuses on concern about the issue of withdrawing from Iraq in what is described as a "no-win" situation and/or the lack of a coherent exit strategy for disengaging from Iraq. The third category in terms of frequency of responses, enunciated by less than one out of five Americans, is the closest to what was stated by Tony Snow. This group says their top concern is that the United States not leave Iraq too early without finishing its mission in order to avoid leaving a "mess."

Republicans clearly are more likely to echo the type of concern highlighted by Snow than are independents and Democrats. Sixteen percent of Republicans volunteer that their biggest concern is the need to send in more troops to finish the mission in Iraq, something President Bush is expected to announce next week. Independents and Democrats are much more concerned about the costs of the war and the difficulty of extracting U.S. forces from the situation there.

By all accounts, in his upcoming speech to the nation on January 10, Bush will focus on the need to finish the mission in Iraq, including the possibility of increasing the number of American armed forces personnel stationed there. The data, however, suggest that to the degree the president wants to address the concerns of the American people as a whole, he should first and foremost discuss the rationale for the high costs of the war in Iraq, particularly in terms of the lives of the men and women stationed there. The data suggest that Bush's second focus should be on plans for the way in which the United States can ultimately withdraw from Iraq. Previous research has shown that at this point the American public feels the costs of the war are not outweighed by the benefits. Thus, from the public's perspective, the president most urgently needs to convince Americans why the continued costs are justified if he is going to announce plans for a continued or expanded presence of U.S armed forces in Iraq.

JANUARY 9
Public Opposes Troop Surge

During President Bush's address to the nation on January 10, he will announce plans for a "surge"—an escalation in the number of American troops in Iraq. The exact way in which the American public reacts to the president's speech is unknown at this point. It will depend on the specific content of Bush's speech, the persuasiveness of his case, and the way in which media coverage of the speech plays out in the hours and days following it.

Going into the speech, however, it is known that the American public in general opposes the concept of an increase in troops in Iraq. A number of polls have shown that when given a choice between alternative ways of handling the troop situation in Iraq, only about 10% of Americans opt for the alternative of increasing troops. The rest opt for withdrawal of troops either immediately, within a 12-month time frame, or taking as much time as needed. At the same time, it would not be unusual to find that support for the president's probable call for more troops in Iraq—once the proposed policy shift is made public—will be higher than this baseline minimum. This assumption is based on the fact that the action will no longer be hypothetical but will have the institutional weight of the presidency behind it after the January 10 speech. A surge will, in essence, have become the stated policy of the country. It is particularly likely that Republicans will increase their support for the policy after the president's announcement.

A new USA Today/Gallup Poll conducted between January 5 and January 7, 2007, provides support for this possibility. The poll finds that only 12% opt for a troop increase using the traditional four-alternatives question, which is little changed from past polling. But the poll included a separate question that summarized a possible "surge" announcement, and found that 36% support the idea of such an increase, while 61% oppose it.

The Anticipated Surge

The exact specifics of what the president will announce in his speech have been leaked to reporters over the last several weeks, a typical process that allows the administration to get an early read on reactions to the speech and to fine-tune the speech before it becomes official. Still, what Bush actually ends up proposing in his Wednesday night speech, and the way in which he says it, will not be known for sure until the speech itself is delivered.

Thus, the weekend USA Today/Gallup Poll of January 5–7 included an approximation of what news accounts indicate is the most likely scenario, phrased as follows:

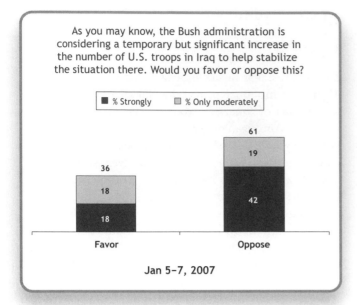

As you may know, the Bush administration is considering a temporary but significant increase in the number of U.S. troops in Iraq to help stabilize the situation there. Would you favor or oppose this?

■ % Strongly   ☐ % Only moderately

Jan 5–7, 2007

Support from the Base

It should be noted that the current poll measures Bush's overall job approval rating at 37%. This suggests that the core support for the pending announcement of a surge essentially mirrors the size of the president's core base. In fact, analysis shows that the 36% support for the surge option is based primarily on strong support from loyal Republicans, two-thirds of whom support it. About a third of independents support it, compared with only 12% of Democrats.

The weekend poll included one additional question pertinent to the president's pending recommendations on Iraq. In this poll, Americans were asked which of the following came closest to their view: The United States can only achieve its goals in Iraq if it increases the numbers of troops it has there; the United States can achieve its goals in Iraq without sending more troops there; or the United States cannot achieve its goals in Iraq regardless of how many troops it has there.

Only about one-quarter of Americans agree with what is likely to be a core component of the president's speech on Wednesday: the argument that the United States can only achieve its goals in Iraq by increasing the number of troops it has there. About half say that U.S. goals can never be achieved regardless of the number of troops it has in Iraq, while another quarter say that U.S. goals can be achieved without sending more troops. If, as expected, Bush announces a surge in U.S. troops in Iraq in his speech this Wednesday night, he will be doing so despite the fact that a majority of Americans oppose such an action. Support for a surge in troops appears likely to be in the one-third range, consisting primarily of the president's political base.

"As you may know, the Bush administration is considering a temporary but significant increase in the number of U.S. troops in Iraq to help stabilize the situation there. Would you favor or oppose this?" This wording includes several salient features: 1) It emphasizes that this will be administration policy; 2) it indicates that the surge will be "temporary"; and 3) it points out that the surge would have a specific purpose ("to help stabilize . . . ").

This pattern of response can be compared with an update on the more general question about what to do next in Iraq that Gallup has been asking for several years, a question that provides four alternatives: 1) withdraw all troops from Iraq immediately; 2) withdraw all troops by January 2008—that is, in 12 months' time; 3) withdraw all troops, but take as many years to do this as are needed to turn control over to the Iraqis; or 4) send more troops to Iraq.

Given these four alternatives, only 12% of Americans opt for the "send more troops" alternative. This is up very slightly from previous surveys in which this question was included. Thus, it appears that support for a troop surge in Iraq at this point ranges from 12% to 36%—depending on the circumstances in which the question is asked and the way in which it is phrased. It is possible, of course, that support may rise even higher than 36% after the president's speech—if, for example, he does a particularly effective job of laying out the rationale for a surge and if media coverage the next morning is particularly positive. Still, the weekend data suggest that it will be a difficult challenge for the president to move the support numbers for a surge above the 50% point, making it likely that his proposed course of action will be opposed by a majority of the American public.

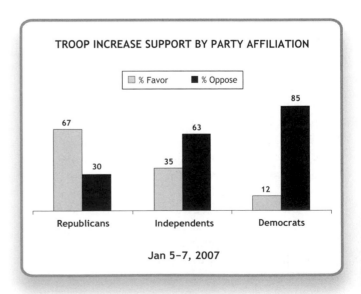

TROOP INCREASE SUPPORT BY PARTY AFFILIATION

☐ % Favor   ■ % Oppose

Jan 5–7, 2007

JANUARY 10

Record Number of Americans Say Situation in Iraq Going "Badly"

Americans' assessment of the situation in Iraq has become progressively more negative in recent months, as the percentage saying things are going "badly" for the United States has jumped to a record high of 71% in the latest USA Today/Gallup Poll. This is up from 64% in October 2006. On the flip side, just 28% think things are going well, down from the previous low of 35% last fall. The latest two readings are markedly more negative than the average sentiment on this question for each of the last three years. From 2004 through 2006, an average of 43% thought the war was going well, while 56% said it was going badly. By contrast, in the first year of the war (2003), an average of 58% thought it was going well, and only 40% perceived that it was going badly.

The recent increase in negative American attitudes about the war in Iraq is also evident in the trend from Gallup's measure of public support for the war, which asks whether the United States made a mistake in sending troops to Iraq. The percentage calling it a mistake is slightly higher today (57%) than it was a month ago (53% in early December) and stands near the high-water mark for this question (59% in September 2005).

The new survey, conducted between January 5 and January 7, also finds the lowest proportion on record (16%) of Americans saying the United States is certain to win in Iraq, although nearly as few (22%) were optimistic about victory in March 2006. The combined percentage saying the United States is either certain or likely to win is 50%. About the same number (46%) now say the United States is either unlikely to win or certain not to win. Last March, the

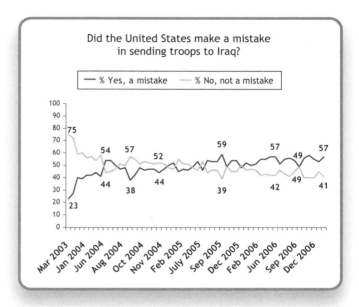

Did the United States make a mistake in sending troops to Iraq?

— % Yes, a mistake   — % No, not a mistake

balance of opinion on this question was slightly more optimistic, with 54% predicting victory and only 41% expecting failure. The extent to which public opinion about Iraq has changed since the beginning of the war is clearly evident in the first readings on this measure in 2003. At that time, as many as 69% of Americans believed the United States was certain to win and another 25% thought victory was likely.

Rationale for More Troops Not Embraced

Public discouragement about the Iraq War is clearly not lost on President George W. Bush, who is scheduled to address the subject in a speech to the nation on January 10. Based on his advance briefings to lawmakers, Bush is expected to propose sending as many as 20,000 more troops to the most troubled areas of Iraq to try to stem

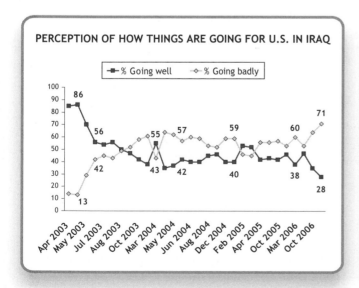

PERCEPTION OF HOW THINGS ARE GOING FOR U.S. IN IRAQ

-■- % Going well   -◇- % Going badly

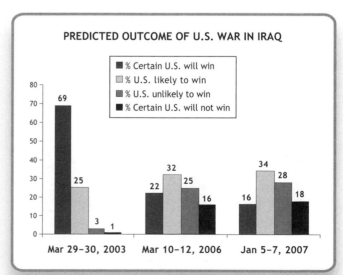

PREDICTED OUTCOME OF U.S. WAR IN IRAQ

■ % Certain U.S. will win
□ % U.S. likely to win
▨ % U.S. unlikely to win
■ % Certain U.S. will not win

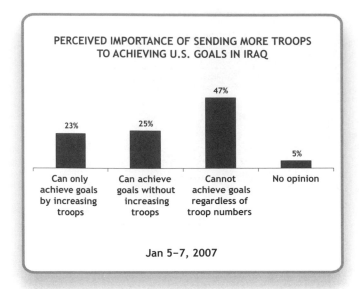

PERCEIVED IMPORTANCE OF SENDING MORE TROOPS
TO ACHIEVING U.S. GOALS IN IRAQ

Jan 5–7, 2007

battle. Only a quarter of Americans (23%) believe sending more troops to Iraq is essential to the United States' achieving its goals there. Another quarter (25%) say U.S. goals can be achieved without sending more troops, while nearly half (47%) say U.S. goals cannot be achieved regardless of how many troops it has there.

Execution of Saddam Hussein Not Seen as Problematic

The taunting Saddam Hussein received from onlookers in the final moments before his execution by the Iraqis on December 30, 2006—something captured on video via cell phone and posted on the Internet—created some concern in the United States that the process was mishandled in a way that could further harm the United States' image in the region. Though he emphasized that Hussein had received justice, President Bush said he wished the execution had been handled in a more "dignified" way. The American public shows rather little concern about this. Asked whether Hussein's execution will help or hurt the United States in achieving its goals in Iraq, only 36% say it will hurt the country, while 43% say it will help. One in five either say it will make no difference (16%) or have no opinion about it (5%). Republicans widely believe Hussein's execution will be helpful to the United States; independents are closely divided, while Democrats are more likely to believe it will harm U.S. interests. However, not even half of Democrats think it will have a negative impact on U.S. efforts.

the sectarian violence plaguing that country. As of January 1, there were approximately 150,000 American troops in Iraq—some 90,000 active forces along with 60,000 reservists. Congressional Democrats are portraying this as a major escalation of the war and indicate they will insist Bush first seek congressional approval, and that they may block funding for it.

The latest poll shows that barely a third of Americans are poised to support Bush's position in this political confrontation. Only 36% say they would favor sending more troops to Iraq if Bush proposes it in his speech; 61% say they would oppose this. Whether Bush is able to expand that support could depend on how well he makes the argument that the new deployment is essential to achieving American goals in Iraq. As of now, he faces a clear uphill

JANUARY 16

Opposition to Troop Increase Unchanged After Bush's Iraq Speech

There has been little change in the public's overall attitudes toward the Iraq War and the administration's proposed plans for an increase in troops in the days following President George W. Bush's speech to the nation on January 10. Americans continue to oppose, by a 59% to 38% margin, the president's plan to increase troops in Iraq. Americans remain unconvinced that it is necessary to send new troops to Iraq to gain victory, as Bush argued, and a majority favor withdrawal of troops within one year. Most Americans also continue to say it was a mistake to send troops to Iraq initially. Americans are split on the issue of congressional action that would block funds for the deployment of additional troops, although there is majority approval for a nonbinding congressional resolution voicing opposition to the surge in troops.

The most basic question included in the poll asked Americans to evaluate Bush's proposal to increase the number of U.S. troops in Iraq.

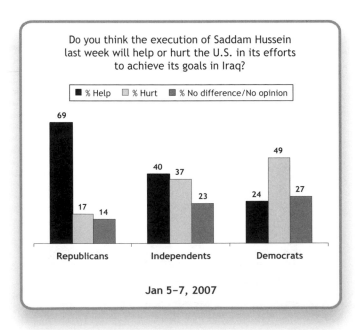

Do you think the execution of Saddam Hussein last week will help or hurt the U.S. in its efforts to achieve its goals in Iraq?

■ % Help   □ % Hurt   ■ % No difference/No opinion

Jan 5–7, 2007

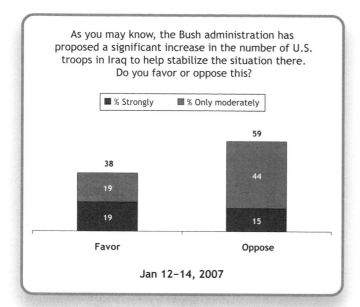

As you may know, the Bush administration has proposed a significant increase in the number of U.S. troops in Iraq to help stabilize the situation there. Do you favor or oppose this?

■ % Strongly   ■ % Only moderately

Jan 12–14, 2007

The results show virtually no change from a poll taken a week ago, on January 5–7, 2007, before the president's speech. In that poll, a similarly worded question that included the phrasing "temporary" showed 36% of Americans favoring a troop increase and 61% opposing it. In short, the data give no indication that the speech and the discussion that followed—including critiques from Democratic leaders—had an impact on American attitudes in either direction. A majority of Americans—56%—favor withdrawal of American troops within 12 months' time; another 29% favor withdrawal over time, but taking as much time as needed; while 13% favor sending in more troops. From a broader perspective, there has been a gradual but slight increase in the percentage of Americans selecting the "send more troops" option, from a low point of 4% in March 2006 to the current 13%.

Despite Bush's arguments in his speech, a majority of Americans say that the United States cannot achieve its goals in Iraq regardless of how many troops it has there. Only 28% agree with the administration's position that the United States can only achieve its goals if it increases the number of troops it has in Iraq, while 17% believe the United States can achieve its goals there without sending in more troops, and 50% say the United States cannot achieve its goals in Iraq regardless of how many troops it has there.

Congressional Action

There has been much discussion about the actions Democratic leaders in Congress could take to signal their opposition to the president's stated intention to send more troops to Iraq. Given the president's constitutional role as commander in chief of the armed forces, Congress has little recourse to stop the president from increasing troop levels should he decide to do so. Two primary options for actions Congress could take have been discussed, however. The first would involve the Democrats in Congress passing a nonbinding resolution opposing the increase in troops in Iraq. The second would be a more dramatic attempt to block funding for the increase in troops. The weekend poll shows a majority of Americans favor the former, but the public is split on the latter. The support for a nonbinding resolution of opposition to the war essentially mirrors the pattern of support for the troop increase itself. This is not a surprising result, suggesting that Americans who oppose the troop surge would be quite willing to see Congress pass a resolution formally expressing such opposition.

Moves to actively block the deployment of more U.S. troops to Iraq are more controversial. House Defense Appropriations Committee chair John Murtha (D.-Pa.)—who had originally voted to authorize the use of force against Iraq in 2002 but came out strongly against the war in November 2005, when he urged immediate withdrawal of U.S. troops—indicated on January 14 that he would introduce legislation to cut off funding for the troop increase. Senate Armed Forces Committee chair Carl Levin (D.-Mich.), however, opposes efforts to deny money for the troop surge, remarking that "I don't think funding is the way you approach this." The American public is apparently just as torn on this issue as are Democratic congressional leaders. Forty-seven percent favor and 50% oppose when Americans are asked their opinion about cutting off funding for the troop increase.

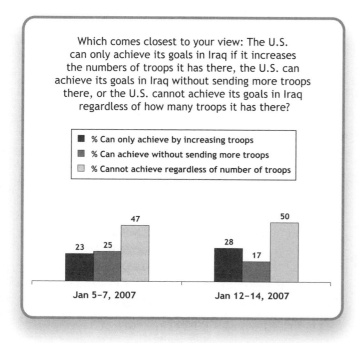

Which comes closest to your view: The U.S. can only achieve its goals in Iraq if it increases the numbers of troops it has there, the U.S. can achieve its goals in Iraq without sending more troops there, or the U.S. cannot achieve its goals in Iraq regardless of how many troops it has there?

■ % Can only achieve by increasing troops
■ % Can achieve without sending more troops
□ % Cannot achieve regardless of number of troops

Jan 5–7, 2007   Jan 12–14, 2007

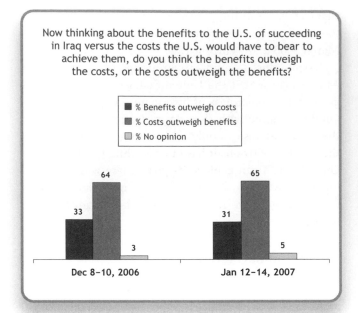

Now thinking about the benefits to the U.S. of succeeding in Iraq versus the costs the U.S. would have to bear to achieve them, do you think the benefits outweigh the costs, or the costs outweigh the benefits?

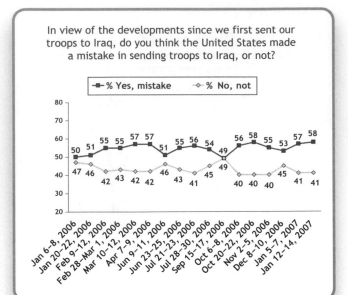

In view of the developments since we first sent our troops to Iraq, do you think the United States made a mistake in sending troops to Iraq, or not?

Benefits vs. Costs

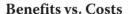

The poll included an update on a key question asking Americans if the benefits to the United States of succeeding in Iraq outweigh the costs. The argument essentially being made by the administration is that the costs of failure in Iraq are so high that any alternative other than pressing for success is unacceptable. However, the American public appears to disagree. By a better than two-to-one margin

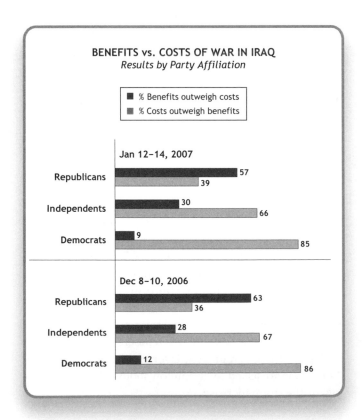

BENEFITS vs. COSTS OF WAR IN IRAQ
Results by Party Affiliation

(65% to 31%), Americans say the "costs of succeeding in Iraq" outweigh the benefits of succeeding. This is almost identical to the results Gallup found when it asked this same question in December 2006.

Views on this question, like most attitudes toward the war, vary greatly by party affiliation. A majority of Republicans, 57%, agree with the administration and say that the benefits of success outweigh the costs, while 39% say the costs outweigh the benefits. Only 9% of Democrats say the benefits outweigh the costs, while the vast majority, 85%, say the costs outweigh the benefits. Most independents say the costs outweigh the benefits. These results are quite similar to the December 2006 poll.

Mistake to Send Troops to Iraq?

One of Gallup's longest-running trend measures regarding the Iraq War is a simple question asking if the United States "made a mistake in sending troops to Iraq" or not. The January 12–14 update on this question finds that the events of the past week have had almost no change on this measure. Fifty-eight percent of Americans say it was a mistake to send troops to Iraq, while 41% say it was not. Prior to the president's speech on Iraq, 57% of Americans said it was a mistake to send troops to Iraq, and 41% said it was not a mistake.

From a long-term perspective, Americans have grown more and more negative about the war in Iraq each year since it began. In 2003, an average of only 32% of Americans said it was a mistake to send troops to Iraq. This average jumped to 46% in 2004, to 51% in 2005, and to 55% in 2006. The average for the two polls conducted so far this year is slightly higher at 58%.

JANUARY 17

Public's Perceptions About Iraq Keeping Down Bush's Job Approval Rating

President George W. Bush's latest job approval rating from the American people remains about where it stood a week earlier—notable because it means his recent televised national address about Iraq on January 10 did nothing to repair his public image. Bush's approval rating for his handling of Iraq specifically is even lower, something that appears to be preventing Bush from getting a broader benefit from the fact that Americans have grown a bit more favorable about his handling of the economy and about economic conditions more generally.

Where's the Traction?

According to the latest USA Today/Gallup Poll, conducted between January 12 and January 14, 2007, 34% of Americans approve of the job Bush is doing, while 63% disapprove. This is similar to the 37% approve–59% disapprove ratings he received in Gallup's January 5–7, 2007, survey. Not only is Bush's overall job approval rating holding steady, but public approval of his handling of Iraq is unchanged. Today, 28% approve of Bush's handling of the situation in Iraq, similar to the 26% found in the last poll. Seven in 10 Americans disapprove of how Bush is handling the Iraq situation.

The latest poll updates Bush's job performance in three additional areas: foreign affairs, the economy, and terrorism. Bush receives his best reviews on terrorism and the economy, for which he receives 46% and 45% approval, respectively. Still, a majority of Americans disapprove of Bush's handling of these issues. Approval of Bush's han-

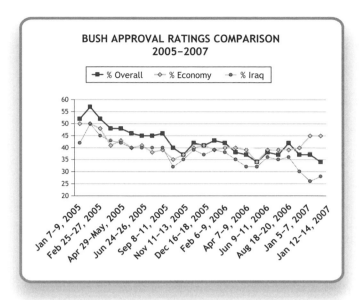

BUSH APPROVAL RATINGS COMPARISON 2005–2007

dling of foreign affairs, at 36%, is similar to his overall job approval rating, while approval of his handling of the situation in Iraq is lower (28%).

Iraq and Economy Ratings Take Different Paths

Gallup's trends for these measures reveal a notable shift in the past several months. For at least the past two years, going back to January 2005, changes in public approval of Bush on the economy and on Iraq closely paralleled changes in his overall approval ratings. However, since late August 2006, Bush's approval rating on the economy has improved slightly—from 39% to 45%—while his overall job approval and Iraq ratings have each declined by eight points. Bush's approval rating on Iraq has fallen

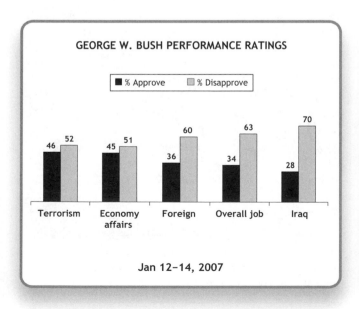

GEORGE W. BUSH PERFORMANCE RATINGS

Jan 12–14, 2007

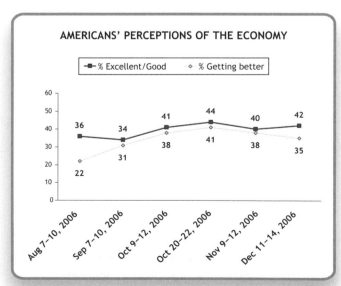

AMERICANS' PERCEPTIONS OF THE ECONOMY

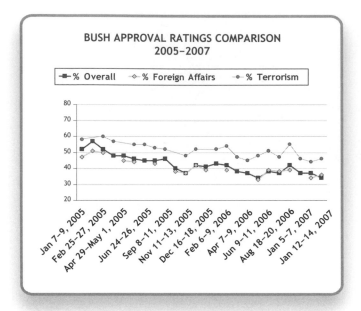

BUSH APPROVAL RATINGS COMPARISON 2005–2007

- % Overall
- % Foreign Affairs
- % Terrorism

from 36% to 28%, and his overall approval rating has fallen from 42% to 34%.

This divergence clearly suggests that Americans' recent evaluations of Bush's overall job performance are now tied more closely to public perceptions about Iraq than to their perceptions of how he is handling the economy. The recent improvement in Bush's economic score is also seen in Gallup's monthly consumer confidence trends, last updated in early December 2006. Between August and December, the percentage of Americans describing economic conditions as "excellent" or "good" rose from 36% to 42%, and the percentage perceiving the economy getting better rose from 22% to 35%.

Nevertheless, Gallup trends show a slight decline in Bush's average monthly overall job approval rating during this period, from 40% in August 2006 and 42% in September 2006 to the 36%–37% range from October 2006 through this month. In contrast to the divergence seen with respect to Bush's handling of the economy, the correlations between the president's overall job approval rating and his approval ratings for foreign affairs and terrorism have remained fairly consistent during the past two years, with all three measures following similar paths.

JANUARY 18

Clinton Remains the Front-Runner Among Democrats

Although the first primaries and caucuses of the 2008 presidential race are still one year away, there has already been a great deal of focus on the election. Several candidates have formally declared their candidacies. Others

have informally indicated that they are likely to be candidates, while still others have set up exploratory committees to help them decide or have already announced that they are not running. News media outlets have planned presidential debates in key primary states as early as March 2007.

Poll results at this point in the race have the great virtue of measuring the inevitable surges in support for various candidates as they enter and leave the race, and as they labor to develop their images and issue positioning in the minds of voters. At the same time, poll results at this point will most likely change—and change significantly—as things happen during candidates' campaigns, and as the field is narrowed during the primary season. As a point of reference, Bill Clinton was in eleventh place among Democratic candidates in a February 1991 poll of Democrats; a little more than a year later he had zoomed to the top of the list. On the other hand, at a similar period in the presidential election cycle, George W. Bush had a commanding lead in Republican polls in late 1998 and early 1999 before winning his party's 2000 presidential nomination. That said, the most recent USA Today/Gallup Poll, conducted between January 12 and January 14, 2007, shows that a pattern of early front-runners is evident in both major parties.

One week after announcing her presidential candidacy, Senator Hillary Clinton speaks in Davenport, Iowa, on January 28, 2007. *(Steve Pope/Landov)*

Democratic Trial Heat

On the Democratic side, New York senator Hillary Clinton remains the clear leader, as she has been in every poll of Democrats that Gallup has conducted since early 2005. Illinois senator Barack Obama is in second place, followed by three other candidates: former senator and 2004 vice presidential candidate John Edwards, former vice president and 2000 presidential candidate Al Gore, and Massachusetts senator and 2004 presidential candidate John Kerry.

The most recent poll was conducted a few days before Obama's January 16 announcement of the formation of his presidential exploratory committee, and shows little change in his positioning compared with the last two polls of 2006. The January poll, which came after the formal announcement of Edwards's candidacy between Christmas and New Year's, does show a slight uptick in Obama's Democratic support. It is possible that support for Obama may increase now that his candidacy appears more certain. At the same time, of course, it is likely that Clinton will announce her candidacy within the next month or two, which could affect *her* positioning. In short, there is still a great deal of potential flux in the standings of these candidates as 2007 unfolds. In order to gain a better understanding of the positioning of the major candidates among Democrats, Gallup combined the results of the most recent three trial heat polls conducted in November, December, and January. This created an aggregated sample of 1,629 Democrats and Democratic leaners. (It should be noted that the precise list of candidates included in each of the three polls differed slightly, which could affect the results.)

IDEOLOGY

The biggest difference across the three major ideological categories—conservative, moderate, and liberal—comes in the vote for Obama, whose percentage of the vote varies from 13% among conservative Democrats to 23% among liberal Democrats. There is little difference across these categories in the vote for Clinton or Edwards.

GENDER

The only gender gap in voter preferences for the major Democratic candidates relates to Clinton, who receives 35% of the vote of female Democrats compared with 26% of the vote of male Democrats.

REPUBLICAN CANDIDATES

Arizona senator John McCain and former New York mayor Rudolph Giuliani remain the two front-runners among Republicans, substantially ahead of any other contenders. Far below these two are former speaker of the House Newt Gingrich and former Massachusetts governor Mitt Romney.

There have been slight fluctuations in the precise level of support given to McCain and Giuliani by Republicans across the last several months, but all of these changes are within the margin of error. There is a great deal of interest in the relative positioning of McCain, given his outspoken support for an increase in troop levels in Iraq. (Giuliani has also supported Bush's recent announcement of a surge.) But as of the dates of this poll, there is no significant change from previous polls in the level of support among Republicans for McCain's candidacy.

Republican Presidential Hopefuls

Gallup recently asked Americans what comes to mind when they reflect on three of the dominant Republican names in the early talk about the 2008 presidential election: Arizona Senator John McCain, former New York Mayor Rudolph Giuliani, and former Massachusetts Governor Mitt Romney. The answers yield mostly positive commentary about McCain and Giuliani—praise for virtuous character, strong leadership, experience, and electability—but relatively little of substance about Romney.

The summary of verbatim responses based on the total sample is remarkably similar to that of Americans who are most relevant to the political futures of these candidates: Republicans (including independents who lean toward the Republican Party). Republicans are slightly less likely than the general public to say something positive when reflecting on McCain (50% of Republicans vs. 55% of national adults) and slightly more likely to say something positive about Giuliani (55% vs. 50%) and Romney (13% vs. 7%)—but these differences are only slight.

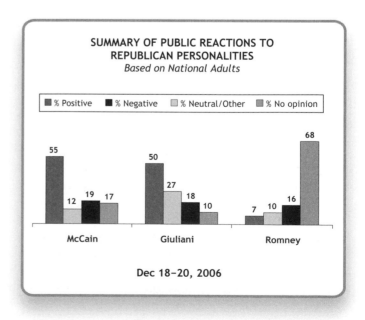

SUMMARY OF PUBLIC REACTIONS TO REPUBLICAN PERSONALITIES
Based on National Adults

■ % Positive   ■ % Negative   □ % Neutral/Other   ■ % No opinion

	McCain	Giuliani	Romney
% Positive	55	50	7
% Neutral/Other	12	27	10
% Negative	19	18	16
% No opinion	17	10	68

Dec 18–20, 2006

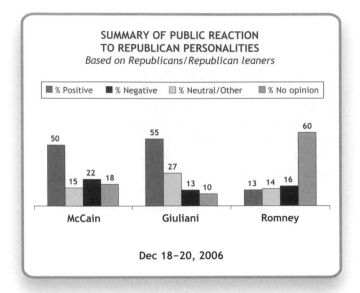

SUMMARY OF PUBLIC REACTION
TO REPUBLICAN PERSONALITIES
Based on Republicans/Republican leaners

■ % Positive   ■ % Negative   ☐ % Neutral/Other   ■ % No opinion

McCain: 50, 15, 22, 18
Giuliani: 55, 27, 13, 10
Romney: 13, 14, 16, 60

Dec 18–20, 2006

McCain and Giuliani Spark Positive Reactions

McCain and Giuliani are running neck and neck at the front of the pack of Republican candidates who are exploring a run for president. According to the January 12–14, 2007, poll, in Gallup's latest trial heat for the 2008 Republican primary, 31% of Republicans say they favor Giuliani and 27% favor McCain. The two are also about evenly matched in terms of the public reactions they provoke.

In answer to Gallup's "What comes to mind" question, the first thing a majority of Americans articulate regarding each of them—59% for McCain and 54% for Giuliani— is generally positive in nature: "He's a good candidate and should run"; "I like him"; "He did a good job after 9/11" (for Giuliani); "He has a good military background" (for McCain). Relatively few Americans (just under 20%) have negative things to say—including criticisms of their character, their politics, or their electability—as their first reaction to either man.

McCain Details

The top three statements made about McCain in the December poll are all positive: He is a good candidate/ He should run (15%); He has a good military background (11%); He is a good man/I like him (11%). Other positive comments are that he has a good track record (5%), is an honorable/trustworthy man (4%), is the best Republican for the job (3%), is okay/all right (3%), has strong beliefs (2%), is experienced (2%), is fair-minded (2%), and has a positive outlook (1%). The most prevalent negative comment is that he is not electable, mentioned by 5% of Americans. Four percent each say he is "wishy-washy" or changes his mind

too much and that they don't like him. Other negatives are that he is too old (2%) or too liberal (2%), his time has passed (1%), he has been disappointing lately (1%), and he is "hotheaded" (1%).

Giuliani Details

The top three statements made about Giuliani are also generally positive: I like him/He is a good guy (13%); The 9/11 terrorist attacks/He did a good job after 9/11 (12%); He is a good candidate/He should run (10%). Some of those mentioning 9/11 do so in a simply factual way, but most also praise his handling of the crisis. Other positive comments about Giuliani are that he has good leadership qualities (6%), is "strong" or "a fighter" (4%), is okay/all right (2%), is honest (2%), has a positive outlook (2%), is qualified (1%), is experienced (1%), and is the Republicans' best choice for president in 2008 (1%).

Negatives about Giuliani are led by the statement that he shouldn't run (6%). Additionally, 4% say they don't like him, and 2% each say he is not qualified, they don't trust him, and he is phony or a "publicity hound." One percent each

At a Senate hearing on global warming on January 30, 2007, Senator John McCain (left) greets Senator Barack Obama (right). *(Chuck Kennedy/Newscom)*

cite his family life including that he was an "adulterer," that he is too liberal, and that he is "overrated." An additional 14% of Americans mention that he was mayor of New York. This is categorized as a neutral comment, as most of these responses merely state this as a fact. Some, however, also mention positive or negative aspects of his role as mayor (about equal numbers for each).

"What's a Romney?"

Romney announced his exploratory committee for president on January 3, 2007, the day before his term as governor expired. He has attracted considerable media buzz through his prominence within Republican political circles and some early fund-raising success. Still, Romney has an extremely low profile with the general public. He garners only 7% support for the Republican nomination in Gallup's latest trial heat. And when asked what his name conjures up in their minds, nearly 7 in 10 Americans can't think of anything. Less than a third of Americans offer a substantive comment about Romney, of whom about half (16%) say something negative and only 7% say something positive.

JANUARY 22
Americans Remain Disgruntled with Nation's Direction

President George W. Bush can be expected to put the best possible face on the country's affairs in his State of the Union speech on January 27—a speech White House press secretary Tony Snow has intimated will not be "typical" in its style. It's unlikely that Bush will admonish the American people for their pessimism with a Jimmy Carter–like "malaise" speech. More likely, he will try to convey a Reaganesque vision of optimism for the country, intended to inspire Americans. Nevertheless, Bush will face an audience in the American public that is firmly dissatisfied with the way things are going in the country and has not been convinced otherwise for the last several years.

According to Gallup's monthly measure of public satisfaction, updated between January 15 and January 18, 2007, only 35% of Americans today are satisfied with the way things are going in the country; 63% are dissatisfied. Positive sentiments are up slightly from the 30% who were satisfied in December. The satisfaction average for all of 2006 was 31%. Still, a majority of Americans have not expressed being satisfied with the direction of the country since January 2004. Except for a brief period following the 2001 terrorist attacks, when Americans expressed elevated levels of satisfaction as part of the broader "rally around the flag" effect triggered by 9/11, public satisfac-

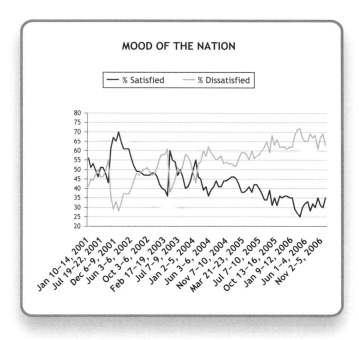

tion with the country has been depressed for most of Bush's presidency.

Iraq and the Economy Are Both Factors

Americans' satisfaction with the country today is highly correlated with how they feel about the Iraq War. According to the latest poll, two-thirds of those who say they favor the war also say they are satisfied with the country's direction. Conversely, the vast majority of those who oppose the war (82%) say they are dissatisfied with the country's direction.

Iraq does not appear to be the sole reason for public dissatisfaction, however. The correlations are just as strong between economic attitudes and satisfaction with the country. Two-thirds (67%) of those whose economic

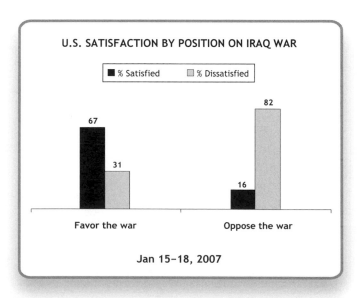

U.S. SATISFACTION BY ECONOMIC OUTLOOK

Jan 15–18, 2007

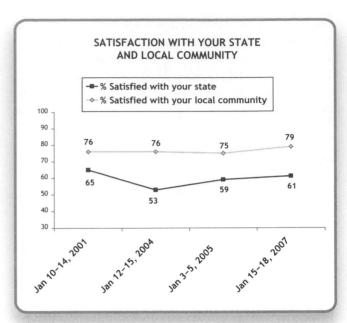

SATISFACTION WITH YOUR STATE AND LOCAL COMMUNITY

outlook is positive are satisfied with the direction of the country, while more than four in five (86%) of those with a negative economic outlook are dissatisfied.

Perhaps more fundamentally, satisfaction is a highly partisan measure these days. Republicans are largely satisfied with the way things are going, while most Democrats are dissatisfied. Political independents fall closer to Democrats in their attitudes; two-thirds of independents are dissatisfied.

The Local View Is Better

The state of affairs looks much brighter to Americans as their focus turns more local. A solid majority—61%—say they are satisfied with conditions in their state; even more—79%—are satisfied with the way things are going in their local community. These attitudes are generally similar to previous readings from 2001, 2004, and 2005.

Satisfaction with affairs at the state level has been fairly constant over the past few years in the Midwest and South. Satisfaction was quite low in the West in January 2004, which Gallup analysts at the time attributed to the broad dissatisfaction in California left over after the recall of Governor Gray Davis a few months earlier. Since then, satisfaction in the West has been on a par with that in the rest of the country. Satisfaction in the East tended to be lower in 2004 and 2005 but is now similar to the national average. Attitudes about affairs at the state level are much less partisan than they are nationally, with only a nine-point difference in satisfaction (69% vs. 60%) between Republicans and Democrats.

State-level satisfaction is somewhat more likely to be tied to people's economic perceptions than it is to party identification, but still not to the same degree as seen with respect to U.S. satisfaction.

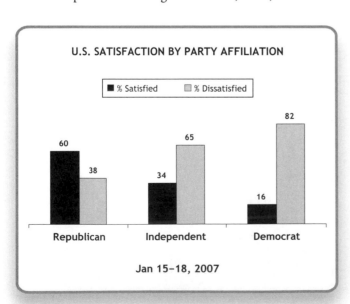

U.S. SATISFACTION BY PARTY AFFILIATION

Jan 15–18, 2007

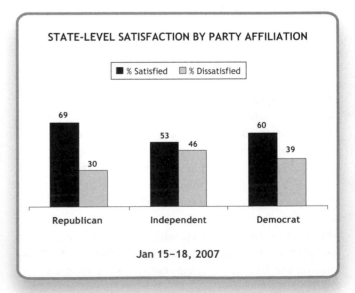

STATE-LEVEL SATISFACTION BY PARTY AFFILIATION

Jan 15–18, 2007

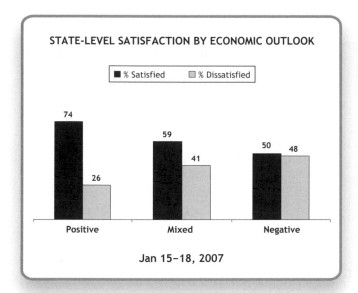

STATE-LEVEL SATISFACTION BY ECONOMIC OUTLOOK

Jan 15–18, 2007

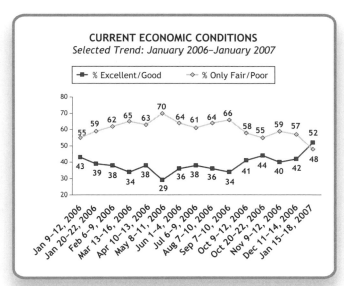

CURRENT ECONOMIC CONDITIONS
Selected Trend: January 2006–January 2007

In contrast with the modest variations seen at the state level, public perceptions of the direction of things in their local communities are uniformly positive, with two-thirds or more of most demographic, political, and regional groups saying they are satisfied.

Americans' Assessments of Economic Conditions Improve Markedly

Gallup's January read on Americans' attitudes about the U.S. economy shows a significant uptick in the assessment of current economic conditions and a modest increase in the view that now is a good time to find a quality job. Both of these measures are now at their highest points since the earliest stages of the Bush presidency. At the same time, a slight majority of Americans continue to say that economic conditions in this country are getting worse. This measure of economic expectations—unlike the assessment of current economic conditions—is little changed from the last several months.

RATINGS OF THE CURRENT ECONOMY

Gallup's January 15–18 update on Americans' views of current economic conditions in the United States shows that 52% rate the economy as excellent or good, 33% rate it as only fair, and 15% rate it as poor.

This reading marks a significant increase in positive perceptions from Gallup's December poll, when just 42% rated the economy as excellent or good. In fact, this assessment is the highest (based on the percentage of Americans rating the economy as excellent or good) since January 2001, which marked the last strongly positive rating at the tail end of the "dot-com" boom. What's behind this significant increase in positive assessments of the

economy? An analysis of trends from the last five months, broken out by party identification, shows an increase in positive perceptions among all three partisan groups, albeit slightly more so among Democrats. Still, a wide gulf remains between the rosy view of Republicans, among whom 78% rate the economy as excellent or good, and Democrats, among whom only 35% rate the economy in one of these two categories.

DIRECTION OF THE ECONOMY

Slightly more than half of Americans, 53%, continue to say the U.S. economy is getting worse, while 38% say it is getting better.

These views of the economy's direction are statistically unchanged from December and are little changed since October. There have been numerous occasions over the past six years in which the assessment of the economy's

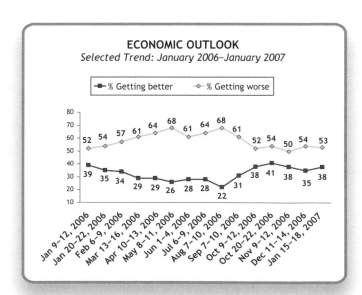

ECONOMIC OUTLOOK
Selected Trend: January 2006–January 2007

Is now a good or bad time to find a quality job?
Selected Trend: January 2006–January 2007

direction has been more positive, including in particular a stretch of time in late 2003 and early 2004, when the percentage saying the economy was getting better was consistently higher than the percentage saying the economy was getting worse. Republicans became slightly more positive about the direction of the economy this month than they were in December, but Democrats' and independents' assessments changed little.

THE JOB MARKET

For the first time since Gallup began assessing Americans' views of the job market in August 2001, more Americans say now is a good time to find a quality job than say it is

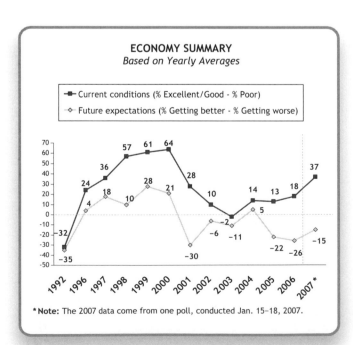

ECONOMY SUMMARY
Based on Yearly Averages

*Note: The 2007 data come from one poll, conducted Jan. 15–18, 2007.

a bad time, by a one-point margin (48% to 47%). This job situation measure has been trending upward. Last month, 44% said it was a good time to find a quality job, while 50% said it was not. The low point on this measure since 2001 came in March 2003, when only 16% of Americans said it was a good time to find a quality job.

Americans' Seemingly Conflicting Assessments of Economic Conditions

For a while now, many economic commentators, as well as Republican stalwarts, have been perplexed by Americans' entrenched negativity toward the U.S. economy, at a time when the stock market is breaking records and unemployment is down. These data on Americans' assessments of current economic conditions reflect what to some people would be an expected uptick in views of the economy. That these data reflect the most positive assessment of the economy since George W. Bush took office in theory represents a major plus for the current administration, which has been touting the improved economy for many months.

It is not entirely clear, however, why Americans would become more positive about current economic conditions while at the same time remaining negative about the overall direction of the economy. In fact, the trend for 2005 and 2006, and now this first reading of 2007, shows a lack of correlation between these two measures, with the current assessment measure staying stable or (in the most recent poll) increasing, while views of the overall future direction of the economy have become more negative.

It is possible that the effect of more positive economic news is felt first in the estimate of current conditions, while Americans are taking longer to reconsider their feelings about longer-term trends—perceptions that would be less susceptible to short-term economic news. It will be important to monitor these measures in the coming months to see whether the expectations measure "catches up" with assessments of the current economy.

JANUARY 24

Clinton's Liabilities: Electability or Likability?

New York senator Hillary Rodham Clinton ended the speculation about when she would step into the race for president—few doubted it would happen—on January 20 by announcing her exploratory committee on her new HillaryClinton.com Web site. This has only fueled the already rampant political discussion about all the reasons Clinton may not succeed in capturing her party's nomination. The theories range from her vote in October 2002 to authorize the Iraq War to the association of her candidacy with

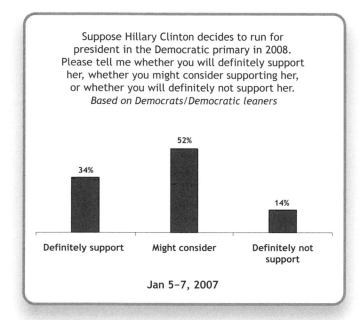

Suppose Hillary Clinton decides to run for president in the Democratic primary in 2008. Please tell me whether you will definitely support her, whether you might consider supporting her, or whether you will definitely not support her.
Based on Democrats/Democratic leaners

Jan 5–7, 2007

her husband, former president Bill Clinton, to her inability to connect with voters on a personal level. A recent USA Today/Gallup Poll suggests that all of these, and more, are factors, but that the paramount ones are her perceived chances of winning in the general election, along with her issue positions. Contrary to the conventional wisdom about the liability of her support for the Iraq War among liberals, Clinton's issue positions are more often raised as a concern by conservative and moderate Democrats than by liberal Democrats.

Clinton's Core Support Hovers Around a Third of Democrats

While most Democrats would likely back Clinton should she win the 2008 Democratic presidential nomination, only about one-third give their unreserved support to her candidacy today. According to a January 5–7, 2007, USA Today/Gallup Poll, only 34% of Democrats and independents who lean to the Democratic Party say they will definitely support Clinton for the nomination. An additional 52% of Democrats say they might consider supporting Clinton, suggesting that she has a pool of as many as 86% of Democrats from which to draw votes. Only 14% rule out supporting her.

The 34% of Democrats saying they would definitely support Clinton for the nomination is close to the 29% who favor her when asked to choose among twelve Democrats listed as possibly running for the nomination. This is according to the latest USA Today/Gallup test election, conducted between January 12 and January 14, 2007. Illinois senator Barack Obama ranks second, with 18%, fol-

lowed by former North Carolina senator John Edwards, at 13%. However, when Democrats are asked whom they would prefer to see win if the race narrows to just Clinton and Obama, only a bare majority (53%) choose Clinton. About 4 out of 10 (39%) prefer Obama, while the remaining 8% are undecided.

Clinton's "I'm In" Launches Media Rush to Judgment

Much of the political analysis surrounding Clinton's announcement—"I'm in"—has been focused on the negative factors that might derail her candidacy in the primaries. One prominent theory is that Democratic voters perceive that Clinton has an electability problem with the general public. Voters may believe she has too many detractors outside of her own party to be a strong presidential candidate.

An editorial in the January 22 *Washington Post* summarized the buzz around this issue by asking, "Is she such a polarizing figure, with such high negatives, that she would be at a disadvantage in the fall campaign?" Gallup's January 5–7, 2007, poll probed Democrats who were not confirmed Clinton supporters about their reasons. Those saying they only might support her for the nomination or would definitely not support her were asked to rate the importance of five different factors as potential grounds for their reluctance. None of the five factors emerges as an overwhelming basis for Democratic aversion to Clinton. On a relative basis, however, her perceived electability is a primary concern. Of Democrats asked the question, 29% say their belief that she cannot win the presidential election is a major reason why they do not definitely support her today. Another 32% say this is a minor reason. Nearly as prominent an explanation is her stand on issues. About a quarter (26%) of non-core Clinton supporters say the fact that they do not agree with her on the issues is a major reason for their reluctance to support her; another 34% say this is a minor reason. Far fewer Democrats in this group cite Clinton's ability to win the Democratic nomination as a major reason (16%) for not fully supporting her at this time. Even fewer cite disliking her personality (11%) or being opposed to sending another Clinton to the White House (10%) as major reasons.

Most Liberals Don't Reject Clinton Based on "the Issues"

Clinton's support for the Iraq War—she voted for the Iraq War resolution, giving President Bush the authority to send troops, in October 2002—has been widely discussed as a potential liability for her with Democrats. However, according to the January 5–7 poll, it is conservative and

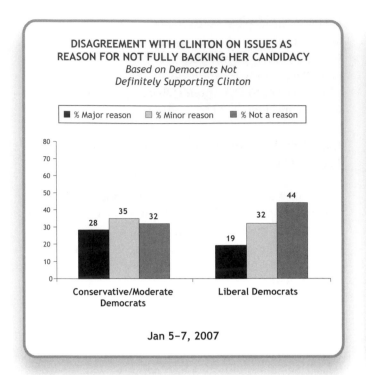

DISAGREEMENT WITH CLINTON ON ISSUES AS
REASON FOR NOT FULLY BACKING HER CANDIDACY
*Based on Democrats Not
Definitely Supporting Clinton*

Jan 5–7, 2007

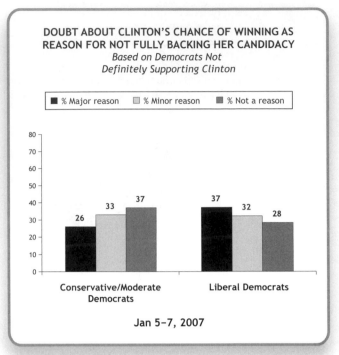

DOUBT ABOUT CLINTON'S CHANCE OF WINNING AS
REASON FOR NOT FULLY BACKING HER CANDIDACY
*Based on Democrats Not
Definitely Supporting Clinton*

Jan 5–7, 2007

moderate Democrats who are most likely to cite disagreement with Clinton over "the issues" as a reason they don't fully back her. Liberals (who tend to be the most opposed to the war) are less likely to give this as a major reason.

Liberals Especially Anxious for a White House Win?

Clinton-averse liberals are much more likely to focus on her electability as their primary concern. Thirty-seven percent of liberal Democrats, compared with 26% of conservative and moderate Democrats, say their doubts about her ability to win the general election are a major reason they don't fully support her. This could conceivably inflate the importance of the electability factor for Clinton if the views of liberal Democrats are disproportionately represented in the primary process next year owing to higher turnout.

Profile of Clinton's Core Supporters

More generally, support for Clinton's candidacy among Democrats comes about equally from conservative/moderate and liberal Democrats: The percentages saying they would definitely vote for her in the primaries are 32% and 38%, respectively. Women are more likely to support her than are men, 37% vs. 29%. Clinton performs best among low-income Democrats: Forty-nine percent of those earning under $30,000 would definitely support her, compared with 30% of those making $30,000 to $74,999 and 26% of those making $75,000 or more. She also receives nearly

twice as much support from nonwhites as from whites, 50% vs. 28%.

JANUARY 25
Americans Troubled by Little Beyond Iraq

If it weren't for the Iraq issue, one might think Americans consider the state of the country today fairly comfortable; only Iraq stands out as a significant concern in Gallup's latest monthly reading of the "most important problem" facing the country. This continues the pattern seen for the last five months, after concerns about immigration and fuel prices in the first half of 2006 largely waned. According to Gallup's January 15–18, 2007, survey, conducted prior to President George W. Bush's State of the Union address on January 27, 36% of Americans cite Iraq as the nation's top problem. No other single issue is mentioned by more than 8% of Americans this month, although all economic issues combined (including the economy in general, unemployment, and taxes) are mentioned by a total of 17% of the public. Additionally, immigration, terrorism, and education are each mentioned by 6%. Unemployment, poverty, and ethical matters each registers 5%.

Gallup's historical trends regarding the country's most important problem show that it is unusual for public concerns to be spread so thinly across a wide number of issues as they are now, with only one issue garnering a substantial number of mentions. This month's results are highly similar to those from November and December 2006. The only exception is the specific category "the economy," which has declined as a concern. After being consistently mentioned by 8% to 11% of Americans from November 2005 through November 2006, it fell to 5% in December 2006 and 4% in the latest poll. All of this belies the fact that the great majority of Americans (63%) are dissatisfied with the way things are going in the country today; only 35% are satisfied. While no single issue is a top concern to the majority of Americans, many Americans (particularly Democrats and independents) may simply be riled by whatever issue they do view as paramount. Also, while only 36% of Americans mention the war in Iraq as a top problem, 6 out of 10 (61%) oppose it.

A Run at the Top

January 2007 represents the 34th consecutive month in which Iraq has held the top spot on Gallup's most-important-problem measure, starting with April 2004. Iraq was also the top-mentioned problem at the start of the war, in 2003. In between, the economy ranked number 1. The record-high response to "most important problem" facing the nation came in October 1978, when 83% of Americans cited "inflation." Just 1% mention this issue today. The second highest response was in October 1945, when 77% cited "unemployment," which 5% cite as an issue today. The 36% mentioning Iraq today matches November 2006 for the highest percentage the Iraq War has registered on this question since 2003. However, it is still much lower than the percentages of Americans citing the Vietnam War at the height of public concern about that conflict, which peaked at 55% in January 1967. Readings of greater than 40% were routine in the early years of the Vietnam War.

Some Historical Context

Gallup has been asking the most important problem question since 1939. The trends show much higher percentages of Americans in the past citing domestic issues that barely occur to Americans as top problems today. For instance, the 8% mentioning healthcare today is nearly a quarter of the percentage (31%) citing this issue in January 1994. The 6% mentioning terrorism today is only a fraction of the 46% citing it in the first month after the 9/11 terrorist attacks. The price of gas, currently at 1% as a concern, has nearly been erased as a top concern since it peaked at 22% last May. Many other issues that currently register minimal public concern—including crime, drugs, unemployment, inflation, racism, and the environment—have each had their day as a dominant problem in the minds of Americans over the past two-thirds of a century.

Presidential Speech Could Have Changed Attitudes

Had President Bush used his 2007 State of the Union speech as an opportunity to rally public concern around a specific issue or two—such as he attempted with Social Security in 2005 and as former President Bill Clinton did with crime and healthcare in 1994—one could have expected to see mentions of those issues rise in public perceptions of the nation's most important problem. In 1994, Gallup recorded a 12-percentage-point increase in mentions of crime as the most important problem within a week of Clinton's State of the Union speech and an 11-point increase in mentions of healthcare. At the same time, there were only minimal changes in other issues. Gallup's surveys several weeks before and after Bush's 2005 State of the Union address found a more than doubling of mentions of Social Security/Medicare as the nation's top problem, from 5% to 13%. In his 2007 State of the Union speech, Bush touched on new solutions to the nation's problems in the areas of education, Social Security, healthcare, immigration, energy, and criminal justice. However, he spent even more time discussing the Iraq War than on all of these issues combined. Clearly, his goal was to raise public confidence in his handling of that issue. As a result, it is unlikely that the speech prompted any significant shifts in Americans' perceptions about the nation's broader roster of problems. Next month's Gallup "most important problem" update will help to confirm that.

Majority of War Opponents Question Its Underlying Rationale

The small group of Americans who favor the war in Iraq generally explain their position by echoing the administration's view that it is part of the war on terror. Those who

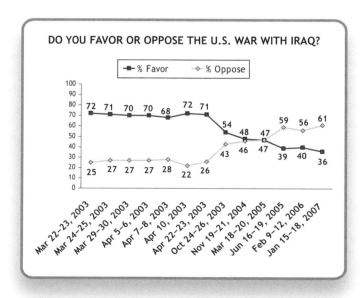

DO YOU FAVOR OR OPPOSE THE U.S. WAR WITH IRAQ?

oppose the war question the initial rationale for going to war and express concern over the war's costs. The most recent Gallup Poll, conducted between January 15 and January 18, 2007, asked Americans if they favored or opposed the war with Iraq, and it then followed up with a question asking them to explain their position in their own words.

The basic data reflect the findings of many other recent surveys: Support for the war in Iraq is at its lowest point since the war began in March 2003.

Why Do Some Americans Favor the War?

Those who favor the war were asked to give their one or two most important reasons. The resulting answers were coded into categories, which grouped similar responses. These responses in general mirror the rationale for the war advanced by the Bush administration. Americans who support the war are most likely to explain their position not by references to the value of the war for the Iraqi people themselves, but in terms of broader concerns—such as the war on terror and keeping the United States safe and secure. More specifically, about 65% of the responses can be categorized as explanations focused on the value of the war in terms of broader considerations outside of Iraq: We need to put a stop to terrorists/terrorism because of 9/11 (34%); We need to help stabilize that region/for safety (13%); To keep our nation safe and secure (12%); To keep the fighting over there and not in the United States (6%). A much smaller percentage, about 30%, of explanations for support of the war can be categorized as ones that focus on the value of the war for the Iraqi people.

Reasons for Opposing the War

The 61% of Americans who oppose the war in Iraq were also asked to explain their position in their own words.

There are two major categories of explanations for opposition to the war in Iraq: the underlying or basic rationale for the United States' being there to begin with and the costs of the war. The most frequently occurring reason given for opposition to the war—mentioned by 67% of those who oppose it—centers on the perception that the initial justification for going to war—that Iraq possessed weapons of mass destruction—was unsound, unjustified, and based on false pretenses. There are no great surprises in the data gathered from the 36% of Americans who support the war in Iraq. These individuals, most of whom identify themselves as Republicans, tend to mirror the administration's position by talking about the value of the war for the United States and other countries in the long term—including the perceived relationship between the war in Iraq and the war on terror—rather than the value of helping the Iraqi people. Less than a third of those who support the war justify that position in terms of its benefit for the Iraqi people.

The reasons given by those who oppose the war are strikingly different from the way the administration has characterized opposition to the war. President Bush, national security adviser Stephen Hadley, and press secretary Tony Snow primarily talk about opposition to the war as based on concern that it is not proceeding well, that progress has been slow, and that the way to victory has not been made clear. These characterizations of opposition to the war implicitly assume that the basic rationale for the war is not being debated—only its progress is. The responses reviewed in this analysis, however, show that opposition to the war is first and foremost based not on its execution but on the underlying reasons for being there in the first place.

FEBRUARY 2007

Throughout February 2007, the potential Republican and Democratic 2008 presidential candidates dominated the media, along with the ongoing Iraq War and other tensions in the Middle East. No candidate drew more coverage than New York senator Hillary Clinton. Although greeted warmly throughout her opening campaign tour, she was repeatedly asked by skeptical voters about her 2002 vote authorizing the use of force in Iraq. Clinton took full responsibility for her vote but said that she would not vote for military action in Iraq again and quickly framed Iraq as "President Bush's war." Her refusal to use categorical phrases, such as "I'm sorry" or "I made a mistake," opened her to criticism, especially from two of her leading Democratic opponents, Illinois senator Barack Obama and former North Carolina senator John Edwards.

Iraq continued to dominate the national news. On February 11, after weeks of internal debate, senior U.S. military officials announced that Iran was supplying Shiite groups in Iraq with sophisticated lethal weapons. Senator John D. Rockefeller (D.-W.V.), the chair of the Senate Intelligence Committee, added that he believed Iranian operatives inside Iraq were training Shiite militias and working against American troops. He also asserted that the White House had a poor understanding of Iranian calculations, and he was concerned that the Bush administration was building a confrontational case against the Tehran government. In a February 1–4, 2007, Gallup survey, 65% responded that Iran was "vitally important" to the United States today, while 22% considered it "important, but not vital."

During February, Gallup released its annual World Affairs Poll. The results found that Republicans and Democrats differ in their overall views of many nations around the world. Republicans, including independents who lean toward the Republican Party, are much more likely than Democrats, including Democratic-leaning independents, to favorably rate Israel (73% vs. 58%), Afghanistan (30% vs. 19%), and Iraq (21% vs. 11%), while Democrats are much more positive about France (69% vs. 40%), Venezuela (47% vs. 33%), and Mexico (65% vs. 45%). Republicans' ratings of Iraq and Afghanistan have declined over the past year, and their ratings of Mexico have been lower over the past two years than at any other point since 2001. Ratings of France among Democrats are at their highest point since the Iraq War began, but are lower among Republicans in recent years and have been relatively steady.

Even though the two party groups differ in their views of several countries around the world, Republicans and Democrats generally tend to agree in their overall rankings of countries. Additionally, the vast majority of Republicans and Democrats have favorable opinions of Australia, Canada, and Britain, and most have negative views toward Iran and North Korea. There has been much controversy about the threats North Korea and Iran pose to the United States in regard to the development of nuclear weapons in these countries. Given the seriousness of the potential threat these countries pose, it is not surprising that Republicans' and Democrats' ratings of these two countries are fairly similar.

The latest poll finds Republicans rating Israel, Afghanistan, and Iraq more positively than do Democrats. But has this always been the case? The following is a detailed look at the trends in favorability ratings of these countries since 2001.

Israel: Republicans have consistently been more positive than Democrats in their overall opinion of Israel since 2001. The largest partisan difference over this period occurred in 2003, about a month prior to the start of the Iraq War. At that time, 78% of Republicans and 53% of Democrats rated Israel favorably, a gap of 25 percentage points. The latest poll finds only a 15-point gap, with ratings among Republicans at 73% and among Democrats at 58%.

CHRONOLOGY

FEBRUARY 2007

February 2   In a grim assessment of the planet, an international network of scientists concludes for the first time that global warming is "unequivocal" and that human activity is the main cause.

February 3   A mammoth truck bomb in Baghdad kills at least 130 people.

February 5   President Bush submits a $2.9 trillion budget to Congress that he claims will eliminate the federal deficit in five years without raising taxes.

February 5   Rudolph Giuliani, former mayor of New York City, files a "statement of candidacy" with the Federal Election Commission, the first step in seeking the Republican presidential nomination.

February 10   Senator Barack Obama of Illinois announces his candidacy for the Democratic presidential nomination.

February 11   Senior U.S. military officials announce that Iran supplies Shiite extremist groups in Iraq with lethal weapons.

February 13   Mitt Romney, former governor of Massachusetts, announces his candidacy for the Republican presidential nomination.

February 16   A sharply divided House of Representatives passes a nonbinding resolution critical of President Bush's decision to send more than 20,000 new combat troops to Iraq.

February 18   Car bombs kill more than 50 people in Baghdad.

February 21   Eight Democratic candidates appear in Carson City, Nevada, at the first Democratic forum of the 2008 presidential race.

February 21   British prime minister Tony Blair announces that up to 1,600 British troops—almost half of Britain's military strength in Iraq—will leave Iraq by the end of 2007.

February 23   Tom Vilsack withdraws from the race for the Democratic nomination for president.

February 24   Vice President Dick Cheney says that "all options are on the table" if Iran continues its nuclear program.

February 25   The film *An Inconvenient Truth*, starring Al Gore, wins the Academy Award for best documentary feature. The film strongly criticizes the Bush administration's policies on global warming.

February 26   A bomb in the Iraqi Ministry of Public Works kills five and injures the Iraqi vice president.

February 28   Senator John McCain of Arizona informally announces his candidacy for the Republican presidential nomination on *The Late Show with David Letterman*.

Afghanistan: Gallup found only slight variations in ratings of Afghanistan in 2002 and 2003 among Republicans and Democrats. Favorable ratings of the country increased among Republicans in 2004 but did not change among Democrats. In 2005, both Republicans' and Democrats' favorable views of Afghanistan reached their highest point, at 49% and 34% respectively, but since then views of the country have deteriorated among both groups.

Iraq: Few Americans—less than 10%—rated Iraq favorably prior to the start of the war in Iraq in March 2003. Then, after the war started, the percentage viewing Iraq favorably increased among both party groups, but much more so among Republicans. Favorable views of Iraq reached their highest point in 2005, with 41% of Republicans and 19% of Democrats holding favorable opinions of

the country. Both Republicans' and Democrats' ratings of Iraq have since declined.

Democrats are much more positive than Republicans in their views of France, Venezuela, and Mexico. Partisan ratings of France and Mexico show some changes in recent years.

France: Republicans' and Democrats' views of France were essentially no different in 2001 and 2002. Favorable views of France dropped substantially among both groups in early 2003, but much more so among Republicans than Democrats. Among Democrats, France's favorable ratings reached a low of 46% in mid-March 2003, while ratings dropped all the way to 20% among Republicans. Since then, ratings of France have improved among both groups, but Democrats still rate the country more favorably than do Republicans. The latest 69% favorable rating among Democrats is the highest Gallup has measured since the Iraq War started, though this is not a statistically significant increase from ratings in recent years.

Mexico: Gallup found essentially no difference between Republicans and Democrats in their ratings of Mexico from 2001 through 2003, and only modest variations in 2004 and 2005. Over the past two years, though, Republicans have become less likely to rate Mexico favorably. From 2001 through 2004, Republicans' favorable ratings of Mexico averaged 72%, while over the past two years, this average has only been 55%. Democrats' views of Mexico have been much more consistent over this period. Republicans' favorable views may have dropped because of their position on the immigration issue in recent years.

Gallup has asked Americans to rate Venezuela only once, that being in this latest poll. The partisan gap in opinions (33% of Republicans vs. 47% of Democrats) may be related to Venezuelan President Hugo Chavez's strong vocal opposition to President George W. Bush and his policies.

FEBRUARY 1

Giuliani, McCain Have Competing Strengths in Republicans' Eyes

A recent Gallup Poll shows former New York City mayor Rudolph Giuliani and Arizona senator John McCain the clear front-runners among the Republican Party's 2008 presidential hopefuls. In the most recent test of rank-and-file Republicans' presidential nomination preferences, 31% said they would be most likely to support Giuliani and 27% said McCain. When asked to choose between the two, Republicans show a slight preference for Giuliani at 50% to 42%.

The latest poll sought to explore Republicans' views of Giuliani and McCain in more depth, asking them to choose which candidate better exemplified certain personal or political characteristics as well as who would be better able to handle specific issues. The results show that Giuliani enjoys a remarkably strong image relative to McCain in terms of his likability. Nearly three-quarters of Republicans

After filing a "statement of candidacy" on February 5, 2007, former New York City mayor Rudolph Giuliani gestures to supporters at a rally in New York. *(Ed Betz/AP Images)*

say Giuliani is the more likable candidate; only 21% choose McCain. Additionally, Giuliani has wide leads over McCain with respect to handling crime, doing the better job in a crisis, uniting the country, understanding the problems of ordinary Americans, being the better public speaker, and being the stronger leader. McCain's strengths center on his handling of "moral values" issues, his ability to handle most foreign policy issues, and his ethical standards.

Giuliani is currently viewed as the candidate more likely to win the presidential election, though Republicans are divided as to which candidate has the better chance of winning the party's presidential nomination. People are also relatively closely divided in their assessment of whether McCain or Giuliani is more qualified to be president—though McCain has a slight edge in this regard.

Candidate Characteristics

The January 25–28, 2007, poll asked Republicans and independents who say they lean to the Republican Party to rate Giuliani versus McCain on each of 15 specific characteristics. Of the 15 characteristics tested, Giuliani is viewed as having a clear advantage on 10 items. McCain "wins" on only three dimensions, and the two candidates are essentially tied on the remaining two.

Giuliani's greatest strength in relation to McCain comes on the following dimensions on which he has at least a 20-point lead over the Arizona senator: Giuliani is perceived as more likable; better in a crisis; more able to unite the country; a better public speaker; better at understanding the problems faced by ordinary Americans; and as the stronger leader. Giuliani does better than McCain, albeit with a slightly smaller lead, on the following: He would perform better in the debates; would more effectively manage the government; has the better chance of beating the Democratic nominee in the 2008 presidential election; and would run the more positive campaign. The two candidates are essentially tied when it comes to who has the better chance of winning the Republican presidential nomination in 2008 and who would be respected more by leaders of other countries. Republicans give McCain the advantage on three characteristics: He is seen as having higher ethical standards; as able to work better with Congress; and as being more qualified to be president. Overall, Giuliani appears to be very well positioned against McCain on many relevant and important dimensions.

Significantly, of course, it is important to note that McCain is viewed by Republicans as more qualified to be president than Giuliani. His strength on working better with Congress undoubtedly flows from his experience as a United States representative from 1983 to 1986 and as a senator since 1987. His advantage with respect to ethical

standards may result both from his own background and from questions about Giuliani's business activities since the end of his mayoralty of New York City, as well as from the events surrounding Giuliani's recent divorce and remarriage. But Giuliani has many perceived strengths, and the distance between Giuliani and McCain on some of these dimensions is very large. For example, there is a 53-point gap in the percentage who consider the former New York City mayor "more likable" than McCain and a 37-point gap regarding who is "most likely to unite the country."

Candidates on the Issues

Giuliani has an advantage on six of the issues tested and McCain has an advantage on four. Giuliani's strengths are primarily in the area of domestic issues, while McCain leads on most international matters. Giuliani's biggest advantage is on crime, for which 78% of Republicans view him as better, compared with 17% who say McCain is. Giuliani, a federal prosecutor prior to being elected mayor of New York City, made crime prevention a focus during his administration, and crime rates in the city fell during his tenure. Giuliani is also viewed as better than McCain on the economy (52% to 38%), education (48% to 38%), healthcare (47% to 39%), and taxes (49% to 37%). The candidates are rated nearly equally on the environment and energy, with 44% saying McCain would do a better job and 43% Giuliani.

McCain, who has long supported an increased U.S. military presence in Iraq, is viewed by Republicans as better able to handle the situation in Iraq by a 53% to 40% margin over Giuliani. (Giuliani has supported recent calls for a troop increase in Iraq.) Republicans also give McCain a 54% to 37% edge on handling "relations with other countries." One international issue in Giuliani's favor is terrorism, on which he has a 53% to 41% edge over McCain. Giuliani's widely praised response to the terrorist attacks of September 11, 2001, while serving as mayor of New York City is the likely reason for this—and is enough to overcome the perhaps more general sense that McCain is better on international matters. McCain's biggest issue advantage is not on an international issue, but with respect to moral values. Fifty-eight percent of Republicans believe he would do the better job on this issue, while 30% believe Giuliani would. Giuliani's past positions in favor of both gay rights and a woman's right to choose an abortion are generally out of step with the views of most rank-and-file Republicans, while McCain's positions have generally been in keeping with the Republican platform.

Republicans' relative ratings of the candidates on the issues do not vary much by their religious commitment or self-described political ideology. As compared with the

Democrats, among whom New York senator Hillary Clinton is clearly the dominant candidate in terms of voter preferences, character dimensions, and issue positioning, the Republicans show more delineation between their leading candidates. Giuliani is viewed favorably by Republicans on key dimensions such as leadership, likability, and electability, while McCain has equally important strengths on foreign policy aptitude, moral values issues, and integrity. But Giuliani's advantages on his strongest issues and characteristics (61 points on crime, 53 points on likability, 40 points on handling a crisis) are much greater than McCain's (28 points on moral values, 15 points on ethical standards).

The poll provides insight into where the candidates stand among party members before campaigning kicks off in earnest: While both McCain and Giuliani have formed presidential candidate exploratory committees, neither has officially announced his candidacy. McCain would do well to emphasize his experience and foreign policy credentials while reminding Republican voters of his traditional views on moral values. For his part, Giuliani apparently would be well advised to remind the voters of his leadership of New York following the September 11 crisis while attempting to capitalize on his more favorable public image.

FEBRUARY 7
Giuliani's Social Views Not Well Known

As former New York City mayor Rudolph Giuliani inches closer to a formal declaration of his candidacy for the 2008 Republican nomination for president, the challenge he faces among Republicans given his support of abortion rights and same-sex civil unions is clear in a recent USA Today/Gallup Poll. Giuliani is extraordinarily well liked and respected by the American public. He also ties or leads Arizona senator John McCain as the front-runner for the Republican presidential nomination in recent Gallup Polls. At the same time, his views on abortion and same-sex civil unions are unknown to most rank-and-file Republicans. Once informed of Giuliani's positions, a sizable minority of Republicans say they would reconsider their support for the otherwise popular and well-respected Republican luminary.

Republicans Unsure of Candidates' Stances on Social Issues

According to a January 5–7, 2007, USA Today/Gallup Poll, three-quarters of Republicans nationwide (including independents who lean to the Republican Party) are unsure whether Giuliani favors or opposes civil unions for same-sex couples. (He favors them, though he opposes

gay marriage.) Nearly two-thirds are unsure whether he is "pro-life" or "pro-choice" on abortion. (He was staunchly pro-choice as mayor.) Republicans are nearly as unfamiliar with McCain's stances on both issues. Only 19% correctly associate McCain with being opposed to same-sex civil unions, and only 28% correctly identify him as pro-life. The vast majority are unsure about his position on both issues.

Giuliani's Candidacy Jeopardized by His Social Platform?

The same January poll asked Republicans whom they would prefer to see win if the Republican nomination narrows down to just Giuliani and McCain. Given this choice, 50% prefer Giuliani while 42% choose McCain. Notably, Giuliani does particularly well with self-described conservative Republicans (52% for Giuliani vs. 39% for McCain), while "moderate" Republicans prefer McCain (52% vs. 43%). However, when Republicans are told in the context of the survey that Giuliani supports same-sex civil unions and holds a pro-choice position on abortion, the net effect on their expressed chances of backing him is negative. Knowing his social views, more than 4 in 10 Republicans indicate a reduced willingness to support Giuliani. Twenty-five percent say they would be less willing to vote for him, and 18% say they would rule out voting for him entirely. Only 13% of Republicans take the contrary tack, saying they are more likely to vote for Giuliani as a result of his being pro-choice and pro–same-sex civil unions. The remainder (41%) say this information about Giuliani does not affect their decision to vote for him one way or another.

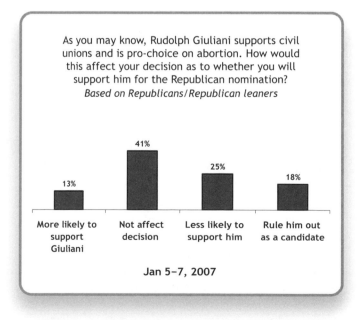

As you may know, Rudolph Giuliani supports civil unions and is pro-choice on abortion. How would this affect your decision as to whether you will support him for the Republican nomination?
Based on Republicans/Republican leaners

More likely to support Giuliani	Not affect decision	Less likely to support him	Rule him out as a candidate
13%	41%	25%	18%

Jan 5–7, 2007

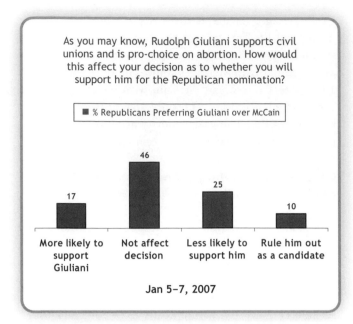

As you may know, Rudolph Giuliani supports civil unions and is pro-choice on abortion. How would this affect your decision as to whether you will support him for the Republican nomination?

■ % Republicans Preferring Giuliani over McCain

17	46	25	10
More likely to support Giuliani	Not affect decision	Less likely to support him	Rule him out as a candidate

Jan 5–7, 2007

The theoretical impact of Giuliani's social views on Republican voter preferences is better seen by looking at the results to this question among Giuliani's own supporters. Of those favoring Giuliani in a two-way match with McCain, a little over one-third (35%) say they would either rule out voting for Giuliani entirely (10%) or be less likely to support him (25%) as a result of knowing his positions on abortion and same-sex civil unions.

If Giuliani lost the support of all those who say they would rule him out as a candidate, his eight-point lead would be erased, and the race would be about tied (45% for Giuliani vs. 47% for McCain). However, if Giuliani were to lose those voters plus all who say they would be "less likely" to support him because of his views, then McCain would have a 27-point lead over Giuliani, 60% vs. 33%. Of course, these numbers represent the high end of Giuliani's potential losses over the issue and assume that all of his former supporters would switch to McCain rather than another Republican in the race. Still, it provides one indication of the magnitude of Giuliani's vulnerability given his positions on certain issues.

Whether Giuliani's positions ultimately derail his candidacy for the nomination partly depends on how much he is able to finesse and fine-tune those views to soften their impact with Republican voters in the months ahead. Although a majority of Republicans tell Gallup they are pro-life (57% according to a January 6–8, 2006, poll) and are against same-sex civil unions (also 57%, as of May 2–4, 2004), sizable minorities share Giuliani's alternative perspectives. Additionally, Giuliani has formidable image strengths, which could well compensate for his potential weaknesses on social policy. As a January 25–28, 2007, Gallup Poll shows, Giuliani is perceived extraordinarily well among Republicans on a number of personality dimensions. Compared with McCain, Giuliani is selected by a huge margin (74% vs. 21%) as the more likable candidate; he is also preferred as the stronger leader (59% vs. 34%) and, importantly, as having the better chance of beating the Democratic candidate in the general election (55% vs. 38%).

FEBRUARY 8

How Do Americans Define "Success" in Iraq?

The Bush administration has repeatedly talked about the need for "success" in Iraq. The Highlights of the Iraq Strategy Review document posted on the White House Web site, www.whitehouse.gov, begins with: "Success in Iraq remains critical to our national security and to success in the War on Terror." In a recent interview with Wolf Blitzer on CNN, Vice President Dick Cheney said: "The bottom line is that we've had enormous successes [in Iraq] and we will continue to have enormous successes." In his State of the Union address on January 23, 2007, President Bush declared: "In the end, I chose this course of action [in Iraq] because it provides the best chance for success."

But the exact definition of what constitutes "success" in Iraq remains unclear. A recent Gallup Poll survey, conducted between January 25 and January 28, 2007, attempted to shed some light on this issue by asking Americans the following open-ended question (responses were recorded verbatim by the interviewer and later coded into categories): "Regardless of whether you support the war, what specific goals or outcomes would the U.S. have to achieve in Iraq in order for you, personally, to consider the war a success?" The responses varied widely but can be divided into five general groupings: Iraq stabilized; Bring troops home/End the war; Nothing/Can never be a success; Get rid of the terrorists/al-Qaeda/Stop terrorism; Win the war/Finish what we started. A majority of respondents define success in Iraq as stabilization of the country, including a stable Iraqi government, Iraqis running their own country, making Iraq secure, peaceful coexistence between the warring factions, and a democratic government in Iraq. About a quarter of Americans more simply define success as U.S. troops returning home and/or an end of the war. Fourteen percent of Americans state that there can never be success there.

Will Success Be Achieved?

Little optimism exists that success will be achieved in Iraq. Respondents were asked, regardless of how they had defined success in response to the open-ended question, to indicate whether they felt that the United States would be likely to achieve success as they defined it. Forty-three percent of respondents say that it is very or somewhat likely that the success goal they mentioned will be achieved, while 57% say it is unlikely. Notably, only 11% say that success is very likely to occur, while more than three times as many say that success is very unlikely to occur. There are, as might be imagined, significant differences in estimates of the likelihood of success based on what is defined as success. In general, those who define success as some form of Iraqi stabilization are most likely to say that success can be achieved. Those who give other responses are much less likely to believe that success in Iraq can be achieved.

The Bush administration has defined success in Iraq as a self-sufficient country able to govern itself in peace, and that this type of success can be achieved. These data suggest that a little less than one-third of those in the sample both define success as some form of Iraqi stabilization and agree that success is at least somewhat likely to be achieved in Iraq. Americans have widely varying definitions of what would constitute "success" in Iraq, but the majority of all respondents mention some aspect of a more stable country—including a self-sufficient Iraq with much less violence, a better economy, and a democratic government. About a quarter of respondents focus on bringing U.S. troops home as their definition of success. Americans in general are not highly optimistic that success—regardless of how it is defined—will be achieved in Iraq. Those who view some form of a stable government as a requirement for success are more likely to believe that this objective can be achieved than those who define success in other ways.

FEBRUARY 12

February Economic Ratings Settle Down After January Uptick

Americans' views of the U.S. economy, after having jumped into significantly more positive territory in January, have settled back down to where they were at the end of 2006. Forty-three percent of Americans now rate the current economy as "excellent" or "good," down nine points from January, but roughly equal to December's reading. Just more than half of Americans continue to say the U.S. economy is getting worse—little changed in recent months—and 45% say now is a good time to find a quality job.

Current Economic Ratings

According to the February 1–4 Gallup Poll, 43% of Americans describe current economic conditions in the country as "excellent" (8%) or "good" (35%). Forty-one percent say

the economy is "only fair" and 16% say it is "poor." These readings represent a decline from the significantly more positive readings of the economy last month, when 52% of Americans described conditions as excellent or good. In essence, the February results have settled back down to levels Gallup measured in late 2006. Still, the latest ratings of the economy are slightly more positive than those measured throughout much of last year. Across 14 polls conducted in 2006 in which Gallup asked Americans to rate current economic conditions, the percentage of Americans saying the economy was excellent or good averaged 38%, with a low of 29% and a high of 44%.

The February data show a decline in ratings of the current economy across all three partisan groups. Sixty-nine percent of Republicans are positive in their assessment of the economy, compared with 36% of independents and 30% of Democrats. Republicans' and independents' ratings of the economy declined over the past month and are back to levels found in late 2006. Democrats are also less positive about the economy this month but are still more positive than they were late last year.

Economic Outlook

There has been little change in Americans' attitudes about the economy's direction in recent months. Even last month, when Americans were more positive about the current economy, attitudes about the economy's direction had remained negative, as they are now. Thirty-eight percent of Americans say the economy is "getting better," while more than half of Americans (52%) say it is "getting worse." These results have been quite stable since the midterm congressional elections in November 2006, but perceptions about the economy's direction are slightly more positive now than they were throughout much of last year. In 2006, the percentage of Americans saying the economy was getting better ranged between 22% and 41%, averaging 32%. Republicans continue to be much more positive about the direction of the economy than are independents or Democrats. Over the past month, there has been little change in partisan ratings on this measure of the economy.

Good Time to Find a Quality Job?

Last month, Americans' perceptions of the job market reached their highest point since 2001 when Gallup began asking the question, with 48% saying it was a good time to find a quality job and 47% saying it was a bad time. These perceptions are slightly more negative in the latest poll and are at roughly the same level Gallup measured in December 2006. Forty-five percent of Americans now say it is a good time to find a quality job and 50% say it is a bad time. The

Is now a good or bad time
to find a quality job?
Selected Trend: January 2006–February 2007

latest results are slightly more positive than in 2006: The "good time" responses averaged 41% last year and the "bad time" averaged 53%.

Republicans have been consistently more likely than independents or Democrats to positively assess the nation's job market. Seventy-two percent of Republicans now say it is a good time to find a quality job, compared with 39% of independents and 31% of Democrats. Over the past month, attitudes among Republicans and Democrats have shown essentially no change, but they have become slightly more negative among independents.

Americans' views of the economy are clearly more positive now than they have been in previous years of this decade, particularly in 2003. But the sharp upward trend found in January of this year—to the highest levels since the end of 2001—has not been sustained in February. Americans did not become more positive in their assessment of the economy's direction in January, and this month's reading on that measure shows little change, either positively or negatively. However, it is too soon to dismiss the January readings as a one-time blip until further data are available in the months ahead that will help establish more stable trends.

FEBRUARY 13

Majority Want Congress to Set Limits on U.S. Troop Presence in Iraq

The American public is more in favor of Congress passing legislation that would set caps on the number of U.S. troops serving in Iraq and a timetable for withdrawal of all troops than they are in favor of Congress passing a nonbinding resolution expressing disfavor with the recently announced troop "surge," while 6 out of 10 Americans oppose the surge.

A majority of Americans continue to say that U.S. military involvement in Iraq was a mistake. Many Americans say that their congressional representative's position on the war will be an important factor in their congressional vote next year, but most do not know what their representative's position on the troop surge is.

What Should Congress Do?

A new USA Today/Gallup Poll, conducted between February 9 and February 11, 2007, includes a series of questions asking Americans about four different actions Congress could take in regard to the war in Iraq. Although the increase in U.S. troops in Iraq is opposed by a 60% to 38% margin, only 40% of Americans want Congress to go so far as to deny funding needed to send those troops to Iraq. Additionally, the idea of Congress passing a "nonbinding resolution to express disapproval of President Bush's plan to send more U.S. troops to Iraq" receives only mixed support; it is favored by a 51% to 46% margin.

Questions asked about a nonbinding resolution in January generally found higher levels of support for the idea. This included a Gallup question asked between January 12 and January 14, 2007, which found that 61% favored the Democrats in Congress passing a resolution to "express their opposition to President Bush's plan to send more U.S. troops to Iraq." That question included this statement: "This resolution, by itself, would not affect Bush's policy, but the Democrats are hoping it will put pressure on him to change his policy." It may be that the currently lower level of support for the resolution is a result of the fact that the surge in troops has in essence become a fait accompli. Some Americans may feel that the time for resolutions is past. At the same time, there are higher levels of support from the public for two more significant congressional measures that would address broader aspects of the war. By a 57% to 40% margin, Americans favor Congress's putting a cap or limit on the number of troops serving in Iraq at any one time; and by a 63% to 35% margin, Americans favor Congress's setting a timetable for withdrawing all U.S. troops from Iraq by the end of 2008.

These data reinforce the finding that the public has perhaps moved beyond a limited focus on the "surge" in troops. There is less support for the two actions proposed in the survey that would address the surge (a resolution of disapproval and denying funding for the surge) than there is overall disapproval of the surge. In other words, some Americans disapprove of the troop increase but do not feel that Congress should be spending time passing resolutions to that effect, or even attempting to pass legislation to hold back funds. That there are higher levels of support for legislation that would put a cap on troops or set a timetable for withdrawal suggests that Americans believe congressional actions should be focused on these more major (and consequential) types of concerns. These findings are consistent with other data that suggest Americans want Congress to be more involved in decisions about the Iraq War. A *Newsweek* poll conducted in late January, for example, found that 64% of Americans believe that Congress has not been assertive enough in challenging the Bush administration's conduct of the war in Iraq.

Frustration over the Senate's Actions?

Most Americans at this point are unaware of where their representative in Congress stands on the Bush plan to increase troops in Iraq. At the same time, about 4 out of 10 say that their representative's position on the war in Iraq will be a "major factor" in their vote in the next congressional elections, with another 28% saying that it will be a "minor factor." Americans who are opposed to the troop surge are somewhat more likely than those who favor it to say that their representative's position on the war will be a major factor in their vote next year. The Senate has tried, unsuccessfully, to debate the war in Iraq, with the ultimate goal being to vote on a nonbinding resolution. The debate has not proceeded because of disagreements about procedural matters surrounding that debate. About one-third of Americans say they are bothered "a great deal" by the fact that Senate attempts to hold a debate on the Iraq War have not been successful; another 28% say they are bothered a "fair amount." Those who favor such a resolution are somewhat more likely to say they are bothered a great deal by the lack of debate in the Senate, but even among this group the percentage of respondents saying they are bothered "a great deal" is less than 50%.

A majority of Americans continue to believe that the initial involvement of the United States in the Iraq War was a mistake. There has been very little change in this measure across three readings so far this year. The all-time high point on the "mistake" question is the 59% that Gallup measured in September 2005. When the United States first initiated the war in March 2003, only 23% said it was a mistake. By June 2004, for the first time a majority of Americans said it was a mistake. This "mistake" percentage dropped back below 50% during the fall of 2004 and the spring of 2005 and has done so on occasion since, but for the most part over the last year a majority of Americans have consistently said that the Iraq War was a mistake. A majority of Americans disapprove of the recent Bush administration decision to send more troops to Iraq. There has been very little change in this sentiment over the last month.

A majority of Americans want Congress to pass legislation that would set a cap on the number of U.S. troops in Iraq and a timetable for withdrawal of all troops by the end of

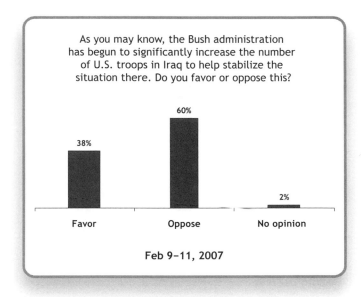

As you may know, the Bush administration has begun to significantly increase the number of U.S. troops in Iraq to help stabilize the situation there. Do you favor or oppose this?

Favor 38%   Oppose 60%   No opinion 2%

Feb 9–11, 2007

2008. There is less interest on the part of the public in having Congress pass a nonbinding resolution of opposition to the troop increase, even though 6 out of 10 Americans oppose the surge. The majority of Americans also oppose legislation that would deny funding for the surge. These attitudes may in part result from the fact that the surge is now already under way, making rhetorical statements of opposition or attempts to deny funding seem less relevant.

FEBRUARY 15

2008 Presidential Battle Closely Contested for Now

Three of the four current front-runners for the Democratic and Republican nominations for president in 2008 can each credibly claim that they would give their party as good a chance as anyone of winning the general election next year. That is no minor point, as Gallup polling suggests voter perceptions of the candidates' national viability could be a crucial factor in determining whom they throw their support to.

According to the new USA Today/Gallup Poll, conducted between February 9 and February 11, 2007, both front-runners for the Republican nomination (Arizona senator John McCain and former New York City mayor Rudolph Giuliani) are nearly tied with the Democratic front-runner (New York senator Hillary Clinton) in hypothetical match-ups for the 2008 fall election. Whether voters are asked to choose between Clinton and McCain or Clinton and Giuliani, the race is within three points. Clinton leads McCain by three points, 50% vs. 47%, and trails Giuliani by two points, 48% vs. 50%. However, given the margin of sampling error for the survey, those leads are not significant.

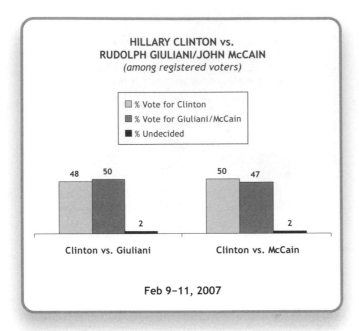

HILLARY CLINTON vs.
RUDOLPH GIULIANI/JOHN McCAIN
(among registered voters)

□ % Vote for Clinton
■ % Vote for Giuliani/McCain
■ % Undecided

Clinton vs. Giuliani: 48, 50, 2
Clinton vs. McCain: 50, 47, 2

Feb 9–11, 2007

The second-place contender for the Democratic nomination—Illinois senator Barack Obama—fares about as well as Clinton does against McCain (tying with him at 48%) but trails Giuliani by a significant nine-point margin: 43% to 52%.

Obama Loses Democrats to Giuliani

When voters are asked to choose between Obama and Giuliani, only 69% of Democrats and Democratic leaners say they would vote for Obama, while 28% say they would vote for Giuliani—while 79% of Democrats prefer Clinton when she is matched against Giuliani. This Democratic defection against Obama largely explains why Obama is currently

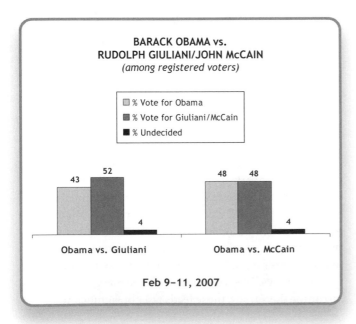

BARACK OBAMA vs.
RUDOLPH GIULIANI/JOHN McCAIN
(among registered voters)

□ % Vote for Obama
■ % Vote for Giuliani/McCain
■ % Undecided

Obama vs. Giuliani: 43, 52, 4
Obama vs. McCain: 48, 48, 4

Feb 9–11, 2007

a weaker opponent for Giuliani than Clinton. Among all voters, Giuliani beats Obama by nine points, but he leads Clinton by only two points, 50 to 48.

Republican preferences in a race that includes Giuliani are about the same, regardless of whether his Democratic opponent is Clinton or Obama. Giuliani is supported by 88% of Republicans when he is matched with Clinton and by 85% when matched with Obama. Republicans are most likely to back their party's nominee in a Clinton vs. Giuliani race (88% would vote for Giuliani); they are least likely to vote Republican when the race is between Obama and McCain (80% would vote for McCain).

The Electability Factor

Voter perceptions of a candidate's chances of winning the general election appear to be influential in their choice of candidate to support for their party's nomination. In January 2004, Gallup asked Democrats: "Which type of candidate would you prefer to see the Democrats nominate for president in 2004: 1) a candidate who agrees with you on almost all of the issues you care about but does not have the best chance of beating George W. Bush, or 2) a candidate who has the best chance of beating George W. Bush but who does not agree with you on almost all of the issues you care about?" The results were unambiguous. When forced to choose, 6 in 10 Democrats (60%) said they would rather support a candidate for the nomination with the best chance of beating Bush. Only 36% opted for the candidate who came closer to sharing their views but did not have the best chance of winning.

In a late January 2007 Gallup Poll, the front-runners of both parties (Clinton for the Democrats and Giuliani for the Republicans) are generally perceived by members of their own parties as being most likely to succeed in the general election. Forty-four percent of Democrats and Democratic-leaning independents say Clinton has the best chance of beating the Republican nominee in the 2008 general election, compared with only 27% choosing former North Carolina senator John Edwards and 21% choosing Obama on this dimension. On the Republican side, Giuliani leads McCain, 55% to 38%, as the candidate perceived to be most likely to win next fall.

FEBRUARY 16
Despite High Visibility, Little Change in Gore's Standing with Public

These are heady times for Al Gore. The former vice president and former presidential candidate recently presented an award at the Grammy Awards; his film, *An*

Inconvenient Truth, has been nominated for an Academy Award; and he has been nominated for a Nobel Peace Prize for his work on global warming. Although Gore has not indicated official interest in running again for the presidency, there are already several Web sites dedicated to trying to bring about that outcome. Yet an analysis of recent Gallup Poll data shows little significant change in Gore's standing with the American public despite his recent high visibility. His favorable ratings are roughly the same as they have been over the last five years, and they remain relatively lukewarm. Although he is tied for third place among Democrats as their favored nominee for the 2008 presidential election, his position is now only slightly higher than it has been in recent months.

Gore's Favorable Rating

Gore's current image in the eyes of Americans stands at 52% favorable and 45% unfavorable. His favorable rating is up four percentage points from June 2006, but that is not a statistically significant change and is also not significantly different from measurements in 2003 and late 2002. Gore's unfavorable rating has not changed at all over this time period.

These data certainly do not reflect any type of major change in Gore's positioning in the minds of Americans. Additionally, his current ratings are not spectacularly positive. Gore is seen in a slightly more positive than negative light, but only by a margin of seven points. By way of comparison, Gore's current favorable rating is significantly below the favorable ratings of other prominent Democrats tested in the most recent Gallup Poll, including former president Bill Clinton (63%), Hillary Clinton (58%), and former president Jimmy Carter (69%).

Gore's favorable rating was above 60% at a number of points when he was vice president. His favorable rating in January 2001, just as he was leaving office after the disputed 2000 election in which he received more popular votes than George W. Bush, was 56%. But since that point, his image has been less positive.

Democratic Trial Heats

Gore is in third place among Democrats when they are asked whom they want to receive their party's nomination in 2008. Gore is essentially tied with former North Carolina senator John Edwards—well behind Hillary Clinton, the front-runner, by a wide margin, and Illinois senator Barack Obama, by a smaller margin. Gore has gained slightly in these trial heat rankings since November 2006, at which time he earned 9% of Democrats' votes. Gore currently garners 14% of the votes of Democrats, essentially the same as Gallup's December reading. Edwards has gained as well during this period. The conclusions from these data suggest that while Gore is well positioned as a third-choice candidate should both Clinton and Obama falter in the months ahead, there is little sign of a major boomlet for his candidacy compared with where he has been in recent times.

FEBRUARY 20

Some Americans Reluctant to Vote for Mormon, 72-Year-Old Presidential Candidates; Strong Support for Black, Women, Catholic Candidates

With arguably the most diverse field of candidates in U.S. history to choose from, Americans will have to decide how comfortable they are electing a person who is not a white Protestant male as president. Whereas in past elections nontraditional candidates were often long shots to win their party's nomination, let alone the presidency, many of the leading candidates in the early stages of the 2008 election process are not cut from the typical presidential cloth, making this issue more salient than ever.

A recent USA Today/Gallup Poll updated a question first asked in 1937 about the public's willingness to vote for presidential candidates across a variety of different demographic dimensions, including gender, religion, and other backgrounds. While Americans overwhelmingly say they would vote for a black, woman, Catholic, or Hispanic president, they are less likely to say they would support a Mormon candidate (such as former Massachusetts governor Mitt Romney), one who is 72 years old (such as Arizona senator John McCain), or one who has been

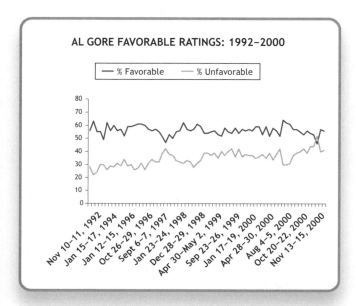

AL GORE FAVORABLE RATINGS: 1992–2000

— % Favorable   — % Unfavorable

Announcing his candidacy for the Republican presidential nomination on February 13, 2007, former Massachusetts governor Mitt Romney rallies supporters in Des Moines, Iowa. *(Charlie Neibergall/AP Images)*

married three times (such as former New York City mayor Giuliani).

The February 9–11, 2007, poll asked Americans whether they would vote for "a generally well-qualified" presidential candidate nominated by their party who was: Jewish, Catholic, Mormon, an atheist, a woman, black, Hispanic, homosexual, 72 years of age, or married for the third time. The Republican front-runner, former New York City mayor Rudolph Giuliani, is Catholic, and Illinois senator Barack Obama, currently running second in the Democratic nomination trial heats, is black. Americans express little hesitation about putting a person with either of those backgrounds in the White House: 95% say they would vote for a Catholic candidate for president, and 94% say they would vote for a black candidate. There is currently no major Jewish candidate running in either party, but if one were, his or her religion would not appear to be a liability: Ninety-two percent of Americans say they would be willing to support a Jewish presidential candidate.

The Democratic front-runner, New York senator Hillary Rodham Clinton, would be the first woman elected president. Nearly 9 in 10 Americans, 88%, say they would vote for a woman for president. Eighty-seven percent also say they would vote for a Hispanic candidate, and New Mexico governor Bill Richardson, a Democrat, is trying to become the first Hispanic president, though his candidacy has not attracted a great deal of support thus far.

The leading Republican candidates, including Giuliani, may run up against a bit more trouble with voter biases, as each has something in his background that may limit his appeal to the electorate. While Giuliani's religion does not appear to be an obstacle, the fact that he has been married three times could be. Though two-thirds of Americans say they would vote for a presidential candidate who is married for the third time, 30% say they would not.

Former Massachusetts governor Mitt Romney's Mormon faith has been widely discussed as he has started campaigning in earnest. Twenty-four percent of Americans say they would not vote for a Mormon presidential candidate, although 72% say they would.

Arizona senator John McCain will be 72 years old at the time of the 2008 election, which would make him the oldest person ever elected president if he is victorious. According to the poll, his age may be a bigger hurdle for McCain than the obstacles Giuliani or Romney would have to overcome. Forty-two percent of Americans say they would not vote for a 72-year-old candidate, even though the majority (57%) say they would. That is about the same willingness found for a hypothetical homosexual candidate (55%). An atheist would seem to have the hardest time getting elected president, as a majority of Americans (53%) say they would not vote for a presidential candidate who was an atheist.

It is important to note that these results mainly give a sense of potential obstacles that candidates face in convincing voters to elect them president, but cannot by themselves predict the chances of a black candidate or a woman candidate being elected, for example. While a woman or a Catholic may have less to overcome than a Mormon in attracting the necessary support to be president, that does not mean a Mormon would always lose to a Catholic or a woman. Each candidate's chances will depend on how well he or she addresses voter concerns during the campaign. For example, when Ronald Reagan (1980, 1984) and Bob Dole (1996) each sought the presidency, roughly two in three Americans said that their advanced age was not a problem—suggesting a lower level of voter trepidation about a candidate's age in specific circumstances than the current poll might indicate is the case in the abstract.

Flashing a broad smile, Senator John McCain prepares to address an audience at an Irish-American awards reception on February 28, 2007. *(Julie Jacobson/AP Images)*

Mormon Faith, Multiple Marriages Could Be Factors in Republican Primaries

While a majority of Americans from the major demographic subgroups would vote for any of these hypothetical candidates (except for an atheist) from heretofore uncommon presidential backgrounds, the likelihood of their doing so varies by political ideology. Conservatives are less willing than moderates or liberals to vote for candidates with several of the characteristics, including being a Mormon or being married three times. This could make things somewhat more difficult for Romney or Giuliani to prevail in the Republican primaries, since conservatives make up the base of the Republican Party. On the other hand, conservatives are as supportive as liberals or moderates of a 72-year-old candidate, if not more so. However, since about as many conservatives would be willing to support a Mormon (66%) or a candidate on his third marriage (60%) as would support a 72-year-old candidate (63%), McCain would not necessarily gain an advantage over his chief rivals for the Republican nomination.

Apart from ideology, there are also differences according to educational attainment in willingness to vote for candidates from unconventional backgrounds. Those who have attended college are in general more likely to support candidates with any of the named characteristics than those with a high school education or less. That is especially the case with regard to candidates who are Hispanic (93% among college-educated versus 76% among non-college-educated respondents), Mormon (79% versus 62%), 72 years of age (63% versus 48%), homosexual (62% versus 43%), or an atheist (52% versus 32%).

Americans Growing More Accepting of a Nontraditional President

Gallup first asked a version of this question—asking whether Americans would vote for candidates who were Jewish, Catholic, or women—in 1937. As one might expect, Americans have become increasingly likely to express support for candidates of these and other diverse backgrounds since then. In 1937, just 60% of Americans said they would vote for a Catholic president, and fewer than half said this with respect to a Jewish (46%) or a woman (33%) president. By the late 1950s, a majority of Americans expressed willingness to vote for a Jewish or woman president, and by 1965 support for a black candidate reached majority status as well. One exception to the general pattern of growing acceptance comes in the case of a Mormon candidate. When Mitt Romney's father, George Romney, sought the Republican presidential nomination in 1968, 75% of Americans said they would vote for a Mormon president. Forty years later, the percentage of Americans willing to support a Mormon for president is essentially unchanged.

Meanwhile, support for homosexual and atheist candidates has grown, though fewer would support either of those types of candidates than would support a Mormon. Only about one in five Americans said they would vote for an atheist when this was first asked in the late 1950s, compared with 45% today. Just 26% said they would support a homosexual presidential candidate in 1978, compared with 55% today.

FEBRUARY 23

Do Highly Religious Americans Believe They Have to Change Society?

Recently collected Gallup Poll data suggest that most highly religious Americans either believe that they can be personally religious without needing to spread their beliefs, or that they can best spread their beliefs by converting others to their religion. Only a small percentage of highly religious Americans—15%—believe that the best way to spread their religion is to change society so that it conforms to their religious beliefs.

These data are important in an environment in which the relationship between religion and society has become more and more of an issue. There is a strong relationship in the United States today between one's religion and one's political beliefs. One of the keys to Republican successes in elections in the early 21st century was the activation of highly religious voters. Protestants, in particular, were concerned about the secularization of society and therefore focused on changing society to reduce instances of abortion and combating same-sex marriages and stem cell research using embryos. The data reviewed here, however, suggest that such interest in imposing change on society on the basis of one's religion is, in theory at least, small. Most highly religious Americans appear content to live the best possible personal life on the basis of their religious beliefs or to engage in traditional attempts at one-on-one conversion.

Basic Data

Two Gallup surveys conducted in the fall of 2006 included a series of questions designed to shed light on what highly religious Americans believe should be the appropriate manifestation of their religious convictions. Three questions were asked in surveys conducted in September and November, and the results were combined to create an aggregate of more than 2,000 interviews. Thirty-seven percent of Americans classify themselves as extremely or very religious. This group of highly religious Americans is split with respect to whether the goal is to live the best possible personal religious life or if it is also necessary to spread their beliefs. Forty-eight percent believe the former; 49% the latter.

More than half of the highly religious Americans who believe it is necessary to spread their beliefs to others say this is best accomplished by converting others to one's religion. This type of traditional evangelical view has, within the Christian tradition over the years, been the basis for such things as Billy Graham's evangelistic crusades and the sponsorship of missionary work in foreign countries. The Mormon religion, as another example, places emphasis on the effort to convert individuals to the Mormon faith, expecting most young men of the faith (and in some instances women) to spend up to two years in missionary work.

A little less than a third of the highly religious Americans who believe in the importance of spreading their beliefs say that this goal is best accomplished by changing aspects

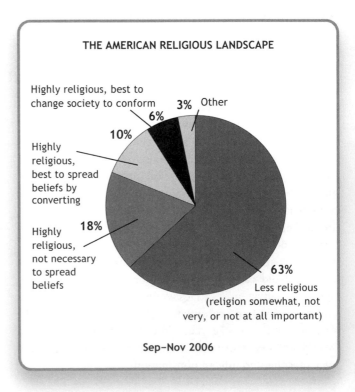

THE AMERICAN RELIGIOUS LANDSCAPE

Highly religious, best to change society to conform   6%

3% Other

10% Highly religious, best to spread beliefs by converting

Highly religious, not necessary to spread beliefs   18%

63% Less religious (religion somewhat, not very, or not at all important)

Sep–Nov 2006

of society to make them consistent with one's religious beliefs and practices. This works out to just 15% of highly religious Americans and only about 6% of the whole adult population. The majority of highly religious Americans believe that they do not need to change the society around them to conform to their religious beliefs, but instead can focus on living the best possible personal religious life, or on one-on-one conversion.

FEBRUARY 26
Giuliani Has Uniquely Broad-Based Political Appeal

Recent USA Today/Gallup presidential heats measures indicate that the 2008 election is not going to be easy for either party. Various pairings of the leading Republican and Democratic contenders generally result in extremely close races. If such early indications are correct, then in order to win, the candidates may need to maximize their support from all sides: their political base, political independents, and even members of the opposing party.

Data from the February 9–11, 2007, survey suggest that the leading candidates have very different chances of accomplishing such a political trifecta. Only one candidate, former New York mayor Rudolph Giuliani, has relatively strong favorable ratings across the political spectrum. New York senator Hillary Rodham Clinton is highly rated by Democrats, but receives relatively weak reviews from independents and Republicans. Arizona senator John McCain and Illinois senator Barack Obama fall somewhere in between.

Clinton and Giuliani Are Favorites with Their Home Teams

Of the leading Republican and Democratic contenders for their party's nominations (those garnering double-digit support), Hillary Clinton is the most popular with members of her own political party: Eighty-seven percent of Democrats view her favorably while only 10% view her unfavorably, resulting in a net +77 image score. Rudolph Giuliani receives nearly as much same-party adulation with a +70 positive image score from fellow Republicans. Al Gore, Barack Obama, and John McCain all cluster well behind these party favorites with positive image scores from their own parties of just 48 or 49 points. Former North Carolina senator John Edwards is even further behind with a +35 score.

Independents Favorable to Giuliani

Democratic adulation is about where Clinton's image strength ends. While she is viewed more favorably than

unfavorably among independents (55% favorable vs. 45% unfavorable), her +10 image score with this group lags well behind the most popular candidates. (Gore's ratings among independents are nearly identical to Clinton's.) Giuliani sets the bar with respect to independents' views of the 2008 presidential candidates: More than two-thirds (68%) of independents view him favorably and only 21% unfavorably, yielding a +47 image score. Obama follows next with +39. McCain and Edwards also fare well, with solidly positive image scores of +30 and +21, respectively. In contrast to Clinton and Gore, none of these candidates are viewed unfavorably by more than 3 in 10 independents.

Republican Front-Runners Have Most Crossover Appeal

Clinton's image is far worse among Republicans: Twenty-eight percent view her favorably and 70% view her unfavorably, yielding a –42 image score. The only other candidate to receive comparably negative ratings from the opposing party is Gore, with a –47 score among Republicans. By contrast, both Republican front-runners—Giuliani and McCain—are viewed more positively than negatively by Democrats, albeit by fairly narrow margins of +18 and +17, respectively. Also proving that people in one political party do not automatically frown on politicians from the opposing party, Obama is viewed more positively than negatively (+10) by Republicans.

Giuliani on Top

The net effect of the candidates' favorable scores according to party affiliation is seen in their overall ratings with the general public. With relatively high ratings from Republicans, independents, and Democrats, Giuliani enjoys the most positive national image of the six presidential front-runners (+44 net favorable). He is followed fairly closely by McCain and Obama. These three also have a sizable number of Americans expressing no opinion of them (at least 12%), which provides a valuable opportunity to improve their ratings as more people get to know them.

Gore has the lowest national image score (+7). Not only does he receive mixed reviews from independents and poor reviews from Republicans, but his image among Democrats is far from optimal. Clinton's national image score (+18) is only slightly better, and only because she is nearly universally applauded by Democrats. Both Clinton and Gore, who have been national figures for more than a decade, have minimal "no opinion" scores. Thus, to improve their favorable scores, they must convert some of their critics into fans. Edwards has the same low net favorable score as

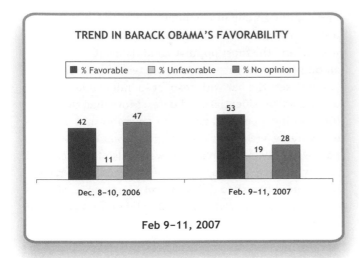

TREND IN BARACK OBAMA'S FAVORABILITY

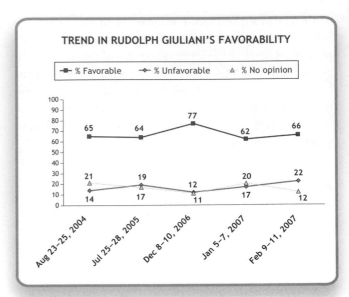

TREND IN RUDOLPH GIULIANI'S FAVORABILITY

Clinton (+18) but is still unknown to 20% of Americans. That may put Edwards in a slightly better position than Clinton in that it is, in theory, easier to move someone from "no opinion" to a favorable view than to convert an unfavorable opinion into a favorable one.

Obama: More Favorables and Unfavorables

For the most part, the candidates' public images have remained fairly stable over the past few months. The favorable ratings of most have fluctuated only slightly up or down since November 2006. The main exception to this is Obama, whose favorable as well as unfavorable ratings have increased as the public has grown more familiar with him. In December 2006, nearly half the general public had no opinion of him. As that proportion declined in the past two months to 28%, the percentage viewing him favorably has risen from 42% to 53%. His unfavorable rating also rose, from 11% to 19%. Thus, his overall net favorable image has

not changed much, rising from +31 in December to +34, where it stands today.

Clinton Rebounds

Views of Hillary Clinton have become slightly more positive since last fall: 58% favorable today, up from 53% in November 2006. Her current rating is notable because it is the highest favorable score she has received from the American public since the end of her tenure as first lady in January 2001. It is also substantially improved over her post–White House low point of 44% favorable and 53% unfavorable, recorded in March 2001.

Giuliani and McCain Fairly Steady

Giuliani's favorable ratings are generally consistent with where they have been since last summer, except for a one-time 77% rating in December 2006. His unfavorable rating has inched up fairly slowly, from 14% in August 2004 to 22% today.

McCain's run for the presidency in 2000 marked his entry onto the national stage, and his favorable ratings that year averaged 61%. Since then, his rating has bounced around some but has averaged 55%, similar to the 57% recorded in the latest poll.

FEBRUARY 28

Americans Predict Bill Clinton Would Be Asset as First Spouse

Former president Bill Clinton will enter uncharted waters should his wife, New York senator Hillary Clinton, succeed

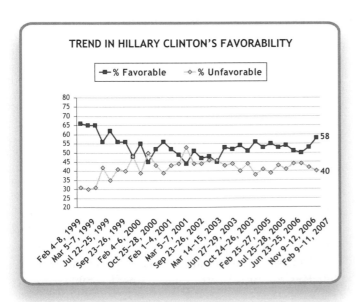

TREND IN HILLARY CLINTON'S FAVORABILITY

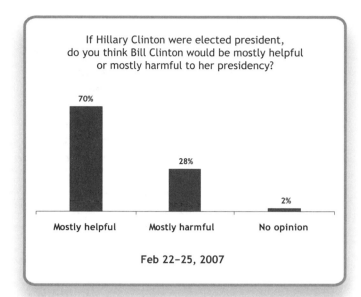

If Hillary Clinton were elected president, do you think Bill Clinton would be mostly helpful or mostly harmful to her presidency?

70%

28%

2%

Mostly helpful   Mostly harmful   No opinion

Feb 22–25, 2007

in capturing the presidency in 2008. Not only would he be the first man in a position that is defined by duties traditionally associated with women, but he would have to make the seemingly awkward transition from the former leader of the United States, with international influence, to a more circumscribed, domestic-oriented post. The latest Gallup survey, conducted between February 22 and February 25, 2007, investigated how Americans say Bill Clinton might write his new resume. Although a majority of Americans (63%) say he should not hold an official government job as policy adviser to a President Hillary Clinton, 61% think he should advise her unofficially. Americans also think Bill Clinton should fill such familiar duties of presidential spouses as hosting White House social events, taking up a charitable cause, and representing the White House abroad at special ceremonies. They do not believe, however, that he should deliver paid speeches before business and industry groups. More generally, Americans predict Clinton would be an asset as a presidential spouse. By a better than two-to-one margin, 70% vs. 28%, Americans believe he would be more helpful than harmful to his wife's presidency.

Bill Clinton's way might be smoothed somewhat by the fact that most Americans believe first ladies have always had some level of influence over the decisions presidents make. About one in five Americans perceive that previous presidential spouses have had "a great deal" of influence, while another 52% believe they have had "a fair amount" of influence. Only 26% minimize the influence first ladies have had with their presidential husbands.

The prevailing view among Americans today is that Bill Clinton would be no different from the norm in the amount of influence he would wield as spouse to the president. Forty percent of Americans predict he would have more

influence than previous presidential spouses. Sixty percent think he would have about the same influence (35%) or even less influence (25%). Republicans and Democrats are fairly similar in their views on this question. About 4 out of every 10 members of each party (including independents who lean toward each) say Bill Clinton would have more influence than the norm. However, Republicans are twice as likely as Democrats to believe Bill Clinton would have less influence than previous presidential spouses.

Americans Expect Bill Clinton to Maintain Traditional Duties

Some of the more visible first lady assignments over the years have been helping to plan White House events and dinners, championing a social issue or cause, and representing the White House at foreign weddings, funerals, and other ceremonies. Additionally, presidents' wives have become important fixtures on the political circuits of their respective parties, helping to raise money and build support for candidates at election time. Most Americans are amenable to Bill Clinton's carrying out all of these familiar roles.

As noted, a majority of Americans also accept the fact that spouses will provide unofficial advice to their partners and believe Bill Clinton should be no different. What Americans don't want to see is Bill Clinton serving in an official government role as a policy adviser to Hillary Clinton: Thirty-five percent favor this, 63% oppose it. By a slimmer margin (45% in favor, 53% opposed), they also think he should not make paid speeches to business and industry groups while his wife is president. If Americans become greatly concerned about Hillary Clinton's presidential powers being usurped by her spouse via "pillow talk," or about controversy over Bill Clinton's role becoming a distraction to her duties, one extreme solution would be for Bill Clinton not to live at the White House. However, nearly 9 in 10 Americans reject this suggestion. Partisan differences are minimal concerning most of the potential roles Bill Clinton could play if his wife were elected president, but larger gaps are evident with respect to his being involved in policymaking or representing the United States in an official capacity.

"No" to Serving Clinton's Senate Term

An entirely different way for Bill Clinton to occupy his time while his wife is president would be to serve the remainder of her term as New York senator. Indeed, state governors commonly appoint a former officeholder's spouse to fill a vacancy created by his or her death or resignation until a new election can be held. In such a scenario, Bill Clinton

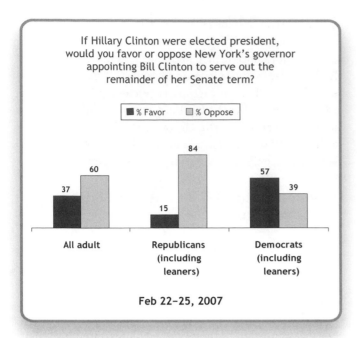

If Hillary Clinton were elected president, would you favor or oppose New York's governor appointing Bill Clinton to serve out the remainder of her Senate term?

■ % Favor   ☐ % Oppose

Feb 22–25, 2007

tives have enthusiastically endorsed this idea should Hillary win the presidency, Americans' initial reactions are negative. Gallup asked, "If Hillary Clinton were elected president, would you favor or oppose New York's governor appointing Bill Clinton to serve out the remainder of her Senate term?" Sixty percent oppose this; 37% are in favor. Republicans and Democrats have sharply different views about this, however. A majority of Democrats and Democratic leaners believe Bill Clinton should serve out his wife's Senate term, while Republicans are in even broader agreement that he should not (although, of course, there is little question that whomever the Democratic governor of New York appointed to replace Hillary Clinton in this scenario would be a Democrat).

Whether Americans would favor Bill Clinton's making an independent run for the Senate is not clear—that is a question for future polling. But public opposition to his serving in an interim capacity, as well as Americans' reluctance to having him continue his lucrative lecture circuit with business and industry, suggests an underlying public concern about conflicts of interest that might extend to a presidential first spouse's serving in the Senate in any capacity.

would serve as New York senator until 2012—that is, for the same four years during which Hillary Clinton would serve as president. While some leading Democratic opera-

MARCH 2007

A poll conducted in Iraq between February 25 and March 5, 2007, for the BBC and other media organizations questioned more than 2000 people in more than 450 neighborhoods and villages across all 18 Iraqi provinces. Similar surveys had been undertaken in 2004 and in 2006. (Gallup conducted two previous surveys of Iraqi residents' view about the war—in 2003 and 2004—as well as a 2002 poll of the Islamic world.) More than 6 in 10 Iraqis now say that their lives are going badly—double the percentage who said so in late 2005—and about half respond that increasing U.S. forces in the country will make the security situation worse. The survey also shows that Iraqis' assessments of the quality of their lives and the future of their country have plunged in comparison with similar polling done in November 2005 and February 2004. When asked to compare their lives today with conditions before the U.S.-led invasion in 2003, the percentage of Iraqis who say things are better now has slipped to 42%, down from 51% in 2005 and 56% in 2004. Thirty-six percent say things in their lives are worse today, an increase of 7% from the 2005 poll, which was conducted during a period of relative optimism prior to the December 2005 parliamentary elections. Twenty-two percent say their lives remain about the same. In 2005, 69% of Iraqis said the situation in their country would be better in 12 months; in 2007 that percentage had fallen to 40%.

In the United States, Iraq continued to rank as the "most important problem" facing the country. In a Gallup survey conducted between March 2 and March 4, 48% responded that the United States can win the war, the lowest such percentage across the nine times this question has been asked since September 2005. Almost 6 out of 10 Americans want troops to be withdrawn within 12 months.

Between March 11 and March 14, Gallup conducted its annual Environmental Poll. (Gallup undertook its first recorded measurement of public attitudes on environmental issues in a February 19–22, 1971, survey, in which 7% of Americans ranked "pollution, ecology" as the "most important problem facing this country today." In the same sample, 28% responded that the war in "Vietnam, Indochina" was the nation's foremost problem.) The results show a five-point increase since March 2006—from 36% to 41%—in the percentage of Americans highly concerned about the issue of global warming, on top of a 10-point increase that occurred between 2004 and 2006. The percentage now worried "a great deal" about global warming is essentially tied for the highest level of recorded concern on this measure with the 40% seen in April 2000. Overall concern about global warming fell from 40% in 2000 to 33% shortly after George W. Bush took office in 2001, mainly because Republicans—who may have been influenced by Bush's skepticism on the issue—became less worried. But concern among Republicans and Democrats has rebounded since 2004. Today, 85% of Democrats and 46% of Republicans worry "a great deal/a fair amount" about global warming.

MARCH 1

Giuliani Edges Out McCain in Perceptions of Viability for Presidency

With former New York City mayor Rudolph Giuliani and Arizona senator John McCain dominating Republican preferences for the 2008 Republican presidential nomination, the Republican race is very much a "Tale of Two Candidates" at this point. A new Gallup survey, conducted between February 22 and February 25, 2007, also finds Giuliani and McCain holding huge advantages over the rest of the Republican field in their perceived chances of winning the general election. Giuliani has the advantage over McCain, however, in public perceptions of each man's chances of becoming president—particularly among

CHRONOLOGY

MARCH 2007

March 1   The three-star general in charge of the Walter Reed Army Medical Center is relieved of his command following disclosures that wounded Iraq War soldiers were living in dilapidated quarters and that outpatients were enduring long waits for treatment.

March 5   Nine American soldiers, most from the 82nd Airborne Division, are killed by bomb blasts in an attack north of Baghdad.

March 6   More than 100 Shiites on a pilgrimage to the holy city of Karbala are killed by Sunni suicide attack bombers and gunmen.

March 6   Lewis "Scooter" Libby, former chief of staff to Vice President Dick Cheney, is convicted of lying to a grand jury and to FBI agents investigating the leak of the identity of a CIA operative in June 2003.

March 8   President Bush leaves for a five-nation tour of Latin America. Protesters await him in each country.

March 11   Fred Thompson, former senator from Tennessee and actor on the television series *Law and Order*, says he is considering a run for the Republican presidential nomination.

March 12   Representative Ron Paul of Texas announces his candidacy for the Republican presidential nomination.

March 12   Republican hopefuls meet for a debate in Myrtle Beach, South Carolina.

March 21   Former vice president Al Gore delivers a blunt message to congressional committees about the dangers of global warming. Senator James Inhofe of Oklahoma, the ranking Republican on the Environment and Public Works Committee, challenges Gore's analysis, saying his pronouncements "are now and have always been filled with inaccuracies and misleading statements."

March 22   Elizabeth Edwards, wife of Democratic candidate John Edwards, announces that her breast cancer has returned in an incurable form. John Edwards's decision to continue his bid for the Democratic presidential nomination receives both support and criticism.

March 22   A mortar shell fired into the heavily fortified Green Zone of Baghdad strikes within 330 feet of visiting United Nations secretary-general Ban Ki-moon while he is holding a press conference.

March 24   The United Nations Security Council votes to tighten economic sanctions on Iran in an attempt to halt its nuclear enrichment program.

March 26   Nine U.S. army officers, including four generals, face disciplinary proceedings as a result of mistakes made in the aftermath of the friendly-fire death of Pat Tilman, an American football player who had left his professional sports career to enlist in the U.S. Army.

March 27   After an impassioned debate, the Senate passes a nonbinding resolution calling on President Bush to set a withdrawal date for troops in Iraq. Senator John McCain, dissenting, says the bill "should be named the 'Date Certain for Surrender Act.'"

March 27   A federal judge dismisses a case of alleged torture against former secretary of defense Donald Rumsfeld brought by former prisoners in Iraq and Afghanistan.

March 28   King Abdullah of Saudi Arabia tells Arab leaders that U.S. occupation of Iraq is "an illegal foreign occupation."

March 29   More than 100 Shiites are killed in Iraq in an extraordinary surge of sectarian violence.

March 29   The Senate passes a resolution that calls for the withdrawal of all U.S. troops from Iraq by March 31, 2008, while funding the war through 2009.

Republicans. Of the top five Republicans in the race—Giuliani, McCain, former Massachusetts governor Mitt Romney, former House speaker Newt Gingrich, and Kansas senator Sam Brownback—Giuliani and McCain are the only two perceived by the public, including by Republicans, to have either an "excellent" or "good" chance of winning the election in November 2008. None of the candidates are viewed by a majority of Americans or Republicans as having "no chance" of winning. But of the top five candidates, the bottom three are generally deemed to have no better than a "slim" chance.

Among the general public, Giuliani's and McCain's chances of winning the presidency in 2008 are rated about equally: 74% say Giuliani has an excellent or good chance and 70% say this about McCain. Former Massachusetts governor Mitt Romney is perceived as highly electable by only 27% of Americans, followed by former House speaker Newt Gingrich (with 23%) and Kansas senator Sam Brownback (with 12%).

The more immediate concern of the candidates as they look ahead to next year's primaries and caucuses, however, is likely to be with regard to perceptions within their own party. Giuliani has a slight advantage over McCain in the percentage of Republicans nationally saying each has an excellent or good chance of winning the presidency: 82% for Giuliani vs. 73% for McCain. Romney ranks third, but with a bit more positive rating among Republicans than among the general public (38% of Republicans say he has an excellent or good chance, compared with 27% of all Americans). Republicans' prognoses for the Gingrich and Brownback candidacies, however, are as low as the general public's ratings.

Giuliani Beats McCain in Head-to-Head Comparison of Electability

Gallup's most recent trial heat measure of Republican preferences for 2008 was conducted between February 9 and February 11, 2007. That poll showed Republicans favoring former New York City mayor Rudolph Giuliani for the nomination over Arizona senator John McCain by a 16-point margin, 40% to 24%. Republicans also have

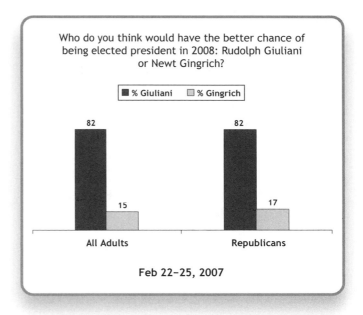

a more positive view of Giuliani, with a net favorable rating (percentage favorable minus percentage unfavorable) of +70 for Giuliani vs. +48 for McCain. According to the new poll, Giuliani also holds an advantage when respondents are asked to choose which of the two leading Republicans has the better chance of winning the election. Giuliani beats McCain by 20 percentage points among Republicans on this measure, 60% vs. 40%. Among the public at large, Giuliani has only a slight lead over McCain on this measure of electability: 53% of Americans choose him while 45% choose McCain. This is because Democrats—and to a lesser degree, independents—are more likely than Republicans to perceive McCain as the stronger candidate.

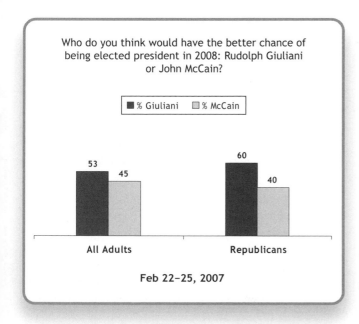

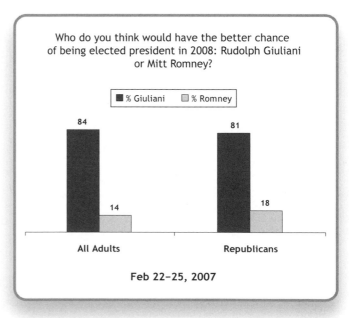

Gingrich and Romney Don't Compete on Viability

The public expresses little doubt about Giuliani's superiority over the third- and fourth-place Republican candidates. Only 14% of Americans think either Gingrich or Romney has a better chance than Giuliani of being elected president in 2008; more than 80% choose Giuliani in each comparison. The numbers are similar among Republicans.

Democrats View Clinton as Most Electable Democratic Candidate

A recent Gallup survey shows that Democrats think New York senator Hillary Clinton has the best chance of being elected president among the Democratic presidential candidates, followed by Illinois senator Barack Obama and former North Carolina senator John Edwards. Even as momentum appears to be building in some political circles for an Al Gore presidential run, less than half of Democrats and only about one-third of Americans think he has a good chance of winning should he run. Overall, Americans are split over which Democrat—Clinton or Obama—has the best chance of being elected, with Republicans giving Obama the better odds. Gallup's February 22–25, 2007, survey asked a representative sample of adults to handicap the 2008 presidential race, giving their views on the chances of several of the prominent Democratic and Republican contenders' winning the presidency. More than 7 in 10 Americans believe Clinton and Obama have an "excellent" or "good" chance of being elected president. At 52%, Edwards is the only other Democrat who is viewed as having a good chance by a majority of the public.

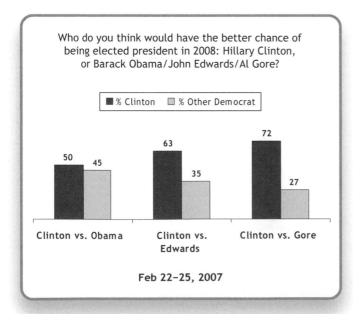

Who do you think would have the better chance of being elected president in 2008: Hillary Clinton, or Barack Obama/John Edwards/Al Gore?

- ■ % Clinton
- ☐ % Other Democrat

	Clinton vs. Obama	Clinton vs. Edwards	Clinton vs. Gore
% Clinton	50	63	72
% Other Democrat	45	35	27

Feb 22–25, 2007

Even after Gore's recent star turn as a presenter at the Grammys and Academy Awards ceremony, only 31% believe the former vice president has a good chance of winning, while 42% believe his chances are slim, and 26% think he has no chance at all. The poll was completed before Gore's documentary on global warming, *An Inconvenient Truth*, was awarded two Oscars on February 25, so the impact of those wins on his chances, if any, is unclear at this point.

New Mexico governor Bill Richardson, Delaware senator Joe Biden, and Connecticut senator Christopher Dodd are thought to have better-than-average odds of winning the presidency by fewer than one in five Americans. To get a better sense of the leading Democrats' perceived electability, Gallup matched Obama, Edwards, and Gore against Clinton, the current front-runner, to see how they fare against her in a direct comparison on the electability dimension. Americans are closely divided in their view of whether Clinton or Obama has the better chance of being elected, with 50% choosing Clinton and 45% choosing Obama. Clinton is seen as having much better odds than either Edwards or Gore, however. She is seen as a more viable candidate than Edwards by a 63% to 35% margin, and by a 72% to 27% margin over Gore.

Partisans See Race Differently

Aside from the long-shot candidates, Democrats think each of their party's candidates has a better chance of winning the presidency than do independents and Republicans. In addition, Republicans and Democrats handicap the race differently. The views of Democrats as to which of their party's candidates has the best chance of winning the November 2008 election will likely be a crucial factor in determining how the candidates perform in next year's presidential primaries and caucuses. At this stage, Democrats view Clinton as the most electable of their party's contenders, with 90% saying she has a good chance of winning, compared to 74% who say this about Obama and 64% who say this about Edwards. Fewer than half of Democrats (44%) believe Gore has a good chance of winning the 2008 presidential election.

In contrast, Republicans think Obama has the best shot of winning: Sixty-six percent think he has a good chance, compared with 58% who say this about Clinton and 41% who say this about Edwards. Only 17% of Republicans believe Gore has a reasonable chance of emerging victorious should he run.

Independents are closely divided in their views: Seventy-one percent think Obama has a good shot to win, while 69% think Clinton does. Even when asked to say which of the two has the better chance, independents split down the middle, with 46% saying Clinton and 45% saying Obama.

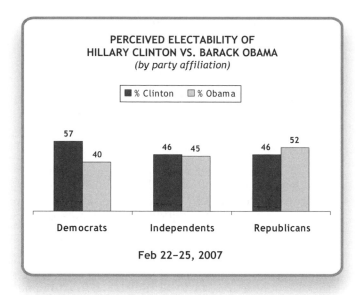

PERCEIVED ELECTABILITY OF HILLARY CLINTON VS. BARACK OBAMA
(by party affiliation)

■ % Clinton ▢ % Obama

Democrats: 57 / 40
Independents: 46 / 45
Republicans: 46 / 52

Feb 22–25, 2007

Clinton's greater perceived electability in comparison with Edwards is largely due to her strength among Democrats. Republicans are only slightly more likely to view her chances of winning as better than Edwards's.

When matched against Clinton, Gore is perceived as having a better chance of winning the presidency by independents (34% choose him) than by either Republicans (22%) or Democrats (25%). Still, independents are nearly twice as likely to believe Clinton has a better shot than Gore of being elected.

Implications

One of the major themes running through political analyses of the 2004 Democratic nomination campaign was the idea of the strategic voter. Exit polls in early primary states showed Democrats believing Massachusetts senator John Kerry had the best chance of beating George W. Bush in the general election, which likely played a big part in his winning the 2004 Democratic presidential nomination. Perceived electability likely also played a major part in Bill Clinton's emergence as the nominee from the 1992 Democratic field. When choosing among candidates who generally share views on issues similar to their own, voters are forced to look for other criteria on which to make their vote decision. And the candidates' chances of winning—in addition to their perceived competence, integrity, and leadership skills—are a reasonable basis on which to make that decision.

The fact that most Americans doubt Gore's chances of winning suggests that he would have an uphill battle for the nomination should he enter the race. Earlier Gallup polling also showed that despite the wave of positive publicity Gore has received in the last year, Americans' opinions of him are improving only marginally, if at all.

With Senator Clinton currently enjoying a strong lead in the Democratic nomination trial heats and given her likely ability to match or exceed her rivals' efforts when it comes to news media coverage, fund-raising, and campaign organization in the key primary states, one possible vulnerability for her in securing the nomination would be a widespread perception that she cannot win the general election. Hollywood executive and loyal Democratic Party supporter David Geffen recently raised that issue while publicly endorsing Obama. At this point, Democrats do not agree with Geffen's doubts about Clinton's electability, but among the general public there is not a consensus that Clinton is a more viable candidate than Obama. Obama's hopes for winning the party's nomination may hinge to a large degree on convincing Democratic primary voters that he has the best chance of winning the general election.

MARCH 2
Americans' Views of the Mormon Religion

Something about the religion of the Church of Jesus Christ of Latter-Day Saints, commonly known as the Mormons, apparently disturbs a significant portion of the American population. Mitt Romney is the first Mormon in a generation to run for president. (His father, George Romney, governor of Michigan and also a Mormon, sought the Republican nomination in 1968, but lost to Richard M. Nixon.) A quarter of Americans in a recent Gallup Poll said they would not vote for an otherwise well-qualified presidential candidate who is a Mormon. A Washington Post/ABC News poll found that 29% of Americans said they would be less likely to vote for a presidential candidate who is a Mormon.

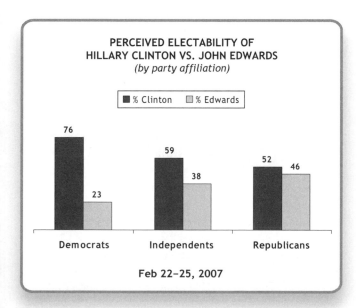

PERCEIVED ELECTABILITY OF HILLARY CLINTON VS. JOHN EDWARDS
(by party affiliation)

■ % Clinton ▢ % Edwards

Democrats: 76 / 23
Independents: 59 / 38
Republicans: 52 / 46

Feb 22–25, 2007

These negative attitudes appear to be based on more than just concerns about the Mormon religion in a presidential context. New Gallup polling shows that 46% of Americans have an unfavorable opinion of the Mormon religion in general, slightly higher than the 42% who have a favorable opinion. Key findings include:

- Americans who are more religious (as measured by frequency of church attendance) and those who are Protestant have highly negative views of the Mormon religion. The differences in views of Mormons among Americans defined by their church attendance are significant. There is a net negative view of −21 points among Americans who attend church weekly, compared with a net positive view of +10 among those who seldom or never attend church.
- Protestants are significantly more negative in their views than Catholics, who are the most positive group by religion.
- There are minor partisan differences: Republicans are slightly more negative in their views of Mormons than are either independents or Democrats.
- There is a major difference by ideological group. Liberals are extremely negative in their views: Twenty-eight percent have favorable opinions and 61% unfavorable opinions. By contrast, conservatives are essentially evenly divided in their views, while moderates break to the positive side, with 48% favorable and 40% unfavorable opinions.
- Opinions of Mormons are better formed in the West, where the preponderance of Mormons live, and are slightly more positive than negative. Only 3% of those living in the West have no opinion whatever of Mormons.

Impressions of the Mormon Religion

To answer the question of what's behind these attitudes, Gallup asked Americans to say what comes to mind first when they think about the Church of Jesus Christ of Latter-Day Saints, also known as the Mormon church. Only 18% of Americans have no opinion or say nothing comes to mind about the Mormon religion. That fact, plus the specificity of the open-ended responses, underscores the idea that Americans appear to have at least some basic associations with the Mormon religion. The impressions in general are widely varied, from the clearly neutral ("Salt Lake City") to the clearly positive ("good people/kind/caring/strong morals") to the clearly negative ("dislike their beliefs/don't agree with their doctrine/false teachings").

MARCH 6
Americans Say Iraq War a Mistake, but Do Not Want Funding Cut

A record-tying number of Americans now say that the Iraq War was a mistake, and less than half say the United States can win the war, a record-low number. Almost 6 out of 10 Americans want troops to be withdrawn within 12 months. At the same time, a majority disapprove of congressional legislation that would cut off funds for troop increases in Iraq or revoke the authority granted the president in 2002. Instead, new USA Today/Gallup Poll data suggest that Americans are in favor of congressional legislation that would set a timetable for withdrawal of all U.S. troops from Iraq by the end of next year. Over three-quarters of Americans also support Congress's requiring U.S. troops to come home from Iraq if Iraqi leaders fail to reduce violence in that country—and mandating that U.S. troops who served in Iraq remain home for one year before being redeployed there.

"Mistake" Trend Ties Highest Level Since War Began

The 59% of Americans who say it was a mistake to send troops to Iraq is tied as the highest percentage since this question was first asked about the Iraq War in March 2003, matching the level from a September 2005 poll. In three prior polls in which this question was asked this year, the mistake percentage has been almost as high, varying between 56% and 58%.

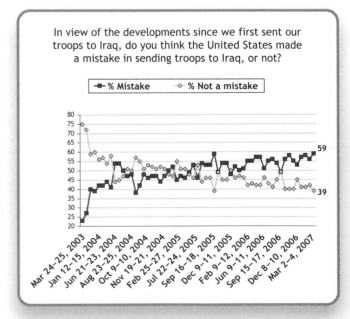

In view of the developments since we first sent our troops to Iraq, do you think the United States made a mistake in sending troops to Iraq, or not?

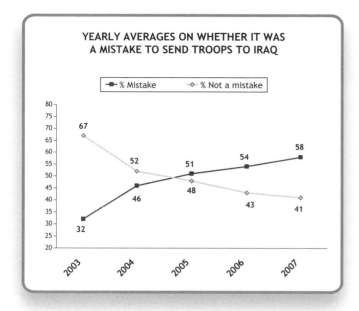

YEARLY AVERAGES ON WHETHER IT WAS
A MISTAKE TO SEND TROOPS TO IRAQ

Which comes closer to your view about the war in Iraq: You think the U.S. will definitely win the war in Iraq; you think the U.S. will probably win the war in Iraq; you think the U.S. can win the war in Iraq, but you don't think it will win; or you do not think the U.S. can win the war in Iraq?

In 2003, only 32% of Americans, on average, said it was a mistake to send troops. This average then increased to 46% in 2004, edged up to 51% in 2005, and averaged 54% last year. So far this year, the average is even higher at 58%.

President Bush's base of Republicans continues to support the administration position on the war; just 29% say the war was a mistake. The vast majority of Democrats, 84%, say it was a mistake to send troops to Iraq, as do 57% of independents.

Can the United States Win?

Just 48% of Americans say that the United States can win the war in Iraq, the lowest such percentage across the nine

times this question has been asked since September 2005. That group of 48% is split among those who say the United States will definitely or probably win (28%) and those who say the United States can win, but won't. The 46% who say the United States cannot win the war is also the highest on record.

Public Opposes Congress's Cutting Iraq Funding

Belief that the war was a mistake does not translate automatically into support for cutting funding for the war—nor into support for revoking the 2002 congressional legislation that authorized the war to begin with. The March 2–4, 2007, poll asked Americans if they favor or oppose Congress's taking six different courses of action with regard to the war in Iraq. Only 37% support Congress's denying the funding needed to send any additional troops to Iraq, and only 44% say they favor Congress's voting to revoke the authority it granted President Bush in 2002 to use military force in Iraq. There is widespread support, at the three-quarters level or higher, for two actions: 1) requiring U.S. troops to come home from Iraq if Iraq's leaders fail to meet their promises to reduce violence in that country and 2) requiring troops returning from Iraq to stay in the United States for at least a year before being redeployed to Iraq. A somewhat lower percentage of Americans—but still a majority—also support setting a timetable for withdrawing all troops from Iraq by the end of next year, as well as putting a cap or limit on the number of troops serving in Iraq at any one time.

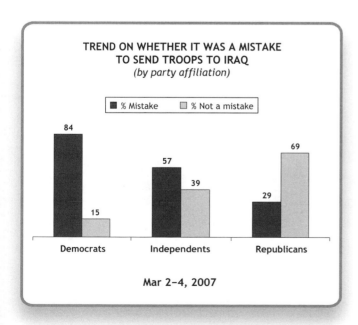

TREND ON WHETHER IT WAS A MISTAKE
TO SEND TROOPS TO IRAQ
(by party affiliation)

Mar 2–4, 2007

There are predictable differences in support for these types of congressional actions by party affiliation. A majority of Democrats support all of the six measures tested, although only a bare majority of 52% support the idea of denying funding for additional troops. A majority of independents support four of the measures. As would be expected, Republicans are less supportive of each measure than Democrats or independents. Still, a majority of Republicans favor requiring troops to stay in the United States for at least a year before returning to Iraq, and requiring troops to come home if Iraq's leaders fail to reduce violence there.

The key question for Congress at this point is what to do about Iraq. The poll tested some of the ideas that have been advanced in recent weeks. The American public seems to have settled on a course of action that would involve a definite commitment to withdrawing troops from Iraq—but not immediately—while rejecting some of the more drastic measures, such as cutting off funds for troops or revoking the initial authority to go into Iraq. Support for the commitment of Americans to congressional legislation mandating withdrawal is found in an update of a separate question in the latest poll that provided Americans with four different proposals about what to do with the troops currently stationed in Iraq. Fifty-eight percent say the government should either withdraw the troops immediately (20%) or within the next 12 months (38%). Twenty-six percent of Americans say the government should work to withdraw troops but should take as long as necessary to do so, and 13% support sending more troops to Iraq.

MARCH 8

Half of Americans Already Tuned In to 2008 Election

Americans are currently giving as much thought to the 2008 presidential election as they might be expected to give a year from now. Twenty months before the United States selects a new president, the latest USA Today/Gallup Poll finds nearly half of Americans (48%) giving "quite a lot" of thought to the next election. This is comparable to the amount of political reflection Americans reported in January 2004 and March 2000—less than a year before each of those years' presidential elections. Gallup did not measure public attention to the 1996 campaign earlier than September of the same year, but the degree of attention reported today is substantially greater than what Gallup found in January 1992 relative to that year's election.

Gallup has only twice previously measured Americans' attention to the campaign a year or more before an elec-

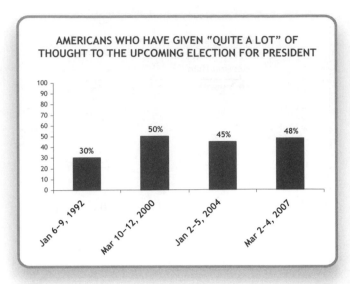

AMERICANS WHO HAVE GIVEN "QUITE A LOT" OF THOUGHT TO THE UPCOMING ELECTION FOR PRESIDENT

tion: in September 1999 and September 1979. (This, in itself, underscores how early the 2008 campaign is getting under way.) In each case, the percentage saying they had given quite a lot of thought to the next election was much lower than the 48% seen today. Together, a majority of Americans today (51%) are paying quite a lot or some attention to the upcoming election, while slightly fewer (48%) are paying only a little or no attention.

Thus, it seems that the 2008 election is sparking an unusual degree of interest from the American public—unusual, but perhaps not surprising. Over the course of several elections, political observers have talked about the emergence of a "permanent campaign"—wherein the first day after an election becomes the first day of the next election cycle. While much of this campaigning goes on behind the scenes—strategizing, fund-raising, building a voter turnout operation—the candidates are directing more of their preliminary activity to the public than ever before: announcing their intention

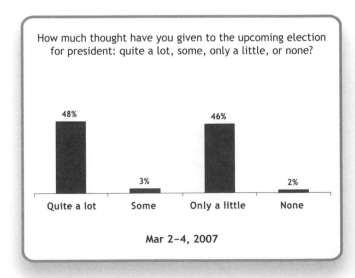

How much thought have you given to the upcoming election for president: quite a lot, some, only a little, or none?

Mar 2–4, 2007

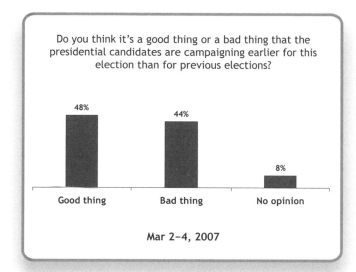

Do you think it's a good thing or a bad thing that the presidential candidates are campaigning earlier for this election than for previous elections?

48% Good thing
44% Bad thing
8% No opinion

Mar 2–4, 2007

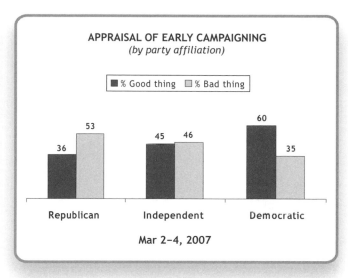

APPRAISAL OF EARLY CAMPAIGNING
(by party affiliation)

■ % Good thing   □ % Bad thing

Republican: 36 / 53
Independent: 45 / 46
Democratic: 60 / 35

Mar 2–4, 2007

to run earlier, seeking major media coverage earlier, and participating in candidate debates earlier.

Split Reaction to the Trend

According to the March 2–4, 2007, survey, Americans are about evenly divided over the impact this acceleration of the election process is having. When asked whether it is a good or bad thing that the presidential candidates are campaigning earlier for this election than in previous years, 48% of Americans say it is a good thing; 44% call it a bad thing.

Democrats tend to consider the trend a good thing, possibly because it allows them to look beyond the Bush administration and focus on the prospect of reinstalling a Democrat in the White House in 2009. By the same token, Republicans tend to call it a bad thing.

On March 12, 2007, Republicans (from left to right) Fred Thompson, Mitt Romney, John McCain, Mike Huckabee, Rudolph Giuliani, and Ron Paul meet for a debate in Myrtle Beach, South Carolina. *(Mary Ann Chastain/AP Images)*

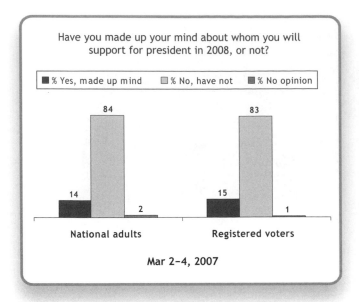

Have you made up your mind about whom you will support for president in 2008, or not?

■ % Yes, made up mind   ☐ % No, have not   ■ % No opinion

National adults: 14, 84, 2
Registered voters: 15, 83, 1

Mar 2-4, 2007

Voter Preferences Still Forming

Though a high number of Americans may be giving advanced thought to the 2008 presidential election, very few have come to a firm conclusion about whom they will vote for. A random half-sample of survey respondents in the latest poll were asked: "Have you made up your mind about whom you will support for president in 2008, or not?" Only 14% of Americans, including 15% of registered voters, responded affirmatively.

The other half-sample was asked: "Which of the following best describes you: You have a good idea about whom you will support for president in 2008; you have thought about it, but you don't have a good idea yet; or

you haven't really thought about whom you will support for president in 2008?"

Many more Democrats than Republicans (22% vs. 6%) are willing to say they have made up their minds about whom they will vote for. The importance of this is unclear, however, as there is little difference between the parties in the percentages saying they have a good idea about whom they will support: 26% of Democrats vs. 23% of Republicans. For now, there is relatively little difference in the percentages of Republicans and Democrats who have given the campaign quite a lot of thought (46% vs. 52%). There is a slightly larger gap between conservatives and liberals (46% vs. 57%), but this is about as large as the differences get. Men are slightly more likely than women to have given a lot of thought to this year's election (51% vs. 45%), and attention is greater among those in upper-income categories than among lower-income categories.

Romney Still Unknown to Many Republicans

One critical measure at this stage of the election campaign is the traditional trial heat that indicates whom Democrats and Republicans want to be their party's nominee for president. A second dimension to the election puzzle is the images of the candidates in the eyes of voters, regardless of whether voters say they would want to vote for them at this point. This is particularly interesting and important at this early stage of the campaign because several candidates began the year with relatively low name identification, meaning that they are still in the process of developing images as the campaign year progresses.

A review of image trends among the major candidates shows that two candidates—Hillary Clinton and Al Gore—have almost universal name identification. At the other end of the spectrum, only 42% of Americans know enough about Mitt Romney to have an opinion about him. The rest of the candidates are known well enough to be evaluated by more than three-quarters of the public. Three candidates have very positive images: Rudolph Giuliani, Barack Obama, and John McCain. Al Gore, Hillary Clinton, and John Edwards have more moderately positive ratings. Mitt Romney is just about as likely to be seen unfavorably as favorably by those who know him. Newt Gingrich is the only candidate tested with a significantly unfavorable image.

Name Identification

Here's a look at where the overall name identification of the major candidates from both parties stands as of early March 2007, based on the percentage who know enough about a candidate to have an opinion:

Which of the following best describes you: You have a good idea about whom you will support for president in 2008; you have thought about it, but you don't have a good idea yet; or you haven't really thought about whom you will support for president in 2008?

■ % Have a good idea
☐ % Thought about it, don't have good idea yet
■ % Haven't really thought about it

National adults: 23, 53, 23
Registered voters: 22, 55, 22

Mar 2-4, 2007

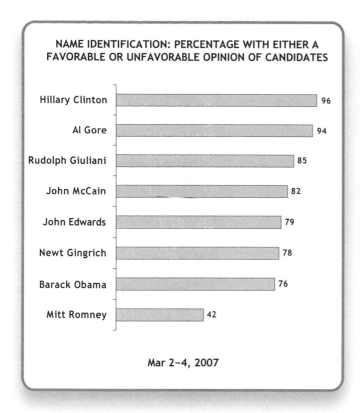

NAME IDENTIFICATION: PERCENTAGE WITH EITHER A FAVORABLE OR UNFAVORABLE OPINION OF CANDIDATES

Hillary Clinton	96
Al Gore	94
Rudolph Giuliani	85
John McCain	82
John Edwards	79
Newt Gingrich	78
Barack Obama	76
Mitt Romney	42

Mar 2–4, 2007

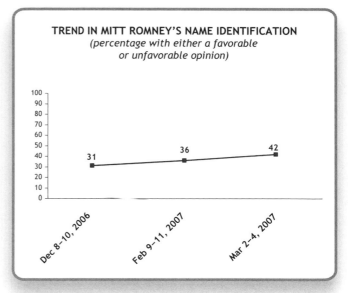

TREND IN MITT ROMNEY'S NAME IDENTIFICATION
(percentage with either a favorable or unfavorable opinion)

Dec 8–10, 2006	Feb 9–11, 2007	Mar 2–4, 2007
31	36	42

Hillary Clinton and Al Gore have near-universal name identification; Mitt Romney is still unknown to over half of Americans. The other five candidates have name identifications between 76% and 85%.

The biggest change in recent months has come in relationship to Barack Obama, whose name identification has risen from 53% in December to 76% today.

Mitt Romney, on the other hand, has seen relatively little growth in his recognition among Americans, rising only 11 percentage points since December. This comes despite the fact that he announced his run for president on February 13 in Michigan, where his father, George W. Romney, served as governor from 1963 to 1969.

Favorable and Unfavorable Ratings

The overall picture of favorable and unfavorable ratings of the candidates among the general population can be grouped as follows:

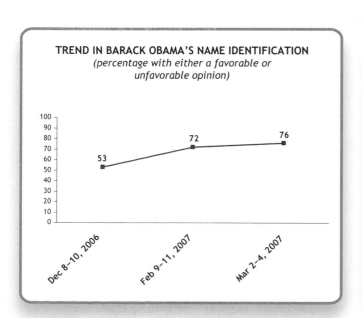

TREND IN BARACK OBAMA'S NAME IDENTIFICATION
(percentage with either a favorable or unfavorable opinion)

Dec 8–10, 2006	Feb 9–11, 2007	Mar 2–4, 2007
53	72	76

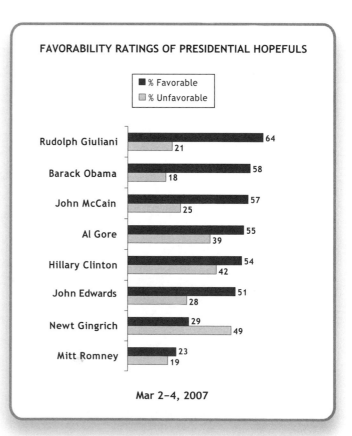

FAVORABILITY RATINGS OF PRESIDENTIAL HOPEFULS

■ % Favorable
☐ % Unfavorable

Candidate	% Favorable	% Unfavorable
Rudolph Giuliani	64	21
Barack Obama	58	18
John McCain	57	25
Al Gore	55	39
Hillary Clinton	54	42
John Edwards	51	28
Newt Gingrich	29	49
Mitt Romney	23	19

Mar 2–4, 2007

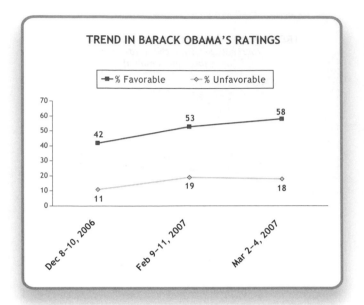

TREND IN BARACK OBAMA'S RATINGS

Very well-liked candidates with high favorable to unfavorable ratios of more than two to one included Rudolph Giuliani, Barack Obama, and John McCain. Moderately well-liked candidates with higher positive than negative ratings included Al Gore, Hillary Clinton, and John Edwards. The one candidate who essentially breaks even between favorable and unfavorable ratings is Mitt Romney, and the disliked candidate with significantly higher unfavorable than favorable rating is Newt Gingrich. Most of these candidates have held on to roughly the same images in recent months. Barack Obama, however, has increased his favorable ratings, while his unfavorable ratings have remained low as he has become better known.

Mitt Romney has also seen some changes over time in the way the public views him: His initially positive image has become slightly less positive. Romney moved from a net positive position in December (albeit among the small group who were familiar with him) to a point in early February where his favorables and unfavorables were evenly matched, to the current situation, in which his favorables are slightly higher than his unfavorables.

Candidate Images Among Partisans

Obama is running second in the trial heats behind Clinton, even though almost one-fourth of Democrats don't know enough about him to rate him. Edwards is in fourth place, but over one-fifth of the Democratic population don't know enough about him to rate him. The major change over time in the ratings of the Democratic candidates among Democrats and Democratic-leaning independents is the increase in net favorable ratings (percentage favorable minus percentage unfavorable) for Obama and Gore. Edwards's net favorable rating has declined over time.

Among Republican candidates, Mitt Romney stands out as the candidate who is significantly less well known than the others. Over half of Republicans say they don't know enough about Romney to be able to rate him. His image among those Republicans who do know him is quite positive. This suggests that if Romney maintains his net positive image among Republicans as the campaign progresses, he could be in a position to become more of a factor in the presidential nomination picture. There has not been a lot of change over time in the net favorable ratings of the Republican candidates among Republicans and Republican-leaning independents. Giuliani had a somewhat more positive image in the late fall of 2006 than he does now, but his image has been steady in the three polls conducted this year.

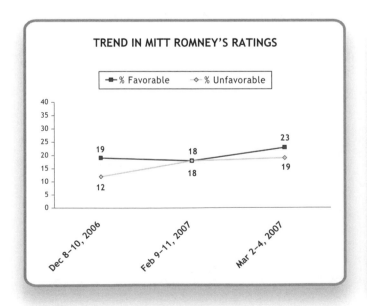

TREND IN MITT ROMNEY'S RATINGS

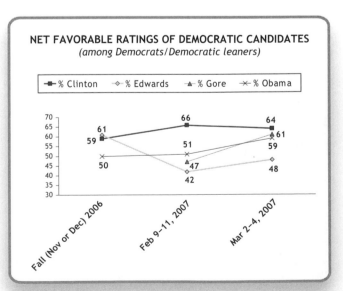

NET FAVORABLE RATINGS OF DEMOCRATIC CANDIDATES
(among Democrats/Democratic leaners)

MARCH 15

Highly Religious Republicans Less Likely to Support Giuliani

Highly religious Republicans, defined as those who attend church weekly, are significantly less likely to support Rudolph Giuliani for their party's nomination than are those who attend church less frequently—though Giuliani, who himself is Catholic, gets higher levels of support from Catholic Republicans than from Republicans who are Protestant. Church attendance makes little difference in the candidate preferences of Democrats, however. Among Democrats, Barack Obama does slightly better among Protestants than among Catholics. These conclusions are based on an aggregated analysis of three recent Gallup Poll presidential preference surveys, conducted on January 12–14, 2007, February 9–11, 2007, and March 2–4, 2007. Even with these combined samples, however, sample sizes in some religious subgroups remain relatively small.

Religious Intensity and Support for Candidates

The relationship between religious intensity and support for presidential candidates has been a significant factor in recent elections, mainly among Republicans. John McCain's poor showing among religious voters contributed to his defeat in the 2000 South Carolina Republican primary, and ultimately derailed his chances of winning his party's nomination. George W. Bush's success in winning the presidency in 2000 and 2004 was in part predicated on a campaign strategy of increasing turnout among the religious Republican Right.

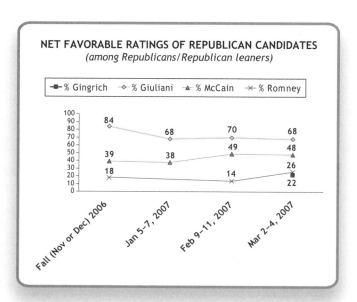

The religion factor has already been raised in the early stages of the 2008 presidential campaign in relation to the presumed impact of the candidates' histories and positions on their support among more religious subgroups of the electorate. This has been particularly the case with respect to the candidacy of Rudolph Giuliani, twice divorced and Catholic. The conservative Richard Land, the head of the Ethics and Religious Liberty Commission of the Southern Baptist Convention, was recently quoted as calling Giuliani's divorce from his second wife a "divorce on steroids" and saying that his candidacy would be "an awfully hard sell" for evangelical Christians.

To investigate the hypothesis that Giuliani is having trouble with more religious Republicans, two recent USA Today/Gallup Polls, conducted on February 9–11, 2007, and March 2–4, 2007, asked Republicans about their views on their party's nomination. There is no agreed-upon definition of "evangelical" among survey researchers, but Gallup analysis has shown that church attendance functions as an excellent broad measure of religious intensity. To that end, our analysis broke Republicans into three subgroups: 1) those who attend church weekly, 2) those who attend church nearly every week or monthly, and 3) those who seldom or never attend church. It is clear that Rudolph Giuliani in fact does receive a lower percentage of the vote from highly religious Republicans than from those who attend church less frequently. At the same time, religious Republicans are only slightly more likely to support John McCain or Newt Gingrich than are less religious Republicans, and neither difference is statistically significant. Religious Republicans are also slightly more likely to indicate support for conservative candidate Sam Brownback. (In fact, all of Brownback's very limited support comes from this highly religious group.)

In sum, Giuliani remains the top candidate among religious Republicans, but he leads John McCain by only seven percentage points among this group. Giuliani's lead among less religious Republicans is much larger: 28 points among those who attend church nearly every week or monthly, and 27 points among those who seldom or never attend church.

Little Difference Among Democrats

There has been much less discussion of the impact of highly religious voters on support for Democratic candidates for president. A Gallup analysis of the relationship between church attendance and support for Democratic candidates indicates that there is in fact little significant relationship between the two. The aggregated polls from January 12–14, 2007, February 9–11, 2007, and March 2–4, 2007, show

Hillary Clinton leading among all three groups by margins ranging from 11 to 16 points.

Religious Identification

Among the three major candidates for the Republican nomination, Giuliani is Catholic, McCain is Protestant, and Romney is Mormon. Therefore, it may not be surprising to find that Giuliani does better among Catholics than among Protestants or those with other religious preference or no religious identity at all. (Giuliani may also do less well among Protestants because they disproportionately tend to be the more religious voters analyzed in the previous section.) Giuliani beats John McCain by an overwhelming 32 percentage points among Republican Catholics, but by 16 points among Protestants. There is no statistical difference in the level of support for other major Republican candidates by religious identity. Former Illinois governor Tommy Thompson is a Catholic and Sam Brownback is a converted Catholic, but neither does better among Catholic Republicans than among other Republicans. Newt Gingrich is Protestant, but again, there is no major difference across these religious categories in his support.

The Democratic Situation

All of the major candidates for the Democratic nomination for president are Protestant: Hillary Clinton, Barack Obama, Al Gore, and John Edwards. Three other Democratic candidates currently drawing minimal support—Joe Biden, Bill Richardson, and former general Wesley Clark— are Catholics. Regardless of the religious identities of these candidates, there is little variation in Democrats' choice of a candidate based on their personal religious identification. Barack Obama does slightly better among Protestant Democrats than among Catholic Democrats. Al Gore does slightly better among "all others" than among those who are Protestant or Catholic. Hillary Clinton wins by margins of between 12 and 21 percentage points among all three of these groups.

MARCH 20
Congress's Job Approval Back Down Again This Month

The modest uptick in approval of the job being done by Congress has dissipated for the most part after only two months. Congress's job approval had risen over the last two months after the Democrats took over control of Congress in early January 2007, fueled in large part by a jump

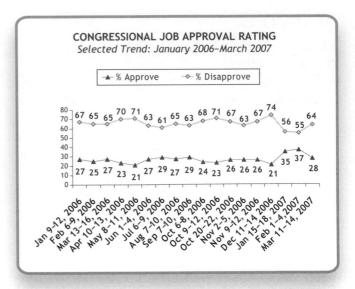

CONGRESSIONAL JOB APPROVAL RATING
Selected Trend: January 2006–March 2007

in approval among rank-and-file Democrats. This month, however, Congress's job approval is back down to levels quite similar to where it was in 2006. Democrats have lost much of the positivity exhibited in the first two months of the year after their party took over. According to Gallup's monthly update on job approval of Congress, in a March 11–14, 2007, national poll, 28% of Americans approve of the job being done by Congress and 64% disapprove. This marks a substantial change from January and February, with approval down nine points and disapproval up nine points.

The current reading suggests that Americans are reverting to their pessimistic attitudes of last year, when Congress's approval ratings were in the 20s for much of the year. The explanation for the increase in job approval ratings for Congress in January and February lies in the fact that Democrats, and to a degree independents, became much

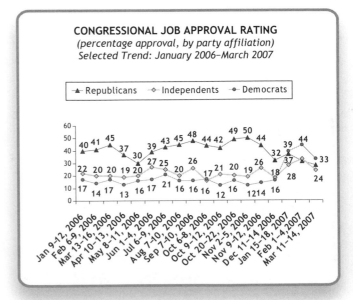

CONGRESSIONAL JOB APPROVAL RATING
(percentage approval, by party affiliation)
Selected Trend: January 2006–March 2007

more positive. This more than offset a drop in approval among Republicans. This month, however, Congress's job approval among Democrats has fallen back, as it has to a lesser degree among independents. Republicans—already much less positive in January and February after their party lost control of Congress—became only slightly more negative this month.

It is difficult to pinpoint precisely what is behind the drop-off in optimism about Congress among Democrats. One possibility is that Democrats are disappointed that their party has been unable to do anything substantive about the Iraq War—the dominant issue in last November's midterm elections. The increase in the price of gas and/or other economic concerns may also be a factor. Overall satisfaction with the way things are going in the United States and ratings of economic optimism are both down in the March Gallup Poll.

MARCH 22
Iraq War Far and Away Top Problem

For three full years, spanning 36 consecutive months since April 2004, the Iraq War has topped Gallup's ranking of the "most important problem" facing the country. Iraq also led the list in early 2003 just before the start of the war, but the issue fell behind the economy for about a year, from March 2003 through March 2004.

The latest data come from Gallup's March 11–14, 2007, survey, in which 35% of Americans identify Iraq (or war generally) as the top problem facing the United States at this time. No other single issue comes close. Healthcare, immigration, and dissatisfaction with government each garner just 8%, making them the second-ranked issues

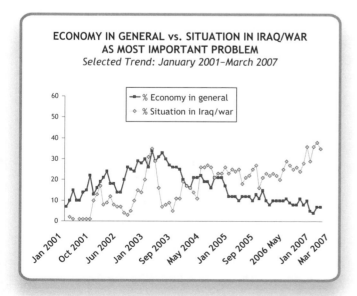

ECONOMY IN GENERAL vs. SITUATION IN IRAQ/WAR AS MOST IMPORTANT PROBLEM
Selected Trend: January 2001–March 2007

behind the situation in Iraq. The only other issues mentioned by at least 5% of Americans are the economy (7%) and ethics, terrorism, and poverty (5% each). The current results differ from last month's by no more than a few percentage points.

Democrats Focus on Iraq

Democrats (including independents who lean Democratic) are especially unified in perceiving Iraq to be the nation's most salient issue. More than 4 in 10 Democrats cite the situation in Iraq as the nation's most important problem, while just about 1 in 10 Democrats mention healthcare, making it this group's second-ranking issue. The war in Iraq and healthcare are followed by dissatisfaction with government, the economy, and education, according to Democrats. Even though it is mentioned by only 25% of Republicans, Iraq is still the leading problem mentioned by that group. There are significant differences, however, in the amount of emphasis placed by Democrats and Republicans on a number of other problems. Thirteen percent of Republicans mention immigration, compared with only 4% of Democrats; 11% of Republicans mention terrorism, compared with 1% of Democrats; 8% of Republicans mention ethical decline, compared with 1% of Democrats; and Republicans are slightly less likely to cite healthcare (5% vs. 9%) and education (2% vs. 6%) as important problems.

During the past several months, only the situation in Iraq has garnered double-digit mentions from the American public in Gallup's "most important problem" surveys. This contrasts with other points during George W. Bush's presidency, when other issues figured much more prominently than they do today. Those that have fallen the most since their high points during Bush's presidency include terrorism, fuel prices, and unemployment. Mentions of immigration, Social Security, education, and energy are also more than 10 points behind their recent high marks.

MARCH 23
Clinton Has Significant Edge Among Democratic Women Age 18–49

Senator Hillary Clinton enjoys a 10-point advantage among Democratic women when their preferences for the Democratic presidential nomination are compared with those of Democratic men. This gender gap is built almost entirely on Clinton's relative strength among 18-to-49-year-old Democratic women. There is little difference by gender in support levels for Clinton among Democrats who are 50 and older.

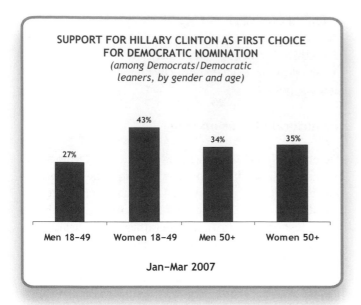

SUPPORT FOR HILLARY CLINTON AS FIRST CHOICE
FOR DEMOCRATIC NOMINATION
*(among Democrats/Democratic
leaders, by gender and age)*

Jan–Mar 2007

BASIC GENDER GAP

These findings are based on aggregated data from three USA Today/Gallup Polls conducted from January through March of this year, surveying a total of 1,495 Democratic voters. Clinton leads the Democratic field among both men and women, but Democratic women are more likely to name Clinton as their preferred choice for the Democratic nomination than are Democratic men (39% vs. 29%, respectively). It does not appear, though, that Democratic men support any candidate other than Clinton in disproportionate numbers. In particular, Democratic men are not significantly more likely to support second-place Senator Barack Obama than are Democratic women.

THE AGE FACTOR

The Democratic gender gap in 2008 preferences is driven almost totally by the disproportionate preference for Clinton's candidacy among 18-to-49-year-old Democratic women. There is essentially no gender gap in preference for Clinton among Democrats age 50 and older. These data are quite remarkable. There is a 16-point difference in the vote preference between men and women who are in the 18-to-49-year-old age demographic—while the gender gap among Democrats age 50 and older is 1 point. Looked at differently, Clinton's highest level of support is among 18-to-49-year-old women; her lowest, among 18-to-49-year-old men. Support for Clinton among men and women age 50 and older comes close to the sample average for all Democrats.

The good news for Clinton is that her support among both men and women 50 and older is relatively strong. She leads second-place Obama by margins of 15 to 18

points among this older age group—which is especially significant given older voters' typically higher turnout levels. The bad news presumably is that Clinton has not yet been able to parlay her gender to special advantage among older women. Among Democratic voters under 50, the good news for Clinton is her great strength among women—a 22-point advantage over Obama. This group—43% of whom choose her as their first choice for their party's nomination—is clearly her most solid base of support. The bad news for the Clinton campaign lies among male Democrats age 18 to 49, which is the only one of these four age and gender groups in which Clinton is statistically tied with Obama.

The accompanying graph displays Clinton's support among four more finely differentiated age groups. The data indicate that the 50-year-mark appears to be the significant dividing point; there is little difference between those 18 to 29 and 30 to 49, and there is little difference between those 50 to 64 and those 65 and older.

Clinton stands in the unique position of having a serious chance to become the first female president in United States history. To accomplish this feat, she will need to secure her party's nomination and then win the November 2008 general election. Previous Gallup analysis has shown that Clinton's favorable rating is higher among women than among men in the general U.S. population. Clinton also does better among Democratic women than among Democratic men—by 10 points—as their first choice for their party's presidential nomination. Although she herself will turn 60 in October 2007, Clinton's gender advantage is built almost entirely off of her significant support among younger Democratic women. Among those 50 and older, her support among women is no greater than among men.

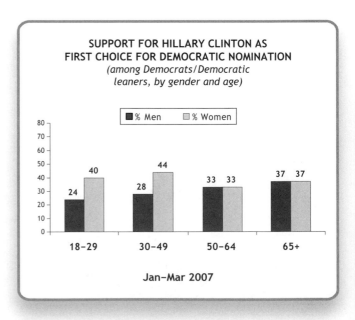

SUPPORT FOR HILLARY CLINTON AS
FIRST CHOICE FOR DEMOCRATIC NOMINATION
*(among Democrats/Democratic
leaders, by gender and age)*

Jan–Mar 2007

From a strategy perspective, this suggests that Clinton's campaign could in theory attempt to trigger more enthusiasm among older women, attempting to create in them the same disproportionate appeal Clinton enjoys among younger women. At the moment, no candidate besides Clinton seems to stand out as having an unusual appeal to Democratic women 50 and older.

Turnout in most primary and general elections skews toward older people. This means that Clinton's strong base of support among younger women may not be fully realized if her campaign does not make special efforts to ensure that these voters actually turn out to vote. The older skew in turnout also underscores the potential importance of an effort on the part of the Clinton campaign to increase her support among older Democratic women. Clinton's campaign consultants presumably have already made or will need to make a strategic decision concerning the campaign's gender focus. One approach would be to focus on her area of strength and push to gain disproportionate turnout among younger women. Another approach would be to focus on addressing the attitudes and concerns of older women and Democratic men in an attempt to tilt those groups' campaign preference more toward her candidacy.

Most national Democratic candidates have done better among women than among men in recent decades—the so-called gender gap that has become a part of American national politics. Women in general are disproportionately likely to vote Democratic, while men are disproportionately likely to vote Republican. The data reviewed here, however, reveal a gender gap in support for Clinton that occurs *within* the ranks of Democrats. This means her appeal to women is not based merely on the usual boost that a Democratic candidate gains among female voters, but is more specific to her particular persona and characteristics. It is unclear to what extent Clinton's gender will be an overt feature of her campaign, or, for that matter, the campaigns of her opponents. But even if Clinton chooses not to openly focus on her gender, it is clear that her appeal has a significant gender skew that will most likely be an important part of campaign dynamics as caucuses and primaries get under way in early 2008.

MARCH 27

Americans Support Edwards's Decision to Continue

The majority of Americans, including two-thirds of Democrats, agree with former senator John Edwards's decision to continue his presidential candidacy despite the recurrence of cancer affecting his wife, Elizabeth. John

At a news conference on March 22, 2007, Democratic presidential candidate John Edwards and his wife Elizabeth announce that her breast cancer has recurred but that he will remain in the race. *(Gerry Broome/AP Images)*

Edwards's favorable rating, however, did not increase significantly after the announcement. At the same time, there is no evidence that Edwards's announcement hurt his standing in the Democratic race, nor is there evidence that it has helped him significantly. A little more than one-third of Americans believe that Edwards will ultimately be forced to withdraw because of his wife's illness. The basic reaction Americans give to Edwards's announcement that he will remain in the race is clear: They support it.

According to the March 23–25, 2007, USA Today/Gallup Poll, Democrats are significantly more likely than Republicans to say Edwards should remain in the race. This likely reflects the underlying reluctance of Republicans to say that any Democratic candidate should stay in the race. Are women disproportionately likely to disagree with Edwards's decision to carry on with his campaign in the face of his wife's serious medical situation? The

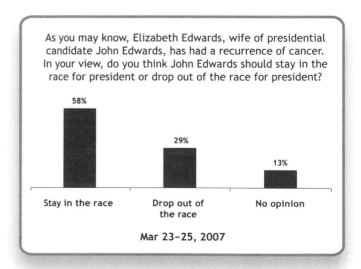

As you may know, Elizabeth Edwards, wife of presidential candidate John Edwards, has had a recurrence of cancer. In your view, do you think John Edwards should stay in the race for president or drop out of the race for president?

58% Stay in the race
29% Drop out of the race
13% No opinion

Mar 23–25, 2007

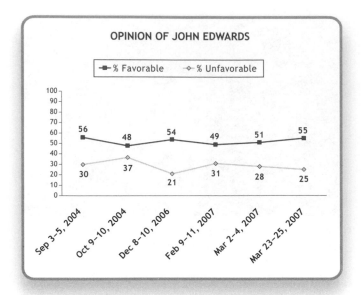

OPINION OF JOHN EDWARDS

—■— % Favorable   —◇— % Unfavorable

MARCH 28

Giuliani Lead in Republican Field Shrinks as Thompson Makes Solid Debut

A new USA Today/Gallup Poll suggests that actor and former Tennessee senator Fred Thompson could be a factor in the race for the Republican presidential nomination, should he decide to enter. Included for the first time in this poll, Thompson places third behind front-runner Rudolph Giuliani and second-place John McCain. There has been little change in the Democratic ballot in recent weeks, other than a slight improvement for John Edwards. Hillary Rodham Clinton remains the Democratic leader, with Barack Obama, Al Gore, and Edwards also getting significant support.

Republican Ballot

One of the major themes running through early media coverage of the Republican campaign is the idea that Republicans are unenthusiastic about the existing field of candidates. The current group of candidates is thought to be either too moderate (Giuliani and McCain), too unknown (Sam Brownback, former Arkansas governor Mike Huckabee, and former Virginia governor Jim Gilmore), or both (Mitt Romney and Nebraska senator Chuck Hagel). There has been constant speculation that some well-known and unquestionably conservative candidate would enter the race to fill this perceived vacuum. Some have long thought that former House speaker Newt Gingrich would be that person, though his unpopularity among the general public casts serious doubt on his ability to win the presidential election. More recently, Thompson, who served in the U.S. Senate from 1994 to 2003 but retired and returned to acting, has said he would consider entering the race.

In Thompson's debut in Gallup's Republican primary trial heat, 12% of Republicans and Republican-leaning independents say they would be most likely to support him for the party's 2008 presidential nomination. That is good enough for third place in the crowded field of 14 candidates, behind Giuliani (31%) and McCain (22%), according to the March 23–25 poll.

Giuliani had held a significant and growing lead over McCain and the rest of the field in the prior two USA Today/ Gallup Polls. While Giuliani still enjoys a significant lead in the current poll, his support has dropped from 44% earlier this month to 31%, and his lead has shrunk from 24 percentage points to 9 points. McCain's support is holding steady at 22%. At 8%, Gingrich is the only other candidate with more than 5% support. Romney has been at 5% or better in each of the prior three polls, but is at 3% in the latest test ballot. Giuliani's shrinking lead in the latest poll stems from both

answer appears to be no. Sixty percent of women support his decision to stay in the race, compared with 55% of men.

Edwards has been firm that his campaign is running full speed ahead. However, there is a risk for Edwards that voters may shy away from supporting him because they assume his departure from the race on account of his wife's health is inevitable. In fact, 38% of Americans believe Edwards will ultimately be forced to withdraw. (Half of Americans are confident he will remain in the race.) There are few differences by partisanship in this perception. Some may have expected at least a temporary uptick in favorable opinions of Edwards as a result of the news coverage he and his wife received last week. However, the new poll does not find this. Edwards's favorable rating edged up four points, but this level of change is not statistically significant.

Impact on Edwards's Trial Heat Standing

Edwards now receives 14% of the vote from Democrats when asked whom they support for their party's nomination. This is up from the 9% he received in early March, but not higher than his standing in January and February, when he received 13% of the vote. (Hillary Clinton remains the leader with 35% of the vote, followed by Barack Obama at 22% and Al Gore at 17%.) Given the lower sample sizes involved when only identifiers with one party are surveyed, small changes in the standings of the candidates are usually not significant. The strongest conclusion from the data, therefore, is that Edwards's announcement certainly did not hurt his standing among Democrats, but there is no evidence that it had a significant positive effect, either.

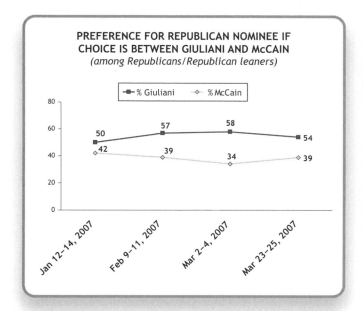

PREFERENCE FOR REPUBLICAN NOMINEE IF
CHOICE IS BETWEEN GIULIANI AND McCAIN
(among Republicans/Republican leaners)

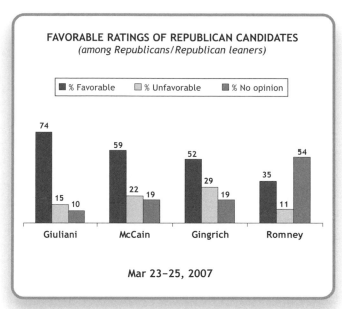

FAVORABLE RATINGS OF REPUBLICAN CANDIDATES
(among Republicans/Republican leaners)

Mar 23–25, 2007

the inclusion of Fred Thompson in the trial heat and a more general drop in support. While Giuliani's 74% favorable rating among Republicans and Republican-leaning independents is down from the prior poll (78%), the four-point drop is not statistically meaningful. However, when the ballot is reconfigured to simulate Thompson's not being in the race (by substituting Thompson voters' second choice), Giuliani's net support is down to 35%, still down nine points from the previous poll.

There has been a slight change in Republicans' preferences when they are asked to choose between Giuliani and McCain in a one-on-one matchup. In the current poll, Giuliani holds a 54% to 39% advantage on this measure of support, compared with 58% to 34% in the prior poll. Giuliani has maintained a significant lead in this head-to-head ballot since February.

Rank-and-file Republicans' ratings of each of the leading candidates provide some evidence that the party base is unenthusiastic about their choice of presidential candidates. Only Giuliani is highly popular with the Republican base, based on his 74% favorable rating among Republicans and Republican-leaning independents. Meanwhile, slightly more than half of Republicans have a positive view of McCain (59%) and Gingrich (52%). Romney remains an unknown quantity to about half of Republicans, but is rated more favorably than unfavorably by those who offer an opinion. (Fred Thompson's favorable ratings were not measured in the current poll.)

McCain has seen a drop in his favorable rating among the party base from an average of 68% in February and early March to 59% in the latest poll. And while the slight drop in Giuliani's rating from the early March poll is not significant, the larger seven-point drop from February is. Meanwhile, Romney's positive scores have inched up as he has

become somewhat better known. McCain's favorable rating is still above the break-even point among all Americans (51%), testifying to his greater appeal among independents and Democrats than what Republican politicians normally enjoy. Giuliani's 60% nationwide favorable rating is the highest among the leading contenders of either party, and he, too, has relatively strong ratings among Democrats. Gingrich is the only major candidate of either party who is viewed more unfavorably (48%) than favorably (29%) by Americans.

Democratic Ballot

Democrats' preferences for their party's 2008 presidential nomination have been fairly stable since early February. In the current poll, 35% of Democrats say they are most likely to support Clinton for the nomination. Obama is next, at 22%. Gore maintains the slightly higher level of support (17%) he received following the Academy Awards ceremony, at which his global warming documentary won two awards. Edwards is now supported by 14%, up from 9% in early March but similar to the levels of support he enjoyed in February. That suggests little effect from the recent news that his wife, Elizabeth, has had a recurrence of cancer and their decision to continue with his presidential campaign.

Outside the four leading contenders, no more than 3% of Democrats support any other Democratic candidate in the latest ballot. Moreover, among the lesser candidates, only Joe Biden has registered as much as 5% in any Gallup Poll this year. Gore has indicated he does not plan to run, but he has not ruled out a bid, either. When Gore voters' second choice is substituted for their Gore vote on the ballot, the results suggest that Clinton's support would increase to 42% and her lead over Obama (24%) would

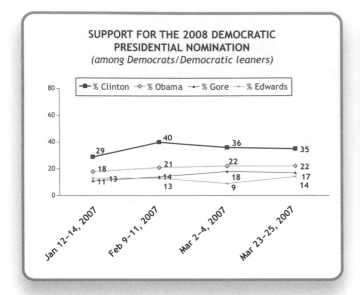

SUPPORT FOR THE 2008 DEMOCRATIC
PRESIDENTIAL NOMINATION
(among Democrats/Democratic leaners)

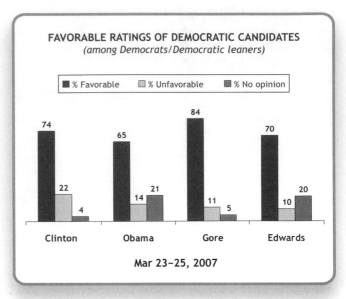

FAVORABLE RATINGS OF DEMOCRATIC CANDIDATES
(among Democrats/Democratic leaners)

Mar 23–25, 2007

stretch to 18 points if Gore were not in the race. Edwards would receive 17% of the vote in this scenario, with every other candidate at 4% or less. Clinton also maintains a significant lead over Obama (56% to 37%) when the two are matched one-on-one. She has led him by a wide margin each time the question has been asked.

Even though Clinton is the clear front-runner, one set of numbers does not work in her favor. In the latest poll, more Democrats and Democratic-leaning independents rate Gore (84%) favorably than they do Clinton (74%). Edwards's favorable rating is 70% among Democrats and Obama's is 65%. Obama's lower rating is attributable to the fact he is less well known, as 21% of Democrats are not familiar enough with him to rate him. That compares with 4% having no opinion of Clinton, 5% of Gore, and 20% of Edwards. In recent weeks, Clinton's favorability rat-

ing among Democrats has declined somewhat, from 80% or better to the current 74%. Meanwhile, Gore's image has improved from 72% in early February to 84% today. Edwards's popularity also received a small boost following the announcement of his wife's recurrence of cancer. Views of Obama have held steady in recent weeks.

At this point, it does not appear that Gore has been able to capitalize on his heightened popularity among Democrats, given the only modest increase in his support in the nomination trial heat in recent weeks and that he still trails Clinton by a wide margin. This could be partly attributable to his apparent reluctance to run, which may cause some Democrats who might otherwise support him not to do so. It could also reflect a desire to nominate "new blood," as Gore was unsuccessful in winning the presidency in 2000 as the Democratic nominee. Of note is that Clinton's favorable rating among all Americans (48%) has dipped below 50% for the first time since early 2003, prior to the release of her autobiography. Gore (56%), Edwards (55%), and Obama (53%) now receive higher favorable ratings among the general public than does Clinton.

Clinton's ability to win the general election is likely to be an issue throughout the campaign. While the sub-50% favorable rating does not mean she is doomed to lose, it does not cast her chances in a favorable light relative to those of her chief rivals.

MARCH 30

The Voters Speak: Reasons Behind Support for Four Front-Runners

Although the presidential campaign is still some nine months away from the first significant caucus or primary

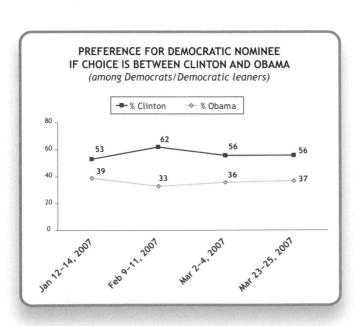

PREFERENCE FOR DEMOCRATIC NOMINEE
IF CHOICE IS BETWEEN CLINTON AND OBAMA
(among Democrats/Democratic leaners)

vote, the incessant campaigning and news coverage that are already taking place allow potential voters to form at least nascent images of the front-running candidates. Recent Gallup polling has asked Americans to talk about the candidates in their own words. A February poll asked respondents to indicate why they felt the major candidates would make good or bad presidents.

Gallup's March 23–25, 2007, poll measures the images of the front-runners in a somewhat different way. Gallup asked Republicans to choose between the two front-runners for their party's nomination—former New York mayor Rudolph Giuliani and Arizona senator John McCain—and then asked respondents to explain the reasons for their choice. Gallup asked Democrats to choose between New York senator Hillary Clinton and Illinois senator Barack Obama and to explain *their* choice. The results give further insights into those dimensions of the candidates that Americans are taking into account at this early stage of the 2008 campaign.

Giuliani vs. McCain

Giuliani maintains his lead over McCain when Gallup asks Republicans and Republican-leaning independents to choose between the two, although Giuliani's lead is down from where it was in early March. It is apparent that a good deal of Giuliani's support among Republicans continues to be based on his perceived leadership abilities, his track record as New York City mayor, and his handling of the aftermath of the 9/11 terrorist attacks. These are the most frequently given responses among his supporters. They also cite Giuliani's personal characteristics and the basic fact that they are familiar with him. Relatively few supporters mention Giuliani's positions on the issues as the reason for their support, consistent with the fact that he has not held any federal elected office and has worked in the private sector since leaving the mayor's office at the end of 2001. A fairly substantial percentage of Giuliani supporters base their support for him mostly on problems they have with McCain—including that McCain changes his mind too much, is a maverick, is too moderate, is not electable, and is too old.

McCain's supporters are considerably less likely than Giuliani's to say that they support their preferred candidate because of the opponent's shortcomings. The relatively few McCain supporters who make specific comparisons with Giuliani focus on the two candidates' ideologies, with McCain being perceived as more conservative than Giuliani by some and more moderate than Giuliani by others. Support for McCain appears to be built mostly on a favorable view of the specific characteristics he is said to exhibit, with his experience and military background

the most frequently cited specific characteristics. Other McCain supporters cite his positions on the issues and his honesty. Eighteen percent of McCain's supporters say their support is simply based on the fact that they are familiar with the candidate. This is a plus for McCain at this point but could be negated to the extent that other Republican presidential candidates become better known during the presidential campaign.

Clinton vs. Obama

As has been the case all year, Clinton has a significant lead over Obama when Democrats and Democratic-leaning independents are asked to choose between the two. Perhaps not surprisingly given Clinton's 15-plus years in the public spotlight, her support is based largely on specifics about her experience and knowledge and her positions on the issues. Her husband, former president Bill Clinton, is mentioned by some supporters, and is presumably seen as a plus by these supporters because of the general experience and exposure to government that his presidency has afforded Hillary. Some Americans support Clinton because she is a woman and would be the first female president in U.S. history if elected. There is some support for Clinton based on a favorable comparison with Obama, but the majority of this support appears to be driven by the fact that these respondents are not familiar with Obama. This may in fact be a plus for Obama, since the familiarity gap will likely close as the campaign moves forward. Support for Obama in the context of this two-person "ballot" is at this point built to a large degree on the fact that he is not Clinton. This should not be surprising because Clinton has been a public figure for so much longer than Obama. Still, it suggests that while Clinton's experience and exposure are pluses in some Democrats' eyes, they represent a negative to others.

The specifics cited by Democrats who are in essence "anti-Clinton" are the simple fact that they do not like Clinton, that Clinton has too much baggage or is too polarizing, and that Clinton is less electable. A small percentage of Obama supporters back him because they believe Clinton's gender is a negative factor hurting her candidacy. There is some support for Obama based on his positions on issues, particularly his opposition to the war in Iraq. A relatively small percentage of Obama's supporters mention the fact that he would be a new, fresh face. This factor has come up in previous open-ended investigations of Obama's appeal to Americans, but is less frequently cited in this context. A number of the reasons given by Americans for their support of these four candidates are similar: the experience of the candidate and his or her positions on the issues and personal characteristics.

Of interest is the fact that Giuliani and Obama supporters are more likely than McCain and Clinton supporters to cite negatives about their preferred candidate's opponent as the reason for their support. This is most likely because McCain and Clinton are better known than the other two, but it suggests that being relatively new on the national scene may have a positive side.

The data support several additional conclusions:

- Giuliani's strength among Republicans is built on the base of his image coming out of New York and the 9/11 aftermath. He benefits at the moment from a positive comparison with his potential opponent, McCain.

- McCain's strength is built on the positive image he has developed among his Republican supporters, including in particular his military background and his general experience. McCain also gains support from those who like his positions on the issues.

- Clinton's strength is her knowledge and experience and her positions on the issues. Her Democratic supporters seem to know her well, and applaud the specifics of her resume—including the fact that her husband was president for eight years—and her stance on issues. Some Clinton supporters explicitly cite Clinton's gender as the reason behind their potential vote.

- Obama at this juncture appears to benefit from Democratic supporters' choosing him over Clinton precisely because he is not Clinton and does not have the baggage and negative image she has developed among these Obama-supporting respondents. Obama gains some support because he is a fresh face with new ideas, and because of his positions on the issues.

APRIL 2007

Recent Gallup polling continues to indicate a favorable political environment for the Democratic Party. Democrats maintained a significant advantage in partisan identification throughout the first quarter of 2007. Additionally, by a sizable margin, Americans say they would rather see the Democrats than the Republicans win the 2008 presidential election. A ray of hope for Republicans exists in that their leading presidential contenders are currently viewed more positively by Americans than the leading Democratic presidential contenders. Also, the Republican candidates are highly competitive with the Democratic candidates in head-to-head matchups.

During the first quarter of 2007, an average of 33% of Americans identified as Democrats, 28% as Republicans, and 38% as independents. Several things are notable about these numbers. First, 28% is the lowest percentage of self-identified Republicans in any quarter since the second quarter of 1999. Yet despite the Democratic Party's advantage over the Republicans, the percentage of Americans identifying with the Democratic Party actually went down this past quarter. After averaging 35% in each of the last three quarters of 2006, Democratic identification is now similar to what it was at the beginning of 2006. The consequent rise in independent identification, from 35% in the final quarter of 2006 to 38% in the first quarter of 2007, pushed that percentage to the highest level it has been since the last quarter of 1999, when 38% also identified as independents. The five-point Democratic edge in party identification over the Republicans is one of the highest observed during the Bush administration, second only to the six-point advantage in the final quarter of 2006. Prior to the Bush presidency, Democratic advantages of this size were not uncommon.

The Democratic edge becomes obvious and more impressive when looking at not just party identification, but also party "leaning." In each poll it conducts, Gallup asks those who identify as independents whether they lean more to the Democratic or Republican Party. Generally speaking, partisan leaners' attitudes and reported behaviors resemble the attitudes and behaviors of party identifiers more than they do those of voters with no party attachment or leaning. These days, a greater proportion of independents express a leaning toward the Democratic Party than toward the Republican Party. When party leanings are taken into account, the 5-percentage-point Democratic advantage on national partisanship from the first quarter grows to 12 points, 52% to 40%. The disproportionate leaning toward the Democratic Party among independents has been evident since early 2005. During the first term of Bush's presidency (2001–5), independents' leanings broke about evenly between the two parties. Democrats had a slightly larger 14-point advantage on leaned-party identification in the final quarter of 2006 than its 12-point edge in the most recent quarter. But those two gaps in favor of the Democrats are the largest Gallup has measured for either party in any quarterly average since it began regularly tracking leaned-party identification in 1991. (Gallup did poll leaned-party identification prior to 1991, though not on a consistent basis. Historical data indicate that Democratic advantages in leaned-party identification even greater than the recent 14-point edge were not uncommon in the 1950s, 1960s, and 1970s.)

In its April 2–5, 2007, poll, Gallup asked Americans if they would rather see the Republicans or Democrats win the 2008 presidential election if the election were held today. The public chose the Democrats by a solid 50% to 35% margin. Democrats show stronger party loyalty on this question than do Republicans: Ninety-six percent of Democrats (and 91% of Democrats and Democratic leaners) want their party's candidate to win, compared with 84% of Republicans (and 80% of Republicans and Republican leaners). That apparent Democratic dominance does not emerge, however, when

CHRONOLOGY

APRIL 2007

April 1 Senator Hillary Clinton's campaign announces that it raised $26 million during the first quarter of 2007, a record amount for this stage of a presidential campaign.

April 1 Mitt Romney's campaign announces it has raised $21 million during the first quarter of 2007, making him the leading Republican fund-raiser.

April 1 Tommy Thompson, former governor of Wisconsin, announces his candidacy for the Republican presidential nomination.

April 1 Senator John McCain leads a Republican congressional delegation to Iraq and says he sees "encouraging signs."

April 2 Representative Tom Tancredo of Colorado announces his candidacy for the Republican presidential nomination.

April 3 Senator Barack Obama's campaign announces it raised $25 million during the first quarter of 2007.

April 5 Rudolph Giuliani says that if elected, he will not seek to make abortion illegal.

April 9 Iran's President Mahmoud Ahmadinejad says that Iran now has the capacity to enrich uranium on a large scale, a critical step on the road to building a nuclear bomb.

April 10 An invitation to Vice President Dick Cheney to be the commencement speaker at Brigham Young University sparks rare protests on the conservative school's campus.

April 12 Two Iraqi members of Parliament and six others are killed by a suicide bomb attack in Iraq's Parliament building, which is located in the American-controlled Green Zone.

April 14 A car bomb kills more than 50 people in Karbala, Iraq.

April 16 In the deadliest shooting by a gunman in American history, a student at Virginia Tech, a university in Blacksburg, Virginia, kills 32 students and teachers.

April 18 Five bombs kill more than 200 civilians in Shiite neighborhoods of Baghdad.

April 18 In a 5–4 decision, the U.S. Supreme Court upholds the 2003 Partial-Birth Abortion Act.

April 19 Attorney General Alberto Gonzales testifies before the Senate Judiciary Committee regarding the firings of federal attorneys. Citing a bad memory, Gonzales fails to answer many questions.

April 25 Senator McCain officially announces his candidacy for the Republican presidential nomination.

April 25 Jim Gilmore, former governor of Virginia, announces his candidacy for the Republican presidential nomination.

April 26 The Senate passes an Iraq spending bill that includes a call for U.S. troops to begin to withdraw from Iraq. Senators Clinton and Obama support the bill; Senator McCain is not present for the vote.

April 26 The first Democratic debate is held at South Carolina State University. All eight Democratic candidates attend.

April 28 A mosque in Karbala is bombed; 55 are killed.

Americans are asked to choose among actual candidates. For example, when Gallup tested preferences between the two leading Republican contenders (former New York mayor Rudolph Giuliani and Arizona senator John McCain) and the two leading Democratic contenders (New York senator Hillary Clinton and Illinois senator Barack Obama), in only one of the four matchups did a candidate have a statistically significant lead among registered voters, and that was a Republican (Giuliani) over a Democrat (Obama). More recent surveys conducted by other polling organizations show the same general pattern: a tight race, if not a Republican lead, in these general election trial heats. In fact, a Democratic candidate leads only when matched against a relatively unknown Republican candidate, such as former Massachusetts governor Mitt Romney or former Tennessee senator Fred Thompson. The relatively poor performance of specific Democratic candidates as compared with the generic ballot may be because, as of now, the leading Republican presidential candidates are viewed more favorably by Americans than are the leading Democrats.

Walking through the Shorja market in Baghdad on April 1, 2007, Senator John McCain reaffirmed his support for the Iraq War. *(Matthew Roe / AP Images)*

Currently, Giuliani has the highest favorable rating of any of the major presidential candidates, at 61%, followed by McCain, at 57%. All of the major Democratic candidates' ratings hover around 50%, including Clinton and former vice president Al Gore, who also have the highest unfavorable ratings. In particular, Clinton's favorable rating has declined in recent weeks; it had been 54% in early March 2007 and 58% in early February. After she released her autobiography in 2003, her favorable rating went above 50%, and it had not gone below that mark until last month. Based on these poll results, it is unclear which party would win if the election were held today. Clearly, the political environment favors the Democrats, given their advantage in party affiliation and the electorate's generic preference for a Democratic president. But partisan political preferences may be less of a factor in presidential elections than in midterm congressional elections—which is supported by the fact that Republican presidential candidates are able to offset, if not completely overcome, the existing Democratic advantage in head-to-head matchups against the Democratic candidates. However, it should be noted that these trial heat matchups are generally not good predictors of what will happen on Election Day this far in advance, particularly when the candidates are not well known.

APRIL 2

Clinton's Gender Gap Most Evident Among Independents

Senator Hillary Clinton has a more positive image among women than among men. This gender gap is most evident among "pure" independents who do not lean toward either party. Clinton's favorable rating among purely independent women is 21 points higher than among independent men. The majority of independent women have a favorable view of Clinton, aligning them with Democrats; most independent men have an unfavorable view of Clinton, aligning them with Republicans. This analysis is based on 10,065 Gallup Poll interviews, conducted between February 2005 and March 2007, in which Clinton's favorable rating was measured.

Gender

The gender gap in opinions of Clinton is highly significant. In this large sample, men are about evenly divided in their opinions of the New York senator, with 49% rating her unfavorably and 47% rating her favorably. Among women, on the other hand, Clinton has a 23-point net favorable rating, 59% to 36%. This gender gap may result from several different factors. One, of course, is that Clinton is a famous female politician with a realistic chance of becoming the first woman president in U.S. history, and thus someone with whom female voters may identify. Another cause is the greater likelihood of women as compared with men to identify with the Democratic Party, coupled with Democrats' tendency to rate Democratic politicians more favorably than do non-Democrats.

APRIL 3

Despite Strength in Poll, Thompson's Image Ill-Defined

A lot of attention has been focused in recent days on the potential candidacy of former Republican senator Fred Thompson. Less than two weeks ago, Thompson indicated that he might jump into the race. When included in the late March USA Today/Gallup Poll shortly thereafter, he came in third among Republicans when asked whom they support for their party's nomination, behind Rudolph Giuliani and John McCain. In addition to being a lawyer and former senator from Tennessee, Thompson is a television and movie actor starring in recent years as a tough district attorney in the top-rated *Law and Order* television series. But the extent to which Thompson's image is dominated by his acting as opposed to his "real world" lawyer and senator roles is unclear. Accordingly, Gallup asked a random sample of Americans to answer this question: "What comes to your mind when you think about former Tennessee senator Fred Thompson?"

The results show that a large number of Republicans (67%) don't know much at all about Thompson. Those who do know him say he would be a good president (6%), but others either talk about his acting career (7%) or offer vague generalities such as "I like him"(7%) or "Nice guy"(5%). What is most interesting about these data is the fact that two-thirds of Americans say that nothing at all comes to mind when they think about "former Tennessee senator Fred Thompson." In other words, despite his acting career, Thompson is not among the ranks of well-known politicians at this point.

The data show that Americans who have an opinion of Thompson are essentially as likely to mention his acting career, including specific mentions of *Law and Order* (15%), as they are other characteristics. References to his thespian activities are followed in rank order by rather vague references to his being a "nice guy" (4%), that "I like him" (also 4%), that he would make a good president (4%), and that he would not make a good president (2%). There is no significant difference in the number of Republicans who are able to come up with any association with Thompson and the number of independents and Democrats; about two-thirds of all three partisan groups draw a blank. Republicans, however,

are slightly less likely to mention Thompson's acting and slightly more likely to mention other dimensions, including the generic "I like him" and "He's a nice guy." Only a small percentage of Republicans mention anything more specific about Thompson. Two percent each say that he is conservative, that he is a good speaker, and that he is honest.

It would appear that the smaller number of Republicans who do know Thompson like him, and 12% obviously like him enough to make him their first choice for the Republican nomination. Thompson's appeal to those Republicans who support him at this point may result from a vague notion that he could be the "conservative who could win" the Republican presidential nomination, rather than from a well-defined picture of his political career or issue positions. And, of course, even among those who know Thompson, his image is built to a certain degree off his acting career. There is little sign here that Republican voters are highly knowledgeable about Thompson's record or his positions on specific issues.

APRIL 4

Republicans and Democrats Seek Similar Qualities in 44th President

Republicans and Democrats are in general agreement about the qualities they are looking for in the next president of the United States, although they do differ on some important specifics. Both sides demand honesty, strong leadership, management skills, and moral integrity in the nation's 44th president. Both sides also put less emphasis on military experience, business experience, political experience, and religious commitment. Beyond these shared views, Republicans are much more likely than Democrats to say marital fidelity is essential in a president. Democrats have a greater interest than Republicans in wanting a president who will consider public opinion when making decisions.

Gallup probed public attitudes about the ideal president in a recent Gallup survey of 1,006 nationally representative adults, conducted between March 26 and March 29, 2007. One question asked respondents to describe, in their own words, what quality they consider most important for the next president to possess. A second question asked respondents to rate the importance of 16 specific qualities a president might have.

Honesty Springs to Mind

With the open-ended measure, Gallup finds honesty to be the top-named quality by Republicans as well as by Democrats. Eleven percent of each group also mention competency in managing the government. Leadership figures in the top five responses for both groups but is mentioned by nearly twice as many Republicans as Democrats. Two qualities in the Republicans' top five that don't appear in the Democrats' are integrity and good moral character. And two qualities in the Democrats' top five that don't appear in the Republicans' are listening to people rather than special interests/political parties and putting domestic interests ahead of foreign interests.

More generally, Republicans appear to attach a bit more importance than do Democrats to the personal qualities of a president, judging from the sum of all personal qualities mentioned in the open-ended results: honesty, integrity, good moral values, intelligence, being honorable, being trustworthy, being a Christian, having common sense, and having charisma. Although these are the most commonly mentioned qualities among both groups, they account for roughly 7 out of 10 mentions among Republicans as compared with less than 6 in 10 among Democrats. Republicans and Democrats are about equally likely to mention qualities more closely associated with the presidency, including leadership, managerial competence, listening to people, having a vision, and being a consensus builder. Democrats are more likely than Republicans to cite taking specific policy positions as being the most important quality they are looking for in a president, almost entirely due to the desire to have the next president put a greater emphasis on domestic issues. Few Americans of either party cite political experience of any kind as the chief quality they are looking for.

No Argument over Importance of Strong Leadership

The second measure asked respondents to rate each of 16 qualities as either "absolutely essential," "important, but not essential," or "not that important." Republicans and Democrats widely agree that it is absolutely essential for a president to be a strong and decisive leader. Most also say it is essential that the next president have good moral character, though Republicans are more likely than Democrats to hold this view. A majority of both groups also agree that the next president must be an effective manager and focus on uniting the country. The bigger partisan differences in favored qualities seem to relate to the public images of the most recent Republican and Democratic presidents. President George W. Bush has been criticized over his Iraq War policy for "staying the course" rather than heeding public opinion polls that show Americans widely opposed to the war. Accordingly, a majority of Republicans (53%) say it is essential that a president has taken consistent issue positions over time, while only 42% of Democrats feel this way. Conversely, half of Democrats consider it essential for a president to pay attention to public opinion when making decisions, compared with only a third of Republicans.

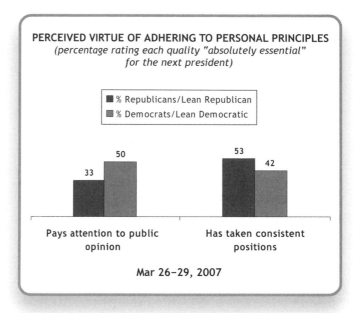

PERCEIVED VIRTUE OF ADHERING TO PERSONAL PRINCIPLES
(percentage rating each quality "absolutely essential" for the next president)

Mar 26–29, 2007

The starkest partisan gap in the poll may stem from opposing perspectives on the marital foibles of former president Bill Clinton, whose affair with a former White House intern while he was in office nearly cost him the presidency. More than twice as many Republicans as Democrats (52% vs. 25%) say it is essential that a president has been faithful to his or her spouse. (Whether this pattern holds if one of the Republican presidential candidates with admitted marital problems becomes nominated remains to be seen.)

Other notable differences by party include Republicans' greater likelihood to consider it essential for a president to regularly attend religious services and to stick closely to the principles of his or her own party. Democrats are more likely than Republicans to want an inspiring speaker.

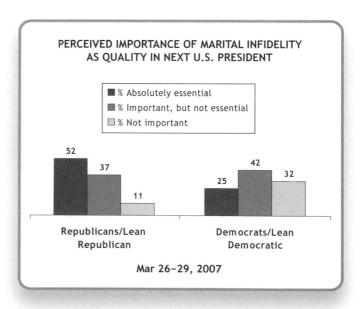

PERCEIVED IMPORTANCE OF MARITAL INFIDELITY AS QUALITY IN NEXT U.S. PRESIDENT

Mar 26–29, 2007

APRIL 10

Clinton Remains Dominant Front-Runner Among Democrats

Hillary Clinton remains the presidential front-runner among Democrats nationally, with twice the support of her nearest challenger. Senator Barack Obama, former North Carolina senator John Edwards, and former vice president Al Gore are tightly bunched in second place, with all other candidates in low single digits. If Gore is removed from the ballot and his supporters' second-place choices substituted, Clinton's lead becomes even more dominant, with Obama and Edwards tied far behind. These data were collected between April 2 and April 5, just as reports of Obama's first-quarter fund-raising success were made public. The survey results suggest that while Obama may have had a great deal of financial momentum in the past quarter, it was not matched by any increase in voter support.

The basic trends over five Gallup Polls conducted among Democrats nationally this year are as follows:

Although the exact percentages vary from poll to poll, as one would expect given the relatively modest sample sizes (between 450 and 500) of Democrats involved in each poll, Clinton remains the dominant leader, far outpacing any of her rivals. The trend for Obama has been relatively static. The Illinois senator ends up in this latest April poll essentially where he was last January: He gets exactly half of the vote given to Clinton. Edwards has held his own during this time: He averaged 13% across the five polls and ended up at 15%. Edwards had one slightly weaker showing in early March, but in the next poll, taken shortly after his announcement that he would continue his campaign despite his wife Elizabeth's recurrence of cancer, his standing recovered.

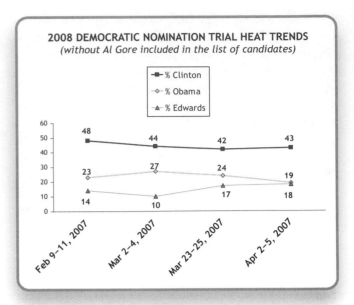

2008 DEMOCRATIC NOMINATION TRIAL HEAT TRENDS
(without Al Gore included in the list of candidates)

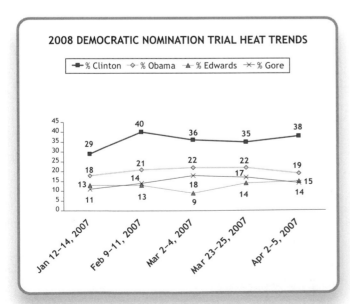

2008 DEMOCRATIC NOMINATION TRIAL HEAT TRENDS

Unannounced candidate Gore pulls in 14% of the vote of Democrats in this poll. He may have received a slight boost in polls conducted after his appearance at the Academy Awards ceremony in February, but the benefits he received appear to have subsided. Whether Gore eventually ends up jumping into the campaign for president is an unknown factor at this point. He has said he has "no plans" to run and has not been campaigning or fund-raising. Among Democrats and Democratic-leaning independents with Gore removed—with the second-place choice of the 14% of Democrats who supported Gore as their first choice substituted for Gore—the extent of Clinton's lead among Democrats becomes even clearer. Clinton is in essence the runaway front-runner, with Obama and Edwards tied far behind for second with less than half of Clinton's support.

The race for the Democratic nomination at this point is still highly fluid. Candidates are dropping in and out of the race, with others hovering in the wings but giving no firm sign yet of their intentions. Clinton's continued dominance as the front-runner across the five Gallup Polls conducted so far this year (and, for that matter, in national polls going back to 2005) is therefore remarkable. There has been some movement from poll to poll, as would be expected, but to this date no other candidate has challenged her hegemony over the process.

There are no signs, either, of any major movement on the part of any of the third tier of announced or potential candidates, including former general Wesley Clark, Delaware senator Joe Biden, New Mexico governor Bill Richardson, and Connecticut senator Christopher Dodd.

The first-quarter fund-raising reports announced last week provided an additional quantitative indicator of where the Democratic candidates stand in the race for

At an informal gathering in Concord, New Hampshire, on April 14, 2007, Senator Joe Biden addresses a small group of prospective voters. *(Lee Mariner / AP Images)*

their party's nomination. Obama received a good deal of positive press for his ability to come close to matching Clinton's first-quarter monetary total. As of early April, the data show that despite holding his own with Clinton on the fund-raising front, Obama continues to trail her by a considerable distance in terms of national Democratic preferences, as do Edwards, Gore, and various third-tier candidates.

APRIL 16

Americans More in Favor of Heavily Taxing the Rich Now Than in 1939

About half of Americans advocate heavy taxation of the rich in order to redistribute wealth, a higher percentage than was the case in 1939. More generally, a large majority of Americans support the principle that wealth should be more evenly distributed in the United States, and an increasing number—although still a minority—say there

are too many rich people in the country. Attitudes toward heavy taxes on the rich are strongly related to one's own income, and Democrats are much more likely to be in favor of income redistribution than are Republicans.

A poll commissioned by *Fortune* magazine in 1939 and conducted by the famous pollster Elmo Roper included a question phrased as follows: "People feel differently about how far a government should go. Here is a phrase which some people believe in and some don't. Do you think our government should or should not redistribute wealth by heavy taxes on the rich?" At that time, near the end of the Great Depression, only a minority of Americans, 35%, said the government should impose heavy taxes on the rich in order to redistribute wealth. A slight majority—54%—said the government should not. (Eleven percent did not have an opinion.) Gallup asked this question again in 1998 and found the percentage willing to say that the government should redistribute wealth had gone up by 10 points, while the "no opinion" responses had dropped to 4% and the negative stayed slightly above 50%.

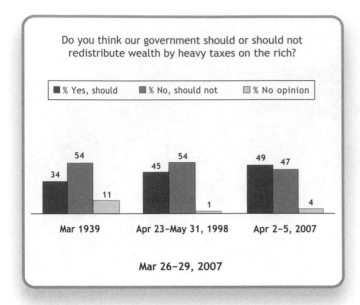

Do you think our government should or should not redistribute wealth by heavy taxes on the rich?

■ % Yes, should   ■ % No, should not   □ % No opinion

Mar 1939 — 34, 54, 11
Apr 23–May 31, 1998 — 45, 54, 1
Apr 2–5, 2007 — 49, 47, 4

Mar 26–29, 2007

Now the attitudes have shifted slightly again, to the point where Americans' sentiment in response to this question is roughly split, with 49% saying the government should redistribute wealth by heavy taxes on the rich and 47% disagreeing.

One must be cautious in interpreting changes between the 1939 poll, which was conducted using different sampling and methods than is the case today, and the current poll. It does appear safe to say, however, that based on this one question, the American public has become at least somewhat more "redistributionist" over the almost seven decades since the end of the Depression. The current results of this question are in line with a separate Gallup question that asks whether various groups in American society are paying their fair share of taxes, or too much or too little. Two-thirds of Americans say "upper-income people" are paying too little in taxes. There is no trend on this question going back to the 1930s, but the super-majority agreement that upper-income people pay too little in taxes has been evident for the last 15 years.

More on Attitudes Toward Wealth and the Rich

The most recent Gallup Poll included two other questions measuring attitudes toward wealth and the rich. One asked: "Do you feel that the distribution of money and wealth in this country today is fair, or do you feel that the money and the wealth in this country should be more evenly distributed among a larger percentage of the people?" The results of this question, asked seven times over the past 23 years, have consistently shown that Americans are strongly in favor of the principle that money and wealth in this country

should be more evenly distributed. The current 66% who feel that way is tied for the highest reading on this measure across this period.

A separate question asked: "As far as you are concerned, do we have too many rich people in this country, too few, or about the right amount?" Here the evidence shows a growing resentment toward the rich. The percentage of Americans who say there are too many rich people in the United States, although still a minority, is up significantly from the two times in the 1990s when this question was asked. In summary, the data show that a significant majority of Americans feel that money and wealth should be distributed more equally across a larger percentage of the population. A significant majority of Americans feel that the rich pay too little in taxes; about half of Americans support the idea of "heavy" taxes on the rich to help redistribute wealth. Almost 4 out of 10 Americans flat-out believe there are "too many" rich people in the country.

Implications

Most societies experience tensions revolving around inequalities of wealth among their members. This seemingly inevitable fact of life has been at the core of revolutions throughout history. American society has been immune from massive revolts of those at the bottom end of the spectrum in part because the public perceives that the United States is an open society with upward social mobility. A recent Gallup Poll found a majority of Americans believing that people who make a lot of money deserve it, and that almost anyone can get rich if they put their mind to it. And a 2003 Gallup Poll found that about a third of Americans, including a significantly higher percentage of younger Americans, believed that they themselves would one day be rich. These findings most likely reflect at least in part the fact that it is easy to advocate greater taxation of the rich, since most Americans do not consider themselves rich. In fact, a 2003 Gallup Poll found that the median annual income that Americans considered "rich" was $122,000. Since the average income in America is markedly below that, it follows that most Americans do not consider themselves rich. (Eighty percent of Americans put themselves in the middle class, working class, or lower class. Only 1% identify themselves as being in the upper class, while 19% are willing to identify themselves as upper middle class.)

The data show that as one gets closer to being what Americans consider rich, one is also less interested in the rich being taxed heavily. This relationship is fairly linear: The more money one makes in general, the more likely one is to say that the government should not be imposing heavy taxes on the rich. There are also political differences in views on heavily taxing the rich. Democrats are more than twice as likely as Republicans to agree that the government should redistribute wealth by heavy taxes on the rich. Americans in general agree with the concept that money and wealth should be distributed more equally in society today, and that the upper-income class of Americans do not pay their fair share in taxes. About half of Americans are willing to go so far as to advocate "heavy taxes" on the rich in order to redistribute wealth. These attitudes are forthcoming despite the belief of many Americans that the rich deserve their money and the hopes Americans themselves harbor that they will be rich some day. From a political viewpoint, these data suggest that a political platform focused on addressing the problems of the lower and middle classes as contrasted with the rich, and including heavier taxes on the rich, could meet with significant approval, particularly among Democrats and those with lower incomes.

APRIL 18

Gallup Summary: Americans and Gun Control

The tragic massacre at Virginia Tech on April 16 has refocused attention on the issue of gun control. It is not yet known where and how the shooter got the weapons used to kill at least 32 students at Virginia Tech, or if stricter gun control laws would have prevented the crime. Still, as was the case after the 1999 Columbine High School tragedy, Americans and their elected officials will once again find themselves wrestling with the issue of how best to attempt to control access to guns in the United States. The Gallup Poll has tracked public perceptions on gun-related issues for several decades. This review helps put the potential renewed focus on gun control in a public opinion context. A Gallup update in January 2007 found that Americans were more satisfied than dissatisfied with the current state of gun laws in the country. Fifty percent of Americans were satisfied with the nation's laws or policies on guns, while 43% were dissatisfied.

More broadly, the issue of guns and gun control was not highly salient in the minds of Americans prior to Monday's tragedy. Few if any Americans spontaneously mention guns or gun control as the most important problem facing the country or as the top priority for the president and Congress to deal with right now. Mention of guns or gun control as the nation's top problem was highest after the Columbine school shooting in 1999—but only 10% mentioned it at that time, and that percentage soon fell.

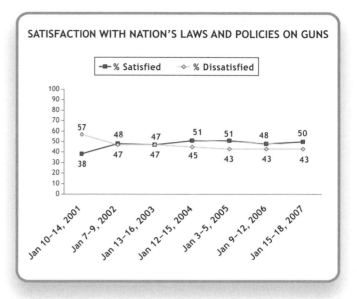

Gun Laws

Gallup has asked Americans 20 times over the last 16 years whether laws covering the sale of firearms should be made more strict, made less strict, or kept as they are now.

In every instance, at least a majority have agreed that gun laws should be made more strict—although the exact level of that sentiment has varied significantly. The high point for agreement with the "more strict" alternative was 78% in 1990, the first time the question was asked. The low point was in October 2002, with only 51% in agreement. These data suggest that if one result of the Virginia Tech shootings is to increase calls for gun control legislation, such calls will be well received by more than half the population.

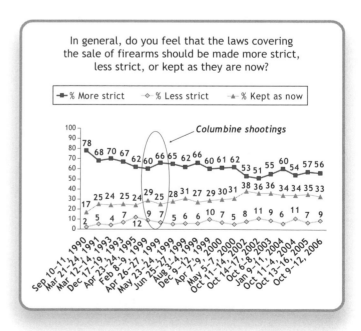

There were slight changes on this measure at the time of the Columbine shootings in April 1999. After that occurrence of gun violence, the percentage of Americans who said that gun laws should be more strict went from 60% in February 1999 to 66% the week after the shootings. This sentiment soon reverted to the 60% range, where it remained until October 2001, following the 9/11 attacks, after which it began to fall slightly. This January's 56% agreement with the "more strict" alternative is roughly average for the last five times the question has been asked since October 2003. Those most in favor of stricter laws include women (66% support stricter gun laws), those living in urban areas (67%), those with postgraduate educations (69%), liberals (70%), Democrats (72%), and those who do not have a gun in the home (70%). A similar question asked by Gallup focuses on a more general question of "gun laws" without reference to "the sale of firearms." The results are not dramatically different from the question referencing the sale of firearms. Fifty-one percent of Americans in a January 2007 poll say gun laws in the country should be more strict, while 14% say less strict and 32% say they should remain as they are now.

The National Rifle Association and other gun advocates often take the position that the correct approach to limiting gun violence is to more fully enforce existing laws rather than create new laws.

Gallup has asked this question four times, and in each instance, a majority has favored the "enforce current laws more strictly and not pass new gun laws" position rather than the "pass new gun laws in addition to enforcing the current laws more strictly" alternative. A comparison of respondents' answers to the last two questions shows that about one-third of those who say gun laws should be made more strict also say that enforcing existing laws is a better approach than passing new laws. This suggests some

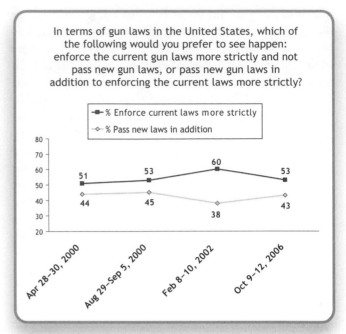

In terms of gun laws in the United States, which of the following would you prefer to see happen: enforce the current gun laws more strictly and not pass new gun laws, or pass new gun laws in addition to enforcing the current laws more strictly?

caution in interpreting survey data showing support for stricter gun laws, because at least some of that sentiment is apparently based on the assumption that this can be done without necessarily passing new laws.

A separate Gallup survey question asks about a law that would ban the possession of handguns, except by the police and other authorized persons.

Two-thirds of Americans reject the idea of such a ban. Opposition to such a ban has been slightly higher in recent years than in the late 1980s and early 1990s. When this question was asked in 1959, 6 out of 10 Americans said they favored a law that would ban the possession of handguns.

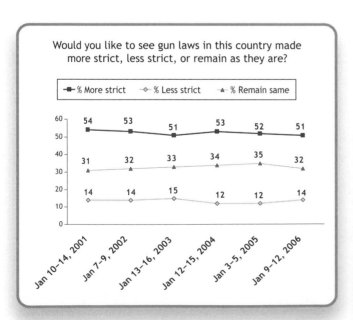

Would you like to see gun laws in this country made more strict, less strict, or remain as they are?

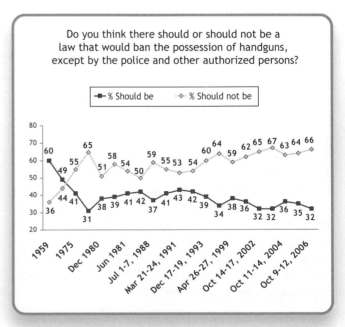

Do you think there should or should not be a law that would ban the possession of handguns, except by the police and other authorized persons?

More than 6 in 10 Republicans say they are satisfied with the nation's laws or policies on guns, while only about one-third of Democrats agree. A strong majority of Democrats feel that gun laws in the United States should be more strict, while only about a third of Republicans feel this way. Slightly less than half of Republicans feel gun laws should remain as they are at the present time. Democrats are also more likely than Republicans to support banning the possession of handguns, though a majority of both groups tend to oppose this. There are also considerable gender differences on this issue. Men are more satisfied with the nation's gun laws and less likely to say that gun laws should be more strict; they are more likely to report owning a gun and are less likely to favor banning possession of handguns. In terms of being able to purchase handguns, more than 9 in 10 Americans support the government's requiring background checks for people purchasing guns. Fifty percent of Americans support and 46% oppose making it illegal to manufacture, sell, or possess the semiautomatic guns known as assault rifles.

Although it is unclear to what degree more rigid gun control laws might have prevented the Virginia Tech tragedy, Gallup's data suggest that the public is, in general, open to the idea of stricter laws governing the sale of firearms and more rigorous enforcement of gun control laws.

APRIL 20

Giuliani and McCain Maintain Hold on Top Two Positions in Republican Field

Former New York City mayor Rudolph Giuliani continues to hold first place in the race for the Republican 2008 presidential nomination with a slightly better than 10-point lead over Arizona senator John McCain, 35% to 22%. After a brief expansion of Giuliani's lead over McCain earlier this month, the race is essentially back to where it was in late March. The latest USA Today/Gallup Poll, conducted between April 13 and April 15, 2007, finds three other candidates jockeying for third place, only one of whom—former Massachusetts governor Mitt Romney—is an announced candidate. Former Tennessee senator Fred Thompson is closely matched with Romney. Former speaker of the House Newt Gingrich, who is openly contemplating a run, is also a contender for third. All other Republicans included in the trial heat question receive 2% or less support from Republican voters. The significance of Romney's current 9% level of support is unclear. Romney has fluctuated between the low and high single digits since January; he was at 8% in early March before falling to 3% in late March. Although his early fund-raising success has given his candidacy considerable credibility at this stage of

With bass guitar in hand, former Arkansas governor Mike Huckabee entertains supporters at an Abraham Lincoln Unity Dinner in Des Moines, Iowa, on April 14, 2007. *(Charlie Neibergall/AP Images)*

the campaign, Romney will need to sustain support near and above the 10% level before establishing himself as a real threat to the top candidates.

There have been no major changes since early April in the relative positioning of the major candidates when factoring in Republicans' second choices for the nomination.

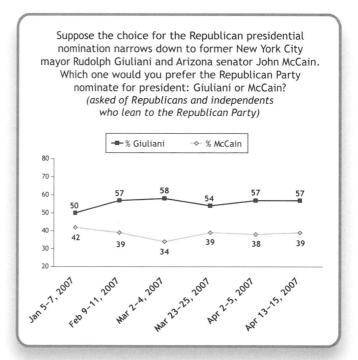

Suppose the choice for the Republican presidential nomination narrows down to former New York City mayor Rudolph Giuliani and Arizona senator John McCain. Which one would you prefer the Republican Party nominate for president: Giuliani or McCain? *(asked of Republicans and independents who lean to the Republican Party)*

Six in 10 Republicans (including independents who lean to the Republican Party) name Giuliani as either their first or second choice; about 4 in 10 name McCain. Thompson is mentioned by 19%, Gingrich by 16%, and Romney by 15%. Even with two opportunities to be chosen, 8 of the 13 candidates listed in Gallup's latest trial heat are named by less than 10% of Republicans. This group is led by former New York governor George Pataki with 6%, former Wisconsin governor Tommy Thompson with 4%, and former Arkansas governor Mike Huckabee with 4%.

Giuliani has led the Republican field in every Gallup trial heat this year, though to varying degrees. Since March, his lead has varied from 9 to 24 percentage points, due mostly to fluctuations in support for his own candidacy: The percentage choosing him has ranged from 31% to 44%, while support for McCain has been, more consistently, in the 16% to 22% range. Despite the volatility of Giuliani's lead in the full trial heat, there has been little change in his dominance over McCain when Republicans are asked to choose between these two candidates in a head-to-head matchup. Giuliani currently leads McCain by 18 points on this measure, one point below his average lead across five polls taken since February.

One-Third Wish Someone Else Would Run

Six in 10 Republicans say they are pleased with the selection of candidates definitely running for the Republican nomination at this point. So far, Giuliani, McCain, Romney, Tommy Thompson, Huckabee, Texas representative Ron Paul, Kansas senator Sam Brownback, Colorado rep-

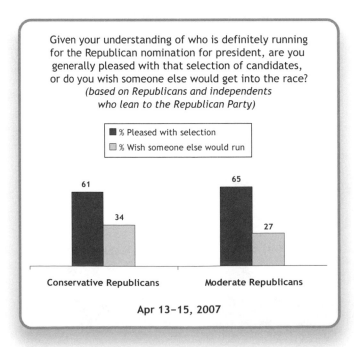

Given your understanding of who is definitely running for the Republican nomination for president, are you generally pleased with that selection of candidates, or do you wish someone else would get into the race?
(based on Republicans and independents who lean to the Republican Party)

■ % Pleased with selection
□ % Wish someone else would run

Conservative Republicans   61   34
Moderate Republicans   65   27

Apr 13–15, 2007

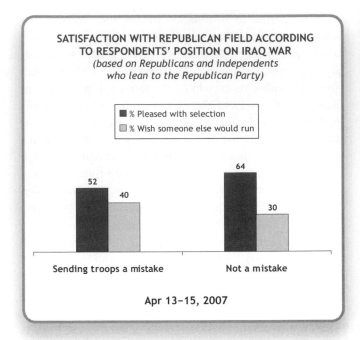

SATISFACTION WITH REPUBLICAN FIELD ACCORDING TO RESPONDENTS' POSITION ON IRAQ WAR
(based on Republicans and independents who lean to the Republican Party)

■ % Pleased with selection
□ % Wish someone else would run

Sending troops a mistake   52   40
Not a mistake   64   30

Apr 13–15, 2007

resentative Tom Tancredo, and California representative Duncan Hunter have announced their intention to run, either officially or unofficially. The list does not include former Virginia governor Jim Gilmore, who thus far has only filed an exploratory committee, nor Gingrich, Pataki, Fred Thompson, or Nebraska senator Chuck Hagel—all of whom have indicated an interest in running, but none of whom has taken formal action to establish his candidacy.

One-third of Republicans say they wish someone else would get into the race, but it is not clear what these potential voters are looking for in such a candidate. That compares with only 18% of Democrats who want another candidate to jump into their race. With Giuliani and McCain both having difficulty burnishing their conservative credentials, particularly on social issues, one might assume that conservative Republicans are especially anxious to have someone else enter the fray. However, moderate and conservative Republicans are similar on this question, with conservatives only slightly more likely (34% vs. 27%) to say they wish someone else would run.

Not much more differentiation is seen according to Republicans' stance on the Iraq War. The desire for an alternative candidate is only 10 points higher (40% vs. 30%) among the minority of Republicans who consider sending troops to Iraq a mistake than it is among the larger group that defends the Bush administration's position on Iraq.

Most Republicans who say they wish someone else would run are nevertheless able to name someone from the current list whom they say they would support for the nomination next year. Only 6% have no opinion or say "none of the above." Also, the basic rank order of candidates is the same among this group as it is among those who say they are pleased

On April 26, 2007, Democrats (from left to right) Mike Gravel, Barack Obama, Christopher Dodd, John Edwards, Dennis Kucinich, Joe Biden, Bill Richardson, and Hillary Clinton meet at South Carolina State University in Orangeburg for the first Democratic debate of the presidential race. *(J. Scott Applewhite/AP Images)*

with the current field. The most notable difference is in the percentages naming Fred Thompson as their first choice for the nomination: Fourteen percent of those who want someone else to run name him, compared with 9% of those who are pleased with the existing field. Also, although Giuliani ranks first among those wanting someone else to run, it is with a somewhat lower 30% than the 37% he receives from Republicans who are satisfied with the field. However, due to the relatively small sample sizes used in this analysis, none of these differences is statistically significant.

APRIL 23

Where the Election Stands, April 2007: A Gallup Poll Review

Polling data suggest the potential for a 2008 presidential election that will generate unusual interest from voters. In fact, early indications are that Americans are already paying as much attention to this election now as they typically do much later in the process. Current political conditions in the United States favor the Democrats. The public is highly dissatisfied with the way George W. Bush is doing his job as president, in large part because of the war in Iraq. As a result, Americans rate the Democratic Party significantly more favorably than the Republican Party, and Democrats hold a large 52% to 40% lead (as of the first quarter, 2007) in the party identification or leanings of the general population. When asked generically about the political outcome of the next election, Americans say they would rather see the Democratic Party than the Republican Party win the 2008 election if it were held today.

Early Measures on the November 2008 Outcome

The devil, however, may be in the details. A major cautionary note for the Democrats at this point in the election cycle is the disparity between Americans' partisan preferences for the next president in the abstract and their preferences between specific candidates being offered up to the voters. When asked to choose between the two major-party front-runners, New York senator Hillary Clinton and former New York City mayor Rudolph Giuliani, Americans divide almost evenly in their support. Test elections between other Democratic and Republican candidates (conducted by a variety of survey firms) show similarly close results. One explanation for this is that in spite of a very favorable Democratic environment, the public views the current Republican front-runners more positively than the current Democratic front-runners. Republicans Giuliani and John McCain typically receive favorable ratings in the mid-50s to low 60s. Ratings of Democrats John Edwards and Barack Obama are generally in the low 50s, and Hillary Clinton's ratings have descended into the 40s. This Republican advantage in candidate popularity at this point may be offsetting the Democratic advantage in the political environment.

The Fight for the Nominations

Poll results at this phase—nine months before the first primaries and caucuses—do not necessarily bear a strong relationship to the reality that unfolds in the election year itself. This has historically been true for the Democratic nomination in particular. Bill Clinton in 1992, Michael Dukakis in 1988, Jimmy Carter in 1976, and George McGovern in

1972 were all virtual unknowns who rose from obscurity to take their party's nomination. Republicans have, on the other hand, been more likely to settle on a nominee early, and stick with him.

In March, three-quarters of voters indicated that they did not yet have a good idea for whom they would vote next year. Only 14% said they had made up their minds about whom they will support. Still, Americans are willing to indicate their preferences even at this early stage of the campaign. Two candidates have developed into the early front-runners for each major party's presidential nomination: Clinton for the Democrats and Giuliani for the Republicans. Clinton's lead over second-place Illinois senator Obama was fairly consistent from January through early April, although it narrowed in a mid-April Gallup Poll. On the Republican side, Giuliani emerged as the leader in early February after having been closely matched with Arizona Senator McCain earlier. McCain has continued to place second in trial heats since February.

There are other announced or semi-announced candidates who in theory may emerge as important factors for each party. None so far has challenged the front-runners in trial heat polling, however. Former North Carolina senator Edwards (a formally announced candidate) and former vice president Al Gore (who has not ruled out a bid but has said he has no plans to run at this time) have been competitive for third place among Democrats. Each has support in the mid- to high teens, not far behind Obama. Three Republicans are competing for third place in terms of Republicans' support for their party's nomination: actor and former Tennessee senator Fred Thompson, former speaker of the House Newt Gingrich, and former Massachusetts governor Mitt Romney. Each of these candidates' support hovers at around 10%. Of these, only Romney has formally announced. None of the other potential or announced candidates in either party has so far received more than a few points in pre-election primary nomination polls. Eight out of 10 Democrats nationwide, compared with only 6 out of 10 Republicans, are satisfied with the choice of candidates for their party's nomination. This relative lack of satisfaction on the Republican side could be seen as a sign of encouragement for unannounced Republicans such as Thompson and Gingrich to officially enter the race. The finding that there is a high level of satisfaction among rank-and-file members of the Democratic Party may suggest less of an opportunity for Gore if he were to decide to enter the Democratic field.

The Candidates' Developing Images

One result of the very early start in the presidential campaign this year is a great deal of exposure of the candidates to potential voters. Some of the candidates had well-developed images before the campaign process began. For these, the campaign process in 2007 will serve to either reinforce or modify what voters already perceive. Others began as virtual unknowns, suggesting that the campaign process will help these candidates build an image from scratch.

Clearly, Clinton is the best-known candidate at this point, with nearly 100% name identification. When asked to comment on Clinton's attributes, voters are especially likely to give her credit for her knowledge and expertise. Her long and highly visible political background also has a downside, as some voters cite her political "baggage" as a reason they would not vote for her. She is also less likely than Obama to be seen as likable. Her husband, former president Bill Clinton, is seen as an asset to a Hillary Clinton presidency rather than a detriment, even among Republicans. Clinton's image has fluctuated considerably over the 14 years since her husband first entered the White House. Earlier this year, her favorable ratings reached 58%, but by mid-April they had dropped to 45%. Among the well-known contenders in both parties, only Gingrich is less popular at this point.

Voters are on a learning curve when it comes to Obama. His familiarity has risen from 53% in December to 79% today. So far, his favorability ratings have remained positive, although his negatives have risen from 11% to 27%. Obama's great appeal to voters is based on his youth and political freshness, according to Gallup open-ended responses. He is also seen as likable. Voters cite his inexperience as his biggest weakness.

Giuliani maintains a positive national image, although by mid-April his favorable rating had fallen by a few points to the lowest in Gallup's three-year tracking history. Still, his favorables are the highest of any candidate from either party, including an 82% favorable rating from Republicans. A March USA Today/Gallup Poll found that a majority of Republicans were unaware of Giuliani's positions on abortion, gun control, and same-sex marriage. Research shows that significant segments of Republicans, particularly more conservative Republicans, are less likely to vote for Giuliani once his positions on these issues are known. Giuliani may also have a problem with religious Republicans in some early primary states. According to a recent Gallup analysis, more intensely religious Republicans were significantly less likely than less religious Republicans to vote for Giuliani, although Giuliani still was the leading candidate among the former group. How Giuliani positions himself on social issues will be one of the early campaign's most important developments.

McCain's supporters cite his "experience" and "qualifications," and see his military background as an asset. McCain's highly public support for the Bush administration's troop surge in Iraq runs counter to the opinion of the majority of Americans. Republicans, however, widely support the surge, and continue to support the war in Iraq. McCain's potential to win the Republican nomination thus could be contingent on perceived progress in Iraq by the end of 2007.

A Different Kind of President?

A number of the leading candidates this year have personal characteristics atypical of past presidents. Clinton is a woman. Obama is black. Giuliani is Catholic and has been married three times. McCain is 70 years old. Romney is a Mormon.

Clinton's gender and Obama's race are obvious factors that voters have presumably already taken into account when reviewing the candidates and giving their candidate preferences. The vast majority of voters say neither gender nor race will factor into their vote. Clinton's gender may be a plus with her base of female Democrats and with female independent voters. Gallup analysis suggests that her gender is a particularly relevant factor for female independent voters. The effects of McCain's age, Giuliani's personal background, and Romney's religion are more difficult to predict. Polling Americans about their reactions to these factors suggests that each could be a problem for sizable segments of the population. Advanced age (a candidate who will be 72 years old on Election Day) generates the most significant negatives, with 4 in 10 voters saying this would be a drawback in a candidate.

Both Obama and Clinton are competing for the black Democratic vote, a minor factor in early primary and caucus states such as New Hampshire and Iowa, but of significant importance in South Carolina and in larger states that have moved their primaries to early February. The best current estimates are that the two leading candidates are fairly closely matched among black Democrats.

With the exception of Gore, Edwards, and Gingrich, most of the other potential candidates for both parties have relatively low name identification. These include Mitt Romney, Fred Thompson, Tommy Thompson, Joe Biden, and Bill Richardson.

Election Issues

Iraq is overwhelmingly seen as the most important problem facing the country today and is the top issue Americans at this point say they will take into account in their 2008 vote. The degree to which Iraq will continue to dominate the election by next year is unknowable. A scenario in which U.S. troops have begun to withdraw from Iraq by 2008 is not out of the question, nor is a scenario in which the recent "surge" in troops is seen as a success. Each of these might significantly affect the presidential election.

Concerns about terrorism will probably continue to be a strong latent issue. The economy is always a factor in an election. Consumer views of the economy became more positive in January, but by March had dropped significantly. This may partly reflect the increasing price of gas. Many aspects of the economy, in addition to energy costs, could come into play next year, including international trade, tax cuts, and income inequality. Healthcare is a rising concern to Americans, who want government involvement but do not want a national healthcare plan. Smaller segments of voters are also concerned about illegal immigration and social issues such as abortion and same-sex marriage.

The Campaign Process

Voters are likely to say that it's good, rather than bad, that the election campaign has started so early. Presumably some Americans believe the grueling process exposes them to the candidates and provides better information with which to make an informed voting decision. Voters are not disturbed by the large amounts of money being raised by the candidates; most say it will not make a difference in the quality of the person who is ultimately elected president.

APRIL 27
Gallup Poll Review: 10 Key Points About Public Opinion on Iraq

With the war in Iraq dominating U.S. news and with a major fight looming between the White House and Congress on new legislation that would fund the Iraq War but simultaneously call for a timetable for troop withdrawal, the opinions of the average American citizen are vitally important. There has been an enormous amount of public-opinion polling on Iraq since the war began in 2003, particularly in the last several months. What follows is a brief outline of 10 important points concerning the American people's views of the war.

1. The Iraq War is an extremely high priority for Americans.

A wide variety of measures show that the war in Iraq is the nation's top problem at this point in time and is by far the top issue with which the public wants its elected representatives in Washington to deal. Unless there is a significant change between now and next year, the war is likely to be one of the top issues in the 2008 presidential and congressional elections. Sixty-two percent of Americans rate Iraq as an "extremely important" issue for the president and Congress, the highest percentage for any issue tested as this year began. Thirty-three percent of Americans regard Iraq as the "most important problem" facing the country

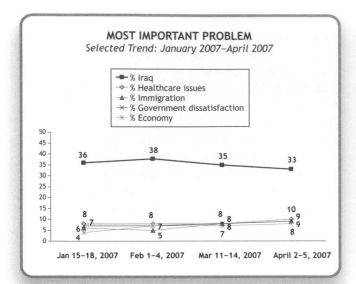

MOST IMPORTANT PROBLEM
Selected Trend: January 2007–April 2007

- % Iraq
- % Healthcare issues
- % Immigration
- % Government dissatisfaction
- % Economy

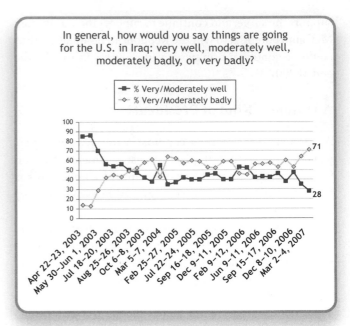

In general, how would you say things are going for the U.S. in Iraq: very well, moderately well, moderately badly, or very badly?

- % Very/Moderately well
- % Very/Moderately badly

today, by far the most dominant issue mentioned. Iraq has been the number one issue on this measure since April 2004. Two out of three Americans choose Iraq as the top priority for the president and Congress to deal with, far and away the most frequently mentioned issue.

2. A majority of Americans say it was a mistake for the United States to have become involved in Iraq.

Americans initially supported the war when it began in March 2003, but by the summer of 2004 a majority said it was a mistake. Perceptions about the war in Iraq remained volatile in 2004 and parts of 2005, but since January 2006, with one exception, at least half of Americans have called sending troops to Iraq a "mistake."

So far this year, an average of 57% of Americans across six polls have said it was a mistake for the United States to send troops to Iraq. It is important to note that opposition to the war in Iraq is not universal. Support for the administration's position on most measures concerning the war, although a minority position, ranges from the mid-30s to the mid-40s.

3. Americans perceive that the war is not going well for the United States.

Since April 2005, a majority of Americans have said things are going badly for the United States in Iraq, and more recently this perception has become even more pronounced. Most Americans also doubt the United States will win the war.

As of January 2007, 71% of Americans in a Gallup Poll said the Iraq War is going badly, including 38% who said it

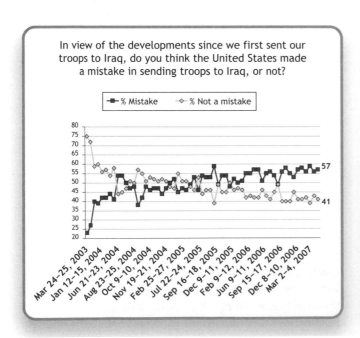

In view of the developments since we first sent our troops to Iraq, do you think the United States made a mistake in sending troops to Iraq, or not?

- % Mistake
- % Not a mistake

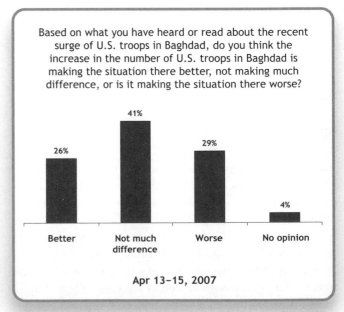

Based on what you have heard or read about the recent surge of U.S. troops in Baghdad, do you think the increase in the number of U.S. troops in Baghdad is making the situation there better, not making much difference, or is it making the situation there worse?

Better	Not much difference	Worse	No opinion
26%	41%	29%	4%

Apr 13–15, 2007

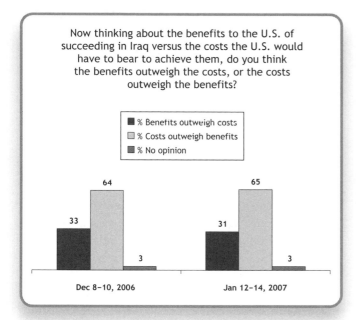

Now thinking about the benefits to the U.S. of succeeding in Iraq versus the costs the U.S. would have to bear to achieve them, do you think the benefits outweigh the costs, or the costs outweigh the benefits?

- % Benefits outweigh costs
- % Costs outweigh benefits
- % No opinion

Here are four different plans the U.S. could follow in dealing with the war in Iraq. Which one do you prefer: Withdraw all troops from Iraq immediately; withdraw all troops by March 2008—that is, in 12 months' time; withdraw troops, but take as many years to do this as are needed to turn control over to the Iraqis; or send more troops to Iraq?

Mar 2–4, 2007

is going very badly; only 28% said it is going well. A CBS News poll conducted in mid-April showed 66% saying the war was going badly. Most Americans do not think the United States will win the war.

4. Americans do not believe the troop surge is having a positive effect.

There are few signs so far that significant numbers of Americans perceive that the troop surge in Iraq is making things in that country better. The majority say the surge is either making no difference or is making things worse.

These attitudes follow earlier poll results showing that the majority of Americans opposed the surge before it was initiated by the administration.

5. Americans perceive that the benefits of winning the Iraq War do not outweigh the costs involved.

With negative perceptions of the war's progress as a backdrop, it may not be surprising that the public sees little upside for Americans in the cost-benefit trade-off of continuing the war. By a more than two-to-one margin, 65% to 31%, Americans say the benefits to the United States of winning the war in Iraq are not worth the costs the United States would have to bear in order to win it.

One attitude associated with the perception that the benefits do not outweigh the costs is that only about a third of Americans believe the threat of terrorism against the United States might increase if American troops withdraw. In an April 9–12, 2007, CBS News poll, 30% of Americans say the threat of terrorism against the United States would increase if the government withdrew its troops from Iraq, while 8% say the threat of terrorism would decrease. Fifty-nine percent say there would be no change. At the same time, a slight majority of Americans interviewed by Gallup in March per-

ceived that when U.S. troops leave Iraq, insurgent attacks in that country will increase. This apparently is not enough of a factor to cause a majority of Americans to support the war.

6. Most Americans support a timetable for removing troops from Iraq within the next year, but not immediate withdrawal.

Despite their overall negativity about the war, only about one in five Americans favor an immediate withdrawal of

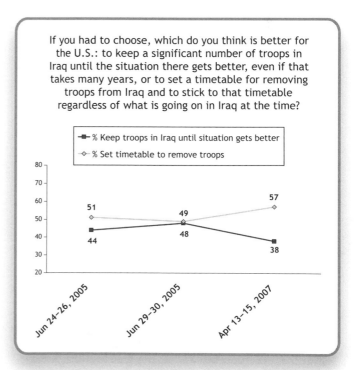

If you had to choose, which do you think is better for the U.S.: to keep a significant number of troops in Iraq until the situation there gets better, even if that takes many years, or to set a timetable for removing troops from Iraq and to stick to that timetable regardless of what is going on in Iraq at the time?

- % Keep troops in Iraq until situation gets better
- % Set timetable to remove troops

troops. Many of the rest support a gradual withdrawal of troops, preferably within a year. The majority of Americans do not favor an open-ended commitment of troops in Iraq.

It thus follows that a wide variety of polls conducted in the last two months indicate a majority of Americans (generally between 55% and 60%) now support a timetable for withdrawal of U.S. troops by next year. Gallup trends show the public about evenly divided on this in 2005, but opinion has now moved to the point that a majority supports a timetable.

A recent NBC News/Wall Street Journal poll specifically included the political entities behind each position in the current battle over withdrawal timetable legislation, and found that Americans preferred the timetable for withdrawal of troops as supported by the "Democrats in Congress" over "President Bush's" administration policy of no timetable for withdrawal, by a 19-point margin.

7. Less than a majority of Americans support cutting funding for the war.

Although some Democrats in Congress suggested cutting funds for the troops in Iraq as a means of forcing a change in U.S. policy, most Americans do not support this. As of late March 2007, 36% favored and 61% opposed denying the funding needed to send any additional U.S. troops to Iraq. Similar results were found in February.

8. Democrats are better positioned than Republicans in regard to handling the issue of Iraq.

Since 2005, the public has perceived that Democrats are better able than Republicans to handle the issue of Iraq.

Prior to this, Americans gave the Republicans the edge. Americans also say they trust the Democrats in Congress more than the administration when it comes to making decisions on Iraq. But that does not mean Americans are satisfied with the way the Democrats have handled the issue. In February, 30% approved of the way congressional Democrats were handling the issue, compared with a 27% approval rating for congressional Republicans. Most also say the Democrats lack a clear plan for handling the situation in Iraq.

9. War views are highly partisan.

Views of the Iraq War are sharply divided along partisan lines. Republicans overwhelmingly support the war; Democrats overwhelmingly oppose it. Independents are more likely to oppose than favor the war. Republicans generally defend the decision to send troops to Iraq: Seventy-four percent say it was not a mistake vs. 24% calling it a mistake. By a 63-point margin (81% vs. 18%), Democrats call sending troops to Iraq a mistake. Sixty-four percent of Republicans oppose a timetable for withdrawal of troops from Iraq, while 81% of Democrats favor it.

Nearly half of Republicans (49%) say the recent troop surge in Baghdad is making the situation there better, while 9% say it is making it worse. Thirty-five percent of Republicans say it is making no difference. Among Demo-

If you had to choose, which do you think is better for the U.S.: to keep a significant number of troops in Iraq until the situation there gets better, even if that takes many years, or to set a timetable for removing troops from Iraq and to stick to that timetable regardless of what is going on in Iraq at the time?
(by party affiliation)

■ % Keep troops in Iraq until situation gets better
□ % Set timetable to remove troops
■ % No opinion

	Republicans	Independents	Democrats
Keep troops	64	38	16
Set timetable	31	57	81
No opinion	5	5	3

Apr 13–15, 2007

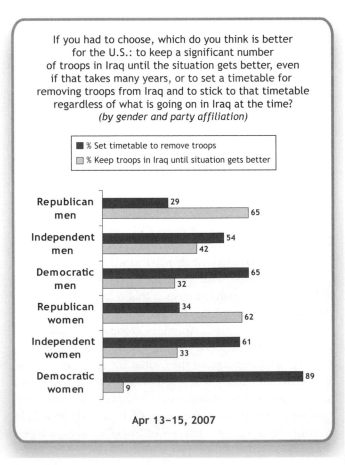

If you had to choose, which do you think is better for the U.S.: to keep a significant number of troops in Iraq until the situation gets better, even if that takes many years, or to set a timetable for removing troops from Iraq and to stick to that timetable regardless of what is going on in Iraq at the time?
(by gender and party affiliation)

■ % Set timetable to remove troops
□ % Keep troops in Iraq until situation gets better

	Set timetable	Keep troops
Republican men	29	65
Independent men	54	42
Democratic men	65	32
Republican women	34	62
Independent women	61	33
Democratic women	89	9

Apr 13–15, 2007

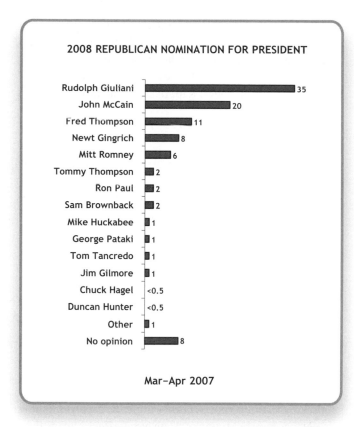

2008 REPUBLICAN NOMINATION FOR PRESIDENT

Candidate	Value
Rudolph Giuliani	35
John McCain	20
Fred Thompson	11
Newt Gingrich	8
Mitt Romney	6
Tommy Thompson	2
Ron Paul	2
Sam Brownback	2
Mike Huckabee	1
George Pataki	1
Tom Tancredo	1
Jim Gilmore	1
Chuck Hagel	<0.5
Duncan Hunter	<0.5
Other	1
No opinion	8

Mar–Apr 2007

crats, just 10% say the troop surge is making the situation better, while 43% say it is making it worse and 45% say it is making no difference. Support for past U.S. wars—including Vietnam—was not as polarized along party lines as with regard to the current war. Gallup data from 1968 and 1969 show that 53% of Americans said it was a mistake to send troops to Vietnam. Fifty-one percent of Democrats agreed with this position at the time, as did 55% of independents and 56% of Republicans.

10. A gender gap exists in views of the Iraq War.

There is a significant gender gap in terms of attitudes toward the war. Women are much more likely than men to say it was a mistake and to support a timetable for removing U.S. troops. Sixty-two percent of women say it was a mistake to send troops to Iraq, compared with 52% of men. Two in three women (66%) support a timetable for removing troops from Iraq; less than half of men (48%) agree. The gender gap is most pronounced among independents and Democrats. Male Republicans are only slightly more likely than female Republicans to favor keeping troops in Iraq and to oppose the idea of a timetable. But gender plays a larger role among independents and Democrats. Sixty-one percent of independent women support the timetable, compared with 54% of independent men. And an overwhelming 89% of Democratic women support the timetable, compared with 65% of Democratic men.

APRIL 30
Inside the Republican Vote for President

Republican presidential candidates square off in their first official debate on May 3, 2007, at the Ronald Reagan Presidential Library in Simi Valley, California. The basic structure of the Republican race has been fairly fixed for several months. Former New York City mayor Rudolph Giuliani is the front-runner, Arizona senator John McCain is in second place, and there is a rough three-way tie for third place between announced candidate Mitt Romney and unannounced candidates Newt Gingrich and Fred Thompson. To provide more insight into the pattern of support for these candidates among Republicans, this analysis is based on an aggregation of the last three polls in which the Republican test ballot was included. These polls were conducted in March and April 2007 and include a total of 1,252 Republicans and Republican-leaning independents.

IDEOLOGY

One of the most intriguing issues in open-nomination battles is the question of how support for the various candidates differs between conservative Republicans and moderate/liberal Republicans. In the race for the 2008 Republican nomination, the candidates span a relatively wide spectrum of views, particularly in terms of their positions on social issues. This is important given the much discussed need for candidates to appeal to conservative Republicans who constitute a key voting bloc in several of the early primary states. At the same time, Gallup data show that while conservatives are the dominant ideological group within the Republican Party, there are a substantial number of moderate/liberal Republicans who cannot be ignored. The data presented in the table below are based

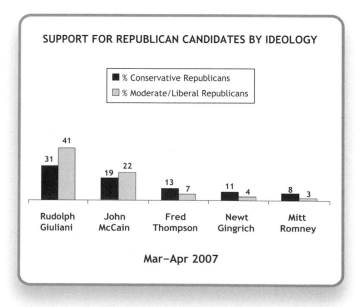

SUPPORT FOR REPUBLICAN CANDIDATES BY IDEOLOGY

- ■ % Conservative Republicans
- ▢ % Moderate/Liberal Republicans

Candidate	Conservative	Moderate/Liberal
Rudolph Giuliani	31	41
John McCain	19	22
Fred Thompson	13	7
Newt Gingrich	11	4
Mitt Romney	8	3

Mar–Apr 2007

on responses to a basic ideology question: "How would you describe your political views: very conservative, conservative, moderate, liberal, or very liberal?" For the purposes of this analysis, Republicans have been divided into two groups: those who are very conservative or conservative, and those who are moderate, liberal, or very liberal:

Front-runner Rudolph Giuliani does a bit better among the combined group of moderate/liberal Republicans than he does among conservative Republicans. On the other hand, Fred Thompson, Newt Gingrich, and Mitt Romney receive more support from conservative Republicans than from moderate and liberal Republicans. John McCain's support is relatively constant across these two groupings. But despite these differences, the basic pattern of the race remains the same among both groups: Giuliani leads and McCain is in second place, regardless of whether one is looking at conservative or moderate/liberal Republicans. Still, it appears that the two leaders—Giuliani and McCain—are more separated from the rest of the pack among moderate/liberal Republicans. Among conservative Republicans, it appears there is more of an interest in voting for alternative candidates, suggesting that conservative Republicans may be less happy with the two leaders than are Republicans who identify themselves as moderate or liberal.

The two candidates with roots in the West—John McCain of Arizona and Mitt Romney from Utah—are better positioned in the West on a relative basis than they are in other regions of the country. Giuliani of New York does less well in the West, so much so that he is essentially tied with McCain. Romney falls in third place (though not statistically ahead of Gingrich or Thompson). Fred Thompson of Tennessee does best in the South. McCain does worse in the South, leading to a situation in which he and Thompson are nearly tied for second place behind Giuliani in that region. Giuliani does slightly better in his home region of the East.

AGE

Five of the prominent Republican candidates are 60 years of age or older, ranging from Mitt Romney at 60 to John McCain at 70. Newt Gingrich is 63, Fred Thompson is 64, and Rudolph Giuliani is 62. There is, it follows, no natural pattern by which a candidate's relative youth might provide him with a particular strength among younger Republicans. Still, the data show that despite his 62 years, Rudolph Giuliani has higher support among younger Republicans, with a 13-point difference between his support among 18-to-29-year-olds and those who are 65 and older. This could spell trouble for Giuliani, since most studies show that younger voters are least likely to actually show up

at the polls to vote. Newt Gingrich and Fred Thompson do better among older Republicans than among younger Republicans. John McCain, who at 72 would be the oldest president to take office in U.S. history, does not do significantly better among older Republicans than he does among those who are younger.

EDUCATION

There are no real differences in support for candidates by education. Those Republicans who have college or postgraduate degrees do not appear to differ substantially from those who have less education in their support for the various candidates.

GENDER

There are no women running for the Republican nomination at this point, so—unlike the case with respect to the Democratic presidential field—there is no obvious hypothesis about a particular candidate getting more support among Republican women than among Republican men. The data show that Republican men tend to be more varied in their choices for the Republican nominee than their female counterparts. Front-runner Rudolph Giuliani's appeal is somewhat higher among female Republicans than among male Republicans by about seven points. There is no difference by gender in support for John McCain: His support is nearly equal among Republican men and women. Republican women are slightly more likely than men to refuse to make a choice at this point.

RELIGION

Being religious in American society today is correlated with being conservative, so it is not surprising to find that the basic patterns of support broken out by church attendance share some similarities to support by ideology. Rudolph Giuliani does slightly better among those who seldom or never attend church, although he still leads among weekly churchgoers. Mitt Romney does slightly better among frequent church attendees, though the differences are not statistically significant. Romney is a Mormon, and Gallup research indicates that Mormons have a higher level of active religiosity (that is, church attendance) than most other major religious groups in America today. Highly religious Republicans may tend to support Romney because they identify with his religious background, or it could more simply be a pattern driven by the underlying relationship between conservatism and frequency of church attendance. There is no discernible pattern of relationship between church attendance and support for McCain, Thompson, or Gingrich.

MAY 2007

On May 1, 2007, President George W. Bush vetoed an Iraqi funding bill that included a timetable for withdrawing U.S. troops from Iraq. This was only the second time Bush had vetoed a congressional bill. In an address to the nation, the president said that setting a date for the pullout of U.S. troops would be "irresponsible" and a "prescription for chaos and confusion." Democratic congressional leaders denounced the veto but were unable to override it. Senate Majority Leader Harry Reid and House Speaker Nancy Pelosi, although highly critical of the president's veto, met with him to discuss negotiating a new funding bill that would win congressional enactment.

The results of a new USA Today/Gallup Poll could embolden congressional Democrats to hold their ground. In line with the Democrats' position, roughly 6 in 10 Americans favor setting a firm timetable for withdrawing U.S. troops from Iraq; just over a third would rather keep a significant number of troops in Iraq until the situation there improves, as President Bush has called for. The results of the May 4–6 poll are similar to those of a month ago, but show somewhat more support for a timetable than was found two years ago. The new results are also consistent with a late-April Gallup survey that found 57% of Americans in favor of setting a timetable for withdrawing troops. Though this puts the public generally on the Democrats' side of the withdrawal debate, it is important to note that the same poll found only 30% of Americans preferring to see troops beginning to return home within six months. An additional 27% would rather have withdrawal start sometime next year or beyond, while 39% oppose withdrawing troops by a date certain.

Critics have chided the Democratic position in favor of a timetable for withdrawal as a "timetable for defeat," and in a newly released videotape, top al-Qaeda operative Sheikh Ayman al-Zawahiri says the Democrats' withdrawal bill "reflects American failure and frustration." This may be disquieting to some, but whether it deters Americans from supporting troop withdrawal may depend on whether they believe the United States would be less safe as a result of withdrawal. At the moment, Americans do not perceive that withdrawing U.S. troops from Iraq on a timetable puts the United States at any greater risk of terrorism than it already faces. According to a pair of parallel questions in the new survey, a majority of Americans (55%) believe new terrorist attacks against the United States will occur if U.S. troops leave Iraq on a timetable, but 51% think such attacks will occur even if U.S. troops remain in Iraq. The answers to a different question in the same poll verify this finding. When Americans are asked whether they believe the United States is more likely to be attacked by terrorists if it keeps its troops in Iraq or if it withdraws its troops from Iraq—or if the status of U.S. troops in Iraq makes no difference—the majority respond that it will make no difference. Additionally, just half of Americans believe pulling U.S. troops out of Iraq by the middle of next year will embolden countries like North Korea and Iran to make threatening moves against the United States. The new poll tested public attitudes about the likelihood of seven outcomes of the Iraq War happening either as a result of the United States's keeping its troops in Iraq for the foreseeable future, or as a result of the United State's removing all of its troops by the middle of next year, or—where applicable—under both scenarios.

While Americans consider the risk of terrorism against the United States to be the same regardless of whether U.S. troops stay in Iraq or leave, they do perceive greater negative consequences stemming from U.S. withdrawal in two areas. One is a full-scale civil war in Iraq: A substantial minority (47%) say this will happen if the United States remains in Iraq, but an even larger percentage (68%) foresee its occurring if the United States leaves the country. The other negative impact relates to the establishment of Iraq as a base of terrorist operations for

CHRONOLOGY

MAY 2007

May 1 President Bush vetoes a congressional Iraq War spending bill because it contained timetables for troop withdrawals.

May 1 Media mogul Rupert Murdock announces that his News Corporation is offering an unsolicited $5 billion to purchase the Dow Jones Corporation, which publishes the prestigious *Wall Street Journal*.

May 3 All 10 Republican candidates meet together for the first time. At the Ronald Reagan Presidential Library, they engage in a vibrant competition to define the party's agenda in a post-Bush era.

May 6 Conservative Nicolas Sarkozy wins the French presidential election, defeating Socialist Ségolène Royal. Sarkozy has promised improved relations with the United States.

May 10 British prime minister Tony Blair announces that he will resign on June 27. Blair has been one of President Bush's closest allies during the Iraq War.

May 10 Attorney General Alberto Gonzales testifies before the House Judiciary Committee on the firing of federal attorneys. He admits the firings were handled poorly but claims that all were justified.

May 14 Inspectors for the International Atomic Energy Agency conclude that Iran is enriching uranium on a far larger scale than had been previously thought.

May 15 Republican presidential candidates debate at the University of South Carolina. Appearing before a conservative audience, they answer repeated questions on abortion, immigration, and government spending.

May 15 Newt Gingrich, former speaker of the House, says there is a strong possibility that he will seek the Republican presidential nomination.

May 21 Governor Bill Richardson of New Mexico announces his candidacy for the Democratic presidential nomination.

May 28 Diplomats from the United States and Iran hold their first talks since 1980, with the topic being the future of Iraq.

---

al-Qaeda: Forty-seven percent say this will happen if the United States stays, while 66% say it will happen if the United States leaves. Americans are also slightly more likely (52% vs. 42%) to believe that a regional Middle East war could break out if the United States leaves Iraq than if it stays. Concern about these consequences of leaving Iraq may be offset by the widespread perception that staying in Iraq indefinitely would spawn increased anti-U.S. hostility throughout the entire region: Sixty-one percent say that if U.S. troops stay, Middle Eastern nations would become much more hostile to the United States.

This appears to be a more persuasive argument for withdrawal than the possibility that the U.S. relationship with its traditional allies could be damaged if it doesn't leave. Only 46% of Americans think allied relations would be severely damaged by staying in Iraq indefinitely. About one in three Americans approve of the way President Bush is handling his job as president so far this year, marking the worst approval rating of his presidency and representing the continuation of a slow and steady decline in this measure since 2002. While Republicans continue to express much higher levels of support for

the president than do Democrats or independents, the president's ratings among all three groups so far this year are at the lowest point of his presidency. Bush's average job approval ratings among independents and Democrats are extremely low and have changed little from last year. Republicans' average ratings of Bush, on the other hand, have declined slightly this year as compared with last year. Conservatives are also more positive than moderates or liberals in their assessment of Bush, but again, average ratings among all three ideological groups are at their lowest level ever.

Bush's job approval rating has averaged 35% over the first five months of this year, the lowest yearly average approval rating of his tenure in the White House and three percentage points lower than last year's average. In Bush's first year in office, 2001, an average of 66% of Americans approved of the job he was doing as president. This average increased to 72% in 2002 but has declined each year since. Bush's yearly average approval rating has been below 50% in 2005, 2006, and, so far, 2007. As is usually the case with respect to presidential job approval ratings, members of the president's own party give him much higher approval ratings than do independents or members of the opposing party. For Bush, this means Republicans express significantly higher levels of support than independents or Democrats. Still, over the six years of his presidency, Bush's ratings have deteriorated among all three partisan groups. So far this year, his ratings have fallen even further among Republicans as compared with last year's average, although they remain well in the positive range. Bush's ratings have remained stable, albeit at extremely low levels, among Democrats and independents.

According to the yearly average data, more than 9 in 10 Republicans approved of the president from 2001 through 2004. Bush's approval rating then started to fall among members of his own party, dropping to an average of 86% in 2005, then to 80% in 2006, and now to 75% so far in 2007. Over the course of his administration, Bush's job approval ratings among Republicans have fallen only 20 points from his high point in 2002 to the latest average, his lowest, in the first five months of 2007. By comparison, Bush's approval rating has dropped 40 points among independents and 45 points among Democrats. Forty-six percent of Democrats, on average, approved of Bush during his first year in office. This increased to an average of 53% in 2002, before dropping to 33% in 2003. Fewer than one in six Democrats approved of Bush in 2004 and 2005, and since then, Democrats' approval ratings for the president have averaged just below 10%. A majority of independents approved of Bush from 2001 to 2003, with a high average of 69% in 2002. Then the president's ratings began to decrease, to 45% in 2004 and 38% in 2005. Bush's rating among independents has averaged 29% in both 2006 and 2007.

Self-described conservatives have consistently been more positive in their assessment of Bush than have moderates or liberals. Ratings among all three groups were at their highest averages in 2002 and at their lowest in 2007. Fifty-nine percent of conservatives, on average, approve of Bush so far in 2007. This average rating is 3 points lower than in 2006, and 26 points lower than Bush's highest rating in 2002. Conservatives' ratings of Bush fell the most between 2005 and 2006, from 70% to 62%. Roughly one in four self-described moderates (26%) approve of the job Bush is doing so far this year, a four-point drop from last year's average. A majority of moderates approved of Bush from 2001 through 2003, but this sentiment has been steadily dropping each year since. An average of just 11% of self-described liberals approve of Bush so far in 2007, the same as last year. Bush's rating among liberals has been quite low in recent years, ranging between 11% and 19% since 2004. Even at their high point, in 2002, only about half of liberals approved of Bush.

MAY 4
Clinton's Image

New York senator Hillary Clinton is one of the best-known political personalities in the country, having been in an intense public spotlight for more than 15 years. Although Clinton has been well known for some time, opinions of her have shifted considerably as the years have gone by. At one point in early 1999, toward the end of her husband's impeachment proceedings, Clinton was viewed favorably by 66% of the American people. But within two years, just after the Clintons left the White House in 2001, her favorable rating had fallen to 44%.

More recently, Hillary Clinton's image has undergone a significant change, becoming steadily less positive as the year has progressed. Gallup's last trend measure showed that 45% of Americans have a favorable view of Clinton while 52% have an unfavorable view. That contrasts with a significantly more positive image—58% favorable, 40% unfavorable—as 2007 began. What's behind Americans' views of Clinton? A recent Gallup Poll asked Americans to say, in their own words, what they particularly like about Clinton, and what they dislike about her. There was no shortage of opinions: About two-thirds of Americans were able or willing to say something positive about Clinton, and about the same percentage were able or willing to say something negative.

Clinton's Positives

It's clear that people who have a positive opinion of Clinton talk about her personal characteristics more than anything else. In particular, it seems that many of those who like Clinton admire her because of her fighting spirit in responding to the many travails and challenges of her life. Along these lines, those who like her mention her strength and stamina, her determination and perseverance, her forthrightness, her standing up for her beliefs, and her aggressiveness. Those who like Clinton also mention her intelligence along with aspects of her political life, including her current campaign for the presidency. Those who have a positive opinion of Clinton offer surprisingly few comments about her positions on the issues. In other words, admiration for Clinton is focused more on inner, dispositional aspects of her persona rather than on more practical or political issue positions. In summary, the top five reasons given by those who have a positive opinion of Clinton are: 1) her strength and stamina; 2) her intelligence; 3) admiration for her campaign for president; and 4) (tie) her political career and leadership, and her knowledge.

Clinton's Negatives

People who dislike Clinton say various things when asked what they don't admire about her—split to a degree between mentions of her personal characteristics and references to her positions on the issues. The biggest contrast between the negative views given by those who dislike Clinton and the positive views given by those who like Clinton is the greater tendency of the former to mention her positions on the issues. Almost one out of four of those who don't like Clinton cite her views on the issues and her liberal positions as what they don't admire about her. Another 11% mention their perception that she wavers too much on the issues and is wishy-washy, while 2% say they don't admire her views on Iraq specifically. That's not to say that her detractors don't mention Clinton's personal characteristics. While those who admire Clinton cite her strength and determination, those who don't like her cite what they perceive to be her "shifty" nature. That includes 14% who say they simply don't trust her, 11% who say she is an opportunist, and 5% who say she has no morals or ethics. Some of the additional responses—that she is too aggressive or arrogant—are essentially mirror images of her positives.

There is little mention of her husband per se by those who don't admire Hillary, but 8% of those who don't like her cite her involvement with past Clinton scandals. Those could, of course, include her husband's White House affair and subsequent impeachment or her own involvement in the Whitewater scandal. In rank order, the top five things people with negative views about Clinton don't admire about her are: 1) her political views and liberal positions on the issues; 2) they generally don't trust her; 3) (tie) they think she is an opportunist, and they think she is too wishy-washy, flip-flopping on the issues; and 5) the past history of the Clintons.

MAY 10

Americans Report Negative Views of Both Bush and Congress on Iraq

Americans report negative views of the way both President George W. Bush and the leaders in Congress are handling the situation in Iraq. A majority of Americans believe the war in Iraq was a mistake, and a clear majority would like to see Congress set a timetable for withdrawal of troops from Iraq. A majority of Americans also want some sort of compromise in the showdown between Bush and Congress on the war. But Americans do not show much consensus about exactly who should yield: Republicans want the Democrats in Congress to compromise and Democrats want Bush to

compromise. Independents—about one-third of the population—tilt toward wanting Bush to move more toward the Democrats' position.

APPROVAL RATINGS ON HANDLING IRAQ

Americans report a low level of approval for the major U.S. political entities involved with the situation in Iraq at this point.

Bush's low level of approval on handling Iraq is not surprising, given his overall approval rating of just 34%. His current 30% rating on handling Iraq is not even the lowest during his administration. That point occurred twice—during the first week of January 2007 and then again in February 2007—when the figure dipped to 26%. (Bush's highest approval rating on handling Iraq [76%] came in April 2003, just about a month after the war began.)

Since the Republicans in Congress have generally mirrored the Bush administration's positions on Iraq, it is not surprising to find that the public also gives them a low approval rating on Iraq. It is perhaps more surprising to find that Americans don't give the Democrats in Congress more than a 34% approval rating on the issue, given that the majority of Americans (59%) favor the general Democratic position of setting a timetable for withdrawal of troops from Iraq. It may be that Americans are frustrated with the fact that the Democratic-controlled Congress and the Bush administration are fighting about what to do about Iraq and are at a virtual stalemate on passing new funding legislation. Buttressing this conclusion is the fact that most Americans want some sort of compromise to get things moving between Congress and the White House on the Iraq issue.

When Americans' responses are combined, the data show that only 4% of Americans think that neither Bush nor the Democrats in Congress should compromise. The problem is that there is no majority agreement about who should do the compromising. Less than one-third of Amer-

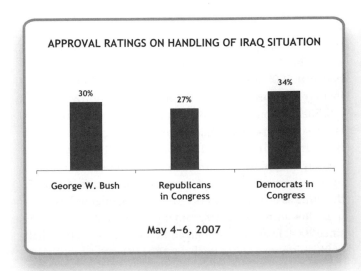

APPROVAL RATINGS ON HANDLING OF IRAQ SITUATION

30%   George W. Bush
27%   Republicans in Congress
34%   Democrats in Congress

May 4–6, 2007

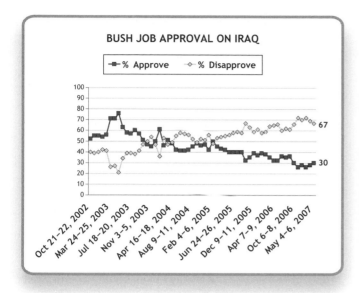

BUSH JOB APPROVAL ON IRAQ

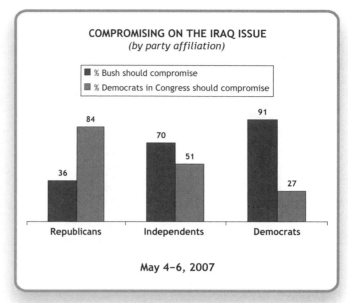

COMPROMISING ON THE IRAQ ISSUE
(by party affiliation)

May 4-6, 2007

icans believe that both sides should compromise, leaving a majority who say that either Bush or the Democratic leaders should compromise, but not the other. Thirty-seven percent say that Bush should compromise, but not the Democrats; 22% say that the Democrats should compromise, but not Bush. The responses to these questions are quite partisan in nature, as would be expected given the highly partisan nature of attitudes toward this war observed over the four years since the conflict began.

The tilt toward the higher overall percentage saying that Bush should compromise is due mainly to the views of independents, who are more likely to say that Bush should yield than that the Democrats should. Also, to a lesser degree, Republicans are slightly less polarized on the issue of who should compromise than are Democrats. The data clearly indicate that Americans want their political leaders in Washington to compromise in order to change the situ-

ation relating to Iraq. This desire for compromise may stem in part from the fact that at the moment Americans are not very positive about the way anyone in Washington is handling the Iraq situation. But large majorities of Republicans and Democrats are firm in saying that it is the other side that should "give" first. These data mirror the difficulties facing the White House and the Democrats in Congress. Both sides have clear views on what should be done next in Iraq, and neither side wants to be the one that capitulates (or what is perceived as capitulating) to the other. Hence, the current stalemate.

It should be noted that Americans clearly want a timetable for withdrawing U.S. troops from Iraq. This finding, coupled with the data that show slightly more Americans want Bush to compromise than want the Democratic leaders in Congress to compromise, suggest that an agreement on the supplemental funding bill that tilts toward some type of timetable for withdrawal would be most acceptable to the American people. This conclusion is reinforced by the findings of a new CNN poll, conducted after President Bush vetoed a funding bill on May 2 that included a timetable for withdrawal of troops from Iraq, which show that a majority of Americans would like Congress to repeat its effort and pass another, similar bill including a timetable for withdrawal.

Experience a Major Reason That Clinton Has Edge over Obama

The latest Gallup polling finds Democratic preferences in the race for the 2008 presidential nomination returning to where they have been for most of the year, with New York senator Hillary Clinton the solid front-runner over

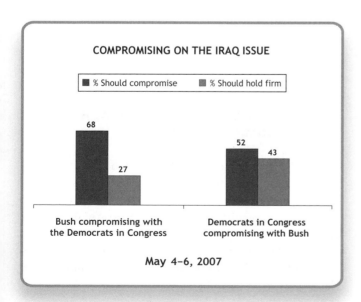

COMPROMISING ON THE IRAQ ISSUE

May 4-6, 2007

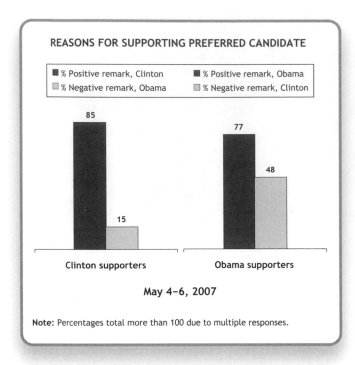

REASONS FOR SUPPORTING PREFERRED CANDIDATE

- ■ % Positive remark, Clinton
- ■ % Positive remark, Obama
- ☐ % Negative remark, Obama
- ☐ % Negative remark, Clinton

Clinton supporters: 85, 15
Obama supporters: 77, 48

May 4–6, 2007

Note: Percentages total more than 100 due to multiple responses.

Illinois senator Barack Obama and the other candidates. Her "experience" in politics is a major reason for her appeal, mentioned most often by Clinton supporters as a reason they back her. "Issue positions" are a top consideration for supporters of both Clinton and Obama. Generally speaking, Clinton supporters' stated reasons for supporting her focus almost exclusively on positive characteristics they see in her. And while Obama supporters mention many things they like about their chosen candidate, a substantial percentage discuss concerns with Clinton as reasons they support Obama.

The May 4–6, 2007, USA Today/Gallup Poll shows Clinton reestablishing a double-digit lead over Obama and the rest of the field of candidates for the nomination, after a mid-April poll showed her with only a 5-point lead. Clinton also beats Obama by a 56% to 37% margin in a hypothetical head-to-head ballot, also a stronger showing than in mid-April (53% to 41%). The current poll asked those who preferred Clinton or Obama in this ballot to give some of the reasons for their choice. Among those who prefer Clinton over Obama, the most common reason given for their choice is that "Clinton is more experienced than Obama," mentioned by 35% of Clinton supporters. Nearly one in four also cite her issue positions and agenda. Seventeen percent say they prefer Clinton because "she is a woman." Ten percent mention the fact that "Bill Clinton was president." Ten percent also say they are more familiar with Clinton than with Obama. Since March, when Gallup first asked this question, there has been little change in the relative frequency with which the various categories of reasons are mentioned.

No single theme dominates Obama supporters' stated reasons for preferring him over Clinton. The most common reasons offered are that his supporters consider him to be "fresh and new," that they agree with his issue positions and agenda, and that they like him or dislike Clinton. A slightly higher percentage of Obama supporters mention the "fresh and new" theme now than did so in March, though this change is not statistically significant. Three other themes, mentioned by between 9% and 11% of Obama supporters, have as much to do with perceived weaknesses of Clinton as with perceived strengths of Obama. These include the idea that "Clinton has too much baggage," that Obama has a better chance of being elected president than Clinton, and that Obama is a less polarizing figure than Clinton.

Generally speaking, it appears that Clinton supporters are highly focused on what they like about her. And while Obama supporters mention many things they like about him, they also have a lot of uncomplimentary things to say about Clinton. Specifically, 85% of Clinton supporters mention something positive about her and only 15% mention something negative about Obama when asked to explain their preference. Seventy-seven percent of Obama supporters say something positive about him, but 48% also mention something negative about Clinton when providing reasons for choosing Obama.

Thus, it appears that the decision-making process for many Democratic primary and caucus voters may largely consist of evaluating the pros and cons of having Clinton as the party's nominee, rather than evaluating the relative merits of Clinton as compared with her rivals for the nomination. That would suggest that Obama, former North Carolina senator John Edwards, lesser-known candidates in the current field, and possibly former vice president Al Gore (should he enter the race) are in a sense vying to be the anti-Clinton candidate. As such, they can expect a good deal of their support to result from opposition to Clinton rather than from enthusiastic support for their own candidacy.

MAY 11

The Age Factor: Older Americans Most Negative About Iraq War

A special Gallup Poll analysis of more than 7,000 interviews conducted this year shows that older Americans are more likely than those who are younger to believe that going to war in Iraq was a mistake. Americans who are 70 and older are particularly more likely to say the war was a mistake. The impact of age on views of the war persists among subgroups of Republicans, independents, and Democrats and also occurs regardless of gender.

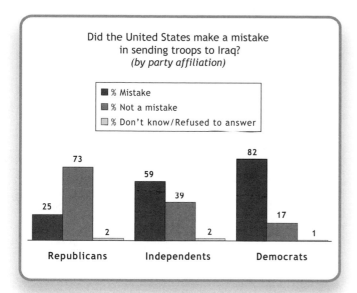

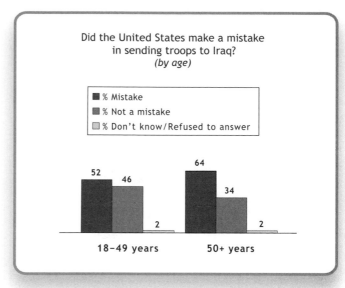

BACKGROUND

Gallup has asked Americans whether U.S. involvement in Iraq was a "mistake" in seven polls taken during the first five months of 2007. Across these more than 7,000 interviews, an average of 57% have said "yes." One already well-established conclusion confirmed by an analysis of this large data set is the unsurprising fact that views on this war are intensely partisan. One of the single best predictors of whether an American views the war as a mistake is his or her political party identification.

The Importance of Age

Beyond this more obvious correlation, one of the more surprising findings in the analysis is the relationship between age and views on the war. Given the indelible images of young people protesting the Vietnam War in the 1960s and early 1970s, and the fact that it is generally young people who are most involved in actually fighting wars, one might hypothesize that opposition to the Iraq War would be highest among younger Americans. That, however, is not the case. Americans age 50 and older are significantly more likely to say the war was a mistake than are those under the age of 50, by a 12-percentage-point margin.

We can look at this relationship between age and views on the war in more detail by breaking age into roughly 10-year age groups.

The differences in the "mistake" percentage among the three age groups below age 50 are not consistent. Americans 30 to 39 years of age are least likely to say the war has been a mistake, while those both younger and older are more likely to say so. Taken as a whole, as noted above, an average of 52% of responses are in the "mistake" cat-

egory. But the pattern of belief that the war was a mistake is somewhat more linear for those age 50 and older. The percentage saying the war was a mistake is similar among those 50 to 59 and 60 to 69, and then increases among those age 70 to 79 and 80 and above. Americans in all four

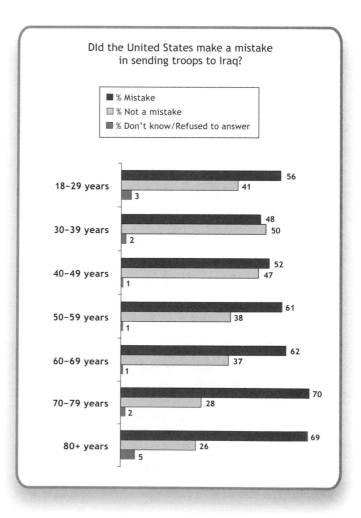

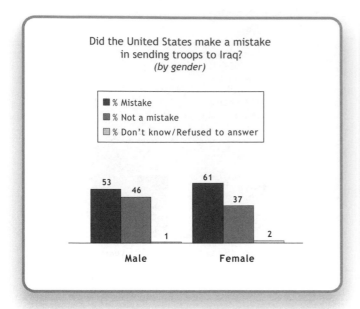

Did the United States make a mistake
in sending troops to Iraq?
(by gender)

■ % Mistake
■ % Not a mistake
☐ % Don't know/Refused to answer

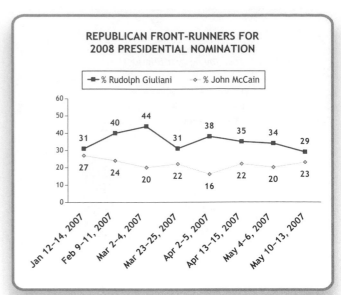

REPUBLICAN FRONT-RUNNERS FOR
2008 PRESIDENTIAL NOMINATION

―■― % Rudolph Giuliani   ―◇― % John McCain

groups age 50 and older show a "mistake" percentage of at least 61%, with an average of 64%.

Gender

Women are more likely than men to say the Iraq War was a mistake. Women are also more predominant in the older age groups in the United States (because women have a longer average life span than men), so it could be conjectured that one reason for the higher percentage of older age groups saying the Iraq War was a mistake is the increasing predominance of women in those groups. The data show, however, that the age difference in the "mistake" percentage persists among both men and women. It is true that within most age groups, women are at least slightly more likely than men to say the war in Iraq was a mistake. But the general pattern of the positive relationship between age and the "mistake" percentage is seen within both gender groups. Women age 50 and older are more likely than women under 50 to say the war was a mistake; the same is true for and men age 50 and older vs. men under 50. Women age 70 and older show the greatest opposition to the war.

MAY 16

New Yorkers Continue to Lead 2008 Nomination Contests

The national front-runners for the 2008 presidential nominations continue to be former New York City mayor Rudolph Giuliani for the Republican Party and New York senator Hillary Clinton for the Democratic Party. Giuliani's pro-choice

views were openly aired during the Republican debate held earlier this month at the Ronald Reagan Presidential Library in California, and he has since tried to clarify them. It is not yet clear whether the resulting controversy has significantly harmed him among Republican voters.

According to a May 10–13, 2007, Gallup Poll, 29% of Republicans favor Giuliani for his party's nomination, giving him a six-point lead over Arizona senator John McCain, with 23%. Clinton holds a nine-point lead in the Democratic race over second-place contender Barack Obama, 35% to 26%. In early March, and again in early April, Giuliani led McCain by more than 20 points, making him a more formidable front-runner than he appears to be in the current poll. More recently, in early May, Giuliani held a 14-point lead over McCain, 34% to 20%. But neither his five-point decline to 29% in the latest poll, nor McCain's three-point increase, are statistically significant changes. Thus it is important to wait until the next poll to see whether the race has truly tightened, or whether the apparently closer race merely reflects random variation because of normal sampling error.

Some of the changes in Giuliani's and McCain's support levels can be attributed to support for actor and former Tennessee senator Fred Thompson, since Gallup added him to the list of potential candidates in late March. However, Gallup's follow-up question, which asks Republican voters whom they would support if the race narrows down to Giuliani and McCain, does not have this complication. The 2007 "narrows down" trend shows Giuliani consistently well ahead of McCain, including in the latest poll, in which he leads by 10 points, 52% to 42%. This is Giuliani's slimmest lead on Gallup's head-to-head measure since January, when he led by only 8 points, but the changes in

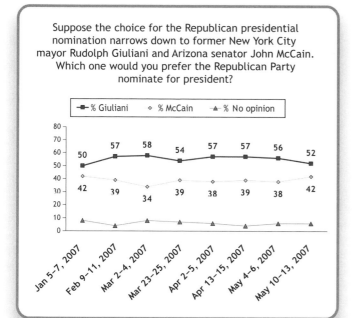

Suppose the choice for the Republican presidential nomination narrows down to former New York City mayor Rudolph Giuliani and Arizona senator John McCain. Which one would you prefer the Republican Party nominate for president?

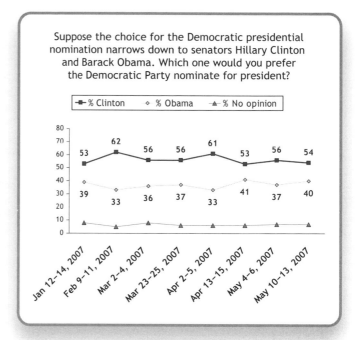

Suppose the choice for the Democratic presidential nomination narrows down to senators Hillary Clinton and Barack Obama. Which one would you prefer the Democratic Party nominate for president?

support for Giuliani and McCain that produced this gap are not statistically significant. Thus it would be premature to say that the race has, indeed, tightened.

Turning back to the Democratic field, Clinton's strongest leads in the race for her party's nomination were 19-point advantages over Obama in mid-February and again in early April. Clinton's nine-point advantage over Obama today, while slimmer than that, is not significantly different from her 15-point lead earlier this month.

Gallup's Democratic head-to-head question, asking Democrats to choose between Clinton and Obama, finds no significant change from earlier this month. Clinton currently leads Obama on this measure by 14 points, 54% to 40%.

The Remaining Democratic Hopefuls

A number of Democratic candidates besides Clinton and Obama have announced their presidential campaigns or intentions to run, but of these, only John Edwards has a meaningful level of support, currently 12%. Al Gore, who has not made any formal announcement about seeking the 2008 nomination, is in a close race with Edwards for third place, with 16%. The remaining candidates all garner no more than 2% support. None of these lower-ranked candidates' positions in the race has changed substantially over the past several months.

Other Republican Contenders

At this point, three Republican candidates are clustered within reach of third place, though Thompson seems to

hold the clearest title to the position. Although his leads over former Massachusetts governor Mitt Romney and former House speaker Newt Gingrich are not great, he has generally maintained a slight edge over both of them across five consecutive Gallup Poll trial heats conducted since March, when Gallup first included him in the mix of Republican names. Romney and Gingrich are closely matched behind him, appearing to vie for fourth place. No other candidate registers more than 2% support from Republicans.

GIULIANI'S IMAGE IN THE SPOTLIGHT

Giuliani stepped into a political briar patch over his abortion views in recent weeks after answering questions about his

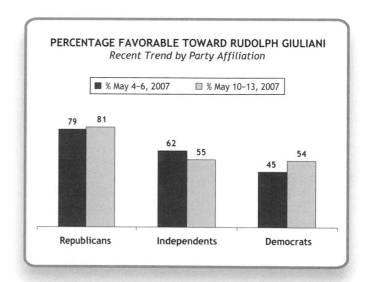

PERCENTAGE FAVORABLE TOWARD RUDOLPH GIULIANI
Recent Trend by Party Affiliation

views at the May 3 Republican debate and then reformulating those answers in post-debate interviews. Giuliani appears to be trying to stake out a nuanced pro-choice position that may not satisfy either side of the debate but won't completely disqualify him among the conservative Right, either. The slight dip in Giuliani's support in the latest poll (though not statistically significant) raises the question whether this controversy is hurting him among Republicans. While support for Giuliani is lower in Gallup's new poll as compared with the previous survey, there has been no decline in Republicans' views of him personally. The percentage of Republicans viewing him favorably stands at 81% today, compared with 79% in early May. At the same time, there has been no significant change in his favorability among independents and a slight improvement among Democrats.

McCain's image has also not changed appreciably over the past month.

MAY 21

Public Divided on "Pro-Choice" vs. "Pro-Life" Abortion Labels

Americans hold a complex set of beliefs about a woman's right to terminate her pregnancy. The majority want the Supreme Court to uphold its 1973 *Roe v. Wade* Supreme Court decision, which protects abortion rights. Most Americans also say abortion should be legal only under certain circumstances and believe there should be a ban on "late-term" or "partial-birth" abortions. But when the entire issue is distilled to the labels most commonly used on each side of the debate—"pro-choice" vs. "pro-life"—the public is split nearly down the middle. According to Gallup's annual Values and Beliefs survey, conducted May 10–13, 2007, 49% of Americans consider themselves pro-choice

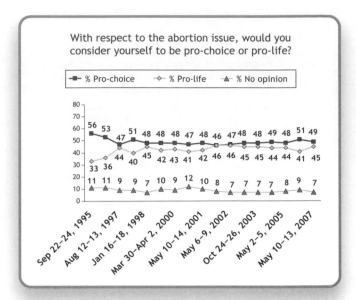

and 45% call themselves pro-life. The balance of opinion on this measure has varied somewhat since Gallup instituted it 12 years ago, in 1995. Since 1998, however, the two groups have been fairly evenly matched in size, with slightly more Americans tending to call themselves pro-choice.

Middle Ground Is Favored

When it comes to Americans' specific attitudes about the right to an abortion, public opinion is somewhat more conservative than its attachment to these labels would suggest. Nearly 6 in 10 Americans (58%) think abortion should either be limited to only a few circumstances or illegal in all circumstances, while just above 4 in 10 (41%) think it should be legal in all or most circumstances.

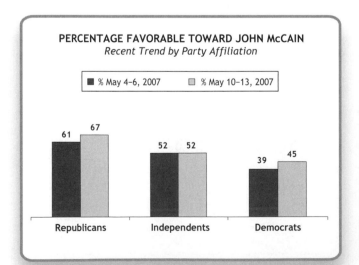

Another way to look at this, however, is that relatively few Americans are positioned at either extreme of the spectrum—believing abortion should be legal in either all circumstances (26%) or illegal in all circumstances (18%). The majority fall somewhere in the middle. Gallup's root question measuring attitudes toward abortion simply asks: "Do you think abortions should be legal under any circumstances, legal only under certain circumstances, or illegal in all circumstances?" The trend, which dates from 1975, shows a majority of Americans have consistently fallen into the middle group.

Abortion is never far from the public mind. Most recently, the focus of attention has been on the Supreme Court's decision in April to uphold a federal law banning partial-birth abortions, as well as on the Republican Party's presidential candidates' views on the issue of abortion more generally.

The latest poll finds most Americans in philosophical agreement with the Court's decision in this case. Seventy-two percent believe the specific abortion procedure known as late-term or partial-birth abortion should be illegal; only 22% believe it should be legal. Americans' views on this issue do not appear to have changed significantly since the question was previously asked in October 2003.

Pro-choice critics of the partial-birth decision see it as a step on the path toward a complete reversal of the 1973 *Roe v. Wade* decision that made abortion broadly legal in the United States. And while Americans would not likely share these critics' disappointment with the partial-birth decision, they would generally agree that *Roe* should remain the law of the land on abortion. Only

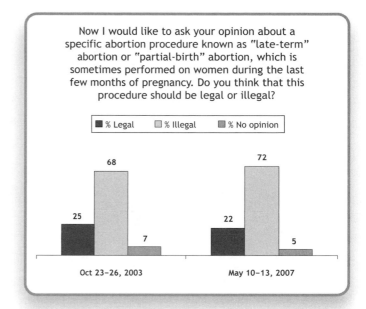

Now I would like to ask your opinion about a specific abortion procedure known as "late-term" abortion or "partial-birth" abortion, which is sometimes performed on women during the last few months of pregnancy. Do you think that this procedure should be legal or illegal?

35% of Americans say they would like to see the Supreme Court overturn this decision; a slight majority, 53%, say they would not like to see it overturned.

The abortion issue could be pivotal in determining the next president of the United States, at least to the degree that it influences Republican voter preferences in nominating their party's candidate. This could play out most dramatically if the current Republican front-runner, Rudolph Giuliani, eventually loses the race for the nomination because of Republican voters' displeasure with his pro-choice views. While most Americans say the abortion issue will factor into their vote, relatively few are single-issue voters on this issue. Just 16% tell Gallup in the latest poll that they will only vote for candidates for major offices who

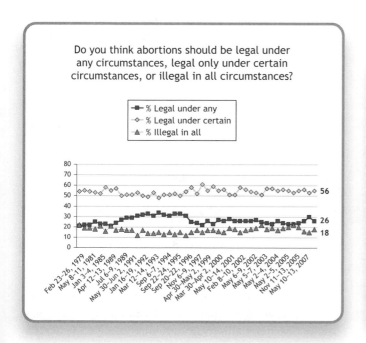

Do you think abortions should be legal under any circumstances, legal only under certain circumstances, or illegal in all circumstances?

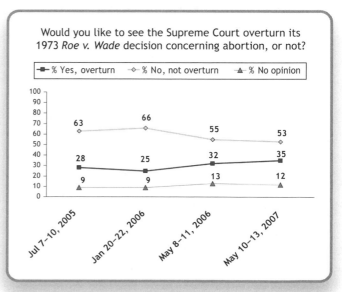

Would you like to see the Supreme Court overturn its 1973 *Roe v. Wade* decision concerning abortion, or not?

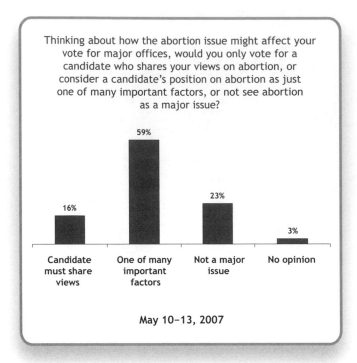

Thinking about how the abortion issue might affect your vote for major offices, would you only vote for a candidate who shares your views on abortion, or consider a candidate's position on abortion as just one of many important factors, or not see abortion as a major issue?

May 10–13, 2007

Americans who identify themselves as pro-life are a bit more likely than those who are pro-choice to identify abortion as a make-or-break issue for them when voting (19% vs. 12%), but this difference is not large. A somewhat greater difference between pro-life and pro-choice adherents is seen among Republicans. Nearly a quarter of pro-life Republicans (22%) identify abortion as a critical voting issue for them, compared with only 8% of pro-choice Republicans. This suggests some intensity among pro-life voters within the Republican Party, at least on a relative basis, which could harm Giuliani during the primaries if it manifests itself in terms of voter turnout.

MAY 22
Gun Ownership and the 2008 Primaries

Gun owners are a powerful force in American politics, and their influence is evident in both the legislative and electoral processes. In general, more gun owners identify as Republicans or lean toward the Republican Party (53%) than identify as Democrats or lean toward the Democratic Party (39%), but there are enough gun owners in each party to make them a force in either party's primaries and caucuses. An analysis of recent Gallup polling suggests that gun owners could be a considerable factor in the Republican nomination process, but less so in the Democratic process. Although Rudolph Giuliani is the front-runner for the Republican nomination, Republican gun owners are less likely than nonowners to support him. On the Democratic side, both gun owners and nonowners rate Hillary Clinton as their top choice for the party's presidential nomination by similar margins over the rest of the Democratic contenders. In two polls conducted this month, Gallup asked partisans their preferences for their party's 2008 presidential nomination and whether they personally own any type of gun. According to the polls, roughly one in three Americans are gun owners, including 41% of Republicans and 24% of Democrats.

The Republican Nomination

Since February, Giuliani has been the established front-runner for the Republican presidential nomination. In the combined May data on rank-and-file Republicans' nomination preferences, he has a 32% to 21% edge over John McCain, and at least a 20-percentage-point advantage over every other candidate. Among Republican gun owners, however, Giuliani's front-running status is not as secure. Twenty-six percent of Republican gun owners say

share their views on abortion. About 6 in 10 say a candidate's position on abortion is just one of many important factors they consider, while 23% do not consider abortion to be a major issue when voting.

The picture is not all that different when looking just at Republicans (including independents who lean Republican). Fewer than one in five Republicans or Republican-leaning independents (17%) say a candidate must share their views on abortion—only slightly greater than the percentage of Democrats (14%) who feel the same way.

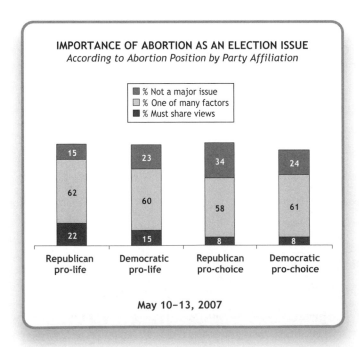

IMPORTANCE OF ABORTION AS AN ELECTION ISSUE
According to Abortion Position by Party Affiliation

- ■ % Not a major issue
- □ % One of many factors
- ■ % Must share views

May 10–13, 2007

Giuliani is their first choice for the nomination, but 22% choose McCain, meaning the candidates are essentially tied, given the margin of error. Fred Thompson, the former Tennessee senator who has not yet decided whether to enter the race, would appear to be a relatively strong candidate among Republican gun owners, as he is named as the top choice by 18% of this group. Mitt Romney's and Newt Gingrich's support among gun owners falls just shy of double digits, and all other candidates are at 2% or below.

While the views of Republican gun owners and non-owners are similar for most of the candidates, there are differences in their support for Giuliani and Thompson. Giuliani's support is 11 points higher among nonowners, while Thompson does better among gun owners by the same margin. Giuliani's slightly weaker standing among gun owners is also evident when looking at preferences between the former New York City mayor and McCain in a one-on-one matchup. Giuliani's 54% to 40% advantage over McCain among all Republicans shrinks to 50% to 45% among Republican gun owners.

The Democratic Nomination

While gun owners are typically aligned with the Republican Party, the fact that nearly one in four Democrats and Democratic leaners owns a gun means they are not an insignificant Democratic constituency. Clinton has a solid lead over Barack Obama, 36% to 24%, among all Democrats in the combined May polls. Her lead is similar among Democratic gun owners (32% to 19%, or 13 points) and nonowners (37% to 26%, or 11 points). Her support is slightly higher among nonowners than gun owners, but the difference is not statistically meaningful. In general, Democrats' nomination preferences are similar among gun owners and nonowners. Obama does slightly better among nonowners and John Edwards among gun owners, but those differences are not statistically significant.

MAY 24

Clinton Leads Obama Among Whites, Blacks, and Most Other Democratic Subgroups

Not only does Hillary Clinton rank first among the leading candidates for the 2008 Democratic nomination in Gallup's national polling, according to data from an aggregated sample of over 3,000 interviews with Democrats conducted by Gallup since March; she dominates at the subgroup level among men, women, whites, blacks, young adults, and seniors. She also leads regardless of Democrats' religious affiliation and political ideology.

Barack Obama is in the unique position of being a former state politician on the national stage for less than three years running against what amounts to a Democratic institution in Hillary Clinton. Obama does well among blacks, but more importantly for his candidacy, he also does well among non-blacks. He has galvanized significant Democratic support around his candidacy across a broad spectrum of the party, in a very short period of time. Perhaps because of Bill Clinton's positive reputation in the black community, however, and Hillary Clinton's own prominence in the party, Clinton also garners a significant share of the black vote. The net result is that Obama trails Clinton among blacks but by only 8 points, compared to a 14-point deficit among whites.

Clinton's widest leads over Obama are with women, seniors, those living in low- and middle-income households, and the non-college-educated. Obama performs best with high socioeconomic groups and among those with more independent leanings, including young Democrats. Only with self-described "Democrats" who aren't really Democrats but rather independents who lean toward the Democratic Party, as well as with college-educated and upper-income Democrats, is Clinton's current hegemony challenged (though not usurped). Among these groups, Obama roughly ties Clinton as the preferred candidate.

Former vice president Al Gore (who has yet to declare he will run) and former North Carolina senator John Edwards have been closely matched for third place since late March, but on average Gore has enjoyed a three-point lead over Edwards. Gore has a significantly better lead than this, however, among Hispanics, as well as among young adults, non-high school graduates, blacks, and self-professed liberals. These findings are based on an aggregate of six Gallup Polls on the Democratic race conducted since early March. The most recent reading, from a May 10–13, 2007, Gallup Poll, yields results nearly identical to those for the entire three-month period, over which Clinton averaged a 12-point lead over Obama.

Clinton's Core Support

Clinton's strongest support comes from groups associated with the traditional working-class base of the Democratic Party: less-educated Americans, Easterners, lower-income Americans, seniors, women, and minorities. In line with this, she also does very well with those who unequivocally associate themselves with the Democratic Party. The data show that Democratic blacks essentially split their vote between Clinton and Obama—offering relatively few votes to Gore, Edwards, or the rest of the field. Thus, both Clinton and Obama do better among blacks than they do among the total sample of Democrats. Obama's greater support among blacks is slightly higher than Clinton's, resulting in an 8-point lead for the New York senator, down from her 12-point lead over Obama in the entire sample.

Obama's Appeal

Obama's support profile is to some extent the flip side of Clinton's. Obama does not lead Clinton by a significant amount among any major subgroup, but he runs about even with her among voters with a postgraduate education, those with a college degree, those in upper-income households, Democrats living in the Midwest (his home turf), and independents who lean Democratic. On a relative basis, he also does fairly well among Democrats age 18 to 29 and among men.

The Race for Third

In the close contest between Gore and Edwards for third place, Gore is the clear leader between these two candidates among Hispanics, young Democrats, and blacks. He also has fairly solid leads in the West (nine points) and East (seven points). Edwards doesn't perform especially well among any subgroups, but on a relative basis he does best in the Midwest and South, and among seniors, Protestants, whites, and conservative Democrats.

Richardson Not Exciting Hispanic Voters

New Mexico governor Bill Richardson is currently the only Hispanic in the field of announced Democratic candidates. Analysis of the March-through-May sample of Democrats, however, shows that so far his ethnic background does not appear to be earning him widespread support among Hispanic voters: Only 6% of Hispanics are supporting Richardson for the nomination. That is more support than he receives from white and black voters, but not enough to raise him out of the ranks of the marginal candidacies at the bottom of the Democratic preference list. (These data do not include Spanish-language interviewing, although polling research has shown that the results of election polling of U.S. citizens who are registered to vote are not substantially altered by the inclusion of Spanish-language interviewing.)

Despite Campaign, Familiarity with Candidates Has Not Changed Substantially

Despite the remarkably early start of the 2008 presidential campaign and the high-visibility presence of the major candidates on television news shows and in televised debates, the name identification of the leading candidates or potential candidates has not changed much so far this year. Hillary Clinton has near-universal name identification, the highest of any of the major candidates. Former New York City mayor Rudolph Giuliani is known by more than 8 in 10 Americans, more than is the case for John McCain or John Edwards. Barack Obama's familiarity is at 75%. There has been little change in any of these candidates' recognition factors over the last several months. The least known of the group of seven political figures included in this analysis are former Tennessee senator Fred Thompson, who despite his acting role on prime time television is known by fewer than 4 out of 10 Americans, and Mitt Romney, whose name identification remains below 50%. Giuliani has the highest net favorable image of any of the major candidates, followed by Obama, Edwards, McCain, Fred Thompson, and finally Clinton and Romney. The net favorable ratings for several of these candidates—including, in particular, Clinton—have shown a decline through April, with a modest recovery in May.

Name Identification

This analysis deals with seven confirmed and potential presidential candidates: Clinton, Obama, and Edwards on the Democratic side, and Giuliani, McCain, Romney, and Fred Thompson on the Republican side. "Name identification" is defined as the percentage of adult Americans who

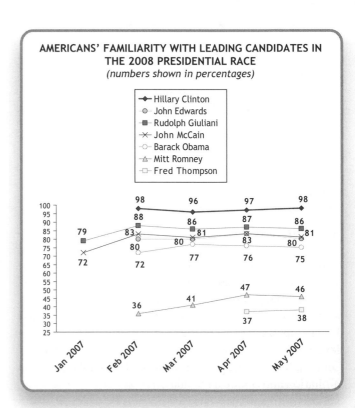

AMERICANS' FAMILIARITY WITH LEADING CANDIDATES IN THE 2008 PRESIDENTIAL RACE
(numbers shown in percentages)

- Hillary Clinton
- John Edwards
- Rudolph Giuliani
- John McCain
- Barack Obama
- Mitt Romney
- Fred Thompson

know enough about the candidate to be able to give an opinion of him or her.

Of these seven, the only one with near-universal name identification is Clinton. The former first lady and current senator from New York is well enough known that almost every American is willing to give an opinion of her. The next most well-known candidate is Giuliani. Seventy-nine percent of Americans knew enough about Giuliani in January of this year to rate him, a figure that rose to 88% by February and has remained essentially constant since. Neither the early media buzz about Giuliani's possible candidacy nor the news coverage of him since he announced have nudged Giuliani into the 90% name recognition range enjoyed by Clinton, however.

About 8 in 10 Americans know McCain and Edwards well enough to have an opinion of them. The name recognition trends for both of these men have shown very little change since February. The 20% of Americans who continue to say they don't know enough about either of these candidates to have an opinion of them is of interest given that both have been in the presidential limelight as candidates in previous election years. McCain was a candidate for president in 2000, at which time his name recognition briefly reached 85%. He is a war hero and a highly visible senator, and has been running hard for the presidency since late last year. Still, his name identification this year has so far remained lower than it was in 2000. Edwards was the Democratic candidate for vice president in 2004 (at which point his name identification in one survey in September 2004 reached 86%). Edwards has also been campaigning almost nonstop this year. He received a great deal of publicity when he and his wife, Elizabeth, made a public announcement in March that her cancer had returned. (Elizabeth was then on the cover of *Time* magazine.) Still, Edwards has yet to reach the levels of recognition he enjoyed in the 2004 campaign.

Slightly below McCain and Edwards on the name identification list is Obama. The Illinois senator burst onto the national scene with a widely praised speech at the Democratic National Convention in 2004, a year in which he won election to the U.S. Senate. Gallup's first test of Obama's name recognition—in December 2006—showed him with a 53% familiarity rating. By this February, Obama's name identification had shot up to 72%, but it has not been much higher since, despite the intense news coverage given him as he has engaged in active campaigning. His current name identification, 75%, is roughly the same as in February. Much less well-known is former Massachusetts governor Mitt Romney. Romney's name identification was 36% in February of this year and has risen to 46%. Still, more than half of Americans do not know enough about Romney to be able to give an opin-

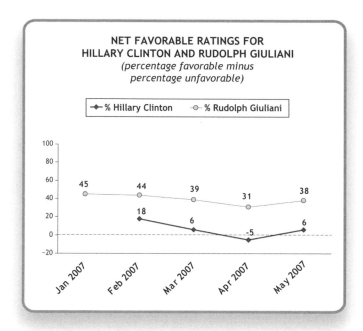

NET FAVORABLE RATINGS FOR
HILLARY CLINTON AND RUDOLPH GIULIANI
*(percentage favorable minus
percentage unfavorable)*

ion of him, with no change between April and May. The least recognized candidate among the seven rated in the present analysis is actor and former Tennessee senator Fred Thompson. Despite his role on the popular TV show *Law and Order* and numerous movie roles over the years, fewer than 4 in 10 Americans know enough about him to have an opinion, and there has been no change in his name identification between April and May.

Images of Clinton and Giuliani

The images of the two front-runners—Clinton for the Democrats and Giuliani for the Republicans—have followed similar trajectories this year. The net favorable ratings for both declined through April and then recovered partially in May. Throughout these months, Giuliani's favorable ratings have remained much more positive than Clinton's. (Keep in mind that these net favorable ratings are with respect to the general public. Both of these candidates do much better among members of their own party.)

The drop in the ratings of these two candidates through April can be explained as part of the natural process by which those running for office lose some of their luster as they are subjected to the intense criticism and media attention that come with campaigning. Why the images of both Clinton and Giuliani recovered in April is unknown, and it will be interesting to track these trends in the summer months to see if the recovery continues, or if their images decline again.

Images of McCain, Obama, and Edwards

All three of these candidates—McCain, Obama, and Edwards—have roughly similar net favorable ratings.

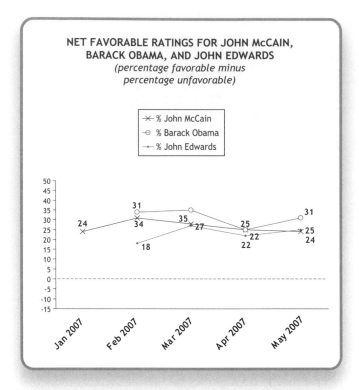

NET FAVORABLE RATINGS FOR JOHN McCAIN, BARACK OBAMA, AND JOHN EDWARDS
(percentage favorable minus percentage unfavorable)

Obama has generally tracked slightly more positively than the other two this year, although their ratings converged in April.

As was true for Clinton and Giuliani, Obama's ratings dropped in April and partially recovered in May. The net favorable ratings for McCain have dropped since his high point in February, with no recovery seen in May. The ratings for Edwards, after jumping in March, are a few points lower in May.

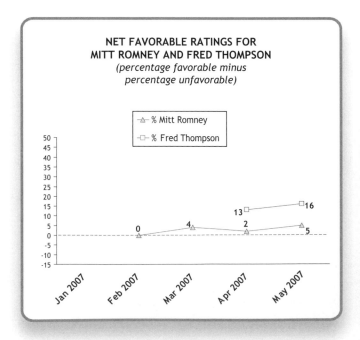

NET FAVORABLE RATINGS FOR MITT ROMNEY AND FRED THOMPSON
(percentage favorable minus percentage unfavorable)

Images of Romney and Thompson

There have been only minor changes in Romney's net favorable ratings since February. He began that month with a lukewarm image: His unfavorable ratings were the equal of his favorable ratings. Since then, his image has moved slightly toward the positive side of the ledger, but with no dramatic upward tilt. Fred Thompson's image is positive, but has not changed significantly in the two months Gallup has measured it.

MAY 25

One-Third of Americans Believe the Bible Is Literally True

About one-third of the American adult population believes that the Bible is the actual word of God and is to be taken literally, word for word. This percentage is slightly lower than it was several decades ago. The majority of those Americans who don't believe that the Bible is literally true believe that it is the inspired word of God, but that not everything in it should be taken literally. About one in five Americans believe the Bible is an ancient book of "fables, legends, history, and moral precepts recorded by man."

Belief in a literal Bible is strongly correlated with indicators of religion, including church attendance and identification with a Protestant or other non-Catholic Christian faith. There is also a strong inverse relationship between education and belief in a literal Bible, with such belief becoming much less prevalent among those who have college educations.

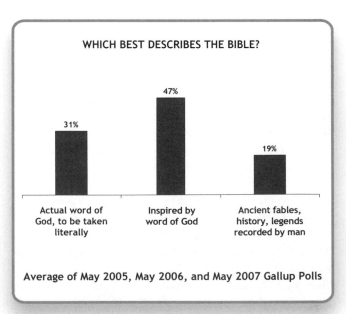

WHICH BEST DESCRIBES THE BIBLE?

Average of May 2005, May 2006, and May 2007 Gallup Polls

Background

A conviction with respect to the authority of the Bible has been and remains a key focal point for many religions today. Some denominations affirm the belief in a literal Bible as a hallmark of their faith. The statement of "Faith and Mission" of the Southern Baptist Convention, for example, states that: "The Holy Bible was written by men divinely inspired and is God's revelation of Himself to man. It is a perfect treasure of divine instruction. It has God for its author, salvation for its end, and truth, without any mixture of error, for its matter. Therefore, all Scripture is totally true and trustworthy." Although even those who believe in a literal Bible can still disagree with respect to exactly what the Bible says about key areas of Scripture and about moral issues, a literal belief structure has been the basis for justifying a variety of important public policy positions in American life—including opposition to evolution and the teaching thereof in public schools (going back to the days of the Scopes "Monkey" Trial in 1925), opposition to gay marriage and homosexuality, the proper relationship between husbands and wives within marriage, observance of a day of rest, the belief that positions as preachers or priests should be reserved for men only, and even such seemingly unrelated topics as immigration.

Beliefs About the Bible

Americans' views of the Bible have not changed materially over the past 16 years. Gallup has asked Americans about their personal views of the Bible nine times since 1991. The percentage saying the Bible is the actual, literal word of God has remained in a relatively narrow range between 27% and 35% across this time period, the average being 31%. Prior to that point, however, the data suggest that Americans' belief in a literal Bible was slightly higher.

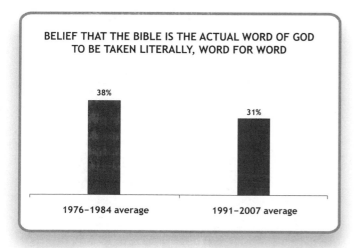

BELIEF THAT THE BIBLE IS THE ACTUAL WORD OF GOD TO BE TAKEN LITERALLY, WORD FOR WORD

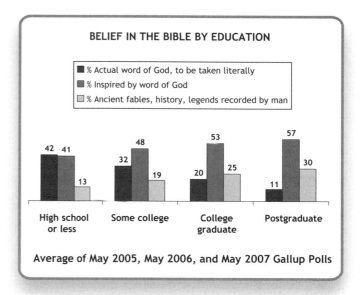

BELIEF IN THE BIBLE BY EDUCATION

- % Actual word of God, to be taken literally
- % Inspired by word of God
- % Ancient fables, history, legends recorded by man

Average of May 2005, May 2006, and May 2007 Gallup Polls

Gallup asked the question seven times between 1976 and 1984, during which time an average of 38% said that the Bible was the actual word of God. At two points during this time period, 40% of Americans agreed with the literal interpretation view of the Bible.

Belief in a Literal Bible Among Subgroups of the Population

To provide a larger and more stable sample for purposes of analyzing the distribution of beliefs regarding the Bible in the American population, Gallup aggregated data from the last three surveys in which Americans were asked about their beliefs regarding the Bible—in May of 2005, 2006, and 2007—for a sample size of 3,010 interviews. The analysis of these data shows one demographic variable that is highly related to views of the Bible: education. The higher the level of education, the less likely the individual is to believe that the Bible is the actual, literal word of God.

Even though those with a postgraduate education are much less likely to believe in a literal Bible, the majority of that group do believe that the Bible is the inspired word of God, rather than solely a human creation. Those who identify as Protestants or other non-Catholic Christians are significantly more likely to believe that the Bible is the literal word of God than are Catholics. Not surprisingly, those Americans who say they have no religious affiliation are much more likely than the other groups to say that the Bible is a creation of human beings. It is interesting to note, however, that 10% of those with no religious identification still believe that the Bible is literally the word of God, and another 26% say it is inspired by God.

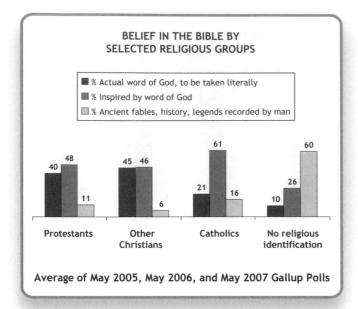

BELIEF IN THE BIBLE BY SELECTED RELIGIOUS GROUPS

- ■ % Actual word of God, to be taken literally
- ■ % Inspired by word of God
- □ % Ancient fables, history, legends recorded by man

Protestants: 40, 48, 11
Other Christians: 45, 46, 6
Catholics: 21, 61, 16
No religious identification: 10, 26, 60

Average of May 2005, May 2006, and May 2007 Gallup Polls

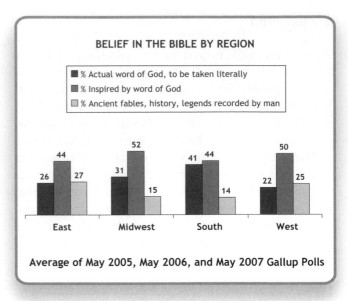

BELIEF IN THE BIBLE BY REGION

- ■ % Actual word of God, to be taken literally
- ■ % Inspired by word of God
- □ % Ancient fables, history, legends recorded by man

East: 26, 44, 27
Midwest: 31, 52, 15
South: 41, 44, 14
West: 22, 50, 25

Average of May 2005, May 2006, and May 2007 Gallup Polls

There is a predictable and highly significant relationship between self-reported church attendance and belief in a literal Bible. Fifty-four percent of those who attend church weekly believe the Bible is the actual word of God. That figure drops in a linear fashion as church attendance falls, to a low point of 8% among those who report never attending church yet believe in a literal Bible.

Church attendance is highest in the South, so it comes as no surprise that Southerners are most likely to believe in a literal Bible. Those in the East are least likely to believe that the Bible is the actual word of God or inspired by the word of God.

Finally, there is not a highly significant relationship between age and belief in a literal Bible.

MAY 31

What Would Americans Tell President Bush to Do About Iraq?

What would Americans say to President Bush if they could talk to him about the situation in Iraq for 15 minutes? The majority of Americans—if they could literally file through the Oval Office and talk to the man they elected to be chief executive and commander in chief—would tell President Bush to focus on developing an exit strategy from Iraq and removing U.S. troops from that country. A smaller group of one in four would tell the president to stay the course or even be more aggressive in Iraq. Six percent would tell the president to own up to his mistakes in Iraq and apologize. About 7% would advise the president to work with study groups or the United Nations to figure out a solution to the Iraq dilemma. Only 5% would have nothing to say to Bush about what Americans currently rank as the nation's most important problem.

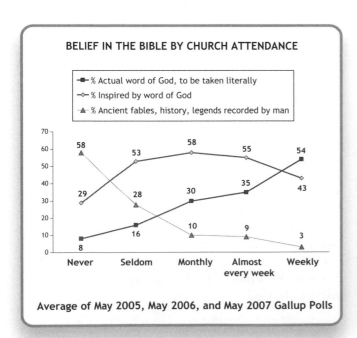

BELIEF IN THE BIBLE BY CHURCH ATTENDANCE

- ■ % Actual word of God, to be taken literally
- ◇ % Inspired by word of God
- ▲ % Ancient fables, history, legends recorded by man

Never: 8, 29, 58
Seldom: 16, 53, 28
Monthly: 30, 58, 10
Almost every week: 35, 55, 9
Weekly: 54, 43, 3

Average of May 2005, May 2006, and May 2007 Gallup Polls

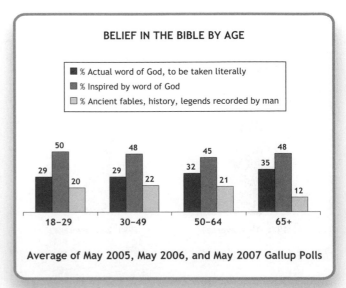

BELIEF IN THE BIBLE BY AGE

- ■ % Actual word of God, to be taken literally
- ■ % Inspired by word of God
- □ % Ancient fables, history, legends recorded by man

18–29: 29, 50, 20
30–49: 29, 48, 22
50–64: 32, 45, 21
65+: 35, 48, 12

Average of May 2005, May 2006, and May 2007 Gallup Polls

JUNE 2007

When Gallup's first question on attitudes toward immigrants and immigration appeared on June 10, 1940—"Should all people who are not United States citizens be required to register with the Government?"—95% of the sample responded in the affirmative. Since then, Gallup has conducted several dozen surveys on "immigrants and immigration" as well as on related topics, such as national identification cards and specific immigration legislation.

On successive cloture votes on June 7 and 28, 2007, the Senate failed to pass the sweeping Comprehensive Immigration Reform Act. Support for the bill had waned after criticism from core Republican voters and from liberal Democrats as well. This legislative defeat came as a setback for President George W. Bush after he had championed the bill with the hope of claiming it as a major domestic policy achievement in the last year and a half of his administration. The derailed immigration measure would have substantially changed U.S. immigration law. It would have provided a path to legal status for most of the some 12 million undocumented immigrants in the United States; authorized a program to legally admit thousands of temporary "guest" workers each year; and established measures to tighten border security and enable tough enforcement of current immigration regulations.

Although a majority of Americans claim that they do not know enough about the controversial immigration bill debated in Congress to have an opinion about it, opposition outweighs support by a three-to-one margin among those who do have an opinion. Among those who say they follow news of the immigration bill most closely, opposition is at the 60% level. There are only minor differences between Democrats and Republicans. Those who oppose the bill mainly say that it provides "amnesty" to illegal immigrants in this country.

Gallup's standard question asking Americans how closely they follow news events shows that only 18% fol-low news about the immigration bill very closely, while another 42% follow it somewhat closely. The 60% who follow the bill very or somewhat closely is exactly the average for all news events tracked by Gallup over the last decade or so. In other words, Americans are not paying a noticeably higher than average level of attention to this bill. Previous surveys conducted by Gallup and other polling organizations presented respondents with specific provisions included in the immigration bill and asked for reaction. In other surveys, various provisions were combined into one broad description of a possible immigration bill. This research has generally shown that a majority of Americans support the provisions tentatively included in the comprehensive bill—including some type of pathway to citizenship for illegal immigrants now in this country. Current Gallup research approached public opinion on the immigration bill in a different way. Rather than explaining or listing the contents of the bill, the research simply asked respondents how closely they were following news about the bill and then asked if they favored the bill, opposed the bill, or "didn't know enough to say."

An important finding here is that a majority of Americans simply don't have an opinion on the immigration bill, despite its prominence in news coverage and talk show discussions in recent weeks. This is consistent with the data showing that only 18% of Americans say they are following news about the bill very closely. The second important finding is that among those who do know enough about the bill to have an opinion, there is roughly a three-to-one level of opposition over support. Additionally, a majority of opponents to the bill feel strongly about their views, while a majority of those who favor the bill say they do not feel strongly about their opinion. In short, there is a core group of about one-third of Americans who are opposed to the immigration bill, counterbalanced by only about one-tenth who support it. This is in the context of the largest group

CHRONOLOGY

JUNE 2007

June 3 CNN hosts the second nationally televised Democratic presidential debate. Iraq is the flash point as the eight Democratic rivals clash on how the war should be handled.

June 5 In a nationally televised debate, the Republican presidential candidates wage verbal combat over pending immigration legislation.

June 6 The leaders of the G8 (the world's leading industrial countries) meet in Germany. Russian president Vladimir Putin surprises President Bush with an offer to build a joint missile defense system against Iran in the former Soviet Republic of Azerbaijan.

June 7 The House of Representatives approves legislation aimed at easing restrictions on federal financing of embryonic stem cell research. The Senate had passed a comparable bill. On June 20, President Bush vetoes the bill, saying, "all human life is sacred."

June 7 The Senate fails to vote on a sweeping immigration reform bill endorsed by President Bush.

June 11 A federal appeals court rules that the president cannot declare civilians to be "enemy combatants" and have the military hold them indefinitely. This ruling rejects the Bush administration's assertion about the scope of executive authority to combat terrorism.

June 12–15 Deadly fighting erupts between the Hamas and Fatah factions of Palestinians. Hamas seizes control of the Gaza Strip, and Fatah holds on to the West Bank.

June 18 The United States ends an economic and political embargo of the Palestinian Authority in an attempt to aid Fatah, the more moderate of the two warring Palestinian factions.

June 19 New York City mayor Michael Bloomberg leaves the Republican Party, encouraging rumors that he is considering an independent presidential run.

June 19 More than 70 are killed when a truck bomb explodes outside a Baghdad mosque.

June 27 Gordon Brown becomes prime minister of the United Kingdom.

June 28 The Senate again fails to bring an omnibus immigration bill to a vote.

June 28 A Democratic presidential debate is held at Howard University, where the candidates focus on domestic issues before a largely African-American audience.

June 29 The Supreme Court reverses itself and agrees to hear claims by Guantánamo Bay prisoners that they have a right to challenge their detention in federal courts.

June 30 Elizabeth Edwards confronts conservative commentator Ann Coulter during a telephone call to MSNBC's *Hardball* program. Edwards asks Coulter to cease "ugly and hateful" personal attacks on her husband, John Edwards.

of Americans—a clear majority—who say they don't know enough about the bill to have an opinion about it. Opposition to the bill is very high—61%—among those who are paying very close attention to it, while only 17% of this group favor it. The ratio of opposition to support drops among those who are following news of the bill somewhat closely, and even more so among the few Americans not paying much attention to the bill but who have an opinion. Interestingly, about one out of five of those who say they are paying very close attention to the bill still say they don't have an opinion on it. That increases to almost 9 out of 10 among those who say they are not paying attention to the bill. There is not a great deal of difference between

Republicans and Democrats in terms of levels of support or opposition to the bill.

Those Americans who either favor or oppose the immigration bill were asked to give some of the reasons in their own words. A substantial percentage of the small number of Americans who favor the bill say they support it because they agree with specific provisions in the bill, including the requirements that immigrants would have to meet to become citizens and the limits the bill would set on who can come into the country. Others do not necessarily agree with all the specifics of the bill but support it on practical grounds, saying that something needs to be done to address the issue and that this bill may be the best compromise that can be achieved. Those Americans who oppose the bill are most likely to volunteer that their opposition is based on the perception that the bill grants amnesty to illegal immigrants now living in this country. Others oppose it because they believe the bill should have stiffer penalties for illegal immigrants, because they believe the new law will not work, or because they have negative feelings about the impact of illegal immigrants in general. The pattern of Americans' attitudes toward illegal immigration, and in particular toward the immigration bill being debated in the Senate, is complex. A good deal of previous research has shown that Americans support the general provisions that are included in the bill, including increased border security and some type of pathway to citizenship for illegal immigrants already in this country—providing that they meet certain requirements.

The political reality, though, is that the current debate on the bill agreed to in principle by President Bush and Senate leaders is taking place in an environment in which the average American simply is not tuned in. Only 18% of Americans are following news about the bill closely, and almost 6 in 10 say they don't know enough about the proposed legislation to have an opinion about it. Those Americans who are following the debate closely are highly likely to be opponents of the bill. Among those who know enough to have an opinion, the bill is opposed by almost a three-to-one margin. Among those who say they are following the news about the bill very closely, opposition outweighs support by almost a four-to-one margin. Politically speaking, it would not be surprising to find that elected representatives who hear from their constituents are highly likely to be getting negative feedback about the bill. The majority who may favor it in principle are not paying much attention at the moment and are generally likely to be silent. House and Senate members, therefore, must in some ways make a decision—to respond to the minority who are making their voices heard, or to the majority whose views are measured in polls but who are not taking the time nor making the effort to voice their sentiments in any other way.

During June, the continuing 2008 presidential election campaign repeatedly focused on the Supreme Court, especially on possible appointments to the Court and possible future Court decisions on abortion—with Democratic candidates supporting the 1973 *Roe v. Wade* decision and Republican candidates, with the exception of former New York City mayor Rudolph Giuliani, favoring overturning the controversial decision that guaranteed a woman's right to an abortion in the first trimester of pregnancy. Gallup's May 2007 poll found that 51% of the public approved of the job the U.S. Supreme Court was doing, down from 60% last fall and on the low side of the range of approval seen over

the last several years. The timing of the poll—one month after the high court, in *Gonzales v. Carhart* (2007), upheld a federal law making it illegal to conduct the late-term abortion procedure known as "partial-birth abortion"—raised questions about whether this high-profile decision played any role in the court's relatively anemic rating. Although the public broadly opposes late-term abortions and thinks the specific procedure known as partial-birth abortion should be banned, Americans also say they do not want to see *Roe v. Wade* overturned. Critics of the court's decision in *Gonzales v. Carhart* say that upholding the federal ban on partial-birth abortion is a step in that direction—and it is possible the public cooled on the court as a result.

JUNE 1

Iraq Still Tops Policy Agenda, but Immigration, Gas Prices Gain

After several months of general stability with respect to Americans' policy agenda for Washington, the public's desire to see the government address immigration and fuel prices grew considerably in May 2007. The percentages naming each of these as one of the top priorities for the federal government to deal with are now at the highest levels seen in at least 10 months. Neither issue has distracted Americans from the war in Iraq, however. Iraq remains by far the public's top-rated priority. Rather, Americans' intensified spotlight on immigration and fuel prices comes at the expense of concern about health care, the economy, and a variety of less prominent issues, on which slight declines are seen.

Each month, Gallup updates Americans' policy "to-do" list for the federal government by asking: "In your view, what one or two issues should be the top priorities for

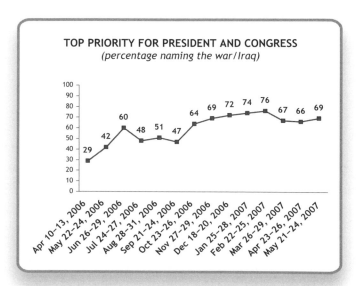

TOP PRIORITY FOR PRESIDENT AND CONGRESS
(percentage naming the war/Iraq)

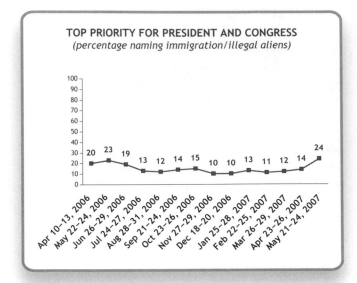

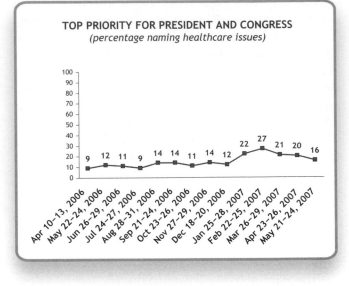

the president and Congress to deal with at this time?" In the most recent Gallup survey, conducted between May 21 and May 24, 2007, nearly 7 in 10 Americans (69%) say the situation in Iraq should be the primary focus, about the same as the 66% recorded in April 2007 and similar to the average percentage mentioning Iraq over the last eight months (70%).

The next most frequently named issue is immigration (24%), followed by fuel prices and energy (17%) and health care (16%). The economy rounds out the top five, mentioned by 10%. No other issue is named by more than 4% of Americans. The 24% citing immigration is the highest seen on this measure since June 2006 (23%). From July 2006 until April 2007, however, the percentage naming immigration averaged only 12%, varying between 10% and 15%.

At 17%, the percentage mentioning some aspect of energy prices is the highest in 10 months, though it is not the record high. That was recorded in May 2006, when

29% of Americans cited fuel prices as the top priority, thus ranking the issue second behind Iraq among Americans' priorities.

The percentage citing some aspect of health care as a priority each month has varied from 9% to 27% over the past year, so the current 16% is about average for this issue.

Finally, mentions of the economy have ratcheted down from a peak of 18% in October 2006 to 10% today. The current figure is the lowest seen for the economy in the 13-month span of this trend.

Differences by Party

Iraq ranks as the top issue for both Democrats and Republicans, although mentions of the situation in Iraq as the top priority for government are somewhat higher among Democrats than among Republicans (76% vs. 62%). Immigration

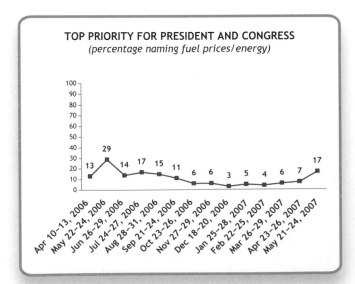

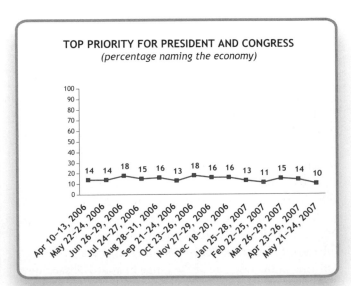

is significantly more likely to be mentioned by Republicans than by Democrats (35% vs. 14%), with independents falling in between (22%). Conversely, health care is mentioned by twice as many Democrats as Republicans (16% vs. 8%). At 17%, independents are as likely as Democrats to name health care as a top priority for government. The three political groups are highly similar in their mentions of fuel prices or the energy situation, with 17% of Republicans, 19% of independents, and 15% of Democrats focusing on these as priorities.

JUNE 8

Candidates' Positions on Iraq Very Important to '08 Vote

The latest USA Today/Gallup Poll finds little change in overall support for the war, with more than half of Americans saying it was a mistake to send troops to Iraq. In terms of the 2008 presidential election, Americans say they would be more likely to vote for a presidential candidate who insists on a timetable for removing U.S. troops from Iraq, and less likely to vote for a candidate who wants to cut off funding for the war. More than 7 in 10 Americans say a candidate's position on the Iraq War will be extremely or very important to their vote next year. Even though a majority of Americans say the United States can win the war in Iraq, fewer than one in three predict it actually will win the war. Americans are somewhat more likely than they were in March to say the country can win the war, but many fewer believe this today than in the prior two years.

Iraq and the 2008 Election

Gallup polling shows that Iraq is clearly the public's number one policy concern, and that it is likely to play a major role in voting decisions in 2008. The June 1–3, 2007, poll finds 33% of Americans saying a candidate's past and current positions on Iraq will be extremely important in determining their vote next year, with an additional 41% saying the candidate's positions will be very important. Only about one in four Americans say these will be somewhat important (19%) or not that important (6%).

Delving further into the possible impact of the Iraq issue on the election, the poll asked Americans how candidates' positions on two of the more controversial policy proposals on the war—a timetable for withdrawing U.S. troops from Iraq and voting to cut off funding for the war, both of which were at the heart of the recent debate on Iraq War funding in Congress—would affect their vote. A majority of Americans, 58%, say they are more likely to vote for a presidential candidate who "only supports legislation on

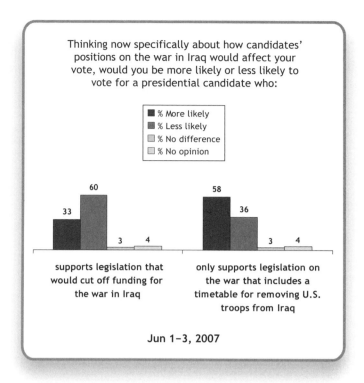

Thinking now specifically about how candidates' positions on the war in Iraq would affect your vote, would you be more likely or less likely to vote for a presidential candidate who:

■ % More likely
■ % Less likely
□ % No difference
□ % No opinion

Jun 1–3, 2007

the war [if it] includes a timetable for removing U.S. troops from Iraq." Thirty-six percent say they are less likely to vote for a candidate who insists on such a provision in future Iraq policy. Only about one in three Americans (33%) say they are more likely to vote for a presidential candidate who "supports legislation that would cut off funding for the war in Iraq," while 60% say they are less likely.

These results accord with previous Gallup polling on Iraq policy, which shows majority support for Congress to enact a troop withdrawal schedule and majority opposition to Congress voting to end funding for the war. The recent vote on a war funding bill on May 24 was a difficult one for some current members of Congress who are running for president—for Republicans who wanted to avoid the perception that they believe the war should continue on its present course indefinitely, and for Democrats who wanted to register their opposition to the war or try to end it while still showing support for the U.S. military. In the end, the leading Republican presidential hopefuls supported the legislation to continue funding the war while not setting a timetable for withdrawal, while most of the Democrats in the Senate who are running for president voted against it. These votes are more or less in line with what the rank and file in their respective parties would support.

A slim majority of Democrats, 51%, say they are more likely to vote for a presidential candidate who supports cutting off funding for the Iraq War, while 39% say they are less likely. The vast majority of Democrats, 78%, say they are more likely to vote for a candidate who insists on a timetable for troop withdrawal. Republicans are disinclined to vote for a candidate who takes either position: Eighty-seven percent say they are less likely to vote for a candidate who would cease funding for the war, and 58% are less likely to support a candidate who would insist on a withdrawal timetable. Independents tend to side with the Democrats on a timetable for troop withdrawal and with the Republicans on cutting off funding for the war. Sixty-one percent of independents say they are more likely to vote for a candidate who insists on a timetable for removing U.S. troops, but 55% say they are less likely to vote for a candidate who supports legislation to cut war funding.

The candidates' votes on this most recent funding bill, as well as their prior positions on the Iraq War, have been a major part of the campaign thus far and will likely continue to be in the future. At this point, it appears the Iraq War issue has potential vulnerabilities for candidates of both parties—in the general election phase if not in the primaries phase—with Republican candidates generally rejecting a timetable for withdrawal that most Americans support, and Democrats voting against funding for the war that most Americans want to continue.

JUNE 11
Majority of Republicans Doubt Theory of Evolution

The majority of Republicans in the United States do not believe the theory of evolution is true and do not believe that humans evolved over millions of years from less advanced forms of life. This suggests that when three Republican presidential candidates in the debate at the Ronald Reagan Presidential Library in California on May 3 stated they did not believe in evolution, they were generally in sync with the bulk of the rank-and-file Republicans whose nomination they are seeking. Independents and Democrats are more likely than Republicans to believe in the theory of evolution. But even among non-Republicans, there appears to be a significant minority who doubt that evolution adequately explains where humans came from.

The data from several recent Gallup studies suggest that Americans' religious behavior is highly correlated with beliefs about evolution. Those who attend church frequently are much less likely to believe in evolution than those who seldom or never attend. That Republicans tend to be frequent churchgoers correlates with their doubts about evolution. The data indicate some seeming confusion on the part of Americans over this issue. About a quarter of Americans say they believe both in evolution's explanation that humans evolved over millions of years and in the creationist explanation that humans were created as is about 10,000 years ago.

Broad Patterns of Belief in Evolution

The theory of evolution as an explanation for the origin and development of life has been controversial for many years—indeed, since the 1859 publication of Charles Darwin's influential *On the Origin of Species*. Although many scientists accept evolution as the best theoretical explanation for diversity in the forms of life on Earth, its validity has become an important issue in the current 2008 presidential campaign. Two recent Republican debates have included questions to the candidates about evolution. Three candidates—Kansas senator Sam Brownback, former Arkansas governor Mike Huckabee, and Colorado representative Tom Tancredo—indicated in response to a question during the May 3 debate that they did not believe in the theory of evolution, although they attempted to clarify their positions in the weeks thereafter.

Several recent Gallup Polls conducted in May and June indicate that a significant number of Americans have doubts about the theory of evolution. One such question was included in a May Gallup survey: "Now thinking about how human beings came to exist on Earth, do you, personally, believe in evolution, or not?" It is important to note that this question included a specific reference to "thinking about how human beings came to exist on Earth," which oriented respondents toward an explicit consideration of the implications of the theory of evolution for humanity's origin. The results may have been different without this introductory phrase. That said, Americans' responses to this question are essentially split down the middle. About half (49%) say they believe in evolution, and about half (48%) say they do not.

A second question included in a June 1–3 USA Today/Gallup Poll asked about evolution side by side with a similar question about creationism: "Next, we'd like to ask about your views on two different explanations for the origin and development of life on earth. Do you think evolution is definitely true, probably true, probably false, or definitely false? Do you think creationism is definitely true, probably true, probably false, or definitely false?" Evolution was defined as "the idea that human beings developed over millions of years from less advanced forms of life," and the results in response to the question were as follows: definitely true, 18%; probably true, 35%; probably false, 16%; definitely false, 28%; no opinion, 3%. Thus, 53% thought evolution was definitely or probably true, while 44% thought it was definitely or probably false.

Creationism was defined as "the idea that God created human beings pretty much in their present form at one time within the last 10,000 years," and the results in response to the question were as follows: definitely true, 39%; probably true, 27%; probably false, 16%; definitely false, 15%; no opinion, 3%. Thus, 66% thought creationism was definitely or probably true, while 31% thought it was definitely or probably false. These results are similar to those from the question asked in May. A little more than half (53%) of Americans say evolution—at least as defined in this question—is definitely or probably true; but even more Americans, two-thirds or 66%, say the theory of creationism is definitely or probably true.

A separate Gallup Poll trend question—also asked in May—gave Americans three choices about human beings' origins. In response, 43% of Americans choose the alternative closest to the creationist perspective: that "God created human beings pretty much in their present form at one time within the last 10,000 years or so." A substantial 38% say human beings evolved, but with God guiding the process. Another 14% favored an interpretation of evolution arguing that God had no part in the process. So a total of 52% replied that humans evolved, with or without God's direction.

To summarize the results of these three questions about evolution and human origins:

Across the three questions, the data show consistently that about half of Americans agree with the theory of evolution, believe that the theory of evolution is probably or definitely true, or believe that humans developed over millions of years with or without God's guidance. Belief in the idea that humans were created pretty much as is within the past 10,000 years is somewhat more dependent on the way in which this concept is measured. A little more than 4 out of 10 Americans, when presented with three alternatives, say they believe that God created humans in their present form within the past 10,000 years. At the same time, two-thirds of Americans, in response to a stand-alone question, say they believe in the theory of "creationism"—defined as the idea that humans were created in their present form within the past 10,000 years.

It might seem contradictory to believe that humans were created in their present form at some time within the past 10,000 years and at the same time believe that humans developed over millions of years from less advanced forms of life. But based on an analysis of the two side-by-side questions asked this month about evolution and creationism, it appears that a substantial number of Americans hold these conflicting views. Twenty-four percent of Americans believe that both the theory of evolution and the theory of creationism are probably or definitely true. Forty-one percent believe that creationism is true and that evolution is false; 28% believe that evolution is true but that creationism is false; and 3% either believe that both are false or have no opinion about at least one of the theories. Without further research, it's impossible to determine the exact thinking process of those who

believe that both the theory of evolution and the theory of creationism are true. It may be, however, that some respondents were seeking a way to express their belief that evolution may have been initiated or guided by God, and told the interviewer that they agreed with both evolution and creationism in an effort to express this more complex attitude.

Importance of Religion and Church Attendance

It is important to remember that all three questions in this analysis included wording that explicitly focused on the origin of human beings. This wording may have made Americans think about the implications of the theory of evolution for the belief in humans beings as special creatures, as reflected in religious teachings generally and in particular in the Judeo-Christian story of human origins as related in the book of Genesis. *USA Today* recently quoted Christian conservative and 2000 Republican presidential candidate Gary Bauer as saying: "Most of us don't think that we're just apes with trousers." Thus it is not surprising to find that many of those who do not believe in the theory of evolution justify that belief with explicitly religious explanations. Those who said they did not believe in evolution were asked: "What is the most important reason why you would say you do not believe in evolution?", and the majority of the responses are clearly religious in nature. It is fascinating to note that some Americans simply justified their objection to evolution by statements of general faith and belief. Although the New Testament does not include many explicit references to the origin of humans in the words of Jesus, 19% of Americans state that they do not believe in evolution because they believe in Jesus Christ. Other religious justifications

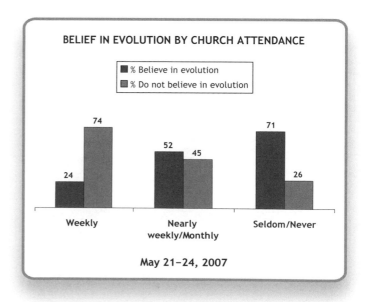

BELIEF IN EVOLUTION BY CHURCH ATTENDANCE

- ■ % Believe in evolution
- ■ % Do not believe in evolution

Weekly: 24, 74
Nearly weekly/Monthly: 52, 45
Seldom/Never: 71, 26

May 21–24, 2007

focus on statements of belief in God, general affirmations of faith, references to the Bible, and the statement that "I'm a Christian." A relatively small percentage of this group justify their disbelief in evolution by saying more specifically that they do not believe that there is enough scientific evidence to prove the theory and/or that they simply do not believe that humans come from beasts or monkeys.

Americans who attend church weekly—about 40% in this sample—are highly likely to reject the theory of evolution. Americans who attend church seldom or never—also about 40%—are strongly likely to accept the theory of evolution.

Republicans Most Likely to Reject Evolution

As noted previously, belief in evolution has already been injected into the political debate this year, with much attention given to the fact three Republican presidential candidates answered a debate question by saying that they did not believe in evolution. It appears that these candidates are, in some ways, "preaching to the choir" in terms of addressing their own party's constituents—the group that matters when it comes to the Republican primaries. Republicans are much more likely to be religious and attend church than independents or Democrats in general. Therefore, it comes as no great surprise to find that Republicans are also significantly more likely not to believe in evolution than independents and Democrats. When the three candidates said that they did not believe in evolution, our analysis suggests that many Republicans across the country no doubt agreed.

It is apparent that many Americans simply do not like the idea that humans evolved from lower forms of life. Americans who say they do not believe in the theory of

evolution are highly likely to justify this belief by reference to religion, to Jesus Christ, or to the Bible. Furthermore, there is a strong correlation between high levels of personal religiosity and doubts about evolution.

JUNE 12
Voter Preferences in Clinton-Giuliani Race Look Fairly "Normal"

If the choice for president in the 2008 election is between New York senator Hillary Clinton running as the Democratic candidate and former New York mayor Rudolph Giuliani as the Republican candidate, the dynamics of voters' preferences could be more similar to recent presidential elections than might be expected. If we remove the fact that Clinton would have the historic distinction of being the first female nominee and that Giuliani would be cast against the Republicans' usual nomination of socially conservative Protestants, the race boils down to a Republican versus a Democrat—and that may have more sway with voters than anything else.

Gallup has run three trial heats this year for the 2008 presidential election in which Hillary Clinton is matched against Rudolph Giuliani, and in all three Giuliani has held a slight lead. Averaging these polls gives Giuliani, the Republican, a five-percentage-point lead (51% vs. 46%) over Clinton, the Democrat, among registered voters nationwide. According to the combined 2007 surveys, Clinton would beat Giuliani among women, blacks, and young voters; in the East and in lower-income households; and among singles, liberals, non-Christians, and, of course, Democrats. Giuliani would beat Clinton among most of these groups' natural counterparts: men, whites, middle-aged adults, seniors, those living in the South and West, upper-income households, married persons, conservatives, Christians, and Republicans.

Given the historic nature of having a female Democrat running in these trial heats against a socially liberal Catholic Republican, it is remarkable how similar it appears these results would be to the 2004 election, in which two white males representing the mainstream politics of the two parties faced off. In that election, President George W. Bush, the Republican, beat Massachusetts senator John Kerry, the Democrat, by about a three-point margin. (This comparison is made using Gallup's final pre-election poll from November 2004, based on the subset of "likely voters" who most closely represent the electorate. In the last six presidential elections, the results based on likely voters have only once deviated by more than a few points from the results based on registered voters.) Most notably, it appears that Clinton would run no stronger among women

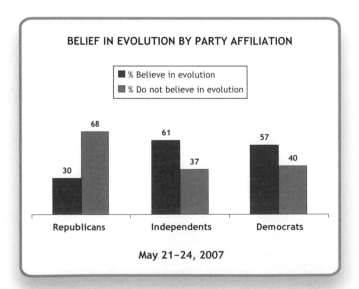

BELIEF IN EVOLUTION BY PARTY AFFILIATION

■ % Believe in evolution
■ % Do not believe in evolution

Republicans: 30 / 68
Independents: 61 / 37
Democrats: 57 / 40

May 21–24, 2007

Claiming she is "ready to lead," Senator Hillary Clinton draws an enthusiastic crowd in Washington, D.C., on June 6, 2007. *(Pablo Martinez Monsivais/AP Images)*

than Kerry did in 2004—or, for that matter, than Vice President Al Gore did when running against Bush in 2000. On average in 2007, women prefer Clinton over Giuliani by a six-point margin (53% to 47%). That is not much different from women's four-point preference for Kerry over Bush in 2004, or from the eight-point preference for Gore over Bush in 2000. A Clinton-Giuliani race may be more striking for its impact on the male vote: Men favor Giuliani over Clinton by a 16-point margin. That compares with a 12-point lead among men for Bush over Kerry among 2004, and a seven-point lead among men for Bush over Gore in 2000.

Clinton's and Giuliani's appeal to voters of various ages, races, regions of the country, and income levels can generally be predicted from the candidate preferences of voters in 2004. There are two important departures, however, in the areas of politics and religion. Those who identify their political views as "moderate" are more likely to support Giuliani in 2008 (51%) than they were to support Bush in 2004 (37%); and a slight majority of independents prefer Giuliani for 2008, whereas a slight majority in 2004 preferred Kerry. In addition, Catholics—a majority of whom

haven't voted for the Republican presidential candidate since Ronald Reagan in 1984—could also switch party loyalties in a Clinton-Giuliani race. Whereas the majority of Catholics backed Kerry in 2004, Gallup's 2007 aggregate data analysis finds a majority backing Giuliani over Clinton for 2008.

It is much too soon to be talking about who will win the 2008 presidential election. It may even be premature to make large wagers on who will be nominated by each party. However, it is not too early to note that the dynamics of national voter support for Clinton are fairly typical for modern Democratic nominees. According to Gallup's 2007 election polling, it appears that if nominated, Clinton—like Kerry and Gore before her—will have to depend on the traditional base of the Democratic Party for her main support, and the outcome will be determined by traditional swing voter groups, such as "independents" and "moderates." At least at this stage, it does not appear that Clinton has a special advantage among women to offset the importance of these groups. If anything, it appears she may face a harder time holding her own among male voters, at least with Giuliani as her opponent.

JUNE 14

An Abiding Relationship: Republicans and Religion

Republicans are significantly more likely than Democrats and independents to report that religion is very important in their lives. This basic relationship is particularly strong among whites and, more generally, among those who report their race or ethnicity as something other than black. Women who are Republicans are more likely to be religious than women who are independents and Democrats. The same relationship between religion and party identification holds among men. The percentage of Americans who say that religion is very important in their lives ranges from 40% among men who are independents to 76% among women who are Republicans. These conclusions are based on a special Gallup analysis of more than 9,000 interviews conducted over the past five years. Roughly 6 in 10 Americans (57%) report that religion is very important in their lives. About one in four (26%) say that religion is "fairly" important, while less than one in six (16%) say that religion is not very important. There have been year-to-year variations in these percentages over the past decades, but the same basic pattern with respect to this measure of religion has stayed stable.

Party Identification and Importance of Religion

An initial look at the basic cross-tabular relationship between party identification and the importance of religion underscores the expected—and important—relationship between religion and political orientation. Those Americans who identify as Republicans are significantly more likely to report that religion is very important than are independents or Democrats. Sixty-six percent of Republicans, 57% of Democrats, and 48% of independents say that religion is very important. That independents are the least likely to find religion important in their lives is not surprising. Americans who identify themselves as independents (i.e., say they do not identify with either the Republican or Democratic Party) are by definition less likely to be involved in politics. The assumption is that they are also less likely to be involved in other social and organizational aspects of life, including religion. Political independents, in other words, may tilt toward being "independent" in their general approach to life.

The Race Factor

The data show that 20% of Americans who identify as Democrats are black, compared with only 2% of Republicans and 8% of independents. Previous research has robustly documented that blacks are the most religious of any identifiable racial or ethnic group in the United States today. This suggests that self-reported importance of religion among Democrats—although lower than among Republicans—may be distinctly different between black Democrats and non-black Democrats. This polling survey investigated this hypothesis by breaking the sample down into six segments, based on the intersection of party identification and race (defined for the purpose of this analysis as blacks and all others). The patterns that emerge are as expected. Fifty percent of non-black Democrats say religion is very important, compared with 83% of black Democrats. In similar fashion, only 45% of non-black independents say that religion is very important, compared with 77% of black independents. (There are too few black Republicans in the sample to allow for meaningful comparison with non-black Republicans.) Considered differently, the data show that the relationship between importance of religion and being a Republican is particularly strong among Americans who are white or in some other non-black ethnic group.

Gender

Past research has shown that women are significantly more religious than men, regardless of the indicator of religiosity being used. In this particular sample, 65% of women in America as measured in these 2004–7 surveys say that religion is very important in their lives, compared with just 49% of men. Women are significantly more likely to be Democrats than are men. Six in 10 Democrats in America today are women, compared to slightly less than half of Republicans and independents.

There are, then, interesting cross-currents tugging at one another in the American population. Women are more likely to be religious than men and more likely to be Democrats; yet Republicans are more likely to be religious than are independents and Democrats. In other words, the less-religious orientation of Democrats in America today exists despite the fact that Democrats are disproportionately composed of women—who are typically more religious. The results show that the impact of two variables—party and gender—appear to operate somewhat independently. Women who identify as Republicans are more likely to report that religion is very important in their lives (76%) than women who identify as Democrats (62%) and independents (57%). And men who identify as Republicans are more likely to report that religion is very important in their lives (58%) than men who identify as or Democrats (48%) and independents (40%). Thus, there is a political party effect within each gender group. One can look at these same data from a different perspective, however, and conclude that there is a noticeable *gender* effect within each *political* group. Women are more religious than men among Republicans, among independents, and among Democrats.

There appears to be a self-selection of sorts in American society. Those women who identify as independents and Democrats are less religious than women who identify as Republicans. The same pattern holds among men. Even though men tend to be less religious overall, those men who identify as Republicans are more religious than men who identify as independents or Democrats. The data reinforce one of the basic conclusions about political life in America today: There is a significant relationship between being religious and identifying with the Republican Party among whites and other non-black groups. Blacks defy this pattern; they are both highly religious and highly likely to identify as Democrats.

This analysis used self-reported importance of religion as the measure of religiosity. A little less than 6 in 10 Americans say that religion is very important in their life, a number that jumps to 66% among Republicans but drops to 50% among non-black Democrats and 45% among non-black independents. Although women are both more religious and more likely to be Democrats than men, the analysis shows that religious women are more likely than less religious women to be Republican. The same pattern holds among men.

JUNE 18

Republican, Democratic Presidential Contests Strikingly Similar

With no incumbent president or vice president running for the 2008 presidential nominations, it is perhaps not surprising that both of the major parties have competitive races, with multiple candidates jockeying for second, if not first, place. Still, the current outlines of voter preferences in the Republican and Democratic nomination battles are remark-

ably similar. According to the latest USA Today/Gallup Poll of national adults, conducted between June 11 and June 14, 2007, each race is characterized by a front-runner attracting about 30% of the potential primary vote nationwide, followed by two candidates garnering about 20% support each in a close contest for second place and a slew of weaker candidates, each supported by no more than 11%. Continuing the parallels, the race for second place in both parties features one announced candidate who has earned fairly steady support throughout the year (but mostly failing to build momentum) and one unannounced candidate with growing support, just recently pulling into a tie for second.

The Democratic Contest

The current Democratic front-runner is New York senator Hillary Clinton. She is favored by 33% of Democrats and independents who lean Democratic—about average for her this year. A USA Today/Gallup Poll conducted earlier this month found Clinton's chief rival, Illinois senator Barack Obama, pulling even with Clinton. However, in the current poll Obama has fallen back to a tie for second place with former vice president Al Gore. At 21%, current support for Obama is near the low end of the support range seen for him since January, while Gore's 18% ties with an early March poll as his best result. Former North Carolina senator John Edwards, once tied with Gore for third place, has been stalled in the 11% to 12% range since May. The only other candidate earning the support of at least 5% of Democrats is New Mexico governor Bill Richardson.

The Republican Contest

On the Republican side, former New York mayor Rudolph Giuliani has managed to hang on to his first-place position through most of 2007 but has a somewhat weaker level of support today than earlier this year. His current 28% of the vote is at the bottom of the support range seen for him since January and is well below the high point of 44% he had in a March Gallup Poll. A stiff battle for second place in the Republican race is now under way between veteran candidate Arizona senator John McCain and newcomer Fred Thompson, the former Tennessee senator who only recently formed an exploratory committee to start raising funds and who has yet to formally announce his candidacy. Support for Thompson has nearly doubled since Gallup's last poll, from 11% in early June to 19% today. McCain is now at 18%. This is similar to the 19% he garnered earlier this month and his average of 22% in two May polls but is well below his high point of 28% last December. Support for former Massachusetts governor Mitt Romney is now at 7%, lower than the 12% seen in early June but typical of the support level he has

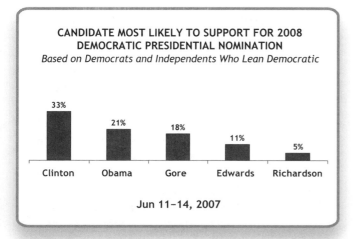

CANDIDATE MOST LIKELY TO SUPPORT FOR 2008 DEMOCRATIC PRESIDENTIAL NOMINATION
Based on Democrats and Independents Who Lean Democratic

Clinton 33%   Obama 21%   Gore 18%   Edwards 11%   Richardson 5%

Jun 11–14, 2007

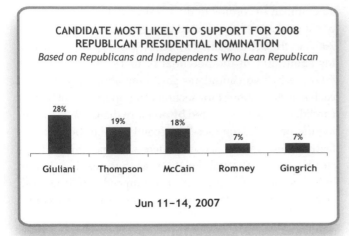

**CANDIDATE MOST LIKELY TO SUPPORT FOR 2008
REPUBLICAN PRESIDENTIAL NOMINATION**
Based on Republicans and Independents Who Lean Republican

Giuliani 28%
Thompson 19%
McCain 18%
Romney 7%
Gingrich 7%

Jun 11–14, 2007

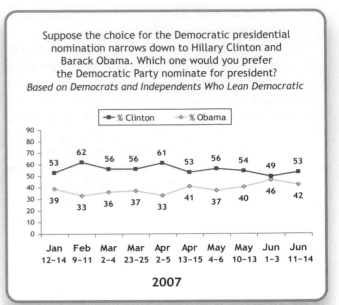

Suppose the choice for the Democratic presidential
nomination narrows down to Hillary Clinton and
Barack Obama. Which one would you prefer
the Democratic Party nominate for president?
Based on Democrats and Independents Who Lean Democratic

% Clinton — % Obama

Clinton: 53, 62, 56, 56, 61, 53, 56, 54, 49, 53
Obama: 39, 33, 36, 37, 33, 41, 37, 40, 46, 42

Jan 12–14, Feb 9–11, Mar 2–4, Mar 23–25, Apr 2–5, Apr 13–15, May 4–6, May 10–13, Jun 1–3, Jun 11–14

2007

received since announcing his candidacy in February. Former speaker of the House Newt Gingrich (whose candidacy is still in question) also comes in at 7%. None of the other eight Republicans named in the poll is supported by more than 3% of Republicans.

"Narrow-Downs"

Not only do Clinton and Giuliani lead their respective races among the full fields of candidates running in their parties, they also are the top choices for their respective parties' nominations when the races are narrowed down to just themselves and one of their leading opponents. On the Republican side, Gallup asked Republicans and independents who lean Republican to name their preference if the choice for the Republican presidential nomination narrowed down to Giuliani and Fred Thompson—the first Giuliani-Thompson face-off Gallup has measured. A slight majority of Republicans (53%) pick Giuliani, while

41% choose Thompson. This 12-point lead for Giuliani is slightly greater than the nine-point lead he has among the full field. (In the early June poll, Giuliani led McCain on this type of measure by 18 points, 56% vs. 38%.)

On the Democratic side, Gallup asked Democrats and independents who lean Democratic to name their preference if the choice for the Democratic presidential nomination narrowed down to Clinton and Obama—a match-up Gallup has been tracking since January. Clinton now leads Obama by 11 percentage points on this measure, 53% vs. 42%—nearly identical to Giuliani's current lead over Thompson. Clinton has held an advantage over Obama on this measure all year, averaging 19 percentage points from January through May but varying quite a bit within that period. Clinton's greatest lead over Obama in this two-candidate matchup was 29 points in mid-February; her smallest was three points in Gallup's early June poll.

JUNE 19
Bush's Job Approval Near Its Low Point

According to a new Gallup Poll, conducted between June 11 and June 14, 2007, just 32% of Americans say they approve of the way George W. Bush is handling his job as president, while 65% disapprove. Bush's current job approval rating is just one point higher than his all-time low as president, measured in May 2006. His current 65% disapproval rating ties for the highest of his entire tenure in the White House, the same as measured in May 2006 and in February 2007. The president's 32% approval rating is little changed since the beginning of May but has been tracking slightly lower than his 35% average for the first six months of the year.

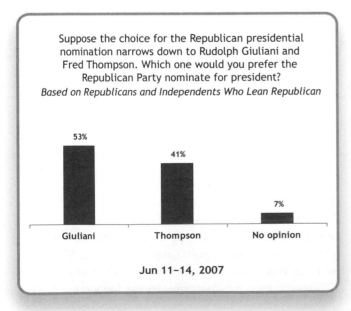

Suppose the choice for the Republican presidential
nomination narrows down to Rudolph Giuliani and
Fred Thompson. Which one would you prefer the
Republican Party nominate for president?
Based on Republicans and Independents Who Lean Republican

Giuliani 53%
Thompson 41%
No opinion 7%

Jun 11–14, 2007

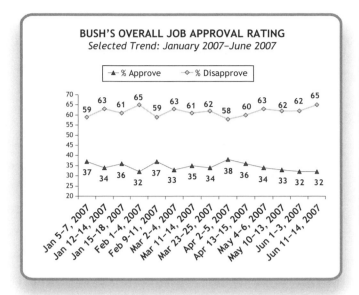

BUSH'S OVERALL JOB APPROVAL RATING
Selected Trend: January 2007–June 2007

Bush's highest rating this year was 38% in early April; his lowest is the 32% recorded in both June polls conducted so far this month.

The president has not had an approval rating above 40% since September 2006, shortly after the five-year anniversary of the 9/11 terrorist attacks. Only former presidents Harry Truman (from October 1950 to December 1952) and Richard Nixon (from July 1973 to August 1974) had approval ratings under 40% for longer periods of time. Bush continues to maintain the support of Republicans and self-identified conservatives, but he has very low ratings among Democrats and independents. Nearly three in four Republicans (73%) approve of the job Bush is doing, compared with 24% of independents and just 8% of Dem-

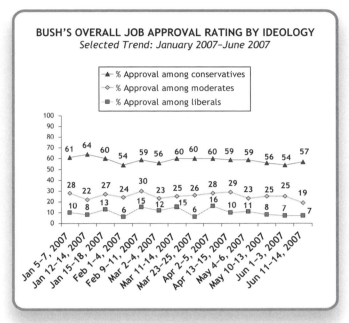

BUSH'S OVERALL JOB APPROVAL RATING BY IDEOLOGY
Selected Trend: January 2007–June 2007

ocrats. Republicans' and Democrats' approval ratings of Bush have not shown much fluctuation over the course of the year, averaging 74% and 8%, respectively. Independents' approval ratings have varied more, averaging 28% and ranging between 22% and 34% since January 2007.

A majority of conservatives, 57%, approve of Bush at the present time, while only 19% of moderates and 7% of liberals share this view. The president's ratings among conservatives and liberals are roughly on average for the year. His ratings among moderates, however, are now at the lowest point of his administration. In May and June 2007, roughly one in four moderates approved of Bush.

Seventy Percent of Americans Say Economy Is Getting Worse

Food and gasoline prices both rose last month. At the pump, gas prices increased about 10% in May and are up almost 40% since January. In addition, average weekly wages for nonsupervisory workers fell, after adjusting for inflation, for the second consecutive month in May. At the same time, the stock market continues at record highs and manufacturing output is edging upward, making factories a tad busier this year. Such conflicting economic reports make it difficult to explain exactly why Gallup's June reading of Americans' economic views remains as negative as seen in May. A modest one in three Americans rate the economy today as either excellent or good, while the percentage saying the economy is getting better fell slightly, from 28% to 23%. Fully 7 in 10 Americans now say the economy is getting worse, the most negative reading in nearly six years. For the first time this year, a majority of Americans are negative about the employment market,

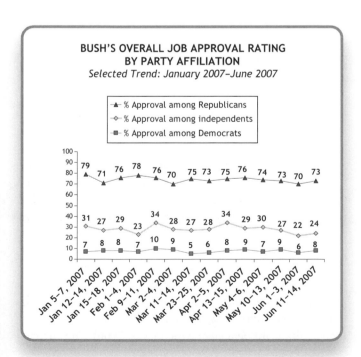

BUSH'S OVERALL JOB APPROVAL RATING BY PARTY AFFILIATION
Selected Trend: January 2007–June 2007

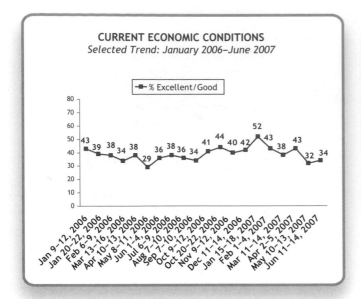

CURRENT ECONOMIC CONDITIONS
Selected Trend: January 2006–June 2007

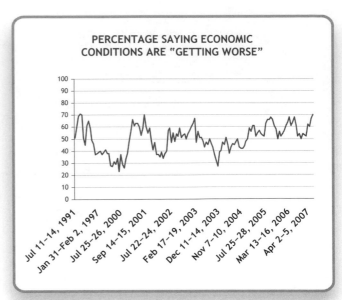

PERCENTAGE SAYING ECONOMIC
CONDITIONS ARE "GETTING WORSE"

saying it is a bad time to find a quality job. Generally, however, this measure remains more positive than in the period from 2002 to 2005.

Current Economic Conditions

According to the June 11–14, 2007, Gallup Poll, 34% of Americans say national economic conditions are "excellent" or "good," while 43% say "only fair" and 23% say "poor." This year, Americans' perceptions of the economy were at their highest levels in January, when 52% of respondents said economic conditions were excellent or good. But such positive views have deteriorated somewhat in the ensuing months. Historically, Americans' positive perceptions of the economy were highest in the late 1990s, with a peak average of 69% in 2000, and lowest in 1992, with an average rating of 13%.

Economic Outlook

The perception that the economy is getting worse has now reached as high a level as at any point since 2001. Seventy percent of Americans say conditions are getting worse. While this is statistically similar to the 67% saying this last month, it is up 10 points since April. Also, just in the past month, there has been a significant five-point drop, from 28% to 23%, in the percentage saying conditions are getting better.

The last time Americans held such negative views was in early September 2001, just before the terrorist attacks on September 11. Since Gallup asked this question, the "getting worse" percentage has been at 70% only four times: twice in 1992, in the September 2001 poll, and in the current poll.

Economy Still Mentioned as the Most Important Problem

This month's replies regarding "the most important problem facing this country today" show little change from previous months in mentions of the economy. Almost one-quarter of Americans (24%) mention some aspect of the economy (fuel and oil prices, the economy in general, jobs, or the federal budget deficit). The most significant trend in perceived problems this year has been the increase in Americans' views that fuel and oil prices are the most important problem the country faces today. In January, just 1% of Americans mentioned oil prices as the most important problem for the nation, compared with 7% in the latest poll. Still, Americans' major concern about fuel prices is much lower today than a year ago, when those citing it as most important peaked at 22% (in May 2006). The current

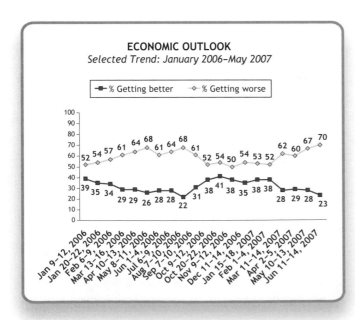

ECONOMIC OUTLOOK
Selected Trend: January 2006–May 2007

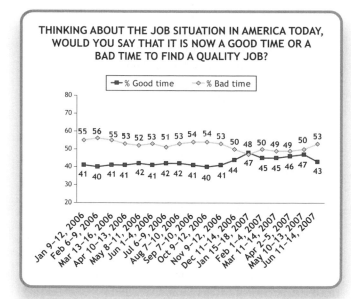

THINKING ABOUT THE JOB SITUATION IN AMERICA TODAY, WOULD YOU SAY THAT IT IS NOW A GOOD TIME OR A BAD TIME TO FIND A QUALITY JOB?

level of concern about this issue is similar to that found in the summer of 2005. The war in Iraq remains the main noneconomic concern for Americans. Thirty-four percent of Americans mentioned the situation in Iraq as the most important noneconomic problem the country faces today, virtually unchanged from May.

Attitudes Toward the Job Situation

Only 43% of Americans say now is a good time to find a quality job, and 53% say it's a bad time. Last month, 47% of Americans said it was a good time to find a quality job, and 50% said it was a bad time. In 2007, public optimism about finding a quality job has ranged from a low of 43% to a high of 48%, but these are still among the most positive ratings since Gallup started to ask this question monthly in August 2001.

A look at yearly averages regarding whether it's a good time to find a quality job shows Americans' positive evaluations have gradually increased. Between 2001 and 2003, fewer than 3 in 10 Americans, on average, said it was a good time to find a quality job. That figure has inched up every year since then and reached 46% in the first six months of 2007. Perceptions of the job market among those who are employed or currently looking for a job are similar to those among the public as a whole. Forty-five percent of employed Americans say it's a good time to find a quality job, compared with 52% who say it's a bad time.

Healthcare Costs Still a Burden

When asked about the most pressing financial problems their family faces today, Americans mention healthcare costs, lack of money or low wages, and oil and gasoline prices. Health-

care costs are mentioned by 16% of Americans, while 13% say low wages and 11% say oil and gasoline prices. These percentages are virtually unchanged from last month. Although the economy is a mixed bag of good and bad news, a growing percentage of Americans appear to be apprehensive about future economic conditions. Seventy percent of Americans think the economy is getting worse, which brings this measure to its lowest level since early September 2001. Oil prices, the overall state of the economy, and jobs are the economic issues of greatest concern to the American public, and for the first time this year, a majority of Americans are saying it's a bad time to find a quality job.

JUNE 21

Americans' Confidence in Congress at All-Time Low

The percentage of Americans with a "great deal" or "quite a lot" of confidence in Congress is at 14%, the lowest in Gallup's history of this measure. It is also the lowest for any of the 16 institutions tested in this year's Confidence in Institutions survey, which covers the military, small business, the police, the church and organized religion, banks, the U.S. Supreme Court and lower federal courts, public schools, the medical system, the presidency, television news, newspapers, the criminal justice system, organized labor, big business, HMOs, and Congress. The public's rating of Congress constitutes one of the lowest confidence measures for any institution tested over the last three decades.

Gallup's annual update on Americans' confidence in institutions shows that confidence ratings are generally down across the board compared with last year. The public's confidence ratings in several institutions, including Congress, are now at all-time low points in Gallup's history of this measure. These low ratings reflect the generally sour mood of the public at this time. Of the 16 societal institutions tested in Gallup's 2007 update, Americans express the most confidence in the military. They have the least confidence in HMOs and Congress. Americans have much more confidence in "small" business than in "big" business.

Basic Data

Gallup's annual update of the public's confidence in institutions—conducted between June 11 and June 14, 2007—shows that all but two of the 16 institutions included in this year's survey have at least slightly lower confidence ratings than last year (although most of these changes are not statistically significant). The largest drops in confidence between 2006 and 2007 are eight percentage points

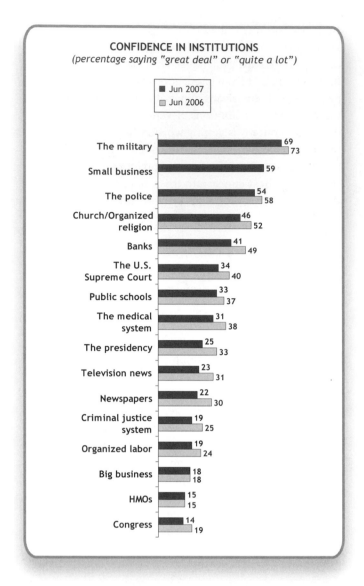

CONFIDENCE IN INSTITUTIONS
(percentage saying "great deal" or "quite a lot")

■ Jun 2007
□ Jun 2006

	Jun 2007	Jun 2006
The military	69	73
Small business	59	
The police	54	58
Church/Organized religion	46	52
Banks	41	49
The U.S. Supreme Court	34	40
Public schools	33	37
The medical system	31	38
The presidency	25	33
Television news	23	31
Newspapers	22	30
Criminal justice system	19	25
Organized labor	19	24
Big business	18	18
HMOs	15	15
Congress	14	19

have confidence ratings in the 40% range—the church/organized religion and banks. All other institutions generate a great deal or quite a lot of confidence from less than 40% of the American population. The five institutions at the bottom of the list—each with confidence ratings below 20%—are the criminal justice system, organized labor, big business, HMOs, and Congress.

Congress and the Other Two Branches of Government

Confidence in the three branches of the U.S. government—executive (the presidency), legislative (Congress), and judicial (the Supreme Court and lower federal courts)—has been drifting downward over the past several years, following historically high ratings in the years immediately after the terrorist attacks of September 11, 2001.

The current confidence rating for Congress—14%—is the lowest in Gallup's history for that institution. Although ratings of Congress have never been high, they were at the 40% level at the time of the Watergate crisis in the 1970s, and again in 1986.

Americans' confidence in the presidency has dropped concomitantly with the drop in Bush's approval ratings. In 2002, 58% were confident in the presidency, compared with the current 25%. President Bush's job approval ratings have fallen from 84% at the beginning of 2002 to 32% today. At 34%, confidence in the Supreme Court, as with Congress, is at its lowest point in Gallup's trend. Confidence in the Supreme Court has been at or above the 50% point at several times during the last several decades. (While confidence in the Supreme Court as an institution is now at 34%, 51% approve of the way the Supreme Court is handling its job.)

for banks, the presidency, television news, and newspapers. There has been no change in the ratings of big business and HMOs.

The drop in confidence in most institutions coincides with a period of time in which Americans have low levels of overall satisfaction with the way things are going in the United States, are giving Congress and President Bush low approval ratings, and are very negative about the direction of the economy. There is little doubt that this same "malaise" is reflected when respondents are asked to rate their confidence in the 16 societal institutions in Gallup's annual update. Whether these low ratings are becoming a permanent fixture of the American psyche or represent a short-term bout of public depression remains to be seen. The general pattern of confidence in institutions has remained similar in recent years. There are three institutions tested this year in which a majority of Americans express a great deal or quite a lot of confidence: the military, small business, and the police. Two institutions tested

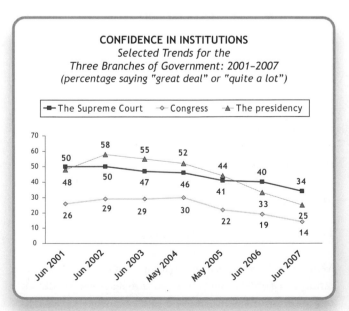

CONFIDENCE IN INSTITUTIONS
Selected Trends for the
Three Branches of Government: 2001–2007
(percentage saying "great deal" or "quite a lot")

■— The Supreme Court ◇ Congress ▲ The presidency

	Jun 2001	Jun 2002	Jun 2003	May 2004	May 2005	Jun 2006	Jun 2007
The Supreme Court	50	50	47	46	41	40	34
Congress	26	29	29	30	22	19	14
The presidency	48	58	55	52	44	33	25

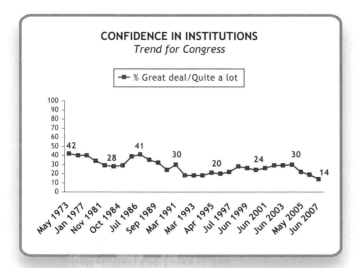

CONFIDENCE IN INSTITUTIONS
Trend for Congress

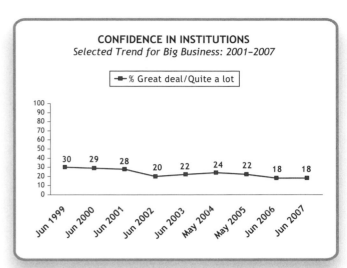

CONFIDENCE IN INSTITUTIONS
Selected Trend for Big Business: 2001–2007

The Military

Americans' confidence in the military has always been relatively high, even in the mid-1970s during the aftermath of the Vietnam War. The military has been near or at the top of the list of institutions tested in each Gallup survey since 1987. The high point for the military—85% expressing a great deal/quite a lot of confidence—came in March 1991, just after the first Persian Gulf War, when the United States swiftly achieved its goal of driving Iraqi forces out of Kuwait. Confidence in the military has been nearly as high at several times since September 11, 2001. The military's current 69% confidence rating, although still the highest of any institution tested this year, is the lowest for the military since 9/11.

Big vs. Small Business

There is an enormous difference in Americans' confidence in business, depending on the adjective placed before the

word "business" when the list is read to respondents. Only 18% of Americans express a great deal or quite a lot of confidence in big business, compared with 59% who express confidence in small business. Confidence in big business has never been high, reaching its maximum of 34% in 1974. Even in the halcyon days of the "dotcom" boom in the late 1990s, only 30% of Americans expressed a great deal or quite a lot of confidence in big business. The current 18% confidence rating in big business is the same as in 2006 and remains the lowest in Gallup history.

The Church and Organized Religion

The 46% confidence rating for the church and organized religion is within one percentage point of being the lowest in Gallup's history.

Ratings for the church fell significantly in the wake of revelations surrounding the priest abuse scandal in the Catholic Church in 2002, and before that they had dropped in the wake

CONFIDENCE IN INSTITUTIONS
Selected Trend for the Military: 2001–2007

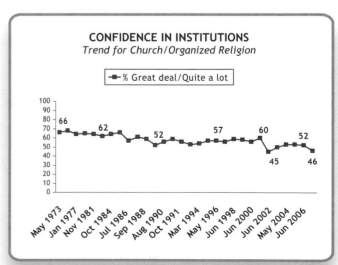

CONFIDENCE IN INSTITUTIONS
Trend for Church/Organized Religion

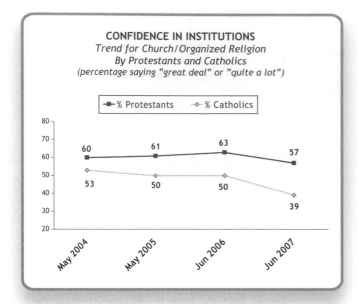

CONFIDENCE IN INSTITUTIONS
Trend for Church/Organized Religion
By Protestants and Catholics
(percentage saying "great deal" or "quite a lot")

of the television evangelism scandals of the late 1980s and early 1990s. Confidence in the church or organized religion is particularly low among Catholics as compared with Protestants. Confidence among Catholics was at 53% in 2004 and has dropped to 39% today. Among Protestants, confidence went from 60% in 2004 to 63% in 2006 and 57% today.

Journalistic Entities

Americans have relatively low levels of confidence in the media and journalism profession. Just 23% of Americans have a great deal or quite a lot of confidence in television news, and only 22% express the same sentiment with regard to newspapers. Neither of these two entities has done exceedingly well in Gallup's history, but both are particularly low this year.

Americans are currently in a very sour mood, a state of affairs that is reflected in the relatively low confidence ratings given many American institutions in Gallup's latest survey. Confidence ratings for Congress are not only at the bottom of this year's list, but represent the lowest confidence rating for Congress in Gallup's history of using this confidence measure. This presumably reflects a confluence of both the historically low standing of Congress in the minds of the public and the overall negative mindset of the American public. Confidence in several other institutions is also at an all-time low point. We assume that the low confidence ratings measured this year are connected to Americans' broader malaise with respect to the state of the country. It is not entirely clear what is behind the currently bad mood on the part of Americans, but Gallup analyses show that the Iraq War and the economy are certainly perceived as major problems. The very low ratings

for Congress suggest that Americans may be upset that their elected representatives have not been able to rectify these concerns.

JUNE 25
Iraq War Impact on the Election

A good deal of the discussion during the 2008 presidential campaign to date has centered on U.S. policy toward the Iraq War. According to recent Gallup Polls, about one in three Americans rate the war as an extremely important issue relative to their vote. Among this group, New York senator Hillary Clinton fares better in a matchup with former New York City mayor Rudolph Giuliani than she does among those for whom the war is a less important issue. Analysis shows that candidates' Iraq War positions seem to have less of an impact on current presidential nomination preferences, though Giuliani and Illinois senator Barack Obama seem to be running slightly better in their respective primaries among those who view the war as a less critical issue.

In two polls conducted this month, Gallup assessed the importance of the Iraq War to Americans' voting deliberations. Specifically, Gallup asked Americans, "How important will a candidate's past and current positions on the war in Iraq be in determining your vote for president in 2008?"

Even though Gallup polling has consistently shown that Democrats are much more likely than Republicans to mention the Iraq War as the most important problem facing the nation and the top priority for the government to deal with, the two groups show only a slight difference in the importance they place on prospective presidential candidates' war positions. Thirty-five percent of Democrats and

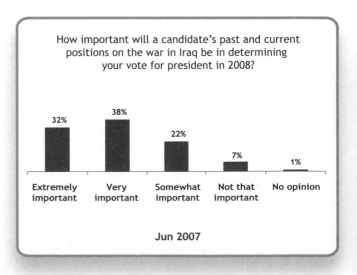

How important will a candidate's past and current positions on the war in Iraq be in determining your vote for president in 2008?

Jun 2007

Democratic-leaning independents say these positions will be extremely important to their 2008 vote, compared with 31% of Republicans and Republican-leaning independents. Democrats who say that the war is extremely important are strongly anti-war, while Republicans who say the war is that important are strongly pro-war.

The War and Nomination Preferences

The Democratic presidential candidates have tried to balance the need to appeal to strong anti-war Democrats whose support will be crucial to winning their party's nomination with not taking positions that are so anti-war that they may turn off voters in the general election. Clinton is the clear front-runner for the party's nomination, and she is the leader both among Democrats who rate the Iraq War as extremely important to their vote and among those who assign less importance to the war. Her support is similar among both groups, and that is the case for nearly all Democrats. One possible exception is Obama, who does slightly better among those who say the war is less important to their vote than among those who say it is extremely important. Though that result is not statistically significant, the net outcome is that Clinton has a much greater lead among Democrats who say the war is extremely important than among those who do not.

Republicans face a different challenge than Democrats on the war, as they must try to appeal to a mostly pro-war Republican base while distancing themselves from the Bush administration's policies, which are widely viewed as ineffective. Giuliani, like Clinton among Democrats, is the front-runner among all Republicans, regardless of their views on the importance of the war. Most Republican candidates—including vocal war supporter Arizona senator John McCain—receive similar support from those who say the war is extremely important and those who do not. The one possible exception to that general pattern is former Tennessee senator Fred Thompson, who fares slightly better among those who assign the highest priority to the war.

The data for nomination preferences in both parties suggest that the Iraq War may not be the defining issue in the primaries, despite the attention it is being given. That might make sense in that the candidates in each party have the same general orientation toward the war. All the Democratic candidates are generally anti-war, and their differences largely lie in the details of how best to remove U.S. troops from Iraq as soon as possible; whereas the Republicans are generally in favor of the war effort (long-shot Texas representative Ron Paul being a notable exception), and they for the most part agree that Iraq should be stabilized before the United States pulls its troops out of the

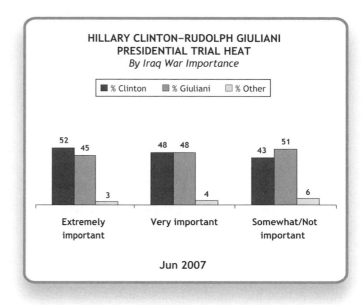

HILLARY CLINTON–RUDOLPH GIULIANI PRESIDENTIAL TRIAL HEAT
By Iraq War Importance

■ % Clinton   ■ % Giuliani   □ % Other

	Extremely important	Very important	Somewhat/Not important
% Clinton	52	48	43
% Giuliani	45	48	51
% Other	3	4	6

Jun 2007

country. It is possible that disagreement over the details of Iraq policy may become more of a factor in voters' candidate preferences as the campaign continues and voters become more familiar with the different candidates and their positions on issues, but at this point the Iraq War is not a major determinant of nominee support.

The War and the General Election

The analysis suggests that the war may be more consequential in the general election phase of the 2008 campaign. In the two polls that asked about the importance of candidates' positions on the Iraq War, Gallup also asked Americans for their preference in a matchup of the two front-running candidates in each party,

Giuliani and Clinton

There is a clear, though modest, linear relationship between Iraq War importance to voters and candidate preference. Clinton leads Giuliani 52% to 45% among those who say the war is extremely important, while the two candidates tie among those who say it is very important. Giuliani has a 51% to 43% advantage among Americans who say the war is only somewhat important or not important.

As mentioned above, the differences are not merely a function of the fact that Democrats attach more importance to the war as a political issue than do Republicans. While this can explain some of the differences observed in the Giuliani-Clinton trial heat, these differences also emerge because Democrats who say the war is extremely important show a stronger preference for Clinton over Giuliani than Democrats who say the war is less important.

Meanwhile, Republicans' support for Giuliani over Clinton is consistent regardless of how important they say the war is. At this early stage of the campaign, it seems that Clinton has emerged as the favorite candidate of those who care most about the Iraq War, within the Democratic Party and in the American electorate more generally.

JUNE 27
The Fights for the Nominations

The 2008 presidential election has gotten off to an unprecedented early start. Many candidates were off and running as the year began. How much has all of the extremely early campaigning for president at this stage of the 2008 race affected voter preferences? On the Democratic side, not much. On the Republican side, not much more.

New York senator Hillary Clinton established her lead among the Democratic candidates early in the process. Since January there have been two occasions when Illinois senator Barack Obama, who has been in second place during most of 2007, came within striking distance of Clinton in Gallup Polls, but she has otherwise maintained her lead, which has ranged from 9 to 19 percentage points. In Gallup's latest poll, conducted between June 11 and June 14, 2007, Clinton leads Obama by 12 points among Democrats (33% to 21%). Former North Carolina senator John Edwards (a formally announced candidate) and former vice president Al Gore (who has not ruled out a bid but has said he has no plans to run at this time) have been competitive for third place among Democrats. Each has the support of at least 10% of Democrats, not too far behind Obama, but there has been little indication that either Gore or Edwards (let alone the other Democrats who are campaigning for the nomination) are making significant enough gains to challenge Clinton.

The Republican race has seen a jockeying of candidates for second place, while there has been little serious threat to the front-runner, former New York City mayor Rudolph Giuliani, since January. Giuliani emerged as the Republican leader in early February, after having been closely matched with Arizona senator John McCain earlier, and he has held that position ever since. Both Clinton and Giuliani have seen the size of their leads in their respective primary races diminish since earlier this year—especially in the case of Giuliani, whose support level just recently fell below 30%—well below his peak of 44% in March. Another change in the Republican field has been the recent increase in support for former Tennessee senator Fred Thompson since his emergence in March as a possible candidate. Thompson scored 12% of the vote the first time Gallup included him in the Republican trial

heats, and in the latest June poll, Thompson receives 19% of the party's vote, earning him a tie for second place with McCain. Support for McCain has hovered around 20% since March—a clear change from January, when he had 27% and nearly tied Giuliani for first place. He has not faded dramatically, however.

In recent weeks, support for former Massachusetts governor Mitt Romney has mostly remained below 10% nationally despite his fund-raising prowess and his strong showing in several early-primary–state polls. Support for former speaker of the House Newt Gingrich—who has said he will not decide for sure whether or not he is running until the fall—is also in this range. None of the other potential or announced candidates in the Republican Party has so far received more than a few percentage points in Gallup's pre-election primary nomination polls. Eight in 10 Democrats nationwide, compared with only 6 in 10 Republicans, are satisfied with the choice of candidates for their party's nomination. This relative lack of satisfaction on the Republican side could be seen as encouraging unannounced Republicans such as Thompson and Gingrich to officially enter the race. Contrariwise, the finding that there is a high level of satisfaction among rank-and-file members of the Democratic Party may suggest less of an opportunity for Gore if he were to decide to enter the Democratic field.

Early Measures on the November 2008 Outcome

Seventeen months before the nation chooses its next president, most signs from the political environment favor the Democratic Party. The Democrats have a clear advantage in party identification among the voting-age population; Americans view the Democratic Party more favorably than the Republican Party; and the basic indicators of the nation's mood are quite negative—something that typically bodes well for the party not currently occupying the White House. Thus, not surprisingly, when asked for their generic party preference for president earlier this year (April 2007), Americans were much more likely to say they would rather see the Democratic Party's candidate win the 2008 election than the Republican Party's candidate. That underlying advantage is evident when specific Democratic presidential candidates are matched up against specific Republican candidates in questions relative to the 2008 election.

McCain and Giuliani would appear to present the toughest matchups for the Democrats at this point. Giuliani is the most positively rated candidate of either party, with a 57% favorable rating in the latest Gallup survey. And while McCain is not rated as favorably overall at 47%, he is potent because he has impressive appeal across political parties—

rated much more positively than negatively by independents, and only slightly more negatively than positively by Democrats. The other Republican contenders, Thompson and Romney, are still unknown to roughly half of Americans and thus are not as well positioned to compete against a well-known Democrat. Despite Giuliani's broad popularity, however, the three leading Democrats are quite competitive with him in national test elections. (As noted, this is likely due to the underlying strength of the Democratic Party over the Republican Party, as seen in trial heats and other public opinion polling questions.) All three Democrats garner 50% of support among registered voters when pitted against Giuliani, with Giuliani getting 46% against Clinton and 45% against both Edwards and Obama. Again, none of these gaps in favor of the Democrats is statistically significant.

Gallup test elections matching McCain against each of the three leading Democrats are too close to call, though Edwards's six-point lead just barely misses attaining statistical significance. Clinton has a three-point edge over the Arizona senator, and Obama has a two-point advantage. Each of the Democratic candidates has statistically significant leads when matched up against Romney. Edwards leads Romney by 29 percentage points (61% to 32%), Obama leads him by 21 points (57% to 36%), and Clinton leads him by 13 points (53% to 40%).

2008 Election Issues

The situation in Iraq is overwhelmingly seen as the most important problem facing the country today, and is the top issue Americans at this point say they will take into account in their 2008 presidential vote. The degree to which Iraq will continue to dominate the election by next year is, of course, unknowable. A scenario in which U.S. troops have begun to withdraw from Iraq by 2008 is not out of the question, nor is a scenario in which the recent "surge" in troops is seen as a success. Each of these might significantly affect the presidential campaign. Terrorism will probably continue to be a strong underlying issue in the campaign. Americans may not talk or even think about it much, but it is a concern that can be easily activated, particularly if there is another major terrorist event. The economy is almost always a factor in an election. Consumer views of the economy became more positive in January but are much more negative in the latest June poll, possibly because of gas prices. Health care is a rising concern among Americans and has been a major issue in past election campaigns. Immigration will likely remain a campaign issue unless and until Congress passes legislation to address the subject of illegal immigration. Immigration ranks second behind the war in Iraq in Gallup's latest update on the most important problem facing the nation.

Early Nomination Polls as Predictors

Poll results at this phase—more than six months before the first primaries and caucuses—are valuable measures of candidate strength and can have an important impact on the campaign. At the same time, the current standings of the candidates are not—nor should they be expected to be—a direct predictor of what will unfold in the election year itself. Volatility with respect to voter preferences has historically been true in the case of the Democratic nomination in particular. Bill Clinton in 1992, Michael Dukakis in 1988, Jimmy Carter in 1976, and George McGovern in 1972 were all virtual unknowns who rose from relative obscurity to take their party's nomination. Republicans have, on the other hand, been more likely to settle on a nominee early and stick with him.

Here's a look at where the election stood at this point—in June, during the year before the election year—in the five previous presidential elections.

In June 2003, Connecticut senator Joe Lieberman outpolled the pack of Democratic hopefuls, with 20% of Democrats supporting Lieberman for their party's 2004 presidential nomination. Fifteen percent supported Missouri representative Dick Gephardt, while 13% supported the eventual nominee, Massachusetts senator John Kerry. No other Democratic candidate received double-digit support that month.

George W. Bush and Al Gore, the Republican and Democratic presidential candidates in 2000, led their party's nomination ballots in June 1999. Gore had an average of 64% of Democrats supporting him for the Democratic nomination that month, with his main challenger, former New Jersey senator Bill Bradley, at just 28% support. Bush averaged 53% support in June 1999. The only other Republican with double-digit support then was Elizabeth Dole, with 11%.

In June 1995, Kansas senator and Senate majority leader Bob Dole, the Republican Party's eventual nominee, led Gallup's Republican nomination ballot by a wide margin over any other candidate. Fifty-one percent of Republicans supported Dole for their party's nomination at that time.

In the summer of 1991, New York governor Mario Cuomo was at the top of the polls for the Democratic nomination, with 22% of registered Democrats' support, followed closely by civil rights activist Jesse Jackson at 18%. Bill Clinton, who eventually won the party's nomination and the general election in 1992, garnered only 5% of the vote among registered Democrats in August 1991.

In June 1987, 39% of Republicans said they supported the eventual Republican nominee and winner, vice president George H. W. Bush, for their party's nomination. Bob Dole was supported by 21% of Republicans at that time. On the

Democratic side, Jesse Jackson had 18% of the votes among Democrats to lead the nomination contest at that time, while the eventual winner, Massachusetts governor Michael Dukakis, had 11%. By then, early front-runner Gary Hart had withdrawn from the field before re-entering later that year.

Early General Election Polls as Predictors

Since World War II, there have been only three elections that replaced a president who had served two four-year terms—in 1960, 1988, and 2000. (In 1952 and 1968, the incumbents were eligible for re-election after having served less than two full terms, but declined to run.) Given the small number and differing outcomes of these similar elections, the historical data do not offer much guidance as to what might happen in 2008. But the data do show that it has not been unusual for the party out of power to lead for much of the year before the "open-seat" election.

George W. Bush held a statistically significant lead over Gore in almost every trial heat poll conducted in 1999; but Bush went on to win a disputed victory in the Electoral College over Gore—who actually won the popular vote—to replace departing Democrat Bill Clinton. In 1987, Democratic front-runner Hart led the elder George Bush for the first several months of the year. Bush took over the lead in late May after news of Hart's extramarital affair derailed his campaign, and Bush subsequently polled better than Hart, Jackson, and Cuomo in late 1987. Bush relinquished the lead the following spring to his eventual challenger, Michael Dukakis, before moving back ahead after the Republican convention and eventually being elected by a comfortable margin to succeed Republican Ronald Reagan as president. In 1959, the various Democratic candidates led for much of the first part of the year, but the tide shifted in the Republicans' favor for much of the presidential preference polling in the latter part of that year. Democrat John Kennedy won a razor-thin victory over Republican Richard Nixon the following year in the contest to succeed Republican Dwight Eisenhower.

JUNE 29

Bush Job Approval Rating: Little Difference Between Whites and Hispanics

There is little difference in President George W. Bush's job approval rating between Hispanics and non-Hispanic whites, despite the fact that Hispanics in the United States today are significantly less likely than non-Hispanic whites to identify with the Republican Party. The president's job approval rating among blacks, few of whom are Republicans, is extremely low. These results are based on interviews

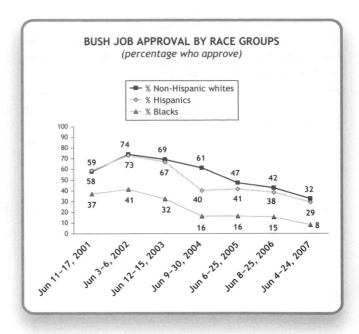

conducted as part of Gallup's Minority Rights and Relations survey, which includes large representative samples of blacks and Hispanics. The poll was conducted between June 4 and June 24, 2007. Bush's job approval rating among non-Hispanic whites in the poll is 32%. Among Hispanics, including those for whom Spanish is their preferred language, Bush's job approval is 29%. Only 8% of blacks in the poll approve of Bush's performance as president. This pattern of similarity between whites and Hispanics in Bush's job approval rating has been evident for the most part over the past six years in the annual Gallup Minority Rights and Relations survey. The only exception was in June 2004, when Bush's job approval ratings among Hispanics were significantly lower than among whites.

The data indicate that the profile of party identification among Hispanics is significantly different from that of non-Hispanic whites, with substantially fewer Republicans (11%) and more independents (39%). One of the reasons for the similarity in job approval ratings between whites and Hispanics is that Hispanic Democrats are much more charitable than white Democrats in their evaluations of Bush. According to the poll, 20% of Hispanic Democrats approve of Bush, compared with just 3% of white Democrats. Six percent of black Democrats approve of Bush. An analysis of various subgroups of Hispanics within the sample indicates little difference in Bush's job approval regardless of age, education, or language of interview. President Bush gets a break of sorts from Hispanics, whose approval of the job he is doing as president is higher than would be expected based on their party identification. Hispanics who identify as Democrats are somewhat more positive about Bush than white or black Democrats, resulting in the higher presidential job approval rating among Hispanics.

JULY 2007

In late June, the Washington Post published a series of articles portraying Dick Cheney as the most influential and powerful vice president in American history. Similarly, John Nichols, Cheney's biographer, argues that "this was not George W. Bush's presidency. It was Dick Cheney's." Gallup's first Dick Cheney poll appeared in May 1989, when 45% of those who had heard of "Richard Cheney" correctly identified him as the then secretary of defense. Since then, Gallup has asked some 300 questions about Cheney. The latest poll, conducted between July 12 and July 15, 2007, finds 30% of Americans approving of the job Cheney is doing as vice president, while 60% disapprove. This is slightly lower than the 34% measured this past March, and the lowest of his entire tenure as Bush's vice president. The same low percentage view Cheney himself favorably.

Although Republicans continue to rate Cheney more positively on both measures than do independents or Democrats, Republicans' ratings also are at their lowest levels to date. In the latest poll, 57% of Republicans say they have a favorable job approval rating of Cheney, compared with 26% of independents and just 12% of Democrats. Throughout the course of the Bush administration, Cheney's job approval rating always has been much higher among Republicans than among independents or Democrats. But his rating is now at its lowest point ever among Republicans and either ties for the lowest or is near the lowest ever among independents and Democrats. Cheney's approval rating reached a high of 68% in January 2002, not long after the 9/11 terrorist attacks that also elevated ratings for President Bush. The vice president's job approval rating subsequently declined to 50% in January 2005. Since the end of 2005, Cheney's rating has been below 50%, averaging just 36%. Americans' overall opinion of Cheney is also at its lowest point: Thirty percent say they have a favorable opin-

ion of the vice president, while 62% have an unfavorable opinion of him. Cheney's favorable rating was somewhat higher earlier this year, at 38% in January and 37% in February.

In July 2000, immediately after Bush announced Cheney as his vice presidential running mate, 51% of Americans rated Cheney favorably and 14% unfavorably, with 35% not familiar enough with him to give an opinion. Cheney's favorable rating reached a high of 67% in January 2002 and remained much more positive than negative until February 2004. Throughout the 2004 re-election campaign, Americans were evenly divided in their views of the vice president. Cheney's favorable rating rebounded somewhat after Bush's 2004 re-election victory, but since October 2005, Cheney's ratings have been more negative than positive. As is the case with respect to Cheney's job approval rating, Republicans have rated the vice president much more favorably than independents or Democrats over the course of his tenure as vice president. Fifty-nine percent of Republicans currently say they have a favorable opinion of Cheney, while 26% of independents and just 9% of Democrats rate him favorably. Republicans' and Democrats' favorable ratings of Cheney are both now at their lowest point, though independents' ratings were lower in the spring of 2006.

Gallup only periodically updates Cheney's job approval ratings and favorable ratings. However, a comparison of the job approval and favorable ratings for Bush and Cheney show similar job approval ratings for the president and vice president over the course of this administration, but consistently higher favorable ratings for Bush than for Cheney. Since 2001, the only time Bush's and Cheney's job approval ratings were not within a few points of each other was in January 2002, when 84% of Americans approved of Bush's handling of his job as

CHRONOLOGY

JULY 2007

July 2   President Bush commutes the 30-month prison sentence of former Cheney aide Lewis "Scooter" Libby for perjury and obstruction of justice.

July 2   Senator McCain dismisses top staffers as his campaign deals with a financial shortfall. McCain's weak fund-raising and campaign overspending have damaged his status as front-runner.

July 5   Former vice president Al Gore says he will not run for public office again.

July 7   A suicide bomber kills more than 150 people in a northern Iraqi village.

July 9   Senator McCain's campaign manager and chief strategist both resign.

July 9   President Bush, citing executive privilege, refuses to give Congress documents relating to the firing of federal attorneys.

July 10   Pakistani troops storm a mosque controlled by radical Islamists. Dozens are killed, including the leader of the militants.

July 12   The NAACP convention hears speeches by presidential hopefuls. Eight Democrats speak but only one Republican, Tom Tancredo, shows up for the event (and receives a standing ovation).

July 14   Republican Jim Gilmore, former governor of Virginia, leaves the Republican presidential race.

July 16   A truck bomb in Kirkuk, Iraq, that targeted a Kurdish political headquarters kills 85 people.

July 17   The United States National Intelligence estimate reports that al-Qaeda has become stronger over the past two years, particularly in Pakistan.

July 23   CNN and YouTube/Google host a Democratic presidential candidates debate in Charleston, South Carolina. Some of the questions are submitted via YouTube.

July 24   The minimum wage rises to $5.85 an hour, the first increase in ten years.

July 25   Two suicide bombers target crowds celebrating Iraq's soccer victory over South Korea.

July 25   The House Judiciary Committee votes to hold former White House counsel Harriet Miers and White House chief of staff Joshua Bolten in contempt for refusing to testify about the firings of federal attorneys.

---

president but only 68% approved of Cheney's performance as vice president. Bush's favorable rating in the current survey is seven points higher than Cheney's, 37% to 30%. Bush's favorable rating has been anywhere from 5 to 16 points higher than Cheney's over the past six years; the current 7-point difference is roughly the average for all such ratings over that period. (In April 2001, the favorable ratings of both were essentially the same: 65%, 64% for Cheney.)

According to the Gallup Poll conducted between July 12 and July 15, 2007, 27% of Americans approve and 66% disapprove of the way Congress is handling its job. Congressional job approval was 24% in June and is now at roughly the same level Gallup measured in May. Still, the public's rating of Congress is lower now than at the start of the year when the Democratic takeover occurred, with roughly one in three Americans approving of Congress in January and February. The current 27% rating is similar to the poor ratings Congress received in 2006, when

Americans elected a Democratic majority after Republicans had controlled both houses of Congress for nearly all of the previous 12 years. So far this year, congressional job approval ratings have averaged 30%—up from an average of 25% in 2006. Since Gallup first started tracking this measure in 1974, the highest yearly average approval rating of Congress was 56% in 2001; the lowest, in 1992, was 18%. Democrats are more positive than Republicans in their current assessment of Congress, although a solid majority of both groups say they disapprove of the job Congress is doing. Roughly one in three Democrats (32%) say they approve of Congress, compared with 18% of Republicans. Independents' approval rating of Congress is 30%. Prior to the transfer of congressional power from Republicans to Democrats in January 2007, congressional job approval ratings were much higher among Republicans than among independents or Democrats; since then, Democrats have become more likely than independents or Republicans to approve of Congress.

JULY 3

Public Assesses Pros and Cons of Possible Clinton Presidency

Former first lady and current New York senator Hillary Clinton remains the front-runner for the Democratic nomination in public opinion polls, and she does no worse than tie the leading Republican candidates in general election trial heat preference surveys. Given that she is a serious contender to be the nation's 44th president, a new Gallup survey asked a nationally representative sample of Americans what they thought would be the best and worst things about a Clinton presidency. More than any other specific comment, Americans cite the historical significance of Clinton being the first female president as the best outcome of her possible election. But a significant percentage say "nothing" positive would result from her being elected. While there is no consensus on what would be the worst thing about a Clinton presidency, issue disagreement with her is a common theme, especially among Republicans. Former president Bill Clinton's possible return to the White House is raised as both a positive and a negative outcome.

Regardless of their views of Hillary Clinton, all respondents in the late June poll were asked to say what would be the "best or most positive thing about a Hillary Clinton presidency." The most frequently occurring specific response—given by 22%—is a reference to the fact that Clinton would be the first female president. The next two most frequent responses mention her ability to deal with two of the key 2008 election issues—healthcare (10%) and Iraq (9%). Seven percent each mention two personal characteristics that respondents think would serve her well in the Oval Office—her experience and that she is capable and competent. Six percent mention the fact that her husband, Bill Clinton, would be back in the White House and able to advise her. Notably, 28% of Americans say there would be "nothing" positive about a Clinton presidency. The fact that Clinton would be the first female president is the most often mentioned aspect of a potential Clinton presidency among all party groups: 25% of Democrats, 24% of independents, and 17% of Republicans. Men (20%) and women (23%) are about equally likely to mention Clinton's becoming the first female president as the best thing about her being elected. And that historic possibility is something that apparently excites younger Americans as well: Thirty-seven percent of 18-to-29-year-olds say her being the first woman to hold the job would be the best thing about her being elected president. That sentiment is shared by 24% of 30-to-49-year-olds but only 12% of those age 50 and older. Not surprisingly, Democrats also commonly cite issues when detailing the benefits of Clinton's being

elected. Nearly as many Democrats mention her personality characteristics.

The most significant partisan difference on this question is that a majority of Republicans, 56%, volunteer that there would no positives in a Clinton presidency, whereas 25% of independents say this and only 7% of Democrats. There is no consensus on the negative aspects of a Clinton presidency; the top five specific mentions are essentially equal from a statistical perspective. These include mentions that she is "too liberal" or "a socialist" (10%), that "Bill Clinton would be back in the White House" (10%), that "she is not qualified" or "would not succeed in the job" (9%), and that the respondent simply dislikes her (7%)—along with mentions of past "Clinton scandals" or "baggage" (7%). There are partisan differences with respect to the specific negative aspects of a potential Clinton presidency. Three of the top five Republican concerns involve issues, including 18% who say she is "too liberal" or "a socialist." Independents (12%) and Democrats (9%) are somewhat more likely than Republicans (7%) to express doubts about her qualifications for the job.

In order to gain more insight into Americans' concerns about Clinton being president, the responses regarding the negative aspects of a Clinton presidency were arranged into broad categories dealing with her issue positions (such as being "too liberal" or her "views on Iraq"), her personality or character ("not qualified" or "don't like her"), or the political implications of Clinton's being elected president ("Bill would be back in the White House" or "Clinton scandals"). Forty-four percent of Republicans mention something about her issue positions or policy preferences when describing the bad things that would result from a Clinton presidency; 27% of Republicans mention something political and 23% mention something about Clinton's personality. By contrast, Democrats and independents are both more likely to mention political considerations as possible downsides than either issues or personality. Whereas 28% of all respondents say there would be nothing good about a Clinton presidency, only 12% say there would be nothing bad about it. Again, there are significant differences by party affiliation with respect to this reply: Twenty percent of Democrats say this, compared with 10% of independents and 4% of Republicans.

JULY 6

"Giuliani Republicans" Less Conservative than the Typical Republican

Since February 2007, former New York City mayor Rudolph Giuliani has led all Gallup Polls of Republicans' preferences for the party's 2008 presidential nomination. He has the highest favorable ratings among the Republican presidential candidates and has raised more money for his campaign in the second quarter of 2007 than any other Republican. Despite this, some experts believe he is far from a cinch to win his party's nomination, in large part because his views on abortion and other social issues are not in step with traditional Republican positions.

Gallup aggregated data from its last three Republican nomination preference ballots to see how the political beliefs of Giuliani's supporters compare with those of Republicans who support other candidates. An analysis of these data finds that Giuliani voters are less likely than other Republicans to identify themselves as conservatives in general and with regard to social issues in particular. There are only minor differences in the two groups' self-described ideology with respect to economic issues. Pro-life Republicans are not eschewing Giuliani completely; in fact, a slight majority of his supporters say they are pro-life rather than pro-choice. However, a much larger proportion of Republicans who support other candidates are pro-life.

Ideology of Republicans

The Republican Party largely consists of Americans who are politically conservative. In the three polls combined for this analysis, 68% of all Republicans and Republican-leaning independents described their political views as either "very conservative" or "conservative." But the subset of Republicans who rate Giuliani as their top choice for the party's 2008 presidential nomination are somewhat less likely than other Republicans to describe themselves in this way. According to the data, 59% of Giuliani Republicans say they are very conservative or conservative, compared with 73% of Republicans who favor other candidates for the nomination. Notably, those who do not support Giuliani are more than twice as likely as Giuliani supporters to say their views are "very conservative" (16% versus 7%). Giuliani voters, by contrast, are more likely to identify themselves as moderates (34% vs. 22%).

To gain additional insight into respondents' ideological orientation, Gallup asked Americans about their ideology with regard to social and economic issues. Overall, Republicans are likely to describe themselves as conservative in both issue areas, and by roughly the same percentages: Sixty-six percent say they are conservative on economic issues and 63% on social issues. Giuliani supporters diverge more from the rest of the party on social issue ideology. Fifty-five percent of Giuliani Republicans say they are conservative on these matters, compared with 66% of all other Republicans. There are, however, only slight differences on economic issues: Sixty-one percent of Giuliani Republicans and 67% of the remainder of Republicans identify

themselves as economic conservatives. This result makes sense given that Giuliani's positions on economic issues are generally in line with those of other Republican candidates, and any differences he has with the others on economic policy have not been highlighted to the extent that his disagreements with them on social issues have been.

Republicans and Abortion

Abortion is a critical issue separating the Republican and Democratic parties. In fact, it has not been uncommon for candidates who held a view in opposition to the majority of their party's rank and file to switch that position prior to entering the presidential nomination race. The most notable example of that in the current election cycle is former Massachusetts governor Mitt Romney's conversion from the pro-choice stand he espoused while running for the U.S. Senate in 1994 and for governor of Massachusetts in 2002 to a pro-life position in the 2008 presidential campaign.

Giuliani, however, has been consistent in his pro-choice views throughout the campaign, and it may be the single issue that most distinguishes him from his main competitors for the nomination. It also distinguishes Giuliani's supporters from his nonsupporters to a significant degree. While Giuliani Republicans are still more likely to identify themselves as pro-life (51%) than pro-choice (44%), the gap is fairly narrow. Among all other Republicans, the gap in favor of the pro-life position is better than two to one, 65% to 29%. The full impact of Giuliani's issue positions on Republicans' preferences is still an unknown. A January USA Today/Gallup Poll found that the vast majority of Republicans were unsure where Giuliani stood on several social issues: Sixty-four percent did not know his position on abortion, and 75% did not know his position on gay civil unions, which he supports. Additionally, about as many Republicans incorrectly said he was pro-life as correctly identified him as pro-choice on abortion. Republicans may be more knowledgeable about Giuliani's positions today, especially because his stand on abortion has been a frequent topic in several Republican candidate debates. The relationship between this potentially heightened awareness and Republican voters' likelihood to support Giuliani is unclear at this point, although it is worth noting that his support for the nomination has dropped to 28% in the most recent poll, the lowest it has been since December 2006.

JULY 9

Gasoline, Jobs, Inflation: Consumers' Top Complaints About Economy

Public optimism about the economy has been in decline since the fall of 2006, dipping to the point where only 23%

said the economy is getting better in a mid-June 2007 Gallup Poll. The question is, why? The latest Gallup survey helped provide an answer by asking respondents who say the economy is either getting better or getting worse to identify the economic indicators they feel support their position. Soaring gasoline prices, unemployment, and rising inflation are the top reasons given by those perceiving an economic downturn. High employment and a healthy stock market are the leading signs behind the views of those who believe the economy is improving. Employment is a major factor on both sides of this perceptual divide, but it is a much stronger element for those saying the economy is improving.

Evidence for Economic Decline

According to the June 25–28, 2007, survey, three major economic negatives are on the minds of those who think the economy is souring. These are high gasoline prices (named by 31% of those who say the economy is getting worse); the job market, including unemployment, layoffs, and outsourcing (30%); and inflation, including rising prices generally and the high price of food and groceries (30%) in particular. Additionally, concerns about the housing market, including sluggish sales and home foreclosures, are cited by 22% of those perceiving an economic downturn. When calculating the total mentions for the job market, inflation, and housing, Gallup counts respondents who name two or more related issues in each category only once, producing a "net" total for each category. Other negative signs named by at least 5% of Americans who consider the economy to be getting worse include the federal budget deficit (10%), healthcare costs (9%), the growing gap between the rich and the poor or middle class (6%), and stagnant wages (5%).

There are some notable distinctions in perspective on this question across different geographic regions. Residents of the South and West are especially concerned about gasoline prices. Those in the Midwest are the most likely to mention job losses and unemployment, while those in the West are least likely to mention this. The housing market and foreclosures are of particular concern in the West. The reasons given for believing the economy is getting worse also differ according to household income—particularly with respect to the housing market (mentioned most frequently by upper-income Americans) and grocery prices (more widely cited by lower-income Americans).

Evidence for Economic Improvement

For the much smaller group of Americans who believe the economy is improving, the dominant factor appears

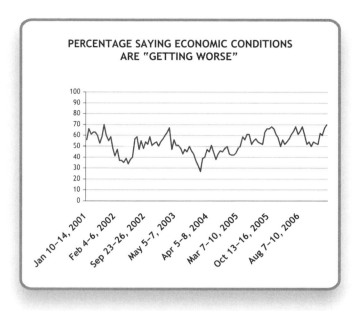

to be the job market. A net total of 44% of economic optimists cite either low unemployment or the availability of jobs as the main sign the economy is improving. Secondarily, 28% mention the strength of the stock market or Wall Street. And 17% of economic optimists see the continued rise in consumer spending as a positive sign for the economy. In direct contrast to the 30% of economic pessimists who cite high inflation as evidence the economy is worsening, 14% of economic optimists cite stable inflation as evidence the economy is improving. Interest rates—cited by 10% of optimists compared with 4% of pessimists—are a somewhat greater factor in the perception of an improving economy. Other signs named by at least 5% of optimists are that business is doing better (10%), that the housing market is picking up (9%), and that gasoline prices are coming down (6%). Consumer confidence has been in short supply for most of the past six years, with the occasional rebounds typically lasting only a few short months. Economic pessimists have outnumbered optimists for more than two years, but the percentage saying the economy is getting worse is now among the highest levels Gallup has seen in monthly tracking since January 2001.

According to the new survey, there is no dominant reason for Americans' believing the economy is getting worse—but the reasons given do tend to cluster into several major categories. Gasoline prices and inflation are particularly associated with negative views of the economy. The job market is seen as a major negative factor among economic pessimists, but it is even more likely to be cited as a positive factor among economic optimists. Weaknesses in the housing market, the federal budget deficit, healthcare costs, and wage inequality figure as relatively minor factors for Americans convinced that the economy is suffering.

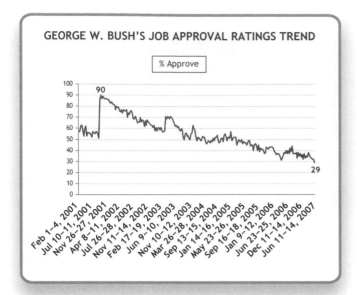

GEORGE W. BUSH'S JOB APPROVAL RATINGS TREND

% Approve

JULY 10

Bush's Job Approval at 29%, Lowest of His Administration

President George W. Bush's job approval rating is now at 29%, the new low point for his administration so far. Bush's current rating ranks in the bottom 3% of more than 1,300 Gallup presidential approval ratings since 1938. Bush's job approval rating was an already low 37% as the year began, and it has dropped gradually since April. The range of job approval ratings over the entire Bush presidency has been extraordinary, from 90% in September 2001 to the current 29%—a decline of 61 percentage points.

Bush's current job approval rating as measured in the July 6–8, 2007, USA Today/Gallup Poll is 29%, down

three percentage points from Gallup's previous measure in mid-June. The newest rating is two percentage points below Bush's previous low point of 31% in May 2006. Bush's rating has been below 50% for more than two years and below 40% since October 2006. The Bush administration received a record-high 90% approval rating in September 2001 in the aftermath of the terrorist attacks on New York City and Washington, D.C.

Bush's ratings have averaged 34% so far this year, reaching only as high as 38% (in April). On a yearly basis, Bush's job approval rating has fallen each year since 2002.

Partisan Ratings

Bush continues to maintain the support of about two-thirds of Republicans, but has low ratings among Democrats and independents.

Sixty-eight percent of Republicans approve of the job Bush is doing, compared with 21% of independents and just 7% of Democrats. Republicans' ratings of Bush are down five percentage points since mid-June 2006. The 68% approval rating among members of his own party ties with a measure obtained in May 2006 as the lowest of his administration. As 2007 began, 79% of Republicans approved of the job Bush was doing as president. Bush's rating among independents also ties for the low of his administration, although independents' ratings of Bush have been in the low 20% range at several points in the past year. Democrats' ratings of Bush show little change in recent months, with approval in the single digits in most polls over the past year.

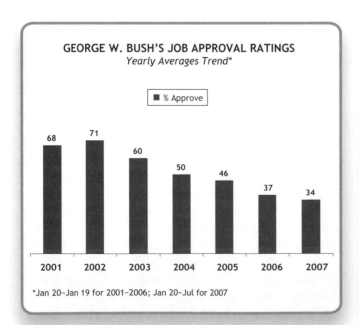

GEORGE W. BUSH'S JOB APPROVAL RATINGS
Yearly Averages Trend*

% Approve

2001	2002	2003	2004	2005	2006	2007
68	71	60	50	46	37	34

*Jan 20–Jan 19 for 2001–2006; Jan 20–Jul for 2007

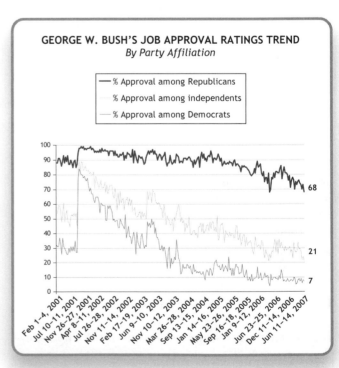

GEORGE W. BUSH'S JOB APPROVAL RATINGS TREND
By Party Affiliation

— % Approval among Republicans
— % Approval among independents
— % Approval among Democrats

Bush's Low in Historical Perspective

Bush's 29% approval rating is low by historical standards. Gallup has recorded 1,325 presidential job approval ratings since 1938, and only 42—or 3%—have been below 30%. Only 32 job approval ratings have been below 29%. Most of these sub-30% job approval ratings were given to two presidents, Harry Truman and Richard Nixon. Jimmy Carter had one rating of 28% and several 29% ratings, and Bush's father, George H. W. Bush, had one rating of 29% in the summer of 1992. Truman received the lowest approval rating in Gallup's history, with 22% of Americans approving of the job he was doing in February 1952. Nixon's 24% approval rating came in the final month of his presidency before he resigned for his role in the Watergate scandal in August 1974.

From a broader perspective, Bush is now one of five presidents since World War II who have recorded at least one job approval rating below 30%, joining Truman, Nixon, Carter, and the elder George Bush. Four additional presidents had administration low points in the 30s: Lyndon Johnson, Gerald Ford, Ronald Reagan, and Bill Clinton. Two presidents did much better: Dwight Eisenhower's low point was 49%, and John F. Kennedy's was 56%, recorded just two months before his assassination in November 1963. President Bush's current job approval rating is not significantly lower than his previous readings. Bush had a 32% rating in mid-June, and his previous low point of 31% in May 2006 was just two percentage points higher than his current rating. The current reading represents, rather, the continuation of a gradual downward drift in the president's ratings going back to 2003, in which each yearly average has been lower than the previous one.

At this point, the public's view of the president has been affected to one degree or another by the conflict in Iraq, Bush's support for the now-aborted immigration bill, the Scooter Libby sentence commutation, and the negative way in which the public views the economy. Future changes in the public's attitudes toward any of these matters could affect Bush's job approval rating going forward. In general, the trajectory of Bush's ratings will depend, to a significant degree, on his ability to hold on to the dwindling support among members of his own party—now down to the two-thirds level.

JULY 11

Latest Poll Shows High Point in Opposition to Iraq War

As an increasing number of Republican senators are questioning the Bush administration's Iraq War policy, and as

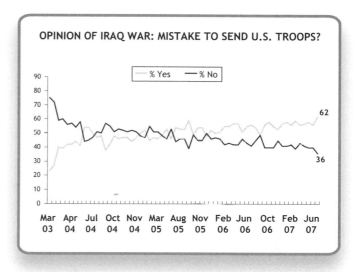

OPINION OF IRAQ WAR: MISTAKE TO SEND U.S. TROOPS?

Democrats again attempt to force an end to the war, the latest USA Today/Gallup Poll shows public opposition to the war at its highest point thus far. Roughly half of Americans say the surge in the number of U.S. troops in Iraq is not making any difference in Baghdad or in Iraq generally. However, the poll suggests that Americans may disagree with Democratic attempts to vote on a new Iraq policy this week: A majority say Congress should hold off on developing a new policy until General David Petraeus, the commander of U.S. forces in Iraq, reports on the progress of the surge in September. At the same time, 7 in 10 Americans say they favor a policy to remove most U.S. troops from Iraq by April 2008.

War Support

The July 6–8, 2007, poll finds 62% of Americans saying the United States made a mistake in sending troops to Iraq; 36% say it was not a mistake. This is the first time Gallup has shown opposition to the war exceeding the 60% level; the previous highs were 59% readings in March 2007 and September 2005.

Since 1950, Gallup has asked a "mistake" question about most wars in which the United States was involved, including the Korean War, the Vietnam War, the Persian Gulf War, and the war in Afghanistan. The only war that compares to the current conflict in terms of public opposition is the Vietnam War. By one measure, opposition to the current war in Iraq has matched and possibly even eclipsed that regarding the Vietnam War. In the period from 1965 to 1973, opposition to the Vietnam War reached a high of 61% in May 1971, compared with the current 62% opposition to the Iraq War. However, in that same 1971 poll the percentage of Americans supporting the Vietnam War—that is, saying it was not a mistake—was 28%, significantly lower than the current 36% support for the Iraq War.

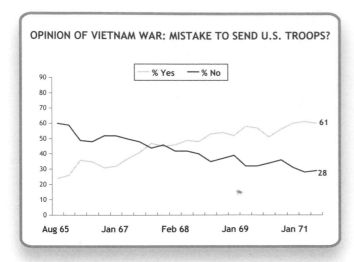

OPINION OF VIETNAM WAR: MISTAKE TO SEND U.S. TROOPS?

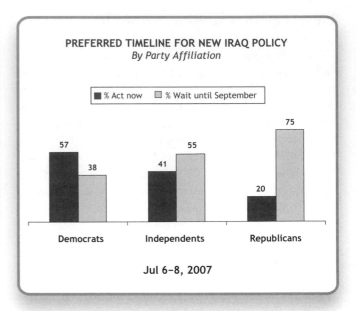

PREFERRED TIMELINE FOR NEW IRAQ POLICY
By Party Affiliation

Jul 6–8, 2007

Ratings for the current Iraq War are still better than several retrospective measures of the Vietnam War as ascertained by Gallup between 1990 and 2000, which showed between 69% and 74% of Americans saying the United States made a mistake in sending troops to Vietnam. The vast majority of Democrats, 84%, think the current war with Iraq is a mistake, as do 66% of independents. Only 28% of Republicans share this view.

The Surge

In early 2007 the Bush administration made a controversial decision to increase the number of U.S. troops in Iraq in order to help secure Baghdad and other parts of Iraq. According to the July 6–8, 2007, poll, only a relatively small minority of Americans believe the surge is making things better in Baghdad or in Iraq at large. Specifically, 17% of Americans say the surge is making the situation in Baghdad better, 30% say it is making it worse, and 49% say it is

not making any difference. That is a slightly more negative assessment than Gallup measured in April, when 26% said the surge was making the situation better, 29% said it was making things worse, and 41% said the increase in troops was not making much difference. The results are generally similar when Gallup asks about the effects of the surge on Iraq as a whole: Twenty-two percent of Americans say the surge is making the situation better throughout Iraq, 25% say it is making things worse, and 51% say the surge is not making much difference.

The success of the surge will be formally assessed in September, when General Petraeus reports to Congress about the progress of the war effort. Even with opposition to the war at a record high, the public seems to endorse a patient approach to developing a new Iraq policy. Fifty-five percent of Americans say Congress should not develop a new policy regarding Iraq until the September progress report, while 40% would prefer to see Congress act now to change Iraq War policy. Views on this matter are highly partisan, however, with a majority of Democrats wanting immediate action to develop a new policy and a majority of Republicans advocating a more patient approach. Most independents are also inclined to wait until September for a new Iraq policy.

The End Game

It is clear that public support for withdrawing troops from Iraq is growing. The July 6–8, 2007, poll finds 71% of Americans in favor of a proposal to remove almost all U.S. troops by April 2008, leaving a limited number of troops for counterterrorism efforts. Twenty-six percent of Americans oppose this scenario. Even though a large majority of Republicans support the war, 42% still favor

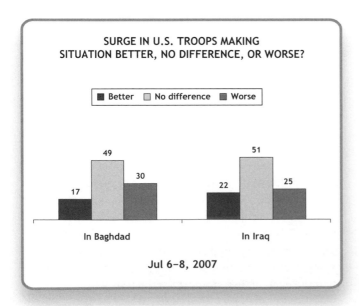

SURGE IN U.S. TROOPS MAKING
SITUATION BETTER, NO DIFFERENCE, OR WORSE?

Jul 6–8, 2007

this proposal for troop removal, while 54% are opposed. Seventy-nine percent of independents and 84% of Democrats would like to see most U.S. troops withdrawn from Iraq by next April. Gallup has consistently found majority support this year among Americans for a variety of proposals that would set timetables for removing U.S. troops from Iraq.

JULY 12

Clinton, Giuliani Still Top Parties' Support for Nominations in 2008

With only about six months remaining before the Iowa caucuses, the races for the Republican and Democratic presidential nominations remain in a steady state. Republican Rudolph Giuliani and Democrat Hillary Clinton continue to hold statistically significant leads over the rest of their respective fields of competitors. The most notable recent change this year has been on the Republican side, where Arizona senator John McCain's recent dip in the polls and former Tennessee senator Fred Thompson's recent gains have resulted in the two switching second and third places. Even though former vice president Al Gore would potentially draw significant support for the Democratic nomination, recent polls suggest his entry would not alter the basic structure of that race.

Democratic Nomination

The July 6–8, 2007, poll asked Democrats and Democratic-leaning independents whom they are most likely to support for the Democratic nomination for president in the next election. Gallup calculated the results both with and without former vice president Al Gore, who has not ruled out a bid but has said he has no plans to run. The ballot excluding Gore was computed by substituting Gore voters' second choice for the nomination. Hillary Clinton leads the pack of Democratic hopefuls on both ballot measures, pulling in 37% support with Gore in the race and 42% with him factored out. Illinois senator Barack Obama places second by a narrow margin with Gore in the race and by a more comfortable margin when Gore's support is reallocated. Gore draws 16%, essentially tying him for third with former North Carolina senator John Edwards at 13%. (Edwards's support is 16% without Gore.) No other candidate receives more than 4% support.

In recent polls, Democrats who would otherwise support Gore have distributed their preferences about equally between Clinton and Obama, with Edwards receiving a smaller slice of the potential Gore voting bloc. In fact, Clinton's advantage over Obama in the current poll is 16 per-

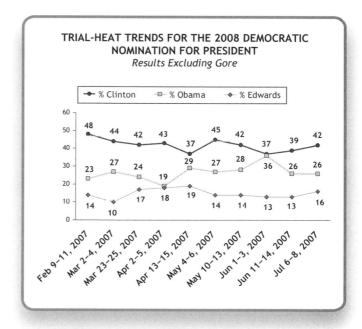

centage points, regardless of whether Gore is in the race or not. Earlier this year, Gore's absence appeared to help Clinton, as she typically received more support from Gore supporters than those of Obama or Edwards. The overall trend in the race has not changed significantly over the course of the year. Clinton has typically led Democrats' preference list for their party's nomination with no less than 37% support (when Gore is excluded), with Obama usually in second place with support in the mid-20s, Edwards in third in the mid-teens, and no other candidate getting more than 5% support in any of these surveys.

With Gore included, the same general pattern holds, although Clinton's support is typically in the mid-30s and Obama's in the low- to mid-20s, with Gore and Edwards vying for third place. Overall, 61% of Democrats name Clinton as their first or second choice for the nomination. (She is the only Democrat above 50% on this measure.) Obama is the first or second choice of 44% of Democrats, while Gore is named by 34% and Edwards by 24%. Clinton has been the first or second choice of a majority of Democrats in every Gallup Poll taken in 2007. Obama reached that mark in an early June poll but more typically has been in the 40% range.

In its last two polls, Gallup has asked Democrats how likely they are to vote in the primaries or caucuses in their state next year. An average of 59% across these polls have said they are "extremely likely" to do so. Among this group of likely Democratic primary voters, the results are very similar to those for all Democrats: Forty-two percent say they are most likely to support Clinton, 28% Obama, and 14% Edwards. With Gore included, the results among likely primary voters are 37% for Clinton, 24% for Obama, 15% for Gore, and 12% for Edwards.

Republican Nomination

Giuliani continues to be the top choice of Republicans for his party's 2008 presidential nomination, with Fred Thompson following next, John McCain in third, and Mitt Romney in fourth. The percentage of support for these candidates varies little depending on whether reluctant candidate Newt Gingrich—the former speaker of the House who is supported by only 6% of Republicans—is included in the race. None of the remaining Republican candidates scores higher than 3% in the poll.

While Giuliani has consistently topped Republicans' preferences for the Republican nomination since February, there have been some changes in the second-place candidate. From February through early June, McCain was a solid second behind Giuliani. In a mid-June poll, Thompson and McCain were essentially tied. Now, as McCain's support has dipped to a low of 16%, Thompson has gained a slight five-point advantage over McCain (and a four-point advantage in a ballot including Gingrich). Also, Giuliani's level of support has fallen from where it was in the spring—even though he continues to maintain a lead.

Giuliani is the first or second choice for the nomination of 52% of Republicans—well ahead of any other Republican on this measure—as he has been all year. Thirty-one percent of Republicans rate Fred Thompson as their first or second choice, 30% name McCain, and 18% name Romney. Republicans' support for Thompson as their first or second choice for the nomination has nearly doubled in recent months, from 16% in late March 2007, when he was first included in Gallup nomination polling, to the current 31%. At the same time, McCain's support has deteriorated, from a high of 47%

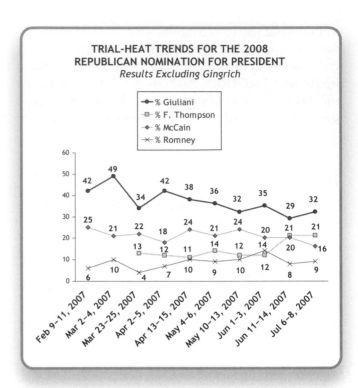

in February to the current 30%. Giuliani's has fallen from 57% to 52%. Turnout may be more of a factor in the Republican primaries than in the Democratic primaries. Among the 61% of Republicans in the last two polls who say they are extremely likely to vote in their state's primary or caucus next year, Giuliani (29%) and Fred Thompson (25%) essentially tie. McCain is third among this group at 18% and Romney fourth at 9%, with all other candidates at 3% or below.

JULY 13

Bloomberg at 12% as Independent for President

If New York City mayor Michael Bloomberg decides to run for president in 2008 as an independent candidate, the latest USA Today/Gallup Poll finds he would start off with a credible level of base support from the American people, drawing most of his votes from the political center. According to the July 6–8, 2007, survey, 12% of registered voters say they would vote for Bloomberg in a three-candidate race that included Hillary Clinton as the Democratic candidate and Rudolph Giuliani as the Republican.

The same poll includes Gallup's first national favorable rating of Bloomberg. In contrast to Giuliani and Clinton, who have near-universal recognition with Americans, more than a third of Americans (37%) don't know enough about Bloomberg to rate him. Among the remainder, he is viewed, on balance, more favorably than unfavorably, 36% vs. 27%. While this suggests that Bloomberg has some opportunity to expand his support just by becoming better known to the

As shown in this cartoon by Gary Markstein, Senator John McCain's campaign hit a low point in July 2007 when both his campaign manager and chief strategist quit, following reports of poor fund-raising. *(Newscom)*

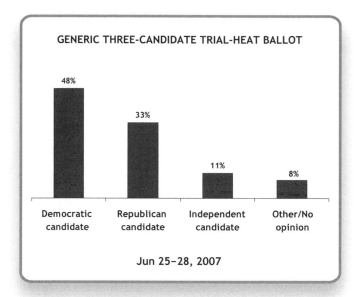

GENERIC THREE-CANDIDATE TRIAL-HEAT BALLOT

48% — Democratic candidate
33% — Republican candidate
11% — Independent candidate
8% — Other/No opinion

Jun 25–28, 2007

public, Gallup's June 25–28, 2007, poll finds that voters may just be more generally open to the idea of any independent candidate running in 2008. That poll included a "generic ballot" question that asked whether they would vote for the Democratic candidate, the Republican candidate, or an independent candidate not affiliated with either party if the 2008 presidential election were held today. Eleven percent of registered voters say they would vote for the independent candidate—very similar to Bloomberg's 12%.

Even at Bloomberg's current level of recognition, his 12% voter support immediately distinguishes Bloomberg from independent presidential contestants of the recent past. Not since Ross Perot drew 19% of the national vote in 1992 on the "United We Stand America" ticket has a third-party presidential candidate garnered double-digit support from America voters. None of the independent or minor party candidates of the last two elections—including Ralph Nader, Pat Buchanan, and the Libertarian Party nominees—have won more than 3% of the vote. Bloomberg's initial support level, though, is not as auspicious as Perot's was in 1992. Gallup's first poll measuring support for Perot's candidacy in late February 1992 found 24% of Americans supporting him. But that was after Perot had already appeared on CNN's *Larry King Live* program declaring his intention to launch a grassroots petition drive to get on the ballot in all 50 states. Whether Bloomberg could similarly excite Americans around his possible candidacy and bring new voters into the process to boost his numbers—Perot peaked at 39% and was in first place in June 1992 before temporarily dropping out of the race—remains to be seen.

Not Necessarily a Spoiler

All candidates for president tend to say they are running to win, but it's clear that some independents, such as Pat

Buchanan in 2004, see their candidacy mostly as a political platform. Theoretically, independent candidates can have some political influence over the issue positions taken by the opponents to whom they pose the greatest threat. Alternatively, by attracting a disproportionate number of Democrats to his Green Party candidacy in 2000, Nader possibly siphoned enough votes away from Al Gore to cost Gore the election.

It's not yet clear what kind of candidate Bloomberg would be—a real contender, or a spoiler who ultimately attempts to push one party or the other in a direction to his liking. In terms of the potential "spoiler" impact of a Bloomberg candidacy, it would initially appear to be minimal. He is supported by 13% of Republicans (including independents who lean Republican) and by 12% of Democrats (including independents who lean Democratic). Clinton's six-point lead over Giuliani in a race that includes Bloomberg is not statistically different from her four-point lead in Gallup's most recent two-way matchup (from mid-June) between Clinton and Giuliani.

Down the road, Bloomberg could, in theory, pose a greater threat to Clinton than to Giuliani, given that he tends to be viewed more favorably by Democrats and liberals than by Republicans and conservatives. Roughly four in 10 Democrats (including Democratic-leaning independents) and liberals say they have a favorable view of Bloomberg. By comparison, only about one in three Republicans (including Republican-leaning independents) and conservatives rate him favorably.

Could Bloomberg Win?

In late spring 2007, Bloomberg left the Republican Party and became unaffiliated with any political party. In a speech on June 19, Bloomberg condemned the current

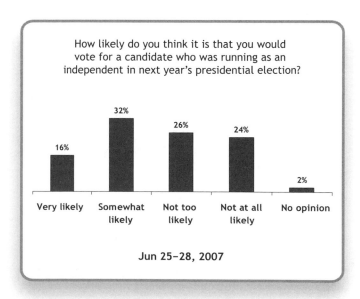

How likely do you think it is that you would vote for a candidate who was running as an independent in next year's presidential election?

16% — Very likely
32% — Somewhat likely
26% — Not too likely
24% — Not at all likely
2% — No opinion

Jun 25–28, 2007

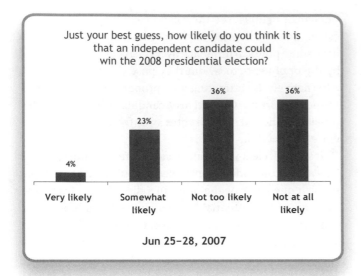

Just your best guess, how likely do you think it is that an independent candidate could win the 2008 presidential election?

Jun 25–28, 2007

partisan politics in Washington, saying, "The politics of partisanship and the resulting inaction and excuses have paralyzed decision-making, primarily at the federal level, and the big issues of the day are not being addressed, leaving our future in jeopardy."

Gallup's latest poll asked Americans if they think the Republican and Democratic parties do an adequate job of representing the American people, or if they do such a poor job that a third major party is needed. Only 33% of Americans say the parties do an adequate job, while a majority of Americans, 58%, say a third party is needed. Bloomberg supporters are much more likely than Clinton or Giuliani supporters to say a third major party is needed: Eighty-one percent of Bloomberg supporters share this view, compared with 56% of Giuliani supporters and 52% of Clinton supporters. Despite majority support for the concept of a third party—and even if Bloomberg can boost his support in the coming months—he still faces an almost insurmountable challenge in terms of actually beating the Republican and Democratic candidates next year. According to the recent Gallup Poll, only about one in six registered voters (16%) say it is "very likely" that they would vote for a candidate who was running as an independent in next year's presidential election. An additional 32% say it is somewhat likely, and 50% say it is not too likely or not at all likely. Fewer voters—only 4%—say it is "very likely" that an independent candidate could win the 2008 presidential election. About one in four voters say that victory by an independent is at least somewhat likely, and 72% say it is not too likely or not at all likely.

JULY 17

Gallup Poll Review: John McCain

For the third national Gallup Poll in a row, Arizona senator John McCain is in third place among Republicans as their

party's preferred nominee—behind former New York City mayor Rudolph Giuliani and former Tennessee senator Fred Thompson. McCain's favorable ratings continue to be significantly lower than they were earlier this year, caused mostly by a drop among independents and moderates. If McCain were to drop out of the race for president, Gallup analysis suggests that front-runner Giuliani would pick up almost half of McCain's votes—far more than any other candidate.

McCain's Position in Republican Field So Far in 2007

The trajectory of McCain's positioning among Republicans has been generally down over the last eight months, although not in a straight or linear fashion. In December 2006, McCain received 28% of the Republican vote, tying him with Giuliani for first place. McCain fell to 16% by April, then rebounded to 23% in a May Gallup Poll, but he has since declined and is sitting at 16% in the last two polls, both conducted in July. This puts McCain in third place behind Giuliani's 30% and Thompson's 20% share of the Republican vote.

Rudolph Giuliani remains the front-runner in our Gallup polling, although his percentage of the Republican vote is not as high now as it was earlier in the year. By way of comparison, McCain has fallen 11 percentage points from his highest percentage of the vote this year to his current position, while Giuliani has fallen 14 percentage points from his highest to his current rating, so it appears that Thompson's inclusion hurt Giuliani more than McCain. But both McCain and Giuliani showed their highest support levels before Gallup began including Thompson in the Republican ballot in late March. While McCain's "free fall" in the polls has been no worse than what Giuliani has experienced, it may appear

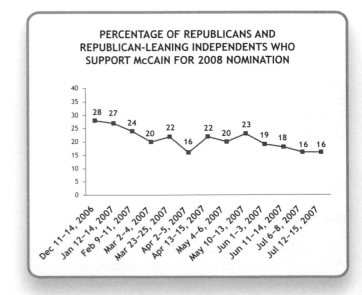

PERCENTAGE OF REPUBLICANS AND REPUBLICAN-LEANING INDEPENDENTS WHO SUPPORT McCAIN FOR 2008 NOMINATION

worse. This is because McCain has, over the course of the year, fallen from a position where he was tied for the lead to a position in which he is in third place, while Giuliani has maintained his first-place position.

McCain's Favorable Ratings

McCain's favorable ratings have fallen significantly compared with earlier in 2007. In two Gallup Polls conducted in February and March, McCain averaged a 57% favorable rating. Now, across the last three Gallup Polls conducted in June and July, his favorable rating has averaged 45%—a drop of 12 percentage points.

If McCain Withdrew?

If McCain were to withdraw from the race for the Republican presidential nomination—something he claims to have no intention of doing—front-runner Giuliani's position would be strengthened, with Fred Thompson and Mitt Romney continuing to run far behind. That conclusion is based on a special analysis that substitutes McCain voters' second choices for their party's presidential nomination in recent Gallup polling. This analysis involved an aggregation of the last four Gallup Polls that included Republican trial heats—conducted between June 1 and June 3, June 11 and June 14, July 6 and July 8, and July 12 and July 16, all in 2007. Across those four polls, McCain averaged 17% of the vote. The results show that Giuliani picks up almost half of McCain's votes, going from a 30% share of Republican choices with McCain on the ballot to 38% with McCain removed. Fred Thompson moves from 17% to 19%, Mitt Romney goes from 9% to 11%, and Newt Gingrich gains a point, from 7% to 8%. Kansas senator Sam Brownback, California representative Duncan Hunter, Texas representa-

tative Ron Paul, former Illinois governor Tommy Thompson, and former Arkansas governor Mike Huckabee all gain one point, but all remain at 3% or less of the vote.

The basic structure of the race is thus unchanged with McCain out, albeit it with a gain in the strength of the lead of front-runner Giuliani. With McCain in, the combined June and July numbers show Giuliani at 30%, McCain and Thompson at 17%, Romney at 9%, and Gingrich at 7%. Without McCain, Giuliani is at 38%, Thompson at 19%, Romney at 11%, and Gingrich at 8%. At the moment, McCain's supporters appear to be most inclined to move to Giuliani if McCain were to drop out, with the result that Giuliani's lead would increase.

JULY 19

Giuliani Would Be Acceptable Nominee to Nearly Three in Four Republicans

Even though Rudolph Giuliani's views on some issues are out of step with most members of his party, nearly three-quarters of Republicans say the former New York City mayor would be an acceptable presidential nominee to them, far more than say this about any other Republican candidate. Meanwhile, roughly eight in 10 Democrats say each of the three leading contenders for their party's nomination—New York senator Hillary Clinton, Illinois senator Barack Obama, and former North Carolina senator John Edwards—would be acceptable to them. There has been relatively little change in Democrats' opinions compared with this time a year ago, but many more Republicans now say that former Massachusetts governor Mitt Romney would be an acceptable presidential nominee.

The June 25–28 survey interviewed nationally representative samples of 536 Democrats (including Democratic-leaning independents) and 426 Republicans (including Republican-leaning independents). Each sample was asked whether the possible candidates for their party's presidential nomination would be acceptable or not acceptable to them as their party's nominee. This provides an upper-limit measure of support—that is, regardless of whether a candidate is a respondent's first, second, third (or lower) choice, would the respondent be comfortable with that candidate as their party's standard-bearer in 2008.

Seventy-four percent of Republicans say Giuliani would be an acceptable Republican presidential nominee in 2008, easily the highest percentage among the current field of candidates. The next tier of Republican contenders is acceptable to smaller majorities of Republicans, with former Tennessee senator Fred Thompson at 59%, Arizona senator John McCain at 57%, and former Massachusetts governor Mitt Romney at 53%. The remaining candidates

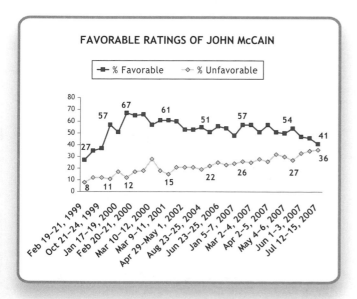

FAVORABLE RATINGS OF JOHN McCAIN

—■— % Favorable   —◇— % Unfavorable

all fall below the majority-support level, with former House speaker Newt Gingrich the highest at 49% and California representative Duncan Hunter last at 16%. A majority of rank-and-file Republicans view six candidates—including Paul, Brownback, Nebraska senator Chuck Hagel, Colorado representative Tom Tancredo, and former Virginia governor Jim Gilmore (who ended his candidacy last week) as well as Hunter—as unacceptable.

Gallup asked this same question one year ago; most of the Republican candidates included in that poll have seen a slight increase in the percentage of Republicans calling them acceptable nominees. McCain is a notable exception, scoring 57% both this year and last. Romney has shown the greatest gain, from 26% in 2006 to 53% in 2007, most of the growth being due to his increased recognition: Thirty-two percent did not have an opinion of Romney in 2006, compared with only 9% this year. Romney's unacceptable ratings dipped only slightly, from 42% to 37%. Another former governor, Arkansas's Mike Huckabee, also posted a double-digit gain on this measure, from 17% to 32%. Nonetheless, more Republicans say they would find him an unacceptable (49%) rather than an acceptable (32%) presidential nominee.

Giuliani's views on abortion, gay civil unions, and gun control run counter to the views of many, if not most, Republicans. The question is whether the party, which includes a large number of religious conservatives and has nominated only pro-life and pro-gun candidates since 1980, could bring itself to nominate the popular former New York City mayor. The poll finds the vast majority of religious Republicans would find Giuliani acceptable as the party's presidential candidate in 2008. Among Republicans who describe themselves as "born again or evangelical," 69% say they would find Giuliani an acceptable nominee, the highest percentage for any candidate among this group. (McCain and Fred Thompson are next at 58% and 57%, respectively.) Among Republicans who attend religious services on a weekly basis, 64% say they would find Giuliani acceptable, with Fred Thompson next at 60%. Giuliani's numbers are better among less religious Republicans; but he clearly does no worse on this measure of potential support than any other candidate among religious Republicans.

On the Democratic side, Clinton has maintained a solid lead over her competitors for the Democratic nomination in Gallup Polls throughout the year. However, nearly as many Democrats say they would find Obama (78%) or Edwards (77%) acceptable choices for the 2008 Democratic presidential nominee as say this about Clinton (82%). Former vice president Al Gore, who may yet enter the race, would be acceptable to 72% of Democrats. The long odds faced by the rest of the field of announced candidates are underscored by the fact that all five are viewed as unacceptable nominees by a majority of Democrats. Most Democratic candidates

have shown little or no gain in their acceptability ratings compared with last year. The exceptions are Clinton, whose ratings have increased 11 percentage points, and Edwards, with an 8-percentage point increase. Gallup did not include Obama, who began pursuing a presidential bid in the fall, in last year's poll. Views of Gore as the nominee have not changed much even though he has been the subject of much publicity in the past year.

JULY 24
Most Top Seed Pairings in 2008 Presidential Election Are Too Close to Call

A recent Gallup Poll assessed the 2008 general election with various pairings of the top two candidates for each party. If, as the question reads, "the election were being held today," a race that includes the top-ranked Republican, Rudolph Giuliani, would be highly competitive, regardless of whether his opponent was the top-ranked Democrat, Hillary Clinton, or the second-place Democrat, Barack Obama. Fred Thompson, newly emergent as Republicans' second choice for the nomination, also matches up closely with Clinton, but trails by a significant margin when matched against Obama. The survey was conducted between July 12 and July 15, 2007. In both trial heats with Giuliani named as the Republican nominee, Giuliani receives 49% of the votes of registered voters nationwide. Running against Giuliani, Clinton receives 46% of the vote, while Obama receives 45%. While Giuliani enjoys a slight lead in both cases, it is within the margin of sampling error for the survey and thus not statistically significant.

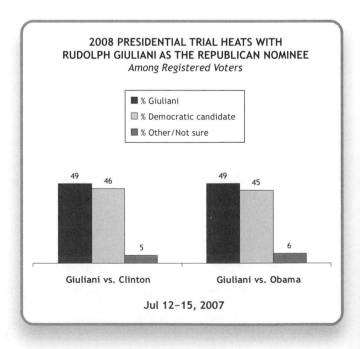

2008 PRESIDENTIAL TRIAL HEATS WITH RUDOLPH GIULIANI AS THE REPUBLICAN NOMINEE
Among Registered Voters

- % Giuliani
- % Democratic candidate
- % Other/Not sure

Giuliani vs. Clinton: 49, 46, 5
Giuliani vs. Obama: 49, 45, 6

Jul 12–15, 2007

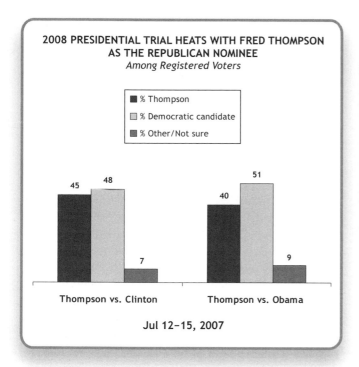

2008 PRESIDENTIAL TRIAL HEATS WITH FRED THOMPSON AS THE REPUBLICAN NOMINEE
Among Registered Voters

■ % Thompson
□ % Democratic candidate
■ % Other/Not sure

Thompson vs. Clinton: 45, 48, 7
Thompson vs. Obama: 40, 51, 9

Jul 12–15, 2007

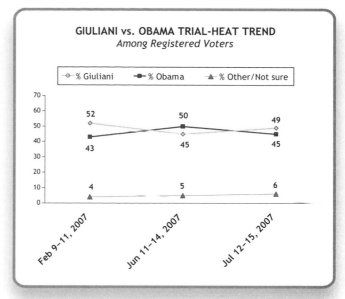

GIULIANI vs. OBAMA TRIAL-HEAT TREND
Among Registered Voters

–◇– % Giuliani   –■– % Obama   –▲– % Other/Not sure

Feb 9–11, 2007: Giuliani 52, Obama 43, Other 4
Jun 11–14, 2007: Giuliani 45, Obama 50, Other 5
Jul 12–15, 2007: Giuliani 49, Obama 45, Other 6

With Fred Thompson headlining the Republican ticket, it appears Clinton would have a slight but not significant lead, 48% vs. 45%, while Obama would lead by a comfortable 51% vs. 40% margin.

The Trends

It is only in the past month that Republicans' support for Thompson has increased to the point where he ties or leads John McCain for second place in the Republican field. Thus, this is the first time Gallup has tested Thompson's strength as the Republican standard-bearer in trial heats against any of the Democrats. However, it is Gallup's fifth measure this

year of a hypothetical Giuliani-Clinton race. In all but one of these Giuliani-Clinton matchups, the race has been too close to call. Giuliani has led in most of them, however, including by a significant seven points in early June. Clinton bested Giuliani only once, in mid-June, and her lead was within the poll's margin of error. Today's three-point lead for Giuliani is also within the margin of error.

This is Gallup's third measure in 2007 of a potential Giuliani-Obama race for president. Giuliani led by a significant nine points in February; the race then reversed to a five-point lead for Obama (within the margin of error) in mid-June, and it is now too close to call, with Giuliani leading Obama by four points.

Weak Republican Link

Of the four hypothetical election ballots tested in the new survey, the Obama-Thompson race stands out because it is the only race in which one of the candidates (Obama) has a healthy lead. Simply put, a Thompson vs. Obama matchup, where Thompson trails by 11 points, presents a much harder race for the Republicans than Giuliani vs. Obama, where Giuliani leads by four points. A comparison of the demographics of voter support in these two matchups reveals that Thompson does less well than Giuliani across the board, but in particular he fails to attract the same level of support from women as Giuliani. Whereas women are about evenly divided in a Giuliani-Obama race (48% vs. 47%), they show a strong preference for Obama in a Thompson-Obama race (54% vs. 36%). Men are also more likely to vote for Obama with Thompson rather than Giuliani as the Republican candidate, though their preference swing is not quite as large.

Perhaps an additional factor explaining why Thompson is relatively weak when paired against Obama is that neither is

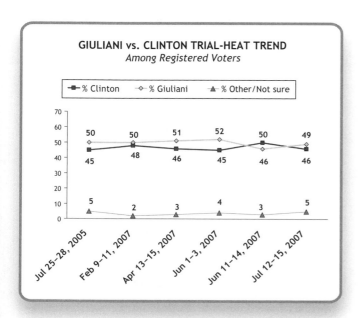

GIULIANI vs. CLINTON TRIAL-HEAT TREND
Among Registered Voters

–■– % Clinton   –◇– % Giuliani   –▲– % Other/Not sure

Jul 25–28, 2005: Giuliani 50, Clinton 45, Other 5
Feb 9–11, 2007: Giuliani 50, Clinton 48, Other 2
Apr 13–15, 2007: Giuliani 51, Clinton 46, Other 3
Jun 1–3, 2007: Giuliani 52, Clinton 45, Other 4
Jun 11–14, 2007: Giuliani 50, Clinton 50, Other 3
Jul 12–15, 2007: Giuliani 49, Clinton 46, Other 5

a fully defined character on the national stage. According to the latest survey, 51% of registered voters don't know enough about Thompson to have an opinion of him, while 21% still haven't formed an opinion of Obama. (This compares with 14% who don't know enough about Giuliani and 4% saying the same of Clinton.) As a result, voter preferences in a matchup between Thompson and Obama may be more influenced than other pairings by voters' fundamental party allegiances, which currently lean more Democratic than Republican by a 50% to 41% margin.

JULY 26

Impact of Religion on Clinton's and Giuliani's Election Chances

A Gallup analysis of the relationship between the religiosity of voters and support for nomination front-runners Rudolph Giuliani and Hillary Clinton finds that religion could play an important but varied role in the presidential primaries and elections. Giuliani's chances of receiving the Republican nomination may be hampered by his weaker performance among highly religious Republicans, who disproportionately say they don't have a candidate to support or else swing toward candidates other than Giuliani. Clinton's chances of getting the Democratic nomination, however, are much less affected by religion; there is little relationship between how religious individual Democrats are and whom they support for their party's nomination.

In a hypothetical general election matchup between Giuliani and Clinton, Giuliani does much better among those who attend church at least monthly than among those who do not—a common pattern for Republican candidates. Among white voters who seldom or never attend church, Clinton defeats Giuliani, primarily owing to the votes of independent voters who don't have strong attachments to either candidate. Among black voters, Clinton wins overwhelmingly against Giuliani regardless of voters' church attendance.

Religion and the 2008 Republican Primaries

Republicans' choices for their party's nominee in the 2008 presidential election are related to how religious they are, as measured by the frequency of church attendance. Only 24% of weekly church attenders say they support Giuliani to win the party's nomination next year. This gives Giuliani a small, statistically insignificant lead over former Tennessee senator Fred Thompson, who has the support of 20% of weekly Republican churchgoers. Sixteen percent of weekly churchgoers support Arizona senator John McCain, 8% pick former Massachusetts governor Mitt Romney, and 7% support former speaker of the House Newt Gingrich. No other Republican candidate garners more than 3% support among weekly Republican churchgoers. (Previous Gallup analysis has shown that—notwithstanding their first-choice preferences—a majority of Republican churchgoers say that Giuliani would be an acceptable nominee.)

Giuliani is much more likely to be the first choice for the Republican nomination among those who attend church less often, with 32% support among those who attend services almost weekly or monthly and 33% among those who seldom or never go to church. Among both groups, Giuliani owns double-digit leads. Who gains in lieu of Giuliani among weekly churchgoers? No one particular candidate. There is little difference by churchgoing frequency in terms of support for the other leading candidates, such as McCain, Thompson, and Romney. A slightly higher percentage of weekly Republican churchgoers say they have no preference at this point, and this group is slightly more likely to support various minor candidates.

Religion and the 2008 Democratic Primaries

Church attendance does not appear to play nearly as significant a role in Democrats' preferences for their party's nominee for president as is the case for Republicans. Clinton leads among Democrats who attend church every week, almost weekly, and monthly—by margins of 15, 8, and 12 points, respectively. Former vice president Al Gore does slightly better among those who seldom or never attend church, and Illinois senator Barack Obama slightly less well—resulting in Gore and Obama being rated evenly among infrequent attenders, while Obama has a substantial lead over Gore among respondents who attend at least monthly.

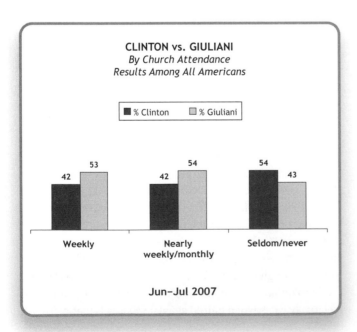

CLINTON vs. GIULIANI
By Church Attendance
Results Among All Americans

■ % Clinton   □ % Giuliani

	Weekly	Nearly weekly/monthly	Seldom/never
% Clinton	42	42	54
% Giuliani	53	54	43

Jun–Jul 2007

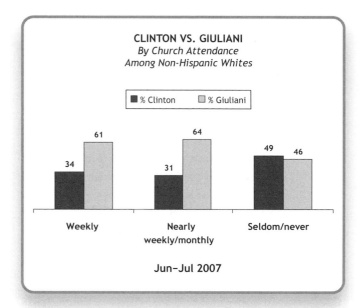

CLINTON VS. GIULIANI
By Church Attendance
Among Non-Hispanic Whites

■ % Clinton   ☐ % Giuliani

Weekly: 34, 61
Nearly weekly/monthly: 31, 64
Seldom/never: 49, 46

Jun–Jul 2007

Clinton vs. Giuliani in the 2008 General Election

In a hypothetical general election matchup between Clinton and Giuliani in which voters are asked which of these two they would prefer to vote for in November 2008, an aggregate of more than 3,000 Gallup Poll interviews collected during June and July 2007 shows the two candidates tied, 48% to 48%. Since highly religious Americans are today significantly more likely to be Republicans than Democrats, it is no surprise to find that Americans who attend church at least monthly are much more likely to vote for Giuliani than for Clinton. Clinton fares much better among those who seldom or never attend religious services.

It is well established that blacks in America are both highly religious and highly likely to be Democrats, thus going against the overall trend in the data. Separate analysis shows that within the subgroup of blacks in the aggregate sample, support for Clinton over Giuliani is overwhelming regardless of the frequency of church attendance. Overall, 85% of blacks prefer Clinton, compared with just 10% for Giuliani. This means that the main source of variation in the relationship between religion and general election candidate choice is among whites. Overall, 54% of whites say they would vote for Giuliani if the election were being held today, while 41% would vote for Clinton. This is testimony in and of itself to the dependence Democrats have on ethnic, nonwhite voters to win elections.

But white voters are by no means monolithic in their support for Giuliani. White frequent churchgoers are particularly likely to support Giuliani over Clinton: Six in 10 whites who attend church at least monthly pick Giuliani, while only about one-third pick Clinton. But among that group of whites who seldom or never attend church, it's a

different story. Clinton has a slight three-point advantage over Giuliani among whites who seldom or never go to church, 49% to 46%.

This relationship between religion and choice of candidate is found for the most part among whites who classify themselves as independents—who are by definition less likely to be firmly attached to the candidate of one party or the other. Among voters who identify as Republicans or Democrats, however, there is substantial party loyalty: A strong majority of both white Republicans and white Democrats, regardless of how frequently they attend church services, say they would vote for their party's candidate. With respect to independents, Clinton does much better among those who seldom or never go to church than she does among those who attend services at least monthly.

These results suggest that to the extent that religion is a factor in a possible Clinton-Giuliani matchup on Election Day 2008, it would play itself out primarily among independents. Clinton's chances in a close race (and the aggregate being used in this article shows that she and Giuliani at this point would run a very close race) might at least partly depend on her ability to make inroads into the Giuliani-leaning propensities of religious white independents.

JULY 31

Public Confidence in Presidential Hopefuls on Key 2008 Election Issues

A new Gallup survey finds each of the five best-known 2008 presidential candidates scoring similarly in ratings of public confidence in their ability to recommend the right course of action with respect to the war in Iraq. This suggests that despite public dissatisfaction with the war, it is not necessarily a winning issue for Democratic candidates. Meanwhile, Republicans Rudolph Giuliani and John McCain have a decided edge over the other candidates on terrorism, while Democrats Hillary Clinton and Barack Obama fare best on healthcare. On the economy, the public is most likely to express confidence in Giuliani, Clinton, and Obama. Ratings of the candidates on all four issues are highly influenced by partisanship, with Clinton's ratings the most polarized along party lines. In general, less well-known candidates Fred Thompson and Mitt Romney do not fare as well as the other candidates on all the issues, primarily because about one in five respondents do not have an opinion on how they would handle each of these issues. The July 23–26, 2007, Gallup Poll asked a representative sample of Americans if they have "a great deal, a fair amount, only a little, or almost no confidence" in the seven leading presidential hopefuls "to recommend the

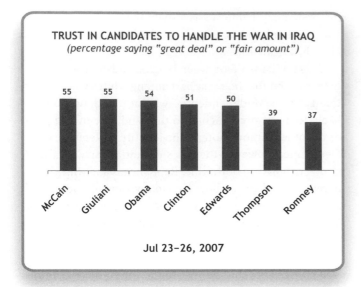

TRUST IN CANDIDATES TO HANDLE THE WAR IN IRAQ
(percentage saying "great deal" or "fair amount")

McCain	Giuliani	Obama	Clinton	Edwards	Thompson	Romney
55	55	54	51	50	39	37

Jul 23–26, 2007

right thing" for each of four issues likely to be key in the 2008 campaign: the war in Iraq, terrorism, healthcare, and the economy.

Unless there is a major shift in Bush administration policy on the war in Iraq between now and the summer of 2008, that issue is likely to dominate the 2008 presidential campaign. But the poll finds none of the major candidates standing out from the others on this issue. Aside from Romney and Thompson, the five other candidates score between 50% and 55% on this measure of public confidence in their ability to choose the proper course of action in Iraq. The failure of the Democratic candidates to score higher confidence levels on Iraq is significant given the fact that a substantial majority of Americans say that the war—initiated and supported by a Republican administration—is a mistake, and that a majority have opposed the Bush administration "surge" that has been supported by both Giuliani and, especially, McCain.

The public usually views the Republican Party as better on terrorism than the Democratic Party, so it is no surprise to see Giuliani and McCain well ahead of the other candidates in public confidence on this issue. Sixty-nine percent of Americans have at least a fair amount of confidence in Giuliani, widely hailed for his response to the 9/11 terrorist attacks while serving as mayor of New York City. Sixty-six percent of Americans express confidence in McCain. Both Clinton and Obama pass the majority threshold on this measure, at 55% and 53%, respectively. Edwards is slightly below that mark, with a 48% confidence score—and nearly as many (47%) say they have little or no confidence in the former North Carolina senator on terrorism.

Even among those who are familiar with Thompson and Romney, these two candidates do not do as well as their Republican colleagues on this issue. Forty-two percent of Americans have at least a fair amount of confidence in Thompson on terrorism, while 36% have little to no confidence in him. Meanwhile, more Americans (44%) say they have little or no confidence in Romney on terrorism than express confidence in him (38%). McCain's relatively positive ratings on terrorism (and Iraq) suggest that despite news reports that his campaign is struggling, he still maintains a strong position in the minds of many Americans on core national security issues.

While the Republicans usually have an edge on terrorism from the public's perspective, the Democrats usually do better on a range of domestic issues such as healthcare. The recent poll is no exception, finding nearly two in three Americans saying they have a great deal or fair amount of confidence in Clinton to recommend the right thing for the nation's healthcare system, slightly higher than the 61% who say this about Obama. A majority of Americans (54%) also express confidence in Edwards.

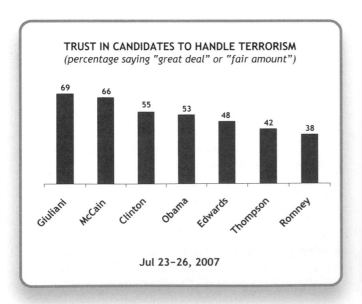

TRUST IN CANDIDATES TO HANDLE TERRORISM
(percentage saying "great deal" or "fair amount")

Giuliani	McCain	Clinton	Obama	Edwards	Thompson	Romney
69	66	55	53	48	42	38

Jul 23–26, 2007

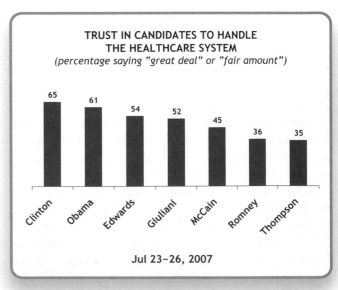

TRUST IN CANDIDATES TO HANDLE THE HEALTHCARE SYSTEM
(percentage saying "great deal" or "fair amount")

Clinton	Obama	Edwards	Giuliani	McCain	Romney	Thompson
65	61	54	52	45	36	35

Jul 23–26, 2007

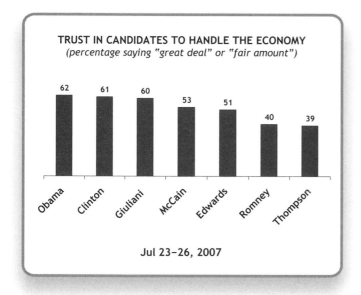

TRUST IN CANDIDATES TO HANDLE THE ECONOMY
(percentage saying "great deal" or "fair amount")

Obama 62, Clinton 61, Giuliani 60, McCain 53, Edwards 51, Romney 40, Thompson 39

Jul 23–26, 2007

Giuliani is the only Republican to get a confidence rating above 50% on healthcare.

A majority of Americans express confidence in each of the five most well-known candidates to recommend the right thing for the economy, but more do so for Obama (62%), Clinton (61%), and Giuliani (60%) than for McCain (53%) and Edwards (51%). Lesser-known candidates fare less well: Forty percent are confident in Romney on the economy, 43% are not, and 18% have no opinion, while 39% are confident in Thompson, 39% are not, and 21% have no opinion.

PARTY DIFFERENCES

Americans' different definitions of the "right thing" to do on Iraq, terrorism, healthcare, and the economy presumably reflect their differing political worldviews. As a result, confidence ratings of the candidates on the issues show wide variation by partisanship.

IRAQ

Republicans express the most confidence in Giuliani to handle Iraq, while Democrats rate Clinton and Obama slightly ahead of Edwards. Independents do not express a high degree of confidence in any of the candidates; Clinton earns their highest rating (55%), but she does not do significantly better than McCain, Obama, or Giuliani among this group.

TERRORISM

Not only do the vast majority of Republicans express confidence in Giuliani and McCain on terrorism, but so do a majority of Democrats. These are the only instances in which a majority of the opposing party expresses confidence in candidates on an issue. Democrats still rate their three leading candidates—Clinton, Obama, and Edwards—ahead of McCain and Giuliani for handling terrorism. This finding suggests that national security issues—so important in the successful presidential campaign of George W. Bush in 2004—could still be a positive factor for the Republican nominee next year.

HEALTHCARE

The Clinton administration's unsuccessful attempt to pass comprehensive healthcare reform in 1993–94 has not shaken Democrats' (or independents') confidence in Hillary Clinton to recommend the right thing with regard to healthcare. Her 91% rating among Democrats on healthcare is the highest for any candidate on any issue within their own party. At the same time, only 33% of Republicans are confident in Clinton on this issue. Republicans put more trust in Giuliani than in any other candidate on healthcare.

ECONOMY

Giuliani also fares the best among Republicans on the economy, by a significant margin over McCain (79% to 66%). With respect to the Democratic candidates, Republicans are more inclined to express confidence in Obama (42%) than in Edwards (29%) or Clinton (27%). Democrats, on the other hand, trust Clinton the most on the economy, at 88%. Independents put more faith in Clinton's and Obama's ability to handle the economy than in any of the other candidates.

PARTY POLARIZATION

Overall, a comparison of the confidence ratings given each candidate by members of both the candidates' own party and the opposing party underscores the highly polarized positioning of Clinton in the minds of many Americans. The average gap in confidence ratings of Clinton between Republicans and Democrats across all four issues is 61 percentage points. That is 18 points more than the next candidate, Edwards, with an average party difference of 43 points. Ratings of confidence in Obama by Democrats and Republicans also show a gap of more than 40 points on average. There are smaller gaps in the ratings of the Republican candidates, suggesting that Republicans rate Democratic candidates worse than Democrats rate Republican candidates. Romney's ratings show the least polarization, in part because of his lower public profile. Among the better-known candidates, confidence ratings of McCain show the smallest differences along party lines.

AUGUST 2007

General David Petraeus, commander of U.S. forces in Iraq, is expected to release his interim report on the progress of the recent surge in U.S. troops in Baghdad and other parts of Iraq in September 2007. President George W. Bush and leading members of both parties in Congress say Petraeus's report will be crucial in determining the future course of U.S. actions in Iraq. The latest USA Today/Gallup Poll, conducted between August 3 and August 5, 2007, finds that Americans are more than twice as likely to rate Petraeus positively than negatively: Forty-seven percent say they have a favorable opinion of Petraeus, while 21% have an unfavorable opinion. One in three Americans (32%) are not familiar enough with Petraeus to rate him.

Petraeus's favorable ratings differ sharply along partisan lines, with Republicans much more likely than Democrats to rate him favorably. Two-thirds of Republicans (67%) have a favorable opinion of Petraeus, while 7% have an unfavorable opinion and 26% do not know enough about him to rate him. Democrats are evenly divided in their view of Petraeus: Thirty-three percent rate him favorably, while 31% rate him unfavorably. Thirty-six percent of Democrats do not know enough about Petraeus to rate him. Independents' ratings closely mirror those of the general population. Military veterans are also very positive in their views of General Petraeus, with 68% of those who have served in the military having a favorable opinion of the general, while 15% have an unfavorable view and 17% have no opinion. Among those who are not veterans, 42% rate Petraeus favorably, 23% rate him unfavorably, and 35% have no opinion.

This is the first time that Gallup asked Americans about their overall opinion of Petraeus, but earlier this year, in April, Gallup asked Americans about the reliability of various leaders as "a source of accurate information about current conditions in Iraq." Eighty percent of Americans said Petraeus was a "very" (43%) or "somewhat" (37%) reliable source of information about conditions in Iraq, while just

13% said he was "not too" or "not at all" reliable. Americans viewed Petraeus as a much more reliable source than any of the other 16 leaders listed in the poll, including President Bush, members of the Bush administration, and leading Republican and Democratic presidential candidates. These results help explain why a majority of Americans, 56%, say Congress should not develop a new policy on Iraq until September, when Petraeus reports on the progress of the U.S. troop surge. Thirty-nine percent of Americans say Congress should act now to develop a new policy on Iraq.

With regard to other issues, healthcare costs are the most important personal financial concern facing Americans today, followed by low wages or lack of money, the cost of owning or renting a home, and high oil and gasoline prices. This list of financial concerns has not changed significantly between November 2006 and July 2007. With expenditures for healthcare rising at two times the rate of inflation and premiums for employer-sponsored health insurance also climbing, it is not surprising that healthcare costs consistently rank at the top of the list when Gallup asks Americans what is the most important financial problem facing their families today. Gallup periodically poses this question about the most important financial problem facing families in its national surveys, most recently in July 2007. Nineteen percent of Americans interviewed in the July 12–15 Gallup Poll say healthcare costs are their top financial concern, with 15% citing lack of money or low wages. These percentages have remained virtually unchanged since last fall. Other financial concerns Americans mention include the cost of owning or renting a home, energy—that is, oil and gasoline prices—and not enough money to pay their debts. Not surprisingly, those with lower annual incomes are more likely to say healthcare costs are the most important financial issue they face. Twenty-two percent of those earning under $30,000 a year say the cost of healthcare is their most important financial problem, compared with only 12% among those making

CHRONOLOGY

AUGUST 2007

August 1   The largest Sunni faction in the Iraqi parliament quits the Iraqi cabinet, citing conflicts with the Shia-dominated government of Prime Minister Nouri al-Maliki.

August 1   An interstate bridge in Minneapolis collapses into the Mississippi River, killing 13. National attention focuses on America's aging transportation infrastructure.

August 5   President Bush signs an antiterrorism law expanding the government's authority to eavesdrop on international telephone calls and read e-mails of American citizens without warrants. Senators Clinton and Obama vote against the bill; Senator McCain is not present for the vote.

August 5   Republican presidential candidates debate in Des Moines, Iowa.

August 7   Democratic presidential candidates meet in Chicago in a debate sponsored by the AFL-CIO.

August 9   Democratic presidential candidates appear at a forum sponsored by the Human Rights Campaign, the nation's largest gay civil rights organization. Republican presidential candidates decline to participate.

August 10   Turmoil in the home mortgage market causes stocks to suffer their biggest one-day decline since February, reflecting growing concerns about tightening credit worldwide.

August 11   Mitt Romney wins the Iowa straw poll. He receives 4,516 votes to John McCain's 101 votes.

August 12   Former Wisconsin governor Tommy Thompson drops out of the race for the Republican presidential nomination.

August 13   Karl Rove, deputy chief of staff to President Bush, announces he will resign at the end of August.

August 14   Truck bombs kill at least 200 people in a Kurdish-speaking area of Iraq near the Syrian border. Apparently the target was Yazidis, a religious minority in Iraq.

August 19   Democratic presidential candidates debate in Des Moines, Iowa.

August 27   Attorney General Alberto Gonzales resigns. Gonzales had been under heavy criticism for his role in the firings of seven U.S. attorneys, allegedly for political reasons.

$75,000 a year or more. Among those in the higher-income group, college expenses are tied with healthcare costs as the top problem, followed by retirement savings. Also not surprisingly, Americans who are 50 and older are significantly more likely than those under 50 to mention health costs as their top financial concern.

Despite the rapid upturn in gasoline prices this year, the percentage of Americans saying energy costs are their top financial problem has stayed remarkably flat this year, rising to 11% in June before settling back to 8% in July. Since November of 2006, most of the other trends in responses to this question have also been quite stable. Healthcare costs have been at the top of the list in every survey in which this question was asked since December 2006, except once. During August, Americans' perceptions of the economy changed course and turned downward. The latest results are from an August 13–16, 2007, survey, conducted before the August 17 stock market surge of 233 points. Gallup saw a slight improvement in Americans' economic outlook in mid-July compared with June; over that time period, the percentage rating current economic conditions as excellent or good rose from 34% to 40%, and the percentage perceiving economic conditions to be getting better increased from 23% to 29%. These gains were more than erased in the mid-August poll, however. The new poll finds current economic ratings down to 33% excellent or good and the percentage saying the economy is improving sinking to 20%. Both measures are now similar to where they were in mid-June 2007.

Regarding a longer-term trend in Gallup's economic measures, public confidence in the economy has been fluctuating in a fairly narrow range over most of George W. Bush's presidency. Positive sentiments about current economic conditions have rarely exceeded 40%, and optimism that the economy is improving has generally been under 50%. Periods of slightly improving perceptions have been consistently followed by a downturn, similar to that seen in the current poll. There is a nine-point decline since July—from 29% to 20%—in the percentage saying the economy is getting better. This is a relatively steep change for this measure, but it is not unprecedented: The measure fell by 10 points between February and March of this year and rose by nine points between last August and September. The 72% now saying the economy is getting worse represents a record level of pessimism on this measure—the highest Gallup has seen since instituting this question in 1991. The previous high was 71% (not statistically different from 72%), recorded in January 1992. Seventy percent of Americans said the economy was getting worse in June 2007.

AUGUST 3

The Best and Worst Aspects of a Possible Giuliani Presidency

Although a substantial percentage of Americans don't know enough about Rudolph Giuliani to be able to predict what would be the best and worst aspects of his potential presidency, the views expressed by those who do have an opinion indicate that prospective voters have a firmly etched image about the former New York City mayor in their minds. Americans with an opinion about Giuliani clearly perceive that the strengths of his presidency would be similar to the type of leadership they think he showed after the terrorist attacks of September 11, 2001: his ability to handle terrorism, his strong leadership, his decisiveness, and his ability to perform in a crisis. On the other hand, the perceived liabilities of a Giuliani presidency appear to fall into three categories: his political inexperience at the national level; his ideological positions on issues—including complaints that he would be both too conservative and too liberal; and questions about his personal traits, including his morality and personal style. Members of Giuliani's own Republican party in particular express concerns about his perceived liberal views and personal morality.

BEST THING ABOUT A GIULIANI PRESIDENCY

A July 23–26, 2007, survey asked a nationally representative sample to name "the best or most positive thing about a Rudolph Giuliani presidency." Almost half of those interviewed were unable to give a response to this question. Recent Gallup Poll research shows that Giuliani's name identification is high: Eighty-four percent of Americans have a basic favorable or unfavorable opinion of him. This result suggests that a substantial percentage of Americans who know enough about Giuliani to have an overall opinion about him still have not reached the point where they are able to express an opinion about the implications of a Giuliani presidency.

The predictions about the positive elements of a possible Giuliani presidency are focused more than anything else on dimensions related to his highly visible role as mayor of New York City during and after the September 11 terrorist attacks. The top three specific categories of responses, mentioned by more than one-quarter of Americans, are that Giuliani would be good in terms of handling terrorism, that he would be a strong leader, and that he would be decisive and able to get things done. A small percentage of respondents say that the best thing about a Giuliani presidency would be that he is "good on crime," a presumed legacy of his days as a prosecutor and New York City mayor. There are more general references to the fact that he is "likable," that he would be good on the economy, and that he is middle of the road, a good communicator, and a Republican. In general, however, the predominant views regarding the positive aspects of a possible Giuliani presidency at this point are a fairly specific direct legacy of the reputation he built in the weeks following 9/11.

WORST THING ABOUT A GIULIANI PRESIDENCY

Gallup also asked respondents to indicate what would be the worst or most negative thing about a Rudolph Giuliani presidency. Of interest is the fact that more Americans were able to answer this negatively oriented question than were able to answer the question about the positives of a Giuliani presidency. Since Gallup Poll data show that Giuliani's overall image is positive (52% of Americans have a favorable opinion of Giuliani, compared with 32% who have an unfavorable opinion), it would not appear that this response arises from an overall negative image of him.

The most frequently occurring specific category of responses to this "worst thing" question is an indication that Giuliani is inexperienced—and that he lacks foreign policy experience in particular. A second broad category of responses deals with issues relating to Giuliani's perceived liberalness: that he is pro-choice on abortion, that he is too liberal or not conservative enough, and that he has supported gay rights. A smaller number of respondents, on the other hand, complain that Giuliani is too conservative, would continue Bush administration policies, would continue the war in Iraq, and is pro–gun control. A third category of responses deals with Giuliani's personal characteristics. The most frequent response in this category is a reference to his moral failings as exemplified by the circumstances surrounding his three marriages. Additionally, some respondents mention their perceptions that Giuliani is dishonest, authoritarian, abrasive, and divisive. In general, the public's concerns about a possible Giuliani presidency seem to coalesce around three themes: his inexperience, his ideological positioning, and his personal characteristics.

Partisan Differences

Not surprisingly, Republicans are more likely to answer the question about the positive aspects of a possible Giuliani presidency than are independents or Democrats. Still, 36% of Republicans have no response when asked to name what would be the most positive thing about a Giuliani presidency, suggesting that he is still not as well positioned among members of his own party as might be optimal for a presidential candidate. By comparison, the analysis of results from Gallup's June survey showed that only 19% of Democrats could not mention anything positive about a Hillary Clinton presidency.

Although there are differences in the exact percentages of responses in each category, all three partisan groups are most likely to mention Giuliani's strength in dealing with terrorism as the best or most positive thing about his prospective presidency. Democrats are slightly more likely than independents and Republicans to answer the "worst thing" question, but not by a large margin. Forty-three percent of Republicans don't have anything to say about the negatives of a Giuliani presidency, compared with 38% of both independents and Democrats. The patterns of response on this negative side of the ledger, however, are more differentiated by party than was the case with regard to the responses to the "best thing" question.

Republicans' top four categories of responses to the worst aspects of a Giuliani presidency question include the following: 1) He is too inexperienced; 2) he is pro-choice on abortion; 3) he is too liberal/not conservative enough; and 4) he has questionable morals and a problematic marital history. These responses give some credence to the oft-mentioned observation that some Republicans will be resistant to nominating Giuliani because of his more liberal values and positions and his troubled marital past. Democrats' top complaints about Giuliani include the following: 1) He is too inexperienced; 2) he would be another Republican in the White House; 3) he has questionable morals and a problematic marital history; 4) he would continue Bush administration policies; and 5) he would continue the war in Iraq. For obvious reasons, Democrats are not concerned about Giuliani's liberal positions, but instead focus on his conservative positions as a Republican who would continue Bush administration policies, particularly those relating to the war in Iraq. In short, the prospect of a Rudolph Giuliani presidency cuts both ways. He would be too liberal for some Republicans, while too conservative for many Democrats.

AUGUST 7

Little Change in Job Ratings of Bush or Congressional Parties

The latest USA Today/Gallup Poll finds the job performance ratings of President George W. Bush and the Republicans and Democrats in Congress essentially unchanged compared with their previous readings, although Bush's job approval rating has now recovered five percentage points since his early-July low point. The president and both congressional parties are all viewed more negatively than positively by a majority of Americans, with the Democrats doing a bit better than the Republicans. While the current ratings of the two major parties in Congress are not significantly lower than they were when last measured in February, they are at their technical low points for the trends that began in 1999. According to the August 3–5, 2007, survey, public approval of the nation's leadership currently stands at 37% for the Democrats in Congress, 34% for Bush, and 29% for the Republicans in Congress. More than 6 in 10 Americans disapprove of Bush and of the Republicans in Congress, while 55% disapprove of the Democrats in Congress.

Gallup's previous job performance rating for Bush was assessed in mid-July. At that time, 31% of Americans approved of the overall job he was doing as president, and 63% disapproved. In early July, Bush reached the low point of his administration, with a job approval rating of 29%. Since May, he has received approval ratings in a relatively narrow range between 29% and 34%, averaging 32%. In the first four months of the year, his ratings averaged a slightly higher 35%.

Gallup's previous approval ratings for the Republicans and Democrats in Congress were measured between February 9 and February 11, 2007. The trend documents a slight decline of four points for each, but this is within the

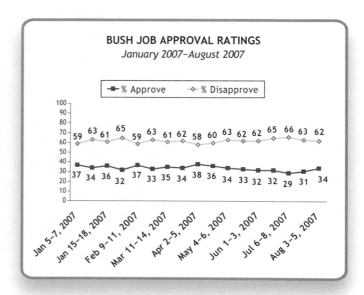

BUSH JOB APPROVAL RATINGS
January 2007–August 2007

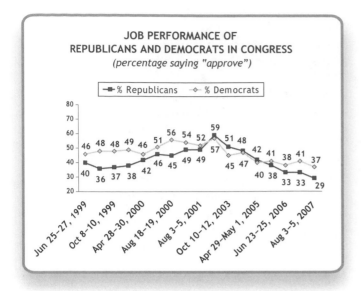

**JOB PERFORMANCE OF
REPUBLICANS AND DEMOCRATS IN CONGRESS**
(percentage saying "approve")

margin of error for comparing results between the two surveys. Thus, there is no sign that the Democrats in Congress are suffering disproportionately from public criticism now that they control Congress. As evident in the longer-term trend, the Democrats in Congress have tended to score higher than congressional Republicans on this measure since the pair of questions was first asked in 1999.

Despite the similarity in overall approval ratings for Bush and the Republicans in Congress, there is not a perfect overlap between the two. Sixty-one percent of respondents who say they approve of the way Bush is handling his job also say they approve of the job the Republicans in Congress are doing—but 36% of those respondents disapprove. Similarly, opposition to Bush does not equate with approval of the Democrats in Congress. Of those who disapprove of the job Bush is doing, only 47% approve of the job the Democrats are doing in Congress, while 45% disapprove.

The public as a whole shows broad dissatisfaction with the nation's leadership, but it has not reached the point where a majority of Republicans and Democrats are critical of their own party's leadership. Partisans still have at least one group they approve of. Fifty-nine percent of Democrats (including Democratic leaners) say they approve of the way the Democrats in Congress are handling their job; a somewhat smaller majority of Republicans/Republican leaners (54%) approve of the way the Republicans in Congress are handling their job. Vastly more Republicans and leaners (71%) than Democrats and leaners (6%) approve of the way Bush is handling his job as president.

Senator Barack Obama makes a point to Senator Hillary Clinton at a forum in Chicago on August 4, 2007. *(Charles Rex Arbogast/AP Images)*

AUGUST 9

Clinton Bounds Further Ahead in Democratic Contest

New York senator Hillary Clinton strengthened her front-runner status in the Democratic field over the past month, pulling 10 points further ahead of Illinois senator Barack Obama than she was in mid-July. According to the August 3–5 USA Today/Gallup Poll, none of the other announced contenders for the 2008 Democratic nomination are within striking distance of Clinton, and only former North Carolina senator John Edwards appears strong enough to potentially compete with Obama for second place. Clinton is now the preferred nominee of 48% of Democrats nationwide, compared with Obama's 26%. Last month, she led by a smaller 12-point margin, 40% vs. 28%. Most of the change is due to increased support for Clinton rather than a decline in support for Obama. Other candidates with at least some support are Edwards with 12%, New Mexico governor Bill Richardson at 4%, Delaware senator Joe Biden at 3%, and Ohio representative Dennis Kucinich at 1%. Connecticut senator Chris Dodd is supported by less than one-half of one percent of Democrats.

These results are based on Democrats and independents who lean toward the Democratic Party and on the assumption that former vice president Al Gore will not be a candidate for the nomination. Should Gore decide to run, it appears he would have limited impact on the race. Gore receives 18% of the vote when included in the list of possible Democratic candidates, but Clinton maintains a sizable lead, and Gore runs neck and neck with Obama for second place.

CLINTON HOLDS SOLID LEAD AMONG LIKELY VOTERS

Although presidential primaries play out in a sequence of state elections that have historically produced some surprises, national polling of partisan preferences usually provides a good indication of which candidates will do well. That forecasting may be improved by focusing on the subset of eligible voters who appear most likely to participate in the primary elections. Gallup's latest survey asked Democrats and Democratic leaners to rate their likelihood of voting in next year's Democratic presidential primary or caucus in their state. Overall, 58% of this group say they are extremely likely to vote, another 25% say they are very likely, 10% say they are somewhat likely, and 7% admit they are not likely to vote.

Looking at the race based on registered Democrats and Democratic leaners who say they are extremely likely to vote (representing 63% of all Democrats and Democratic leaners), Clinton still dominates the field, although by a bit smaller margin than among all Democrats. Support for

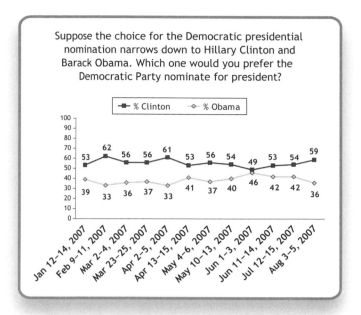

Suppose the choice for the Democratic presidential nomination narrows down to Hillary Clinton and Barack Obama. Which one would you prefer the Democratic Party nominate for president?

Clinton remains about the same, at 47%, but the percentage choosing Obama is slightly higher, at 31%. This tightening of the race, albeit slight, reflects the fact that a smaller percentage of Clinton's voters than Obama's (62% vs. 75%) say they are extremely likely to vote.

CLINTON PULLS AHEAD IN TWO-PERSON FIELD

Clinton's improved standing in the latest poll is also reflected in a separate question asking Democrats whom they would vote for should the Democratic field narrow down to just Clinton and Obama. Clinton now leads Obama by a 23-point margin on this measure, 59% to 36%. Last month she held a much smaller 12-point lead, though the current spread is similar to where she stood earlier this year.

Not only is Clinton generally preferred for the nomination over Obama, but in a new question asking Democrats which of the two candidates would do the better job handling four specific foreign policy responsibilities, Clinton wins hands down on each. The survey was conducted after Obama's widely publicized August 1 foreign policy speech in which he took a hard line against Al-Qaeda, saying that as president he would not wait for approval from Pakistan's government to authorize any military action he felt was warranted against terrorist sites in Pakistan. He also said he would meet with the leaders of hostile countries such as Cuba and North Korea, something his opponents have seized on to reinforce the perception that Obama lacks the experience necessary to be president. Thus, it is notable that the poll finds Clinton leading Obama by her widest margins yet in perceived handling of international terrorism, regarding "relations with nations that are unfriendly to the United States," and with respect to two other issues. This could possibly explain Clinton's recent rise in the polls.

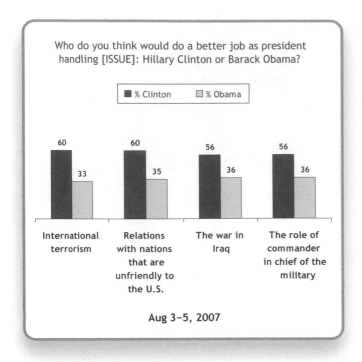

Who do you think would do a better job as president handling [ISSUE]: Hillary Clinton or Barack Obama?

■ % Clinton   □ % Obama

	International terrorism	Relations with nations that are unfriendly to the U.S.	The war in Iraq	The role of commander in chief of the military
% Clinton	60	60	56	56
% Obama	33	35	36	36

Aug 3–5, 2007

Giuliani Maintains Lead as Republican Presidential Preferences Stabilize

Republicans' presidential preferences have remained highly stable in each of the last three Gallup Polls, with support for the leading candidates varying by not more than a percentage point. The latest survey, conducted between August 3 and August 5, 2007, shows Rudolph Giuliani as the established front-runner, with still unannounced candidate Fred Thompson solidifying his second-place standing, Arizona senator John McCain solidly in third, former Massachusetts governor Mitt Romney in fourth, and the remaining candidates at 2% or less support nationwide. The results differ very little when looking at Republicans versus Republican-leaning independents, and also among those who say they are extremely likely to vote in the Republican primary or caucus in their state next year.

In the poll, Giuliani draws the support of 33% of Republicans and Republican-leaning independents, followed by former Tennessee senator Fred Thompson at 21%, McCain at 16%, and Romney at 8%. These results exclude support for former House speaker Newt Gingrich, who has not ruled out a bid but also has not taken steps toward a formal candidacy (unlike his fellow unannounced candidate, Thompson). Prior to this poll, Gallup had regularly reported results including Gingrich, who is supported by 10% of Republicans when he is included in the ballot.

Most interviews in the poll were conducted before the Republican debate on July 29 in Iowa, though so far the presidential debates have not moved the numbers much

On August 5, 2007, nine Republican candidates gather for a debate at Drake University in Des Moines, Iowa: (from left to right) Tom Tancredo, Tommy Thompson, Sam Brownback, John McCain, Rudolph Giuliani, Mitt Romney, Mike Huckabee, Ron Paul, and Duncan Hunter. *(Kevin Sanders/AP Images)*

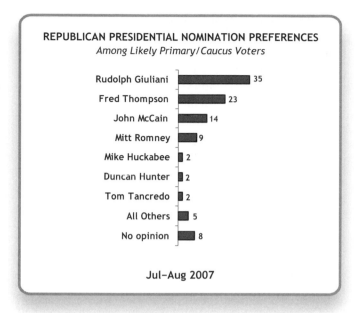

REPUBLICAN PRESIDENTIAL NOMINATION PREFERENCES
Among Likely Primary/Caucus Voters

Rudolph Giuliani   35
Fred Thompson   23
John McCain   14
Mitt Romney   9
Mike Huckabee   2
Duncan Hunter   2
Tom Tancredo   2
All Others   5
No opinion   8

Jul–Aug 2007

on either the Republican or Democratic side. Because the results have been so stable, the data can be combined into a larger sample of Republicans in order to analyze the preferences of various Republican subgroups. The following analyses are based on interviews with over 1,200 Republicans and Republican-leaning independents taken from July and August Gallup Polls. First, among the roughly 6 in 10 Republicans who say they are "extremely likely" to vote in their state's presidential primary or caucus next year, Giuliani remains the leader, maintaining the same 12-point margin over Fred Thompson.

Candidate support also varies little among those who identify as Republicans versus those who identify as inde-

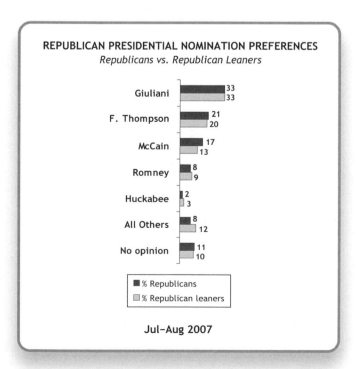

REPUBLICAN PRESIDENTIAL NOMINATION PREFERENCES
Republicans vs. Republican Leaners

Giuliani   33 / 33
F. Thompson   21 / 20
McCain   17 / 13
Romney   8 / 9
Huckabee   2 / 3
All Others   8 / 12
No opinion   11 / 10

■ % Republicans
▢ % Republican leaners

Jul–Aug 2007

pendents but say they lean Republican. In many states, only those who are registered as Republicans can vote in the primaries, though some states allow independents to participate and others allow party declaration on the same day as the primary or caucus. This distinction makes little difference when it comes to candidate support, however: McCain is the only candidate who shows even a hint of doing better among Republicans than among Republican leaners.

Because there is a bit of a "favorite son" dynamic in presidential nominating politics, particularly in the early stages of the campaign when not all the candidates are well known, the patterns of candidate support vary significantly by region. Generally speaking, most candidates are running best in their home region of the country. Still, the only region in which Giuliani is not the top candidate is the South, where Thompson edges him out, though not by a statistically significant margin. Romney performs somewhat better in the Northeast and West than in the Midwest and South.

An analysis of candidate preferences in the combined data set also yields these insights: Churchgoing Republicans are less likely to favor Giuliani than nonchurchgoing Republicans, but Giuliani is the number one candidate among all Republicans regardless of their churchgoing habits. Among Republicans who report attending church at least monthly, 29% support Giuliani, 22% Thompson, 18% McCain, and 8% Romney; among Republicans who seldom or never attend church, 38% name Giuliani as their top choice for the nomination, 19% Thompson, 13% McCain, and 9% Romney. Also, Giuliani fares better among younger Republicans (age 18–34, 40%) than among middle-aged (35–54, 34%) or older Republicans (27%). In contrast, Thompson fares much better among middle-aged (23%) and older Republicans (24%) than he does among younger Republicans (13%). Finally, there is a decided gender gap in support for Fred Thompson: Twenty-six percent of male Republicans support him compared with 16% of female Republicans.

AUGUST 10

Examining Obama's Strong Appeal to Highly Educated Americans

Illinois senator Barack Obama has a much greater appeal to highly educated Americans than to those with less education. Part of the explanation for this phenomenon is that Obama is better known among those with higher levels of education. An additional causal factor is that highly educated Americans are more likely to be Democrats. But Gallup analysis shows that Obama has a particularly

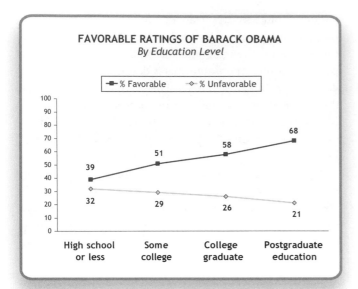

FAVORABLE RATINGS OF BARACK OBAMA
By Education Level

between education and favorable rating for Obama is based on an aggregated sample of more than 4,000 interviews derived from four Gallup Polls conducted in June, July, and August of this year.

Obama's favorable rating climbs from 39% among Americans with a high school education or less to 68% among those with a postgraduate education. The percentage of Americans with unfavorable opinions of Obama does not go down in inverse proportion to the increase in favorable opinions. In other words, part of the reason the percentage of favorable views of Obama increases with education is that the greater the education level, the higher the percentage of people who have an opinion of Obama—and this increase appears to come predominantly among those with favorable opinions.

It is clear that Obama's name identification does indeed increase with education.

On this measure, among those who have an opinion of him, Obama receives a favorable rating from 55% of those with a high school education or less. This figure climbs to 76% among those with a postgraduate education who have an opinion. Clearly, then, the higher favorable ratings Obama receives among those with higher levels of education are not solely because he is better known among those with more education. Among those who are familiar with him, his appeal is stronger for those with higher levels of education.

Is this education skew in Obama's appeal to highly educated Americans a phenomenon common to other candidates? Among the four Democrats the Gallup Polls tracked—Obama, Clinton, Gore, and Edwards—three exhibit a somewhat similar education skew. This pattern is most evident for Obama, however. As noted, Obama's favorable rating jumps 21 percentage points between those with a high school education and those with a postgraduate education. This compares with increases of 14 percentage points for Gore and five percentage points for Edwards, and a three-percentage-point decline for Clinton. In short, the skew in appeal by education exhibited by Obama is evident for two other Democrats, although not to the extent evident for Obama. Only Clinton has no increase in appeal among those with higher levels of education.

strong appeal as well to independents and Republicans with higher levels of education, a pattern that is not duplicated by New York senator Hillary Clinton, former North Carolina senator John Edwards, or former vice president Al Gore.

Obama's greater appeal to highly educated Americans is evident in the basic balloting among Democrats. He essentially ties Clinton among Democrats with a postgraduate education but loses to her by more than 30 percentage points among Democrats with a high school education or less. And the appeal of Obama to Americans with higher levels of education is not confined to Democrats but is evident among the national population as a whole, based on the Gallup Poll's favorable/unfavorable rating scale. The fundamental nature of the correlation

Underlying Factors

There is little question that some of this skew in appeal for these Democrats is because Americans with postgraduate degrees are significantly more likely to identify as Democrats. To control for that effect, Gallup looked at the relationship between education and favorable opinions within partisan groups. Among Democrats, a positive relationship

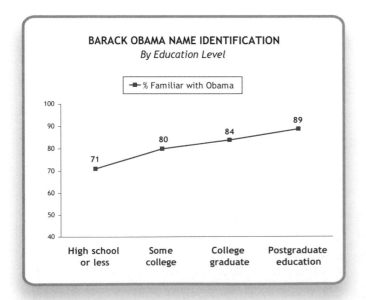

BARACK OBAMA NAME IDENTIFICATION
By Education Level

between education and favorable ratings is evident not just for Obama, but also for Edwards and Gore. Obama's favorable ratio among Democrats with a postgraduate education is no higher than it is for Gore, and just slightly higher than it is for Edwards and Clinton. In other words, Obama does not occupy a uniquely positive position among highly educated Democrats.

There is a different pattern evident in the data among independents and Republicans, however. Obama has a stronger appeal to those independents and Republicans with a postgraduate education than any of the other three leading Democratic candidates. Independents also rate Obama more favorably regardless of education level. Edwards and Gore have a somewhat similar increase in appeal to those with a postgraduate education compared with those with lower levels of education among independents. Among Republicans, Obama's skew in appeal by education appears to be unique among these four Democratic personalities.

In sum, Obama enjoys a particularly positive image among Americans who have high levels of education. This is due in part to the fact that he is a Democrat, and Americans with postgraduate levels of education are more likely than others to identify as Democrats. In fact, controlling for party and name identification, the data show that Obama does not have an unusually strong appeal to highly educated Democrats as compared with other Democratic personalities. But Obama's appeal is stronger among independents and Republicans with higher levels of education than the other Democrats surveyed. This is particularly true among Republicans with a postgraduate education, among whom Obama enjoys a slightly more positive than negative image—unusual for a Democratic presidential candidate.

Public Rates Giuliani Most Favorably of Eight Presidential Hopefuls

The latest USA Today/Gallup Poll finds Americans most positive in their assessment of former New York City mayor Rudolph Giuliani out of eight possible presidential candidates in the 2008 election. The public is also more positive than negative in their ratings of Illinois senator Barack Obama, former North Carolina senator John Edwards, and former Tennessee senator Fred Thompson, whereas their views of New York senator Hillary Clinton, Arizona senator John McCain, and former vice president Al Gore are equally positive and negative, and their ratings of Massachusetts governor Mitt Romney are more negative than positive. In recent weeks, McCain's and Obama's unfavorable ratings have increased significantly and are now the highest Gallup has ever measured for these men.

Candidate Ratings

Giuliani is the only candidate who has a majority favorable rating: Fifty-five percent of Americans rate him favorably, while 32% rate him unfavorably. Giuliani also has the highest "net favorable rating"—percentage favorable minus percentage unfavorable— of any of the candidates, at +23. Three other presidential hopefuls also have high net favorable ratings: Obama +14, Edwards +12, and Thompson +11. Gore's net favorable rating is +2. Americans' views of McCain and Clinton are evenly divided, yielding net favorable ratings of –1 for McCain and –2 for Clinton. Romney is rated more negatively than any of the other candidates on this measure, with a net favorable rating of –9.

McCain's overall favorability rating is now at its lowest point this year, with 41% rating him favorably and 42% unfavorably. McCain's net favorable rating was fairly positive over the first five months of the year, but it has dropped in each poll since the beginning of June. This is the first time since February 1999, when Gallup first tested opinions of McCain, that his positive ratings have not exceeded his negative ratings.

Although Obama's net favorable rating is still one of the most positive of any candidate in the poll, his +14 net rating is his lowest since the beginning of the year and marks a continued decline in his net ratings since mid-May. Obama's rating was highest in early March at +40 and has averaged +28 over the course of the year.

McCain's and Obama's favorable ratings have not declined over the past month: rather, a higher percentage of Americans now rate each candidate unfavorably, leading to a lower net favorable rating. Typically, Americans' ratings of relatively unknown candidates are more favorable than unfavor-

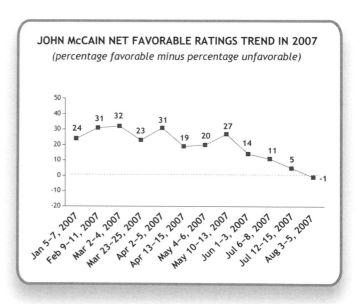

JOHN McCAIN NET FAVORABLE RATINGS TREND IN 2007
(percentage favorable minus percentage unfavorable)

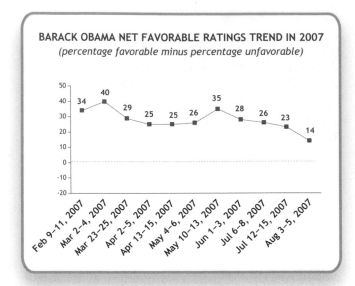

BARACK OBAMA NET FAVORABLE RATINGS TREND IN 2007
(percentage favorable minus percentage unfavorable)

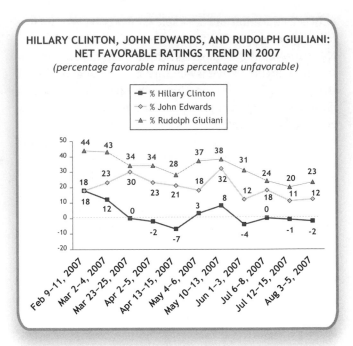

HILLARY CLINTON, JOHN EDWARDS, AND RUDOLPH GIULIANI:
NET FAVORABLE RATINGS TREND IN 2007
(percentage favorable minus percentage unfavorable)

able in the early stages of their campaign. But opinions of Romney have never been much more positive than negative; his highest net favorable was only +8 this past May. As he has become somewhat better known in recent months, his ratings have become on balance negative, and his current net favorable rating is –9 (22% favorable, 31% unfavorable). About half of Americans remain unfamiliar with him.

Thompson—the other still relatively unknown candidate—fits the more typical pattern of being viewed more positively than negatively. His net favorable ratings have been consistent since Gallup first measured his ratings in April, ranging between a +10 and a +16 net favorable rating over this period of time. Currently, he has a 31% favorable rating and a 20% unfavorable rating, for a net score of +11. Forty-nine percent of Americans remain unfamiliar with the actor and former Tennessee senator.

Americans' ratings of Clinton, Edwards, and Giuliani have not shown much significant change in recent months. However, ratings of all three candidates have been higher at earlier points this year. Giuliani's and Clinton's net favorable ratings were highest in February, at +44 and +18, respectively, while Edwards's peaked at +32 in May. Giuliani and Edwards have consistently had net positive ratings, while Clinton's ratings have been more divided.

CANDIDATE RATINGS BY PARTISANSHIP

Perhaps not surprisingly, Republicans and Democrats alike are much more likely to rate their own party's candidates favorably. Giuliani, by far, is the most positively rated Republican candidate among rank-and-file Republicans, with a +64 net favorable rating. Thompson has a +35 net favorable rating among Republicans; McCain and Romney have similar +17 and +16 net favorable ratings, respectively. Among independents, Giuliani scores the highest, with a net favorable rating of +17, and Romney scores the worst, with a –13 net favorable rating. Independents are divided in their views of Thompson and McCain. Among Democrats, Thompson and Giuliani fare better than the other Republican candidates. Clinton has the highest net favorable rating among Democrats at +71. Gore's net favorable rating is +56, only slightly above Edwards's +53; Obama's is slightly lower, at +45. Among independents, Obama and Edwards are rated the highest, with net favorable ratings of +18 and +14, respectively. Independents are divided in their view of Gore (+3), and are more negative than positive in their views of Clinton

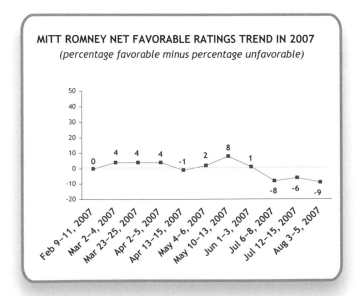

MITT ROMNEY NET FAVORABLE RATINGS TREND IN 2007
(percentage favorable minus percentage unfavorable)

(–9). All four Democrats receive net negative ratings from Republicans, with Clinton rated the worst.

Republicans and Democrats differ significantly in their views of all eight candidates measured in this poll, but the largest variations are found in ratings of Clinton. Only 13% of Republicans rate Clinton favorably, while 84% rate her unfavorably. The exact opposite is the case among Democrats: Eighty-four percent rate Clinton favorably and 13% unfavorably. The smallest partisan difference is seen in ratings of Romney and Thompson (neither of whom is well known by a majority of Democrats) and McCain.

AUGUST 14

Gallup Poll Review: Key Points About Public Opinion on Iraq

With the war in Iraq dominating American news and with a potential fight looming between the White House and Congress when General David Petraeus, commander of U.S. forces in Iraq, reports on the progress of the troop surge in September, the opinions of the average American citizen are vitally important. There has been an enormous amount of public opinion polling on Iraq since the war began in 2003, particularly in the course of the last year. What follows is a brief updated outline of key aspects of Americans' views of the war.

1. The Iraq war is an extremely high priority for Americans.

A wide variety of measures show that the war in Iraq is perceived by the American public as the nation's top problem at this time, and as the top priority for government. Unless there is a significant change between now and next year, the war is likely to be one of the top issues in the 2008 presidential and congressional elections. Thirty-five percent of Americans name Iraq as the "most important problem" facing the country today, by far the most dominant issue mentioned. Iraq has been the number one issue specified in response to this question since April 2004. Nearly 7 in 10 Americans choose Iraq as the top priority for the president and Congress to deal with, far and away the most frequently mentioned issue in response to this question. Iraq has also topped this list since this question was first asked by Gallup in April 2006.

Two-thirds of registered voters say the war in Iraq will be "extremely important" or "very important" to their 2008 presidential vote.

2. A majority of Americans continue to say it was a mistake for the United States to have become involved in Iraq.

In Gallup's latest poll, conducted in early August, 57% of Americans said it was a mistake to send troops to Iraq,

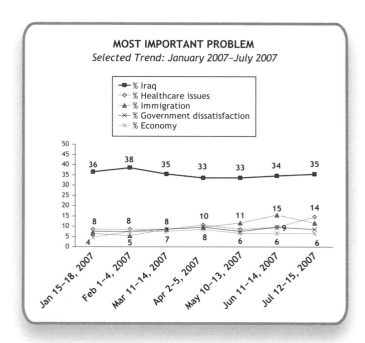

MOST IMPORTANT PROBLEM
Selected Trend: January 2007–July 2007

while 42% said it was not. That is typical of the responses to this "mistake" question all year. In fact, no less than 48% of Americans have called the war a mistake in every Gallup Poll taken since August 2005.

Gallup has been using a "mistake" question of this sort to measure public opinion about wars going back to the Korean War in the early 1950s. Less than a majority of Americans called the Korean War a mistake for most of its duration, but a majority of Americans consistently called the war in Vietnam a mistake from August 1968 on. In contrast to the war in Iraq, most Americans continue to be supportive of U.S. military action in Afghanistan, as

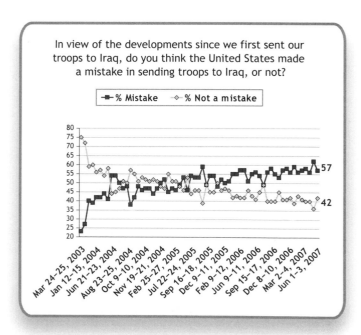

In view of the developments since we first sent our troops to Iraq, do you think the United States made a mistake in sending troops to Iraq, or not?

they have been since it began in October 2001. Twenty-five percent of Americans in the early August poll said it was a mistake to undertake military action in Afghanistan, while 70% said it was not a mistake.

3. A majority of Americans perceive that the benefits of winning the war in Iraq do not outweigh the costs involved, and Americans are not convinced that the war is a part of the war on terrorism. Still, there are mixed views of the impact on terrorism if the United States withdraws its troops from Iraq.

With negative perceptions of the war's progress as a backdrop, it may not be surprising that the public sees little upside for Americans in the cost-benefit trade-off of continuing the war in Iraq. By more than a two-to-one margin, 65% to 31%, Americans in January of this year said the benefits to the United States of winning the war in Iraq were not worth the costs the United States would have to bear in order to win it.

Asked in mid-June 2007 if the war in Iraq was part of the war on terrorism, 43% of Americans said it was, while a slight majority, 53%, said it was an entirely separate military action. A recent CNN poll showed that 42% of Americans say the war with Iraq has made the United States safer from terrorism, while a slightly higher percentage, 49%, say it has made the country less safe. But Americans' views of the impact of withdrawing U.S. troops from Iraq on the war on terrorism are more sharply divided. The CNN poll found that just about as many Americans say that the chances of a terrorist attack in the United States would be higher if the country withdraws troops from Iraq as soon as possible as say the chances of a terror-

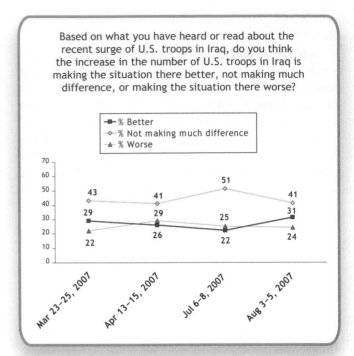

ist attack would be higher if the United States keeps its troops in Iraq.

4. There has been a recent increase in the percentage of Americans saying that the war is making things better in Iraq, although a majority of Americans still do not agree that the troop surge is having a positive effect.

Gallup's early August poll showed that 31% of Americans said the recent surge of U.S. troops in Iraq is making the situation there better. That's a nine-point increase (up from 22%) since early July. Still, the majority of Americans say the troop surge is not making much of a difference or is actually making the situation worse.

5. Americans are apparently conflicted on the issue of when and how best to remove troops from Iraq.

While most Americans support the broad principle of a timetable for removing troops from Iraq within the next year, relatively few believe that all troops should be withdrawn immediately. Public support remains high for the general concept of a timetable to withdraw most U.S. troops from Iraq: According to the early August Gallup Poll, 66% of Americans favor removing all U.S. troops from Iraq by April 2008, except for a limited number that would be involved in counterterrorist operations. Last month, 71% favored this proposal. But previous Gallup polling shows that relatively few Americans want immediate withdrawal of troops from Iraq. And a recent ABC News/Washington Post poll finds that only about one-third of Americans support the concept of the United States withdrawing all of its troops now. The rest say the United States should begin to withdraw troops, keep troop levels the same, or increase troop levels.

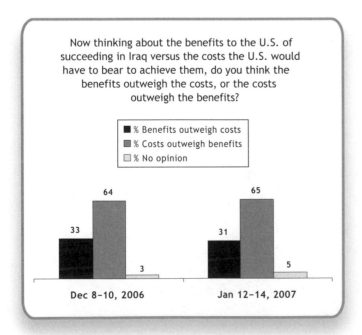

6. A majority of Americans do not want Congress to take action on Iraq until the mid-September report of General David Petraeus, who is highly respected.

Notwithstanding their sustained opposition to the war and majority support for some type of timetable to withdraw U.S. troops from Iraq, Americans say they are willing to wait until September before setting a new course in Iraq. At that time, General Petraeus reports to Congress about the progress of the war effort. Fifty-six percent of Americans are inclined to wait until then for a new Iraq policy, while 39% say Congress should develop a new policy now. These views are little changed from last month. More generally, Americans have more positive than negative views of General Petraeus, by about a two-to-one ratio—although 32% of Americans are not familiar enough with Petraeus to rate him. Opinions about General Petraeus are already highly political. Republicans with an opinion are overwhelmingly positive about Petraeus; Democrats are split.

Earlier this year, a Gallup survey showed that Petraeus had a higher credibility rating on Iraq than any of 16 other individuals tested—including President Bush, Vice President Dick Cheney, Secretary of Defense Robert Gates, or such presidential candidates as Hillary Clinton, Rudolph Giuliani, John McCain, and Barack Obama.

7. The Democrats are better positioned than the Republicans on handling the issue of Iraq.

Since 2005, the public has perceived that Democrats are better able than Republicans to handle the issue of Iraq. Prior to this, Americans gave the Republicans the edge. Americans also say they trust the Democrats in Congress more than the administration when it comes to making decisions on Iraq. But a recent CBS News/New York Times poll finds that while Americans are more likely to approve of the way the Democrats in Congress rather than the Republicans in Congress are handling the situation in Iraq,

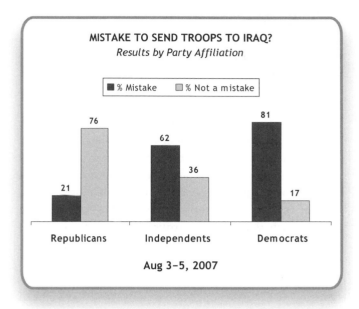

MISTAKE TO SEND TROOPS TO IRAQ?
Results by Party Affiliation

■ % Mistake   ☐ % Not a mistake

Republicans: 21, 76
Independents: 62, 36
Democrats: 81, 17

Aug 3–5, 2007

approval ratings for both parties are dismal. Thirty percent of Americans approve of the way the Democrats in Congress are handling the situation in Iraq, while 22% approve of the way the Republicans in Congress are handling the problem. These results are typical of what Gallup and other polling firms have found this year.

8. Views on the war are highly partisan.

Views of the Iraq War are sharply divided along partisan lines—perhaps not surprisingly, given the degree to which the war is identified with the Republican Bush-Cheney administration. Republicans overwhelmingly support the war; Democrats overwhelmingly oppose it. Independents are more likely to oppose than favor the war. About three-quarters of Republicans say that sending troops to Iraq was not a mistake; Democrats, by a 60-point margin, say it was a mistake.

The same partisan differences emerge when Americans are asked to evaluate the impact of the recent troop surge in Iraq. Sixty percent of Republicans say the surge is making the situation in Iraq better, while 7% say it is making it worse. Among Democrats, just 7% say the troop surge is making the situation better, while 39% say it is making it worse and 51% say it is making no difference. Similarly, upwards of 9 in 10 Democrats support removing all U.S. troops from Iraq by April 2008, but only 41% of Republicans support this plan. Nearly three in four Republicans say Congress should wait until General Petraeus's report on the progress of the troop surge to develop a new policy on Iraq; Democrats are more divided as to whether Congress should act now (50%) or wait until September (44%).

Support for past U.S. wars—including the war in Vietnam—was not as polarized along party lines as with respect to the current war. Gallup data from 1968 and 1969 show

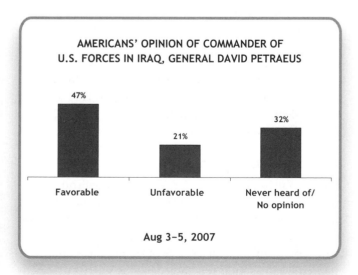

AMERICANS' OPINION OF COMMANDER OF
U.S. FORCES IN IRAQ, GENERAL DAVID PETRAEUS

Favorable: 47%
Unfavorable: 21%
Never heard of/ No opinion: 32%

Aug 3–5, 2007

that a little more than half of Americans said it was a mistake to send troops to Vietnam—and while 51% of Democrats agreed with this position at the time, so did 55% of independents and 56% of Republicans. In short, there was remarkably little differentiation.

9. Men are more likely to support the war in Iraq than are women.

There is a significant gender gap in terms of attitudes on the war. Women are more likely than men to say it was a mistake and to support a timetable for removing U.S. troops. This is probably because women are more likely to identify as Democrats than are men, but in general women are less likely than men, regardless of party identification, to favor military action. Sixty-one percent of women say it was a mistake to send troops to Iraq, compared with 52% of men. Slightly more than 7 in 10 women support a timetable for removing troops from Iraq by April 2008; 59% of men agree.

AUGUST 16

Obama's Appeal to the Well-Educated Not Conducive to Winning Nomination

Illinois senator Barack Obama is clearly in second place behind New York senator Hillary Clinton in the race for the Democratic presidential nomination, but he is highly competitive with Clinton among the most educated segment of the party. That appeal may be one reason he has met or surpassed Clinton's fund-raising totals despite not gaining much ground in voter support this year: Well-educated Americans tend to have greater income. An analysis of historical Gallup Poll data on rank-and-file Democrats' nomination preferences shows that at least one candidate has exhibited a pattern similar to Obama's education skew in each election cycle since 1988, but that candidate usually does not end up winning the Democratic presidential nomination.

Democratic Candidate Support by Education

According to combined data from Gallup's national Democratic nomination trial heat polls conducted in July and August 2007, Obama's support rises from 19% among Democrats with a high school education or less to 28% of those who attended college but did not finish and 33% among college graduates. By contrast, Clinton's support shows a downward trend by education level, as 51% of Democrats with a high school education or less, 45% of those with some college education, and 33% of college graduates support her. Thus, while Clinton leads Obama by 32 percentage points (51% to 19%) among Democrats with

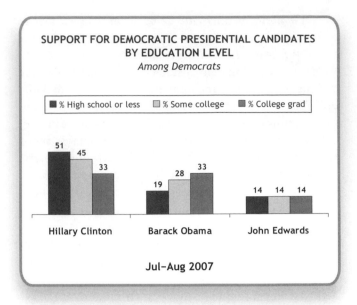

SUPPORT FOR DEMOCRATIC PRESIDENTIAL CANDIDATES BY EDUCATION LEVEL
Among Democrats

% High school or less   % Some college   % College grad

Hillary Clinton: 51, 45, 33
Barack Obama: 19, 28, 33
John Edwards: 14, 14, 14

Jul–Aug 2007

the least formal education, she merely ties him among the most educated Democrats. Former North Carolina senator John Edwards's support is a consistent 14% among Democrats of all education levels.

Analysis of historical Gallup Poll data leading up to the Iowa caucuses shows that Obama's support pattern by education is not uncommon. The analyses rely on combined results of available data from national polls conducted in the November, December, and January prior to the Iowa caucuses, usually held in mid-to-late January of the presidential election year. Thus, the figures show where the nomination contest race stood among all Democrats before actual voting took place. In some cases, such as in 1988, 1992, and 2004, the pre-Iowa figures were not predictive of the eventual outcome, as the candidate leading the national polls did not win the nomination. In 1996, President Bill Clinton was unchallenged for the nomination, so there are no data for that election. To ensure comparability across elections and maintain robust sample sizes, the analysis compares the preferences of Democrats without any college education and those who attended college. In the current campaign, Hillary Clinton's support is 51% among Democrats without any college education and 45% among those who attended college. Obama's support is 19% among non-college-educated Democrats and 28% among Democrats who attended college.

THE 2004 ELECTION

By the fall of 2003, former Vermont governor Howard Dean was able to translate his fund-raising success—fueled in large part by Internet donations—into front-runner status for the 2004 Democratic nomination. Prior to the Iowa caucuses, 23% of Democrats nationwide named Dean as their top choice for the party's presidential nomination, followed by retired general Wesley Clark at 16%, Connecticut senator Joe Lieberman at 12%, and eventual nominee Massachusetts senator John Kerry, tied with Missouri representative Dick Gephardt, at 9%. Dean's support showed a decided education skew: Sixteen percent of non-college-educated Democrats and 27% of Democrats with some college education (including 33% of college graduates) supported him. Although Kerry's pre-Iowa national support was still limited, college-educated (9%) and non-college-educated Democrats (9%) were equally likely to support him. Kerry surprised everyone by winning the Iowa caucuses while Dean finished a disappointing third. Kerry followed up his Iowa win by defeating Dean in New Hampshire, seriously crippling the former front-runner's candidacy.

THE 2000 ELECTION

Vice President Al Gore was the clear front-runner in 2000, and his only notable challenger was former New Jersey senator Bill Bradley. Gore had a significant lead over Bradley in pre-Iowa national polls, including among all education groups. Bradley did get greater support from college-educated Democrats (36%) than from non-college-educated Democrats (29%). Bradley's support was as high as 41% among Democrats with a postgraduate education, but he still trailed Gore (49%) among this group. After a decisive victory for Gore in the Iowa caucuses, he edged out Bradley in New Hampshire, one of the few states in which experts thought Bradley could defeat Gore. Gore wound up winning every Democratic primary and caucus that year.

THE 1992 ELECTION

The 1992 Democratic field was largely filled with unknown candidates after better-known candidates such as former New York governor Mario Cuomo, Bradley, and Gore declined to run. Indeed, no front-runner had emerged before Iowa and New Hampshire. Former California governor Jerry Brown, out of office for nearly 10 years and who had twice unsuccessfully sought the presidency, was the best known and had a slight edge over Arkansas governor Bill Clinton in rank-and-file Democrats' preferences as 1992 began. Some believed that former Vietnam veteran and then Nebraska senator Bob Kerrey might emerge from the field. Kerrey showed the greatest education skew among the candidates, with support nearly twice as high among Democrats who had attended college (15%) as among those with a high school education or less (8%). Kerrey finished a distant third behind Massachusetts senator Paul Tsongas and Clinton in New Hampshire, but went on to win the South Dakota caucuses. He performed poorly in the remaining primaries and caucuses before ending his campaign in early March.

THE 1988 ELECTION

In 1988, two Democratic candidates appealed more to college-educated than to non-college-educated party members. One was Illinois senator Paul Simon; the other was the eventual nominee, Massachusetts governor Michael Dukakis. Dukakis's support was twice as high among college-educated Democrats nationally (15%) than among non-college-educated Democrats (7%). Simon's appeal was three times greater among college-educated Democrats (13%) than among non-college-educated Democrats (5%). (Former Arizona governor Bruce Babbitt's support also showed an education skew, but only 2% of Democrats supported him, so he is not included in this analysis.)

Colorado senator Gary Hart had left the campaign in May 1987 due to accusations of marital infidelity, but he renewed his presidential bid in December and immediately regained his front-runner status nationally. His national support did not foreshadow his dismal performance in New Hampshire, where he finished seventh, with Dukakis winning that primary. A spirited campaign saw most candidates win at least one state's primary or caucus during the process before Dukakis emerged as the nominee.

IMPLICATIONS OF THE ANALYSIS

Obama and future candidates who have a stronger appeal to more highly educated Democrats can look to Dukakis's campaign as a model for success in achieving the party's nomination, while attempting to avoid the more common fate among past candidates whose support increased with respondent education level. It is not entirely clear why those candidates whose support is positively correlated with education level have not fared better in recent campaigns. But at the most basic level, these candidates were typically not that well positioned at the start of the primary and caucus season and thus started out at a disadvantage. Dean is an obvious exception to that, but Bradley and Kerrey, for example, were well behind the front-runners in their respective campaigns and were never able to gain the momentum needed to catch or overtake them. This may be due in large part to name recognition. Especially early in a campaign, Democrats with a college education are probably more likely than Democrats without a college education to be familiar with the lesser-known candidates. Name identification is a critical factor in candidate support, because respondents are not likely to support a candidate they know little about. Much of the battle for the candidates is to become known, and once they do become known, their campaign can play out differently from how it starts.

At this point in the 2008 campaign, Hillary Clinton is nearly universally known among all Democrats, regardless of education level. On the other hand, Obama is much more familiar to highly educated Democrats than to those with less formal education. An alternative explanation is that candidates whose support increases with education level may share similarities—such as in their issue positions or personal style—that appeal to highly educated Democrats but may not attract the broader base of the party. Or candidates who exhibit an education skew in their support may just have run bad campaigns—Bradley, Dean, Kerrey, and Simon were all thought to have run lackluster campaigns. Dukakis is the obvious exception to this. It is also important to note that the candidate with greater appeal to educated Democrats often is not even the top choice among this group. While college-educated Democrats were more likely to support Bradley, Kerrey, Dukakis, and Simon than non-college-educated Democrats, college-educated Democrats still preferred Gore to Bradley, Jerry Brown or Bill Clinton to Kerrey, and Gary Hart or Jesse Jackson to Dukakis and Simon at the outset of their respective campaigns. While Obama's pattern of support certainly does not mean his candidacy is doomed, he would be bucking the recent historical trend of Democratic nomination outcomes should he win.

AUGUST 20
Romney Posts Modest Gains

Republican presidential candidate Mitt Romney has posted modest gains over the last two weeks, both in his favorable rating and in his positioning in the race for the Republican presidential nomination. One presumption is that Romney's gains reflect the visibility that followed his win in the Iowa Republican Party straw poll on August 11, although data in the new Gallup Poll show that only a third of Republicans nationwide are aware that Romney won this unofficial contest.

Romney now receives 14% of Republicans' votes when they are asked whom they would like as their party's presidential nominee, up from 8% in each of the two previous Gallup Polls conducted in July and early August. Romney's current positioning puts him slightly behind front-runner Rudolph Giuliani and unannounced candidate Fred Thompson but slightly ahead of John McCain, who slips to 11% in this poll. Romney's positioning is not a new high point for the former Massachusetts governor; he was at 14% in a Gallup Poll in early June. At that time, however, McCain had a clear claim on second place, while Romney was roughly tied with Thompson for third. These data do not include preferences for former speaker of the House Newt Gingrich. When the ballot is adjusted to reflect only the currently declared candidates (thus excluding not only Gingrich but also Thompson and Iowa senator Chuck

Hagel), Giuliani is supported by 39% of Republicans, Romney by 17%, McCain by 15%, and former Arkansas governor Mike Huckabee—who finished second in the Iowa straw poll—by 7%. Giuliani and McCain did not participate in the straw poll.

Romney's Favorable Rating

Romney's favorable rating has jumped from 22% to 33% over the past two weeks, while his unfavorable rating has fallen from 31% to 24%. Romney's favorable rating had been in the 22% to 23% range over the previous three Gallup Polls conducted in July and August, with a higher unfavorable than favorable rating in each of these polls. Although his favorable rating had been as high as 27% in May, the current 33% is his highest to date.

Forty-nine percent of Republicans now have a favorable opinion of Romney, compared with 36% in the prior poll. At the same time, Romney's unfavorable rating among Republicans has dropped from 20% to 16%. And Romney's name identification among Republicans—the percentage who have an opinion of him—jumped by nine points over the last two weeks. Still, despite these gains for Romney, his favorable rating among Republicans remains below Giuliani's and McCain's, and although his favorable rating is similar to Thompson's, his unfavorable rating is more than twice as high. Romney is, however, better known than Thompson (despite the latter's film and TV exposure), and much better known than Huckabee or Kansas senator Sam Brownback.

Awareness of Romney's Iowa Straw Poll Victory

Romney won the Iowa straw poll on August 11 with 32% of the vote of Republicans who cast straw poll ballots, followed by Huckabee with 18%. One might assume that Romney's image and vote gains in the August 13–16 Gallup Poll reflect in part the positive visibility he received as a result of that victory. That may be the case, but a separate question asked at the end of the poll shows that only a third of Republicans could name Romney as the winner in Iowa.

The sample size of Republicans who were aware that Romney had won the Iowa straw poll is quite small, but it is of interest to look at the candidate preferences among this group. The data show that Thompson has a slight lead over Romney among this group, with Giuliani slightly further behind. This finding may reflect the pre-existing preferences of the group most likely to follow Republican politics closely, or those of Republicans who were paying attention specifically to the Iowa straw poll. But it is true that Romney does better (as does Thompson) among Republicans who were aware of Romney's victory in Iowa than among those who were not. The general finding is that Romney has enjoyed a modest improvement in his standing among Republicans, and that this improvement coincides with the time of his victory in the Iowa straw poll.

AUGUST 22

Clinton Maintains Expanded Lead for Democratic Nomination

A new Gallup Poll finds New York senator Hillary Clinton's strengthened front-runner status in the Democratic field for the 2008 Democratic presidential nomination holding firm, following an early August survey in which she stretched her mid-July 12-point lead over Illinois senator Barack Obama to 22 points. The latest Gallup Poll, conducted between August 3 and August 16, 2007, finds public support for the Democratic nomination at 48% for Clinton and 25% for Obama, giving Clinton a 23-point lead. Support for former North Carolina senator John Edwards, in third place with 13%, is similar to what he has received since May. However, support for the bottom tier of candidates appears to be dropping off compared with June and July. At 2%, support for New Mexico governor Bill Richardson is not lower by a statistically significant margin than the 4% he received in early August, but it is lower than his readings of 5% in June and July. Delaware senator Joe Biden's current 1% is his weakest showing of the year, and below his high of 4% in July. Ohio representative Dennis Kucinich and Connecticut senator Chris Dodd remain mired in the 1%–2% range.

These results are based on responses from Democrats and independents who lean toward the Democratic Party, and on the assumption that former vice president Al Gore will not be a candidate for the nomination. With Gore included as a possible candidate, Clinton still enjoys a solid

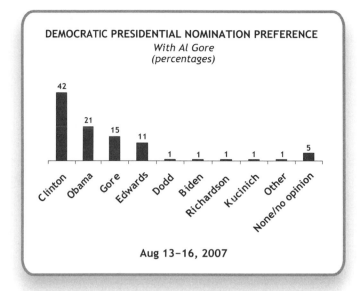

DEMOCRATIC PRESIDENTIAL NOMINATION PREFERENCE
With Al Gore
(percentages)

Aug 13–16, 2007

21-point lead over Obama (42% vs. 21%), while Gore competes with Edwards for third place. These results are also very similar to those found earlier in August.

Clinton has led Obama by a significant margin in all but one Gallup Poll trial heat since February 2007. She started off the year with a 25-point lead over Obama. That narrowed to an average of 12 points between mid-April and July, including one June survey in which Gallup found the race essentially tied. However, support for Clinton surged earlier this month to 48%, up from 40% in June, and it remains at that level in the latest poll. Support for Obama has been more stable, in the 25%–28% range. Gallup also observes this pattern in a separate question asking Democrats whom they would vote for should the Democratic field narrow down to just Clinton and Obama. Clinton now leads Obama by 27 points on this measure, 61% to 34%. In mid-July, she held a much smaller 12-point lead, though the current spread is similar to where she stood earlier this year.

According to combined data from the two August surveys, Clinton leads Obama for her party's nomination among Democratic women as well as Democratic men, among all age groups, and in all four major regions of the country. On a relative basis, she is particularly strong among women, in the East and South, and among older Democrats. In particular, Clinton has a substantial lead among women and men 50 years of age and older, and a sizable lead among younger women as well. However, she is in a near tie with Obama among 18- to 49-year-old men. She does about equally well among Democratic voters who say they are extremely likely to vote in next year's primaries and those who indicate they are less likely to vote.

Gallup's early August survey was conducted shortly after a widely publicized foreign policy speech by Obama in which he made some statements about the war on terrorism and relations with leaders of hostile countries that drew

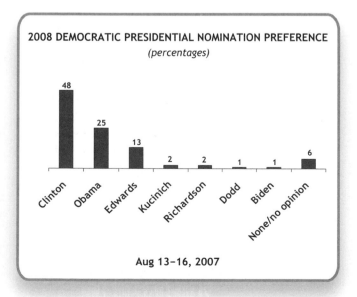

2008 DEMOCRATIC PRESIDENTIAL NOMINATION PREFERENCE
(percentages)

Aug 13–16, 2007

a broad range of criticism from both sides of the political aisle. The extent to which that firestorm was responsible for the increase in support for Clinton's candidacy noted at the time is unclear. Given the results of the new poll, one thing is clear, however: Clinton's surge was neither a fluke of sampling error nor merely a fleeting reaction by voters to something on the campaign trail.

Gallup Poll Review: Karl Rove's Assertions About Clinton

White House adviser Karl Rove—who announced he would be leaving his post at the end of August—has during the last week made a number of statements about New York senator Hillary Clinton's image and electability, in some instances invoking specific mentions of Gallup Polls. The thrust of Rove's assertions is that Clinton's "unfavorable" ratings are at record levels for a presidential candidate, and that as a result she is "fatally flawed" in her quest to be elected in November 2008. Rove is correct in noting that Clinton's unfavorable ratings are high, and unusually so for a candidate this far in advance of the election. However, a review of historical Gallup data suggests that contrary to Rove's assertions, her current image ratings do not necessarily spell defeat. Clinton's current unfavorable ratings are in reality not much different from what other candidates have had in the year they won both the nomination and the election. Second, her image has been more negative than positive several other times during the past 15 years, but she has often recovered and she could do so again. And finally, despite Clinton's high unfavorables, she remains competitive with the Republican candidates in Gallup's presidential test elections.

One of the first statements by Rove that attracted attention was his comment on the syndicated Rush Limbaugh radio program on August 15. Asked about Clinton's election prospects, Rove said: "I'll simply repeat what I said publicly on the record. I think she's likely to be the nominee, and I think she's fatally flawed," which was followed by this explanation: "There is no front-runner who has entered the primary season with negatives as high as she has in the history of modern polling. She's going into the general election with, depending on what poll you look at, in the high forties on the negative side, and just below that on the positive side, and there's nobody who has ever won the presidency who started out in that kind of position." A few days later, Rove was asked about his statements on NBC's *Meet the Press*. Rove reiterated his basic position, albeit this time mentioning the Gallup Poll specifically: "She enters the general election campaign with the highest negatives of any candidate in the history of the Gallup Poll. . . . She enters the presidential contest with higher negatives. . . . Hers are at 49—the only other candidate to

come close was Al Gore with 34, I believe." On the CBS program *Face the Nation*, Rove said, "She enters the primary season with the highest negatives of any front-runner since the history of polling began." Chris Wallace on *Fox News Sunday* pressed Rove a little more on his statements, asking, "Well, but what makes her fatally flawed? I understand she has high negatives. George W. Bush had high negatives going into the 2004 campaign—didn't beat him." To which Rove responded: "Yeah, but look. First of all, they were nowhere near as high as hers. In fact, I think the next highest is Al Gore going into the 2000 campaign."

Since Rove has made his assertions in off-the-cuff comments in broadcast interview settings, it is not surprising that they vary somewhat in comparative precision. In some instances Rove references the primary election season, while in others he references the general election. In particular, Rove appears to make reference to "entering" the primary or general election season—a relatively vague time frame, particularly this year when campaigning essentially began as the 2004 election ended. Despite some uncertainty about the precise details of Rove's contentions, it appears that his basic points are clear. Rove is asserting that Clinton has higher unfavorable ratings now than other presidential candidates in previous election cycles—and, according to the historical record, will be "fatally" unable to win the general election in 2008 should she gain the Democratic nomination.

As noted, it is impossible to determine what the level of unfavorable ratings was for other presidential candidates as they were "entering" the election season, since there is no clear consensus as to when each campaign began. But in order to put Clinton's current image in historical perspective, Gallup reviewed data from previous elections and searched for the highest unfavorable ratings given to major candidates in each. The results show that several other presidential candidates were at some points during their campaigns in essentially the same position as Clinton is today, with an unfavorable rating just below 50%. This includes George W. Bush in 2004 and Bill Clinton in 1992, both of whom went on to win both their party's nomination and the election.

Hillary Clinton's precise current ratings are 47% favorable and 48% unfavorable. A careful review of past data shows that there is no reason to assume Clinton will maintain these high unfavorable ratings as the election draws closer. As the above data suggest, a number of candidates have had relatively high unfavorable ratings at some point in the election campaign but managed to improve them at least somewhat by Election Day. But there have also been numerous examples in recent years of more dramatic change—when well-known politicians' favorability ratings have shifted from net-negative to net-positive. Sometimes these changes have occurred in a very short time span. What is most relevant is the fact that Hillary Clinton's own favorable ratings have

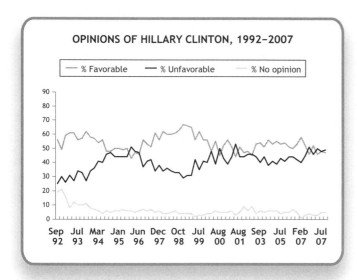

OPINIONS OF HILLARY CLINTON, 1992–2007

— % Favorable   — % Unfavorable   — % No opinion

shown dramatic shifts since she entered national public life in 1992. As recently as April 2007 a majority of Americans rated Clinton unfavorably, but a month later her favorable rating had increased eight percentage points while her unfavorable rating had dropped seven points. Clinton benefited from the release of her autobiography in June 2003, which erased some of the negative feelings toward her stemming from the Clintons' messy White House departure in early 2001. Clinton's favorable ratings also improved following the 1996 and 2000 elections.

It is true that many Americans have made up their mind about Clinton and will forever view her negatively, and there are many Americans who will continue to view her positively no matter what. But there is also a sizable percentage of Americans whose opinions of Clinton are not seemingly set in stone—enough so that her overall rating can shift from being generally positive to generally negative, as occurred earlier this year. Rove's hypothesis that Clinton's candidacy is doomed may rest on the assumption that candidates' negatives increase as the campaign progresses. That is usually the case, but probably results from the fact that Americans become more familiar with the candidates and increasingly view them as partisan figures over the course of a campaign. Clinton is already known to almost all Americans, and opinions of her are already divided along partisan lines, so the normal campaign dynamics likely do not apply to her. Still, just as it is possible for Clinton's image to improve during the campaign, it could also get worse. But that would more than likely be the result of a specific negative incident, rather than being just a function of the normal dynamics of a presidential campaign.

While a candidate's favorables are a strong predictor of possible electoral success, they are also an indirect measure. One important direct measure is the assessment of Americans' actual voting preferences. And on this mea-

sure, Clinton—even with her currently high unfavorable ratings—is competitive with all of the leading Republicans. For example, the latest Gallup general election trial heat shows 50% of registered voters preferring former New York City mayor Rudolph Giuliani while 46% prefer Clinton when the two are matched one-to-one. In the prior poll, Clinton had a slight edge over Giuliani (50%–46%), though in neither case was the lead statistically significant. It is notable that Giuliani stands as the most positively rated 2008 presidential candidate in terms of favorable ratings, at 59% (with a 27% unfavorable rating), but still does not beat Clinton in a trial heat "if the election were held today."

Clinton also was competitive with McCain in a June matchup, and she led Romney as well. In that June poll, Clinton did no worse against McCain and Giuliani than her chief Democratic competitors, Illinois senator Barack Obama and former North Carolina senator John Edwards. She did slightly worse against Romney than either Obama or Edwards, but she still led the former Massachusetts governor by a statistically significant margin in that poll. Karl Rove's assertion that Clinton's candidacy is "fatally flawed," then, runs counter to the historical finding that candidates' images often change, sometimes dramatically, as the campaign progresses. In other words, Clinton's ultimate electability will likely be determined more by what happens in the next 15 months, while she campaigns, than by what Americans think of her now. It is clear that Americans have been willing to revise their opinions of Clinton over time in response to current events, just as they have, historically, changed their views of other presidential candidates. Typically, a winning presidential candidate's favorable rating is only slightly more positive than negative on the eve of an election. Clinton would need to boost her positives by only a few points to achieve that position.

AUGUST 23
Veterans and the 2008 Election

In past presidential elections, many candidates had served in the U.S. military, so their military records were not a campaign issue. But as baby boomers have replaced the World War II generation as the source of presidential candidates, service to the country has been something candidates with military experience (such as John McCain and John Kerry) tout, and lack of military service, or of an appropriate type of service, has been the topic of investigation and criticism (as with Bill Clinton and George W. Bush). In the 2008 election campaign, military service is the exception rather than the rule on the resumes of White House aspirants: McCain stands alone among the leading presidential candidates of both political parties as having served in the military.

McCain and his nonveteran rivals for the presidency will do their best to court the roughly one in six Americans who have served in the military. Many of the candidates, for example, addressed the Veterans of Foreign Wars convention in late August. According to combined data from the three most recent Gallup Polls, U.S. military veterans nationwide have the most positive views of Rudolph Giuliani, McCain, and Fred Thompson among the leading 2008 presidential candidates. Veterans' preferences with respect to the parties' presidential nominations are very similar to those of nonveterans. One exception is that Thompson is slightly more likely to be supported by veterans than by nonveterans affiliated with the Republican Party.

Veterans' Views of the Presidential Candidates

According to data from more than 3,000 combined interviews in July and August 2007 Gallup Polls, Republican candidates are generally rated more positively by veterans than Democratic candidates. In fact, each of the four leading Republicans is rated more positively by veterans than nonveterans, and each of the three leading Democrats is rated more positively by nonveterans than by veterans. Giuliani has the highest favorable rating among veterans at 64%. Thompson is also viewed quite favorably by veterans: His favorable rating (40%) is roughly twice as high as his unfavorable rating (21%). But 39% of veterans are not familiar enough with the actor and former Tennessee senator to rate him. McCain, the former Vietnam prisoner of war, is also rated more positively (52%) than negatively (40%) by veterans. Veterans' views of Barack Obama, John Edwards, and Mitt Romney are about equally positive and negative. Hillary Clinton is the only candidate who is viewed much more negatively (59%) than positively (37%) by veterans. Clinton would seem to be at a decided disadvantage among veterans, given that roughly 9 in 10 veterans in this sample are men.

Veterans' affinity for Republican candidates is clear, with only Romney not rated substantially more positively than negatively by this group. This is partly due to party identification: Overall, 49% of veterans identify with or lean to the Republican Party, compared with 41% who are Democratic in their political orientation. Among nonveterans, the figures are essentially reversed: 50% Democratic and 39% Republican. But veteran status can transcend political orientation. This is especially evident in ratings of McCain, who is rated more positively by veterans than nonveterans of the same party affiliation. Specifically, 63% of Republicans and Republican-leaning independents who served in the military rate McCain favorably, compared with 51% of Republicans who did not serve. Among Democrats and Democratic-leaning independents, 43% of veterans and 35% of nonveterans rate McCain positively.

Veterans and the 2008 Nominations

Veterans are usually a key target voting bloc for Republican presidential nomination hopefuls, given the group's usual alignment with the Republican Party. As of now, Giuliani (28%) and Thompson (25%) essentially tie among veterans who identify with or lean to the Republican Party when they are asked to name their top choice for the 2008 presidential nomination. This is markedly different from nonveteran Republicans' preferences, which show a strong tilt toward Giuliani. While McCain's favorable ratings among veterans are higher than his ratings among nonveterans, support for McCain as the Republican presidential nominee is no better among veterans (13%) than among nonveterans (14%). And not only does that 13% support figure among veterans leave McCain trailing both Giuliani and Thompson by significant margins; it leaves him in a tie with Romney—who has been criticized for his and his sons' lack of military service—for third place among the veteran vote. None of the other Republican candidates receives more than 3% of the vote from veterans, including California representative Duncan Hunter, Iowa senator Chuck Hagel, and Texas representative Ron Paul—all of whom served in the military.

On the Democratic side, Clinton's strong positioning for the party's presidential nomination is evident from the fact that she is the top choice even among Democratic veterans, a group that in general does not view her all that positively. Her lead over second-place Obama is not as large among veterans (11 percentage points) who identify or lean to the Democratic Party as it is among nonveterans (20 points), but she maintains a sizable lead among both groups. None of the other Democratic candidates shows much difference in their appeal to veterans and nonveterans. As might be expected, then, veterans are not likely to be a key voting group in the Democratic nomination contest. However, they could very well tip the scales in the Republican primaries and caucuses to Giuliani or Thompson, assuming the latter officially enters the race. Veterans will likely rally around the Republican nominee in the general election phase of the campaign, particularly if Clinton is the Democratic nominee.

Are Clinton and Giuliani Coasting on High Name Identification?

Given the early start of the 2008 presidential campaigns, one of the uncertainties hanging over the process has been the degree to which voter preferences for the Democratic and Republican nominations might change as some of the candidates inevitably become more familiar to the public. Do the early front-runners have a greater chance of being overtaken than early front-runners in previous elections? Gallup's initial polling on the 2008 race was conducted at a time when, among the current contenders for the Democratic nomination, only Hillary Clinton was universally familiar to Democrats. By February 2007, 98% of Democrats had either a positive or negative view of her, while somewhat smaller numbers knew enough about her chief rivals to rate them: Eighty percent could rate John Edwards, and 72% could rate Barack Obama. None of the other active contenders for the Democratic nomination has received more than a few percent of the vote, and they can all be assumed to have had even lower name recognition.

According to Gallup's most recent survey, 94% of Democrats are familiar enough with Clinton to rate her, 85% can rate Edwards, and 84% can rate Obama. Based on an aggregate of three polls conducted in July and August, 77% of Democrats are familiar with all three of these candidates, while 23% are not familiar with at least one of the three (generally either Edwards or Obama). This adds up to good news for Clinton. Among all Democrats, Clinton currently leads the Democratic field by about a two-to-one margin over Obama. Furthermore, Clinton leads with 43% of the vote among those who are familiar with all three top contenders, compared with 30% for Obama. Clinton also leads with 53% of the vote among Democrats who are unfamiliar with one or both of her chief rivals. In short, although Clinton's lead shrinks among Democrats who are familiar with all three of the top contenders, she is still on top. The implication of these data is clear: Even as Obama and Edwards build their name identification among Democrats, it would appear unlikely that this increasing public familiarity alone will upset Clinton's lead.

Republican Race Appears Less Stable

The picture is quite different on the Republican side. There are currently four candidates with double-digit support for the 2008 Republican nomination: Rudolph Giuliani, Fred Thompson, John McCain, and Mitt Romney. Among these, only Giuliani and McCain have widespread name identification in their party, currently 91% and 87% of Republicans, respectively. Only 64% and 56% of Republicans are able to rate Romney and Thompson, respectively, either favorably or unfavorably.

As a result, a much higher proportion of Republicans than Democrats fall in the category of being unfamiliar with one or more of their leading contenders for the 2008 presidential nomination. Fewer than half of Republicans (46%) are familiar enough with the candidates to rate all four, while 54% cannot rate at least one of them. Giuliani has been the front-runner for the Republican nomination since the start of the year, and according to Gallup's latest poll (conducted between August 13 and August 16, 2007), he leads Thompson, his chief rival, by 13 percentage points—32% vs. 19%, respectively. According to Gallup's analysis of the relation-

ship between candidate familiarity and voter choice over the past three polls, Giuliani is the clear favorite among Republicans who are not familiar with all of the other candidates in the field: He leads this group with 38% of the vote, compared with 18% for McCain, 12% for Thompson, and only 6% for Romney. However, among the slightly smaller group of Republicans who are familiar with all four candidates, the leader is Thompson, with 33%. Giuliani ranks second with 25%, followed by Romney (16%) and then McCain (9%). This represents a stark contrast to the stability of voter choices on the Democratic side. The implication is that Giuliani is at greater risk than Clinton of losing support as the campaign progresses and his opponents become better known.

The leading contenders for the Democratic nomination are people generally familiar to Democrats. Clinton is the most well known, but Obama and Edwards currently enjoy broad name recognition as well. Clinton maintains her front-runner status both among Democrats who are familiar with all three candidates and among those who know her, but not one or both of her opponents. This suggests less room for a natural decaying of support for Clinton as the visibility of her opponents increases.

The Republican field is characterized by two well-known candidates: Giuliani—who is, and has been, the clear front-runner—and McCain, whose support has faded. There are also two lesser-known candidates garnering significant levels of support, either of whom could eventually challenge Giuliani for the nomination. According to recent data, Giuliani's position is quite strong among Republicans who are less familiar with the broader field; but among those who are familiar with all four, he actually trails Thompson. One cannot simply project the Republican numbers into the future, on the assumption that Thompson's and Romney's strength will automatically grow along with their name recognition. For one thing, the candidates could become less liked—just as easily as better liked—as they become more well known. Additionally, Republicans currently familiar with Thompson and Romney may represent a unique group of voters who are simply more apt to support those candidates; that intensity of support could dissipate as they become better known. But the current pattern suggests the possibility for a significant shift in Republican voter preferences as the campaign continues—and as Romney and Thompson inevitably gain more visibility.

AUGUST 29

Most Say That Presidential Candidates Should Refuse Lobbyist Money

The issue of accepting campaign contributions from Washington lobbyists has become a significant part of the current campaign strategy of Democratic candidates John Edwards and Barack Obama. Both have stated that they will not accept such contributions—and both have criticized front-runner Hillary Clinton for not taking the same pledge. As Edwards says on his campaign Web site: "John Edwards [has] challenged the entire Democratic Party to reform itself and end the practice of taking campaign money from Washington lobbyists." New Gallup Poll data suggest that this has the potential to be an effective strategy for Edwards and Obama. It appears that presidential candidates are closely in tune with American public opinion when they decry the influence of lobbyists and vow to avoid taking lobbyist money. Asked about acceptable ways for candidates to raise money, more than three-quarters of Americans say that raising campaign money from contributions made by Washington lobbyists is unacceptable—the least acceptable in a list of six ways for raising money. Furthermore, two-thirds of Americans say that candidates who accept money from Washington lobbyists cannot change the way things are done in Washington; and overwhelming majorities say that candidates—and Hillary Clinton in particular—should not accept money from lobbyists.

Acceptable Ways to Raise Money

The August 23–26, 2007, Gallup survey asked Americans in several different ways to give their views on the acceptability of presidential candidates accepting money from lobbyists. In all instances, no matter how the question is asked, a large majority of Americans say it is unacceptable. One question sequence included in the poll asked Americans to rate how acceptable it would be for presidential candidates to raise money from six different sources. Accepting contributions from Washington lobbyists came in last on the list.

Americans overwhelmingly approve of candidates, accepting money from individual citizens or from the candidate's own savings and wealth. There are mixed feelings about accepting money from political action committees. A majority also say that public financing from the federal government is unacceptable. And three-quarters say that accepting money from Washington lobbyists is unacceptable. Republicans, Democrats, and independents do not differ significantly in their views regarding acceptable ways for presidential candidates to raise money for their campaigns. The issue of accepting money from lobbyists has been more prominent in the debate among Democratic presidential contenders this year than among Republicans—manifesting itself in particular in the pledges by Edwards and Obama not to accept such contributions. But rank-and-file Democrats (of whom only 26% say it is acceptable) are little different from Republicans (29%) in their views on this matter.

A strong majority of Americans, when they are asked about it directly, say that presidential candidates should refuse to take contributions from Washington lobbyists. The Gallup survey included two variants of questions on this issue. A random half of the sample was asked about a generic presidential candidate refusing to accept lobbyist contributions, while the other random half was asked directly whether or not Hillary Clinton should refuse to accept such contributions. Eighty percent of Americans say that a generic candidate for president should refuse to accept campaign contributions from Washington lobbyists; only 18% say it is okay to accept these donations.

Again, there is little difference between Republicans and Democrats on this question. Support for refusing to accept lobbyists' contributions is 75% among Republicans, 80% among Democrats, and 85% among independents. The other random half sample was asked the same question about accepting money from Washington lobbyists, but with reference specifically to Hillary Clinton. The question included a reminder that two of Clinton's competitors for the Democratic nomination—Edwards and Obama—had made public statements that they would refuse to accept campaign contributions from Washington lobbyists.

Seventy-two percent of Americans say that Clinton should refuse to accept money from lobbyists. This issue has become one that Clinton has found it necessary to address directly. On Monday, she countered the criticisms from Edwards and Obama by saying that she has a long track record of fighting for different issues—and, in particular, for a national health-care plan—without being influenced by special interests, despite accepting lobbyist money. Even Clinton's base supporters, however—rank-and-file Democrats—say the New York senator should refuse to accept campaign contributions from lobbyists. Sixty-nine percent of Democrats say Clinton should refuse lobbyist contributions—not much different from the 71% of Republicans and 75% of independents who share this point of view. More broadly, Americans appear to agree with the argument put forth by Obama and Edwards that candidates who accept money from Washington lobbyists would not be able to change the way things are done in Washington should they be elected president.

Democrats are more likely than Republicans to agree with this notion, suggesting it could be an effective theme for Obama and Edwards to pursue as they try to defeat the heavily favored Clinton for the party's nomination. Sixty-nine percent of Democrats say candidates who accept money from lobbyists would not be able to bring about change in Washington, as compared with 57% of Republicans; while just 28%—as compared with 36% of Republicans—say they would be able to change the way things are done. Independents' responses are very similar to Democrats' responses.

SEPTEMBER 2007

According to a new USA Today/Gallup Poll, more than three in four Americans plan to take time out on September 11, 2007, to reflect on the tragic events that occurred on that day six years ago. Most say they will recognize it informally, such as by saying a prayer, observing a moment of silence, or watching retrospective news coverage of 9/11; but some will take part in more formal observances, such as by attending a memorial service. September 11 appears to have had an enduring, but not necessarily deep, impact on the American public. Seventy-one percent of adults describe 9/11 as the most memorable news event of their lifetime, and 50% believe Americans have permanently changed the way they live as a result; however, only 29% say their own lives are permanently changed. The percentage perceiving that 9/11 has had a lasting impact on Americans' lives is only slightly lower today than it was six months after the attacks: 50% today, compared with 55% in March 2002.

While the poll finds that Americans are fairly uniform in their perceptions of the impact 9/11 has had on Americans generally, it finds a notable gender difference in those reporting that their own lives have changed. Women overall are more likely than men to say their lives have changed (35% vs. 21%), though this is most pronounced among women under 50. The greatest difference with respect to whether 9/11 is the most memorable news story of respondents' lives is by age. Nearly four in five of those 18 to 34 (79%) see it as such, as do 74% of those 35 to 54; but the figure drops to 60% among those 55 and older. According to the September 7–8, 2007, survey, Americans widely believe the level of attention given to the anniversary of 9/11 is warranted. About half the public says Americans do the right amount to recognize the anniversary and 29% say they do too little, while just 16% say they do too much. People who define their political views as "conservative" are more than twice as likely as "liberals"—38% vs. 16%—to say Americans do too little.

Despite the broad impact of 9/11, many Americans know fairly little about the Muslim world or what Muslims think about America. As part of the Gallup World Poll, Gallup conducted surveys from 2005 through 2007 in countries with predominantly Muslim or substantially Muslim populations that together make up 90% of the global Muslim population. These surveys were based on in-home, in-person interviews with randomly selected national samples (urban and rural) of approximately 1,000 adults, age 15 years and older. The Gallup World Poll found that despite widespread anti-American sentiment, only a small minority of Muslims saw the 9/11 attacks as morally justified. Even more significantly, there was no correlation between level of religiosity and extremism among respondents. Among the 7% of the population that fits in the politically radical category—those who saw the 9/11 attacks as completely justified and have an unfavorable view of the United States—94% said religion is an important part of their daily lives—as did 90% among those in the moderate majority. And no significant difference exists between radicals and moderates in mosque attendance.

Gallup probed respondents further and asked both those who condoned and those who condemned extremist acts why they said what they did. The responses fly in the face of conventional wisdom. For example, in Indonesia, the largest Muslim-majority country in the world, many of those who condemned terrorism cited humanitarian or religious justifications for their response. On the other hand, not a single respondent in Indonesia who condoned the attacks of 9/11 cited the Quran as justification. Instead, this group's responses were markedly secular and worldly. For example, one Indonesian respondent said, "The U.S. government is too controlling toward other countries, seems like colonizing."

Those who condone terrorist acts differ from others with respect to politics, not piety. For example, the politi-

CHRONOLOGY

SEPTEMBER 2007

September 2   Christopher Hill, the U.S. negotiator with North Korea, announces that North Korea will disable all of its nuclear facilities by the end of the year.

September 3   President Bush makes a surprise visit to Iraq to meet with Prime Minister Nouri al-Maliki. The president is accompanied by Secretary of State Condoleezza Rice and Defense Secretary Robert Gates. The president announces that an American troop reduction in Iraq is now possible.

September 5   Fox News sponsors a Republican presidential candidate debate in New Hampshire.

September 5   Fred Thompson announces his candidacy for the Republican nomination. Thompson is a former Tennessee senator and has been an actor in films and on the television series *Law & Order*. His first political advertisement airs in the middle of the Republican presidential debate that he is not attending.

September 7   Terrorist Osama bin Laden releases a video in which he promises to continue targeting the United States.

September 9   Democratic presidential candidates debate in Coral Gables, Florida. The debate is sponsored by a Spanish-language media company. Immigration is the main topic.

September 10   General David Petraeus, commanding general of the Multi-National Force in Iraq, tells Congress that progress is being made but that more time is needed to secure peace in Iraq.

September 14   Former diplomat and political activist Alan Keyes announces his candidacy for the Republican presidential nomination. In 2004, Keyes ran unsuccessfully against Barack Obama for the U.S. Senate seat in Illinois.

September 16   At least 17 Iraqi civilians are killed by employees of Blackwater USA while escorting a diplomatic convoy in Baghdad.

Blackwater, a private firm, provides security to American officials.

September 17   President Bush chooses Michael Mukasey to replace Alberto Gonzales as attorney general.

September 25   Speaking at Columbia University, Iranian president Mahmoud Ahmadinejad accuses the United States of supporting worldwide terrorism. During the speech Ahmadinejad defends his right to deny the Holocaust and says there are no homosexuals in Iran.

September 26   The government of Myanmar begins a brutal suppression of pro-democracy protests. The harsh crackdown leads to international condemnation.

September 26   Democratic presidential candidates debate at Dartmouth College in Hanover, New Hampshire.

September 29   Former speaker of the House Newt Gingrich announces that he will not run for the Republican presidential nomination.

---

cally radical often cite "occupation and U.S. domination" as their greatest fear for their country, and only a small minority of them agree that the United States would allow people in the region to fashion their own political future or that it is serious about supporting democracy in the region. Also, among this group's top responses was that to improve relations with the Muslim world, the West should respect Islam and stop imposing its own beliefs and policies. In contrast, moderates most often mentioned economic problems as their greatest fear for their country; they see economic support and investments, along with respecting Islam, as ways for the West to improve relations. Moderates are also more likely than the politically radical to believe that the United

States is serious about promoting democracy. While the politically radical are as likely as the moderate majority to say that better relations with the West are of personal concern to them, they are much less likely to believe that the West reciprocates this concern, and therefore much less likely to believe that relations will ever improve. In short, perceptions of being under siege characterize those who sympathize with extremism.

From many Muslims' point of view, the conflict with the West is about policy, not principles. Moreover, despite intense political anger at some Western powers, Muslims do not reject Western values wholesale. Citizens of countries from Saudi Arabia to Morocco, from Indonesia to

Pakistan, express admiration for Western democratic values, such as freedom of the press and government accountability, as well as for Western technology. The politically radical are actually more likely than the moderate majority to say that greater democracy will help Muslims progress.

SEPTEMBER 4

Democrats Express Decided Preference for Change over Experience

The Democratic presidential nomination could well be decided on the basis of whether Democratic primary and caucus voters prefer an experienced candidate or one who would make changing the way things are done in Washington his or her top priority. New York senator Hillary Clinton—with a comfortable lead in nomination preference polling at this point—is making her case for the nomination on the basis of her extensive experience in Washington, including her eight years as first lady and her six-plus years as a U.S. senator. Her closest competitors, Illinois senator Barack Obama and former North Carolina senator John Edwards, have much less federal government experience: Edwards served one six-year term in the U.S. Senate, and Obama is in his third year as a U.S. senator. Not surprisingly, Obama and Edwards are attempting to portray themselves as Washington outsiders and are focusing their campaign message on their ability to bring change to the nation's capital.

In spite of Clinton's comfortable lead in nomination preference polls, a recent Gallup survey finds that—in theory, at least—Democrats by a large margin consider it more important that a candidate can bring about change than that he or she has experience. The August 23–26 Gallup survey results of Democrats and Democratic-leaning independents were lopsided in favor of "change": 73% of Democrats said changing the system would be more important to their decision about whom to support, while only 26% opted for "experience." A separate question in the poll, on the other hand, suggests that it may not be a matter of "either/or." When asked how desirable or undesirable certain characteristics would be for the next president to have, an overwhelming 96% of Democrats say it would be desirable to have a candidate who "would bring about change in Washington" as the next chief executive. But a majority of Democrats, 59%, still think "a lot of experience in Washington" is a desirable characteristic, while only 11% say it is undesirable and 29% say it doesn't matter either way. Even with the strong preference for change, most Democrats do not value a candidate's having only limited experience in Washington. Just 18% say it is desirable, while 44% believe it is undesirable and 37% say it does not matter.

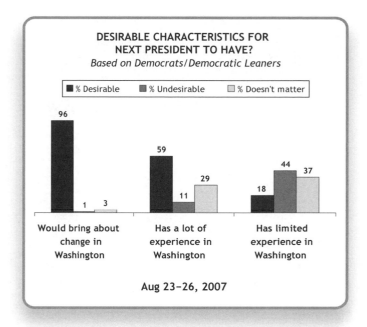

The ability to bring about change is not something that only Democrats are seeking in the next president; 93% of all Americans think this would be a desirable characteristic for the 44th president, including 89% of Republicans. Fifty-six percent of Americans (including 53% of Republicans) believe a lot of experience is desirable.

While change is more important than experience to Democrats by both measures, the results suggest that Democrats still value experience and see a lack of experience in Washington as a drawback. Thus, Democrats may not view Obama and Edwards as experienced enough to handle the job of president. The Clinton campaign seized upon Obama's promise, in a recent debate, to meet without preconditions with leaders of nations unfriendly to the

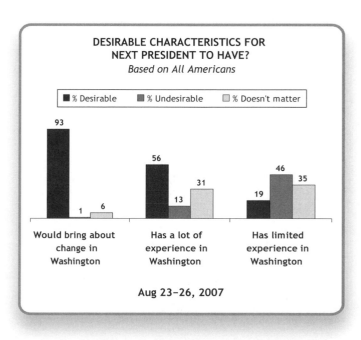

To highlight his support for the Iraq War, Senator John McCain undertook a "No Surrender" tour in September 2007. Here he addresses a Veterans of Foreign Wars rally in Rochester, New Hampshire. *(Cheryl Senter/AP Images)*

United States as a "rookie mistake" that a more experienced political hand like herself would not have made. Other factors might also help explain why Clinton is leading the race for the Democratic nomination even though the desire for change is much stronger than that for experience. For one thing, in addition to touting her experience, Clinton is also promoting herself as an agent of change in Washington, so many Democrats hungry for change may see Clinton as capable of delivering that change and possibly as better able to do that than Obama or Edwards. Thus, while most, if not all, "experience" voters may naturally align themselves with Clinton, many "change" voters may do so too.

Furthermore, even though levels of reported attention to the campaign are high, Americans may not be closely tuned in to the nomination fight to the point where they have well-formed opinions of the candidates and their messages. Thus, the crucial association that Obama and Edwards need to make to succeed—that each is the "change candidate"—may not yet have been made in voters' minds. Finally, Clinton's lead may not be as solid as her wide margin suggests. Many polls show that many prospective primary voters have yet to make up their minds about whom they will vote for.

SEPTEMBER 10

Public Confident in Petraeus, but Wants Iraq-Withdrawal Timetable

As General David Petraeus, commander of U.S. forces in Iraq, prepares to testify before Congress on the situation in Iraq on September 10 and 11, it is unclear to what extent his report will change American minds on the war. A new USA Today/Gallup Poll finds that while a majority of Americans have confidence in Petraeus's recommendations about what to do next in Iraq, most expect that rather than being an objective assessment of the situation in Iraq, the report will be biased to reflect what the Bush administration wants the public to believe. Only about one-third of Americans say the surge of U.S. troops in Iraq is making the situation there better, and most continue to favor a timetable for the withdrawal of U.S. troops from Iraq.

According to the September 7–8 poll, the public has more trust in Petraeus's recommendations for what to do next in Iraq than it does in other key leaders involved in developing U.S. policy there. Sixty-three percent of

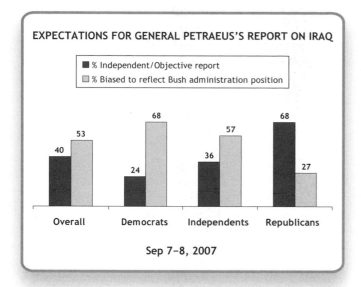

EXPECTATIONS FOR GENERAL PETRAEUS'S REPORT ON IRAQ

■ % Independent/Objective report
□ % Biased to reflect Bush administration position

Sep 7–8, 2007

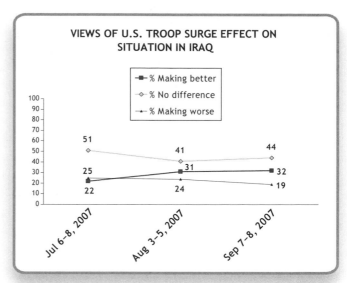

VIEWS OF U.S. TROOP SURGE EFFECT ON SITUATION IN IRAQ

—■— % Making better
—◇— % No difference
—▲— % Making worse

Americans say they have a great deal (27%) or a fair amount (36%) of confidence in Petraeus's recommendations. Fifty-eight percent have confidence in what the "Joint Chiefs of Staff and other military leaders at the Pentagon" would recommend. Americans have far less trust in political leaders than in military leaders when it comes to Iraq policy. Only 38% have at least a fair amount of confidence in President Bush's recommendations for the future course of action in Iraq. Congress fares slightly better than Bush on this measure, with 44% saying they are confident in congressional Democrats' recommendations, and 41% saying the same about those of congressional Republicans. Americans are least confident in what Iraq's political leaders might recommend: Just 27% have confidence in their plans.

Despite the relatively high level of trust in Petraeus's recommendations, most Americans suspect that his report will largely reflect what the Bush administration wants the public to believe about Iraq (53%), rather than believing it will be "an independent and objective report on the current situation in Iraq" (40%). A recently released ABC News/Washington Post poll found a similar result, with 53% of Americans saying Petraeus's report will "try to make things look better than they really are," and 39% believing his report will "honestly reflect the situation in Iraq." It is unclear how much, if any, impact that attempts by the Democratic Party's leadership to cast doubt on Petraeus's testimony have had on these attitudes. The Democrats have been referring to Petraeus's update as the "Bush report." It is not surprising to find that opinions on this matter are highly partisan, with the vast majority of self-identified Democrats in the Gallup Poll expecting a political speech, and the vast majority of Republicans expecting an honest accounting of conditions in Iraq.

Independents are more likely to believe the report will be political in nature rather than objective.

According to the September 7–8 USA Today/Gallup Poll, 32% of Americans believe the surge is making the situation in Iraq better—similar to what Gallup found last month, but a more favorable evaluation than as of earlier this year. A plurality of Americans, 44%, continue to believe the increased troop levels are not making any difference, and 19% say they are making things worse.

One in three Americans say they are now more confident that the United States will achieve its goals in Iraq as a result of the surge; 61% are not more confident.

Americans' Views on Iraq War Policy

Given the public's lack of confidence in the success of the surge to date, it is understandable that the majority of Americans, 60%, continue to favor a timetable for removing troops from Iraq, while 35% would rather see the United States keep a significant number of troops in Iraq until the situation there gets better. These results are in line with public opinion throughout this year. Based on combined results of three questions concerning what to do about troop levels in Iraq, whereas the majority of the public favor a timetable for withdrawal, only about one in five Americans believe the United States should start that process immediately. The greatest number of Americans, 39%, favor a timetable calling for a gradual withdrawal of U.S. troops. Those opposed to a timetable are more likely to favor maintaining troop levels for the time being over a reduction in forces. News reports have suggested that General Petraeus would prefer to maintain troop levels, though it is believed he might go along with a proposal for at least a small drawdown in troop levels in early 2008.

In all, 23% of Americans oppose a timetable and prefer that troop levels be kept the same, while 9% oppose a timetable but think the United States is in a position to begin a reduction in troop levels.

The complexity of Iraq policy is underscored by the finding that even though Americans favor a timetable for withdrawal, they also believe the United States has "an obligation to establish a reasonable level of stability and security in Iraq before withdrawing all of its troops." Sixty-seven percent say this, while 29% disagree. General Petraeus's report is likely to focus on U.S. military efforts in Iraq, but most Americans (56%) believe the United States should do more to address the situation through the political process. Meanwhile, the public is largely divided in its views of whether the United States is adequately dealing with the situation from a military perspective.

Petraeus's report before Congress is required by legislation passed earlier this year that provided continued funding for the war. That legislation also laid out a series of goals or benchmarks for the Iraqi government to meet as a condition for receiving continued economic and military aid from the United States. The poll finds Americans are dubious about the Iraqi government's ability to meet those goals and benchmarks. Only 36% believe it is capable of meeting them. When asked whether they believe the Iraqi government is sincere about achieving them, only 38% of Americans say yes. All told, only about one in five Americans can be considered optimists—believing that the Iraqi government is both capable of achieving the goals and sincere about doing so. About two in five are pessimistic on both counts.

Among the other major findings of the poll are that a majority of Americans, 54%, continue to oppose the war, calling it a "mistake" for the United States to have sent troops. This percentage is slightly lower than what Gallup measured as recently as July 2007, when opposition reached a high of 62%. Only 32% of Americans believe the United States will "definitely" or "probably" win the war, while 62% believe the United States will not win. And consistent with opinion since 2005, Americans are more likely to say the war has made the United States less safe (49%) rather than safer (40%) from terrorism. About half of Americans (46%) say Congress is not doing enough to oversee Iraq policy, 26% say it is doing the right amount, and 22% say it is doing too much. Over the past year, during which partisan control of Congress shifted from the Republicans to the Democrats, Americans have become less likely to believe Congress is not doing enough (56% said this in September 2006), and more likely to believe it is doing too much (14% in September 2006).

SEPTEMBER 12
Thompson's Official Bid Changes Little in Republican Nomination Race

A new USA Today/Gallup Poll finds little change in Republicans' preferences for their party's 2008 presidential nomination. Former New York City mayor Rudolph Giuliani continues to lead other Republican candidates. Former Tennessee senator Fred Thompson, who formalized his bid for the Republican nomination for president on September 5, follows in second place in the latest polling. Americans' overall opinions of Thompson increased to their highest level this year following his official announcement, while their ratings of former Massachusetts governor Mitt Romney have settled back down after a brief improvement following his win in the Republican Iowa straw poll on August 11. Americans' ratings of Giuliani also fell since last month and are now close to their lowest levels this year. Slightly more Republicans say they are pleased with the selection of candidates in the race than did so earlier this year.

Republican Nomination Ballot

The September 7–8, 2007, poll asked Republicans and Republican-leaning independents whom they would be most likely to support for the Republican nomination for president in 2008. Giuliani leads, with 34% of Republicans supporting the former New York City mayor for the nomination. Following next is Thompson at 22%, Arizona senator John McCain at 15%, and Romney at 10%. No other Republican candidate garners more than 5% of the vote. Thompson officially announced his bid for the White House on *The Tonight Show* with Jay Leno, but Thompson's announcement has done little to change the overall structure of the race for the Republican nomination. Thompson's current level of support (22%) is his highest to date, but it is not significantly better than it had been over the course of the summer before his official entry in to the race.

Following his win in the Iowa straw poll, Romney's support increased from 8% in early August to 14% in mid-August. Now, in the latest poll, Republicans' support for Romney has dipped to 10%, but this decline falls within the poll's margin of error. Still, there is no evidence in this poll of a continuation of post-Iowa momentum for Romney. And Republicans' support for Giuliani and McCain has not shown much significant change in recent weeks. Overall, 59% of Republicans say it is "extremely likely" they will vote in the Republican primary or caucus in their state when it is held next year. Among those who are extremely likely to vote in their state's primary or caucus, 33% say they plan to

Five days after announcing his candidacy for the Republican presidential nomination, former senator Fred Thompson greets supporters in Columbia, South Carolina, on September 10, 2007. *(Mary Ann Chastain/AP Images)*

vote for Giuliani, 26% plan to vote for Thompson, 12% for McCain, and 11% for Romney. No other Republican candidate garners double-digit support among this group.

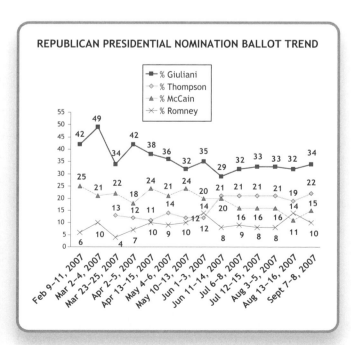

REPUBLICAN PRESIDENTIAL NOMINATION BALLOT TREND

The poll also asked Republicans about whom they prefer to win the Republican nomination if the race narrows down to Giuliani and Thompson or, alternatively, Giuliani and Romney. A majority of Republicans pick Giuliani in both instances, with Thompson faring better than Romney in these head-to-head matchups against the former New York City mayor. By a 53% to 40% margin, Republicans say they would prefer Giuliani to win the nomination rather than Thompson. Thompson's support is six points higher now than in mid-August, but these results are at roughly the same level Gallup measured in June.

Sixty-eight percent of Republicans pick Giuliani rather than Romney to win the nomination next year, while 23% choose Romney over Giuliani. Though only fourth among Republicans on the all-candidate ballot, Romney is the leading fund-raiser and has led statewide polls in the key early states of Iowa and New Hampshire. Republicans are now showing somewhat greater enthusiasm for their choice of candidates running for the Republican nomination than they did in April. In the current poll, 70% of Republicans say they are pleased with the selection of candidates running for the nomination, while 26% say they wish someone else would get into the race. Earlier this year, 61% said they were pleased with the choice of candidates, while 33% said they wished someone else would enter the race.

Favorability Ratings of Republican Hopefuls

Republicans rate Giuliani more positively than any of the other three candidates. Seventy-five percent say they have a favorable opinion of Giuliani; sixty percent of Republicans rate McCain favorably, and 53% rate Thompson favorably. Romney's ratings are the lowest among the four leading Republicans, at 45%. This is the first time that a majority of Republicans have rated Thompson favorably. As Republicans have become more familiar with Thompson over the course of the year, their views of him have become generally more positive. His unfavorable ratings have remained quite low, ranging only between 6% and 13% since April. Among all Americans, Giuliani is rated more favorably than the other leading Republicans. Fifty-three percent of Americans say they have a favorable opinion of Giuliani, compared with ratings of 46% for McCain, 36% for Thompson, and 27% for Romney. More than 4 in 10 Americans do not know enough about Thompson or Romney to rate them.

Following his official entry into the race, Americans are now more familiar with Thompson than at any other point this year. However, 45% of Americans still do not know enough about him to rate him. At the same time, Thompson's favorable rating is at its highest point to date (36%); his previous high was 31% in early August. Thompson's ratings have consistently been more positive than negative since Gallup first measured them in April 2007. Romney's image received a boost last month after he won the Iowa straw poll, but that more positive evaluation has quickly dis-

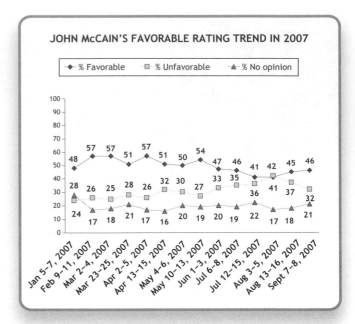

sipated. After a 33% favorable and 21% unfavorable rating in mid-August, his ratings are now 27% favorable and 28% unfavorable. Aside from that one August poll, Romney's ratings have been about equally positive and negative since the summer. The public's rating of Giuliani is also lower now than in mid-August, having dropped from 59% to 53%. His current rating is also among the lowest this year; it was lower only once in July, when 52% rated Giuliani favorably and 32% unfavorably.

Americans' views of McCain have improved since early August, when the public was as likely to rate him unfavorably (42%) as favorably (41%). In the latest poll, Americans are much more likely to view McCain favorably than unfavorably, 46% to 32%. Still, his ratings were higher earlier

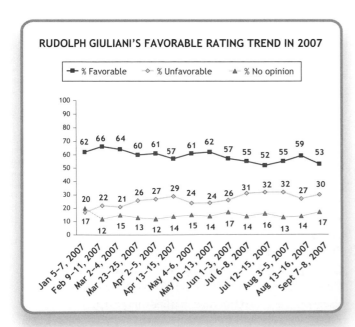

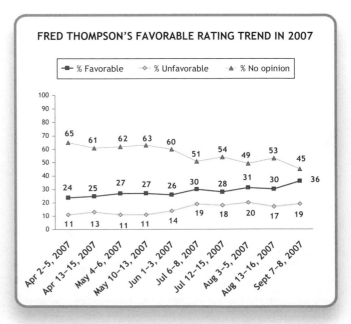

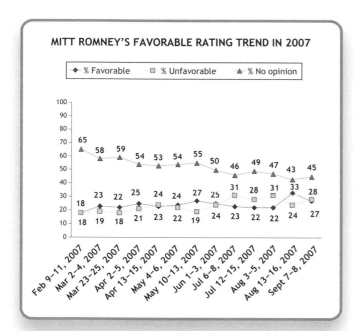

MITT ROMNEY'S FAVORABLE RATING TREND IN 2007

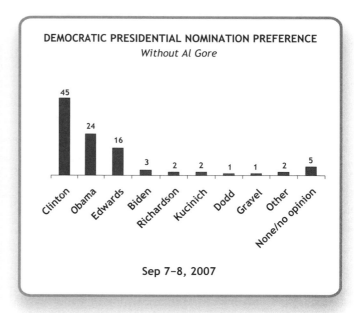

DEMOCRATIC PRESIDENTIAL NOMINATION PREFERENCE
Without Al Gore

Sep 7–8, 2007

in the year, with a high favorable rating of 57% at several points in the first few months of the year.

SEPTEMBER 13

Clinton Retains Strong Lead in Democratic Field

For the third consecutive time since early August, a Gallup Poll finds Senator Hillary Clinton leading her closest competitor for the 2008 Democratic presidential nomination, Barack Obama, by more than 20 points among Democrats nationwide. Clinton enjoys sizable leads in all major regions of the country as well as among men, women, and the subset of Democrats who say they are most likely to vote in the Democratic primary in their state next year. Clinton is currently favored by 45% of Democrats for the nomination, but her broad favorable ratings underscore the fact that a majority of Democrats would ultimately be willing to support her.

According to the new USA Today/Gallup survey, conducted between September 7 and September 8, former Senator John Edwards continues to rank third in national Democratic preferences. The 16% support he receives from Democrats (including independents who lean Democratic) is within the margin of error of the 12% to 13% support levels he earned in August. But if current preferences for the top three candidates are maintained in a subsequent survey, it would represent a slight improvement in Edwards's standing, putting him within single digits of Obama for second place. Other Democratic candidates, including Delaware senator Joe Biden and New Mexico governor Bill Richardson, continue to receive nominal support, as they have throughout the campaign.

Gore Maintains Tie for Third; Has Little Impact on Race

These results are all based on the assumption that former vice president Al Gore will not be a candidate for the nomination. With Gore included in the field, Clinton still enjoys a solid 20-point lead over Obama (39% vs. 19%), while Gore

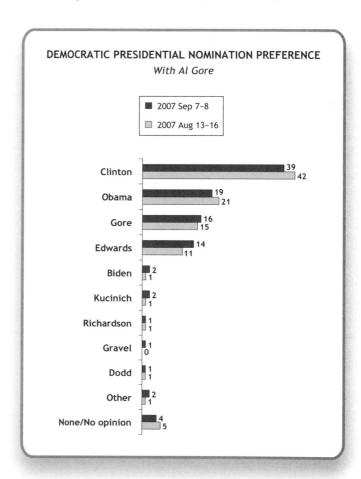

DEMOCRATIC PRESIDENTIAL NOMINATION PREFERENCE
With Al Gore

about ties with Edwards for third place. Although Gore has made it increasingly evident that he does not intend to run for the nomination, his current 16% support is no different from the 15% he received in mid-August.

The Race in Detail

According to the latest Gallup Poll, Clinton leads Obama for the nomination among Democratic women as well as Democratic men, and in all four major regions of the country. Gallup's early reading on voter interest in the primary elections suggests that Obama does not enjoy some hidden potential of achieving an upset victory by virtue of voter turnout. The percentage of his supporters saying they are extremely likely to participate in their state's primary election or caucus next year is higher than Clinton's (63% vs. 54%), but not by a statistically significant margin. Also, the higher the turnout, the less possibility there appears to be for such an advantage, as a similar percentage of both groups (79% of Clinton supporters and 76% of Obama supporters) say they are either extremely likely or very likely to vote.

Clinton is proving to be a formidable front-runner, as not only has she led Obama by a significant margin in all but one Gallup Poll trial heat since February, but she enjoys high favorable ratings in the Democratic Party that extend well beyond her current 45% support level. Three-quarters of Democrats and Democratic leaners have a favorable view of the former first lady, while only 20% have an unfavorable view of her. Obama and Edwards lag behind in favorability because more people are not familiar with them.

Additionally, at least 63% of Democrats are willing to vote for Clinton in the Democratic primaries next year, the

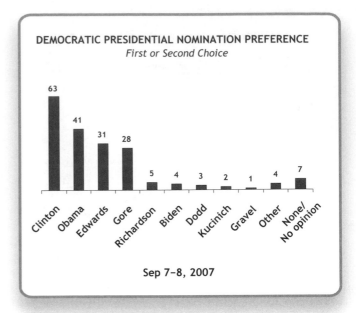

DEMOCRATIC PRESIDENTIAL NOMINATION PREFERENCE
First or Second Choice

Sep 7–8, 2007

same percentage naming her as either their first or second choice for the nomination. The total percentage willing to support Obama, Edwards, or Gore is much lower. Even when given two chances to be named as voters' preferred candidates, none of the bottom-tier candidates is named by more than 5% of Democrats.

Clinton's 63% potential support is identical to the percentage favoring her for the nomination when respondents are given a narrowed-down choice of either her or Obama. This is similar to her showing on this measure in mid-August and represents a slight improvement for her from earlier in the summer.

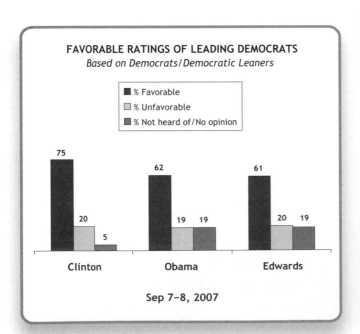

FAVORABLE RATINGS OF LEADING DEMOCRATS
Based on Democrats/Democratic Leaners

■ % Favorable
▨ % Unfavorable
▨ % Not heard of/No opinion

Sep 7–8, 2007

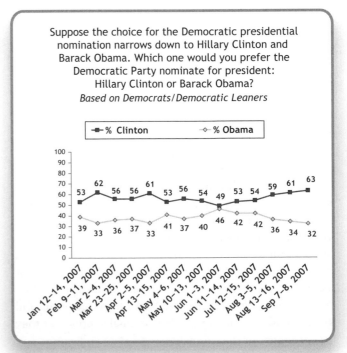

Suppose the choice for the Democratic presidential nomination narrows down to Hillary Clinton and Barack Obama. Which one would you prefer the Democratic Party nominate for president: Hillary Clinton or Barack Obama?
Based on Democrats/Democratic Leaners

■ % Clinton　　◇ % Obama

SEPTEMBER 14

Bush Approval Continues to Hold Steady in Low 30s

The American public's evaluation of the job President George W. Bush is doing has been generally stable over the past four months, fluctuating across nine polls only within a narrow five-point range between 29% and 34%. The most recent USA Today/Gallup measure of Bush's job approval rating—33%—comes from a September 7–9, 2007, poll, conducted just before the beginning of the high-profile congressional testimony of General David Petraeus on September 10–11 and Bush's September 13 speech to the nation on Iraq. Sixty-two percent of Americans currently disapprove of Bush's job performance as president; 5% abstain from giving an opinion. Bush began the year with a job approval rating of 37%, but the rating was at 34% by mid-January—little different from where it is now. His 2007 high point of 38% came in early April, and his low point of 29% was measured in early July.

In a broader context, Bush's average job approval rating for the four years of his first term was a much higher 62%, fueled by the high ratings he received after the terrorist attacks on September 11, 2001. His average rating for 2005, the first year of his second term, fell to 46%, and it declined further, to 37%, for 2006. Bush has averaged a 34% job approval rating so far this year. It appears that approval of Bush has solidified into starkly different patterns by party affiliation: There is more than a 60-percentage-point difference between the approval rating Republicans and Democrats give Bush. At this point, more than three-quarters of those who identify with Republicans continue to say they approve of the job he is doing; only 9% of Democrats approve. About a quarter of independents approve.

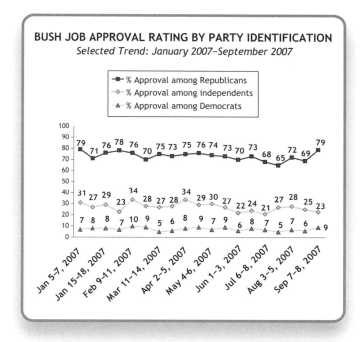

These partisan ratings of Bush have scarcely changed throughout 2007. All but three Gallup Polls this year have shown Republican ratings of Bush in the 70% range (the other three were in the 60s), and all but one poll has shown Democratic ratings of the job Bush is doing at under 10%. The average job approval rating for all the presidents Gallup has measured since World War II is 55%; this puts Bush's current ratings at the low, negative end of the historic job approval spectrum. Bush's current 33% job approval rating, however, is still above the all-time lows reached by Harry Truman in 1951 and 1952 and Richard Nixon in 1974—both near the ends of their administrations.

SEPTEMBER 17

Which Characteristics Are Most Desirable in the Next President?

A recent Gallup Poll asked Americans to indicate whether each of 20 "characteristics"—including candidates' background, profession, and stance on issues—would be desirable or undesirable for the next president to have. The results show that the most desirable trait of those tested would be to bring about change in Washington. A majority of Americans also say it would be desirable for the next president to be successful in business, to have served in the military or Congress, and to have a lot of experience in Washington. On the other hand, more than half of Americans say it would be undesirable for the next president to have worked as a lobbyist or to be 70 years of age or older. Certain characteristics—like a candidate's religion, marital history, race or ethnicity, financial background, and

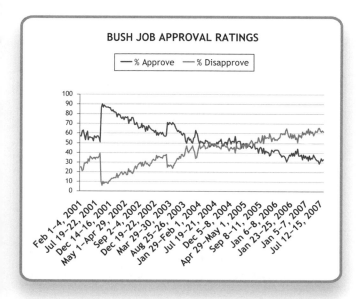

gender—are viewed as neither desirable nor undesirable by most Americans.

From the list included in the survey, 93% of Americans view the ability to bring about change in Washington as desirable. A solid majority of Americans, 71%, also say it would be desirable for the next president to have been successful in business. Other characteristics seen as desirable by a majority of Americans include having personally served in the military (58%), having served in the U.S. House or Senate (57%), and having a lot of experience in Washington (56%). Half say having been a state governor is desirable.

One interesting finding is the fact that a majority of Americans apparently think that both being able to bring about change in Washington and having experience in Washington would be desirable. This is of interest given the current positioning battle within the Democratic Party, as challengers John Edwards and Barack Obama attempt to argue that they would bring about change in Washington as opposed to Hillary Clinton, given her long tenure as a Washington insider.

Americans react most negatively to two presidential characteristics: that a candidate would have worked as a government lobbyist; and that he or she would be 70 years of age or older. Fifty-two percent say each of these two characteristics would be undesirable. Pluralities with respect to each characteristic consider having only limited experience in Washington (46%), having strained relationships with his or her children (45%), and having changed positions on issues over time (42%) to be undesirable traits.

The public views nine of the characteristics tested as neutral: That is, a majority say, in each case, that it does not matter to them either way. These include: being a Catholic (86% say it does not matter either way), having been divorced (81%), belonging to a racial or ethnic minority group (77%), being personally wealthy (73%), being a Mormon (72%), being a woman (68%), working as a lawyer (58%), having a child who has served in the military (55%), and having been mayor of a large city (55%). Still, more than one in five Americans say that two of these characteristics—being a Mormon (22%) and being a lawyer (23%)—are undesirable traits for a president, suggesting that these could have a negative impact in close primary races or in the general election.

Republicans, independents, and Democrats differ significantly on several of the attributes that would be desirable in the next president. Many of these differences may be due to characteristics possessed by current presidential candidates in the Republican and Democratic fields. Still, the most desirable characteristic among all three party groups is bringing about change in Washington—a view shared by 89% of Republicans, 94% of independents, and 96% of Democrats.

There are five characteristics that Republicans are substantially more likely than independents or Democrats to say would be desirable in the next president. Seventy-one percent of Republicans say military service would be a desirable characteristic for the next president, while only 56% of independents and 49% of Democrats share this view. Of all of the leading presidential candidates in either party at this point, only Arizona senator John McCain has previous military service. Republican candidate Duncan Hunter and Democratic hopeful Christ Dodd also served in the military. Nearly 6 in 10 Republicans say serving as a state governor would be desirable; fewer than half of independents (48%) or Democrats (45%) say this. Two Republican candidates, Mitt Romney (Massachusetts) and Mike Huckabee (Arkansas), and one Democratic candidate, Bill Richardson (New Mexico), have been or are state governors. The leading Republican candidate, Rudolph Giuliani, is the former mayor of New York City, so it is not surprising that Republicans (49%) are more inclined than independents (35%) or Democrats (32%) to say that having been mayor of a large city would be a desirable characteristic. Of the other candidates, only Dennis Kucinich, currently a congressman from Ohio, has been a large-city mayor, having served as mayor of Cleveland from 1977 to 1979.

Republicans are slightly more likely than independents or Democrats to say that having a son or daughter who has served in the military would be a desirable trait in the next president. McCain has two sons serving in the military, and Delaware senator and Democratic candidate Joe Biden has a son who is being deployed to Iraq next year. Romney has been criticized for his sons' lack of military service.

Although a majority of all three party groups say success in business would be a desirable attribute, a higher percentage of Republicans (80%) than of independents (68%) or Democrats (67%) say this would be desirable. Several presidential candidates have become relatively wealthy through various business enterprises—especially Romney (Bain Capital), but also Edwards (in the legal field, and with other business associations since leaving the Senate in 2004), Giuliani (various consulting firms and other arrangements), Thompson (acting), and Clinton (book deals).

One area that stands out as a potential problem for Giuliani among his party faithful is his strained relationship with his two adult children. A majority of Republicans, 54%, say this would be an undesirable characteristic in the next president; by comparison, only about 4 in 10 independents and Democrats say this would be so. A majority in both of these groups says this does not matter either way.

Democrats, meanwhile, are substantially more likely than Republicans to say that being 70 years of age or older would be an undesirable characteristic in the next president. Sixty-five percent of Democrats say a president 70 or older would be undesirable, compared with 38% of Republicans. (A majority of independents say this would be undesirable as well.) Two Republican candidates—McCain and Texas representative Ron Paul—are over 70 years old.

Democrats also are slightly more likely than independents or Republicans to say that having a lot of experience in Washington and having served in Congress would be desirable characteristics in the next president. Sixty-three percent of Democrats say it would be desirable for the next president to have a lot of experience in Washington— slightly higher than the 51% among independents and 56% among Republicans who hold this view. Similarly, 63% of Democrats, compared with 52% of independents and 55% of Republicans, say having served in Congress would be a desirable characteristic. All the Democratic candidates are serving or have served in Congress.

Although a solid majority of all three party groups say it would not matter to them if the next president was a member of a racial minority group or a lawyer, Democrats are more inclined than independents and Republicans to consider these two characteristics desirable. One in six Democrats (17%) say it would be desirable if the next president was a member of a minority group, while only 7% of independents and 6% of Republicans say this. Being a lawyer is likewise somewhat more desirable to Democrats (26%) than it is to independents (17%) or Republicans (13%). Each of the three leading Democrats—Clinton, Edwards, and Obama—is a lawyer, and all three had careers in the legal field before entering politics. On the Republican side, leading candidates Giuliani and Thompson are both lawyers. Democrats and independents (each at 22%) are twice as likely as Republicans (11%) to say it would be undesirable for the next president to be personally wealthy, but most in each group say this does not matter to them. As noted above, a number of the candidates are financially well off, with Romney's personal wealth having been estimated at well above $100 million.

The three party groups do not differ that much regarding the desirability of eight attributes: being likely to bring about change in Washington; having changed positions on issues over time; having worked as a government lobbyist; having limited experience in Washington; being a Catholic, a woman, or a Mormon; and having been divorced. Many of the current presidential candidates have been answering questions about their backgrounds, but for many Americans, this involves attributes that are neither desirable nor undesirable in the next president. Solid majorities of Americans say it does not matter to them if the next president is a Catholic, divorced, a member of a racial or ethnic minority, wealthy, a Mormon, a woman, a lawyer, or a

parent of a child who has served in the military—or if he or she has served as mayor of a large city. Still, that a substantial minority of Americans view some of these characteristics as undesirable may be enough to tilt an otherwise close race. For example, that one out of five Americans look negatively on a candidate who is a Mormon could affect Romney's chances in a close Republican primary race. What the public most desires is a president who will bring about change in Washington—something Republicans, independents, and Democrats agree about strongly. Somewhat paradoxically, however, a majority of Americans also say that having experience in Washington is a plus for a presidential candidate.

There are certain factors that loom as larger negatives for some candidates. Having served as a government lobbyist, as recently announced candidate Fred Thompson has done intermittently throughout his career, and being 70 years of age or over, as is true of McCain and Paul, are viewed as undesirable characteristics by a majority of Americans. Limited experience in Washington, which applies to Obama and Edwards, and flip-flopping on issues, which several candidates—particularly Romney—have been criticized for doing, also has the potential to hurt these candidates' chances in this race. Giuliani's strained relationship with his children is also frowned upon by the public—including by a majority of Giuliani's core Republican constituency.

SEPTEMBER 18
McCain Gains While Romney Fades

Former New York City mayor Rudolph Giuliani continues to lead the national race for the Republican presidential nomination, although his support has faded to one of its lowest readings of the year. Former Tennessee senator Fred Thompson, who recently announced his candidacy, holds steady in second place, 8 percentage points behind the front-runner. Meanwhile, Arizona senator John McCain has continued to recover from his early August doldrums and is in third place, only 4 points behind Thompson and more than 10 points ahead of former Massachusetts governor Mitt Romney. Romney's minibounce after the Iowa straw poll in early August appears to have been short-lived. In general, support for McCain has shown gradual improvement over the past month, and Americans' opinions of McCain are at their highest point since May. McCain is now rated as favorably by Americans as Giuliani, and more so than the less well-known Thompson or Romney.

The September 14–16, 2007, Gallup Poll survey finds Giuliani maintaining a significant lead over the eight other announced Republican candidates, with 30% of

Republicans (and Republican-leaning independents) supporting the former New York City mayor for the nomination. Following next is Thompson at 22%, McCain at 18%, and Romney at 7%. Former Arkansas governor Mike Huckabee and Texas congressman Ron Paul each get 4% of the vote. These figures represent some modest changes in Republicans' preferences for their party's nomination compared with just a month ago.

Although Giuliani remains in first place, his current level of support—30%—is among his lowest so far this year. (His 29% support in June was the lowest.) Still, it is not significantly lower than what Gallup has tracked in recent months. Since July, Giuliani's support has averaged 32%. Public support for Romney nearly doubled after his win in the Iowa straw poll in early August, from 8% to 14%. Since then, however, Republican support for Romney has waned, dropping to 7% in the latest poll, his lowest level of support in any poll since April. Thus, on the national level, Romney has not been able to capitalize on his Iowa win to move to a position in which he is challenging the front-runners. The pattern of Republican preference for McCain is just the opposite. He faded to his low point of the year in early August (11%), coincident with Romney's Iowa win and amid widespread publicity about troubles within his own campaign. McCain has recovered his positioning within the ranks of the Republican Party since then, however, moving to 15% in early September and 18% in the current poll. He appears to have solidified a strong third-place showing in the race and is only four points behind Thompson in this poll.

Despite the hoopla surrounding Thompson's official announcement in early September that he was running

Still considered the front-runner for the Republican presidential nomination, Rudolph Giuliani interrupts his speech to the National Rifle Association to take a call from his wife on September 21, 2007. *(Gerald Herbert/AP Images)*

for president, Republicans' support for his candidacy has barely moved in recent months, generally registering 21% to 22% since mid-June. Thus, while Thompson's standing has improved somewhat in relation to Giuliani, his own level of support has not increased significantly. There is a bit of good news for Thompson in the poll, however. He fares better among those Republican voters who appear most likely to vote in the primaries this year than he does among Republicans and Republican leaners in general. Overall, 61% of Republicans say it is "extremely likely" that they will vote in the Republican primary or caucus in their state when it is held next year; Giuliani and Thompson are essentially tied among this group, with McCain a solid third place. No other Republican candidate receives double-digit support among this group of voters.

Republican Candidates' Images

For most of the year, Giuliani has been the most favorably rated Republican candidate in the eyes of the American public. But in the current poll, McCain's ratings have moved up to the point where he is essentially tied with Giuliani as the most positively evaluated of the four leading Republican candidates. More than half of Americans have a favorable opinion of McCain (53%) and Giuliani (52%); 38% rate Thompson favorably, and 27% favorably rate Romney. (It should be noted that the lower favorable ratings for Thompson and Romney are in part due to voters' overall lack of familiarity with them: 39% of Americans have no

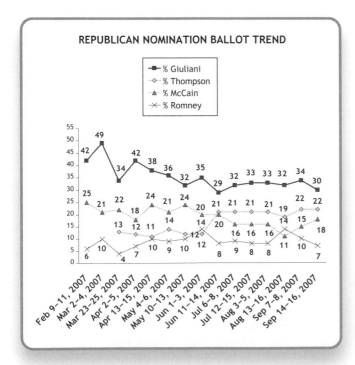

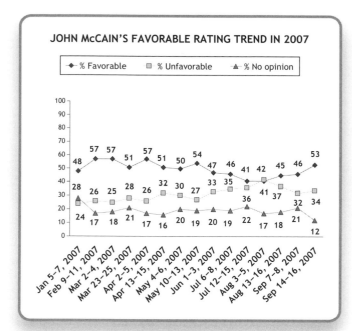

JOHN McCAIN'S FAVORABLE RATING TREND IN 2007

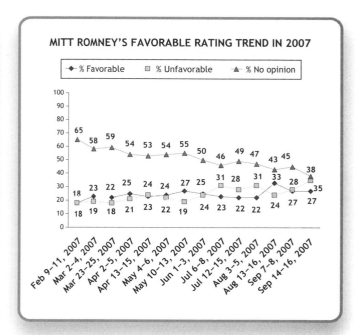

MITT ROMNEY'S FAVORABLE RATING TREND IN 2007

opinion of Thompson and 38% have no opinion of Romney.) Americans' ratings of McCain have become much more positive in recent weeks and are now at their highest level since May. McCain's favorable rating fell under 50% in June and dropped to as low as 41% in August, when Americans were as likely to rate him unfavorably as favorably. McCain's rating has been improving modestly since then, and it is now above 50% again, with his unfavorable rating dropping to 34%.

The public's familiarity with Thompson continues to rise. When Gallup first tested Americans' familiarity with him in April of this year, only 35% knew him well enough to have an opinion; that number is now 60%. Thompson's favor-

able rating is at 38%—its highest point to date, although not much higher than his 36% rating from earlier this month. His unfavorable rating (now at 22%) is also at its highest point, although it has been close to this level in previous months.

While Romney's favorable rating is the same as it was earlier this month, his unfavorable rating has increased and is now at its highest point to date. Romney's ratings had improved following his win in the Iowa straw poll in August, after which 33% rated him positively and 24% negatively. Since then, his ratings have quickly deteriorated. Romney now has a net negative image in the eyes of Americans (27% favorable, 35% unfavorable), as was the case in several polls this summer.

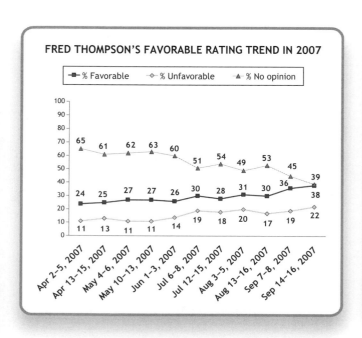

FRED THOMPSON'S FAVORABLE RATING TREND IN 2007

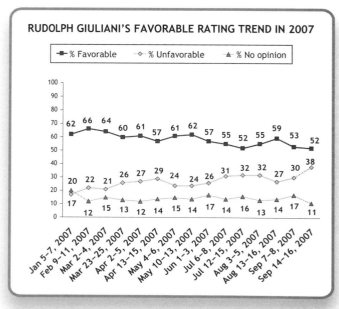

RUDOLPH GIULIANI'S FAVORABLE RATING TREND IN 2007

Giuliani's favorable rating also shows little change from earlier this month, but now ties for his lowest this year. His current unfavorable rating (38%) is the most negative Gallup has recorded for Giuliani over the course of the year and is eight points higher than it was earlier in the month.

Giuliani is the most favorably rated of the four leading Republicans among the party faithful, followed closely by McCain. More than one-third of Republicans don't know enough about either Thompson or Romney to have an opinion about either man. At the same time, Thompson has the least negative baggage among members of his own party. Only 9% of Republicans have an unfavorable opinion of Thompson, giving him the best positive-to-negative ratio of any of these four candidates. The other three candidates are roughly tied with negative ratings between 22% and 25% among Republicans, although Giuliani and McCain have much higher favorable ratings than does Romney, who has the lowest positive-to-negative-ratio among Republicans of any of these four leading candidates.

SEPTEMBER 20

Congress's Approval Rating Rises Slightly

Gallup's 2007 polling from January through August chronicled a nearly relentless decline in public approval of the job Congress is doing. However, after sinking to a record-tying low of 18% last month, Congress's approval rating has rebounded to 24%—the largest one-month increase in support for Congress seen since the Democrats took majority control of both the Senate and the House of Representatives in January.

Nearly all of the recent increase is due to improved ratings of Congress among Republicans. The percent-

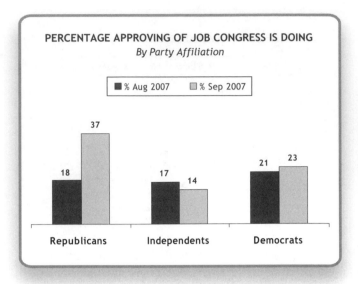

age of Republicans approving of the job Congress is doing rose from 18% in August to 37% in September. At the same time, there was only a two-point increase in approval among Democrats, and a three-point decline among independents (neither of which is statistically significant).

The September 14–16, 2007, poll was conducted just days after General David Petraeus, the commander of U.S. forces in Iraq, testified before Congress on the war in Iraq. It is notable that the House and Senate were in recess for most of August, and thus Petraeus's testimony represents the only significant news out of Congress for the period between Gallup's mid-August and mid-September surveys. Although Democrats did their share of grilling Petraeus during his testimony—and some questioned the general's independence from the Bush administration—just seeing Congress listening to Petraeus deliver his fairly upbeat report on the situation in Iraq may have warmed some Republicans toward Congress. However, other findings from the new poll indicate that the improved ratings of Congress are specific to that body, and not tied to a more fundamental improvement in the public's mood.

Americans' approval of President George W. Bush is now at 36%, the highest since April 2007 and slightly higher than his 33% job approval average since that point. An early September Gallup Poll found Bush's approval rating at 33%, indicating that General Petraeus's testimony occasioned at most a three-point increase in Bush's approval score. It has now been a full year since Bush last had an approval rating above 40%. (That was a 44% approval rating in September 2006.) Public satisfaction with the direction of the country also remains close to where it was in August, increasing by a small but not statistically significant four points—from 24% to 28%. It was

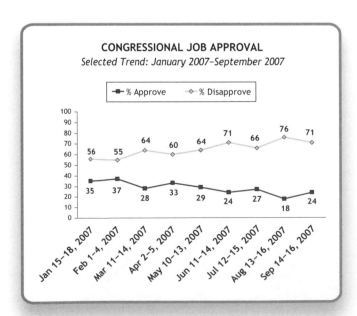

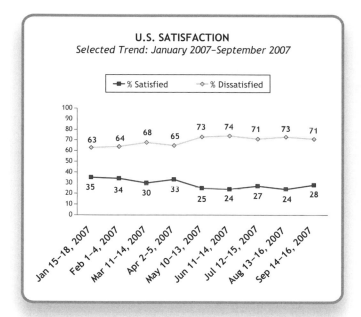

U.S. SATISFACTION
Selected Trend: January 2007–September 2007

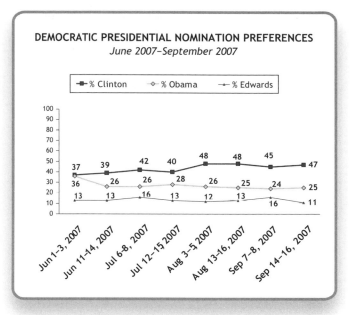

DEMOCRATIC PRESIDENTIAL NOMINATION PREFERENCES
June 2007–September 2007

nearly as high in July as it is today, but it has otherwise been in the 24% to 25% range since May.

Though improved, Congress's approval rating continues to be anemic, still registering on the extremely low end of the historical range of Gallup approval scores for Congress dating back to 1974. A Gallup survey in August 2007 identified disappointment with congressional inaction as one of the public's leading complaints against Congress. Another, mentioned mainly by Democrats, is its failure to bring the war in Iraq to a close. Democrats' approval of Congress has barely changed since August, suggesting that neither of these concerns was alleviated over the past month. Republicans, on the other hand, may, as noted, have simply been pleased to see Petraeus given an attentive congressional audience for his message of staying the course in Iraq.

Clinton as Dominant Among Democratic Union Members as Among Nonmembers

Gallup's latest poll finds Hillary Clinton maintaining the better-than-20-percentage-point lead for the Democratic Party's 2008 presidential nomination that she has enjoyed since early August. Combined data from recent nomination preference polls show that her dominance extends to a key Democratic constituency—labor union members. Even though John Edwards has experienced some success in securing labor union endorsements, Clinton has a substantial lead over both Barack Obama and Edwards among Democratic union members. Generally speaking, Edwards does only slightly better among union members than among nonmembers, while the opposite is true for Obama. Clinton's support is strong and similar among Democrats regardless of their union status.

National Preferences for the Democratic Nomination

Gallup's latest poll, conducted between September 14 and September 16, finds 47% of Democrats and Democratic-leaning independents nationwide naming Clinton as their first choice for the 2008 presidential nomination. Obama is second at 25%, 22 points behind Clinton. Edwards is in third place; his 11% showing in the current poll is down from 16% in the prior poll and is his worst showing in any poll since a 10% reading in March. All other candidates for the Democratic nomination are at 5% or less.

Clinton has had a sizable lead in nearly every poll Gallup has conducted this year. From mid-June through July, Clinton's lead over Obama ranged from 12 to 16 percentage points in three different polls. Her lead expanded in early August to more than 20 points and has remained above 20 points since then, varying between 21 and 23 points. This expanded lead is mainly attributable to an increase in support for Clinton, rather than a decline in support for Obama. Clinton has averaged 47% support since August, compared with 40% from mid-June to July. The respective averages for Obama are 25% since August and 27% from mid-June to July.

DEMOCRATIC UNION MEMBER PREFERENCES

Combined data from the last five Gallup Polls—consisting of more than 5,000 interviews conducted between mid-July and mid-September—finds just 8% of Americans reporting that they belong to a labor union. Another 6% reside in a household with a labor union member. Even given the limited extent of union membership in the United States, however, labor unions are known to effectively organize their members for political purposes, so their influence may be greater than their numbers might suggest, particularly within the Democratic Party. Labor union members are a key Democratic constituency, given their strong support for the party. According to combined Gallup data, 63% of labor union members identify with or lean toward the Democratic Party, while only 28% identify with or lean toward the Republican Party. All told, about one in six Democratic identifiers or leaners are union members or live in a union household.

All the Democratic presidential candidates are pro-union, and each has aggressively pursued labor union endorsements. National unions are now beginning to give their endorsements to the various candidates. So far, Edwards, Clinton, and Chris Dodd have won prominent union endorsements. But the data show that rank-and-file union members who identify with or lean toward the Democratic Party are solidly behind Clinton for the party's presidential nomination at this point—and they differ little from nonunion Democrats in their presidential preferences. The data show that 45% of Democratic union members favor Clinton for the nomination, nearly identical with her 46% support among non–union members. Obama does slightly worse among union members (19%) than he does among nonmembers (26%). Even with significant union backing, Edwards's support is only slightly higher among union members (17%) than nonmembers (13%). The net effect is that Obama (19%) and Edwards (17%) essentially tie for second among union members, but both are well behind Clinton. All other Democrats are at 4% or below among union members.

The three leading Democratic candidates are viewed fairly similarly among Democratic union members: Seventy-seven percent have a favorable view of Clinton, while 72% view Obama positively and 71% regard Edwards favorably. Opinions of Clinton are similar among Democratic union members and nonmembers, but Edwards and Obama are viewed more positively by union members than by nonmembers aligned with the party. This may merely result from union members' being more likely to be familiar with Obama and Edwards than non–union members, rather than the two candidates' having a greater appeal to Democrats with connections to organized labor. Thus, Democratic union members would likely accept any of the leading Democratic candidates as the party's presidential nominee. But the Democratic candidates don't look quite as strong in a general election context among all union members—which includes those who do not affiliate with the Democratic Party.

Obama, Edwards, and Clinton have favorable ratings in the mid-to-high 50s among all union members. But Republican Rudolph Giuliani's favorable rating also exceeds 50%

among this group, and John McCain's is close to that mark. Nearly half of union members are not familiar enough with Fred Thompson to rate him, but among those who do, more view him favorably than unfavorably. Mitt Romney is the only presidential candidate who is viewed more negatively than positively among union members.

SEPTEMBER 21
Americans Deeply Dissatisfied with Nation's Governance

Americans—especially Democrats and independents—remain deeply dissatisfied with the way the nation is being governed today. The current level of satisfaction is the lowest it has been this decade and is as low as at any point at which the question was asked since September 1973. There is no indication that Democrats have become less dissatisfied as a result of their takeover of Congress after last November's election. The question at issue in this analysis is straightforward: "On the whole, would you say you are satisfied or dissatisfied with the way the nation is being governed?" Gallup has asked this question every September since 2001, and before then in the early 1970s, in 1984, and in 1991.

Sixty-seven percent of Americans are dissatisfied with the way the nation is being governed today, while only 31% are satisfied. This marks the most negative assessment of governance in response to this question since Gallup's September 1973 poll, conducted in the midst of the ongoing Watergate scandal then engulfing the Nixon administration. (At that time, 26% were satisfied and 66% were

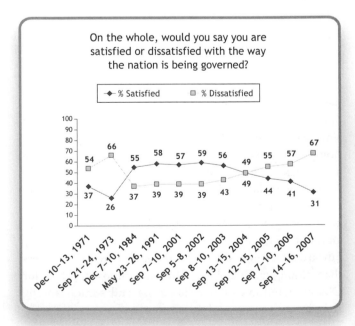

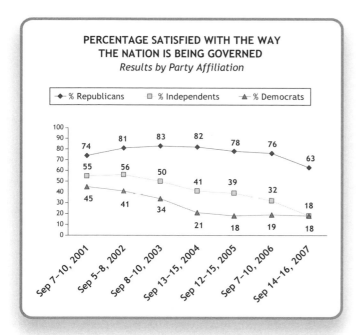

PERCENTAGE SATISFIED WITH THE WAY THE NATION IS BEING GOVERNED
Results by Party Affiliation

◆ % Republicans ◻ % Independents ▲ % Democrats

dissatisfied.) Since 2002, there has been a steady decline in satisfaction with the way the nation is being governed. This is not a surprise, of course, given the fact that most measures of presidential and congressional approval have declined throughout that same time period. Still, these data provide further confirmation of the fact that the status of the national government in the eyes of average Americans is now extremely low.

PARTISAN DIFFERENCES

There is a deep divide in the response to this governance question by partisanship. While more than 6 out of 10 Republicans say they are satisfied with the way the nation is being governed, only 18% of independents and Democrats agree.

While this partisan rift has been evident in each poll conducted since 2001, it has become more exaggerated in recent years. For example, there was a gap of 29 percentage points between the satisfaction level of Republicans and Democrats in September 2001, compared with the 45-point gap today. One might have expected that Democrats' satisfaction with the way the nation is being governed would have improved this year given that Democrats took over control of the House and the Senate at the beginning of 2007. But this did not occur—Democrats are as negative now as they have been in the past two years. It may be that respondents think solely about the presidency in answering this question. Or it may be that Democrats have decided that their party's control of Congress has made little difference in the overall direction of the country and the way in which it is being governed. At any rate, it is also

important to note that Republicans' satisfaction with the way the nation is being governed (63%), although high on a relative basis compared with that expressed by independents and Democrats, is the lowest it has been across the seven September Gallup Polls beginning in 2001—and is also 13 points lower than last year.

Iraq Remains Top Problem Facing the Nation

Three in 10 Americans say that the war in Iraq is the most important problem facing the country—the lowest percentage naming the war since October 2006. Americans are much more likely to say they trust the Democratic Party rather than the Republican Party to handle the nation's top problem; earlier in the Bush presidency, Americans were equally likely to trust the two parties. The war in Iraq is the most important problem in the minds of both Republicans and Democrats, although Democrats mention the war much more frequently than Republicans do. The vast majority of Republicans and Democrats say they trust their own party to better handle the nation's top problem, but Republicans' level of trust in their party is at its lowest point since George W. Bush was elected president.

Most Important Problem

The September 14–16, 2007, poll afforded a monthly update of Gallup's longstanding question that asks Americans to

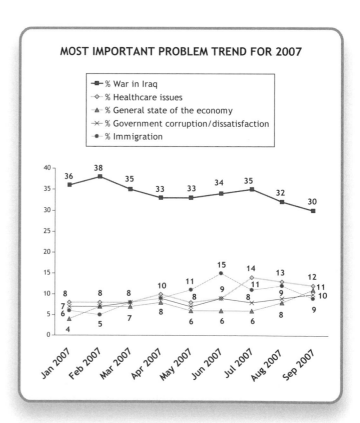

MOST IMPORTANT PROBLEM TREND FOR 2007

■ % War in Iraq
◇ % Healthcare issues
▲ % General state of the economy
✕ % Government corruption/dissatisfaction
● % Immigration

name, in their own words, the most important problem facing the country at this time. The war in Iraq continues to be the dominant problem in the eyes of the public, named by 30% of Americans. Following next are healthcare issues (12%), the general state of the economy (11%), government corruption and dissatisfaction with government (10%), and immigration (9%). Between 3% and 5% of Americans mention terrorism, ethics and morality, education, poverty and homelessness, and the environment. Americans have been most likely to mention Iraq as the nation's top problem since the spring of 2004, but there have been modest variations in the percentage naming it in recent months.

The extent of Americans' belief that Iraq is the nation's most important problem has gradually declined over the past two months and is now at the lowest point so far this year. In July, 35% of Americans said Iraq was the top problem, followed by 32% in August and 30% in the latest poll. (The two-percentage-point decrease since last month falls within the poll's margin of error.) The last time the percentage naming Iraq as the nation's top problem was lower than it is now was in October 2006—when 28% said the war was the top problem. The belief that Iraq was the nation's most important problem was most prevalent this year in February, at 38%—which was the highest percentage since the war began.

The percentage of Americans naming healthcare issues, the economy, and government corruption and dissatisfaction with government as the most important problem facing the country has increased slightly, but not significantly, in recent months. The belief that immigration is the nation's top problem peaked in June, at 15%, and that percentage has gradually declined since then, with 9% now saying it is their top concern. Analysis of an aggregated sample of more than 3,000 interviews conducted in July, August, and September 2007 shows that Iraq remains the top problem regardless of party identification. However, the percentage of each partisan group naming Iraq does vary significantly, from 42% of Democrats to 31% of independents and 26% of Republicans. Democrats (16%) are also more likely than Republicans (11%) to say that healthcare is the top problem. Republicans, meanwhile, are more inclined than Democrats to mention immigration (15% vs. 5%, respectively), terrorism (10% vs. 2%), or ethics and morality (8% vs. 5%) as the most important problem facing the country. The party groups are roughly equally likely to name the economy, government corruption, education, poverty, or unemployment as the nation's top problem.

REPUBLICANS VS. DEMOCRATS AS BETTER PARTY TO HANDLE THE MOST IMPORTANT PROBLEM

The latest poll also asked those who identify a most important problem whether the Republican Party or the Demo-

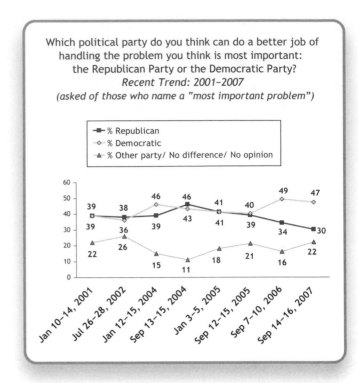

cratic Party can do a better job of handling that problem. Americans are much more likely to say that the Democratic Party (47%) rather than the Republican Party (30%) would do a better job handling the problem they think is most important. Twenty-two percent volunteer that it makes no difference or that the other party could better handle it, or offer no opinion. Those who say Iraq is the nation's most important problem are twice as likely to say they trust the Democratic Party rather than the Republican Party to handle the war. These results are quite similar to those Gallup recorded in 2006, but between most of 2001 and 2005, Americans were about equally likely to say they trusted the Democratic Party to handle the nation's top problem as they were to say they trusted the Republican Party.

Since Gallup first asked this question in 1956, however, the "party best able to handle" results have shown substantial fluctuation. In 1956, Americans were more inclined to say they trusted Republicans rather than Democrats to handle the nation's top problem, which at that time revolved around concerns about war, international aid, and racism. Then, from 1960 through 1984 (with the exception of one poll in 1968), Americans expressed more trust in the Democratic Party than in the Republican Party to handle the nation's top problem, with between 37% and 44% not offering an opinion. Republicans were more trusted than Democrats from 1984 through 1986 and throughout much of George H. W. Bush's presidency—until the 1992 presidential election got under way, when Americans expressed greater trust in the Democrats. Republicans were more

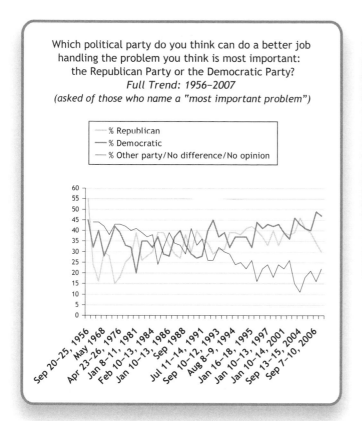

Which political party do you think can do a better job handling the problem you think is most important: the Republican Party or the Democratic Party?
Full Trend: 1956–2007
(asked of those who name a "most important problem")

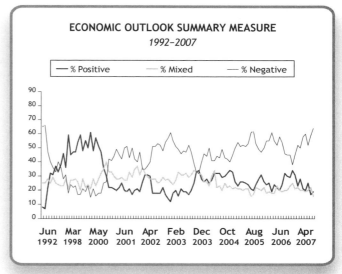

ECONOMIC OUTLOOK SUMMARY MEASURE
1992–2007

trusted than Democrats again in 1994, when Republicans eventually took over control of both houses of Congress in the midterm elections that year, and both parties were equally trusted earlier in the current Bush administration.

The vast majority of Republicans (73%) and Democrats (86%) say they trust their own party to do a better job handling the most important problem as they identify it. Since 2001, there has been little change in Democrats' view of which party they trust to handle the nation's top problem, with the exception of a 2002 poll when this sentiment dipped to 74%, most likely due to the aftermath of the 9/11 terrorist attacks. Republicans, however, are much less likely to trust their party now than at any other time since Bush was elected president in 2000. Since 2004, independents have shown more trust in the Democratic Party than in the Republican Party, with a significant percentage not offering an opinion. Prior to that, independents were equally likely to trust the two parties.

SEPTEMBER 24
Public's Economic Outlook Remains Gloomy

The Federal Reserve Board responded to growing concerns about the economy by lowering interest rates on September 18. The latest Gallup Poll makes clear that concerns about the economy extend well beyond the few who set monetary policy in the United States. Sixty-four percent of Americans

have what can be considered a negative outlook on the economy—they say current conditions are "only fair" or "poor" and are not improving—one of the highest levels Gallup has measured since 1992. Evaluations of the job market are also beginning to show some signs of decline, and the economy is approaching the war in Iraq in terms of Americans' perception of the most important problem facing the country.

The Economy

Each month, Gallup asks Americans for both their assessment of current economic conditions and their view of the direction in which the economy is headed. In the latest poll, conducted between September 14 and September 16, 2007 (prior to the Federal Reserve Board's interest rate cut), just 19% of Americans have a positive economic outlook, 16% have mixed opinions on the economy, and 64% have a negative outlook. Gallup has not observed a more negative economic outlook since September 1992, when 66% rated the economy negatively. Since then, there have been several readings in the 60s—including last May when gas prices spiked, in February 2003 during the run-up to the war in Iraq, and in the fall of 2005 following Hurricane Katrina—but none higher than the current 64%.

This highly negative economic evaluation is mostly driven by the widespread belief that the economy is headed in the wrong direction. Seventy-one percent of Americans now believe the economy is getting worse, while only 20% say it is getting better. It is unclear what impact the Federal Reserve Board's interest rate cut may have on Americans' confidence going forward, but this is the second month in a row in which Americans have been very downbeat about the economy's momentum. Last month, 72% said the economy was getting worse; this is the highest Gallup has measured since it first began asking this question in 1991.

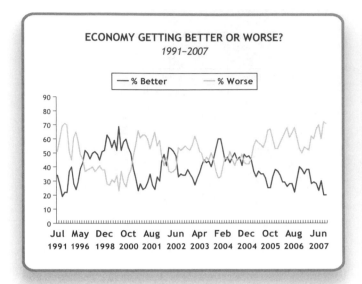

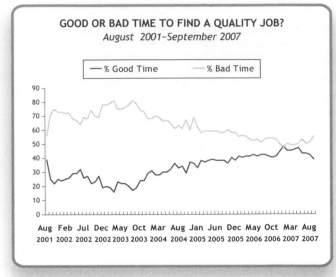

Americans' assessment of current economic conditions are not very positive, either. Thirty-one percent of Americans rate current economic conditions as either excellent or good, while 23% say they are poor. Forty-six percent describe them as only fair. Those percentages are little changed from last month (33% excellent or good, 20% poor), but much worse than what Gallup measured at the beginning of the year, when 52% of Americans rated economic conditions as excellent or good. In fact, the 31% currently rating the economy in positive terms is the lowest since May 2006—when gas prices sharply rose and only 29% rated it as such.

At times, Americans have been much more negative about current economic conditions than they are now. For example, just 18% rated the economy in positive terms in February 2003. Even further back, less than one in five Americans rated economic conditions positively during 1992 and much of 1993, including a low of 10% in early September of 1992.

The Job Market

Gallup's monthly economic polling also asks Americans for their evaluations of the job market. Thirty-nine percent say it is now a good time to find a quality job, which is the first reading below 40% in nearly two years (since December 2005). Positive assessments of the job market were as high as 48% in January 2007 and 47% as recently as May 2007. Evaluations of the job market have been much worse in the past. Since Gallup first began tracking this question in 2001, the low point was a 16% reading in March 2003.

The Economy as the Nation's Top Problem

Even with economic concerns running high, the war in Iraq continues to overshadow the economy in Americans' perception of the most important problem facing the country.

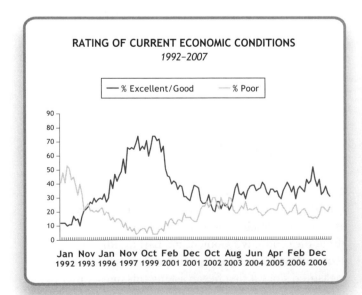

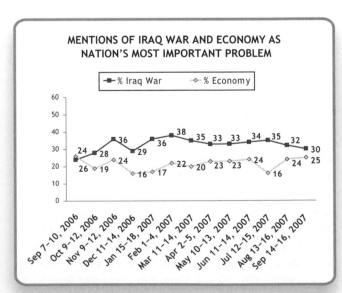

However, the gap between the percentage who mention these two issues is narrowing. In the current poll, 30% of Americans mention the war in Iraq when asked to name the most important problem facing the country, while 25% mention some aspect of the economy, including general mentions of the economy, unemployment, inflation, and gas prices. That five-point difference is the lowest Gallup has found since September 2006, when the two were mentioned about equally. Since last October, the gap in mentions of Iraq versus the economy has averaged 12 percentage points.

SEPTEMBER 25

Democratic Party Maintains Solid Image Advantage over Republicans

Public attitudes toward the two major political parties have not changed much in recent months. That's good news for the Democratic Party, which moved into a superior image position when compared with the Republican Party more than a year ago. Americans not only continue to view the Democratic Party more favorably than the Republican Party in general terms, but they also choose the Democratic Party as the preferred party for maintaining the nation's economic prosperity. And in a departure from recent history, Americans see the Democrats as the political party better able to protect the country from terrorism. According to a Gallup annual survey, conducted between September 14 and September 16, 2007, the Democratic Party enjoys a 15-point lead over the Republicans in overall favorability, 53% vs. 38%.

These ratings are nearly identical to those obtained during July 2007. Gallup's frequent measurement of party favorability in recent years shows that favorable views of the two major parties were fairly balanced between January 2003 and February 2005. In this two-year period, positive ratings of both parties typically ranged between 47% and 55%, with a high rating of 56% for the Republicans in 2003 (shortly after the start of the Iraq War) and a high rating of 59% for the Democrats in January 2004 (immediately following the New Hampshire Democratic primary). However, starting in the second half of 2005, the public's positive image of the Republican Party began to show signs of decline. Since April 2006, the Democrats have maintained a consistently strong advantage in favorability, averaging about 14 points.

The recent gain in the Democratic Party's image advantage is due primarily to a sharp decline in Americans' favorable perceptions of the Republican Party more than to an improvement in the public's perception of the Democrats. This is particularly evident when looking at annual aver-

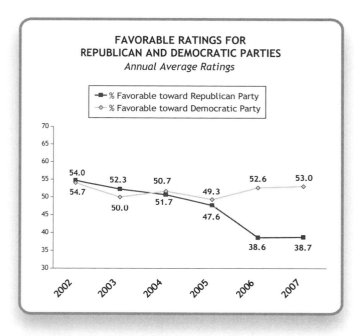

FAVORABLE RATINGS FOR
REPUBLICAN AND DEMOCRATIC PARTIES
Annual Average Ratings

ages of the favorable ratings for each party. Between 2002 and 2007, the percentage of Americans with a favorable view of the Republican Party fell from 54.7% to 38.7%—a 16-percentage point decline. (This was after a sharp rise in Republican Party ratings between 2001 and 2002 following the 9/11 terrorist attacks.) Over the same period, the Democrats' average favorable rating barely changed, falling by one percentage point (from 54.0% to 53.0%).

PARTY OF PROSPERITY

For more than a half century, Gallup has asked Americans whether the Republican Party or the Democratic

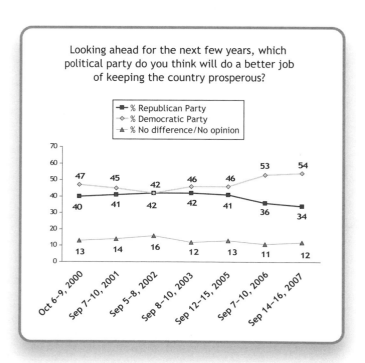

Looking ahead for the next few years, which political party do you think will do a better job of keeping the country prosperous?

Party would do a better job keeping the country prosperous. Since 2001 the Democratic Party has either tied or led the Republicans on this measure. However, that lead expanded significantly between September 2005 and September 2006, from 5 points to 17 points, and it is currently 20 points. Fifty-four percent of Americans now say the Democrats would do the better job, compared with only 34% who choose the Republicans.

PARTY OF NATIONAL SECURITY

Through this period of decline in the Republicans' overall favorability, one enduring strength has been the perception that it is the better party for handling international terrorism and national defense. One year after the 9/11 attacks, the Republicans had a 19-point lead over the Democrats in this area. That lead gradually sank to a statistically insignificant two-point lead in 2006. This year, for the first time since Gallup started asking this question in 2002, more Americans say the Democratic Party will do a better job than the Republican Party of protecting the country from security threats, 47% vs. 42%. These results mirror those Gallup obtained in October 2006 when it found a 46%–41% advantage for "the Democrats in Congress" over "the Republicans in Congress" when Americans were asked which representatives do a better job handling terrorism. Thus, Democrats likely gained the upper hand on the terrorism issue last fall just before the elections, and they have been able to maintain that slim advantage since then.

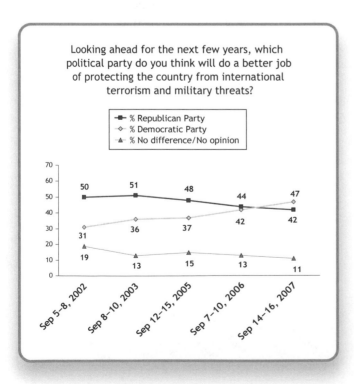

Looking ahead for the next few years, which political party do you think will do a better job of protecting the country from international terrorism and military threats?

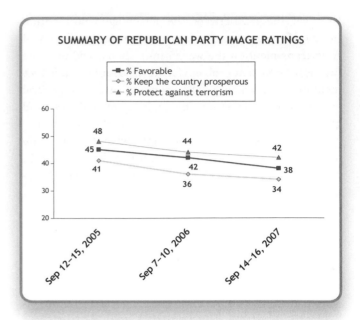

SUMMARY OF REPUBLICAN PARTY IMAGE RATINGS

Tethered to the Party Leader

The recent declines in public preferences for the Republican Party on the economy and terrorism run parallel to the decline in the Republican Party's overall favorability. In turn, public perceptions of the Republican Party appear to be strongly linked to the popularity of the most visible face of the party for Americans, President George W. Bush. In fact, for most of the past several years, the Republican Party's favorable ratings and Bush's job approval rating have been nearly identical.

That strong link has not always been the case. In the period from 9/11 until the end of 2003, Americans rated President Bush much more positively than they did the Republican Party generally, even though both received an image boost post-9/11.

Should Bill Clinton Play an Active Policy-Making Role as First Spouse?

What role would the American public want former president Bill Clinton to play in the White House if his wife, Hillary Clinton, is elected president in November 2008? A recent USA Today/Gallup Poll asked Americans about Bill Clinton's possible role as First Spouse and found a slim majority of Americans saying they would like him to play an active policy-making role in his wife's administration. Prior to Bill Clinton's inauguration as president in 1993, Americans were less supportive of Hillary Clinton's having an active policy-making role in his administration. The public is more likely to express worry that Bill Clinton would have too large rather than too small a role in his wife's

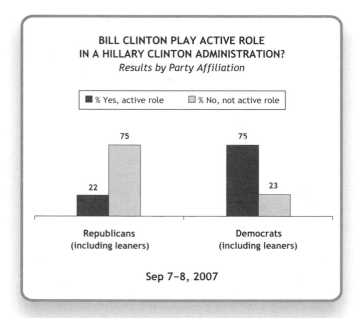

BILL CLINTON PLAY ACTIVE ROLE
IN A HILLARY CLINTON ADMINISTRATION?
Results by Party Affiliation

Sep 7–8, 2007

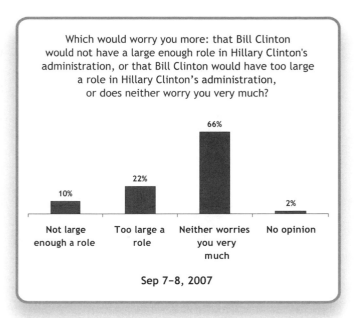

Which would worry you more: that Bill Clinton
would not have a large enough role in Hillary Clinton's
administration, or that Bill Clinton would have too large
a role in Hillary Clinton's administration,
or does neither worry you very much?

Sep 7–8, 2007

administration, although the vast majority of Americans say neither scenario worries them very much. These results are essentially the same as those Gallup measured with respect to Hillary Clinton following her husband's election in 1992. The September 7–8, 2007, poll asked Americans if they would like to see Bill Clinton play an active role in policy-making in Hillary Clinton's administration. More than half of Americans, 53%, say they would like him to play an active role, while 44% say they would not.

Gallup asked the same question regarding Hillary Clinton's potential role in husband Bill's administration following his victory in the 1992 presidential election. In December 1992, a plurality of Americans said Hillary Clinton should play an active role in Bill Clinton's administration. But by January 1993, a slim majority of Americans said she should not play an active policy-making role in her husband's White House.

The opinions of Republicans (including independents who lean toward the Republican Party) and Democrats (including Democratic-leaning independents) differ dramatically as to whether or not Bill Clinton should play an active role in policy-making in his wife's possible White House administration. Just 22% of Republicans would want Bill Clinton to play an active role in Hillary Clinton's administration, while 75% would not want him to play an active role. Democrats' views are nearly the mirror image: Seventy-five percent would want Bill Clinton to play an active policy-making role, while 23% would not. The poll also asked Americans what scenarios would worry them more: that Bill Clinton would have too large a role in Hillary Clinton's presidential administration or that he would not have a large enough role, or if neither worried them

very much. Americans are slightly more likely to say they would worry that Bill Clinton would have too large a role in his wife's administration (22%) rather than not have a large enough role (10%). But most Americans (66%) say that neither scenario worries them very much.

These results are very similar to Americans' views about Hillary Clinton's role in her husband's administration 15 years ago. In November 1992, 26% of Americans said they were more worried that Hillary Clinton would have too large a role in her husband's administration, 4% worried that she would not have a large enough role, and 67% said neither scenario worried them very much. Republicans express a higher level of concern than Democrats that Bill Clinton would have too large a role in his wife's administration. Forty-four percent of Republicans say they worry more that Bill Clinton would have too large a role, while

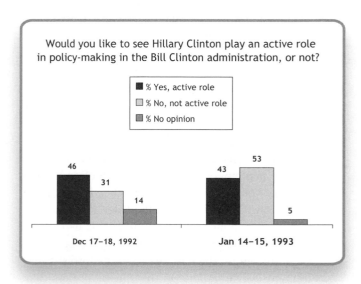

Would you like to see Hillary Clinton play an active role
in policy-making in the Bill Clinton administration, or not?

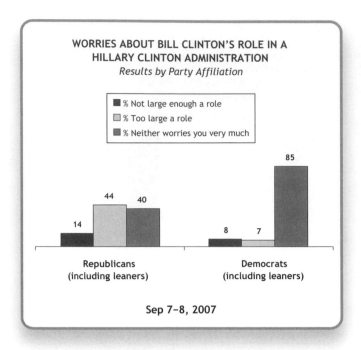

WORRIES ABOUT BILL CLINTON'S ROLE IN A HILLARY CLINTON ADMINISTRATION
Results by Party Affiliation

- ■ % Not large enough a role
- ■ % Too large a role
- ■ % Neither worries you very much

Sep 7–8, 2007

14% worry about his not having a large enough role and 40% say neither scenario worries them much. The vast majority of Democrats—85%—say they are not worried about the extent of Bill Clinton's involvement in his wife's administration.

SEPTEMBER 26

Low Trust in Federal Government Rivals Watergate-Era Levels

A high degree of public trust in elected leaders is one of the basic underpinnings of representative government. Gallup's annual Governance Survey shows that trust in the federal government has continued to decrease this year after showing noticeable signs of decline over the past two years. Americans now generally express less trust in the federal government than at any point in the past decade, and trust in many federal government institutions is now lower than it was during the Watergate era in the early 1970s, generally recognized as the low point in American history for trust in government. Gallup has asked multiple questions about trust in government since 1972 and has done so on a regular basis for the past 10 years, including each September since 2001. Gallup conducted this year's poll between September 14 and September16 and found that barely half of Americans, 51%, say they have a "great deal" or "fair amount" of "trust in the federal government to handle international problems." While this percentage is not appreciably different from what Gallup has found at other points within the past year, it is the lowest single measurement ever obtained on this question. Less than

half of Americans, 47%, now have at least a fair amount of "trust in the federal government to handle domestic problems." Gallup found a sub-50% reading on this measure only one other time, in 1976. (Gallup did not ask this question between 1977 and 1997, and it is possible that lower readings than today's might otherwise have been obtained during this period.)

Given President George W. Bush's flagging approval ratings, it comes as no surprise that "trust in the executive branch of government" is on the low end of the historical spectrum. In fact, the 43% who now express trust in the executive branch is only slightly better than the 40% who did so in April 1974, four months before Richard Nixon resigned as president amid the Watergate scandal. "Trust in the legislative branch of the federal government" continues to erode, dropping six percentage points in each of the last two years (from 62% in 2005 to 50% today). The current level of trust in Congress is significantly lower than any other such measurement Gallup has obtained.

The candidates running for president in 2008 will be trying to win over a skeptical public. Just 55% of Americans express trust in the "men and women in political life in this country who either hold or are running for public office." That matches the low that Gallup found in 2001. Americans continue to express a high—but diminished—level of trust in the "American people as a whole when it comes to making judgments under our democratic system about issues facing the country." Currently, 70% of Americans trust the public's ability to perform its role in a democratic government, which is down from 78% two years ago when we last asked the question and is significantly lower than any other reading Gallup has taken. The one part of the federal government that has been able to maintain public confidence is the judicial branch, headed by the Supreme Court. Sixty-nine percent of Americans have a great deal or fair amount of "trust in the judicial branch," in line with what Gallup has observed since 2003. The poll indicates that the public's lack of trust seems to be directed primarily at the federal government. There has been no observable decline of "public trust in state and local governments." Sixty-seven percent of Americans now express trust in their state government, matching the levels of 2004 and 2005. Sixty-nine percent also trust their local government, similar to what Gallup has found since 2001.

Return to Watergate?

There have been two watershed events in terms of public trust in government in the past four decades. The first was the Watergate scandal in 1972–74, which shook public trust in government and eventually led to Richard Nixon's resignation as president. The second was the September

Still considered the front-runner for the Democratic presidential nomination, Senator Hillary Clinton addresses a crowd of 10,000 supporters in Oakland, California, on September 30, 2007. *(Jakub Mosur/AP Images)*

11, 2001, terrorist attacks, which spawned a nationwide rally behind government leaders and produced record-high approval ratings and levels of trust in government.

Trust in government now rivals the low ebb during the Watergate era. In fact, levels of most of the "trust" items inquired about in this survey are significantly lower today than they were in 1974, though the decline in trust at that time was mostly limited to ratings of the executive branch and of the federal government's ability to handle domestic problems. Clearly, trust has dropped dramatically compared with where it stood in the period after September 11. In particular, the public's "trust in the executive branch" and belief in "the federal government's ability to deal with international and domestic problems" have fallen off by about 30 percentage points in the past six years.

Although such high levels of trust as existed in 2001–2 would be difficult to sustain, the recent declines suggest much more than a return to "normal" levels of trust. For example, "trust in the executive branch" today is down

20 points from its immediate pre-September 11 figure of 63%. There have also been significant drops in the public's "trust in the federal government to deal with international problems" (down 17 points from 68% pre–September 11) and with domestic problems (down 13 points). There are myriad explanations for today's low levels of trust in the federal government: the ongoing war in Iraq, for which the end seems nowhere in sight; uneasiness with some of the methods the Bush administration has used in its attempts to prevent terrorism; and a rash of scandals involving members of Congress, which helped push Republicans out of power in 2006. Additional reasons include a contentious relationship between the Democratic Congress and the Republican president that has produced little in the way of substantive legislation on key issues facing the country this year; and economic uncertainty, exemplified by a volatile stock market and problems in the housing market.

Of course, one of the lessons of the Watergate era is that the American system of government is resilient enough that it can withstand low levels of trust in government. But trust in government is not necessarily easy to restore, and the conditions that have given rise to the decline in trust today seem unlikely to improve substantially in the near term. To some extent, the 2008 election campaign may be the kind of fresh start the public requires to regain its trust in the federal government.

SEPTEMBER 27
Clinton Stays on Top

Since August, Senator Hillary Clinton has consistently led the 2008 Democratic presidential field by a better than 20-point margin over Senator Barack Obama. With a lead of that size—unless the race were highly polarized, which it is not—it's logical that she would also dominate the race among most major Democratic subgroups. And she does. In the four Gallup presidential election surveys conducted in August and September, Clinton has led Obama by an average of 22 points (47% to 25%). Former senator John Edwards holds third place with about half of Obama's level of support, while no other candidate is favored by more than 3% of Democrats and independents who lean Democratic. For the time being, Edwards appears to be firmly planted in third place, with considerable distance between himself and Obama and no one barking at his heels. This assumes, however, that former vice president Al Gore does not eventually decide to seek the nomination. Gallup's test elections that include Gore show him closely matched with Edwards for third.

CLINTON LEADS IN EVERY SUBGROUP OF DEMOCRATS

According to aggregated data from the four most recent surveys, Clinton holds a commanding lead among nearly every major subgroup of potential Democratic primary voters. (This includes all adults who consider themselves Democrats as well as independents who lean to the Democratic Party.) There are certainly differences in the size of Clinton's lead over Obama among various subgroups of the Democratic population. However, neither of the unique factors that characterizes this primary race—that Clinton is the first woman to lead either party's presidential nomination contest, and that Obama is one of the first black Americans to have a solid chance of winning the nomination—skews Democrats' preferences enough to make Obama the leader among either blacks or men. Clinton is widely favored for the nomination by women, whites, seniors, core Democrats, the non-college-educated, those living in low- and middle-income households, self-described conservatives, and residents of both the East and

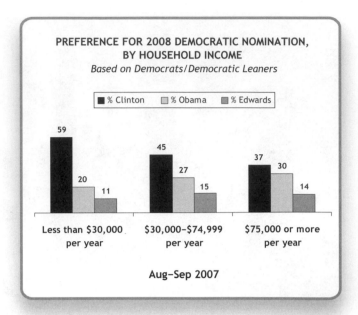

West. And she also leads Obama by smaller but still double-digit margins among most of the natural counterparts to these groups: men, blacks, young adults, independents, college graduates, self-described moderates and liberals, and residents of the South and Midwest.

All of these patterns are nearly identical to what Gallup found this spring in a similar aggregate data review. Thus, while Clinton has expanded her overall lead since that point, it appears that nothing in the course of the campaign thus far has produced any fundamental changes in the appeal of Clinton or Obama to various Democratic groups. As was the case earlier this year, upper-income Democrats represent one of Clinton's few weak links. Among those living in households with an annual income of $75,000 or more, she leads Obama by only seven points (37% vs. 30%). This may help explain Obama's competitiveness with Clinton in fund-

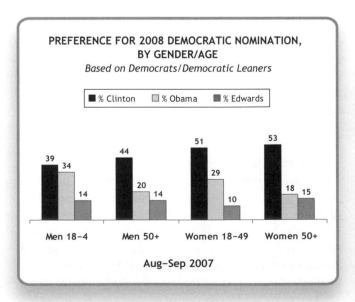

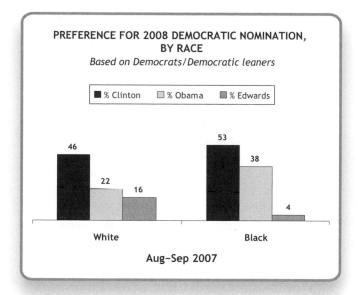

PREFERENCE FOR 2008 DEMOCRATIC NOMINATION, BY RACE

Based on Democrats/Democratic leaners

■ % Clinton   □ % Obama   ■ % Edwards

White: 46, 22, 16
Black: 53, 38, 4

Aug–Sep 2007

tions are more likely than those with no college experience to support Obama. On a much smaller scale, the highly educated are also more prone to support New Mexico governor Bill Richardson.

By rebuilding her strong lead in the Democratic race after it had withered somewhat this spring, Clinton is establishing an air of inevitability around her candidacy. That could make it difficult for Obama or Edwards to pull off an upset in the upcoming primaries. That neither Obama nor Edwards leads among even one significant voter subgroup only accentuates the point.

SEPTEMBER 28

Giuliani Leading Among Most Republican Subgroups

raising—even though he has not been competitive with her in national Democratic nomination preference polls.

Clinton is also in a relatively stiff battle for votes among younger Democratic men. Whereas she leads Obama by 35 points, for example, among women age 50 and older (53% to 18%), she leads by only five points among men under the age of 50 (39% to 34%).

Nearly 4 in 10 blacks favor Obama for the nomination, compared with fewer than one-quarter of whites (38% vs. 22%). However, blacks' support for Obama does not come at the expense of their support for Clinton. In fact, blacks are more likely than whites to support Clinton. Rather, blacks steer their support to the top two candidates, giving less support to the lower-ranked candidates—particularly Edwards.

There is some variation in Democratic preferences according to education level. Those with college educa-

Rudolph Giuliani has led the field of Republican candidates for the 2008 presidential nomination in every Gallup Poll since January 2007. In the most recent nationwide poll of Republicans, 30% name Giuliani as their first choice for their party's nomination, giving him an eight-point lead over second-place Fred Thompson, who registers 22% support. John McCain is in third place at 18%, and Mitt Romney is in fourth at 7%, with the five other announced candidates all polling at 4% or less. While nowhere near as dominant as the Democratic front-runner, Hillary Clinton, Giuliani, like Clinton, leads among most subgroups within his party. In fact, Giuliani does no worse than tie for first in each of a number of key Republican demographic groups. But some of Giuliani's weakest showings are among subgroups of the party not likely to embrace his current or past pro-choice, pro–gay rights, and pro–gun control positions: Southerners, weekly churchgoers, Protestants, and men—in particular, married men.

IDEOLOGY

Republicans are roughly twice as likely to describe their political views as "conservative" than as either "moderate" or "liberal." Giuliani has a lead among conservative Republicans as well as among moderate and liberal Republicans, but his lead is much larger within the latter group (21 points vs. 7 points). Thompson and McCain tie for second place among moderate and liberal Republicans, but Thompson is a clear second choice among the much larger conservative group.

RELIGION

For more than two decades, the Republican Party has been closely aligned with conservative religious individuals and groups. There has been considerable media speculation that religious Republicans are not very enthusiastic about

PREFERENCE FOR 2008 DEMOCRATIC NOMINATION, BY EDUCATION

Based on Democrats/Democratic Leaners

■ % Clinton   □ % Obama   ■ % Edwards   ■ % Richardson

High school or less: 56, 18, 14, 1
Some college: 44, 30, 12, 3
College graduate: 45, 27, 14, 4
Postgraduate: 39, 28, 13, 6

Aug–Sep 2007

any of the leading Republican candidates for the 2008 nomination, given some of their past positions on moral and values issues. While their ballot choice cannot speak to that directly, the data do show that Giuliani does not fare as well among religious Republicans as he does among other constituencies within the party. Specifically, Giuliani (27%) and Thompson (24%) are running about neck and neck among the most religious Republicans—those who attend church on a weekly basis. McCain is third among this key group, while Romney and former Arkansas governor and ordained minister Mike Huckabee essentially tie for fourth. Among less religious Republicans, Giuliani is the clear leader, with double-digit leads.

Historically, every Republican nominee for president to this point has been of a Protestant faith. So it is notable that the group of leading contenders for next year's nomination includes a Catholic (Giuliani) and a Mormon, or member of the Church of Jesus Christ of Latter-day Saints (Romney). Giuliani leads the field by a wide 26-point margin among Republican Catholics. But he has a much smaller, five-point lead among Republican Protestants (including those who identify as "Christian" but do not mention a specific Christian denomination). Romney is supported by 8% of Republican Protestants, not appreciably worse than his showing among Republicans generally. That is notable because Gallup research has shown that a majority of Protestants have a negative view of the Mormon religion.

REGION

Much of the Republican Party's success in electoral politics can be attributed to its strength in the South. Thus, it is important for a Republican presidential candidate to demonstrate an appeal to Southerners. Giuliani and Thompson have been running even among Republicans living in the South, with McCain and, especially, Romney trailing by significant margins there. As is usually the case in nomination campaigns, there is a strong "native son" effect in support of various candidates. Thompson (the South), Giuliani (the Northeast), and McCain (the West) all have the greatest support in their home regions. Romney's best showings are in the Northeast—the home region for the former Massachusetts governor—and in the West, which has a large population of Mormons and where he is known for his leadership of the 2002 Winter Olympics in Salt Lake City, Utah.

OCTOBER 2007

Americans consistently rank healthcare as one of the top domestic issues they want the president and Congress to focus on. Not surprisingly, nearly all of the leading 2008 presidential candidates have put forth position papers or plans for reforming the nation's healthcare system. These include various Democratic proposals for government-funded healthcare programs as well as various Republican proposals for making private health insurance more affordable and accessible. From September 24 to September 27, 2007, Gallup evaluated public support for 12 of these plans and, remarkably, found majority support for all of them. The implication? Americans may be receptive to almost any remedy for improving the nation's healthcare system.

Americans generally support all of the healthcare proposals Gallup tested, ranging from a national healthcare system akin to the Canadian and European systems to government deregulation of healthcare aimed at increasing competition among private healthcare providers. However, support levels span a wide range, from 53% to 94%. Additionally, some of the plans are more controversial than others, with a majority of Democrats favoring them and a majority of Republicans opposed. The broadest support levels are generally seen for proposals aimed at expanding Americans' access to private health insurance, with relatively modest levels of government funding. There is near-universal support (94% in favor) for giving tax breaks to small businesses to allow them to provide health insurance for their employees. Nearly as many (86%) favor allowing American workers to keep the same medical insurance when they change jobs. About four in five Americans (81%) favor requiring large companies either to offer health insurance coverage to their employees or to pay into a pool that would be used to pay for health insurance. Along the same lines, 77% favor reducing government regulation to allow more health insurance providers to compete in the system. Seventy-six percent favor providing government subsidies to help lower-income Americans buy health insurance. And 81% of Americans favor providing incentives in health insurance plans for those who can demonstrate that they live healthy lifestyles. Three proposals are favored by approximately two-thirds of Americans. Nearly 7 in 10 (69%) favor so-called tort reform laws that would limit the amount of money awarded in malpractice suits against doctors, and 68 percent favor providing American families with a $15,000 tax credit to allow them to buy private health insurance. The same percentage (68%) favor having the federal government help fund state-run healthcare programs that attempt to address the health insurance situations of each state.

The three least-favored approaches, though still supported by a majority of Americans, were 1) establishing a national healthcare system funded by the government, similar to those in Canada and Europe (54% in favor); 2) repealing the federal income tax cuts passed in 2001 and 2002 and using that money to pay for new healthcare programs (54%); and 3) requiring every American to carry some form of health insurance (53%). Notably, these three proposals are the only proposals measured that do not receive bipartisan public support. They are each supported by a majority of Democrats, but by fewer than half of Republicans. By contrast, the most popular programs on the list receive broad bipartisan support, with nearly equal levels of Republicans and Democrats favoring them. The proposals can also be arrayed on a government-private continuum, where a national health system run by the federal government is the most extreme government solution, and reducing government regulation of healthcare to allow for more competition among health insurance providers is the most extreme private solution. Yet, there is no clear ideological pattern in the support levels for these proposals. Whereas only 54% of Americans favor a national

CHRONOLOGY

OCTOBER 2007

October 2 Senator Hillary Clinton's campaign announces it has exceeded Senator Obama's donations since July, stripping him at least temporarily of a crucial political advantage.

October 3 President Bush vetoes the Children's Health Insurance Program. In his veto statement, the president says that "the bill moves our health system in the wrong direction."

October 6 Pakistani president Pervez Musharraf is overwhelmingly re-elected president of Pakistan by that nation's legislature. Key opposition leaders boycott the vote.

October 9 Republican presidential candidates debate in Dearborn, Michigan.

October 12 Former vice president Al Gore wins the Nobel Peace Prize for his work warning of the dangers of global warming. He shares the prize with the Intergovernmental Panel on Climate Change, a scientific group that evaluates the risk of climate change caused by human activity.

October 14 Republican presidential candidates debate in Manchester, New Hampshire.

October 17 The Senate Judiciary Committee begins confirmation hearings for Michael Mukasey, President Bush's choice to become attorney general.

October 18 Former prime minister Benazir Bhutto arrives in Pakistan to excited crowds. She escapes an attack that kills more than 100 people.

October 18 Oil prices reach $90 a barrel.

October 19 Sam Brownback drops out of the race for the Republican presidential nomination.

October 20 Republican Bobby Jindal, age 36, is elected governor of Louisiana, the first Indian-American governor in the United States. He is seen as a rising star in the Republican Party.

October 21 Fox News hosts a Republican presidential debate in Orlando, Florida.

October 21 ABC News and the *New Hampshire Union Leader* host a Democratic presidential debate in New Hampshire.

October 30 Democratic presidential candidates debate in Philadelphia.

---

healthcare system, 68% favor another approach that also sounds "government-heavy": state-run programs paid for in part by the federal government. And that is roughly the same level of support offered for one of the most popular private reforms: placing limits on the amount of money awarded in medical malpractice suits (69%).

Previous Gallup polling has shown that most Americans who have health insurance say they are satisfied with their own healthcare coverage and are even satisfied with the costs they pay for that coverage. However, Gallup has documented that healthcare is viewed as one of the nation's top domestic problems and is also one of the top three issues Americans say will be the basis for their vote in the coming presidential election. Additionally, healthcare is cited near the top of the list when Americans are asked to name the biggest financial problems facing their families. For these reasons, healthcare presents itself as an attractive issue for political candidates to champion. Indeed, as found in the most recent poll, Americans are amenable to a broad array of proposals aimed at improv-

ing the nation's healthcare system. And they are not especially ideological in their preferences. Policy makers eager to make some progress on healthcare reform might consider focusing their efforts on expanding access to private health insurance, as these proposals tend to receive the highest and most bipartisan support. There is likely to be much more resistance—particularly from Republicans—when it comes to major government expenditures or a government takeover of healthcare. Still, even establishing a national healthcare plan is currently favored by more than half the American public.

OCTOBER 1
Who Likes Clinton, and Who Doesn't?

Americans' opinions about New York senator Hillary Clinton mirror the underlying partisan divide in the American population today. According to an analysis of a special aggregated sample of more than 7,000 interviews in which

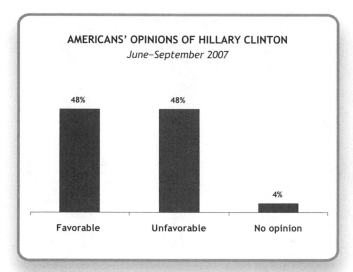

AMERICANS' OPINIONS OF HILLARY CLINTON
June–September 2007

48%	48%	4%
Favorable	Unfavorable	No opinion

Americans were asked to rate Clinton, all conducted between June and September 2007, the public is split precisely down the middle when asked whether its opinions of Clinton are favorable or unfavorable.

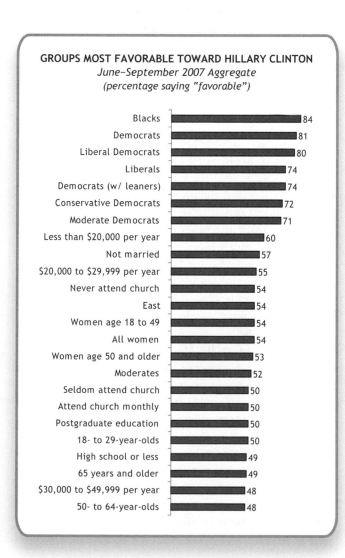

GROUPS MOST FAVORABLE TOWARD HILLARY CLINTON
June–September 2007 Aggregate
(percentage saying "favorable")

Blacks	84
Democrats	81
Liberal Democrats	80
Liberals	74
Democrats (w/ leaners)	74
Conservative Democrats	72
Moderate Democrats	71
Less than $20,000 per year	60
Not married	57
$20,000 to $29,999 per year	55
Never attend church	54
East	54
Women age 18 to 49	54
All women	54
Women age 50 and older	53
Moderates	52
Seldom attend church	50
Attend church monthly	50
Postgraduate education	50
18- to 29-year-olds	50
High school or less	49
65 years and older	49
$30,000 to $49,999 per year	48
50- to 64-year-olds	48

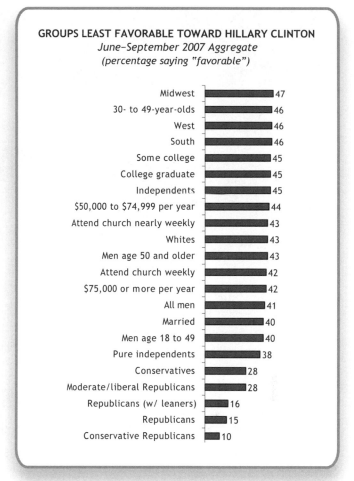

GROUPS LEAST FAVORABLE TOWARD HILLARY CLINTON
June–September 2007 Aggregate
(percentage saying "favorable")

Midwest	47
30- to 49-year-olds	46
West	46
South	46
Some college	45
College graduate	45
Independents	45
$50,000 to $74,999 per year	44
Attend church nearly weekly	43
Whites	43
Men age 50 and older	43
Attend church weekly	42
$75,000 or more per year	42
All men	41
Married	40
Men age 18 to 49	40
Pure independents	38
Conservatives	28
Moderate/liberal Republicans	28
Republicans (w/ leaners)	16
Republicans	15
Conservative Republicans	10

Forty-eight percent of Americans have a favorable opinion of Clinton; 48% have an unfavorable opinion. Only 4% don't have an opinion of Clinton, making her one of the nation's most well-recognized (and polarizing) political figures. But just who is most likely to have a favorable opinion of Clinton, and who is least likely to have a favorable opinion? To help answer that question, Gallup analyzed opinions of Clinton among a large number of subgroups of the American population, defined by age, gender, education, race, region, church attendance, income, marital status, partisanship, and ideology.

It is immediately apparent that there are three major variables highly related to opinions of Clinton in today's America: the respondent's race, party identification, and self-reported ideology. Beyond members of groups defined by these three variables, however, differences in favorable ratings of Clinton across these subgroups are relatively small: Most ratings are fewer than 10 points above the 48% average for the sample. Women, for example, have a favorable rating of Clinton just six points above the national average (54%). While this is significantly different from the rating among men (41%), the gender gap is much, much

Former president Bill Clinton and daughter Chelsea listen as Senator Hillary Clinton speaks at a birthday celebration in New York City on October 25, 2007, a day before her 60th birthday. *(Frank Franklin II/AP Images)*

smaller than the party or ideology gap. Similarly, those who live in the East—which encompasses New York, the state Clinton represents—give Clinton a favorable rating just six points higher than the average (54%). Many of the observed differences are statistically significant, given the large size of the data set. But a rating six points above the average seems of only modest importance, especially when evaluated against the large differences by party and ideology.

Once again, it is apparent that party affiliation and ideology are the major factors driving Americans' opinions of Clinton. The groups at the bottom—that is, those with the least favorable opinions of Clinton—are Republicans (15%) and conservative Republicans (10%).

OCTOBER 2

Churchgoing Protestants Not Embracing Romney

In order to win the 2008 election, it is important for the Republican presidential candidate to fare well among religious Protestants, a core party constituency. Former Massachusetts governor Mitt Romney, a member of the Church of Jesus Christ of Latter-day Saints, faces a unique challenge in trying to win the support of these voters, who have a decidedly negative view of the Mormon Church. An analysis of recent Gallup Poll data shows that Romney is viewed almost as negatively as positively by churchgoing Protestants, while the other major Republican contenders are viewed much more positively than negatively by this group. National Gallup Polls also show Romney fares worse among churchgoing Protestants than among the party more generally when Republicans are asked for their preferred presidential nominee.

PROTESTANTS AND THE MORMON RELIGION

Differences in their views of Jesus Christ and of scripture have divided Mormons from adherents of other Christian faiths. In fact, because of these differences, some Christians do not consider Mormonism to be a Christian faith at all, even though Mormons share with conventional Christians the basic belief in Jesus Christ as Savior. In February 2007, a Gallup Poll found that 52% of Protestants had a negative opinion of the Mormon Church, and an even higher 64% of Protestants who attend church weekly did so. That compares with a 46% negative rating among all Americans.

That negativity carries over to the political sphere to a large degree: Combined data from February and March Gallup Polls found 37% of churchgoing Protestants saying they would not vote for a qualified Mormon candidate for president, significantly higher than the 26% of all Protestants and 22% of all Americans who said the same. Churchgoing Protestants did not show similar opposition to voting for either a Catholic or a Jewish presidential candidate.

Thus it is clear that Romney has a lot to overcome to win the support of religious Protestants, and recent Gallup Poll data make clear that, to this point, he has not been very successful in doing so. The following analyses are based on combined data from the last three Gallup Polls that included respondents' religious affiliation, their reported churchgoing behavior, and their ratings of the leading presidential candidates. All told, the data include interviews with more than 3,000 Americans, including 1,700 Protestants, conducted between August 13 and September 16, 2007.

OPINIONS OF ROMNEY AMONG CHURCHGOING PROTESTANTS

Gallup gauges overall candidate appeal by asking Americans whether they have a favorable or unfavorable opinion of a candidate. Thirty-two percent of churchgoing Protestants view Romney favorably, and 29% view him unfavorably—resulting in a net favorable rating of +3 among this subgroup. That net favorable rating among churchgoing Protestants, however, is far worse than the ratings of his chief rivals for the Republican presidential nomination: former Tennessee senator Fred Thompson (+26), Arizona senator John McCain (+21), and former New York City mayor Rudolph Giuliani (+19). Even worse for Romney, two Democratic presidential candidates—Illinois senator Barack Obama (+10) and former North Carolina senator John Edwards (+9)—have better net favorable ratings among this traditionally Republican group than does Romney. Only New York senator Hillary Clinton is viewed more negatively by churchgoing Protestants than Romney.

As a Catholic who has taken liberal positions on many social issues, Giuliani may have his own challenges in gaining religious Protestants' support. Because of his pro-choice position on abortion in particular, some religious conservatives have threatened to consider supporting a third-party candidate if neither major party presidential nominee supports the pro-life platform. Yet, Giuliani's +19 favorable rating among churchgoing Protestants is still one of the best ratings of any of the leading candidates among this subgroup, and differs little from his +23 rating among all Americans. Romney fares only slightly better when looking at the smaller subgroup of churchgoing Protestants who identify as Republicans (including independents who lean to the Republican Party). Among this group, Romney's net favorable rating is +15 (41% favorable, 26% unfavorable). However, that still pales in comparison with the net favorable ratings that churchgoing Protestant Republicans give to Thompson (+46), Giuliani (+45), and McCain (+41).

OPINIONS OF ROMNEY AMONG OTHER RELIGIOUS GROUPS

Romney's relatively poor showing among churchgoing Protestants has apparently more to do with respondents' religious affiliation than with their level of religious commitment. For example, practicing Catholics view Romney substantially more positively (40%) than negatively (24%), resulting in a +16 net favorable rating. Despite the generally positive review from practicing Catholics, though, Romney is still rated less positively than the other Republican contenders among this group, although he rates as well as or better than all of the Democratic candidates. Practicing Catholics even seem willing to overlook Giuliani's liberal social views, as his net favorable rating among this group is the highest, at +38. Winning over religious Protestants might not be Romney's greatest challenge in terms of being elected president, however. He is easily the lowest-rated presidential candidate among those who express no religious affiliation, with twice as many rating him unfavorably (37%) as favorably (18%). Nonreligious Americans tend to be disproportionately Democratic in their political orientation; they generally view the Democratic candidates more positively than the Republicans. Nevertheless, their views of Giuliani and McCain are still slightly more positive than negative.

Support for the Republican Nomination

Romney is currently running in fourth place in preference polls for the Republican presidential nomination, with 10% of support among Republicans nationwide. As one would expect in light of the above analysis, his support is lower among churchgoing Protestants (7%) than among all other Republicans (12%). Giuliani's potential struggles among religious Protestants are evident in these data: His 23% support among this group compares with 36% support among all other Republicans. Thus, while Giuliani is rated just as favorably as Thompson and McCain by religious Protestants, they are less likely than other Republicans to support him for the nomination. Thompson has a slight but not statistically significant lead among this group, 26% to Giuliani's 23%. McCain is in third place at 16%, followed by Huckabee (10%)—an ordained minister who is outpolling Romney among churchgoing Protestants even though he receives the support of just 4% of all Republicans—and Romney.

When Gallup asked Americans earlier this year about their willingness to vote for a nontraditional presidential candidate, it was clear that a Mormon presidential candidate would have a tougher time getting elected than a black candidate, a woman, a Catholic, or a Hispanic, even though a large majority of Americans say they would vote for a qualified presidential candidate with any of those characteristics. The challenge for Mitt Romney is even greater because one of the groups least likely to embrace a Mormon presidential candidate makes up a critical component of his party's base. So far, Romney has been successful at fund-raising, which has helped him win support in key early primary states. Even if Romney eventually wins the Iowa caucus or the New Hampshire primary, however, his candidacy could stall in the subsequent southern state primaries and caucuses unless he can improve his standing among religious Protestants.

OCTOBER 3

Americans Favor Both Bush's and Democrats' Troop Withdrawal Proposals

It has been well established that Americans favor the initiation of the withdrawal of U.S. troops from Iraq. While all sides in the political debate seem to favor some type of withdrawal, the question has now shifted to how soon withdrawal will occur and how many troops will be withdrawn. New Gallup polling suggests that Americans are not necessarily finely attuned to the nuances of various proposals to withdraw troops. The poll, conducted between September 24 and September 27, 2007, included separate questions asking Americans about two sharply different plans for withdrawal of troops from Iraq. The first was a short description of the plan put forward by General David Petraeus and President George W. Bush to withdraw about 40,000 troops by summer 2008, but not to make a commitment to further withdrawals until that time. The other was a basic description of a plan introduced in the Senate by Democratic senators that calls for the withdrawal of most U.S. troops within nine months, with the remaining troops to serve only in support roles (a proposal that failed to pass in the Senate). The short-term impact of these two plans would be very different. One would still leave 130,000 troops in Iraq by next summer; the other would have most troops withdrawn by that point.

Yet, the results from the poll show that similar, large percentages of Americans favor both plans. Two-thirds of Americans favor the Petraeus-Bush plan, while almost as many (63%) favor a version of the plan introduced in the Senate by Democrats. Only 13% of Americans oppose both plans, meaning that the vast majority of Americans agree

with at least one of these two plans to withdraw troops from Iraq. Nearly half (45%) of Americans say they favor both plans. Twenty percent favor only the Petraeus-Bush plan; 17% favor only the Democrats' plan. There are differences in support for the plans among political groups, as would be expected, but there are also broad areas of crossover support. Seventy-two percent of Republicans support the Petraeus-Bush plan, compared with 62% of Democrats and 64% of Independents; 82% of Democrats support the Senate Democrats' plan, compared with 40% of Republicans and 67% of independents.

The most interesting finding is the substantial support among Democrats for the Petraeus-Bush plan, which would withdraw some troops now but would leave 130,000 troops in place by next summer, with no commitment to withdraw more. A smaller but still substantial percentage of Republicans support the more fast-moving Democratic plan to withdraw "most" troops within nine months. (It is important to note that the polling question did not identify the political origins of either plan.) After respondents had given their opinions of both troop-withdrawal plans, they were asked to choose between the two. When respondents are forced to make this choice, there is a slight preference for the more aggressive Democratic plan to withdraw most troops within the next nine months—53% as opposed to 44% for Petraeus-Bush. It appears, though, that Americans are less rigid about the precise details of the speed with which U.S. troops are withdrawn from Iraq than might have been thought, as long as at least some withdrawal is under way.

While elected officials in Washington, D.C., make fine-tuned distinctions between the various ways in which troops could be withdrawn from Iraq, these data suggest that average Americans are not nearly as specific in their wishes. Almost half of Americans support both of two different plans for withdrawal. Factoring this group together with the smaller groups that support just one or the other plan, the results show that either of the plans for withdrawal of troops tested in this research has majority support from the American public. One interpretation of these findings is that any plan that includes withdrawal has a good chance of gaining at least initial support from Americans. The way the basic questions about the two plans were framed, respondents may have assumed not that they were being asked if one plan was better than another, but rather about each plan as an option in and of itself. Some opponents of the war, in other words, may have felt that any plan to begin withdrawing troops from Iraq was better than no plan at all. The data show a slight preference for the plan that speeds up troop withdrawal to the point where most troops would be gone within the next nine months—but that preference is apparently not so rigid that many of those who favor that option would not support a slower plan as well. In general, the data suggest that Bush administration policy in Iraq is well within the acceptable range for the American public. The results seem to suggest that so long as the administration is beginning the process of withdrawing at least some troops from Iraq, a majority of the American public will be satisfied.

OCTOBER 4
Democrats Prefer Clinton to Her Rivals to Handle Most Policy Issues

Senator Hillary Clinton, who currently leads the Democratic race for the 2008 presidential nomination by more than 20 percentage points in a USA Today/Gallup Poll, is also chosen by Democrats (including Democratic-leaning independents) as the candidate best able to handle many national issues. In fact, according to the latest Gallup survey, Democrats perceive Clinton as the best prepared of the top three Democratic contenders to handle 13 of 17 different challenges that could face the next president: "being commander in chief of the military"; "energy and the environment"; "healing political divisions in the country"; "taxes"; "the economy"; "immigration"; "reforming the way the government in Washington works"; "healthcare"; "terrorism"; "the situation in Iraq"; "crime"; "inspiring Americans"; "education"; "relations with other countries"; "gay marriage"; "abortion"; and "race relations." While Clinton dominates on core policy issues, Senator Barack Obama does relatively well on the handful of items included that tap into the candidates' ability to relate to people and heal divisions in the country. Democrats do not consider former senator John Edwards the best candidate on any issue.

Clinton Walks Away with Top Policy Issues

When given the choice of the top three Democratic candidates— Clinton, Obama, and Edwards—an outright majority of Democrats say Clinton would do the best job on five out of 17 issues measured in the poll. This includes some of the major domestic policy issues that Americans typically rate among those having the most important bearing on their vote for federal offices: healthcare (65%), the economy (60%), and education (58%). It also includes two of the leading "values" issues in today's culture: abortion (61%) and gay marriage (51%). Clinton is preferred by a solid plurality of Democrats on an additional seven issues. Among these are terrorism (49%) and the situation in Iraq (47%). She also holds solid leads on taxes (48%), energy and the environment (43%), and crime (43%), and somewhat smaller leads on immigration (39%) and being commander in chief of the military (38%).

Obama's Strength Is on the Personal Dimension

A majority of Democrats prefer Obama on only one issue: race relations (58%). He also leads Clinton and Edwards with a sizable plurality as the candidate best able to inspire Americans (44%). While being inspiring could be a valuable asset to a candidate, particularly as campaigning picks up closer to the first primaries, Obama's existing lead in that area is evidently not enough to compensate for Clinton's overwhelming advantage on policy issues. Otherwise, he might not be trailing Clinton by as much as 22 points in Gallup's latest trial heat.

Obama's image as someone who can move people is also evident in his relatively strong scores for healing political divisions in the country (37%); he edges out Clinton by a statistically insignificant three points on this item. Obama also ties Clinton as the candidate most likely to be perceived as "reforming the way the government in Washington works"(37%)—something that could require as much interpersonal as political skill. (Reform has been a focal point of the Obama campaign, so the fact that he only ties Clinton among Democrats on this issue is notable.)

Edwards Is Shut Out

Edwards, currently in third place for the Democratic nomination, is not regarded as best able to handle any of the 17 issues. Notably, Edwards receives his highest score—28%—for being commander in chief of the military. This is much higher than his average score of 18% for all 17 issues. The fact that Edwards receives his highest rating on the commander in chief dimension may say more about what Democrats think of Clinton and Obama on this issue than about what they think of Edwards. Clinton could be underperforming on the commander-in-chief item because she is a woman. This is suggested by the fact that she is much more widely chosen for "handling relations with other countries" than for being "commander in chief of the military": 54% vs. 38%.

For his part, Obama may not be the perfect commander-in-chief alternative to Clinton for Democrats. He went on record this summer saying that, as president, he would consider a unilateral invasion of Pakistan to root out terrorists, and he promised to engage in diplomacy with the leaders of nations hostile to the United States. This earned Obama considerable criticism from his Democratic rivals, and it may explain Clinton's expanded lead in Gallup's trial heat polls in the past two months. Indeed, the percentage choosing Obama as best able to handle relations with other countries fell by five points between January 2007 and today.

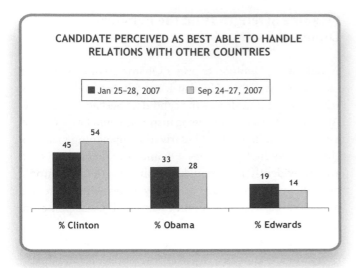

CANDIDATE PERCEIVED AS BEST ABLE TO HANDLE
RELATIONS WITH OTHER COUNTRIES

■ Jan 25–28, 2007   □ Sep 24–27, 2007

45   54   33   28   19   14

% Clinton   % Obama   % Edwards

As a result of these potential liabilities for Clinton and Obama, some Democrats could be naming Edwards as their preferred choice for commander in chief by default. The fact that Clinton does relatively worse on the personal dimensions tested in this poll—for being inspiring and healing divisions in the country (34%)—raises the question of her broader personal appeal. When Gallup last asked Democrats which candidate they preferred on the issues, in January 2007, a parallel question was asked comparing the candidates on personal qualities that might be desirable in a president. In that poll, at a time when Clinton led Obama by a smaller margin than she does today, her ratings on personal qualities were highly mixed: She prevailed on leadership items such as being a strong leader, managing the government, and performing well in a crisis, but as is likewise seen in the current poll, she did worse on interpersonal dimensions.

OCTOBER 5

Republicans Divided over Which Candidate Best on Abortion Issue

Republicans are mixed on which of the four leading contenders for their party's presidential nomination would do the best job on issues likely to face the next president, according to a recent Gallup survey. In particular, there is a decided lack of consensus over which candidate would best handle the abortion issue. Generally speaking, current front-runner Rudolph Giuliani seems to fare better than his rivals, having a clear advantage on some issues, especially in the areas of crime (62%), terrorism (49%), race relations (48%), and being able to inspire Americans (50%). John McCain has a perceptible advantage with respect to serving as commander in chief of the military (43%). Fred Thompson and Mitt Romney—still relative unknowns—

do not fare particularly well on any of the issues. But on most issues, no candidate has a clear advantage over his competitors.

No Clear Leader on Most Issues

The September 24–27 Gallup survey asked a nationally representative sample of Republicans and Republican-leaning independents which of the four leading candidates for the party's presidential nomination would do the best job on each of 17 key issues. While Giuliani appears to have a clear lead on seven of these issues—crime (62%), race relations (48%), inspiring Americans (50%), terrorism (49%), healing political divisions in the country (35%), the economy (34%), and energy and the environment (28%)—on the other ten issues no Republican appears to have much of a lead, if any. When Gallup asked the same question of Democrats about their party's nominees, Hillary Clinton was the clear leader on almost every issue.

The abortion issue has probably been the most controversial in the Republican primary campaign to this point. Giuliani's pro-choice position puts him at odds with the majority of his party, and conservative religious leaders recently threatened to support a third-party candidate if the Republican Party nominated a pro-choice candidate for president. Giuliani is not the only candidate who has had to defend his abortion views. Romney has taken a pro-choice position in past campaigns and has had to answer questions about his recent "conversion" to a pro-life viewpoint. Thompson, who reliably took pro-life positions as a senator, has had to explain his work as a lobbyist for a pro-choice interest group. Even though McCain may have the most consistent record of supporting pro-life legislation, the general perception of him as a moderate may create the misperception that he is moderate on the abortion issue as well.

The poll finds 23% of Republicans saying Thompson would do the best job on abortion, with 20% saying Romney would, 19% Giuliani, and 15% McCain. Notably, the greatest number of Republicans, 24%, do not have an opinion as to which candidate would best handle abortion. That high "no opinion" figure seems to underscore the notion that many Republicans have doubts about the candidates' commitment to the pro-life position long favored by the party. There is a similarly high "no opinion" with respect to another key moral values issue: gay marriage. More than one in five Republicans have no clear idea regarding which candidate would best handle this issue. Giuliani has a slight but not statistically significant 27% to 22% advantage over Thompson on gay marriage, with Romney next at 18%. The results may be surprising given that Giuliani's past pro–gay rights positions are out of step with the Republican base.

But his edge on gay marriage may result from the likelihood that pro–gay rights Republicans choose him over the other candidates, whereas Republicans less supportive of gay rights may not recognize one candidate as superior to the others on this issue.

Healthcare—which may not be as important an issue in the Republican primary as moral values issues—is another issue on which Republicans do not perceive any candidate as having a particular advantage. On healthcare, Giuliani (24%), Romney (23%), and Thompson (22%) are basically even. As governor of Massachusetts, Romney helped to transform the healthcare system for residents in his state, and healthcare yields his highest score on any single issue. The lack of Republican consensus as to which of their party's candidates would do the best job on healthcare stands in stark contrast to the Democrats, among whom Hillary Clinton is clearly seen as best on this issue.

Arguably, the Iraq war will be the most important issue for the next president. Giuliani (31%) and McCain (30%) essentially tie on Iraq. Eighteen percent give Thompson the nod on this issue, while only 9% say Romney would best handle it. Giuliani (30%) and McCain (26%) are also closely matched on a more general foreign policy issue, handling "relations with other countries." Republicans view Giuliani (28%) and Thompson (27%) as best able to reform the way government in Washington works. This is Thompson's strongest showing on any of the 17 issues. While in the Senate, Thompson chaired the Governmental Affairs Committee, which oversees the way the Senate conducts business. Giuliani has slight edges on immigration (an eight-point advantage over McCain and Thompson), taxes (a seven-point advantage over Thompson), and education (an eight-point advantage over Romney), but not large enough margins to suggest that he is viewed as superior to his competitors in any overall sense.

GIULIANI'S PERCEIVED STRENGTHS

Giuliani is currently viewed as the clear leader on seven issues. His signature issues are crime (a 48-percentage-point advantage over the next-highest-rated candidate), race relations (a 34-point advantage), inspiring Americans (30 points), and terrorism (28 points)—all issues he is likely perceived as having dealt with as mayor of New York City. Giuliani has double-digit advantages on several more issues, including healing political divisions in the country (11 points), the economy (11 points), and energy and the environment (10 points). Thompson typically comes in second on these issues, though McCain does on terrorism.

MCCAIN'S PERCEIVED STRENGTHS

McCain is the only other candidate who can claim a sizable advantage on an issue: Forty-three percent of Republicans

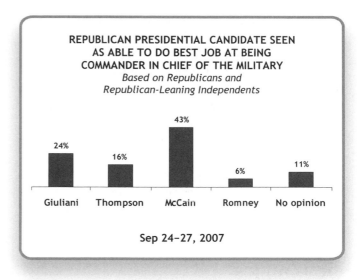

REPUBLICAN PRESIDENTIAL CANDIDATE SEEN AS ABLE TO DO BEST JOB AT BEING COMMANDER IN CHIEF OF THE MILITARY
Based on Republicans and Republican-Leaning Independents

Giuliani 24% | Thompson 16% | McCain 43% | Romney 6% | No opinion 11%

Sep 24–27, 2007

believe McCain—the only one of the four leading candidates who served in the U.S. military—would do the best job as commander in chief of the military. Giuliani is a distant second at 24%, and only 6% say Romney would do a good job as military leader, one of his worst showings.

Of the four leading Republicans, McCain clearly has the strongest foreign policy credentials because of his leadership on military issues during his 20-plus years in the U.S. Senate, as well as his own military service. That is likely why he fares relatively well on the three issues dealing with international matters. However, McCain's standing on foreign policy issues relative to Giuliani has slipped since earlier this year. In January, a Gallup Poll pitted McCain against just Giuliani on a similar battery of issues. McCain scored better than Giuliani on two of the three foreign policy issues tested in that poll (the situation in Iraq and relations with other countries, but not terrorism). In the current poll, McCain is viewed as superior to Giuliani on only one of four foreign policy issues (being commander in chief) while losing his former advantage on Iraq and relations with other countries. He continues to trail Giuliani on terrorism. Those losses may merely reflect the changing structure of the race. In January, McCain and Giuliani were closely matched as Republicans' preferred presidential nominee, but Giuliani emerged as the front-runner in February and has remained in first place ever since. So McCain's slide in the polls may have also brought down his ratings on issues, including those that are his usual strengths.

That Republicans do not perceive any of the candidates as having an advantage on more than half of the issues tested in the poll adds further weight to the notion that the Republican presidential nomination contest is likely to be a wide-open affair. Even though Giuliani has led in polls of rank-and-file Republicans' nomination preferences most of this year, his status as front-runner seems far from secure. Although he shows strength on issues he is likely perceived to have dealt with, such as crime, terrorism, and race relations, he has not convinced Republicans that he is the best candidate to handle many other important issues. Also, his vulnerabilities on moral values issues could end up overshadowing his strengths. By contrast, on the Democratic side, Clinton both has a large lead in the polls and is viewed by Democrats as best able to handle nearly every one of the issues Gallup tested. The Republican candidates' ability to bolster their credentials on core conservative issues such as abortion, gay marriage, and immigration could be crucial in determining the eventual Republican nominee.

OCTOBER 8

Republicans Remain Deeply Distrustful of News Media

Republicans in the United States today remain deeply distrustful of the national news media—in sharp contrast to Democrats, who have a great deal more trust in the media's accuracy. Overall, less than half of Americans, regardless of partisanship, have a great deal or a fair amount of trust in the mass media. Nearly half of Americans—including over three-quarters of Republicans—perceive the media as too liberal, while fewer than one in five say the media are too conservative. Americans are less likely to perceive bias in their local news media than in the national news media.

In general, how much trust and confidence do you have in the mass media—such as newspapers, TV, and radio—when it comes to reporting the news fully, accurately, and fairly: a great deal, a fair amount, not very much, or none at all?

Gallup's annual Governance Poll, updated between September 14 and September 16, 2007, uncovered high levels of distrust on the part of Americans about most aspects of their government, and found a continuation of the high level of dissatisfaction with the way things are going in the country seen for the past two years. Given this generally negative environment, it is not surprising to find that Americans also give the mass media low trust and confidence ratings. The survey shows that only 9% of Americans say they have a great deal of trust and confidence in the mass media to report the news "fully, accurately, and fairly," while another 38% say they have a "fair amount" of trust in the media to do this. This combined 47% great deal/fair amount rating is down slightly from the media trust ratings from 2003.

However, these recent ratings are all lower than the ratings Gallup obtained in surveys conducted in the late 1990s through 2003, in which at least half of Americans said they had a great deal or a fair amount of trust in the accuracy of the news media. Gallup had previously asked this "trust in media" question in the 1970s, when trust levels were much higher than they are today. In fact, in one Gallup survey conducted in 1976, 72% of Americans said they had a great deal or fair amount of trust in the news media.

PARTISAN DIFFERENCES

There are profound differences between Americans who identify themselves as Republicans and those who identify as Democrats regarding trust in the news media to report the news fully, accurately, and fairly. In this year's survey, nearly half as many Republicans as Democrats say they have a great deal or a fair amount of trust in the news media. Independents tend to be closer to the largely cynical views of Republicans than to the more trusting views of Democrats.

The differences between Republican and Democratic views of the media have been evident throughout this decade, although in the September 2002 Gallup survey—one year after the 9/11 terrorist attacks—the gap between Republicans and Democrats was not nearly as large as it has been in the past four surveys. Gallup's June 1976 survey on trust in the media by party showed a much different picture. The gap in trust levels between Republicans and Democrats was not nearly as large then as it is today: In 1976, 63% of Republicans told Gallup interviewers they had a great deal or a fair amount of trust in the accuracy of the news media, compared with 75% of Democrats. One reason for this general distrust of the media is the fact that only about a third of Americans today say that the news media are "just about right" when it comes to

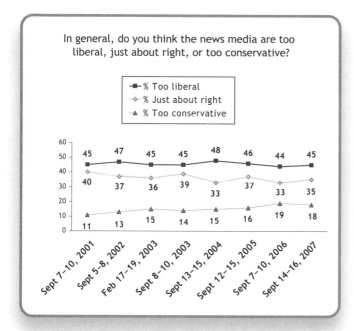

In general, do you think the news media are too liberal, just about right, or too conservative?

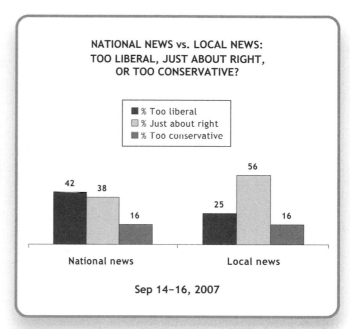

NATIONAL NEWS vs. LOCAL NEWS: TOO LIBERAL, JUST ABOUT RIGHT, OR TOO CONSERVATIVE?

ideological balance. More than twice as many Americans say the news media are too liberal (45%) rather than too conservative (18%).

This is not a new phenomenon. The tendency on the part of Americans to perceive the news media as too liberal has been observed in each Gallup survey in which this question has been asked since 2001. Still, if there is a perceptible trend, it is the finding that the "too conservative" number has been climbing slightly throughout the decade—from 11% in 2001 to 19% and 18% over the last two years. Americans' views of the bias in news media

are highly related—as would be expected—to underlying political orientation.

Over three-quarters of Republicans perceive the news media as being too liberal; that percentage drops to 43% among independents and only 16% among Democrats. One might expect that Democrats would "return the favor" to Republicans and view the news media as too conservative, but that is not the case. Only 22% of Democrats say the media are too conservative. The majority say the news media are about right. In short, while Republicans are highly likely to perceive the media as being biased toward the left, Democrats are much less likely to perceive the media as being biased toward the right. Whether or not this reflects reality (i.e., whether the media are in reality more Democratic and more liberal in their orientation) is an open question not answerable by these data.

LOCAL VS. NATIONAL

There's at least one bit of good news for the news media in this research. Americans are quite a bit more convinced of the neutrality of their local news media than they are of the national media's neutrality.

Over half of Americans say their local news media are about right in terms of ideological balance, while the remaining respondents have much more mixed views of the local media: Twenty-five percent say they are too liberal, but 16% say they are too conservative. This is consistent with a number of Gallup findings over the years to the effect that Americans tend to perceive conditions in their local communities more positively than they do conditions across the country more generally.

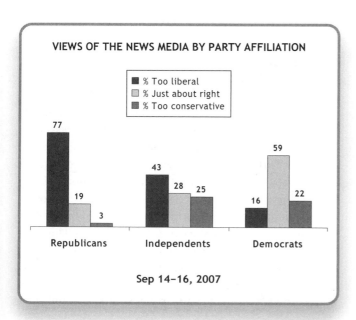

VIEWS OF THE NEWS MEDIA BY PARTY AFFILIATION

OCTOBER 9
Bush's Approval Rating Returns to Low 30s

According to a new Gallup Poll, conducted between October 4 and October 7, 2007, President George W. Bush's job approval rating from the American public is an anemic 32%. That is slightly below his previous reading of 36% from mid-September but is identical to his average approval score for all Gallup Polls conducted thus far in the second half of the year. Nearly two out of three Americans currently disapprove of Bush's job performance. Public approval of the job Bush is doing averaged a slightly higher 35% in the first half of this year, peaking at 38% in April. His lowest score of the year thus far—and also the lowest score of his presidency—was 29%, in July.

Bush's Conservative and Republican Base Giving Him Near-Record Low Support

President Bush continues to be rated approvingly by the two political groups that have traditionally formed his most supportive base: Republicans, and Americans who define their political views as "conservative." But the level of approval from each of these groups is currently at or near the lowest points seen since he became president. The 67% of Republicans approving of Bush today is slightly below the average 71% Republican approval since July, and approaches his term low point of 65% approval from Republicans three months ago. Support from Bush's party is now significantly below where it stood at the beginning of the year (averaging 75% in January).

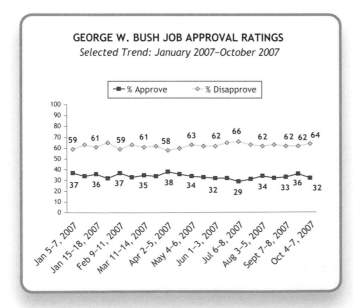

GEORGE W. BUSH JOB APPROVAL RATINGS
Selected Trend: January 2007–October 2007

While Bush's ratings from independents and Democrats have varied during the year, they are currently quite similar to where they have been since the start of July. Independents have averaged a 26% approval rating since July and are now at 27%. Democrats have averaged a 7% approval rating, exactly where they are in this latest poll. Both groups' current approval ratings for Bush are very similar to what they were at the beginning of the year (29% and 8%, respectively).

Similarly, just 51% of self-described conservatives approve of Bush today, the lowest rating of his presidency from this group (although it was a statistically indistinguishable 52% at one point earlier this year). His current 51% is below his 56% average approval rating from conservatives since the start of July, and even further below his average approval from this group in January.

Other Demographic Ratings Are Stable

Approval ratings of Bush by gender, age, and region are fairly similar to what they have been in recent months. As in the past few months, the new poll shows Bush's approval ratings are only slightly higher among men (34%) than among women (29%). There are also fairly small differences by age, with young adults (18 to 29 years of age) being relatively less approving (29%) than those 30 and older (34%). As is typically the case, whites are more positive about Bush than is the much more Democratic-oriented nonwhite population (37% vs. 13%, respectively). Throughout his presidency, Bush has typically received higher ratings in the South and Midwest than in the East and West, and that is seen in his average ratings since July. But in the current poll, only the South (38%) exhibits higher approval than the poll average, while the Midwest is similar (26%) to the East (29%) and West (30%).

Giuliani Still on Top as Republicans Prepare to Debate in Michigan

As the Republican presidential candidates square off in the latest in a series of debates—this time in Dearborn, Michigan, on October 9—new Gallup polling shows former New York City mayor Rudolph Giuliani continuing to hold onto his status as front-runner, 12 points ahead of former Tennessee senator Fred Thompson and 16 points ahead of John McCain. Thompson—for whom this will be the first national debate since he officially declared his candidacy—is still less well known to Republicans nationwide than Giuliani and McCain, suggesting that the debate could be an important opportunity for him to fill in the blanks in the minds of Republican primary voters. The poll also

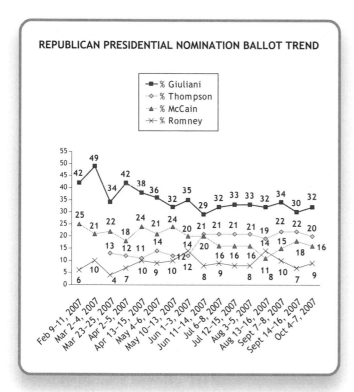

REPUBLICAN PRESIDENTIAL NOMINATION BALLOT TREND

- ■ % Giuliani
- ◇ % Thompson
- ▲ % McCain
- ✕ % Romney

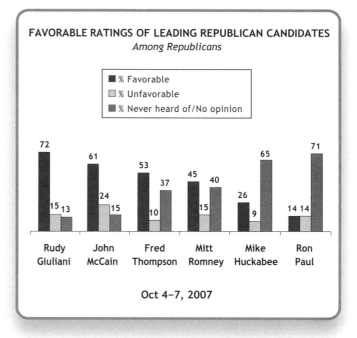

FAVORABLE RATINGS OF LEADING REPUBLICAN CANDIDATES
Among Republicans

- ■ % Favorable
- □ % Unfavorable
- ■ % Never heard of/No opinion

Oct 4–7, 2007

finds former Arkansas governor Mike Huckabee moving to within two points of former Massachusetts governor Mitt Romney, whose nationwide support among Republicans remains mired in single digits.

The basic structure of the national Republican race for president has remained relatively stable since early September. A new Gallup update, based on interviews conducted between October 4 and October 7, shows that Rudolph Giuliani remains the front-runner, followed by Fred Thompson and John McCain.

If there has been a change of note over the last several months, it has been the failure of Romney to capital-

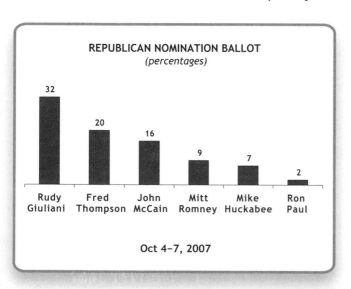

REPUBLICAN NOMINATION BALLOT
(percentages)

Rudy Giuliani	Fred Thompson	John McCain	Mitt Romney	Mike Huckabee	Ron Paul
32	20	16	9	7	2

Oct 4–7, 2007

ize on his minisurge when he won the Iowa straw poll in early August. McCain has, at the same time, recovered his standing after slipping in August. There has been a slight but steady increase in support for Huckabee, despite his very low name identification: He has gone from 1% of the vote as recently as May to 7% today, within two points of the better-known (and much better-financed) Romney, thereby clearly separating himself from the other "minor" candidates competing for the Republican nomination.

Giuliani's share of the national Republican vote has been in the 30% to 34% range since July. The former New York City mayor had attracted as much as 49% of the Republican vote in March (prior to the inclusion of Thompson on the ballot), but his share has settled back down and has shown little change in recent months. Giuliani is the best known of the major candidates among Republicans and is also the best liked, with a 72% favorable rating and only a 15% unfavorable rating.

Some news media reports have focused on Thompson's failure to catch on with voters after declaring his candidacy, and indeed, Gallup data show that while Thompson's vote share has not decreased in polling going back to mid-June, it has also not increased. The former movie and television actor now attracts 20% of the Republican vote, within a few points of where he has been in every Gallup Poll since the middle of June. Thompson's name identification among Republicans is still relatively low. Thirty-seven percent of Republicans nationwide say they don't know enough about Thompson to have either a favorable or an unfavorable opinion, which is far higher than the corresponding figures for Giuliani (13%) and McCain (15%), and about equal to

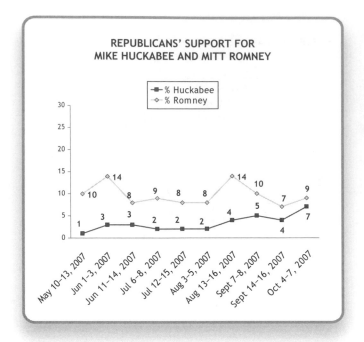

REPUBLICANS' SUPPORT FOR MIKE HUCKABEE AND MITT ROMNEY

— ■ — % Huckabee
— ◇ — % Romney

Romney values: 10, 14, 8, 9, 8, 8, 14, 10, 7, 9
Huckabee values: 1, 3, 3, 2, 2, 2, 4, 5, 4, 7

May 10–13, 2007
Jun 1–3, 2007
Jun 11–14, 2007
Jul 6–8, 2007
Jul 12–15, 2007
Aug 3–5, 2007
Aug 13–16, 2007
Sept 7–8, 2007
Sept 14–16, 2007
Oct 4–7, 2007

Texas representative Ron Paul addresses the Iowa Republican Party's annual Reagan Dinner in Des Moines on October 27, 2007. *(Charlie Neibergall/AP Images)*

that for Romney (40%). Among those who do know Thompson, however, his image is quite positive, with a better than five-to-one ratio of favorable to unfavorable opinions.

McCain is in third place among Republicans nationwide with 16% of the vote. With the exception of one Gallup Poll conducted in mid-August, this is essentially where he has been since July. In one mid-August poll, conducted shortly after Romney had won the Iowa straw poll, McCain fell behind Romney into fourth place with only 11% of the vote, but he has since recovered. Still, McCain is nowhere near the 26% to 28% of the national Republican vote he was receiving in late 2006 and in Gallup's first poll of 2007, at which time he was essentially tied with Giuliani as the party's front-runner. McCain's image, although still quite positive on balance, is the most mixed of any of the major candidates among Republicans. The former naval officer has a 61% favorable and 24% unfavorable rating among this group.

These national data show few signs of change in the positioning of Romney. The former head of Bain Capital is in fourth place with only 9% of the Republican vote, just a couple of points ahead of Huckabee. The gap between Romney and fifth-place challenger Huckabee is the smallest of the year, and the trend lines of vote support between the two have generally been growing closer together. It does not appear outside the realm of possibility that Huckabee could surpass Romney at some point in the future and climb into fourth place nationally among Republicans.

Despite the large amount of national publicity Romney has received, including a recent cover story in *Newsweek* magazine, he is still not all that well known among Republicans: 40% say they don't know enough about him to

have either a positive or negative opinion. Among those who do have an opinion, Romney's image is favorable by a three-to-one ratio. Potentially good news for Huckabee, the former governor of Arkansas who lost more than 100 pounds in a highly publicized weight loss campaign, is that two-thirds of Republicans don't know enough about him to rate him. (His image is 26% favorable and 9% unfavorable among those who do know him.) This means Huckabee has the opportunity to make significant advances if he continues to make favorable impressions as the campaign progresses.

Texas representative Ron Paul, who made waves last week with a strong fund-raising performance in the third quarter, still has not gained any traction in the polls. The Texas congressman and former medical doctor is now supported by just 2% of Republicans nationwide, even after the widespread reporting of his recent $5 million campaign haul. To date, his top performance in nationwide Republican polls has been 4% in a mid-September poll. Paul has a very substantial name-identification problem among Republicans, 72% of whom say they don't know enough about him to have either a positive or negative opinion.

OCTOBER 10

Clinton Maintains Commanding Lead in Latest Election Update

The latest Gallup Poll of nationwide Democrats' preference for their party's 2008 presidential nomination shows New York senator Hillary Clinton continuing to hold a commanding lead over Illinois senator Barack Obama and the remainder of the Democratic field. Clinton's lead over Obama is 21 percentage points in the current poll and has exceeded 20 points in each of five Gallup Polls conducted since the beginning of August.

The October 4–7, 2007, poll finds 47% of Democrats and Democratic-leaning independents favoring Clinton for the nomination, with 26% supporting Obama. Former senator John Edwards is the only other candidate in double digits, at 11%. Those three candidates account for 84% of the vote, leaving little support for the remaining contenders, led by New Mexico governor Bill Richardson at 4%. These results are nearly identical to those Gallup found in mid-September: Each candidate's support is the same or varies by only 1 percentage point compared with a September 14–16, 2007, poll. For that matter, Gallup's poll results have been quite stable since August. In an August 3–5, 2007, Gallup Poll, Clinton's support increased from the roughly 40% it had been in June and July to 48%, and she has averaged 47% in the five polls since then.

The rise in support for Clinton has not come disproportionately at the expense of any one challenger; rather, most candidates have seen a very slight drop in their support since August. The nomination contest is little different when looking only at the preferences of Democrats who say they are extremely likely to participate in their state's presidential primary or caucus next year. Among this group (representing about 60% of Democrats), Clinton's lead dips just below 20 points, with 48% preferring her, 29% Obama, and 10% Edwards.

Clinton's advantage over Obama and Edwards is also evident in Democrats' basic opinions of the candidates. Eighty-one percent have a favorable opinion of Clinton, compared with a 70% favorable rating for Obama and 69% for Edwards. Clinton's higher favorable rating does not merely reflect the fact that she is better known than Obama or Edwards, since her net favorable rating (which excludes those without an opinion and is calculated by subtracting the percent unfavorable from the percent favorable) also surpasses those of her chief rivals by double digits. The one area where Clinton appears weak in comparison with Obama and Edwards is in her net favorable rating among all Americans. While Clinton (51%), Obama (54%), and Edwards (48%) have similar favorable ratings, Clinton's high negatives—a 44% unfavorable rating—leave her with

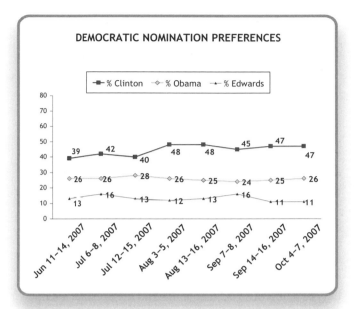

a net favorable rating of just +7. In contrast, Obama has a +27 net favorable rating and Edwards a +17 among the general public.

Clinton's relatively low net favorable rating reflects Americans' polarized opinions of her: Republicans are about as negative toward her (19% favorable, 78% unfavorable) as Democrats are positive. But her weak showing on this measure compared with Obama and Edwards may not be a fatal flaw in her quest for the presidency. She still performs just as well as, if not better than, Obama and Edwards against the leading Republican candidates in general election trial heat matchups. Additionally, as far as Clinton is concerned, the greater challenge for her presidential viability may not be outperforming Obama and Edwards on favorable ratings but rather keeping her net favorable rating in positive territory. Notably, the current

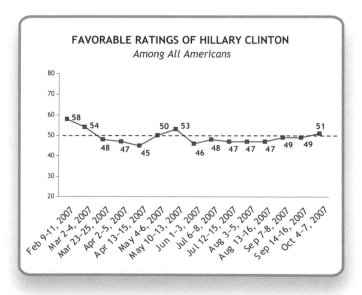

poll finds Clinton with a favorable rating above 50% among all Americans for the first time since May.

Usually, presidential candidates' favorable ratings decline and their unfavorable ratings climb over the course of the campaign as they become better known and are increasingly viewed by the public in a strongly partisan light. As a result, in recent elections, the major party presidential nominees have had favorable ratings not much above 50%. Even though Obama and Edwards have much greater positive than negative ratings now, if either is the Democratic nominee he would likely see his positive ratings decline substantially by November 2008. But the usual campaign dynamic may not apply to Clinton, who is already nearly universally known and has been seen through a partisan lens for a long time. As a result, her favorable ratings may not change much over the course of the campaign. In fact, her current scores are similar to what the presidential nominees' scores will likely be next November.

Clinton's favorable ratings have shown some movement this year at the margins, which has pushed these ratings above and below the 50% level. There is no historical precedent for a candidate winning the presidency with a favorable rating below 50%, but some have been very close to that mark. For example, only 51% of Americans had a favorable view of George W. Bush in late October 2004. It would seem unlikely that Americans would elect a president whom they view more negatively than positively, and indeed Bush won only a narrow victory over John Kerry (who had a similar favorable rating to Bush) in 2004. Thus, a favorable rating above 50% could be one important indicator of Clinton's ability to win the presidential election.

OCTOBER 16
Giuliani Generates Most "Enthusiastic" Support from Republicans

Republicans are more enthusiastic about the candidacy of former New York City mayor Rudolph Giuliani to be their party's nominee for the 2008 presidential election than they are about any of the other leading Republican contenders. Not only does Giuliani continue to lead the pack when Republicans are asked whom they support for the nomination, but he is also the candidate Republicans are most likely to say they would vote for enthusiastically in the general election should he win the nomination.

There are no signs in the latest USA Today/Gallup Poll that any of the major candidates for the Republican nomination gained standing as a result of the debate that took place in Dearborn, Michigan, on October 9; the race has remained remarkably steady. At the same time, a majority of Republicans who express a candidate preference say

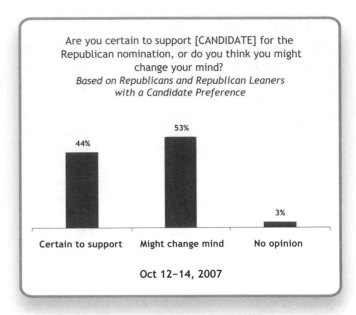

Are you certain to support [CANDIDATE] for the Republican nomination, or do you think you might change your mind?
Based on Republicans and Republican Leaners with a Candidate Preference

Oct 12–14, 2007

they might change their minds about whom they will support. Republicans appear to be least enthusiastic about the potential candidacy of former Massachusetts governor Mitt Romney. The possibility of Arizona senator John McCain's gaining the nomination is also viewed less enthusiastically by Republicans than would be the candidacy of Giuliani or former Tennessee senator Fred Thompson.

Republican Nomination Ballot

The new October 12–14, 2007, USA Today/Gallup Poll finds that the Republican debate—the first in which Thompson took part—did little to change the basic makeup of the Republican race. Giuliani continues to lead the pack of Republican contenders, with 32% of Republicans and Republican-leaning independents currently supporting him for the nomination. Giuliani is now 14 points ahead of Thompson, who gets 18% of the vote. Fourteen percent of Republicans favor McCain, and 10% prefer Romney as the party's presidential nominee. No other Republican candidate garners more than 6% support. None of the changes compared with Gallup's last poll is statistically significant.

The basic structure of the race has remained virtually unchanged since September, and from a broad perspective has not changed a great deal since June, when Thompson first jumped above 20% in the Republican preference poll. However, the race remains—at least in theory—quite fluid. A majority of Republicans with a candidate preference tell Gallup that they might change their minds about whom they will support between now and next year's primaries and caucuses. Just 44% of Republicans say they are certain to support their candidate, while 53% might change their minds.

By comparison, 57% of Democrats (including Democratic-leaning independents) say they are certain to vote for their preferred candidate; only 42% say they might change their minds. These findings give further support to the assumption that the Republican race is in flux, while the Democratic race is more and more coalescing around the candidacy of Hillary Clinton.

Voter Enthusiasm

The latest poll also asked Republicans to indicate their overall enthusiasm about voting for each of the four top contenders if they were to win their party's nomination. Republicans would be most enthusiastic about voting for Giuliani if he were to win the nomination. Fifty-one percent of Republicans say they would vote for him enthusiastically, while 38% would vote enthusiastically for McCain and 37% for Thompson. Only 25% would enthusiastically vote for Romney. Some of the observed differences in the enthusiastic vote measure are attributable to higher "no opinions" when it comes to Thompson and Romney. Still, it is telling to note that in Romney's case, more Republicans say they would vote for him "mainly as a vote against the Democrat" than say they would enthusiastically vote for him should he be the nominee. Additionally, 22% of Republicans flat-out say they would vote against Romney or not vote at all if he were the nominee. (The percentage who would not vote for the other three is roughly 15% each.) In short, Romney at this point is not only garnering just 10% of the Republican vote, but is also in the position of having Republicans saying they would end up voting for him should he win their party's nomination more to avoid voting for a Democrat than out of enthusiasm for his candidacy in its own right.

If the Republican nominee were McCain, the percentages who would vote for him enthusiastically and who would vote for him "mainly as a vote against the Democrat" are essentially equal, suggesting a lack of Republican fervor for his candidacy as well. Republicans seem more inclined to cast their votes for Thompson and especially Giuliani, whom they would vote for "happily" rather than mainly to defeat the Democrat.

In terms of overall image, Republicans continue to rate Giuliani more favorably than McCain, Thompson, or Romney. In the latest poll, 67% of Republicans have a favorable opinion of Giuliani—higher than the 61% for McCain, 53% for Thompson, and 41% for Romney. Roughly one in three Republicans are not familiar enough with Thompson or Romney to rate them. Thompson's rating among Republicans did not change meaningfully in the current poll compared with the pre-debate poll in early October: His favorable rating went up by three points, but his unfavorable rating also went up, by five points. In other words, he

became slightly better known, but his image did not move strongly in one direction more than the other. The bottom line for Thompson's first debate appearance seems to be that it had little immediate effect on his standing among Republicans in terms of either his image or his standing in the trial-heat poll.

Even After Nobel Prize, Support for Gore Presidential Bid Remains Limited

Former vice president Al Gore has added the Nobel Peace Prize to the collection of awards he has won this year, which also includes an Academy Award and an Emmy. Speculation about his presidential intentions has only increased following his Nobel Prize win on October 12, 2007. A new USA Today/Gallup Poll, conducted between October 12 and October 14 just after Gore was awarded the Nobel Peace Prize, shows a slight bump in Gore's favorable rating. But there had not been a large groundswell of support for him to run for president prior to last week, and that remains the case. Gore's standing in Gallup's Democratic nomination trial heats is little improved following the Nobel Prize announcement; he remains in third place, and his support is no better now than it has been throughout much of this year. Still, Americans are more inclined to say Gore deserved to win the Nobel Peace Prize than to say he did not deserve to win it.

The most visible effect of Gore's Nobel Prize is in the public's overall opinions of him. The October 12–14 poll finds 58% of Americans saying they have a favorable view of Gore, up from 50% in the prior reading taken in August 2007. That is Gore's high favorable rating for the year and his best in any Gallup Poll since September 2000. Gore's favorable rating had been around 50% most of this year,

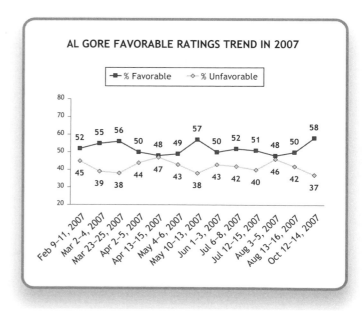

aside from a brief period in the mid-50s range following his Academy Award victory on February 25, 2007.

Gallup has tracked opinions of Gore since 1992, and his favorable rating peaked at 64% on two occasions—immediately following the Democratic National Conventions in 2000 (at which he was nominated for president) and 1992 (at which he was nominated for vice president). Gore's highest unfavorable rating was 52% in December 2000, when he was challenging the Florida presidential election results in the courts. Democrats have very positive views of Gore, and these views improved following his Nobel Peace Prize. Seventy-nine percent of Democrats now have a positive opinion of Gore, compared with 73% in the August survey. Even with the improvement, however, Gore's favorable rating among Democrats is not as good as that of Senator Hillary Clinton, of whom 84% of Democrats have a favorable opinion. But Gore now has a better favorable rating than Senator Barack Obama and former senator John Edwards, who were viewed similarly to Gore by Democrats prior to last week.

Gore for President?

Americans' opinions about Gore as a presidential candidate were changed little by his Nobel Prize—neither in terms of the desire to see him enter the race nor with respect to Democrats' support for him for the party's 2008 presidential nomination. Just 41% of Americans say they would like to see Gore run for president; the majority, 54%, are opposed to a Gore candidacy. That is essentially the same result that Gallup found in March 2007, when 38% expressed a desire for a Gore presidential bid. Even Democrats seem tepid to the idea of Gore running for president: Just 48% favor such a move, while 43% are opposed. As one would expect, Republicans (24% in favor) and independents (43%) are mostly opposed to Gore's running for president.

In the new update of national Democrats' and Democratic-leaning independents' preferences for the Democratic presidential nomination, only 14% select Gore as their first choice when he is included in a list along with the eight announced Democratic candidates. Clinton leads with 44%, while Obama is next at 19%. Gore finishes slightly ahead of Edwards, who is supported by 10% of rank-and-file Democrats. (With Gore support factored out—as per Gallup's standard reporting of the Democratic ballot—Clinton leads Obama by 50% to 21%.) In the pre–Nobel Prize poll, taken between October 4 and October 7, 10% of Democrats chose Gore as their first choice, so the win may have increased his support slightly, but the four-percentage-point bump is within the poll's margin of sampling error. Any bump Gore received appears to have come at Senator Obama's expense, as Obama is the only candidate to show evidence of a drop from the prior poll. Gore's current 14% support is on the low end of what he has received since February, when the Democratic field largely took shape. His high, however, recorded in several polls, was just 18%.

Did He Deserve to Win the Prize?

Some critics have questioned the Nobel Committee's selection of Gore for the Nobel Peace Prize, wondering how his campaign to raise awareness of climate change is deserving of a prize usually given in recognition of humanitarian or diplomatic work. Most Americans do not share that skepticism: Forty-three percent say Gore deserved the award, while 26% say he did not and 31% do not have an opinion either way. A majority of Democrats, 62%, endorse the selection of Gore, while only 10% question it. Contrariwise, 40% of Republicans say Gore did not deserve to win and only 24% believe that he should have received the award.

OCTOBER 17
Fifty Percent of Democrats Now Back Clinton

The latest USA Today/Gallup Poll finds Senator Hillary Clinton extending her already sizable lead over Barack Obama in Democrats' 2008 presidential nomination preference polling. Half of Democrats say they are most likely to support her for the nomination, and her 29-point lead over Senator Barack Obama is the largest she has held to date. Additionally, a majority of Clinton supporters say they are certain to support her for the presidential nomination, and nearly

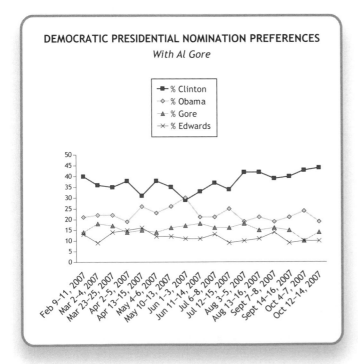

DEMOCRATIC PRESIDENTIAL NOMINATION PREFERENCES
With Al Gore

- ■ % Clinton
- ◇ % Obama
- ▲ % Gore
- ✕ % Edwards

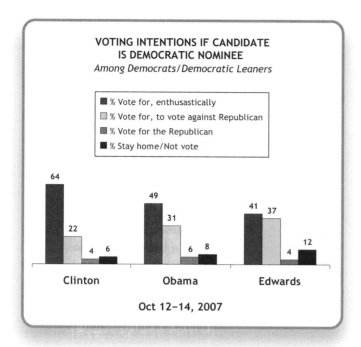

VOTING INTENTIONS IF CANDIDATE IS DEMOCRATIC NOMINEE
Among Democrats/Democratic Leaners

- ■ % Vote for, enthusastically
- ☐ % Vote for, to vote against Republican
- ▨ % Vote for the Republican
- ■ % Stay home/Not vote

Oct 12–14, 2007

two-thirds of Democrats say they would vote for her enthusiastically in November 2008 if she were indeed the party's nominee. Leads greater than 20 percentage points have been rare in past Democratic campaigns, but historically those who have enjoyed such a large lead in Gallup Polls this late in the year have won the nomination the following year.

The October 12–14, 2007, update finds 50% of Democrats (including independents who lean to the Democratic Party) supporting Clinton for the nomination, her best showing so far. Obama is a distant second at 21%, followed by former senator John Edwards at 13%. The five other active presidential candidates are supported by 4% or less of Democrats. Clinton has never trailed at any point in the campaign, and has led Obama by at least 20 percentage points since August. Her lead has expanded from 21 points in the previous poll to 29 points as a result of a slight increase in support for her (from 47% to 50%) and a slight dip in support for Obama (from 26% to 21%). Both changes are within the polls' margins of sampling error.

All told, 57% of Democrats who express a candidate preference say they are certain to support that candidate, much better than the 44% of Republicans who say they are certain to support their first choice for the Republican nomination. But the Democratic number is inflated by Clinton supporters: Sixty-seven percent of Democrats who name Clinton as their first choice say they are certain to support her, compared with just 44% of Democrats who support any of the other Democratic presidential candidates. Thus, it appears that the Democrats' advantage in candidate enthusiasm over Republicans is largely attributable to heightened excitement among Clinton backers. That idea is further underscored by the fact that 64% of all

Democrats say they would vote for Clinton "enthusiastically" if she were the party's presidential nominee in 2008, significantly higher than the comparable percentages for Obama (49%) and Edwards (41%).

Clinton's standing within her own party is much stronger than that of the Republican front-runner, former mayor Rudolph Giuliani. Fifty-one percent of Republicans say they would vote enthusiastically for Giuliani if he were the Republican nominee in the 2008 presidential election.

Clinton's Lead in Historical Perspective

Since the 1972 campaign—when the power to choose the party's nominees was shifted from national convention delegates to voters in state primaries and caucuses—Democrats have rarely had a front-runner as dominant as Clinton. In four of eight contested nomination campaigns from 1972 to 2004, no candidate had a lead of 20 points in a Gallup Poll at any point during the year prior to the election. In two of these campaigns, this occurred just once during that time. Only in 1979 (Massachusetts senator Edward M. Kennedy) and 1999 (former vice president Al Gore) were front-runners able to sustain a lead of that magnitude over several polls. The majority of the historical 20-point leads occurred in 1999, when Vice President Gore was challenged only by former senator Bill Bradley of New Jersey for the 2000 Democratic nomination.

So far in this pre-election year, Clinton has held a lead of 20 points or more in 8 of 18 Gallup Polls, including the last six polls. Clinton is just the fifth Democratic presidential candidate since 1972 to hold a 20-point lead at any point in the year prior to the election. The others were Kennedy in June and July 1979, former vice president Walter Mondale in November 1983, former senator Gary Hart of Colorado in April 1987, and Gore for most of 1999. Kennedy and Hart ultimately lost their nomination bids, but their large leads came much earlier in their respective campaigns. Kennedy's candidacy lost its steam when Jimmy Carter's popularity surged in late 1979 following the Iran hostage crisis and the Soviet invasion of Afghanistan. Hart's 20-point lead occurred in the last poll taken before he suspended his campaign after the press was able to confirm rumors that he was having an extramarital affair. Both Mondale and Gore, who like Clinton held their large leads much later in the campaign, went on to win the Democratic presidential nomination. Moreover, Mondale and Gore both saw their leads expand between the start of the election campaign and the Iowa caucuses. Both then won the Iowa caucuses, though Mondale would subsequently lose the New Hampshire primary to Hart and see his lead disappear. Mondale recovered and had the nomination well in hand by April 1984. Gore won the 2000 New Hampshire primary over Bradley and easily won the nomination.

Clinton is also just the third Democratic presidential candidate to have reached 50% support on Gallup's national ballot in the year prior to the election, joining Kennedy in 1979 and Gore in 1999. Gore's long run of support in excess of 50% is partly attributable to the fact that he had just one challenger for the nomination. Large leads and support in excess of 50% have been much more common on the Republican side. In fact, every Republican presidential nominee since 1972 has led his challengers by 20 or more points at least once in the year prior to the election. All but Gerald Ford in 1975 and George H. W. Bush in 1987 reached 50% support on Gallup's national ballot the year before the election. Giuliani has yet to reach 50% (his high was 49% in March), but he has led the field of Republican challengers by better than 20 points, in March and April 2007. His support has declined since that time, however, and his lead has averaged just 12 points.

By now, it is obvious that Clinton is extremely well positioned to win the 2008 Democratic presidential nomination. Her status as the front-runner seems to be solidifying at an opportune time, with the Iowa caucuses less than three months away. It is not beyond the realm of possibility that she could stumble and not win the nomination, as did Kennedy and Hart, but those cases occurred under rather extreme circumstances. Those candidates also held their large leads long before any votes were cast. Because of Clinton's large lead this close to the first official contest, one would expect the Clinton campaign to "play it safe" and not take the sort of risks that could derail her campaign. Indeed, the perception is that she is already "moving toward the center" by taking more moderate positions on issues—positions that Democratic primary voters may not necessarily endorse, but that may position her better for the general election campaign against the Republican. At the same time, Clinton's chief rivals, Obama and Edwards, find themselves in a position where they may have no choice but to step up their attacks on her in an effort to weaken her standing.

OCTOBER 18

Public: Situation in Iraq Getting Worse for United States

The majority of Americans believe the situation in Iraq is getting worse for the United States rather than better, and 6 out of 10 say U.S. involvement in the war was a mistake. Although attitudes about the war in Iraq remain highly partisan, as they have been since its inception more than four years ago, well under half of Republicans at this point say the war is getting better. Only slightly more than half of Americans are aware that the United States is planning to begin removing troops from Iraq during the next several months.

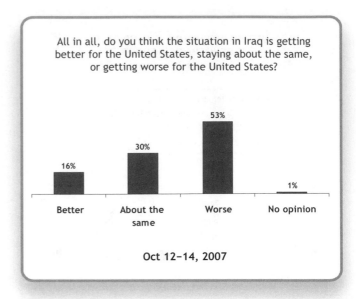

All in all, do you think the situation in Iraq is getting better for the United States, staying about the same, or getting worse for the United States?

Better 16% About the same 30% Worse 53% No opinion 1%

Oct 12–14, 2007

The Bush administration and other Republicans recently began talking up progress in Iraq, partially in reaction to the harsh comments about the situation in Iraq by retired lieutenant general Ricardo Sanchez. White House press secretary Dana Perino recently said, "I think that, by any measure, if you look at Iraq today, where we've been because of the surge, where we've come because of the surge, we're in a much better place today." Republican senator Mitch McConnell of Kentucky said on ABC's *This Week* on October 1: "I think the vast majority of people who are unhappy about the war are unhappy about it because they don't think it's been handled very well, and they now look at it and see we're actually making progress toward having an acceptable conclusion." A new USA

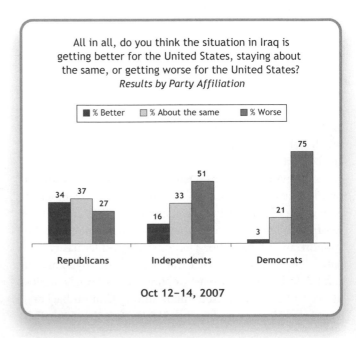

All in all, do you think the situation in Iraq is getting better for the United States, staying about the same, or getting worse for the United States?
Results by Party Affiliation

■ % Better   ☐ % About the same   ■ % Worse

Republicans 34 37 27   Independents 16 33 51   Democrats 3 21 75

Oct 12–14, 2007

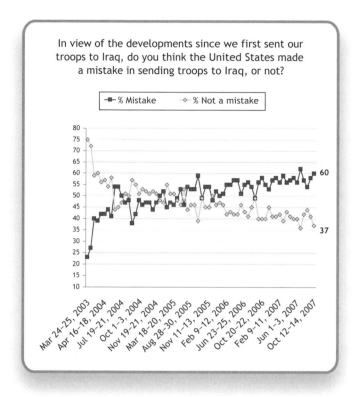

In view of the developments since we first sent our troops to Iraq, do you think the United States made a mistake in sending troops to Iraq, or not?

Iraq War a Mistake?

Gallup has asked Americans since the war began in March 2003 whether or not they believe the United States made a mistake in sending troops to Iraq. The latest results from the October 12–14, 2007, poll show that 60% of Americans believe U.S. involvement in the war was a mistake. This is within two percentage points of the highest such result on record; 62% of Americans said the war was a mistake in July 2007.

Although there have been fluctuations in the responses to this question from March 2003 to today, at least a majority of Americans have said the decision to send troops to Iraq was a mistake since December 2005, with the exception of one survey in September 2006. A majority of Americans first said the war was a mistake a little more than a year after the war began, in June 2004. Belief that U.S. involvement in Iraq was a mistake is highly related to views about current progress in the war. More than 7 in 10 Americans who say the war was a mistake also say things are getting worse for the United States in Iraq. But even among those who do not believe the war was a mistake, only 36% say the war is getting better for the United States at this point, while 40% say it is staying the same and 23% believe it is getting worse.

Awareness

The poll asked Americans about their knowledge of changes in the status of U.S. troop levels in Iraq. In fact, the United States is beginning to draw down the number of troops in Iraq, with reported plans to reduce the number to 130,000 by the summer of 2008. But apparently only about half of Americans are aware of these plans; the rest think the number of U.S. troops in Iraq is either increasing or staying the same. (Some of the controversy regarding current administration plans in Iraq revolves around whether or not dropping troop levels back to the point where they were before the surge is a "real" reduction or not. It is possible that some individuals who were aware of the current reductions still answered that the troop levels are being "kept the same" for that reason.) Public awareness that the United States is beginning to decrease the number of troops in Iraq is somewhat related to opinions about how the war in Iraq is going for the United States.

The small percentage (17%) of Americans who think the United States is increasing troop levels are significantly more likely to say things are getting worse for the United States in Iraq (68%). It is unclear whether or not these individuals' high level of pessimism is driven by their perception that troop levels are increasing, or whether their pessimism about the direction of the war causes them to

Today/Gallup Poll finds that relatively few Americans agree with these assessments—at least in response to a general question asking Americans' views about whether the situation in Iraq is getting better or getting worse for the United States.

The wording of the question did not explain to the respondents exactly what reference point to use in answering. It may be that some respondents were taking a broad time perspective and answering in terms of a comparison to the beginning of the war more than four years ago. Other questions asking only about the impact of the recent "surge" in Iraq may elicit different response patterns. But the responses to this general wording show that only 16% of Americans say the situation in Iraq is getting better for the United States, about one-third (30%) say it is staying about the same, and a majority (53%) say it is getting worse.

Even Republicans are apparently not able to generate much enthusiasm for the proposition that the situation in Iraq is getting better for the United States. While 27% of Republicans say the situation in Iraq is getting worse for the United States, only one-third (34%) say it is getting better, and the rest say it is staying about the same. Democrats are much more negative, as would be expected in this highly partisan environment; three-quarters say things are getting worse for the United States in Iraq. The attitudes of independents are somewhere in between, with 51% saying things are getting worse.

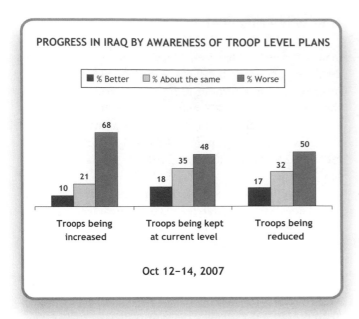

PROGRESS IN IRAQ BY AWARENESS OF TROOP LEVEL PLANS

■ % Better   □ % About the same   ■ % Worse

Troops being increased: 10, 21, 68
Troops being kept at current level: 18, 35, 48
Troops being reduced: 17, 32, 50

Oct 12–14, 2007

perceive that things are going badly. About half of those who say the number of troops is either staying the same or decreasing still believe that the war is getting worse for the United States in Iraq.

OCTOBER 23
Gallup Election Review: October 2007

The first official vote in the 2008 presidential primaries will be cast in early January, just a little more than two months away. This presidential campaign is one of the longest in recent history. At this point in the race, candidates have been actively campaigning for almost a year; a long series of debates have already been held; and voters, particularly in key early caucus and primary states, have become used to the type of intense campaign rhetoric usually heard only much later in the campaign. The process began so early this year that some candidates officially announced they were running, campaigned furiously, and then withdrew before the first caucus or primary had been held. Gallup has conducted more than 24,000 interviews since January 2007 relating to the election, and an analysis of the trends evident in the data suggest certain patterns that in some instances give us an excellent indication of how the race is likely to shape up.

Political Landscape Favorable for the Democrats

The political environment in which the 2008 presidential election will take place has been and continues to be favorable for the Democratic ticket, whomever it will finally

include. In a broad sense, the American public's assessment of the state of the nation continues to be negative. Such a negative evaluation usually results in Americans' wanting to hold the party in the White House accountable, suggesting the possibility that the Republican presidential candidate—although not himself an incumbent—will face an uphill battle in getting elected unless conditions change between now and the fall of 2008. Consider these indicators of the mood and state of the nation. President George W. Bush's job approval rating is currently at 32% (according to the October 12–14, 2007, USA Today/Gallup Poll) and has been below 40% since September 2006. The last two quarterly averages for Bush's job approval rating have been among the lowest in Gallup Poll history. It is possible that the president's approval ratings may recover between now and November 2008, but as of now, there is a significant potential for the president's problems to negatively affect the Republican presidential ticket. Furthermore, only 26% of Americans say they are satisfied with the way things are going in the country at this time. (Seventy-two percent are dissatisfied.) Although higher than the record low of 12% on this measure, this low satisfaction level again suggests potential trouble for the Republicans. Just 33% of Americans describe economic conditions in the country today as "excellent" or "good," while 23% say they are poor. Also, the majority (66%) say the economy is getting worse rather than better (23%). Historically, a perceived negative economic environment has been a key indicator of trouble for an incumbent president seeking re-election, including Gerald Ford in 1976, Jimmy Carter in 1980, and George H. W. Bush in 1992. The current president Bush is not seeking re-election, but the economic situation, if it continues to be perceived equally negatively next year, will certainly present a challenge to any Republican candidate attempting to hold the White House for the party.

The number one problem facing the nation today, according to Gallup Polls, is the war in Iraq. By all measures, the American public perceives that the war in Iraq is going badly and was ill-conceived initially. The public is also more likely to perceive that the Democrats would do a better job on Iraq than the Republicans. Hence it would appear that the Iraq situation could be used to the Democratic candidate's advantage next year, although ambivalence on the part of the public about what to do now in Iraq may make it difficult for the Democratic nominee to stake out a clear position on this issue.

A number of indicators suggest that the image of Republicans, taken as a whole, is in poor shape at this time. Fifty-nine percent of Americans have an unfavorable view of the Republican Party, while just 38% have a favorable one. At the same time, 53% of Americans rate the Democratic Party favorably, versus 43% unfavorably. Americans have rated the Democrats more positively than the Republicans since April 2005 (by at least one point in each poll over the past two and a half years).

Thus, it is not surprising to find Democrats faring well in "generic ballot" matchups against Republicans for the 2008 presidential election. For instance, in an October 12–16 CBS News Poll, 48% of voters said they would "probably" vote for the Democratic presidential candidate, while only 33% indicated a likely vote for the Republican candidate. A CNN/Opinion Research Corporation poll conducted between October 12 and October 14 found the "generic" Democrat ahead of the "generic" Republican by 13 points. However, the election is much closer when specific candidates are matched in hypothetical trial-heat ballots. In fact, Democratic candidates hold statistically significant leads at this point over only the lesser-known Republican candidates (Thompson and Romney). The trial heats are essentially tied in matchups of Clinton or Obama versus Giuliani or McCain. The October 12–14 CNN/Opinion Research Corporation poll finds 49% of voters supporting New York senator Hillary Clinton in a hypothetical matchup against Rudolph Giuliani, who garnered 47% support. A Fox News/Opinion Dynamics poll from October 9–10 shows a close race between Clinton and Giuliani (47% for Clinton to 43% for Giuliani), and Clinton and McCain (47% to 44%). Clinton performs much better against Romney and Thompson (50% to 38% against either). And an early-October National Public Radio poll has Giuliani in an essential dead heat with both Clinton (who beats him, 47% to 44%) and Obama (44% to 44%). Both Democratic candidates do better against Thompson.

The Democratic Race: Conditions Auspicious for Clinton to Win

Gallup's 2007 national presidential polling strongly points to Clinton's winning the 2008 Democratic nomination. Barring something unusual or otherwise unexpected, she is well positioned for the 2008 Democratic primaries. Obama has not been an insignificant rival: He came within single digits of tying Clinton for the lead on two different occasions this spring. But he has recently lost ground and is now in the weakest position relative to Clinton that he has been in all year. No other announced or potential Democratic candidate has come close to threatening Clinton's front-runner status since the campaign began, including former vice president Al Gore and former North Carolina senator John Edwards. When 2008 is history and one looks retrospectively at where the race stands today, the key factors forecasting Clinton's success will likely be the following:

CLINTON HAS HAD A CONSISTENT RUN AT THE TOP

Clinton has led the Democratic pack in every Gallup Poll conducted between November 2006 and October 2007. For most of this time, Clinton has led Obama by a double-digit margin. Her lead over Obama has expanded to nearly 30 points (50% to 21%) in Gallup's latest poll, conducted between October 12 and October 14. Gallup polling on Democratic nominations going back to the 1972 election shows that, by historical standards, a lead of even 20 points is large for Democratic candidates. The two candidates who held this distinction in the fall months before the election year (Gore in 1999 and Walter Mondale in 1983) eventually won the Democratic nomination. Also, and importantly, two-thirds of Democrats who prefer Clinton for their party's nomination say they are certain to vote for her in the primaries, a higher percentage than is found for supporters of the other Democratic candidates.

CLINTON'S SUPPORT RUNS DEEP

Clinton holds a commanding lead among nearly every major subgroup of potential Democratic primary voters. Some of her strongest showings are among women, non-whites, those in lower-income households, those with less formal education, and Southerners.

Clinton enjoys high favorable ratings in the Democratic Party that extend well beyond the 40% to 50% of Democrats typically naming her as their top choice for the nomination. Eighty-two percent of Democrats and Democratic leaners have a favorable view of the former first lady, while only 16% have an unfavorable view of her. Obama (70% favorable among Democrats) and Edwards (63% favorable) lag behind Clinton on this measure, in part because fewer Democrats are familiar with them. Democrats also rate Clinton as the candidate most likely to defeat the Republican in the general election—a key perceptual advantage given that primary voters are trying to distinguish among candidates with largely similar issue positions. Additionally, 64% of Democrats say they would vote for Clinton enthusiastically in November 2008 should she be the party's nominee. Forty-nine percent say this about Obama and 41% about Edwards.

CLINTON'S IMAGE STRONG ON TOP POLICY ISSUES

According to the September 24–27, 2007, Gallup Poll, Democrats and Democratic-leaning independents choose Clinton as the candidate best able to handle a wide variety of national issues. In fact, even when given the choice of the top three Democratic candidates—Clinton, Obama, and Edwards—an outright majority of Democrats say Clinton would do the best job on 6 out of 17 issues measured in the poll. This includes some of the major nuts-and-bolts policy issues Americans generally rate as most important to their vote for federal offices: healthcare, the economy, and education. It also includes two of the leading "values" issues in today's culture: abortion and gay marriage. Clinton is preferred by a solid plurality of Democrats on an additional seven issues. Among these are terrorism and the situation in Iraq—two of the most hotly debated issues of the election, potentially crucial to voters. She also holds sizable leads on taxes and energy, and somewhat smaller leads on crime, immigration, and being commander in chief of the military. Obama is preferred by a majority of Democrats on only one issue: race relations. He also leads Clinton and Edwards with a sizable plurality as the candidate best able to inspire Americans.

Clinton's nomination seems almost inevitable, but Ted Kennedy (1980) and Gary Hart (1988) provide some caution that under extreme circumstances, a strong Democratic candidate can blow a big lead. Kennedy's and Hart's big leads came much earlier in the campaign, however. Of note as well: Mondale saw his large lead from the fall of 1983 disappear after Hart's win in the 1984 New Hampshire primary, before Mondale recovered and went on to secure the nomination. Some have speculated that Americans might be uncomfortable with Bill Clinton returning to the White House after scandal marred his presidency, but polling data suggest this is not the case—at least not now.

The Republican Nomination

The Republican presidential nomination race at this point looks to be much more competitive than the Democratic contest, and atypical compared with past Republican nomination campaigns. Former New York City mayor Rudolph Giuliani has held a statistically significant lead in every Gallup national preference poll since February, averaging a 12-point lead over former Tennessee senator Fred Thompson over the past three months. Arizona senator John McCain is third, usually just a few points behind Thompson. Former Massachusetts governor Mitt Romney has not gained much traction in national polls. In the most recent Gallup Poll, just 10% of Republicans chose him for the Republican presidential nomination. Former Arkansas governor Mike Huckabee has seen his support pick up a little in the past few months, but he remains in single digits. Kansas senator Sam Brownback's departure from the race—announced this past weekend—will almost certainly have little direct effect, as he consistently polled at only 1% or 2% of the vote.

Romney's campaign team is banking on an initially strong performance in key early caucus and primary states to overcome their candidate's relatively poor showing among Republicans nationwide. Romney in fact does lead all recent polls in the key early states of Iowa and New Hampshire (more comfortably in Iowa than in New Hamp-

Three days before Halloween, Republican candidate Rudolph Giuliani poses with a pumpkin painted to resemble him in Hollis, New Hampshire. *(Jim Cole/AP Images)*

shire). Huckabee also outperforms his national numbers in Iowa, and is currently vying with Giuliani and Thompson for second place in that state.

Fifty-one percent of Republicans nationwide say they would vote enthusiastically for Giuliani in November 2008 should he be the party's nominee. McCain, Thompson, and Romney are not generating the same level of enthusiasm among the party base. But the level of enthusiasm toward Giuliani is significantly lower than that generated by Democratic front-runner Clinton. Republicans continue to rate Giuliani more positively than his leading competitors on Gallup's favorability measure, but he by no means dominates on this measure. Sixty-seven percent of Republicans and Republican leaners have a favorable opinion of Giuliani, compared with 61% for McCain, 53% for Thompson, and 41% for Romney. Romney's and Thompson's lower ratings are due in large part to the fact that they are not as well known as Giuliani (and McCain); roughly one in three Republicans do not have an opinion of Thompson or Romney. Thus, Giuliani's +40 net favorable rating (67% favorable minus 27% unfavorable) is roughly the same as the lesser-known Thompson's +36 (53%

favorable minus 17% unfavorable). Giuliani's favorable rating among Republicans has also declined: It was 74% as recently as August and has in the past been in the 80% range.

Religious Republicans' dissatisfaction with the party's field of presidential candidates has been a major story line during the campaign. There have been many questions raised about Giuliani's conservative credentials, and he does not fare as well among religious Republicans as he does among less religious party supporters, though he remains the leader among both groups. Also, Romney's Mormon faith is proving to be a significant obstacle in his ability to appeal to churchgoing Protestants—a key Republican constituency—who view him about as negatively as positively.

Beyond the size of Clinton's lead versus the size of Giuliani's, evidence that the Republican nomination contest is more unsettled comes from the fact that a majority of Republicans in a recent USA Today/Gallup Poll said they may change their minds about voting for their currently preferred candidate, while a majority of Democrats said they were certain to support their chosen candidate. Republicans have expressed less satisfaction than the Democrats with their field of presidential candidates throughout the campaign.

In past presidential nomination campaigns, Republicans have typically coalesced around a candidate early in the campaign, and that candidate has usually won the nomination without much competition. Every Republican presidential nominee since 1972 has led his challengers by 20 or more points at some time during the year before the election. All but Gerald Ford in 1975 and George H. W. Bush in 1987 reached 50% support on Gallup's national ballot during the year before the election. Giuliani has yet to reach 50% (his high was 49% in March), but he did lead the field of Republican challengers by better than 20 points in March and April 2007. Giuliani departs from past Republican history, however, in that in most cases the leading candidate (and eventual nominee) had a much larger lead during the autumn, before the primaries began, than Giuliani does now.

Early General Election Polls as Predictors

Since World War II, there have been only three elections that replaced a president who had served two four-year terms—in 1960, 1988, and 2000. (In 1952 and 1968, the incumbents, Harry Truman and Lyndon Johnson, respectively, were eligible for re-election after having served less than two full terms but declined to run.) Given the small number and differing outcomes of these similar elections, the historical data do not offer much guidance as to what might happen in 2008. But the data do show that it has not been unusual for the party out of power to lead for much of the year before the "open-seat" election. George W. Bush held a statistically significant lead over Gore in almost every trial-heat poll conducted in 1999. Republican Bush went on the following year to win a disputed victory over Gore in the Electoral College to replace departing Democrat Bill Clinton.

In 1987, Democratic front-runner Gary Hart led George H. W. Bush for the first several months of the year. Bush took over the lead in late May after news of Hart's extramarital affair derailed his campaign, and Bush polled better than Hart, Jesse Jackson, and Mario Cuomo in late 1987. Bush relinquished the lead the following spring to his eventual challenger, Michael Dukakis, before moving back ahead after the Republican convention and eventually being elected by a comfortable margin to succeed Republican Ronald Reagan as president. In 1959, the various Democratic candidates led for much of the first part of the year, but the tide shifted in the Republicans' favor for much of the latter part of that year's presidential preference polling. Democrat John Kennedy won a razor-thin victory over Republican Richard Nixon the following year in the contest to succeed Republican Dwight Eisenhower.

OCTOBER 24

Most Voters Not Moved by Winfrey's Endorsement of Obama

Presidential candidates will take almost any help they can get in their quest for the Oval Office. Senator Barack Obama is getting a highly publicized assist from popular talk show host Oprah Winfrey in his presidential bid, based on her formal endorsement of his candidacy this past May. The value of this type of endorsement is unclear, however, as most Americans say endorsements are not an important factor in their presidential vote. More to the point, relatively few Americans say Winfrey's specific endorsement increases the likelihood that they will vote for Obama. Support for Obama as the Democratic nominee has not changed much over the course of the year, and in fact has dipped to one of its lowest points in the most recent Gallup update.

The October 12–14, 2007, poll asked Americans how Winfrey's endorsement of Obama for president would affect their voting decision next year. The vast majority—81%—say her endorsement will make no difference to their vote for president. There is little difference between the percentage of Americans who say they are more likely to vote for Obama (8%) and the percentage who say they are more likely to vote against him (10%) because of the endorsement. More generally, most Americans do not consider endorsements from prominent people to be an important factor in helping to determine which candidate they will support for president. Only 16% say such endorsements are "very important" to them, while an additional 21% say they are "somewhat important." A majority of 61% say that endorsements are "not too" (23%) or "not at all" (38%) important. The poll finds that Democrats (41%) are somewhat more likely than Republicans (30%) to say that endorsements are important; but a majority of both groups say endorsements are not that important an influence on their voting choice.

This result and the fact that Winfrey is endorsing a Democrat suggest a potentially greater impact of the endorsement than would be the case if she were endorsing a Republican. (It is important to note that this analysis does not factor in how blacks in particular feel on this matter, because this poll's sample size for the black population is too small to analyze.)

Americans' Opinion of Winfrey Down

The current poll finds that 66% of Americans say they have a favorable opinion of Oprah Winfrey, while 26% have an unfavorable opinion of her. Winfrey's favorable rating is lower now than in any of the four polls in which Gallup has measured the public's opinion of her; Winfrey's ratings were 7 to 12 percentage points higher in previous polls.

Winfrey's favorable rating is down among most subgroups of Americans, but the decline appears to be greater among Americans age 50 and older. Among that age group, 61% of adults have a favorable opinion of Winfrey in the latest poll; prior to that, Winfrey's favorable rating among this group was between 72% and 75%. Among adults age 18 to 49, Winfrey's rating has remained quite stable over this period of time; it is currently at 71%, down only slightly from 74% in the prior two readings. Democrats have consistently rated Winfrey more favorably than Republicans over the years; but Winfrey's endorsement of Obama represented a more explicit identification of herself with the Democratic Party. Republicans' favorable opinions of her have indeed declined, from 69% in January to 59% in the current poll; but Democrats' opinions of Winfrey have also become less positive, showing a drop of seven points, from 78% to 71%. Thus, it is not clear that Winfrey's Obama endorsement is the reason for her slightly lower favorable rating. Overall, younger women and blacks are the groups most likely to rate her favorably: Eighty-five percent of women between the ages of 18 and 49 and 83% of blacks say they have a favorable opinion of her. At least three out of four Americans in the following groups rate her favorably: nonwhites (79%), women (77%), those living in urban areas (77%), self-described liberals (75%), and parents with children under 18 (75%). (The 83% figure for blacks who rate Winfrey favorably is based on the average results of the three polls conducted from 2003 to 2007.)

It is difficult to measure the precise impact of Winfrey's endorsement on Obama's standing in the Democratic nomination race. He averaged 23% in four polls from February, March, and early April—all conducted before Winfrey endorsed him—and has averaged 24% in the four

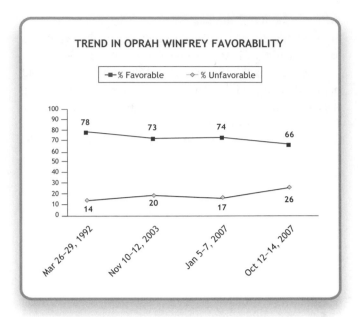

most recent Gallup election polls. So support for Obama is essentially unchanged since before her endorsement. In fact, though likely not because of Winfrey's involvement in his candidacy, Obama's fortunes may be beginning to turn downward. In the most recent Gallup Poll election update, 21% of Democrats supported Obama for the Democratic presidential nomination, one of his worst showings to date. His current 29-point deficit in relation to Clinton on the national test ballot is the largest he has yet faced.

Winfrey's endorsement of Obama will likely aid his candidacy only at the margins, and that would not be enough for him to overcome his current large deficit in relation to Clinton. But Winfrey's appeal to certain groups—such as women—could help Obama perform better among those groups than he otherwise would. Among groups of voters that view both Obama and Winfrey favorably, such as blacks, the endorsement may not change minds but may primarily reinforce existing views. That reinforcement could help motivate voters to turn out to vote or to work in support of Obama's candidacy.

Analysis of Support for Obama

About a year ago, Illinois senator Barack Obama made known his intention to run for president in the 2008 election. His showing thus far has not met the high expectations many had held for the young and charismatic senator. Though he has consistently placed second in Democratic nomination test ballots, his levels of support have been pretty flat since he entered the race. Yet, based on his favorable ratings among all Americans, he rates as one of the most popular presidential candidates, if not the most popular. Blacks and young adults are among his greatest supporters, both in the

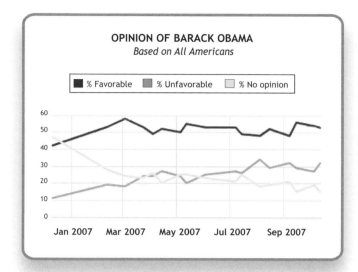

OPINION OF BARACK OBAMA
Based on All Americans

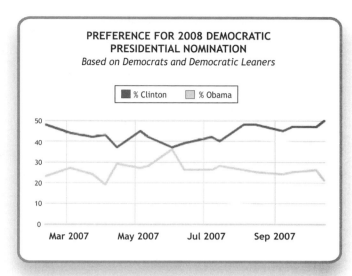

PREFERENCE FOR 2008 DEMOCRATIC
PRESIDENTIAL NOMINATION
Based on Democrats and Democratic Leaners

country at large and within Democratic ranks. Over the past two months, Obama has averaged a 53% favorable rating and a 30% unfavorable rating across four Gallup Polls. Seventeen percent are still not familiar enough with Obama to offer an opinion of him. His favorable rating edges out those of Hillary Clinton and Rudolph Giuliani and is the highest among the leading presidential candidates of both parties, as is his +23 net favorable rating (% favorable minus % unfavorable). Clinton, currently the comfortable front-runner for the Democratic presidential nomination, has only a +5 net favorable score, as her relatively strong favorable rating is offset by the highest unfavorable rating of any candidate.

Presidential candidates usually see their unfavorable rating climb over the course of a campaign, as they become clearly identified with one party or the other in Americans' minds. That dynamic has applied to Obama as well, who has seen his unfavorable score rise from 18% in March to 32% in the most recent poll, with most of that increase coming among Republicans. Obama's initial 42% favorable rating from last December quickly increased to 58% by early March, before falling back to the low 50s in late March. It has been in the high 40s to mid-50s range since that time.

Within his own party, though, Obama does not rate as positively as Clinton, and not much more positively than John Edwards. Obama's deficit in relation to Clinton on this measure is a key weakness in his quest for the party's nomination. Even so, Democrats, as would be expected, are one of the groups that offer the most positive ratings of Obama. His other core support groups—all of which accord him net favorable ratings in excess of +30—include blacks, college graduates, and young adults, in particular young women.

Obama's Support for the Democratic Nomination

At this point, Obama's standing in the Democratic nomination race is most relevant to gauging his presidential

fortunes, and those fortunes may be beginning to turn downward. In the most recent USA Today/Gallup Poll election update, 21% of Democrats supported Obama for the Democratic presidential nomination, one of his worst showings to date. His current 29-point deficit in relation to Clinton on the national test ballot is the largest he has faced. His support has been in the 25% range since late June, and has exceeded the 30% level only once this year.

Given that Clinton has such a commanding lead, it is no surprise that she leads Obama among all major Democratic subgroups, according to combined data from the four most recent Gallup election surveys, conducted in September and October. Obama's support averaged 24% among all Democrats across these surveys. Several of the groups within the general population that view Obama most favorably are also among the Democratic constituencies most likely to name Obama as their number one choice for the 2008 Democratic presidential nomination. Obama's strongest showing is among black Democrats—40% favor him for the nomination—but he still trails Clinton by nine points among this group. Obama's support also skews toward younger Democrats: Thirty-five percent of those age 18 to 34 favor him for the nomination, compared with 25% of 35- to 54-year-olds and only 15% of Democrats age 55 and older.

And Obama fares relatively better among Democrats in the Midwest, younger males, and those with children under 18 than among Democrats generally.

Implications for the Obama Campaign

Obama and his other Democratic rivals have their work cut out for them in trying to defeat Clinton for the Democratic nomination. The fact that Clinton leads not only among Democrats nationwide but also among every key Democratic subgroup makes targeting one's campaign efforts a challenge. Obama's relatively strong appeal to black and young Democrats is something of a double-edged sword, because those groups are usually among the least likely to turn out to vote. But Obama's ability to inspire people may help him capitalize on his strengths among these groups. His relatively weak support among older Democrats (and older Americans generally) is somewhat of a liability, because this is one of the groups most likely to vote. Should Obama survive the Democratic primaries, he may be fairly well positioned to win the presidency, given his relatively high favorable ratings and a political environment that currently advantages the Democratic Party.

OCTOBER 29

Women Key to Growing Clinton Lead Among Democrats

Gallup polling has in recent months demonstrated a definite increase in support for Senator Hillary Clinton as the favored 2008 Democratic presidential nominee. Her support has increased from roughly 4 in 10 Democrats and Democratic leaners to close to half of this group, including a high reading of 50% in the most recent USA Today/Gallup Poll. As a result, her lead over second-place Barack Obama has grown to 29 percentage points, the largest of the campaign.

Analysis of Gallup Poll data reveals that most Democratic subgroups show increased support for Clinton during the last two months as compared with the summer. Her support has grown more among Democratic women than men, and the increases have been especially great among college-educated women and unmarried women. Other Democratic subgroups that have shown considerable movement toward Clinton's candidacy in recent months are rural residents, young adults, and those without children under 18. These findings are derived from two aggregated data sets of Gallup polling on 2008 Democratic presidential nomination preferences. The first data set spans three polls conducted from mid-June through July, just before the increase in Clinton support was first evident. Clinton averaged 40% of the Democratic vote in those polls. The second data set includes the four most recent Gallup election polls, all conducted in September and October, when Clinton averaged a 48% share of the Democratic vote.

Sources of Clinton's Support

Nearly every Democratic subgroup has shown some increase in support for Clinton over the past several months. (Two that have not are blacks and Midwesterners—which are two of Obama's stronger constituencies.) The largest increases in support for Clinton have come from among rural residents (a 20% increase in support), women with a college degree (+15%), single women (+13%), younger women (+12%), and women with no children under 18 (+12%). Obviously there is much overlap in membership among these groups—but a stronger appeal to certain subgroups of women within the Democratic Party has clearly been a key to Clinton's expanded lead.

Overall, 52% of women who identify themselves as Democrats or as leaning to the Democratic Party rate Clinton as their top choice for the party's 2008 presidential nomination, compared with 41% of Democratic men. Clinton's support is slightly higher among unmarried women (55%), women without a college education (55%), and younger women (54%), all three of which figure as some of Clinton's strongest constituencies. Democrats residing in low-income households (56%) and Easterners (53%) also rank among the subgroups showing the highest levels of support for Clinton. Clinton's weakest showing among any of the subgroups analyzed is among college-educated men, of whom just 34% support her candidacy. Even so, Clinton maintains a slim advantage over Obama (who receives 30% support) among this group of Democrats. Notably, Clinton's support varies little according to Democrats' self-reported political ideology. Fifty percent of conservative Democrats, 48% of liberal Democrats, and 46% of moderate Democrats choose Clinton as their preferred nominee.

Clinton Sweeps Candidate Healthcare Ratings

Of the seven Republican and Democratic candidates currently receiving the most support for their respective parties' 2008 nomination for president, Senator Hillary Clinton receives the most favorable public reviews for having good healthcare proposals. Though she outshines her chief Democratic rivals on this score, it's the Republicans who fare the worst. According to Gallup's September 24–27 survey, Clinton is the only candidate whom a majority of Americans commend for having "good ideas about how to address the healthcare system in the United States." Fifty-three percent say she has good ideas, while 38% disagree. (The poll was conducted shortly after Clinton unveiled the latest installment of her healthcare plan in September, but she has generally scored well on the healthcare issue throughout the campaign.) Clinton's leading Democratic opponents—Senator Barack Obama and former senator John Edwards—are the next most highly rated on healthcare, with roughly 4 in 10 Americans saying each has good ideas. All four Republicans rated—former mayor Rudolph Giuliani, Senator John McCain, former governor Mitt Romney, and former senator Fred Thompson—fall below Edwards and Obama, with Giuliani scoring the best (31% say he has good ideas) and Thompson the worst (18%).

Much of the variation in these ratings can be explained by the percentages of Americans with no opinion of the respective candidates' healthcare plans. For instance, whereas only 9% of Americans have no opinion about Clinton's ideas, 22% have no opinion about Obama's and 41% have no opinion about Thompson's. Still, even when limiting the assessment to informed opinions of each candidate, Clinton is the only candidate receiving mostly positive reviews. Obama and Edwards are viewed equally positively and negatively, and all four Republicans are viewed more negatively than positively.

There are other notable differences in the ratings of the candidates on healthcare by political party. Of course, the Democratic candidates receive more praise from Americans identifying themselves as Democrats (including independents who lean Democratic) than from those identifying as Republicans (and Republican leaners), and vice versa. However, the Democrats receive much more praise from members of their own party than the Republicans do from members of theirs. Whereas a majority of Democrats say that each of the three leading Democrats has good ideas on healthcare, none of the four leading Republican candidates receives majority approval from Republicans nationwide. This is most stark in terms of the party front-runners. While 83% of Democrats say their party's front-runner (Clinton) has good ideas about addressing healthcare, only 47% of Republicans say this with respect to the top-ranked Republican, Giuliani.

Republican Healthcare Ideas Fare Better Than Candidate Ratings Might Suggest

The Democratic advantage on healthcare seen in the candidate ratings, however, is not nearly as obvious in public reaction to the healthcare proposals emanating from the various campaigns. The most popular proposal tested in the poll comes from the Clinton campaign: giving tax breaks to small businesses to allow them to provide health insurance for their employees. More than 9 in 10 Americans (94%) favor this. One of the key elements in all three of the leading Democrats' plans is also among the most popular tested in the poll: requiring large companies to offer health insurance to their employees or pay into a pool used to fund it. Approximately 8 in 10 Americans favor this, including 89% of Democrats and 72% of Republicans.

At the same time, four of the most popular proposals tested include two elements championed by former governor Mike Huckabee: allowing workers to maintain their medical insurance when they change jobs (86%) and providing incentives in health insurance plans for those who can demonstrate a healthy lifestyle (81%). Romney's proposal for reducing government regulation of health insurance providers is favored by 77% of Americans. Both Romney's and Obama's plans include provisions for government subsidies to help lower-income Americans buy private health insurance, a position favored by 76% of Americans. Additionally, 7 in 10 Americans like Republican-backed proposals to institute caps on medical malpractice awards (69%), give American families a $15,000 tax credit to buy private health insurance (68%), and have the federal government help fund state-based healthcare programs (68%).

On the other hand, all three of the least well-reviewed proposals—although still favored by more than half of Americans—come from the Democrats. Representative Dennis Kucinich's proposal for establishing a national healthcare system funded by the government is supported by 54% of Americans, including 76% of Democrats but only 27% of Republicans. Requiring all Americans to carry some form of health insurance, something several of the Democratic plans include, is favored by 53% of Americans. However, because the candidates generally link this mandate to income-based government subsidies to help make health insurance affordable, public support for the intent of this proposal might actually be higher. Similarly, the percentage of Americans saying they favor repealing the federal income tax cuts passed in 2001 and 2002 to pay for new healthcare programs might be higher than the 54% of Americans found in the survey if the question specified that this would apply only to higher-income Americans—as is the case in the Clinton, Obama, and Edwards plans.

In general, the Democratic candidates—those leading the field as well as those lagging in the polls—tend to favor policies that will result in "universal" healthcare coverage, either by a combination of public and private initiatives or through a new national healthcare plan. The Republican candidates tend to speak in terms of expanding healthcare access and coverage by focusing on free-market reforms to the existing private-based healthcare system. Both approaches have potential strengths and weaknesses in terms of winning public support. But the playing field is not as level as public reaction to assorted elements of the various healthcare reform plans might indicate. Perhaps the Democrats have been more vocal about their plans, or more successful in explaining them; perhaps by virtue of the fundamental images of the two parties, Americans are just more willing to believe that Democrats can deal with healthcare. (Recent Gallup polling has given the Democratic Party a strong advantage over the Republicans on this issue, with the Democrats chosen by about 2 to 1 over the Republicans as the party better able to handle healthcare.) Whatever the reason, when it comes to healthcare, Americans clearly have much greater confidence in the leading Democratic candidates—and in Clinton in particular—than in the Republican candidates.

NOVEMBER 2007

The Gallup Poll constantly updates its analysis of the American public's priorities for their elected representatives in Washington—the men and women sent to the nation's capital to do the people's bidding. The Top 10 Priorities list is based on an analysis of open-ended responses to questions asking Americans to name the top priorities for the government along with the most important problem facing the nation today—and to a series of additional questions in response to which respondents give priority to the issues and concerns facing the nation today. Each of the Top 10 Priorities listed below is accompanied by a capsule summary. As the year 2007 comes to a close and voters prepare to go to the polls in caucuses and primaries across the country, these summaries explain what the American public wants its representatives to do with respect to each of these issues.

1. Iraq

Iraq is clearly the dominant policy issue on Americans' minds: It has been at the top of Gallup's Most Important Problem list since March 2004. By a wide margin over any other issue, Americans say it should be the president's and Congress's top priority. In general, Americans have been more likely over the past two years to say that U.S. involvement in the war was a mistake than to say they favor it. In September 2007, 58% of Americans said the Iraq War was a mistake, four points below the highest percentage giving that answer since the war began in March 2003—62% in July 2007. A majority of Americans believe that the United States can win the war in Iraq, but only about a third think it actually will win the war. A majority of Americans opposed the Bush administration's 2007 "surge" in troops, and by September 2007 only about a third believed that the surge was making things better in Iraq. It is clear that Americans want the process of withdrawing U.S. troops from Iraq to

begin now: A majority favor setting a timetable for removing U.S. troops. But there is disagreement regarding how soon and how fast troops should be withdrawn. In late September 2007, Gallup polling showed that Americans approved of a plan to lower the troop level to 130,000 by summer 2008, with no further commitment to withdrawal at that time, and also approved of a plan to withdraw "most" troops within nine months. At the same time, Americans do not favor Congress's passing a resolution to deny funding for the war.

Americans trust General David Petraeus to make the appropriate recommendations about what to do next in Iraq more than they trust other leaders in Washington, including President Bush and the Republican and Democratic leaders in Congress. More than 7 in 10 Americans say the United States is not doing enough to hold the Iraqi government accountable for taking control of the situation in their country. Views on the war are sharply divided along party lines, with Republicans generally supportive and Democrats strongly opposed.

2. Terrorism and National Security

Terrorism is to a significant extent a latent concern for Americans. Along with the Iraq War, terrorism emerges as a top election or public policy concern when Americans are asked to rate the importance of a battery of specific issues. But the public is less likely to name terrorism in open-ended questions asking for the nation's most pressing problem or for the top issues for Congress to deal with. Typically, less than 10% volunteer "terrorism" in response to these questions.

Overall, Americans show fairly broad tolerance for strong antiterrorism measures. Relatively few Americans think the Patriot Act "goes too far" in compromising civil liberties to fight terrorism; a majority either think

CHRONOLOGY

NOVEMBER 2007

November 2 President Bush vetoes the Water Resources Development Act, which would fund a variety of programs for improvements to rivers and harbors, including rebuilding areas damaged by Hurricane Katrina in 2005. His veto is overridden by the House (November 6) and the Senate (November 8). This is the first Bush veto overridden by Congress.

November 3 Pakistani president Perez Musharraf declares a state of emergency, arresting hundreds of opposition leaders. Widespread demonstrations occur across the country. President Bush calls upon Musharraf to restore civilian rule. At the end of the month, Musharraf steps down as military chief but remains Pakistan's president.

November 5 A strike by the Writers Guild of America begins over the issue of sharing residual rights and Internet-based profits. It will last until February 12, 2008.

November 7 A suicide bomber kills dozens of people in Afghanistan, including six members of the parliament.

November 8 The Senate confirms Michael Mukasey as attorney general.

November 15 Democratic presidential candidates debate in Las Vegas. CNN, which sponsors the debate, is criticized for using Clinton supporter James Carville in its post-debate commentary.

November 28 CNN and You-Tube host a Republican presidential debate in St. Petersburg, Florida.

November 30 A disturbed man claiming to have a bomb strapped to his chest takes over Hillary Clinton's campaign office in Rochester, New Hampshire, and holds several hostages for six hours.

---

it is about right or would like it to go further. A majority oppose the use of torture with terrorist suspects and oppose assassinating the leaders of foreign governments that sponsor terrorism. A majority favor requiring CIA agents to adhere to Geneva Convention guidelines when interrogating prisoners. A slight plurality oppose trials in which terrorist suspects are not allowed to see evidence obtained using classified or secret methods. More than half of Americans have said the Guantánamo Bay prison facility in Cuba should be kept open. Americans favor the Bush administration's efforts to wiretap telephone calls of suspected terrorists without a court order. The majority of Americans at this point do not connect the Iraq War with the war on terrorism and are slightly more likely to say the war in Iraq has made the United States less safe, rather than more safe, from terrorism.

3. Economy

American concern about the economy as a top issue has been fairly low during 2007, but taken as a whole, Americans who are dissatisfied with the way things are going in the country today are more likely to mention aspects of the economy than any other issue. Americans' ratings of current economic conditions became more positive in January 2007, but slipped again as 2007 progressed and by summer had become among the most negative that Gallup has measured since the early 1990s. Gallup's September 2007 poll found that roughly 7 in 10 Americans believe the economy is getting worse.

Americans are more positive about their personal financial situation than about the economy as a whole. The hierarchy of personal financial problems that Americans face—and presumably, therefore, that they want government to address—centers on simply not having enough money, having too much debt, the impact of rising costs and inflation, the price of gasoline, healthcare costs, college, retirement, and home ownership. It follows that when asked why they believe the economy is getting worse, Americans are most likely to say it is because of gasoline prices, the poor job and employment situation, inflation, the housing market, and the growing gap between rich and poor. Asked what they would do to improve the economy, Americans advocate, more than anything else, the creation of more and better jobs. While Americans believe they pay too much in taxes, they do not appear to prioritize tax cuts as the primary cure for economic problems. Seven in 10 Americans say they are worried that the recent problems in the home mortgage-lending industry, such as home foreclosures and subprime mortgages, will have a negative effect on the economy; fewer are worried about how this will affect their own personal financial situation. Americans also express concern about the federal deficit, and some data suggest that the public would favor reducing the deficit rather than cutting taxes. Americans are suspicious of big business and tend to favor almost any economic proposal that puts the onus of reform on business.

4. Energy

Americans' concern about energy varies to a significant degree depending on the price of gasoline at the pump. At points in the spring and summer of 2006, Americans rated the energy situation as more serious than they have in several years, and energy and fuel prices began to show up with high frequency as the nation's most important problem and as the top priority for government to deal with. By the summer of 2007, however, the measure of this concern about energy had not risen dramatically, suggesting that the public was becoming accustomed to high gas prices.

When asked which of two approaches to addressing the energy situation they prefer—more production or more conservation—Americans have consistently chosen conservation by a wide margin. The percentage favoring opening up the Alaskan Arctic National Wildlife Refuge gradually increased from 2002 through 2006, with nearly half endorsing it last year; but in 2007 this percentage dropped back down, with only about four in 10 supporting it.

Americans' anger about the energy situation seems mostly directed at the oil and gas industry. Of 25 business and industry sectors rated in 2007, the oil and gas industry receives the most negative ratings. This suggests that government efforts aimed at controlling and regulating the oil industry will be met with high levels of public approval. Large majorities of Americans favor more stringent emissions standards for autos, business, and industry, along with setting mandatory limits on greenhouse gas emissions and developing alternative sources of fuel for automobiles. About half favor expanded use of nuclear power as an energy source, though only about 4 in 10 support constructing nuclear power stations in their own communities.

5. Illegal Immigration

Immigration became a growing concern for Americans in 2007. By the summer of 2007, nearly three in 10 Americans named immigration as the top priority for Congress and government, second only to those who named Iraq. But after attempts to reform immigration policy were defeated in Congress this summer, fewer Americans viewed this as the top government priority, with just 16% mentioning it in September 2007.

Generally speaking, Americans view the effects of immigration positively, but less so than has been the case in the past. Americans are particularly less likely now to say that immigration helps the country culturally and economically. Few Americans want to see immigration levels increased; slightly more want them decreased rather than kept at their present levels. The debate in Congress earlier this year focused on illegal immigration: Proposed legislation has sought to control the flow of illegal immigrants into the country and to develop a plan to deal with illegal immigrants already in the country. Americans think both are important goals. A substantial majority of Americans favor most efforts to stem the flow of illegal immigrants into this country. Throughout the debate over new immigration legislation this year, a majority of Americans favored a plan that would allow illegal immigrants the opportunity to become U.S. citizens if they meet certain requirements over a period of time; but many Americans did not pay attention to the fight over the immigration bill, and among the minority that did, the bill was significantly more likely to be opposed than favored. Americans are somewhat conflicted on some aspects of immigration: They believe illegal immigrants are a drain on taxes and services but also acknowledge the contribution of illegal immigrants to the labor force.

6. Healthcare

Healthcare is among the top domestic concerns of Americans. Medical costs are among the top financial problems facing American families, and healthcare is considered one of the top economic problems for the country as a whole. Healthcare costs and access to healthcare are volunteered as the top specific health problems facing the country, rather than diseases such as AIDS or cancer. Despite these very high levels of concern, however, there is little consensus on exactly what Americans want done to curb healthcare costs. Americans favor each of various alternative solutions by substantial majorities, including offering tax deductions to businesses that provide healthcare coverage, expanding low-income federal assistance to purchase health insurance, lowering the Medicare eligibility age to 55, offering tax deductions to the uninsured, and requiring businesses to offer health insurance. Gallup polling in September 2007 showed that a slight majority of Americans at this time go so far as to favor a national healthcare plan run by the government, similar to the systems in Canada and Great Britain. Americans agree that it is the responsibility of the federal government to make sure that all Americans have healthcare coverage. In general, Americans favor almost any proposal that would force businesses to take more responsibility for providing healthcare coverage for their employees.

7. Education

Americans are more positive about the job being done by their local public schools than they are when asked to rate schools in general across the country. The public tends to believe that it is the responsibility of public schools to try to close the achievement gap between white students and black and Hispanic students. Americans believe that more than anything else, reducing the number of students per classroom while at the same time increasing the number and quality of teachers is the best way to improve public education. Americans also recognize that schools need more funding. They advocate a return to more basics in the curriculum and favor extending the school day in public schools by one hour a day. Contrary to current trends in public education, according to which local school districts are increasingly subject to federal and state mandates, Americans want control of the schools to be at the local school board level, not at the state or federal government level. Half of Americans are not familiar with the most massive attempt to improve public education in recent years, the 2001 No Child Left Behind Act (NCLB). Those who are familiar with NCLB are just as likely to believe that it has hurt public schools as to believe that it has helped. A majority of Americans favor the concept of charter schools. Americans strongly believe that preschool programs for low-income students would improve their school performance.

8. Morality

The acceptable patterns of behavior relating to sexual relations, marriage, reproduction, and matters of life and death are fundamental aspects of any society. As such, they are tightly intertwined with the fundamental beliefs and value structures, particularly as buttressed by religious traditions, subscribed to by members of that society. Moral issues thus have the potential to be extremely powerful in affecting citizens' beliefs about what their elected representatives should be doing. Still, it is rare that legislation relating to moral issues is at the top of the public's agenda for its elected representatives, who are more likely to be subject to intense pressure from smaller interest and values groups on both sides of these issues.

Americans have long been concerned about the state of morality in the United States. More than eight in 10 Americans rate the state of moral values in the United States as only fair or poor (44% say poor), and more than

eight in 10 say that moral values are getting worse rather than better. Moral issues consistently appear in Gallup's monthly measurement of the most important problem facing the country. Morality is a vast domain covering many different aspects of Americans' personal and social lives, however, and it is thus impossible to pass simple legislation that will broadly increase the perceived level of morality in this country. Lawmakers attempting to address the public's concerns about moral issues are faced with the need to deal with these concerns on an issue-by-issue basis.

9. Fixing Government

Concerns about the way government is working now rank among the top five issues when Americans are asked to name the most important problem facing the country. At this juncture in history, Americans are very negative in their views of their elected representatives in Congress: Job approval ratings of Congress are only in the mid-20% range, among the lowest that Gallup has ever observed going back to the 1970s. The public now has the lowest level of confidence in Congress in Gallup's history, and Americans rank the federal government near the bottom of the list of industry or business sectors. Americans continue to believe that political officeholders at the federal level are not highly honest and ethical: As many Americans say most members of Congress are corrupt as say they are not. In 2006, half of Americans said corruption in government was an extremely important issue bearing on their vote for Congress in 2006, ranking second only to the war in Iraq in a list of issues facing the nation. Americans say the Democrats are better able to handle corruption than the Republicans, but only about a third give either party high marks on this issue. It appears that Americans in general favor almost any effort to remedy this situation. Most support campaign finance laws proposed to help fix the election process. The majority of Americans also believe Congress would do a better job if it paid more attention to public opinion and less attention to its members' own personal views.

10. Environment

The environment is not highly likely to be mentioned spontaneously by Americans as a top problem facing the United States at this time, and is also has a low presence when the public is asked about priorities for government. The environment is seen as more important when Americans are presented with a list of issues. A majority of Americans say the government is doing too little to protect the environment, and many worry about environmental conditions. A significant majority believe that the quality of the environment is getting worse, not better.

There has been an increase in Americans' general concern about the environment and in their awareness of global warming. Most Americans take global warming seriously, but only about four in 10 Americans believe that immediate, drastic action is needed to deal with the problem, and just 28% say the impact of global warming will be "extreme" in 50 years if efforts to address the problem are not increased. At this point, 55% of Americans say protection of the environment should be given priority over economic growth, and a majority of Americans believe that protection of the environment should be favored over energy source development. Americans are not opposed to policy initiatives aimed at improving the environment, but they are not pressing for them at this time. The environmental policy initiatives Americans would most welcome appear to be those with the most direct impact: maintaining the safety of drinking water, curbing toxic waste, and improving water and air quality.

NOVEMBER 1

Public Gives Clinton Best Odds of Being Elected President

In Americans' judgment, New York senator Hillary Clinton has the best odds of all the main contenders for the 2008 Democratic presidential nomination of winning the general election in November 2008. The percentage rating her chances of being elected as excellent or good is significantly higher than for any other candidate, and on a comparative basis, Americans say she has a better chance of being elected than Illinois senator Barack Obama, former North Carolina senator John Edwards, and even former vice president Al Gore. Democrats give Clinton better odds of winning than do Republicans and independents, but even a majority of Republicans believe she has a good chance of being elected and say she has a better chance than any of her competitors. These findings are based on a Gallup Poll conducted between October 25 and 28. Clinton's electability was a significant issue in an October 30 debate involving the Democratic presidential candidates. It is unclear to what extent that debate and the ensuing media coverage of it will affect Americans' views of Clinton's candidacy, but even before the debate it was clear that Americans widely believed Clinton to be a viable presidential candidate. The poll asked Americans whether each of the top five announced Democratic candidates had an excellent, good, or slim chance, or no chance, of being elected president in 2008. The ordering of the candidates' perceived electability generally follows their rank order in Gallup's Democratic nomination trial heats: Clinton is the clear leader, with Obama second and Edwards third.

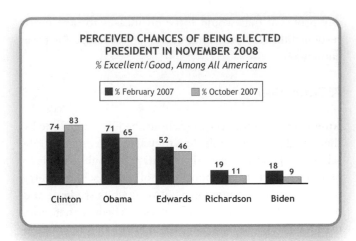

PERCEIVED CHANCES OF BEING ELECTED PRESIDENT IN NOVEMBER 2008
% Excellent/Good, Among All Americans

■ % February 2007   ▪ % October 2007

	Clinton	Obama	Edwards	Richardson	Biden
Feb 2007	74	71	52	19	18
Oct 2007	83	65	46	11	9

More than eight in 10 Americans say Clinton has an excellent or good chance of being elected president next year. Close to two-thirds also believe Obama has at least a good chance of being elected, even though he is now further behind Clinton in national Democratic nomination trial heats than he was only a few months ago. Clinton, Obama, and former New York City mayor Rudolph Giuliani are the only candidates of either party whom most Americans view as having an excellent or good chance of being elected president. Edwards falls just short of the 50% mark on this measure, and only about one in 10 Americans believe that New Mexico governor Bill Richardson or Delaware senator Joe Biden has a better than slim chance of being elected. A February 2007 Gallup Poll asked the same question about each of these candidates. Since that time, Americans have grown more confident in Clinton's chances while becoming less likely to believe any of the other Democratic candidates can win. Clinton and Obama were essentially even on this measure back in February, but Clinton now has an 18-point advantage.

Perceptions by Party

All three major party groups—Democrats, independents, and Republicans—perceive Clinton as having the best chance of winning the presidency. However, within that pattern, Democrats rate the leading Democratic candidates' chances better than do Republicans. Presidential long shots Richardson and Biden are given about equally slim odds of winning by all partisan groups. Currently, 90% of Democrats say Clinton has an excellent or good chance of being elected, the same percentage as in February. But now 46% of Democrats say she has an excellent chance, while in February a slightly smaller percentage, 37%, gave her the best odds. Democrats have downgraded Edwards's chances since February, but Obama's perceived odds are holding steady. The increase in Clinton's perceived chances observed from February to the present among all Americans, then, has come from Republicans (+15 since February) and independents (+14). The decrease in Obama's chances has come more from Republicans (−13) than independents (−6). Republicans, like Democrats, are now less likely than they were in February to see Edwards as a good bet for winning the presidency (−11), while independents' ratings of Edwards have changed little in the past eight months.

Head-to-Head Matchups

In addition to getting a read on each candidate's perceived chances in isolation, the poll also tested Clinton's perceived strength in a series of comparative measures pitting her against each of her strongest rivals for the Democratic nomination, including former vice president Al Gore. Gore, who recently won the Nobel Peace Prize for his work on climate change, has maintained that he has no plans to run for president. Even so, there are organized efforts to urge him to do so, and he has yet to definitively rule out a run. Gore consistently receives double-digit support when included in Gallup's national preference polls for the Democratic nomination, usually placing behind Obama but ahead of Edwards for third place. Democrats, Republicans, and independents show an increased belief in Gore's chances against Clinton, even though all three groups still rate Clinton's chances as better.

Americans believe Clinton has a better chance of being elected president than each of her three leading competitors. The one who comes closest is Gore. Since February, Clinton's advantage over Obama and Edwards has increased, but she has lost some ground to Gore. Clinton and Obama were essentially tied in February, but she has now opened up a wide lead over him. In February, Republicans were more likely to say Obama had a better chance of being elected than Clinton, 52% to 46%. Now, Republicans have revised their thinking and believe Clinton has the better chance by a better than two-to-one margin, 64% to 31%. Democrats were the only party group that thought Clinton had the better chance than Obama in February (57% to 40%), and they still do, but by a much wider 76% to 22% margin.

Clinton's lead in national preference polls has expanded since the summer, and that has helped foster the belief that her nomination as the Democratic candidate for president is likely, if not almost certain. Indeed, there have been reports that she is already campaigning in "general election" mode by trying to move toward the center of the ideological spectrum, whereas Democratic candidates usually try to position themselves more on the liberal side during the primary contests. Obama and Edwards used the October 30 debate to increase their attacks on Clinton in hopes of cutting into her lead. One of the issues raised was her electability. From this survey, conducted before that debate, it is clear that Americans—including both Democrats and Republicans—believe not only that she is electable but that she has a better chance of winning than any other Democratic candidate running for president.

NOVEMBER 2
Public: Giuliani Has Best Chance of Defeating Clinton

The vast majority of Americans say former New York City mayor Rudolph Giuliani has an excellent or good chance both of being elected president and of defeating Hillary Clinton in the November 2008 general election if Clinton is the Democratic presidential candidate. None of the other leading Republican candidates comes close to Giuliani on either measure. Americans give Giuliani, Arizona senator John McCain, and former Massachusetts governor Mitt Romney slightly better chances of "being elected president" than of "defeating Hillary Clinton." Giuliani also has an advantage in perceived electability over the rest of the Republican field in a series of head-to-head electability comparisons against McCain, Romney, and former Tennessee senator Fred Thompson. Giuliani has at least a 40-point electability advantage in each of these comparisons. Democrats, independents, and Republicans all rate Giuliani as the Republicans' best bet in 2008.

Electability of Republican Candidates

The October 25–28, 2007, Gallup Poll asked Americans one of two questions about the chances of six Republican candidates' winning the presidency in November 2008. Half of the respondents were asked about the candidates' chances "of being elected president in November 2008." The other half were asked about the candidates' chances of "defeating Hillary Clinton for president in November 2008 if she is the Democratic candidate." Giuliani is the only candidate who a majority of Americans (79%) say has an excellent or good chance of "being elected president" in 2008. McCain (47%) and Romney (45%) fall just below the 50% level on this measure. Only 31% of Americans view Thompson, who has consistently placed second in national Republican nomination preference polls, as having an excellent or good chance of being elected. The public does not give dark-horse candidates Mike Huckabee, the former governor of Arkansas, and Representative Ron Paul from Texas good odds.

Americans give the leading Republicans—Giuliani, McCain, and Romney—a slightly worse chance of "defeating

Hillary Clinton for president" than of being elected president. Giuliani continues to be perceived as strongest, with 71% saying he has an excellent or good chance of beating Clinton. No other Republican exceeds 40%, with McCain (40%), Romney (37%), and Thompson (34%) closely matched for second. Just 16% of Americans think Huckabee stands a good chance of defeating Clinton, and only 12% think that of Paul. The vast majority of Republicans—86%—say Giuliani has an excellent or good chance of defeating Clinton in next year's general election. More than half of Republicans also say Romney (55%) and Thompson (52%) stand a good chance of defeating Clinton, and 48% say the same about McCain. Giuliani is the only candidate who a majority of independents and Democrats say has a good chance of defeating Clinton in November 2008. In general, Republicans give their party's presidential candidates essentially the same odds of being elected president as they do of defeating Clinton. Independents and Democrats typically give the four leading Republicans better odds of being elected president than of defeating Clinton.

Forty-five percent of Americans now judge that Romney has an excellent or good chance of winning the presidency, up from 27% since February, while belief that McCain can win the election has decreased by an even larger margin, from 70% to 47%. In both polls, more than 7 in 10 Americans have said Giuliani has a good chance of winning the election. The results show a similar pattern among Republicans. Independents and Democrats have also downgraded McCain's chances compared with the February results and upgraded Romney's chances. The slide over the course of the year in Republican support for McCain to win the party's nomination may explain why fewer Americans say he is electable. And while Romney's support in these trial heat polls has not risen dramatically, more Americans may say he is electable because of his successful fund-raising efforts this year.

The poll included a series of questions that paired each of the four leading Republican candidates against one another and asked respondents to choose which of the two would have the best chance of being elected president in November 2008. Giuliani maintains at least a 40-point lead over the three other leading Republican candidates in these head-to-head comparisons—77% to 20% against Thompson, 75% to 21% against Romney, and 69% to 29% against McCain. McCain fares next best on this series of measures, outpolling both Thompson (61% to 36%) and Romney (57% to 39%). Romney edges out Thompson in their one-on-one matchup, 50% to 43%.

In February, Gallup asked the Giuliani versus McCain and Giuliani versus Romney electability comparison questions, with Giuliani winning both matchups. Now, however, fewer Americans say McCain has a better chance than

Giuliani of being elected president than did so in February, and slightly more Americans say Romney has a better chance than Giuliani of being elected president. Among Republicans, Giuliani easily wins the comparison matchups over Romney (75% to 22%), Thompson (74% to 25%), and McCain (70% to 28%). But in matchups between other candidates, Republicans are essentially divided as to which candidate has the better chance of winning the presidency next November. There have been some slight variations in the Republican matchups between Giuliani and McCain and Giuliani and Romney since February, but most of those differences fall within the polls' margins of error.

Clinton Considered Presidential on 11 Dimensions

The U.S. Constitution spells out the legal duties of the president, but other roles presidents are expected to fill are more rooted in norms established by the nation's earliest officeholders. Nowhere in the Constitution does it specify that the president must be inspiring or dignified or safeguard the nation's economy, but these are now among the responsibilities many political scientists and citizens find necessary. In his influential study *The American Presidency*, first published in 1956, presidential scholar Clinton Rossiter outlined seven basic roles of the president: chief of party, chief legislator, chief of state, chief diplomat, chief executive, guardian of the economy, and commander in chief. In a Gallup Poll conducted between October 25 and 28, 2007, Americans were asked to consider how well the front-runner for the 2008 Democratic nomination—Senator Hillary Clinton—would handle each of 11 responsibilities associated with Rossiter's seven presidential roles should she be elected president next year. Clinton scores well on all 11. No less than 53% of Americans think she would do an "outstanding" or "good" job of handling any of the responsibilities, while the minority describes her as doing a "poor" or "terrible" job. Her positive scores average 66% across all 11 areas and reach as high as 83% on one dimension. As might be expected, Clinton's strongest scores are in two areas relying on interaction within her own party. More than 8 in 10 Americans think she would do a good or outstanding job of serving as leader of the Democratic Party—a de facto position that comes with holding the highest office in the land, what Rossiter calls "chief of party." Similarly, with both houses of Congress now controlled by the Democrats, it is logical that 73% of Americans believe Clinton would do a good or outstanding job of working with Congress, in her role as "chief legislator."

Two-thirds or more of Americans are positive about the job Clinton would do in proposing new domestic policy legislation, preserving the dignity of the office of the president, and representing the United States abroad, spanning the roles identified by Rossiter as "chief legislator," "chief of state," and "chief diplomat." Between 62% and 65% of Americans also have positive expectations for Clinton in the areas of managing the federal government and appointing Supreme Court justices and federal judges (both "chief executive"), managing the economy ("guardian of the economy"), and managing U.S. foreign policy ("chief diplomat"). Clinton's lowest scores—though a majority of Americans still rate her positively—are in the areas of inspiring Americans and bringing people together (also "chief of state") and handling the responsibilities of commander in chief of the military.

SHARP PARTISAN DIFFERENCES

Serving as leader of the Democratic Party and working with Congress are the only presidential roles included in the survey in which a majority or near majority of Republicans believe Clinton would do a good or outstanding job (65% and 47%, respectively). On all others, a large majority of Republicans have negative predictions of Clinton's performance. That ranges from 66% saying she would do a poor or terrible job of proposing domestic legislation to 84% saying she would perform badly as commander in chief. The rank order is about the same when looking just at the percentages calling her likely performance "terrible" in each area.

Whether Republicans would be as critical of the potential leadership of other Democratic candidates can't be answered from the poll, but their overall view of Clinton is certainly more negative than is their opinion of Senator Barack Obama and of former senator John Edwards. In a mid-September Gallup Poll, only 17% of Republicans said they had a favorable view of Clinton, while 81% had an unfavorable view. Forty percent of Republicans, on the other hand, had favorable opinions of Obama and Edwards. By contrast, most Democrats have a favorable view of Clinton (81% in mid-September); unsurprisingly, the overwhelming majority of Democrats are positive in their predictions about Clinton's possible presidential leadership—their expectations varying in a narrow range between 86% saying she would do a good or outstanding job as commander in chief to 98% saying she would excel as leader of the Democratic Party. Significantly more variation is seen in Democratic attitudes, however, in terms of the percentages specifically calling her performance outstanding. This highest praise is accorded the prospects of her representing the United States abroad (47% predict she would do an outstanding job) and maintaining the dignity of the office of president (47%), along with her leadership of the Democratic Party (45%). It is awarded by fewer than a third of Democrats with respect to her serving as commander in chief (28%), working with Congress (30%), and managing the federal government (31%). Importantly for Clinton, the roughly one-third of Americans who consider themselves political independents are positive about Clinton on all 11 dimensions—aligning them much more closely with Democrats' views of Clinton than with Republicans'.

How well a candidate is seen as likely to fulfill the basic duties of the presidency, however, is only one aspect of the political calculus Americans use to elect a president. The appeal of the various candidates on personal grounds, how closely Americans agree with the candidates on specific issues, the national popularity of the Republican and Democratic parties, and the particular challenges facing the country at the time of the election all factor in as well. From the data reviewed here, Clinton clearly passes a basic test of presidential leadership. The vast majority of her own party members, as well as a majority of political independents, are confident she could carry out the fundamental duties associated with the job. Republicans' rather harsh expectations are, in fact, consistent with their mostly unfavorable opinions of her. But the net result is positive scores from a majority of Americans on all 11 dimensions. Whether Clinton's potential presidential leadership is more highly rated than that of her Democratic opponents or of any of the potential Republican nominees is another matter—perhaps fodder for future polling.

NOVEMBER 5

Religious Whites Still Tilt Toward Republican Party, Bush

An extensive Gallup analysis of more than 90,000 interviews conducted from 2004 to 2007 shows that highly religious Americans are not drifting away from the Republican Party any more than are Americans generally, or than nonreligious Americans specifically. All Americans have become less likely over the last three years to identify with the Republican Party and less likely to approve of the job President Bush is doing. Highly religious Americans have followed this same pattern, but no more—and no less—than anyone else. This is particularly true among highly religious white Americans, who have constituted a core base for the Republican Party. Thus, the gap between religious white Americans and whites who are not religious in terms of Republican identification and Bush approval is just as large today as it was in 2004 and 2005. Highly religious white Americans remain one of the strongest pockets of support for the Republican Party in the United States.

BACKGROUND

In "The Evangelical Crackup," an October 28, 2007, article in the *New York Times Magazine*, David Kirkpatrick advanced the hypothesis that "the extraordinary evangelical love affair with [President George W.] Bush has ended, for many." Kirkpatrick built most of his article around interviews with conservative Christian pastors and religious leaders, but bolstered his argument using poll data: "Today the president's support among evangelicals, still among his most loyal constituents, has crumbled. Once close to 90 percent, the president's approval rating among white evangelicals has fallen to a recent low below 45 percent, according to polls by the Pew Research Center. . . . And the dissatisfaction extends beyond Bush. For the first time in many years, white evangelical identification with the Republican Party has dipped below 50 percent."

But to what degree has the "love affair" between highly religious white Americans and the Republican Party really ended? Is the president's support really crumbling among evangelicals? And does it appear that a degree or type of disaffection is occurring among religious Americans that is distinct from what is occurring among the broader national population? To help answer these questions, Gallup assembled a data set of more than 90,000 interviews from approximately 90 national surveys conducted between January 2004 and October 2007. Each survey included questions asking respondents about their church attendance, their political identification, and their approval of President Bush. (The analysis that follows focuses exclusively on white respondents, given the near-monolithic identification with the Democratic Party and disapproval of President Bush among blacks.) The analysis underscores first and foremost the degree to which both the Republican Party and President Bush have slipped significantly in their standing among *all* white Americans between 2004 and 2007.

The percentage of white Americans identifying themselves as Republicans has fallen by seven points from 2004 to 2007, from 39% to 32%. The percentage of white Americans approving of the job Bush is doing as president of the

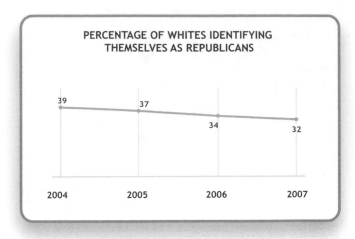

PERCENTAGE OF WHITES IDENTIFYING THEMSELVES AS REPUBLICANS

2004	2005	2006	2007
39	37	34	32

United States has fallen by 19 points, from 56% in 2004 to 37% after the first 10 months of 2007. These conclusions are based on a comparison of more than 25,000 interviews with white Americans that Gallup conducted in 2004 and more than 18,000 interviews with white Americans conducted between January and October 2007. The fact that the poll data cited in Kirkpatrick's article show Republican identification and Bush approval dropping among evangelicals is not in and of itself surprising—because Republican identification and Bush approval have been falling in general. The more important issue is the *degree* of this change relative to that observed among other groups within the population. The question becomes: Has the Republican Party suffered disproportionate losses among religious whites, or do the changes among this group appear to reflect broad, general trends?

For the purposes of this analysis, church attendance is being used as the measure of religiosity. (Church attendance is highly correlated with other measures of religion, includ-

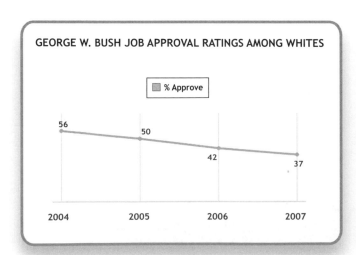

GEORGE W. BUSH JOB APPROVAL RATINGS AMONG WHITES

■ % Approve

2004	2005	2006	2007
56	50	42	37

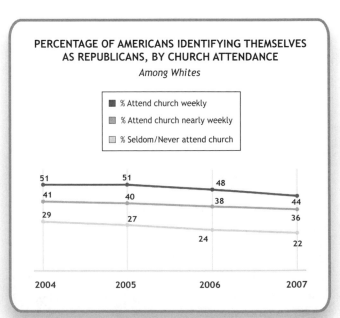

PERCENTAGE OF AMERICANS IDENTIFYING THEMSELVES AS REPUBLICANS, BY CHURCH ATTENDANCE
Among Whites

■ % Attend church weekly
■ % Attend church nearly weekly
□ % Seldom/Never attend church

	2004	2005	2006	2007
% Attend church weekly	51	51	48	44
% Attend church nearly weekly	41	40	38	36
% Seldom/Never attend church	29	27	24	22

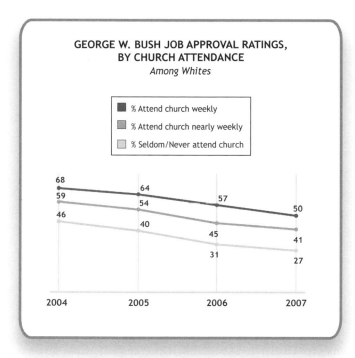

GEORGE W. BUSH JOB APPROVAL RATINGS, BY CHURCH ATTENDANCE
Among Whites

- ■ % Attend church weekly
- ■ % Attend church nearly weekly
- □ % Seldom/Never attend church

	2004	2005	2006	2007
Weekly	68	64	57	50
Nearly weekly	59	54	45	41
Seldom/Never	46	40	31	27

ing the self-reported importance of religion in one's daily life.) Based on 2007 Gallup Poll data, 29% of white Americans go to church weekly. Twenty-three percent of whites say they attend church almost every week or monthly and 47% say they attend seldom or never.

The data show that there has been no diminution in the relative advantage that Bush and the Republican Party enjoy among highly religious whites over less religious whites in 2007, compared to what it was in 2004. The overall level of Republican/Bush identification has declined over these three years, so that now each group defined by church attendance has lower Republican identification and lower Bush approval than it did in 2004. But the relative gap between these groups has remained constant. The gap in Republican identification between highly religious whites and nonreligious whites was 22 points in 2004, and is exactly the same—22 points—in 2007. The gap in Bush job approval between highly religious whites and nonreligious whites was 22 points in 2004 and is 23 points in 2007.

It appears likely that highly religious white Americans have been affected by the same issues, events, and trends that have weakened the position of the Republicans and President Bush across all of American society. Identification with the Republican Party and support for Bush have fallen among religious whites, but on a proportionate basis— and Republicans continue to enjoy a significant advantage among religious whites compared with less religious whites, as they have in the past. It is true that the Republican leanings of highly religious whites did drop. They were not immune to the pressures that have negatively affected the Republican Party since 2004. But religious whites did

not succumb at a disproportionately greater rate than other white Americans. Thus, to this day they continue to be one of the subgroups most likely to identify with the Republican Party and most likely to approve of the job Bush is doing as president. It appears not that there has been a unique falling off of Republican/Bush support within the highly religious segment of the population, but rather that this group has drifted away from the Republican Party and Bush to the same degree as everyone else.

Majority of Americans Pleased with Presidential Field

The presidential election is just a year away, though the candidates have been campaigning in earnest for many months. Just over half of Americans say they are pleased with the field of candidates running for president, similar to what Gallup found four years ago, in advance of the 2004 election. However, the overall stability of this measure hides the fact that Democrats are much more pleased now than they were in 2003, and Republicans are much less pleased. The poll also finds that the Iraq War rates as the top issue for Americans by a significant margin over healthcare and the economy.

EVALUATION OF 2008 CANDIDATES

According to an October 12–14 USA Today/Gallup Poll, 56% of Americans say they are "generally pleased with the field of candidates running for president," while 36% "wish someone else was running." Gallup's measurement prior to the 2004 election—taken in October 2003—showed nearly the same result, with 52% of Americans expressing satisfaction with the field of candidates and 39% expressing displeasure. At that time, George W. Bush was seeking a second term in office, and a large field of Democratic candidates lacking the star power of the current field was seeking to run against him. The relative stability in the overall measure of candidate satisfaction, however, belies

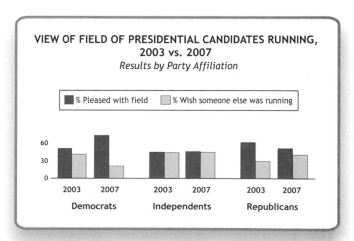

VIEW OF FIELD OF PRESIDENTIAL CANDIDATES RUNNING, 2003 vs. 2007
Results by Party Affiliation

- ■ % Pleased with field   ■ % Wish someone else was running significant change beneath the surface. Compared with 2003, Democrats are now much more likely to express satisfaction with their crop of presidential candidates, Republicans' enthusiasm is down somewhat, and independents' perceptions are similar now to what they were in 2003.

Other Gallup polling this year has found similar gaps in Republican versus Democratic enthusiasm when each party's supporters are specifically asked about their level of satisfaction with the candidates running for their party's presidential nomination.

Important Election Issues

The recent poll also asked the subsample of registered voters which issues will be most important to them when deciding whom to vote for next year. Thirty-eight percent mention Iraq, easily the top issue. Healthcare and the economy are next, mentioned by 18% and 15% of registered voters, respectively. No other issue reaches double digits, including terrorism-related concerns. Iraq is the top issue among Democrats, independents, and Republicans, but Democrats are most likely to mention it. Democrats are also significantly more likely than Republicans to mention healthcare. Gallup asked the same question in April 2007. The only substantial change since then has been an increase in the percentage of registered voters mentioning healthcare—at 18% today, up from 10%. The Iraq War will likely be the dominant issue in the 2008 election, more so than it was in 2004. Heading into that election, the economy rated as the top concern. Iraq was second, but was mentioned by only about half as many as now.

These results further bolster the notion that the Democratic Party is heading into the 2008 election year with a distinct advantage. First, rank-and-file Democrats are much more enthusiastic about their candidates than are Republicans, which should encourage Democrats to turn out on Election Day. Second, the three dominant issues—Iraq, healthcare, and the economy—are all issues that the public currently views the Democrats as better able to handle than the Republicans, according to other recent polling. The Republicans are certainly not doomed—the political winds can shift and a year is a long time in politics—but the party faces an uphill climb.

NOVEMBER 7

Clinton's Big Lead in Democratic Race Unchanged

New USA Today/Gallup polling conducted between November 2 and November 4 shows few signs that front-runner Senator Hillary Clinton's standing among Demo-

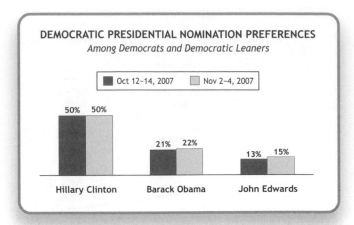

DEMOCRATIC PRESIDENTIAL NOMINATION PREFERENCES
Among Democrats and Democratic Leaners

■ Oct 12–14, 2007   ☐ Nov 2–4, 2007

Hillary Clinton	Barack Obama	John Edwards
50% 50%	21% 22%	13% 15%

crats nationally was affected by the Democratic candidates' debate at Drexel University in Philadelphia on October 30. Clinton continues to lead all contenders as Democrats' first choice for the nomination with half of the Democrats preferring her—more than double the support of her nearest challenger, Senator Barack Obama. Former senator John Edwards, the trial lawyer whose forceful approach to Clinton during the debate has become the subject of considerable discussion, saw no change in his position as the Democrats' third-place candidate.

Clinton's 50% of Democratic support, Obama's 22%, and Edwards' 15% are virtually unchanged from Gallup's October 12–14 poll and are representative of the general structure of the race for the Democratic nomination since August. New Mexico governor Bill Richardson has 4% of the vote, while Delaware senator Joe Biden, Ohio representative Dennis Kucinich, and Connecticut senator Christopher Dodd each have only 1% of the Democratic vote.

Last week's debate at Drexel University was notable in that it was the first such event to see sustained criticism of the front-running Clinton by her challengers. Some observers opined in print and on the air that Clinton had in fact "lost" the debate by virtue of the way she responded to questions about Iran and about a plan to allow illegal immigrants in her home state of New York to obtain drivers' licenses. This poll did not ask Democrats whether they saw the debate or news coverage of it, and thus did not measure directly any perceived gain or loss by candidates as a result of the debate or of the news coverage that followed. But the stability in Gallup's nomination preference trends more indirectly suggests that the debate had little impact on the standing of the candidates in the minds of Democrats nationwide. Clinton's lead remains formidable.

Images of the Candidates

Nationally, Clinton is viewed favorably by 52% of Americans and unfavorably by 45%. This is almost precisely what

Gallup measured in two October 2007 polls. In similar fashion, there has been no statistically significant change in the images of either Obama or Edwards among Americans when the results before and after the debate are compared. Among Democrats there have been slight changes in the candidates' images, but none that are statistically meaningful. Clinton continues to have the highest favorable ratings of the three leading candidates, although Obama and Edwards suffer in comparison not because they have higher unfavorable ratings, but because there are higher percentages of Democrats who, even at this point in time, don't know enough about them to have an opinion. Clinton had an 84% favorable image among Democrats in the Gallup Poll conducted before the debate and has an 82% favorable image in the current poll. Edwards's image became slightly more favorable between the two polls, but not enough to be statistically meaningful.

At this point in the race for the Democratic nomination, after 10 months of arduous campaigning, the structure of the race appears pretty well established, and it may take a powerful confluence of events to change it. Some observers saw the October 30 debate in Philadelphia as such an event—but the latest Gallup Poll data suggest that the debate had little, if any, impact on the race. Clinton remains the dominant front-runner and has the highest favorable image of any of the leading candidates among Democrats nationwide.

Giuliani Leads; Close Race for Second Among Republicans

The latest USA Today/Gallup update on national Republicans' preferences for the party's 2008 presidential nomination shows former New York City mayor Rudolph Giuliani maintaining a significant lead, with three candidates closely matched for second place. The November 2–4 poll finds Giuliani the top choice of 34% of Republicans and Republican-leaning independents, followed by Arizona senator John McCain at 18%, former Tennessee senator Fred Thompson at 17%, former Massachusetts governor Mitt Romney at 14%, and former Arkansas governor Mike Huckabee at 6% support, with all other active candidates at 1% or less of the vote.

At least 30% of Republicans have named Giuliani as their first choice for the nomination in all but one poll this year. He has led in every Gallup Poll since February 2007, with an average lead of 14 percentage points. Thus, his current 16-point edge over McCain is in line with his typical standing. Romney's 14% showing in the current poll ties his best to date, from early June and following his victory in the Iowa straw poll in mid-August. But in both those instances, Romney failed to sustain positive momen-

tum in the national polls. His support dropped to 8% in the next poll following his 14% reading from June, and to 10% following that same reading in August. Meanwhile, Thompson's support is below 20% for a second consecutive poll after being at or above 20% in all but one poll from mid-June to early October.

Views of the Candidates

Giuliani is also well ahead of his competitors in terms of having the most positive overall image among Republicans. Seventy-four percent of Republicans and Republican leaners have a favorable opinion of Giuliani, and his net favorable rating of +57 (percentage favorable minus percentage unfavorable) is nearly 20 points better than that of McCain, who is the second most positively rated candidate. One-third or more of Republicans are still not familiar enough with Romney, Thompson, or Huckabee to have formed an opinion of them. But all three are viewed more positively than negatively by Republican partisans.

Among the general public, the leading Republican candidates' ratings lag behind those of the leading Democrats. Each of the three leading Democrats has a net favorable rating among all Americans, with Hillary Clinton at +7, Barack Obama at +23, and John Edwards at +19. Only Giuliani and McCain can claim this distinction among the leading Republicans. Thompson, Huckabee, and Romney—though they are all still relative unknowns to most Americans—currently get about as many negative evaluations as positive ones. Notably, however, the Republican front-runner (Giuliani) is much more favorably viewed by the general public than is the Democratic front-runner (Clinton). In fact, Giuliani currently ties Obama as the most popular candidate nationally. In recent weeks, Thompson's image has suffered greatly. When he officially entered the race in early September, his net favorable rating was +17 (36% favorable, 19% unfavorable) among all Americans and +41 (54% favorable, 13% unfavorable) among Republicans. Now, barely two months into his official campaign, his ratings have fallen to +1 (29% favorable, 28% unfavorable) and +29 (47% favorable, 18% unfavorable), respectively. It is not uncommon for presidential candidates' negatives to grow as they campaign for the presidency. But in the cases of Giuliani and Obama, though their negatives have grown over time, they are still on balance rated positively. During this time, Thompson's support for the Republican nomination has fallen slightly but perceptibly, from 22% to 17%.

With the Iowa caucuses less than two months away, the Republican field is showing some movement. Thompson has fallen back into a tie for second place with McCain, and Romney is nipping at their heels. Romney will attempt to sustain positive poll momentum for the first time during the campaign. He remains the leader in polls of Iowa and New Hampshire Republicans, and strong showings there will likely improve his national standing. Giuliani, however, continues to lead in national polls and remains well positioned, especially given that Republicans have traditionally selected the national front-runner as the party's presidential nominee.

NOVEMBER 8

Clinton Eclipses Giuliani in National Election Indicators

The political climate continues to look positive for Senator Hillary Rodham Clinton. Not only is she holding a considerable lead for the 2008 Democratic presidential nomination—chosen by a more than two-to-one margin over second-place contender Senator Barack Obama—but she has once again moved slightly ahead of the Republican front-runner, Rudolph Giuliani, in Gallup's national ballot for the general election. According to the latest USA Today/Gallup Poll, conducted between November 2 and November 4, Clinton now leads Giuliani by six percentage points—51% to 45%—as the candidate whom registered voters would support for president next November. This is a change from August, when Clinton trailed Giuliani by four points. Gallup's trial-heat polls pitting Clinton against Giuliani have shown the race to be tight all year, with the "lead" changing several times back and forth between the two. Giuliani had small leads in polls conducted in February, April, and early June; Clinton moved into the lead in a mid-June poll. Giuliani regained the lead

in August, and now Clinton is ahead. None of these leads has been large.

Clinton and Giuliani currently receive equal levels of support from members of their own party in this one-on-one ballot: 89% of Democratic registered voters prefer Clinton for president, while 88% of Republicans choose Giuliani. Independents break about evenly: 48% for Giuliani and 46% for Clinton. Clinton's lead in the poll is due to the somewhat greater proportion of Americans calling themselves Democrats than Republicans in this survey.

Some Added Assurance for Clinton

The current poll also included a measure of the likelihood that Americans would vote for each of seven presidential candidates in the general election. At 32%, Clinton is the recipient of the highest percentage saying they will "definitely" vote for her—money in the bank, as it were. That is a high percentage considering the party nominations have not even been decided yet, perhaps indicating that voters are more certain of Clinton's winning her party's nomination than of anyone else earning a spot on the ballot next fall. Both Giuliani and Obama run at least 10 points behind Clinton on this early indicator of electoral strength, with 22% and 19%, respectively, saying they will definitely vote for each. The even lower percentages for former senator John Edwards, Senator John McCain, former senator Fred Thompson, and former governor Mitt Romney on this measure follow the rank order in which they are favored for their respective party nominations in the same poll.

The only asterisk to Clinton's advantage on this measure—and a potentially significant one—is that more voters say they "might consider" voting for Giuliani and Obama than say this about her. As a result, these three top contenders for the 2008 presidency run about evenly in the percentage of voters saying they will either definitely vote for or might consider voting for each. Edwards and McCain both get a considerable boost from those saying they might consider supporting each in the general election, putting them equal or close to their respective parties' front-runners.

Thompson and Romney lag well behind, with no more than 39% of voters identifying themselves as potential voters for each; indeed, a majority of Americans put themselves into the "definitely not vote for" column for each. However, a standard caveat applies to interpreting these ratings: Thompson and Romney are both much less well known than the other leading contenders for the Democratic and Republican nominations, and accordingly are at a disadvantage on all candidate strength measures. In principle, they could become more competitive if and when they become better known during the campaign.

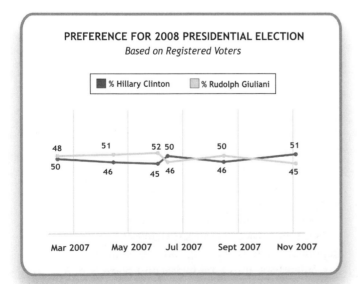

PREFERENCE FOR 2008 PRESIDENTIAL ELECTION
Based on Registered Voters

■ % Hillary Clinton   □ % Rudolph Giuliani

48   51   52 50   50   51
50   46   45 46   46   45

Mar 2007   May 2007   Jul 2007   Sept 2007   Nov 2007

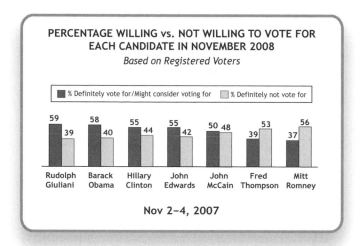

PERCENTAGE WILLING vs. NOT WILLING TO VOTE FOR EACH CANDIDATE IN NOVEMBER 2008

Based on Registered Voters

■ % Definitely vote for/Might consider voting for   □ % Definitely not vote for

Rudolph Giuliani: 59 / 39
Barack Obama: 58 / 40
Hillary Clinton: 55 / 44
John Edwards: 55 / 42
John McCain: 50 / 48
Fred Thompson: 39 / 53
Mitt Romney: 37 / 56

Nov 2–4, 2007

Gallup had previously asked this voting likelihood question about Clinton in a January 2006 survey; at that time, only half as many registered voters said they would definitely vote for her as say this today. More said they might consider voting for her than do today, but on balance the current poll offers a more positive picture for her. Nearly two years ago, 48% said they would definitely or possibly vote for Clinton for president; today that figure is 55%. Conversely, it would seem that Clinton has crossed an important electability threshold, with only 44% of voters now (compared with 51% in January 2006) saying they would definitely not vote for her.

Despite currently trailing in the head-to-head matchup with Clinton, Giuliani has as deep a well as Clinton's, if not a deeper one, into which to dip for voters, but he needs to do a better job of dipping. That is the essence of what Gallup's latest set of national election figures says about the election. Nearly 6 in 10 voters express a willingness to vote for Giuliani in November 2008, compared with Clinton's 55%. Yet Giuliani currently trails her by six percentage points in Gallup's head-to-head ballot test. A key problem for him is that he is attracting a much smaller share of his potential voters than Clinton is of hers.

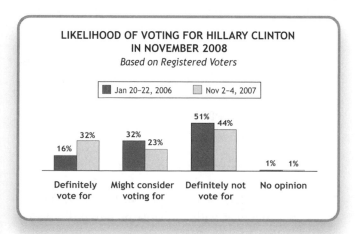

LIKELIHOOD OF VOTING FOR HILLARY CLINTON IN NOVEMBER 2008

Based on Registered Voters

■ Jan 20–22, 2006   □ Nov 2–4, 2007

Definitely vote for: 16% / 32%
Might consider voting for: 32% / 23%
Definitely not vote for: 51% / 44%
No opinion: 1% / 1%

NOVEMBER 12

Clinton, Giuliani, and Obama Tie on Presidential Leadership

Despite Senator Hillary Clinton's position as the dominant front-runner for the Democratic Party's presidential nomination, Americans rate Clinton and competitor Senator Barack Obama roughly the same when asked about the candidates' leadership qualities and about their agreement with the candidates on the issues, with former senator John Edwards not too far behind. This conceals the fact that Clinton is more positively evaluated by those in her own party than is Obama or Edwards, while she does worse than her competitors among Republicans. On the other hand, former mayor Rudolph Giuliani, who is the front-runner for the Republican Party's nomination, does better than either former governor Mitt Romney or former senator Fred Thompson on both dimensions, maintaining his advantage among Republicans as well as Democrats. These findings from the November 2–4, 2007, USA Today/Gallup Poll suggest that while Clinton is well respected by Democrats, she lags behind her Democratic challengers among Republicans—which, if that persists, could have implications for the general election. (The same poll shows Clinton leading Giuliani among registered voters by a six-point margin, so it is not a fatal problem for her at the moment, but it could explain why she is not doing even better in the face-off.)

More Perceive Leadership in Candidates Than Shared Policy Positions

Gallup asked respondents whether each of the six candidates rated in the survey "has the personality and leadership qualities a president should have" and whether they agree or disagree with each candidate "on the issues that matter most to you." Americans are slightly more likely to say Clinton has the personality and leadership qualities needed in a president than to say they agree with her on the issues, though a majority of Americans answer yes to both statements. Giuliani and Obama receive nearly the same ratings as Clinton on both dimensions. Edwards trails only slightly behind Obama on these measures. Romney and Thompson, on the other hand, have much lower scores—in part because of lower name identification, but also because they have higher negatives on these measures.

Americans' perceptions of the personality and leadership strengths of the top-ranked candidates for president, as well as their agreement with them on the issues, closely follow their overall opinions of these candidates as measured by Gallup's standard favorability question. At least half the public views Clinton, Obama, Giuliani, and Edwards favorably; unsurprisingly, a majority of Americans

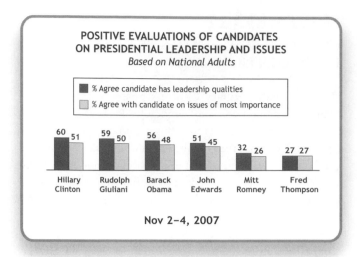

POSITIVE EVALUATIONS OF CANDIDATES
ON PRESIDENTIAL LEADERSHIP AND ISSUES
Based on National Adults

■ % Agree candidate has leadership qualities
▢ % Agree with candidate on issues of most importance

	Hillary Clinton	Rudolph Giuliani	Barack Obama	John Edwards	Mitt Romney	Fred Thompson
Leadership	60	59	56	51	32	27
Issues	51	50	48	45	26	27

Nov 2–4, 2007

say each has "the personality and leadership qualities a president should have," and about half say they agree with each on the most important issues.

Romney and Thompson have much lower favorable scores—in part because a substantial segment of the public is not familiar with them—and consequently their ratings with respect to leadership qualities and issue positions are quite low. Romney and Thompson have more to overcome than low name identification, however; nearly half of Americans say each man lacks the leadership qualities a president should have and does not share their views on the issues. Fewer than 4 in 10 Americans say this on either dimension with respect to Giuliani, Obama, and Edwards, or regarding Clinton relative to leadership qualities. However, 44% say she does not share their views on the most important issues.

Partisan Differences

While several of the candidates cluster together at the top of the rankings with respect to leadership and issues agreement, considerable differentiation is seen according to partisanship. Consistent with her strong front-runner status in the Democratic Party, Clinton is the clear favorite of Democrats on both dimensions, well ahead of Obama and Edwards as well as of the Republicans rated. Similarly, among Republicans, Giuliani far outpaces not only Clinton, Obama, and Edwards but the other two Republicans included in the survey: Romney and Thompson. (Senator John McCain was not rated on these leadership and issues questions, so it is unclear whether he would be more competitive with Giuliani on these dimensions than Romney or Thompson.)

Naturally, their partisan supporters give the front-runners for each party's presidential nomination—Clinton for the Democrats and Giuliani for the Republicans—high marks on both dimensions. However, Clinton is rated

slightly higher by Democrats than Giuliani is by Republicans, particularly with respect to agreement with the candidates on the issues: Eighty-eight percent of Democrats say Clinton has the personality and leadership qualities necessary to be president, compared with 81% of Republicans saying this about Giuliani; and 85% of Democrats say they agree with Clinton on issues that are most important to them, compared with 75% of Republicans saying this of Giuliani. At the same time, Giuliani has greater crossover political appeal on both dimensions. Only 22% of Republicans say Clinton has presidential leadership qualities, compared with 39% of Democrats saying this of Giuliani; similarly, only 11% of Republicans agree with Clinton on the most important issues, compared with 29% of Democrats who agree with Giuliani. These differences in crossover appeal could obviously play an important role if Clinton and Giuliani emerge as the nominees for their respective parties next year.

Obama also has relatively high crossover appeal, as Republicans' positive ratings of him on both dimensions are about as twice as high as those for Clinton. That could speak to the comparative viability of Clinton in the general election versus that of Obama if he became the nominee.

NOVEMBER 13
Giuliani, Moral Values, and the Republican Nomination

A major story line throughout the presidential campaign has been Republican front-runner Rudolph Giuliani's potential vulnerability because of his pro-choice views on abortion and pro–gay rights stance, positions that are generally out of step with most Republican voters. Giuliani has led national preference polls for the Republican nomination for much of the year, but it is unclear to what extent Republican voters know about his positions on these issues and, more importantly, how that might play out in the nomination battle. A review of recent Gallup Poll data finds that while most Republicans are unaware of Giuliani's positions on abortion and gay rights, they nevertheless generally perceive him to be liberal or moderate on moral values issues. In the most recent Gallup Poll, most Republicans expressed a preference for a nominee who is conservative on such issues—but even among these voters, Giuliani had more support for the nomination than any of his competitors.

Knowledge of Giuliani's Positions

A recent USA Today/Gallup Poll revealed that most Republicans are unfamiliar with Giuliani's precise positions on

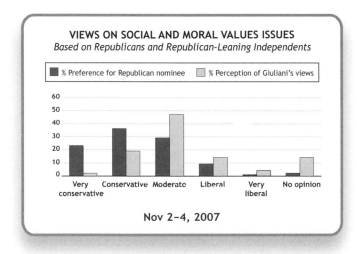

VIEWS ON SOCIAL AND MORAL VALUES ISSUES
Based on Republicans and Republican-Leaning Independents

■ % Preference for Republican nominee   ▢ % Perception of Giuliani's views

Nov 2–4, 2007

abortion (55%) and gay civil unions (74%). Republicans are more knowledgeable about Giuliani's position on abortion, but not about his position on civil unions, than they were earlier in the year. In January, 64% of Republicans were unsure of his position on abortion, and those who responded were as likely to characterize him as being pro-life (16%) as pro-choice (20%). Now, Republicans clearly identify him as pro-choice, by a 37% to 8% margin.

At the same time, even if most Republicans are unable to specify Giuliani's positions on these issues, there is a perception that his views on "social and moral values issues" fall somewhere in the middle of the ideological spectrum. The November 2–4 USA Today/Gallup Poll shows that most Republicans perceive Giuliani as moderate (47%) or liberal (18%) on social and moral values issues. Just 21% believe he is conservative. The challenge for Giuliani is that most rank-and-file Republicans would prefer the party nominate a candidate with conservative or very conservative (59%) rather than liberal or moderate (39%) positions on these issues.

Among Republicans who prefer a conservative values candidate for the 2008 presidential nomination, Giuliani does not fare as well as he does among those who prefer a moderate or liberal candidate. But he still tops the list among the former group, even though his lead over second-place Fred Thompson is not statistically significant. He is the solid choice among Republicans who prefer a nominee with liberal or moderate social issues positions, with a 25-point lead over second-place John McCain. Some analysts believe that Giuliani may fail to win the Republican nomination on account of his views on moral values issues, and the fact that a majority of Republicans do not know his precise views on those issues lends some weight to that argument. But as the above analysis makes clear, he is at worst competitive and at best the leader among Republicans who would be disinclined to support a candidate with his social and moral values issues profile.

Results of other Gallup Polls provide some possible hypotheses as to why moral values issues have not, to this point, derailed Giuliani's campaign:

1. On the most basic level, Giuliani passes the "likability" test better than his Republican competitors. His 74% favorable rating among Republicans is 12 points higher than the Republican rated next most positively, McCain.

2. Giuliani benefits when the campaign focus shifts away from issues and onto other relevant dimensions, such as the candidates' personal characteristics. For example, Republicans widely perceive Giuliani to be a stronger leader than Romney and Thompson, and 63% of Republicans say Giuliani's "leadership style" makes them more likely to vote for him.

3. Giuliani is currently well positioned among "strategic" Republican voters—those who are most likely to support the candidate who they perceive has the best chance of winning. A recent Gallup Poll found that Republicans do in fact rate Giuliani as the candidate with the best chance of being elected president and, separately, as the candidate with the best chance of defeating Hillary Clinton in the November 2008 election. Even though a majority of Republicans, 57%, say they want the party to nominate the candidate closest to them on the issues, a substantial minority of 38% of Republicans prefer the party nominate the candidate with the best chance of beating the Democrat, even if that candidate does not agree with them on the issues they care about. Giuliani is the top choice among these "strategic Republicans" and fares better among this group than he does among "issues voters."

4. Republican primary and caucus voters will likely take many issues into account when deciding which candidate to support, and Giuliani may look more appealing on other issues than he does on moral values. For example, a September Gallup Poll showed Giuliani with significant advantages over his chief Republican rivals on terrorism and crime. Also, in the November 2–4 poll, Giuliani looks to be a better fit with the party rank and file on economic issues—64% of Republicans want the party to nominate an economic conservative, and 41% view Giuliani in those terms—than on moral values. Perhaps most importantly, though, moral values issues may not be as crucial to deciding the Republican nominee as some pundits perceive. In the October 12–14 poll, 61% of Republicans say Giuliani's views on abortion and gay rights either make no difference in whether they will vote for him for president or make them more likely to vote *for* him. Twenty-eight percent say Giuliani's views make them more likely to vote against him, including 17% who say "much more likely."

The Republican presidential candidates will certainly do their best to remind voters about Giuliani's views on abortion and gay marriage, because those positions are an

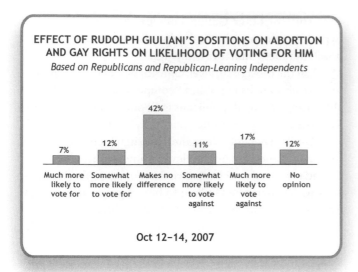

EFFECT OF RUDOLPH GIULIANI'S POSITIONS ON ABORTION AND GAY RIGHTS ON LIKELIHOOD OF VOTING FOR HIM

Based on Republicans and Republican-Leaning Independents

42%

7%   12%   11%   17%   12%

Much more | Somewhat | Makes no | Somewhat | Much more | No
likely to | more likely | difference | more likely | likely to | opinion
vote for | to vote for | | to vote | vote |
| | | against | against |

Oct 12–14, 2007

obvious weakness for him. But it likely will take much more than that to defeat the current front-runner. Televangelist Pat Robertson's endorsement of Giuliani on November 7 shows that even strongly religious Republicans will not necessarily disqualify the former New York City mayor on those grounds.

What's Behind Republican and Democratic Party Identification?

One of the most important variables in understanding Americans' political attitudes is partisanship, or the political party with which a voter identifies. There is no more compelling example of this than the cross-tabulation of candidate choice (in a hypothetical matchup between Hillary Clinton and Rudolph Giuliani) and party identification. Almost 9 in 10 of those who identified as Democrats in an early November Gallup Poll said they were going to vote for Clinton, while almost exactly the same percentage of those who identified as Republicans said they were going to vote for Giuliani. (Independents split down the middle.) This reflection of the key importance of partisanship is typical of all presidential elections for which Gallup has survey data.

Because of the importance of political partisanship as a predictor of political attitudes, its sources have been the subject of much study and debate among survey researchers and political scientists over the years. There is broad agreement that one's identification with a political party is due to a combination of one's upbringing, one's ethnicity or race, one's geographic location, and one's socioeconomic status. In addition to these factors, Americans also align themselves with a party based on the party's basic ideology or specific issue positions. To help gain a better understanding of all of these factors, a recent Gallup Poll asked Americans—after they identified as Republicans or

Democrats (or said they leaned to one or the other party if they initially said they were independents)—to explain in their own words just what it was about their chosen party that appealed to them most.

The Appeal of the Republican and Democratic Parties

Republicans appear to justify their allegiance to their party most often with a reference to its conservatism generally and its conservative stances on moral issues in particular. Beyond that, Republicans mention the party's conservative economic positions, its preference for smaller government, and, in smaller numbers, a variety of other considerations.

The pattern of rationales or justifications that Democrats invoke is somewhat different. Compared with the percentage of Republicans who mention conservatism as their rationale for identifying with the Republican Party, the percentage of Democrats who mention liberalism is relatively small. Instead, Democrats are most likely to mention that the Democratic Party appeals to them because it is for the working class, the middle class, or the "common man." Democrats also tend to mention issues or party stances in general, and to a lesser extent specific issues such as the party's anti-war, pro-healthcare, and pro-environment stances.

Ideological Groups Within the Parties

The vast majority of Americans—more than 9 in 10—identify with or lean to one of the two major parties. Each of the major political parties, then, constitutes a relatively "big tent," comprising a number of subgroups that may have different reasons for identifying themselves with that party. One important distinction among Republicans is between those who describe their views on political issues as "conservative" (about 76% of Republicans in this sample) and those who describe their views as either "moderate" or "liberal" (about 24%). Polling results show that the large group of Republicans who have identified themselves as conservatives are especially likely to say the party appeals to them precisely because it is conservative in general and, in particular, conservative on moral issues. There is little difference between the two groups in terms of mentioning the appeal of the Republican Party because of its conservative economic policies. The smaller group of Republicans who identify themselves as moderate or liberal are more likely than conservative Republicans to say the appeal of the party lies with its focus on individual self-reliance. Importantly, the data also show that moderate and liberal Republicans are more likely to say they don't have a reason for liking the Republican Party, and in general are less likely to offer any response to this question (regarding why the party appeals to them), though it allowed up to three different answers from each respondent. This could suggest that moderates and liberals who identify with the Republican Party are, in a broad sense, less certain of why they are Republicans than are those who are conservative.

Democrats can be divided in a slightly different fashion: between those who are conservative or moderate in their issue orientation (58% of Democrats in this sample) and those who are liberal (42%). As might be expected, liberal Democrats are more likely than conservative or moderate Democrats to mention that the appeal of the Democratic Party is that it is liberal. But otherwise there are not large differences in the reasons given for party identification. Both groups also appear to offer responses with roughly the same frequency and to have similar "don't know" patterns.

The appeal of the Republican and Democratic parties to those who identify with each is based first and foremost on broad views of each party's general ideology and orientation, rather than on specific issues. Republicans more than anything else say they like the Republican Party because it is conservative; Democrats say they like the Democratic Party because it favors the common man, the middle class, and the working class. The finding that the appeal of the Republican Party is based above all else on its conservatism would seem to leave moderate and liberal Republicans at least somewhat out in the cold. The data seem to confirm that. The latter group of Republicans is less likely than conservative Republicans to be able to give a reason for their party identification.

NOVEMBER 14

Americans Widely Disappointed With Democrats in Congress

Amidst a swirl of public dissatisfaction about the Iraq War, the economy, and government corruption—and with President Bush more generally—Americans went to the polls in November 2006 and voted enough Republicans out of office to give the Democrats majority control of Congress. A year later, Americans are as negative about the job Congress is doing as they were leading up to the 2006 midterm elections. And according to recent Gallup polling, Americans are distinctly negative about the Democrats' handling of several major policy issues. The latest Gallup survey, conducted between October 25 and October 28, 2007, asked Americans to say whether they are "pleased," "neutral," "disappointed," or "angry" about the way the Democrats in Congress have been dealing with seven major issues confronting the nation: the federal budget, terrorism, Iraq, immigration, the economy, government reform, and healthcare.

Overall, relatively few Americans—ranging from 7% for the federal budget deficit to 17% for terrorism—are pleased with the Democrats' performance on any of these issues. Between 12% and 26% say they are angry about how the Democrats are handling these issues. However, most Americans fall in between, with a plurality generally saying they are disappointed with congressional Democrats' performance on each of the issues. Another way to evaluate these findings is to combine the percentages saying they are pleased or neutral and contrast these totals with the percentages saying they are disappointed or angry (two clearly negative categories). Judged this way, Democrats receive their best ratings on terrorism and their worst on Iraq and immigration.

More specifically, a majority of Americans are pleased or neutral about the way the Democratic Congress has dealt with terrorism, and close to half are pleased or neutral about Congress's handling of the economy and government reform. These relatively positive ratings could reflect some of the Democrats' early successes in passing the antiterrorism recommendations of the September 11, 2001, commission, raising the minimum wage, and reforming a variety of ethics and lobbying laws. They may also reflect the absence of major terrorist acts or highly publicized terrorist threats this year. But on four other issues, the public offers more clearly negative assessments. Six in 10 Americans are disappointed or angry with the Democrats' performance on healthcare and the federal budget deficit. About two-thirds have a negative reaction to their handling of immigration and Iraq. Iraq is the most negatively evaluated of all—perhaps reflecting not only the degree to which Iraq is seen as the nation's top problem today, but also the expectation that a new, Democratic-controlled Congress would have been more effective in changing course in Iraq.

If this lackluster evaluation of the Democratic Congress were highly partisan—with Republicans mostly negative and Democrats mostly positive—the House and Senate leadership could at least be satisfied that it is meeting the expectations of its base supporters. However, that is not the case. Democrats are less negative than Republicans, but they are still somewhat negative about the performance of their own party's leadership in Congress. A majority of Democrats are positive or neutral about the Democratic Congress on three issues (terrorism, government reform, and the economy), but a majority are negative on another three (the federal budget deficit, immigration, and Iraq). Democrats are about equally divided (at 50% vs. 49%) in their assessment of congressional Democrats on healthcare.

The two issues at the bottom in Democrats' rankings of Congress—immigration and Iraq—both apparently tap Democratic frustration with congressional inaction or failure to prevail over the Republicans. With a comprehensive immigration reform bill dying in late June, it is perhaps not surprising that 16% of Democrats say they are "angry" about congressional Democrats' handling of immigration. Similarly, the Democrats' failure to force President Bush to pull out of Iraq, or at least to establish a timetable for withdrawing troops, perhaps explains why 17% of Democrats are angry with congressional Democrats on the Iraq issue. As would be expected, Republicans are even more critical of the Democratic-controlled Congress than are Democrats, with a majority of Republicans saying they are disappointed or angry with congressional Democrats on all seven issues. On most issues, the views of independents fall somewhere between those of the two party groups.

Democrats took power in January 2007 with a declared agenda of what they would accomplish in the first 100 legislative hours, while also offering the customary promises about working in a bipartisan fashion to do the nation's business. At the time, 37% of Republicans and 39% of Democrats approved of the job Congress as a whole was doing. As of October 2007, only 25% of Republicans and 26% of Democrats approve. The data reviewed above indicate some of the causes for today's depressed ratings. Of the major issues Congress has wrestled with during this session, Iraq and immigration appear to be producing the most flak for congressional Democrats, with a majority of rank-and-file Democrats as well as Republicans generally critical of their job performance. The Democrats' taking a stand on these issues and then failing to deliver has produced substantial bipartisan irritation with Congress.

NOVEMBER 16

Giuliani Leads; Four More at or Above 10% in Republican Contest

The latest Gallup Poll update on national Republicans' preferences for the party's 2008 nomination shows former New York City mayor Rudolph Giuliani continuing to lead the field, although his support has dropped below 30% for the first time since June, and his nine-point lead is on the low end of the leads he has held since February. Four other Republican candidates now register double-digit support, including former Arkansas governor Mike Huckabee, who now has his highest level of support to date. In general, the Republican field appears more tightly bunched than at other times this year, suggesting the possibility of a highly competitive race for the party's presidential nomination.

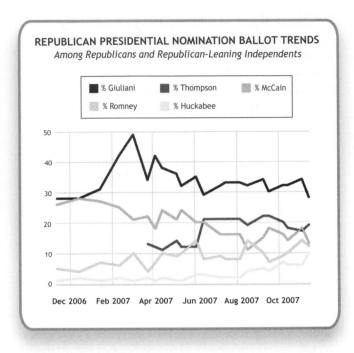

REPUBLICAN PRESIDENTIAL NOMINATION BALLOT TRENDS
Among Republicans and Republican-Leaning Independents

■ % Giuliani   ■ % Thompson   ■ % McCain
■ % Romney   ■ % Huckabee

The November 11–14 Gallup Poll finds 28% of Republicans and Republican-leaning independents nationwide naming Giuliani as their first choice for the party's 2008 presidential nomination. Former Tennessee senator Fred Thompson is second, at 19%. Thompson appears, for the moment, to have halted some negative momentum, as his numbers had fallen slightly in each of the three prior polls. Thompson received a key endorsement from the National Right to Life Committee on November 13, although it is unclear whether that boosted his support. Arizona senator John McCain (13%), former Massachusetts governor Mitt Romney (12%), and Huckabee (10%) are closely matched for third place. Texas representative Ron Paul places sixth with 5% support. This marks the first time Huckabee's support has reached double digits in a Gallup Poll. He currently places second in several polls of Republicans in the state of Iowa, site of the first Republican caucus. The leader in Iowa polls is Romney, who for the first time has seen his national support in double digits for three successive polls. Since February 2007, Giuliani has led every Gallup Poll of Republican presidential preferences by a statistically significant margin. His largest lead during this time was 28 points in early March (before Thompson's support was measured), and his smallest lead of 8 points occurred on three separate occasions in May, June, and September.

On November 7, televangelist Pat Robertson endorsed Giuliani for president. The poll sought to gauge the possible impact of that endorsement by asking Republicans whether Robertson's endorsement would make them more likely to vote for Giuliani or less likely to do so, or would not affect their vote. Typically, poll respondents say endorsements do not sway their vote, and that is the case here: Seventy-six percent say their vote will be unaffected. Nearly as many Republicans say Robertson's endorsement makes them less likely to vote for Giuliani (9%) as say it makes them more likely to do so (12%).

Among the roughly six in 10 Republicans in the current poll who say they are "extremely likely" to vote in their state's 2008 presidential primary or caucus, Giuliani (25%) and Thompson (21%) are essentially tied. McCain (13%), Romney (12%), and Huckabee (12%) tie for third among this group. In the prior poll, 31% of "likely" Republican primary or caucus voters favored Giuliani, with Thompson and McCain both at 20%. Given the small sample sizes of likely primary voters in a single poll, these changes are not statistically significant. With the Iowa caucuses less than two months away, the campaign is beginning to heat up. As Republicans begin to focus more attention on the candidates, their preferences could begin to show change. Already it appears that Romney and Huckabee have improved their national standing in recent months. Giuliani has led for much of the year, and while his support is down in the current poll, it is unclear at this point whether that is the beginning of a trend toward a tighter race or just reflects a temporary variation in his support.

Clinton Sustains Huge Lead in Democratic Nomination Race

In the national standings of the Democratic presidential candidates seeking their party's nomination next year, New York senator Hillary Clinton continues to hold a strong 27-point lead over second-place rival Illinois senator Barack Obama, according to a new Gallup Poll. Former North Carolina senator John Edwards remains further behind in third place. According to the November 11–14, 2007, poll, 48% of Democrats say they are most likely to support Clinton for the party's presidential nomination in 2008, followed by Obama at 21% and Edwards at 12%. No other candidate garners more than 4% support.

Democrats' preferences for the nomination have shown little significant change since August 2007. In every poll since then, Clinton has maintained at least a 20-point lead over Obama, with her support fluctuating between 45% and 50% over this period. Her biggest lead occurred in mid-October, when 50% supported Clinton and 21% Obama. From a longer-term perspective, in all but one survey this year, Clinton has had a statistically significant lead over the other leading contenders.

There is little difference in the dynamics of the Democratic race among the 58% of Democrats and Democratic leaners who say they are "extremely likely" to vote in next

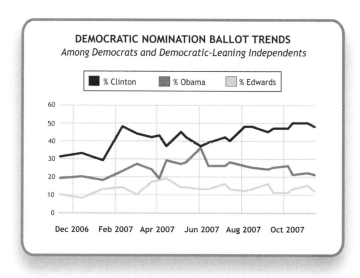

DEMOCRATIC NOMINATION BALLOT TRENDS
Among Democrats and Democratic-Leaning Independents

■ % Clinton   ■ % Obama   □ % Edwards

year's Democratic primaries or caucuses: Forty-eight percent support Clinton, while 23% support Obama and 11% Edwards. None of the other candidates garners double-digit support. Clinton's support is slightly lower among Democratic-leaning independents than it is among core Democrats, but she still commands a strong lead among both groups. Across the two surveys conducted this month, 52% of Democrats support Clinton for the nomination, compared with 45% of Democratic-leaning independents. None of Clinton's competitors fares better among Democratic-leaning independents than among Democrats; rather, several candidates—Obama, Edwards, Biden, and Kucinich—are at most four points lower among the former group. If former vice president Al Gore were to enter the race to win the Democratic nomination—something he has repeatedly said he has no plans to do—he would be tied with Obama for second place. Clinton would still have a substantial lead over both Gore and Obama, with 42% of Democrats supporting Clinton for the nomination. Seventeen percent would support Gore, 16% Obama, and 9% Edwards.

NOVEMBER 26

Democratic Candidates Look Good in Latest 2008 Trial Heats

A Gallup Poll of registered voters conducted nationwide between November 11 and November 14, 2007, finds Senator Hillary Clinton with a slim but not statistically significant advantage over both former New York City mayor Rudolph Giuliani and Senator John McCain in head-to-head matchups for the 2008 general election for president. Clinton has much more substantial leads over former senator Fred Thompson and former governor Mitt Romney. Senator Barack Obama also has significant

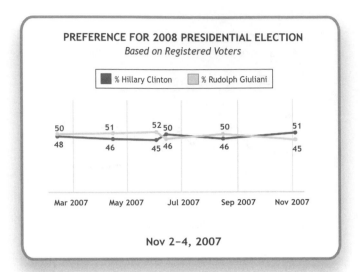

PREFERENCE FOR 2008 PRESIDENTIAL ELECTION
Based on Registered Voters

■ % Hillary Clinton   □ % Rudolph Giuliani

50   51   52 50   50   51
48   46   45 46   46   45

Mar 2007   May 2007   Jul 2007   Sep 2007   Nov 2007

Nov 2-4, 2007

leads over Thompson and Romney, but essentially ties with Giuliani and McCain. Clinton—the dominant front-runner for the Democratic presidential nomination—would appear to have at least a slight advantage among registered voters over any Republican candidate if the election were held today. She has a five-point edge over Giuliani (49% to 44%)and a six-point edge over McCain (50% to 44%), but neither lead is statistically significant. Clinton runs much more strongly against the lesser-known Thompson (53% to 40%) and Romney (54% to 38%).

Gallup previously tested these same matchups in June (Clinton versus Giuliani, McCain, and Romney) and July (Clinton versus Thompson). Since then, Clinton's standing against Giuliani, McCain, and Romney has remained about the same, while she now fares much better against Thompson. In July, 48% of registered voters preferred Clinton versus 45% for Thompson. Gallup has most frequently tested matchups between the Democratic and Republican front-runners, Clinton and Giuliani. Clinton has held a slight edge in three of the last four polls, but none of these leads was statistically significant. Prior to that, Giuliani had a slight advantage.

The results for Obama matched up against the Republican candidates are largely similar to those for Clinton: He has substantial leads over both Thompson and Romney, and is highly competitive with McCain and Giuliani. Though Clinton's margins of support over McCain (six points) and Giuliani (five points) are larger than Obama's margins of support against the same candidates (three points and no points, respectively), the differences are not large enough to be considered statistically meaningful. Obama has not improved his standing against any of the leading Republican candidates, however, compared with poll results from the summer. Obama already enjoyed a sizable lead over Thompson in the summer and continues to do so in the latest poll, so Clinton's improvement versus the actor and

former senator mainly catches her up with Obama in their respective matchups with Thompson.

At this stage in the campaign, Clinton and Obama are at worst competitive with the leading Republicans and at best hold a statistically significant lead over them. In a broad sense, that is consistent with the numerous indicators showing a political environment favorable to the Democratic Party, including an unpopular Republican president, dissatisfaction with the direction of the country, and more positive ratings of the Democratic Party than of the Republican Party. However, the fact that neither leading Democratic candidate has a commanding lead over the best-known Republican candidates could be perceived as troubling for the Democrats. Trial heat matchups this far away from the election are generally not predictive of the eventual outcome, but they do give an indication that the Democratic nominee—whoever that may be—will begin the campaign with less of an advantage over the Republican nominee than one would expect.

NOVEMBER 28
What Is Behind Anti-Clinton Sentiment?

Hillary Clinton's status as a candidate for president in 2008 is certainly contributing to the widespread interest in the campaign. Even sitting vice presidents who sought the office did not have nearly as universal name recognition as Clinton, and few candidates have ever begun the campaign with such polarized ratings. Much of the discussion in both the Democratic and Republican nomination campaigns has centered on the candidates' attempts to derail the Clinton White House Express. But what exactly is driving the attitudes of those who have negative views of the former first lady and current senator from New York? To help answer that question, a November 2–4 USA Today/Gallup Poll explored in detail the views of Americans who can be considered Clinton detractors—defined as the 44% of registered voters who say they definitely would not vote for Clinton for president in 2008. This anti-Clinton group was then asked to explain in their own words why they would not vote for her.

The most common specific explanation offered—simple dislike of her—is probably also the most basic, mentioned by 25% of Clinton nonsupporters. Bill Clinton is also on the minds of many of his spouse's critics: Thirteen percent mention their dislike of him or their disapproval of his presidency as a reason for not supporting his wife for president. Policy disagreements also figure prominently in Clinton detractors' reasoning. Seventeen percent mention general disagreement with her on issues, in addition to the relatively small percentages who cite specific disagreements with her on healthcare, Iraq, and immigration.

Along the same lines, 6% describe her more generally as a "radical" or "socialist," and 5% say she is "too liberal." Four percent cite her Democratic Party affiliation as a reason they would not vote for her.

There are also several character concerns with Clinton, including perceived dishonesty, a lack of the proper experience to be president, and the notion that she is a "flip-flopper" who takes issue positions that are politically expedient. In the end, Clinton detractors are about equally likely to give a reason falling into one of the three broad categories of responses described above: basic dislike of her or her husband (38%), policy disagreements (39%), and character concerns (34%). One response that doesn't quite fit those broad categories—mentioned by 8% of Clinton nonsupporters—involves reservations about a woman being elected president. This includes respondents who say they themselves don't favor a woman in the role, as well as those who perceive the country as not ready for a female in the highest elected office.

Views of the Bush-Clinton Dynasty

The poll also asked respondents for their views on the possibility of the continuation of a Bush family–Clinton family White House succession pattern. If Hillary Clinton is elected in 2008, a Bush or a Clinton will have served as president for six consecutive presidential terms, or 24 years (1989–2013), by the end of Clinton's first term. A majority think a continuation of the Bush-Clinton dynasty in the Oval Office would not make much difference to the country. Those who think it would have a negative impact outnumber those who think it would have a positive impact by more than a two-to-one margin (31% to 13%).

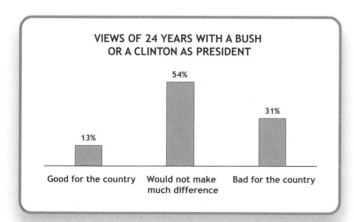

VIEWS OF 24 YEARS WITH A BUSH OR A CLINTON AS PRESIDENT

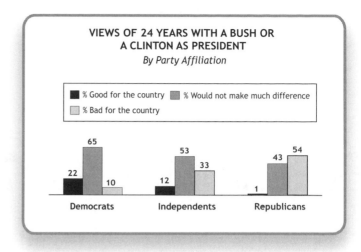

VIEWS OF 24 YEARS WITH A BUSH OR A CLINTON AS PRESIDENT
By Party Affiliation

Responses to this question are largely driven by one's support for Hillary Clinton for president. A majority of Republicans (most of whom say they definitely would not vote for Clinton) think keeping the Bush-Clinton family succession going is bad for the country, whereas a majority of Democrats (most of whom say they definitely will vote for Clinton or would consider doing so) say it would make little difference to the country. Democrats are twice as likely to say it would be good for the country as to say it would be bad. Most independents have a neutral stance on this question, but they are more likely to say it would be bad rather than good for the country.

Starting out the campaign with close to half of voters solidly against her candidacy does not seem like a good position to be in, but other candidates (Mitt Romney and Fred Thompson) have even greater numbers of detractors in the poll, and Clinton's numbers are not appreciably worse than those of Rudolph Giuliani, Barack Obama, or John Edwards. The apparent theme of the 2008 election campaign has been Clinton's electability. She does have unusually high unfavorable ratings for a candidate this early in the campaign. However, that might just be due to the fact that she is universally known a year before the election, something most presidential candidates cannot claim. Clinton's unfavorable ratings and the percentage who say they definitely would not vote for her are not unusual compared with those of other presidential candidates near the end of a campaign. So as long as her negatives don't continue to grow, she may be as well positioned to win in November 2008 as Obama, Edwards, or the Republican candidate would be.

DECEMBER 2007

The year 2007 has been an extraordinary one in presidential politics, with vigorous campaigning for both the Republican and Democratic presidential nominations over essentially the entire year. Throughout 2007, the Gallup Poll has tracked Americans' knowledge and evaluations of the candidates, their voting intentions, and the general mood of the country. The overall "mood" environment in which the campaigning took place became increasingly negative in 2007. As a number of the major candidates became much better known to the American public in the course of the year, their images often became more negative—owing perhaps to both the intense media focus on their backgrounds and positions and to attacks and criticisms from their opponents. As the year ended, Senators Barack Obama of Illinois and John McCain of Arizona and former senator John Edwards of North Carolina had the most positive images of the major candidates from both parties. On the Democratic side, the year 2007 began and ended with the same front-runner, Hillary Clinton. In contrast, the national rank ordering of candidate support on the Republican side was significantly different—and more muddled—in December than it had been in January.

Mood of the Nation at the End of 2007

The public's overall mood at the end of 2007 was the same as when the year began—negative. Only 27% of Americans in December said they were satisfied with the way things were going in the United States, up slightly from the year's low point of 20% in November but below January's 35% satisfaction level. Americans' rating of the U.S. economy also dropped as the year progressed, from 52% saying it was excellent or good in January to just 28% saying so in December.

Party Identification in 2007

Democrats maintained a slight lead over Republicans in party identification in most Gallup surveys in 2007. At the year's end, 33% of Americans identified themselves as Democrats, while 27% identified as Republicans. The largest percentage of Americans in 2007, however, said they were independents and did not identify with either party (although many said, after further questioning, that they "leaned" toward one party or the other.) At several points throughout the year, as many as 43% of Americans said they were independent; the "independent" figure was at 39% at year's end.

Changes in Americans' Awareness of the Candidates Throughout 2007

New York senator Hillary Clinton began and ended 2007 with virtually universal name identification: Close to 100% of Americans know enough about her to have an opinion. Clinton's top competitor for the Democratic nomination, Barack Obama, gained visibility as the year progressed but still ended the year substantially below Clinton in terms of overall national recognition. Obama's name identification was at 72% in early 2007 (up from 53% in December 2006, when Gallup first measured him) and had risen to 87% by year's end. Although Edwards was the Democratic vice presidential candidate in 2004, he began 2007 with just 80% name identification—and after a year of active campaigning, Edwards's name identification had risen only marginally, to 86%. Former New York City mayor Rudolph Giuliani and Senator John McCain remained the most well known candidates seeking the Republican nomination throughout the year, with some increase in their name recognition as the year progressed. Ninety-one percent of Americans

CHRONOLOGY

DECEMBER 2007

December 1 Five presidential candidates attend the Heartland Presidential Forum in Des Moines, Iowa, sponsored by nonprofit organizations that work on such issues as farming, immigration, and urban poverty. While all candidates were invited, only Democrats Dodd, Edwards, Kucinich, and Obama appear at the event. Clinton participates via telephone.

December 2 The United Russia party of President Vladimir Putin wins 60% of the vote in parliamentary elections.

December 3 A U.S. National Intelligence Estimate says that Iran halted its nuclear weapons program in 2003. President Bush reiterates that Iran still remains a dangerous nation.

December 4 National Public Radio hosts a radio debate for Democratic presidential candidates in Des Moines, Iowa. Bill Richardson is unable to attend.

December 6 Mitt Romney, a Mormon, delivers a speech on his religious faith at the George H. W. Bush Presidential Library.

December 9 Univision, a Spanish-language media company, hosts a debate for Republican presidential candidates. Tom Tancredo, a strong opponent of illegal immigration, refuses to attend.

December 12 The *Des Moines Register* sponsors a debate for Republican presidential candidates in Johnston, Iowa.

December 13 The *Des Moines Register* sponsors a debate for Democratic presidential candidates in Johnston, Iowa. Six Democratic candidates—Biden, Clinton, Dodd, Edwards, Obama, and Richardson—were invited; Kucinich and Gravel were excluded on the grounds that they had no serious campaign presence in Iowa.

December 14 President Perez Musharraf ends a six-week state of emergency and restores the constitution in Pakistan.

December 20 Tom Tancredo drops out of the race for the Republican presidential nomination.

December 27 Benazir Bhutto, opposition leader and former prime minister of Pakistan, is killed in a bomb attack during a campaign rally. Riots erupt throughout Pakistan.

December 29 General David Petraeus says that the recent success in reducing violence has restored the image of the United States with Iraqis.

---

were familiar enough with Giuliani to have an opinion of him in December, compared with 79% in January. Eighty-four percent of Americans were familiar with McCain at year's end, up from 72% in January.

The biggest gains in name identification among the Republican candidates in 2007 were for former Massachusetts governor Mitt Romney and former Arkansas governor Mike Huckabee. Fewer than 4 out of 10 Americans knew enough about Romney to rate him at the beginning of the year; by December, Romney's name identification was at 67%. Gallup first asked Americans about Huckabee in August, at which time he had 31% name identification; by December his name identification had risen to 58%. Americans' awareness of actor and former Tennessee senator Fred Thompson also rose substantially throughout the year. Still, despite extensive news coverage and publicity

during 2007, at year's end a third or more of Americans still said they didn't know enough about Thompson to rate him. Thompson had less than 40% name identification in April when Gallup first evaluated him and was at 64% by year's end.

Changes in Americans' Opinions of the Candidates

The public's ratings of two of the three leading Democratic candidates for president in 2008 have shown significant changes as the year progressed. Throughout the year, Hillary Clinton's net favorable rating (the percentage rating her favorably minus the percentage rating her unfavorably) has consistently been more negative than that of Obama or Edwards. Clinton's +18 favorable rating had fallen to +3 by the end of the year, having been in net negative territory at several points before that. Obama's ratings have been the most positive among these three Democratic contenders in each national Gallup Poll conducted in 2007; still, his ratings ended the year slightly more negative than in the early months of the year. John Edwards's net favorable rating stayed essentially constant as the year progressed.

Americans' opinions of the leading Republican candidates have shown significant fluctuation this year. At points early in the year, Giuliani's and McCain's net favorable ratings were higher than Romney's, and they were initially higher than Thompson's and Huckabee's ratings when those two candidates were initially measured by Gallup in April and August, respectively. But Giuliani's net favorable rating dropped as the year progressed, going from a +45 in January to a +9 in December. McCain's ratings suffered in the summer but by December had recovered to the point where his net favorable was on par with where it was as the year began. That put McCain at a higher point (+25) than any of the other three leading Republican candidates at year's end. Romney's net ratings have fluctuated above and below zero all year, ending up at −3. Thompson's rating fell to −4 by December. And Huckabee, first measured in August, saw his ratings rise significantly by Gallup's late November/early December poll, only to fall in the last poll of the year, conducted in mid-December.

Preferences Among Democrats and Republicans for Their Parties' Nominations

The race for the Democratic nomination remained remarkably consistent at the national level over the course of the year. Clinton has led in every national Gallup Poll conducted this year, with the exception of one poll in early June. Obama has consistently been in second place and Edwards in third place. Clinton's lead has been large throughout the final four months of 2007. In Gallup's year-end national poll, conducted in mid-December, 45% of Democrats and Democratic leaners said they supported Clinton for the nomination, while 27% supported Obama and 15% Edwards.

The race for the Republican nomination, on the other hand, became more complex as the year progressed. Giuliani maintained a lead in Gallup's national polls throughout the year after eclipsing McCain in the early months of 2007. But Giuliani's share of the vote dropped as the year progressed. The most significant change of the year on the Republican side came in the positioning of Huckabee, who rose from a consistent 1% to 2% of the vote in the first six months of the year to a year-ending 16%, putting him in a statistical tie with McCain, Romney, and Thompson. McCain's percentage of the vote dropped as the year pro-

gressed, going from 27% in January to a year-ending 14%. Romney's vote percentage went from 7% to a year-ending 14%. Thompson, first measured by Gallup nationally at 13% in March, rose to a high point of 22% in September, only to fall to 14% by the end of the year.

DECEMBER 4
Giuliani Still Leads Nationally, but Huckabee Is Gaining

The latest national USA Today/Gallup Poll shows that former New York City mayor Rudolph Giuliani remains in the lead for the Republican nomination, although his percentage of the vote is trending downward. Meanwhile, former Arkansas governor Mike Huckabee has moved into a four-way tie for second place, only nine points behind Giuliani. Giuliani received 25% of the Republican vote in the November 30–December 2 poll. That's down three points from mid-November and nine points from his recent high point of 34%, which he has reached twice since September. Technically, the 25% share of the vote for Giuliani is the lowest Gallup has recorded since November 2006, when it began tracking national Republicans' nomination preferences—although it is not statistically different from the 28% recorded in November of this year and at two points in late 2006.

The big news among Republicans revolves around the minisurge of Huckabee, who has been the center of much national news coverage as the result of his strong showings in polls of likely Iowa caucus goers, and who has been deemed by critics to have performed well in recent Republican debates. There is little doubt that this publicity has

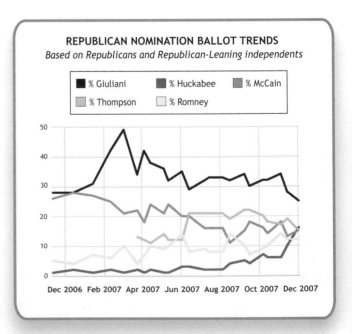

REPUBLICAN NOMINATION BALLOT TRENDS
Based on Republicans and Republican-Leaning independents

■ % Giuliani   ■ % Huckabee   ■ % McCain
■ % Thompson   ■ % Romney

Dec 2006 Feb 2007 Apr 2007 Jun 2007 Aug 2007 Oct 2007 Dec 2007

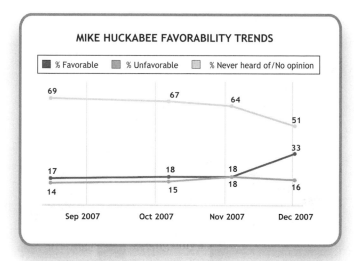

MIKE HUCKABEE FAVORABILITY TRENDS

been behind the national gains measured in Gallup's weekend poll. Huckabee gets 16% of the Republican vote in the poll—up from 6% at the beginning of November and only 2% as recently as August. As a result, Huckabee, former Tennessee senator Fred Thompson (15%), Arizona senator John McCain (15%), and former Massachusetts governor Mitt Romney (12%) are essentially tied for second place.

Huckabee's Name Identification

Huckabee has seen a significant increase in his name recognition and positive image among all Americans over the last several weeks. Gallup first asked Americans about Huckabee in August, and at that point 31% knew enough about him to have an opinion. Now, 49% have an opinion, and those opinions have become much more favorable than unfavorable.

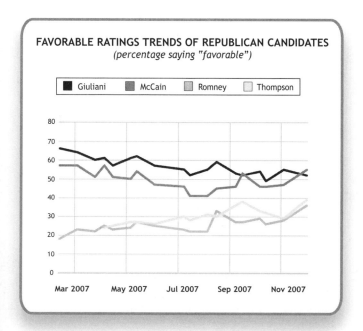

FAVORABLE RATINGS TRENDS OF REPUBLICAN CANDIDATES
(percentage saying "favorable")

At the same time, there have been more modest increases in Americans' favorable ratings of McCain, Thompson, and Romney in this poll compared with previous surveys. Those Republicans' favorable ratings, like Huckabee's, are at or near their 2007 highs. But Americans have become slightly less positive about Giuliani.

Among Republicans, Huckabee's image has improved and become competitive with those of Romney and Thompson. Although slightly fewer Republicans know Huckabee than know either of these other two candidates, their favorable percentages are comparable. Indeed, Huckabee's negatives are actually smaller than those for the other two. McCain has both higher positive and higher negative ratings than Romney, Thompson, and Huckabee—as does Giuliani, who, as befits the front-runner, has the highest positive image of any candidate.

One of the key questions in the Republican presidential race at this point is the impact of the early caucus and primary outcomes on the position of front-runner Rudolph Giuliani at the national level. If Giuliani does not make a strong showing in Iowa and New Hampshire—as the polls in those states would suggest may well be the case—the focus will be on the damage done to his front-runner status as the primaries progress. At present, trend data at the national level show that Giuliani's lead is shrinking, suggesting that he is far from invulnerable. The current data would make it hard to argue that any one of the other candidates is in a demonstrably better second-place position than the others. Four candidates are within four points of each other behind Giuliani. There has been some movement this year in the national Republican picture. John McCain, for example, went from 27% of the Republican vote at the beginning of the year to a low point of 11% in August, only to recover modestly to 15% in the current poll. So it would not be unusual to find Huckabee's support moving either up or down once again in the weeks to come, particularly as his candidacy attracts increased media scrutiny. But at the moment, about one month before the Iowa caucuses on January 3, 2008, Huckabee clearly is the Republican candidate with the most momentum.

Clinton Still Has Big Lead Despite Drop in Support

A new USA Today/Gallup Poll finds Senator Hillary Clinton continuing to lead the field of Democratic candidates for the party's 2008 presidential nomination, though her support has dropped to its lowest level since June. Thirty-nine percent of Democrats and Democratic-leaning independents support Clinton in the November 30–December 2 poll, with Senator Barack Obama second at 24% and former senator John Edwards third at 15%.

Can she do it? A selection of buttons festoons the shirt of a Clinton supporter in Story City, Iowa, in December 2007 on the eve of the Iowa caucuses. *(Charlie Neibergall/AP Images)*

Clinton's support had been at 48% in the prior poll, conducted between November 11 and November 14, and had been near 50% since mid-September. The drop in her support did not seem to disproportionately benefit any one of her rivals; instead, most of the other Democratic candidates appear to have picked up at least some support since the last poll was taken. Clinton's 15-point lead over Obama is about half of what it was when she enjoyed her largest

advantage—29 points in an October 12–14 poll (50% to 21%). Clinton has led in every Gallup Poll of nationwide Democrats' nomination preferences since November 2006 and has held a statistically significant advantage over all of her competitors in all but one of these polls.

One positive sign for Clinton is that her lead over Obama is larger among core Democrats (those who identify with the party rather than those who initially identify as independents but say they lean to the Democratic Party). Among those who identify as Democrats, 47% favor Clinton and 21% Obama. In many states, only those who have officially registered as Democrats can vote in the primaries.

Views of the Candidates

Clinton (74%) has a slightly higher favorable rating than Obama (70%) or Edwards (67%) among Democrats and Democratic leaners. But Clinton also has slightly higher negatives (i.e., unfavorable ratings) among this group than either of her closest pursuers. One in seven Democrats are still not familiar enough with Obama and Edwards to rate them. Among the general public, opinions of Clinton have

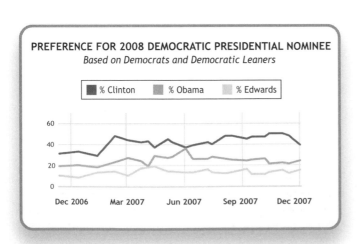

PREFERENCE FOR 2008 DEMOCRATIC PRESIDENTIAL NOMINEE
Based on Democrats and Democratic Leaners

■ % Clinton   ■ % Obama   ■ % Edwards

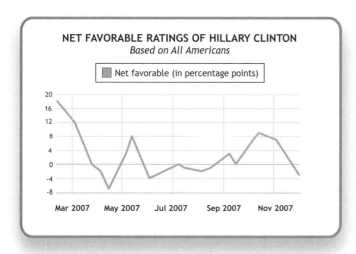

NET FAVORABLE RATINGS OF HILLARY CLINTON
Based on All Americans

Net favorable (in percentage points)

been closely divided throughout the year, switching from net-positive to net-negative ratings on several occasions. In the latest poll, the ratings are once again tilting negative, with 47% rating her favorably and 50% unfavorably, after being more positive than negative throughout the fall months.

By comparison, Obama and Edwards have substantial favorable ratings among the general population, with Obama at +20 (53% favorable, 33% unfavorable) and Edwards at +15 (50% favorable, 35% unfavorable). Both candidates have had net-positive scores throughout the campaign. Even with a drop in support in the latest poll, Clinton remains the solid front-runner for the Democratic Party's nomination. Her strong positioning in the polls to this point has made her the prime target of the other candidates' attacks, which have become more frequent with the first official votes now just one month away. The stepped-up attacks are likely one reason for the dip in support for Clinton. While the Iowa caucuses are always important in presidential nomination campaigns, they are widely viewed as a critical race only for the Democratic candidates—much more so than for the Republicans. With Clinton enjoying such a consistently large lead in national polls and leading in nearly every state primary pre-election poll, some believe Iowa is Edwards's and Obama's best and possibly only chance to change the dynamics of the race. Polls of likely Iowa caucus voters suggest Clinton is locked in a tight race with Obama and Edwards in that state. A win in Iowa would probably help bolster Clinton's standing in the races that follow, and make an Obama or Edwards nomination seem less probable.

DECEMBER 6

Huckabee's Name Identification and Favorable Ratings Surge over Past Month

As Americans have become more familiar with former Arkansas governor Mike Huckabee in the past few weeks,

their assessments of him have become much more positive, with Americans about twice as likely to rate him favorably as unfavorably in the latest USA Today/Gallup Poll. Even with the increased attention to his candidacy, however, a slim majority of Americans still say they are not familiar with Huckabee. When Americans are asked what comes to mind when they think of Huckabee, a sizable majority cannot name anything, but those who can name something tend to say that they like him, that he is a good prospect and a rising star, and that he is a nice, down-to-earth guy. Few Americans say anything negative about him. In the past month, support for Huckabee as the Republican nominee for president has increased significantly, from 10% to 16%. Huckabee is now essentially tied for second place with Fred Thompson, John McCain, and Mitt Romney behind front-runner Rudolph Giuliani in the contest to win the Republican Party's 2008 presidential nomination.

According to the November 30–December 2, 2007, poll, 33% of Americans say they have a favorable opinion of Huckabee, while 16% have an unfavorable opinion and 51% say they are not familiar enough with Huckabee to rate him. This is a rather dramatic change from early November, when Americans were equally divided between positive (18%) and negative (18%) views of Huckabee. As he has become better known, Huckabee's favorable rating has increased substantially, while his unfavorable rating has held steady. As would be expected, Republicans are much more positive than independents or Democrats in their views of Huckabee; still, his positive ratings among all three groups have increased significantly in the past month. A slight majority of Republicans, 53%, say they have a favorable opinion of Huckabee, up 26 points since early November. Republicans have consistently rated Huckabee more positively than negatively since August, when Gallup first asked about him. Even though Democrats' ratings of Huckabee are at their most positive level to date, Democrats are still about equally likely to rate Huckabee unfavorably (21%) as favorably (20%). But that is an improvement compared with the October and early November ratings, when Democrats were on balance negative toward him. Huckabee's favorable rating among independents has increased by 11 points since early November and, for the first time, is significantly more positive than negative. From August through early November, independents were about evenly divided in their views of Huckabee.

AMERICANS' THOUGHTS ON HUCKABEE

Gallup's November 26–29, 2007, poll asked Americans to say, in their own words: "What comes to mind when [they] think about former Arkansas governor Mike Huckabee." Key findings from this survey are that 1) a majority of Americans at the time of this survey were not familiar enough with

Huckabee to say anything about him; 2) most of what Americans did say about Huckabee was positive; and 3) few Americans mentioned anything negative about him. Sixty-five percent of Americans in this Gallup survey were not able to say anything about Huckabee. In a heated political environment, things change on a daily basis, and it is likely that Americans are quickly becoming more familiar with Huckabee.

Given the lack of a well-defined image of Huckabee, it is not surprising that no common themes emerge in response to the open-ended question. Americans most commonly say about Huckabee that they like him or view him favorably (mentioned by 6%); that he is a good prospect, a rising star, and is becoming popular (4%); that he has good Christian values and is religious (3%); that he is a nice guy and down to earth (3%); and that he is conservative (3%). Fewer Americans mention Huckabee's perceived honesty, their dislike of him, their agreement with his views, that he is unlikely to win, that he has lost a lot of weight, or that he was endorsed by action film star Chuck Norris. One emerging pattern in the open-ended responses is that positive comments far outweigh the negative. Nineteen percent of Americans mention something clearly positive about Huckabee, while just 3% mention something clearly negative. Four percent mention something that could be positive to some and negative to others: that he is a conservative, that he is a Republican, and that they are familiar with the pro-Huckabee commercial featuring Chuck Norris.

Nationally, Choices for Party Nominees Still Wide Open

Democrats are a little more likely than Republicans to say they have made up their minds about whom they will support for their party's presidential nomination. Democrats who have made up their minds are also more likely than Republicans to have decided on one particular candidate—Hillary Clinton—while Republicans who have made up their minds spread their preferences across a number of different candidates. But a large majority of those who identify with both parties choose the option "have not made up [my] mind yet" when that option is explicitly presented, underscoring the significant potential for change in the national races as the caucus and primary season gets under way.

The rise of former Arkansas governor Mike Huckabee in national and Iowa polls of Republicans is a reminder of how quickly the shape of an election can change in the period before actual voting begins. Many Americans will choose a candidate when they are asked for whom they would vote "if the election were being held today," and the evidence shows that when these choices are made close to an election, they are excellent predictors of actual voting behavior. But early in the

process, the election is many months away, and it is understood that while these measures provide an excellent portrait of an election's current landscape, a lot can still change.

The potential for such change is made clear when the results of a question from a November 26–29 Gallup survey are examined. Representative samples of Republicans and Democrats were asked: "Thinking now about the candidates running for the [Republican/Democratic] nomination for president in 2008, as of today, have you decided which candidate you plan to support, or have you not made up your mind yet?" This question did not prompt respondents with the names of any candidates and explicitly invited them to opt out of making a choice if they had not made up their minds yet. The results show that a large majority of both Republicans and Democrats opt for the "not made up [my] mind yet" alternative, leaving just a minority claiming to have decided whom they will support for their party's nomination.

There are some slight differences in the responses by party. Democrats are slightly more likely than Republicans to say they have made up their mind, and Democrats who have decided are more settled on one specific candidate (Clinton). By contrast, the smaller number of Republicans who have settled on a candidate are less unified in their choices. But the broad picture is quite clear: There is a significant potential for movement in voter preferences in both parties.

REPUBLICANS

Seventy-four percent of Republicans say they have not yet made up their mind whom they will support for the their party's nomination. Among those who do claim to have made up their mind, no single candidate dominates. Rudolph Giuliani, Mitt Romney, Fred Thompson, Mike Huckabee, Texas representative Ron Paul, John McCain, and California representative Duncan Hunter are all named by between 1% and 5% of Republicans. These data are somewhat at odds with the results of the traditional horse race question in which voters are given a list of names and asked for whom they would vote. Giuliani has led all year in Gallup's national polls of this kind, although his lead has shrunk to just nine points in the most recent such poll, ahead of a tightly bunched group of four candidates: Huckabee, Thompson, McCain, and Romney. However, in response to Gallup's question asking Republicans without prompting to name the candidate they support, Giuliani has no lead, and all five of these candidates get roughly the same percentage of the Republican vote choice.

DEMOCRATS

Sixty-nine percent of Democrats say they have not made up their minds about whom they will support for their party's nomination. Among those who have made up their minds, Clinton dominates; she is chosen by more than twice as many Democrats as any other candidate. Behind Clinton are Barack Obama and John Edwards, with no other candidate getting more than 1% of the vote. Clinton has led in most polls of Democrats all year, often by substantial margins, so it may be no surprise to find that Democratic voters who claim to have made up their mind are most likely to mention her as the candidate they will support. Still, one way of looking at these results is to say that more than 8 out of 10 Democrats either have decided on a candidate other than Clinton, or have not yet decided whom they will support—underscoring the enormous potential for change in the Democratic contest as the election campaign progresses.

DECEMBER 7

Democratic Party Winning on Issues

Less than a year before Americans go to the polls to choose the next president and the 111th Congress, Gallup finds the Democrats holding a considerable advantage over the Republicans in public perceptions of which party can handle a variety of national issues. Overall, the Democratic Party is perceived as better able to handle 6 of 10 issues that are likely to be heavily debated in the 2008 campaign, the Republican Party leads on two issues, and the two parties roughly tie on another two. According to the new USA Today/Gallup Poll, conducted between November 30 and December 2, 2007, the Democrats' strongest issue areas include healthcare, the housing market, protecting Americans' rights and freedoms, corruption in government, the economy, and Iraq. The Republicans lead on which party can better handle illegal immigration and terrorism, but not by as much as the Democrats lead on their best issues. The two parties are roughly tied on moral values and taxes.

The Republican Party was in a much stronger position on issues in January 2004, 10 months before President George W. Bush won re-election and the Republicans retained their majority position in Congress. At that time, the party held large leads on terrorism (+30 percentage

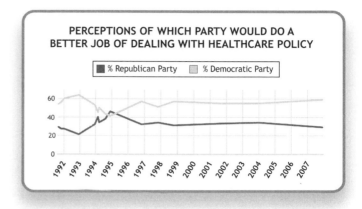

PERCEPTIONS OF WHICH PARTY WOULD DO A BETTER JOB OF DEALING WITH HEALTHCARE POLICY

points) and Iraq (+16), and closely matched the Democrats on the economy (−4)—three of the most important issues to voters in that election. Republicans' advantage on terrorism has since fallen to only 10 points; they now lose to the Democrats on Iraq by 10 points and on the economy by 12 points. At the same time, the Democrats' advantage on healthcare has expanded from 21 to 30 points.

DEMOCRATS FAR AHEAD ON THE ECONOMY

Gallup's long-term trend for which party can better handle the economy finds the Democrats doing well on a historical basis. Gallup has been taking this measure periodically since 1982, and in most polls the Democrats have led the Republicans in perceptions of which party can better handle the economy—but not often by as large a margin as they do today (52% to 40%).

Across all 18 ratings by party on the economy, the Democrats have averaged a 2-point lead, 44% vs. 42%. Furthermore, the Democrats consistently tied or led the Republicans on the economy within the year before each of the last four presidential elections, two of which Democrat Bill Clinton won (1992 and 1996), and two of which Republican George W. Bush won (2000 and 2004). In January 1992, the Democrats led the Republicans by 7 points as the party better able to handle the economy; in October 1996, the Democrats led by 9 points; in May 2000, the Democrats led by 4 points (within the margin of error); and in January 2004, the Democrats again led by 4 points (also within margin of error). In short, while it is not unusual for the Republicans to be roughly tied with or behind the Democrats on this measure, their current 12-point deficit is on the high side. If a disadvantage this large persists in 2008, it could spell trouble for the party if the economy figures as a major issue for voters.

DEMOCRATS' LEAD ON HEALTHCARE NOT UNUSUAL

From a historical perspective, the Democrats' current advantage over the Republicans on healthcare policy is

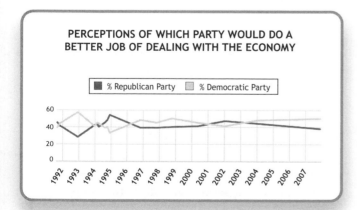

PERCEPTIONS OF WHICH PARTY WOULD DO A BETTER JOB OF DEALING WITH THE ECONOMY

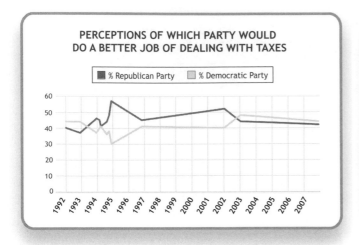

PERCEPTIONS OF WHICH PARTY WOULD
DO A BETTER JOB OF DEALING WITH TAXES

■ % Republican Party   □ % Democratic Party

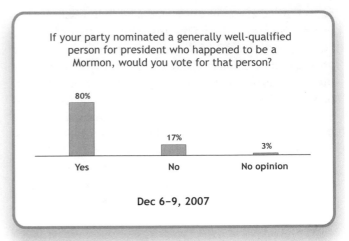

If your party nominated a generally well-qualified
person for president who happened to be a
Mormon, would you vote for that person?

80%

17%

3%

Yes   No   No opinion

Dec 6–9, 2007

less striking. Except for a period in 1994, the Democrats have typically led by a wide margin on healthcare. Their current 30-point advantage is similar to their 33-point lead in January 1992 and not much higher than the 21- to 26-point leads seen in recent years.

PARITY ON TAXES IS NOT UNUSUAL, EITHER

The lead in perceived handling of taxes has shifted back and forth between the Democrats and Republicans over the years. Thus, the fact that the parties are roughly at parity today is not particularly notable. The Republican Party enjoyed 5- to 10-point leads on this measure leading up to November 1994, when Republicans won a historic takeover of Congress. This was followed by a sharp spike in preference for the Republicans on taxes in a late November 1994 poll. However, at most other times the two parties have been closely matched, as they are today.

In January 2004, 10 months prior to that year's presidential election (which Bush won), the Republican Party dominated public preferences for which party could better handle terrorism and Iraq, was at parity with the Democrats on the economy and taxes, and was well behind the Democrats on healthcare. Today, some 11 months before the 2008 presidential election, the Republicans hold at best modest leads over the Democrats on immigration and terrorism; they tie the Democrats on taxes; trail by 10 or more points on the housing market, the economy, and Iraq; and are substantially behind on healthcare. Lacking their previous dominance on terrorism and Iraq, and failing to beat the Democrats on every economic or pocketbook issue tested, the Republicans have a lot of ground to make up on issues. It seems unlikely that their 7-point lead on illegal immigration—the only issue besides terrorism for which the Republicans are preferred—positions them to do that.

DECEMBER 11
Percentage Unwilling to Vote for a Mormon Holds Steady

A new Gallup Poll finds about one in six Americans, including similar percentages of Republicans and Democrats, indicating they would not support their party's nominee for president if that person were a Mormon.

The poll was conducted in the days immediately following a major speech on December 6 by Republican presidential candidate and former Massachusetts governor Mitt Romney, in which he attempted to quiet voter concern about his Mormon religion. The speech appeared to be a response to the political situation in Iowa, where former Arkansas governor Mike Huckabee, who has made his Christian faith a centerpiece of his Republican presidential campaign, has taken the lead in the Iowa caucus polls. According to the December 6–9 Gallup survey, Americans are about as likely today (80%) as they were in March (77%) to say they would vote for a Mormon if their party nominated someone of that faith for president. At that time, 19% said they would not vote for a Mormon presidential candidate. However, in early February, just before Romney officially declared his candidacy for president, the percentage saying they would not vote for a Mormon was somewhat higher, at 24%. Over the long term, attitudes have changed little on this question, with 17% in 1967 and 1999 saying they would not support their party's nominee for president if that person were a Mormon. The 1967 poll was conducted as Romney's father, former Michigan governor George Romney, was himself seeking the presidency.

PARTISAN DIFFERENCES IN WILLINGNESS TO SUPPORT A MORMON CANDIDATE

At this point, Romney may care most about how his speech played among Republicans in Iowa; but Gallup's post-speech survey finds no difference nationally between Republicans and Democrats in their reaction to a Mormon presidential

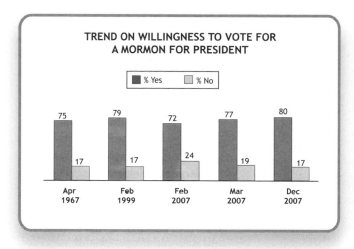

TREND ON WILLINGNESS TO VOTE FOR A MORMON FOR PRESIDENT

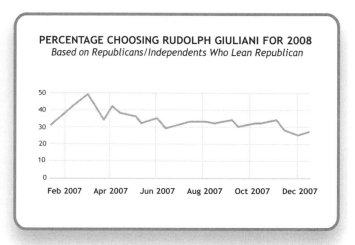

PERCENTAGE CHOOSING RUDOLPH GIULIANI FOR 2008
Based on Republicans/Independents Who Lean Republican

candidate. Eighteen percent of both groups say they would not vote for a Mormon, similar to the 20% to 21% saying this in March. Republicans showed more widespread opposition to voting for a Mormon candidate in Gallup's February 2007 poll, at which time 30% of Republicans, compared with 23% of Democrats, expressed this view. However, the current results for both parties are similar to those from February 1999. Up to 14% of Republicans have supported Romney for his party's nomination at various times since June 2007. Still, he clearly faces some anti-Mormon opposition to his candidacy within the Republican Party as well as among the general public. Various Gallup measures put the national figure at around 20%.

Public reaction with regard to the Mormon issue may have been harshest when Romney first entered the race—when Republicans, in particular, were especially likely to resist the idea of supporting a Mormon as their party's nominee. But that outlook has abated, and attitudes are now no different toward a Mormon candidate such as Romney than they were in March. While his Mormon affiliation is a potential problem for Romney, particularly in some primaries, it has to be considered in the context that other biases are potentially harmful to other candidates in the race from both major parties. Four percent of Americans (including 3% of Republicans) say they would not vote for a Catholic, 5% would not vote for a black, 12% would not vote for a woman, and 12% would not vote for a Hispanic. Earlier this year, Gallup found 28% of Americans saying they would not vote for someone who is in his third marriage, and 40% would not vote for someone who is 72 years of age.

DECEMBER 18

Giuliani Leads Republican Race; Huckabee, Others Tie for Second

After a recent surge in national Republican support for Mike Huckabee for the 2008 Republican presidential nomi-

nation, propelling him from a distant fifth place in early November into a tie for second at the end of the month, a new USA Today/Gallup Poll, conducted between December 14 and December 16, finds that Huckabee's rapid rise has leveled off. The latest poll results are nearly identical to what they were in Gallup's late November/early December survey. More than a quarter of Republicans and independents who lean Republican favor Rudolph Giuliani for the nomination, while Huckabee, John McCain, Fred Thompson, and Mitt Romney are closely matched in second place. Former ambassador Alan Keyes, who announced his current bid for the Republican nomination three months ago, is tied with Ron Paul in distant sixth place. The 27% currently supporting Giuliani is a bit below Giuliani's average 34% support level for 2007 and is the third consecutive reading since mid-November in which his share of the vote has fallen below 30%. At the same time, Giuliani's current 11-point lead is no worse than it was two weeks ago, suggesting that his recent erosion among Republicans nationally has—at least for the moment—been stemmed.

It is important to note that five Republican candidates (Giuliani, Huckabee, McCain, Thompson, and Romney) all now register a significant amount of support for the nomination, each garnering at least 14% of the vote. For most of the year prior to now, only one or two candidates besides Giuliani registered national support of at least 13%. The result is more competition for Giuliani today than at any previous time. However, since May, Giuliani's lead over his various chief rivals has not varied substantially. In recent months it has ranged from 8 percentage points to 16 points, with his current 11-point advantage over Huckabee about average.

The Huckabee Challenge

Giuliani's position today would seem stronger if he were not so far behind in the polls in the early voting states—particularly Iowa, where Huckabee recently replaced

Romney as the leader in the polls. Most of the Iowa polls currently show Giuliani in third place, well behind the two leaders. It was Huckabee's swift—and, to many, surprising—ascent to the top of the pack in Iowa between October and November 2007 that gave him a valuable blitz of media attention and helped fuel his support among Republicans nationally by late November. He has since taken the lead in a number of recent polls conducted in South Carolina and is inching up in New Hampshire. The current USA Today/Gallup Poll, however, provides some evidence that Huckabee's national bounce may have leveled off, at least for the time being. Gallup's previous measure of the national Republican race was conducted in late November/early December, but several polls conducted by other firms since then have shown Huckabee tied or nearly tied with Giuliani for first place, with both candidates receiving 21% to 24% of the vote. (Other surveys in the same time frame showed Giuliani still ahead by as much as eight points.)

Different Angles, Same Picture

About two-thirds of Republicans and Republican leaners nationally say they are "extremely likely" to vote in their states' Republican presidential caucus or primary in 2008. The preference ranking of Republican candidates among this group of likely voters is essentially the same as it is among all Republicans and Republican leaners. The picture is also similar when factoring in voters' second choices. Combining Republicans' first and second choices for the nomination, Giuliani is the most widely favored, chosen by 47%. McCain, Romney, Huckabee, and Thompson are closely matched for second place, with between 24% and 29% choosing each.

Giuliani is also Republicans' first choice for the nomination when paired against Huckabee and Romney in separate measures of Republican voters' preferences if the race narrowed down to just two candidates. Giuliani

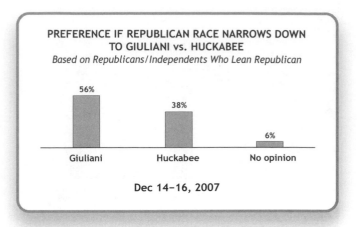

leads Huckabee by 56% to 38% and leads Romney by 57% to 37%.

While Giuliani's lead is substantial in both cases, Gallup trends from earlier this fall on the Giuliani vs. Romney matchup indicate that Giuliani has lost some ground, not dissimilar to the decline in support for him on the overall ballot over the same period. In early September and early October (when 34% and 32% of Republicans, respectively, named Giuliani as their top choice for the nomination), about two-thirds said they would rather see Giuliani nominated for president than Romney. Today, when 27% choose Giuliani on the full Republican ballot, 57% choose him over Romney.

As the first caucuses and primaries of 2008 come into view, their impact on national preferences for the election is becoming increasingly magnified, as is their potential for transforming the race. Giuliani has led the Republican field continuously since February and remains the front-runner. But he is now in his weakest position nationally all year, in part because the field of competitive candidates is getting more crowded. However, even with all the attention paid to Huckabee in recent weeks, a majority of Republicans still say they would prefer Giuliani in a two-way race between him and either Huckabee or Romney, suggesting that it's still Giuliani's race to lose.

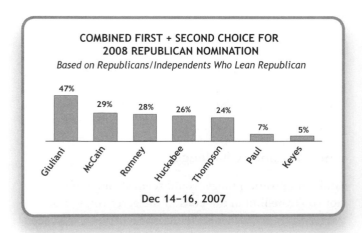

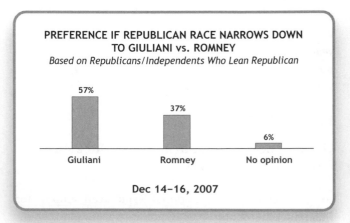

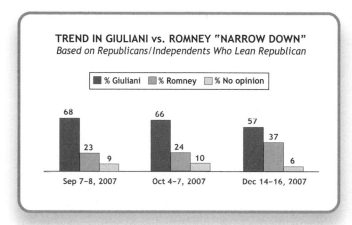

TREND IN GIULIANI vs. ROMNEY "NARROW DOWN"
Based on Republicans/Independents Who Lean Republican

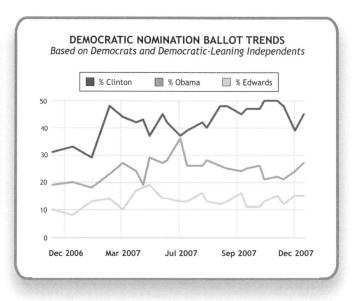

DEMOCRATIC NOMINATION BALLOT TRENDS
Based on Democrats and Democratic-Leaning Independents

Clinton Maintains Large Lead over Obama Nationally

Despite extensive recent news coverage of Illinois senator Barack Obama's growing support in Iowa and New Hampshire, there has been little change in the positioning of the Democratic presidential candidates on a national level, according to a new USA Today/Gallup Poll. New York senator Hillary Clinton continues to have a substantial lead over the group of Democrats vying to win the party's nomination for president in 2008. Obama remains a solid second, as he has been all year, with former North Carolina senator John Edwards continuing to hold down third place. Clinton's support improved modestly from a dip earlier this month and is nearly back to her high levels from the late summer and early fall. Obama's support has shown a gradual improvement in the past month and has returned to its late-summer/early-fall levels.

Democratic Nomination Ballot Trends

The December 14–16, 2007, poll shows that Clinton continues to have a large lead over her competitors, with 45% of Democrats and Democratic-leaning independents saying they support her for the nomination. Twenty-seven percent of Democrats support Obama and 15% support Edwards. Senator Joe Biden (3%), Governor Bill Richardson (2%), and Representative Dennis Kucinich (2%) are well behind in what has pretty much been a three-person race throughout the entire campaign.

The pattern of Democrats' overall support for their party's nomination has not shown much significant change in months and has in a broad sense been fairly stable through most of 2007. In recent weeks, there has been some variation in Democrats' support for the two leading contenders—Clinton and Obama—but nothing major enough to affect the race dramatically. Clinton's support edged up from 39% in late November/early December to 45% in the

latest poll. Her current support level is close to what Gallup measured from August through mid-November, ranging between 45% and 50% during that time. Democrats' support for Obama has gradually increased in the past month, rising from 21% in mid-November to 27% in the latest poll. Obama's support was highest in early June, when 37% of Democrats supported Clinton and 36% Obama, with the rest split among the other candidates.

If the race for the Democratic nomination narrows down to just Clinton and Obama, 55% of Democrats say they would prefer Clinton, while 38% would prefer Obama. Clinton has maintained a double-digit lead over Obama on this measure in all but one poll this year. Her largest lead was 31 points in early September (63% to

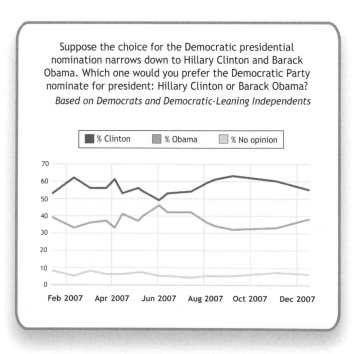

Suppose the choice for the Democratic presidential nomination narrows down to Hillary Clinton and Barack Obama. Which one would you prefer the Democratic Party nominate for president: Hillary Clinton or Barack Obama?
Based on Democrats and Democratic-Leaning Independents

32%), and her smallest lead was just three points in June (49% to 46%).

Clinton also maintains a substantial lead among the 55% of Democrats who say they are "extremely likely" to vote in next year's caucuses and primaries. Forty-five percent of these Democratic voters support Clinton to win the party nomination, while 26% support Obama and 17% Edwards. The poll also asked Democrats whether they were certain to support their preferred candidate in next year's caucuses and primaries or whether they were not certain. Nearly two in three Democrats, 64%, say they are certain to support their candidate, while 34% say they are not certain. By comparison, Republicans interviewed in the same poll are somewhat less likely to be certain about their current candidate preference: Fifty-seven percent of Republicans and Republican leaners say they are certain to vote for their preferred candidate and 43% are not. Clinton and Obama supporters are overwhelmingly likely to say they are certain to vote for their preferred candidate. Seventy-three percent of Clinton supporters say they are certain to vote for her, while 24% are not certain. Among Obama supporters, 66% are certain to vote for him, while 34% are not.

DECEMBER 19

Whom Would Americans Vote for in November 2008?

Hypothetical 2008 general election matchups between Democratic and Republican presidential candidates suggest that the Democrats would continue to have an edge if the election were held today. Specifically, Barack Obama does better than Hillary Clinton against two out of three Republican candidates, while Rudolph Giuliani does better than either Mike Huckabee or Mitt Romney against the Democrats. Additionally, the new poll shows that the Democrats are comfortably ahead of the Republicans when voters are asked for which party's candidate for the House of Representatives they will vote next November.

Presidential Matchups

The December 14–16 USA Today/Gallup Poll pitted Clinton and Obama against Giuliani, Romney, and Huckabee—yielding six separate matchups. The results show that among registered voters the two Democratic candidates are tied with or lead the three Republican candidates in all six pairings—albeit across a range from just 1 point (Clinton versus Giuliani) to a robust margin of 18 points (Obama versus Romney). The Democratic candidates get between 49% and 57% of the national vote across these six matchups; the Republican candidates get between 39% and 48%.

Obama does as well as or better than Clinton against the three Republican candidates. These results are of interest against a backdrop that shows that an increasing number of Democrats are interested in nominating a candidate who has the best chance of beating the Republican in the November 2008 election. (In November 2007, 36% of Democrats chose that alternative, versus nominating a candidate whom they agree with on the issues; now, just a month later, 45% of Democrats prefer to nominate a candidate who has the best chance of beating the Republican.) It is also of interest that Clinton's name identification—based on the percentage of Americans who know enough to have either a favorable or an unfavorable opinion of her—is at 98% in our latest poll. Obama's national name identification is lower, at 87%. Yet he does as well as or better than she does when pitted against the Republican candidates. Giuliani does better than his two Republican counterparts when voters are asked to choose between the Republicans and the two Democratic candidates. That could be because he is much better known than the other Republican candidates included in the poll. Perhaps the most interesting observation one can make from a comparison of the Republican performances is that Huckabee—whose name identification at 58% is lower than Romney's at 67%—still manages to match the latter's performance in these general election trial heats.

All in all, it can be said that at this point, the Democrats maintain at least a slight edge across these hypothetical matchups. Also, Obama tends to fare better against the Republicans than does Clinton, and Giuliani tests better against the Democrats than does Huckabee or Romney. There have been some changes in these results across time, however, and it appears that the trends are to some degree moving in opposite directions. While Clinton has lost ground against Giuliani since early November, Obama has been gaining ground. A somewhat similar pattern holds with respect to matchups of the two Democratic candidates against Romney. Romney now does better against Clinton than he did in November, while Romney's position against Obama has not changed since then.

Congressional Ballot

All 435 seats in the House of Representatives are up for grabs in 2008, as they are every two years. Gallup typically gauges the potential for a change in the relative distribution of seats between the two major parties by asking a "generic ballot" question. At this point, the Democrats have a sizable 13-point edge among registered voters. That compares with an 11-point lead among registered voters in Gallup's final 2006 pre-election poll. Democrats gained 30 seats in that election and wrested control of the House from the Republicans. If the type of broad Democratic edge that Gallup now measures continues through next fall, the odds are high that the Democrats will continue to control the House when the dust settles after the November 4, 2008, election.

DECEMBER 20
Is Clinton Electable?

At the Democratic debate in Philadelphia on October 30, Connecticut senator Christopher Dodd said: "Whether it's fair or not fair, the fact of the matter is that [with respect to] my colleague from New York, Senator Clinton, there are 50% of the American public that say they're not going to vote for her. I'm not saying anything that people don't know already. I don't necessarily like it, but those are the facts. We as a party certainly have to take that into consideration." Questions about Hillary Clinton's ability to win a general presidential election have followed her from the moment she announced her 2008 presidential election bid. Now that Democrats are poised to actually select their party's nominee, the questions have resurfaced with some intensity. The issue is addressed most directly by national surveys asking voters whether they would be more likely to vote for Clinton or for one of her Republican opponents in the November 2008 election. Out of eight such trial heats Gallup has conducted this year in which Clinton was paired against Republican front-runner Rudolph Giuliani, Clinton led in two, was statistically tied in four, and trailed in two.

Clinton has tended to perform better in matchups with less prominent Republican candidates. For example, in Gallup's latest poll, conducted between December 14 and December 16, 2007, Clinton effectively ties Giuliani (49% for Clinton vs. 48% for Giuliani), but she leads Mike Huckabee by a nine-point margin (53% vs. 44%) and leads Mitt Romney by six points (52% vs. 46%). Whether Clinton could win the 2008 general election would also depend on voter turnout. If equal proportions of Republicans and Democrats come out to vote, the results on Election Day should look very much like the national polls. Under that scenario, Clinton is clearly capable of winning. However, if a much higher proportion of Republicans come out, that could tilt an otherwise close election against her.

CLINTON'S IMPACT ON TURNOUT

Would Clinton's presence on the ballot next fall as the Democratic nominee for president trigger a Republican stampede to the polls? Recent Gallup data addressing this don't provide a clear answer. One question on the new poll asks registered voters whether, assuming circumstances arose that would make it difficult for them to get to the polls, they would make a greater effort to vote next fall if Clinton or, alternatively, Barack Obama were the Democratic nominee for president. Most voters say they would make the same effort regardless. Among the rest, twice as many say they would make a greater effort to vote if Clinton were the nominee than if it were Obama, 16% vs. 7%. However, given the responses by party affiliation, the possible effect on the election outcome appears to be nil. With Clinton as the nominee, Democrats are about as likely to be energized to get to the polls (presumably to support her) as are Republicans (presumably to support her opponent).

THE FEAR FACTOR

In contrast to this finding, a question included in the November and December Gallup Polls finds a majority of Republicans alarmed by the prospect of a Clinton presidency—and insufficient positive sentiment among Democrats to neutralize Republicans' alarm. Asked whether they would be "excited," "pleased," "disappointed," or "afraid" if each of various candidates became president, more than half of Republicans (62%) say they would be afraid if Clinton were elected. Barely half as many Democrats (35%) say they would be excited by this outcome.

No other candidate from either party generates as much cross-party fear as Clinton does among Republicans. The closest are John Edwards with 31% of Republicans saying they would be afraid if he became president, Obama with 30%, and Giuliani with 29%. Because the percentage of Republicans who would be fearful of a Clinton presidency is higher than the percentage of Democrats who would be excited, there may be greater potential for a surge of Republican turnout against Clinton than for a surge of Democratic turnout in support of her. Still, Clinton does generate more excitement from within her own party than any other leading Republican or Democrat does from their own party.

The same patterns are seen, only a bit less starkly, with a question from the December 14–16 USA Today/Gallup Poll that asks Americans to say what kind of president each candidate would make: "great," "good," "average," "poor," or "terrible." Of the eight candidates rated, Clinton generates the most extremely negative reactions from members of the opposing party: Forty-three percent of Republicans say she would be terrible, compared with only 20% of Republicans saying this of Edwards and 13% of Democrats saying this of Fred Thompson. Clinton also generates the most positives from members of her own party regarding the likelihood of her being a "great" president—substantially more than her major challengers for the Democratic nomination and more than any of the leading Republican candidates are accorded by Republican voters.

Taking these results at face value, Clinton looks as electable as anyone running for president today, if not more so. She appears particularly strong vis-à-vis the Republicans in November, beating Giuliani and other Republican candidates by significant margins. In more recent polling, she does no worse than tie Giuliani. Additional assurances about her electability can be found in Gallup data showing that while Republicans may be more motivated to get out and vote on Election Day with Clinton, rather than Obama, on the ticket, Democrats are as well, thus nullifying any likely effect on the outcome. Still, the 62% of Republicans who are fearful of a Clinton presidency is a startling figure. Without an equal proportion of Democrats somehow counterbalancing that, there is at least the *potential* for a substantial Republican effort in the general election to keep Clinton out of office, whether that means unprecedented levels of donations or volunteers, or higher than usual turnout on Election Day.

DECEMBER 21

Romney Has Slim Lead in New Hampshire

A new USA Today/Gallup Poll of New Hampshire voters who are likely to vote in the January 8, 2008, Republican primary shows that Mitt Romney—former governor of next-door Massachusetts—has a narrow seven-point lead over Arizona senator John McCain. Despite the intense media focus on former Arkansas governor Mike Huckabee's rise to prominence in Iowa, in New Hampshire he is essentially tied with former New York mayor Rudolph Giuliani and Texas representative Ron Paul for third place. Republicans in New Hampshire say illegal immigration and the economy are the top issues they will be most likely to take into account in deciding on their vote, although at the same time a slight majority of Republicans say the leadership skills and vision of the candidates are more important than their stances on specific issues.

The USA Today/Gallup Poll, conducted between December 17 and December 19, isolated a sample of likely New Hampshire Republican primary voters and determined the candidate for whom they said they would be most likely to vote. Romney's lead is not surprising. He has been ahead in various polls of New Hampshire Republicans all year long, a position most often attributed to the visibility he gained as governor of neighboring state Massachusetts. McCain, who won the 2000 New Hampshire primary and is hoping to repeat that success in 2008 to propel his campaign, is in second place. Huckabee has gained widespread visibility in recent weeks as a result of his strong showing in polls of Iowa caucus goers and his gains in national polls. Still, at the moment, he comes in essentially tied with Giuliani

and Paul behind the two leaders. Huckabee only recently began to campaign in New Hampshire, and Giuliani has spent little time there, instead setting his sights on the large states voting on February 5.

A little more than half of likely Republican voters in New Hampshire say they are certain to vote for their first choice, leaving quite a bit of room for change between now and the January 8 primary. The poll asked Republican voters about their second choice, and the results show that Huckabee does not do any better as a second choice than he did as a first choice. Romney ends up with 53% of the combined first- and second-choice votes, McCain gets 44%, Giuliani gets 36%, and Huckabee trails with just 20%. The sequence of events next month has the Iowa caucuses taking place on January 3, followed by the New Hampshire primary just five days later. If Huckabee indeed does have a strong showing in Iowa, it is possible that the resulting publicity could alter the votes of New Hampshire Republicans. But the second-choice data reviewed here suggest that Huckabee could have a difficult time pulling out a strong showing in New Hampshire regardless of his performance in Iowa.

Issues Important to Republican Voters

The poll asked Republicans to choose, from among a list of six issues, which would be the most important in determining their vote: illegal immigration, economic conditions, terrorism, the situation in Iraq, healthcare, and taxes. No single issue out of these six dominates the responses of Republicans, although illegal immigration and economic conditions appear to be somewhat more important than the others. Importantly, Iraq is fairly low on the list, in sharp contrast to the responses of New Hampshire Democrats, for whom Iraq is number 1. It should be noted, however, that when asked to say which will be most important to their vote—issues or "leadership skills and vision"—Republicans come down on the side of the latter, perhaps suggesting that the various issues the candidates talk about will be less important in the final analysis than the overall impression they make on the minds of voters.

Candidate Perceptions

Republicans were asked which of the major candidates best fits each of six descriptive phrases: has new ideas to solve the country's problems; has the best chance of beating the Democrat; shares your values; can get things done in Washington; stands up for what he believes in; and is in touch with the average American. Although Romney leads the overall balloting among Republicans in New Hampshire, he does not lead on all of these dimensions.

He is more likely than any other candidate to be identified as having new ideas, having the best chance of beating the Democrat, and sharing "your values." McCain, on the other hand, is most likely to be seen as the candidate who can get things done in Washington, as standing up for what he believes in, and as being in touch with average Americans. Romney maintains a small lead among likely Republican voters in New Hampshire, with McCain close behind in second place. Huckabee, the recipient of the most publicity of any Republican candidate in recent weeks, is tied for third with Giuliani and Paul. The degree to which the results of the January 3 Iowa caucuses will affect these candidate standings in New Hampshire is unknown.

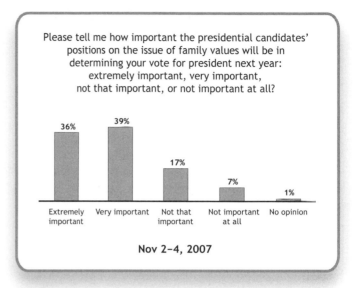

Please tell me how important the presidential candidates' positions on the issue of family values will be in determining your vote for president next year: extremely important, very important, not that important, or not important at all?

Nov 2–4, 2007

DECEMBER 26
"Family Values" Important to Presidential Vote

A recent USA Today/Gallup Poll finds three in four Americans saying the positions of the presidential candidates on family values will be an important factor in determining their vote for president in November 2008, with just more than one in three saying they will be "extremely" important. When asked what the words "family values" conjure up for them in the context of a political campaign, Americans most often say the family unit, family structure, or strong families. Americans also frequently say the issue of family values represents a political ploy or a way to win votes—or, alternatively, that it relates to healthcare issues, as well as to the issues of abortion, gay rights, and gay marriage.

The November 2–4, 2007, poll asked Americans whether the presidential candidates' positions on family values will be extremely important, very important, not that important, or not important at all in determining their vote for president next year. The vast majority of Americans say the candidates' positions on this issue will be extremely (36%) or very (39%) important to their vote. Only about one in four say the candidates' positions will not be important.

"Family values" resonates more with some groups of Americans—such as Republicans, self-described conservatives, and women—than it does with others. Republicans (86% extremely or very important) are more likely than independents or Democrats to say the family values issue will be important to their vote for president next year—but strong majorities of both independents (71%) and Democrats (72%) also say this issue will be important. Eighty-eight percent of conservatives say the candidates' positions on family values will be extremely or very important to their vote next November, much higher than

the 75% of moderates and, especially, the 58% of liberals who say this. Women (79%) are somewhat more likely than men (70%) to say the presidential candidates' views on family values will be extremely or very important to their vote for president.

The poll asked Americans to explain, in their own words, what they think the words "family values" mean in the context of a political campaign. The most common answers respondents give in essence repeat the word "family" or some variant of it. Thirty-two percent of Americans respond in this way, basically restating the term "family values." Twelve percent of Americans reply cynically that the notion of family values is a political ploy, a way to win votes, or a phony issue. Eleven percent say "family values" connotes healthcare and health insurance to them. Ten percent mention morals and morality, and another 10% say abortion. Smaller percentages of Americans mention things like education, religion and Christianity, honesty and integrity, marriage, gay marriage, and taxes. There are only minor variations by partisanship in views of what "family values" means in the context of a political campaign: Republicans, independents, and Democrats most frequently mention some aspect of the family unit. The only two statistically significant variations involve healthcare and abortion: A higher percentage of Democrats (15%) than of Republicans or independents (9% each) say healthcare comes to mind when they think of "family values" in a political campaign, while Republicans are more likely than Democrats to say abortion, 14% to 7%.

The perceptions of conservatives, moderates, and liberals regarding family values are similar to the extent that the top response for each group relates to the family, including the family unit, family structure, and strong families. But liberals (18%) are more likely than conservatives (8%) to say "family values" is just a political ploy and a way to win votes. By comparison, conservatives (13%) and moderates (15%) are more likely than liberals (5%) to say "family values" in the context of a political campaign represents healthcare issues, and conservatives (13%) are more likely than moderates (8%) or liberals (7%) to mention the abortion issue.

DECEMBER 27

Clinton Excels Among Seniors, Low-Income Democrats

Barack Obama's newfound momentum in the Iowa and New Hampshire Democratic presidential contests—he rose from second or third place into competition with Hillary Clinton for first—seems to have reset national Democratic preferences for Obama and Clinton to where they were in late summer and early fall. After a period from mid-October to mid-November when Gallup's national polling found Clinton's lead over Obama rising from about 22 points to nearly 30 points, Clinton now leads Obama by just shy of 20 points, similar to her standing in September and early October. Though Obama's national position among Democrats (including independents who lean Democratic) has recovered somewhat since November, Clinton still leads by enough that she continues to dominate the race at the subgroup level. Obama runs more strongly with some groups than others, but Clinton outpaces him among nearly every major demographic and political subgroup. According to aggregated data from Gallup's two most recent national surveys, conducted between late November and mid-December, Clinton's strongest leads for the nomination are among seniors, women, lower- and middle-income as well as less educated Democrats, easterners (the East being Clinton's current region as U.S. senator from New York), and southerners (the South being her former region as first lady of Arkansas). Clinton's advantage over Obama among these groups ranges from 22 to 35 points. Clinton also enjoys solid leads among non-Hispanic whites, blacks, Westerners, and pre-seniors (age 50 to 64). Obama does best among men, voters under 50, upper-income and highly educated Democrats, and those living in the Midwest (the region of his home state of Illinois). However, he does no better than tie Clinton among any of these groups.

Political Patterns of Support

On the basis of partisanship, Clinton is preferred to Obama by a 24-point margin among rank-and-file Democrats (48% vs. 24%), but by only a 2-point margin (32% vs. 30%) among

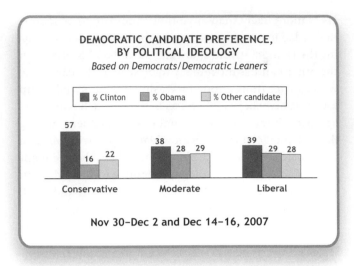

independents who lean Democratic. Gallup also finds a sharp difference in candidate preference according to Democrats' self-described political ideology. Only one in five Democrats consider themselves "conservative" politically, but those who do are overwhelmingly in Clinton's corner. Clinton has much smaller leads (10 points each) among "moderate" and "liberal" Democrats.

The Age and Gender Divide

The influence of gender and age on voter preferences between the two leading Democratic candidates is evident when looking at the four major age/gender categories of voters. Clinton is most popular among women and seniors: She has a 30-point lead over Obama among women age 50 and older but trails Obama by 2 percentage points (not a statistically significant margin) among men age 18 to 49. (This is one of the few subgroups among whom Obama comes close to leading Clinton.) Age appears to prevail over gender when it comes to the other two age/gender subgroups: Clinton has a 21-point lead among older men, compared with a 14-point lead among younger women.

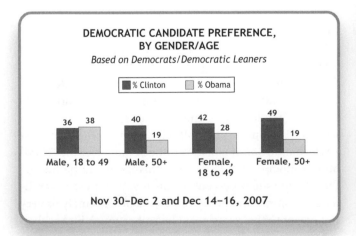

Although Edwards is polling well in Iowa—possibly well enough to win that state's caucuses when they are held on January 3, 2008—he and all other Democratic contenders remain far behind Clinton and Obama in terms of being major contenders for the Democratic nomination. Still, there are a few noteworthy distinctions in the demographic support patterns for some of the less prominent candidates. Edwards is supported by 18% of non-Hispanic white Democrats but by only 3% of blacks. Support for Delaware senator Joe Biden is highly correlated with age, with the percentage choosing him rising from 2% of Democrats age 18 to 49 to 6% of those 50 and older. Biden's support is also more concentrated among moderate Democrats (6%) than among liberal (2%) or conservative (2%) Democrats.

Patterns of Support for the Republican Contenders

As the first actual voting in the 2008 presidential race draws near, it is a good time to review the patterns of support for the Republican presidential candidates among various subgroups of the national Republican population. The analyses that follow are from two Gallup Polls conducted in late November/early December and in mid-December, yielding an aggregated sample of more than 800 Republican voters. Several of the candidates, the analysis shows, have fairly distinctive patterns of support. Former New York City mayor Rudolph Giuliani does best among moderate/liberal Republicans, those who seldom or never attend church, and younger Republicans (despite the fact that he is 63). Arizona senator John McCain has a more even distribution of support, although he does at least slightly better among moderate/liberal Republicans. Former Arkansas governor Mike Huckabee does much better among conservative Republicans, frequent church attenders, those who are older, and those who live in the South and Midwest. Former Massachusetts governor Mitt Romney's appeal is higher among conservative Republicans and is slightly higher among older Republicans and those with college degrees. Former Tennessee senator Fred Thompson's appeal is higher among conservatives and in the South.

IDEOLOGY

There are significant differences in candidate preference by the self-reported ideology of Republicans. Four candidates—Huckabee, Giuliani, Thompson, and Romney—essentially tie among conservative Republicans. Giuliani leads among moderate/liberal Republicans, followed by McCain. Hard-core Republicans—those who identify with the party as opposed to independents who lean toward it—are stronger in their support for Thompson than are

independents who lean Republican. There is relatively little difference across the other candidates.

RELIGION

Religion is a variable that provides important differentiation within the Republican Party in today's political environment. Republicans who are very religious—based, in this analysis, on self-reported church attendance—often show significantly different voting patterns than do Republicans who are less religious (that is, those who attend church less regularly). The biggest differences by church attendance come in terms of support for Giuliani and Huckabee. The former—a Roman Catholic who has been divorced twice—has twice as much support among Republicans who seldom or never attend church as among those who are weekly church attenders. On the other hand, Huckabee—an ordained Baptist minister who attended a Baptist college in Arkansas and went to seminary for one year before dropping out to work for a televangelist—has over three times as much support among weekly church attenders as among those who seldom or never attend church. Indeed, Huckabee would be the winner if a national election were held only among Republicans who attend church weekly. On the other hand, an election among Republicans who seldom or never attend church would find Giuliani winning in a relative landslide.

THE AGE FACTOR

The leading Republican presidential candidates this year are relatively old. Four of these five candidates are 60 years of age or older: McCain is currently 71; Giuliani, 63; Thompson, 65; and Romney, 60. That leaves the youthful Huckabee—now 52—as the lone below-60-year-old candidate in this group.

However, the age of the candidates does not appear to be related to differences in their support by age. Huckabee's support is higher among Republicans 50 years or older than it is among those under 50. At the same time, the strongest disproportionate support among younger Republicans is for the 63-year-old Giuliani, whose support level is 10 points higher among those under 50 than among those over 50.

REGION

Not surprisingly, presidential candidates generally tend to do better among voters living in the regions of the country from which they come than they do elsewhere. Huckabee—from Arkansas—does best in the South and the Midwest. Thompson, from Tennessee, does best in the South. But front-runner Giuliani, who is from New York, has a fairly consistent appeal across regions, except for a somewhat lower level of support in the South. Romney also has a fairly even distribution of support across regions, except for a slightly lower level of support in the South, which is the one region to which he does not have any direct tie (Romney attended Brigham Young University in Utah and is famous for his work on the 2002 Salt Lake City Winter Olympics; his father was governor of Michigan in the Midwest; and he more recently resided in and served as governor of Massachusetts.)

EDUCATION

There are no major differences in candidate support by education; the support for most of these candidates is generally fairly consistent across educational categories. Republicans with college degrees tend to be more likely than those with less education to say they support Romney.

JANUARY 2008

In the early part of January, Iowa and New Hampshire voters cast the first official votes of the 2008 presidential election. Until recently, the party nominating races have been fairly stable at the national level, with New York senator Hillary Clinton enjoying a sizable lead over Illinois senator Barack Obama and the rest of the Democratic field, and former New York City mayor Rudolph Giuliani consistently leading the Republican field, though by not as large a margin as Clinton's lead over her Democratic competitors. Some recent national polls suggest that Giuliani has slipped into a tie nationally with former Arkansas governor Mike Huckabee, former Massachusetts governor Mitt Romney, or Arizona senator John McCain.

A review of Gallup historical data on national Republican and Democratic presidential nomination preferences shows that the results of the Iowa caucuses and New Hampshire primary have the potential to shift national preferences, sometimes dramatically. Gallup has polled Republicans' and Democrats' presidential nomination preferences nationally since 1936; but it was not until 1972 that primary and caucus voters had a meaningful say in choosing their respective parties' nominees. Since then, it has not been uncommon for national nomination preferences to quickly change following the Iowa and New Hampshire contests. This has especially been the case when the Iowa caucuses or the New Hampshire primary produced an unexpected result, as in the case of Jimmy Carter's and John Kerry's surprise wins in 1976 and 2004, respectively. In those two elections, the race was transformed in favor of the victorious candidate. Sometimes, though, the "bounce" a candidate receives from winning Iowa or New Hampshire has proven only temporary.

What follows is an election-by-election review of Gallup data on national presidential nomination preferences before and after the Iowa caucuses and New Hampshire primary, beginning with the 1976 election. Because the Iowa and New Hampshire contests have often occurred within days of each other, in many cases the analysis compares pre-Iowa numbers with post-Iowa, post–New Hampshire numbers.

1976

Jimmy Carter is often credited with making the Iowa caucuses the significant contest they are today. He targeted his early campaign efforts at that state, and those efforts paid off, as Carter's win in Iowa on January 26, 1976, helped the former Georgia governor rise out of obscurity to become a serious contender for, and eventual winner of, the 1976 Democratic nomination. Prior to the Iowa caucuses, just 4% of national Democrats said they were likely to support Carter for the nomination, well behind Hubert Humphrey (27%) and George Wallace (22%). Gallup did not poll on the Democratic race again that year until after the New Hampshire primary on February 24, which Carter also won. By that time, Carter was running neck and neck nationally with Humphrey. Republican candidates did not compete in the Iowa caucuses in 1976, but incumbent president Gerald Ford managed only a narrow victory of 50.6%–49.4% over challenger Ronald Reagan in the New Hampshire primary. Ford had led Reagan 55%–35% nationally prior to New Hampshire, but immediately following that contest his lead was cut in half, to 51%–41%. Though Reagan went on to win several state primaries that year, he never got much closer to Ford on the national ballot.

1980

An unpopular President Carter sought re-election in 1980 and faced a challenge for the Democratic nomination from Massachusetts senator Edward Kennedy. Kennedy led throughout much of 1979 as Carter's approval ratings

CHRONOLOGY

JANUARY 2008

January 1 Over 900 American soldiers died in Iraq during 2007, making it the deadliest year since the 2003 invasion. However, casualties declined during the last quarter of the year.

January 3 The Iowa caucuses are held, the first step in the process of electing each party's delegates to the presidential nominating conventions. Barack Obama wins the Democratic caucuses with 38% to John Edwards's 30% and Hillary Clinton's 29%. Mike Huckabee wins the Republican caucuses with 35% to Mitt Romney's 25%, Fred Thompson's 13%, John McCain's 13%, Ron Paul's 10%, and Rudolph Giuliani's 4%.

January 3 Joe Biden and Christopher Dodd drop out of the race for the Democratic presidential nomination after their poor showing in the Iowa caucuses.

January 5 ABC hosts Republican and Democratic presidential debates at Saint Anselm College in New Hampshire. Republican Duncan Hunter and Democrats Dennis Kucinich and Mike Gravel are excluded because of their poor showings in national and local polls.

January 5 Mitt Romney wins the Republican caucus in Wyoming.

January 6 A Republican forum for presidential candidates is hosted by Fox News in Milford, New Hampshire. Ron Paul is not included.

January 8 Hillary Clinton wins the first-in-the-nation New Hampshire Democratic primary with 39% of the vote to Obama's 37% and Edwards's 17%. McCain wins the New Hampshire Republican primary with 37% of the vote to Romney's 32%, Huckabee's 11 percent, Giuliani's 8%, and Paul's 8%.

January 10 Bill Richardson drops out of the race for the Democratic presidential nomination.

January 10 Fox News hosts a Republican debate in Myrtle Beach, South Carolina. Duncan Hunter and Alan Keyes do not participate.

January 15 Clinton, Edwards, and Obama, the three leading Democratic candidates, debate in Las Vegas. Kucinich did not meet debate host MSNBC's criteria for inclusion; a legal suit by the Kucinich campaign was rejected by the Nevada Supreme Court.

January 15 Romney wins the Republican primary in Michigan. Clinton wins the Democratic primary in Michigan, but because Michigan had moved up its primary date without the national Democratic Party's permission, most Democratic candidates removed their names from the ballot.

January 19 Romney wins the Republican caucuses in Nevada.

---

were hovering around 30%. In November, the public rallied around Carter after the Iranians seized U.S. hostages, and Kennedy's lead evaporated. Carter won a decisive victory in Iowa on January 21, 1980, and saw his 14-point national lead (51%–37%) surge to 34 points (63%–29%). His lead would decline by the time of the Democratic convention that summer, but he maintained a significant lead over Kennedy for the duration of the campaign. Ronald Reagan entered the 1980 Republican presidential nomination contest as the clear front-runner and dominated the party's national preference polls throughout 1979. But he suffered a narrow defeat to former CIA director George H. W. Bush in Iowa, and Bush surged in the polls as a result. Immediately following Iowa, Bush and Reagan were tied in the polls. Bush's surge did not last, however, and within a week, Reagan had regained a slim national lead of seven points. After winning the New Hampshire primary on February 26, Reagan regained his dominant position over the rest of the Republican field.

1984

Former vice president Walter Mondale entered the 1984 campaign as the clear front-runner for the Democratic nomination and probable challenger to President Reagan. Mondale won easily in Iowa on February 20 but lost in an upset in New Hampshire on February 28 to Colorado senator Gary Hart. Gallup did not poll between the Iowa

Clinton gains more votes than Obama in the Nevada caucuses among Democrats, but caucus rules result in Obama's winning more delegates.

January 19   Duncan Hunter drops out of the race for the Republican presidential nomination.

January 21   Clinton, Edwards, and Obama debate in Myrtle Beach, South Carolina.

January 21   Stock market values drop in Europe and Asia by as much as 7%.

January 22   To forestall further stock market declines, the Federal Reserve cuts interest rates by three-quarters of a percent, the largest single reduction in its history. The Dow Jones Industrial Average recovers to end down only 1%.

January 22   McCain wins the Louisiana caucuses, although the "Pro-life/Uncommitted" slate actually receives more votes.

January 22   Fred Thompson drops out of the race for the Republican presidential nomination.

January 24   The House of Representatives votes for an economic stimulus plan created in negotiations with President Bush. The plan will give middle- and working-class families rebate checks of up to $600 for individuals, $1,200 for couples, and, for families, an additional $300 per child.

January 24   MSNBC hosts a Republican debate in Boca Raton, Florida. Giuliani, Huckabee, McCain, Paul, and Romney participate.

January 24   Dennis Kucinich drops out of the race for the Democratic presidential nomination.

January 26   Obama wins the South Carolina primary with more than half the vote.

January 27   Senator Edward Kennedy endorses Obama. Kennedy's endorsement attracts widespread media attention and helps to add to Obama's momentum.

January 29   McCain wins the Republican primary in Florida. Clinton wins the Democratic vote— but, as in the case of Michigan, the national Democratic Party has ruled that the Florida vote will not count.

January 30   John Edwards drops out of the race for the Democratic presidential nomination. Rudolph Giuliani drops out of the race for the Republican presidential nomination.

January 30   The *Los Angles Times* and CNN host a Republican debate at the Ronald Reagan Presidential Library in Simi Valley, California. As the Republican field shrinks, only Huckabee, McCain, Paul, and Romney participate.

January 31   The two remaining Democratic contenders, Clinton and Obama, debate in Hollywood, California. This is the last debate before the Super Tuesday primaries on February 5.

---

caucuses and the New Hampshire primary that year, but Mondale's once formidable lead essentially disappeared after those two contests. Prior to Iowa, he had held a 36-point lead. After New Hampshire, Hart surged from 3% to 30% nationally and pulled into a statistical dead heat with Mondale. Hart and Mondale remained locked in a tight battle in national Gallup Polls for the next month, before Mondale began to pull away on his way to winning the nomination.

1988

Gallup polled national Democratic and Republican presidential nomination preferences before Iowa but did not do so again until after Iowa, New Hampshire, and that year's "Super Tuesday" Southern primaries. As a result, it is not possible to isolate the impact of the Iowa caucuses and New Hampshire primary on national nomination preferences in 1988.

1992

In 1992, Democrats did not contest the Iowa caucuses because Iowa senator Tom Harkin was a presidential candidate, making the February 18 New Hampshire primary the first critical test of strength that year. Arkansas governor Bill Clinton had emerged as the national Democratic front-runner by the time of the New Hampshire primary, but his campaign was nearly derailed by accusations of marital infidelity. Nevertheless, he managed a strong second-place finish to former Massachusetts senator Paul Tsongas in that primary. That was enough to help Clinton maintain his national front-runner status, even though Tsongas's national support more than tripled after he won in New Hampshire. Incumbent president George H. W. Bush was challenged for the Republican nomination by commentator Patrick Buchanan. Bush held a commanding lead throughout the campaign, even after Buchanan gave him a serious challenge in the New Hampshire primary.

1996

Kansas senator Bob Dole, who had unsuccessfully sought the Republican nomination in 1980 and 1988, was the solid front-runner entering the 1996 election year. Despite a narrow win in Iowa on February 12 and a narrow loss to Buchanan in New Hampshire on February 20, Dole remained the clear leader in national preference polls. The main effect of the 1996 Iowa and New Hampshire results was to reorder the relative standings of the second-tier candidates (publisher Steve Forbes, Buchanan, and former Tennessee governor Lamar Alexander).

2000

The 2000 Iowa caucus results did little to move the national numbers, largely because the front-runners (Vice President Al Gore and Texas governor George W. Bush) each comfortably won their respective party's caucuses. Prior to the January 24 Iowa caucuses, Gore led former New Jersey senator Bill Bradley 60% to 28%, and he led 67% to 22% after winning there. There was also little shift in the national numbers after Gore defeated Bradley in New Hampshire on February 1. The Republican race also changed little after the 2000 Iowa caucuses, but it changed more substantially following New Hampshire. Front-runner George W. Bush led Senator John McCain 64%–17% before the Iowa caucuses and 64%–15% after winning there. McCain then upset Bush in New Hampshire, and while Bush maintained a sizable lead nationally, his support fell (to 56%) and McCain's increased (33%). That was as close as McCain would get to Bush during that campaign.

2004

Prior to the January 19, 2004, Iowa caucuses, former Vermont governor Howard Dean had emerged as the Democratic front-runner, with 25% national support, and General Wesley Clark appeared to be his strongest challenger at 19%. Massachusetts senator John Kerry was supported by

just 9% of national Democrats, about the same level of support as Missouri representative Dick Gephardt (8%), Connecticut senator Joe Lieberman (7%), and North Carolina senator John Edwards (6%) received. Kerry won an upset victory in Iowa and followed that up with a solid victory in New Hampshire on January 27. After his win in those two contests, Kerry became the overwhelming choice of national Democrats, with 47% supporting him. Edwards and Dean tied for second at 13% in the first post-Iowa/post–New Hampshire national poll.

Implications of the Data

It is clear that rank-and-file Democrats and Republicans nationwide pay attention to the results of the Iowa caucuses and New Hampshire primary, as national preferences have often changed in response to the outcomes of these two contests. That has especially been the case when the Iowa or New Hampshire results deviated from expectations—after which the winning candidate has often surged in the national polls. Those surges have likely been fueled by the positive media attention that is showered on the winners, perhaps in conjunction with more critical coverage of the candidates who failed to meet expectations. Those post-Iowa, post–New Hampshire surges have propelled back-of-the-pack candidates like Carter and Kerry to their party's nomination (in 1976 and 2004, respectively). But in other cases, as with Bush in 1980 and Hart in 1984, the post-Iowa or post–New Hampshire surge was short-lived, and the previous front-running candidate recovered and went on to win the nomination. In still other cases, such as for the Democrats in both 1980 and 2000, the national front-runners won the Iowa and New Hampshire contests, and as a result the national numbers were largely unaffected. And for the Democrats in 1992 and the Republicans in 1996, the front-runners did not win (or win decisively) in the key early contests, but they did not suffer much in the national polls.

The historical data, then, do not yield any clear insight into how or even whether the national numbers might change following this year's Iowa caucuses and New Hampshire primary. Usually, the performance of the various candidates in these contests is evaluated in terms of how well they meet expectations rather than how they finish in relation to their competitors. But even those expectations are somewhat murky this year, as most recent state pre-election polls of Iowa and New Hampshire voters predict very close contests on both the Republican and Democratic sides. Still, the potential is certainly there for national preferences to be shaken up in the coming days, particularly if one of the candidates scores a decisive victory in Iowa or New Hampshire.

JANUARY 2

Americans Speculate About Iowa's Impact

The January 3 Iowa caucuses are positioned to transform the dynamics, if not the outcome, of the major parties' presidential nomination races, particularly if the results defy expectations. An upset win by a candidate in this first contest of the season could sway New Hampshire primary voters on January 8, and from there it's anybody's guess what happens. Gallup recently asked Americans to adopt the role of political pundit and speculate about how various possible outcomes in Iowa and New Hampshire might affect the candidacies of the winners and losers. According to the December 10–13, 2007, Gallup survey, Americans tend to play up the significance of Barack Obama possibly winning in Iowa, as well as the significance of hypothetical back-to-back defeats for Rudolph Giuliani in Iowa and New Hampshire. Americans play down the significance of a John Edwards win in Iowa, and also of Hillary Clinton potentially winning in both Iowa and New Hampshire. Americans have mixed views about what winning in Iowa would mean for the campaigns of Mitt Romney and Mike Huckabee.

Speculation on the Democratic Race

Most polls of likely Iowa Democratic caucus-goers show a highly competitive race among Clinton, Obama, and Edwards, making it appear that any of the three could win Iowa. That's a much different position for Clinton than is the case in the national polls, where she leads Obama by a considerable margin and Edwards is in a distant third place. What effect do Americans think losing Iowa would have on Clinton's shot at the nomination? Seven in 10 Americans, including 84% of Democrats, believe that losing Iowa would be only "a temporary setback" for Clinton's campaign. Fewer than one-third think that it would be "a sign that her campaign is in serious trouble." At the same time, and somewhat inconsistently, most Americans—including

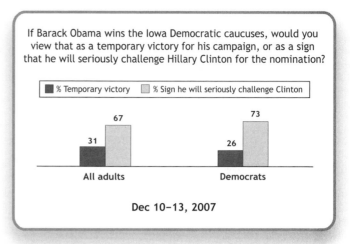

If Barack Obama wins the Iowa Democratic caucuses, would you view that as a temporary victory for his campaign, or as a sign that he will seriously challenge Hillary Clinton for the nomination?

Dec 10–13, 2007

nearly three in four Democrats—believe an Obama win in Iowa would be "a sign that he will seriously challenge Hillary Clinton for the nomination" and not just a "temporary victory" for him. Thus, the impact of a potential Obama victory in Iowa on the psychology of the race is a bit unclear. Americans say it would make him a force to be reckoned with; at the same time, they don't seem to believe it would seriously derail the "Clinton Express." The public is less likely, on the other hand, to consider a potential Edwards victory in Iowa to be a significant indication of his ability to challenge Clinton. Four in 10 Americans (including 47% of Democrats) say Edwards's winning Iowa would be a sign that he will seriously challenge Clinton for the nomination; the majority tend to believe that this would be only a temporary victory for Edwards. While Clinton has a lot to lose in Iowa, particularly from an Obama victory, winning in both Iowa and New Hampshire doesn't guarantee her candidacy a sense of inevitability with the public. Fifty-six percent of Americans, and the same percentage of Democrats, say that if Clinton wins both the Iowa caucuses and the New Hampshire primary, another candidate could still win the Democratic nomination; only a little over 40% say the nomination would be essentially decided.

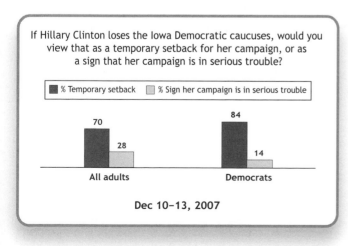

If Hillary Clinton loses the Iowa Democratic caucuses, would you view that as a temporary setback for her campaign, or as a sign that her campaign is in serious trouble?

Dec 10–13, 2007

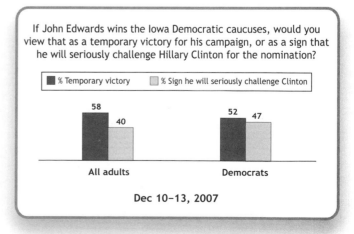

If John Edwards wins the Iowa Democratic caucuses, would you view that as a temporary victory for his campaign, or as a sign that he will seriously challenge Hillary Clinton for the nomination?

Dec 10–13, 2007

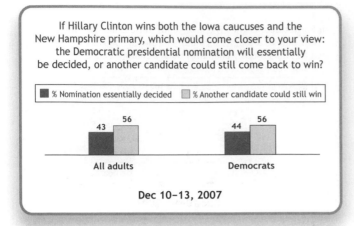

If Hillary Clinton wins both the Iowa caucuses and the New Hampshire primary, which would come closer to your view: the Democratic presidential nomination will essentially be decided, or another candidate could still come back to win?

% Nomination essentially decided   % Another candidate could still win

All adults: 43, 56
Democrats: 44, 56

Dec 10–13, 2007

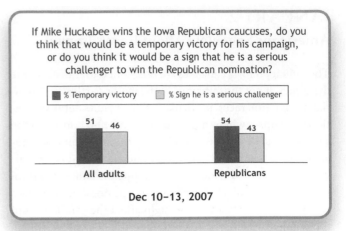

If Mike Huckabee wins the Iowa Republican caucuses, do you think that would be a temporary victory for his campaign, or do you think it would be a sign that he is a serious challenger to win the Republican nomination?

% Temporary victory   % Sign he is a serious challenger

All adults: 51, 46
Republicans: 54, 43

Dec 10–13, 2007

Republican-Based Prognostications

With Giuliani essentially conceding Iowa to his competitors, the race to win the Republican caucuses in Iowa is down to Romney, Huckabee, and—to a lesser extent—John McCain and Fred Thompson. Most polls now show Huckabee and Romney with significant leads over the other candidates in Iowa, and recent national Republican polls show Romney and Huckabee challenging Giuliani's front-runner position there. Thus, for both Huckabee and Romney, winning Iowa has major significance with respect to their positions nationally, not just in the early primary states. Americans are divided almost evenly over whether winning the Iowa caucuses would be a temporary victory for Romney (51%) or a sign that he is a serious challenger to win the Republican nomination (46%). Republicans tend to take a Romney win a bit more seriously, with a slight majority (53%) saying winning Iowa would be a significant sign of Romney's strength as a challenger.

Americans on the whole are also closely divided over the meaning of a Huckabee win in Iowa: Fifty-one percent say it would be a temporary victory for him, while 46% say it would

be a sign that he is a serious challenger for the Republican nomination. Republicans are no more likely than the public as a whole to believe that a Huckabee win in Iowa would be significant. Thus, our respondents view the possible impact of a Huckabee or Romney victory in Iowa as uncertain. Republicans—the constituency that counts in the short term—are slightly more likely to consider a potential Romney victory in the Hawkeye state as significant than would be the case for a Huckabee victory, but views are split in both situations.

Rudolph Giuliani has explained that he is running minimal campaigns in Iowa and New Hampshire in an effort to focus on the voting that will take place on February 5, when 22 states, including delegate-rich California and New York, will hold their contests. Given Giuliani's recent decline in the national polls, however, this would appear to be a risky strategy—and one that voters won't buy into should he lose Iowa and New Hampshire, as is expected. Only 28% of Americans believe that losing both contests would be just a temporary setback for Giuliani; 71% say it would be a sign his campaign is in serious trouble. Republicans are not much more forgiving: 38% say it would be a temporary setback, while 61% say it would be a sign of serious trouble.

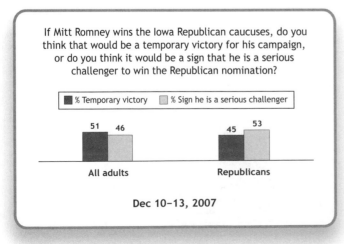

If Mitt Romney wins the Iowa Republican caucuses, do you think that would be a temporary victory for his campaign, or do you think it would be a sign that he is a serious challenger to win the Republican nomination?

% Temporary victory   % Sign he is a serious challenger

All adults: 51, 46
Republicans: 45, 53

Dec 10–13, 2007

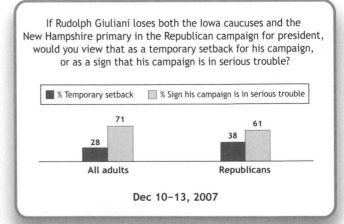

If Rudolph Giuliani loses both the Iowa caucuses and the New Hampshire primary in the Republican campaign for president, would you view that as a temporary setback for his campaign, or as a sign that his campaign is in serious trouble?

% Temporary setback   % Sign his campaign is in serious trouble

All adults: 28, 71
Republicans: 38, 61

Dec 10–13, 2007

With his slogan "Change we can believe in," Senator Barack Obama addresses a victory party in Des Moines after winning the Democratic caucuses in Iowa on January 3, 2008. *(Rick Bowmer / AP Images)*

The real fallout from the Iowa caucuses will depend on the precise results, the media coverage and spin, and the way the candidates handle the outcome in the days following the vote. Still, the attitudes reported here offer some clues as to how Americans might react. On the Democratic side, the potential impact of a Clinton loss in Iowa appears to be mixed: Democrats say losing Iowa would be only a temporary setback for her campaign, but at the same time say an Obama win there would be a sign that he was seriously challenging Clinton's front-runner position. On the Republican side, the data suggest that the situation for Giuliani is more grave than his campaign would like to acknowledge. As much as he is trying to manage expectations for the early contests, a majority of Republicans say that back-to-back losses for Giuliani in Iowa and New Hampshire would spell serious trouble for his campaign.

JANUARY 4

Americans Taking Front-Loaded Primaries in Stride

Americans are taking the acceleration of the primary process leading to the 2008 presidential election in stride. Although the first nominating elections are in January, and

the identity of the 2008 nominees will likely be known by early February, these are not vexing developments to most Americans. In fact, for a plurality, these are good things. At worst, most Americans are neutral about the front-loaded nature of the 2008 primaries. About half (49%) say that having the caucuses and primaries begin in January is a good thing, and another 27% say it is neither good nor bad, leaving less than one-quarter calling it bad. Americans are slightly more negative about having the races essentially decided by early February, with 36% calling this a bad thing; more (45%), however, consider it a good thing. Of course,

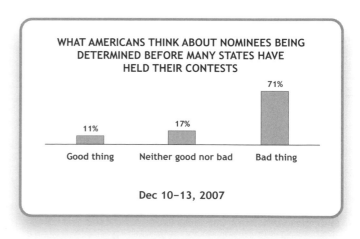

WHAT AMERICANS THINK ABOUT NOMINEES BEING DETERMINED BEFORE MANY STATES HAVE HELD THEIR CONTESTS

Good thing	Neither good nor bad	Bad thing
11%	17%	71%

Dec 10–13, 2007

the flip side of knowing early on in the process who the nominees will be is that the states that go to the polls later in the primary season have little or no impact on choosing the nominees. Despite their relatively positive reactions to having the nominations decided early, most Americans consider the limited influence of states with later primaries and caucuses a bad thing.

Americans are generally ambivalent about Iowa and New Hampshire being the states that traditionally begin the presidential primary season. Nearly as many Americans consider the two states' initiation of the primary season

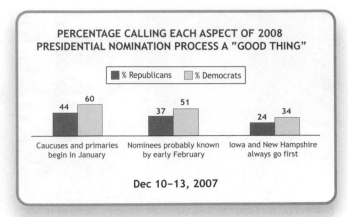

PERCENTAGE CALLING EACH ASPECT OF 2008 PRESIDENTIAL NOMINATION PROCESS A "GOOD THING"

Dec 10–13, 2007

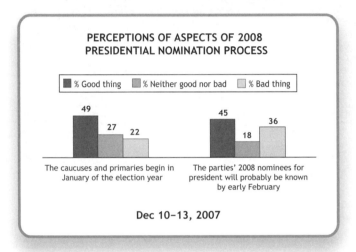

PERCEPTIONS OF ASPECTS OF 2008 PRESIDENTIAL NOMINATION PROCESS

Dec 10–13, 2007

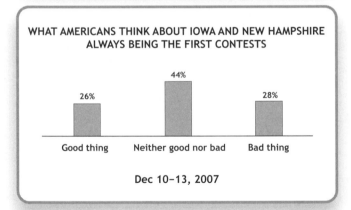

WHAT AMERICANS THINK ABOUT IOWA AND NEW HAMPSHIRE ALWAYS BEING THE FIRST CONTESTS

Dec 10–13, 2007

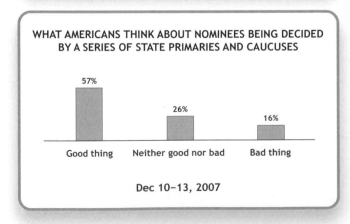

WHAT AMERICANS THINK ABOUT NOMINEES BEING DECIDED BY A SERIES OF STATE PRIMARIES AND CAUCUSES

Dec 10–13, 2007

good as call it bad, while most say it is neither. Regardless, most Americans like choosing the party nominees for president through a system of state primaries and caucuses.

Democrats More Positive About the Nomination Process

Republicans and Democrats nationwide are equally supportive of the general primary system in place to choose presidential nominees: Sixty percent of both groups call it a good thing. Both groups also view the potential irrelevancy of states holding later primaries as a bad thing. However, in terms of starting the process in January, identifying the nominees by early February, and beginning the political season in Iowa and New Hampshire, Democrats are generally more positive about the 2008 nominating season than are Republicans.

JANUARY 7

Obama, McCain Lead Among New Hampshire Likely Voters

With his victory in the Iowa caucuses on January 3, Senator Barack Obama has taken a substantial lead over Senator Hillary Clinton among Democrats likely to vote in the New Hampshire primary, to be held on January 8. Senator John McCain, who placed fourth in Iowa, now has a modest lead among likely Republican voters. Obama does particularly well among independents who say they will vote in the Democratic primary. And Democratic voters' choice of Obama as the Democratic candidate best able to win the November presidential election has surged since mid-December.

On the other hand, despite his highly publicized victory in the January 3 Iowa caucuses, former Arkansas governor Mike Huckabee only marginally improved his status among Republicans compared with Gallup's mid-December poll, and he is in third place—significantly behind McCain and

After his surprise win in the Republican caucuses in Iowa on January 3, 2008, Mike Huckabee addresses a victory party in Des Moines. His wife, Janet, is behind him. *(Evan Vucci/AP Images)*

Mitt Romney—in New Hampshire. These results are from a USA Today/Gallup Poll of likely voters in New Hampshire, conducted between January 4 and January 6.

THE NEW HAMPSHIRE DEMOCRATIC PRIMARY

Senators Obama and Clinton were essentially tied among both registered voters and likely voters in New Hampshire in the December 17–19 USA Today/Gallup Poll. By this past weekend, after the Iowa caucuses, Obama had moved slightly ahead of Clinton among registered voters, but had jumped more significantly ahead among likely voters. Obama now has a substantial 13-point (41%–28%) lead over Clinton among likely voters, with Senator John Edwards following in third place, with 19% of the vote. This marks a dramatic shift from just two and a half weeks ago.

All in all, Obama's share of the vote among likely voters went up by nine points between the two polls, while Clinton's dropped by four points, Edwards's share went up by one point, New Mexico governor Bill Richardson's dropped by two points, and Ohio representative Dennis Kucinich's share stayed the same. The "no opinion" or "other" percentage went from 2% to 3% between the two polls. (The mid-December USA Today/Gallup Poll included the names of Senators Joseph Biden of Delaware and Christopher Dodd of Connecticut—both of whom dropped out of the race after the Iowa caucuses. These two candidates had 5% support between them in the December poll.)

The USA Today/Gallup polls in New Hampshire included a question that asked Democratic voters to indicate which candidate best fit each of a list of "characteris-

tics" or descriptions. The percentage of likely Democratic voters selecting Obama went up at least a little on each of the six dimensions. The largest shift came in Democratic voters' perception of the candidate who "has the best chance of beating the Republican in November." Obama jumped by 19 points on this dimension between the two polls, while Clinton fell by 13 points. Whereas Clinton led Obama on this dimension by 21 points in mid-December, Obama now leads Clinton by 11 points after Iowa. These data underscore the conclusion that one significant effect of Obama's Iowa win was the apparent transformation of the first-term Illinois senator's image from that of a new kid on the block competing against Clinton's vast organization and experience to a candidate who has the best chance of winning against the Republican nominee in November.

THE NEW HAMPSHIRE REPUBLICAN PRIMARY

A key question since Huckabee's dramatic win in the Iowa caucuses has been its potential impact on New Hampshire Republican primary voters. Iowa, with a significant proportion of evangelical Christians, was fertile ground for the former Baptist minister's campaign, but it has been unclear whether more secular New Hampshire would be as receptive to his appeal. There are indications that Huckabee has moved up sharply among Republicans nationally since the Iowa vote. But the January 4–6 weekend poll in New Hampshire shows little sign that Huckabee has been able to transform his Iowa victory into anything approaching the type of surge seen for Obama among New Hampshire Democrats. Huckabee had 9% of the vote in mid-December and 13% in the weekend, post-Iowa poll, a gain of just four percentage points.

The more significant change that occurred between the two polls was in the relative positioning of the two front-runners in the Republican field—Romney and McCain. Whereas Romney led McCain among likely New Hampshire primary voters by seven points in mid-December, McCain now leads Romney by four points. That lead is not statistically significant, but it suggests that McCain has a real chance of coming away from New Hampshire with a victory, as he did in 2000. Rudolph Giuliani's share of the New Hampshire vote dropped by three points, and he is tied with Texas representative Ron Paul for fourth place in the poll. Former Tennessee senator Fred Thompson, who tied McCain for third in Iowa, looks to be an afterthought in New Hampshire.

There has been some movement in the percentage of Republican voters in New Hampshire selecting various candidates as best fitting each of the six descriptive phrases included in the survey. As was the case on the Democratic side, the biggest change here involved perceptions as to who is the candidate best able to win in November. McCain gained on this dimension, while Giuliani, who did not compete in Iowa, and Romney both fell.

Composition of the Turnout

The success of both new front-runners—Obama and McCain—in New Hampshire will depend on the impact of independents who vote in the respective primaries. Both of these candidates do better among "undeclared" voters than among registered voters of either the Democratic or Republican parties; Clinton and Romney do better among their respective parties' more hard-core faithful. While Obama leads Clinton among registered voters, it is a significantly smaller lead than among all Democratic voters. McCain and Romney tie among registered Republicans.

Obama has followed his dramatic victory in the Iowa caucuses with a jump to front-runner status among likely Democratic voters in the January 8 New Hampshire primary. Obama, tied with Clinton in mid-December, is now ahead of her by 13 points. Obama has gained a significant advantage among those New Hampshire voters whom Gallup deems most likely to actually turn out and vote in the Democratic primary. (He has only a small lead over Clinton among all registered Democratic voters in New Hampshire.) Obama enjoys relative strength among independents who lean toward the Democratic Party. Obama's victory in Iowa apparently helped convince large numbers of New Hampshire Democratic likely voters that he can win in November if he is the Democratic nominee. He trailed Clinton in mid-December by 21 points as the

Senator Hillary Clinton sheds a tear in a Portsmouth café on January 7, 2008, a day before the New Hampshire primary. *(Elise Amendola/AP Images)*

candidate perceived to have "the best chance of beating the Republican in November," but now leads her on this dimension by 11 points.

The post-Iowa change on the Republican side has not been quite as dramatic. Romney led McCain by seven points in December; McCain now leads Romney by four points. Of note is the fact that the Iowa winner, Huckabee, appears unlikely to duplicate his feat in New Hampshire. He gained only four points in the post-Iowa poll in New Hampshire and is in third place, far behind the two Republican front-runners. The relatively close nature of the race is reflected in the fact that McCain and Romney are now essentially tied as the candidate Republican voters in New Hampshire see as most likely to be able to win in November. A big change here was the decline of Giuliani, who has dropped significantly on this dimension since December.

Huckabee, Obama Gain at National Level

Republican Mike Huckabee and Democrat Barack Obama—both winners in the January 3 Iowa caucuses—have gained support at the national level among those who identify with their respective parties. Huckabee now has a five-percentage point advantage in the Republican race nationally, while Obama is tied with Hillary Clinton. These results are from the latest USA Today/Gallup Poll of national adults, conducted between January 4 and January 6, 2008. All interviews were conducted following Huckabee's and Obama's caucus wins in Iowa. Results from tomorrow's New Hampshire primary may, of course, produce still further changes in the national standing of the candidates.

Among Republicans, Huckabee has jumped from 16% of the vote in December 2007 to 25% as of this polling. Coupled with the loss of support for former front-runner Rudolph Giuliani, Huckabee is now the leader among Republicans nationally, with a 5-point lead over Giuliani and a 6-point lead over John McCain (who has gained 5 points since December). Mitt Romney, after failing to win in Iowa, is now in fifth place nationally with just 9% of the vote, which is his lowest percentage since early October.

On the Democratic side, Iowa winner Obama has moved into a tie with Clinton: Both now have 33% of the vote. This represents a 6-point gain since December 2007 for Obama and a 12-point loss for Clinton. John Edwards has gained 5 points since December, moving from 15% to 20% support among Democrats. Edwards is now closer to the front-runner among Democrats than he has been at any point since Gallup began tracking the Democratic race more than a year ago. This is also the first time since June that Clinton has not held a statistically significant lead over the rest of her competitors; she had led by 27 points as recently as mid-November.

JANUARY 8
Obama, Huckabee Surge in Latest National Poll

The political jolt created by the January 3 Iowa caucuses is causing a change in voter preferences in both the New Hampshire Democratic and Republican primaries—and thereby transforming the national presidential election race as well. The latest USA Today/Gallup national poll was conducted in the days immediately after the Iowa caucuses, from January 4 to 6. According to that survey, the winners out of Iowa—Republican Mike Huckabee and Democrat Barack Obama—have now pulled even or slightly ahead in their respective primary races and among voters nationwide. Prior to winning the Iowa Democratic caucus, Obama was mired in second place behind Hillary Clinton, and Huckabee was tied for second with several Republicans behind then front-runner Giuliani.

OBAMA RISING

The survey finds Obama tied with Clinton for first place, his best showing in months. Both candidates are now chosen by 33% of Democrats and Democratic-leaning independents nationwide as their preferred candidate for the nomination. This is a major shift from mid-December 2007, when Clinton led Obama by 18 points, 45% to 27%. Much of the shift toward Obama is because of a 12-point decline in support for Clinton over this period. But not all of those voters have gone directly to Obama; some have shifted to John Edwards. Support for Obama has grown by 6 points since mid-December, while Edwards has picked up 5 points over the same period, going from 15% to 20%. This represents the highest level of support for Edwards in any Gallup election poll over the past year.

Obama's post-Iowa public image reflects the important perception that he is the man to beat for the nomination. Forty-six percent of all Americans, including 42% of Democrats, believe Obama is the candidate most likely to win the Democratic nomination for president. Slightly fewer—35% of Democrats—pick Clinton, while only 14% pick Edwards. This finding is no doubt due to the extraordinarily high publicity given to the events in Iowa over the past week, resulting in more than three-quarters of Americans, and 81% of Democrats, being able to correctly name Obama as the winner of the Iowa Democratic caucuses. When asked if they happen to know who won, most of those who don't name Obama say they don't know; only a small fraction (1% each) incorrectly name Clinton or Edwards.

THE REPUBLICAN PICTURE

Following Huckabee's Iowa win, 25% of Republicans nationwide now rate him as their top choice for the 2008

Republican presidential nomination, up from 16% in mid-December. Senator John McCain also saw his support increase during that time, from 14% to 19%. After losing the expectations game in Iowa by coming in second, Romney is now suffering a decline in national support, putting him well out of range for the lead. His current 9% of the vote is his worst showing in the race since early October. Support for Giuliani, who chose not to compete in Iowa and has hence been out of the media spotlight, has also dropped, from 27% to 20%. Fred Thompson and Ron Paul are essentially holding steady at 12% and 4%, respectively. Huckabee's five-point advantage over Giuliani and six-point edge over McCain still fall within the poll's margin of error, so from a strict statistical perspective, the three are essentially tied.

The January 4–6 poll marks the first time in nearly a year that Giuliani has not held a significant lead on the national ballot, though he clearly had been losing ground, slipping below the 30% mark in November and December. In late 2006 and early 2007, McCain and Giuliani were essentially running even. Giuliani then surged into the lead in February, and he had remained in first place ever since. The 20% support for him in the current poll also marks his low point since Gallup began tracking the national numbers in November 2006. While Giuliani has reached his low point, Huckabee is now enjoying his highest level of national support since the campaign began. (Huckabee was in the low single digits in national polls throughout much of 2007. He did not reach double digits until mid-November.) Huckabee's rise is reminiscent of other dark-horse candidates in previous nomination campaigns who rose from low single digits in national polls during the early stages of the campaign to become real factors—if not winners. Jimmy Carter in 1976, George H. W. Bush in 1980, Gary Hart in 1984, Michael Dukakis in 1988, and Bill Clinton in 1992 are examples. Carter, Dukakis, and Clinton all went on to win their party's nomination, while Bush and Hart seriously challenged their party's front-runners, although both eventually lost the nomination. Huckabee's current front-runner status is bolstered by the poll's finding that 33% of Americans, including 36% of Republicans, think he will win the Republican nomination for president. Eighteen percent each believe McCain or Giuliani will prevail, while 14% believe Romney will emerge as the Republican nominee.

JANUARY 9

After New Hampshire, What's Next for Democrats, Republicans?

Senators John McCain and Hillary Clinton emerged as the winners of the January 8 New Hampshire primary.

For both, it is their first win of the 2008 campaign season. (Neither won the January 3 Iowa caucuses.) The results have thrown the respective Democratic and Republican presidential nomination races into a fascinating and historically unique situation. Gallup's January 4–6 national polling on Democratic and Republican nomination preferences had shown significant movement as a result of the Iowa caucuses. Barack Obama had moved into a tie with Clinton, and Mike Huckabee had edged ahead of former front-runner Rudolph Giuliani (and of McCain, who polled one point behind Giuliani). Now, with the McCain and Clinton victories, more change can be expected. Gallup has usually observed significant shifts in national nomination preferences when the Iowa and New Hampshire results go against the conventional wisdom. The results have certainly defied expectations this year, with the pre-Iowa national Democratic front-runner Clinton losing in Iowa; Huckabee winning by a large margin over the Republican front-runner in Iowa, Mitt Romney; Romney—governor of next-door Massachusetts—losing again in New Hampshire; and Senator Clinton winning in New Hampshire in the face of pre-election polls that pointed to an Obama win.

Typically in past elections, a Democratic candidate who swept both Iowa and New Hampshire emerged as the national leader (or, in the case of Carter in 1976, a co-front-runner). A split decision between Iowa and New Hampshire has been rare in Democratic nomination campaign history during the primaries era: Only in 1984 and 1988 did the two contests produce different winners. So it is unclear, based on prior history, how this year's Iowa and New Hampshire results might affect the national Democratic polls and subsequent primary voting. (Gallup did not do any immediate post–New Hampshire polling in 1988; in 1984, Hart's win in New Hampshire brought him within three points of Mondale.)

A key to national reactions to the New Hampshire outcome is expectations. Given the widespread expectation that Obama would win—based on his Iowa win and on almost every New Hampshire pre-election poll, including Gallup's—observers have interpreted Clinton's narrow win as a surprise victory. One plausible scenario is that the impact of her win may thus be amplified in the post-election analysis, and that voters outside of New Hampshire will see it as a more significant victory than if a close contest had been predicted.

The 2008 Republican campaign marks the first time in the primaries era that the national front-runner going into Iowa (in this case Giuliani) has lost both of the early contests. That result was no doubt due in part to Giuliani's having not competed vigorously in Iowa and New Hampshire; he decided instead to concentrate his campaign efforts on the larger states that come later in the campaign, where he believes he has a better shot at winning. The candidates have divided the spoils from the early states: Huckabee and Romney placing first and second, respectively, in Iowa, and McCain and Romney leading the field in New Hampshire. Given that Huckabee enjoyed a bounce in the national polls after Iowa, one might expect that McCain, too, will enjoy a bounce after his New Hampshire victory.

From another perspective, an Iowa–New Hampshire sweep, while common in Democratic campaigns, has never occurred in a Republican nomination campaign when both were contested, making this year's results "business as usual," in a sense, for the Republican Party. But historically, when the pre-Iowa national front-runner scored a victory in either Iowa or New Hampshire, he was usually able to keep the lead. For example, in 1980, following his win in Iowa, George H. W. Bush pulled into a statistical tie with Ronald Reagan, before Reagan regained his dominant lead with a win in New Hampshire. Of course, this year's pre-Iowa front-runner, Giuliani, has not won yet. Gallup's January 4–6 national poll (conducted after Iowa but before New Hampshire) showed Huckabee moving to the front of the Republican pack, with 25% support, compared with 20% for Giuliani and 19% for McCain. As noted, if any Republican is going to get a bounce out of New Hampshire, it would most logically be McCain, just as he did following his victory there in 2000. If that happens, the key will be how big a bump, and whether McCain is able to ride it to victory in Michigan and South Carolina next week. Both of these are "open primary" states where independents can vote, and pre-election and exit poll data show that McCain did particularly well among independents in New Hampshire. And indeed, in 2000, McCain won the Michigan Republican primary.

JANUARY 14

Republican Identification in 2007 Lowest in Last Two Decades

The percentage of Americans who identified as Republicans in 2007 is the lowest for any of the 20 calendar years since 1988, when Gallup began conducting its interviewing primarily by telephone. An average of 27.7% of Americans identified as Republicans, based on more than 26,000 Gallup interviews in 2007. The previous low in Republican identification was 28.1% in 1999. Meanwhile, 32.5% of Americans identified as Democrats and 38.6% as political independents in 2007. The latter percentage is on the high end of what Gallup has measured over the last two decades, surpassed by only the 39.1% independent identification average for 1995. The high point for

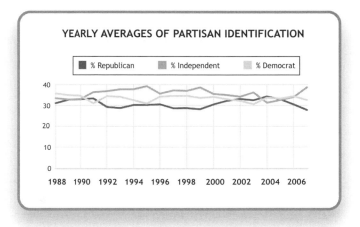

Democratic identification came in 1988, when 35.6% said they were Democrats.

Republican identification has dropped by roughly two percentage points in each of the last three years and is now nearly seven points below the 20-year high of 34.2% in 2004. Democratic identification also dropped by about two percentage points in 2007—from 34.3% in 2006—while the proportion of independents rose significantly, from 33.9% in 2006 to 38.6% last year. The current rise in the number of political independents is consistent with a cyclical pattern with respect to party identification that corresponds with the political calendar. Gallup typically observes a rise in the percentage of independents during the year between national elections. Conversely, Gallup has seen a dip in independents in the third quarter of years in which national elections occur. (Gallup observed such a decline, for example, in 1992, 1996, 1998, 2000, 2004, and 2006). At that stage, people are presumably more tuned in to political matters, the major parties are holding their conventions, and voters are staking out their sides in the election.

The net effect of the recent changes is that Democrats now have a nearly five-point advantage in party identification, up from roughly four points in 2006, when the Democrats prevailed in the midterm elections. In 2004 and

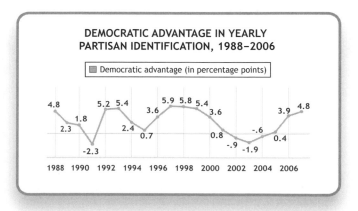

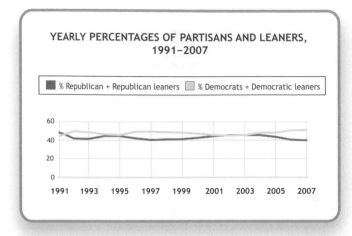

YEARLY PERCENTAGES OF PARTISANS AND LEANERS, 1991–2007

■ % Republican + Republican leaners ☐ % Democrats + Democratic leaners

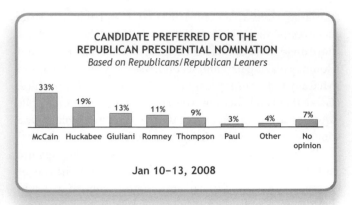

CANDIDATE PREFERRED FOR THE REPUBLICAN PRESIDENTIAL NOMINATION

Based on Republicans/Republican Leaners

Jan 10–13, 2008

2005, roughly equal proportions of Americans identified as Republicans and Democrats. The Democratic advantage is even greater when taking into account the partisan leanings of independents. In addition to the 32.5% of Americans who identified as Democrats in 2007, another 18.1% initially said they were independents but expressed a Democratic leaning, for a total of 50.6% Democrats and Democratic leaners. A total of 39.6% of Americans identified with, or leaned to, the Republican Party. This 11-point gap in partisan leaning is the largest Gallup has observed since it began regularly measuring partisan leanings in 1991, topping the previous high gap of 10.2 points from last year.

The Democrats not only maintained but increased their partisan advantage over the Republicans in 2007, at a time when the ranks of independents were also swelling in the mid-phase of the two-year party identification cycle. As a result, Democrats are heading into the presidential election year in a position of strength relative to the Republican Party. History suggests that the percentage of Americans identifying as independents will dip later this year, most likely over the summer. The question is by how much, and whether either party will grow proportionally larger as a result.

JANUARY 15
Updating the Nominations After New Hampshire

A new USA Today/Gallup Poll finds the winners of the New Hampshire primaries leading their respective fields for the Republican and Democratic nominations. More broadly, the Democratic race is similar to where it was at the beginning of December 2007, while the Republican race has been transformed. According to the new survey, conducted between January 10 and January 13, John

McCain now leads the Republican field with 33% of the vote of Republicans and Republican-leaning independents. Mike Huckabee is in second place with 19%, and Rudolph Giuliani about ties Mitt Romney for third, with both men in the low double digits (13% and 11%, respectively). Fred Thompson lags slightly behind with 9%.

McCain is now the favorite among both men and women; among middle-aged and older Republicans; among lower-, middle-, and upper-income Republicans; and among all Republican identifiers—as well as among independents who lean Republican. He leads Huckabee 47% to 12% among self-described "moderate" Republicans, but the two are about tied among "conservatives" (26% for McCain vs. 24% for Huckabee). More generally, conservative preferences in the race are highly dispersed across the five top-ranked candidates, while close to half of moderates choose McCain. A 51% majority of Republicans and Republican leaners name McCain as either their first or second choice for the nomination—potentially important for him when lesser-ranked candidates start to drop out. The next closest candidate in total support is Huckabee, with 36%, followed by Giuliani with 34%.

The Democrats Post–New Hampshire

On the Democratic side, Hillary Clinton leads Barack Obama among Democrats and Democratic-leaning inde-

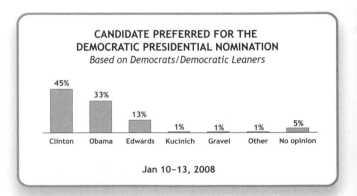

CANDIDATE PREFERRED FOR THE DEMOCRATIC PRESIDENTIAL NOMINATION

Based on Democrats/Democratic Leaners

Jan 10–13, 2008

A day after endorsing Senator Barack Obama for president, Senator Edward Kennedy appears with him at a rally at American University in Washington, D.C., on January 28, 2008. *(Chip Somodevilla/Newscom)*

pendents by a 12-point margin: 45% vs. 33%. John Edwards trails in third place with 13%. Clinton leads Obama by substantial margins among whites, women, middle-aged adults, seniors, and people who identify themselves as Democrats—as well as among self-described conservatives, moderates, and liberals. Obama leads—and leads big—among young adults and blacks. The two are closely matched among men and among independents who lean Democratic. Factoring in second choices, Clinton and Obama are nearly evenly matched in total support among Democrats—70% for Clinton and 64% for Obama—suggesting just how nip and tuck this race could be if they keep swapping wins in the early primary states.

McCain's Big Comeback

Stepping back and comparing the Republican race today to where it was in Gallup's last poll prior to the Iowa caucuses—conducted between December 14 and December16, 2007—the big winner is McCain, whose support has more than doubled in less than a month. His unexceptional

fourth-place showing in Iowa made little impression on national voters, according to a January 4–6 Gallup Poll; but his big win in New Hampshire has now catapulted him into first place.

The clear losers—at least for now—appear to be Giuliani and Thompson, both of whom have seen their support shrink since December. Giuliani's tenuous front-runner position in December rapidly disintegrated through the period of early elections that he chose not to contest. Support for Thompson, at 9% in the new poll, has faded from the 14% recorded in December and is his worst showing since he entered the race last spring. Romney reportedly hoped to gain more from the initial rounds of state voting, so to the extent he didn't, that could be perceived as a loss. In terms of straight numbers, however, his current support registers about what it was prior to Iowa—in the low double digits. Support for Huckabee surged nationally following his Iowa victory, putting him briefly in first place, but his support has since fallen back to about where it was in mid-December. Ron Paul, California representative Duncan Hunter, and former ambassador Alan Keyes share the support of 6% of Republican voters among them, the same as in mid-December.

Clinton Back on Top

The millions of dollars spent in pursuit of the Democratic presidential nomination, along with back-to-back dramatic election nights in Iowa and New Hampshire, have resulted in little net change in the Democratic race nationally since December. At 45%, Clinton's support is exactly the same today as it was in mid-December. The interim Gallup Poll, conducted immediately after the Iowa caucuses in early January, showed Clinton and Obama tied at 33%. Edwards, who edged out Clinton for second place in Iowa, rose to 20% in that same poll. However, following Clinton's unexpected win in New Hampshire, her national support has rebounded and that of Edwards has receded—also to December's level. Obama's support level is the same as it was post-Iowa. Since December, Bill Richardson, Joe Biden, and Christopher Dodd have all dropped out of the race, and at least by the overall numbers, it appears that their support has mostly gone to Obama. The only remaining lower-ranked candidates still in the race are Dennis Kucinich and Mike Gravel, both with 1%.

Politically speaking, McCain is back, and Huckabee, Clinton, and Obama all survived the grueling Iowa and New Hampshire contests; but Giuliani and Thompson are on life support. The near-term fates of Romney and Edwards seem most uncertain following their Iowa and New Hampshire losses, depending in part on the expectations that develop for their candidacies in the coming primaries. But one shouldn't look back, or perhaps even take too much stock in the present. The upcoming contests in Michigan, Nevada, South Carolina, and Florida offer fresh opportunities for more drama and turmoil in what is developing into a most interesting pair of races.

Huckabee, McCain Lead Among Highly Religious Republicans

Highly religious Republicans continue to support former Arkansas governor Mike Huckabee more than they do any other Republican candidate, but just barely. In the wake of Arizona senator John McCain's win in the New Hampshire primary, his support has risen among religious Republicans to the point where he is just below Huckabee. Religious Republicans' support for former front-runner Rudolph Giuliani has fallen precipitously, while support for former Massachusetts governor Mitt Romney has remained constant at a relatively weak level. About 36% of Republicans nationwide report attending church every week, which Gallup has taken as defining a high level of overall reli-

giosity. The presidential preferences of a group this large can be significant in the political process, and Republican candidates have, to varying degrees, attempted to win their allegiance as the 2008 campaign has progressed.

This year's Republican nomination contest has an unusual variety of religions represented among the major candidates, as they include a Mormon (Mitt Romney), a Catholic (Rudolph Giuliani), and an ordained Baptist minister and former seminarian (Mike Huckabee). Perhaps not surprisingly, Huckabee in recent months has gained the strongest allegiance from highly religious Republicans (that is, weekly churchgoers). Among this group, Huckabee has been the top choice for the nomination in each of four Gallup Polls conducted since late November. Despite his religious background, however, Huckabee by no means has a lock on the support of highly religious Republicans. In Gallup's November/early December 2007 Poll, Huckabee was just four percentage points ahead of former Tennessee senator Fred Thompson among this group. In December, he was just three points ahead of Rudolph Giuliani, and in the current January 10–13 survey, he is only four points ahead of John McCain. Only in the January 4–6 survey— conducted in the immediate aftermath of Huckabee's dramatic victory in the Iowa caucuses—did he enjoy a sizable lead over every Republican contender.

The pattern of religious support for the other Republican contenders has followed their overall national popularity at any given time.

- John McCain's support from religious Republicans has risen in January, particularly in the latest survey conducted after his win in New Hampshire.
- Rudolph Giuliani has seen his support erode among religious Republicans concomitant with his loss of support nationwide, which in turn reflects his strategic decision not to focus on winning the Iowa or New Hampshire contests.
- Mitt Romney's support has been basically flat over the past two months.
- Fred Thompson was, as noted above, at one point close to enjoying a lead among Republicans generally. Along with his downward drift among all Republicans, his support among religious Republicans has dropped to the 10% level in both of Gallup's January surveys.

The short-term impact of the vote of highly religious Republicans will likely vary from state to state as the primary season unfolds. Huckabee did well in Iowa, which has a strong cadre of evangelical Republican voters, but did relatively poorly in New Hampshire, where the rate of church attendance is one of the lowest of any state in the union. It can be predicted that Huckabee will do better in states that have a more religious population—including South Carolina, which has one of the highest church-going percentages in the nation—and in selected southern states on February 5.

John McCain has generated significant support among highly religious Republicans coming off his victory in New Hampshire. Whether he can maintain this level of support remains to be seen, and the upcoming primary contests in Michigan, Nevada, and South Carolina will be important tests of his ability to sustain it. Rudolph Giuliani and Mitt Romney perform relatively less well among religious Republicans at this point—although history shows that Giuliani has done well among this group in the past and therefore presumably has the potential to gain among them in the future.

After losing the Florida primary on January 29, 2008, Rudolph Giuliani (left) formally withdraws from the Republican presidential race the next day and endorses John McCain (center). McCain's wife, Cindy, looks on. *(Jim Ruymen/Newscom)*

JANUARY 17

Just What Types of Change Do Americans Want?

One of the most frequently heard mantras on the presidential campaign trail this year has been the call for "change." Several of the leading presidential candidates have adopted "change" as a campaign theme and have rushed to claim that they are the candidate of change. Barack Obama has made change the central motif of his campaign from the beginning, saying he is for "real change in Washington." Former president Bill Clinton responded to Obama's attempt to own the "change" theme by saying that Obama was the "establishment" candidate and would engender only the "feeling of change." Republican Mitt Romney put out a press release entitled "Governor Mitt Romney Calls for Change." A recent news story about John McCain carried the title "McCain Also Calls Himself 'Agent of Change,'" quoting McCain as saying, "I've made the greatest change."

Given Americans' low levels of satisfaction with the way things are going in the United States, their very low ratings of Congress and the president, and their low level of satisfaction with the way government in this country works, the desire for change—and candidates' perception of the desire for change—is not surprising. At a time when George W. Bush's job approval rating has been stuck in the 30% to 35% range for many months, it is abundantly clear that Americans want a change from the Bush presidency. A question included in the January 10–13 USA Today/Gallup Poll found that almost 8 out of 10 Americans want the next president to change direction from Bush's policies. But exactly what form that desired "change" should take has been a little murky. Change is such a broad concept that—as with a Rorschach inkblot test—an individual can read into the word what he or she wants. One can seek a change from the way in which the Bush administration (or Congress) operates, a change with respect to specific policy decisions, or perhaps just a more general change in the type of leadership the country has.

To help understand the desire for "change" a little better, the January 4–13 USA Today/Gallup Poll included this open-ended question: "As you may know, a common theme in this year's presidential election has been a desire for change in this country. What type of change would you, personally, most like to see the next president bring about?" First and foremost, it is clear from these results that when Americans look ahead to the "change" they hope the next president could bring about, they have in mind specific problems and concerns, not more general changes in the structure or systems of government. In fact, these results to a significant degree mirror those found when Gallup asks Americans each month to name the most important problem facing the nation. The top four problems Americans mention in our January "most important problem" update are Iraq, the economy, healthcare, and immigration—matching the top four specific areas in which Americans want to see "change" take place, according to the January 10–13 poll. This finding is significant. It suggests that when Americans say they want the next president to bring about change, they are mainly thinking about solving what they perceive to be the nation's significant problems. There is very little discussion in these open-ended questions of a desire to bring about more fundamental changes in the way Washington operates, in the process of governing, and so forth.

It is possible, of course, that Americans view more fundamental changes in the process as being necessary to solve problems. A January 4–6 survey tracked Americans' satisfaction with "our system of government and how well it works" and found that the latest results continue a trend of declining satisfaction in recent years. Back in 2001, before the 9/11 terrorist attacks, satisfaction with the government was at 68%. That rose in January 2002 to 76% but has been declining ever since, to the current 53%. So the responses to the open-ended question about change do not in and of themselves preclude a desire for changes more fundamental to our system of government. Gallup's question asked Americans what they wanted the next president to change, and the responses might have been different had the question had specifically asked about desired changes in Washington, or in government more generally. But the results reviewed here do suggest that the first reaction of Americans, when they hear discussion of the "change" a new president could bring about, is to focus on change that very specifically involves solving the nation's problems.

Americans Are Tuned In to the Election

Almost two-thirds of Americans already report giving "quite a lot" of thought to the presidential election this year, the highest such number Gallup has recorded in January of an election year, including in 2004, 2000, and 1992. Some of this enthusiasm for the election this year may be a result of the early start of the caucuses and primaries. In 2004, for example, only 45% of Americans said they had given quite a lot of thought to the election in early January, but by the end of that month—when the primary season was getting under way in earnest—the percentage giving quite a lot of thought to the election had jumped to 58%, not too far behind where it is today. In January 2000, a year before President Bill Clinton left office, the percentage giving quite a lot of thought remained low throughout the month. It picked up only a little in early February (to 39%) following the Iowa caucuses and New Hampshire

primary that year, perhaps because Vice President Al Gore was largely a shoo-in for the Democratic nomination, and Texas governor George W. Bush was a strong front-runner on the Republican side.

There are only slight differences by party in this "thought given" measure this year. Independents, predictably, are slightly less likely to say they have given quite a lot of thought to the election than are Republicans and Democrats. There are a number of plausible explanations, in addition to the early start, for why Americans are paying more attention to the election in 2008. This year is the first election since 1928 in which neither a sitting president nor a sitting vice president is seeking his party's presidential nomination, leaving true "open" contests within both major parties. There is also the fact that the cast of characters in 2008 is widely varied and interesting, including the first major runs of a woman and an African-American candidate for their party's nomination, and the first-ever candidacy of a former president's spouse.

JANUARY 22
Voters Not Clamoring for Third-Party Candidacy This Year

New York City mayor Michael Bloomberg continues to mull over the possibility of running for president as an independent candidate, much as fellow billionaire Ross Perot did in 1992. Last week, Bloomberg said, "I am not a candidate." But speculation that he might jump into the presidential race continues unabated, in part because his personal wealth would make it easy for him to begin a campaign without the usual rounds of fund-raising, and in part because he refuses to rule out the possibility and expresses obvious interest in running.

There has been much discussion this year about the American public's desire for "change," at a time when a significant majority of Americans indicate that they are dissatisfied with the way things are going in the United States today, and when there is growing concern about the economy. At the same time, change after the 2008 election is inevitable, given that the incumbent president and vice president are not running for re-election. Additionally, recent Gallup polling has assessed some of the public's attitudes that could be related to the ultimate success of an independent or third party candidate running against the two major party candidates in 2008. The data show that Americans are quite positive about the candidates running for president so far and believe they have suggested good solutions to the nation's problems, marking a sharp contrast with what these same measures showed in early 1992. Thus, while dissatisfaction in general is high, the

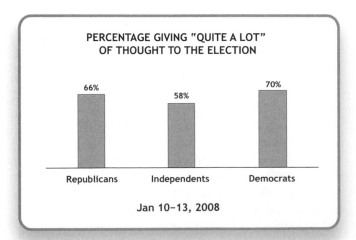

PERCENTAGE GIVING "QUITE A LOT" OF THOUGHT TO THE ELECTION

Republicans 66%   Independents 58%   Democrats 70%

Jan 10–13, 2008

American public does not appear to believe it is important or necessary for an independent candidate outside of the traditional two major parties to step into the race in order to save the nation.

Is There a Candidate Running Who Will Make a Good President?

One key finding comes from an analysis of responses to the question, "Is there any candidate running this year that you think would make a good president, or not?" The most interesting comparison here is between the responses to this question in 1992 and this year's responses. More than twice as many Americans in 2008 say there is a candidate they think would make a good president as said so in January 1992. In terms of the political environment, there are, of course, a number of differences between the two election years that might explain the large gap. In early January 1992, an incumbent Republican president with low job approval ratings, George H. W. Bush, was seeking re-election, while no nationally known candidate was running on the Democratic side. Bill Clinton emerged as the front-runner and eventual nominee only after the primary season had begun—which it had not at the time of the January 6–9, 1992, poll. In 2008, on the other hand, there are open races in both major parties; high-profile and well-liked candidates are running in both parties; there has been active campaigning for over a year; and the primaries season began particularly early. Still, whatever the reasons, voters are much more enthusiastic about the cast of characters running this year than was the case in January 1992, which suggests that voters' desire for a third party candidate to enter the race is considerably weaker in 2008 than it was 16 years ago.

Talking About Issues You Care About?

Another question in Gallup's January 10–13 poll asked Americans whether the presidential candidates are talking about issues they really care about. The 72% who say "yes" in 2008 is higher than the figures at comparable points in 2000 (54%) and 1992 (60%). In fact, the percentage saying "yes" this year is almost as high as it has been in October of previous election years—a time when positive responses to these types of questions usually rise.

Have Candidates Come Up with Good Ideas for Solving the Country's Problems?

Almost 6 out of 10 Americans say the presidential candidates have come up with good ideas for solving the country's problems. On a comparative basis, again, this is twice

as high as the comparable measure obtained in January 1992, and one of the highest Gallup has ever measured at any point during an election year.

There is no way at this point of estimating the potential impact or success of a third party or independent candidate were one to jump into the race. Much would presumably depend on how the remainder of the primary campaign plays out, on who the eventual major party nominees are, and on what the state of the nation is by later this spring or into the summer. When Ross Perot jumped into the campaign in the spring of 1992, he moved to the top of the national horse race polls, pulling in more potential voters than either President Bush or Bill Clinton. Perot later left the race and then re-entered it, creating a highly unusual set of campaign dynamics; he ended up winning 19% of the 1992 popular presidential vote. The data suggest that the environment would not be nearly as propitious this year as it was for Perot that year. It is true that Americans are broadly dissatisfied this year with both the state of the nation and the economy, as they were in 1992. But Americans at this juncture seem much more willing to say that the current crop of candidates running in the major parties have proposed good solutions to the nation's problems—and as a result, there is a high level of satisfaction with those currently running. Thus, were Bloomberg to jump into the race, his first job would be to convince voters that he would bring to the table something that the major party candidates have not.

JANUARY 25
Huckabee's Challenge

What's ahead for former Arkansas governor Mike Huckabee? Huckabee dominated national news coverage after his win in the Iowa Republican caucuses on January 3, but he subsequently lost primaries in New Hampshire, Nevada, Michigan, and South Carolina and has since slipped from the forefront of national news coverage. Gallup polling conducted this week shows that Huckabee is still in second place among Republicans nationally—roughly tied with Mitt Romney, but behind John McCain by about 10 points. Huckabee's long-shot chance to win the nomination, of course, depends on his being able to chalk up more wins soon. But Gallup analysis suggests that how well Huckabee—an ordained Southern Baptist minister—can do in a state's Republican primary is highly related to how religious that state is. Based on this criterion, Huckabee's chances of doing well in Florida are not particularly strong. And although on "Super Tuesday," February 5, when 24 states hold primaries and caucuses, his chances look good in certain Southern states, he will be challenged to do well in

Standing with former first lady Nancy Reagan (far right), the four remaining Republican candidates (from left to right) Mitt Romney, John McCain, Ron Paul, and Mike Huckabee meet for a debate at the Ronald Reagan Presidential Library in Simi Valley, California, on January 30, 2008. *(Justin Sullivan/Newscom)*

the big-prize states of California, New York, Arizona, and New Jersey.

HUCKABEE'S RELIGIOUS BASE

Huckabee's support, on both the state and national levels, is strongly related to church attendance. His win in Iowa, as widely noted, was based to a large degree on his ability to attract the strong support of more religious Iowa Republican caucus-goers. In contrast, his lackluster third-place showing in New Hampshire was related to the fact that there simply weren't enough highly religious Republicans in that state to vote for him. For example, Gallup Polls conducted before the New Hampshire primary showed that while weekly church attenders constitute 39% of national Republicans (according to Gallup's January 4–6 poll), they make up only 24% of New Hampshire Republicans. In fact, for Huckabee, New Hampshire was probably the worst state in which to try to sustain his momentum after his win in Iowa. A 2006 Gallup analysis of more than 68,000 nationwide interviews showed that New Hampshire, along with its neighboring state of Vermont, had the lowest level of self-reported church attendance of any state measured. The average in the United States was 42% weekly, or almost

every week, church attendance—but only 24% of New Hampshire residents said they attended weekly or almost every week. (Iowa was above the average, at 46%.) Indeed, New Hampshire exit polls showed that while Huckabee had some strength among Republicans who were frequent church attenders, he had very little among anyone else. Huckabee got 34% of the vote among those who said they attended more than once a week, winning among that group. He received 21% among those who attended once a week—somewhat behind McCain and Romney. But Huckabee received only 6% among the rest of New Hampshire Republican primary voters.

South Carolina was, predictably, a different story, as the state has the highest estimated church attendance of any state in the union. Sure enough, Huckabee came in a strong second in that state last week, three points behind McCain. The Edison-Mitofsky exit poll conducted after South Carolina voting last Saturday showed that among weekly church attenders, Huckabee beat McCain by a 43% to 27% margin. Still, Huckabee's margin among this religious group of Republicans was not high enough to offset McCain's performance among those who were less religious, resulting in Huckabee's three-point loss. Nevada has one of the lowest rates of average church attendance in the United States, and Huckabee tied for fourth in that state's caucuses, with 8% of the vote. (He did not actively campaign there.) Florida's church attendance is slightly below average at 39%, so Huckabee—everything else being equal—wouldn't be expected to do particularly well there. (Maine, with one of the lowest church attendance averages in the country, has caucuses February 1. Huckabee will likely not do well in that state.)

Five of the Super Tuesday states—Alabama, Arkansas, Georgia, Tennessee, and Utah—have church attendance levels that average above 50%, well ahead of the national average. Except for Utah, which should belong to Mitt Romney given the Mormon connection, these states could be fertile territory for the Huckabee campaign. Even if Huckabee does well in the Southern states on February 5, however, the results will most likely be overwhelmed by the attention given to the delegate-rich states of California, New York, Arizona, Illinois, and New Jersey. Of these five, Illinois ties the national average on church attendance, while the other four are all well below average. And, of course, Arizona is home to McCain, further diminishing Huckabee's chances in that state.

Highly religious Republicans constitute Huckabee's main source of voting strength. A Baptist minister, he went to a Baptist college in Arkansas and attended Southwestern Baptist Theological Seminary in Fort Worth, Texas. And he has been able to parlay that background into a strong appeal to religious Republicans around the country, which worked well in the more religious state of Iowa. But that positioning works less well in states that have below-average levels of religiosity. Huckabee and his advisers are no doubt aware of these realities and have tried to expand his appeal beyond moral and values issues—talking instead about taxes and emphasizing a more general populist message compatible with his working-class background. At the same time, Huckabee's ability to win continues to depend on his ability to activate religious voters, something he was not able to do at a sufficiently high level in South Carolina to gain a victory. A Gallup analysis of church attendance levels in forthcoming primary states suggests that, everything else being equal, Huckabee will have a hard time doing well in Florida and that he will be deeply challenged in the big Super Tuesday states like New York, California, Arizona, and New Jersey.

FEBRUARY 2008

Gallup daily tracking polls show that consumer confidence in the first part of February 2008 is down from the same period in January, particularly among middle-income consumers. Confidence began to deteriorate during the first two weeks of January, reaching its lowest level between January 16 and January 27—about the time of the Federal Reserve Board's emergency interest rate cut. There was a slight recovery in late January, but consumer perceptions of the U.S. economy remain more negative now than they were when the year began, and show no signs—at least so far—of responding to the interest rate cuts or to the Bush administration's newly passed economic stimulus package.

In Gallup's February 6–12 polling, one in three consumers rated current economic conditions as "poor"—up significantly from the 27% "poor" rating in the January 6–12 polling (and the 24% who said the economy was "poor" as the year began). This represents the highest percentage of consumers rating the U.S. economy as "poor" since February 2003—more than five years ago, just before the war with Iraq began—when 34% of consumers reported a similar view. Comparing the February 6–12 and January 6–12 data, the largest decline in ratings of the economy took place among middle-income consumers. In January, 39% of lower-income consumers (those making less than $24,000 a year) rated current economic conditions as "poor," compared with 27% of middle-income consumers (those with annual incomes of $24,000 to $60,000). By early February, the percentage of lower-income consumers saying the economy was poor had increased by 2 percentage points to 41%, while the percentage of middle-income consumers saying "poor" had surged by 10 points to 37%.

In early February, only 14% of American consumers said current economic conditions were "getting better," while 79% thought they were "getting worse." This represents a slight decline in consumer expectations from the January 6–12 polling (17% getting better, 77% getting worse), and

a greater decrease from the first few days of January (20% getting better, 73% getting worse). More importantly, it means current consumer economic expectations remain below their prewar (March 2003: 23% better, 67% worse) and pre-9/11 (September 2001: 19% better, 70% worse) levels. From early January to early February, the economic outlook of consumers making less than $90,000 a year grew more pessimistic. In contrast, among those with annual incomes of at least $90,000, the percentage saying conditions were getting worse actually declined, by 4 percentage points (from 77% to 73%).

Gallup's polling shows that consumer confidence—in terms of both how consumers rate the current economy and their expectations for the economy's direction—deteriorated in early February as compared in particular with early January. The large number of consumer interviews that Gallup's daily polling entails—more than 6,000 so far in February—affords added reliability to estimates that consumer perceptions of the economy are deteriorating. It also allows a more in-depth look at consumer perceptions and gives evidence that the greatest deterioration in consumer confidence is taking place among middle-income consumers. In turn, this implies that the financial squeeze that has played such havoc with lower-income consumers in recent years is now spreading to middle-income consumers. Of course, none of this is good news for the nation's retailers, or for the outlook for the U.S. economy in the months ahead.

FEBRUARY 1

Clinton's Gender Advantage over Obama Narrows

New York senator Hillary Clinton, the first woman to become a front-runner for her party's presidential nomina-

CHRONOLOGY

FEBRUARY 2008

February 1   The Bureau of Labor Statistics reports that the nation's employers eliminated some 17,000 jobs in January, raising fears of a recession.

February 1   Two female suicide bombers kill almost 100 people in Baghdad.

February 2   Republican Mitt Romney wins the Maine Republican caucuses.

February 5   Twenty-four states hold elections in the "Super Tuesday" primaries. Barack Obama wins 13 of the contests, although he gains only slightly more delegates than Hillary Clinton, who wins the big prize of California. John McCain wins nine Republican contests, handily defeating Romney, his closest challenger.

February 7   Romney drops out of the race for the Republican presidential nomination.

February 9   Obama sweeps the day's primary elections, winning in Washington, Louisiana, and Nebraska. Mike Huckabee wins the Republican caucuses in Kansas and

receives the most votes in Louisiana (although with no clear majority, so Republican state party rules give him no committed delegates).

February 10   Obama wins the Maine Democratic caucuses.

February 12   Obama and McCain win primaries in Virginia, Maryland, and Washington, D.C.

February 12   The Senate votes to broaden the government's spying powers and to give legal protection to telephone companies that cooperated with President Bush's program of eavesdropping without a warrant. Senator McCain votes for the measure; Senators Clinton and Obama are not present for the vote.

February 17   The ethnic Albanian province of Kosovo declares independence from Serbia. The United States backs Kosovo, creating tension with Russia, a strong supporter of a united Serbia.

February 18   Pakistan president Pervez Musharraf's political supporters are defeated in parliamentary elections. Almost all of the leading figures in Musharraf's political party that had governed for the last five years lose their seats.

February 19   Obama wins primaries in Wisconsin and Hawaii; McCain wins in Wisconsin.

February 19   Fidel Castro resigns as president of Cuba, and his brother, Raul, replaces him.

February 21   Clinton and Obama debate in Austin, Texas. The debate, hosted by CNN and Univision, stresses immigration issues.

February 23   The comedy show *Saturday Night Live* airs a sketch suggesting that the media treat Obama more kindly than Clinton. The sketch attracts widespread media notice, encouraged by the Clinton camp.

February 24   Ralph Nader announces that he will run for president as an independent.

February 26   NBC News moderates a debate between Clinton and Obama in Cleveland.

February 28   The Clinton campaign releases its "3:00 A.M." television commercial that shows a telephone ringing in the middle of the night and suggests Obama would not be ready to respond to an international crisis.

---

tion, has enjoyed disproportionately strong support from female voters. For example, an analysis of 11,794 interviews conducted with Democratic voters since January 2, 2008, shows that Clinton receives the vote of 48% of women, compared with 38% of men. But in recent days, the overall gap between Clinton and her only remaining serious competitor, Illinois senator Barack Obama, has been closing, and an analysis of the patterns of voter choice by gender

shows that Obama's gains over the last 10 days have come disproportionately among women. Clinton has been losing more support from women than from men, in essence moving closer to a point where the "gender playing field" has been leveled.

Comparing the three-day average of polls conducted between January 18 and January 20 with the three-day average of polls conducted between January 28 and January

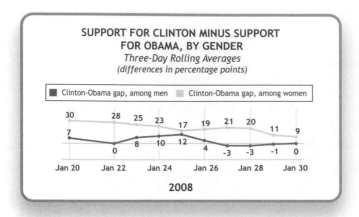

SUPPORT FOR CLINTON MINUS SUPPORT FOR OBAMA, BY GENDER
Three-Day Rolling Averages
(differences in percentage points)

30 shows that while Clinton's level of support among men has essentially stayed the same, she has lost 8 points among women. At the same time, Obama has gained 6 points among men but has gained even more—13 points—among women. While there was a 13-point difference between female and male support for Clinton in the January 18–20 interviewing, there is now just a 6-point gap. Obama was operating with a 10-point deficit among women as compared with his support among men roughly 10 days ago, but that gender gap is now just 3 points. In general, the patterns of support for the two candidates by gender are much closer to one another than they were just 10 days ago. Gender now appears to make less of a difference. The narrowing of the race by gender is apparent in most key subgroups of women, including by age, race, education, and marital status. The major trend evident in the Gallup Poll daily tracking data over the last 10 days has been the narrowing of the race for the Democratic nomination. Obama has been gradually chipping away at Clinton's lead, to the point where he trails her by just a few points. A detailed analysis of the patterns evident in the trend data over the last 10 days shows that Clinton's loss of support has occurred disproportionately among Democratic women. Clinton is the first female to become a major party's front-running candidate for the presidential nomination, and her particular appeal to female voters has long been considered one of her political strengths. If Obama continues to increase his appeal to women to the point where Clinton's gender gap is neutralized, she will have lost one of her most reliable bases of support going into the all-important "Super Tuesday" vote on February 5.

FEBRUARY 3

Clinton and Obama Tied: Both Are Satisfying to Democrats

A USA Today/Gallup Poll conducted between January 30 and February 2 finds Hillary Clinton and Barack Obama in a statistical tie for the Democratic presidential nomination, with Clinton preferred by 45% of Democrats nationally and Obama by 44%. In the Republican contest, Arizona senator John McCain leads former Massachusetts governor Mitt Romney by 42% to 24%, and former Arkansas governor Mike Huckabee is in third place with 18%. Given the current state of both races, the Super Tuesday elections on February 5 have tremendous potential for solidifying McCain's position as the probable Republican nominee and for clarifying who is likely to win the Democratic prize. The new Gallup Poll indicates that whatever the outcome, Democrats nationwide will be equally satisfied with their nominee. They show equal levels of enthusiasm for either Clinton or Obama being on the ballot in November: Fifty-five percent of Democrats (including independents who lean Democratic) say they would vote for Obama "enthusiastically" in November were he the Democratic nominee; 53% say the same with respect to Clinton.

In addition, Democrats are no more likely to believe that one of the candidates is more electable in the fall than the other. Forty-five percent of Democrats think Clinton has the better chance of beating the Republican candidate for president in November; 43% say that of Obama. By contrast, Gallup finds more lopsided attitudes among Republicans—and they are tilted strongly in McCain's favor. Republicans are less enthusiastic about voting for each of their leading potential nominees than the Democrats are about theirs; however, McCain is the clear leader on this score over Romney. McCain also beats Romney handily in perceptions of which of the two has the better chance of winning in November. Just under half of Republicans (including independents who lean to the Republican Party) say they would vote enthusiastically for McCain in the fall, and only 35% are enthusiastic about potentially voting for Romney. Republicans choose McCain by nearly three to one—68% to 24%—as the Republican more likely to beat the Democrat in November.

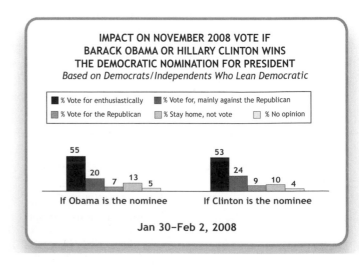

IMPACT ON NOVEMBER 2008 VOTE IF BARACK OBAMA OR HILLARY CLINTON WINS THE DEMOCRATIC NOMINATION FOR PRESIDENT
Based on Democrats/Independents Who Lean Democratic

Jan 30–Feb 2, 2008

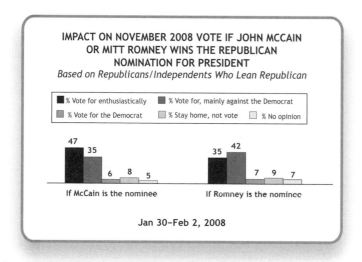

IMPACT ON NOVEMBER 2008 VOTE IF JOHN MCCAIN
OR MITT ROMNEY WINS THE REPUBLICAN
NOMINATION FOR PRESIDENT
Based on Republicans/Independents Who Lean Republican

- ■ % Vote for enthusiastically
- ■ % Vote for, mainly against the Democrat
- ■ % Vote for the Democrat
- ■ % Stay home, not vote
- □ % No opinion

If McCain is the nominee: 47, 35, 6, 8, 5
If Romney is the nominee: 35, 42, 7, 9, 7

Jan 30–Feb 2, 2008

Democratic Enthusiasm for Clinton and Obama Is Fairly Broad

Enthusiasm among Democrats for Clinton and Obama as their party's potential nominees is fairly high among most subgroups of the party. While there has been much media attention regarding Clinton's appeal to Democratic women and Obama's to black Democrats, at least half of both groups say they would enthusiastically vote for the other candidate. Obama has been performing particularly well with younger voters in Gallup's election polls. In the latest poll, he leads Clinton by nearly 20 points among 18- to 29-year-old Democrats: 56% for Obama vs. 37% for Clinton. Young Democrats are more likely to say they would vote enthusiastically for Obama in the fall than to say this about Clinton: 56% vs. 46%. Still, nearly half of young Democrats would be enthusiastic about voting for Clinton. Democrats age 65 and older—who favor Clinton by a substantial 57% to 31% margin in the new poll—are more enthusiastic about voting for Clinton than for Obama in the fall, but by only 10 points: 57% vs. 47%.

There are clear differences in support among political independents. Independents who lean toward the Democratic Party—and who thus may be voting in the open Democratic primary elections this year—favor Obama over Clinton by 52% vs. 35%. While 51% of Democratic leaners say they would vote enthusiastically for Obama in the fall, only 38% feel this way about Clinton. This compares with roughly 6 in 10 Democratic identifiers who are enthusiastic about both candidates.

Republican Enthusiasm Seen for McCain, but Not for Romney

McCain has turned his first-place showing in the January 8 New Hampshire primary into a full-scale comeback,

rising to the top of national Republican preference polls and scoring crucial wins in South Carolina on January 19 and in Florida on January 29. Some leading voices in the Republican conservative movement have since come out swinging against him. How influential they've been at convincing rank-and-file Republicans that McCain would unravel the "Reagan revolution" and be a greater political ally to Democratic senator Edward Kennedy of Massachusetts than to House Republican leader John Boehner of Ohio is unclear. Yet, Republican conservatives generally are as enthusiastic as Republican moderates about voting for McCain in the fall (47% and 48%, respectively). They are also more enthusiastic about voting for McCain than for Romney (47% vs. 40%).

At 47%, overall Republican enthusiasm for McCain is a bit lower than Democratic enthusiasm for both Clinton and Obama, but it registers above 40% among most major subgroups of Republicans. In contrast, enthusiasm for Romney's being on the ballot in November averages 35%, and dips below 30% among moderates, liberals, and independent Republican leaners. The Democratic primary race between Clinton and Obama is too close to call—not just as far as the horse race is concerned, but also with respect to Democratic perceptions of which candidate has the better chance in the general election, and in terms of the enthusiasm Democrats voters feel for the candidates. One disparity between the front-runners—and it could be an important one—is that independents who lean Democratic are much more enthusiastic about voting for Obama than for Clinton in the fall. There is much more clarity on the Republican side to the effect that McCain is the strongest candidate. He has extended his

By February 2008, Senator John McCain emerged as the front-runner for the Republican presidential nomination. *(Don Emmert/Newscom)*

lead over Romney to nearly 20 points, is widely viewed as having a better chance than Romney of winning in November, and generates more enthusiasm for his candidacy—from Republican identifiers and conservatives as well as from Republican leaners and moderates—than does Romney.

FEBRUARY 6

Four in 10 Democrats: Bill Clinton Attacked Obama Unfairly

A substantial minority of Democrats believe that Hillary and Bill Clinton have unfairly attacked Barack Obama during the presidential campaign. In turn, Democrats are much less likely to think Obama has attacked Hillary Clinton unfairly. There is not a widespread belief among Republicans that Mitt Romney or John McCain has attacked the other unfairly. Bill Clinton's public image has declined in the past few months—mostly among Democrats—possibly because of his controversial remarks during the campaign.

WHEN DEMOCRATS ATTACK

The January 30–February 2 Gallup Poll asked Democrats (including Democratic-leaning independents) for their views on the way the leading candidates have conducted their campaigns. Democrats are more likely to perceive that Hillary Clinton has been unfairly attacking Obama (35% say this) than to say the reverse (23% believe Obama has attacked Clinton unfairly). But Democrats are most likely to believe that former president Bill Clinton has attacked Obama unfairly: 41% of Democrats believe this. It is important to note that while greater proportions of Democrats think the Clintons are attacking Obama unfairly than the other way around, more Democrats believe the Clintons are *not* attacking Obama unfairly than believe they are. In fact, the majority of Democrats (55%) say Hillary Clinton has not attacked Obama unfairly.

One of the major stories of the campaign has been the controversial remarks Bill Clinton has made about Obama while campaigning for Hillary. They include his references to Obama's stated opposition to the Iraq War as a "fairy tale," and his attempts to downplay Obama's South Carolina primary win on January 26 by pointing out that Jesse Jackson had also been victorious in that state during the presidential primaries in 1984 and 1988. These remarks may be a reason the former president's favorable rating has taken a slight dip in recent months. His rating is down to 50% in the current poll, compared

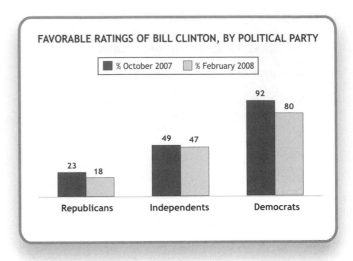

with a 56% reading in October 2007, the last time the favorability question was asked with respect to Bill Clinton. His favorable rating has dropped a substantial 12 percentage points among Democrats during that time. Perceptions of unfairness are in the eyes of the beholder. However, more than half of Obama supporters believe the Clintons are attacking their preferred candidate unfairly, while only about 1 in 10 Obama backers think he has been unfair toward Hillary Clinton. Likewise, Clinton supporters are more likely to believe Obama has been unfair toward Hillary Clinton than to believe either Hillary or Bill has been unfair toward Obama. The tone of this year's Democratic campaign is apparently more negative than what Democrats perceived in the 2000 nomination contest between Vice President Al Gore and New Jersey senator Bill Bradley. A mid-January CNN/USA Today/Gallup Poll from that year found just 23% saying Bradley was attacking Gore unfairly, and only 15% saying Gore was being unfair to Bradley.

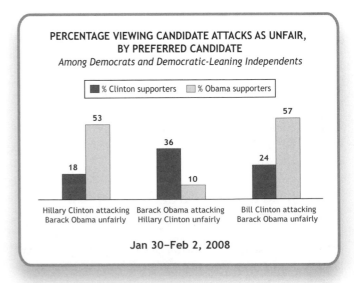

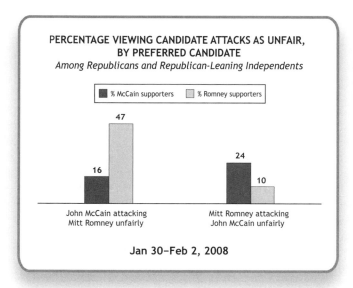

PERCENTAGE VIEWING CANDIDATE ATTACKS AS UNFAIR,
BY PREFERRED CANDIDATE
Among Republicans and Republican-Leaning Independents

■ % McCain supporters   □ % Romney supporters

47
16
24
10

John McCain attacking
Mitt Romney unfairly

Mitt Romney attacking
John McCain unfairly

Jan 30–Feb 2, 2008

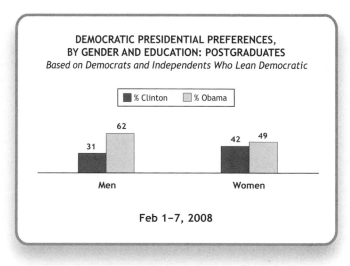

DEMOCRATIC PRESIDENTIAL PREFERENCES,
BY GENDER AND EDUCATION: POSTGRADUATES
Based on Democrats and Independents Who Lean Democratic

■ % Clinton   □ % Obama

62
31
42
49

Men   Women

Feb 1–7, 2008

WHEN REPUBLICANS ATTACK

There is not as large a gap in Republicans' perceptions about either of their leading presidential candidates engaging in unfair attacks on his opponent. Twenty-six percent of Republicans (including Republican-leaning independents) say McCain is attacking Romney unfairly, while 21% believe Romney is doing so with respect to McCain. This in spite of the fact that one of the story lines in media coverage of the January 30 Republican debate was the candidates' pointed remarks to each other. McCain and Romney supporters both are, predictably, more likely to believe that their preferred candidate is being attacked unfairly and is not attacking the other unfairly. In fact, nearly half of Romney supporters believe McCain is attacking their man unfairly—perhaps a result of McCain's recent claims that Romney has come out in favor of timetables for ending the war in Iraq. Republicans today are about as likely to say McCain is attacking Romney unfairly (24%) as they were to say McCain was attacking George W. Bush unfairly in 2000. At that time, relatively few Republicans believed that Bush was attacking McCain unfairly. It should be pointed out that those data were collected before the very contentious South Carolina primary that year.

FEBRUARY 9

Education and Gender Help Predict Democratic Preferences

Gender and education are both strong predictors of Democrats' preferences for their party's presidential nominee. Generally speaking, the more education a Democrat has, the less likely he or she is to support

Hillary Clinton and the more likely to support Barack Obama. Additionally, women are more likely than men to support Clinton, while men are more likely than women to support Obama. An aggregate of Gallup Poll daily election tracking interviews with Democrats, conducted from February 1 through February 7, shows that these two variables combine to become a powerful predictor of a Democrat's vote. Among the most highly educated Democrats—those with postgraduate educations—both men and women are more likely to support Obama than Clinton. Among the least educated—those with no college education—both men and women are more likely to support Clinton than Obama.

The range of support for the candidates according to education and gender is as follows: Obama beats Clinton by a two-to-one margin, 62% to 31%, among men with postgraduate educations. Although the margin is much smaller (49% vs. 42%), Obama also beats Clinton among women with postgraduate degrees. In other words, the strength of Obama's appeal to highly educated Democrats seems to be stronger than the pull of gender (i.e.,

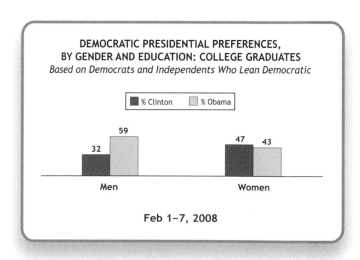

DEMOCRATIC PRESIDENTIAL PREFERENCES,
BY GENDER AND EDUCATION: COLLEGE GRADUATES
Based on Democrats and Independents Who Lean Democratic

■ % Clinton   □ % Obama

59
32
47
43

Men   Women

Feb 1–7, 2008

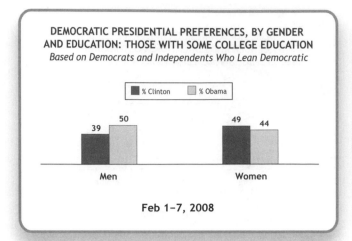

**DEMOCRATIC PRESIDENTIAL PREFERENCES, BY GENDER
AND EDUCATION: THOSE WITH SOME COLLEGE EDUCATION**
Based on Democrats and Independents Who Lean Democratic

Feb 1–7, 2008

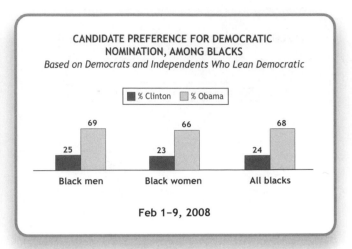

**CANDIDATE PREFERENCE FOR DEMOCRATIC
NOMINATION, AMONG BLACKS**
Based on Democrats and Independents Who Lean Democratic

Feb 1–9, 2008

of Clinton's appeal to women). Among those with college degrees but no postgraduate education, Obama wins over Clinton among men, but women in this group tilt slightly toward Clinton, by a 47% to 43% margin. Among those with some college education (but not a four-year degree), Obama still wins among men (50% vs. 39%), while women show a slight preference for Clinton (49% vs. 44%). Finally, in the group of Democrats with high-school diplomas or less, the impact of education is strong: Clinton beats Obama overwhelmingly among both men and women in this group. In short, education is a highly significant predictor of Democrats' vote choices, particularly among the two groups at the extreme ends of formal education—those with postgraduate degrees and those with high school educations or less. Gender, too, is a predictor, but it is essentially overwhelmed by the impact of education in the two extreme groups, so that both men and women with postgraduate educations prefer Obama, while both men and women who have no formal education beyond high school fairly strongly support Clinton.

FEBRUARY 11

Black Men, Women Equally Likely to Support Obama

The gender gap in Democratic preferences for Hillary Clinton versus Barack Obama—with a greater share of women than men supporting Clinton—is evident among whites and Hispanics, but not among blacks. Blacks' overwhelming support for Obama to be the 2008 Democratic presidential nominee is just as strong among women as it is among men. In Gallup Poll daily tracking interviews conducted between February 1 and February 9, only a quarter of black men (25%) and black women (23%) say they support Clinton for the nomination, while about two-thirds of each group favor Obama. This is based on blacks who are Democrats or independents who lean to the Democratic Party. During the same period, Gallup finds white Democrats of both sexes more likely to favor Clinton than Obama. However, among white Democratic women, the margin in favor of Clinton is 28 points, 59% vs. 31%, com-

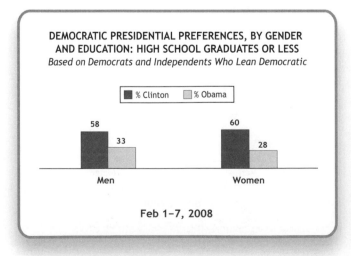

**DEMOCRATIC PRESIDENTIAL PREFERENCES, BY GENDER
AND EDUCATION: HIGH SCHOOL GRADUATES OR LESS**
Based on Democrats and Independents Who Lean Democratic

Feb 1–7, 2008

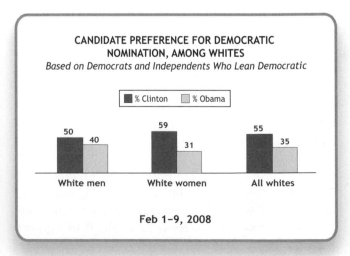

**CANDIDATE PREFERENCE FOR DEMOCRATIC
NOMINATION, AMONG WHITES**
Based on Democrats and Independents Who Lean Democratic

Feb 1–9, 2008

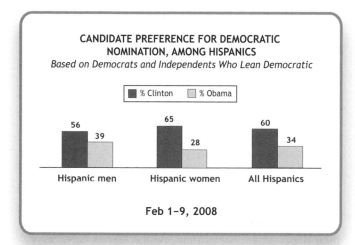

CANDIDATE PREFERENCE FOR DEMOCRATIC NOMINATION, AMONG HISPANICS
Based on Democrats and Independents Who Lean Democratic

■ % Clinton   ▢ % Obama

	Hispanic men	Hispanic women	All Hispanics
% Clinton	56	65	60
% Obama	39	28	34

Feb 1–9, 2008

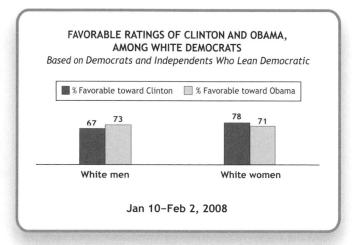

FAVORABLE RATINGS OF CLINTON AND OBAMA, AMONG WHITE DEMOCRATS
Based on Democrats and Independents Who Lean Democratic

■ % Favorable toward Clinton   ▢ % Favorable toward Obama

	White men	White women
% Favorable toward Clinton	67	78
% Favorable toward Obama	73	71

Jan 10–Feb 2, 2008

pared with a 10-point margin (50% vs. 40%) among white Democratic men. In short, the gender gap is significant among whites. A gender gap of similar scope is seen among Hispanic Democrats—who, overall, have been supporting Clinton to an even higher degree than have whites. Hispanic women favor Clinton by a 37-point margin, compared with the 17-point margin seen among Hispanic men.

Blacks as Favorable Toward Clinton as Toward Obama

The Gallup Poll daily tracking survey does not measure favorability toward the candidates, but according to two USA Today/Gallup Polls from January through early February, blacks' preference for Obama does not necessarily amount to a rejection of Clinton. Her favorability scores among black Democrats are about as high as Obama's. Thus, it appears that blacks' uniformly high support for Obama is not because of any major contrast in their perceptions of Obama versus Clinton, but because of the greater appeal of his candidacy. Similarly, white Democratic wom-

en's support for Clinton does not necessarily constitute a rejection of Obama. In fact, Clinton's favorability score among white Democratic women in these recent polls is only slightly higher than Obama's (78% vs. 71%).

There are major differences in Democrats' support for Clinton versus Obama based on race, ethnicity, and gender. Blacks overwhelmingly support Obama. Hispanics and women disproportionately support Clinton. It can be hypothesized that the cross-voting pressures of gender and race on voters may be particularly strong on black women. The appeal of supporting a woman for president could draw them to Clinton, while the tug of supporting a black could draw them toward Obama. Gallup analysis shows that a bias for supporting the female candidate may be in play among white and Hispanic Democratic women. However, whatever desire black women may have to vote for someone who could become the first woman president in U.S. history is outweighed by their apparently stronger desire to support Obama—who could become the first black president in U.S. history.

FEBRUARY 12

McCain Holds His Own Against Obama, Clinton

John McCain essentially holds his own when pitted against either of the two leading Democratic candidates for president in hypothetical general election trial heats. This is despite the fact that Democrats have a decided advantage on several measures of party strength and positioning. The USA Today/Gallup Poll conducted between February 8 and February 10 shows that McCain leads Hillary Clinton by one point, 49% to 48%, in a hypothetical general election matchup among likely voters. He trails Barack Obama by four points, 46% to 50%. Both of these differences are within the poll's margin of error. The results suggest that if the election were held today, it would be a close race if

FAVORABLE RATINGS OF CLINTON AND OBAMA, AMONG BLACK DEMOCRATS
Based on Democrats and Independents Who Lean Democratic

■ % Favorable toward Clinton   ▢ % Favorable toward Obama

	Black men	Black women
% Favorable toward Clinton	81	84
% Favorable toward Obama	83	84

Jan 10–Feb 2, 2008

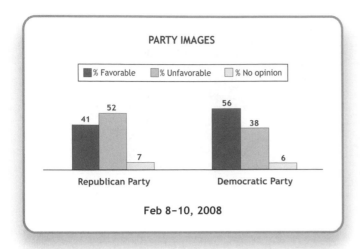

PARTY IMAGES

■ % Favorable   ■ % Unfavorable   □ % No opinion

Republican Party: 41, 52, 7
Democratic Party: 56, 38, 6

Feb 8–10, 2008

Democrats have double-digit leads over Republicans in recent Gallup Polls. Within the current sample, 54% of those interviewed either identify with or lean toward the Democratic Party, compared with just 39% who identify with or lean toward the Republican Party. And on generic presidential election questions, in which respondents are asked which party's candidate they would prefer to win the presidency next fall (without naming names), the Democrats have typically been winning by double-digit margins.

In short, there appears to be a significant advantage for the Democrats over the Republicans on several general measures of party image and strength, suggesting a propitious political environment for the Democrats. Nevertheless, McCain, the front-running Republican nominee, is outperforming what would otherwise be predicted in general election trial heats and testing quite well against the two leading Democratic candidates, beating Clinton by one point and losing to Obama by four points. (Both gaps are within the margin of error.) Many things can and will change, however, between now and Election Day. If these types of numbers hold through the fall, the coming election could be a close one, regardless of voters' apparently negative attitudes toward the Republican Party.

McCain were the Republican nominee and either Obama or Clinton were the Democratic nominee. They also indicate that despite vigorous debate regarding whether Clinton or Obama would be most electable in November, Obama has at best a slight advantage over Clinton on that dimension.

At the same time, a number of recent measures included in the Gallup Poll and other polls show that the Democrats in theory have some strong structural political advantages at this point. In terms of the parties' favorable images,

Despite losing primary elections in Maryland, Virginia, and Washington, D.C., on February 12, 2008, Senator Hillary Clinton vows that night at the University of Texas in El Paso to triumph in the upcoming contest in Texas. *(Rick Gershon/Newscom)*

Democrats Much More Enthusiastic About Their Candidates

The 2008 presidential election will be remembered for the historic Democratic nomination battle between a female candidate and a black candidate. But beyond those distinctions, Democrats currently view the election as historic in terms of the quality of their leading candidates. Six in 10 say both Senators Obama and Clinton are better than most presidential candidates who have run during their lifetimes. In contrast, most Republicans view Senator John McCain as neither better nor worse than prior candidates, and barely half of the party's supporters say they would be satisfied if he won the party's presidential nomination. It is unclear how this gap in candidate enthusiasm may play out in the general election, given that McCain is closely matched with both Democrats in Gallup's latest trial heats. The February 8–February 10 USA Today/Gallup Poll asked Americans to evaluate the leading presidential contenders against "all the people who have run for president during your lifetime." The results show a substantial difference by party affiliation. Most Democrats say Clinton (62%) and Obama (60%) are better than most presidential candidates who have run during their lifetime, including 12% who rate each as the "best presidential candidate" of all such. In stark contrast, only about half as many Republicans (34%) rate McCain as better than most candidates during their lifetime. The majority of Republicans, 52%, believe McCain is not much different from prior candidates.

Because independents and Republicans rate Obama more positively on this measure than they rate Clinton, he is rated the best overall, in that he scores highest among all Americans. Republicans' disdain for Clinton is clear: Nearly three in four rate Clinton as worse than most (34%) if not *the* worst (40%) presidential candidate in their lifetime. But it is important to point out that Democrats—despite the positive momentum now swirling around Obama's candidacy—are as likely to give Clinton a positive historical review as they

are Obama. McCain's ratings on this measure are not all that different by party: The majority of independents, Democrats, and Republicans see him as a "run-of-the-mill" candidate. The poll provides further evidence of Republican unease with McCain as the party's presidential nominee. Updating a Gallup trend question asked in the 1988 and 1992 elections, barely half of Republicans and Republican-leaning independents (51%) say they would be satisfied if McCain ends up the winner in the Republican race; 45% say they would prefer to see one of the other Republican candidates win. In 1988 and 1992, Republicans were much more enthusiastic about George H. W. Bush as the party's standard-bearer. In 1988, 68% said they were satisfied that Bush was the Republican winner; in 1992, 80% were.

This question was also asked of Democrats in 1988 and 1992. Republicans' ratings of McCain are a little worse than what Democrats (and Democratic-leaning independents) said in June 1992 about Bill Clinton's nomination (58% were satisfied with him as the likely nominee at that point in the campaign) and in June 1988 about Michael Dukakis's nomination (62% were satisfied).

McCain does, however, fare about as well on a basic likability test within his party as do the Democrats in theirs. Seventy-one percent of Republicans have a favorable opinion of McCain—essentially the same as Obama's 72% favorable rating among Democrats. Clinton is rated slightly higher by her Democratic supporters, with a 78% favorable rating. The Democratic race has attracted a great deal of attention from the media and the public, as two historic candidates continue to be locked in a tight battle for their party's presidential nomination. The Republican nomination is all but decided in favor of McCain, but Republicans apparently are not overly thrilled with the outcome. It is unclear, however, if another Republican candidate would have generated any more enthusiasm among the party than McCain currently does. It is also unclear whether the apparent lack of Republican enthusiasm will sink the party's chances of winning the November election.

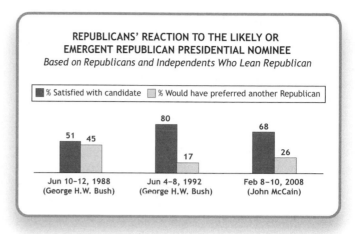

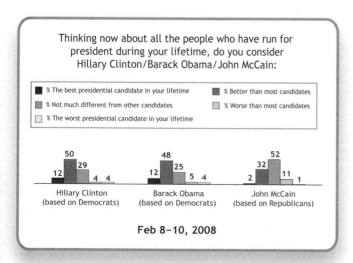

FEBRUARY 13

Iraq and the Economy Are Top Issues to Voters

More than 40 candidate debates and forums have been held in the 2008 presidential election cycle thus far—at least 20 for each party. Factoring in the speeches, interviews, and position papers coming out of the campaigns, there already has been a tremendous flow of information on national issues—and the general election campaign has not yet started. This may be fortunate, because new Gallup data suggest that Americans are interested in having a lot of information available as they make their voting decisions. According to the latest USA Today/Gallup Poll, most Americans rate candidates' positions on 14 issues—all of the issues listed in the February 8–10 poll—as either "extremely" or "very" important in their decision-making in choosing a new president. Although none of the issues is considered extremely important by a majority of Americans (the situation in Iraq registers the highest level, at 43%), all of them are rated as either extremely or very important by at least 60%. The situation in Iraq and the economy tie as the issues Americans say are most important to their vote; the environment and illegal immigration tie for the least important.

POSITIONS ON TERRORISM MOST IMPORTANT TO REPUBLICAN VOTERS

With Senators Hillary Clinton and Barack Obama still battling for the Democratic nomination and Senator John McCain yet to officially win the Republican nomination, the current discussion of issues in the election remains focused on how the candidates' positions compare with

IMPORTANCE OF ISSUES IN INFLUENCING REPUBLICANS' VOTE FOR PRESIDENT

	Extremely or very important
	%
Terrorism	50
Moral values	39
Corruption in government	37
The economy	35
The situation in Iraq	35
Illegal immigration	34
Taxes	31
Energy, including gasoline prices	26
Healthcare	25
Education	24
Social Security	21
The federal budget deficit	18
Medicare	18
The environment, including global warming	12

Feb 8–10, 2008

what voters in their respective parties are looking for. Some of the strongest distinctions among issues within each party cohort are seen at the "extremely" important level. On this basis, the top issue for Republicans is clear: terrorism. Fully half of Republicans say the candidates' positions on terrorism are extremely important to their vote, suggesting a possible reason that McCain, with his military background and tough antiterrorist positions, has been successful in recent weeks in filling the void created when former New York City mayor Rudolph Giuliani's campaign deflated early in the primary season. Republicans' particular focus on terrorism was widely considered to be one of the factors that helped George W. Bush activate his "base" in 2004 and win re-election—and it is likely to be important again this fall in energizing Republicans around their party's nominee. No other issue so unites Republicans.

At least a third of Republicans rate an assortment of other issues as extremely important, led by moral values at 39%. The relatively high ranking of this issue can help explain why Mike Huckabee has continued to present a challenge to McCain in some states, and why he has pledged to stay in the race even if it is only to give voters a clearly conservative alternative to McCain.

NUMEROUS ISSUES IMPORTANT TO DEMOCRATS

For Democrats, the top issue of importance to their vote is a tie between the situation in Iraq and healthcare—Iraq being an issue that Obama and Clinton are highly competitive on, healthcare one that most Democrats perceive as a strength of Clinton. However, the economy, education, corruption in government, and energy all follow closely behind these two

IMPORTANCE OF CANDIDATES' POSITIONS ON EACH ISSUE IN INFLUENCING AMERICANS' VOTE FOR PRESIDENT

	Extremely or very important	Extremely important	Very important
	%	%	%
The economy	89	48	41
The situation in Iraq	87	44	43
Education	81	46	35
Corruption in government	79	39	40
Healthcare	79	42	37
Energy, including gasoline prices	79	43	36
Terrorism	77	37	40
Social Security	73	43	30
The federal budget deficit	73	43	30
Moral values	69	36	33
Medicare	69	40	29
Taxes	69	42	27
The environment, including global warming	62	35	27
Illegal immigration	60	34	26

Feb 8–10, 2008

IMPORTANCE OF ISSUES IN INFLUENCING DEMOCRATS' VOTE FOR PRESIDENT

	Extremely or very important
	%
The situation in Iraq	50
Healthcare	48
The economy	45
Education	44
Corruption in government	43
Energy, including gasoline prices	43
Social Security	39
The federal budget deficit	39
Medicare	39
The environment, including global warming	38
Terrorism	36
Moral values	29
Taxes	29
Illegal immigration	22

Feb 8–10, 2008

in perceived importance, and at least a third of Democrats rate an additional five issues as extremely important. Of interest are the relatively low positioning of terrorism and moral values on this issues list among Democrats, in sharp contrast to their high rankings among Republicans.

ECONOMY AND THE WAR LOOM LARGE FOR INDEPENDENTS

Come the fall, both nominees will be striving to attract independent swing voters. Right now, the most highly rated issues for independents are the economy, the situation in Iraq, and corruption in government—all issues that rank

IMPORTANCE OF ISSUES IN INFLUENCING INDEPENDENTS' VOTE FOR PRESIDENT

	Extremely or very important
	%
The economy	42
The situation in Iraq	41
Corruption in government	41
Terrorism	38
Energy, including gasoline price	36
Healthcare	35
Education	34
Moral values	33
The federal budget deficit	31
The environment, including global warming	29
Social Security	28
Medicare	28
Illegal immigration	24
Taxes	22

Feb 8–10, 2008

fairly high among Democrats as well. However, the more Republican-oriented terrorism issue ranks a close fourth. In general, most Americans are reluctant to say that any of the issues tested in the new poll are less than very important to their vote for president this year. However, on a relative basis, the economy and Iraq are likely to be most influential. These are top-rated by both Democrats and independents, and are fairly important to Republicans as well. The key to how the issues play out in the election could be whether independents come to favor the Republican or the Democratic candidate's approach to their key issues, which at the moment appear to be the economy, Iraq, and corruption in government, with terrorism not far behind.

FEBRUARY 14

How Does McCain's Support Compare Historically?

Most observers now say that with Senator John McCain's primary victories on February 12 in Virginia, Maryland, and the District of Columbia, he is all but certain to be the Republican nominee this year, based on calculations of the number of delegates necessary to win the nomination. But Mike Huckabee continues to campaign vigorously against McCain, and the news media spend a substantial amount of time highlighting the alleged rifts within the Republican Party in terms of conservative unwillingness to support McCain as their party's nominee.

Gallup Poll daily election tracking makes it possible to place McCain's current status as his party's presumptive nominee in historical perspective by providing the basis for a comparison with the support that other front-runners have enjoyed in previous elections. At some point in every election, once a party's nominee is essentially known and agreed upon, Gallup has stopped asking members of that party about the nomination process and has moved on to asking about the general election. So the "final" nomination survey each election year serves as an interesting indicator of the overall support level that a nominee was receiving among members of his party at the time he was deemed (by Gallup editors, at any rate) to have the nomination sewn up. McCain is not quite at that point yet. But analysis of where previous front-runners were when they were assumed to have the nomination in hand provides a framework to use in calibrating just how "wounded" a nominee McCain may be. At this point, it can be said that while McCain's current 51% level of support among Republicans for his presumptive candidacy is not overwhelming based on Gallup's historical record, it is not unprecedentedly low, either. And there is still room for McCain to improve his standing in the days ahead. The following are several presidential election year examples of where things stood for a presumptive nominee in previous elections:

2004

Gallup's last 2004 primary nomination survey in which Democratic candidates were pitted against one another was conducted between February 16 and February 17. In that survey, John Kerry (who at that point was the presumptive nominee) received the support of 64% of the respondents, compared with John Edwards's 18%. Incumbent President George W. Bush was unchallenged for the Republican nomination.

2000

Gallup's last primary nomination survey for both parties in 2000 was conducted between February 25 and February 27. Al Gore, who as incumbent vice president was all but assured of getting the nomination but who had some primary opposition, ended up in that final survey with 65% of Democratic support to Bill Bradley's 28%. On the Republican side, George W. Bush, despite having been the leading Republican on track to get his party's nomination extending well back into 1999, was receiving a relatively modest 57% of Republican support. Who was in second place? None other than McCain, who at 34% had a slightly higher level of Republican support than Huckabee does now.

1996

Kansas senator Bob Dole, the eventual Republican nominee in 1996, had 58% of his party's support in Gallup's last primary survey of that year, conducted between March 8 and March 10. Commentator Pat Buchanan and publisher Steve Forbes trailed, each with 15% of Republican support. Bill Clinton was the incumbent Democratic president seeking re-election and had no opposition.

1992

Arkansas governor Clinton had 71% of Democratic support in Gallup's final primary survey of 1992, conducted between March 20 and March 22; former California governor Jerry Brown received 25%. On the Republican side, incumbent President George H. W. Bush received 86%, with Pat Buchanan behind at 11%. (The final Republican nomination survey in 1992 was conducted between March 11 and March 12.)

1988

Massachusetts governor Michael Dukakis received 69% support in Gallup's final primary Democratic primary poll in 1988, conducted between May 13 and May 15, with Jesse Jackson second at 21%. On the Republican side, Vice President George H. W. Bush was in the lead by a virtually identical margin, 69% to 22% over Bob Dole at the time of Gallup's last Republican primary poll, conducted between March 10 and March 12.

1984

Gallup's last primary survey in 1984 was conducted between May 18 and May 21—even later than the final survey of 1988—and showed that former vice president Walter Mondale (who won the nomination) was ahead of Colorado senator Gary Hart by a relatively small margin, 46% to 34%, with Jackson at 10%. (Mondale's 46% was the lowest margin recorded by any likely nominee in a final Gallup survey from 1980 through 2004.) Ronald Reagan was the incumbent president running for re-election on the Republican side and was not seriously challenged.

1980

Gallup's final primary nomination survey of 1980 was conducted between February 29 and March 3. Reagan received 55% of the vote in that survey, followed by George H. W. Bush (the man who became his vice president) with 25%. Jimmy Carter was the Democratic incumbent president seeking re-election.

Implications of the Data

These data show that at 51%, McCain's current support level is relatively low compared with the support that presumptive nominees in either party have enjoyed since 1980 as of when Gallup finished its primary polling. In fact, only Mondale in 1984 had a lower level of support in that final Gallup survey. Polling over the next several days will show whether McCain's support picks up after news of his three primary wins on February 12—or whether it drops, given the news that Huckabee did well in Virginia among religious and conservative Republicans. If McCain's support climbs to at least 55%, then he will at least be able to say that his support is where Ronald Reagan's was in 1980 at the point when he was assumed to have won his party's nomination.

FEBRUARY 19

Obama Gaining Among Middle-Aged, Women, Hispanics

The momentum in the Democratic nomination race has clearly swung toward Barack Obama. Not only has he won all of the primary contests since Super Tuesday

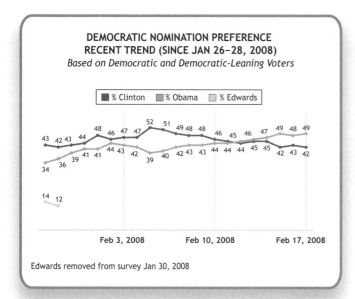

**DEMOCRATIC NOMINATION PREFERENCE
RECENT TREND (SINCE JAN 26–28, 2008)**
Based on Democratic and Democratic-Leaning Voters

Edwards removed from survey Jan 30, 2008

DEMOCRATIC NOMINATION PREFERENCE, BY VOTER AGE GROUP				
Based on Democratic Voters				
	Clinton Feb 5–9	Obama Feb 5–9	Clinton Feb 13–17	Obama Feb 13–17
18 to 34 years old	37%	57%	34%	61%
35 to 54 years old	49%	42%	42%	51%
55 years and older	58%	32%	51%	37%

on February 5—Louisiana (February 9), the District of Columbia (February 12), Maryland (February 12), and Virginia (February 12)—but he has steadily gained in Gallup Poll daily tracking to the point where he has overtaken Hillary Clinton for the first time, holding a statistically significant lead in each of the last three daily polls.

Obama's standing has improved among most Democratic subgroups over the past several days. But one of the more substantial shifts has been the changing preferences of middle-aged Democratic voters, who have moved away from Clinton and toward Obama in the past week. Obama has also made gains among three other groups that have favored Clinton throughout much of the campaign—women, Hispanics, and self-identified Democrats. Obama and Clinton are now running even among these three key groups in the most recent Gallup data. These findings are based on a comparison of Democratic voters' nomination preferences in February 5–9 polling with those in February 13–17 polling. Each of these five-day tracking periods consists of interviews with roughly 2,000 Democratic voters nationwide. Overall, in the February 5–9 data, Clinton led Obama by an average of 49% to 42%. In the most recent five days (February 13–17), the candidates' standings have basically flipped, with Obama leading Clinton by an average of 49% to 43%.

THE AGE EFFECT

Throughout the campaign, exit polls have shown that Obama has appealed to younger voters and Clinton to older voters. Even as the momentum has swung in Obama's favor, that basic pattern at opposite ends of the age spectrum still holds. The change in recent days has been in middle-aged Democratic voters' preferences. In the February 5–9 period, Clinton led among Democratic voters age 35 to 54

by a 49% to 42% margin. Now, Obama is the leader among this group by 51% to 42%. This suggests that middle-aged voters will be a key swing group to monitor in the remaining Democratic primaries and caucuses. For the moment, Obama has captured their allegiance.

THE GENDER GAP

Clinton's primary victories to date have been fueled in large part by support from female voters. The former first lady and current New York senator has always demonstrated a particular appeal to women. When Obama closed the gap with Clinton nationally—as he did in the days leading up to Super Tuesday—he usually did so by reducing her lead among women. In the days immediately after Super Tuesday, Clinton rebuilt her lead among women, enjoying a 53% to 38% lead in the February 5–9 polling. But her gender advantage has once again dissipated. In the February 13–17 data, female Democratic voters are about as likely to say they prefer Obama as Clinton (46%).

HISPANICS

Many credited Clinton's strong appeal to Hispanics with helping her win the important February 5 California primary, and her support among this key group gives the campaign hope for a comeback victory in the March 4 Texas primary. But the tracking data suggest that her advantage among Hispanics may be eroding, at least on a national level. In the February 5–9 data, Clinton led Obama by nearly two-to-one, 63%–32%, among Hispanic Democratic voters. In the February 13–17 data, the two are essentially tied among this constituency, with 50% preferring Obama and 46% Clinton.

DEMOCRATIC NOMINATION PREFERENCE, BY GENDER				
Based on Democratic Voters				
	Clinton Feb 5–9	Obama Feb 5–9	Clinton Feb 13–17	Obama Feb 13–17
Men	44%	48%	39%	54%
Women	53%	38%	45%	45%

DEMOCRATIC NOMINATION PREFERENCE, BY HISPANIC ETHNICITY
Based on Democratic Voters

	Clinton Feb 5–9	Obama Feb 5–9	Clinton Feb 13–17	Obama Feb 13–17
Hispanic	63%	32%	46%	50%
Non-Hispanic	47%	44%	42%	49%

PARTY IDENTIFICATION

Clinton looked like a solid bet for the nomination early in the campaign process not only because of her consistent lead, but also because she was typically the preferred choice among core Democrats (those who identify as Democrats when asked to give their party affiliation). Meanwhile, Obama tended to fare better among those who initially identify as independents but then say they "lean" to the Democratic Party. In the February 5–9 data, Clinton continued to lead Obama, 51% to 41%, among Democratic identifiers, while trailing slightly (48% to 42%) among independents. In the February 13–17 data, Obama expanded his lead among independents (58% to 36%) while achieving parity with Clinton among core Democrats (46% Obama, 45% Clinton).

OTHER DEMOCRATIC VOTER GROUPS

Obama has further expanded his dominant position among black Democrats. In the February 5–9 data, Obama led Clinton 68% to 24%. In the February 13–17 data, Obama expanded his lead among this group to 77% to 20%. Both candidates have maintained their leads among their core supporters by education level: Clinton among those with less formal education (February 5–9: Clinton 60%, Obama 30%; February 13–17: Clinton 53%, Obama 38%) and Obama among college graduates (February 5–9: Obama 53%, Clinton 40%; February 13–17: Obama 56%, Clinton 37%). The middle group of those who attended college but did not graduate shows movement toward Obama in the latest polling (February 5–9: Obama 48%, Clinton 44%; February 13–17: Obama 57%, Clinton 35%). Married Democratic voters have shifted from a Clinton-leaning to an Obama-leaning group (February 5–9: Clinton 51%, Obama 40%; February 13–17: Obama 49%, Clinton 43%). Clinton's

leads among Democrats have dissipated in the Northeast (February 5–9: Clinton 53%, Obama 39%; February 13–17: Clinton 47%, Obama 45%) and the West (February 5–9: Clinton 52%, Obama 42%; February 13–17: Obama 54%; Clinton 39%).

FEBRUARY 21

Democrats Have Significant Identification, Image Advantage

Americans are now more likely to identify themselves as Democrats than at any time since the year 2000. Forty percent of Americans in the February 11–14 Gallup Poll—in response to the question "In politics, as of today, do you consider yourself a Republican, a Democrat, or an independent?"—said they identified with the Democratic Party, while 26% identified with the Republican Party and 34% with neither. (Most of these considered themselves independents.) The 40% Democratic identification figure is unusually high. The last time 40% of Americans identified as Democrats was in August 2000. Before that, there were just a handful of Gallup Poll telephone surveys, going back to 1985, in which 40% or more of Americans identified as Democrats. The highest Democratic identification in a Gallup telephone poll was 42% in July 1987.

The gap between Democratic and Republican identification—now at 14 percentage points—is also almost a record high. The gap was higher only in December 1998—immediately after President Bill Clinton had been impeached by the Republican-controlled House of Representatives—when 41% of Americans identified as Democrats and only 20% as Republicans. The highest level of identification with the Republican Party, 39%, has been reached at three points: in May 1991 (a few months after the first Persian

DEMOCRATIC NOMINATION PREFERENCE, BY PARTY AFFILIATION

	Clinton Feb 5–9	Obama Feb 5–9	Clinton Feb 13–17	Obama Feb 13–17
Democrat	51%	41%	45%	46%
Independent/ Lean Democratic	42%	48%	36%	58%

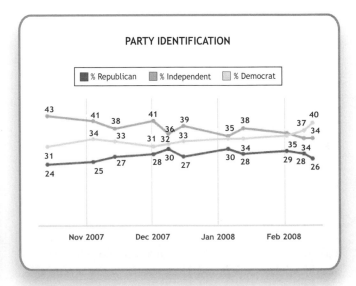

PARTY IDENTIFICATION

■ % Republican   ■ % Independent   □ % Democrat

Nov 2007   Dec 2007   Jan 2008   Feb 2008

Gulf War), in December 2003 (just after Saddam Hussein's capture), and in September 2004 (after a successful Republican convention at which President George W. Bush was nominated for a second term in office).

In 2007, as often happens in a year in which there is no national election, Americans were increasingly likely to identify as independents. This year, as presidential election voting has begun in primaries and caucuses, Democrats have been the beneficiary as Americans have become more likely to express identification with a party. As 2007 ended, an average of two Gallup Polls conducted in December showed 32.5% of Americans identifying as Democrats, 37.5% as independents, and 28.5% as Republicans. Now, the shift is evident. Identification with the Republican Party and with no party has slipped slightly, while identification with the Democratic Party has gained. There are several other indications that the Democratic Party is riding high at the moment. First, the percentage of Americans with a favorable image of the Democratic Party (56%) is significantly higher than is the case for the Republican Party (41%). In addition, a February 8–10 USA Today/Gallup Poll asked Americans to say whether three specific dimensions applied or did not apply to the two parties. The dimensions were 1) can bring about the changes this country needs; 2) is able to manage the federal government effectively; and 3) has mostly honest and ethical members in Congress.

In each instance, the American public was more likely to say the characteristic applies to the Democratic Party than to the Republican Party. The biggest difference—almost 20 points—is on the dimension of bringing about change, perhaps not surprising given the strong emphasis on change in Barack Obama's campaign (and, to some degree, that of Hillary Clinton). Also, because there has been a Republican administration in the White House since 2001, it may be natural for Americans to say the Democratic Party would be more able to bring about change were its standard-bearer to move into the White House in 2009.

These data underscore the strong position of the Democratic Party at this point in the election year: A near-record number of Americans indicate that they currently identify as Democrats; the image of the Democratic Party is much more favorable than that of the Republican Party; and Americans say the Democratic Party is better positioned to bring about change and is more likely to be able to manage the government effectively. These things can change, of course, between now and Election Day. In addition, recent polling has shown that John McCain, the likely Republican nominee, does relatively well when pitted against the two leading Democratic candidates, suggesting that the Republican Party's image troubles don't necessarily transfer directly to specific candidates (or, at any rate, to John McCain).

FEBRUARY 22

Clinton Has Edge Among Highly Religious White Democrats

Hillary Clinton enjoys a significant edge in support over Barack Obama among white Democrats who are highly religious. In interviews conducted between February 15 and February 20 as part of Gallup Poll daily election tracking, 57% of white, non-Hispanic Democratic voters who attend church weekly support Clinton, while only 29% support Obama. Among those who attend church less frequently or never, Clinton's support drops, while Obama's climbs. This analysis is based on white Democrats. There is less of a relationship between candidate support and religion among black Democrats, who are both highly religious and highly likely to support Obama.

Much of the attention to the relationship between religion and the election this year has been focused on the Republican primaries. Baptist preacher Mike Huckabee has consistently performed disproportionately well among highly religious Republicans in polls and primary voting, and prior to his leaving the race, Mitt Romney faced questions about his Mormon faith and about how well his candidacy would play among evangelical Christians. But in the current data, religion makes a difference on the Democratic side of the election as well. Underlying demographic patterns help account for this relationship. Church attendance is related to gender, and women are more likely than men to support Clinton. (In this sample of white Democrats, 44% of men support Clinton, compared with 54% of women.) An analysis of the support patterns for Clinton and Obama by religion and gender, however, shows that it is not just the gender factor that accounts for the overall relationship. Men who attend church weekly are more likely to support Clinton and less likely to support Obama than are men who attend less frequently or not at all. Women who attend church weekly are also somewhat more likely to

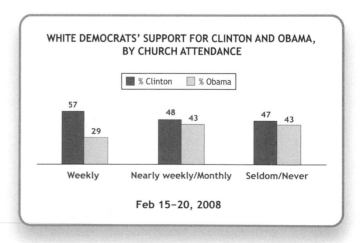

WHITE DEMOCRATS' SUPPORT FOR CLINTON AND OBAMA, BY CHURCH ATTENDANCE

% Clinton   % Obama

Weekly: 57, 29
Nearly weekly/Monthly: 48, 43
Seldom/Never: 47, 43

Feb 15–20, 2008

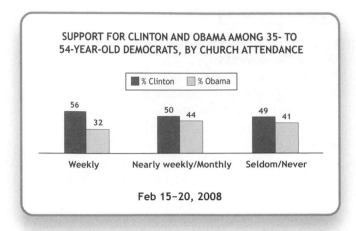

SUPPORT FOR CLINTON AND OBAMA AMONG 35- TO
54-YEAR-OLD DEMOCRATS, BY CHURCH ATTENDANCE

Feb 15–20, 2008

support Clinton over Obama than are women who attend less frequently or never, although the difference is not as pronounced.

Another underlying demographic factor that helps account for the relationship is age. Church attendance is positively correlated with age. (In this sample of white Democratic voters, for example, the percentage attending church weekly more than doubles, from 16% to 34%, in a comparison between those who are 18 to 34 and those who are 55 and older.) In addition, older Democrats are more likely than younger Democrats to support Clinton. There are too few 18- to 34-year-olds who attend church weekly in this sample to provide a basis for meaningful analysis. But the relationship between religiosity and support for Clinton does hold among 35- to 54-year-old white Democrats. Among those in this age group who attend church weekly, 56% support Clinton compared with 32% who support Obama. Among those who attend less frequently, the gap is narrower. Even among the 55-and-older group of white Democrats, who tend to strongly support Clinton, there is a modest relationship between religiosity and candidate choice. The Clinton-over-Obama gap among weekly church attenders 55 and older is 37 points—61%

to 24%—while it is a somewhat smaller 24 points (56% to 32%) among those in this age group who seldom or never attend.

Gaining the allegiance of highly religious voters can be a significant plus in an election. Religious voters are strongly attached to their positions, highly motivated, and easy to reach through targeted media and church contact, and can form an important core of a winning election strategy. Most of the attention in recent elections has been focused on the Republicans' ability to mobilize this group in support of their candidate, based in part on specific values issues. Hillary Clinton, as seen in this analysis, at this point in the campaign has been able to disproportionately gain the support of religious white Democrats. Whether this national pattern can bolster her efforts to prevail over Obama as the Democratic nominee is less clear. For one thing, the percentage of the white Democratic electorate that is highly religious is smaller than is the case among Republicans. (In the sample used for this analysis, 25% of white Democrats attend church weekly, while 57% say they seldom or never attend church.) Thus, the allegiance of highly religious white Democrats has limited impact in that they constitute a minority of white Democratic voters. Still, in a close election, small voter segments can make a difference. Additionally, of course, the current targets for Clinton are the March 4 Texas and Ohio primaries, and it is unclear to what degree the relevant national patterns are replicated in these two states. In general, one does not typically associate Clinton with conservative positions on the values issues that the typical religious voter cares about: abortion, gay marriage, and stem cell research. But Democratic voters in the remaining primary states may have other concerns that she can tap into, and if the Clinton campaign is able to devise a strategy for nurturing her connection to religious voters, it could make a difference.

FEBRUARY 25

Public Views Obama, McCain as Unifying Candidates

Most Americans think Barack Obama and John McCain would unite rather than divide the country as president, but view Hillary Clinton and Mike Huckabee as potentially more divisive chief executives. These results are based on a February 8–10 USA Today/Gallup Poll, which asked Americans if they think the four leading presidential candidates "would do more to unite or more to divide the country as president." The public is most likely to view Obama as a unifying force, with 66% believing he would do more to unite the country and 30% saying he would do more to divide it if he were elected. McCain is a close second, with

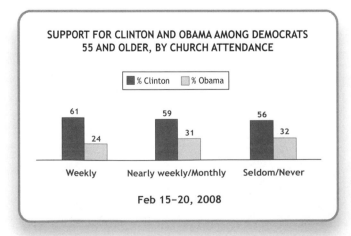

SUPPORT FOR CLINTON AND OBAMA AMONG DEMOCRATS
55 AND OLDER, BY CHURCH ATTENDANCE

Feb 15–20, 2008

After addressing a crowd in Austin, Texas, on February 28, 2008, Barack Obama holds a youthful supporter. *(Ben Sklar/Newscom)*

Americans viewing him as more of a uniter than a divider by a 59% to 36% margin.

On the other hand, Americans believe Clinton and Huckabee are more likely to divide Americans than bring them together. Forty percent say Clinton would unite Americans as president, but a majority, 57%, say she would do more to divide them. One of the reasons Clinton may be seen as more of a divider is her long history as a partisan politician in the public eye. Huckabee's attempts to rise above negative campaigning have not necessarily enhanced his image as a unifying candidate: Thirty-eight percent believe he would do more to unite Americans, but 47% believe he would do more to divide them.

Generally speaking, party identifiers are more likely to rate their party's candidates as uniters rather than dividers. But a closer examination of the results by party affiliation suggests that these ratings are more than just knee-jerk partisan reactions. For example, Democrats are signifi-

cantly more likely to view Obama (79%) than Clinton (65%) as a unifying candidate. Likewise, more Republicans think McCain (79%) would unite the country than think Huckabee (57%) would. By better than two-to-one margins, independents think both Obama and McCain would tend to bring Americans together. But independents think Clinton would maintain or create divisions by nearly the same two-to-one margin, 62% to 35%. Republicans are far more critical of Clinton than Obama on this measure. In fact, those who identify with the Republican Party are more than six times as likely to believe Clinton would tend to divide the country (85%) as unite it (13%). Meanwhile, Republicans are just as likely to say Obama would bring the country together as to say he would drive it apart.

In 2000, many Americans were looking to heal the partisan divisions of the prior eight years. George W. Bush promised to be more of a uniter than a divider, but whatever Bush's intentions, his policies and governing style may in the end leave the country more divided than it was when he took office. A public yearning to move past party divisions may help explain the success of Obama and McCain in their respective parties' nomination campaigns to date and may set up a general election between what the public perceives to be two unifying candidates. However, the realities of the general election phase of a presidential campaign may work against the candidates' desires to unite the country. Obama's and McCain's "unifying" images could be put to a strong test if they wind up on the giving or receiving end of the partisan attacks so common in a tightly contested campaign. Thus, the challenge for both would be to maintain the perception, for the duration of the campaign, that they would bring the country together.

McCain Competitive with Democrats in Latest Trial Heats

Democratic front-runner Barack Obama and likely Republican nominee John McCain are essentially tied in likely voters' preferences for president if the general election were held today. Forty-eight percent of likely voters say they prefer McCain for president, and 47% Obama, according to a USA Today/Gallup Poll, conducted between February 21 and February 24. The two have been closely matched each of the three times the question has been asked of likely voters this year. The contest would be about as tight if Hillary Clinton were the Democratic nominee. In that test ballot, 50% of likely voters choose McCain and 46% Clinton.

The Democratic candidates do slightly better among all registered voters, but the two hypothetical races are still a statistical tie among this larger group of voters. These close contests occur in a political environment

Do you think each of the following candidates would do more to unite or more to divide the country as president?

■ % More to unite   ☐ % More to divide

	% More to unite	% More to divide
Barack Obama	66	30
John McCain	59	36
Hillary Clinton	40	57
Mike Huckabee	38	47

Feb 8–10, 2008

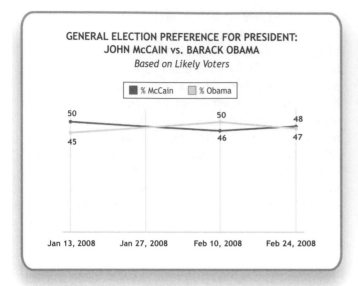

GENERAL ELECTION PREFERENCE FOR PRESIDENT:
JOHN McCAIN vs. BARACK OBAMA
Based on Likely Voters

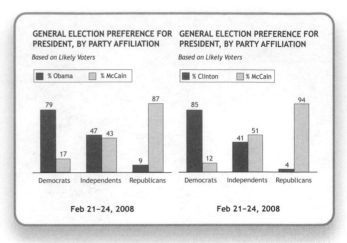

GENERAL ELECTION PREFERENCE FOR PRESIDENT, BY PARTY AFFILIATION
Based on Likely Voters

GENERAL ELECTION PREFERENCE FOR PRESIDENT, BY PARTY AFFILIATION
Based on Likely Voters

Feb 21–24, 2008   Feb 21–24, 2008

that is currently quite favorable to the Democratic Party: Democrats have a significant edge in terms of current party identification; the Democratic Party has much higher favorable ratings than the Republican Party; and when various polling organizations ask a "generic ballot" question, Americans decisively say that in theory they would prefer a Democrat to a Republican as president. Thus, it appears McCain is doing better than what might be expected of a Republican nominee in general. One reason for this is that McCain is able to attract support beyond just Republican Party loyalists. McCain currently attracts more support among likely voters who identify as Democrats than either Democratic candidate attracts among Republicans who are likely to vote. Also, McCain is competitive with Obama among politically independent likely voters and leads Clinton by 10 percentage points among this group.

Gallup polling on the presidential election thus far has indicated that the contest may be quite close, and the outcome could be similar to what occurred in the prior two presidential elections. This is in spite of the fact that everything else being equal, the Democratic candidate this year should be leading the Republican candidate. As these data show, John McCain is able to transcend party identification to some degree, because he has more crossover appeal than either Democrat. Also, the general election campaign is just getting started. Over the next eight months, Democrats will attempt to link McCain to an unpopular incumbent president and to hold the Republican Party responsible for a faltering economy and for Americans' general discontent with the way things are going in the country. If they are successful in doing so—assuming Americans' attitudes do not improve considerably between now and November—then the prospective Democratic candidates may run stronger in future general election trial heats. At the same time, of course, Republicans will be attacking the Democratic nominee. All in all, a lot can change between February and November.

FEBRUARY 26

Democrats, Republicans: Obama Likely to Win Nomination

Both Republicans and Democrats appear convinced at this point that Barack Obama is going to win the Democratic presidential nomination. Not only does Obama enjoy this perceptual aura of inevitability, but he also is widely seen as the candidate who would provide the stiffer challenge for John McCain in November. Republicans say he would be tougher for McCain to beat, and Democrats say he would have the best chance of beating McCain come November. The February 21– 24 USA Today/Gallup Poll asked Americans which candidate "will win the

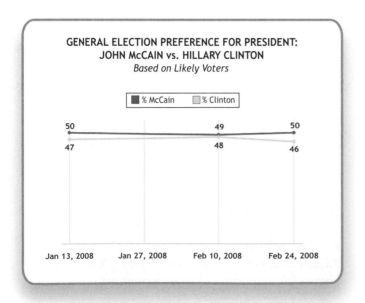

GENERAL ELECTION PREFERENCE FOR PRESIDENT:
JOHN McCAIN vs. HILLARY CLINTON
Based on Likely Voters

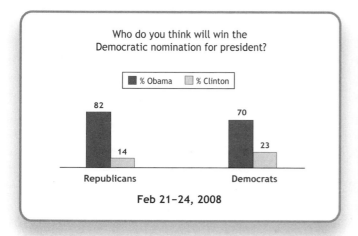

Who do you think will win the
Democratic nomination for president?

Feb 21–24, 2008

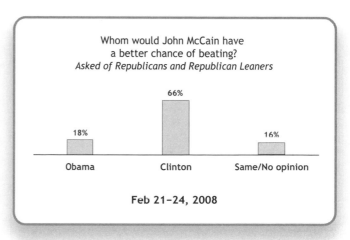

Whom would John McCain have
a better chance of beating?
Asked of Republicans and Republican Leaners

Feb 21–24, 2008

Democratic nomination this year," Hillary Clinton or Obama. There's little question about Americans' feelings on this issue. Almost three-quarters say Obama will win his party's nomination, compared with only 20% who say Clinton will win. That perception of inevitability is present among both Republicans and Democrats: 82% of Republicans and 70% of Democrats say Obama will win. Only 23% of Democrats believe Clinton will win their party's nomination—despite the fact that in this sample, about 4 out of 10 Democrats say they personally support Clinton. In fact, only half of Democrats who support the former first lady believe she will win the nomination; 43% believe she will not. Only 5% of Democrats who support Obama think Clinton will be the nominee; 91% think their candidate, Obama, will win.

Gallup first asked Americans in early January 2008 who they thought would win the Democratic nomination. At that point, just after the Iowa caucuses that Obama had swept, the American public was much less certain that Obama would win his party's nomination; Democrats in particular were almost as likely to say Clinton would win (36%) as to say Obama would win (41%). Not only does a

significant majority of Americans now see Obama's securing of the Democratic Party's nomination as inevitable; both Republicans and Democrats perceive him as the candidate who would present the more formidable challenge to presumptive Republican nominee McCain.

Democrats, by more than a two-to-one margin (63% to 30%), say Obama, rather than Clinton, "has the best chance of beating the Republican in November." Democrats no doubt would be pleased to find out that Republicans are much more fearful of Obama than of Clinton. A separate question asked of Republicans found them saying by an overwhelming 66% to 18% margin that McCain would have an easier time beating Clinton than Obama. It appears that a substantial majority of Americans have concluded that Obama is going to be the Democratic Party's nominee this year—even before he has won the required number of delegates and before voting takes place in the crucial March 4 primary states of Texas and Ohio. Importantly, close to half of Democrats who say they support Clinton concede that Obama is going to win their party's nomination. Another sign of Obama's strength is the perception of Democrats and Republicans alike that Obama would be the more difficult opponent for McCain to beat in November. These perceptions can change, but the data show that Obama currently has the strong edge in both perceptions and momentum. This puts even more pressure on Clinton not only to do well in the March 4 primaries, but to win impressively.

FEBRUARY 27

Few Democrats Say "Experience" Is Critical to Their Vote

According to a USA Today/Gallup Poll, conducted between February 21 and February 24, more than four in five Democrats (including independents who lean

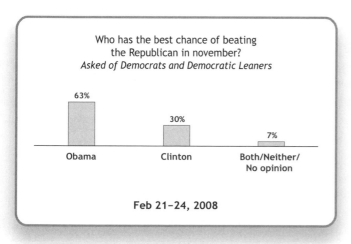

Who has the best chance of beating
the Republican in november?
Asked of Democrats and Democratic Leaners

Feb 21–24, 2008

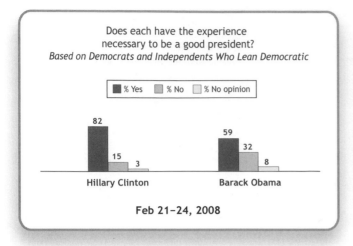

Does each have the experience
necessary to be a good president?
Based on Democrats and Independents Who Lean Democratic

■ % Yes   □ % No   □ % No opinion

Feb 21-24, 2008

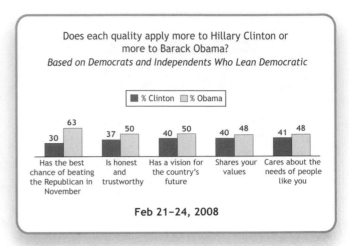

Does each quality apply more to Hillary Clinton or
more to Barack Obama?
Based on Democrats and Independents Who Lean Democratic

■ % Clinton   □ % Obama

Feb 21-24, 2008

Democratic) believe Hillary Clinton has "the experience necessary to be a good president." Only about three in five Democrats say the same of Barack Obama. Clinton thus seems to have won the argument in the Democratic Party over whether she or Obama has the better résumé to be president, but that is just one of many issues in their nomination battle, and not one in which Democrats put a tremendous amount of weight. Democrats also believe Clinton is more apt than Obama to "get things done," to offer "a clear plan for solving the country's problems," and to be a "strong and decisive leader." On the other hand, Obama beats Clinton among Democrats in perceptions that he cares about the needs of people like themselves, shares their values, has a vision for the country's future, is honest and trustworthy, and has the best chance of beating the Republican candidate for president in November. Obama's better than two-to-one lead over Clinton in electability is the strongest advantage seen for either candidate on any issue or dimension measured in the poll. The two are closely matched (Obama 47%, Clinton 43%) in ratings of who better "understands the problems Americans face in their daily lives."

What Matters Most?

In the new poll, Democratic voters were asked to say which of three qualities—leadership skills and vision, positions on the issues, or experience—is most important to their vote for president. Of these, it turns out, experience is last by a significant margin. The top-ranked quality, rather, is leadership skills and vision. Both candidates have perceptual strengths with voters that speak to different aspects of this dimension. As noted, Clinton gets the higher marks for such leadership qualities as being able to "get things done," offering "a clear plan for solving the country's problems," and being "a strong and decisive leader." Obama beats Clinton by 10 points on having a vision for the country's future. Regarding "positions on the issues," which Democrats rank second in importance, the two candidates are nearly at a draw in Democratic perceptions of who is better on each of seven national issues. Clinton and Obama are quite close when Democrats are asked to say which of the two would better handle five specific issues: energy, Iraq, the economy, the environment, and terrorism. Obama has a strong advan-

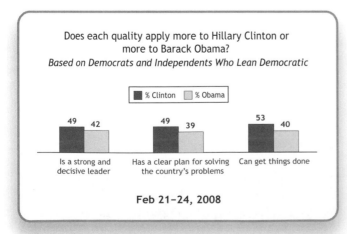

Does each quality apply more to Hillary Clinton or
more to Barack Obama?
Based on Democrats and Independents Who Lean Democratic

■ % Clinton   □ % Obama

Feb 21-24, 2008

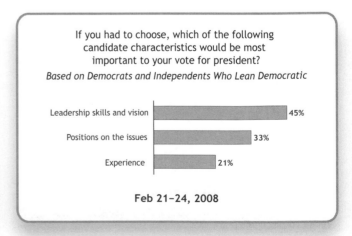

If you had to choose, which of the following
candidate characteristics would be most
important to your vote for president?
Based on Democrats and Independents Who Lean Democratic

Feb 21-24, 2008

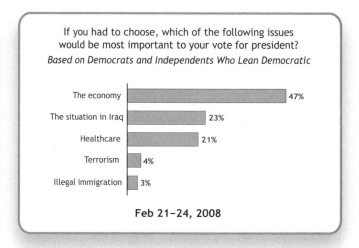

Regardless of which presidential candidate you support, please tell me if you think Hillary Clinton or Barack Obama would better handle each of the following issues.
Based on Democrats and Independents Who Lean Democratic

Feb 21–24, 2008

If you had to choose, which of the following issues would be most important to your vote for president?
Based on Democrats and Independents Who Lean Democratic

Feb 21–24, 2008

tage on handling corruption in government (leading Clinton by 24 points), but this is matched by Clinton's strong advantage on her signature issue, healthcare (on which she leads Obama by 21 points).

Putting this all in context, Democrats attach much more importance to the economy—an issue on which Obama and Clinton are about tied—than to healthcare. Clinton beats Obama in Democrats' perceptions of the two candidates' experience and leadership skills; Obama has solid advantages on Democrats' perceptions about his vision, values, and honesty and enjoys a big advantage on electability. He and Clinton are about evenly matched in voter perceptions of their handling of major issues, though Obama captures the outsider image as the one who can better clean up corruption in government, while Clinton has a big advantage on healthcare. Although it is not entirely clear how much Obama's perceived deficits on "experience" and healthcare hurt him with Democrats, or how much his perceived strengths on vision, fighting corruption, and electability help him, it all seems to balance out in his favor. The same poll producing these

findings shows Obama favored for the nomination by a 12 percentage point margin over Clinton, 51% to 39%.

FEBRUARY 28

The Gender Gap and Other Divides in the 2008 Election

The gender gap in voting for president may be significantly larger if Hillary Clinton rather than Barack Obama is the Democratic nominee. But this is not because Clinton would perform significantly better among female voters than Obama would. Rather, it is because male voters are much more likely to prefer the Republican John McCain in a matchup with Clinton than they would be in an Obama-McCain contest. That is just one example of several possible differences in how

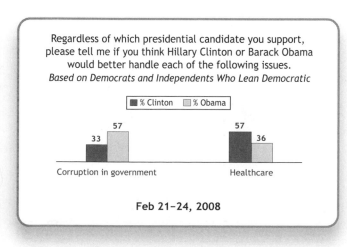

Regardless of which presidential candidate you support, please tell me if you think Hillary Clinton or Barack Obama would better handle each of the following issues.
Based on Democrats and Independents Who Lean Democratic

Feb 21–24, 2008

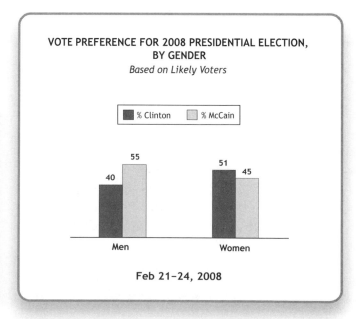

VOTE PREFERENCE FOR 2008 PRESIDENTIAL ELECTION, BY GENDER
Based on Likely Voters

Feb 21–24, 2008

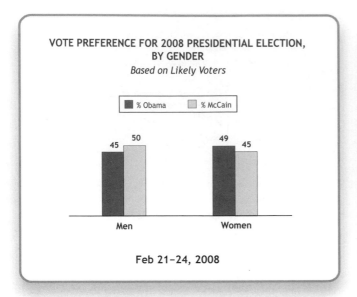

VOTE PREFERENCE FOR 2008 PRESIDENTIAL ELECTION,
BY GENDER
Based on Likely Voters

Feb 21–24, 2008

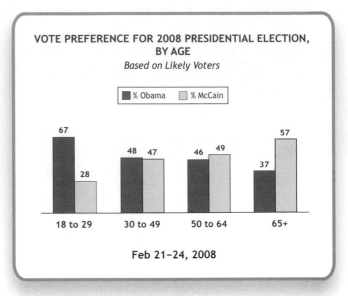

VOTE PREFERENCE FOR 2008 PRESIDENTIAL ELECTION,
BY AGE
Based on Likely Voters

Feb 21–24, 2008

various demographic groups might vote in the 2008 presidential election under the two possible scenarios Clinton vs. McCain or Obama vs. McCain. These results are based on the latest USA Today/Gallup Poll, which interviewed a large sample of 1,653 Americans who are considered likely voters. This larger sample allows for an in-depth look at current candidate preference by subgroup.

A contest pitting the 71-year-old McCain against the 46-year-old Obama would surely offer a stark contrast by age. But regardless of whether the Democrats nominate Obama or Clinton to face McCain, initial indications are that voting by age will be highly partisan this November, with younger voters more likely to support the Democrat and older voters McCain. But the generational divide would be much wider if Obama is the Democratic candidate instead of Clinton. For example, McCain's advan-

tage over the Democratic candidate among senior citizens would be 10 percentage points if he were running against Clinton but 20 points versus Obama. At the other end of the age spectrum, Obama's advantage over McCain among the youngest voters is 39 points, compared with a 15-point Clinton edge in this group.

Obama owes many of his Democratic primary and caucus wins thus far to the support of college-educated voters. According to the current Gallup Poll, Obama's appeal to college-educated voters may extend to the general election phase of the campaign. In an Obama-McCain matchup, voters who attended college prefer Obama, while those who did not attend college prefer McCain. The poll suggests that there would be essentially no educational dimension to the voting in a Clinton-McCain matchup.

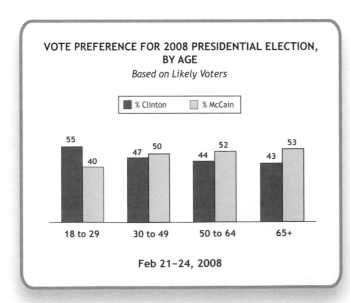

VOTE PREFERENCE FOR 2008 PRESIDENTIAL ELECTION,
BY AGE
Based on Likely Voters

Feb 21–24, 2008

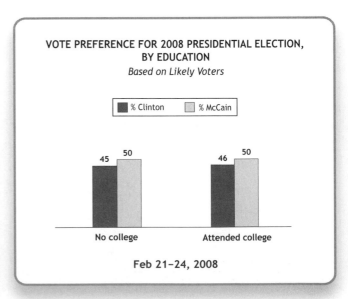

VOTE PREFERENCE FOR 2008 PRESIDENTIAL ELECTION,
BY EDUCATION
Based on Likely Voters

Feb 21–24, 2008

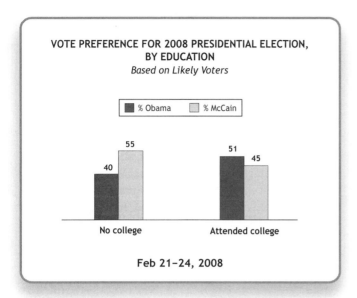

VOTE PREFERENCE FOR 2008 PRESIDENTIAL ELECTION,
BY EDUCATION
Based on Likely Voters

■ % Obama   ▨ % McCain

No college: 40, 55
Attended college: 51, 45

Feb 21–24, 2008

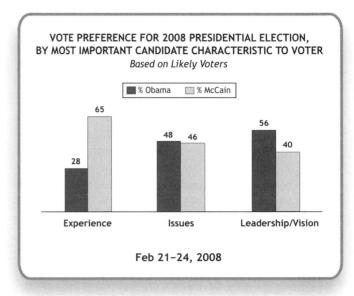

VOTE PREFERENCE FOR 2008 PRESIDENTIAL ELECTION,
BY MOST IMPORTANT CANDIDATE CHARACTERISTIC TO VOTER
Based on Likely Voters

■ % Obama   ▨ % McCain

Experience: 28, 65
Issues: 48, 46
Leadership/Vision: 56, 40

Feb 21–24, 2008

Voters were also asked which of the following characteristics would be most important to their vote—experience, candidate issue positions, or the candidate's perceived leadership skills and vision. In a Clinton-McCain contest, the candidates would essentially tie among both "experience" and "leadership" voters, but McCain would have an edge among "issues" voters. A McCain-Obama matchup would present voters with a clear choice on the experience and leadership dimensions, with those valuing experience overwhelmingly preferring McCain for president, and those preferring leadership firmly in Obama's camp. Whereas McCain has an advantage over Clinton with "issues" voters, he and Obama essentially tie among this group.

These are a few examples in which support patterns may differ significantly in the fall. However, many other key subgroups would probably vote for the same party's candidate regardless of whether the Democrats nominate Clinton or Obama, including subgroups defined by race, ideology, religiosity, marital status, and veteran status. Also, a McCain-Clinton contest would likely be more of a partisan fight than a McCain-Obama contest, in which many party-aligned voters may choose to vote for the candidate of the other party.

McCain's Age Seen as Less Problematic Than Dole's in 1996

More Americans said Kansas senator Bob Dole was too old to be president when he ran in 1996 than say John McCain is too old this year. Twenty-seven percent of American adults in February 1996 said Dole was too old to be president; 20% this year say McCain is too old. Dole was slightly older during his run for the presidency than McCain is this year. Dole was born in July 1923, making him 72 and 73 during the course of the 1996 campaign year. McCain was born in August 1936, making him 71 now and 72 in the fall. (McCain would be the oldest president to be

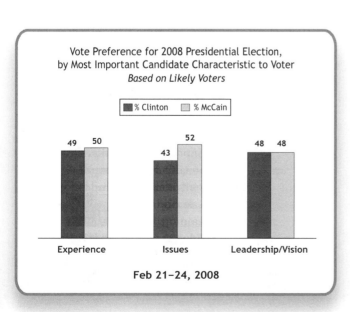

Vote Preference for 2008 Presidential Election,
by Most Important Candidate Characteristic to Voter
Based on Likely Voters

■ % Clinton   ▨ % McCain

Experience: 49, 50
Issues: 43, 52
Leadership/Vision: 48, 48

Feb 21–24, 2008

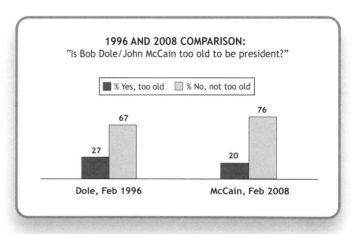

1996 AND 2008 COMPARISON:
"Is Bob Dole/John McCain too old to be president?"

■ % Yes, too old   ▨ % No, not too old

Dole, Feb 1996: 27, 67
McCain, Feb 2008: 20, 76

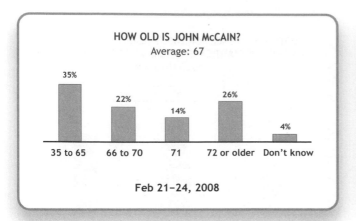

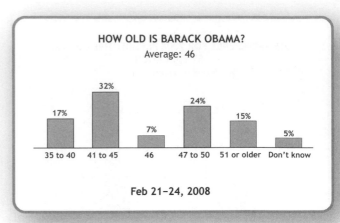

elected for the first time if he were to win in November.) Of some comfort to McCain is the fact that Americans on average perceive him to be slightly younger than his real age. When the public is asked to guess McCain's age, the average of all guesses puts McCain at 67, and a majority of Americans—57%—guess that he is 70 or younger. There is a partisan difference in perceptions of the impact of McCain's age. Twenty-eight percent of Democrats say McCain is too old to be president, compared with 11% of Republicans.

Counterbalancing McCain's older age is Barack Obama's relative youth. Obama was born in August 1961, making him 46 now and 47 next fall. (Obama would not be the youngest president were he to win in November; John Kennedy was 43 when he was inaugurated in January 1961 and Theodore Roosevelt was 42 when he ascended to the presidency upon the death of William McKinley in 1901.) Only 13% of Americans, however, say Obama is too young to be president. Republicans are only slightly more likely than Democrats to say Obama is too young. Americans are quite accurate in their estimates of Obama's age. The average guess is his actual age, 46. Seventeen percent of

Americans guess that Obama is 40 or younger, while 15% say he is 51 or older.

Hillary Clinton is between McCain and Obama in age. She was born in October 1947, making her 60 now and 61 before Inauguration Day for the next president in January 2009. The recent Gallup Poll did not ask Americans whether Clinton was too young or too old to be president, but did ask them to guess her age. There's presumed good news for Clinton in the results: The average guess is a youthful 56, and 66% of Americans guess that she is under 60, including about 4 in 10 who believe she is 55 or younger. Only 12% of Americans say she is 61 or older.

FEBRUARY 29

Republicans Split on Whether Huckabee Should Drop Out

Although Arizona senator John McCain is all but certain to be the Republican nominee for president this year, Repub-

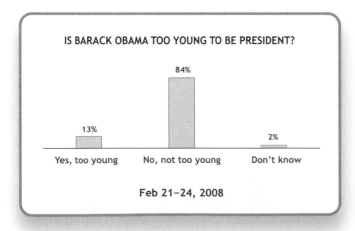

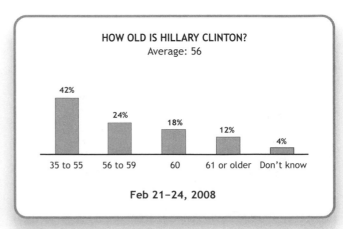

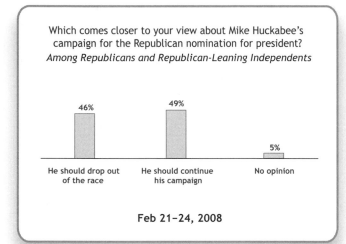

Which comes closer to your view about Mike Huckabee's campaign for the Republican nomination for president?
Among Republicans and Republican-Leaning Independents

46%
He should drop out
of the race

49%
He should continue
his campaign

5%
No opinion

Feb 21–24, 2008

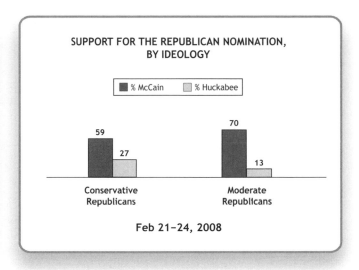

SUPPORT FOR THE REPUBLICAN NOMINATION,
BY IDEOLOGY

■ % McCain   ▨ % Huckabee

59
27
Conservative
Republicans

70
13
Moderate
Republicans

Feb 21–24, 2008

licans remain split on the issue of whether challenger Mike Huckabee should give up or should continue to campaign against McCain in upcoming primaries. The results show that there is no strong majority sentiment on the part of Republicans that Huckabee should leave the race. Forty-six percent say he should drop out, while 49% say he should continue.

According to media reports and many political observers, one of McCain's biggest challenges at this point is to woo the conservative wing of the Republican Party. It is not surprising, therefore, to find some differences by ideology in views of Huckabee's staying in the race. Conservative Republicans say Huckabee should stay in the race, by a 54% to 42% margin. Moderate Republicans, on the other hand, say by a 57% to 38% margin that Huckabee should quit. Gallup Poll daily election tracking data show that about a quarter of Republicans nationwide continue to support Huckabee. Another 5% support Texas representative Ron

Paul or former ambassador Alan Keyes, and 9% volunteer the name of another candidate (such as Barack Obama, Hillary Clinton, or Mitt Romney) or don't have a choice. That currently leaves McCain with the support of about 6 in 10 Republicans nationwide.

In general, McCain's nomination support is lower among conservative Republicans and higher among moderate Republicans. But the differences are perhaps not as large as might be expected, given all of the attention paid to McCain's presumed problems with the conservative wing of his party. In the February 21–24 USA Today/Gallup Poll, Huckabee receives 27% support among conservative Republicans to McCain's 59%, but only 13% among moderate Republicans vs. McCain's 70%. In addition to his service as former governor of Arkansas, Huckabee is a Baptist minister and former seminarian, and exit polls in primaries this year have shown that he does best among highly religious voters. That continues to be the case now. The differences are not huge, but

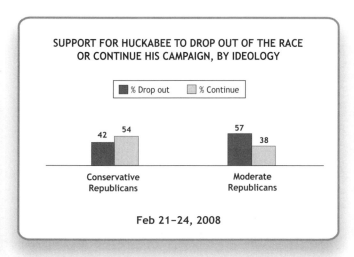

SUPPORT FOR HUCKABEE TO DROP OUT OF THE RACE
OR CONTINUE HIS CAMPAIGN, BY IDEOLOGY

■ % Drop out   ▨ % Continue

42   54
Conservative
Republicans

57   38
Moderate
Republicans

Feb 21–24, 2008

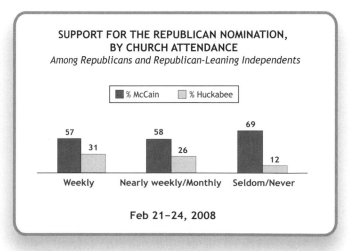

SUPPORT FOR THE REPUBLICAN NOMINATION,
BY CHURCH ATTENDANCE
Among Republicans and Republican-Leaning Independents

■ % McCain   ▨ % Huckabee

57   31
Weekly

58   26
Nearly weekly/Monthly

69   12
Seldom/Never

Feb 21–24, 2008

Huckabee's support drops from 31% among Republicans who attend church weekly to only 12% among those who seldom or never attend. McCain's support, on the other hand, moves from 57% among weekly churchgoers to 69% among those who seldom or never attend church.

There are relatively few other variations within subgroups that distinguish Huckabee's Republican support from that of McCain. Huckabee does slightly better among Republican women than among men. (Republican men, interestingly, are more likely than Republican women to support Paul and Keyes.) Huckabee does particularly well among 18- to 49-year-old women, and in general does better among Republicans under 50 than among those who are 50 and above.

MARCH 2008

The percentage of Americans saying they worry "a great deal" about the economy has surged by more than 20 points over the past year, moving the issue from 10th on the list of 12 national issues measured in 2007 to essentially tied today with healthcare. Gallup updates public concern about major issues confronting the country each March. The only other issue for which Americans' level of concern increased a significant amount since 2007 is unemployment, a major economic subissue. Concern about the remaining 10 issues either held steady (as did energy, the environment, and race relations, among others) or declined slightly (healthcare, illegal immigration, and hunger/homelessness).

Aside from the economy's ascension to the top of this year's list, the 2008 ranking of issues is similar to that of 2007. Healthcare remains a dominant concern. Last year it was ranked number one, with 63% worried a great deal, far ahead of Social Security, in second place with 49%. This year, healthcare nearly ties the economy for first, with only a two-point difference in the percentage worried about each: 60% for the economy, 58% for healthcare. Several issues are clustered in the 40% to 49% range as secondary concerns this year: crime and violence, energy, Social Security, drug use, the environment, illegal immigration, and possible terrorism against the United States. Slightly fewer than 40% of Americans say they worry a great deal about hunger and homelessness or about unemployment. Only 18% rate race relations as a major concern. Race relations is the only issue about which the majority of Americans say they worry only a little or not at all.

Economic anxiety has grown fairly uniformly across various segments of the American public. In March 2007, fewer than half of all men and women, of adults in all major age groups, and of Republicans as well as Democrats were worried a great deal about the economy. In March 2008, half or more in each of these demographic categories say

they worry a great deal about it. For each of the past two years, women have been more likely than men to say they worry about the economy (64% vs. 57% in 2008), and Democrats have been much more likely than Republicans to be worried (72% vs. 52%). Other areas for which Gallup finds significant gender differences—all with women more concerned than men—are healthcare, crime, the environment, drug use, the possibility of terrorist attacks, unemployment, and hunger/homelessness.

The "worry ratings" for most issues are characterized by significant partisan differences. There are seven in addition to the economy about which Democrats express more concern than Republicans: healthcare, energy, Social Security, the environment, hunger/homelessness, unemployment, and race relations. Republicans express more concern than Democrats about only two issues: illegal immigration and the possibility of future terrorism against the United States. Republicans and Democrats express about equal levels of

---

RECENT TREND IN WORRY ABOUT MAJOR NATIONAL ISSUES
(percentage worry a "great deal")

	March 2007	March 2008	Change
	%	%	pct. pts.
The economy	39	60	21
Unemployment	25	36	11
Energy	43	47	4
Crime and violence	48	49	1
Possible terrorism against the U.S.	41	40	-1
Race relations	19	18	-1
Drug use	45	43	-2
Social Security	49	46	-3
The environment	43	40	-3
Healthcare	63	58	-5
Illegal immigration	45	40	-5
Hunger/Homelessness	43	38	-5

CHRONOLOGY

MARCH 2008

March 2   Dozens are killed during fighting between Israeli forces and Hamas militants in Gaza.

March 4   Mike Huckabee drops out of the contest for the Republican presidential nomination, making John McCain the presumptive nominee.

March 4   Hillary Clinton wins contests in Ohio and Rhode Island; Barack Obama wins in Vermont. Texas splits, with Clinton winning the popular vote and Obama winning the caucuses. Clinton's win in Ohio slows Obama's momentum and breathes new life into her campaign, although Obama maintains a lead in delegates.

March 7   Clinton adviser and former Democratic vice presidential nominee Geraldine Ferraro asserts that Obama's race is helping his campaign: "If Obama was a white man he would not be in this position." Ferraro resigns as a formal Clinton adviser on March 11, but she does not retract her initial statement.

March 8   Obama wins the Wyoming caucuses.

March 8   President Bush vetoes a bill that would have banned harsh interrogation techniques such as waterboarding.

March 10   Protests by Tibetan monks against China's occupation of Tibet are harshly repressed by China's security forces. The protests, and the ensuing brutality, attract international attention.

March 11   Obama wins the Mississippi primary.

March 14   Jeremiah Wright, Obama's former minister, attracts media attention when snippets of his controversial sermons surface. Clips showing Wright being highly critical of America become a major news story.

March 16   The Federal Reserve approves a $30 billion credit line to JPMorgan Chase so that it can purchase Bear Stearns, one of the nation's largest underwriters of mortgage bonds. Stock markets around the world tumble.

March 17   In recounting an episode as an example of her foreign policy experience, Clinton talks about evading sniper fire during a 1996 trip to Bosnia. Her account is challenged by news organizations.

March 18   Obama delivers a sweeping assessment of race relations in America as he seeks to defuse the furor created by Reverend Wright's inflammatory statements. Obama's speech has been watched more than 4 million times through the campaign's official YouTube channel.

March 21   Bill Richardson endorses Obama. James Carville, a former aide to Bill Clinton, compares Richardson to Judas, "who sold out for 30 pieces of silver."

March 23   An explosive device kills four soldiers in Iraq, bringing America's total dead from the five-year conflict to 4,000.

March 25   Clinton admits to "misspeaking" when she recalled ducking sniper fire in Bosnia.

March 25   Iraqi troops, backed by United States forces, attempt to oust the militia of Moktada al-Sadr from Basra. The operation has only limited success and ends in a negotiated truce six days later.

concern regarding the issues of crime and drug use. The 81% of Americans who say the economy is getting worse (in a poll conducted between March 25 and 27), while still a very pessimistic assessment of the economy's direction, is the least negative rating Gallup has measured so far in March: Each day in March, at least 8 in 10 Americans have said the economy is getting worse. At the start of 2008, Americans were slightly less pessimistic, with 73% believing the economy was headed in the wrong direction. The public continues to be more likely to rate the current health of the economy as "poor" (39%) rather than "excellent" or "good" (19%).

Five years after the United States invaded Iraq, 42% of Americans believe history will judge the conflict a success, while 54% predict it will be remembered as a failure. This generally negative indictment of the Iraq War jibes with the view 59% of Americans now hold that sending U.S. troops to Iraq in the first place was "a mistake." Only 42% of Americans considered sending troops to have been a mistake shortly after the first anniversary of the invasion that began on March 19, 2003, but by 2005 the figure was regularly 50% or more, and it has approached 60% for about the past year. Public opposition to the Iraq War does not appear to be based on perceptions that the Iraqi people have suffered from the conflict. As troubled as Iraq is today as a result of sectarian violence and damage to the nation's infrastructure from the war, two-thirds of Americans (67%) believe Iraq will be better off in the long run than it was before the U.S. invasion. Still, five years after President George W. Bush directed the U.S. military to launch major air strikes on Iraq to drive Saddam Hussein out of power, a majority of Americans believe he overstated the dangers of that regime. More specifically, 53% agree with the statement that "the Bush administration deliberately misled the American public about whether Iraq had weapons of mass destruction," while 42% disagree. A majority of Americans came to this damning conclusion about Bush in 2005, and a majority have continued to maintain it.

Aside from whether Americans believe the Bush administration lied about the threat Iraq posed, many Americans simply believe the threat didn't exist. More than half of those who consider the war a mistake (representing 32% of Americans) say they hold that view because they believe the United States lacked sufficient justification to invade Iraq in the first place. Significantly fewer (18% of Americans) cite mishandling of the war effort as the main reason they consider it to have been a mistake. Another 8% say both reasons are equally important to their criticism of the invasion. In a special one-night reaction poll conducted on March 20, 2003, Gallup found 76% of Americans saying they approved of the decision to go to war with Iraq, including 60% who strongly approved. Only 8% predicted the conflict would last more than a year, and only 11% thought more than 1,000 troops would be killed. A majority of Americans at that time said that simply removing Saddam Hussein from power—even if he escaped capture—would qualify as "success." Five years and roughly 4,000 American deaths later, the country got more than it bargained for, and it shows in diminished support for the war.

MARCH 4

Public Divided on Whether Obama Has Necessary Experience

The most recent USA Today/Gallup poll finds 46% of Americans saying Illinois senator Barack Obama has the experience necessary to be president, and another 46% saying he does not. The February 21–24 poll finds a sharp contrast between these attitudes about the three-year senator from Illinois and the comparable beliefs about his rivals for the presidency, Washington veterans Senators

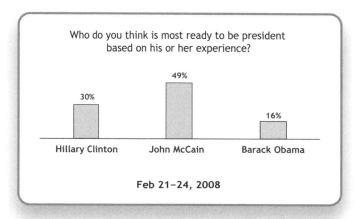

John McCain of Arizona and Hillary Clinton of New York. Seventy percent of Americans believe McCain has the necessary experience to be president, slightly more than say this about Clinton (65%). When Americans are asked to choose which among the three candidates is most ready to be president based on his or her experience, McCain, the presumptive Republican nominee, wins more decisively, with Obama a distant third.

McCain's advantage on this dimension is not entirely because Clinton and Obama "split" the Democratic vote. McCain dominates among Republicans as expected, but he also leads by a wide margin among independents. A majority of Democrats say Clinton is most ready to be president, with Obama and McCain closely matched for second.

The expected party differences occur when Americans are asked to rate each candidate individually on having the necessary experience to be president. These differences are most evident in the case of Clinton, with 85% of Democrats saying she has the necessary experience but only 33% of Republicans agreeing. A majority of all three major political groups—Democrats, Republicans, and independents—

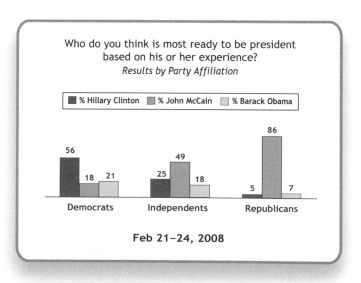

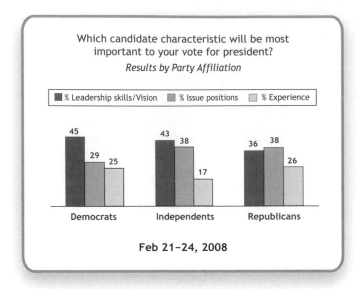

Which candidate characteristic will be most
important to your vote for president?
Results by Party Affiliation

■ % Leadership skills/Vision   ■ % Issue positions   □ % Experience

Democrats — 45, 29, 25
Independents — 43, 38, 17
Republicans — 36, 38, 26

Feb 21–24, 2008

think McCain has sufficient experience. Democrats are about as likely to say McCain has the necessary experience as say this about Obama.

While experience is often an important item on a candidate's résumé, it may not be what voters are most looking for this year. When asked which of three candidate characteristics is most important to their 2008 vote, only 22% of Americans say experience. Thirty-four percent say the candidate's issue positions, and the most, 42%, say the candidate's leadership skills and vision. These importance ratings show mild variation by party. Democrats choose leadership skills and vision by a wide margin over both issue positions and experience, something clearly working in Obama's favor. Independents choose leadership by a slim margin over issue positions, while Republicans' preferences are almost evenly divided between issue positions and leadership.

Obama's relative lack of experience has been an issue in the presidential campaign to date, and it could become a bigger issue if he becomes McCain's Democratic opponent in the general election. As many Americans believe Obama, the three-year U.S. senator, lacks the experience needed to be president as believe he possesses it. However, experience does not seem to be very high on Americans' list of qualifications for the next president, so this apparent weakness for Obama may not be fatal. Americans are more likely to be looking for a candidate with leadership skills and vision, characteristics with respect to which Obama has obvious strengths.

MARCH 5
State of the Election After March 4 Voting

After Hillary Clinton's March 4 primary victories in Texas, Ohio, and Rhode Island, the outcome of the race for the Democratic presidential nomination will depend on the

votes of the shrinking number of Democrats who have yet to cast a ballot in their states' primaries and caucuses, and on the votes of party "superdelegates" at the Democratic National Convention in August. The sentiments of rank-and-file Democrats across the country provide an important indicator of whether Clinton or Barack Obama would be most satisfying to those who will be expected to support him or her in the November presidential election. Those sentiments have shown a great deal of change this year. Frequently, the race has been very close. But at one point in January, Clinton led Obama by 20 points among Democratic voters. Recently, Obama had pulled ahead by 8 points. At the moment, Clinton has a slight 4-point edge over Obama in terms of national Democratic support, 48% to 44%. This is based on data collected largely before the results of the March 4 voting became known.

Meanwhile, although the assumption is that Clinton and Obama will continue to campaign, discussion will continue regarding the possibility that one or both candidates might take some other action—including announcing a joint ticket. The polling information suggests that Democrats broadly support Clinton continuing her candidacy. An ABC News/Washington Post poll conducted before the March 4 voting found that 67% of Democrats favored Clinton's staying in the race if she won in either Texas or Ohio's. Given that she won both primaries, the former by 3 points and the latter by 10, it seems safe to assume that rank-and-file Democrats want the race to continue.

When asked on an early morning CBS talk show on March 5 about the possibility of sharing a ticket with Obama, Clinton, said: "Well, that may, you know, be where this is headed. But, of course, we have to decide who's on the top of the ticket." The limited data Gallup has on the possibility of a shared Clinton-Obama ticket come from a February 8–10 poll. Most Democrats and Democratic-leaning independents say they would welcome a joint ticket, with

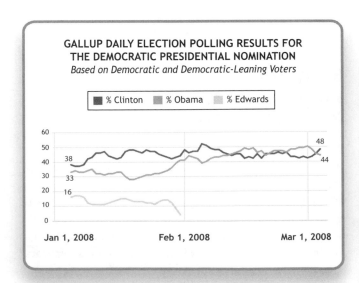

**GALLUP DAILY ELECTION POLLING RESULTS FOR
THE DEMOCRATIC PRESIDENTIAL NOMINATION**
Based on Democratic and Democratic-Leaning Voters

■ % Clinton   ■ % Obama   □ % Edwards

38 ... 48
33 ... 44
16

Jan 1, 2008   Feb 1, 2008   Mar 1, 2008

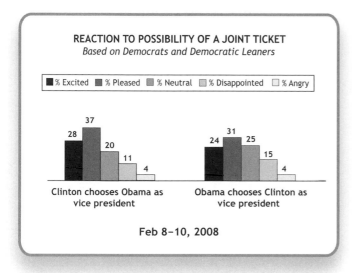

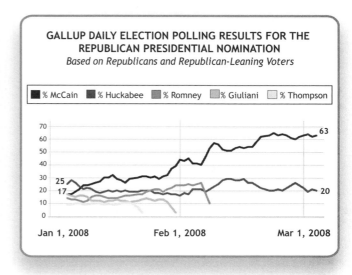

slightly more (at the time of the poll) saying they would be "excited" or "pleased" with a Clinton-Obama ticket (65%) than with an Obama-Clinton one (55%). The aforementioned ABC News/Washington Post poll also found that if they assume Obama wins the nomination, Democrats are much more likely to mention Clinton as their preferred vice presidential nominee than any other individual. Meanwhile, exit poll data from the March 4 voting confirm that the patterns of voter support for Clinton and Obama are clearly established at this point. Obama's strength is a coalition based primarily on support from a significant majority of black Democratic voters, coupled with the support of young voters and voters who are upscale educationally. Clinton's strength comes from Democrats who have less education, those who are older, Hispanic Democrats, and,

At a Rose Garden reception at the White House on March 5, 2008, President George W. Bush endorses presumptive Republican nominee John McCain for president. (Roger L. Wollenberg/Newscom)

more generally, white Democrats. She also continues to do better among women than among men.

On the Republican side, the final Gallup tracking poll of contenders for the Republican nomination shows that former Arkansas governor Mike Huckabee, who bowed out of the race for his party's nomination on March 4, maintained the support of 20% of Republicans. His voter base until the end was skewed toward conservatives and those who attend church frequently, as well as those who are younger. Huckabee led the Republican field briefly after his win in Iowa on January 3, but McCain moved ahead in Gallup Poll daily tracking after he won the New Hampshire primary five days later. McCain never relinquished that lead—which, in fact, continued to grow as former Tennessee senator Fred Thompson, former New York City mayor Rudolph Giuliani, and former Massachusetts governor Mitt Romney dropped out.

Gallup's latest measures of Americans' preferences between McCain and the two likely Democratic candidates in hypothetical general election trial heats were obtained in late February and showed close contests between McCain and either Obama or Clinton. Once the Democratic nominee is known, the major focus will be on changes in support for the two parties' nominees as the campaign moves through the predictable phases of vice presidential announcements, party conventions, and the intense campaigning that can be expected in September and October.

MARCH 7

Almost Half of Americans Say Military Is Not Strong Enough

A record proportion of Americans—47%—say the country's national defense is not strong enough. Another 41% say the country's defense is about right, while 10% say it is

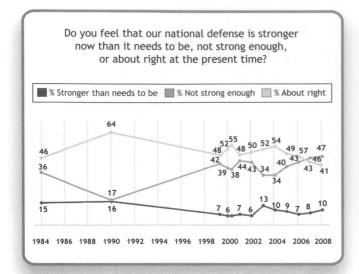

Do you feel that our national defense is stronger now than it needs to be, not strong enough, or about right at the present time?

- ■ % Stronger than needs to be
- ■ % Not strong enough
- □ % About right

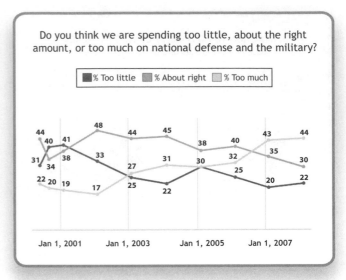

Do you think we are spending too little, about the right amount, or too much on national defense and the military?

- ■ % Too little
- ■ % About right
- □ % Too much

stronger than it needs to be. Gallup has asked this question consistently every February since 2001. In February 2001—seven months before the 9/11 terrorist attacks—44% of Americans said the nation's defense was not strong enough. In February 2002, the number was virtually the same. But in February 2003 and 2004, the "not strong enough" number dropped to 34%. It has risen slightly each year since to the current 47%, the highest in Gallup's history. Gallup asked this question on an infrequent basis several times before 2001. The low point for the "not strong enough" sentiment was 17% in January 1990, at which time almost two-thirds of Americans said that the national defense was about right. There are modest differences in views on the state of the country's national defense by partisan orientation.

Democrats are slightly more likely than Republicans to believe that the nation's defense is stronger than it needs to be, but the two parties are about equal in terms of those believing that the national defense is not strong enough. Even

as almost half of Americans say the national defense is not as strong as it should be, there is an increasing feeling on the part of Americans that the government in Washington spends too much for national defense and military purposes.

In February 2001, just as President Bush took over the presidency from President Bill Clinton, 38% of Americans said the amount being spent on defense and the military was about right, 41% said too little was being spent, and only 19% said "too much." Despite or perhaps because of the 9/11 terrorist attacks and the wars in Afghanistan and Iraq, the percentage of Americans saying too much is being spent on the military and defense has increased over the past seven years. Now, in the February 2008 survey, 44% of Americans say the U.S. is spending too much on the military and on defense, while just 22% say the country is spending too little.

There have been widely varying views on the question of military spending over the years prior to 2001. The all-time high point of sentiment that too much was being spent on the military came in November 1969, in the middle of the Vietnam War (the first time Gallup asked the question using this wording), when 52% said this. In January 1981, just as President Ronald Reagan was taking office, a little more than half of Americans said the United States was spending too little on defense, perhaps as a reaction to Reagan's presidential campaign position that the military needed strengthening. By 1987, in the middle of Reagan's second term, only 14% said the United States was spending too little. There is a major difference in current attitudes on the issue of military spending by partisan orientation. Democrats are more than three times as likely as Republicans to say the government is spending too much on national defense and the military, while Republicans are much more likely to say the government is spending about the right amount or too little.

Is the U.S. national defense stronger than it needs to be, not strong enough, or about right?

- ■ % Stronger than needs to be
- ■ % Not strong enough
- □ % About right

	Republicans	Independents	Democrats
% Stronger than needs to be	3	10	15
% Not strong enough	46	48	46
% About right	50	40	37

Feb 11–14, 2008

MARCH 10

Obama Recaptures Lead Among Democrats

Based on Gallup polling conducted between March 7 and March 9, 49% of Democratic voters nationally support Barack Obama for the Democratic nomination compared with 44% backing Hillary Clinton, giving Obama a slight but statistically significant lead.

Between March 2 and March 9, Clinton and Obama had been very close in national Democratic support, but preferences have now returned to where they stood in late February, when Gallup Poll daily tracking found Obama consistently ahead by a five- to eight-point margin. This comeback for Obama started prior to his victory in the Wyoming caucuses on March 8, thus blunting Clinton's winning streak coming off of the March 4 primaries. Obama has led Clinton on each of the individual days included in today's three-day rolling average, from March 7 to March 9.

Clinton Supporters Favor Quick Creation of "Dream Ticket"

Fifty-nine percent of Hillary Clinton supporters favor a quick decision to form a "dream ticket" of both Clinton and Obama, while a majority of Obama supporters oppose the idea and would rather the campaign for the nomination continue. Among all Democratic and Democratic-leaning voters, the March 6–9 Gallup Poll shows 51% of Democrats favoring immediately settling on a joint ticket of the two candidates, while 45% of Democrats think the candidates should soldier on. (Four percent have no opinion on the issue.) One possible reason Clinton supporters are more likely than Obama supporters to favor negotiating a joint ticket now is that Clinton supporters may be more worried that she will lose if the campaigning continues. (Obama is

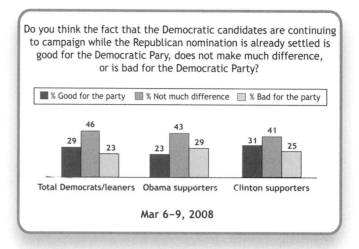

Do you think the fact that the Democratic candidates are continuing to campaign while the Republican nomination is already settled is good for the Democratic Pary, does not make much difference, or is bad for the Democratic Party?

■ % Good for the party   ▨ % Not much difference   ▢ % Bad for the party

	Total Democrats/leaners	Obama supporters	Clinton supporters
Good	29	23	31
Not much difference	46	43	41
Bad	23	29	25

Mar 6–9, 2008

currently ahead in the number of pledged delegates, and most experts believe Clinton will have difficulty erasing that lead if the remaining primaries and caucuses are close contests.) But a poll question asking who is most likely to win the nomination shows that both candidates' supporters believe their candidate will win, although there is slightly more optimism among Obama supporters: 71% of Clinton supporters say they believe she will win the nomination, compared with 83% of Obama supporters who say he will prevail. (More generally, 51% of all Democrats and Democratic leaners believe Obama will win, while 42% think Clinton will. But this marks a decrease in perceptions that Obama will emerge the victor; prior to Clinton's wins in the crucial Ohio and Texas primaries on March 4, 70% of Democrats thought Obama would win.)

The battle for the Democratic nomination could last at least as long as the Pennsylvania primary on April 22 and conceivably could continue into the summer and even up to the Democratic convention in August. Some argue that this would be good for the Democrats, because it keeps their race in the media spotlight and would therefore result in less coverage of the Republican nominee, John McCain. Others argue that the continuing campaign, with both Obama and Clinton focusing on the other candidate's negatives and faults, could end up hurting the eventual nominee, while at the same time allowing McCain to sail above the fray, raise funds, and in general focus on the November election. National Democrats clearly have mixed feelings regarding the pluses and minuses of a continuing Democratic campaign. A plurality of 46% of Democrats say that the fact that the Democrats are continuing to campaign while the Republicans have decided on their nominee doesn't make much difference. Another 23% say it is bad for the party, while 29% say it is good for the party. There is little significant difference between Clinton and Obama supporters in responses to this question.

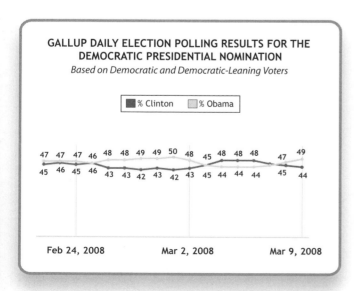

GALLUP DAILY ELECTION POLLING RESULTS FOR THE DEMOCRATIC PRESIDENTIAL NOMINATION
Based on Democratic and Democratic-Leaning Voters

■ % Clinton   ▢ % Obama

% Obama: 47 47 47 46 48 48 49 49 50 48 45 48 48 48 47 49

% Clinton: 45 46 45 46 43 43 42 43 42 43 45 44 44 44 45 44

Feb 24, 2008   Mar 2, 2008   Mar 9, 2008

MARCH 11

Democrats Divided over How Superdelegates Should Vote

Rank-and-file Democrats are fairly evenly divided between those saying superdelegates should vote for the candidate with the most delegates after all the primaries and caucuses are concluded, and those saying superdelegates should vote for the candidate they believe would make the better president. Clinton and Obama supporters take opposing views on the matter.

There is a real possibility that the Democratic Party superdelegates—party activists, officeholders, and elders who are free to support any candidate they choose—will ultimately decide who the nominee is. That it is because it is unlikely that either Obama or Clinton will amass enough pledged delegates in the primaries and caucuses to clinch the nomination. A Gallup Poll conducted between March 6 and March 9 asked Democrats how superdelegates should vote if one candidate has more delegates at the time of the convention but they believe the other candidate would be a better president. Fifty percent believe superdelegates should side with the voters and choose the leader in the delegate count, while 45% believe superdelegates should vote their consciences and cast their ballots for the candidate they think would be the better president. The odds are that Obama will have more delegates at the time of the convention, and the data suggest that Democrats are aware of this and respond accordingly. By a two-to-one margin (64% to 32%), Democrats who support Obama believe superdelegates should vote for the candidate with more pledged delegates. Meanwhile, Clinton supporters take the opposing view and say by nearly the same margin, 60% to 35%, that superdelegates should vote for the candidate they think would be the better president.

Clinton's wins in the March 4 Ohio and Texas primaries eliminated the possibility of an early conclusion to the Democratic nomination fight and increased the possibility of the nomination's being decided at the Democratic convention in late August. The subsequent split over how superdelegates should vote is not surprising, given that Democrats have been fairly evenly divided for most of 2008 between preferring Clinton or Obama as the party's nominee. Many Democrats understand the implications of the decision facing the superdelegates for each candidate, and thus tend to favor an approach that works in their preferred candidate's best interests.

Democrats Favor Compromise on Florida, Michigan Delegates

The Democratic Party's rank and file favor allowing Florida and Michigan Democratic delegates to participate in this year's presidential nominating convention, but there is a considerable lack of consensus over exactly what the solution to this controversy should be.

In general, most Democrats (55%) favor some compromise that would allow the two states' delegates to participate, rather than excluding those states' delegates entirely (23%), which is the current plan. (Twenty-two percent do not have an opinion either way.) But those who favor a compromise divide almost equally between a "do-over" primary or caucus to be held in those states between now and the convention, and finding a way to abide by the results of the January contests, in which neither Clinton nor Obama actively campaigned (in Michigan, Obama was not even on the ballot) and no delegates were officially at stake.

Six in 10 Democrats say they are paying very or somewhat close attention to the controversy over the conven-

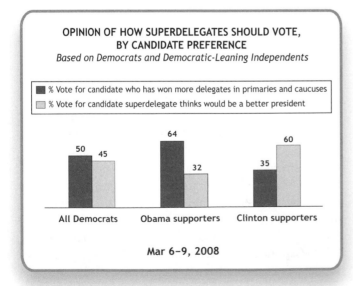

OPINION OF HOW SUPERDELEGATES SHOULD VOTE, BY CANDIDATE PREFERENCE
Based on Democrats and Democratic-Leaning Independents

■ % Vote for candidate who has won more delegates in primaries and caucuses
□ % Vote for candidate superdelegate thinks would be a better president

All Democrats: 50, 45
Obama supporters: 64, 32
Clinton supporters: 35, 60

Mar 6–9, 2008

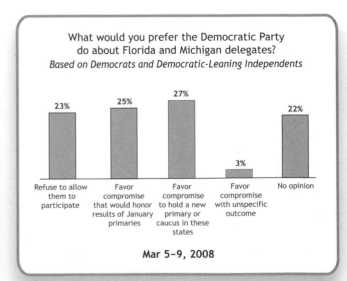

What would you prefer the Democratic Party do about Florida and Michigan delegates?
Based on Democrats and Democratic-Leaning Independents

Refuse to allow them to participate: 23%
Favor compromise that would honor results of January primaries: 25%
Favor compromise to hold a new primary or caucus in these states: 27%
Favor compromise with unspecific outcome: 3%
No opinion: 22%

Mar 5–9, 2008

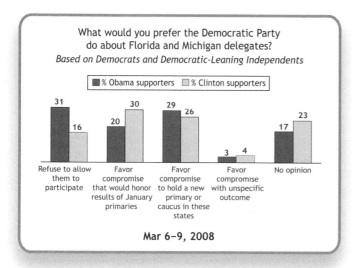

What would you prefer the Democratic Party do about Florida and Michigan delegates?
Based on Democrats and Democratic-Leaning Independents

■ % Obama supporters   □ % Clinton supporters

Mar 6–9, 2008

results, while Obama supporters who favor a compromise are more inclined to support a second binding primary or caucus in those states.

The Democratic rank and file does not provide much guidance to its party leaders as to how the party should ideally proceed in resolving the Florida/Michigan controversy, although there is a clear preference that something should be done to allow Michigan and Florida delegates to have a say at the convention.

MARCH 12

Before Spitzer Scandal, Mixed Ethics Reviews for Governors

Despite New Yorkers' apparent shock over their corruption-fighting governor's involvement with a prostitution ring, Americans may not be surprised to see another governor in ethical trouble. As of December 2006, just 22% of Americans held state governors in high esteem for their moral character or judged their honesty and ethics as high or very high.

Still, only 26% of Americans said the honesty and ethics of governors were low or very low—most said they were average—meaning, presumably, that scandals like the one now befalling New York governor Eliot Spitzer could risk lowering the reputation of governors even further. Gallup conducts an annual rating of the perceived honesty and ethical standards of people serving in various professions but does not include all professions on the list every year. State governors were last included in December 2006, at which time nurses were the most well-regarded profession, with 84% rating them highly, and car salesmen the least respected, at 7%. Governors were positioned in the bottom half of the 2006 list, ranking 14th out of 23 professions rated based on the percentage giving them a high ethics rating. Yet, relative to other categories of politicians, state governors are among the most well regarded. In 2006, they were viewed as more ethical than senators (ranked 18th)

tion delegates from Florida and Michigan. The Democratic National Committee had said it would refuse to seat a state's delegation at the convention if that state—other than Iowa, New Hampshire, South Carolina, or Nevada—held its primary or caucus before Super Tuesday on February 5. Florida and Michigan Democratic Party leaders defied that order by proceeding to hold their primaries in January. The Democratic National Committee is holding firm in its position, and now those two states are faced with the possibility of having no voice at the convention. With the contest so close and every delegate important to the outcome, there is now considerable pressure on the Democratic National Committee to find an acceptable solution. Supporters of both candidates favor some sort of compromise; Clinton supporters are slightly more likely than Obama supporters to favor a compromise. That in part reflects the reality of the situation: Because Clinton "won" both of these states' contests, Obama supporters (31%) are understandably more likely to favor excluding those states altogether than are Clinton supporters (16%). Clinton supporters who favor a compromise tend toward advocating an outcome that would honor the January

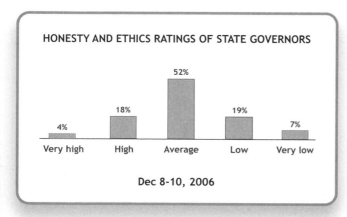

HONESTY AND ETHICS RATINGS OF STATE GOVERNORS

Dec 8–10, 2006

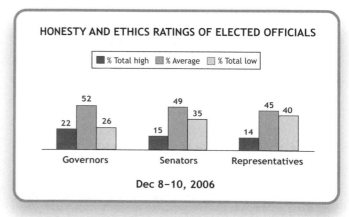

HONESTY AND ETHICS RATINGS OF ELECTED OFFICIALS

■ % Total high   ■ % Average   □ % Total low

Dec 8–10, 2006

and representatives (19th). The contrast was especially sharp in terms of the percentage saying each group had low ethics: 26% for state governors, compared with 35% for senators and 40% for representatives.

Gallup's 2007 "honesty and ethics" list included "state officeholders," at which time this broad category (which could include governors along with other state officials) was rated highly by only 12% of Americans. On the few occasions that Gallup has included both state governors and other state officeholders in the same survey, state governors received the higher scores. For example, in 1999, 24% of Americans rated the ethics of state governors high or very high, compared with 16% for other state officeholders. Gallup trends show generally little change in the ratings of state governors since they were first included in Gallup's honesty and ethics of professions survey in 1999. Positive ethics ratings for governors were higher in November 2000 (30%) but have otherwise been in the 22% to 26% range.

MARCH 13

Obama, Clinton Equally Matched vs. McCain

Although the November presidential election is still eight months away, the results of Gallup Poll daily tracking show that if the election were held today, the outcome would be quite tight, with both Barack Obama and Hillary Clinton running within two percentage points of Republican nominee John McCain. These results are based on interviews with 4,355 registered voters nationwide between March 8 and March 12. All voters were asked their preferences in both pairings: McCain vs. Obama and McCain vs. Clinton, with the order of the pairings randomly rotated across the sample. There are two notable findings in these data. First, despite the fact that the Democratic Party is generically better positioned than the Republican Party at this point in time, the Republican nominee is running neck and neck with the two possible Democratic nominees. Second, despite the continuing focus on the relative electability of Obama and Clinton , there is no difference in the way the two stack up against McCain. Furthermore, it is possible that the Democrats are handicapped to a degree by the fact that their final nominee has not yet been determined, and that the Democratic candidate's strength against McCain will increase once the Democratic nominee is determined.

The preferences for their nominee among Democrats nationally are very close.

The latest Gallup Poll daily tracking update on Democratic nomination preferences, based on March 10–12 polling, shows 48% of national Democratic voters favoring Obama and 46% Clinton. There was no sign in Gallup's

March 12 interviewing that Obama picked up any major surge in support nationally as a result of his strong win in the Mississippi primary on March 11.

Americans on Iraq: Should the United States Stay or Go?

Americans are as divided today as they have been since September 2007 about this country's troop presence in Iraq: 41% favor setting a timetable for gradually pulling out of Iraq, while 35% want to maintain troops there until the situation improves. Only 18% of Americans favor an immediate withdrawal of all U.S. troops.

Looking at the same data differently, 60% of Americans want the United States to set a timetable for removing troops from Iraq rather than maintaining an indefinite military commitment. But there is no national consensus on how soon the United States should start pulling out. Eighteen percent of Americans favor immediate withdrawal, 41% favor gradual withdrawal on a timetable, and 35% favor no withdrawal. (An additional 1% favor a timetable but have no opinion about whether withdrawal should be immediate or gradual.) Regardless of what they may personally want to happen, a slight majority of Americans—52%—believe the United States will continue to have a significant number of troops in Iraq for at least another four years. Only 39% predict the major U.S. troop deployment will end within the next three years.

One reason most Americans object to maintaining troop levels indefinitely may be that, to many, it is unclear that the troops are achieving their goals. While 40% of Americans believe that the 2007 U.S. troop surge in Iraq is having a positive effect on the situation there, nearly as many (38%) say the surge is not making much difference, and 20% say it is making things worse. This is a much more positive balance of opinion about the U.S.

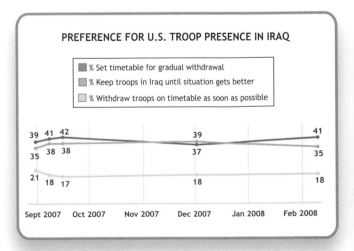

PREFERENCE FOR U.S. TROOP PRESENCE IN IRAQ

■ % Set timetable for gradual withdrawal
■ % Keep troops in Iraq until situation gets better
□ % Withdraw troops on timetable as soon as possible

	Sept 2007	Oct 2007	Nov 2007	Dec 2007	Jan 2008	Feb 2008
Set timetable	39	41	42		39	41
Keep troops	35	38	38		37	35
Withdraw	21	18	17		18	18

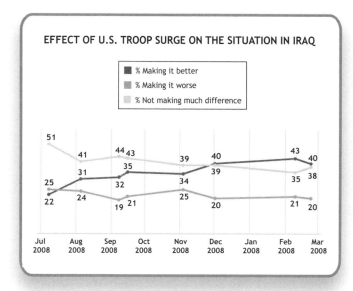

EFFECT OF U.S. TROOP SURGE ON THE SITUATION IN IRAQ

■ % Making it better
■ % Making it worse
■ % Not making much difference

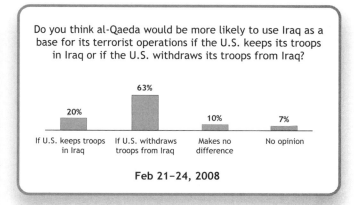

Do you think al-Qaeda would be more likely to use Iraq as a base for its terrorist operations if the U.S. keeps its troops in Iraq or if the U.S. withdraws its troops from Iraq?

Feb 21–24, 2008

troop surge than Gallup found in July 2007, when as many Americans thought the surge was making matters worse as said it was improving things. Positive attitudes about the surge grew last summer and fall—rising from 22% in July to 40% in late November/early December—but have failed to expand any further.

MARCH 14

Americans Concerned About Impact of Leaving Iraq

Most Americans think the United States has an obligation to remain in Iraq until a reasonable level of stability and security has been reached. Although about 60% of Americans believe that the United States' initial involvement in the Iraq War was a mistake, fewer than 20% say the United States should initiate an immediate withdrawal of troops. Why is this the case? A review of the responses to several questions on Iraq in a recent USA Today/Gallup poll provides some indication of the reasons that an apparently

conflicted American population is hesitant to recommend immediate withdrawal despite its basic feeling that U.S. involvement there has been a mistake. Almost two-thirds of Americans believe the United States has an obligation to establish a reasonable level of stability in Iraq before withdrawing all troops.

The poll did not ask Americans directly if they felt that such a "reasonable level of stability" had yet been reached. But a recent CBS News/New York Times poll found that a majority of Americans believe things are going badly for the "U.S. in its efforts to bring stability and order to Iraq." This suggests that Americans don't feel stability is yet the norm in Iraq, and therefore—based on the attitudes measured by the Gallup Poll question—that it is necessary for troops to remain in Iraq until such stability is achieved. Additionally, more than 60% of Americans feel that al-Qaeda would be more likely to use Iraq as a base for its terrorist operations if the United States withdrew its troops than if it kept its troops there, mirroring one of the Bush administration's (and presidential candidate John McCain's) most frequently used arguments against an immediate withdrawal of troops from Iraq. A majority of Americans (57%) also believe that more Iraqis would die from violence in that country if the U.S. withdrew its troops than would be the case if it kept its troops there.

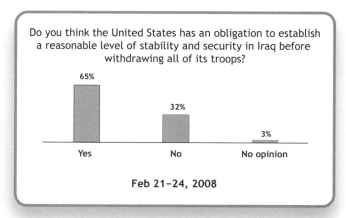

Do you think the United States has an obligation to establish a reasonable level of stability and security in Iraq before withdrawing all of its troops?

Feb 21–24, 2008

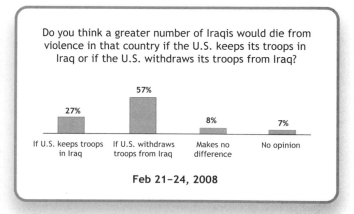

Do you think a greater number of Iraqis would die from violence in that country if the U.S. keeps its troops in Iraq or if the U.S. withdraws its troops from Iraq?

Feb 21–24, 2008

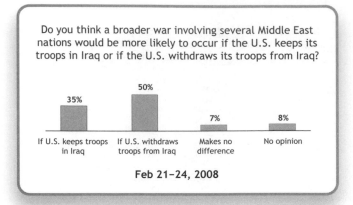

Do you think a broader war involving several Middle East nations would be more likely to occur if the U.S. keeps its troops in Iraq or if the U.S. withdraws its troops from Iraq?

| If U.S. keeps troops in Iraq | If U.S. withdraws troops from Iraq | Makes no difference | No opinion |
| 35% | 50% | 7% | 8% |

Feb 21–24, 2008

And half of Americans say the likelihood of a broader Middle East war would increase if the United States withdrew its troops from Iraq, while just 35% say that prospect is more likely if the United States kept its troops in Iraq. Americans are not convinced, however, that the likelihood of terrorist attacks against the United States would increase if the country withdrew its troops from Iraq: About as many say such attacks are more likely if the United States keeps troops in Iraq (40%) as say they are more likely if the U.S. withdraws its troops (38%).

Americans have—perhaps inevitably, given the complex nature of the war in Iraq—a set of somewhat ambivalent attitudes about the situation there. In Gallup's latest poll, 59% of Americans say U.S. involvement in the war in Iraq was a mistake. One might think, therefore, that a similar majority would favor an immediate withdrawal of troops from that country. But that's not the case. Less than 20%, in fact, say the U.S. should withdraw its troops immediately. The rest say either that troops should stay in Iraq as long as necessary, with no timetable for withdrawal, or that there should be a gradual timetable for withdrawal.

The data suggest that there are reasons Americans hesitate to recommend an immediate withdrawal of troops. A majority of Americans believe that withdrawing troops from Iraq would lead to a greater possibility of al-Qaeda's using Iraq as a base for terrorist operations, a greater number of Iraqi deaths from violence, and a greater likelihood of a broader Middle East war. Additionally, Americans believe the United States has an obligation to remain in Iraq until that country is stable, and recent poll results suggest that a majority of Americans do not believe an acceptable level of stability has yet been reached. (Americans are not inclined to believe there would be an increased chance of terrorist attacks against the United States if its troops were withdrawn.) The next U.S. president, then, will face this confused landscape. Americans obviously are negative about the entire Iraqi enterprise—a majority say history will judge the U.S. involvement in Iraq to have been a failure—but, perhaps realistically, they believe the attempt to extricate the U.S. military from that country is not going to be a simple or straightforward matter.

MARCH 16
McCain 47%, Obama 44%

The latest Gallup Poll daily tracking update on registered voters' general election preferences for president finds that John McCain has opened up a slight advantage over Barack Obama, 47% to 44%, while McCain and Hillary Clinton remain tied at 46% each. Those results are based on interviews with over 4,000 registered voters nationwide conducted between March 11 and March 15. This marks the first time since Gallup began reporting these general election results on March 7 that McCain's relative positioning against Obama and Clinton has not been exactly the same. McCain's three-percentage-point advantage over Obama is not statistically significant, and it remains to be seen if the differentiation between the two Democratic candidates when pitted against McCain will continue in the days ahead. Meanwhile, the race for the Democratic nomination remains close, with Gallup Poll daily tracking showing that 48% of Democratic voters nationwide prefer Obama and 45% Clinton. This three-point lead for Obama is the same as shown in the March 7–10 polling and is not statistically significant.

MARCH 17
U.S. Satisfaction Dips to 19%

A March 6–9, 2008, Gallup Poll finds only 19% of Americans satisfied with the way things are going in the United States today. This is similar to the 20% found in early February and in November 2007 but is technically the lowest Gallup has recorded since August 1992. Gallup initiated the U.S. satisfaction measure in 1979 and has been track-

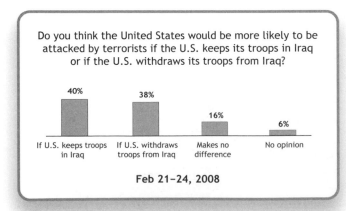

Do you think the United States would be more likely to be attacked by terrorists if the U.S. keeps its troops in Iraq or if the U.S. withdraws its troops from Iraq?

| If U.S. keeps troops in Iraq | If U.S. withdraws troops from Iraq | Makes no difference | No opinion |
| 40% | 38% | 16% | 6% |

Feb 21–24, 2008

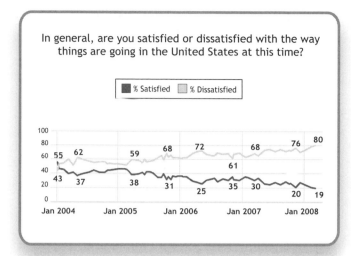

In general, are you satisfied or dissatisfied with the way things are going in the United States at this time?

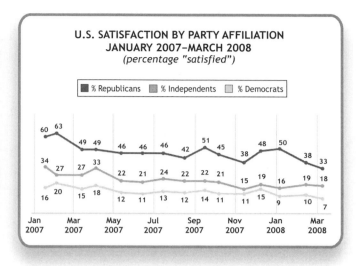

U.S. SATISFACTION BY PARTY AFFILIATION
JANUARY 2007–MARCH 2008
(percentage "satisfied")

ing it monthly since October 2000. The low point came in July 1979, when only 12% of Americans were satisfied with the state of the country. Americans' mood sank to nearly this level in 1992, when 14% declared themselves satisfied in June of that election year and 17% in August. The high points of satisfaction—70% and 71%—came in January and February 1999 (under a booming economy) and in the post-9/11 period in December 2001 (when Americans were rallying in support of the country). The last time a majority of Americans were satisfied with the direction of the country was in January 2004. After some volatility in 2004 and early 2005, satisfaction with the way things are going in the United States has essentially been in decline continuously since September 2005.

Since January 2007, satisfaction with the direction of the country has dropped by nearly half, from 35% to 19%. However, it has dropped much more among Republicans (from 60% to 33%) than among Democrats (from 16% to 7%). The 33% of Republicans satisfied with the country today is the lowest Gallup has found for members of President Bush's party since he took office in 2001.

MARCH 18

McCain's Favorable Rating Highest in Eight Years

John McCain's 67% favorable rating is the highest of any of the three major candidates running for president, and ties for his highest in Gallup polling history. McCain's favorable rating matches the 67% he received in February 2000, when he was in the middle of his first run for president. But since that point, McCain's image in the eyes of Americans has undergone significant shifts. The Arizona senator had favorable ratings in the 57% range as he began his presidential campaign last winter, but as his campaign floundered in the summer of 2007, his favorable rating dropped as low as 41%. At that point, many observers had written off his campaign. But McCain rebounded, winning the New Hampshire primary in January 2008 and then clinching the Republican nomination two months later. His current favorable rating represents a gain of 26 points since summer 2007, includ-

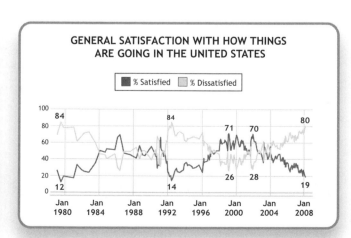

GENERAL SATISFACTION WITH HOW THINGS ARE GOING IN THE UNITED STATES

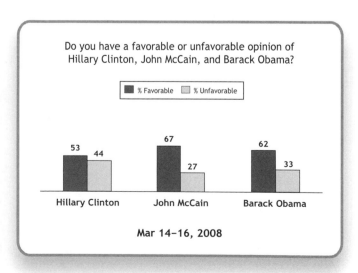

Do you have a favorable or unfavorable opinion of Hillary Clinton, John McCain, and Barack Obama?

Mar 14–16, 2008

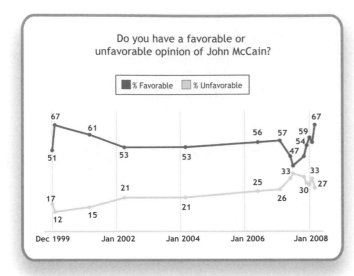

Do you have a favorable or unfavorable opinion of John McCain?

ing an 11-point increase since he won enough delegates to ensure his nomination on March 4, 2008.

Illinois senator Barack Obama's favorable rating is now at 62%, the highest by one point that Gallup has recorded for Obama since Gallup's first reading in December 2006 (at which point almost half of Americans did not know enough about him to give him a rating). Obama's ratings have been fairly stable in recent months, ranging between 58% and 62% across five Gallup Polls conducted since January 2008.

Hillary Clinton's favorable rating of 53% is significantly lower than the favorable ratings of the other two candidates, in part no doubt because of her long history in the public eye, including eight years as first lady in her husband's administration from 1993 to 2001. Still, this is Clinton's highest favorable rating since October 2007.

Over the years, Clinton has seen a number of ups and downs in her image. Her highest favorable rating of 67% came in December 1998, just as her husband was being impeached

for charges relating to his involvement with a White House intern. Since then, however, her rating has fallen as low as 44% in March 2001 and 45% as recently as April 2007. Her current rating represents an increase of five points since late February 2008 (prior to her wins in the crucial Ohio and Texas primaries on March 4). Both Obama and Clinton have slightly higher favorable ratings among Democrats now than they had in February 2008, suggesting that the negative infighting that has characterized the Democratic campaign in recent weeks is not damaging either candidate's image in the eyes of the party faithful.

One reason for the higher favorable ratings McCain and Obama enjoy is their crossover appeal to Americans who identify with the other party. McCain gets an extraordinarily high 52% favorable rating from Democrats and independents who lean Democratic, while Obama gets a 39% favorable rating from Republicans and Republican leaners. Clinton, on the other hand, receives only a 20% favorable rating from Republicans and Republican leaners. McCain is also helped by the fact that he receives an 87% favorable rating from Republicans, higher than the 80% and 79% that Clinton and Obama, respectively, currently receive from Democrats.

Obama Seeks to Bridge Racial Divide Among Democrats

Barack Obama's major speech on race in Philadelphia on March 18 was a reminder of the continuing, and highly charged, impact of race in American society in general and in this presidential campaign in particular. Obama, confronted with the continuing controversy over statements made by his former minister, Reverend Jeremiah Wright, tried to limit the damage by discussing what he called "a misunderstanding that exists between the races." Obama's speech presumably had the objective of shoring up as much white support for his presidential candidacy as possible among Democratic voters—particularly in the large state of Pennsylvania, the location for his speech and a state that holds its Democratic primary on April 22. There is certainly a large racial divide in the Democratic presidential campaign at this point. In Gallup Poll daily election tracking, race is the single issue that divides the Democratic electorate more than any other. In an aggregate of 6,721 interviews Gallup has conducted between March 1 and March 16, 80% of black Democrats support Obama while only 15% support Hillary Clinton. Non-Hispanic whites split 53% for Clinton and 38% for Obama, while white Hispanics are even stronger for Clinton, 59% to 37%. While Obama's focus at this point is on winning the Democratic nomination, his viability in the general election (should he win the nomination) will presumably be affected by white voters' views of his candidacy. At this time, however, there is very little racial divide between Obama and Clinton in

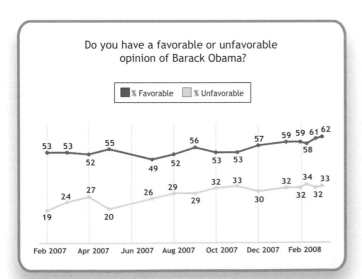

Do you have a favorable or unfavorable opinion of Barack Obama?

After controversial remarks by his pastor received wide coverage, Senator Barack Obama delivers a speech on race in Philadelphia on March 18, 2008. *(Alex Brandon/ AP Images)*

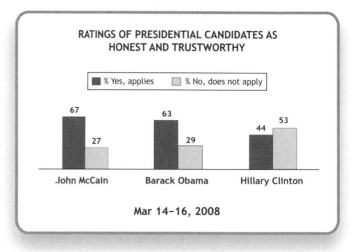

RATINGS OF PRESIDENTIAL CANDIDATES AS HONEST AND TRUSTWORTHY

■ % Yes, applies   □ % No, does not apply

	John McCain	Barack Obama	Hillary Clinton
% Yes, applies	67	63	44
% No, does not apply	27	29	53

Mar 14–16, 2008

Gallup's general election matchups. Blacks overwhelmingly support either Democratic candidate over John McCain, as would be expected given historical voting patterns. Indeed, there is little significant difference in black or white support for the Democratic candidate against McCain, whether that candidate is Obama or Clinton.

Perceived Honesty Gap a Problem for Clinton vs. Obama and McCain

Hillary Clinton is rated as "honest and trustworthy" by 44% of Americans, far fewer than say this about John McCain (67%) and Barack Obama (63%). The USA Today/Gallup poll conducted between March 14 and March 16 asked Americans to rate the presidential candidates on honesty and trustworthiness and on nine other character and leadership dimensions: "cares about the needs of people like you," "is a strong and decisive leader," "shares your values," "has a clear plan for solving the country's problems," "has a vision for the country's future," "can manage the government effectively," "understands the problems Americans face in their daily lives," "would work well with both parties in Washington to get things done," and "is someone you would be proud to have as president." The 23-point gap separating Clinton (44%) and McCain (67%) on honesty and trustworthiness is the largest between any two candidates with respect to any dimension tested in the poll.

In addition to his strong showing on honesty, McCain fares well on leadership. Sixty-nine percent of Americans describe the Arizona senator as "a strong and decisive leader," giving him an advantage over both Clinton (61%)

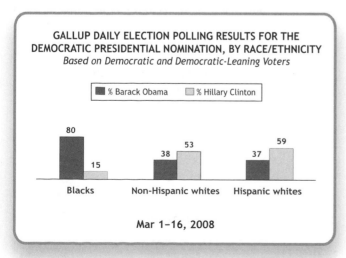

GALLUP DAILY ELECTION POLLING RESULTS FOR THE DEMOCRATIC PRESIDENTIAL NOMINATION, BY RACE/ETHNICITY
Based on Democratic and Democratic-Leaning Voters

■ % Barack Obama   □ % Hillary Clinton

	Blacks	Non-Hispanic whites	Hispanic whites
% Barack Obama	80	38	37
% Hillary Clinton	15	53	59

Mar 1–16, 2008

RATINGS OF PRESIDENTIAL CANDIDATES ON CHARACTER AND QUALITY DIMENSIONS

	McCain	Obama	Clinton
Cares about the needs of people like you	54	66	54
Is a strong and decisive leader	69	56	61
Is honest and trustworthy	67	63	44
Shares your values	46	51	45
Has a clear plan for solving the country's problems	42	41	49
Has a vision for the country's future	65	67	68
Can manage the government effectively	60	48	51
Understands the problems Americans face in their daily lives	55	67	58
Would work well with both parties in Washington to get things done	61	62	49
Is someone you would be proud to have as president	55	57	47

Note: Figures are percentages saying each characteristic applies to the candidate.

Mar 14–16, 2008

and Obama (56%) in this regard. Obama's strengths lie in his perceived empathy: Two in three Americans say he "understands the problems Americans face in their daily lives" and "cares about the needs of people like you." Clinton and McCain are in the mid-50s on both of these dimensions. Obama (51%) also edges McCain (46%) and Clinton (45%) on "shares your values."

Clinton is the leader on what proves to be a weakness for both McCain and Obama—having "a clear plan for solving the country's problems." Forty-nine percent say Clinton does, compared with 41% for Obama and 42% for McCain. Clinton has tried to emphasize this theme in her campaign in order to draw a distinction between herself and Obama, and it rates as Obama's (and McCain's) lowest score.

Clinton has been less successful in convincing voters that she can better navigate her way through the Washington policy process than the other candidates. McCain (60%) leads both Clinton (51%) and Obama (48%) on being able to manage the government effectively. Likewise, Obama (62%) and McCain (61%) finish well ahead of Clinton (49%) with respect to being able to "work well with both parties in Washington to get things done." All three candidates are rated well with respect to having a vision for the country's future: Sixty-eight percent say this about Clinton, 67% about Obama, and 65% about McCain. One final dimension, however, underscores another potential vulnerability for Clinton: Only 47% of Americans say she is someone they would be proud to have as president. (Fifty-one percent say they would not be proud to have Clinton as president.) Obama (57%) and McCain (55%) both score above the 50% level on this measure—a further indication that both tend to fare better on basic likability measures than Clinton.

It is clear that voters are able to distinguish among the three major presidential candidates and rate some areas as strengths and some as weaknesses for each. Clinton would appear to have more weaknesses in the public's eyes than McCain or Obama, though that might reflect the fact that she is a better-known figure and has lower favorable ratings. Currently, she holds a significant lead over Obama on only 2 of the 10 character dimensions evaluated here ("strong and decisive leader" and 'having a clear plan for solving the country's problems") and over McCain on only one (having a clear plan). Despite this, she remains competitive with McCain in general election matchups, and she has held off Obama's attempts to wrap up the Democratic nomination.

MARCH 21
Clinton 47%, Obama 45%

Hillary Clinton's recent lead over Barack Obama in national Democratic nomination preferences has dwindled so

that the two are now nearly tied, with Clinton at 47% and Obama at 45% in March 18–20 Gallup Poll daily tracking. Clinton moved seven percentage points ahead of Obama in Gallup's March 19 report and retained a significant five-point lead on March 20. Her gains were coincident with the controversy over Obama's former pastor and "spiritual mentor," Reverend Jeremiah Wright. However, the surge in Democrats' preference for Clinton that Gallup detected earlier in the week has started to move out of the three-day rolling average, and the race is back to a near tie. It is possible that Obama's aggressive efforts to diffuse the Wright story, including a major speech about race on March 18, have been effective. Still, Obama has yet to recover fully from the apparent damage done by the Wright controversy. It was only one week ago that Obama led the race by a significant six-point margin over Clinton, 50% to 44%. And this turmoil on the Democratic side may be slightly beneficial to the Republicans' White House aspirations, at least for the time being. In separate trial heats for the fall election, John McCain continues to hold slim advantages over Clinton and Obama among national registered voters. Earlier in March, both Democrats held a slight edge.

MARCH 24
Clinton, Obama Closely Matched Among Jewish Democrats

Jewish Democratic voters show a slight preference for Hillary Clinton (48%) over Barack Obama (43%) for the party's 2008 presidential nomination. The five-point Clinton advantage is within the margin of error for this sample of Jewish Democrats. The data are based on interviews with Jewish Democratic voters conducted in Gallup Poll daily tracking between March 1 and March 22. (So far this month, all Democratic voters regardless of religious affiliation are equally divided—46% each—in supporting Clinton or Obama.) Obama's ability to win votes in the Jewish community has been questioned, given indications that many believe he does not support Israel

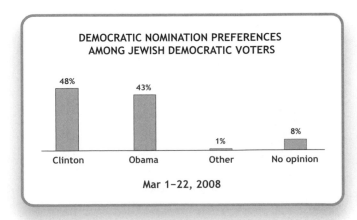

DEMOCRATIC NOMINATION PREFERENCES AMONG JEWISH DEMOCRATIC VOTERS

Clinton	Obama	Other	No opinion
48%	43%	1%	8%

Mar 1–22, 2008

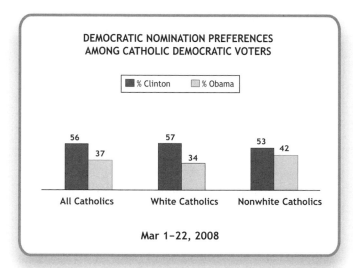

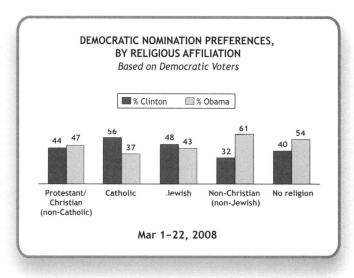

as strongly as other candidates. Some of Obama's supporters (including the Reverend Jeremiah Wright, former pastor of Obama's church) and some of his foreign policy advisers are regarded as anti-Israel. Obama has met with Jewish leaders to reassure them of his commitment to Israel.

While the candidates run about evenly among Jewish Democrats, Clinton does better among Catholic Democratic voters, leading Obama by nearly 20 percentage points, 56% to 37%, in the March data among this group. Clinton out-polls Obama among both white Catholics (57% to 34%) and nonwhite Catholics (53% to 42%). The latter group largely comprises Hispanics, a core Clinton support group.

Democratic voters who are Protestant (including those who say they are "Christian" but provide no specific denomination) divide about equally between Obama (47%) and Clinton (44%). But the overall Protestant numbers hide a deep racial gap, with Clinton leading by more than 20 points among white Protestant Democratic voters (56% to 34%) and Obama holding an even larger 45-point lead

among nonwhite Protestant Democratic voters (70% to 25%). With Jewish and Protestant Democrats basically split in their preferences, and Catholics strongly in Clinton's corner, Obama is able to make up the difference by running better than she does among Democrats with no religious preference (54% to 40%) and among those who practice non-Christian religions (61% to 32%; this subgroup is defined as not including Jews).

MARCH 26

If It's McCain vs. Obama, 28% of Clinton Backers Go for McCain

A sizable proportion of Democrats would vote for John McCain in the presidential election next November if he is matched against the candidate they do not support for the Democratic nomination. This is particularly true of Hillary Clinton supporters, more than a quarter of whom currently

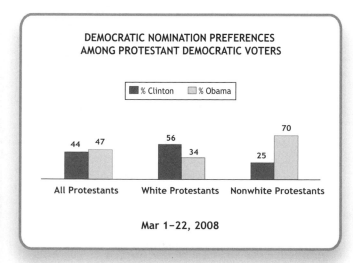

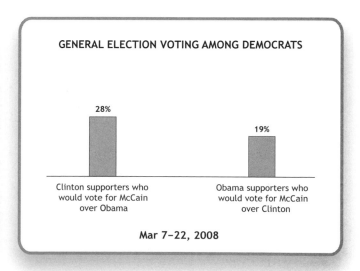

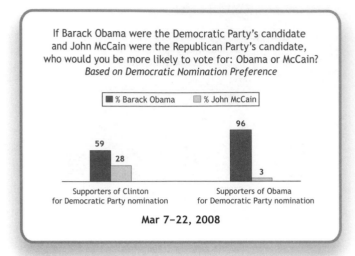

If Barack Obama were the Democratic Party's candidate
and John McCain were the Republican Party's candidate,
who would you be more likely to vote for: Obama or McCain?
Based on Democratic Nomination Preference

Mar 7–22, 2008

say they would vote for McCain if Barack Obama is the Democratic nominee.

These conclusions are based on an analysis of Democratic voters' responses to separate voting questions in March 7–22 Gallup Poll daily election tracking. In each day's survey, respondents are asked for their general election preferences in McCain-Clinton and McCain-Obama matchups. Democratic voters are then asked whom they support for their party's nomination.

As would be expected, almost all Democratic voters who say they support Obama for their party's nomination also say they would vote for him in a general election matchup against McCain. But only 59% of Democratic voters who support Clinton say they would vote for Obama against McCain, while 28% say they would vote for the Republican McCain. This suggests that some Clinton supporters are so strongly opposed to Obama (or so loyal to Clinton) that they would go so far as to vote for the other party's candidate next

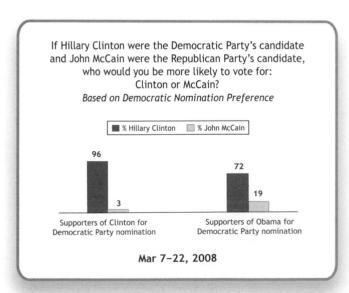

If Hillary Clinton were the Democratic Party's candidate
and John McCain were the Republican Party's candidate,
who would you be more likely to vote for:
Clinton or McCain?
Based on Democratic Nomination Preference

Mar 7–22, 2008

November if Obama is the Democratic nominee. The results follow the same pattern, but not quite to the same extent, when the relationship between Democratic nomination preference and a general election matchup between Clinton and McCain is examined. Here again, as expected, almost all of those who support Clinton for the Democratic Party's nomination say they would vote for her against McCain. Seventy-two percent of those who support Obama for the party's nomination would vote for Clinton against McCain, while 19% would vote for the Republican.

The data suggest that the continuing and sometimes fractious Democratic nomination fight could have a negative impact for the Democratic Party in next November's election. A not insignificant percentage of both Obama and Clinton supporters currently say they would vote for McCain if he ends up running against the candidate they do not support. What is unknown, however, is how many Democrats would actually carry out their stated attention and vote for a Republican next fall if their preferred candidate did not become the Democratic nominee. The Democratic campaign is in the heat of battle at the moment, but by November there will have been several months of attempts to build party unity around the eventual nominee—and a focus on reasons the Republican nominee needs to be defeated.

Additionally, there is often some threat of deserting the party while party nomination battles are waged, but this threat can dissipate. For example, in answer to a recent Gallup question, 11% of Republicans said they would vote for the Democratic candidate or a third-party candidate next fall if McCain does not choose a vice president who is considerably more conservative than he is. (And another 9% said they just wouldn't vote.) These results suggest that it may be normal for some voters to threaten early on in the process—perhaps out of frustration—that they will desert their party if the results of the nomination process are not to their liking. And it may be equally likely that they fall back into line by the time of the general election. It is worth noting that historically, in Gallup's final pre-election polls from 1992 to 2004, 10% or fewer of Republicans and Democrats typically vote for the other party's presidential candidate. Still, when almost 3 out of 10 Clinton supporters say they would vote for McCain over Obama, it suggests that divisions are running deep within the Democratic Party. If the fight for the party's nomination continues until the Denver convention in late August, the Democratic Party could suffer some damage as it tries to regroup for the November general election.

Obama 47%, Clinton 46%

Barack Obama and Hillary Clinton remain in a statistical tie in the preferences of national Democratic voters,

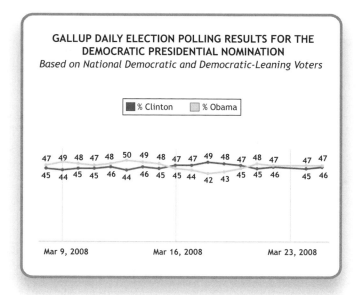

GALLUP DAILY ELECTION POLLING RESULTS FOR THE DEMOCRATIC PRESIDENTIAL NOMINATION

Based on National Democratic and Democratic-Leaning Voters

■ % Clinton   □ % Obama

47 49 48 47 48 50 49 48 47 47 49 48 47 48 47 47 47
45 44 45 45 46 44 46 45 45 44 42 43 45 45 46 45 46

Mar 9, 2008   Mar 16, 2008   Mar 23, 2008

with Obama at 47% support and Clinton at 46%. These results are based on interviews conducted on March 22 and on March 24 and 25, with no interviews conducted on Easter Sunday, March 23. After the political changes that occurred over the last two weeks spanning the Reverend Jeremiah Wright controversy, the Democratic race appears to have settled down, at least for the time being. Clinton's share of Democratic support has been either 45% or 46% over the last four Gallup Poll daily tracking reports, while Obama's share has been either 47% or 48%. Voters' preferences in two hypothetical November general election matchups are also very stable. In separate trial heats for president, John McCain has a two-percentage-point lead over both Obama and Clinton.

MARCH 27

Which Democratic Groups Are Most at Risk of Deserting?

Democrats are most at risk of losing the support of independents, conservative Democrats, and, among Hillary Clinton supporters, less well-educated Democrats if those voters' preferred candidate—whether Clinton or Barack Obama—does not win the party's nomination. Black Democrats appear loyal to the party regardless of who wins the nomination.

The finding that sizable percentages of Democrats say they would vote for Republican John McCain next November if the Democratic nominee is not their preferred candidate raises interesting questions about exactly whom the Democrats are most at risk of losing within the general election. To answer those questions, Gallup analyzed the basic relationship between Democratic candidate support and the current general election vote within various subgroups of the population.

CLINTON SUPPORTERS

There are clear differences by subgroup in self-reported intention to vote for McCain under an Obama-wins-the-nomination scenario. In other words, it appears that if Obama is on the ticket, some groups of Clinton-supporting Democrats are more likely to bolt the party and vote for the Republican nominee next fall than are others. The average "defection rate" of Clinton-supporting Democrats away from Obama and to McCain in the general election matchup is 28%. The two groups of Clinton-supporting Democrats who are significantly above this average are independents who lean Democratic and conservative Democrats.

The groups that are significantly below average in potential defection to McCain if Obama runs against him are blacks, liberal Democrats, those with postgraduate educations, and core Democrats (i.e., those who identify as Democrats when asked their party identification). Clinton-supporting Democrats with the most education are the least likely to say they would vote for McCain if he ran against Obama next fall. Those with less formal education are most likely to vote for McCain. There are only small differences by gender and no significant differences by age among Clinton supporters in voting for McCain if Obama is on the ticket.

VOTE FOR JOHN McCAIN IF THE GENERAL ELECTION CONTEST IS McCAIN vs. BARACK OBAMA

Based on Democrats Who Support Hillary Clinton for the Democratic Nomination

	% who say they will vote for John McCain
Independents/Lean Democratic	39
Conservative Democrats	38
High school education or less	30
Moderate Democrats	30
Men	30
Non-Hispanic whites	29
Hispanic whites	29
18–34 years old	28
35–54 years old	28
Some college education	27
55+ years old	27
Women	26
College graduate	25
Democratic identifiers	24
Postgraduate education	21
Liberal Democrats	18
Non-Hispanic blacks	15

Mar 7–22, 2008

OBAMA SUPPORTERS

The percentages of Democratic voters who support Obama for the nomination but who would vote for McCain if Clinton is the nominee are lower across most subgroups than is the case with respect to Clinton supporters in the event of a McCain-Obama race. This is a reflection of the basic finding that Obama supporters are less likely to abandon their preferred party and vote for McCain—even if their candidate does not get the Democratic nomination—than is the case for Clinton supporters in the reverse scenario. But there are differences across subgroups of Obama supporters in their intentions to vote for McCain. Obama supporters who would be most likely to support McCain in a McCain-Clinton race are independents who lean Democratic, conservative and moderate Democrats, and non-Hispanic whites. Those least likely to bolt the party and vote for McCain are blacks, liberal Democrats, and core Democrats. There are no significant age differences.

Across the board, the data show that Democratic voting in the general election is more at risk among some subgroups of voters than among others. In particular, independent voters who lean Democratic are more likely than any other subgroup tested to say they would vote for McCain if their candidate does not gain the nomination. Conservative Democrats appear to be less attached to the party than are liberal Democrats, and likewise more willing to say

they would vote for McCain if their candidate is not the nominee. Almost 4 out of 10 Clinton supporters in these two groups say they would vote for McCain if Obama is the nominee. The percentages are still high, but 10 to 15 points lower, for voters in these groups who support Obama when they are asked if they wold vote for McCain in a McCain-Clinton contest.

These findings are not necessarily surprising, but they underscore Democrats' vulnerability with voters who are positioned somewhere in the middle of the political or ideological spectrum. This may also reflect McCain's strong appeal to independent voters, who may not need much nudging to shift their vote from a Democratic candidate to McCain. Black Democratic voters, on the other hand, regardless of whom they support, seem prepared to remain quite loyal to the Democratic Party. Fifteen percent of blacks who support Clinton would vote for McCain if Obama is the nominee, and only 10% of blacks who support Obama would vote for McCain if Clinton is the nominee. In other words, there is little apparent risk of the Democrats' losing a substantial proportion of black voters regardless of who the nominee is.

This last finding is significant. Obama has the overwhelming support of black Democratic voters at this point, and there has been discussion of the backlash that could occur if Obama were to lose the nomination to Clinton. But these data suggest that Clinton could still expect to receive the vote of most black Obama supporters were she to win and face McCain in the fall. (The data do not address the issue of motivation or turnout, which could be lower among blacks if Obama is not the nominee; nor do the data address the implications of how Clinton might win the nomination. If Clinton were to win by the vote of superdelegates, for example, the backlash from black Obama supporters might be greater than if she were to win by gaining a higher percentage than Obama of the popular vote cast in primaries and caucuses.) The data show an inverse relationship between education and the potential defection of Clinton voters to McCain if Obama is the nominee. Thus, Obama's winning the Democratic nomination runs a risk of the Democratic Party's losing support in November from less well-educated Democrats who support Clinton.

There is no significant gender difference evident in the data. Both men and women tend to mirror the overall sample patterns in terms of projected vote for McCain, with only minor differences. This may be surprising to some who might expect that women who support Clinton (who would be the first female president in U.S. history if she is nominated and wins the election) would be less loyal to the party if their candidate did not win the nomination. But this does not seem to be the case at this time.

VOTE FOR JOHN McCAIN IF THE GENERAL ELECTION CONTEST IS McCAIN vs. HILLARY CLINTON

Based on Democrats Who Support Barack Obama for the Democratic Nomination

	% who say they wll vote for John McCain
Independents/Lean Democratic	29
Conservative Democrats	25
Moderate Democrats	25
Non-Hispanic whites	24
Hispanic whites	21
Men	21
College graduate	20
35–54 years old	20
High school education or less	19
Postgraduate education	19
18–34 years old	19
55+ years old	19
Some college education	18
Women	18
Democratic identifiers	15
Liberal Democrats	11
Non-Hispanic blacks	10

Mar 7–22, 2008

Although there are no significant differences in willingness to vote for McCain across age groups, a more detailed analysis suggests a greater hesitation to vote for the Democratic candidate as age increases if the voter's candidate is not the nominee. This occurs because the "undecided" vote goes up with age. Older Democrats are no more likely to vote for McCain if their candidate does not win than are those who are younger, as noted in the previous sections of this analysis. However, it appears that older voters *are* less likely to vote for the Democratic candidate if he or she is not the one they support. In other words, instead of declaring a vote for McCain in this situations, these older voters are more likely to be undecided. The basic difference between Clinton and Obama supporters is observed across all three age groups. In each instance, Clinton supporters are less likely to support Obama against McCain than are Obama supporters to support Clinton against McCain.

MARCH 30
Obama 52%, Clinton 42%

Barack Obama has extended his lead over Hillary Clinton among Democrats nationally to 52% to 42%, Obama's largest lead of the year so far and the third consecutive Gallup Poll daily tracking report in which he has held a statistically significant lead. These results are based on Gallup Poll daily tracking conducted between March 27 and March 29. (Obama did particularly well in interviewing conducted on March 29.) This marks the first time either candidate has held a double-digit lead over the other since Gallup's February 4–6 poll, at which point Clinton led Obama by 11 percentage points. According to tracking interviews from March 25–29, John McCain continues to hold a small four-point lead over Clinton among national registered voters. McCain leads Obama by three points, 47% to 44%.

APRIL 2008

The percentage of Americans who are satisfied with the way things are going in the United States is now at only 15%, according to the latest Gallup Poll. This marks the lowest reading on this measure since June 1992, and the third lowest that Gallup has recorded since 1979. Satisfaction with the way things are going has been falling each month in 2008, beginning with an already low 24% in January and dropping to 20% in February, 19% in March, and now this month's 15%. Just before George W. Bush took office as president in January 2001, 56% of Americans were satisfied with the way things were going in the United States. That percentage soared to a near-record high 70% in December 2001, a few months after the September 11 terrorist attacks and the aggressive U.S. response in Afghanistan. (The record-high satisfaction rating across the 29 years in which Gallup has been using this measure was 71%, which came in February 1999 as President Bill Clinton was acquitted by the U.S. Senate on impeachment charges.) The average satisfaction rating for all of 2001 was 55%. Satisfaction for each year since then has declined, culminating in a 28% average for 2007 and a 20% average satisfaction in the first four months of 2008.

Gallup began asking this satisfaction question in February 1979, and in July of that year recorded what still stands as the all-time low on this measure, 12%, in the midst of worries about the economy and skyrocketing gasoline prices. The second-lowest measure of 14% came in June 1992, in the final year of the George H. W. Bush administration and during another time of perceived economic recession.

One does not have to go much further than the daily newspaper headlines or the lead stories on cable news channels to discern likely causes for the extraordinarily low levels of satisfaction with the way things are going in the United States today. But Gallup's monthly measure of what Americans themselves perceive to be the most important problem facing the country provides precise figures that help explain why the public is so negative about the current state of affairs in the United States. There has been a steady rise in the percentage of Americans mentioning some aspect of the economy as the nation's top problem over the past six months, from 22% in October 2007 to 61% in this most recent April 2008 measure. About two-thirds of these mentions are simply "the economy," with an additional 9% naming the price of gasoline, 6% unemployment, and 4% the high cost of living and inflation. The second most commonly mentioned problem is Iraq, at 23%. The percentage mentioning Iraq as the nation's top problem has held fairly constant since November 2007, even as the percentage of Americans mentioning the economy has increased monthly. Other problems mentioned by 5% or more of Americans include healthcare, dissatisfaction with government, and immigration.

Gallup data—and a review of news headlines—suggest that the most important reason so many Americans are dissatisfied with the way things are going in the United

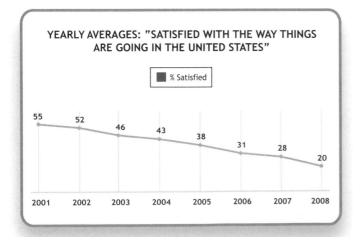

YEARLY AVERAGES: "SATISFIED WITH THE WAY THINGS ARE GOING IN THE UNITED STATES"

■ % Satisfied

2001	2002	2003	2004	2005	2006	2007	2008
55	52	46	43	38	31	28	20

CHRONOLOGY

APRIL 2008

April 6 Hillary Clinton's chief campaign strategist, Mark Penn, resigns.

April 8 Iran announces that it will expand its production of enriched uranium.

April 8 General David Petraeus tells Congress that progress in Iraq has been "significant" but is "fragile and reversible."

April 13 Hillary Clinton and Barack Obama discuss personal values and religion at a forum in Pennsylvania. The candidates appear separately and take questions from moderators and the audience.

April 15 Bombs in three Iraqi cities kill at least 60 people.

April 16 Clinton and Obama appear at their final debate, hosted by ABC News. Moderators Charles Gibson and George Stephanopoulus are criticized for the trivial nature of some of their questions.

April 19 Iraqi forces take control of Basra from the militia of Moktada al-Sadr.

April 22 Clinton wins the Pennsylvania primary.

April 27 Afghan President Hamid Karzai survives an assassination attempt by Taliban militants.

April 29 Housing prices continue to fall across the country, with the Standard & Poors/Case-Shiller Index showing an annual decline of 12.7%.

States is the economy. The number of Americans mentioning some aspect of the economy as the nation's top problem has almost tripled in the last six months, and the economy now far eclipses the war in Iraq as the American public's dominant perceived problem. Additionally, Gallup's tracking measures of the economy continue to show consumer confidence at or near all-time lows. Not surprisingly, the last two occasions when satisfaction levels were lower than the current 15% were also times when the U.S. economy was perceived to be the dominant problem facing the nation, in 1979 and 1992. The current low satisfaction level coincides with President Bush's lowest job approval rating of his administration. Low satisfaction levels in 1979 and 1992 were major factors in Jimmy Carter's and George H. W. Bush's respective failures to be re-elected to second terms as president. The current President Bush cannot run for re-election. It remains to be seen whether voters will take out their frustrations by electing a Democrat to the presidency, but if they are inclined to punish Bush's party, it could make John McCain's presidential bid an uphill challenge (though he currently is highly competitive with the Democratic candidates in presidential election trial heats). Democrats currently control both houses of Congress, but Gallup's generic ballot tests of congressional election voting preferences suggest that voters still favor Democratic control of Congress and thus may not hold congressional Democrats accountable for the current situation.

APRIL 2

Obama, Clinton Leverage Different Groups vs. McCain

Gallup Poll daily tracking results for the general election have shown that both Illinois senator Barack Obama and New York senator Hillary Clinton are essentially tied with Arizona senator John McCain among registered voters nationwide. At this point, then, there would appear not to be a major difference in the overall strength that either Democratic candidate would bring to bear in the general election against McCain. But an analysis of the voting patterns within different subgroups of the population shows that the way in which the two Democratic candidates arrive at that parity with McCain is quite different. A new Gallup

GENERAL ELECTION PREFERENCE
Among Registered Voters

	% Obama	% McCain
Liberal Democrats	85	8
Moderate Democrats	72	18
Conservative Democrats	61	28
Pure independents	29	42
Moderate/Liberal Republicans	18	75
Conservative Republicans	6	90

Mar 7–29, 2008

GENERAL ELECTION PREFERENCE
Among Registered Voters

	% Clinton	% McCain
Liberal Democrats	86	8
Moderate Democrats	77	16
Conservative Democrats	73	21
Pure independents	23	48
Moderate/Liberal Republicans	14	81
Conservative Republicans	4	92

Mar 7–29, 2008

analysis of 19,076 interviews conducted between March 7 and March 29 divides registered voters into a number of subgroups, based on partisan identification and ideology.

In a broad sense, the difference in voting patterns for the two Democratic candidates by partisan/ideological group follows a predictable pattern. The two candidates do best among liberal Democrats, and then progressively worse among moderate Democrats, conservative Democrats, "pure" independents (who do not lean toward one party or the other), and moderate/liberal Republicans. They do worst among conservative Republicans. The analysis can be continued with a more detailed examination of the electorate, separating voters into three groups based on race and ethnicity. Given the dominant percentage of non-Hispanic whites—relative to white Hispanics and non-Hispanic blacks—in the sample, our analysis breaks down the votes of non-Hispanic whites into partisan and ideological categories.

Here, Obama's margin over McCain among non-Hispanic black registered voters is 85 points, while Clinton's margin is 69 points. In other words, while both Democrats dominate McCain among black voters, Obama has a significantly larger margin over McCain than does Clinton. (It appears that black voters are both less likely to say they would vote for Clinton against McCain and more likely to say they don't have a preference between the two.) Clinton does slightly better than Obama against McCain among Hispanics. And there are different, and interesting, patterns in the relative performances of Clinton and Obama against McCain among whites across party and ideological groups. In general, Clinton does better against McCain among all three groups of white Democrats than does Obama; the difference between Obama and Clinton is largest among conservative white Democrats. In fact, among this group, Obama manages to get only 50% of the vote to McCain's 35%, while Clinton wins by a much larger 68% to 25% margin. Obama makes up for this, however, with a stronger relative performance among independents and Republicans. While McCain outpolls both Clinton and

Obama among "pure independents," Obama is somewhat more competitive with him among this group (trailing by 22 points, compared with 32 points for Clinton). McCain, of course, beats both candidates by significant margins among the two groups of Republicans identified in this analysis. But again, Clinton loses by slightly larger margins than does Obama.

At this point in the election cycle, there are more Democrats and Democratic-leaning independents than there are Republicans and Republican-leaning independents. McCain has been able to hold his own against the two Democratic candidates in general election trial heat ballots in the face of this disparity, mostly because he does very well among conservative Republicans and wins among independents.

The two Democratic candidates offer different profiles of strengths and weaknesses when pitted against the Republican McCain in the general election. Obama's strength is his appeal to black voters and his somewhat greater appeal than Clinton's among independents and Republicans. On the other hand, Clinton has a stronger appeal to white Democrats, particularly white conservative Democrats, only half of whom at this point say they would vote for Obama if he were the nominee pitted against McCain. Clinton has a slight advantage over Obama in the matchup with McCain among Hispanics.

When the votes of all registered voters are averaged, as noted previously, the two Democratic candidates end up performing about the same against McCain. Clinton appears better able to gain the support of the Democratic base, particularly conservative Democrats, while Obama builds his coalition with a stronger appeal to independents, Republicans, and black voters. Obama enjoys the traditionally high support from black Democrats that all recent Democratic nominees have received. However, Obama would have the challenge of shoring up his support among white Democrats if he were the nominee, while Clinton would need to expand her support among independents and "soft" Republicans (while at the same time motivating black voters). Looking ahead to the fall election, it is not clear at this point whether one of these profiles of support is better, from a strategic campaign perspective, than the other.

APRIL 3

Clinton Less Appealing than Obama as Potential Vice President

Only 42% of Democrats nationwide want Hillary Clinton to be the Democratic vice presidential nominee if Barack Obama wins the presidential nomination, while 55% think he should pick someone else. By contrast, the majority of Democrats—58%—would like to see Obama nominated as vice president if Clinton heads the ticket.

Thus, if the Democratic electorate has its way, Obama will be on the Democratic presidential ticket this fall, as either president or vice president. Clinton's chances of being on the ticket seem more likely to end if she loses the nomination—at least judging by Democrats' weak support for an Obama-Clinton unity ticket. The reason for the disparity is that a relatively small number of Obama supporters—just 29%—favor Obama's choosing Clinton as a possible running mate; 70% percent say they would rather he choose someone else. In contrast, a majority of Clinton supporters—53%—would want Clinton to choose Obama for vice president if she is nominated. Similar percentages—a majority of both Clinton supporters and Obama supporters—say they would want their own candidate selected for vice president should the other candidate win the Democratic nomination for president.

Former New York governor Mario Cuomo, among other Democratic Party elders, has recently argued that the only way for Democratic voters to come together in the fall will be for the two candidates to come together on a Democratic unity ticket. Gallup has reported that Obama supporters are more likely to remain loyal to the Democratic ticket in the fall than are Clinton supporters if their respective candidates are not nominated for president. However, according to the vice presidential preferences reported here, party loyalty and party unity are not one and the same. Most Obama supporters may be willing to bury the hatchet and vote for Clinton for president, but they don't seem eager to embrace Clinton as Obama's running mate for the sake of party unity.

APRIL 5
Obama 49%, Clinton 44%

Barack Obama continues to hold a five-percentage-point, 49% to 44%, advantage over Hillary Clinton in national Democratic voters' nomination preferences. Obama's current margin is based on Gallup Poll daily tracking interviews conducted between April 2 and April 4. The major election news on April 4 was the release of Hillary and Bill Clinton's tax returns for the past eight years, showing combined income of over $100 million during that time period (an average of $12.5 million per year). What impact, if any, this information will have on Democratic voters' preferences will become clearer in the days ahead.

Registered voters' preferences in the general election have shifted slightly, to the point where Obama now ties the presumptive Republican nominee, John McCain, at

45% support each, among national registered voters, while McCain edges out Clinton by a 47% to 45% margin. Both trial heats have shown close races since the tracking program began on March 7, with McCain usually holding slight leads. The current Obama-McCain 45% to 45% tie marks one of the few times when McCain's support has dropped to the point where his support is only equal to that of either Democratic candidate.

APRIL 8
Iraq War Attitudes Politically Polarized

Republicans reject the idea of a timetable for withdrawing U.S. troops from Iraq by a better than two-to-one margin, 65% to 32%. Democrats show an even greater margin in favor of a timetable: 81% in favor, 15% opposed. Political divisions on the war have long been evident in Gallup polling data on Iraq, and those divisions continue today. Three national elections since the war began—the 2004 and 2008 presidential elections and the 2006 midterm elections—have shone a bright spotlight on those differences. In general, Republicans tend to support the war and oppose plans to end it before the situation is stabilized, while Democrats oppose it and seek an end to U.S. involvement. This political divide on Iraq will be in clear public view on April 8, when General David Petraeus, commander of U.S. forces in Iraq, testifies before Congress. Among his questioners will be the three leading presidential candidates: Republican senator John McCain and Democratic senators Hillary Clinton and Barack Obama. The candidates' views on the war are in line with the rank and file of their parties.

OPINIONS ON THE WAR IN IRAQ, BY POLITICAL PARTY				
	All Americans	Democrats	Independents	Republicans
Does U.S. have obligation to establish security in Iraq?				
Yes, does	65%	54%	62%	83%
No, does not	32%	43%	34%	16%
Will Iraq be better off in long run than before war?				
Yes, better off	67%	58%	62%	84%
No, worse off	26%	35%	29%	11%
Did U.S. make a mistake in sending troops to Iraq?				
Yes, made a mistake	59%	82%	63%	24%
No, did not	39%	16%	34%	74%

Feb 21–24, 2008

In addition to the desirability or not of a troop with-drawal timetable, partisans have differing views on how successful the surge of U.S. troops in Iraq has been. Most Republicans, 70%, believe it is making the situation in Iraq better. In contrast, only 21% of Democrats say the surge is improving the situation, with nearly half (47%) saying it is not making much of a difference and 31% saying it is mak-ing matters worse. Independents are about evenly divided as to whether the surge is making the situation better (37%) or not making much of a difference (40%). And positions regarding a withdrawal timetable and the progress of the surge are just two examples of the wide political gaps in opinions about the war. The largest partisan difference is on whether the United States made a mistake in sending troops to Iraq: 82% of Democrats say it did, whereas just 24% of Republicans agree.

As a whole, Democrats are opposed to the war, and their attitudes differ little regardless of their political ideology. But Republicans of different ideological stripes differ on several matters relating to the war. For example, liberal or moderate Republicans are divided as to whether the United States should set a timetable for withdrawing from Iraq, while conservative Republicans overwhelmingly oppose a timetable. Moderate and liberal Republicans are also twice as likely as conservative Republicans (40% to 19%) to say the United States made a mistake in getting involved in Iraq, and they are somewhat less optimistic that the surge is making things better (52%) than are conservative Repub-licans (78%). On the Iraq issue, McCain is closely aligned with the conservative wing of the party—which is notable given that conservative leaders have criticized McCain's positions on several issues, including immigration, taxes, and campaign finance reform.

Implications for the (Post-election) Future

The 2008 presidential election will present voters with a clear choice on Iraq, with Republicans putting forth one of the Senate's fiercest supporters of the war and Democrats choosing one of two leading Senate opponents—includ-ing Obama, who has made his opposition to the war from the beginning a major focus of his campaign. If McCain is elected, U.S. policy on Iraq will likely continue as it has under the Bush administration, with slower troop drawdowns tied to progress in establishing security in Iraq. If either Obama or Clinton is elected, finding a quick end to the war will likely be the new president's top priority. In general, the public tends to side with the Democrats with respect to favoring a timetable, but relatively few advocate a quick withdrawal. And most seem sympathetic to the Republican argument that the United States needs to establish a certain level of security in Iraq before withdrawing its troops.

About One in Four Democrats Have Switched Candidates

Roughly one in four Democrats nationally say their prefer-ence as to whether Hillary Clinton or Barack Obama wins the Democratic presidential nomination has changed at least once since the start of the primary season in January 2008. Most of the switchers—19% of all Democrats and Democratic leaners—have moved out of Clinton's ranks and into Obama's, while 7% have taken the reverse path, moving from Obama to Clinton. According to a March 24–27 Gallup Poll, a third of Democrats and independents who lean Democratic say they have consistently preferred Obama for the nomination and another third say they have consistently preferred Clinton, while a total of 26% say they previously supported Clinton or Obama but now favor the other candidate. Switchers are found across the spectrum of Democratic voters but are more heavily concentrated among nonwhites than among whites (34% vs. 22%). Most of the switching among nonwhites has benefited Obama: Twenty-nine percent of those nonwhites now support him, compared with only 5% of the switchers currently support-ing Clinton.

National Democratic support for Clinton and Obama has shifted at various times in 2008, often in reaction to specific primary election results or to controversies beset-ting the candidates. In mid-January, the Gallup Poll daily tracking of Democratic preferences found Clinton lead-ing Obama by a 20-percentage-point margin, 48% to 28%. More recently, Obama has been in front, with his lead over Clinton reaching 10 points (52% to 42%) in late March.

APRIL 9

Obama Dominates Clinton Among College Graduates

National Democrats remain strongly divided by educa-tion with respect to their preference for their party's presi-dential nomination, with less well-educated Democrats supporting Hillary Clinton, while those with college and postgraduate educations are just as strongly skewed toward Barack Obama. Both major Democratic candidates are Ivy League–educated lawyers—Clinton with a law degree from Yale, Obama with a law degree from Harvard. Both have embraced populist rhetoric on the campaign trail, pushing for higher taxes on the rich and emphasizing government programs that would be designed to help the less fortu-nate. Yet the two candidates' support levels have been and remain significantly influenced by voter education levels. Among all Democratic voters interviewed in the first seven days of April as part of Gallup Poll daily tracking, Clinton leads by a 13-point margin among those who have a high school educations or less (53%–40%). Obama, on the other hand, leads among all other groups—that is, those with some college, college graduates, and postgraduates, including a 34-point margin among Democrats with postgraduate educations (64%–30%).

This general pattern is not new. In August 2007, for example, a review of Democratic voting data showed that, just as is the case today, Clinton led Obama by a large margin among all Democrats with high school educations or less, while the two were tied among those with postgraduate educations. (At that time, of course, there were other candidates in the race.)

White Democrats

Black Democrats strongly favor Obama regardless of their educational level. Among non-Hispanic white Democrats, on the other hand, the difference in support for the two candidates remains large, both among those with postgraduate educations and among those with high school educations or less. Among white Democrats with high school educations or less, Clinton beats Obama by roughly a two-to-one margin. She still wins, although by a much-reduced margin, among white Democrats with some college education. Among college graduates, Obama wins. And among white Democrats with postgraduate educations, Obama beats Clinton by almost a two-to-one margin—the mirror image of what is found among Democrats with high school educations or less.

This existing pattern is a continuation of trends in the data evident as long ago as last summer. It seems that from the moment he appeared on the national scene as a serious Democratic contender, Obama's appeal has been strongly skewed toward those with high levels of education, while Clinton has been the dominant favorite of those with less education. Educational attainment is correlated with age,

and it is known that Clinton does best among older voters. But Gallup analysis shows that the relationship between candidate support and education persists even among Democrats who are 50 years of age and older. One possible explanation for the substantial differences in support for the two candidates by education is that Democrats with less education have a greater objection to a black presidential candidate. A December 2007 Gallup Poll, however, showed only a slight difference by education in, at least, the stated acceptance of a black candidate for president. Ninety-seven percent of those with college degrees said they would vote for a "generally well-qualified person for president who happened to be black," compared with 91% of those with high school educations or less. This seeming lack of objection to a black candidate across the educational spectrum would not seem to support a theory that racism is the source of the educational differences.

Jeremiah Wright

One of the most significant issues in the Democratic campaign this year was the focus on the controversial sermons of Obama's former minister, the Reverend Jeremiah Wright of the Trinity United Church of Christ in Chicago. Even though overt objections to Obama's race do not appear to underlie the differences in support by education among white Democrats, it is possible that the focus on the Wright controversy affected the support for Obama among Democrats with lower levels of education, as some have suggested. In order to investigate that possibility, Gallup analyzed the voting patterns of white Democrats in its daily tracking data for the seven-day period March 9–15 (as the Wright controversy was unfolding) and the most recent seven-day period, April 1–7. The results show little change in the pattern of support among white Democrats with high school educations or less. This group supported Clinton over Obama by 33

PREFERENCE FOR DEMOCRATIC PARTY NOMINATION, BY EDUCATION
Among Non-Hispanic White Democrats and Democratic Leaners

	Hillary Clinton	Barack Obama	Clinton minus Obama
	%	%	%
All	52	39	13
High school education or less	62	29	33
Some college education	49	40	9
College graduate	44	51	–7
Postgraduate education	43	51	–8

Mar 9–15, 2008

PREFERENCE FOR DEMOCRATIC PARTY NOMINATION, BY EDUCATION
Among Non-Hispanic White Democrats and Democratic Leaners

	Hillary Clinton	Barack Obama	Clinton minus Obama
	%	%	%
All	50	43	7
High school education or less	61	31	30
Some college education	49	43	6
College graduate	40	52	–12
Postgraduate education	32	61	–29

Apr 1–7, 2008

points in the March 9–15 period and supports her by a 30-point margin now. This suggests that as race arguably became a bigger factor in the campaign, less-educated white Democrats were not affected. The biggest change, in fact, came about among those with postgraduate educations, who went from an 8-point margin for Obama in the March sample to a 29-point margin now. Thus, Obama's relative support level among those with high levels of educational attainment has actually increased over this period—and the data show little support for the hypothesis that less well-educated Democrats have swung to Clinton as a result of the Wright controversy.

Another explanation could be that Obama is less well-known than Clinton among those with lower education levels, and that Clinton does best among this group because of her higher relative name identification. But March Gallup Poll data show that both Obama and Clinton have near-universal name identification across all educational levels. The Gallup analysis from last August 2007 reviewed the fact that "new" candidates—such as Howard Dean in 2004, Bill Bradley in 2000, and Michael Dukakis in 1988—have traditionally excited more interest from highly educated Democrats. It could be that less well-educated voters are simply more comfortable with candidates who have been around for a long time (like Clinton in this year's race), while Democratic voters with higher education levels are more comfortable supporting someone who is new on the scene. All in all, the underlying reasons for the extraordinary differences in Democratic candidate support by education are not entirely clear at this point. The basic facts, however, are these: Clinton is the highly favored candidate among Democrats with lower levels of education, while Obama is highly favored among those with college and, especially, postgraduate educations.

APRIL 10
Obama 50%, Clinton 42%

Barack Obama continues to lead Hillary Clinton in national Democratic preferences for the Democratic presidential nomination, now by an 8-percentage-point margin of 50% to 42%. This is the fourth consecutive day of Gallup Poll daily tracking in which Obama has held a significant lead, ranging from 8 to 10 points, over his competitor. Obama has also led Clinton by at least 1 point in every three-day rolling average reported by Gallup since March 18–20. There has been little change in the highly competitive nature of the general election, based on Gallup Poll daily tracking of registered voters nationwide. Presumptive nominee John McCain is within 1 point of both Obama

and Clinton: It's currently Obama 46%, McCain 45%, and McCain 45%, Clinton 44%.

APRIL 11
Bush Job Approval Lowest of His Administration

President George W. Bush's job approval rating has dropped to 28%, the lowest of his administration. Bush's approval is lower than that of any president since World War II with the exceptions of Jimmy Carter (who had a low point of 28% in 1979) and Richard Nixon and Harry Truman, who suffered ratings in the low- to mid-20s range in the last years of their administrations.

Bush's lowest job approval rating had been 29%, reported in a July 2007 Gallup Poll. Since that time, Bush's approval ratings have been generally in the low-30s range, averaging 32.5% across the eight polls conducted this year before the most recent poll, which was conducted between April 6 and April 9. Bush's average for his first seven years in office was 52%, reflecting a slide from high ratings in his first two years (68% and 71%, respectively) to very low ratings (37% and 33%, respectively) in his sixth and seventh years and in the first months of 2008. Bush's highest job approval rating was 90%, recorded in September 2001 just after the September 11 terrorist attacks, and it is the highest job approval rating in Gallup Poll history.

Bush's low rating in the current poll is the result of an extraordinarily low average approval rating from Democrats, a low level of support from independents, and support from just two-thirds of his Republican base. When Bush received a 29% rating in Gallup's July 6–8, 2007, poll, the partisan approval ratings were similar to today's: 68% approval among Republicans, 21% among independents, and 7% among Democrats.

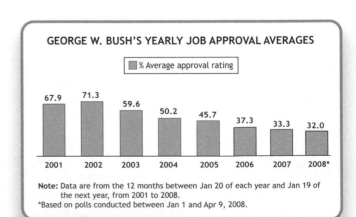

GEORGE W. BUSH'S YEARLY JOB APPROVAL AVERAGES

■ % Average approval rating

	2001	2002	2003	2004	2005	2006	2007	2008*
	67.9	71.3	59.6	50.2	45.7	37.3	33.3	32.0

Note: Data are from the 12 months between Jan 20 of each year and Jan 19 of the next year, from 2001 to 2008.
*Based on polls conducted between Jan 1 and Apr 9, 2008.

Historical Comparisons

Bush's current 28% job approval rating is at the very low end of the spectrum of approval ratings Gallup has recorded across the 11 presidents who have served since World War II. The average presidential job approval rating over that period has been 55%. The highest reading, as noted, was the 90% for the current President Bush in September 2001; the lowest was 22%, for Truman in February 1952. Only three presidents in Gallup Poll history have received job approval ratings of 28% or lower:

- Truman recorded a number of readings below 28% in 1951 and 1952 as his administration was beset—somewhat similarly to Bush today—with problems relating to the economy and an unpopular war (in Korea).
- Nixon had two readings of 24% in July and August 1974, the latter just prior to his leaving office as a result of the Watergate scandal.
- Carter's low point of 28% was measured in late June and early July 1979, as the country underwent significant gasoline shortages and amid perceptions of a failing economy.

Of note is that George W. Bush has now descended below the low point of his father, George H. W. Bush: The senior Bush had readings of 29% in July and August 1992. The former president also recorded a high point of 89% (just after the Persian Gulf War), the highest on record until his son's 90% in September 2001. Both Bushes, in short, have undergone radical 60-point drops in job approval in the course of their administrations.

Presidential Approval Ratings in Context

Presidents who receive job approval ratings in the 20s range are generally beset by economic concerns, wars, or scandals. Truman, who has the dubious distinction of having obtained the lowest job approval rating in Gallup Poll history, had the triple whammy of a bad economy, an unpopular war, and hints of scandal in the last years of his administration. Nixon, of course, was primarily laid low by Watergate, although he had been the steward of an unpopular war for most of the years after he took office in January 1969. Carter was in the middle of a bad economy and sharply rising gasoline prices when he suffered a 28% job approval rating in the summer of 1979. Now, George W. Bush, the current president, has obtained a 28% job approval rating at a time when Americans are extraordinarily worried about the economy, when gas prices have risen to historical high points, when the country is engaged in a war that the majority of Americans say was a mistake,

and at a time when only 15% of Americans say they are satisfied with the way things are going in the United States.

APRIL 15
Obama 51%, Clinton 40%

Barack Obama is maintaining his lead over Hillary Clinton among Democrats nationally in the latest Gallup Poll daily tracking, with a 51% to 40% margin in the April 12–14 average. The current 11-percentage-point lead is the largest for Obama this year, and marks the ninth consecutive day in which Obama has led Clinton by a statistically significant margin. The current Gallup Poll daily tracking average is based on interviewing conducted from April 12 to April 14, after the initial reports of Obama's controversial remarks about "bitter" small-town residents began to be reported in the news media. The two Democratic candidates will hold a nationally televised debate in Philadelphia on April 16, and it is possible that this confrontation—along with any delayed impact of Obama's controversial remarks—will affect Democratic voters' perceptions in the days to come. In general election trial-heat matchups, both Democratic candidates now have identical, slight 46% to 44% margins over presumptive Republican nominee John McCain.

APRIL 16
Obama Support Among "Bitter" Voters Unchanged

As Barack Obama and Hillary Clinton prepare for the April 16 debate in Philadelphia, Gallup's daily tracking indicates that Obama's support has yet to suffer following his widely reported remarks about small-town voters being "bitter." The remarks were first reported on April 11. Obama said in essence that small-town voters are bitter because the government has not been able to help their economic plight. As a result, they "cling" to religion and drift toward narrow issues such as gun rights and anti-trade or anti-immigration policies instead of attending to their larger economic interests.

Clinton has criticized Obama's comments on the campaign trail in recent days and is sure to remind Pennsylvania voters of those remarks in the forthcoming debate. Clinton and other Obama critics have characterized his remarks as being insensitive to less well-educated, lower-income, and religious voters. If his comments affect any voters, presumably it would be voters in these subgroups. But an in-depth analysis of Gallup Poll daily tracking data collected both before and after the controversy shows little or no change

In efforts to appeal to blue-collar voters, Senator Hillary Clinton downs a shot of whiskey at a bar in Crown Point, Indiana, while Senator Barack Obama rolls a gutter ball at a bowling alley in Altoona, Pennsylvania. *(Carolyn Kaster/AP Images; Alex Wong/Newscom)*

in support for Obama as the Democratic nominee among these types of Democratic voters.

The analysis is based on tracking data of Democratic voters' nomination preferences immediately before (April 8–10) and immediately after (April 12–14) Obama's remarks became a major campaign issue. Although Gallup's tracking data do not have a variable that identifies small-town residents per se, it can identify a number of groups that have suffered economically and are presumably the types of voters to whom Obama was referring.

INCOME

Democratic voters at the lower end of the economic spectrum have disproportionately backed Clinton for the nomination, but her standing among these voters has not changed since Obama's remarks. Obama's support among voters making $24,000 or less a year has shown a slight drop of three percentage points in recent days, but that is not statistically significant.

EDUCATION

Gallup has reported on the "education gap" in voting in the Democratic primary race, with Obama running strongly among those with a college degree or postgraduate education and Clinton doing better among those with less formal education. Obama's remarks may have offended voters who did not attend college, but if they did, it has not materially affected his support among this group, which has dropped just one point since the controversy began. Because Clinton's support among those with a high school education or less also dipped slightly, the relative positioning of the candidates among this group has not changed.

FINANCIAL WORRY

Education and income are essentially surrogates for lower socioeconomic status, and that may not necessarily indicate economic distress. The Gallup tracking poll can help address the issue directly because it asks voters if they worry about money. Though Clinton tends to appeal to voters with less education and income, Obama runs better among Democratic voters who say they are worried about money. That could be because blacks, who overwhelmingly support Obama, are more likely to worry about money. Obama led by 15 points among Democratic voters who said they were worried about money before his remarks were publicized, and has essentially the same lead (14 points) since then.

RELIGION

Obama hypothesized that many of the voters he was talking about "cling" to religion because of their frustration with their economic state. But there is no evidence that more religious Democratic voters have shifted their support away from Obama as a result of his statement. Prior to the controversy, 49% of Democrats who say religion is an important part of their lives supported Obama and 42% preferred Clinton—and Obama maintains a similar five-point lead among religious Democrats in the more recent data.

BLACK VERSUS WHITE DEMOCRATS

The above analysis looks at subgroups among the Democratic electorate as a whole. But since whites are more likely than blacks to live in small towns, Obama probably had white voters in mind when he made his remarks. Polling has established that Obama receives overwhelming support among blacks, so it is possible he has lost support among lower-educated white Democrats in recent days but offset those losses with gains among lower-educated black Democrats. But our analysis finds no evidence that whites have reacted to the controversy in a different way from blacks.

Implications

It certainly appears that, as of Gallup's April 14 interviewing, Obama's remarks have not hurt him—either among the Democratic electorate as a whole or among the Democratic constituencies Obama was referring to. The April 16 debate may shine a spotlight on those comments and make them known to a wider audience, so the possibility remains that Obama has not completely weathered the storm. Conceivably, Obama could be hurt more in a general election context, where voters with the characteristics he describes might already be inclined to vote Republican, and such remarks could nudge them more in that direction. But Gallup's general election tracking data, as with our data regarding the Democratic nomination contest, have so far shown no deterioration in Obama's standing versus presumptive Republican nominee John McCain.

APRIL 17

Obama 49%, Clinton 42%

The latest Gallup Poll daily tracking update shows Barack Obama with a 49% to 42% lead over Hillary Clinton in national Democratic voters' nomination preferences. This 7-percentage-point margin, though down slightly from Obama's high-water mark of an 11-point lead in Gallup's April 12–14 average, represents the eleventh consecutive day on which Obama has held a statistically significant lead over Clinton. The current average is based on interviewing conducted between April 14 and April 16. The two Democratic candidates held their final debate before the April 22 Pennsylvania primary on April 16 in Philadelphia, and any impact of the debate—and of the media spin that will inevitably follow—will begin to be reflected in the tracking averages over the next several days. There is little change in the results of Gallup's tracking of the general election. Forty-six percent of registered voters say they would vote for Obama if he were matched against John McCain and the election were held today, while 44% would choose McCain. The Clinton-McCain trial heat has Clinton at 46% and McCain at 45%.

APRIL 19

Clinton 46%, Obama 45%

Gallup Poll daily tracking shows that Hillary Clinton now receives 46% of the support of Democrats nationally com-

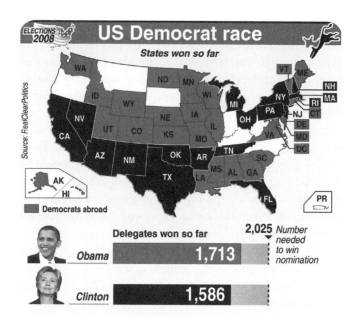

The Democratic presidential race remained close throughout the spring. This election map shows Senator Barack Obama with a slight lead in delegates over Senator Hillary Clinton on April 21, 2008, a day before the Pennsylvania primary. *(RealClear Politics/Newscom)*

pared with 45% for Barack Obama, marking the first time Obama has not led in Gallup's daily tracking since March 18–20. These results are based on interviewing conducted between April 16 and April 18, including two days of interviewing after the contentious April 16 debate in Philadelphia and the media focus that followed. Support for Clinton has been significantly higher in both of these post-debate nights of interviewing than in recent weeks. The two Democratic candidates are now engaged in intensive campaigning leading up to the April 22 Pennsylvania primary and are under a continual and hot media spotlight, increasing the chances for change in the views of Democrats in the days ahead. There has been no change in the general election trial heats, with Obama's margin over Republican John McCain at 45% to 44% among registered voters nationally, and Clinton's margin at 46% to 44%.

APRIL 22

Democrats Split on Whether Campaign Is Hurting the Party

Democrats are split right down the middle on whether the protracted campaign for the Democratic nomination is hurting the Democratic Party: 48% say it is hurting the party and 48% say it is not. The reason for these split sentiments on the impact of the campaign is clear when the views of Obama supporters and Clinton supporters are separated from one another. A majority of Obama supporters say the campaign is hurting the party and that party leaders should get together to back one of the candidates. A majority of Clinton supporters, on the other hand, say the continuing campaign is not hurting the party and should continue. Since Obama leads in terms of earned delegates, popular vote, and national polling at the moment, it is perhaps not surprising that his supporters would be happy to see the race come to a close, presumably under the assumption that he would be declared the winner. Clinton supporters, it can be assumed, prefer the idea of continuing the campaign in the hope that Obama will stumble, leaving an opening or rationale for superdelegates to support Clinton.

Democrats were also asked if the campaign for their party's nomination is too negative, with evenly divided results: Forty-seven percent of Democrats say it is, while 49% say it is not. But there are again big differences among Democrats based on candidate preference. Obama supporters by a three-to-two margin agree that the campaign is too negative, while Clinton supporters just as strongly believe it is not. Many observers have commented that *both* campaigns have been negative in the days leading up to the April 22 Pennsylvania primary. But Obama supporters who say things are too negative believe Clinton is mostly to blame. Clinton supporters who say things are too negative, on the other hand, blame both campaigns.

Implications for the Nomination Process

All in all, Democrats are divided on the impact of the continuing and protracted campaign for the Democratic nomination. The reasons for this division are clear. Clinton supporters, apparently realizing that their candidate's best hope of winning is to continue to campaign and hope something happens that breaks in her favor, are fine with a continuing campaign, are not worried about its negativity, and do not think it is bad for the party. Given the fact that Obama is ahead in the race for the nomination at the moment, it is not surprising that his supporters would like to have the race wrapped up and believe that its protracted length is hurting the party overall. As a result, it would appear difficult at this time for Democrats nationally to come to a consensus on ending the Democratic race. As long as Clinton can maintain a substantial base of support, her supporters will likely advocate continuing the race, in order to keep open the possibility that she can win the nomination.

Only 26% Say Obama Looks Down on Americans

Most Americans reject the suggestion that any of the leading presidential candidates look down on the average American—though more say it applies to Hillary Clinton (32%) than to Barack Obama (26%) or John McCain (22%). Nearly identical results are produced when the question asks specifically about "working-class" Americans rather than "average" Americans.

The campaign flap over how the candidates perceive average Americans stems from Obama's recent comments about the psychology of working-class, small-town voters in Pennsylvania, saying: "And it's not surprising [that] they get bitter, they cling to guns or religion or antipathy to people who aren't like them or anti-immigrant sentiment or anti-trade sentiment as a way to explain their frustrations." Senators Clinton and McCain have both labeled these comments "elitist," and Clinton, in particular, has tried to capitalize on them leading up to the crucial April 22 Pennsylvania primary election. But as noted, according to the new USA Today/Gallup Poll, conducted between April 18 and April 20, only 26% of Americans believe Obama "looks down on the average American"—a smaller percentage than say this of Clinton—while 69% think he "respects" the average American.

Gallup finds no difference in perceptions of Obama's outlook between high- and low-income Americans. There are also virtually no differences among Democrats in the percentages saying Obama or Clinton look down on average Americans—15% and 18%, respectively. The "elitism" charge could play a bigger role in the national election—where it could work against the Democrats—as roughly half of Republicans perceive that both Clinton and Obama look down on average Americans. Less than a third of Democrats say this about McCain.

Bush's 69% Job Disapproval Rating Highest in Gallup History

President George W. Bush's disapproval rating is at 69%—which is not only the highest of the Bush administration, but the highest disapproval rating in Gallup Poll history. President Bush's approval rating now is at 28%, which ties for the lowest of his administration but is not the lowest in Gallup Poll history: Harry Truman received a 22% approval rating in 1952, and Richard Nixon had two 24% job approval scores in 1974. In other words, although Bush's disapproval rating is the highest in Gallup history, his approval rating is not the lowest. This seeming anomaly is mostly because of differences over the years in the percentage of respondents who say "Don't know" or offer no opinion when asked to rate a president. Thus, Truman's 22% approval rating was accompanied by a 64% disapproval rating, leaving 14% of those interviewed who did not offer an opinion about his job performance. Nixon's two 24% job approval ratings in 1974 were paired with 63% and 66% disapproval ratings,

HIGHEST FIVE DISAPPROVAL RATINGS IN GALLUP HISTORY

	Dates of Gallup Poll	Disapproval rating
George W. Bush	Apr 18–20, 2008	69%
Harry Truman	Jan 6–11, 1952	67%
George W. Bush	Apr 6–9, 2008	67%
Richard Nixon	Aug 2–5, 1974	66%
George W. Bush	Jul 6–8, 2007	66%

leaving 13% and 10% with no opinion. But in the most recent poll, Bush's approval rating is 28% while his disapproval rating is 69%, leaving only 3.5% (rounded to 4%) who don't have an opinion.

There is no single explanation for why the percentage who decline to give an opinion of the president's job performance is lower now than in the past. However, it is possible that when Gallup polled in the Truman and Nixon years, respondents may have been more likely to say they didn't have an opinion in lieu of saying they disapproved of the president. In other words, respondents who did not approve of the president's performance, rather than flat-out saying they disapproved, may have simply told interviewers they didn't have an opinion. Today, Americans appear to be more willing to give a negative response, resulting in the situation in which Bush's disapproval rating is at a record high while his approval rating is not at a record low.

Interviewing in the Truman and Nixon years was conducted in respondents' homes rather than by telephone, which may be related to differences in the percentages of respondents who gave "No opinion" answers to the job approval question. But an interesting contrast is provided by polling conducted in the administration of the current president's father, George H. W. Bush, who in one poll in 1992 had a 29% approval rating, only one point higher than his son's current approval rating. In that 1992 poll, the senior Bush had only a 60% disapproval rating, leaving 11% with no opinion, similar to the "No opinion" percentages in the Truman and Nixon polls. Yet the 1992 poll was conducted by telephone in similar fashion to polling today, suggesting that the mode of interviewing per se is perhaps not the sole explanation for the "No opinion" differences

BUSH, NIXON, AND TRUMAN JOB PERFORMANCE RATINGS

President	Dates of Gallup Poll	Approve	Disapprove	No opinion
George W. Bush	Apr 18–20, 2008	28%	69%	4%
Richard Nixon	Jul 12–15, 1974	24%	63%	13%
Richard Nixon	Aug 2–5, 1974	24%	66%	10%
Harry Truman	Feb 9–14, 1952	22%	64%	14%

over the years. It may well be that the current president Bush is simply a more polarizing figure, one who generates strong opinions in a negative direction and therefore fewer ambivalent, "No opinion" responses than was the case for George H. W. Bush, Truman, or Nixon at the nadirs of their administrations. The bottom line remains that—perhaps for several reasons—the 69% disapproval rating generated by the current president is the highest such rating recorded over the years in which Gallup has been measuring the public's approval and disapproval of each president's job performance.

APRIL 23
The Day After the Pennsylvania Primary

Hillary Clinton's 54.7% to 45.3% win over Barack Obama in the April 22 Pennsylvania primary, while not necessarily surprising, suggest three key points of interest from a national polling perspective as the campaign moves forward.

CLINTON'S COALITION

Initial analysis of the Edison-Mitofsky exit poll from the Pennsylvania primary shows that Clinton won by doing well among women (who constituted almost 6 out of 10 voters, according to the exit poll), older voters, whites, Catholics, lower-income voters, and voters with less education. These are the same basic patterns that occur in Gallup's analysis of Democratic candidate support nationally.

It appears that the coalitions of the two candidates are fairly well established at this point. To a significant degree, Clinton was able to win in Pennsylvania because of the state's demographic composition, and the existence of these same patterns of support nationally suggests that her chances of victory over Obama will be related more to the types of voters who live in each remaining primary state rather than to the nature or effectiveness of future campaigning.

ELECTABILITY

Much of Clinton's current campaign positioning is based on her claim that she is more electable against John McCain next November. Analysis of Gallup data, however, does not find empirical justification for this claim at this point. In head-to-head matchups against presumptive Republican nominee McCain, Clinton and Obama perform almost exactly the same. In Gallup's latest tracking of the general election, based on interviewing conducted between April 18 and April 22, McCain has a one-point lead over both Clinton and Obama. In the April 18–20 USA Today/Gallup Poll, both Clinton and Obama were slightly—but almost identically—ahead of McCain among likely voters. In neither instance is there any meaningful difference in how the two candidates stack up against McCain. Clinton has argued that her wins in states like Pennsylvania and Ohio underscore her ability to win possible swing states in the general election next November. But a recent Gallup analysis of the vote patterns in states that were competitive in the 2004 election shows that Obama and Clinton perform exactly the same when paired against McCain in those states—again giving no indication that either of the two Democratic candidates at this point is more "electable" than the other. Furthermore, in that analysis, Obama did slightly better than Clinton versus McCain in both reliably Democratic and reliably Republican states.

Implications of the Pennsylvania Results

Clinton had long been the leader in Pennsylvania polls, and her win on April 22 was not unexpected. It did solidify her determination to continue to pursue the Democratic nomination—something that Gallup data show is certainly pleasing to her supporters while just as equally displeasing to Obama supporters. The lasting negative impact, if any, of the long campaign is yet to be determined, but Gallup analysis continues to show that a sizable minority of both Clinton and Obama supporters say they would vote for McCain if their nominee does not win, suggesting some possible negative fallout. When asked specifically about the impact of the long and divisive campaign, Clinton supporters are unworried, while Obama supporters wish the campaigning were over and say it is hurting the party.

The demographic coalitions of support put together by the two candidates appear firmly in place by this point in the campaign, and it's likely that the winners in the states to come will be determined more by the composition of the population in those states than by the effectiveness of the candidates' campaigning. At the same time, Clinton's argument that she is more electable in the fall does not appear at this juncture to have support in national data; both she and Obama fare equally well when pitted in polling against McCain.

APRIL 24
Democratic Gap Narrows, Obama Stays Ahead

The Gallup Poll daily tracking update based on April 21–23 interviewing shows Barack Obama holding a narrower advantage over Hillary Clinton than he has had in recent days, 49% to 44%, in nationwide Democratic nomination preferences. These are the first results to include any interviewing following Clinton's impressive victory in the Pennsylvania primary on April 22. Though the gap between the two has narrowed—down to 5 percentage points from 10- and 8-point Obama leads on the prior two days—Obama remains ahead. Notably, he outpolled Clinton slightly in interviewing on the night of April 23, the first night of post–Pennsylvania primary data collection. The full impact of the Pennsylvania results will be apparent in the coming days. Though the initial indications are that it has helped Clinton, so far her win has not dramatically altered the dynamics of the race at the national level.

The candidates have turned their attention to the May 6 primaries in Indiana and North Carolina, with Indiana perhaps becoming Clinton's latest "last stand" contest. Clinton was able to keep her campaign alive by winning previous "last stand" contests in New Hampshire, Ohio, and Texas, and now Pennsylvania. Both Democrats are running exactly even with John McCain in Gallup's presidential trial heats among registered voters, with the McCain-Obama contest at 45% to 45% and the McCain-Clinton matchup at 46% to 46%.

Opposition to Iraq War Reaches New High

The most recent USA Today/Gallup Poll finds 63% of Americans saying the United States made a mistake in sending troops to Iraq, a new high mark, by one percentage point, in yes answers to that question.

The new high in Iraq War opposition is also notable because it is the highest "mistake" percentage Gallup has ever measured for an active war involving the United States—surpassing by two points the 61% who said in May 1971 that the Vietnam War was a mistake. At that time, however, Gallup found greater uncertainty (11% with no opinion) and lower outright support for the Vietnam War (28% said it was *not* a mistake) than it found with respect to the Iraq War today (36% saying it was not a mistake), so it is not clear-cut which war has been less popular with the American public. When Gallup has asked about Vietnam retrospectively over the years since that war ended, as many as 74% of Americans (in 1990) said it was a mistake. In February and March 1952, a majority of Americans also said the United States had made a mistake in sending troops to Korea, the only other U.S. intervention since 1950 that has registered majority opposition. In summer 2007, by way of comparison, just 25% said the United States had made a mistake in sending troops to Afghanistan. Opposition to the first Persian Gulf War reached only as high as 30%, in January 1991 (before actual fighting began; after fighting commenced, the high was just 21%).

By now, public opposition to the Iraq War is pretty well established. Gallup has found at least half of Americans

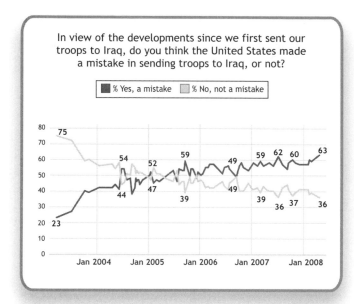

In view of the developments since we first sent our troops to Iraq, do you think the United States made a mistake in sending troops to Iraq, or not?

■ % Yes, a mistake   ☐ % No, not a mistake

Do you feel that the distribution of money and wealth in this country today is fair, or do you feel that the money and wealth in this country should be more evenly distributed among a larger percentage of the people?

Based on Annual Income

	Distribution is fair	Should be more evenly distributed
	%	%
Less than $30,000	19	78
$30,000 to $74,999	26	70
$75,000 +	35	63

Apr 6–9, 2008

calling the war a mistake in all but one survey since December 2005. The average percentage saying the war is a mistake has increased every year of the conflict—and is nearly twice as high thus far in 2008 (the sixth year of the conflict) as it was in its initial year.

Implications for the Iraq War

Even though majority opposition to the Iraq War is well established, other Gallup polling has found that the public does not necessarily advocate a quick end to the war. While a majority now favor a timetable for withdrawing troops, only about one in five Americans think the withdrawal should begin immediately and be completed as soon as possible. The public will implicitly choose one path on Iraq this fall, given the choice between Republican presidential candidate John McCain (who supports the war and argues that the consequences of withdrawal would be severe) and either of the two Democratic presidential candidates, Hillary Clinton or Barack Obama, both of whom oppose the war and want to end it as quickly as they deem prudent.

APRIL 25

Many Americans Okay with Increasing Taxes on Rich

Slightly over half of Americans believe the government should redistribute wealth by means of heavy taxes on the rich. The percentage holding this view (51%, vs. 43% opposed) is similar to that found in Gallup polling last year, is up from 1998, and in particular is higher than was

found in a Roper poll conducted for *Fortune* magazine back in 1939. Although the methods and sampling techniques of polling done in the 1930s may differ significantly from those of today, the rough comparison suggests that Americans appear to have become even more "redistributionist" in their views than they were at the tail end of the Great Depression.

Other recent Gallup Poll questions underscore the finding that Americans are generally open to the idea of some type of effort to distribute wealth more evenly. Asked if the distribution of money and wealth in this country is fair or if money and wealth need to be distributed more evenly, about two-thirds of Americans agree with the latter response. This is up slightly from last year and, by two points, is the highest "more evenly distributed" response to this question that Gallup has found over the eight times it has been asked since 1984. The results of another question Gallup asks each April find 63% of Americans saying that upper-income Americans pay "too little" in taxes (although this percentage is down slightly from previous polling). One reason it may be easy for Americans to readily agree with wealth redistribution and increased taxes on the rich is that most Americans do not perceive themselves to be rich and therefore presumably assume they have nothing

Do you think our government should or should not redistribute wealth by heavy taxes on the rich?

Based on Annual Income

	Yes, should redistribute	No, should not redistribute
	%	%
Less than $30,000	56	38
$30,000 to $74,999	54	41
$75,000 +	46	52

Apr 6–9, 2008

to fear—financially—from such new policies. Analysis of the responses to these two questions by income shows that there are some differences by respondents' income, but these differences are not large. One issue here is that the top income category Gallup uses is $75,000 and higher, representing a little more than a quarter of the population. Clearly, results might have been different had it been possible to isolate a sample of those making, for example, $200,000 a year or more.

The possibility of some type of political policy that would institute higher tax rates on high-income households was discussed in the April 16 Philadelphia debate between the two Democratic contenders, and both Hillary Clinton and Barack Obama appeared to agree with some variant of this type of policy (although both are multimillionaires, according to their recently released tax statements). The public opinion data reviewed here suggest that a majority of Americans would be receptive to such a policy.

APRIL 27
Clinton and Obama Remain Tied at 47%

Gallup Poll daily tracking finds that national Democratic voters' preferences for their party's nomination remain evenly split, with Barack Obama and Hillary Clinton each receiving 47% support. These results, based on April 24–26 polling, are the second such in which all interviews have been conducted after Clinton's April 22 Pennsylvania primary win, and suggest that Democratic voters are, for the moment at least, divided right down the middle as to which candidate they most want to represent their party in November's general election. Obama led the race for a number of days prior to Pennsylvania; Clinton has now

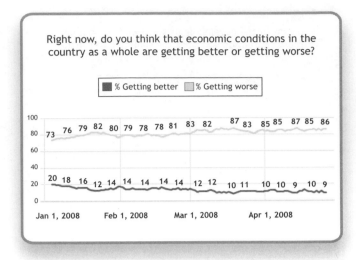

Right now, do you think that economic conditions in the country as a whole are getting better or getting worse?

■ % Getting better ☐ % Getting worse

erased his lead, but so far has not been able to translate her primary win—and the subsequent media coverage of her "Never say die" campaigning—into a lead of her own. The close nature of the race at this point gives even more importance to the outcome of the North Carolina and Indiana primaries on May 6. Meanwhile, Clinton maintains her slight 47% to 44% advantage over John McCain in general election preferences among national registered voters in the latest, April 24–26, results. Obama and McCain are tied at 45% each.

Americans Deeply Pessimistic About Economy

Eighty-six percent of Americans say the U.S. economy is getting worse, while 44% rate the current economy as "poor" and only 15% rate it as "excellent" or "good." These consumer sentiments represent a continuation of the strongly negative views of the economy measured by Gallup Poll daily tracking over the last two months.

APRIL 28
McCain Widely Recognized as a "War Hero"

The 5½ years John McCain spent as a prisoner of war in Vietnam, enduring solitary confinement and torture and at one point refusing to be sent home ahead of other POWs, have earned him the mantle of "war hero" in the eyes of 66% of Americans. This is according to a USA Today/Gallup Poll of the nation's adults, conducted between April 18 and April 20. In contrast to the situation regarding the previous Vietnam War veteran to seek the presidency—Democratic senator John Kerry in 2004—there is bipartisan public agreement that McCain deserves this acclaim. Whereas nearly 6 in 10 Democrats (58%) currently say McCain is a war hero, in September

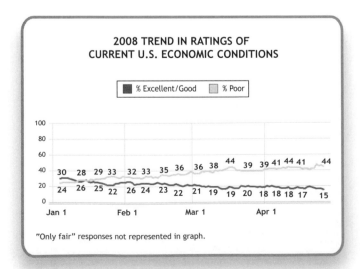

2008 TREND IN RATINGS OF CURRENT U.S. ECONOMIC CONDITIONS

■ % Excellent/Good ☐ % Poor

"Only fair" responses not represented in graph.

2004 only 29% of Republicans called Kerry a hero. There is also more universal agreement among Republicans today about McCain's war service than there was among Democrats four years ago about Kerry's. (As a result, fewer than half of Americans overall in 2004—48%—considered Kerry a war hero.)

Indeed, McCain's broad-based reputation as a war hero may be a factor in his current success in going toe-to-toe with his likely Democratic opponents in Gallup Poll daily trial heats for the fall election. McCain's relatively strong showing comes at a time when his Republican Party is facing its worst image crisis in a decade, with Americans' ratings of the party near the lowest seen in the past decade; President George W. Bush's approval ratings are at near-record lows for any president in over half a century; and the administration is fighting an unpopular war in Iraq that McCain supports. When asked specifically how McCain's military service affects their vote for president, a fairly substantial 38% of Americans say it makes them more likely to vote for him, including 15% who say his service is a "major factor" in their decision. About a quarter of Republicans say it is a major factor, as do 14% of independents and 10% of Democrats. If sustained, this could be a critical advantage for McCain in attracting swing voters in a close election.

McCain: Basic Favorability

Another significant factor explaining why McCain is competitive with the Democrats for president at the moment is, no doubt, his general popularity as a public figure. Sixty percent of Americans have a favorable view of him; only 33% hold an unfavorable view. This immediately distinguishes McCain from President Bush, who is currently viewed much more unfavorably (66%) than favorably (32%). Not only is McCain's favorable rating from Americans nearly twice as high as Bush's, but a majority of independents (62%) as well as more than a third of Democrats (36%) view him positively. McCain's favorability is critical for his candidacy because both of his Democratic opponents are also well liked by Americans. McCain and Obama are tied in favorability—each with a 60% favorable rating, including relatively high ratings from independents and members of the opposing party. Clinton has lower appeal among independents (only 48% have a favorable view of her) but is still viewed favorably by 53% of all Americans.

A Maverick?

In addition to his military experience, another explanation for McCain's popularity may be his well-established reputation inside the nation's capital as a political maverick—as someone who has bucked the Republican Party on such issues as the 2001 Bush tax cuts and regulation of the tobacco industry, and as one who has forged alliances with Democrats on climate change legislation, judicial nominations, and campaign finance reform. However, it is not clear how much this aspect of his career is helping to differentiate him from the troubled Republican Party. In answer to a question designed to determine whether the public perceives McCain to be a maverick, only 45% of Americans say he is "a different kind of Republican." Slightly more, 48%, say he is "basically the same as most other Republicans." Sixty percent of Republicans consider McCain a different kind of Republican, compared with just under half of independents (46%) and only a third of Democrats (34%). Thus, in contrast to the bipartisan view that McCain is a war hero, his maverick image is more a matter of political debate.

On paper, 2008 is a formidable year for a Republican to be seeking the presidency. Yet, since January, McCain has been roughly tied with both Clinton and Obama in trial heats for the fall election. Two prominent theories as to why McCain has been able to rise above his party's image problems are his having established himself as a political maverick who can work with Democrats, and his heroism in Vietnam. According to the new poll, it appears that the latter may be the more influential of the two factors. While his war image may not directly translate into votes for his candidacy, it may help explain why the same Gallup Poll finds two-thirds of Americans calling McCain "honest and trustworthy," and about half saying he is someone who "cares about the needs of people like you" and "is someone you would be proud to have as president." All of those perceptions are likely to contribute to McCain's overall favorability with the American public—and that, in turn, makes him a competitive candidate.

APRIL 29

Education Clearly Divides Preferences of White Democrats

Hillary Clinton leads Barack Obama by 21 points among non-Hispanic white Democratic voters who don't have a college degree (56% to 35%), while Obama leads Clinton by a 19-point margin among white Democratic voters who do have a college degree (56% to 37%). This difference in support by education is evident across all age groups, although it is somewhat stronger among middle-aged white Democrats. Among this subgroup, we find that Clinton's lead among those without a college degree swells to 27 points, while Obama leads among those with

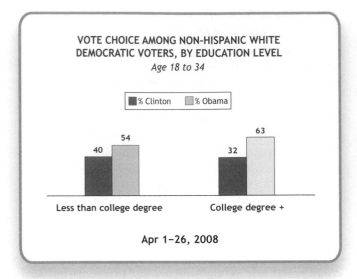

VOTE CHOICE AMONG NON-HISPANIC WHITE
DEMOCRATIC VOTERS, BY EDUCATION LEVEL
Age 18 to 34

Apr 1–26, 2008

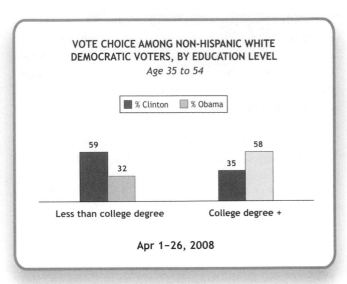

VOTE CHOICE AMONG NON-HISPANIC WHITE
DEMOCRATIC VOTERS, BY EDUCATION LEVEL
Age 35 to 54

Apr 1–26, 2008

a college degree by an almost as large 23 points. In short, the candidate preference of these 35- to 54-year-old white Democratic voters essentially flips based on the single variable of education.

Much has been made in recent weeks of Obama's failure to connect with blue-collar or working-class white Democrats, in part because of his much-publicized comments about the bitterness of small-town Democrats in Pennsylvania. But an analysis of the pattern of support for the two candidates among the 35- to 54-year-old age group by employment status shows that the strong impact of education persists regardless of whether or not the individual is employed. Thus, it may be a mistake to assume that being a worker per se is involved in the equation when Obama's appeal is analyzed. In fact, education is a predictor of candidate support—among these middle-aged white voters—regardless of employ-

ment status. The strength of support for Clinton is not as dramatic among whites under age 35 without a degree as it is among whites 35 to 54. And Obama's youth appeal is evident regardless of education in this younger voter category. Still, slight differences remain between these younger voters with no college degree and those who do have a college degree. (Among younger white voters who are employed, the impact of education is even less.) Among white voters 55 and older (the majority of whom are not employed), Clinton wins by an overwhelming 31-point margin among those with less than a college degree, while Obama holds a seven-point margin among those with a college degree.

In the overall sample of 7,999 non-Hispanic white Democratic voters Gallup interviewed between April 1 and April 26, Clinton beats Obama by a 49% to 42% margin. As seen above, Clinton gains this winning mar-

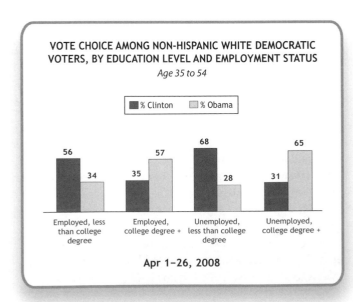

VOTE CHOICE AMONG NON-HISPANIC WHITE DEMOCRATIC
VOTERS, BY EDUCATION LEVEL AND EMPLOYMENT STATUS
Age 35 to 54

Apr 1–26, 2008

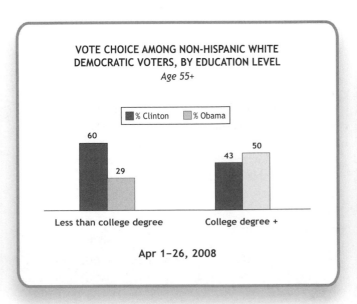

VOTE CHOICE AMONG NON-HISPANIC WHITE
DEMOCRATIC VOTERS, BY EDUCATION LEVEL
Age 55+

Apr 1–26, 2008

gin in part because of her very high percentage of support among those with lower education levels. Obama's support among the well educated is not strong enough to counteract Clinton's strength among the less well educated. These relationships are particularly strong among white middle-aged Democrats between 35 and 54. Although there has been a lot of discussion about Clinton's and Obama's differential appeal to blue-collar workers or members of the "working class," this analysis suggests that for middle-aged voters, education is a powerful predictor of preference regardless of working status. The relationship persists among those 55 and older, the majority of whom do not work. Whether Obama is able to change this pattern by convincing working-class white voters that he deserves their support remains to be seen. Furthermore, the current analysis is based on national Democratic voters, whereas patterns of support can vary on a state-by-state basis.

One in Five Americans Expect Gasoline to Hit $5 per Gallon

While 9 in 10 Americans expect gasoline prices at the pump to hit $4 a gallon in their local area this summer, one in five expect gasoline to hit $5 a gallon, and 1 in 20 expect gasoline prices to reach $6 a gallon. On April 28, in the nation's capital, American truckers protested high fuel prices. But the squeeze people find themselves in at the moment is not limited to those who drive big rigs. Nearly three in four Americans say today's record gasoline prices are creating a hardship for them personally (20%) or have caused them to adjust their usual spending and saving habits in significant ways (52%).

When asked in an open-ended format which one or two issues should be the top priorities for the president and Congress to deal with at this time, 22% of Americans say gasoline and energy prices. That is twice the level of a month ago and is well above mentions of any other specific economic issue, including healthcare (at 16%). (The top overall issue mentioned is the economy in general, at 48%.) While in reality most government efforts to deal with rising gasoline prices may do more harm than good, doing nothing as gasoline prices significantly disrupt the living standards of most Americans is likely to be politically unacceptable, particularly in an election year.

APRIL 30
Candidate Perceptions in Depth

Over the course of the presidential campaign, Americans have become increasingly likely to view John McCain as too old and Hillary Clinton as dishonest. Barack Obama is much better known today than before the campaign began, but the dominant perceptions of him (as being young and inexperienced, but also as a fresh face with new ideas) have changed little. These findings are based on results from the latest Gallup survey, which asked respondents to describe in their own words "what comes to mind" when they think of the three leading presidential candidates. The question had been previously asked in late November 2006, before the candidates officially announced their intentions to run for president. The current data show that the most commonly mentioned characteristics associated with John McCain are that he is "too old," that he is a "good man"/"likable," that he would give the country more of the same/be another George W. Bush, and that he had a good military background—along with a basic dislike of him. Apparently, Americans have become more cognizant of McCain's age, as only 2% mentioned this in November 2006. Another major change in volunteered responses about McCain is a not unexpected decline in the percentage of Americans who say he is "a good candidate" who "should run." Another new perception of McCain is that he is a "war hawk" given his positions on the Iraq War, which were probably not as well known when the question was last asked. Also, back in November 2006 no one had specifically thought of McCain as potentially representing what amounts to a third Bush term.

Barack Obama was not well known when the open-ended question was first asked. In November 2006, 36% of Americans were either not familiar enough with Obama to provide a response or had no opinion of him. Now, just 9% fall into these categories. Yet, even with the increase in familiarity with Obama, the most commonly held perceptions about him have not changed: namely, that he is "young and inexperienced" as well as "a fresh face with new ideas." Equal percentages volunteer that they like and dislike him. Perhaps the most notable change in perceptions of Obama is that he is "dishonest." Five percent now mention this, though it was not volunteered in November 2006. Other newly offered characterizations of Obama are that he lacks substance/is all talk and no action, and that he is an "elitist" or a "snob." There is some disagreement expressed with his religious views—a possible outgrowth of his previous membership in the Reverend Jeremiah Wright's church. But none of these views is widely held.

The most commonly held perceptions of Hillary Clinton are that she is dishonest or not trustworthy, that she is qualified and capable, and that she is strong—along with an association with her of past scandals or "baggage" associated with husband Bill Clinton, and a basic dislike of her. Since the question was last asked about her, there have been significant increases in perceptions of Hillary Clinton as being dishonest and of the baggage Bill Clinton brings.

On the bright side for her, there has been an increase in the percentage who mention that she is experienced, and a significant decline in the percentage who believe she is merely "riding Bill's coattails."

Praise and Criticism for the Candidates

As the specific comments make clear, the candidates receive a fair amount of both praise and criticism from the American public. By characterizing each of the specific open-ended categories as representing either positive, negative, or neutral responses (the last usually meaning a purely descriptive or objective characterization, such as "a Democrat"), one can get a sense of whether these volunteered comments focus more on positive or negative qualities associated with each candidate. The results show that Americans tend to give many more negative than positive responses about Hillary Clinton. In fact, more than half mention something negative about Clinton, nearly twice as many as the 30% who say something positive about her. John McCain and Barack Obama, on the other hand, receive about equal percentages of positive and negative comments.

In part, these differences reflect the basic favorable ratings of each candidate. In the most recent USA Today/Gallup Poll, both Obama (at 60%) and McCain (also 60%) had higher favorable ratings than Clinton (53%). But Clinton's favorable rating was on balance more positive than nega-tive. The lopsided negative comments about Clinton in response to the open-ended question may reflect a more intense dislike of her by her critics. Or they may reflect a stronger association of negative characteristics with her—these tend to be the most accessible ones when people are asked what comes to mind when they think of her. This largely negative characterization of Clinton has not changed much since November 2006. In that poll, 33% of all mentions of her were positive in orientation and 51% negative—only slightly better than what the current poll shows.

Although the other candidates' current positive/negative ratios are currently better than Clinton's, they both have worsened significantly since the last time the question was asked. In November 2006, twice as many Americans mentioned something positive (34%) as negative (18%) about Obama, compared with the roughly even distribution today. McCain's ratio has suffered even more, dropping from a 55% to 19% positive/negative split to the even split found today. This suggests that in the world of politics, familiarity may breed contempt. As the candidates campaign and become better known, the public finds out a lot that it doesn't like about each one, and (at least in the case of McCain) fewer things that it does like. This could be a natural result of campaigning—where the goal is to generate a base of support, but in doing so, a candidate also generates a well of opposition.

MAY 2008

After steadily deteriorating since January 2008, Americans' economic mood is stabilizing so far in May, albeit at last month's very dismal levels. Aggregated Gallup Poll daily tracking data from May shows 43% of Americans describing current economic conditions as "poor," identical to the average for all of April. Pessimism about the direction of the economy also remains high, as 86% of Americans polled from May 1 to May13 say the economy is getting worse, similar to the 85% who said so in April.

An overall assessment of Americans' views of the economy can be derived by creating an economic mood measure based on responses to the two questions discussed here. Respondents who say the economy is either "excellent" or "good" and getting better (or who volunteer that it is staying the same) are considered "positive" about the economy. Those who say the economy is "only fair" or "poor" and staying that way or getting worse are considered "negative." All others are considered "mixed" in their economic views. The majority of Americans—65%—were already negative about the economy in January. But that proportion swelled to over three-quarters of Americans by April. The percentage considered "positive" has nearly vanished, dropping from 12% in January to 7% in April and May. And the percentage of "mixed" responses has dwindled from 20% to 13%.

Negative economic views are not only widespread but also hold across all demographic subgroups. According to the aggregate of May 1–13 Gallup Poll daily tracking, Americans living in high-income households, Republicans, and residents of the Southwest and the Rocky Mountain states are a bit more likely to have a positive economic outlook than are others; but the vast majority of these groups, too, are negative about the economy. Americans have had little reason to feel good about the economy in 2008—what with tremendous stock market volatility, a crisis in the housing and credit markets, rising unemployment, and skyrocketing fuel prices. Mounting problems in many of these areas have brought about a steady decline in Americans' ratings of the economy since January. Yet as bad as the current ratings are, there is still opportunity for them to get worse, if the remaining 20% of Americans now categorized as either positive or mixed in their views on the economy move into the "negative" column. Thus, if there is any good news in Gallup's daily tracking of Americans' views of the economy, it's that confidence hasn't gotten any worse in May. The bad news is that it is holding at the very negative level reached in April.

A recent USA Today/Gallup Poll finds 36% of Americans—a majority of the 57% of Americans who had travel plans this summer—reporting that they are changing their summer vacation plans as a result of the rise in gasoline prices, significantly more than the 21% who say they are sticking to their plans. Forty-one percent say they did not plan on traveling much during the summer and are thus relatively unaffected by the price of gasoline. The poll was conducted between May 2 and May 4, and since then gasoline prices have continued to rise, so it's possible that an even higher percentage of Americans have decided to alter their plans.

Although gasoline prices are now the highest in history, a comparison of reactions to this question today and in June 2006 shows that the current results are somewhat, but not dramatically, more negative than they were two years ago: In 2006, 33% of Americans said they were changing their plans, while 28% said they were not. Then, as now, a majority of those who had plans to travel said they were changing them because of the price of gasoline. What exactly are those who are changing their plans doing to make up for the high price of gasoline? An open-ended question included in the poll asked just that question. The results suggest somewhat more draconian responses to gasoline prices than was the case in June 2006. Over a

CHRONOLOGY

MAY 2008

May 3 A cyclone devastates Myanmar, killing more than 100,000 people. The country's secretive junta is slow to react and interferes with international attempts to deliver aid.

May 6 Barack Obama solidly wins the North Carolina primary and narrowly loses in Indiana. Commentators begin to declare the race over. NBC News Washington bureau chief Tim Russert states, "We now know who the Democratic nominee's going to be." The *New York Post*'s headline reads "TOAST," referring to Hillary Clinton.

May 7 In a *USA Today* interview, Clinton says that she has a better chance of winning the presidential election, in part because of her support from "hard-working Americans, white Americans." The Obama camp strongly criticizes this perceived racially charged remark.

May 7 Dmitri Medvedev becomes Russia's new president. The next day, Vladimir Putin is overwhelm-ingly chosen prime minister by the nation's parliament.

May 9 The State Department renews Blackwater Worldwide's contract to provide security for American diplomats in Iraq. Blackwater guards were responsible for killing 17 Iraqi civilians in a 2007 incident.

May 12 Oil surges to a record high of $130 a barrel.

May 12 A 7.9-magnitude earthquake strikes China, centered in Sichuan Province. More than 60,000 people are killed.

May 13 Clinton wins the West Virginia primary by a large margin, but Obama continues to gain more superdelegates and remains ahead in the Democratic delegate count.

May 14 John Edwards endorses Obama for the Democratic presidential nomination.

May 15 The California Supreme Court rules that same-sex couples have a constitutional right to marry. This decision makes California the second state, after Massachusetts, to allow such unions.

May 20 Obama wins the Oregon presidential primary; Clinton wins the Kentucky presidential primary.

May 20 Senator Edward Kennedy is diagnosed with a brain tumor.

May 23 Commenting on why she's remaining in the presidential race, Clinton recalls how late in the year previous Democratic nomination races had been decided. As an example, she mentions Senator Robert F. Kennedy's assassination in June 1968. Her statement is interpreted by some as a suggestion that an assassination or some other tragedy might befall Obama.

May 31 The Democratic National Committee decides to seat the disputed Michigan and Florida delegates, but will allow them only half a vote per delegate. It also assigns the "uncommitted" voters in Michigan to Obama, as Obama, following Democratic Party rules, had withdrawn his name from the Michigan ballot. This ruling is seen as a victory for Obama.

---

third of those who are changing their plans this summer, 37%, say they are canceling their vacation plans altogether, compared with 26% two years ago. Another 24% this year say they are changing their destination in order to make the trip shorter, while 20% say they are cutting down on the number of trips they are taking. Two years ago, those changing their plans were most likely to be cutting down on the number of trips they would be taking. About 4 out of 10 Americans apparently will not be affected by rising gasoline prices this summer as far as their vacations are concerned because they did not plan on traveling much to begin with. But among those who did plan on travel-ing, a majority say they will be changing their plans, and over a third of that group say they will be canceling their vacation plans altogether.

MAY 1

Clinton's vs. Obama's Strengths in the General Election

Gallup Poll daily tracking over the past month indicates that the 2008 presidential election could be another nail-biter of the sort seen in 2000 and, to a lesser extent, 2004. Both Democratic contenders are closely matched against John McCain in trial heats for the general election. But while the broad outlines of voter support for New York senator Hillary Clinton and Illinois senator Barack Obama are highly similar—both candidates attract traditional Democratic constituencies—there are some differences that could be important in assessing which of the two has the better chance of beating Arizona senator John McCain.

A Mostly Traditional Democratic Coalition for Clinton

According to an aggregate of Gallup Poll daily tracking from between April 21 and April 27, including interviews with more than 6,000 registered voters, a Clinton-McCain race looks highly typical of recent elections, with the Democrat widely favored by women, blacks, adults under 30 years of age, Easterners, low-income, low-education-level Americans, Catholics, Hispanics, secular Americans, unmarried adults, and Democrats. Two important differences from recent general elections are Clinton's especially strong performance among women and her relatively weak performance among black Americans. Her 12-point advantage over McCain among women (52% vs. 40%) contrasts with single-digit advantages among women for John Kerry (2004), Al Gore (2000), and Bill Clinton (1996) in the previous three presidential elections. And her 78% level of support from blacks contrasts with more than 90% support among blacks for those three candidates. The latter level of support clearly highlights the risk the Democratic Party faces with blacks (the overwhelming majority of whom are Democrats who support Obama for the Democratic nomination) should Clinton win the nomination by the votes of the superdelegates or by some other means that Obama's black supporters perceive as unfair or undemocratic. Also, only 82% of Democrats currently say they would vote for Clinton in the fall, whereas recent Democratic presidential candidates have received no less than 89% of the vote from their party.

Obama Charting a Different Course

An Obama-McCain race differs from a Clinton-McCain one mainly in terms of degrees of support for the Democrat among various subgroups. Obama beats McCain among nearly all of the aforementioned core Democratic constituencies. But his margin of support is lower among women, Easterners, low-income Americans, Catholics, Hispanics, and self-identified Democrats. (Obama also does less well than Clinton in the South, although both lose to McCain in that region.) Obama largely offsets these losses by doing better than Clinton among blacks and among high-income Americans. He also does slightly better among the one-third or so of voters who consider themselves political independents. Obama's near-universal support among blacks

is the more typical pattern for a Democratic presidential candidate than is the lower support Clinton receives.

Thus, as between the two likely Democratic candidates, Clinton performs especially well relative to Obama among Americans of lower and lower-middle incomes and among those with lower levels of education (i.e., no college experience)—and among Democrats generally, seniors, and Hispanics. Obama's distinguishing strengths are his stronger performance among blacks and higher-income Americans, although he also performs slightly better among independents. The most recent weekly aggregate of Gallup Poll daily tracking finds Clinton doing just as well as Obama among voters age 18 to 29. This marks a sharp reversal for Clinton, who had been trailing Obama among young voters for most of March and April—but it is not clear whether the current data are an anomaly or represent a dramatic shift in younger voters' preferences.

Obama Falls Short Among Conservative Democrats

Given the apparent willingness of many blacks to forsake Clinton in November if she is the Democratic Party's nominee—either by voting for McCain or by not voting at all—it may seem surprising that Clinton still outperforms Obama among Democrats, 82% vs. 74%. The reason for this is Obama's relatively poor performance among conservative Democrats. Only 62% of Democrats who describe their political views as "conservative" choose Obama in a race between Obama and McCain; by contrast, 74% of conservative Democrats would vote for Clinton in a Clinton vs. McCain race. Obama does just as well as Clinton among liberal Democrats and nearly as well among moderate Democrats. His great weakness is, and has been since early March, among conservative Democrats. These observations are made as the protracted battle for the Democratic

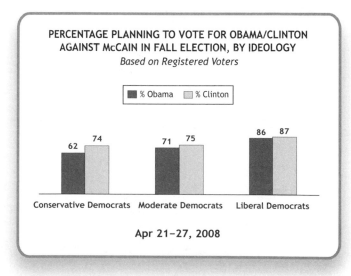

PERCENTAGE PLANNING TO VOTE FOR OBAMA/CLINTON AGAINST McCAIN IN FALL ELECTION, BY IDEOLOGY
Based on Registered Voters

■ % Obama   □ % Clinton

	Conservative Democrats	Moderate Democrats	Liberal Democrats
% Obama	62	71	86
% Clinton	74	75	87

Apr 21–27, 2008

nomination gets increasingly contentious, and before the eventual nominee has had the opportunity to heal party wounds. Much could change. At present, it seems that both Clinton and Obama would win the support of traditional Democratic constituencies in the fall election if they were nominated for president. However, compared with previous Democratic nominees, Clinton seems poised to do historically well among women and less well among blacks. Obama could have trouble holding blue-collar and conservative Democrats but could compensate for that if he maintains his strong appeal to blacks and upper-income Americans and continues to match McCain among political independents.

MAY 2

Is the Ongoing Democratic Campaign Good or Bad for the Party?

Six out of 10 Democrats say the continuing campaign for the Democratic presidential nomination is doing more harm than good for the Democratic Party, up slightly from the percentage who felt this way last month. This overall negative view of the impact of the continuing campaign among Democrats masks significant variations in attitudes based on candidate preference. Democrats who support Barack Obama are well above the overall Democratic average in their belief that the continuing campaign is doing more harm than good. This is no doubt because Obama is the current leader in both the popular vote (excluding Florida and Michigan) and the overall delegate count. Continuing to campaign has very little upside potential for Obama and a lot of downside potential—as may be occurring now, with Obama having to deal with continuing controversy surrounding his relationship with the Reverend Jeremiah Wright.

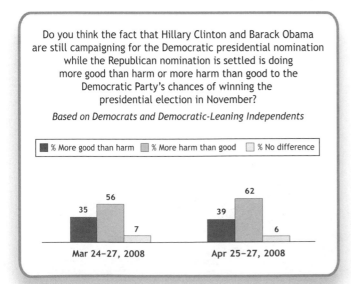

Do you think the fact that Hillary Clinton and Barack Obama are still campaigning for the Democratic presidential nomination while the Republican nomination is settled is doing more good than harm or more harm than good to the Democratic Party's chances of winning the presidential election in November?

Based on Democrats and Democratic-Leaning Independents

Legend: % More good than harm / % More harm than good / % No difference

Mar 24–27, 2008: 35, 56, 7
Apr 25–27, 2008: 39, 62, 6

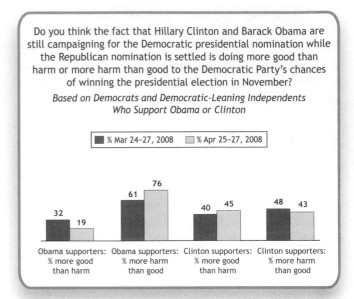

Do you think the fact that Hillary Clinton and Barack Obama are still campaigning for the Democratic presidential nomination while the Republican nomination is settled is doing more good than harm or more harm than good to the Democratic Party's chances of winning the presidential election in November?

Based on Democrats and Democratic-Leaning Independents Who Support Obama or Clinton

Legend: % Mar 24–27, 2008 / % Apr 25–27, 2008

Obama supporters: % more good than harm: 32, 19
Obama supporters: % more harm than good: 61, 76
Clinton supporters: % more good than harm: 40, 45
Clinton supporters: % more harm than good: 48, 43

These recent events probably contribute to Obama supporters' even greater likelihood than was the case a month ago of viewing the continuing campaign as harmful. On the other hand, Democrats who support Hillary Clinton have much more mixed views. A slight plurality of 45% say the continuing campaign is doing more good than harm, while 43% agree that it is harmful—again, given that Clinton's only realistic chance of winning the nomination is to continue to campaign and hope that events will help convince Obama-committed superdelegates to switch and vote for her. And in the opposite direction from that measured among Obama supporters, Clinton supporters have become slightly more positive about the impact of the continuing campaign than they were a month ago.

These data reinforce the degree to which two groups of Democrats, as defined by the candidate they support, view the continuing campaign from significantly different perspectives. On average, Democrats appear to agree that the continuing campaign is harming their party's chances of winning in November. Obama supporters have become even more hardened in this view over the past month as they have watched the negative news that has surrounded their candidate. In contrast, Clinton supporters have become a little more likely to believe that the continuing campaign may not be so harmful after all.

MAY 5

Clinton Supporters Believe Jeremiah Wright Is Relevant to Campaign

Democrats nationally who have followed the controversy surrounding the relationship between Barack Obama and

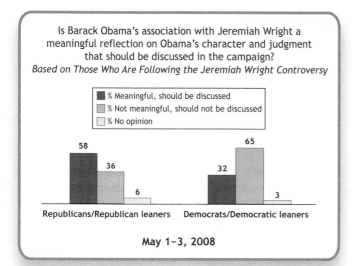

Is Barack Obama's association with Jeremiah Wright a meaningful reflection on Obama's character and judgment that should be discussed in the campaign?
Based on Those Who Are Following the Jeremiah Wright Controversy

May 1–3, 2008

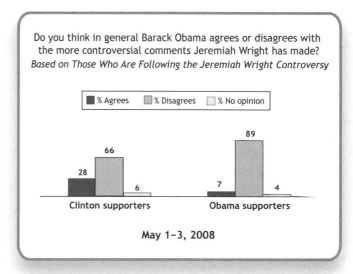

Do you think in general Barack Obama agrees or disagrees with the more controversial comments Jeremiah Wright has made?
Based on Those Who Are Following the Jeremiah Wright Controversy

May 1–3, 2008

his former minister, the Reverend Jeremiah Wright, say by a two-to-one margin that Obama's association with Wright is not meaningful and should not be discussed in the campaign, while a majority of Republicans disagree.

About three-quarters of Democrats who are Hillary Clinton supporters and 8 out of 10 Obama supporters say they have followed the Jeremiah Wright controversy. Perhaps not surprisingly, there is a significant difference in the way Democrats view this matter based on the candidate they support. Clinton supporters who have followed the controversy believe, by a slight majority, that the story should be discussed in the campaign because it is a meaningful reflection on Obama's character. (On this they agree with Republicans.) Even though Obama himself admitted on NBC's *Meet the Press* on May 4 that his relationship with Wright is a legitimate campaign topic, Obama sup-

porters overwhelmingly say it should not be discussed in the campaign.

The major short-term interest with regard to the Wright controversy has been its potential impact on the race for the Democratic nomination. It is clear from the USA Today/Gallup Poll data that it could be having some impact, because Clinton supporters appear to be at least somewhat prone to take the controversy into account in assessing Obama—certainly more so than are Obama's supporters. Almost 3 out of 10 Clinton supporters who have followed the controversy say Obama agrees with the more controversial comments Wright has made—whereas the vast majority of Obama supporters, almost 9 out of 10, believe that Obama disagrees with Wright's more controversial statements. Additionally, 9 out of 10 Obama supporters believe Obama has handled the controversy well,

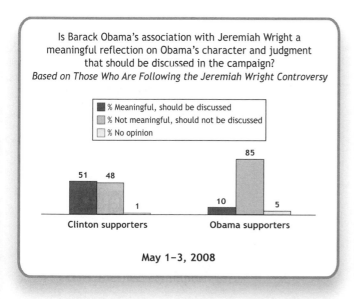

Is Barack Obama's association with Jeremiah Wright a meaningful reflection on Obama's character and judgment that should be discussed in the campaign?
Based on Those Who Are Following the Jeremiah Wright Controversy

May 1–3, 2008

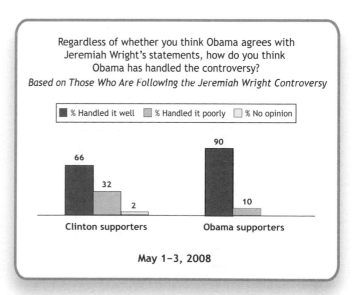

Regardless of whether you think Obama agrees with Jeremiah Wright's statements, how do you think Obama has handled the controversy?
Based on Those Who Are Following the Jeremiah Wright Controversy

May 1–3, 2008

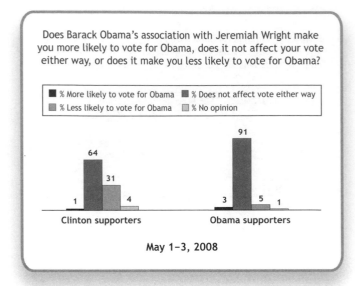

Does Barack Obama's association with Jeremiah Wright make you more likely to vote for Obama, does it not affect your vote either way, or does it make you less likely to vote for Obama?

■ % More likely to vote for Obama   ■ % Does not affect vote either way
■ % Less likely to vote for Obama   ■ % No opinion

Clinton supporters   Obama supporters

May 1–3, 2008

a sentiment that a lower percentage—albeit still a majority (66%)—of Clinton supporters agree with.

Asked directly whether Obama's association with Wright has made them more likely or less likely to vote for Obama, or whether it does not affect their vote, Obama supporters overwhelmingly say it makes no difference to them. On the other hand, a little less than a third of Clinton supporters say the association between Wright and Obama has made them less likely to vote for Obama. (These answers are among all Clinton and Obama supporters, regardless of how closely they have been following the controversy.)

Impact of the Controversy

The May 1–3 poll shows that Obama's unfavorable rating (21) is up slightly from last month (15%) among Democrats. A detailed look at the trends on Obama's favorables by nomination preference show that Obama became slightly less popular among Clinton supporters, while his almost universally favorable rating among his own supporters stayed the same. It is sometimes difficult to tease out the specific impact of a high-profile news event on the fortunes of candidates in the middle of a heated presidential campaign. The data reviewed above indicate that the Wright controversy certainly seems to have had at least some impact on Democrats who support Clinton and who have followed the controversy. These voters say by a slight majority that the controversy is a legitimate topic for news media to discuss, and a not insignificant minority say Obama agrees with Wright's more controversial statements. About a third of all Clinton supporters say the relationship has made them less likely to vote for Obama. Additionally, Clinton supporters in this latest poll have a slightly less favorable view of Obama than they did two weeks ago. Of course, it

is not known whether the Wright controversy has actually caused some Obama supporters to defect and move into Clinton's camp, or whether it has simply reinforced Clinton supporters' pre-existing attitudes. Whether the controversy will affect the results of the May 6 Indiana and North Carolina primaries remains to be seen.

MAY 6
Most Democrats Not Eager for Either Candidate to Drop Out

Heading into the important presidential primaries on May 6 in North Carolina and Indiana, 6 in 10 Democrats say Hillary Clinton and Barack Obama should continue their presidential campaigns. Of the minority who would like to see either Clinton or Obama drop out and concede the nomination, more call for Clinton to step down than for Obama to do so. These results are based on the May 1–3 USA Today/Gallup Poll. There have indeed been calls for Clinton to drop out, given Obama's lead in pledged delegates, which he built up in a string of primary and caucus victories in February. Those calls have been quieted to some extent with Clinton's big wins in the March 4 Ohio and Texas primaries and the April 22 Pennsylvania primary. Even so, she is unlikely to overcome the delegate deficit unless she can convince a disproportionate amount of undecided superdelegates to support her candidacy.

Democrats' opinions about the desirable next steps in the campaign are, not surprisingly, highly influenced by the candidate they currently favor. Obama supporters are about evenly divided between favoring a continuation of the campaign and wanting to see Clinton drop out and concede to Obama. Most Clinton supporters favor having the campaign continue, obviously in order to allow Clinton

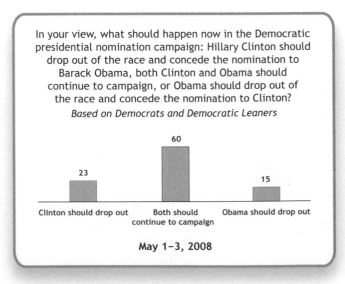

In your view, what should happen now in the Democratic presidential nomination campaign: Hillary Clinton should drop out of the race and concede the nomination to Barack Obama, both Clinton and Obama should continue to campaign, or Obama should drop out of the race and concede the nomination to Clinton?

Based on Democrats and Democratic Leaners

Clinton should drop out   Both should continue to campaign   Obama should drop out

May 1–3, 2008

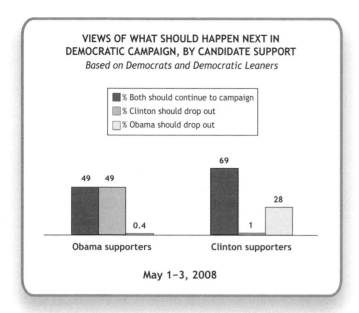

VIEWS OF WHAT SHOULD HAPPEN NEXT IN DEMOCRATIC CAMPAIGN, BY CANDIDATE SUPPORT

Based on Democrats and Democratic Leaners

■ % Both should continue to campaign
▨ % Clinton should drop out
□ % Obama should drop out

Obama supporters: 49, 49, 0.4
Clinton supporters: 69, 1, 28

May 1–3, 2008

a chance to catch up to Obama, while the remainder say Obama should drop out. If the remaining contests play out as the prior contests have, with the candidates fairly evenly matched, then the decisions of the remaining uncommitted superdelegates will determine the party's presidential nominee.

The poll asked Democrats for their views on when the undecided superdelegates should decide whom to support for the nomination. Most would seem to agree with Democratic National Committee chairman Howard Dean that all superdelegates should commit to a candidate by the end of June. This includes 24% who want superdelegates to decide immediately (after the May 6 primaries) and an additional 45% who seem willing to allow the superdelegates until the end of the primary and caucus season to make up their minds. (The last contests are scheduled for June 3.) Only about one-fourth of Democrats say the superdelegates should be able to decide at the party's nominating convention in late August. Here again, Democrats' preferences vary according to their candidate of choice. Obama supporters are twice as likely as Clinton supporters to say undecided superdelegates should make up their minds this week, while Clinton supporters are twice as likely to say the superdelegates should be able to stay undecided, if they so choose, until the convention. Just under half of both Obama supporters and Clinton supporters say superdelegates should make up their minds after the primaries and caucuses are over.

The results suggest that a majority of Democrats are willing to allow the primary and caucus schedule to play out. That is somewhat at odds with earlier Gallup polling showing that the party rank and file believed that the ongoing campaign was doing more harm than good to the Democrats' chances of winning the November election. The sentiments expressed in the most recent poll may reflect a belief in letting all voters have their say. Indiana and North Carolina are the two largest contests remaining, so if the results of these primaries are not decisive (which they are not likely to be unless Obama sweeps both), then it seems most likely that the primary campaign will go on for another month until the final contests in Montana and South Dakota on June 3.

MAY 7

Obama Beats McCain Among Jewish Voters

Barack Obama is faring better than might be expected among Jewish voters, beating John McCain in Gallup Poll daily general election matchups and trailing Hillary Clinton only slightly in Jewish Democrats' preference for the Democratic nomination. This is according to an aggregate of Gallup Poll daily tracking from April 1 to April 30, including interviews with close to 800 Jewish voters and nearly 600 Jewish Democratic voters. Gallup Poll daily tracking also finds no recent decline in the percentage of Jewish Democrats favoring Obama for the Democratic presidential nomination. Jewish Democrats continue to favor Hillary Clinton, but by only a slim margin over Obama: 50% to 43% in April, compared with 51% to 41% in March. In terms of the general election, Jewish voters nationwide are nearly as likely to say they would vote for Obama if he were the Democratic nominee running against the Republican McCain as to say they would vote for Clinton (61% vs. 66%, respectively).

According to Gallup's aggregated tracking data for all of April, 61% of Jewish voters would vote for Obama, much higher than the national average of 45% of all registered voters. Rather than declining between March and April, support for Obama versus McCain among Jewish voters has increased slightly, from a 23-point margin in favor of Obama (58% to 35%) to a 29-point margin (61% to 32%). The results are similar for Clinton, who received 66% of the vote from Jewish Democrats in April compared with 27% for McCain—a 39-point lead. Clinton led McCain by 29 points in March, 61% to 32%. Evidence of Obama's concern about Jewish support for his candidacy stretches back to at least January, when he first publicly refuted false Web-fueled rumors that he was or had been a Muslim—the implication of the rumors being that he would be sympathetic to Muslim political concerns and anti-Israel in his worldview. At the same time, he also repudiated the anti-Semitic remarks of Nation of Islam leader Louis Farrakhan, and he recently disassociated himself from his former pastor, the Reverend Jeremiah Wright. Thus, any damage to Jews' perceptions of Obama as someone who would be unsympathetic to their interests could have occurred much earlier in the campaign. However, despite recent events—particularly the ongoing controversy about why Obama would have belonged to a church led by someone with Wright's anti-Israel views (among other criticisms of Wright)—Gallup trends suggest that Obama's Jewish support is holding up.

Obama's Support Similar to Kerry's in 2004

Barack Obama's current level of support among white voters in a head-to-head matchup against John McCain is no worse than John Kerry's margin of support among whites against George W. Bush in the 2004 presidential election. Much of the talk following the May 6 primaries, in which Obama convincingly won North Carolina and narrowly lost Indiana to Clinton, has focused on just how electable Obama—now the highly probable nominee—will be in the general election. The Clinton campaign has argued that Obama's weaknesses among white voters and blue-collar voters will hurt him against McCain in the fall. But it appears that the way Obama stacks up against McCain at this point is similar to the way in which Kerry performed against Bush in 2004 among several key racial, educational, religious, and gender subgroups. This conclusion is based on an analysis of exit poll data from 2004 compared with the Obama-McCain matchup in 4,000 Gallup Poll daily tracking interviews conducted during the first five days of May 2008.

Kerry, the Democratic nominee in 2004, lost to the Republican Bush by a 51% to 48% margin in the popular vote. In Gallup Poll daily tracking data from May 1 to 5, 2008, Obama is losing to McCain among registered voters by a 46% to 45% margin. Although there is a sizable component of undecideds in the Gallup Poll tracking data (and obviously there are no undecideds in the 2004 exit poll data), the margins in these two races are quite similar, with Kerry losing by three points and Obama by one point. This overall comparison, in and of itself, suggests that Obama,

assuming he captures the Democratic nomination, begins the general election contest in roughly the same position at which Kerry ended his unsuccessful quest in 2004—that is, with the prospect of a very close race. The more specific comparison of Obama's positioning versus Kerry's among various subgroups of the electorate suggests that the basic dynamic of the general presidential election is fairly predictable, based on past patterns.

SPECIFICS OF THE OBAMA-KERRY COMPARISON

Obama would be the first African-American candidate to receive a major party nomination in United States history, which could have racial implications in the voting. Some observers have argued that Obama has a particular liability among white voters, whom exit polls showed voted for Clinton in both North Carolina and Indiana.

The general election exit poll in 2004 showed that Kerry lost the white vote to Bush by a 17-point, 58% to 41% margin. At the moment, in Gallup's tracking of the general election across the first five days of May (with a sample of more than 4,000 registered voters), Obama is losing the white vote to McCain by a 53% to 37% margin, or 16 points. In short, Obama's relative performance among white voters—at least at the moment—is similar to Kerry's in 2004. Democratic candidates at the presidential level have traditionally received the overwhelming majority of black votes. In 2004, Kerry defeated Bush among blacks by 88% to 11%. At this point, Obama is leading McCain among blacks by a 91% to 5% margin. So there is little difference in how Obama fares among blacks compared with how Kerry did in 2004, in part because of the already very high "pre-existing" Democratic tilt of black voters as seen in previous presidential elections.

Another issue that has arisen in the course of the Democratic nomination campaign this year is the so-called blue-collar vote. In the primary campaigns, Obama has clearly done better than Clinton among those with a college degree, and worse among those without a college degree. But a comparison of Obama's performance against McCain among educational subgroups with Kerry's performance against Bush suggests that Obama is not at an unusual deficit among those with lower levels of education. Obama loses by a four-point, 47% to 43%, margin among those with no college education; Kerry lost to Bush among those with no college education by a similar, six-point (53% to 47%) margin. Kerry and Bush tied among college graduates in 2004; in Gallup Poll daily tracking, Obama wins by 50% to 44% among college graduates. Among those with post-graduate educations, Kerry won over Bush by 55% to 44%, or 11 points; Obama is beating McCain by 57% to 38%, or 19 points, among this group. The comparative data cer-

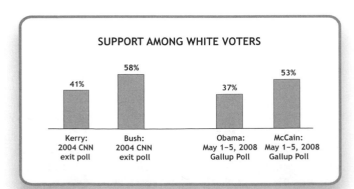

SUPPORT AMONG WHITE VOTERS

41% — Kerry: 2004 CNN exit poll
58% — Bush: 2004 CNN exit poll
37% — Obama: May 1–5, 2008 Gallup Poll
53% — McCain: May 1–5, 2008 Gallup Poll

tainly suggest that Obama is relatively strong among well-educated voters. So at the moment it would appear that Obama's problems with less well-educated voters—emphasized heavily by the Clinton campaign—are no worse than were Kerry's in 2004, and are more than made up for by Obama's strength among those with college degrees.

There has been a significant gender gap in presidential voting for at least three decades. As would be predicted, Obama wins among women by four points, 47% to 43%, in the Gallup Poll tracking data. This is very close to the three-point margin by which Kerry beat Bush among women in 2004. Obama loses among men by five points, while Kerry lost among men in 2004 by 11 points.

One of the fundamental verities of American political life is the significant religion gap in party identification and in presidential voting: Republicans typically do much better among those with high self-reported church attendance. In 2004, Bush beat Kerry by 61% to 39% among those who attend church weekly. McCain is beating Obama by 55% to 36% among this group. Among those who never attend church, Kerry won big in 2004, 61% to 36%. Obama wins among this group, 54% to 36%. It appears that the religion gap is slightly smaller this year than it was in 2004.

Each presidential campaign takes place in a new and different environment, with a new cast of characters and issues. If, as expected, Obama wins the Democratic nomination this year, the campaign will have an even more distinctive "newness" to it, as Obama would represent the first black major party candidate in the country's history. Still, the analysis reviewed here suggests that the basic outlines of an Obama-McCain campaign would in many ways resemble those of the 2004 race between Kerry and Bush. At the moment, Gallup Poll daily tracking indicates that this November's election could be close, as was the popular vote in 2000 and 2004. In other words, just as 2004 was in many ways a replay of 2000, this year's election could be a replay of 2004, with minor changes around the edges. Certainly the current data show that the patterns of support for Obama among various key racial, educational, religious, and gender groups when he is pitted against McCain do not look like they have changed dramatically from those that characterized the 2004 contest between Kerry and Bush.

MAY 8

Bush Approval Rating Down to 60% Among Republicans

At a time when President George W. Bush's job approval rating has fallen to 28%, just 6 in 10 Republicans approve of the job he is doing, the lowest of his administration. Bush has had a 28% overall job approval rating in each of the

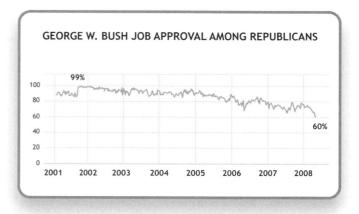

last three Gallup Polls—the worst of his administration, and the worst for any president since Jimmy Carter's 28% approval rating in 1979. In the most recent poll, conducted between May 1 and May 3, Bush's approval rating among his own party's supporters has dropped to 60%. Throughout his presidency, Bush has averaged 85% approval among Republicans, including a robust 92% in his first term and 77% thus far in his second term. So the current figures among the Republican faithful represent a significant departure from the norm for the Bush presidency. Lower support among Republicans primarily accounts for the erosion in Bush's overall job approval rating in recent weeks. His approval ratings among Democrats and independents are already at low levels and do not seem to be deteriorating much further.

While discouraging for Bush, his 60% approval rating among his natural political base is similar to the low points for several recent presidents, including Bill Clinton, George H. W. Bush, and Gerald Ford. Dwight Eisenhower and John F. Kennedy never had very low overall approval ratings, so

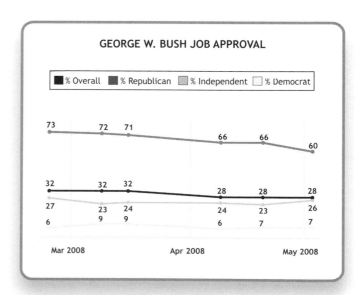

LOWEST APPROVAL RATINGS BY OWN POLITICAL PARTY FOR PRESIDENTS FROM EISENHOWER TO BUSH

President	Party	Lowest approval by own party	Dates	Overall approval rating in poll
Eisenhower	R	79%	Mar 6–11, 1958	51%
			May 28–Jun 2, 1958	54%
			Jul 16–21, 1960	49%*
Kennedy	D	71%	Sept 12–17, 1963	56%*
Johnson	D	48%	Aug 7–12, 1968	35%*
Nixon	R	48%	May 10–13, 1974	25%
			Jun 21–24, 1974	26%
Ford	R	57%	Jan 10–13, 1975	37%*
Carter	D	34%	Jun 29–Jul 2, 1979	28%*
			Oct 5–8, 1979	29%
Reagan	R	67%	Jan 21–24, 1983	37%
G.H.W. Bush	R	57%	Jul 31–Aug 2, 1992	29%*
Clinton	D	63%	Jun 5–6, 1993	37%*
G.W. Bush	R	60%	May 1–3, 2008	28%*

*Lowest approval rating while president

even their lowest ratings among their own party were still quite high (above 70%). While Ronald Reagan's job approval rating among all Americans did fall as low as 35% overall, Republicans' approval of him never fell below 67%.

Carter is the president with the dubious distinction of having received the lowest job approval rating from his own party since 1953, when Gallup began to compile presidential approval ratings by party affiliation. (Harry Truman had some of the lowest historical approval ratings, including 22% and 23% in late 1951 and early 1952. In those polls, his approval ratings among Democrats ranged between 42% and 44%. But Gallup did not compile approval and disapproval ratings for all political parties until the Eisenhower administration.) Only 34% of Democrats approved of Carter in a pair of 1979 Gallup Polls. Carter's overall ratings at that time were similar to Bush's current overall ratings, but his ratings were not nearly as polarized along party lines as Bush's are: He did much better among Republicans than Bush is doing now among Democrats, and also did slightly better among independents than Bush is currently doing. Lyndon Johnson and Richard Nixon also had troubled presidencies and are the only other presidents whose approval rating among their own party's supporters fell below 50%.

George W. Bush's overall job approval rating had been running about 33% for quite a while, but it has now fallen below 30% as some Republicans have stopped backing him. The most likely explanation for this loss in support could be rising gasoline prices, which historically have been shown to depress presidential approval ratings. Bush's job approval rating remains six percentage points above Harry Truman's all-time low. If it falls below that, it will most likely do so as a result of further losses in support from his Republican base.

MAY 10
Obama 49%, Clinton 44%

According to the Gallup Poll daily tracking three-day rolling average for May 7–9, Barack Obama has widened the gap over Hillary Clinton to a 49% to 44% margin. These results are the first three-day aggregate in which all interviews have been conducted after the May 6 North Carolina and Indiana primaries. Although Obama's margin over Clinton is now larger than it has been over the last several days, he has yet to move into a significant or commanding lead, despite much discussion about the inevitability of his becoming the Democratic nominee. Hillary Clinton is maintaining a 48% to 44% lead over John McCain in the current tracking of general election preferences, slightly larger than Barack Obama's 46% to 45% slim, one-percentage-point margin over McCain.

MAY 12
Bush May Be as Harmful to McCain as Wright Is to Obama

President Bush may do as much damage to John McCain's chances of being elected as Jeremiah Wright does to Barack Obama's, according to results of a recent USA Today/Gallup Poll. The May 1–3 poll finds 38% of likely voters saying McCain's association with Bush makes them less likely to vote for McCain, while 33% say Obama's association with Wright diminishes their likelihood of voting for him. The Bush-McCain relationship does have more upside than the Obama-Wright association, though, as 7% say they are more likely to vote for McCain because of his association with Bush, while only 1% say they are more likely to vote for Obama because of his association with Wright. Importantly, a majority of voters in both questions say the personal association will not affect their vote either way.

The nature of the two relationships is clearly different: Wright was Obama's former pastor, while Bush and McCain were rivals for the 2000 presidential nomination, though Bush has endorsed McCain in the 2008 election. But both present problems for the candidates—Wright on account of his incendiary sermons and controversial remarks, which have raised questions about Obama's beliefs and personal judgment, and Bush owing to his low approval ratings, which hurt the Republicans in the 2006 elections and may well do so again in 2008. The poll also asked how former president Bill Clinton might affect vot-

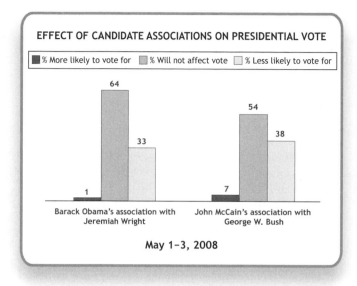

EFFECT OF CANDIDATE ASSOCIATIONS ON PRESIDENTIAL VOTE

■ % More likely to vote for   ■ % Will not affect vote   □ % Less likely to vote for

May 1–3, 2008

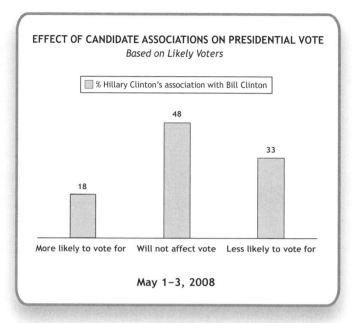

EFFECT OF CANDIDATE ASSOCIATIONS ON PRESIDENTIAL VOTE
Based on Likely Voters

□ % Hillary Clinton's association with Bill Clinton

May 1–3, 2008

ers' propensity to vote for Hillary Clinton. While the 33% who say it makes them less likely to cast a ballot for Hillary for president rivals the percentages found in connection with the McCain-Bush and Obama-Wright associations, the 18% who say it makes them more likely to vote for Hillary means Bill also helps attract support for his wife. Just under half say the Clintons' association would not affect their vote.

The percentages of voters saying they are less likely to vote for a candidate because of one of their personal associations probably overstates the true negative impact on the candidates, mainly because voters who might not seriously consider voting for a candidate in the first place (e.g., Democrats with respect to McCain or Republicans in the case of Obama) often respond that they are "less likely" to vote for that candidate on account of a given association. So it is instructive to see how the results compare when considering voters who are generally inclined to support a candidate—specifically, the rank and file of the candidate's party. From this perspective, the data suggest that Wright may be more detrimental to Obama's candidacy than Bush is to McCain's. Nearly one-fifth of Democrats, 19%, say they are less likely to vote for Obama because of his ties to Wright (only 2% say the Wright-Obama connection increases their odds of voting for Obama). Meanwhile, just 10% of Republicans say they are less likely to vote for McCain because of his association with Bush; about the same percentage (12%) say this relationship makes them more likely to vote for McCain. It is important to note that the question asks about the likelihood of voting for a candidate—so a respondent may say that Obama's association with Wright makes him or her less likely to vote for Obama, but might still vote for Obama. So in addition to measuring voter intention, the question probably also functions as a

measure of enthusiasm for the voter's preferred candidate. As such, the actual percentages may best be thought of as a rough gauge of the risks that each of these controversial associations poses to the respective candidate.

In general, the results are mixed as to whether Wright or Bush is a greater threat to, respectively, Obama's or McCain's presidential ambitions. Among the entire electorate, the two appear to be about equally damaging; in particular, Bush could hinder McCain's ability to attract independent and Democratic voters. However, the poll suggests that Obama may have a harder time holding his natural base of support given his association with Wright, so that may make Wright a greater threat to Obama than Bush is to McCain.

MAY 13

After Indiana and North Carolina Primaries, Democrats Still Okay with Continuing Campaign

A new USA Today/Gallup Poll shows that 55% of Democrats say both Hillary Clinton and Barack Obama should continue campaigning for the Democratic presidential nomination, while 35% say Clinton should drop out. The poll was conducted between May 8 and May 11, after the May 6 North Carolina and Indiana primaries and amid much discussion in the news media about the inevitability of Obama's being the nominee, given his current delegate and popular vote count. Compared with a May 1–3 poll conducted prior to last week's primaries, there has been an increase in the percentage of Democrats who say Clinton

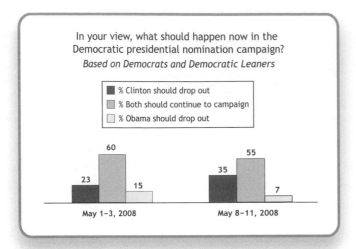

In your view, what should happen now in the Democratic presidential nomination campaign?
Based on Democrats and Democratic Leaners

- ■ % Clinton should drop out
- ■ % Both should continue to campaign
- □ % Obama should drop out

should drop out and a decrease in the already small percentage who say Obama should drop out. Still, the overall pattern of Democratic views has remained the same, with a majority in both of the May polls comfortable with a continuation of the campaign.

There is, not surprisingly, a major difference in views on this issue between supporters of the two candidates. Three-quarters of Clinton supporters say that she should stay in the race and the campaign should continue (and only 14% say Obama should drop out); 6 out of 10 Obama supporters, on the other hand, say Clinton should drop out, although this still leaves 39% who favor a continuation of the campaign. On the issue of whether Obama, if he wins the nomination, should choose Clinton as his running mate, a slight majority of Democrats say "yes." Fifty-five percent of Democrats say this would be a good idea, compared with 38% who think Obama should choose someone else. There are again big differences in views on this issue between Obama supporters and Clinton supporters. Clinton supporters are enthusiastic about the idea of an Obama-Clinton "dream ticket," with 73% saying they favor the idea; just 19% of her supporters reject it. Obama supporters, on the other hand, are much less enthusiastic: 52% oppose the idea, though a sizable 43% minority say they would favor it.

MAY 14

Obama, McCain Highly Competitive for Independent Vote

Barack Obama (44%) and John McCain (42%) are essentially tied in presidential vote choice among independents. The two candidates have been closely matched among independents since mid-March, with the advantage switching between McCain and Obama several times. These results

are based on weekly aggregates of Gallup Poll daily tracking data, with the most recent covering data collected between May 5 and May 11. Since Gallup began compiling weekly aggregates in mid-March, Obama's support among independents has ranged between 40% and 45%, and McCain's between 41% and 48%. Each candidate wins the vast majority of votes from his own party, with Obama currently holding a 76% to 15% edge over McCain among Democratic registered voters and McCain leading Obama by 84% to 12% among Republican registered voters.

The candidates' support within their own party has been very stable thus far this year, with Obama's share of the Democratic vote ranging from 73% to 76% since mid-March and McCain's share of the Republican vote ranging between 84% and 87%. Obama is able to hold his own against McCain despite receiving less support from his fellow party members because significantly more Americans currently identify as Democrats than as Republicans. In fact, among all registered voters in May 5–11 tracking polling, Obama led McCain by 47% to 43%. The competition for the independent vote would look quite different if Hillary Clinton somehow emerged as the Democratic nominee: McCain has consistently led Clinton among independents. But Clinton would also be competitive with McCain among all voters, because she wins a greater share of the Democratic vote versus McCain than Obama does. In the most recent data, 84% of Democrats said they would vote for Clinton over McCain, compared with the 76% Democratic support Obama receives. Clinton's Democratic support has not fallen below 80% in the weekly aggregates, while Obama has yet to achieve that mark. McCain does hold more of his own party versus Clinton than he does versus Obama, getting 88% of the Republican vote in the recent data, and a range of 86% to 91% since mid-March.

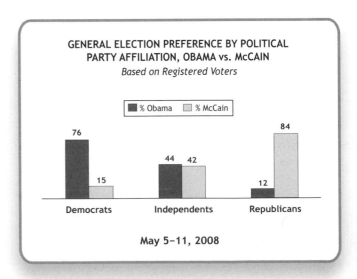

GENERAL ELECTION PREFERENCE BY POLITICAL PARTY AFFILIATION, OBAMA vs. McCAIN
Based on Registered Voters

- ■ % Obama   □ % McCain

May 5–11, 2008

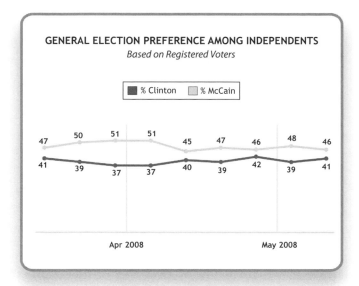

GENERAL ELECTION PREFERENCE AMONG INDEPENDENTS
Based on Registered Voters

■ % Clinton   ☐ % McCain

Apr 2008   May 2008

The Role of the Independent Vote

Independents are usually one of the most closely watched swing voter groups in each presidential election. However, contrary to expectations, they are not always decisive, in part because turnout among independents is usually lower than it is among those with a political party affiliation. According to Gallup historical data from prior presidential elections, George W. Bush in 2004, Al Gore in 2000, Jimmy Carter in 1976, and John F. Kennedy in 1960 all won the popular vote despite losing among independents. It would seem more critical that McCain prevail among independents in order for him to win the November election, given the Republican deficit in voter identification and voting enthusiasm relative to the Democrats.

MAY 17

Obama Opens Up 51% to 42% Lead Over Clinton

Barack Obama has reopened a significant lead over Hillary Clinton among national Democrats and now leads by a 51% to 42% margin, according to Gallup Poll daily tracking from May 14 to 16. Obama's nine-percentage-point lead is a strong showing for the Illinois senator in Gallup's May 16 interviewing. For the past few days, news coverage of the 2008 election has been dominated by the back-and-forth between Obama and the presumptive Republican nominee, John McCain, involving critical comments by McCain regarding statements by Obama on relations with Iran and dealing with the Israeli-Palestinian conflict, on the one hand, and attempts by Obama to underscore the links between McCain and President Bush, on the other.

Using two eggs, artist John Lamouranne creates an "egghead" sculpture of Senator Barack Obama. *(Newscom)*

Also implicit in this news coverage has been the assumption that Obama will be the Democratic nominee, with correspondingly much less news coverage of Clinton—despite the fact that she continues to campaign against Obama as the May 13 primary voting in Kentucky and Oregon approaches. Some news accounts suggest that Obama may "declare victory" after the voting on May 20. Both Obama's strong attacks on McCain and the Bush administration and the fact that Clinton has in some ways been shoved aside in news coverage of the campaign may have contributed to Obama's strong performance among Democrats in Gallup Poll daily tracking on May 9. Meanwhile, the latest Gallup Poll daily tracking data on the national election, from May 12 to 16, finds McCain remaining slightly ahead of Obama, 47% to 44%, among registered voters, while Clinton—despite the widespread assumption that she will not be the Democratic nominee—is doing better than Obama against McCain, with a slight two-point advantage over the Arizona senator, 47% to 45%.

MAY 20

Key Clinton Constituencies Moving Toward Obama

Gallup Poll daily tracking has documented a surge in Democratic voters' support for Obama over Clinton in recent days, swelling from a 4-percentage-point lead for Obama during the first part of May to a record 16-point lead for him in polling from May 16 to May 18. Obama's previous largest lead over Clinton was 11 percentage points, achieved briefly in mid-April. However, for most of the past month, Clinton and Obama have been fairly closely matched, with neither sustaining a significant lead for more than a few days. It thus remains to be seen whether this improvement in Obama's standing is a variation on the same pattern or represents a turning point in the race.

Obama Swamps Clinton Among Young Voters and Others

The broadening of Obama's appeal for the nomination seen in Gallup's May 16–18 polling is fairly widespread, with the percentage favoring him increasing among most demographic categories of Democratic voters. As a result, certain groups that were already highly supportive of Obama for the nomination—men, 18- to 29-year-olds, postgraduates, and upper-income Democrats—are now overwhelmingly in his camp. Obama is currently favored among these groups by a two-to-one margin over Clinton. At the same time, support for Clinton among some of her

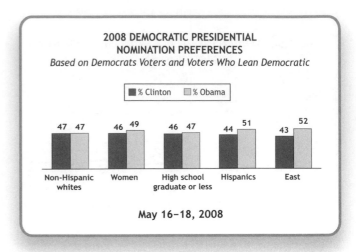

2008 DEMOCRATIC PRESIDENTIAL NOMINATION PREFERENCES
Based on Democrats Voters and Voters Who Lean Democratic

May 16–18, 2008

traditionally stalwart support groups—women, Easterners, whites, adults with no college education, and Hispanics—has fallen below 50%. The only major demographic group in which a majority still support Clinton is women age 50 and older. This group's preferences have changed little during May, at the same time that Clinton's support among younger men (age 18 to 49) has declined by nearly 10 points.

After nearly 20 grueling weeks on the campaign trail since he shook up the Democratic primary race by winning the Iowa caucuses, Obama has finally stretched his lead over his chief rival into the teens. Having previously captured close to a maximum level of support from black voters, Obama has achieved his latest gains from among a broad spectrum of rank-and-file Democrats. At least for now, he has expanded his position as the preferred candidate of men, of young adults, and of highly educated Democrats, and he has erased Clinton's advantages among most of her prior core constituency groups, including women, the less well educated, and whites.

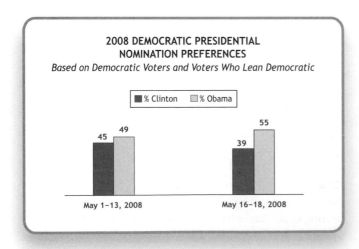

2008 DEMOCRATIC PRESIDENTIAL NOMINATION PREFERENCES
Based on Democratic Voters and Voters Who Lean Democratic

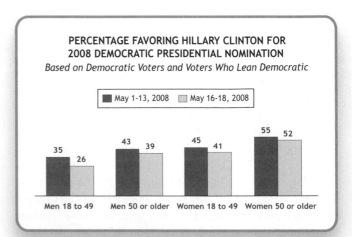

PERCENTAGE FAVORING HILLARY CLINTON FOR 2008 DEMOCRATIC PRESIDENTIAL NOMINATION
Based on Democratic Voters and Voters Who Lean Democratic

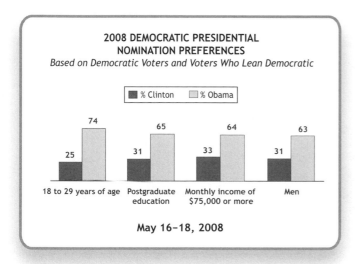

2008 DEMOCRATIC PRESIDENTIAL NOMINATION PREFERENCES
Based on Democratic Voters and Voters Who Lean Democratic

■ % Clinton   □ % Obama

	18 to 29 years of age	Postgraduate education	Monthly income of $75,000 or more	Men
% Clinton	25	31	33	31
% Obama	74	65	64	63

May 16–18, 2008

MAY 21

Obama Faces Uphill Climb Versus McCain Among White Voters

Barack Obama, the presumed Democratic nominee, will likely enter the general election with more of a handicap among white voters than would have been the case if Hillary Clinton had been the nominee, mainly because of Clinton's stronger performance among white women. A new Gallup Poll analysis of daily tracking data collected between May 1 and May 17 shows that Clinton's edge among white voters is not, as some have hypothesized, based on Obama's problems with blue-collar white men, but more reflects the fact of Clinton's strength among white women.

White Male Voters

In general, Obama and Clinton perform exactly the same among non-Hispanic white men when pitted against presumptive Republican nominee John McCain. Both Obama and Clinton lose to McCain among this group by 21-point margins, 36% to 57%. There has been discussion of Obama's presumed problem among blue-collar white males should he win the Democratic nomination. The current analysis, however, shows that relative to Clinton, Obama does not suffer from a large "blue-collar male" deficit as has been hypothesized. Obama loses to McCain in a hypothetical matchup among non-college-educated white men by 25 points, while Clinton loses by 20 points. Additionally, Obama shows compensatory strength among white-collar men, defined here as those with a college education. Among this group, Obama loses to McCain by 13 points, while Clinton loses by 22 points.

Collectively, these data suggest that the Democrats' probable nomination of Obama rather than Clinton does not mean Democrats will enter the general election with a bigger deficit among white men than they would have if Clinton were the nominee. The data from May suggest that Clinton might do only slightly better than Obama against McCain among blue-collar white men, and that this slight advantage likely would be offset by Obama's slight advantage among college-educated men.

White Female Voters

Among non-Hispanic white women, on the other hand, there is a significant difference in the way the two Democratic candidates perform against McCain. Both Obama and Clinton do better among white women than among white men against McCain—a typical pattern for Democratic presidential candidates. But there are differences between the two Democratic candidates. While Obama loses to McCain by a nine-point margin among white women, Clinton wins, by a three-point margin. This difference persists when white women are segmented into two groups by education. While Obama loses to McCain by 16 points among non-Hispanic white women with no college education, Clinton ties McCain. And while Obama does manage to squeak out a 4-point advantage over McCain among college-educated white women, Clinton wins, by an 11-point margin.

Although there has been a great deal of discussion of the problems that await Obama among white men should he win the Democratic nomination, this analysis suggests that while McCain certainly is strong among this group, it is no more of a strength against Obama than it would be against Clinton. Clinton's slight advantage among blue-collar white men is offset by Obama's advantage among white-collar white men. The bigger issue appears to be Obama's problems among white women, when compared with how Clinton would perform among this group. Clinton does better than Obama against McCain among both blue-collar and white-collar white women.

All in all, although both Democrats are to a degree handicapped against McCain among white voters, Clinton would perform better than Obama in a general election matchup among non-Hispanic whites. If we combine data from white voters of both genders, the current analysis shows that McCain wins against Obama among whites, 53% to 38%, and beats Clinton by a considerably smaller 51% to 42% margin. It is important to note that Obama runs about as well against McCain as Clinton does, and both Democrats currently maintain a slight advantage over McCain in general election trial heats. So any weaker relative performance by Obama versus McCain among a particular demographic group (such as white women or lower-educated voters) is made up for by a stronger relative performance among another group (such as blacks or higher-educated voters).

MAY 23

Typical Marriage Gap Evident in Early 2008 Vote

The Democratic candidates lead Republican John McCain among unmarried voters, while McCain bests both Barack Obama and Hillary Clinton among married voters. These results, based on interviews with more than 18,000 registered voters from Gallup Poll daily tracking in May, are similar to what Gallup has observed in recent presidential elections. In the last three presidential elections, the Republican candidate has fared better among married voters of either gender—except married women in 1996, when Bob Dole lost narrowly to Bill Clinton. Meanwhile, the Democratic candidate has won among unmarried voters of both genders in all three elections since 1996. (Gallup does not have data for voting by marital status prior to the 1996 election.)

Usually, among the four marriage-by-gender groups, married men show the greatest support for the Republican candidate and unmarried women most strongly back the Democrat. The degree to which those relationships hold in 2008 may depend in part on which candidate the Democrats eventually nominate. If, as seems likely, Obama is the Democratic nominee, he would enter the general election phase of the campaign with commanding leads among both unmarried men and unmarried women: He leads McCain by 23 percentage points among unmarried women and by 16 points among unmarried men. In turn, McCain outpolls Obama by a wide 17-point margin among married men, but holds a smaller 6-point advantage among married women.

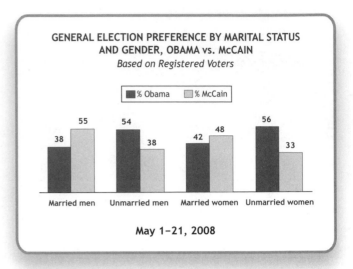

GENERAL ELECTION PREFERENCE BY MARITAL STATUS AND GENDER, OBAMA vs. McCAIN
Based on Registered Voters

May 1–21, 2008

The picture looks somewhat different on the assumption that Clinton is the Democratic nominee. She, like Obama, leads McCain among both unmarried groups, but by a larger margin among unmarried women (31 points) and by a smaller margin among unmarried men (6 points). McCain would fare just as well among married men against Clinton as he does against Obama, but these data suggest that Clinton and McCain would be highly competitive for the votes of married women. No doubt these relationships reflect Clinton's appeal to female voters, who have been among her most reliable supporters in the Democratic primaries. It is unclear whether Obama would be able to increase his standing among female voters if he were the Democratic nominee. But he has tended to make up for any disadvantage he has among female voters with greater support among blacks and young people.

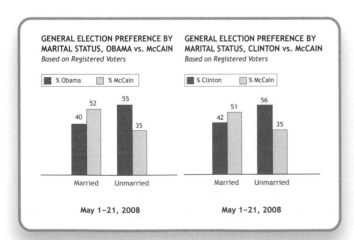

GENERAL ELECTION PREFERENCE BY MARITAL STATUS, OBAMA vs. McCAIN
Based on Registered Voters

May 1–21, 2008

GENERAL ELECTION PREFERENCE BY MARITAL STATUS, CLINTON vs. McCAIN
Based on Registered Voters

May 1–21, 2008

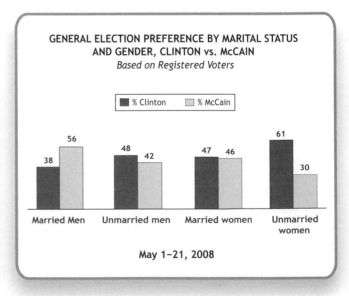

GENERAL ELECTION PREFERENCE BY MARITAL STATUS AND GENDER, CLINTON vs. McCAIN
Based on Registered Voters

May 1–21, 2008

These results suggest that the marriage gap evident in the past few elections will likely persist in 2008 as well, with McCain typically leading among married voters and the Democratic candidate leading among unmarried voters. Of the four marriage-by-gender groups, married women seem to be the most competitive, with Clinton and McCain essentially running even and McCain holding only a modest lead versus Obama among this group.

MAY 25

Clinton Maintains Lead Over McCain

Gallup Poll daily tracking from May 20 to May 24 finds Clinton maintaining a significant 49% to 44% lead over McCain when registered voters are asked about their preference in the fall general election, while McCain has a slight 47% to 45% advantage over Obama. Thus, although Obama is considered to be the highly probable Democratic nominee, Gallup Poll daily tracking continues to show that, at the moment, Clinton is performing better against presumptive Republican nominee McCain. Clinton's five-percentage-point lead over McCain is statistically significant. Yet, while Clinton is enjoying stronger support than Obama against McCain in a hypothetical general election matchup, she continues to lose to Obama among national Democrats. The most recent May 22–24 three-day rolling average has Obama at 50% and Clinton at 45%, a slightly smaller margin than in previous days.

MAY 27

Six in 10 Democrats Confident of Victory in 2008 Election

Democrats are much more confident that their party will win the November presidential election than are Republicans. A new Gallup survey, conducted between May 19 and May 21, finds 61% of Democrats saying they are confident their party will win the election, including 35% who are "very confident." Meanwhile, only 39% of Republicans are confident, with only 13% saying they are very confident. Thus, rank-and-file Republicans are aware that their party faces an uphill battle to retain the White House, given the problems in the economy, an ongoing and unpopular war, and an incumbent Republican president with some of the lowest job approval ratings in Gallup Poll history.

While Republicans generally agree that their odds of winning are long, a majority (58%) believe that likely presidential nominee John McCain gives the party the best chance among any of this year's Republican candidates of winning the election. Thirty-seven percent believe another candidate would have increased the party's odds of winning, with former Massachusetts governor Mitt Romney and former Arkansas governor Mike Huckabee mentioned most often (by 16% and 9% of Republicans, respectively).

Democrats are likewise secure in the belief that their likely candidate, Barack Obama, gives the party the best chance of winning the presidential election. Sixty-two percent of Democrats say this—though 34% disagree, and the vast majority of these Democrats believe Hillary Clinton would give the party a better chance of winning. Clinton herself has raised doubts about Obama's ability to deliver the White House to the Democrats in the fall, citing her success in the primaries in large swing states such as Ohio and Pennsylvania and her greater appeal to blue-collar voters, a key Democratic constituency. Notably, Democrats who prefer Obama for the nomination are much more confident in the party's chances of winning the November presidential election than are Clinton supporters, by a 70% to 49% margin. As would be expected, a majority of Clinton supporters believe Clinton would give the party the best chance of winning in November; only 22% of Clinton supporters believe Obama gives the Democrats the best chance of victory.

A Positive Outlook for the Democrats

Rank-and-file Democrats are optimistic that the current political environment, which is favorable to them, will allow them to win the presidency, in the same way it allowed them to take control of Congress in the 2006 midterm elections. Several important political indicators underscore the Democratic advantage heading into the 2008 election, including party identification, favorability ratings for the two political parties, and party members' enthusiasm about voting in the fall election. Turnout in Democratic primaries this year has also dwarfed that in Republican primaries, even in the early months when both contests were competitive. Republican Party leaders are hoping that their supporters' pessimism does not result in depressed turnout on Election Day. Republican leaders can perhaps take some solace in the fact that the rank and file believe the party will nominate the candidate who gives their party the best chance of winning, however long the odds may be.

MAY 28

Clinton's Swing-State Advantage

In the 20 states where Hillary Clinton has claimed victory in the 2008 Democratic primary and caucus elections, she has led John McCain in Gallup Poll daily trial heats for the general election over the past two weeks of Gallup Poll daily tracking by 50% to 43%. In those same states, Barack Obama is about tied with McCain among national registered voters, 45% to 46%. In contrast, in the 28 states and the District of Columbia where Obama has won a higher share of the popular vote against Clinton in the 2008 Democratic primaries and caucuses, there is essentially no difference in how Obama and Clinton each fare against McCain; both Democrats are statistically tied with him for the fall election. All of this speaks to Clinton's claim that her primary-state victories over Obama indicate her potential superiority in the general election. The results are based on aggregated data from Gallup Poll daily tracking from May 12 to May 25, including interviews with more than 11,000 registered voters nationwide. Across this period, Gallup has found Clinton performing marginally better than Obama in separate trial heats for the general election against McCain. Clinton has led McCain by an average of three percentage points, 48% vs. 45%; Obama has trailed McCain by an average of one point, 45% vs. 46%.

Clinton's popular-vote victories thus far include the three biggest Electoral College prizes: California (a solid Democratic state), New York (another sure bet for the Democrats), and Texas (a solid Republican state). (Although Obama won more delegates in Texas, Clinton's vote total exceeded Obama's by nearly 100,000 votes.) However, her victories also include several of the largest swing states that both parties will be battling to win in November: Pennsylvania and Ohio, as well as wins in the disputed Florida and Michigan primaries. As a result, Clinton's 20 states represent more than 300 Electoral College votes, while Obama's 28 states and the District of Columbia represent only 224 Electoral College votes. (Note that the findings with Michigan and Florida data removed are virtually identical to those shown above: Clinton runs five percentage points better than Obama versus McCain in the states she has won [51% vs. 46%], excluding Michigan and Florida; Obama has virtually no advantage over Clinton versus McCain in the states he has won.) The question is, do Clinton's popular victories over Obama in states that encompass three-fifths of national voters mean Clinton has a better chance than Obama of winning electoral votes this fall? That's the argument she and her campaign have been making, including at a campaign stop in Kentucky 10 days ago (prior to the Kentucky and Oregon primaries), where she was quoted as saying: "The states I've won total 300 electoral votes. If we had the same rules as the Republicans, I would be the nominee right now. We have different rules, so what we've got to figure out is who can win 270 electoral votes. My opponent has won states totaling 224 electoral votes."

As the Gallup analysis shows, Clinton is currently running ahead of McCain in the 20 states where she has

prevailed in the popular vote, while Obama is tied with McCain in those same states. Thus, at this stage in the race (before the general election campaigns have begun), there is some support for her argument that her primary-state victories indicate she would be stronger than Obama in the general election. The same cannot be said for Obama in the 28 states and the District of Columbia where he prevailed in the popular vote. As of now, in those states, he is performing no better than Clinton in general election trial heats versus McCain. Thus, the principle of primary-state victories translating into greater general election strength, while apparently operative with respect to the states Clinton has won, does not seem to apply at the moment to states Obama has won.

Red States, Blue States, Swing States

The picture described above is somewhat muddied by the fact that the sets of states Clinton and Obama have each won include reliably "red" (solid Republican) and "blue" (solid Democratic) states. A relative advantage for either Democratic contender in the primaries in such states won't matter come the fall, given that the general election outcome in these states is almost a foregone conclusion. Removing reliably red and blue states from the analysis leaves just the swing or "purple" states that could be competitive for both parties. Gallup defines these as states that favored neither George W. Bush nor John Kerry in the 2004 presidential election by more than five percentage points. Additionally, Arkansas—one of Clinton's home states—is considered a potential swing state should she become the nominee. And Missouri is considered a swing state because although Bush beat Kerry in that state by seven points in 2004, Missouri has switched sides in the three most recent national elections, voting Democratic in 1996 and Republican in 2000 and 2004. (Other states have also switched sides in the last three elections, but the 2004 vote margins in these states were well beyond 10 points for either Bush or Kerry.)

Clinton's 2008 swing-state victories include Nevada, Pennsylvania, Ohio, New Hampshire, New Mexico, Arkansas, and—based solely on popular vote (not delegates)—Florida and Michigan, for a total of 105 electoral votes. Thus far in May, Gallup has found Clinton leading McCain in these states by six percentage points, 49% to 43%, whereas McCain holds a slight edge over Obama in these states, 46% to 43%. Thus, as of today, Clinton is clearly the stronger Democratic candidate in this cluster of states in which she beat Obama in the popular vote.

With Florida and Michigan removed from the group of purple states in which Clinton has won the popular vote—leaving Arkansas, Nevada, Pennsylvania, Ohio,

New Hampshire, and New Mexico, with a total of 61 electoral votes—her relative advantage over Obama expands slightly: Clinton beats McCain in this group of states by 10 percentage points, 51% to 41%, whereas McCain leads Obama by the same three-point margin, 46% to 43%. Obama's swing-state victories include Colorado, Oregon, Minnesota, Iowa, Wisconsin, and Missouri, for a total of 54 electoral votes. Obama leads McCain in these states by eight percentage points, while Clinton falls one point behind McCain—the reverse of the pattern observed in Clinton's swing states. The only other difference seen in the two candidates' general election performances is in the seven safe (mostly Southern) Republican states won by Clinton in the primaries. Clinton loses to McCain by four points in these states, while Obama loses to McCain by 14 points. The two candidates fare equally well in the red states Obama won, as well as in the blue states each candidate won. Of course, as noted, relative advantages in the blue states are less important to the presidential election, assuming the outcome is assured regardless of which Democratic candidate is nominated.

Commentary: Swing-State Advantages

According to Gallup's May 12–25 tracking polling, Clinton is running stronger against McCain than is Obama in the 20 states where Clinton won popular-vote victories in the Democratic primaries and caucuses. By contrast, Obama runs no better against McCain than does Clinton in the 28 states plus the District of Columbia where he prevailed. On this basis, Clinton appears to have the stronger chance of capitalizing on her primary-election strengths in the general election. However, just focusing on the swing states in Clinton's and Obama's respective win columns, the two run fairly similarly against McCain. Clinton beats McCain in her purple (swing) states (including Florida and Michigan) by 49% to 43%, while Obama slightly trails McCain (43% to 46%) in those states—a nine-point gap in Clinton's favor. Conversely, Obama beats McCain in his purple states 49% to 41%, while Clinton trails McCain by one point, 45% to 46%, in those states—an identical nine-point gap in Obama's favor.

Clinton's main advantage is that her states—including Florida and Michigan—represent nearly twice as many Electoral College votes as Obama's. However, removing Florida and Michigan from the equation, her purple states are about comparable to Obama's in cumulative electoral vote total, and thus the two appear more evenly positioned. What gives Clinton an additional boost in her national support among Democrats—but is not likely to increase her chances of winning Electoral College votes in November—is her superior performance over Obama in

the reliably red states where she has captured the popular vote in the primaries. These include such typically safe Republican states as Oklahoma, Texas, Indiana, and Arizona.

MAY 29

Public Says Media Harder on Clinton than on Obama or McCain

Although Americans in general think that news media coverage of the three major presidential candidates has been "about right," they are more inclined to say the media has been "too hard" on Hillary Clinton and "too easy" on Barack Obama and John McCain. These results are based on the latest Gallup survey, conducted between May 19 and May 21. Bill and Hillary Clinton are two of the most prominent people to suggest that the news media have been unfairly critical of her and her campaign. The overall sentiment of the American public seems to tilt in agreement, with significantly more Americans saying the media have been too hard on Clinton than say that about the coverage of either Obama or McCain. Clinton's supporters generally share this negative view of her treatment by the media: A majority (56%) of Democrats who support Clinton for the presidential nomination say the media has been too hard on her—nearly double the percentage of Obama supporters who agree.

Some, including the Clintons, have also argued that the media were not taking a critical enough look at Obama, though that talk has subsided to some degree given the attention paid to the controversy over his association with the Reverend Jeremiah Wright and his remarks about "bitter" rural voters. Most Obama supporters seem satisfied with the coverage of their candidate: Fifty-three percent say it has been about right, while 33% say it has been too harsh. On the other hand, Clinton supporters are more than twice as likely to say media coverage has been too easy on Obama as to say it has been too hard on him.

In addition to assessing voters' views of the coverage of the presidential candidates, the poll asked Americans to evaluate news coverage of the political parties during the campaign. The public is slightly more inclined to think the Democratic Party has gotten more favorable or at least less unfavorable coverage, as 23% say the media have been too hard on the Republican Party, compared with 16% who say this about coverage of the Democratic Party.

More generally, Americans are roughly equally divided as to whether they approve (47%) or disapprove (52%) of the job the news media are doing in covering the election. When those who disapprove were asked to explain why they feel so, their comments focused more on general criticisms than on the treatment of specific candidates. The most common responses involved general accusations of bias, and of not being completely truthful. Other criticisms included that coverage was too "shallow" and did not pay attention to important issues, instead focusing too much on negative stories; and some faulted the media for too much coverage of politics in general. Republicans who disapprove of media coverage are most likely to say it is because the coverage is biased or too focused on the Democrats. Democrats, on the other hand, tend to disapprove because media coverage is too shallow and does not cover important issues, and because there is too much focus on the negative.

Views of the Media in Context

Although slightly more Americans disapprove than approve of media coverage of the election, a plurality of respondents say the coverage of each presidential candidate and of both political parties has been "about right." Americans have not always been very charitable in their ratings of the media, so the current ratings, while not overly positive, are not necessarily bad when considered in that context. The media to some extent are saddled with the perception that they do not treat a person's preferred candidate as well as they treat other candidates. This is apparent in the ratings of Clinton's and Obama's media treatment by their respective supporters, and it also applies to ratings of McCain's media coverage by Republicans.

Partisan Gap on Global Warming Grows

The slight upward trend in Americans' concern about global warming over the past decade masks a more significant trend: the growing gap between Republicans and Democrats over this issue. In 1997, Republicans and Democrats were equally likely to say the effects of global warming had "already begun to happen" (47% and 46%, respectively). In sharp contrast, this year's Gallup Environment Poll finds only 41% of Republicans saying the effects of global warming have already begun, compared with three-quarters of Democrats (76%). At the same time, during the past decade, Republicans have become much more likely to believe that news of global warming is "generally exaggerated" (from 34% in 1997 to 59% this year), while far fewer Democrats agree with that view, ranging from 23% in 1997 to 18% in 2008.

The scientific consensus regarding the reality and causes of global warming has grown stronger over the past decade,

as reflected in the widely publicized reports of the Intergovernmental Panel on Climate Change (IPCC). Interestingly, both Republicans and Democrats have become more likely to accept that "most scientists believe that global warming is occurring," although Gallup's trend data are more limited on this question, and hence caution is called for in drawing firm conclusions. The percentage of Republicans holding this view increased from 39% in 1997 to 56% in 2001, and it remains at that level in 2008. For Democrats the increase in those agreeing has been somewhat larger, from 51% in 1997 to 70% in 2001 and 74% today.

Although increasing proportions of both Republicans and Democrats accept that a majority of scientists believe global warming is occurring, the pattern is very different with respect to the second key conclusion of the IPCC: that human activities are contributing to global warming. Gallup's trend data show that Republicans have become less likely over the past half-decade to accept the idea of humans contributing to global warming: The percentage believing that global warming is due more to "the effects of pollution from human activities" than to natural environmental changes has declined by 10 percentage points, from 52% in 2003 to 42% in 2008. In contrast, Democrats may have become slightly more likely to attribute global warming to human activities, with the percentage giving this response increasing from 68% to 73% over the same period (although this shift is within the margin of error for the two Democratic samples).

Finally, and perhaps reflecting a synthesis of views on the foregoing issues, the trends reveal a modest increase in the gap between Republicans and Democrats over the threat posed by global warming. There has been a modest increase in the percentage of Republicans who believe global warming "will pose a serious threat" during their lifetimes, from 21% in 1997 to 29% today. The increase among Democrats, from 36% to 50%, is somewhat larger. The result is that while fully half of Democrats see global warming as a serious threat, this is true of less than a third of Republicans.

Explaining the growing partisan gap in public views of global warming will require extensive analyses. As shown, Republicans harbor more widespread skepticism of news coverage of global warming than they did a decade ago, and that could be driving down their willingness to believe environmental reports about the phenomenon. Those doubts could be fueled, in turn, by the skepticism about global warming currently expressed by party leaders and conservative commentators. It will be particularly interesting to see whether Republican presidential candidate John McCain's "greener" stance on the issue, including his support for policies to limit human-induced climate change, influences rank-and-file Republicans over the coming months.

JUNE 2008

Gallup's annual update on confidence in institutions finds just 12% of Americans expressing confidence in Congress—the lowest of the 16 institutions tested this year, and the worst rating Gallup has measured for any institution in the 35-year history of this question. Gallup first asked about confidence in institutions in 1973, repeating the question biannually through 1983 and obtaining annual

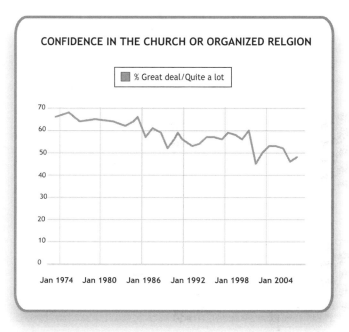

updates since then. This year's update comes from a June 9–12 Gallup Poll.

In the latest update, Congress ranks just below HMOs, for whom 13% of Americans express "a great deal" or "quite a lot" of confidence. Big business, the criminal justice system, organized labor, newspapers, television news, and the presidency all receive relatively low confidence ratings. In contrast, Americans express the most confidence in the military, as they have each year since 1988 (with the exception of 1997, when small business edged it out). Small business ranks second in the current poll, just ahead of the police. These are the only three institutions for which a majority of Americans express a high degree of confidence. From 1973 through 1985, organized religion was the highest-rated institution. Today, just 48% of Americans express confidence in organized religion, one of its lowest ratings ever. The lowest

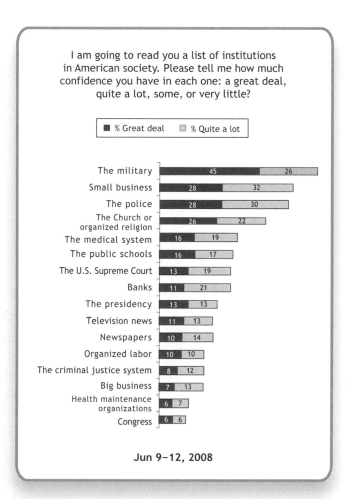

I am going to read you a list of institutions in American society. Please tell me how much confidence you have in each one: a great deal, quite a lot, some, or very little?

Jun 9–12, 2008

CHRONOLOGY

JUNE 2008

June 1   The United States military announces that during May, 19 American soldiers were killed in Iraq, the lowest level since hostilities began in 2003.

June 1   Hillary Clinton wins the Puerto Rico primary.

June 3   Barack Obama wins the Montana primary; Clinton wins the South Dakota primary. With all the primary and caucus contests complete, Obama has a clear majority of delegates. His status as the Democratic presidential nominee seems assured.

June 5   The Senate Select Committee on Intelligence reports that the Bush administration exaggerated the threat posed by Iraq in order to justify the war. The White House calls the report a "selective view."

June 7   Clinton suspends her campaign for the Democratic presidential nomination and concedes to Obama. In her speech she asks her supporters "to join me in working as hard for Barack Obama as you have for me."

June 12   The Supreme Court rules that detainees in Guantánamo have a constitutional right to appeal their imprisonment to a federal court.

June 13   Taliban forces assault a jail in Kandahar, Afghanistan. Hundreds of Taliban prisoners escape.

June 17   A bus filled with explosives kills more than 60 people in Baghdad.

June 19   Obama declares that he will not use federal matching funds for the general election campaign. This decision removes the limit that would have been placed on his fund-raising.

June 26   The Supreme Court rules that the Second Amendment protects an individual's right to keep a loaded handgun at home for self-defense.

June 27   Obama and Clinton hold a joint event in Unity, New Hampshire, pledging to work together to defeat John McCain in November.

---

score for religion to date was 45% in 2002, at the height of the Catholic Church's priest sex abuse scandal.

Prior to this year's 12% confidence rating for Congress, HMOs had registered the lowest historical score, 13% in

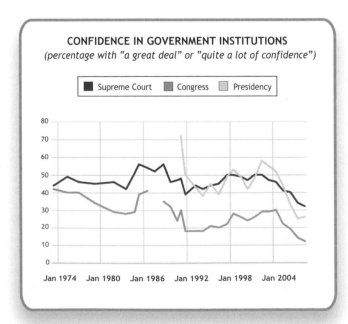

CONFIDENCE IN GOVERNMENT INSTITUTIONS
(percentage with "a great deal" or "quite a lot of confidence")

■ Supreme Court   ■ Congress   □ Presidency

2002. The 12% rating for Congress does not include the 45% of Americans who now say they have "some" confidence in Congress; a nearly equal proportion—41%—say they have "little" or "no" confidence in Congress. Even though the Supreme Court (32% "great deal" or "quite a lot" of confidence) and presidency (26%) are rated more positively than Congress, all government institutions are at or near their lowest ratings to date. The rating for the presidency is just one percentage point above its worst rating of 25% from 2007, while the Supreme Court's rating is its worst ever. Government institutions are not alone in experiencing a decline in public confidence. While only one nongovernmental institution (banks) has seen a significant decline in confidence over the past year, all have dropped compared with 2004, the last presidential election year. Banks and the three branches of government have had the greatest drops in confidence over that time, while the military and big business have seen the least change.

With respect to these confidence measures, long-term changes are usually more evident than year-to-year changes, and the current data are no exception. There has been little change from the 2007 ratings, aside from a

CHANGE IN CONFIDENCE IN INSTITUTIONS, 2004-2008 *(percentage with "a great deal" or "quite a lot of confidence")*	2004	2008	Change
The presidency	52	26	-26
Banks	53	32	-21
Congress	30	12	-18
The U.S. Supreme Court	46	32	-14
The criminal justice system	34	20	-14
Organized labor	31	20	-11
The medical system	44	35	-9
The public schools	41	33	-8
Newspapers	30	24	-6
Television news	30	24	-6
The police	64	58	-6
The Church or organized religion	53	48	-5
Health maintenance organizations	18	13	-5
The military	75	71	-4
Big business	24	20	-4

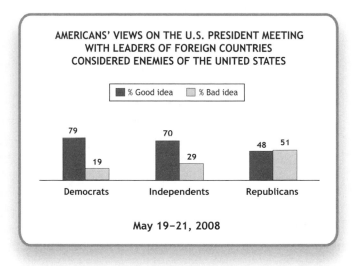

AMERICANS' VIEWS ON THE U.S. PRESIDENT MEETING WITH LEADERS OF FOREIGN COUNTRIES CONSIDERED ENEMIES OF THE UNITED STATES

May 19–21, 2008

9-point drop in confidence for banks (from 41% to 32%). Beyond that, the only other significant changes are modest increases in reported confidence in the police (58%, up from 54%) and the medical system (35%, up from 31%), but both cases mainly reflect a rebound to 2006 levels after they experienced declines in 2007. The poor economy and the lack of effective government action on important issues such as gasoline prices, the Iraq War, and immigration have helped contribute to the erosion of trust and confidence in government institutions. These confidence-in-institutions ratings underscore the public's frustration and signal an electorate that may be hungry for change in Washington come the fall elections.

JUNE 2

Americans Favor President Meeting with U.S. Enemies

Large majorities of Democrats and independents, and even half of Republicans, believe that the president of the United States should meet with the leaders of countries that are considered enemies of the United States. Overall, 67% of Americans say this kind of diplomacy is a good idea.

Although separate Gallup polling shows that few Americans view Iran favorably and that Iran leads Americans' list of top U.S. enemies in the world, the new Gallup survey also finds high public support for presidential-level meetings between the United States and Iran. About 6 in 10 Americans (59%) think it would be a good idea for the president of the United States to meet with the president of Iran. This includes about half of Republi-

cans, a majority of independents, and most Democrats. Both positions enjoy broad popular appeal, with majorities of men, women, younger and older Americans, and those from different regions of the country all saying direct presidential-level talks with Iran and with other enemy nations are a good idea. The issue of undertaking presidential diplomacy with U.S. enemies distinguishes Illinois senator Barack Obama from the presumptive Republican presidential nominee, Arizona senator John McCain, and even from his opponent for the Democratic nomination, New York senator Hillary Clinton. Obama is the only one of the three who has said he would personally meet as president with the leaders of countries like Iran, Syria, Cuba, and Venezuela, and he recently defended his position by saying that "strong countries and strong presidents talk to their adversaries." Clinton has criticized Obama's approach as "naïve," and McCain has been unrelenting in his attacks on the issue, accusing Obama of being dangerously inexperienced and having "reckless judgment."

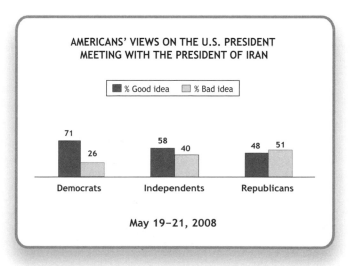

AMERICANS' VIEWS ON THE U.S. PRESIDENT MEETING WITH THE PRESIDENT OF IRAN

May 19–21, 2008

McCain may eventually persuade more Americans that there is nothing for the president of the United States to discuss with hostile foreign leaders like Iranian president Mahmoud Ahmadinejad, and that to do so only undermines U.S. efforts to destabilize such regimes. However, for now, whether it's the leader of an "enemy" country generally or the president of Iran specifically, Americans think it's a good idea for the president of the United States to meet directly with the nation's adversaries.

JUNE 3

Clinton Maintains Loyalty of Democratic Women

The Democratic primary season is ending with Barack Obama maintaining an overall advantage in national Democratic nomination preference, but with continuing evidence of a significant gender gap. Hillary Clinton is the clear favorite of Democratic women, among whom she leads Obama by a 49% to 45% margin, while Obama leads over Clinton among Democratic men by a 20-point margin, 57% to 37%. The Gallup analysis of more than 12,000 Gallup Poll daily tracking interviews conducted among Democratic voters in May finds that Clinton's relative advantage among women is evident not only among all Democrats, but also among certain key subgroups of the Democratic electorate.

As has been well demonstrated this year, there are enormous differences among Democratic racial and ethnic groups in candidate preference between Obama and Clinton, but the current analysis shows that Clinton's disproportionate appeal among women (and Obama's among men) persists even when race and ethnicity are

controlled for. Obama has an overall lead of 70 points over Clinton among non-Hispanic black Democratic voters. He wins by a 75-point margin among black men, compared with a slightly slimmer 67-point margin among black women. Among non-Hispanic whites, the gender gap is more pronounced: Obama wins among white men by 7 points but loses among white women by a 20-point margin. Among white Hispanics, the gap is similarly large: Obama loses to Clinton among Hispanic men by six points and loses among Hispanic women by 30 points.

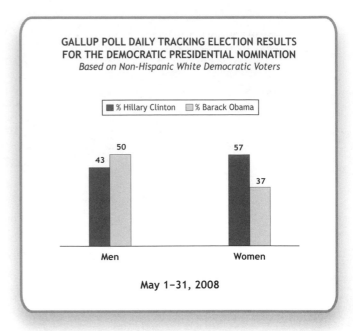

GALLUP POLL DAILY TRACKING ELECTION RESULTS FOR THE DEMOCRATIC PRESIDENTIAL NOMINATION
Based on Non-Hispanic White Democratic Voters

May 1–31, 2008

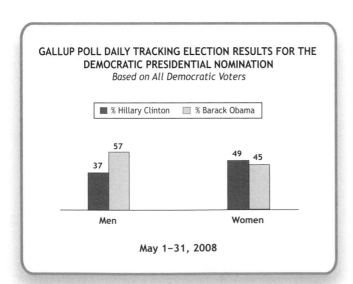

GALLUP POLL DAILY TRACKING ELECTION RESULTS FOR THE DEMOCRATIC PRESIDENTIAL NOMINATION
Based on All Democratic Voters

May 1–31, 2008

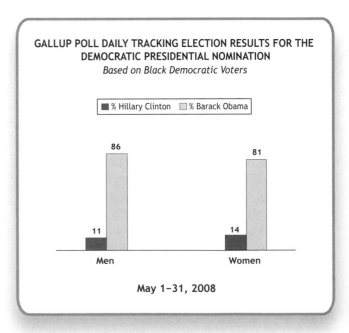

GALLUP POLL DAILY TRACKING ELECTION RESULTS FOR THE DEMOCRATIC PRESIDENTIAL NOMINATION
Based on Black Democratic Voters

May 1–31, 2008

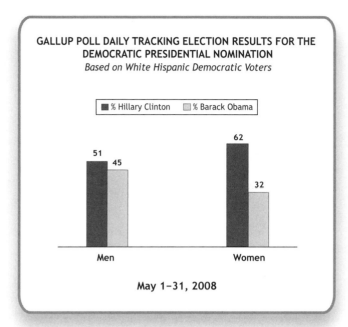

GALLUP POLL DAILY TRACKING ELECTION RESULTS FOR THE DEMOCRATIC PRESIDENTIAL NOMINATION
Based on White Hispanic Democratic Voters

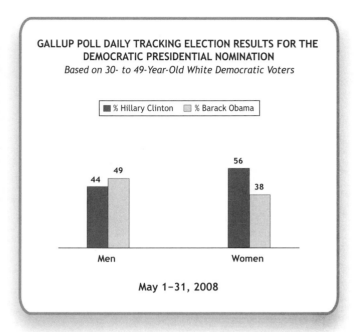

GALLUP POLL DAILY TRACKING ELECTION RESULTS FOR THE DEMOCRATIC PRESIDENTIAL NOMINATION
Based on 30- to 49-Year-Old White Democratic Voters

The other demographic dimensions that have clearly differentiated patterns of support among Democrats this year are age and education. Overall, Obama has great strength among younger Democrats and among Democrats with higher levels of education, while Clinton's support is stronger among older, less well-educated voters. Even though Obama wins among 18- to 29-year-old Democratic voters of both genders, there is still a significant gender gap: He beats Clinton among 18- to 29-year-old white men by a very large 43 points, but wins among white women age 18 to 29 by a much smaller 12-point margin. And among the oldest group of white Democrats, those 65 and older (arguably Clinton's core constituency), Obama loses to Clinton among white males by 19 points but by a more substantial 36 points among white females.

Clinton has demonstrated strength among Democratic voters who are not college graduates, while Obama does well among those who have graduated from college. But there is a gender gap of 22 points among non-college-educated white Democrats, with Obama losing to Clinton by only 8 points among men in this group, but by 30 points among women. Among college graduates, Obama wins

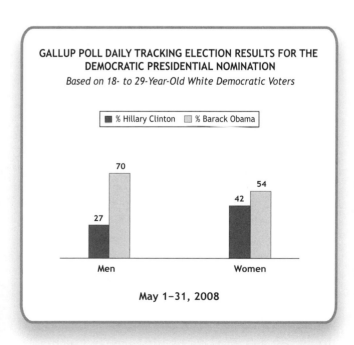

GALLUP POLL DAILY TRACKING ELECTION RESULTS FOR THE DEMOCRATIC PRESIDENTIAL NOMINATION
Based on 18- to 29-Year-Old White Democratic Voters

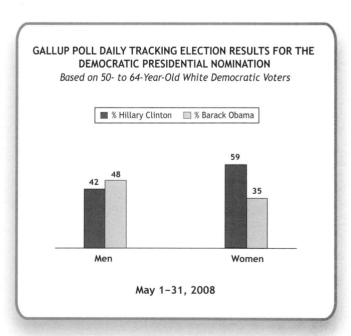

GALLUP POLL DAILY TRACKING ELECTION RESULTS FOR THE DEMOCRATIC PRESIDENTIAL NOMINATION
Based on 50- to 64-Year-Old White Democratic Voters

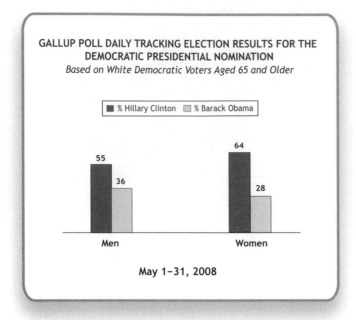

GALLUP POLL DAILY TRACKING ELECTION RESULTS FOR THE
DEMOCRATIC PRESIDENTIAL NOMINATION
Based on White Democratic Voters Aged 65 and Older

May 1–31, 2008

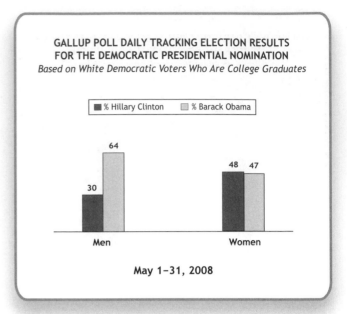

GALLUP POLL DAILY TRACKING ELECTION RESULTS
FOR THE DEMOCRATIC PRESIDENTIAL NOMINATION
Based on White Democratic Voters Who Are College Graduates

May 1–31, 2008

among men by 34 points, while Clinton edges him by one point among women, for a gender gap of 35 points.

Implications for the General Election

Democrats traditionally do better among women than among men in general election presidential matchups. Assuming that Obama gains the Democratic nomination, as appears all but certain, he will need to depend on a strong turnout among women to ensure his victory—or, conversely, he will need to alter the typical pattern by which men skew toward voting for the Republican presidential candidate. The data reviewed here among Democratic voters clearly show the degree to which Clinton, the

first major party female presidential candidate to make it this far in the process, has capitalized on the strength of Democratic women as a core constituency. This suggests that Obama has the general election challenge of gaining strength among the women who have favored Clinton, or capitalizing on the opportunity provided by the men who have supported his candidacy. Some observers have suggested that Obama could face a backlash of sorts among Democratic women and thus run the risk of losing their votes in the general election.

An analysis of more than 25,000 interviews Gallup conducted among registered voters in May reveals the expected gender gap in Obama's and Clinton's performance against presumptive Republican nominee John McCain. Obama loses to McCain by 6 points among men while winning by 6 points among women; Clinton loses among men by 9 points and wins among women by 14 points. Doing the math on these numbers shows why Clinton was able to do slightly better than Obama against McCain overall in May: She generated stronger support among women that more than compensated for her weaker level of support among men. Obama's challenge is to increase his margin among Democratic women closer to the 14 points Clinton enjoys (from his current 6-point margin), while in the process gaining a few points against McCain in the overall general election balloting. In a close race, this could be enough to be the difference between a win and a loss.

Record-High 55% of Americans "Financially Worse Off"

A majority of Americans say they are worse off financially than a year ago, marking the first time in Gallup's 32-

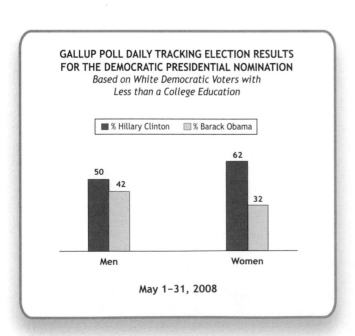

GALLUP POLL DAILY TRACKING ELECTION RESULTS
FOR THE DEMOCRATIC PRESIDENTIAL NOMINATION
*Based on White Democratic Voters with
Less than a College Education*

May 1–31, 2008

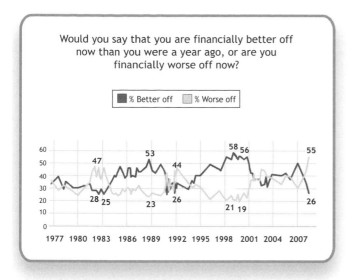

Would you say that you are financially better off now than you were a year ago, or are you financially worse off now?

■ % Better off   □ % Worse off

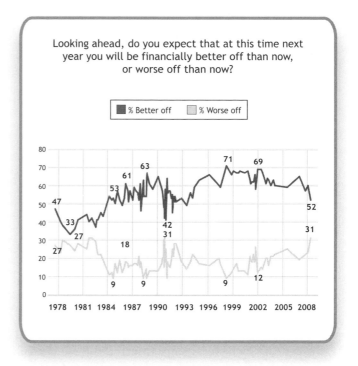

Looking ahead, do you expect that at this time next year you will be financially better off than now, or worse off than now?

■ % Better off   □ % Worse off

year history of asking the question that more than half of Americans give this pessimistic assessment. The previous high on this "worse off than a year ago" measure was back in 1982, in the first years of the Reagan administration, when 47% of those interviewed said they were worse off. When Gallup last asked this question in late January/early February 2008, 44% said they were worse off. Only 26%

of Americans now say they are *better* off financially than they were a year ago—which is one point shy of the all-time low reading on this measure, 25%, recorded several

Claiming victory in his quest for the Democratic presidential nomination, Senator Barack Obama bumps fists with his wife, Michelle, at a rally in St. Paul, Minnesota, on June 3, 2008. *(Scott Olson/Newscom)*

times from 1982 to 1990. At the same time, Americans remain, on a relative basis at least, somewhat optimistic about the future. Fifty-two percent believe they will be better off financially a year from now, while just 31% say they will be worse off. This "optimism" measure is actually quite a bit more positive than it has been at other times. The lowest reading on the "will be better off" measure was 33%, recorded in 1979, and the readings have been below 50% at several other points since then. The highest optimism reading occurred in March 1998, when 71% said they anticipated being better off in a year than they were at the moment.

Commentary

The bad news from these data is clear: A record number of Americans have become convinced that their personal financial situation has deteriorated over the last year. Perhaps the high price of gasoline and the impact it is having on Americans' budgets is a major factor in these perceptions (although it should be noted that the negative result for this measure is worse than at other times when there was a sudden run-up in the price of gasoline). Because Americans are usually more positive about their personal situation than about the more general situation "out there," the record-high negative reading when the public is asked about its own financial situation suggests that the current economic downturn is having a significant personal impact. The good news is that Americans have not lost their typical pattern of optimism: A little more than half retain some optimism that their financial situation will get better in the year ahead. In fact, a review of the history of asking these two questions shows that optimism is certainly the rule. There has never been a time when Americans have been more pessimistic than optimistic about their future financial situation; and despite the sharp uptick in negative mood, that generally optimistic attitude continues today.

JUNE 4

As Primary Campaign Ends, Clinton's Image Mostly Intact

Hillary Clinton is emerging from the bitterly contested Democratic primary campaign with her public image among Democrats largely intact. More than three-quarters of Democrats (74%) still view her favorably—the same percentage of Democrats who view Barack Obama favorably. For most of 2007, 80% or more of national Democrats said they had a favorable view of Clinton. Positive views of her dipped below 80% in January and February 2008,

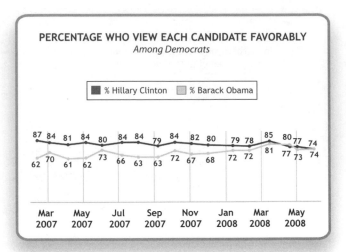

PERCENTAGE WHO VIEW EACH CANDIDATE FAVORABLY
Among Democrats

rebounded to 85% in March, but have since been in the mid- to high 70s. Over the same period, Obama's favorability rating rose by 12 points, from 62% last February to 74% today. This was as Obama became better known nationally, and more people were able to rate him. While Clinton's favorable rating among Democrats is slightly lower today than it once was, it has remained nearly flat among political independents. Also, after about a year of receiving minimal favorable ratings from Republicans (ranging from 12% to 19%), she is now viewed favorably by a slightly more robust 24% of Republicans, similar to the 21% to 28% seen in February and March 2007.

Beyond maintaining fairly strong favorability ratings among Democrats, Clinton also continues to be highly competitive in USA Today/Gallup general election trial heats against Republican John McCain. Although this is quickly becoming irrelevant in terms of her efforts to convince superdelegates to back her nomination bid, it is an additional example of how her general appeal with the public has held up in spite of her impending Democratic

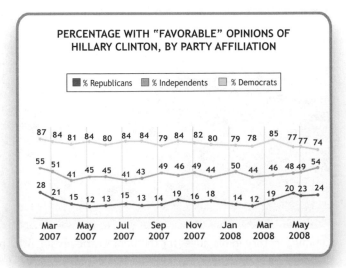

PERCENTAGE WITH "FAVORABLE" OPINIONS OF HILLARY CLINTON, BY PARTY AFFILIATION

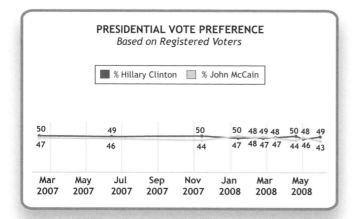

PRESIDENTIAL VOTE PREFERENCE
Based on Registered Voters

■ % Hillary Clinton   ☐ % John McCain

| 50 | | 49 | | | | 50 | | 50 | 48 | 49 | 48 | | 50 | 48 | | 49 |
| 47 | | | 46 | | | | 44 | | 47 | | 48 | 47 | 47 | | | 44 | 46 | 43 |

| Mar 2007 | May 2007 | Jul 2007 | Sep 2007 | Nov 2007 | Jan 2008 | Mar 2008 | May 2008 |

defeat. In February 2007, Clinton was favored by 50% of national registered voters to McCain's 47%. Today she holds an even stronger, six-point lead on the same presidential ballot question, 49% to 43%. Of course, these positive indicators of Clinton's popularity belie the fact that national Democrats now favor Obama over Clinton for the Democratic nomination by a substantial margin. The latest USA Today/Gallup Poll on the Democratic nomination, conducted between May 30 and June 1, 2008, finds Obama leading Clinton in national Democratic preferences by 13 points, 53% to 40%. About a year ago, Clinton led second-place Obama by 14 points, 42% to 28%, with former North Carolina senator John Edwards the choice of 14%. And at the height of Clinton's front-runner position, in October 2007, she led Obama by 29 points, 50% to 21%.

Thus, whereas Clinton's overall favorability among Democrats has declined by 13 points from its high point in February 2007, her position relative to Obama in national Democratic preferences has swung by as much as 42 points. It was anticipated that the year 2008 would be dominated by complaints that the front-loaded primary schedule (exemplified by "Super Tuesday") allowed the party front-runners to sew up their respective nominations too early. The disproportionate influence of Iowa and New Hampshire, as compared with the more populous and nationally representative states that would hold their elections as "late" as March or April, would also, it was assumed, again be in the forefront of criticism. Instead, the political discourse in 2008 has focused on examining how Clinton, a candidate with a substantial lead in national Democratic preferences heading into the primaries and overwhelming advantages in party support, could lose the elected delegate war. One thing is clear: Clinton did not lose on the basis of greatly diminished popular appeal—not within her party, not among political independents, and not among all registered voters. She still has considerable strengths in those areas.

General Election Shaping Up as Change vs. Experience

When Americans are asked why they would support either Barack Obama or John McCain in November's general election, Obama supporters are most likely to stress that he would bring about change and a fresh approach, while McCain supporters are most likely to mention that he is the most experienced. Now that Obama and McCain have become the presumptive nominees of their respective parties, the question becomes one of ascertaining exactly what themes, concerns, and issues will be on voters' minds as they choose between the two candidates. There are clear differences in the demographic characteristics of the two candidates' supporters, and polling shows that both will begin the general election race with their respective parties' traditional base groups of voters. But what's inside the minds of each candidate's supporters at this point? A recent May 19–21 Gallup survey included an open-ended question asking Americans which candidate they wanted to see win the general election, and then asking those in each group to explain in their own words why they chose their particular candidate. An analysis of the results suggests the following conclusions:

1. First and foremost, the reasons Americans give for supporting the two presumptive nominees show that they have picked up on the nominees' dominant themes as expressed in their campaign speeches, advertisements, and public pronouncements so far: Obama would bring about needed change, while McCain brings needed experience. These themes are articulated by more than one out of four of each candidate's supporters.

2. As is typically the case in presidential elections, a significant percentage of Americans supporting the two candidates explain their preference in more generic ways, centering on partisanship or party identification or ideological positioning of the candidates, along with general likes or dislikes of the candidates and their personalities. Obama supporters in particular are likely to mention their desire to prevent a Republican from continuing to occupy the White House as a reason for their support.

3. Obama appears to be more of a lightning rod for his opponents than is true for McCain. The data show that McCain supporters are more likely to mention Obama (in a negative way) as their reason for supporting McCain than Obama supporters are to mention McCain as the reason they support Obama.

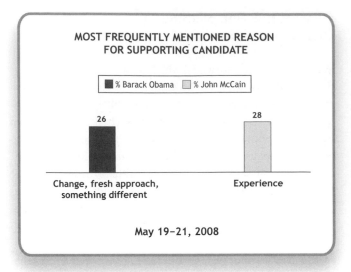

MOST FREQUENTLY MENTIONED REASON
FOR SUPPORTING CANDIDATE

■ % Barack Obama   □ % John McCain

26   28

Change, fresh approach,   Experience
something different

May 19-21, 2008

Please tell me in your own words why you want
Barack Obama to win the presidential election.
Based on Respondents Who Want Obama to Win the Election

Would bring change/fresh approach/something different	26%
Do not want another Republican/more of the same/third Bush term	17%
Vote Democratic/Respondent is a Democrat	10%
Agree with Obama's policies/ideas (nonspecific)	10%
Obama is the better candidate	9%
Down to earth/Cares about people	5%
Do not like McCain	4%
Honest/Has integrity	4%
Iraq war issue (would stop war)	3%
Intelligent	3%
Time for a black president	3%
Obama is lesser of two evils	2%
Can unite Americans	2%
Healthcare issue	1%
Do not trust McCain	1%
Economy/Better for the economy	1%
Other	2%
No reason in particular	1%

May 19-21, 2008

Note: Percentages add to more than 100 due to multiple responses.

4. At this early point in the campaign, few Americans supporting either candidate mention issue positions as the reason for their support—although, as indicated above, many do say they generally agree or disagree with a candidate's ideology or party platform. Among specific issues for either candidate, Iraq is the most frequently mentioned, although by relatively few supporters.

5. McCain supporters appear slightly more likely to mention their candidate's issue positions or specific traits as a reason for their vote than is the case for Obama supporters.

6. The most frequently occurring explanations centering on Obama's personal characteristics are that he is "down to earth" and "cares about people," that he is honest, his leadership, and his intelligence.

7. The most frequently occurring explanations centering on McCain's personal characteristics are that he is conservative, his war record and military service, and his leadership abilities.

DETAILS: OBAMA SUPPORTERS

Obama supporters most frequently base their support on Obama's ability to bring about change and a fresh approach to governing, echoing the central theme of the Obama campaign so far this year. Beyond this specific response, however, the next four categories of responses from Obama supporters are more generic or partisan in nature, rather than being specific to Obama's attributes or policy positions: not wanting another Republican or a "third" Bush term (the latter, of course, echoes an often-heard refrain from Obama on the campaign trail), a straightforward partisan explanation that the respondent is a Democrat and always votes Democratic, general agreement with Obama's policies, and a generic "Obama is the better candidate" response. Relatively small percentages of Obama's supporters give more

specific explanations focusing on his personal characteristics, issue positions, or other matters. These include the perception that Obama is "down to earth" and "cares about people," that he is honest or has good leadership qualities, that he would end the war in Iraq, that he is intelligent, that it is time for a black president, and that he would unite Americans. The most frequently mentioned issue positions are Obama's stance on the Iraq War, mentioned by 3% of Obama supporters, and healthcare and the economy, each supplied by just 1% of Obama's supporters.

DETAILS: MCCAIN SUPPORTERS

McCain supporters are most likely to say they support the Arizona senator's candidacy because of his experience or Obama's lack of experience. This—as is the case with Obama's supporters—echoes a central McCain campaign theme. Beyond that, there is a category of explanations built around partisan or generic issues relating to McCain's overall persona: general agreement with McCain on the issues, McCain is a Republican, McCain is a conservative, McCain is "the better candidate," and McCain is the lesser of two evils. McCain supporters are more likely to mention their dislike for Obama than are Obama supporters to mention their dislike for McCain. Six percent of McCain supporters say they do not like Obama (vs. 4% of Obama supporters who do not like McCain), 4% say they do not trust Obama (vs. 1% in the other direction), and 3% say Obama is too liberal (vs. less than 1% in the other direction). Some McCain

Please tell me in your own words why you want
John McCain to win the presidential election.
Based on Respondents Who Want McCain to Win the Election

Experience (McCain has/Obama lacks)	28%
Agree with McCain on issues (nonspecific)	12%
Vote Republican/Respondent is a Republican	9%
McCain is conservative	8%
McCain is the better candidate	7%
Do not like Obama	6%
Military service/background	6%
McCain is lesser of two evils	6%
Leadership qualities	6%
Iraq War issue	5%
Do not trust Obama	4%
Obama is too liberal	3%
Economy/Fiscal policy	3%
Gun rights/Second Amendment	2%
Abortion issue (McCain is pro-life)	2%
Taxes	1%
Honest/Has integrity	1%
Other	3%
No reason in particular	2%

May 19–21, 2008

Note: Percentages add to more than 100 due to multiple responses.

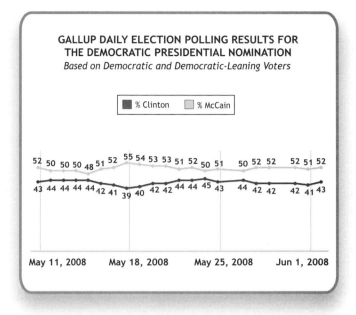

**GALLUP DAILY ELECTION POLLING RESULTS FOR
THE DEMOCRATIC PRESIDENTIAL NOMINATION**
Based on Democratic and Democratic-Leaning Voters

■ % Clinton   ■ % McCain

52 50 50 50 48 51 52 55 54 53 53 51 52 50 51   50 52 52   52 51 52
43 44 44 44 44 42 41 39 40 42 42 44 44 45 43   44 42 42   42 41 43

May 11, 2008   May 18, 2008   May 25, 2008   Jun 1, 2008

supporters mention his military background and his leadership qualities. In terms of specific issues, 5% of McCain's supporters mention Iraq, while smaller numbers say they support him because of his position on the economy, gun rights, abortion, or taxes.

Americans have clearly picked up, then, on the "change" versus "experience" themes enunciated by Obama and McCain in the nascent stages of the general election campaign. Additionally, a number of Obama supporters echo the Obama campaign theme that they do not want a third term of Republicans in the White House. Beyond these explanations for candidate support, there are the usual partisan and generic explanations observable in any presidential election. It appears that McCain supporters are more specifically negative about Obama than is the case the other way around, and that McCain supporters offer somewhat more specific explanations for their support based on their candidate's issue positions and personal characteristics than is the case with respect to Obama supporters.

Gallup Daily: Voters Evenly Split Between Obama, McCain

After winning one of the most competitive nomination battles in history, Barack Obama faces what looks to be an equally tough general election for the presidency. Gallup Poll daily tracking from May 29 and from May 31 to

June 3 shows Obama one point behind John McCain in national registered voter preference, 45% to 46%. Obama announced enough new superdelegate supporters on June 3 to put him over the 2,118-vote threshold needed to win a majority of delegates to the 2008 Democratic National Convention, thus virtually assuring him the party's nomination. Hillary Clinton, who has not yet conceded the nomination to Obama, continues to fare well in Gallup Poll general election daily tracking versus McCain: She leads McCain 48% to 45%. At the same time, indicative of the difficulty she ran into in the Democratic delegate contest, Clinton continues to trail Obama in national Democratic preference for the nomination by a nine-percentage-point margin. In Gallup Poll daily tracking from June 1 to June 3, Clinton is favored by 43% of national Democratic voters, compared with Obama's 52%.

JUNE 5

An Early Gallup Road Map to the McCain-Obama Matchup

As the general election campaign between Barack Obama and John McCain unofficially gets under way, many of the typical Democratic-Republican divides in the electorate—such as those by religion, gender, marital status, and income—already appear to be in place. Additionally, some of the special appeal each candidate had for certain groups of voters in the nomination phase of the election (on the basis of age, education, race, and political affiliation) seems to be carrying over into the general election. These findings are based on aggregated data from Gallup Poll daily tracking in May, consisting of more than 25,000 total interviews with registered voters nationwide. Obama

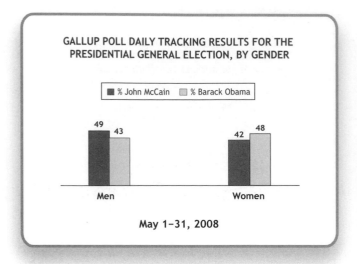

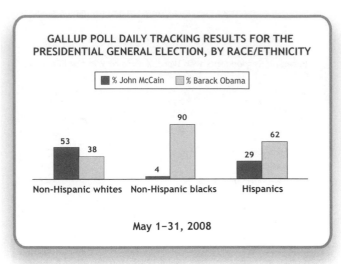

(supported by an average of 45.6% of national registered voters) and McCain (favored by 45.4%) were essentially tied in the full May dataset.

GENDER

As is typically the case in presidential elections, the Republican candidate is running better among male voters, while the Democrat fares better among women. The data show McCain with a 6-point advantage over Obama among men, and Obama leading McCain by the same margin among women.

AGE

Perhaps one of the greatest divides aside from race in the 2008 election will be along age lines, with Obama demonstrating great appeal to younger voters but not faring as well among senior citizens. Obama leads McCain by 23

points among voters age 18 to 29, while trailing McCain by 12 points among those 65 and older. The two run about evenly among the two middle-aged groups.

RACE

It is no secret that Obama owes his nomination in large part to overwhelming support among blacks, and that same high level of support will likely be evident in the general election. Roughly 9 in 10 blacks say they would vote for Obama if the election were held today, while McCain's support among blacks is in the low single digits. Blacks are typically a strong Democratic constituency, so the impact of the first black presidential candidate on a major party ticket may be more evident in terms of motivating high black turnout than in overwhelming support for the Democrat on Election Day. Obama did not fare well against Hillary Clinton among Hispanics in the 2008 primaries, but the early indications are that he will do well among this increasingly Democratic ethnic group in the general election. The May data show Obama with a 62% to 29% advantage over McCain among Hispanics. McCain currently maintains a strong advantage over Obama among non-Hispanic white voters, 53% to 38%.

EDUCATION

Highly educated voters were another key group helping to propel Obama to the Democratic nomination. The two candidates run about evenly among all education groups except those with postgraduate education, among whom Obama currently leads by a significant margin. It is notable that McCain runs competitively with Obama among voters with a high school education or less, which is normally a solid Democratic group. Obama offsets that by running evenly with McCain in a usually strong Republican group: voters with a four-year degree but no postgraduate education.

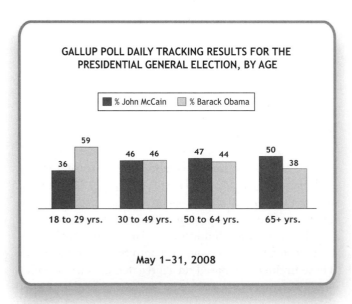

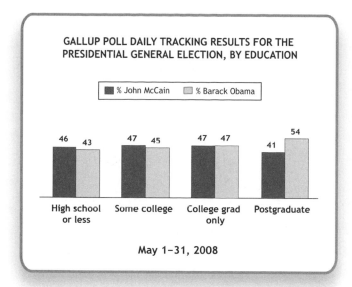

GALLUP POLL DAILY TRACKING RESULTS FOR THE PRESIDENTIAL GENERAL ELECTION, BY EDUCATION

May 1–31, 2008

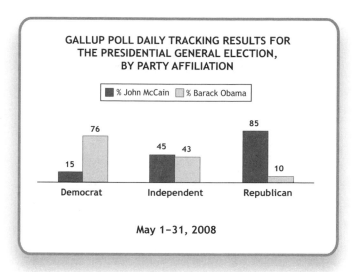

GALLUP POLL DAILY TRACKING RESULTS FOR THE PRESIDENTIAL GENERAL ELECTION, BY PARTY AFFILIATION

May 1–31, 2008

INCOME

While Obama does not fare as well among traditionally Democratic lower-education voters, he does do well among traditionally Democratic lower-income voters, beating McCain by double digits among this group. The two are competitive among middle- and upper-income voters, with McCain doing slightly better among wealthier voters.

REGION

McCain—like Republican candidates before him—is the heavy favorite in the South; Obama leads McCain in the East and West. The Midwest may be the most competitive region in this election, with Obama currently maintaining a slight advantage in his home region.

PARTY IDENTIFICATION

Both McCain and Obama can thank independents for helping them gain their respective parties' presidential nominations. And the two candidates are closely matched among independents in general election matchups. As far as the two major political party groups are concerned, McCain is securing greater party loyalty at the moment, holding 85% of his fellow Republicans as compared with 76% support for Obama among Democrats. But because at this point in the campaign, more Americans identify themselves as Democrats than as Republicans, it is more critical to McCain's fortunes to hold his base than it is for Obama.

IDEOLOGY

Liberals overwhelmingly support Obama, with 8 in 10 saying they would vote for him. McCain gets the support of

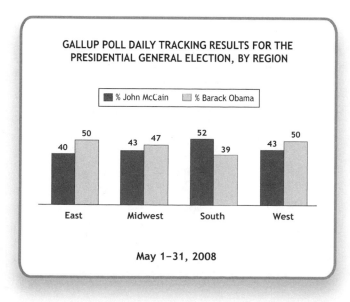

GALLUP POLL DAILY TRACKING RESULTS FOR THE PRESIDENTIAL GENERAL ELECTION, BY REGION

May 1–31, 2008

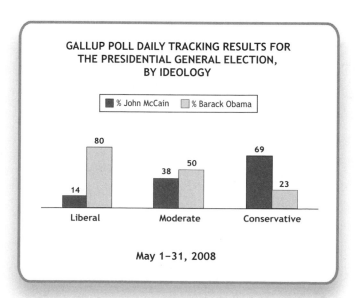

GALLUP POLL DAILY TRACKING RESULTS FOR THE PRESIDENTIAL GENERAL ELECTION, BY IDEOLOGY

May 1–31, 2008

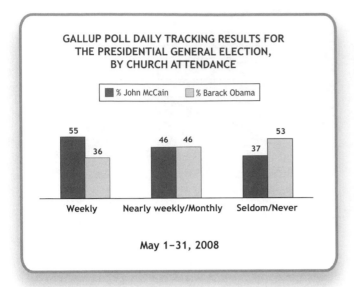

GALLUP POLL DAILY TRACKING RESULTS FOR THE PRESIDENTIAL GENERAL ELECTION, BY CHURCH ATTENDANCE

May 1–31, 2008

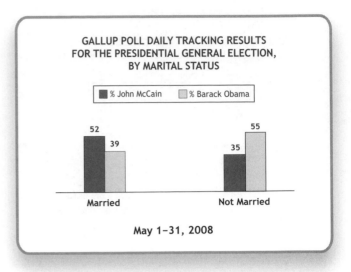

GALLUP POLL DAILY TRACKING RESULTS FOR THE PRESIDENTIAL GENERAL ELECTION, BY MARITAL STATUS

May 1–31, 2008

69% of conservatives. In this case, however, because more Americans identify themselves as conservatives than as liberals, Obama needs to keep his fellow ideologues in the fold more than McCain does. Obama has a significant lead over McCain among political moderates, 50% to 38%.

RELIGIOSITY

Religious commitment has proven to be one of the greatest dividing lines in U.S. politics, with highly religious voters aligning themselves with the Republican Party and non-religious voters tending to vote Democratic. That pattern is apparent in the 2008 campaign, with McCain holding a 19-point lead among voters who attend religious services weekly and Obama leading by 16 points among those who rarely or never attend church. The two candidates are evenly matched among the middle group that attends church on a nearly weekly or monthly basis.

RELIGIOUS PREFERENCE

McCain leads Obama by 10 points among Protestants and other non-Catholic Christians, the largest religious group in the United States; McCain's lead would be even larger except for the facts that blacks are most likely to be Protestant and overwhelmingly support Obama. Catholics are a traditional swing group, and McCain and Obama are evenly matched among them at this point. Obama has significant leads among two reliably Democratic groups: Jewish voters and voters with no religious affiliation.

MARITAL STATUS

In recent presidential elections, married voters have tended to vote Republican, and unmarried voters Democratic. That relationship appears as if it will hold in 2008, with McCain up by 13 points over Obama among those currently married, while Obama has a 20-point lead among those who are not married.

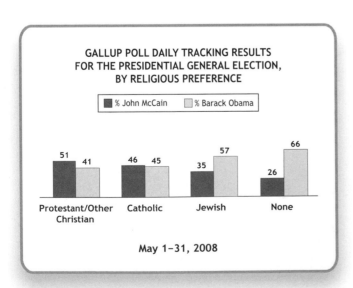

GALLUP POLL DAILY TRACKING RESULTS FOR THE PRESIDENTIAL GENERAL ELECTION, BY RELIGIOUS PREFERENCE

May 1–31, 2008

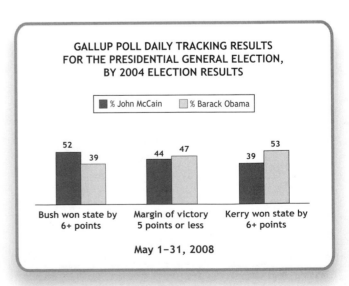

GALLUP POLL DAILY TRACKING RESULTS FOR THE PRESIDENTIAL GENERAL ELECTION, BY 2004 ELECTION RESULTS

May 1–31, 2008

RED VS. BLUE STATES

As of now, both candidates are running comparably strongly among voters in states that their respective parties won by comfortable margins in 2004. Obama currently holds a slim advantage among voters in swing states—those where the winning candidate won a narrow victory of five percentage points or less.

JUNE 6

Among Blacks, Clinton's Image Sinks over Last Year

In an election year in which race is front and center, American blacks have grown more negative toward Hillary Clinton, while blacks' favorable opinions of Barack Obama have soared. Blacks have also become more negative toward John McCain. A new USA Today/Gallup survey, conducted between May 30 and June 2, 2008, shows that blacks in the United States are significantly more likely now than they were a year ago to have an unfavorable opinion of Clinton. While in June 2007, an overwhelming 84% of blacks said their opinion of Clinton was favorable, that has dropped to 58% today. Unfavorable opinions of Clinton among blacks have jumped from 10% last June to 36% today.

The last year, of course, witnessed the rise of Obama from a little-known Illinois senator to his now being poised to be the first black candidate to win a major party's nomination for president in U.S. history. During that time, Clinton, formerly part of a political power coupled with very strong ties to the black community, became redefined as Obama's

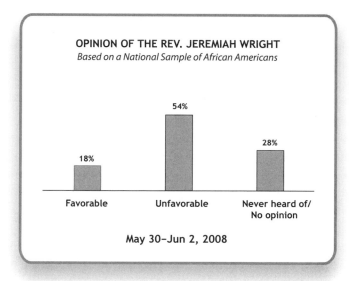

OPINION OF THE REV. JEREMIAH WRIGHT
Based on a National Sample of African Americans

May 30–Jun 2, 2008

opponent, and it appears that a perhaps inevitable fallout from that occurrence was a drop in her standing in the eyes of blacks across the country. Indeed, blacks' opinions of presumptive Democratic nominee Obama have become more positive as he has become better known over the past year. Obama's image among blacks was an already very positive 68% favorable and 8% unfavorable last year at this time; now it is 86% favorable and 9% unfavorable. (In addition, year-to-year data show that among black Democrats, Clinton went from being competitive with Obama as first choice for the Democratic Party's nominee last year—42% for Obama, 43% for Clinton—to an overwhelming majority of 82% of black Democrats favoring Obama in the current survey, compared with 15% for Clinton.)

Clinton can perhaps take some comfort in the fact that the presumptive Republican nominee, McCain, has also seen his image become more negative in the eyes of black Americans over the last year. In June 2007, McCain's image

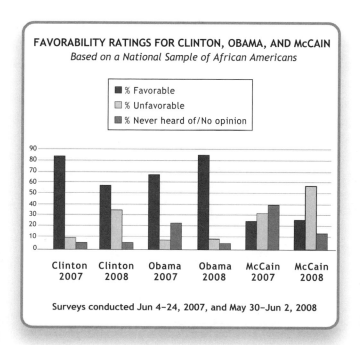

FAVORABILITY RATINGS FOR CLINTON, OBAMA, AND McCAIN
Based on a National Sample of African Americans

■ % Favorable
□ % Unfavorable
■ % Never heard of/No opinion

Surveys conducted Jun 4-24, 2007, and May 30–Jun 2, 2008

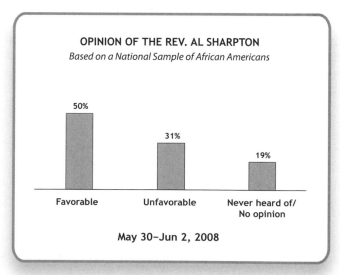

OPINION OF THE REV. AL SHARPTON
Based on a National Sample of African Americans

May 30–Jun 2, 2008

among blacks was 26% favorable and 33% unfavorable, with 41% saying they either didn't have an opinion or had never heard of McCain. Now, as he has become better known, blacks' opinions of McCain have moved decidedly into the negative column: Fifty-eight percent are now unfavorable and 27% favorable.

Considerable news coverage has been given over to Obama's former minister, the Reverend Jeremiah Wright, over the past several months. Wright, for many years the minister of Trinity United Church of Christ in Chicago, was vaulted into the national spotlight when video excerpts of his sermons surfaced on the Internet. His image became even more controversial after a fiery speech at the National Press Club in Washington. The new USA Today/Gallup survey suggests that Wright certainly cannot claim to have the allegiance of the majority of blacks in this country: 54% of blacks say they have an unfavorable opinion of the controversial minister, while only 18% say their opinion is favorable. By contrast, blacks' opinions of another controversial minister, the Reverend Al Sharpton, are significantly more positive.

Blacks, Young Adults Sense Security Risks for Obama

Safety is always a paramount concern for presidents and those who seek the office of president. In the 2008 general election campaign, 57% of black Americans believe Barack Obama faces even greater security risks than other candidates who have run for president in recent years. The majority of (non-Hispanic) whites think he is at no greater risk of being harmed. These relative apprehensions aside, only 16% of blacks and 7% of whites say they are "very worried" about Obama's safety. Among those who are very worried, 15% of blacks and about half of whites (which

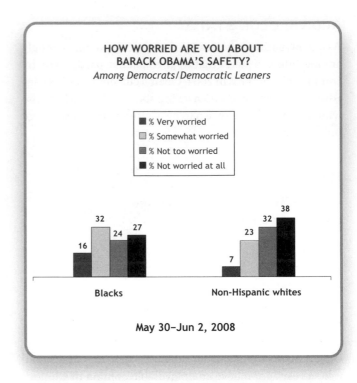

translates to a minuscule 2% of blacks and 3% of whites overall) say they are so worried that, given the chance early on in the campaign to advise Obama, they would have urged him not to run. Most, however, say they would have advised Obama not to let these concerns stand in his way.

GENERATIONAL DIFFERENCES

Older Americans may clearly remember the 1968 assassination of Martin Luther King, Jr., as well as the Kennedy assassinations of the 1960s. Yet, it is young Americans—the age group giving the greatest support to Obama's candidacy—who are most likely to believe Obama is at greater security risk than other candidates. A slight majority of

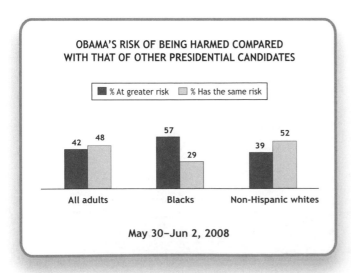

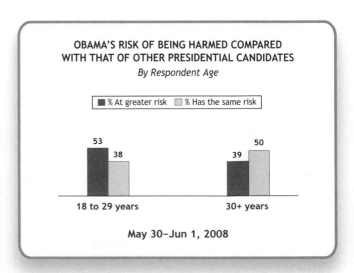

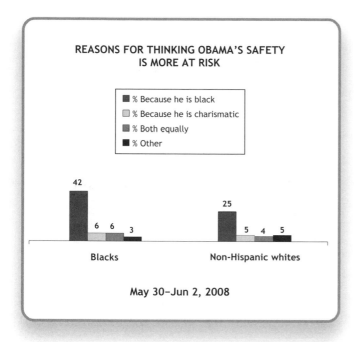

REASONS FOR THINKING OBAMA'S SAFETY IS MORE AT RISK

- ■ % Because he is black
- □ % Because he is charismatic
- ■ % Both equally
- ■ % Other

Blacks: 42, 6, 6, 3
Non-Hispanic whites: 25, 5, 4, 5

May 30–Jun 2, 2008

young adults (53%) say Obama is at greater risk, compared with 39% of those 30 and older. (There is no difference between the views of middle-aged and older Americans.) Among blacks, there is no generational divide in perceptions of Obama's safety between those 18 to 49 and those 50 and older. Close to 6 in 10 in both groups (58% and 57%, respectively) think he is at greater risk.

WHY THE RISK?

Obama himself has said, "I face the same security issues as anybody." Yet in May 2007, the Secret Service announced that Obama was being placed under its protection at the campaign's request, nearly a year before other recent candidates have received this level of security, and the earliest for any presidential candidate. Is it Obama's race or the striking similarities to John F. Kennedy and Robert F. Kennedy in terms of charisma and the highly charged crowds of supporters the candidate attracts that evoke these concerns? Forty-two percent of blacks and 25% of whites identify Obama's race as the primary reason they believe he is in greater jeopardy than the average candidate. Only 6% of blacks and 5% of whites point to Obama's charisma and large following as the principal reason they believe he is a greater target, while 6% and 4%, respectively, say that his race and his charisma are equally important.

Gallup Daily: Obama 46%, McCain 45%

Barack Obama and John McCain continue to run about even in presidential preferences for the fall election, with Obama favored by 46% of national registered voters and

McCain by 45%. This finding, based on Gallup Poll daily tracking from June 1 to June 5, is consistent with the close nature of the Obama-McCain race for the past week. The latest results include two nights of interviewing since Obama declared victory over Hillary Clinton in the Democratic delegate contest on June 3. Although interviewing on June 4 showed no immediate bounce in national support for Obama versus McCain, the results on June 5 were quite favorable to Obama. It will be important to see if Obama can maintain this support over the coming days.

To Be or Not to Be Vice President?

The question of whether Obama will select Hillary Clinton to be his vice presidential running mate has replaced the drama of the primary election. According to Gallup Poll daily interviewing from June 4 to June 5, exactly half of national Democratic voters (including independents who lean Democratic) would like him to select Clinton; 36% want him to choose someone else, and the remaining 14% are unsure.

JUNE 9
Most Say Race Will Not Be a Factor in Their Presidential Vote

A large majority of blacks, 78%, and an even larger 88% of whites say the fact that Barack Obama is black makes no difference in terms of their likelihood of voting for him for president. This may appear to be a surprisingly high percentage of blacks saying Obama's race makes no difference, given that his nomination will mark a historic moment in American political history: the first black

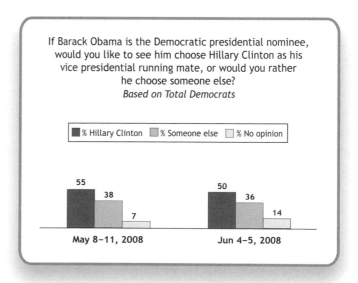

If Barack Obama is the Democratic presidential nominee, would you like to see him choose Hillary Clinton as his vice presidential running mate, or would you rather he choose someone else?
Based on Total Democrats

- ■ % Hillary Clinton
- ■ % Someone else
- □ % No opinion

May 8–11, 2008: 55, 38, 7
Jun 4–5, 2008: 50, 36, 14

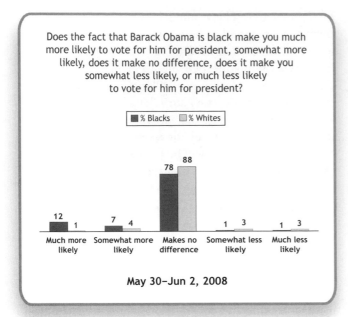

Does the fact that Barack Obama is black make you much more likely to vote for him for president, somewhat more likely, does it make no difference, does it make you somewhat less likely, or much less likely to vote for him for president?

May 30–Jun 2, 2008

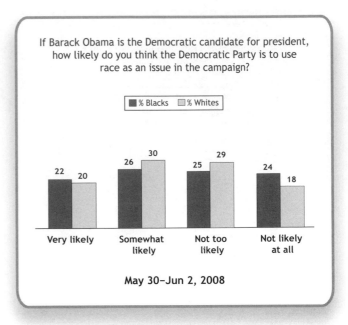

If Barack Obama is the Democratic candidate for president, how likely do you think the Democratic Party is to use race as an issue in the campaign?

May 30–Jun 2, 2008

candidate to capture a major party's nomination. Without question, blacks are going to vote for Obama in overwhelming numbers; the latest Gallup tracking shows that Obama gets 93% of the black vote when pitted against Republican John McCain in a hypothetical trial heat.

So on the one hand, black voters say Obama's race makes no difference to them; yet at the same time, about 9 out of 10 blacks say they will vote for Obama. But the high percentage of the black vote going to Obama is not unusual. Gallup polling estimated that John Kerry received 93% of the black vote in 2004 and Al Gore received 95% in 2000. So it may be that black voters are accurately self-reporting that

they would be voting for the Democratic candidate regardless of his or her race, and Obama's race is not a deciding factor for them.

Whites are even less likely than blacks to say Obama's race would be a factor in their vote: 88% of non-Hispanic whites say his race makes no difference. Six percent of whites say they are less likely to vote for Obama because of his race; 5% say they are more likely to vote for him. There has been discussion this year of a "hidden" race factor according to which certain groups of white voters will end up not voting for Obama because he is a black candidate. What these data show is that more than 9 in 10 whites,

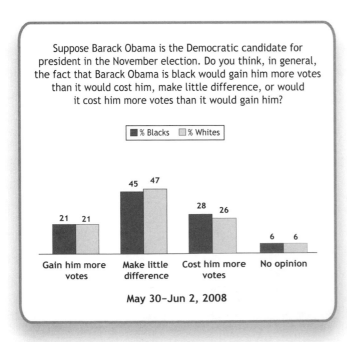

Suppose Barack Obama is the Democratic candidate for president in the November election. Do you think, in general, the fact that Barack Obama is black would gain him more votes than it would cost him, make little difference, or would it cost him more votes than it would gain him?

May 30–Jun 2, 2008

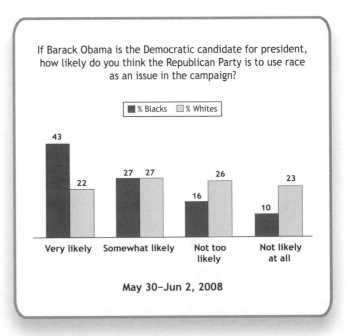

If Barack Obama is the Democratic candidate for president, how likely do you think the Republican Party is to use race as an issue in the campaign?

May 30–Jun 2, 2008

when asked directly about Obama's race, deny that it will be a negative factor in their vote.

A separate poll question measured the perceived impact of Obama's race by asking respondents to speculate about the impact of race on the electorate more generally. In this case, there is more variation in opinions, among both blacks and whites. Blacks are quite divided in their responses to this question. A little more than a quarter, 28%, say Obama's race will cost him more than it will gain him in the election; but 21% of blacks give the opposite response and say Obama's race will be a net plus for his candidacy. Most of the rest, 45%, say it will make little difference. The responses among whites to this question are remarkably similar to those among blacks, differing by just a few percentage points. A third set of questions asked about the potential use of race (the "race card" one hears so much about in campaign coverage) by the two political parties.

Blacks appear to believe that race will be a factor in how the election campaign is run by both Republicans and Democrats, but far more so for the former than for the latter. Forty-eight percent of blacks say the Democrats' campaign will make race a factor this year, while 70% say Republicans will use race as an issue. Whites are much more uniform in their responses to this question: About half say each party will use race as an issue in the campaign. The question did not ask respondents specific follow-up questions about how race would be used in the campaign, so it is unclear whether respondents who believe race will be made an issue think this is good or bad. Most blacks identify themselves as Democrats, making the precise meaning of the fact that half of blacks interviewed think the Democratic Party will use race as a factor in the campaign even less clear. It can be hypothesized that the strong majority of blacks who say Republicans will use race as an issue view that possibility in a negative light.

The Uncertain Effect of Race

Blacks overwhelmingly have favored the Democratic candidate in past elections, while the Republican candidate has typically won the majority of the white vote. General election voting data so far in this campaign show that this pattern is continuing this year: Blacks are overwhelmingly likely to vote for Obama, while the majority of non-Hispanic whites indicate that they will vote for McCain. Race is a strong factor in projected voting for Obama against McCain, as it was in Obama's Democratic primary race against Hillary Clinton. The critical analytic question becomes one of ascertaining whether the historic nature of Obama's nomination as a major party black candidate will have an impact above and beyond the usual patterns of racial differences in voting. The data reviewed here suggest that while most voters deny that

Obama's race affects them personally, many do think it will have an effect on other voters—that is, on the electorate as a whole—either helping Obama or hurting him. Still, there is no consensus on the part of the average voter with respect to whether Obama's race will be a net plus or a net minus. Thus, there is little guidance from the voters themselves in seeking to determine the ultimate impact of Obama's race on the campaign this year.

Four in 10 Americans See Their Standard of Living Declining

Forty-three percent of Americans say their standard of living is worse now than it was five years ago, nearly matching the percentage (45%) who say their standard of living has gotten better during that time. These results are based on a May 30-June 1 USA Today/Gallup Poll. In the same poll, Gallup for the first time found a majority of Americans saying their personal finances are worse now than a year ago. Lower-income Americans, those age 50 and older, and those without college educations are among the subgroups who are most likely to believe their standard of living has deteriorated during the past five years. Politics apparently color one's views on this question, as a majority of Democrats (57%) and liberals (53%), compared with fewer than half of Republicans (23%) and conservatives (12%), report a diminished standard of living while a Republican occupies the White House.

Americans are typically optimistic about how things will be in the future, and that applies in this case. When asked to project five years into the future, 62% say they expect their standard of living to be better; only 25% think it will be worse. There is little variation with respect to future expectations by demographic subgroup, with the notable exception of age. Senior citizens, many of whom live in retirement on fixed incomes, are not optimistic about the future, with just 35% expecting an improved standard of living and 39% expecting a worse one.

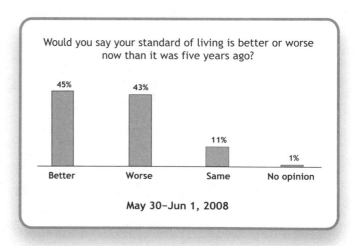

Would you say your standard of living is better or worse now than it was five years ago?

Better 45%   Worse 43%   Same 11%   No opinion 1%

May 30–Jun 1, 2008

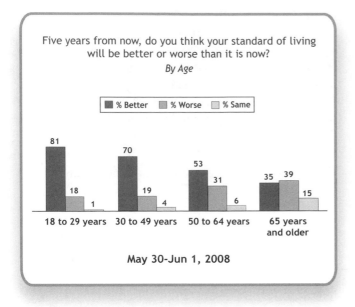

Five years from now, do you think your standard of living
will be better or worse than it is now?

By Age

■ % Better   ■ % Worse   □ % Same

81
18
1
18 to 29 years

70
19
4
30 to 49 years

53
31
6
50 to 64 years

35 39
15
65 years
and older

May 30-Jun 1, 2008

is better than their parents' was at the same age, including 38% who say theirs is much better than their parents'; only 18% say their standard of living is worse than that of their parents. Americans are all that optimistic, however, that their children will have a better quality of life than they do: Forty-five percent expect their children's standard of living to be better than theirs is, 20% say it will be the same, and 28% believe it will be worse. Younger adults are among the most optimistic about their children's economic situation, with 60% of 18- to 29-year-olds expecting their children to have a better standard of living than they do. That compares with just 38% of those age 50 and older expecting a more comfortable financial situation for their children. The problems in the economy are taking their toll on American consumers, with about as many now reporting a diminished standard of living as an improved one. Nevertheless, by and large, Americans still expect things to improve over the next five years.

In addition to asking Americans to compare their standard of living with the recent past and the anticipated near future, the poll asked respondents to compare where they are now financially to where their parents were at the same age, and where their children will be. Sixty-three percent of Americans report that their current standard of living

JUNE 11
Obama Gains Among Women After Clinton Exit

Since Hillary Clinton decided to concede the Democratic nomination to Barack Obama on June 7, Obama

After one of the hardest-fought primary battles in American history, Senator Hillary Clinton suspends her campaign at the National Building Museum in Washington, D.C., on June 7, 2008. *(Ron Edmonds/AP Images)*

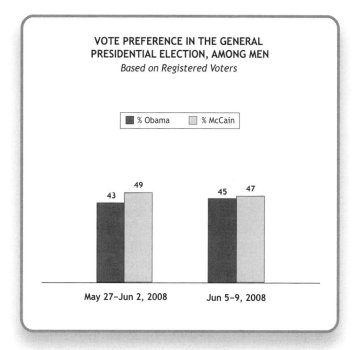

**VOTE PREFERENCE IN THE GENERAL
PRESIDENTIAL ELECTION, AMONG MEN**
Based on Registered Voters

■ % Obama   □ % McCain

43 49   45 47

May 27–Jun 2, 2008   Jun 5–9, 2008

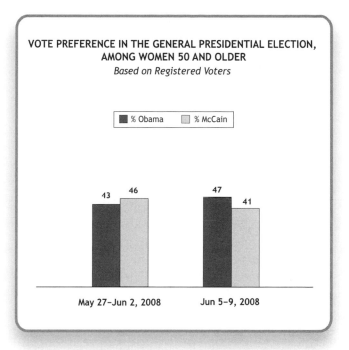

**VOTE PREFERENCE IN THE GENERAL PRESIDENTIAL ELECTION,
AMONG WOMEN 50 AND OLDER**
Based on Registered Voters

■ % Obama   □ % McCain

43 46   47 41

May 27–Jun 2, 2008   Jun 5–9, 2008

has established a lead over Republican John McCain in general election polling. Obama's gains have come more from women than from men, though he has picked up support among both groups in recent days. Obama's lead among women has now expanded from 5 percentage points to 13, while his deficit among men has shrunk from 6 points to 2. These figures are based on aggregated Gallup Poll daily tracking interviews with national registered voters conducted between May 27 and June 2 (the week immediately before Obama clinched the nomina-

**VOTE PREFERENCE IN THE GENERAL
PRESIDENTIAL ELECTION, AMONG WOMEN**
Based on Registered Voters

■ % Obama   □ % McCain

48 43   51 38

May 27–Jun 2, 2008   Jun 5–9, 2008

tion on June 3), which showed Obama and McCain tied at 46%, and between June 5 and June 9 (the five days after it was reported that Clinton would suspend her campaign), which showed Obama ahead, 48% to 42%. Obama clinched the nomination on the evening of June 3, and the news media reported that Clinton would suspend her campaign on the evening of June 4. Thus, the data give a clear picture of voter support before and after Clinton's exit.

While campaigning for president, Clinton demonstrated an especially strong appeal to women. She led McCain by 52% to 40% among women in her final full week as a candidate, exactly equal to her average in such matchups since mid-March. By comparison, Obama held only an average 47% to 42% lead over McCain among women during the same time span. At least for now, however, he seems to be matching Clinton's performance among women versus McCain, judging by his current 13-point lead among female voters.

One of Clinton's core groups of supporters during the nomination phase of the campaign was older women. During the last few days of her active candidacy, Clinton led McCain by 51% to 41% among women age 50 and older, while Obama *trailed* McCain among this group, 46% to 43%. Since Clinton suspended her campaign, however, older women's vote preferences have shifted toward Obama, so that he now enjoys a 6-point advantage over McCain.

Obama had always run much better among younger women, in large part because of his strong appeal to younger voters generally. But his support among women age 18 to 49 has also risen in the past few days, further expanding his already formidable 52% to 40% lead over McCain in this cohort to 56% to 35%. Obama has made major gains in the past few days among married women, erasing McCain's former 52% to 40% lead in favor of a 45% to 45% tie. Meanwhile, the vote preferences among married men (a solid McCain group) and unmarried men and women (solid Obama groups) have changed little since Clinton decided to end her White House bid.

Obama has also seen his support among non-Hispanic white women increase modestly, though McCain still holds a slim 46% to 43% advantage among this group; prior to Clinton's departure, McCain led Obama by 50% to 41% among white women. Interestingly, while white women were a major part of Clinton's constituency in the primaries, she maintained only a slim advantage, if any, in general election trial heats versus McCain among this group. In the last week of her campaign, she only tied McCain among white women, at 47%. Thus, her strong performance against McCain among all female voters in presidential trial heats was primarily because of strong support from minority women.

Implications for the General Election

Obama's recent gains in the polls have been greatly aided by increased support from female voters. Now that Clinton is no longer campaigning and the focus of voters' decision-making is a choice between Obama and McCain, female voters may be taking a second look at Obama. Indeed, his current 13-point advantage over McCain among women is essentially the same advantage that Clinton held over McCain throughout her active candidacy. Obama's challenge in the general election campaign will be to bring core Democratic groups that did not strongly support him in the primaries—women, voters with less formal education, and conservative Democrats—back into the fold. He appears to be already doing that among women. However, it is not clear whether this is just a temporary rally in support for Obama upon his clinching the nomination, or whether he will be able to sustain a high level of support from female voters for the duration of the campaign.

Gallup Daily: Obama 48%, McCain 42%

Barack Obama continues to hold a lead over John McCain in Gallup Poll daily tracking—48% to 42% in the June 8–10 polling of registered voters nationwide. This marks the third consecutive day that Obama has held a significant lead, as he enjoys a modest boost in support following Hillary Clinton's decision to concede the nomination. Obama's six- and seven-percentage-point advantages over McCain in recent days have been his best margins

to date. Obama has held significant leads over McCain at other points since mid-March (when Gallup first began tracking general election preferences), but for the most part the two candidates have been locked in statistical dead heats.

JUNE 12
Large Democratic Base Provides Big Advantage for Obama

The current political landscape, with Americans identifying themselves as Democrats outnumbering by a substantial margin those who identify as Republicans, provides a significant advantage for Barack Obama's presidential chances. These data are based on 5,299 interviews with registered voters conducted as part of Gallup Poll daily tracking during the six-day period of June 5–10, representing the period since the general election matchup of Obama versus McCain became definite. Thirty-seven percent of Americans identify themselves as Democrats, compared with 28% who identify as Republicans. Another 34% say they are independents or don't choose (in response to this initial question) to identify with either party.

Following very well-established patterns in American presidential elections, voter identification as a Republican or Democrat is strongly, but not totally, correlated with support for the two parties' candidates. Those who identify as Republicans appear at this juncture to be a bit more loyal to their party's candidate, with 85% supporting McCain compared with the 78% of those who identify as Democrats supporting Obama; or, one could say, Democrats have a slightly higher defection rate at this point than do Republicans. (Although these data were collected after Clinton's announcement that she was suspending her campaign, it is possible that the Democratic defection rate represents some residual anger among Clinton-supporting

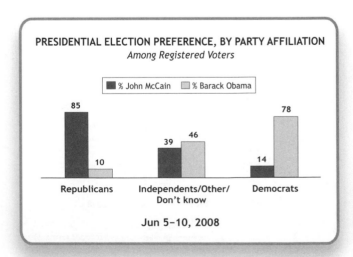

PRESIDENTIAL ELECTION PREFERENCE, BY PARTY AFFILIATION
Among Registered Voters

■ % John McCain   ▢ % Barack Obama

Republicans: 85, 10
Independents/Other/Don't know: 39, 46
Democrats: 14, 78

Jun 5–10, 2008

Senator Joe Lieberman (right) appears with Senator John McCain in Pemberton, New Jersey, on June 13, 2008. Lieberman, the Democratic candidate for vice president in 2000, had endorsed McCain for president in December 2007. *(L. M. Otero/AP Images)*

Democrats—anger that may dissipate between now and November.) Independents—who initially do not identify with either party—break toward Obama by a 46% to 39% margin. (McCain and Obama have been competitive for the independent vote since March.)

When all of these data for June 5–10 are put together, the overall vote pattern for this period among registered voters adds up to a six-point margin for Obama over McCain, 48% to 42%. The margin is in Obama's favor in part because there are more Democrats than Republicans in the sample, which helps compensate for the fact that Democrats are slightly less loyal to Obama than are Republicans to McCain. Obama's margin is also based on his ability to swing independents slightly in his direction. Hypothetically speaking, if there were no independents in the race, Obama would still win by a five-point margin, 49% to 44%, reflecting the higher percentage of Democratic identifiers in the voting population.

All in all, for McCain to win the popular vote in November, some combination of the following would need to occur: an increase in the percentage of the voting population who identify as Republicans, an increase in the percentage of Republicans who support McCain, an increase in the percentage of the vote McCain receives from those who identify as Democrats, an increase in the support McCain receives among independents; and a much higher turnout rate for McCain supporters than for Obama supporters. It appears that McCain's chances of increasing his support among independents may not be extremely high. The accompanying table shows the split in party identification when the 34% who are independents

are asked if they "lean" one way or the other. This more detailed analysis provides a better understanding of why Obama is leading among independents. When pressed to say which way they lean, the 34% who initially identify as independents tilt toward identifying with the Democratic Party by a significant margin: 15% lean Democratic, 11% lean Republican, and 8% remain "pure" independents and refuse to indicate which way they lean. Looked at another way, 44% of the initial independent segment leans Democratic, compared with just 33% who lean Republican.

Furthermore, these "leaners" are essentially as loyal to the candidate of the party they lean to as are those who initially identified with a party without being prompted. Eighty-one percent of independents who lean Republican support McCain—compared with 85% of Republican identifiers—while 83% of those who lean Democratic support Obama—more than the 78% of Democratic identifiers who support the party's candidate. McCain gets a slightly higher 84% of Republicans with leaners than Obama's 80% of Democrats with leaners, but the significantly higher percentage of Democrats in the electorate gives Obama his overall edge. What about the small sliver of "pure independents" who do not admit to leaning toward one party or the other? This group constitutes only 8% of the voting electorate, and is largely an apolitical group. They are much more likely to be undecided than other voters, but the basic tilt is 35% to 26% for McCain over Obama. This, of course, is not nearly enough to compensate for the larger number of Democratic identifiers.

Republicans Sour on Nation's Moral Climate

Republicans have grown more critical of the state of moral values in the United States, with the percentage rating present moral conditions "poor" rising from 36% in 2006 to 51%

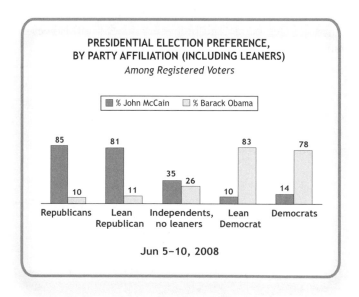

PRESIDENTIAL ELECTION PREFERENCE, BY PARTY AFFILIATION (INCLUDING LEANERS)
Among Registered Voters

% John McCain   % Barack Obama

	Republicans	Lean Republican	Independents, no leaners	Lean Democrat	Democrats
% John McCain	85	81	35	10	14
% Barack Obama	10	11	26	83	78

Jun 5–10, 2008

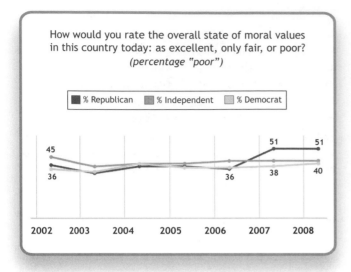

How would you rate the overall state of moral values in this country today: as excellent, only fair, or poor?
(percentage "poor")

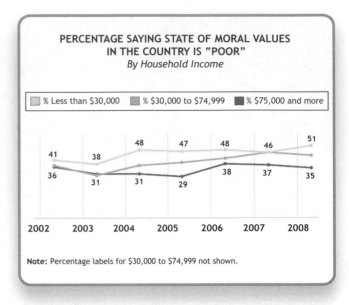

PERCENTAGE SAYING STATE OF MORAL VALUES IN THE COUNTRY IS "POOR"
By Household Income

Note: Percentage labels for $30,000 to $74,999 not shown.

in 2007, and remaining at that level today. No comparable change is seen among independents or Democrats. Thus, Republicans are now significantly more negative about moral values than independents or Democrats, which marks a change from the recent past. These findings come from Gallup's annual Values and Beliefs survey, updated between May 8 and May 11, 2008. The overall results to the question about the state of moral values show that, as has been the case consistently throughout the decade, few Americans give the country's moral climate high marks. Only 15% consider moral values to be "excellent" or "good," while 41% call them "only fair," and 44% consider them to be "poor." A follow-up question asks respondents whether moral values are getting better or getting worse, and yields an equally negative answer: Only 11% of Americans perceive that values are improving, while 81% say things are getting worse.

It is unclear why Republicans' views about the state of the nation's moral values would have soured sometime between the May 2006 and May 2007 Gallup surveys, while those of Democrats and independents did not. However, since 2002, in response to the second question about moral

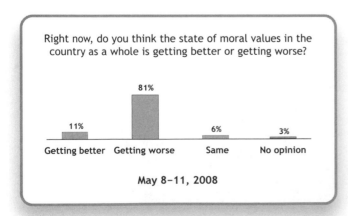

Right now, do you think the state of moral values in the country as a whole is getting better or getting worse?

May 8–11, 2008

values, all three partisan groups have grown increasingly pessimistic about the direction in which the country's moral values are headed. For example, in May 2003, Gallup found 29% of Republicans saying moral values were getting better and 64% saying they were getting worse; in 2004, the "getting worse" number jumped to 77%, and by 2005 it had reached 82%. For the past two years, about 9 in 10 Republicans have said the state of moral values is getting worse. The pattern is similar for independents and Democrats, although their pessimism in 2007 and 2008 has been lower than that of Republicans.

Gallup finds only minimal differences between men and women and among adults of different age categories regarding trends in their perceptions about the current state of moral conditions. These ratings have been fairly negative but flat, while their outlook on the direction of moral values has been growing worse. There does seem to be a widening income divide in perceptions of moral values—just not in the direction one might expect, given Republicans' increasing discontent with the state of moral values. Since 2002, low- and middle-income Americans (both groups with disproportionately lower average incomes than Republicans) have become more likely to think moral conditions are poor, while there has been no change among upper-income Americans.

Americans are reliably negative when it comes to rating moral values in the country: Since 2002, a majority of Americans have consistently said the state of moral values is less than good and getting worse. Apart from this general pattern, Republicans' disaffection with the nation's moral climate (but not Democrats' or independents') has increased over the past two years. A number of "values" issues have been in the news in recent years, including gay marriage, pop star misbehavior, and reports of high-profile elected officials involved in sex-related scandals, but it is unclear that any of these is responsible for this pattern in the data. Whatever the cause, Republicans' increasing disaffection may signal that they will be particularly anxious to elect a new president this November who will help to uphold or restore the values they now see as lacking in the country.

JUNE 13

Public Faults Bush for Lack of Action on Energy

In the midst of record high gasoline prices, just 17% of Americans say President Bush is doing enough to solve the country's energy problems, a significant decline from already low figures in 2006. Additionally, nearly half of Americans, 49%, say the Bush administration deserves a great deal of blame for the country's energy problems, up from 38% in 2006 and just 20% in May 2001, when rolling blackouts in California focused national attention on the issue. Of the seven government and business institutions tested in the poll, the Bush administration ranks second on the blame list, behind only U.S. oil companies at 60%. Oil companies have topped the list each time Gallup has asked this question, and—like Bush—are blamed more now than they were in 2006.

Even though these results find oil companies being blamed to a greater degree than in 2006, results of a recent Gallup Poll suggests that Americans are becoming more aware that high gasoline prices are a result of many factors beyond simple oil company greed. While "oil company greed" remains the most commonly mentioned reason for high gasoline prices, the percentage offering this explanation has dropped significantly in the past year. Rather, Americans are more likely to cite a variety of other factors—such as greater demand for oil, the declining value of

the U.S. dollar, and market speculators—as reasons for high gasoline prices. This increase in those blaming "big oil" from 49% to 60% may also reflect a more general pattern of the public assigning greater responsibility to all government and business institutions for the country's energy problems. All six institutions tested in the 2006 and 2008 Gallup Polls showed higher levels of blame this year.

Over the past two years, the public has increasingly looked to government to solve the nation's energy problems. Forty-nine percent of Americans now say the government should have the primary responsibility for developing alternative sources of energy to gasoline, up from 38% in 2006. Currently, 30% say oil and energy companies should have the main responsibility, nearly the same as in 2006.

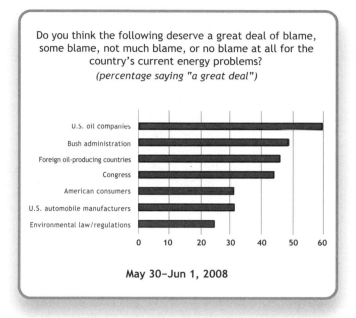

Do you think the following deserve a great deal of blame, some blame, not much blame, or no blame at all for the country's current energy problems?
(percentage saying "a great deal")

May 30–Jun 1, 2008

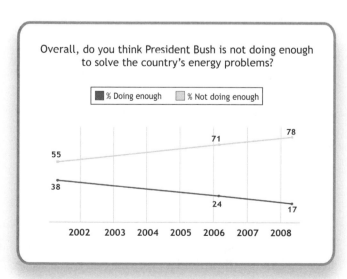

Overall, do you think President Bush is not doing enough to solve the country's energy problems?

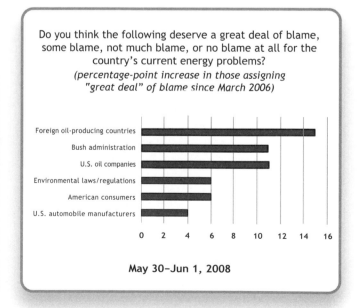

Do you think the following deserve a great deal of blame, some blame, not much blame, or no blame at all for the country's current energy problems?
(percentage-point increase in those assigning "great deal" of blame since March 2006)

May 30–Jun 1, 2008

Only 12% now believe that automobile companies should be primarily responsible, half as many as in 2006.

The Bush administration and Congress have taken action on energy in recent years, but those steps were largely targeted toward energy usage in the future and did little to address the more immediate concern of high gasoline prices. Bush himself has said there is no "magic wand" he can wave to cut gasoline prices. Though Americans may be more aware of the complex reasons for high gasoline prices, they still hold their elected officials accountable. That may be why the already low approval ratings of Bush and Congress have eroded further in recent months.

Religious Americans Prefer McCain over Obama

John McCain beats Barack Obama in a general-election trial heat by a 47% to 42% margin among voters who say religion is an important part of their daily lives, while Obama wins by an overwhelming 58% to 33% margin among voters who say religion is not an important part of their daily lives. This analysis is based on a sample of more than 5,000 registered voters interviewed between June 5 and June 10, all of the interviews being completed since Obama's status as the Democratic nominee became a near certainty after the final Democratic primaries. The data show that Americans' self-reporting of the importance of religion in their lives is powerfully predictive of their voting preferences in the coming general election. Thirty-five percent of Americans at this time say religion is *not* an important part of their daily lives; among this group, support for Obama's candidacy is 10 points higher than in the sample as a whole (Obama led McCain overall by a 48% to 42% margin during this period), and support for McCain is 9 points lower. This

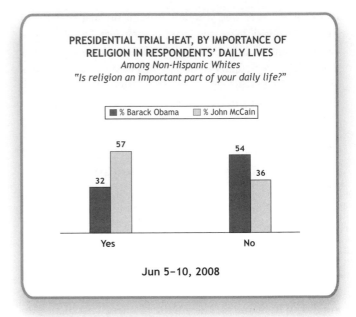

PRESIDENTIAL TRIAL HEAT, BY IMPORTANCE OF RELIGION IN RESPONDENTS' DAILY LIVES
Among Non-Hispanic Whites
"Is religion an important part of your daily life?"

Jun 5–10, 2008

results in a swing from a 6-point overall lead for Obama among all voters to a lead of 25 points among less religious voters. Among the group of Americans for whom religion is important, on the other hand—amounting to 64% of the sample—the swing is from the Obama 6-point lead to a McCain lead of 5 points.

The relationship between the importance of religion and candidate preference, powerful as it is, is mitigated by the fact that the black Americans included in the sample are both highly religious and highly likely to support Obama. It therefore follows that the relationship between the self-reported importance of religion and the respondent's expected general-election vote is stronger when the sample is restricted only to whites. McCain wins overall among non-Hispanic whites by a 49% to 40% margin, a common pattern for Republican candidates in recent presidential races. But among whites, as is true for the overall sample, religion remains a very strong dividing variable.

Among white voters for whom religion is an important part of their daily lives, McCain's margin stretches to a very large 25 points, 57% to 32%. Among white voters for whom religion is not an important part of their daily lives—about 37% of all white voters—Obama wins by an 18-point margin, 54% to 36%. There is, then, an extraordinary 43-point differential in candidate preference among non-Hispanic whites between those who are religious and those who are not; the importance of religion is thus a powerful predictor of white voters' presidential vote intentions. The reasons for this relationship are complex. Self-reported importance of religion is itself highly related to a number of other demographic variables, which in turn are related to political orientation. Younger voters, for example, are less likely than those who are older to say religion is important

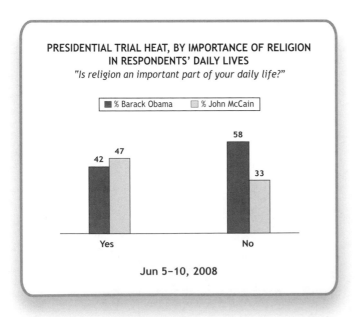

PRESIDENTIAL TRIAL HEAT, BY IMPORTANCE OF RELIGION IN RESPONDENTS' DAILY LIVES
"Is religion an important part of your daily life?"

Jun 5–10, 2008

in their lives, and younger voters are among Obama's largest support groups. Unmarried voters are also less likely to say religion is important in their lives and more likely to support Obama. Likewise, highly educated voters are less likely to say religion is important in their lives (although they attend church as frequently as those with less education), and highly educated voters constitute another strong voter bloc for Obama. At the same time, importance of religion is related to a number of social and values attitudes that are themselves related to political orientation.

Thus, it is difficult to pinpoint exactly what is driving the religion–voter preference relationship. It may be that religion per se is less important than some underlying causal factor—either demographic or attitudinal—that is correlated with both religion and voting propensity. Still, the fact remains that a person's answer to a simple question about the importance of religion in his or her life is a strong indication as to how that person will vote in the November general election.

JUNE 16

Americans Expect Obama Will Be Next President

Barack Obama and John McCain are now about tied in Gallup Poll daily tracking of voter preferences for the general election—but in a June 9–12 Gallup Poll, Obama leads McCain 52% to 41% in public perceptions of who will win in November. Democrats are slightly more confident that their presumptive nominee will prevail in November—76% say Obama will win—than Republicans are about McCain's chances (67% believe he will win). What tips the balance of national opinion more strongly in favor of Obama is that,

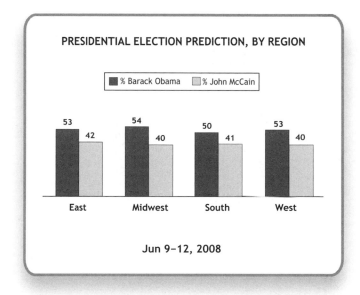

by a 9-percentage-point margin, independents join Democrats in believing Obama is likely to win. Gallup Poll daily tracking of the presidential election over the same period as the June 9–12 Gallup Poll shows Obama beating McCain among registered voters in the East and West, while he roughly ties McCain in the Midwest and trails McCain by a substantial margin in the South. Nevertheless, roughly half of voters in all four regions believe Obama is the more likely of the two to win.

Similarly, perceptions of Obama's electability by age don't exactly line up with his presidential support patterns across age cohorts. Thus, Gallup Poll daily tracking spanning June 9–12 shows adults age 18 to 34 to be his strongest support group: They give him a 24-point lead over McCain, compared with a virtual tie between Obama and McCain among those age 35 to 54 and a 6-point lead

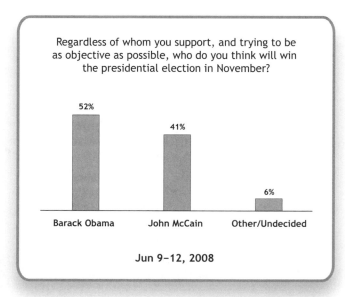

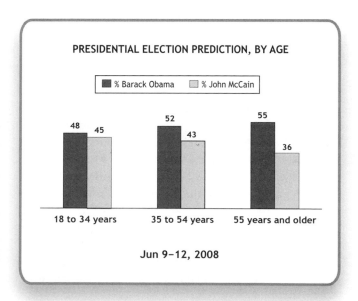

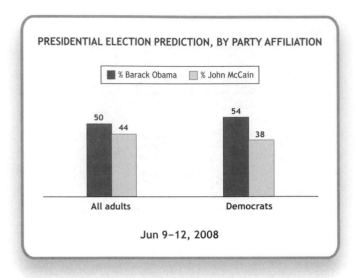

PRESIDENTIAL ELECTION PREDICTION, BY PARTY AFFILIATION

Jun 9–12, 2008

for McCain among those 55 and older. One might expect younger Americans, then, to be the most optimistic about the chances of the first black nominee from either major party winning the presidency—yet they are in fact the least likely to believe he will win. Adults age 18 to 34 are essentially divided between Obama and McCain as the likely winner: 48% percent predict an Obama win vs. 45% for McCain. By contrast, a majority of Americans age 35 to 54 and an even more substantial majority of Americans 55 and older say Obama will win. Gallup Poll daily tracking shows women backing Obama over McCain, 50% to 38%, while men prefer McCain to Obama, 48% to 42%. Nevertheless, both genders are more likely to believe Obama rather than McCain will win the election.

JUNE 17

Gasoline Prices Having a Ripple Effect on Americans' Lives

Most Americans are able to list specific ways in which the high price of gasoline has affected them personally, and many say that the rising cost of gasoline has had a ripple effect on their personal and financial lives outside of things directly related to driving or travel. The answers given in response to the question "What are the most important ways that the high price of gasoline has affected you personally?," asked in a recent June 9–12 Gallup Poll, are diverse and suggest that there is no one single effect of rising gasoline prices that comes to Americans' minds when they are asked to enumerate its impact. Instead, it appears that the consequences of gasoline prices can be classified into three main categories: direct impact on Americans' normal driving and travel plans and patterns; impact on Americans' financial lives more generally (out-

side of issues relating directly to gasoline or travel), including the perceived impact of the rising price of gasoline on inflation and the rising price of food; and a "no impact" category, reflecting in which the responses of those who say they haven't been affected or are unable to mention a specific way in which gasoline prices have affected them. The responses included in the first of these categories are to be expected, but the significant number of Americans who talk about the ways in which the high price of gasoline is beginning to affect their lives outside of cutting back on driving underscores the impact of high gasoline prices on many aspects of American society today.

The overwhelming majority of Americans are able to give an answer when asked about the impact of high gasoline prices on their personal lives, and the vast majority of these answers reflect some sort of negative consequence. While a number of Americans are most likely to mention that the rising price of gasoline has forced them to modify their driving patterns in some fashion, many talk about the injurious impact of gasoline prices on their general financial situation and/or the way that the rising price of gasoline has caused the prices of non-gasoline goods and services to increase. Of course, these open-ended responses do not give an indication of the severity of the impact of gasoline prices. Cutting back on spending may mean one thing to a millionaire and another thing entirely to a family making only $30,000 a year. Still, the harsh nature of many of the types of responses given—including response categories with labels like "cannot afford the cost of driving," "have little or no disposable income," "am hurting financially," and "don't visit family as often"—suggest that the public is enduring fairly harsh consequences of the unprecedented rapid increase in the price of gasoline.

JUNE 18

Forty-Somethings May Hold Key to Election

Barack Obama's appeal to younger voters and John McCain's support among older voters may have created a situation wherein the outcome of the election will turn on the preferences of middle-aged voters—particularly those in their 40s. Since Hillary Clinton suspended her campaign earlier this month, McCain and Obama have tied at 46% support among registered voters between the ages of 40 and 49, according to an analysis of Gallup Poll daily tracking data from June 5 to June 16. During that time, Gallup interviewed nearly 10,000 registered voters nationwide, including 1,637 in their 40s. Obama led McCain by an average of 47% to 42% among the entire sample of registered voters.

In addition to exactly tying among voters in their 40s, the candidates are also competitive among voters in their 50s,

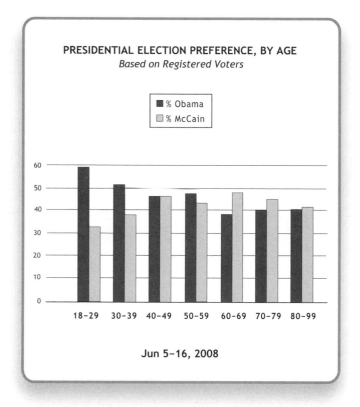

PRESIDENTIAL ELECTION PREFERENCE, BY AGE
Based on Registered Voters

Jun 5–16, 2008

with Obama holding a slight 47% to 43% advantage. Obama currently holds a commanding lead among younger voters, beating McCain 59% to 32% among voters under 30 and 51% to 38% among voters in their 30s. Currently, McCain's highest support is found with voters between the ages of 60 and 69, among whom he leads Obama by 10 percentage points, 48% to 38%. McCain also currently holds slim edges among voters in their 70s and 80s. Forty-something voters are a politically interesting group because some of the common political divides in the American electorate are not evident within this particular age group. For example, there is almost no gender gap in voting preferences among

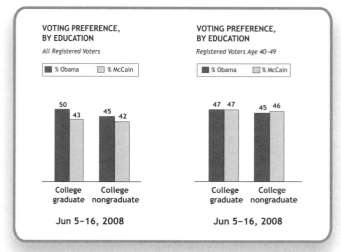

VOTING PREFERENCE, BY EDUCATION
All Registered Voters

VOTING PREFERENCE, BY EDUCATION
Registered Voters Age 40–49

Jun 5–16, 2008

Jun 5–16, 2008

those in their 40s—though there is a noticeable gender gap among all registered voters. Similarly, the candidates fare equally well among college graduates (normally a strong Obama group) and among those without college education (usually a better group for McCain).

That is not to say that the usual political differences do not apply to this group: Obama still leads overwhelmingly among Democrats, liberals, and nonwhites in their 40s, while McCain has the edge among Republicans, conservatives, whites, and higher-income voters between the ages of 40 and 49. And voter preferences may actually vary more by marital status among those in their 40s than among all voters. In this dataset, McCain held a 53% to 39% advantage among married voters in their 40s (compared with a 49% to 40% advantage among all registered voters who are married), while Obama had a commanding 62% to 28% lead among unmarried voters in this age bracket (compared with a 56% to 32% lead among all unmarried voters).

JUNE 20

Republicans, Democrats Differ on Creationism

There is a significant political divide in this country in beliefs about the origin of human beings, with 60% of Republicans saying humans were created in their present form by God 10,000 years ago, a belief shared by only 40% of independents and 38% of Democrats. Gallup has been asking this three-part question about the origin of humans since 1982. Perhaps surprisingly to some, the results for the broad sample of adult Americans show very little change over the years. During this 26-year time period, between 43% and 47% of Americans have agreed with the creationist view that God created human beings pretty much in their present form at one time within the last 10,000 years or

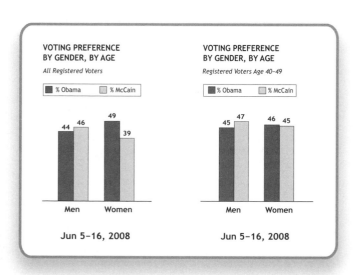

VOTING PREFERENCE BY GENDER, BY AGE
All Registered Voters

VOTING PREFERENCE BY GENDER, BY AGE
Registered Voters Age 40–49

Jun 5–16, 2008

Jun 5–16, 2008

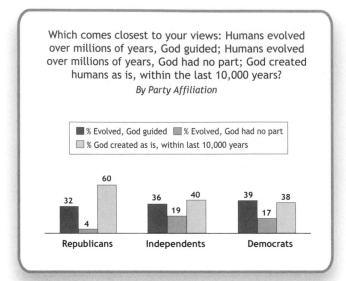

Which comes closest to your views: Humans evolved over millions of years, God guided; Humans evolved over millions of years, God had no part; God created humans as is, within the last 10,000 years?

By Party Affiliation

■ % Evolved, God guided   ■ % Evolved, God had no part
□ % God created as is, within last 10,000 years

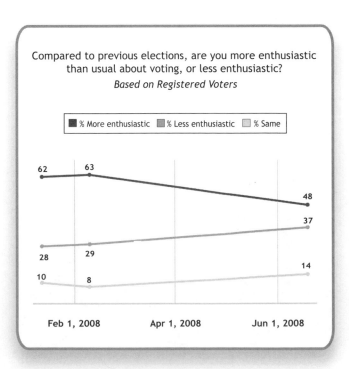

Which comes closest to your views: Humans evolved over millions of years, God guided; Humans evolved over millions of years, God had no part; God created humans as is, within the last 10,000 years?

By Church Attendance

■ % Evolved, God guided   ■ % Evolved, God had no part
□ % God created as is, within last 10,000 years

so. Between 35% and 40% have agreed with the alternative explanation that humans evolved, but with God guiding the process; while only 9% to 14% have chosen a pure secularist evolution perspective, that humans evolved with no guidance by God. The significantly higher percentage of Republicans who adopt the creationist view reflects in part the strong relationship between religion and views on the origin of humans. Republicans are significantly more likely to attend church weekly than are others, and Americans who attend church weekly are highly likely to accept the creationist explanation for the origin of humans.

Implications for the Election

Although evolution is not a front-burner issue (particularly in light of the economy and the price of gasoline), the issue

of teaching evolution in schools came up on the campaign trail last year and could resurface in one way or another between now and the November election. Presumptive Republican nominee John McCain is facing the challenge of gaining the confidence and enthusiasm of conservative Republicans; turnout among this group could be an important factor in determining the final outcome in a number of key swing states. A majority of Republicans accept the creationist explanation of the origin of humans, and if the issue of what is taught in schools relating to evolution and creationism surfaces as a campaign issue, McCain's response could turn out to be quite important.

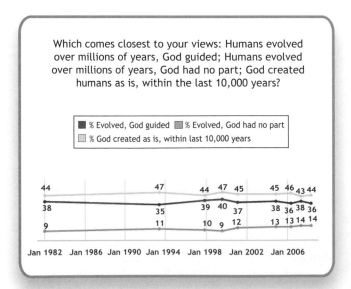

Which comes closest to your views: Humans evolved over millions of years, God guided; Humans evolved over millions of years, God had no part; God created humans as is, within the last 10,000 years?

■ % Evolved, God guided   ■ % Evolved, God had no part
□ % God created as is, within last 10,000 years

Compared to previous elections, are you more enthusiastic than usual about voting, or less enthusiastic?

Based on Registered Voters

■ % More enthusiastic   ■ % Less enthusiastic   □ % Same

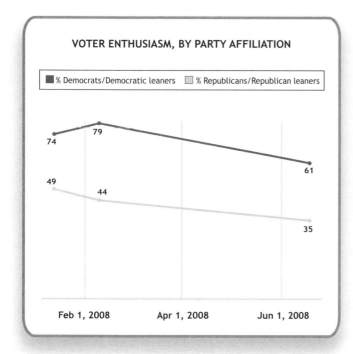

VOTER ENTHUSIASM, BY PARTY AFFILIATION

■ % Democrats/Democratic leaners   □ % Republicans/Republican leaners

74   79   61

49   44   35

Feb 1, 2008   Apr 1, 2008   Jun 1, 2008

JUNE 22

Gallup Daily: Election Preferences Are Stable

National registered voters' preferences for the general election remain closely divided between Democrat Barack Obama (46%) and Republican John McCain (44%). Gallup Poll daily tracking for June 19–21 shows the same results Gallup reported the prior two days, with Obama holding a slight but not statistically significant advantage over McCain. Obama has not trailed McCain in the last 15 Gallup Poll daily reports (beginning with the June 1–5 polling), but he has held a statistically significant advantage in less than half of these (6 out of 15). His lead during this time has been as large as seven percentage points.

JUNE 23

Election Enthusiasm Dips After Primaries

A new USA Today/Gallup Poll finds a sharp drop in voter enthusiasm. Forty-eight percent of registered voters say they are "more enthusiastic than usual about voting," compared with 63% who said this in a poll conducted just after the Super Tuesday presidential primaries and caucuses in early February 2008. The drop has occurred among both Republicans and Democrats, though the decline has been greater among Democrats, in large part because Republican enthusiasm was relatively low to begin with. Democrats continue to hold a wide advantage (61% to 35%) on voter enthusiasm.

A post-primary voter hangover is not unprecedented, but Gallup did not observe as large a decline in enthusiasm in 2000 or 2004 after the presidential nominees were essentially decided. Between January 2000 and March 2000, enthusiasm about voting dropped by six percentage points among both Republicans (from 51% to 45%) and Democrats (from 39% to 33%). In 2004, Democrats' enthusiasm dropped from late January to March (59% to 51%), while Republicans' enthusiasm basically stayed the same (53% to 52%). The lack of change in Republican enthusiasm in 2004 could have resulted from the fact that George W. Bush, seeking a second term, was running unopposed for the party's nomination. The poll does not provide many clues as to why the drop may have been greater this year than in previous election years. For example, although polls have shown that the majority of Republicans and Democrats are satisfied with their parties' chosen nominees, it is possible that those who strongly supported one of their challengers (such as Hillary Clinton or Mitt Romney) may be disappointed in the outcome and thus less excited about voting in November than if their chosen candidate had won the nomination. If that is the case, however, it is not apparent from the candidates' favorable ratings: Both John McCain and Barack Obama are viewed more favorably now by those who identify with their respective parties than they were in February 2008. It is important to note that the overall drop in enthusiasm since February does not mean that Americans are any less engaged in the campaign. In the new poll, 75% say they have given "quite a lot of thought" to the election, essentially the same as the 76% who responded that way in February. At least 7 in 10 Americans have reported giving this high degree of attention to the election since late January. In fact, the current level of attention paid to the election is significantly higher than it was in June 2004 (an average of 67%) and much higher than in June 2000 (an average of 45%).

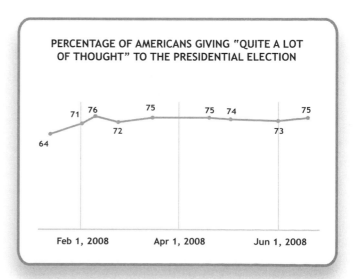

PERCENTAGE OF AMERICANS GIVING "QUITE A LOT OF THOUGHT" TO THE PRESIDENTIAL ELECTION

64   71   76   72   75   75   74   73   75

Feb 1, 2008   Apr 1, 2008   Jun 1, 2008

MORE/LESS ENTHUSIASTIC THAN USUAL ABOUT VOTING,
Republicans and Republican Leaners, Historical Trend

	% More enthusiastic	% Less enthusiastic	% Same
2000 Jan 7–10	51	32	16
2000 Mar 10–12	45	32	22
2004 Jan 29–Feb 1	53	31	15
2004 Mar 26–28	52	27	20
2004 Jul 19–21	51	32	15
2004 Jul 30–Aug 1	62	27	11
2004 Aug 23–25	60	30	9
2004 Sep 3–5	69	18	13
2004 Oct 14–16	68	19	12
2008 Jan 10–13	49	37	12
2008 Feb 8–10	44	48	8
2008 Jun 15–19	35	51	13

Enthusiasm in a Historical Context

At 35%, the percentage of Republicans who say they are more enthusiastic than usual about voting is the lowest Gallup has measured for Republicans at any time during the last three presidential election years. (It is just two points higher than the low for either party—33% for Democrats, in March 2000.) The prior Republican low was detected in the post–Super Tuesday poll earlier this year. Republicans were much more enthusiastic about voting in 2004 when George W. Bush was seeking re-election. In February, a record 79% of Democrats said they were more enthusiastic than usual about voting. Even with the decline to 61%, Democratic enthusiasm remains relatively high from a historical perspective.

Implications for the Election

Though the public is still highly engaged in the election, that engagement is apparently more subdued than it was

earlier this year, judging by the drop in the percentage of registered voters who report being more enthusiastic than usual about voting. Voter enthusiasm may well pick up again as the campaign moves closer to Election Day, as occurred in 2004. Gallup's long history of relating the degree of "thought" Americans are giving to an election to voter turnout suggests that 2008 will be another high-turnout election year.

Gallup has less historical data on the "more enthusiastic than usual about voting" question, and thus far it has not established a strong link between enthusiasm and voter turnout. However, it generally has been the case in presidential and midterm election years that the party with the relative advantage in enthusiasm does better in the election. So even if Democratic enthusiasm has dropped since Obama clinched the party's presidential nomination, the fact that Democrats maintain a wide lead in enthusiasm over Republicans is a positive sign for the Democratic Party.

JUNE 24
Obama Has Edge on Key Election Issues

Americans see Barack Obama as better able than John McCain to handle energy issues and the economy—the two most important election issues in the public's eyes, according to a recent Gallup survey. Six other issues were tested in the poll, with the two candidates positioned roughly evenly on Iraq, moral values, and illegal immigration, while Obama has an edge on healthcare and taxes. McCain's only advantage is on terrorism. The June 15–19 USA Today/Gallup Poll asked Americans to rate the importance of the

MORE/LESS ENTHUSIASTIC ABOUT VOTING THAN USUAL
Democrats and Democratic Leaners, Historical Trend

	% More enthusiastic	% Less enthusiastic	% Same
2000 Jan 7–10	39	42	17
2000 Mar 10–12	33	47	19
2004 Jan 29–Feb 1	59	34	6
2004 Mar 26–28	51	35	13
2004 Jul 19–21	68	20	12
2004 Jul 30–Aug 1	73	21	6
2004 Aug 23–25	60	30	10
2004 Sep 3–5	62	29	7
2004 Oct 14–16	67	23	10
2008 Jan 10–13	74	19	6
2008 Feb 8–10	79	15	6
2008 Jun 15–19	61	25	13

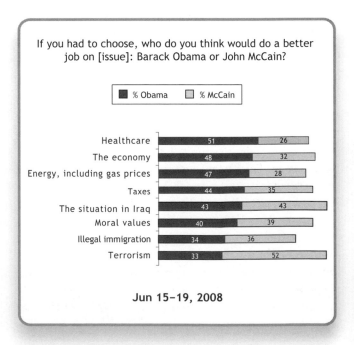

If you had to choose, who do you think would do a better job on [issue]: Barack Obama or John McCain?

■ % Obama   ☐ % McCain

	% Obama	% McCain
Healthcare	51	26
The economy	48	32
Energy, including gas prices	47	28
Taxes	44	35
The situation in Iraq	43	43
Moral values	40	39
Illegal immigration	34	36
Terrorism	33	52

Jun 15–19, 2008

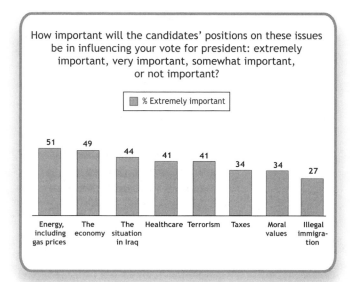

How important will the candidates' positions on these issues be in influencing your vote for president: extremely important, very important, somewhat important, or not important?

■ % Extremely important

| Energy, including gas prices | The economy | The situation in Iraq | Healthcare | Terrorism | Taxes | Moral values | Illegal immigration |
| 51 | 49 | 44 | 41 | 41 | 34 | 34 | 27 |

presidential candidates' positions on eight policy issues: energy, the economy, the situation in Iraq, healthcare, terrorism, taxes, moral values, and illegal immigration. The poll then asked respondents questions designed to measure the degree to which they perceive Obama and McCain as able to handle each of the eight issues.

A majority of Americans believe that the candidates' positions on all eight issues will be either "extremely" or "very important" to their vote—not a surprising finding, given that each issue included in the list has received significant attention in the 2008 campaign. The proportion of Americans who rate each issue as "extremely" important in influencing their vote for president, perhaps a better test of each issue's likely impact this fall, ranges from 27% to 51%. Two issues top the list: energy, including gasoline prices, and the economy. (Energy has escalated in importance to voters in recent months as gasoline prices have risen to the $4-per-gallon level.) Obama has a clear advantage over McCain on both of these top two issues. Americans give Obama a 19-point edge over McCain as better able to deal with energy, with 47% choosing Obama and 28% McCain. On the economy, Obama has a 16-point margin over McCain, 48% to 32%.

The next tier of issues—Iraq, healthcare, and terrorism—receive "extremely important" ratings from 41% to 44% of Americans. The positioning of the candidates on these three issues is mixed. Obama and McCain are tied as to who would be better able to handle Iraq; Obama wins by a substantial 25-point margin on healthcare; and McCain wins on terrorism by 19 points. (Terrorism is the only issue of the eight tested on which McCain has a significant advantage over Obama in voter perceptions.) The bottom tier of issues—taxes, moral values, and illegal immigration—is seen as extremely important by approximately a

third of Americans or less. On two of these issues—moral values and illegal immigration—Obama and McCain are essentially tied; Obama has a 9-point lead over McCain on taxes.

Implications for the Election

Obama is leading McCain by six points among registered voters in the head-to-head matchup included in the current USA Today/Gallup Poll, and there are significantly more Americans at the moment who identify themselves as Democrats than as Republicans. So it is not surprising that Obama is rated as better able to handle more of the tested issues than is McCain. Whatever the cause, the finding that Obama has significant strength on domestic issues is potentially quite meaningful in this year's election, given that gasoline prices and the economy are the two issues the public is most likely to see as important in choosing between the two candidates. In fact, further analysis of the poll results shows that less than half of Americans believe McCain would be able to do a good job of handling either problem, while 59% say Obama would be able to do a good job on both of these issues. Iraq, on which the two candidates have sharply divergent positions, is not too far behind energy/gasoline prices and the economy in terms of imputed importance. As of now, however, Americans are equally likely to choose Obama or McCain as likely to do a better job on this problem.

The poll points to one undisputed strength for McCain: terrorism. Slightly less than half of Americans say Obama would do a good job of handing terrorism, while 70% say that about McCain. But terrorism is slightly less important as a voting issue in Americans' eyes than are economic issues, gasoline prices, and Iraq. These data would suggest that from a campaign perspective, Obama would be advised to play off his domestic strengths, particularly in terms of the economy, to try to neutralize McCain's strength on terrorism and increase his (Obama's) perceived strength on Iraq. McCain, on the other hand, is strongly positioned on national security but needs to move into a more competitive position with Obama in terms of critical domestic issues relating to the economy and gasoline prices.

JUNE 25

McCain vs. Obama as Commander in Chief

John McCain's life experience has earned him a solid national reputation as someone who can serve as the nation's commander in chief, with 80% saying he can handle the responsibilities of this important role. Barack Obama lags well behind on the same measure, but does pass the 50%

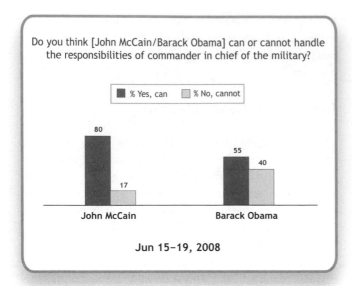

Do you think [John McCain/Barack Obama] can or cannot handle the responsibilities of commander in chief of the military?

■ % Yes, can   □ % No, cannot

Jun 15–19, 2008

public confidence threshold. Whereas McCain is viewed as qualified to be commander in chief by large majorities of Republicans (94%), independents (79%), and Democrats (71%), perceptions of Obama as commander in chief are more divided along partisan lines. Most Democrats and a solid majority of independents say Obama can handle the responsibilities of commander in chief of the nation's military; most Republicans, however, say he is not qualified.

The same June 15–19 USA Today/Gallup Poll finds much smaller advantages for McCain over Obama on the narrower questions of which candidate Americans trust more to make decisions about sending U.S. troops into combat generally, and into Iran specifically. McCain leads Obama by 53% to 40% as the candidate more Americans say they would trust if a situation arose that required the president to make a decision about sending U.S. troops into combat. The overwhelming majority of Republicans choose McCain on this measure, as do over half of independents

and nearly a quarter of Democrats. In terms of Iran specifically, however, Obama and McCain are nearly tied in public trust ratings. McCain's five-percentage-point lead on this measure, 48% to 43%, is not statistically significant. Nearly as many Republicans and Democrats prefer McCain to make a decision regarding sending troops into Iran as do so on the general sending troops into combat measure, but he has less support from independents. Whereas 54% of independents choose McCain as the candidate they trust more to make decisions about sending troops into combat generally, only 44% trust him more as far as sending troops to Iran is concerned. The differences reflect Americans' general agreement with Obama regarding U.S. diplomacy with Iran. As Gallup previously reported, almost 6 in 10 Americans (59%) think it would be a good idea for the president of the United States to meet with the president of Iran—a position Obama has espoused and McCain has roundly criticized.

McCain clearly enjoys a more broad-based positive reputation with Americans with respect to military matters than does Obama, but it is unclear how this will benefit him in the election. McCain gets significantly more crossover support from Democrats as being able to fulfill the duties of commander in chief than Obama does from Republicans, but this is unlikely to win him many crossover votes. More importantly, even though independents express greater confidence in McCain than in Obama as a commander in chief, more than half do have confidence in Obama in this regard. And although more independents choose McCain as the candidate they trust to send U.S. troops into combat generally, they are divided between McCain and Obama when it comes to sending troops into Iran. In short, while defense issues are potentially one of McCain's strong suits, the more the issue is framed in terms of sending U.S. troops into combat, and particularly into Iran, the less helpful this advantage may be to his candidacy.

JUNE 26

Obama Holds Slim Advantage over McCain Among Catholics

Among major American religious groups, Catholic voters are most closely divided in their presidential voting preferences, with Barack Obama holding a narrow 47% to 43% advantage over John McCain. McCain leads Obama among Protestants (48% to 41%) and Mormons (70% to 23%), while Obama holds the upper hand among Jewish voters (62% to 29%) and those with no religious affiliation (65% to 25%). These results are based on aggregated Gallup Poll daily tracking data from June 5 to June 23, with all 14,000+ interviews conducted after Hillary Clinton decided to end her presidential bid.

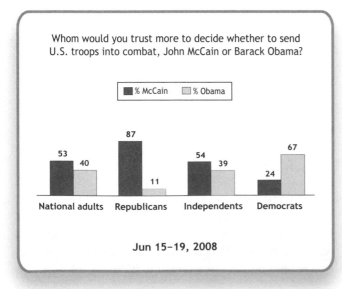

Whom would you trust more to decide whether to send U.S. troops into combat, John McCain or Barack Obama?

■ % McCain   □ % Obama

Jun 15–19, 2008

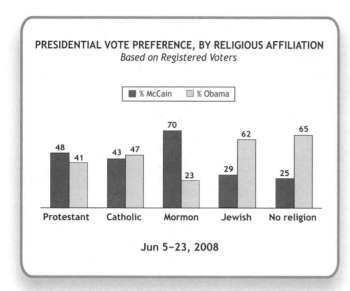

PRESIDENTIAL VOTE PREFERENCE, BY RELIGIOUS AFFILIATION
Based on Registered Voters
Jun 5–23, 2008

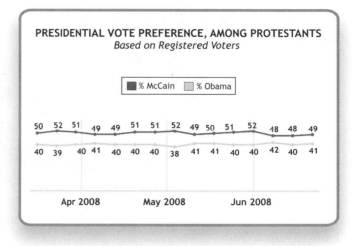

PRESIDENTIAL VOTE PREFERENCE, AMONG PROTESTANTS
Based on Registered Voters

During this time, Obama averaged a 46% to 43% lead over McCain among all registered voters. Catholics have traditionally been a key swing voter group, and the 2008 election is proving to be no exception. Since Gallup began tracking general election voting preferences in early March, the largest advantage either candidate has had among Catholics in any given week has been only 5 percentage points. Obama's appeal to minority voters, including Hispanics, helps to push him ahead of McCain among Catholics. In these data, roughly one in seven Catholic registered voters report being of Hispanic ethnicity, and they prefer Obama by a 66% to 25% margin. Among non-Hispanic Catholics, McCain has a 46% to 43% advantage.

Support Among Other Religious Groups

Obama's overwhelming support among blacks helps him stay within hailing distance of McCain among Protestant

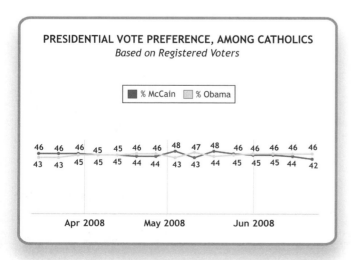

PRESIDENTIAL VOTE PREFERENCE, AMONG CATHOLICS
Based on Registered Voters

voters. Currently, McCain leads Obama by 7 points among all Protestants, but white Protestants solidly back McCain (56% to 32%) and nonwhite Protestants overwhelmingly favor Obama (77% to 15%, including the support of more than 9 in 10 black Protestants). Only about 2% of Americans identify their religious affiliation as the Church of Jesus Christ of Latter-day Saints, or Mormons. They have become a reliably Republican group, and McCain leads Obama by a better than three-to-one margin among Mormon voters, 70% to 23%. Americans of Jewish faith are about as prevalent as Mormons, with roughly 2% of Americans identifying themselves as Jews. They have been a traditionally strong Democratic group, but they have taken on somewhat added significance because of questions that have been raised about Obama's support for the Jewish state of Israel, in response to which Obama has taken steps to reassure Americans of his support for Israel. He currently leads McCain by 62% to 29% among Jewish voters, and has typically held a sizable advantage against McCain among this voting group.

Implications for the Election

As the general election campaign has gotten under way, the traditional political/religious alliances already seem to be in place. That includes Mormons overwhelmingly supporting the Republican candidate, Protestants (especially white Protestants) backing the Republican, and Jewish and nonreligious voters favoring the Democrat. Catholics continue to be the primary religious battleground group, and McCain and Obama will do their best to persuade Catholic voters, who have tended to back the winner in presidential elections more often than not. For McCain, that will likely entail an emphasis on the moral positions he shares with Catholics (pro-life, anti–gay rights). For Obama, his desire to help out the less fortunate will appeal to many Catholic voters.

At a unity rally in Unity, New Hampshire, on June 27, 2008, Senator Hillary Clinton endorses Senator Barack Obama for president. *(Elise Amendola/AP Images)*

Obama, McCain Still Tied, Now at 44%

Gallup Poll daily tracking from June 23 to June 25 finds Barack Obama and John McCain tied for the second straight day in national registered voter preferences for the fall election, with each winning 44% of the vote. The results are consistent with the June 25 finding of a tie at 45%. Additionally, Obama and McCain have been roughly tied in each individual day's results including in today's three-day rolling average, indicating some stability in the race since June 23. The gap in support for the two presumptive major party nominees over the past week has been less than the four-percentage-point margin of sampling error needed for one of the candidates to demonstrate a statistically significant lead, so the race has been very close. However, until the tie on June 25, based on interviewing conducted between June 22 and June 24, Obama held a slight advantage.

JUNE 27

Numerous Polls Show Obama Leading in Close Race

Gallup Poll daily tracking over the past week or so, along with a USA Today/Gallup Poll conducted last week with 1,600 national adults, indicates that the race for the presidency at this point is quite close. Barack Obama has held a modest lead for the most part, but over the past several days, even that small lead has evaporated to the point where Obama and John McCain are tied among registered voters. In fact, the tie has now persisted for two straight Gallup Poll daily tracking reports (each report consisting of a three-day rolling average of more than 2,600 registered voters). Indeed, Gallup's tracking results have been quite steady over the past weeks—spanning thousands of interviews—showing little dramatic change from day to day or week to week. A Time magazine poll conducted between June 19 and June 25 also shows the race close, with a slight 47% to 43% lead for Obama. A Fox News poll from June 17 to June 18 shows a close race as well, with Obama at 45% and McCain at 41%. Yet, two other polls released over the past week—Los Angeles Times/Bloomberg (June 19–23) and Newsweek (June 18–19)—both show Obama with a double-digit lead over McCain.

Well-done scientific polls measuring voter sentiment more typically than not yield roughly the same estimates, so the difference in estimates between these polls and the Gallup Polls is unusual. Specifically looking at the differences between the various polls, the estimate of Obama's share of the vote in the latest Gallup tracking poll from June 23 through June 25 is 44%. This compares with the 49% estimate for Obama in the Los Angeles Times/Bloomberg poll and the 51% estimate in the Newsweek poll (and with the 48% estimate among registered voters in our USA Today/Gallup Poll conducted between June 15 and June 19). Gallup's present tracking estimate of McCain's current percentage of the vote is also 44%; the USA Today/Gallup Poll from last week had it at 42%. But McCain was at 36% and 37% in the Newsweek and Los Angeles Times/Bloomberg polls. The interviewing for these polls was conducted over different time periods. The interviewing period for the Los Angeles Times/Bloomberg poll stretched from June 19 through June 23, and it found Obama at 49% and McCain at 37%. The combined Gallup tracking for these same five days (involving more than 4,000 interviews with registered voters) shows Obama with 46% of the vote and McCain with 44%. So an apples-to-apples comparison (based on the same interviewing period) shows a three-percentage-point difference in estimates of Obama's share of the vote, and a seven-point difference in estimates of McCain's share of the vote.

As is always the case, there are also some slight differences in the way the polls were conducted. The Los Angeles Times/Bloomberg poll asks a "right direction/wrong direction" question before the ballot question; our Gallup Poll daily tracking screens for registered voters before the ballot. The Los Angeles Times/Bloomberg poll includes the phrase "or would you vote for a candidate from some other party?" The Gallup Poll does not include this option. It is unclear whether or how the order or content of questions may affect the polling results. Extensive Gallup polling of the electorate simply did not pick up any major Obama surge over McCain in recent days. Broadly speaking, according to our data, the two candidates remain closely matched among registered voters.

Obama Beats McCain on Most Character Ratings

The June 15–19 USA Today/Gallup Poll finds Obama swamping McCain in Americans' perceptions of who has a

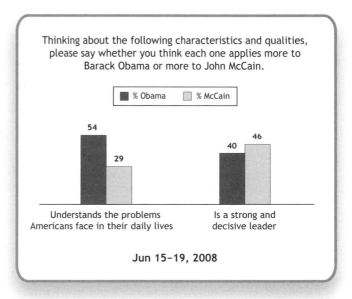

Thinking about the following characteristics and qualities, please say whether you think each one applies more to Barack Obama or more to John McCain.

Jun 15–19, 2008

better grasp of the problems Americans face, while McCain leads Obama by a slight margin as a "strong and decisive leader." More generally, Obama is the more highly regarded of the two candidates on a number of positive personal and leadership characteristics, ranging from his empathy for average Americans to his political independence and his ability to solve the nation's problems. He leads McCain by significant margins on 7 of 10 characteristics tested in the recent poll; he roughly ties McCain on 2 and trails McCain on only 1.

EMPATHY AND INDEPENDENCE

The two dimensions on which Obama does best relative to McCain—understanding the problems Americans face in their daily lives and caring about "the needs of people like you"—both concern his perceived empathy for average Americans. He outscores McCain by more than 20 percentage points on both of these characteristics. Obama also leads by double digits on two dimensions that reflect Americans' perceptions of the candidates' political independence: being independent in his thoughts and actions and standing up to special interests. Obama and McCain are more closely

BARACK OBAMA VS. JOHN McCAIN ON INDEPENDENCE CHARACTERISTICS

	Obama	McCain
Is independent in his thoughts and actions	52%	36%
Would stand up to special interests, including those aligned with his party	48%	34%

Jun 15–19, 2008

BARACK OBAMA VS. JOHN McCAIN ON EFFECTIVENESS CHARACTERISTICS

	Obama	McCain
Would work well with both parties to get things done in Washington	48%	35%
Has a clear plan for solving the country's problems	41%	31%

Jun 15–19, 2008

BARACK OBAMA VS. JOHN McCAIN ON VALUES/MORAL CHARACTERISTICS

	Obama	McCain
Shares your values	47%	39%
Is honest and trustworthy	39%	35%

Jun 15–19, 2008

BARACK OBAMA VS. JOHN McCAIN ON LEADERSHIP/COMPETENCE CHARACTERISTICS

	Obama	McCain
Can manage the government effectively	42%	42%
Is a strong and decisive leader	40%	46%

Jun 15–19, 2008

matched when it comes to their personal ethics or values. Obama leads McCain, but only slightly, on the "shares your values" dimension, while the two are nearly tied in perceptions of who is more "honest and trustworthy." Again, many Americans do not see either candidate as superior on the honesty dimension—though both candidates score well on this attribute when rated individually.

EFFECTIVENESS AND LEADERSHIP

Obama also performs well on two dimensions related to his effectiveness in achieving public policy objectives: working well with both parties to get things done, and having a clear plan for solving the country's problems (though on this latter dimension, a substantial 28% do not express a preference for either candidate). McCain is slightly more likely than Obama to be regarded as a "strong and decisive leader." He also ties Obama in perceptions of which candidate can better manage the government effectively.

While neither dimension constitutes a strong advantage for McCain, his relatively good performance on these two characteristics signals that Americans see him as someone who can lead people and oversee government agencies. These are core responsibilities of the presidency, and ones on which he at least measures up to Obama.

Implications for the Election

Obama clearly wins on most of Gallup's character ratings; the question is whether he wins by large enough margins on the dimensions that are most important to Americans when electing a president. Obama's six-point lead in the horse race in the same poll is an important summary indicator suggesting that he does.

Americans Place Priority on the Economy over Terrorism

Confidence in a presidential candidate's ability to handle terrorism may not be enough to satisfy American voters in 2008. A majority of Americans say they prefer a candidate whose greatest strength is fixing the economy (56%) rather than one whose greatest strength is protecting the country from terrorism (39%).

This week, Charles Black, a senior McCain adviser, reignited the debate over the politics of national security and the appropriateness of propagating campaign messages based on fear after being quoted in *Fortune* magazine stating that another terrorist attack on U.S. soil "would be a big advantage" for McCain. Despite the criticism Black received, President Bush echoed a similar theme, saying McCain is the only presidential candidate "who knows what it takes to defeat our enemies." The

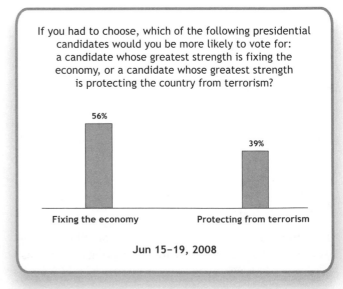

If you had to choose, which of the following presidential candidates would you be more likely to vote for: a candidate whose greatest strength is fixing the economy, or a candidate whose greatest strength is protecting the country from terrorism?

56% Fixing the economy

39% Protecting from terrorism

Jun 15–19, 2008

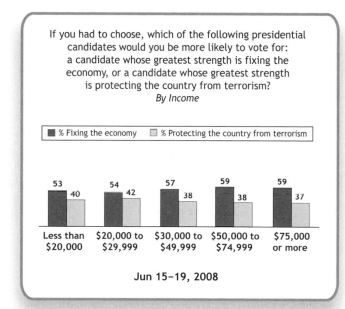

If you had to choose, which of the following presidential candidates would you be more likely to vote for: a candidate whose greatest strength is fixing the economy, or a candidate whose greatest strength is protecting the country from terrorism?
By Income

■ % Fixing the economy   □ % Protecting the country from terrorism

Less than $20,000	$20,000 to $29,999	$30,000 to $49,999	$50,000 to $74,999	$75,000 or more
53 / 40	54 / 42	57 / 38	59 / 38	59 / 37

Jun 15–19, 2008

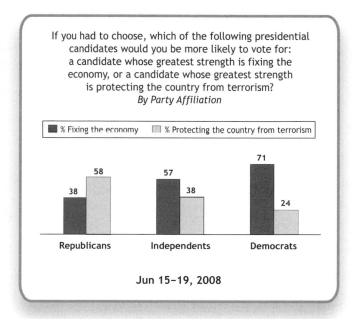

If you had to choose, which of the following presidential candidates would you be more likely to vote for: a candidate whose greatest strength is fixing the economy, or a candidate whose greatest strength is protecting the country from terrorism?
By Party Affiliation

■ % Fixing the economy   □ % Protecting the country from terrorism

Republicans	Independents	Democrats
38 / 58	57 / 38	71 / 24

Jun 15–19, 2008

rationale behind these statements is clear. Out of eight key election issues tested in a recent USA Today/Gallup Poll, McCain's number one perceived strength is his ability to handle terrorism, while Barack Obama outperforms McCain on his perceived ability to handle energy prices and the economy—which outrank terrorism as priority issues for most Americans. And a majority of Americans, regardless of income, say they prefer a candidate who is best at fixing the economy.

Given the candidates' perceived respective strengths on the economy and terrorism, voters' preferences for the most part correspond to their perceptions of which is the more important issue. But preference for the economy over security as a priority is not a perfect vote predictor. A full one-quarter of those who prefer a candidate who can protect the country from terrorism say they will vote for Obama, and a nearly identical percentage of those who prefer a candidate who can fix the economy say they will vote for McCain. That said, independents decisively prefer a candidate whose greatest strength is fixing the economy, by a 57% to 38% margin over one whose greatest strength is protecting against terrorism. In fact, their preference with respect to fixing the economy is as strong as the preference among Republicans for a candidate who can protect the country from terrorism. It is also worth noting that more than a third of Republicans opt for the "fixing the economy" candidate.

The McCain campaign faces the dilemma of positioning a candidate whose perceived strength, combating terrorism, is currently not in sync with Americans' most important priority, the economy. While the statements from Charles Black and President Bush did serve to reintroduce terrorism into the campaign conversation, Ameri-

cans' financial worries are not going away. With the ripple effect of high gasoline prices taking a direct toll on many Americans' lives, the economy remains the more decisive factor in their vote, and in that respect, Obama currently has the advantage.

JUNE 30

Democrats Favored to Retain House in November

The Democratic Party is in a good position to retain its majority status in the House of Representatives this November. Democrats lead the Republicans by 51% to 40% in party preferences for House candidates among all registered voters, and by 52% to 42% among likely voters. This

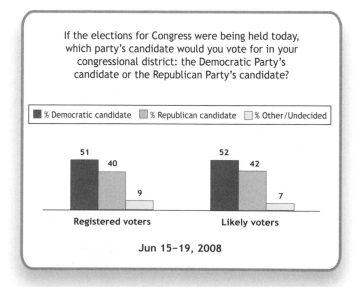

If the elections for Congress were being held today, which party's candidate would you vote for in your congressional district: the Democratic Party's candidate or the Republican Party's candidate?

■ % Democratic candidate   ■ % Republican candidate   □ % Other/Undecided

Registered voters	Likely voters
51 / 40 / 9	52 / 42 / 7

Jun 15–19, 2008

is according to Gallup's "generic ballot" question, asking Americans which party's candidate they would vote for in their congressional district if the election were held today. The USA Today/Gallup survey was conducted between June 15 and June 19, 2008. The Democrats' 11-point advantage among registered voters is slightly less than what Gallup found in mid-February—at that time, the Democrats led by 55% to 40%—but it still puts them in a comfortable position heading into the fall.

The current registered voter results are identical to those from Gallup's final pre-election survey in 2006. In that election, the Democrats wrested majority control of the House of Representatives from the Republicans, winning 53% of all votes cast nationally for congressional candidates to the Republicans' 45%. The implication, of course, is that the Democrats are on track to hold on to their House majority in the 2008 elections.

Voter turnout typically does help the Republicans narrow any Democratic advantage seen in pre-election polls based on all registered voters. That was the case in 2004, when the Republicans trailed the Democrats by 4 percentage points among registered voters in Gallup's final pre-election survey, 45% to 49%, but the Republicans went on to win 47% of the national popular vote and a 30-seat majority in the House. Since the 2004 election, however, the Republicans have generally trailed the Democrats on the generic congressional ballot by a much larger margin. The 11-point gap Gallup now sees in the Democrats' favor is very close to the average Democratic lead for all of 2006. Although the balance of power in the House of Representatives will be determined by 435 individual congressional elections, Gallup's generic-ballot measure of national support for the two major parties—more specifically, the final pre-election generic ballot based on likely voters—has proven to be a strong predictor of the actual percentage of votes cast nationally for all Republican and Democratic candidates. This, in turn, has borne a close relationship to the number of seats won by each party.

About One in Four Voters Are "Swing Voters"

According to the most recent USA Today/Gallup survey, 23% of likely voters can be considered "swing voters"—including 6% who do not have a preference between Barack Obama and John McCain for president and 17% who currently support either McCain or Obama but say they could change their minds between now and Election Day. Obama's 7-point advantage over McCain among voters who have made up their minds (42% to 35%) is similar to the 6-point advantage (50% to 44%) he enjoys among all likely voters in the June 15–19 poll. This is Gallup's first measurement in this election cycle of swing voters in the

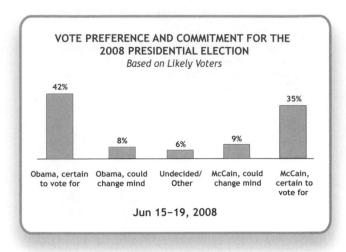

U.S. electorate. At no point in 2004—a year when swing voters were somewhat scarce from a historical perspective—did Gallup find as high a proportion of swing voters as it finds today. The high mark in swing voters in 2004 was just 18% in May, and in the final pre-election poll only 9% of likely voters had not made a firm candidate choice.

WHO ARE THE SWING VOTERS?

In a typical election year, political independents and moderates are among those most likely to fall into the swing voter group. And that is the case as well in 2008. In this year's election, it appears that swing voters are less likely to come from subgroups that show strong support for Obama, which is a positive sign for Obama. As shown in the accompanying graphs, liberals are the least likely of the ideological groups, and Democrats of the party affiliation groups, to fall into the swing voter group. Additionally, only 12% of voters under age 30 are swing voters, compared with roughly a quarter of those age 30 or older; throughout the campaign, young adults have supported Obama overwhelmingly. Also, white voters (26%) are more likely than nonwhites (18%) to be uncommitted at this point—and Obama has typically held the support of more than 90% of blacks and 60% of Hispanics.

SWING VOTERS TEND TO LIKE BOTH MCCAIN AND OBAMA

In general, swing voters seem to be positively disposed toward both candidates: 50% have a favorable opinion of both McCain and Obama, while only 11% view both negatively. By comparison, just one-quarter of committed voters have a positive opinion of both candidates. In July 2004, just 25% of swing voters viewed both John Kerry and George W. Bush favorably, while 13% had negative opinions of both. That indicates that in this election, swing voters

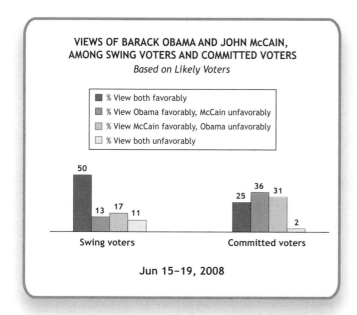

VIEWS OF BARACK OBAMA AND JOHN McCAIN,
AMONG SWING VOTERS AND COMMITTED VOTERS
Based on Likely Voters

■ % View both favorably
■ % View Obama favorably, McCain unfavorably
■ % View McCain favorably, Obama unfavorably
□ % View both unfavorably

Swing voters: 50, 13, 17, 11
Committed voters: 25, 36, 31, 2

Jun 15–19, 2008

uncommitted voters, they may find a receptive audience. Half of swing voters have a positive opinion of both Obama and McCain, far more than had a favorable image of both Bush and Kerry in 2004. The candidates' messages, their choices of vice presidential running mates, and their performance in the fall debates all have the potential to bring undecided voters into their camps.

Gallup Daily: Obama Leads McCain, 47% to 42%

After more than a week of Barack Obama and John McCain being tied in Gallup Poll daily tracking, Obama now holds a statistically significant five-percentage-point lead in the preferences of national registered voters, 47% to 42%, slightly larger than the 46% to 42% lead for Obama recorded on June 29. This is according to Gallup Poll daily tracking interviews from June 26 through June 29, with no surveys conducted on June 27. Obama previously led McCain by a statistically significant margin—peaking at seven points—right after Hillary Clinton suspended her campaign for the Democratic nomination in early June. However, this lasted for only three days—a mini-bounce—after which the margin narrowed to three points and more recently to an exact tie, before expanding to a four-point lead for Obama on June 29. While the race has been consistently competitive for most of the past two months, McCain has not led Obama by a significant margin since early May.

are much more likely to choose between two appealing (to them) options rather than trying to pick "the lesser of two evils."

With a greater proportion of swing voters up for grabs in this year's presidential election than in 2004, the campaigns may not wish to follow the famous Bush 2004 strategy of concentrating resources on mobilizing existing supporters instead of persuading undecideds. If the campaigns choose to devote a substantial share of resources to winning over

JULY 2008

Weekly averages of Gallup Poll daily consumer ratings show that, after being essentially flat for most of June and July 2008, Americans' outlook with respect to the economy improved slightly during the last week of July. This is seen in positive ratings of current economic conditions (16% now call them excellent or good) as well as in perceptions of the economy's direction (12% say it is getting better). The net result is that the overall percentage of Americans holding "positive" views about the economy (based on a combination of their answers to the two questions) has inched up to 7%, from 5% at the start of the month. Another 14% have mixed views about current and future economic conditions, while 77% have solidly negative views. The weekly aggregates are based on nationally representative samples of approximately 3,500 adults and thus have a high degree of statistical reliability. The 12% now saying that economic conditions in the country are getting better is the highest this indication of positive consumer sentiment has reached since late February/early March. Still, it is only slightly more than half of its level as of January (which, relative to long-term trends, was already a depressed period for consumers). Similarly, the 16% calling current conditions excellent or good and the 7% net "positive" today are about half the parallel figures for early January.

The stock market and fuel prices at the pump have to some degree played tag team against consumer confidence this year. The stock market dropped sharply in early to mid-January, leveling off during much of February before continuing to trend downward through mid-March. It recovered somewhat in April and May, only to fall into a deep descent in June. It has thus far been quite volatile in July. Gasoline prices began to take off in mid-February, reaching the $4-per-gallon mark in early June. The average price then leveled off at just over $4 for several weeks, but it

has receded slightly in the past two weeks. A special Gallup analysis shows that the decline in public perceptions of the economy in the first quarter of 2008 (through mid-March) closely paralleled both the increase in gasoline prices and the decline in the stock market. Since then, consumer attitudes have been less closely related to shifts in the stock market, but they remain highly correlated with changes in gasoline prices. In just the past two weeks (from July 14 through July 27), gasoline prices and consumer attitudes both improved slightly, while the stock market fluctuated.

Multiple aspects of the economy are problematic right now, including the housing market, the mortgage industry, various retail sectors, and the labor market, in addition to energy costs and a tumultuous stock market. Americans could be forming their overall economic views based on the news about any or all of these factors—but gasoline prices may currently be having the most influence. While a majority of Americans have money invested in the stock market, only 24% in January/February told Gallup that the sharp decline in the market at that time was having a "very negative" impact on their family's financial situation. This contrasted with the 57%—even then—saying that the rise in gasoline and home heating prices was having a very negative impact on them. More recently, gasoline prices ranked number one in a July Gallup Poll as Americans' most important financial problem, and large majorities say they are cutting back on their spending as a result. The uptick in consumer confidence this month is only a marginal improvement in an otherwise grim picture. It is a positive change, however, and one that appears to reflect a slight sigh of relief on the part of Americans at the pump. Given the 2008 trends, further declines in gasoline prices this year could be just what it takes to keep consumer confidence moving in a positive direction, which could in turn have a positive ripple effect on retail spending, the

CHRONOLOGY

JULY 2008

July 1   More American and coalition troops died in Afghanistan in June than during any other month since the U.S.–led invasion began in 2001.

July 6   Jesse Jackson is recorded making disparaging remarks about Barack Obama. Beyond vulgarities, Jackson says that Obama "was speaking down to black people." Jackson later apologizes for his critical comments.

July 9   The Senate approves a major expansion of the federal government's surveillance powers, giving President Bush another victory in a series of clashes with Democrats over national security issues. Senator Obama votes for the law; Senator Clinton votes against it. Senator McCain expresses his support but was campaigning and did not vote.

July 14   A satirical *New Yorker* magazine cover depicts Obama and his wife Michelle as fist-bumping, flag-burning terrorists in the Oval Office. The *New Yorker* argues that the cover makes fun of extremist views, but the Obama camp is critical.

July 18   Former Texas senator Phil Gramm, McCain's chief economic adviser, leaves the campaign after controversial remarks dismissing concerns about the troubled economy by referring to it as merely a "mental recession." He also said that the United States had become "a nation of whiners."

July 19   International talks on Iran's nuclear program end in deadlock. The presence of a senior American diplomat at the conference was one of the most important encounters between the United States and Iran since relations were severed nearly three decades ago.

July 21   Obama begins an overseas tour with planned stops in Afghanistan, Iraq, and Europe.

July 23   The House of Representatives votes to give the Treasury Department broad authority to protect the nation's two largest mortgage companies, Fannie Mae (the Federal National Mortgage Association) and Freddie Mac (the Federal Home Mortgage Association), from financial collapse.

July 24   Obama speaks before a crowd of 200,000 people in Berlin,

July 30   The McCain campaign reacts to Obama's positive reception abroad by releasing a commercial comparing Obama to celebrities Paris Hilton and Britney Spears. "He's the biggest celebrity in the world. But is he ready to lead?" Paris Hilton later issues her own spoof ad referring to McCain as "a white-haired dude."

housing market, employment, and, ultimately, the gross domestic product.

JULY 1

Americans Worry McCain Would Be Too Similar to Bush

A recent USA Today/Gallup Poll finds about two in three Americans concerned that John McCain would pursue policies as president that are too similar to what George W. Bush has pursued. Nearly half—49%—say they are "very concerned" about this. McCain faces a challenge in trying to convince voters to allow him to follow an unpopular president of the same party. Democratic candidate Barack Obama has attempted to link McCain to Bush by saying

that electing McCain would effectively lead to a "third Bush term." Although McCain remains competitive in head-to-head matchups with Obama, the poll suggests that McCain may have more work to do to distance himself from Bush. That is clearly a delicate balancing act for McCain, as Bush remains relatively popular with the Republican base. While only 28% of Americans approve of the job Bush is doing as president, a majority of Republicans (60%) still do approve. Bush's approval rating among current McCain supporters is slightly lower, at 55%.

Bush is deeply unpopular with Democrats (only 6% approve of the job he is doing as president), and 9 in 10 Democrats say they are concerned that McCain's policies would be too similar to those of Bush. And among independents—a group to which McCain has demonstrated appeal—two-thirds share that concern, including nearly

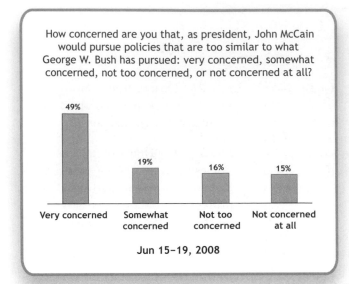

How concerned are you that, as president, John McCain would pursue policies that are too similar to what George W. Bush has pursued: very concerned, somewhat concerned, not too concerned, or not concerned at all?

Jun 15–19, 2008

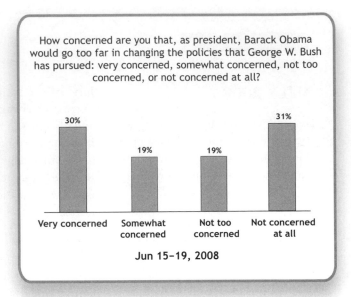

How concerned are you that, as president, Barack Obama would go too far in changing the policies that George W. Bush has pursued: very concerned, somewhat concerned, not too concerned, or not concerned at all?

Jun 15–19, 2008

half who are very concerned. Even one in five Republicans are very concerned about the McCain-Bush similarities. A recent CBS News poll asked registered voters what they thought McCain would do—continue Bush's policies, change to more conservative policies, or change to less conservative policies. A plurality of 43% believe he would continue Bush's policies, but more expect some change—either in a more conservative (21%) or less conservative (28%) direction. Thus, while most voters express concern about McCain being too much like Bush, a majority do not necessarily expect this to happen. While most Democrats (65%) believe that McCain would generally continue Bush's policies, only 34% of independents and 20% of Republicans do. Independents are about evenly divided as to whether McCain would be more conservative or less conservative

than Bush, while nearly half of Republicans think he would be less conservative.

Obama and "Change"

Obama is running as the "change" candidate, and while that would seem to be advantageous positioning in an election to replace an unpopular incumbent, there is risk in advocating more change than Americans might be comfortable with. To the extent that McCain and the Republican Party can paint Obama as seeking to accomplish too great a departure from the status quo, they can make McCain seem like a safe alternative. The USA Today/Gallup Poll asked Americans how concerned they are that Obama would go too far in changing policies that Bush has pursued. About half say they

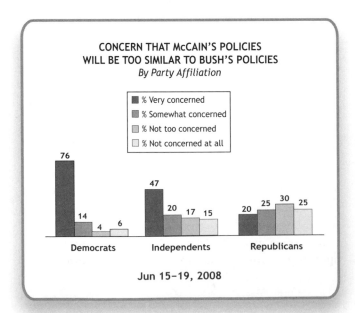

CONCERN THAT McCAIN'S POLICIES WILL BE TOO SIMILAR TO BUSH'S POLICIES
By Party Affiliation

- ■ % Very concerned
- ■ % Somewhat concerned
- □ % Not too concerned
- □ % Not concerned at all

Jun 15–19, 2008

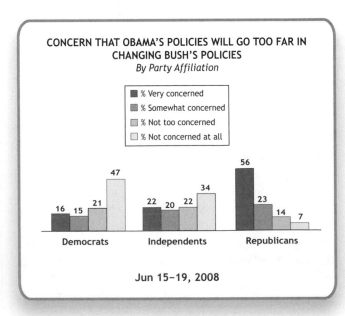

CONCERN THAT OBAMA'S POLICIES WILL GO TOO FAR IN CHANGING BUSH'S POLICIES
By Party Affiliation

- ■ % Very concerned
- ■ % Somewhat concerned
- □ % Not too concerned
- □ % Not concerned at all

Jun 15–19, 2008

are concerned, including 30% who are very concerned. One in three Americans—predominantly Democrats—are not concerned at all. Most Republicans—who likely will vote for McCain anyway—are concerned about Obama's bringing about too much of a departure from Bush. Less than half of independents are, including only 22% who say they are very concerned (compared with 47% of independents who are very concerned about McCain's being too similar to Bush).

Implications for Election Strategy and Prospects

At this point, Americans seem more concerned about not getting enough change than about getting too much with the next president, which works to Obama's benefit. But the campaign has barely begun, and Republicans will do their best to make the case that Obama is too liberal to be trusted. (Obama had the highest liberal voting score of any senator in 2007, according to the *National Journal*'s annual report.) McCain does have enough disagreements with Bush to make the argument that he will not represent a third Bush term perhaps seem credible. At the same time, on major issues such as the economy and Iraq, McCain's and Bush's positions are essentially the same.

JULY 2

Hispanic Voters Solidly Behind Obama

Hispanic registered voters' support for Barack Obama for president remained consistent and strong in June, with Obama leading John McCain by 59% to 29% among this group. While Hispanics generally preferred Hillary Clinton

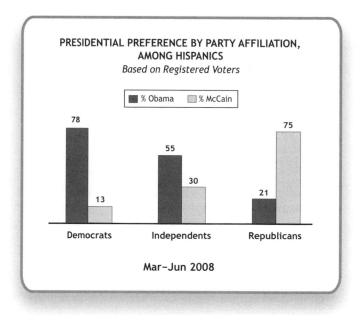

to Obama for the Democratic presidential nomination, a solid majority of Hispanics have consistently backed Obama against McCain in general election trial heats. Obama has led McCain by about a two-to-one margin since Gallup began tracking general election voting preferences in early March. Gallup has interviewed more than 4,000 Hispanic registered voters during this time period. An analysis of candidate support by subgroup within the Hispanic electorate reveals that many of the well-established divisions in this year's campaign—such as the gender gap and the marriage gap—are weak or nonexistent among Hispanic voters; rather, Hispanics of differing demographic backgrounds all tend to solidly support Obama. It thus appears that there isn't much beyond a shared Hispanic ethnicity or

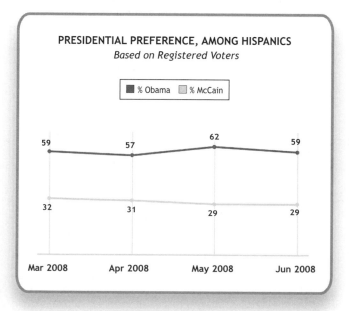

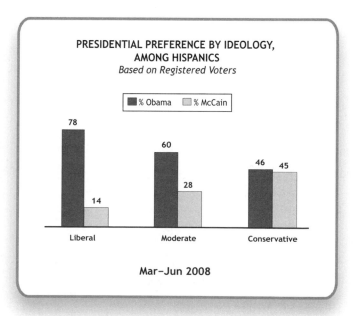

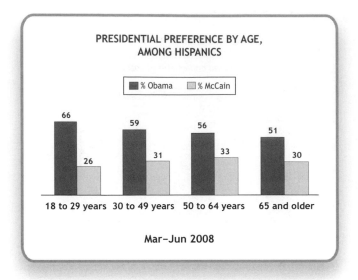

identity that explains Hispanic voting patterns. Perhaps the only exceptions to this general pattern are the minorities of Hispanic voters who identify themselves as Republicans (18%) or who say they have conservative political views (36%). McCain leads Obama handily among Hispanic Republicans and is about even with him among Hispanic conservatives. In an election pitting one of the younger recent presidential candidates against the oldest candidate ever, candidate preferences by age group have varied. Differences in the Hispanic vote by age, however, are fairly small. While younger Hispanic voters show greater support for Obama than do older subgroups, support for McCain increases only slightly among older Hispanics.

PRESIDENTIAL PREFERENCE BY DEMOGRAPHIC SUBGROUP, AMONG HISPANICS
Based on Registered Voters

	% Obama	% McCain
Men	60	32
Women	59	29
College graduate	60	32
College nongraduate	59	29
Married	55	35
Not married	63	25
Attend church weekly	51	34
Attend church monthly	61	30
Seldom/Never attend	63	27
East	64	25
Midwest	63	25
South	52	36
West	62	29

Mar–Jun 2008

Implications for the Election

Some political experts assumed that Obama's largely unsuccessful struggle to attract widespread Hispanic support in the Democratic primaries would carry over into the general election campaign against the Republican candidate. But Hispanics have become a reliable Democratic voting bloc, and have so far shown little difficulty in transferring their loyalties from Clinton to Obama. Obama continues to lead McCain by about a two-to-one margin among Hispanic voters, as he has since March—and Hispanic voters could be crucial in key swing states such as New Mexico, Colorado, and Florida. While George W. Bush made a strong push for the Hispanic vote in the 2000 and 2004 elections, McCain faces an uphill battle to attract Hispanics' support, given their consistent and solid support for Obama in recent months.

As Independents Shrink, Democrats Gain

The extraordinary 2008 election year is proving to be quite ordinary in at least one respect: the downward trend in the percentage of Americans identifying themselves as political independents. The proportion of independents in Gallup Poll surveys averaged 36% in the latest quarter (from April to June), down from 39% last fall and 40% last summer. This conforms to a pattern evident in Gallup's long-term party identification trends, whereby the percentage of Americans identifying themselves as political independents typically dips in the months leading up to presidential and midterm congressional elections and peaks sometime between election years.

While the percentage of independents has shrunk a bit since late 2007, Gallup trends show relatively little change in Americans' identification with the Republican Party over the same period: It has generally held at 27%, while Democratic identification increased from 31% at the end of 2007 to 36% today. This skew toward one party in the redistribution of voters in an election year is not unprecedented. However, by the third quarter (from July to September), it

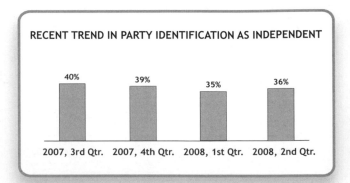

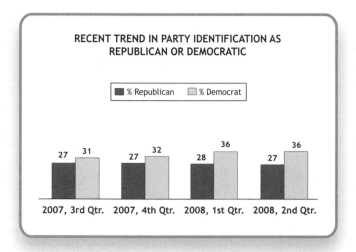

RECENT TREND IN PARTY IDENTIFICATION AS REPUBLICAN OR DEMOCRATIC

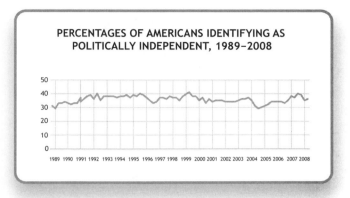

PERCENTAGES OF AMERICANS IDENTIFYING AS POLITICALLY INDEPENDENT, 1989–2008

would be unusual not to see some heightened public identification with both parties. If the percentage of Americans identifying themselves as Republican does not pick up, the Democrats will have their strongest structural advantage in 20 years going into the November election. Party identification with either party was virtually the same in both the first quarter of 2008 (64%) and the second (63%).

Trends in Election-Year Declines in Independents

The cyclical decline in Americans' identifying themselves as politically independent has been seen in the first quarter of prior presidential election years, spanning Gallup Polls conducted each year from January through March. In previous elections the figures continued to drop in the second and third quarters. In the fourth quarter of 1995, for example, 39% of Americans identified themselves as political independents; in the first quarter of 1996 this dipped to 37%, and by the third quarter it had fallen to 33%. In the fall of 1999, Gallup found 38% calling themselves independent, a percentage that fell to 35% at the start of 2000 and to 33% by the third quarter. From October to December 2003 only 37% of Americans considered themselves independent, but this fell to 35% in early 2004 and to only 29% by the third quarter. The pattern did not hold for the 1992 election, a year when a viable third-party candidate (Ross Perot) helped maintain higher levels of public identification as independent. In all of the last four presidential election years, the percentage of independents started to rebound in the fourth quarter, spanning October to December Gallup polling.

Implications

Party identification is an important backdrop to elections, establishing the base level of support for the major party candidates. But party identification is not static; elections routinely stimulate some otherwise independent-oriented Americans to identify with one or the other party, at least temporarily. The Democratic Party entered the 2008 election season with a solid advantage in party identification (32% to 27% in the fourth quarter of 2007), but as a result of independents' becoming more partisan in their thinking during the election, the Democrats now lead by a larger, nine-percentage-point margin, 36% to 27%, tying with the third quarter of 1997 for their widest advantage in the past 20 years. History suggests that independents will continue to decline over the next three months. The question is: Will they continue to flock to the Democrats, or will they divide more evenly between the two parties?

JULY 3
States Differ in Their Economic Outlook

Americans across the country are very negative about the economy, but this negativity is not distributed equally. Residents of states such as Utah, North Dakota, and Texas are well below average in their negative views. Residents of other states, such as Rhode Island, Maine, and Michigan, are well above average. These conclusions are based on an analysis of 96,822 interviews conducted over the last six months as part of the Gallup Poll daily tracking program. During that time, 8% of Americans on average could be classified as "positive" about the economy. This is based on a Gallup calculation taking into account views of both the current economy and the direction of the economy going forward. A much higher 73% can be classified as negative on the economy. (Seventeen percent are "mixed.") A net negativity measure results when the percentage who are positive is subtracted from the percentage who are negative. For the country as a whole, the net negativity for the first six months of 2008 is 64. Not all states are created equal in this regard, however.

**NET NEGATIVE VIEWS OF THE U.S. ECONOMY:
MOST NEGATIVE AND MOST POSITIVE STATES**

*Net negativity = % negative about
U.S. economy minus % positive*

Most negative states	Net negativity (pct. pts.)	Most positive states	Net negativity (pct. pts.)
Rhode Island	84	Utah	49
Maine	77	North Dakota	52
Michigan	75	Texas	52
Vermont	75	Wyoming	54
Massachusetts	74	New Mexico	54

Jan–Jun 2008

**NET NEGATIVE VIEWS OF THE U.S. ECONOMY
IN BATTLEGROUND STATES**

*Net negativity = % negative about
U.S. economy minus % positive*

Battleground state	Net negativity
	pct. pts.
Michigan	75
Pennsylvania	69
Ohio	68
Nevada	68
Florida	67
New Hampshire	66
Oregon	65
NATIONAL AVERAGE	64
Wisconsin	64
Minnesota	64
Colorado	63
Iowa	61
New Mexico	54

Jan–Jun 2008

Although in every state, many more residents view the economy negatively than view it positively, there is significant variation across states. At the low end of the negative range (i.e., states that are least negative) are Utah, North Dakota, Texas, Wyoming, and New Mexico. The net negative rating in each of these states is 10 or more points below the overall average for the United States.

At the high end of the negative range (i.e., states in which residents are the most negative about the economy) are Rhode Island, Maine, Michigan, Vermont, and Massachusetts. Each of these has an average net negative rating that is 10 or more points higher than the national average. The difference in net negativity between the two extreme groups of states is large. The average net negativity for the five least negative states is 52; the average net negativity for the five most negative states is 76. The single most negative state, Rhode Island, has a net negative rating that is 35 points higher than the net negative rating of the least negative state, Utah—49.

Battleground States

The economy is shaping up to be the top issue in this presidential election year. There is thus a natural interest in the economic sentiments of residents living in the "battleground" states in which the candidates will be targeting the majority of their campaigning. The table above right displays the net negative views of the economy within the 12 battleground states in which neither George W. Bush nor John Kerry had more than a five-point margin of victory in the 2004 popular vote. Many of these states are close to the national average net negativity value of 64. But the data show that the candidates would want to be particularly focused on the economy in a state like Michigan, and perhaps a little less so in a state like New Mexico.

By historical standards, Americans at this juncture are very negative about the economy. Gallup calculations show that subtracting the percentage of Americans who are positive from the percentage who are negative yields a net negative gap of 64 points. There are, however, variations in views of the national economy by region. The questions on which this measure is based ask about the national economy, not individual state or local economies. Still, residents of certain states—including those benefiting from the spike in energy prices, such as Texas and Wyoming—are much less negative in their views of the U.S. economy than are residents of Northeastern states and of Michigan, the latter hit hard by the downturn in the auto industry.

Residents of most of the 12 battleground states that will be key focus points in this year's presidential campaign are neither significantly more positive nor more negative than the national average in their views of the economy. This suggests that in terms of their campaign rhetoric and proposals on the economy, the candidates can approach most swing states in a manner that is no different from their national pronouncements on the subject. There are two exceptions: The battleground state of Michigan has residents who are among the most negative of any state, while residents of the battleground state of New Mexico are among the least negative.

Obama 47%, McCain 43%

The race for president remains "steady as she goes," with Barack Obama maintaining a modest 47% to 43% advantage over John McCain among registered voters in the

June 30–July 2 Gallup Poll daily tracking results. As would be expected from any methodology involving repeated sampling from a large population, there have been slight fluctuations in the daily reports of Gallup Poll daily tracking rolling averages (each based on three days' worth of interviewing of over 2,500 registered voters), but little indication for weeks now of any substantive change in the structure of the race. The preferences of registered voters with respect to the two major party candidates remain closely divided, with Obama usually polling within a few percentage points of 46% and McCain polling within a few points of 43%.

JULY 6

Gallup Daily: Obama Leads, 48% to 42%

Barack Obama continues to maintain a slim margin over John McCain, 48% to 42%, according to Gallup Poll daily tracking conducted between July 2–3 and July 5. Today's three-day rolling average is based on interviewing conducted in the two days before the July 4 holiday and on Saturday, July 5 (no interviewing was conducted on July 4). About 5% of voters say they will not vote for either major party candidate, while an additional 6% are undecided.

News organizations over the last several days have given extensive play to the precise wording of various Obama statements concerning what he would do regarding withdrawal of troops from Iraq were he to be elected president. So far, there is little sign in the Gallup Poll daily tracking data that this has made a difference in the preferences of registered voters. Of course, it is to be expected that voters' attention is turned elsewhere over a holiday weekend, so a major shift in the standing of the two candidates would be an unusual occurrence. Until the vice presidential nominees are announced and/or the Democratic National Convention begins in late August, the concurrent efforts both of the campaigns to influence voter perceptions of the race and of the news media to find something new and compelling to say about the race will be competing for what could be sparse voter attention.

JULY 7

July Leader Lost in 6 of Last 9 Competitive Presidential Elections

In 9 of the past 15 presidential elections, the candidate who was leading in Gallup polling roughly four months before the election ultimately won the popular vote for president. However, narrowing the set of 15 races to the 9 that were competitive, the early polling proved prescient in only 3

GALLUP PRE-ELECTION POLLS FROM EARLY TO MID-JULY* IN "COMPETITIVE" ELECTIONS

Date of survey	Leader in early/mid-July	Popular vote winner	Winner's +/– in early/ mid-July	Winner's +/– on Election Day
2004 July 8-11	Kerry, 51%–44%	Bush	–7	+3.0
2000 July 14-16	Bush, 43%–41%	Gore	–2	+0.5
1992 July 6-8	Bush, 35%–28%	Clinton	–7	+5.5
1988 July 8-10	Dukakis, 47%–41%	Bush	–6	+7.7
1980 July 11-14	Reagan, 37%–34%	Reagan	+3	+9.8
1976 July 16-19	Carter, 62%–29%	Carter	+33	+2.0
1968 June 29–July 3	Humphrey, 50%–44%	Nixon	–5	+0.7
1960 June 30–July 5+	Kennedy, 50%–44%	Kennedy	+6	+0.2
1948 July 16-21+	Dewey, 48%–37%	Truman	–11	+4.4

Note: Results based on registered voters, except as noted below.

* Except for 1968 and 1960, which are late June to early July.

+ Based on national adults.

of those. (In 1976, Jimmy Carter, who won that election, was ahead by 33 points in mid-July, but the race narrowed significantly by Election Day, and he won by only 2 points. Thus, for purposes of this analysis, the 1976 race is classified as competitive.) With Barack Obama leading John McCain by no more than 6 percentage points in Gallup's early July polling, the 2008 race currently fits best into the "competitive" category. Given that assumption, Gallup's election trends from a comparable point in previous presidential election years offer no strong indication of whether Obama or McCain is headed for victory in November. In the six other elections since 1948—all but one of which involved the successful re-election of an incumbent—the eventual winner was leading by at least 16 points at this stage of the campaign and retained a wide lead right through the election. On this basis, these six races can be considered "noncompetitive."

The category of competitive elections (in which the early to mid-July leader was not necessarily the eventual winner) can usefully be grouped into two subcategories, but it

GALLUP PRE-ELECTION POLLS FROM EARLY TO MID-JULY IN "NONCOMPETITVE" ELECTIONS

Date of survey	Leader in early/mid-July	Popular vote winner	Winner's +/– in early/ mid-July	Winner's +/– on Election Day
1996 July 18-22	Clinton, 50%–33%	Clinton	+17	+8.3
1984 July 13-16	Reagan, 55%–39%	Reagan	+16	+18.2
1972 July 14-17	Nixon, 56%–37%	Nixon	+19	+23.1
1964 July 5-7	Johnson, 62%–26%	Johnson	+36	+22.6
1956 July 12-17	Eisenhower, 61%–37%	Eisenhower	+24	+15.6
1952 July 13-18	Eisenhower, 58%–33%	Eisenhower	+25	+10.8

Note: Results based on registered voters.

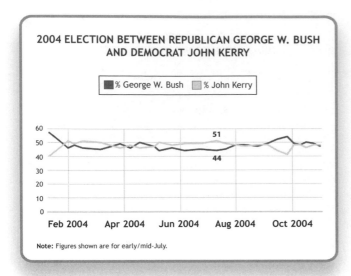

2004 ELECTION BETWEEN REPUBLICAN GEORGE W. BUSH AND DEMOCRAT JOHN KERRY

■ % George W. Bush   ☐ % John Kerry

Note: Figures shown are for early/mid-July.

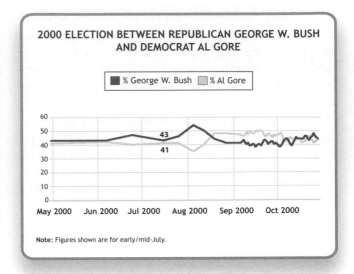

2000 ELECTION BETWEEN REPUBLICAN GEORGE W. BUSH AND DEMOCRAT AL GORE

■ % George W. Bush   ☐ % Al Gore

Note: Figures shown are for early/mid-July.

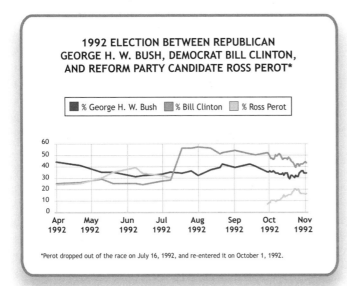

1992 ELECTION BETWEEN REPUBLICAN GEORGE H. W. BUSH, DEMOCRAT BILL CLINTON, AND REFORM PARTY CANDIDATE ROSS PEROT*

■ % George H. W. Bush   ■ % Bill Clinton   ☐ % Ross Perot

*Perot dropped out of the race on July 16, 1992, and re-entered it on October 1, 1992.

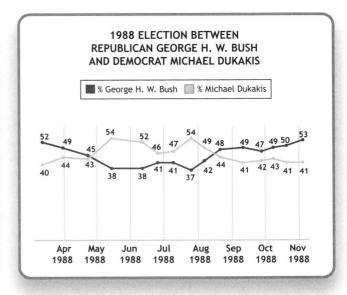

1988 ELECTION BETWEEN REPUBLICAN GEORGE H. W. BUSH AND DEMOCRAT MICHAEL DUKAKIS

■ % George H. W. Bush   ☐ % Michael Dukakis

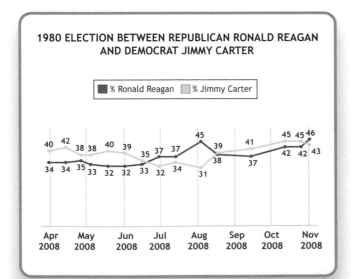

1980 ELECTION BETWEEN REPUBLICAN RONALD REAGAN AND DEMOCRAT JIMMY CARTER

■ % Ronald Reagan   ☐ % Jimmy Carter

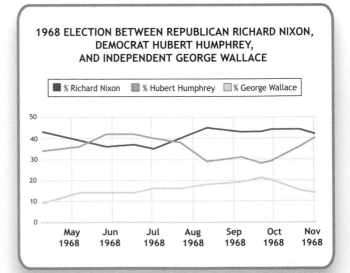

1968 ELECTION BETWEEN REPUBLICAN RICHARD NIXON, DEMOCRAT HUBERT HUMPHREY, AND INDEPENDENT GEORGE WALLACE

■ % Richard Nixon   ■ % Hubert Humphrey   ☐ % George Wallace

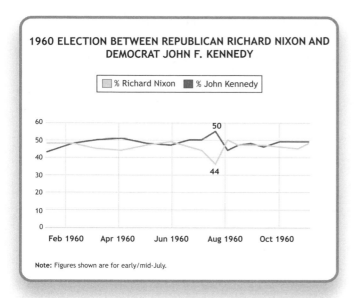

1960 ELECTION BETWEEN REPUBLICAN RICHARD NIXON AND DEMOCRAT JOHN F. KENNEDY

% Richard Nixon   % John Kennedy

Note: Figures shown are for early/mid-July.

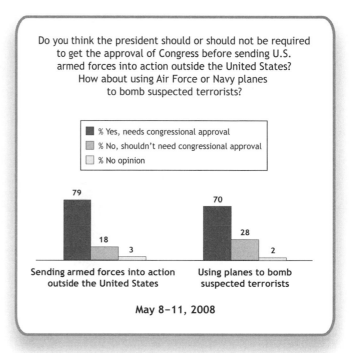

Do you think the president should or should not be required to get the approval of Congress before sending U.S. armed forces into action outside the United States? How about using Air Force or Navy planes to bomb suspected terrorists?

% Yes, needs congressional approval
% No, shouldn't need congressional approval
% No opinion

Sending armed forces into action outside the United States: 79, 18, 3
Using planes to bomb suspected terrorists: 70, 28, 2

May 8–11, 2008

is too soon to say which category this year's race falls into In four elections—2004, 2000, 1980, and 1960—either the race remained closely contested for the entire campaign or the lead switched back and forth between the two major candidates throughout the summer and/or fall. In three elections—1992, 1988, and 1968—one of the parties' national conventions late in the summer proved to be a turning point in the race, vaulting one of the candidates into a lead, however small, that extended through the duration of the campaign. The 1976 presidential election was in a class all by itself. Jimmy Carter enjoyed large double-digit leads throughout the spring and summer, but Gerald Ford narrowed the gap in the fall to single digits and almost won the election. The 1948 election was also a singular case wherein nearly all of Gallup's pre-election polls, including the final pre-election poll conducted more than a week before the election, showed the eventual winner (Harry Truman) trailing his opponent, Thomas Dewey. As a result of this failure to provide an accurate forecast of the race, Gallup quickly instituted a number of major and important changes to its pre-election polling methods, including identifying "likely voters" and polling right up to Election Day.

Commentary

Barack Obama has consistently led John McCain in Gallup Poll daily tracking for the past month, but by an average of only three points among registered voters. His largest lead since July 1 has been six points, although in the latest Gallup report, based on interviews conducted on July 3 and between July 5 and July 6, it is just four points, 47% to 43%. History provides no clear indication of the relationship between this narrow margin and the eventual outcome in November. The pattern that occurred in several presidential years suggests that the convention period could be

crucial for either cementing Obama's slight advantage or establishing McCain as the new front-runner. This year's Democratic convention will be held in Denver from August 25 to August 28, followed by the Republican convention in Minneapolis/St. Paul from September 1 to September 4. If neither convention succeeds in transforming the election, the race could very well remain close right through the home stretch.

Public Wants Congress to Approve Military Action, Bombings

An overwhelming 79% majority of Americans believe the president should get the approval of Congress before

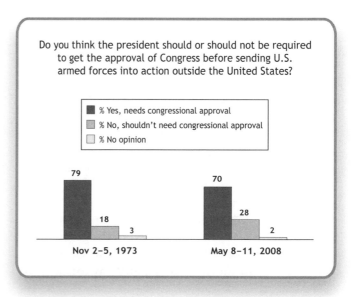

Do you think the president should or should not be required to get the approval of Congress before sending U.S. armed forces into action outside the United States?

% Yes, needs congressional approval
% No, shouldn't need congressional approval
% No opinion

Nov 2–5, 1973: 79, 18, 3
May 8–11, 2008: 70, 28, 2

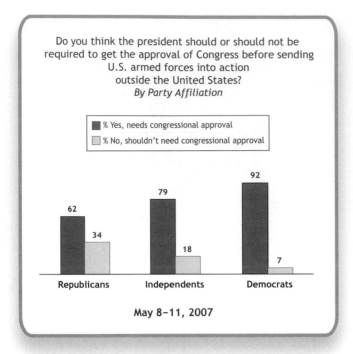

Do you think the president should or should not be required to get the approval of Congress before sending U.S. armed forces into action outside the United States?
By Party Affiliation

May 8–11, 2007

tinue to be matters of dispute. This uncertainty led to the formation of a National War Powers Commission in 2007, created to review relevant legal and historical issues and, ultimately, to make a recommendation on how the executive and legislative branches should approach war situations. (The commission, headed by two former secretaries of state, James Baker and Warren Christopher, is set to make its final report on July 8.) The recent Gallup Poll shows that while there is some difference of opinion by party affiliation on the idea that the president be required to get congressional approval, a majority of every political group agrees.

Specific Situations

The current poll asked Americans about the necessity for the president to gain the approval of Congress before sending U.S. armed forces into action in five specific situations. There is significant variation across these hypothetical situations. Half or more of Americans do *not* believe the president needs to get congressional approval before committing U.S. forces into action if the United States is attacked, if American citizens are in danger or in need of rescue abroad, or in order to conduct a humanitarian mission in response to a natural disaster. On the other hand, there is widespread public agreement that the president needs congressional approval to send troops into action even if he or she does not think a combat operation would last a long time, or in a situation in which the president wants to use Air Force or Navy planes to bomb suspected terrorists. Democrats are significantly more likely than Republicans to agree that the president needs congressional approval before bombing suspected terrorists; still—as

sending U.S. armed forces into action outside the United States, and 70% believe congressional approval should be required before the president decides to bomb suspected terrorists. According to Gallup trends, there has been little change over the last 35 years in the basic sentiment that the president needs congressional approval before sending U.S. troops into combat overseas.

The year 1973 was significant in the history of debate over presidential war powers. That year, U.S. involvement in the Vietnam War was drawing to a close, and Congress acted in an attempt to bring clarity to the war powers issue—enacting over President Nixon's veto the War Powers Act, which stated: "The President, in every possible instance, shall consult with Congress before introducing United States Armed Forces into hostilities or into situations where imminent involvement in hostilities is clearly indicated by the circumstances, and after every such introduction shall consult regularly with the Congress until United States Armed Forces are no longer engaged in hostilities or have been removed from such situations." At that time, Congress was clearly reflecting the will of the people. Seventy-nine percent of Americans in a November 1973 Gallup Poll agreed that Congress needed to give its stamp of approval before the president committed U.S. troops into action on foreign soil. Now, some 35 years later, as the United States is involved in another drawn-out war, the percentage of Americans agreeing with this sentiment is a bit lower, at 70%. What the U.S. Constitution's framers intended in terms of the war powers of the governmental branches and how exactly the nation should react in today's changed and fast-moving international environment con-

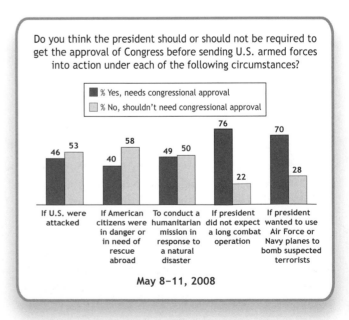

Do you think the president should or should not be required to get the approval of Congress before sending U.S. armed forces into action under each of the following circumstances?

May 8–11, 2008

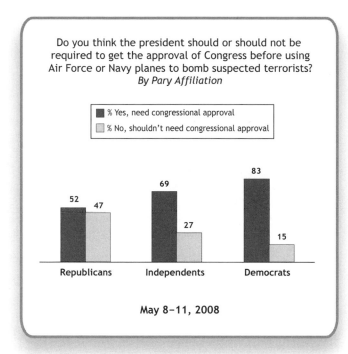

Do you think the president should or should not be required to get the approval of Congress before using Air Force or Navy planes to bomb suspected terrorists?
By Pary Affiliation

■ % Yes, need congressional approval
□ % No, shouldn't need congressional approval

May 8–11, 2008

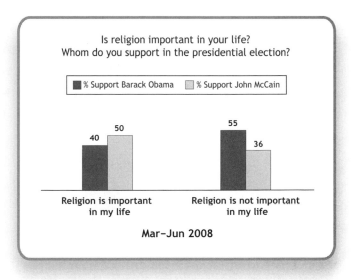

Is religion important in your life?
Whom do you support in the presidential election?

■ % Support Barack Obama   □ % Support John McCain

Mar–Jun 2008

is the case with respect to the basic war powers question—even a slight majority of Republicans agree that congressional approval is needed in this scenario.

JULY 8

Religious Intensity Predicts Support for McCain

Americans who say religion is an important part of their daily lives support John McCain over Barack Obama for president, 50% to 40%, while their less religious counterparts support Obama over McCain, 55% to 36%. The finding that the Republican candidate does better among more religious Americans is not a new one. White evangelical Christian voters, for example, have traditionally been among the most reliable Republican voters. The current analysis shows that the divide in voter preferences based on religiosity is not confined to white Protestants, but also occurs among non-Hispanic white Catholics. Indeed, the relationship between religiosity and voter choice is apparent among other groups that may not have been traditionally thought of in this regard, including in particular American Jews and, to a slight degree, those who identify with non-Christian and non-Jewish religions. There are exceptions to the correlation between religiosity and the inclination to vote Republican. The strong support for Obama among Hispanic Catholics, black non-Catholic Christians, and those who do not have a specific religious identity appears to be little affected by self-reported importance of religion.

The relationship of religion to voter choice is most clearly seen in the large segment of Americans who are white and identify themselves as either Protestant or affiliated with some other non-Catholic Christian religion. Among those in this group who say religion is important in their daily lives, McCain beats Obama by a 36-point margin, 63% to 27%. Among those in this group who say religion is not important, McCain and Obama are essentially tied, at 46% for McCain and 45% for Obama. The same pattern, although not quite as dramatic, is seen among non-Hispanic white Catholics. Those in this group for whom religion is important prefer McCain to Obama by a 16-point margin. Non-Hispanic white Catholics for whom religion is not important give Obama a slight, two-point margin over McCain, 47% to 45%. These patterns, so starkly evident among white Christians, essentially disappear among Catholics who are Hispanic, and among non-Catholic Christians who are black. Cultural considerations

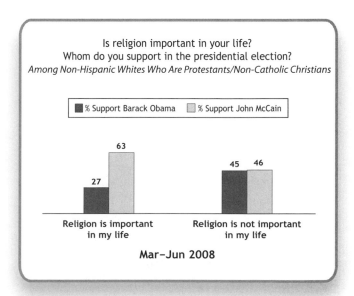

Is religion important in your life?
Whom do you support in the presidential election?
Among Non-Hispanic Whites Who Are Protestants/Non-Catholic Christians

■ % Support Barack Obama   □ % Support John McCain

Mar–Jun 2008

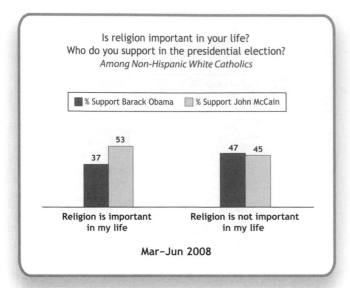

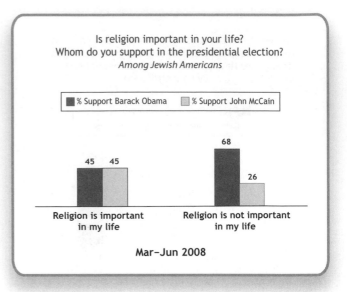

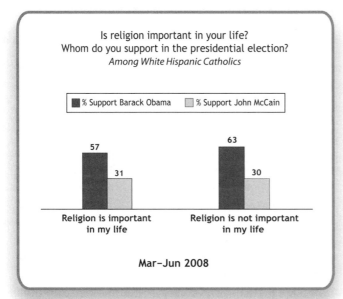

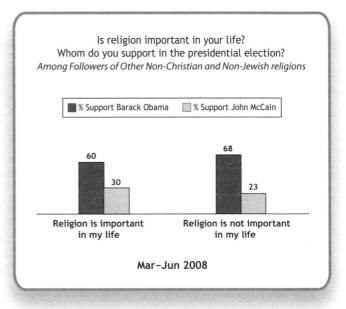

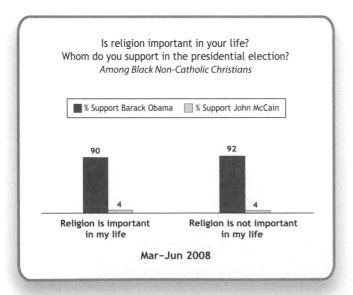

deriving from ethnicity and race are likely the dominant factors influencing voter decision among these groups. The differential impact of personal importance of religion within these groups, it appears to follow, is much smaller than it is among other groups examined in this analysis.

Only 39% of Jews report that religion is important in their daily lives, well below the overall national average. Among the smaller group of religious Jews, however, Obama and McCain break even, 45% to 45%. This compares with Obama's 68% to 26% lead among the majority of Jews for whom religion is not important. The importance of religion has a modest impact among Americans who report identification with non-Christian, non-Jewish religions. Obama wins by a significant margin among these individuals regardless of whether they report religion to be important in their daily lives or not, but the Obama over McCain margin is larger among those for whom religion is not important (a 45-point margin versus a 30-point margin.) Finally, there is the group of about 12% of Americans who say that they have no specific religious identity or affiliation. This group is strongly likely to support Obama, and there is no substantive difference in the pattern of support for Obama over McCain among the small group of 11% of this voter segment who say religion is important in their daily lives.

Summary: Religiosity and Voter Choice in This Election

It has been well established from analysis of previous survey data that certain groups of highly religious Christians—usually defined as "evangelicals"—are reliably Republican in their presidential vote preferences. The current analysis expands the exploration of this relationship between religiosity and voter choice, taking advantage of a large sample of almost 95,000 interviews conducted as part of the Gallup Poll daily tracking program from March through June. The data confirm that among non-Hispanic white Christians—both Catholics and non-Catholics—those who report that religion is important in their daily lives are significantly more likely to report voting for McCain over Obama than are those who say religion is not important.

Significantly, the analysis suggests that the presence of this relationship between religious intensity and presidential vote choice can be extended to include Jews and to some degree those who identify with a non-Christian, non-Jewish religion. In both of these groups, those who say religion is important are more likely to support McCain than are those who say religion is not important in their daily lives. At the same time, the data show that for two voter groups, Hispanic Catholics and black non-Catholic Christians, there is little evidence of a relationship between the importance of religion and voter choice; these two groups appear to be strong Obama supporters regardless of whether they report being personally religious or not. And among the small segment of Americans who do not report identification with any religion, support for Obama is also strong, and relatively unaffected by the self-reported importance of religion.

JULY 9

Obama Gaining Among Voters with Less Formal Education

In June, voters with a high school education or less were as likely to prefer Barack Obama as John McCain for president. That represents a change from earlier in the campaign. McCain has led Obama among this group over the last three months, though by diminishing margins. Voters with less formal education have been a core Democratic constituency in the last four presidential elections, preferring Bill Clinton, Al Gore, and John Kerry to their respective Republican opponents. But it is a group that Obama—who has unusually strong appeal to well-educated voters—has struggled to appeal to, both in the primaries against Hillary Clinton and in the early part of the general election campaign versus McCain. In recent months, he has clearly begun to make gains among voters with less education—even though, historically, his performance still trails that of other Democratic presidential candidates.

Since March, Obama has become increasingly competitive with McCain among both men and women with less formal schooling, as among both white and nonwhite voters with less formal schooling. Among each of these subgroups of voters, the Obama-McCain gap has moved 6 or 7 points in Obama's favor over the past four months. As a result, Obama now holds a lead over McCain among women with less formal education and trails McCain by just 4 points among men of similar educational attainment. Obama still trails McCain by a considerable 17 points among whites with less education, but has expanded his already formidable lead among nonwhites with high school education or less. Overall, Obama's gains in the polls since March (from an average 1-point deficit in March to a 3-point lead in June among all registered voters) have come disproportionately from voters with less formal education. Among other educational groups, his support has stayed relatively constant or gained only a little in recent months. But Obama was already competitive with McCain among voters with differing levels of postsecondary education when Gallup began tracking general election preferences in March. Now he is

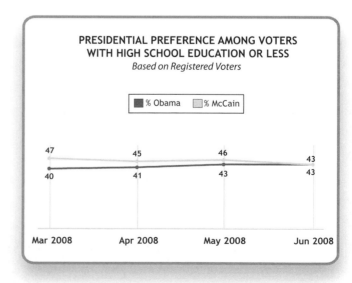

PRESIDENTIAL PREFERENCE AMONG VOTERS WITH HIGH SCHOOL EDUCATION OR LESS
Based on Registered Voters

■ % Obama   ▢ % McCain

47	45	46	43
40	41	43	43
Mar 2008	Apr 2008	May 2008	Jun 2008

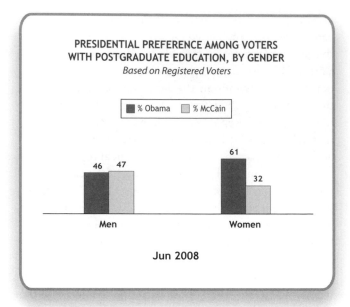

PRESIDENTIAL PREFERENCE AMONG VOTERS
WITH POSTGRADUATE EDUCATION, BY GENDER
Based on Registered Voters

Jun 2008

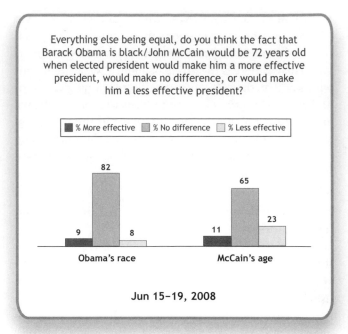

Everything else being equal, do you think the fact that
Barack Obama is black/John McCain would be 72 years
old when elected president would make him a more effective
president, would make no difference, or would make
him a less effective president?

Jun 15–19, 2008

competitive with McCain among all educational groups—
and he holds a wide lead among those with the most formal
education (those with postgraduate educations).

Just as they potentially appear to be in the general election
phase, highly educated voters were a key part of Obama's
winning coalition in the primaries, and much has been made
of his appeal to this group throughout the campaign. But his
strong support among highly educated voters is driven by his
specific appeal to women with postgraduate educations. In
June, Obama led McCain by 29 points among these voters,
while running about even with McCain among men with
postgraduate educations. These patterns have been highly
stable each month during the election campaign.

Implications for the General Election

Obama's gains among less educated voters are surely
a positive sign for his campaign and certainly help allay
some of the concerns about his electability, specifically
regarding his struggles in appealing to this core Democratic group. While he is on track to do less well than other
recent Democratic presidential candidates among voters
with less formal education, his great appeal to college-educated voters (and even more so, to those whose schooling
continued after getting a college degree) helps to offset
that. Women with high educational attainment appear to
be one of Obama's strongest constituencies.

McCain's Age Seen as More of a Problem Than Obama's Race

Twenty-three percent of Americans say John McCain's
age would make him a less effective president were he to

win in November, while only 8% say Barack Obama's race
would make him less effective. These results derive from
two questions included in a July 15–19 USA Today/Gallup
Poll. One question asked respondents whether Obama's
race would make him more effective, would make him less
effective, or would make no difference if he were to be
elected president. A parallel question asked about the perceived impact of the fact that McCain would be 72 when
inaugurated next January, were he to win.

More than 8 out of 10 Americans say Obama's race would
make no difference in terms of his effectiveness in the White

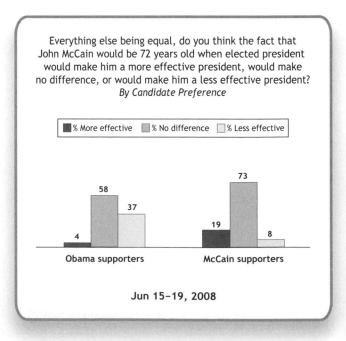

Everything else being equal, do you think the fact that
John McCain would be 72 years old when elected president
would make him a more effective president, would make
no difference, or would make him a less effective president?
By Candidate Preference

Jun 15–19, 2008

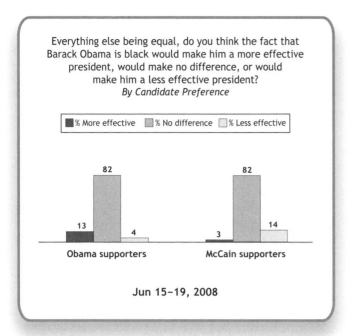

Everything else being equal, do you think the fact that Barack Obama is black would make him a more effective president, would make no difference, or would make him a less effective president?
By Candidate Preference

■ % More effective   ■ % No difference   □ % Less effective

Jun 15–19, 2008

Everything else being equal, do you think the fact that John McCain would be 72 years old when elected president would make him a more effective president, would not make any difference, or would make him a less effective president?
By Respondent Age

	More effective	No difference	Less effective
	%	%	%
18 to 29 yrs. old	11	62	26
30 to 49 yrs. old	9	67	23
50 to 64 yrs. old	9	64	26
65+ yrs. old	14	64	21

Jun 15–19, 2008

House. Of the rest, just as many say his being black would make him more effective as president as say it would make him less effective. Thus, as far as the public is concerned, Obama's race appears to be a wash in terms of perceptions about his ability to serve effectively as president.

There is more expressed concern about McCain's age. As is the case with respect to Obama's race, the majority of Americans say that McCain's being 72 next January would not make any difference in terms of his effectiveness in the White House. But 23% say McCain would be less effective as a result of his age, while only 11% say he would be more effective. The net result is a slightly negative view of the impact of McCain's advanced age. Over a third of Obama voters in the poll's sample say McCain's age would make him a less effective president, although that leaves a majority who still say it would make no difference. On the other hand, just 19% of McCain's own supporters say his age would make him more effective. (Only 8% say it would make him less effective.) Exactly the same percentage—82%—of both Obama voters and McCain voters say Obama's being black would make no difference in terms of his effectiveness as president. But, importantly, only 14% of McCain voters have a negative view of the impact of Obama's race, compared with the 37% of Obama voters who view the impact of McCain's age negatively.

There is a slight tendency for Obama voters to say Obama's being black would be a plus, while McCain voters are slightly more likely to say it would be a negative than Obama voters are to say it would be a positive, but these are not major differences. Independents, the key group that both campaigns are heavily targeting, basi-cally reflect the opinions of voters generally in their views of the impact of Obama's race and McCain's age.

The Views of Older Americans and Black Americans

One might expect that older Americans would be more likely than younger Americans to be less negative about the impact of McCain's age, but in fact the differences by age group are slight. Even among Americans 65 and older, McCain's age is seen as a net negative, with 21% saying it will make him less effective and only 14% saying it will make him more effective; their views are only slightly less negative, and slightly more positive, than those of younger age groups. By the same token, young Americans, age 18

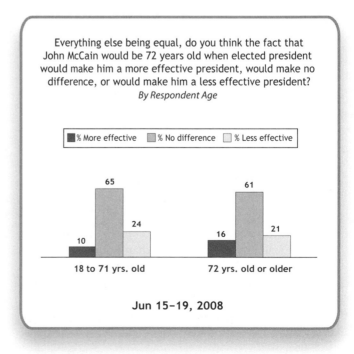

Everything else being equal, do you think the fact that John McCain would be 72 years old when elected president would make him a more effective president, would make no difference, or would make him a less effective president?
By Respondent Age

■ % More effective   ■ % No difference   □ % Less effective

Jun 15–19, 2008

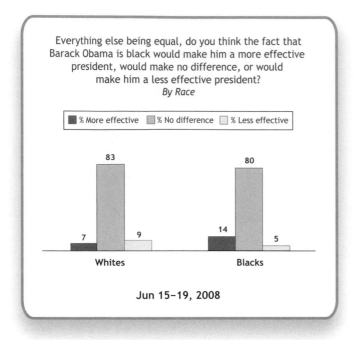

Everything else being equal, do you think the fact that Barack Obama is black would make him a more effective president, would make no difference, or would make him a less effective president?
By Race

■ % More effective   ▨ % No difference   ☐ % Less effective

Whites: 7 — 83 — 9
Blacks: 14 — 80 — 5

Jun 15–19, 2008

no strong endorsement of the positive impact of age from older Americans who are at least the age he will be in January. A majority of those who themselves are 72 and older say McCain's age will make no difference to his presidency; but among those who do have an opinion, slightly more say it will make him less effective as president than say it will make him more effective.

It might be expected that black Americans would see Obama's race as a plus for his effectiveness in the White House—for example, in terms of his ability to reach across racial lines in addressing problems involving race in this country. But there is little evidence of such attitudes in these data. Black Americans are as likely as white Americans to say Obama's race will make no difference, and only a small 14% of blacks say Obama would be more effective as a result of his race. At the same time, an even smaller 5% of blacks say Obama's race would make him less effective, suggesting little concern that he might face resistance to his presidency as a result of his race.

JULY 10
Obama Retains Small Advantage

Barack Obama continues to hold a slight advantage over John McCain, 46% to 43%, in the latest Gallup Poll daily tracking presidential election trial heat update. These results are based on interviews conducted between July 7 and July 9 with more than 2,600 registered voters nationwide. Both candidates are actively out on the campaign trail and news media continue to devote substantial resources to coverage of the campaign, but there is little sign at this point in the summer that voters are radically shifting in their preferences. Since Gallup's June 24–26 polling, when the candidates were even at 44%, the percentage favoring Obama has ranged only from 46% to 48%, while the percentage preferring McCain has varied just as little, from 42% to 44%.

Fewer Americans Favor Cutting Back Immigration

A new Gallup Poll finds 39% of Americans in favor of reductions in immigration, down from 45% a year ago. Currently, the public is just as likely to favor maintaining the status quo on immigration as it is to favor a decrease. Only a relatively small minority of 18% of Americans believe immigration levels should be increased. These results are based on Gallup's annual Minority Rights and Relations Survey, conducted between June 5 and July 6 of this year and consisting of interviews with more

to 29, are basically no more negative about McCain's age than are those in older age groups. A separate analysis looked only at respondents who themselves are age 72 or older—the group presumably most likely to be aware of the implications of McCain's age on his ability to serve effectively as president. Among this group, there is a little more sentiment that McCain's age would make him less effective than there is that his age would make him more effective, while 6 out of 10 say it would make no difference. Black Americans are little different from whites in their views of the impact of Obama's race. Blacks are slightly more likely than whites to perceive that Obama's race would be a net plus with respect to his effectiveness as president, but the difference, as noted, is not large at all. Eight out of 10 or more of both whites and blacks perceive that Obama's race would make no difference.

Summary: Age and Race in This Election

The majority of Americans appear to believe that neither McCain's age nor Obama's race will make a difference in terms of either candidate's effectiveness as president should he be elected this November. Among those who do think these factors would make a difference, however, there is somewhat more concern about McCain's age than there is about Obama's race. This is fueled in part by the views of Obama supporters, more than a third of whom say McCain's age would make him less effective. McCain, who has often referred to the health and vitality of his elderly mother as an indication of the fact that older people can be alert and effective, may be discouraged to find that he gets

than 1,900 adults nationwide, including large samples of blacks and Hispanics. (The poll sample is weighted to be representative of the entire adult population.) During much of this decade, a plurality if not a majority of Americans have favored cutbacks in immigration, reaching as high as 58% shortly after the Sept. 11, 2001, terrorist attacks. But the current percentage in favor of reduced immigration levels is within a percentage point of the lowest Gallup has measured in the last 20 years or so (a 38% reading, in the year 2000; the all-time low was 33%, way back in 1965). In 2006, 39% also favored decreased immigration.

The post–September 11 reading was not the historical high point in calls for reduced immigration; in the mid-1990s—during a backlash against immigrants symbolized by the passing of California's Proposition 187, which denied government benefits to illegal immigrants, in 1994—roughly two in three Americans wanted to see less immigration. The apparent softening on immigration is also evident in the fact that 64% of Americans now say immigration is a good thing for the country today, up from 60% last year and marking the second highest reading in the now eight-year history of the Minority Rights and Relations Survey.

One reason anti-immigration sentiment has diminished somewhat may be that immigration has receded as an issue this year as Americans have focused on the struggling economy and record-high gasoline prices. In a June Gallup Poll, just 4% named immigration as the most important problem facing the country, down from 11% at the beginning of the year. Also in June, just 27% of Americans said illegal immigration would be an extremely important issue relative to their vote for president this year, ranking it dead

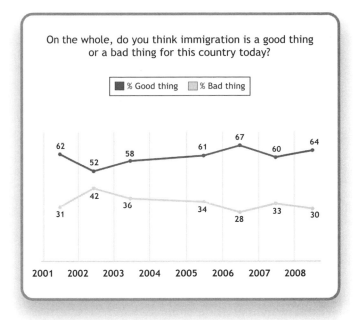

last of eight issues tested. President Bush and Congress failed in their attempt to pass comprehensive immigration reform last year, and the issue has been put on the back burner during this presidential election year.

Immigration and the Economy

The June 5–July 6 poll finds that Americans have mixed views on some of the precise effects of immigration on the economy. On the one hand, by a two-to-one margin, the public says immigrants cost taxpayers too much by

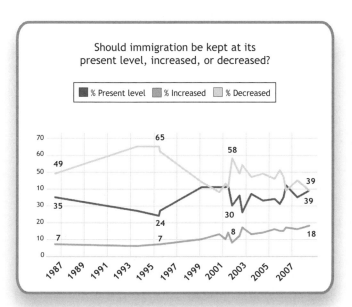

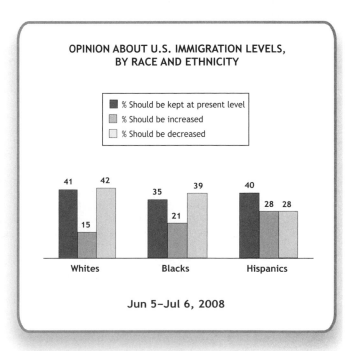

using government services as opposed to becoming productive citizens who pay their fair share of taxes. These views are essentially unchanged from 2006. But on the other hand, Americans by an even wider margin see some economic benefit from immigrants, based on the perception that illegal immigrants tend to take low-paying jobs that Americans don't want (79%) as opposed to taking away jobs that would otherwise go to Americans (15%). Again, these sentiments have not changed materially since 2006.

Immigration Attitudes by Subgroup

Of the major racial and ethnic groups, Hispanics tend to be the most supportive of immigration. This is not surprising, given that nearly half of the Hispanics in the poll are themselves immigrants. Only 28% of Hispanics favor decreased immigration, compared with 39% of blacks and 42% of non-Hispanic whites. Additionally, 70% of Hispanics say immigration is good for the country today, compared with 62% of whites and 57% of blacks. Hispanics also break with most other Americans in rejecting the notion that illegal immigrants are a drain on taxpayer resources. Whereas solid majorities of whites (71%) and blacks (62%) believe that illegal immigrants cost taxpayers too much money, only 30% of Hispanics agree. Nearly two in three Hispanics hold the view that illegal immigrants become productive citizens who pay their fair share of taxes.

As expected, there are political differences in attitudes toward immigration, but these tend to be stronger according to one's ideological inclination than by political party affiliation. A majority of self-identified conser-

IMMIGRATION ATTITUDES, BY POLITICAL IDEOLOGY			
	Liberal	Moderate	Conservative
Immigration Levels			
Should be kept at present level	45%	39%	35%
Should be increased	22%	22%	12%
Should be decreased	30%	37%	51%
Effect on the Country			
Good	71%	64%	59%
Bad	25%	28%	35%
Effect on Taxes			
Immigrants in long run pay fair share	50%	31%	17%
Immigrants cost taxpayers too much	46%	64%	76%
Jobs Immigrants Take			
Mostly jobs Americans want	8%	16%	17%
Mostly low-paying jobs Americans don't want	87%	79%	74%

Jun 5–Jul 6, 2008

vatives believe immigration levels should be reduced, while only 30% of liberals agree. Close to half of liberals favor keeping the status quo. Liberals are much more likely than conservatives to say immigration has been good for the country, and to believe that immigrants eventually become productive citizens and pay their fair share of taxes.

The Uncertain Status of the Immigration Issue Today

As the illegal immigration issue has faded from the public consciousness, Americans have become somewhat less likely to take anti-immigration stances. It is unclear at this point whether that means the public is coming to terms with the immigration issue and with the complexities involved in dealing with illegal immigrants living in the United States, or whether the public might become somewhat less tolerant of immigration should elected leaders take up the issue again.

JULY 13
Presidential Preferences Remain Consistent

Barack Obama wins the support of 46% of national registered voters interviewed in Gallup Poll daily tracking from July 10 to July12, while John McCain is not far behind with 43%. This marks the 14th straight Gallup Poll daily tracking report in which 46% to 48% of voters favor Obama and

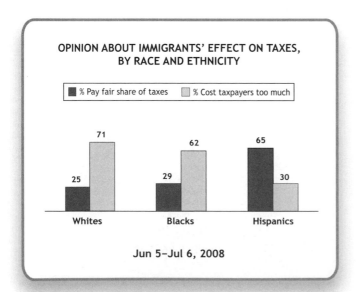

OPINION ABOUT IMMIGRANTS' EFFECT ON TAXES, BY RACE AND ETHNICITY

■ % Pay fair share of taxes   ■ % Cost taxpayers too much

Whites: 25, 71
Blacks: 29, 62
Hispanics: 65, 30

Jun 5–Jul 6, 2008

between 42% and 44% favor McCain. This narrow "zone" has given Obama a continuous, but fairly slim, lead over the two-week period. Obama also held a slim lead for most of June (averaging three percentage points), although he led by a six- to seven-point margin for three days at the start of June. The two candidates were tied for a brief period in late June, but the last time McCain held a significant lead over Obama was in early May.

JULY 14

"Black Spokesman" Title Still Up for Grabs

Twenty-nine percent of black Americans name Barack Obama as the individual or leader in the United States whom they would choose as their spokesman on issues of race, but 49% name someone else and nearly a quarter offer no name at all. The issue came up last week after controversial remarks the Reverend Jesse Jackson made about Obama. Jackson criticized Obama's campaign message urging African Americans to take personal responsibility as "talking down to black people." He claimed that Obama has not adequately emphasized the need for the government to take on more responsibility and take action to help blacks. The June 5–July 6 poll, conducted before the Jackson controversy erupted, finds that Obama is clearly the most dominant individual blacks think of in terms of representing their views on racial matters. He far outpaces the Reverend Al Sharpton, mentioned by 6%; Jackson himself (with 4%); Bill and Hillary Clinton, each with 3%; and an array of academic, political, religious, and entertainment icons of the black community. However, consistent with Obama's efforts to downplay the racial symbolism of his candidacy, most blacks don't think of Obama as their racial spokesman. A total of 49% cite someone else—including 6% who name themselves.

These results are from Gallup's annual Minority Rights and Relations Survey, conducted each June. The 2008 survey comprised nationally representative interviews with 1,935 adults, including more than 700 non-Hispanic whites, more than 600 blacks, and more than 500 Hispanics, all weighted to represent their correct proportions in the population. The results do not suggest that black Democrats are not excited about Obama's candidacy or that they don't hold out high hopes for what an Obama victory could achieve for black Americans. A remarkable 90% of black Democrats—compared with 64% of non-Hispanic white Democrats and 36% of all Republicans—say they are "more enthusiastic" about voting than usual this year. Additionally, the Minority Rights and Relations Survey shows that a 59% majority of blacks

If you had to name one individual or leader in the United States to speak for you on issues of race, who would that be? *Among African Americans*	
	%
Barack Obama	29
Al Sharpton	6
Jesse Jackson	4
Bill Clinton	3
Hillary Clinton	3
Oprah Winfrey	2
Maya Angelou	1
Colin Powell	1
Louis Farrakhan	1
Bill Cosby	1
Tavis Smiley	1
Cornel West	1
My minister/pastor	1
Me/Myself	6
Other	18
No one	7
No opinion	16

Jun 5–Jul 6, 2008

say they would view Obama's winning the presidency as one of the most important advances of the past century for blacks—compared with a slightly smaller 48% of non-Hispanic white Americans, and 50% of adult Americans generally, who view the prospect of putting the first black

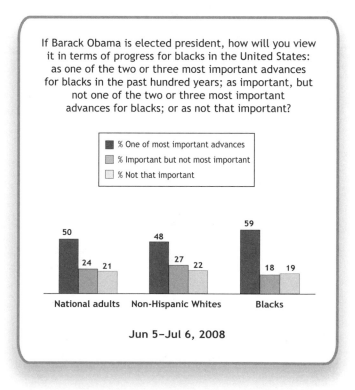

If Barack Obama is elected president, how will you view it in terms of progress for blacks in the United States: as one of the two or three most important advances for blacks in the past hundred years; as important, but not one of the two or three most important advances for blacks; or as not that important?

- ■ % One of most important advances
- ▨ % Important but not most important
- ▢ % Not that important

National adults: 50, 24, 21
Non-Hispanic Whites: 48, 27, 22
Blacks: 59, 18, 19

Jun 5–Jul 6, 2008

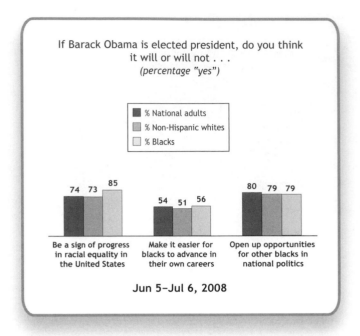

If Barack Obama is elected president, do you think
it will or will not . . .
(percentage "yes")

■ % National adults
■ % Non-Hispanic whites
□ % Blacks

	Be a sign of progress in racial equality in the United States	Make it easier for blacks to advance in their own careers	Open up opportunities for other blacks in national politics
	74 73 85	54 51 56	80 79 79

Jun 5–Jul 6, 2008

American in the White House as marking a key civil rights milestone.

Overwhelming majorities of whites (73%) and blacks (85%) believe an Obama win would be a sign of progress toward racial equality in the United States. Most whites and blacks also believe it would open up national political opportunities for other blacks, and majorities think it would make it easier for blacks to advance in their own careers. Now that Obama has become the first African-American to be a major party's presumptive nominee for president, one might ask how black America will react if he doesn't win. Only a third of blacks (34%) predict that race relations in the country would worsen (either a little or a lot) if Obama loses. While only 18% say relations would improve, a plurality, 45%, say they would not change. Whites generally agree, with a slim majority saying race

If Barack Obama loses the presidential election, do think
race relations in this country will get a lot better,
get a little better, not change, get a little worse,
or get a lot worse?

	Get a lot better	Get a little better	Not change	Get a little worse	Get a lot worse
	%	%	%	%	%
National adults	3	12	53	22	8
Non-Hispanic whites	2	11	53	22	8
Blacks	5	13	45	16	18

Jun 5–Jul 6, 2008

relations will not change if Obama loses, but with more saying they will get worse than saying they will get better. At the same time, blacks have muted expectations for how much an Obama win would improve race relations. Although two-thirds of blacks think it would improve race relations to some degree, only 23% say race relations would "get a lot better."

Implications: Race and Obama in the General Election

Twenty-nine percent of blacks name Obama as the individual or leader in the United States whom they would choose as their spokesman for race issues, far more than name any other individual, including the 4% who mention Jesse Jackson. This suggests a passing of the baton with respect to the political leadership of black Americans, which some have suggested may be what is troubling Jackson.

In discussing Jackson's controversial remarks about Obama recently, Sharpton said, "Senator Obama is running for president of all Americans, not just African Americans." To the extent that is true, it is not curtailing black Americans' willingness to support Obama for president. According to Gallup Poll daily tracking in the first week of July, 90% of black registered voters say they are voting for him, compared with only 4% backing McCain. And, as noted, blacks are almost universally enthusiastic about the election.

However, the poll does suggest that black Americans see beyond race when thinking about Obama. By not heavily associating Obama with the "black spokesman" role (49% name someone else, and nearly a quarter name no one), and by holding somewhat muted expectations regarding the capacity of an Obama victory to improve race relations, blacks seem to agree with the essence of Sharpton's commentary: Obama is more than "the black candidate for president"; he is a candidate for president who happens to be black.

JULY 15
Gallup Daily: Obama Maintains Slight Advantage

The latest Gallup Poll daily tracking update shows Barack Obama maintaining a slight advantage over John McCain, with 47% of registered voters saying they would vote for Obama and 43% for John McCain if the presidential election were held today. McCain's percentage of the vote has been remarkably steady of late, varying only two percentage points, between 42% and 44%, over a two-week period. In fact, McCain has received precisely 43% of the vote in each of the last four Gallup tracking reports. Obama's percentage of the vote has varied slightly more but has generally been at 46%, 47%, or 48% for weeks. Whatever the gap between the two candidates, however, there has not been much change in the nature of the race. This lack of change has occurred in an environment replete with a vast amount of news coverage of the candidates, their campaigns, and their statements, coupled with active campaigning by both candidates through these "dog days" of summer, and the fact that the candidates are saturating the airwaves with commercials in key swing states. The bottom line: At this point, the presidential race appears to remain quite competitive.

Making Sense of the Campaign Doldrums

The presidential race is in the doldrums. The "doldrums" is a nautical description for a place where the winds are calm, meaning a sailing ship just sits there. In this instance, the term is used to suggest that the presidential election is essentially becalmed, with few winds pushing the presidential election ship in either direction. This is not unexpected. There was an incredible flurry of high winds from January through May, propelled by the jet stream of primary activity (to continue the nautical analogy). Now there is no jet stream. Looking to the horizon, we expect the winds—perhaps winds of hurricane force—to pick up as we approach the conventions.

　This isn't to say that the campaigns aren't attempting to turn up the wind machines. No doubt, each campaign is haunted by the specter of Michael Dukakis in 1988. Upon receiving the Democratic nomination at the convention in July, Dukakis returned home to Massachusetts to attend to being governor. That was fine in principle. But his absence from the presidential campaign trail coincided with the total evaporation of the 17-percentage-point post-convention lead over George H. W. Bush that Dukakis enjoyed immediately after the Democratic convention. So Dukakis dutifully toiled away in Boston; the Republicans held their own convention in August; Bush emerged with an 8-point lead by early September; and Bush won the election in November. Consequently, neither campaign is allowing its candidate to rest: Barack Obama and John McCain are campaigning ceaselessly. The news media are doing their part, breathlessly looking for any morsel of campaign news to report. Indeed, campaign news still fronts the newspapers, leads newscasts, and is the dominant talk on cable news shows.

　The campaigns may argue that the real purpose of their campaigning at this point is not to change voters' minds but to lay the groundwork for the "brand positioning" for their candidate so that he is better able to withstand the

Appropriate or inappropriate? Artist Barry Blitt's July 21, 2008, *New Yorker* front cover provoked controversy by portraying Barack and Michelle Obama as fist-bumping, gun-toting, flag-burning terrorists standing in the Oval Office. Blitt titled his illustration "Politics of Fear." *(Sipa Press/Newscom)*

inevitable battles to come. If that's the case, then the results of the effort won't be known until later this summer and fall; voters at this point simply aren't changing their minds. Gallup Poll daily tracking essentially shows no substantive or structural change in the standing of the two candidates in trial heat measures for more than a month now.

JULY 16
Obama Maintaining Support Among Liberals

Barack Obama's support among political liberals has not declined in recent weeks, and in fact shows evidence of a modest uptick. Currently, 82% of self-identified liberals

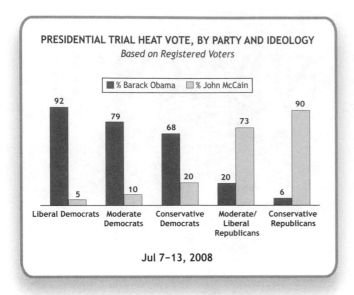

PRESIDENTIAL TRIAL HEAT VOTE, BY PARTY AND IDEOLOGY
Based on Registered Voters

■ % Barack Obama   ☐ % John McCain

Jul 7–13, 2008

Party supporters for his past or present moderate positions on campaign finance reform, illegal immigration, and tax cuts. But as has been the case with respect to Obama, this criticism has done little to faze the party rank and file, as McCain's support among conservative Republicans in presidential trial heats versus Obama has always been very high and quite stable. Currently, Obama and McCain do about equally well in attracting support from the most ideological supporters of their respective parties.

Commentary

It is clear that any perceived shifts by Obama toward the middle on specific issues have not brought about a decline in support for him among the more ideological wing of his party. There are many possible reasons for this. For one thing, a substantial number of liberals may not be aware of Obama's apparent movement toward the center. On the other hand, they may realize that it is common for presidential candidates to shift toward more moderate positions during a general election campaign in order to build a winning electoral coalition. Even though liberals who are upset with Obama's recent issue positions have other voting options this fall, including independent candidate Ralph Nader and Green Party candidate Cynthia McKinney, they may not necessarily view those long-shot candidates as viable alternatives to Obama. As such, they may continue to back Obama despite some policy disagreements with him.

(including 92% of liberals who identify themselves as Democrats) say they would vote for Obama rather than John McCain if the election were held today. His support from both groups is the highest to date in Gallup Poll daily tracking. Some on the political Left have criticized Obama for his recent centrist-leaning positions on some issues—positions that appear to be a departure from what he advocated earlier in the campaign. For example, Obama previously said he would oppose legislation providing immunity to telecommunications companies that provided customer data to the federal government as part of its anti-terrorism efforts. But when an anti-terror bill came up last week that provided telecommunications companies with this type of immunity, he voted in favor of it. Obama has also said that he may refine his position on the war in Iraq after he tours the country and meets with U.S. military leaders. Some took this as a signal that he may be backing away from his call for withdrawing U.S. troops from Iraq within 16 months of taking office, although Obama responded by reiterating his support for his withdrawal timetable.

Despite questions about Obama's commitment to a "progressive" agenda, Gallup Poll daily tracking data show that rank-and-file liberal Democrats are no less likely to support Obama now than they were earlier in the campaign. Obama's performance among liberals compares favorably with that of his former Democratic nomination rival, Hillary Clinton, when she was still an active candidate. In March-to-June presidential trial heats matching Clinton against McCain, Clinton's support topped out at 81% among all liberals and 89% among liberal Democrats, both slightly below where Obama currently stands. Obama is not alone in receiving complaints about his issue positions from party ideologues. McCain, too, has been criticized by some prominent (conservative) Republican

Congressional Approval Hits Record-Low 14%

Congress's job approval rating has dropped five percentage points over the past month, from 19% in June to 14% in July, making the current reading the lowest congressional job approval rating in the 34-year Gallup Poll history of asking the question. The previous low was 18%, last reached in May. The 75% currently disapproving of Congress is just shy of the record-high 78% in March 1992. These results, from a July 10–13 Gallup Poll, follow 18 months of dismal job approval ratings for Congress, during which approval has usually registered below 30% and has averaged only 25%. Still, the 14% approval rating is extraordinary. Approval of Congress has fallen below 20% only six times in the 34 years Gallup has measured it. Including the latest reading, four of those have come in the past year: in July, June, and May 2008 and in August 2007. The two additional below-20% readings were from March 1992 (in the midst of the bank check-kiting scandal in the House of Representatives) and June 1979 (during an energy crisis that resulted in surging gasoline prices and long gasoline lines), when 18% and 19% of Americans, respectively, approved of the job Congress was doing. The most recent decline comes almost

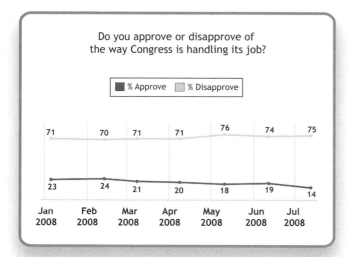

Do you approve or disapprove of
the way Congress is handling its job?

exclusively from Democrats, whose approval of Congress fell from 23% in June to 11% in July, while independents' approval of Congress fell two points and Republicans' rose four points. As a result, Republicans are now more likely than Democrats to approve of the job the Democratic-controlled Congress is doing (19% vs. 11%).

The 11% of Democrats now approving of Congress is slightly lower than Gallup found in 2006, toward the end of the Republican-led 109th Congress. Democratic approval of Congress initially surged after the Democratic takeover of the House and Senate, from 16% in December 2006 to 44% in February 2007; but by August 2007 it had fallen to 21%. Democrats' approval of Congress rebounded to 37% later that year but has since been in nearly continuous decline. Republicans' approval of Congress dipped at the point of transition from Republican to Democratic control after the 2006 midterm elections, from 50% in November 2006 to 31% in February 2007, and has continued to trend downward, except for a brief spike last fall after General David Petraeus's testimony before Congress in September 2007.

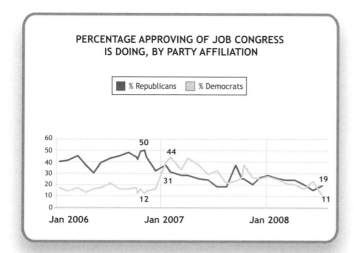

PERCENTAGE APPROVING OF JOB CONGRESS
IS DOING, BY PARTY AFFILIATION

Commentary

Gallup's latest monthly update with respect to public approval of Congress suggests several observations:

1. As economic conditions in the country are worsening, Congress is taking the brunt of public dissatisfaction. Since the start of the year, public approval of Congress has fallen from 23% to 14%, while approval of President George W. Bush has been more stable: Thirty-two percent approved of the job he was doing in early January versus 31% today, with a range of just 28% to 34%.

2. One reason for the growing approval gap between Congress and Bush is that the latter benefits from a core group of Republicans who continue to stick by him (67% of Republicans approve of Bush in the latest Gallup Poll) and who, at this point, are likely to remain supportive of him through the close of his term. This contrasts with the paltry 11% of Democrats who currently approve of the job Congress is doing. By its nature, Congress may simply be less able to engender this kind of political loyalty—it typically trails the sitting president in approval—and so the current Democratic Congress lacks a reliable pool of Democratic support to keep its approval ratings afloat.

3. Still, the Democratic Congress has received much less intraparty support for its leadership of the kind that the Republican Congress enjoyed from Republicans in 2006. The mild honeymoon that the current Congress enjoyed with its own party at the start of last year quickly faded as Democrats grew upset with congressional inaction on Iraq and immigration reform.

4. Finally, 2008 now looks an awful lot like 1979, and for some of the same reasons: mounting inflation, record-high gasoline prices, and a looming recession. Public approval of President Jimmy Carter in mid-July 1979 was 29%, very similar to Bush's current 31%. And approval of Congress was also comparable: 19% in June 1979 vs. 14% today.

JULY 17

Two Attractive Options . . . So Far

The 2008 election is shaping up thus far as a contest between two well-liked candidates. The latest figures show favorable ratings of 64% for Barack Obama and 59% for John McCain. Obama's is the highest Gallup has measured for a presidential candidate in mid-June in the past four presidential election years, and McCain's also ranks as one of the highest. In fact, as of mid-June, one in three Americans had a favorable opinion of both candidates, much higher than what Gallup found at similar points in the 2004 (17%), 2000 (24%), and 1996 (24%) election years.

So the high-intensity and highly front-loaded primary process seems to have worked from the standpoint that most Americans like the options the parties put before them, apparently much more so than in recent election years. Usually, as the campaign wears on, favorable ratings tend to move toward the 50% mark, so it will be interesting to see where Obama and McCain are in late October/early November. But if the factors driving favorable ratings down are no stronger in 2008 than in prior election years, there may well be a significant percentage of Americans who would be satisfied with the election of either candidate.

Bush Quarterly Average Establishes New Low: 29%

George W. Bush will end his 30th quarter in the White House with just a 29.0% average approval rating for the last three months, the worst of his presidency. President Bush's previous low quarterly average was 31.3%, in the prior (29th) quarter. During his 30th quarter (spanning the period from April 20 through July 19), Bush's six individual Gallup Poll approval ratings ranged between 28% and 31%. (The 31% figure is from the most recent update, based on a July 10–13 Gallup Poll.) High gasoline prices, numerous economic problems, and ongoing U.S. military action in Iraq and Afghanistan all contributed to Bush's recent low ratings, which rank among the lowest Gallup has measured historically. (The lowest single rating for any president was Harry Truman's 22% job approval rating in February 1952.) Bush has achieved a personal low of 28% five times, three of which occurred in his most recent quarter in office. Bush spent a good part of 2001 and 2002 at the opposite end of

the spectrum, registering some of the highest approval ratings in Gallup's polling history, including a record-high 90% from a poll conducted shortly after the September 11 terrorist attacks. Since then, Bush's approval rating has steadily declined.

Gallup has measured only eight presidential quarterly averages lower than Bush's current 29% since it regularly began tracking presidential approval ratings in 1945—all eight registered either by Truman in 1951 and 1952 or by Richard Nixon in 1973 and 1974. Jimmy Carter joins Bush, Truman, and Nixon as presidents with the 15 worst quarterly averages. Bush is only the fifth president since World War II to have served a 30th quarter in office, and he now rates as the president with the worst average approval rating among these five presidents during this period of his presidency. Truman previously had the lowest 30th-quarter average, at 32%, while Dwight Eisenhower, Ronald Reagan, and Bill Clinton all averaged above 50%.

SIXTEEN LOWEST QUARTERLY APPROVAL AVERAGES, GALLUP POLLS, 1945–2008

Rank	President	Dates	Quarter in office	Average rating	# of polls
251	Truman	Oct 20, 1951–Jan 19, 1952	27	23.0	2
250	Nixon	Jul 20–Aug 9, 1974	23	24.0	1
249	Truman	Jan 20–Apr 19, 1952	28	25.0	3
247 (tie)	Nixon	Apr 20–Jul 19, 1974	22	26.0	7
247 (tie)	Truman	Apr 20–Jul 19, 1951	25	26.0	3
246	Nixon	Jan 20–Apr 19, 1974	25	26.0	7
245	Truman	Jan 20–Apr 19, 1951	24	26.3	4
244	Nixon	Oct 20, 1973–Jan 19, 1974	20	28.0	5
243	G.W. Bush	Apr 20–Jul 19, 2008	30	29.0	6
242	Truman	Apr 20–Jul 19, 1952	29	29.8	4
240 (tie)	Carter	Apr 20–Jul 19, 1979	10	30.7	6
240 (tie)	Truman	Jul 20–Oct 19, 2008	26	30.7	3
239	G.W. Bush	Jan 20–Apr 19, 2008	29	31.3	8
238	Carter	Jul 20–Oct 19, 1979	11	31.4	7
236 (tie)	G.W. Bush	Apr 20–Oct 19, 2007	26	31.8	6
236 (tie)	Nixon	Jul 20–Oct 19, 1973	19	31.8	6

GEORGE W. BUSH QUARTERLY JOB APPROVAL AVERAGES

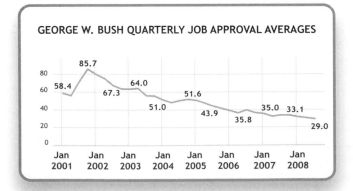

PRESIDENTS' 30TH-QUARTER APPROVAL AVERAGES, GALLUP POLLS, 1945–2008

President	Dates of 30th quarter	Approval rating	# of polls
Truman	Jul 20–Oct 19, 1952	32.0%	3
Eisenhower	Apr 20–Jul 19, 1960	58.8%	5
Reagan	Apr 20–Jul 19, 1988	50.3%	6
Clinton	Apr 20–Jul 19, 2000	58.0%	7
G.W. Bush	Apr 20–Jul 19, 2008	29.0%	6

Implications for the Election: Uncertain

With just eight months and two quarters left in his presidency, Bush is clearly limping toward the finish line, and unless national conditions improve significantly, he will likely leave office with low ratings (even if he gets a post-election bounce, as outgoing presidents typically do). His historically low approval ratings are a challenge for John McCain and for the Republican Party's hopes of retaining the presidency. The closest historical parallel to the current situation is the 1952 election, when Democratic candidate Adlai Stevenson unsuccessfully sought to succeed the unpopular Harry Truman as president. But an outgoing president's approval ratings are not generally very predictive of the outcome of a presidential election. Among the more popular presidents in the late stages of their terms, only Reagan was succeeded as president by a member of his party.

JULY 20

Obama Has Three-Point Edge

The latest Gallup Poll daily tracking report for July 17–19 shows Barack Obama maintaining a slight advantage over John McCain, 45% to 42%. This marks the third report in a row in which Obama's support, at 45%, is slightly lower than his overall average for the last month and a half. The percentage of registered voters interviewed who do not make a choice between the two candidates has increased slightly; McCain's support level remains no higher than it has been. Obama began his highly publicized international trip just as the last interviews in this three-day rolling average were being collected. It remains to be seen whether the intense publicity Obama will receive as a result of the trip will make a difference in overall voter preferences as the week progresses. So far this summer, it appears that not much has been able to induce substantial change in voter support for the two major party candidates.

JULY 23

Obama Has Modest Four-Point Lead

Barack Obama maintains a modest 46% to 42% lead over John McCain among registered voters nationally in Gallup Poll daily tracking, with no sign yet of a significant "bounce" from Obama's high-visibility world tour. Gallup also finds 6% of voters saying they won't vote for either candidate, while another 6% are still undecided. The big news from Gallup Poll daily tracking is the continuing stability of this race. Many observers (including, based on its reaction, the McCain campaign itself) have hypothesized

At his home in Kennebunkport, Maine, former president George H. W. Bush (left) praises presumptive Republican nominee John McCain on July 21, 2008. *(Carolyn Kaster/ AP Images)*

that Obama might benefit from a major breakthrough in voter sentiment as a result of the streaming video, photos, and news coverage of the Illinois senator with U.S. troops, military commanders, and foreign leaders abroad. Perhaps the signal event of Obama's overseas trip will be a forthcoming speech before tens of thousands in Germany later this week. It remains to be seen whether or not news coverage of this speech will alter the support patterns among American voters.

Britons, French, Germans Solidly Back Obama

Substantial majorities of citizens in France, Germany, and the United Kingdom say that they would like to see Barack Obama rather than John McCain elected U.S. president, and also that it makes a difference to their country who is elected. Obama, along with a small group of other senators, visited Afghanistan and Iraq this week as part of an official congressional fact-finding mission, and he is now set to visit with the leaders of the United Kingdom, Germany,

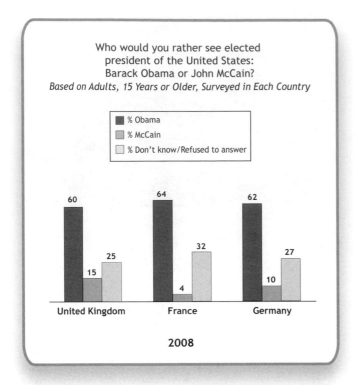

Who would you rather see elected
president of the United States:
Barack Obama or John McCain?

Based on Adults, 15 Years or Older, Surveyed in Each Country

2008

would rather see Obama than McCain elected president this fall. The majorities that favor Obama in these countries compare with the small advantage Obama currently holds in Gallup Poll's U.S. daily tracking. It is also clear that the residents of these European countries believe they have more than a passing interest in the November election. A solid majority in each say that the results of the election will make a difference to their country. In each of these countries, Gallup recorded in 2007 abysmally low approval of U.S. leadership: just 8% approval in Germany, 9% in France, and 20% in the United Kingdom. Much of this likely stems from opposition to the U.S.–led Iraq War, but it could also result from U.S. policy on global warming or reported human rights abuses in Guantánamo Bay.

Obama's current strength in these countries may be an outcome of the early publicity surrounding his nomination, particularly the fascinating and dramatic primary contest between Obama and the well-known Senator Hillary Clinton. As a result of the extended Democratic primary season, for much of the spring McCain received far less international media attention than Obama. It is possible, therefore, that McCain could gain some support overseas as the visibility of the two U.S. presidential candidates in the worldwide media becomes more equal over the next three months. Still, there is no question that Obama has become something of a "rock star" in many countries, and whether it is simple name recognition or an awareness of and agreement with his policy positions, he is clearly the favorite at this point.

and France as he moves into a campaign-oriented segment of his overseas trip.

If the choice of U.S. president were up to citizens of these countries, Obama would defeat McCain in a landslide. Even with relatively high no-opinion percentages in each country (ranging from 25% to 32%), solid majorities of residents in the United Kingdom, France, and Germany

These results suggest that residents of the three major European nations Obama visited will likely pay attention to the outcome of the U.S. election. Given these countries' strongly favorable views of Obama, his election could go a long way toward restoring U.S. prestige in Europe. That is not to say McCain could not also improve this country's image; given the low regard in which Europeans hold U.S. leadership today, they would likely welcome almost any change. However, Europeans do seem positively disposed to the Democratic presidential nominee at this point, and he might not need to work as hard to earn their favor as McCain would, assuming he maintains his positive image through November. The Obama campaign at the same time recognizes some risk to his being so widely adored in Europe, which some Americans may not view as a plus—although Gallup's 2008 update on the images of the United Kingdom, France, and Germany in this country shows that a significant majority of Americans now have a favorable image of each.

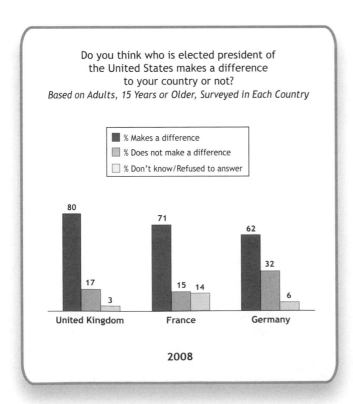

Do you think who is elected president of
the United States makes a difference
to your country or not?

Based on Adults, 15 Years or Older, Surveyed in Each Country

2008

Obama Gains over McCain in Swing States Since June

Since Barack Obama clinched the Democratic nomination in early June and moved into a front-running posi-

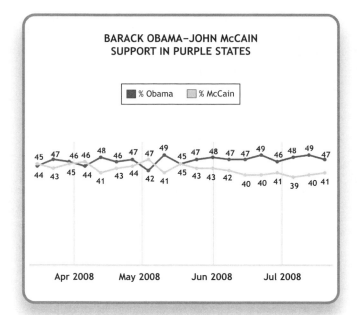

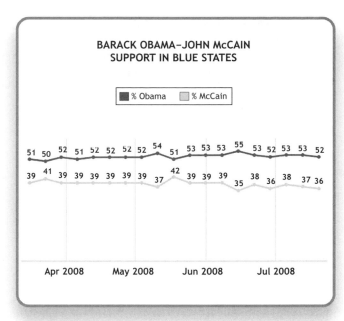

tion in the general election campaign, he has seen his standing versus John McCain improve among voters in red states, blue states, and competitive (or purple) states. Obama has gained at least 3 points over McCain in all three state groupings compared with voter sentiments in March through May of 2008.

Before Obama secured the Democratic nomination in early June, he and McCain were running even nationally, with each averaging 45% of the total vote in Gallup Poll daily tracking from March through May. Since then, Obama has gained a slight upper hand, averaging a three-percentage-point national advantage over McCain (46% to 43%) in June and July polling. These results are based on data from tens of thousands of interviews with registered voters in all 50 states plus the District of Columbia, so the changes, despite their relatively small size, are statistically meaningful. Obama's gains have come across the political and geographic spectrum, as he has improved his relative positioning versus McCain in "red states" (defined as those Republican George W. Bush won by 6 percentage points or more in 2004), "blue states" (those Democrat John Kerry won by 6 percentage points or more in 2004), and "purple states" (those in which the margin of victory for the winning candidate was less than 6 points).

While Obama has gained slightly within each of these state groupings, he has gained somewhat more in the most competitive states, seeing his lead expand in these states by 6 points, as opposed to 3-point gains versus McCain in red and blue states. Since early June, he has averaged a 16-point lead over McCain in blue states and an 8-point lead in purple states, while trailing McCain by an average of 10 points in red states. (McCain trails by only 3 points overall, given

the greater number of voters in red states.) And while the changes in voter preferences have not been great, Obama has clearly established himself as the consistent leader in purple states since late May, whereas the two candidates were more competitive in these states prior to then. Meanwhile, McCain has always enjoyed a comfortable lead in red states, while Obama has done the same in blue states.

Despite his growing deficit in the competitive states, McCain has been able to remain close to Obama on the national level because more voters reside in red states (40%) than in blue states (31%). Thus, while McCain would merely need to break even with Obama in the most competitive states in order to win (indeed, he could win even

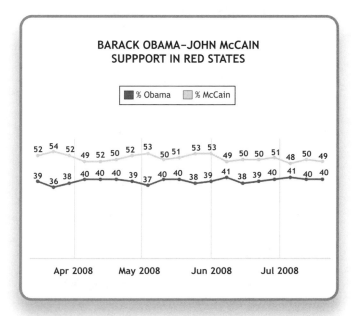

if he trails Obama by a couple of points in those states), Obama needs to score at least a modest advantage in purple states in order to win the popular vote. Thus, the key to the remainder of the campaign is not *whether* Obama has the lead over McCain in these states, but *by how much*. Of course, the winner of the actual election is determined by electoral votes. This analysis groups all competitive states together and assumes that the better Obama does in the popular vote in these states, the better his chances of winning a greater share of the votes in these states and consequently their electoral votes.

JULY 25

Gallup Daily: Obama by Six, Is There a Europe Effect?

Barack Obama has expanded his lead over John McCain in the July 22–24 Gallup Poll daily tracking rolling average and now has a 47% to 41% advantage over his Republican challenger. Obama's current lead matches his lead in the Gallup Poll daily tracking rolling average for July 18–20. His six-percentage-point lead, also measured at several other points in July and June, is the highest Obama has enjoyed since he had a seven-point advantage over McCain in early June (which was Obama's largest lead of the campaign).

The key question at this particular point in the campaign concerns the impact, if any, of this unusual week, during which Obama conducted his highly publicized world tour while McCain attempted to recover some of the media spotlight by engaging in domestic campaign events and taking the opportunity to make critical comments about his presumed Democratic opponent. European residents certainly evince a strong sentiment in favor of Obama's winning the U.S. presidency—much higher than the pro-Obama sentiment here at home. (Residents of the United States have been favoring Obama by just about three points.) Gallup polling shows that residents of Germany, France, and the United Kingdom, by very large margins, would rather see Obama win instead of McCain. The key is the degree to which the sentiments of European residents might "rub off" on American voters as they absorb news coverage of Obama's trip.

In a broad sense, there are several ways that Obama's European trip could affect American voters:

1. Obama's trip could end up being the basis for a shift in voter preferences to the point where he pulls into a sustained lead over McCain. This could occur on a delayed basis: It's possible that Obama's trip, while not having an immediate effect on tracking numbers, could lay the groundwork in the minds of voters to the point where they are more open to an Obama presidency at some point in the future (such as the Democratic convention). In particular, this might occur if his trip removes doubts voters might have about Obama's ability to handle international affairs.

2. Voters may simply not pay much attention to the trip, and its net impact could end up being very minor. The data so far this summer have shown little significant movement in voter numbers, suggesting that voters may, to some degree, be tuning out the election coverage regardless of the candidates' efforts to stimulate interest.

3. Voters might pay attention to Obama's trip but decide that the trip, per se, did not demonstrate anything justifying a fundamental shift in their voting preferences. While the news media have made a great deal out of the trip, it's conceivable that it may not appear to be significant to the majority of voters.

4. Voters could pay attention to the trip but shift support *away* from Obama if they viewed the trip, or the way Obama conducted himself, in a negative light. Conserva-

Senator Barack Obama addresses a massive rally in Berlin, Germany, on July 24, 2008. *(Jae C. Hong/AP Images)*

tive commentators—and of course the McCain campaign itself—have certainly been arguing that there are negatives associated with the trip, including a potential perception of presumptuousness on the part of a presidential nominee making a speech more appropriate for an actual president, the belief that the content of his speeches did not contain anything new, or criticism to the effect that the real issues facing the voters are domestic, not international.

The evidence is certainly mixed at this point as to which of these scenarios may end up being closest to reality. Obama's six-point lead over the past weekend initially suggested that he was perhaps on the cusp of a jump in support as a result of (or at least coinciding with) his trip. But that lead was not sustained, and the Gallup averages reported in the middle of this week have been in and around the average three-point advantage Obama has maintained for the last month and a half. Now, on the basis of a strong showing in Gallup interviewing on July 24, Obama is back to a six-point margin over McCain. That night Obama made his highly anticipated speech in Berlin, Germany, to a crowd estimated to be larger than 200,000, and it is not implausible that it might have affected enough voters to move his overall advantage in the horse race tracking a few points. The dropoff in Obama's support earlier this week, however, suggests caution in assuming that the trip will have any lasting impact on the contours of the race; we will have to wait until the tracking results through the weekend and into next week are monitored carefully. To signify a real difference in the support patterns of voters in the United States, the data would need to show either a sustained six-point-plus lead for Obama over a number of days—or conversely, John McCain moving into the lead (something he has not done since early June) and sustaining that lead.

Previous election year polling shows that the conventions have a high (but not 100%) probability of shaking up the race. The impact of events prior to the conventions is certainly more difficult to pin down. As noted, the structure of the race this year appears to have snapped into place in early June after Hillary Clinton dropped out of the race for the Democratic Party's nomination, and it simply has not changed much since.

JULY 28

Gallup Daily: Obama 48%, McCain 40%

Barack Obama leads John McCain by a 48% to 40% margin among registered voters in Gallup Poll daily tracking conducted between July 25 and July 27. Obama gained ground over McCain in each of the last three tracking updates, but today's average shows no further gains and a slight drop in Obama's percentage of the vote from 49% to 48%. Obama's progress coincided with his highly visible foreign tour, and it is not unreasonable to expect that his lead over McCain may settle back to a margin closer to what Gallup has measured for most of the summer as the impact of the trip fades. At the same time, McCain and his surrogates have engaged in sharp attacks on Obama in their attempt to blunt the impact of his trip, and some of that effort could have an effect on voters. The basic structure of the race so far this summer has been remarkably stable, and it remains to be seen if either candidate can alter it for a sustained period of time before the conventions in late August and early September.

JULY 29

Assessing the Impact of Obama's Trip

Could John McCain benefit from Barack Obama's much-publicized foreign trip? Several observations from the just-completed USA Today/Gallup Poll suggest that this is a possibility. Americans' overall reaction to the trip was muted, as shown in the accompanying results. Thirty-five percent had a positive opinion of the Obama trip, while 26% had a negative opinion, with the rest—more than a third—saying they didn't know enough about the trip to be able to say. Not surprisingly, there were highly partisan reactions to the trip. Notably, Democrats are slightly less likely than Republicans to have an opinion on the trip at all.

The slightly higher degree of attention Republicans paid to the trip could in part reflect the fact that Republican leaders—including McCain himself and, in particular, conservative commentators—were highly vocal in their efforts to blunt the impact of the trip and were quick to criticize

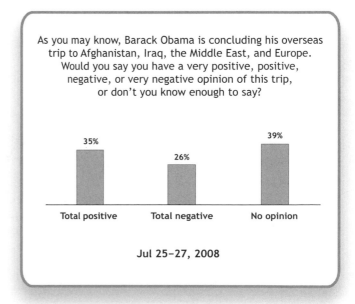

As you may know, Barack Obama is concluding his overseas trip to Afghanistan, Iraq, the Middle East, and Europe. Would you say you have a very positive, positive, negative, or very negative opinion of this trip, or don't you know enough to say?

Total positive — 35%
Total negative — 26%
No opinion — 39%

Jul 25–27, 2008

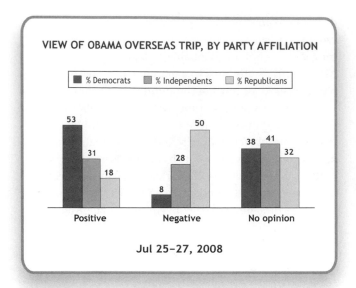

VIEW OF OBAMA OVERSEAS TRIP, BY PARTY AFFILIATION

■ % Democrats   ■ % Independents   □ % Republicans

Positive: 53, 31, 18
Negative: 8, 28, 50
No opinion: 38, 41, 32

Jul 25–27, 2008

and politicize it, finding fault with Obama, for a number of reasons, at almost every stop.

The heavy coverage of the trip may have fueled speculation (or reinforced pre-existing attitudes) regarding alleged news media bias in Obama's favor. A separate set of questions in the current poll asked Americans about their views of the news media's coverage of the two major party candidates. Americans are more than twice as likely to say that media coverage of Obama is unfairly positive as to say it is unfairly negative. With respect to McCain, the opposite is true, with many more seeing coverage of him as unfairly negative than as unfairly positive.

There are huge partisan differences between those voting for McCain and those voting for Obama in their views of the media coverage of the candidates. In general, McCain

voters largely believe their candidate is being treated unfairly while Obama is getting overly friendly media coverage—whereas Obama voters tend to see the media coverage of both candidates as even-handed. Since the previous USA Today/Gallup Poll, Obama's image has suffered to some degree, while McCain's has slightly improved. In the June 15–19 poll, 64% of Americans had a positive view of Obama, compared with 61% today; over the same period, McCain's favorable rating has increased from 59% to 62%. While these changes are not large, the most interesting finding is that the change in opinions of Obama has come only among Republicans and independents; Democrats' views of Obama (and of McCain, for that matter) have not changed. These changes, which are all relatively slight, may reflect the type of normal fluctuation one sees in election seasons, or perhaps emerging negative reactions to Obama's recent trip. The trip may also be responsible for the difference in the preferences of likely versus registered voters found in the new USA Today/Gallup Poll. McCain gains among likely voters compared with registered voters in this poll, something he has not done in previous USA Today/Gallup Polls this year.

The reasons for the discrepancy between registered and likely voters in this poll as compared with previous polls are not entirely clear, but the data show that in this poll, Republicans have become slightly more likely to say they are giving quite a lot of thought to the election, while independents and Democrats are giving less thought to it than they have throughout this year. In other words, Republicans have become more attentive to the election on a relative basis, which increases their percentage of the likely voter pool. A Democratic advantage in thought being given to the election (and indeed in qualifying as a likely voter, according to Gallup's model) is not the norm historically, so in some ways, after the excitement of the Democratic nomination campaign has subsided, the current poll may suggest that the electorate is returning to a more usual state of affairs.

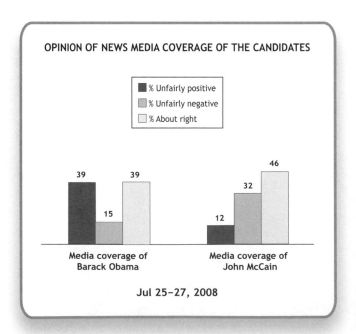

OPINION OF NEWS MEDIA COVERAGE OF THE CANDIDATES

■ % Unfairly positive
■ % Unfairly negative
□ % About right

Media coverage of Barack Obama: 39, 15, 39
Media coverage of John McCain: 12, 32, 46

Jul 25–27, 2008

OPINION OF NEWS MEDIA COVERAGE OF THE CANDIDATES

	Unfairly positive	Unfairly negative	About right
McCain supporters			
Coverage of Obama	61%	9%	24%
Coverage of McCain	5%	49%	40%
Obama supporters			
Coverage of Obama	21%	21%	53%
Coverage of McCain	18%	18%	55%

Jul 25–27, 2008

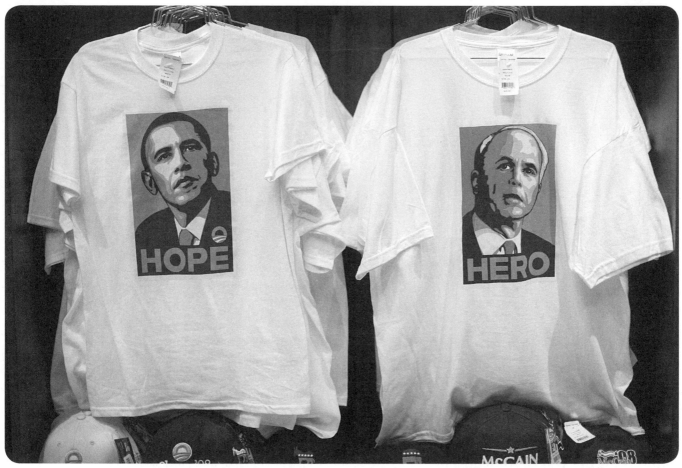

Competing T-shirts of presumptive candidates Barack Obama (left) and John McCain (right) hang in a gift shop in Washington, D.C. *(Jae C. Hong/AP Images)*

It is difficult to pinpoint the exact causes of any of the changes in voter perceptions discussed above. But the available data show that Republicans are strongly convinced that the media are much too positive in their coverage of Obama and too negative in their coverage of McCain. The media's coverage of Obama's foreign trip, coupled with

a strong reaction from McCain and other conservatives, may have had the seemingly paradoxical effect of increasing Republicans' energy and excitement about voting for McCain. If this is the case, the degree to which this effect is short-term versus long-term is still not clear.

JULY 30

Afghan War Edges Out Iraq as Most Important for United States

By a slim margin, Americans say the war in Afghanistan is more important for the United States than is the conflict in Iraq. This question was asked for the first time in the July 25–27 USA Today/Gallup Poll, so there is no historical record of changes over time, if any, in the public's views of the relative importance of these two wars. President Bush in essence began both wars, sending U.S. troops into Afghanistan in the fall of 2001 and into Iraq in March 2003. Faced with a choice between the two, however, Republicans tilt toward saying the Iraq conflict is more important. Independents and Democrats say the Afghan war is more

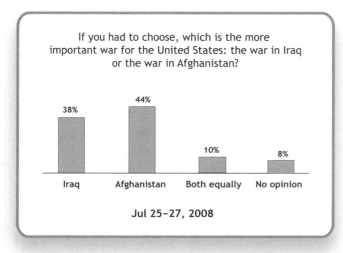

If you had to choose, which is the more important war for the United States: the war in Iraq or the war in Afghanistan?

38% Iraq
44% Afghanistan
10% Both equally
8% No opinion

Jul 25–27, 2008

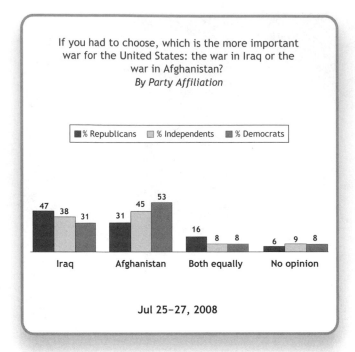

If you had to choose, which is the more important war for the United States: the war in Iraq or the war in Afghanistan?
By Party Affiliation

Jul 25–27, 2008

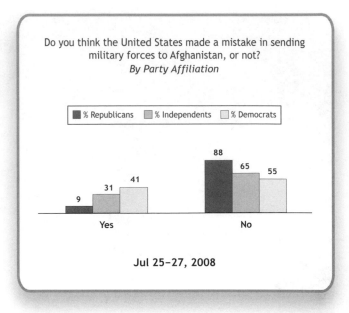

Do you think the United States made a mistake in sending military forces to Afghanistan, or not?
By Party Affiliation

Jul 25–27, 2008

important. These results reinforce the conclusion that the Iraq War has been the more politicized (and controversial) of the two wars.

Support for the War in Afghanistan

Americans appear to strongly support the initial decision to go to war in Afghanistan, based on responses to Gallup's classic "mistake" question (which has been asked about U.S. conflicts since the Korean War in the early 1950s). Two-thirds (68%) affirm that sending military forces to Afghanistan was not a mistake. There is a significant difference in the way the three partisan groups respond to this question, although

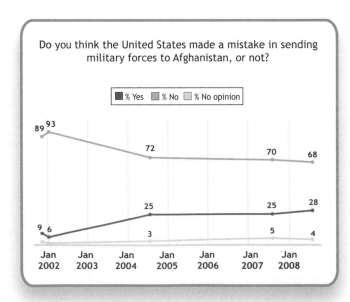

Do you think the United States made a mistake in sending military forces to Afghanistan, or not?

less than half of any group says the Afghanistan intervention was a mistake. Support for U.S. military involvement in Afghanistan decreased between 2002 and 2004 but has remained fairly constant since that point. The poll showing that two-thirds of Americans say the war in Afghanistan was *not* a mistake can be contrasted to polling in recent years showing that the majority of Americans have consistently said the war in Iraq *was* a mistake.

There has been a good deal of negative publicity in recent months about the way things are going for the United States in Afghanistan, but the current poll shows only a slight increase in the percentage of Americans who say things are going badly there. In general, views of the way the war is going are split.

Deploy More Troops in Afghanistan?

Should the United States send additional troops to Afghanistan, as has been advocated by some? The answer is a clear "yes" in the context of using those troops to combat terrorists. The July 25–27 poll included a question in which a random half of respondents were asked whether they favored or opposed sending additional U.S. troops from Iraq to Afghanistan to fight al-Qaeda and Taliban terrorist operations. The other half were asked about sending U.S. troops to Afghanistan to fight terrorists, but with no mention of where those troops would come from. The results show that it makes little difference whether the "from Iraq" phrase is included in the question wording; a majority favor sending additional troops in either case. There has been little change in these responses since last summer.

There are interesting differences by party in response to this question about sending more troops to Afghanistan.

Republicans are more in favor of sending troops when there is no mention of the troops coming "from Iraq"; Democrats are more in favor when "from Iraq" is included. The evidence reviewed here shows that Democrats feel the war in Afghanistan is more important than the war in Iraq, while Republicans believe the opposite. Republicans favor sending more troops to Afghanistan regardless, but a little less so if it means taking them away from Iraq. Democrats are more likely to approve of sending troops to Afghanistan if they come from Iraq.

Gallup Daily: Presidential Race Tightens to Four Points

After moving into a nine-percentage-point lead over John McCain in Gallup Poll daily tracking of national registered voters between July 25 and July 27, Barack Obama now leads by just four points, 46% to 42%. Today's results are based on Gallup Poll daily tracking from July 27 to July 29. The percentage of voters favoring Obama for president swelled from 45% in July 21–23 tracking, conducted at the outset of Obama's weeklong visit to Europe and the Middle East, to 49% in July 24–26 interviewing, conducted at the height of the publicity surrounding the tour. At the same time, McCain's support ebbed from 43% to 40%, and the percentage of undecided voters fell from 7% to 4%. With Obama now back on U.S. soil and taking up less of the nightly news, voter preferences have reverted to their pre-trip levels.

Obama Retains Strength Among the Highly Educated

Barack Obama has by far his greatest strength among voters with postgraduate education, while John McCain has his highest level of support among voters who have a college degree but no postgraduate education. This analysis is based on Gallup's detailed assessment of the vote within educational subgroups. The latest update, consisting of more than 6,000 interviews conducted between July 21 and July 27, shows that the relationship between education and the Obama-versus-McCain margin in the presidential vote is a U-shaped curve of sorts. Presumptive Democratic nominee Obama does well compared with McCain among those without a college degree and among those with postgraduate education. McCain enjoys his strongest support among those with a college degree.

There is also an interesting trend in the proportion of each educational group that is undecided. The percentage of undecided voters is highest among those with the least formal education and shrinks among groups with higher average educational attainment. The data indicate that McCain's strength among college graduates, compared with his standing among those with less than a college education, is based on his gaining as the percentage of undecideds decreases. Obama's percentage of the vote is relatively constant across all three groups of those with college educations or less.

WHITES, BY EDUCATION

Obama wins overwhelmingly among blacks across all educational levels. An analysis of voter preference by education among whites, however (with blacks and Hispanics taken out of the equation), shows the same basic pattern as is the case among all voters. Overall, as has been well established, McCain does much better against Obama among whites in general than he does among nonwhites. The presumptive Republican nominee in fact "wins" among each educational group of whites except those with postgraduate education. But as is the case with respect to all voters, McCain's relative advantage is greatest among college graduates, and the data to a degree reflect the same U-shaped curve evident among all voters.

Education and Voter Preference Across Elections

The overall pattern of voter preference by education this summer is roughly consistent with that of the last presidential election in 2004, although the margins within each group vary across elections. In 2004, Gallup's final analysis of the vote showed John Kerry winning among voters with high school educations or less and winning among those with postgraduate education—similar to Obama's edge among these groups today. Bush won among those with college degrees (but no postgraduate education) in 2004, as does McCain today (but by a slimmer margin). The biggest difference between the two years: Bush won strongly among those with some college in 2004, whereas Obama leads among that group at this point this year.

JULY 31
Nearly Half of Adults Now Applaud the Iraq Surge

A new USA Today/Gallup Poll finds nearly half of Americans saying the U.S. troop surge in Iraq, now over, has made the situation there better, up from 40% in February and just 22% a year ago. Similarly, the percentage believing the surge "is not making much difference" has declined from 51% a year ago and 38% in February to just 32%. The net result is that, for the first time, Americans are about evenly divided in their overall assessment of the surge: Forty-eight

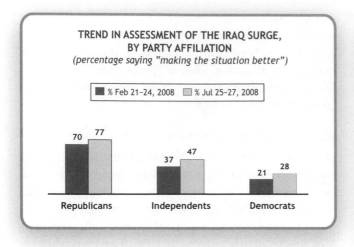

TREND IN ASSESSMENT OF THE IRAQ SURGE, BY PARTY AFFILIATION
(percentage saying "making the situation better")

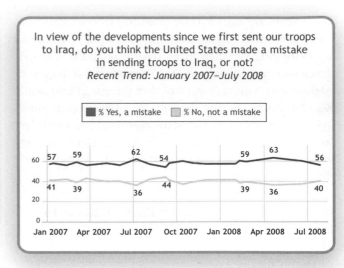

In view of the developments since we first sent our troops to Iraq, do you think the United States made a mistake in sending troops to Iraq, or not?
Recent Trend: January 2007–July 2008

percent say it is making the situation better, while a combined 49% indicate it is not. Although this balance of views is still not highly positive, it is more of an endorsement of the surge than what Gallup has previously found. Gallup's very first reading on this question, from July 2007, was the most negative, with half of Americans (51%) believing the surge was having no impact and as many saying it was making matters worse as that it was improving things. Since then, the percentage crediting the surge with making things better has gradually increased, and the percentage saying it is having no impact has decreased. There has been less change in the percentage blaming the surge for creating more problems, which has varied within an eight-point range, from 25% to 17%. Americans' views about the surge have been, and remain, highly politicized. However, all three partisan groups—Republicans, independents, and Democrats—have grown more likely since February to believe the surge is helping.

NO RIPPLE EFFECT ON WAR VIEWS

Americans' growing confidence in the surge does not appear to be softening their broader criticism of the Iraq War. Although close to half of Americans now believe the surge is helping the situation in Iraq, the majority continue to say that sending troops to Iraq was a "mistake," and that things there are going "badly" for the United States. Neither of these views has changed much in recent months. The 56% saying the war is a mistake in the July 25–27 poll is similar to the 60% last month and the 59% in February. In fact, despite some fluctuation, views on this question have not changed substantively for the past 18 months.

Gallup now finds 46% of Americans saying things are going very or moderately well for the United States in Iraq, while 51% say things are going moderately or very badly. The last time this question was asked, in November/December 2007, a similar number (43%) said things were going well, while slightly more (56%) said they were going badly. However, today's results are not much different from those recorded in January 2006. In what could be Gallup's final assessment of the U.S. troop surge in Iraq that started in 2007 and ended earlier this month, Americans credit the surge with bringing about some progress in Iraq—but not enough to convince them that the war is going well for the United States, or that sending troops there initially was the right course of action.

AUGUST 2008

Over the first eight months of 2008, Democrats have consistently rated the economy more poorly than Republicans have, while independents have tended to align more closely with the Democrats rather than the Republicans on this issue. Although respondents from all three political groups have become somewhat less pessimistic about the economy during the first half of August, Democrats remain highly negative about current conditions, with 54% rating the economy "poor"—more than twice the 25% "poor" rating of Republicans. Independents' views of the economy (46% "poor") align more closely with Democrats' views than with those of Republicans. Democrats are also highly pessimistic about the future direction of the economy, with 86% in early August saying things are getting worse. This is far higher than the 64% of Republicans who answer similarly but aligns fairly well with the 81% of independents who hold a similar view. At the same time, all party groups' assessments both of current economic conditions and of the economic outlook have become more positive in the first part of August as compared with July. "Poor" ratings of the economy are down 6 points among Democrats, 5 points among independents, and 3 points among Republicans. During the same period, there have been declines of between 5 and 12 points among the three groups in the percentage saying the economy is getting worse.

Gallup polling over the first eight months of 2008 has shown Democrats and independents to be consistently more negative than their Republican counterparts about the condition of the economy and its prospects. This finding has continued over the past several weeks, even as overall consumer perceptions have become somewhat less negative in response to falling gasoline prices. They clearly indicate that views of the economy are heavily influenced by partisanship.

The nation's economic distress is likely to be the top issue at the Democratic National Convention. It would appear that Democrats are well positioned to pick up independent support after their convention, since the two groups seem to share a great deal of pessimism about the future direction of the economy. However, this does not necessarily mean that the majority of Americans will share the Democrats' enthusiasm about their specific proposals for reinvigorating the economy. For example, Americans generally share the Democrats' view that the "wealthy" do not pay enough in taxes. On the other hand, when given a choice about how government should address the numerous economic difficulties facing consumers today, 84% of Americans prefer that the government focus on improving overall economic conditions and jobs, while only 13% prefer that the government respond by taking steps to distribute wealth more evenly. How Democrats end up balancing these two seemingly contradictory views may play a significant role in how they fare this November.

AUGUST 1
Views of Obama on International Matters Little Changed

A clear aim of Barack Obama's overseas trip in late July—to Europe, Afghanistan, and Iraq and other Middle Eastern countries—was to demonstrate to Americans who questioned his foreign policy credentials that he is up to the job of commander in chief of the military and can handle key matters of foreign policy. However, at least in the short term, the trip does not appear to have accomplished that goal. Just 52% say Obama can handle the job of commander in chief, compared with a 55% reading before the trip. Additionally, Americans are no more likely now than before Obama's trip to believe he would do a good job as president of handling the issues of terrorism and the Iraq War. These findings are based on the July

CHRONOLOGY

AUGUST 2008

August 7–13 Fighting breaks out in South Ossetia and Abkhazia, two disputed areas inside Georgia. Russian troops intervene in both places and engage Georgian forces. The United States and other nations condemn the intervention, and a ceasefire is arranged on August 13.

August 8 Former presidential candidate John Edwards admits to having had an affair with a campaign worker.

August 8–24 The Olympic Games are held in Beijing, China.

August 16 Barack Obama and John McCain appear, back-to-back but separately, at Saddleback Church in Orange County, California. The forum is hosted by Saddleback's popular preacher and nationally known author Rick Warren.

August 18 Pervez Musharraf, long a U. S. ally, resigns as Pakistan's president.

August 20 McCain is criticized by the Obama camp for being out of touch with the problems of regular Americans when he is unable to say how many homes he owns during an interview with the Web site Politico.com. Later McCain says he owns seven homes.

August 22 A United States air strike, intending to target Taliban militants, accidentally kills dozens of civilians in Afghanistan.

August 23 Obama selects Delaware senator Joe Biden as his vice presidential running mate.

August 25–28 The Democratic National Convention is held in Denver.

August 26 Hillary Clinton receives a standing ovation during her speech to the Democratic convention. She tells her supporters to give their votes to Obama.

August 28 Obama gives his acceptance speech outdoors to a crowd of 80,000 at Invesco Field.

August 29 McCain chooses Alaska governor Sarah Palin as his vice presidential running mate.

25–27 USA Today/Gallup Poll, conducted just as Obama was ending his trip abroad. The lack of positive momentum in perceptions that Obama can handle the military or key international issues means that Republican presidential candidate John McCain still retains a significant advantage over Obama in terms of being commander in chief and dealing with terrorism. This is not unexpected, given the extensive foreign policy and military experience

McCain has accrued while serving in Congress for more than two decades (and in the U.S. Navy for most of the rest of his adult life). Obama did not serve in the military and has been in the Senate for only four years, though he does serve on the Senate Foreign Relations Committee.

The two candidates are more evenly matched on the Iraq War issue, even as McCain continues to criticize Obama for not backing the surge of U.S. troops to Iraq, which by most accounts appears to have worked. At least on this issue, Obama is able to offset McCain's experience in foreign policy matters because of his long-held opposition to the war, which appeals to the majority of Americans who consider the war to have been a mistake.

One area of international relations in which Obama appears to have an advantage over McCain is diplomacy. When asked to rate how each candidate would handle "relations with other countries," a total of 62% say Obama would do a good job, while 55% say McCain would. But when respondents are asked to choose which of the two would do a better job in this area, Obama wins by a comfortable 52% to 37% margin. This particular question was not asked prior to the Obama trip, so it is unclear whether his standing is any better or worse than it was

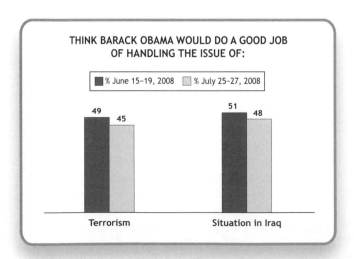

THINK BARACK OBAMA WOULD DO A GOOD JOB OF HANDLING THE ISSUE OF:

■ % June 15–19, 2008   ▨ % July 25–27, 2008

Terrorism: 49, 45

Situation in Iraq: 51, 48

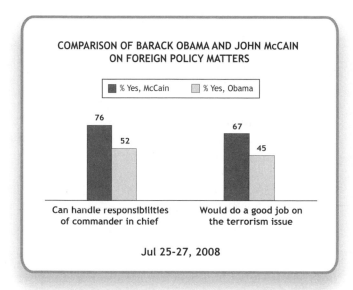

COMPARISON OF BARACK OBAMA AND JOHN McCAIN
ON FOREIGN POLICY MATTERS

Jul 25-27, 2008

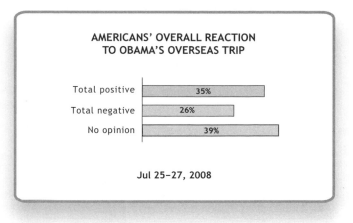

AMERICANS' OVERALL REACTION
TO OBAMA'S OVERSEAS TRIP

Jul 25-27, 2008

before his overseas tour. Many of the images of Obama's trip showed him meeting with foreign leaders, so it would not be surprising if the trip did help him somewhat in this regard.

In addition to assessing the candidates' perceived competence with respect to foreign policy matters, the poll asked for Americans' judgments about the candidates' ability to handle two major domestic issues: the economy and energy. On both of these domestic issues, more Americans say Obama would do a good job than say McCain would—by margins of 54% to 43% on energy, and 50% to 39% on energy and gas prices.

Implications for the Obama Campaign

Clearly, Obama still has some work to do to convince Americans he can handle some of the international

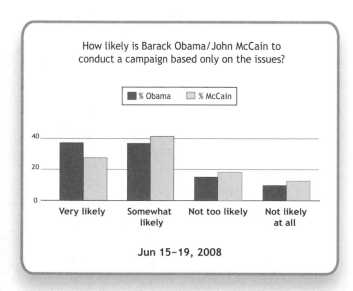

How likely is Barack Obama/John McCain to
conduct a campaign based only on the issues?

Jun 15-19, 2008

responsibilities of the presidency. While Obama already is viewed as being better than McCain at handling "relations with other countries," McCain has wide advantages over Obama in perceptions that he would be able to handle the job of commander in chief and would do a good job with respect to handling terrorism. Even though fewer Americans say Obama is able to handle the role of commander in chief than say this about McCain, a majority of Americans do think the Illinois senator is up to the task. In some ways, it may not be as important for Obama to close this perceptual gap with McCain as it is to keep his own percentage above the majority level. That may especially be true in an election year when Americans rate domestic issues like the economy and energy as the top issues that will affect their vote. Thus, Obama could in theory win the election on the basis of his perceived strengths on domestic issues, so long as Americans don't disqualify him for perceived weaknesses on military and defense issues.

AUGUST 3

Gallup Daily: Obama 45%, McCain 44%

Democrat Barack Obama and Republican John McCain remain statistically tied in the latest Gallup Poll daily tracking update for July 31–August 2, with Obama at 45% and McCain at 44% among registered voters. The results reflect a fairly steady pattern of voter sentiment over the last several days, with the two candidates either tied in an absolute sense or, as in today's average, statistically tied. As has been the case all summer, the race appears to be settling back into a pattern where Obama has a small margin over McCain. The overall average margin for June and July has been three percentage points in Obama's favor, despite some brief periods when Obama led statistically within the margin of error and other times when the race was tied. Obama has been unable to sustain a significant lead over

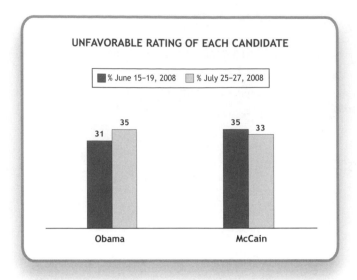

UNFAVORABLE RATING OF EACH CANDIDATE

% June 15–19, 2008   % July 25–27, 2008

Obama: 31, 35
McCain: 35, 33

McCain, and the latter has been unable to achieve even a small lead over Obama.

AUGUST 5

Voters Not Strongly Backing Incumbents for Congress

In a year when approval of Congress has reached a new low, just 36% of registered voters say most members of Congress deserve re-election. This is among the lowest ratings Gallup has measured in any recent presidential or congressional election year. These results are based on a July 25–27 USA Today/Gallup Poll of 900 registered voters nationwide. The poll was conducted before Congress began a month-long recess late last week. Gallup has found ratings in the neighborhood of the current 36% in three other election years: 1992, 1994, and 2006. The elections in all of these years brought about significant change in the membership of Congress. In the 1994 and 2006 midterm election years, when only 38% of registered voters said most members of Congress were deserving of another term, enough seats switched party hands that control of Congress switched from one party to the other—from the Democrats to the Republicans in 1994 and from the Republicans to the Democrats in 2006. In the presidential election year of 1992, when only 29% of registered voters said most members deserved re-election, Congress experienced considerable turnover, but Democrats retained party control and the actual change in the party composition of Congress was much less than in 1994 or 2006. That may have been because a large number of incumbent members retired rather than run for re-election in 1992—or simply because the congres-

sional elections were overshadowed by the presidential election that year.

DOES YOUR REPRESENTATIVE DESERVE TO BE RE-ELECTED?

Voters are usually much more charitable when asked whether their own member of Congress—as opposed to most members—deserves to be re-elected, and that is the case in the latest poll: 57% of registered voters say the U.S. representative from their own congressional district deserves to be re-elected. Still, that is at the low end of what Gallup has historically measured with respect to one's own representative: slightly higher than the 1994 and 2006 readings (both 54%), and somewhat better than the all-time low of 48% recorded in 1992. Both questions (with respect to most members and your own representative) seem to show similar changes from one poll to another, and low ratings in both responses tend to presage significant turnover in Congress. Accordingly, congressional incumbents may be in for a bumpy ride during this fall's campaign, as many try to hold on to their seats in a year when voters are looking to change the government.

On a variety of measures, 2008 looks like a better year for Democrats than for Republicans. But at the same time, Democrats have control of both houses of Congress. So it is not immediately clear which party's incumbents might be more vulnerable if voters want to change Congress. The poll sought to get some traction on this question by asking voters to report whether their member of Congress was a Republican or a Democrat. That gives a sense of whom voters have in mind when they say their member of Congress does or does not deserve re-election. In fact, a fairly large proportion of voters (35%) are unsure whether their member of Congress is a Democrat or a Republican. But among those who are aware of that, the data suggest that Democratic members might be a little safer this year than Republicans. Among voters who report that their member of Congress is a Democrat, 64% say he or she deserves re-election, compared with 57% who say their Republican representative deserves another term. Among the roughly one in three voters who are unsure whether a Republican or a Democrat represents their district, barely half (51%) say their member deserves to be re-elected.

Implications for the Election

One major theme of the 2008 election thus far has been "change." Most of the presidential candidates sounded that theme during their campaigns, but voters apparently are in the mood to change Congress as well. Typically, when lower percentages of voters say their member of Congress and most members of Congress deserve re-election, the membership of Congress is shaken up on Election Day. There are, however, countervailing forces that make the direction of the coming change somewhat unpredictable this year. The Democrats hold the majority of seats in Congress in a year when Congress is historically unpopular, but the political environment in 2008 seems to favor the Democrats. Our data suggest that the favorable political environment may be the stronger force at work, given that voters with a Democrat representing them are more likely to say that that representative deserves another term than are voters with a Republican representing them.

AUGUST 6

Independents Remain Split Between Obama and McCain

Barack Obama's lead over John McCain in Gallup Poll daily tracking of national registered voters fell from an average of six percentage points for the week of July 21–27 (47% vs. 41%) to an average of just one point from July 28 to August 3 (45% vs. 44%). Obama's slightly elevated support from July 21 to July 27 included his widest three-day rolling average lead over McCain to date: a nine-percentage-point lead in Gallup Poll daily tracking conducted between July 24 and July 26, 49% to 40%. Voter preferences on an average weekly basis have been highly stable since early June. However, with more than 6,000 registered voters underlying each set of weekly numbers, the contraction of the race between the last two full weekly aggregates is statistically significant. More recently, Gallup Poll daily tracking reports from August 4 to August 6 have tended to show Obama with a slight lead. The aggregated dataset for July 21–27 showed Obama enjoying slightly higher than usual levels of support from women, Hispanics, the non-college-educated, and conservative Democrats. But in the most recent weekly aggregate, from July 28 to August 3 Obama's support levels from these groups have reverted to what can be considered the norm.

Still, throughout both periods, Obama maintained broad levels of support among his standard core constituency groups: Democrats, liberals, moderates, women, 18- to 29-year-olds, blacks, Hispanics, those with no religious affiliation, and postgraduates. He holds solid leads over McCain among all of these groups in Gallup tracking from July 28 to August 3. In contrast to these electoral

advantages for Obama, McCain does reliably well among men, seniors, whites, conservatives, Protestants, and, of course, Republicans. Major subgroups of the population affording neither candidate a large or consistent edge include 30- to 49-year-olds, 50- to 64-year-olds, college graduates, those with some college education, those with no college education, political independents, and Catholics. The weekly trends in the candidate preferences of these "swing" groups since June show just how close the race is among these groups. Perhaps most important is the tight nature of the race among independents. Also of note, Obama held a slight edge among Catholics in mid- to late July, but those gains were erased in tracking from July 28 to August 3. The aggregated weekly data for the other swing groups show no clear shifts over time in favor of either Obama or McCain.

In terms of building a winning coalition this November, McCain and Obama each start with nearly universal support from their political bases in the Republican and Democratic parties. Initial Republican concerns that McCain would have difficulty retaining the support of conservatives have not panned out, nor have fears that Hillary Clinton's supporters would defect from the party in droves should Obama be nominated. This seems to shift the focus of the contest primarily to political independents—long known to be a McCain strength, but also fertile ground for Obama, given his strong appeal to young, generally independent voters. Gallup's weekly aggregate trends document how close the election has been, and remains, among the politically unanchored middle, as well as among certain age, educational, and religious subgroups. If the race starts to change, it will most likely do so among these voters.

AUGUST 11

Candidates Have Received Poll Bounces After Naming Vice Presidents

With Barack Obama and John McCain poised to announce their vice presidential running mates in the coming weeks, a review of Gallup Poll data finds that, since 1996, presidential candidates have received slight bumps in support in the polls after naming their vice presidential running mates. Historically, presidential nominations were decided at the party conventions, as a result of which vice presidential running mates were also selected at the conventions. That made it difficult to disentangle the effect on a candidate's support of naming a vice presidential running mate from the "convention bounce" that presidential candidates have typically received. This situation has changed in recent elections. With the nominees known long before the conventions take place, presidential candidates have been announcing their vice presidential choices in advance of the conventions. And now that these vice presidential announcements are separate events from the conventions, polling can better isolate any impact the announcement of a running mate has on presidential preferences.

Since 1996, Gallup has conducted polls in the small window of time *after* the announcement of a presidential candidate's running mate but *before* the convention has taken place. During this time, there have been four instances of nonincumbent presidential candidates choosing a running mate: the announcements by Bob Dole in 1996, George W. Bush and Al Gore in 2000, and John Kerry in 2004. A comparison of the multi-night polls taken before and after these candidates announced their vice presidential running mates shows an average five-point increase in the candidate's support.

1996

In 1996, Bill Clinton was seeking a second term as president and Gore a second term as vice president, with Republican Dole challenging them. Dole selected former congressman and secretary of housing and urban development Jack Kemp as his running mate on August 11. Clinton had a commanding lead in the polls through much of the summer, and the last poll before Dole chose Kemp (conducted between August 5 and August 7) showed Clinton with a 52% to 30% lead over Dole among registered voters. The next Gallup Poll, conducted between August 14 and August 15, confirmed an increase in Dole's support (which had been evident in a one-night reaction poll conducted on August 11). The August 14–15 poll showed Dole's support increasing nine points, from 30% to 39%, cutting Clinton's lead in half. A Gallup Poll conducted immediately after the Republican National Convention showed Dole narrowing the gap even further, with Clinton holding just a 48% to 41% lead.

Clinton's own support varied little during this time, ranging between 48% and 52%. Thus, the Dole surge seemed to come mostly at the expense of Reform Party candidate Ross Perot, whose support was 12% before the Kemp announcement and 7% afterward. Dole's surge proved to be short-lived, however. A week after the Republican convention concluded, Clinton had re-established a double-digit lead (50% to 38%), and he, too, received a bounce after his party's convention in late August (55% to 34%), which essentially put the race back where it was at the beginning of August. Clinton went on to win the election by 49% to 41%.

2000

Republican Bush and Democrat Gore vied to succeed Clinton as president in the 2000 election. On July 24, Bush decided to name the chairman of his vice presidential search committee, Dick Cheney, as his running mate. The last Gallup Poll prior to this date showed Bush (43%) and Gore (41%) essentially tied among registered voters. A July 25–26 poll showed Bush doing slightly better than before he chose Cheney, leading Gore 46% to 41%, which was a three-point increase in Bush's support. (A one-night poll conducted July 24 showed Bush getting a larger, six-point bounce.) The modest bump Bush got after the selection of Cheney presaged an even larger convention bounce for Bush (from 46% to 54%). Similar to the pattern seen with Clinton in 1996, support for Gore held steady during Bush's vice presidential selection phase (at 41%), meaning that Bush's expanded support came from undecided voters and minor party–candidate supporters.

Gore announced his vice presidential running mate, Connecticut senator Joe Lieberman, just a few days after the Republican National Convention in 2000, and the announcement helped to blunt the impact of the Republican convention bounce for Bush. Gore's support among registered voters increased by five points in the August 11–12 Gallup Poll. (A one-night poll conducted on August 7, the night Gore selected Lieberman, showed an eight-point increase in Gore's support.) So while Gore still trailed Bush by a considerable margin, Gore's standing clearly improved after his naming of Lieberman. Like Bush, Gore got a significant convention bounce, and immediately after the Democratic National Convention he had overtaken Bush in the polls. Bush and Gore continued their hotly contested campaign throughout the fall and into December, when Bush finally won the election.

2004

Kerry was the Democratic challenger to Bush in 2004, and Kerry chose his nomination rival, John Edwards, as his running mate on July 6, several weeks before the Democratic National Convention. Kerry, who was essentially tied with Bush among registered voters in late June, saw his support increase by four points after he named Edwards (from 46% to 50%), according to a July 8–11 Gallup Poll. As a result, Kerry moved into an eight-point lead over Bush. About 10 days later, Gallup's pre–Democratic convention poll found Kerry still holding an advantage over Bush, though it had narrowed to four points. Kerry's share of the vote in the polls was down slightly to 47%, compared with 46% before he chose Edwards. Thus, any benefit Kerry received from announcing Edwards diminished rather quickly, and by the time the Democratic convention had ended, Bush had moved back into a statistical tie with Kerry, as Kerry received no convention bounce. Bush went on to win a narrow victory over Kerry on Election Day.

Implications for the Campaign: Uncertain

Gallup election trends suggest that recent nonincumbent presidential candidates have received a boost in the polls, ranging from three to nine points (and averaging five points), after naming their vice presidential running mates. This "vice presidential bounce" is separate from and precedes the usual convention bounce. Even though it is unclear whether vice presidential candidates materially aid a presidential candidate's election fortunes, the vice presidential announcements are among the most talked about and anticipated events of the campaign.

When a candidate announces his choice of running mate, he can expect to dominate the news with what is usually very positive coverage. And such a wave of positive coverage can usually fuel a bounce in the polls, as it does around the conventions. Of course, the vice presidential announcement is quickly overtaken by other campaign events, such as the conventions themselves and, later, the debates. Perhaps as a result, at least in recent years, any impact of the vice presidential announcement has proven to be short-lived. So far in the 2008 campaign, McCain and Obama have remained fairly closely matched. These data suggest the potential for their vice presidential announcements to shake up, at least temporarily, the structure of the race.

AUGUST 12

Support for Third-Party Candidates Appears Limited Thus Far

A new Gallup Poll finds only 2% of registered voters naming a third party candidate when asked in an open-ended fashion whom they will vote for this fall. The question, part of an August 7–10 Gallup Poll, allowed respondents to name any candidate or political party, without any prompting of specific names from Gallup interviewers. This is a different approach than Gallup takes in its daily tracking polling and USA Today/Gallup Polls, in which voters are asked whether they would vote for Barack Obama or John McCain for president if the election were held today. With the open-ended question used in the new poll, 83% of registered voters named either Obama (45%) or McCain (38%) as their preferred candidate. Obama's seven-point advantage over McCain on the open-ended ballot is similar to the five-point lead he currently holds in Gallup's daily tracking

poll. Another 1% of voters mentioned Hillary Clinton, who conceded the Democratic nomination to Obama in early June after a long and intense campaign but who retains a loyal following. An additional 1% mentioned one of several other candidates (mainly Republicans) who are ineligible to run (George W. Bush) or have long since ended their campaigns (Mitt Romney, Mike Huckabee, and Ron Paul) and will not appear on the ballot this fall. Thirteen percent of registered voters are either undecided (6%) or say they do not plan to vote (7%).

That leaves only about 2% who say they plan to vote for a third-party candidate in November—not much different from the 1% in Gallup Poll daily tracking who typically volunteer that they will vote for someone other than Obama or McCain. On the open-ended question, 1% specifically name Libertarian Party candidate Bob Barr and 1% name Ralph Nader, who is running as an independent this year after unsuccessful presidential bids in 1996, 2000, and 2004. Less than 1% mention the name of Cynthia McKinney, the Green Party's nominee. No other organized third parties running a presidential candidate were named by poll respondents. It is important to note that Gallup interviewers accepted either the actual name of the candidate *or* the candidate's party affiliation as a valid response. So, for example, if a supporter of the Libertarian Party was not aware that Barr was the party's candidate but still volunteered the name of the party, his or her response would still be registered as a Libertarian vote.

Measuring Third-Party Support

There are certainly trade-offs in trying to get an accurate read on third-party candidate support. Each election year, Gallup uses a variety of approaches, including third party candidate name identification, the open-ended question reported here, and prompted ballots, in which the names of all candidates who will appear on the ballot in most states are read, to try to assess the level of third-party voting. These questions not only help inform Gallup about the level of third-party voting, but also indicate whether a third-party candidate merits inclusion in Gallup's standard presidential trial heat question. The standard closed-ended Gallup trial heat question used in Gallup Poll daily tracking and USA Today/Gallup polling has thus far in 2008 not included the names of minor party candidates. Doing so runs the risk of overestimating their actual support and affecting poll accuracy, based on a comparison of final pre-election poll estimates with the actual vote on Election Day. Typically, unless there has been a well-known and well-funded third party candidate running (like Ross Perot in 1992 and 1996), minor party candidates have accounted for about 1% to 2% of the actual vote on Election Day. Recent polls by other firms that have included the names of minor party candidates in their presidential trial heats find total third-party support ranging from 5% to 10% among registered voters.

Even though Gallup does not read the names of minor party candidates in its standard closed-ended question, it does accept volunteered responses of minor party candidates (about 1% in tracking so far this year). Still, it is possible that individual respondents might think they can choose only from among the names read when the standard question is asked, and thus may not realize that they can volunteer the name of a third-party candidate. The open-ended question gets around this potential pitfall by putting all candidates on an equal footing, so to speak. No names are read, and therefore there can be no presupposition that the respondent must choose between the two major party candidates. Thus, if there is significant unmeasured support for a candidate outside of the two major parties that is not being detected through volunteered responses to the standard closed-ended question, the open-ended question should pick it up—particularly if voters are highly committed to voting for a particular third-party candidate.

Gallup's standard measure of listing the candidates when asking the presidential trial heat question dates back to the 1936 election and attempts to mimic the act of voting as closely as possible. When voters cast their ballots on Election Day, the candidates' names and party affiliations are listed on the ballot for them to see. The open-ended question thus requires a higher level of knowledge of the candidates running than does voting itself, but is a useful secondary approach to make sure the standard ballot is not missing any undetected third-party support. While it is not out of the question that third-party voting could be higher this year than it has been in most recent elections, the new Gallup Poll clearly suggests there is no unmeasured groundswell of support for any of the minor party candidates running at this point in the campaign.

AUGUST 13

Gender Gap Among White Voters Larger Now Than in 2004

John McCain continues to have a significant advantage over Barack Obama among non-Hispanic white males but does much less well among white females—winning among the former by a 20-point margin while only tying Obama among the latter. This finding, based on Gallup Poll daily tracking interviews with more than 8,200 non-

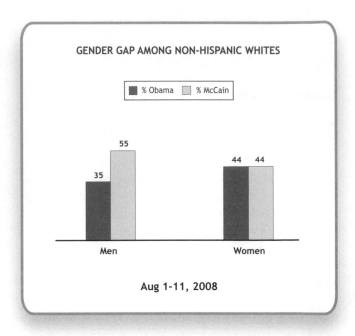

GENDER GAP AMONG NON-HISPANIC WHITES

■ % Obama □ % McCain

Men: 35, 55
Women: 44, 44

Aug 1-11, 2008

Hispanic white registered voters conducted from August 1 to August 11, shows that McCain now does slightly better among white men as compared with George W. Bush's final position against John Kerry in the 2004 election. But McCain is doing worse than Bush among white women. The net effect of this expanded gender gap is to give Obama a slightly better position among whites than was the case for Kerry in 2004.

Gender Gap Among Whites in Historical Perspective

Democratic presidential candidates have generally done less well among white men than among white women in recent elections. But the gap between the two genders among whites is significantly larger this year than it was in 2004. In Gallup's final poll of registered voters in late October 2004, Kerry trailed Bush by 9 points among non-Hispanic white women and by 16 points among non-Hispanic white men. That produced a 7-point gender gap, about one-third the size of this year's 20-point gap.

McCain's relative advantage among men is slightly better this year than was Bush's in 2004. But McCain has lost ground to Obama among white women: Bush's 9-point lead over Kerry among this group four years ago has evaporated. The larger gender gap overall is giving Obama a modest boost as compared with the final positioning of the 2004 candidates. In Gallup's late–October 2004 poll, Kerry was behind Bush by 12 points among non-Hispanic white registered voters; this year, Obama trails McCain by a modestly smaller 9-point margin. Obama's gains among white women more than compensate for his slight loss of positioning among white men.

EDUCATION

The impact of education in patterns of support for Obama and McCain plays out differently between white men and white women. Among men, McCain leads regardless of education. He does particularly well among white men with some college and those who are college graduates, slightly less well among those who have high school educations or less, and least well among white men with postgraduate educations (among whom he wins by just 6 points). The pattern is somewhat different among non-Hispanic white women. Obama trails McCain by 7 points among white women with high school educations or less, and then does progressively better among those with higher levels of formal education. Obama beats McCain by a slight margin among white women who are college graduates; remarkably, Obama has a very large 25-point margin among white women with postgraduate degrees.

Implications for the Election

The slightly weaker position for McCain in comparison with Obama among whites is not a major shift, but does represent a loss for McCain compared with his fellow Republican's performance among whites in 2004. The data show that the explanation lies with Obama's stronger showing among white women. Whereas Bush led Kerry by 9 points among white women in 2004, McCain and Obama are now tied among this group. This gain by Obama is partially mitigated by the fact that he does slightly less well among white men than did Kerry, but the net impact of the widening gender gap overall is a gain for Obama among whites.

There has been much talk about Obama's relative problems this year in appealing to white men, particularly those with less than a college education. The data reviewed here from early August show that Obama in general does indeed trail McCain significantly among white men, particularly those who have a college degree or less. This white male deficit appears to be slightly larger than it was for Kerry in 2004. But Obama's relative strength among white women, particularly those with postgraduate educations, has to this point more than made up for his deficit among white men.

AUGUST 19

Veterans Solidly Back McCain

With both presidential candidates addressing the Veterans of Foreign Wars convention this week, Gallup finds that registered voters who have served in the U.S. military solidly back McCain over Obama, 56% to 34%. This is based on aggregated data from August 5–17 Gallup Poll daily tracking, involving interviews with more than 11,000 registered voters, including 2,238 military veterans. Veterans are defined as those who are or have been members of the U.S. military. Obama leads McCain 46% to 43% among all registered voters during this time.

The veteran vote is of some interest this year given McCain's notable service in the navy, including several years as a prisoner of war in North Vietnam. Obama did not serve in the military. But even without the distinction provided this year by McCain's well-known military service, veterans tend to be Republican in their political orientation, and Republican candidates generally fare better than Democratic candidates among this voting group. For example, in Gallup's final pre-election poll in 2004, 55% of registered voters who had served in the military backed George W. Bush, compared with 39% who supported John Kerry. It is notable, then, that McCain is doing only about as well among military veterans as Bush did in 2004, despite the two Republican candidates' very different military backgrounds. (Bush was in the Texas Air National Guard but did not serve overseas.) Veterans' affinity for the Republican Party is confirmed by the finding that 47% of those who have served in the military currently identify with or lean to the Republican Party, while 39% identify with or lean to the Democratic Party. By comparison, 48% of all adults are Democratic in their party orientation and 37% are Republican. Even without the common bond of shared military service, veterans' alignment with McCain would not be surprising, given the demographic composition of the group. Veterans are overwhelmingly male (91% of the veterans in the sample are men) and tend to be older (the majority are age 50 or above). Those also happen to be two of McCain's stronger voting constituencies in this campaign.

Effect of Being a Veteran on the Vote

But how much does being a veteran influence one's choice for president? Does McCain's support among veterans reflect some effect borne of their shared military service, or does it merely reflect veterans' alignment with the Republican Party? Given the large sample size of veterans, one can assess the relative importance of the two factors by looking at veterans' candidate preferences while taking into account their party affiliation. The data show that there is a small effect of being a veteran over and above party affiliation, but party is clearly the dominant factor influencing vote choice. Among Republicans and Republican leaners, McCain is the choice of 89% of veterans compared with 83% of nonveterans, a difference of six percentage points. There is also a six-point difference in McCain's support among Democrats and Democratic leaners who have served in the military (17%) as opposed to those who have not done so (11%), but Obama is the overwhelming choice of Democratic supporters regardless of military service.

Summary: Military Service and Voter Preference

McCain clearly holds an advantage over Obama among veterans, but that is probably more because veterans tend to be Republicans than because McCain himself served in the military and is regarded by some as a war hero. Veterans showed similarly strong support for Bush in the 2004 presidential election. The data suggest a separate effect of military service on candidate preference, but it is rather small and is overwhelmed by the influence of party affiliation.

AUGUST 20

McCain Still Dominant Among the Highly Religious

John McCain continues to dominate Barack Obama among religious Americans, winning among those who attend worship services weekly by a 53% to 37% margin, and losing to Obama among those who seldom or never attend church by 54% to 34%. Both presidential candidates appeared on August 16 at a "Civil Forum on the Presidency" at Saddleback Church in California, moderated by the church's pastor, Rick Warren. The candidates answered questions about their faith and about other campaign and policy issues. The Gallup data reviewed here (from a Gallup aggregate of interviews conducted between August 11 and August 17) show that among those in attendance at the church, McCain was likely more well appreciated than Obama, as he no doubt was to religious voters around the country who watched on television. Not only does McCain do much better against Obama among those who attend church frequently, but he also beats Obama by an 8-point margin among Americans who say religion is important in their lives, while Obama wins by a 22-point margin among those for whom religion is not important.

This strong relationship between religiosity and voter behavior is not new. In 2004, Gallup data from late October showed that George W. Bush was ahead of John Kerry by a 19-point margin among registered voters who were weekly church attenders, while Kerry was ahead by a 24-point margin among registered voters who seldom or never attended church. Black Americans, however, are both highly religious and highly likely to vote Democratic

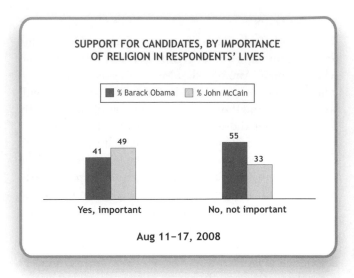

SUPPORT FOR CANDIDATES, BY IMPORTANCE OF RELIGION IN RESPONDENTS' LIVES

■ % Barack Obama   ▢ % John McCain

Yes, important: 41 / 49
No, not important: 55 / 33

Aug 11–17, 2008

in presidential contests—so when the data are restricted just to whites, the relationship between religion and voter preference is even more pronounced. Among whites, McCain has a very large 39-point margin among those who attend church weekly, while Obama still manages to win among whites who seldom or never attend church, albeit by a more modest 9-point margin. (In this same weekly aggregate, McCain beats Obama overall among whites by a 51% to 37% margin.)

Implications for the Election

The relationship between religiosity and identification with the Republican Party has been so strong in recent years that there is little question McCain will do well among this group in November. The relevant question is more about the degree to which highly religious white Americans are excited by the McCain candidacy and therefore willing to work for his election and to turn out on Election Day. At this point, the estimate is that McCain is doing about as well among registered voters who are weekly church attenders as Bush did in 2004.

Conventions Typically Result in Five-Point Bounce

To the extent that history is a guide, Barack Obama and John McCain can both expect to see some increase in voter support after their nominating conventions, an effect observed after nearly all of the 22 national conventions held since 1964. The median increase in support has been 5 percentage points. This "convention bounce" is an important part of the presidential campaign narrative. Gallup has data enabling it to reasonably estimate each presidential candidate's convention bounce dating back to 1964. All but two candidates—George McGovern in 1972 and John Kerry in 2004—saw their support among registered voters increase after their party's convention.

The largest bounce in Gallup's polling history was a 16-point increase for Bill Clinton after the 1992 Democratic National Convention, as Clinton and the Democrats successfully linked George H. W. Bush to the country's economic woes. Clinton seized the lead after that convention and never relinquished it on his way to winning the election. (Third-party candidate Ross Perot dropped out of the race while the convention was in progress, which created a political vacuum that Clinton helped fill; but the 16-point bounce is based on a comparison of Bush versus Clinton trial heats before and after the Democratic convention. Perot re-entered the 1992 presidential race on October 1.) Of course, it can be risky to predict the future based on historical patterns. In 2004, neither Kerry (whose support actually dropped by 1 point after his party's convention) nor George W. Bush (whose support increased by just 2 points) got a significant boost from their parties' conventions. Both fell well below the historical norm of 5-point increases, and they now rank as the single worst post-convention showings of any presidential candidate of their respective parties.

It is unclear at this point whether 2004 marks the start of a trend away from post-convention bounces or is a historical anomaly. One thing that distinguished 2004 from earlier elections is that voters were already tuned in to the campaign well before the conventions took place and likely already had given some thought to how they would vote. Thus, events at the conventions arguably might have had little effect on their preferences, whereas in earlier elections the conventions may have been the first time that many voters began to pay attention to the presidential race, and thus their preferences may have been more subject to change. So far, 2008 looks more like 2004 than like earlier elections in terms of pre-convention voter interest levels—so if the convention bounces of 1964 through 2000 were largely a product of low pre-convention levels of voter attention, then there might not be big surges in candidate support this year.

Factors Affecting the Size of the Bounce

History shows that a 5-point convention bounce has been typical, no matter which party's convention was involved, whether or not an incumbent candidate was running, or the order of the conventions. (The average or mean bounce of 6 points is slightly higher than the median 5-point bounce, but the mean is unduly influenced by the large 1992 Clinton result; the mean excluding that data

point is equivalent to the median of 5 points.) On average, Democratic candidates have enjoyed slightly larger bounces than Republicans (6.2 points to 5.3), but that difference is entirely due to the 1992 Clinton bounce; if that one example is taken out, then the parties' average bounces are virtually the same (5.2 Democratic, 5.3 Republican). What does distinguish the parties is the much greater variability in the size of Democratic bounces. Democrats can claim the four largest bounces (Clinton in 1992, Carter in 1976 and 1980, and Mondale in 1984) but also three of the four smallest (Humphrey in 1968, McGovern in 1972, and Kerry in 2004), so their bounces have ranged from −1 to +16 points. Republicans' convention bounces have fallen more narrowly between +2 and +8 points.

The political tradition is that the party currently occupying the White House holds its convention second. Thus, this year, Obama and the Democrats will lead off the back-to-back convention weeks, with McCain and the Republicans following. Going first or second doesn't seem to confer any advantage or disadvantage in terms of the size of the convention bounce, however. The average bounce for first conventions in an election year is 6.3 points (5.3 excluding 1992) and for second conventions is 5.2 points.

Implications for This Election

The conventions are one of the most anticipated events of the political calendar, and their potential to shift voter preferences is significant. In 1988 and 1992, the conventions were the turning points in the campaign, moving the formerly trailing candidate ahead for the duration. In other years, such as 1980 and 2000, the conventions changed the front-runner but not permanently, as subsequent events (in particular, the debates) led to changes later in the campaign. Typically, Gallup finds candidates gaining 5 points in the polls after their conventions, though it is far from certain that the candidates will receive bounces of that size in 2008. There are a number of factors that could lead to smaller than usual convention bounces this year, most notably the tightly compressed convention schedule, with the Republican convention beginning just four days after the Democratic convention ends. Also, it is rumored that McCain will announce his vice presidential running mate the day after the Democratic convention ends, stealing away some of the political spotlight from Obama the day after he gives his presidential nomination acceptance speech. Lastly, the high level of early voter attention may reduce the potential for significant shifts in voter preferences after the conventions.

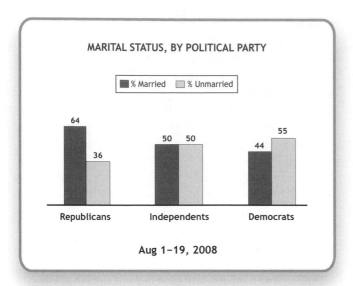

MARITAL STATUS, BY POLITICAL PARTY

■ % Married   □ % Unmarried

Aug 1–19, 2008

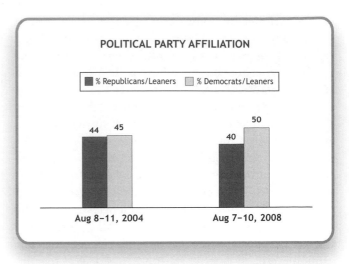

POLITICAL PARTY AFFILIATION

■ % Republicans/Leaners   □ % Democrats/Leaners

AUGUST 21

The Marriage Gap in Support for McCain and Obama

Among American registered voters who are married and whom Gallup interviewed between August 1 and August 19, John McCain is leading Barack Obama by 13 points; among unmarried American voters, Obama has a 22-point margin. A large part of the explanation for this marriage gap resides in the basic fact that the two major political parties are fundamentally divided by marital status. Almost two-thirds of Americans who identify with the Republican Party are married, while a majority of Democrats are unmarried.

Demographic Differences

This marriage gap is one of several such demographic gaps in support for the two major party candidates. There is,

for example, a significant gender gap (Obama does better among women; McCain among men) and a significant age gap (Obama does better among younger Americans). Since men are significantly more likely than women to be married in America today, and since those under age 35 are significantly more likely to be unmarried than are those who are older, could it be that the marriage gap is merely a reflection of these other two basic demographic characteristics? An analysis of Gallup's August data would answer "no" to that question: The differences in support by marital status persist across gender and age groups. Although women are in general somewhat stronger in their support for Obama than men are for McCain, married women tilt more toward McCain (by 46% to 42%), while unmarried women favor Obama. The same pattern holds for men.

Younger Americans in general are among Obama's strongest supporters. Yet among those 18 to 34 who are

PREFERENCE FOR THE GENERAL ELECTION
By Marital Status and Age

	Obama	McCain
18 to 34 married	43%	47%
18 to 34 unmarried	63%	27%
35 to 54 married	38%	52%
35 to 54 unmarried	56%	33%
55+ married	36%	52%
55+ unmarried	48%	38%

Aug 1–19, 2008

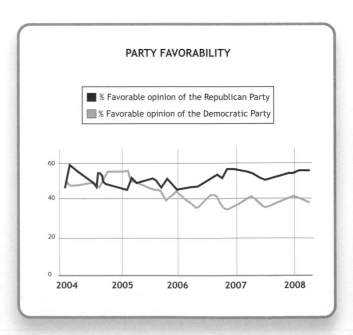

PARTY FAVORABILITY

■ % Favorable opinion of the Republican Party
□ % Favorable opinion of the Democratic Party

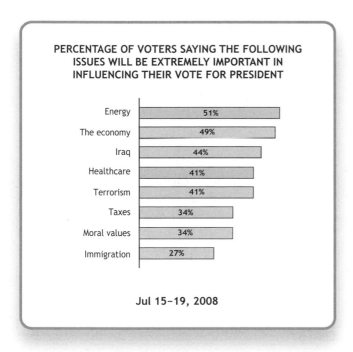

PERCENTAGE OF VOTERS SAYING THE FOLLOWING ISSUES WILL BE EXTREMELY IMPORTANT IN INFLUENCING THEIR VOTE FOR PRESIDENT

Issue	Percentage
Energy	51%
The economy	49%
Iraq	44%
Healthcare	41%
Terrorism	41%
Taxes	34%
Moral values	34%
Immigration	27%

Jul 15–19, 2008

married, McCain manages to best Obama by 4 points (47% to 43%), while among 18- to 34-year-olds who are unmarried, Obama wins by an overwhelming 36-point margin (63% to 27%). The same pattern holds among those who are older. Among both 35- to 54-year-olds and those 55 and older, those who are married skew toward McCain while those who are not married skew toward Obama.

AUGUST 23

Biden Does No Harm, but May Not Help Much

Barack Obama's selection of Delaware senator and former presidential candidate Joe Biden as his running mate is not generating much of an immediate reaction from the nation's voters. Just 14% of registered voters interviewed in a new USA Today/Gallup Poll say Biden makes them more likely to vote for Obama in November and 7% say they are less likely, while 72% say he will not have much effect on their vote. This results in Biden's potentially having a net impact on voter support for the Democratic ticket of +7 percentage points—small by comparison with other recent vice presidential selections.

- A net 17% of nationwide registered voters said they were more likely to vote for John Kerry in 2004 on the basis of his selection of John Edwards as his running mate (24% more likely and 7% less likely).
- A net 12% of voters reported being more likely to vote for Al Gore in 2000 on account of his

choosing Joe Lieberman (16% more likely and 4% less likely).
- A net 18% of voters indicated they were more likely to vote for Bob Dole in 1996 on the basis of his choice of Jack Kemp to complete the ticket (26% more likely and 8% less likely).
- A net 25% of voters were more likely to vote for Bill Clinton in 1992 on account of his choice of Al Gore (33% more likely and 8% less likely).

The only recent vice presidential choices to spark less voter response than Biden were Dick Cheney in 2000 (net 4%, with 14% more likely and 10% less likely) and Dan Quayle in 1988 (net score of 0, with 10% more likely and 10% less likely). It should be noted that all of these poll figures represent initial public reaction to new vice presidential selections. Voters' reactions to Biden could well change as the campaign progresses. The only vice presidential nominee who appeared to be an actual drag on a presidential ticket around convention time was Quayle in August 1992 (then the sitting vice president), when 6% of voters said they were more likely to vote for Bush because of Quayle and 25% said they were less likely—a 19-point *negative* differential. One possible reason for Biden's minimal impact on voter support for Obama so far is that more than half of voters have no views on the six-term senator from Delaware, either not knowing enough about him to express an opinion or say-

Senator Barack Obama (left) and his vice-presidential running mate, Senator Joe Biden, appear together in Springfield, Illinois, on August 23, 2008. *(M. Spencer Green/AP Images)*

ing they have never heard of him. In this regard, Biden looks very much like Lieberman in 2000.

Biden Is Seen as "Qualified"

Biden does pass a basic public opinion hurdle in terms of being seen as qualified to serve as president. His 57% "qualified" score is similar to the vice presidential choices from the last three elections and clearly separates him from the dreaded category occupied by Dan Quayle, the only recent vice presidential selection whom a majority of Americans said was "not qualified" (32%). More generally, 16% of voters consider Biden an "excellent" choice for vice president, 31% a "pretty good" choice, 21% "only fair," and 12% "poor." The total of 47% viewing him as excellent or pretty good is lower than the immediate post–vice presidential announcement ratings of Edwards in 2004, and Lieberman and Cheney in 2000—in part because of the high percentage (20%) with no opinion of the Biden choice.

With Obama consistently getting a lower share of support from Democrats than John McCain gets from Republicans, Biden's contribution to the ticket might be most important in terms of his ability to bring in more of the traditional Democratic base.

Democrats' initial reaction to Biden is positive, but not extraordinarily so. Half of Democrats say they have a favorable view of Biden (with nearly half having no opinion), 64% think he is an excellent or pretty good choice for vice president, and 70% think he is qualified to be president. Perhaps most importantly, 21% say they are more likely to vote for Obama as a result of Biden's presence on the ticket. (By way of comparison, a net 34% of Democrats said they were more likely to vote for Kerry on the basis of Edwards's being selected in 2004, and a net 23% of Democrats said they were more likely to vote for Gore on account of Lieberman's presence on the ticket.) Only 2% say they are *less* likely to vote for Obama because of the Biden choice. It is unclear whether these numbers are enough to sufficiently increase Obama's support within the party.

Implications for the Election

One approach to picking a vice president is to seek to "do no harm." Perhaps with Quayle's possibly negative impact on his father's unsuccessful 1992 re-election campaign in mind, George W. Bush was quoted in 2000 as saying, "You want . . . somebody who's not going to hurt you." Obama's own campaign manager recently echoed this sentiment, saying, "Whether someone helps win you an election, I think, is kind of a side benefit. You certainly want to pick someone who doesn't hurt you." The initial evidence is that Biden won't hurt Obama in the election, but with only 14% of voters saying they are more likely to vote for the ticket with Biden on it and 7% less likely, he is not positioned at this point to help Obama much, either.

Election Remains a Statistical Dead Heat

Barack Obama and John McCain remain nearly tied in Gallup Poll daily tracking, with Obama favored by 46% of national registered voters and McCain by 44%. Today's result, based on August 20–22 interviewing, represents the last Gallup Poll daily tracking update on the presidential race based on interviewing conducted entirely before Obama's selection of Joe Biden to be his running mate was announced early this morning. The full immediate impact on voters of that decision will not be reflected in Gallup's continuous three-day rolling average results until August 26. Obama has not held a statistically significant lead over McCain in any Gallup Poll daily tracking report since August 13, or 10 reporting days. This is the longest stretch with Obama leading by no more than three percentage points since before Obama clinched the Democratic nomination in early June. While Obama clearly hopes that the publicity from the upcoming Democratic convention will help him break out of the present deadlock—and historical poll trends show that a five-point bounce in support for a presidential candidate is typical after each nominating convention—the fact that neither presidential candidate in the 2004 election received a significant convention bounce puts a question mark over the inevitability of that happening in 2008.

AUGUST 25

Obama Holds Lead over McCain on Top Issue of Economy

As the Democratic National Convention gets under way, voters, by a 52% to 40% margin, believe Barack Obama is better able than John McCain to handle the economy. And the economy easily tops the list when voters are asked which of five issues will be most important to their vote for president. Obama's 12-percentage-point advantage over McCain on the economy marks a significant improvement from early February, when Gallup last asked this question; at that time, his advantage was 46% to 43%. More recently, Gallup asked slightly different questions about the candidates' economic aptitudes and found Obama faring significantly better than McCain in these polls as well. Broadly, voters clearly see the candidates as having opposing areas of strength. They give Obama the advantage on each of the four domestic issues tested in the poll, and McCain the advantage on all three international issues. Obama's biggest issue advantage versus McCain comes with regard to healthcare policy (56% to 34%), a traditionally strong issue for the Democratic Party. The candidates have spent much time on the campaign trail discussing the nation's energy challenges and their ideas for solving them, and so far registered voters rate Obama as better able to handle the issue, 51% to 40%. On taxes, Obama holds only a slight edge, 47% to 44%.

McCain leads Obama by double digits on the three international issues tested, with the largest margin a 24-point advantage in reference to terrorism. The presumptive Republican nominee also outpolls Obama on U.S. policy toward Russia, 52% to 35%. This issue has emerged in the campaign due to Russia's recent invasion of the former Soviet republic of Georgia (a U.S. ally), a move the United States government strongly opposed. This international flare-up may be one reason that McCain has pulled closer to Obama in presidential trial heat polls in recent days. Despite giving McCain a clear advantage on international issues, a slim majority of voters, 53%, say Obama can handle the responsibilities of commander in chief. That pales in comparison with the 80% who believe McCain is up to the role, but it is an important threshold for Obama to meet, given his relatively thin experience in dealing with international issues. Even if voters believe Obama is better able to address the economy, they could conceivably disqualify him for the job if they do not believe he is capable of handling the president's international responsibilities. Obama's selection of Senator Biden as his vice presidential running mate adds significant expertise on foreign policy and national defense to the Democratic ticket.

Implications for the Campaigns

Obama's perceived advantage over McCain with regard to handling the economy is a major plus for the Democrat's campaign. However, even with that advantage, the overall presidential race remains close, which may reflect McCain's superior perceived credentials on international issues and concerns about Obama's lack of experience. Obama may never overtake McCain in terms of being perceived as better able to handle international issues, so the Illinois senator's challenge may be to convince voters that he is competent to deal with such issues. Currently, a slim majority of voters believe he is, and a key goal

for Obama's acceptance speech on August 28 will be to maintain or improve that level while retaining his perceived advantage over McCain on voters' top issue of the economy. Meanwhile, McCain may not need to burnish his international credentials during the Republican convention, but he needs to convince voters that he can do as well as or better than Obama on the economy.

Michelle Obama's Speech Could Make a Difference

Michelle Obama's speech on the first night of the Democratic convention in Denver might have an effect on the election, as over half of Americans say a presidential candidate's spouse is an important factor in their vote. Overall, Republicans are slightly more likely to say the candidate's spouse matters than are Democrats (56%–48%). Michelle Obama will be making her speech before a national audience that has significantly more favorable than unfavorable views of the Harvard law graduate who has been married to Barack Obama since 1992. Michelle Obama's favorables are more than twice as high as her unfavorables, and only 22% of Americans say they have never heard of her or do not know enough about her to have an opinion. Over the summer, Michelle Obama's favorable ratings have increased slightly, while her unfavorable ratings have gone down.

Although Michelle Obama's name identification is lower than that of her husband, the ratio of favorable to unfavorable impressions of the two Obamas is roughly comparable. In other words, Michelle Obama does not appear to have a distinctly different overall image in

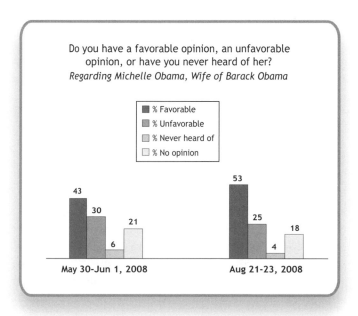

Do you have a favorable opinion, an unfavorable opinion, or have you never heard of her?
Regarding Michelle Obama, Wife of Barack Obama

- ■ % Favorable
- ■ % Unfavorable
- ■ % Never heard of
- □ % No opinion

May 30-Jun 1, 2008: 43, 30, 6, 21
Aug 21-23, 2008: 53, 25, 4, 18

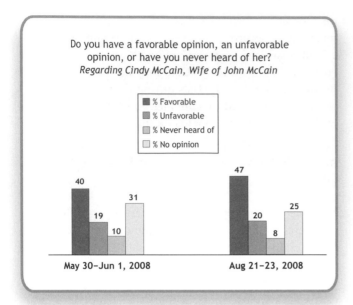

Do you have a favorable opinion, an unfavorable opinion, or have you never heard of her?
Regarding Cindy McCain, Wife of John McCain

- ■ % Favorable
- ■ % Unfavorable
- □ % Never heard of
- □ % No opinion

May 30–Jun 1, 2008: 40, 19, 10, 31
Aug 21–23, 2008: 47, 20, 8, 25

the eyes of Americans than does her husband. Michelle Obama is a little better known than John McCain's wife, Cindy, who has 67% name identification compared with Michelle Obama's 78%. The overall ratio of favorable to unfavorable opinions of the two possible first ladies is roughly comparable. (Cindy McCain is scheduled to speak on September 3 at the Republican convention in St. Paul, Minnesota.) Michelle Obama is, of course, better known and has a much more positive image among Democrats than among Republicans. However, it appears that Michelle Obama has engendered more negative reactions from those who identify with the opposing party than is the case for Cindy McCain with respect to Democrats. Almost half of Republicans and Republican leaners say they have an unfavorable opinion of Michelle Obama, compared with just a third of Democrats and Democratic leaners who say they have an unfavorable opinion of Cindy McCain.

AUGUST 26

Hillary Clinton's Stock Still High Among Democrats

The intense battle for the Democratic nomination between Hillary Clinton and Barack Obama seems to have done little to diminish Democrats' affinity for the New York senator. Eighty percent of Democrats have a favorable opinion of her, compared with 74% just before Obama clinched the presidential nomination in early June and 82% before the primaries began, when she was considered the strong front-runner for the nomination. Her favorable rating among all

Americans is 54%, the most positive since just after she officially announced her candidacy in early 2007. At the same time, Obama rates above Clinton on basic favorability—among both the general public (63%) and the Democratic rank and file (86%). Obama has typically rated higher than Clinton among the general public since the presidential primaries got under way in January. But Obama's higher favorable rating among Democrats is a more recent development. Clinton typically had higher favorable ratings than Obama throughout this presidential campaign season—but that to a large degree reflected Democrats' greater familiarity with Clinton than with Obama (until recently, a substantial minority of Democrats did not have an opinion of Obama), rather than a more negative evaluation of Obama.

In any case, Democrats still see a future for Clinton in the Democratic Party. Seventy-nine percent want her to be a major national spokesperson for the party over the next four years as she completes her second term in the Senate; just 18% of Democrats would prefer she have a less prominent role within the party. Additionally, 75% of Democrats say they would like to see Clinton run for president again someday. Overall, Americans are not as enthusiastic about a second Clinton presidential bid, with 52% in favor. That includes 50% of independents and only 24% of Republicans.

Will Clinton's Supporters Back Obama?

During the primaries, there was significant concern within Democratic ranks that large numbers of the eventual loser's supporters would not back the nominee and thus hurt the party's chances of winning in November. In the latest USA Today/Gallup Poll, 16% of registered Democrats who say they supported Clinton in the primaries say they would vote for John McCain if the election were held today, and another 14% are undecided. One of Obama's—and, indeed, one of Clinton's—challenges during the Democratic convention is to reduce those numbers. The vast majority of former Clinton supporters (70%) say they would back Obama, and they have a predominantly positive view of him (78% favorable, 18% unfavorable). Even today, however, there remain concerns among Clinton backers that Obama does not give the Democratic Party the best chance of defeating McCain and the Republicans in the presidential election. But a CNN/Opinion Research poll conducted between August 23 and August 24 found the two running similarly in trial heats versus McCain, with Obama and McCain tied (47% to 47%) and Clinton having a slim but not statistically significant advantage over McCain (49% to 46%).

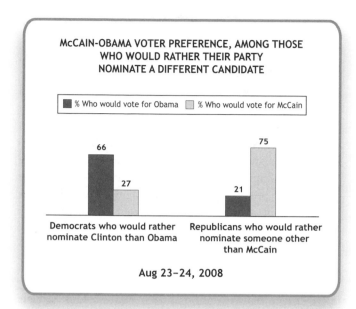

McCAIN-OBAMA VOTER PREFERENCE, AMONG THOSE WHO WOULD RATHER THEIR PARTY NOMINATE A DIFFERENT CANDIDATE

Aug 23-24, 2008

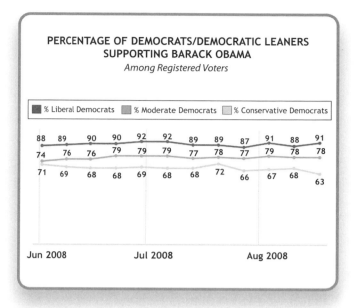

PERCENTAGE OF DEMOCRATS/DEMOCRATIC LEANERS SUPPORTING BARACK OBAMA
Among Registered Voters

Even if many Democrats believe their odds of victory might be slightly better with Clinton rather than Obama heading the ticket, there does not seem to be widespread support among the Democratic rank and file for denying Obama the nomination. The same CNN/Opinion Research poll finds 59% of Democrats saying that if the choice of Democratic nominee were up to them, they would choose Obama, while just 37% would anoint Clinton. That's about at least as strong an endorsement as Republicans give McCain (57% would nominate him, 42% someone else), despite the fact that McCain won his party's nomination in a shorter, and perhaps less contentious, campaign than the Democratic contest.

A key question is to what extent those favoring another nominee will defect and vote for the other party in the general election. For the most part, party supporters will likely remain loyal. As noted, the USA Today/Gallup Poll finds 70% of former Clinton supporters saying they would vote for Obama if the election were held today (though only 47% say they are certain to do so). Additionally, the CNN/Opinion Research poll finds 66% of those who would have preferred Clinton backing Obama versus McCain. That leaves a nontrivial percentage who would cross party lines: Among Democrats who say they would nominate Clinton if the choice were up to them, 27% would vote for McCain if the election were held today. But the Republicans face a similar problem, as 21% of those who would rather the party nominate someone other than McCain say they would vote today for Obama in the general election.

Implications for the Election

Obama and Clinton are doing their best to heal any remaining wounds within the Democratic Party left over from their protracted nomination battle. In general, Democrats still view Clinton positively and would welcome a prominent role for her within the party in the future. While some Clinton supporters have yet to fall in line and support Obama for president, for the most part Clinton supporters have a positive opinion of Obama (as well as a largely negative view of McCain). So it is still not out of the question that they will "come home" by Election Day. But it is important to note that unifying the party is not a challenge unique to the Democratic Party, as many Republican supporters who are not enthusiastic about McCain have yet to return to the Republican fold.

AUGUST 27

Conservative Democrats Peeling Away from Obama

Barack Obama has been struggling to maintain his Democratic base thus far in August, and according to weekly averages of Gallup Poll daily tracking, the problem seems to be with conservative Democrats. Within the Democratic Party, Obama's losses are primarily evident among the relatively small group that describes its political views as conservative. The 63% of conservative Democrats supporting Obama over McCain in the August 18–24 polling is the lowest support Obama has received since he clinched the Democratic nomination in June. At the same time, there have been no similar drops in support for Obama among liberal or moderate Democrats. As a result, support for Obama among all Democratic registered voters fell from 81% in early August (August 4–10) to 78% last week (August 18–24). Obama's support from Republicans over

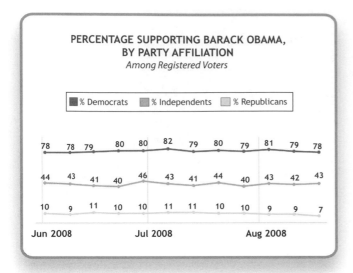

PERCENTAGE SUPPORTING BARACK OBAMA,
BY PARTY AFFILIATION
Among Registered Voters

■ % Democrats   ■ % Independents   □ % Republicans

78 78 79 80 80 82 79 80 79 81 79 78

44 43 41 40 46 43 41 44 40 43 42 43

10 9 11 10 10 11 11 10 10 9 9 7

Jun 2008   Jul 2008   Aug 2008

this period also dipped, from 9% to 7%, while 42% to 43% of independents have consistently supported him. The 78% of Democrats backing Obama from August 18 to August 24 ties for the lowest seen since early June, and the 7% of Republicans for Obama is the lowest to date (since the start of Gallup Poll daily tracking of the Obama-McCain race in March). Among Republicans, Obama has mainly seen his support eroding among moderate and liberal Republicans, from 19% to 13% during August. Obama's support from conservative Republicans, at 4% to 6% in July and early August, could not go much lower.

More generally, recent weekly averages of Gallup Poll daily tracking show the race for president tightening just prior to the Democratic convention. Whereas Obama led McCain 47% to 42% earlier this month and 45% to 43% from August 11 to August 17, from August 18 to August 24 the race was exactly tied at 45%. The large sample sizes (more than 6,000 registered voters) included in each weekly aggregate mean there is greater reliability that these changes are real than if they were seen on only a day-to-day basis. (Notably, most of the interviews included in the August 18–24 weekly aggregate took place before Obama's August 23 announcement that Senator Joe Biden would serve as his vice presidential running mate, so the week's results should not be interpreted as reflecting public reaction to that decision.) The presidential contest has remained close in subsequent days, and McCain took a slight (though not statistically significant) lead this week in the August 25 tracking report, 46% to 44%. Obama's troubles are also evident among married women. Between August 4 and August 10 and between August 18 and August 24, the percentage of married women backing Obama fell from 46% to 39%, while support from unmarried women fell from 58% to 55%. At the

same time, there has been no decrease in the percentage of married or unmarried men supporting Obama.

Obama held the slight upper hand in the race from early June through mid-August. His failure to maintain that lead last week—instead averaging a tie with McCain at 45%—can be largely explained by some defections from the conservative wing of the Democratic Party, as well as less crossover support from moderate and liberal Republicans. Given these contradictory partisan trends, and the fact that Gallup finds no clear pattern in the recent weekly presidential preference trends by religion, there does not seem to be a coherent ideological or religious basis for the shift (as, for example, the controversy over Obama's views on abortion). It will be important to see whether Obama's erstwhile supporters—particularly conservative Democrats—come back to the fold this week as they watch the Democratic convention and take a fresh look at their nominee for president.

Bill Clinton's Image Has Taken a Hit, but His Legacy Is Largely Intact

Former president Bill Clinton's controversial remarks against Barack Obama earlier this year were a major part of the 2008 campaign narrative. Some political observers wondered whether Clinton was harming his legacy while campaigning on his wife's behalf. The latest USA Today/Gallup Poll suggests that this is not the case. Nearly half of Americans believe history will regard Clinton as an outstanding or above-average president, little changed from his last pre-campaign rating and indeed constituting his most positive review to date.

Clinton will address the Democratic convention Wednesday night (August 27). He and Obama have had

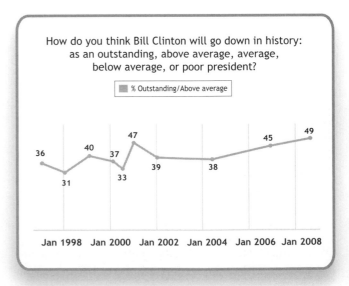

How do you think Bill Clinton will go down in history: as an outstanding, above average, average, below average, or poor president?

■ % Outstanding/Above average

36 31 40 37 47 33 39 38 45 49

Jan 1998   Jan 2000   Jan 2002   Jan 2004   Jan 2006   Jan 2008

an uneasy relationship, in part because of remarks Clinton made against the Illinois senator while campaigning for Hillary Clinton, including describing Obama's campaign narrative as a "fairy tale" and apparently dismissing Obama's South Carolina primary victory in January by reminding people that Jesse Jackson had also won the state's primary in 1984 and 1988.

In Gallup's last pre-campaign reading, from December 2006, 45% of Americans said Clinton would go down in history as an outstanding or above-average president. With 49% saying that today, the public evidently does not believe his legacy has been damaged. Notably, Obama supporters are largely positive when assessing Bill Clinton's historical significance. Among Democrats and Democratic-leaning independents who say they supported Obama in the primaries, 60% say Clinton will be regarded as an outstanding or above-average president. That figure pales in comparison with the 80% above-average or better ratings from Democrats who supported Hillary Clinton during the primaries, but it is little different from the 65% of all Democrats in 2006 who said Bill Clinton would get a favorable historical review.

Yet even though perceptions of Clinton's historical legacy have not suffered, there has been some short-term damage to the former president's image during the last several months. Currently, 52% of Americans say they have a favorable opinion of him. He has averaged just a 51% favorable rating in four 2008 readings, all of which were taken after Clinton's most controversial remarks. That compares with an average 60% favorable score last year.

The poll provides some suggestive evidence that the decline in Clinton's favorable rating may primarily be due to more negative assessments from Obama supporters. In the October 2007 poll—the last reading before the prima-

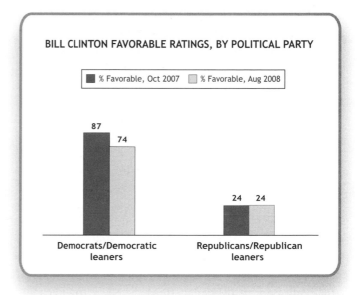

BILL CLINTON FAVORABLE RATINGS, BY POLITICAL PARTY

% Favorable, Oct 2007 ☐ % Favorable, Aug 2008

Democrats/Democratic leaners: 87, 74
Republicans/Republican leaners: 24, 24

ries began—87% of all Democrats and 24% of all Republicans rated Clinton favorably. In the latest poll, Clinton's favorable rating remains 24% among Republicans but has declined to 74% among Democrats. And when Democrats in the current poll are subdivided according to their candidate of choice in the primaries, Obama backers give Bill Clinton an average 64% favorable score, compared with 90% among Hillary Clinton supporters.

AUGUST 28

Obama Still Lags Behind McCain as Leader, Commander in Chief

John McCain has an edge over Barack Obama in the public's eyes as a strong and decisive leader, and McCain is also significantly more likely to be viewed as able to handle the job of commander in chief. These facts underscore an area of weakness for Obama that McCain has attempted to exploit in recent campaign ads, and that Obama could in theory fruitfully address in his high-visibility acceptance speech at the Democratic convention.

The latest USA Today/Gallup Poll, conducted between August 21 and August 23, asked Americans to indicate whether various characteristics and qualities best fit Obama or McCain. Obama beats McCain by a 7-point or larger margin on four dimensions: caring "about the needs of people like you," being able to work well with both parties to get things done, being independent, and sharing the respondent's values. The two are essentially tied in perceptions that they put the country's interests ahead of their own, that they are honest and trustworthy, and that they are able to manage the government

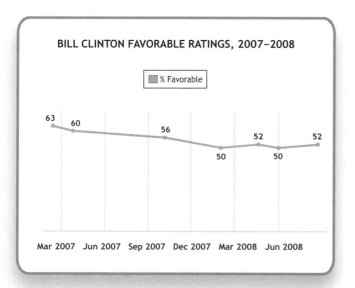

BILL CLINTON FAVORABLE RATINGS, 2007–2008

% Favorable

63, 60, 56, 50, 52, 50, 52

Mar 2007   Jun 2007   Sep 2007   Dec 2007   Mar 2008   Jun 2008 effectively. McCain is significantly ahead on a single, but important, dimension: "is a strong and decisive leader." Not coincidentally, this has been a key focus of recent McCain attack ads against Obama. (Despite the ads, there has been almost no change since mid-June in perceptions of who is the better leader.)

Questions included in the recent poll asked respondents to indicate whether they believe Obama and McCain could "handle the responsibilities of commander in chief of the military." Obama clearly operates at a decided perceptual deficit compared with McCain on this dimension: Eighty percent of Americans say McCain could handle the responsibilities of being commander in chief, compared with 53% for Obama. These views have not changed throughout the summer. McCain's edge almost certainly reflects in part that he was a graduate of the U.S. Naval Academy and an officer in the U.S. Navy for decades, while Obama did not serve in the military. It may also reflect the fact that McCain is older, has more experience in the Senate and the federal government, and has taken a leading role in the Senate on many foreign policy issues, most notably the Iraq War. If these are in fact the major underlying facts informing Americans' opinions about the candidates, then it is unclear to what extent Obama's rhetoric or McCain's campaign ads could change the existing perceptions. But polling data from four years ago suggest that the views of the public on this dimension can change. George W. Bush and John Kerry scored similarly on the commander-in-chief item in two polls conducted in June and late July/early August of 2004. But from September on, after the two conventions and particularly the now famous "Swift Boat" attack ads on Kerry, Bush had a significant advantage on the commander-in-chief dimension.

Implications for the Election

Previous Gallup analysis reviewed data showing that Obama has the edge over McCain in the eyes of Americans on domestic issues such as the economy, healthcare, and energy, while McCain does better on international issues such as terrorism, the situation in Russia, and Iraq. Coupled with the data reviewed here on personal characteristics and qualities, it is clear that Obama has a cluster of strengths relating to "soft" dimensions such as caring and values, along with domestic issues. McCain has a "harder" image: He is seen as being a strong leader and potential commander in chief, and as being able to handle international issues. This positioning of the two candidates is not unusual and reflects broad Republican versus Democratic strengths in recent elections (although, as noted, for a period of time early in the 2004 campaign Kerry was tied with Bush on the commander-in-chief dimension).

Gallup Daily: Obama Moves Ahead, 48% to 42%

Barack Obama has gained ground in the latest Gallup Poll daily tracking average from August 25 to 27 and now leads John McCain among registered voters by a 48% to 42% margin. This directly coincides with the first three days of the Democratic convention in Denver, and is no doubt beginning to reflect the typical convention "bounce" that Gallup has observed after most party conventions in recent decades. There is a lag of sorts involved in the daily tracking, however, as interviewing is conducted in most parts of the country before that evening's high-focus speeches have taken place. Thus, the current three-day average would reflect any impact of Monday night's speech by Michelle Obama and Tuesday night's speech by Hillary Clinton, but would not completely reflect Wednesday night's lineup of speakers, including John Kerry, former president Bill Clinton, and vice presidential nominee Joe Biden—nor the appearance on stage at the end of the evening by Barack Obama himself.

Gallup's interviewing for August 22–24, the last three days before the convention officially began, showed the race at a 45% to 45% tie. Thus, there is already a six-percentage-point bounce evident in the data, although the final, "official" postconvention bounce used in comparison with other recent conventions will not be tabulated by Gallup until interviewing is completed on August 29–31. The dynamics of the race in the forthcoming days will be of keen interest this year, as McCain, by all accounts, will attempt to pounce on the Democrats' bounce by announcing his vice presidential

Which of the following characteristics and qualities applies more to Barack Obama or more to John McCain?			
	Obama	McCain	Advantage (pct. pts.)
Cares about the needs of people like you	53%	33%	Obama +20
Would work well with both parties to get things done in Washington	51%	38%	Obama +13
Is independent in his thoughts and actions	50%	37%	Obama +13
Shares your values	47%	40%	Obama +7
Puts the country's interests ahead of his own political interests	44%	42%	Obama +2
Is honest and trustworthy	39%	39%	Even
Can manage the government effectively	43%	44%	McCain +1
Is a strong and decisive leader	40%	48%	McCain +8

Aug 21–23, 2008

At Invesco Field in Denver, Colorado, Barack Obama delivers his speech accepting the Democratic nomination for president on August 28, 2008. *(Ron Edmunds/AP Images)*

running mate the day after the Democratic convention concludes, and with attention turning quickly in any case to the Republican convention, which is set to begin on September 1 in St. Paul. Also in the mix of possibly influential factors this year will be an act of nature. If Tropical Storm Gustav becomes a hurricane and makes landfall on the Gulf Coast sometime on September 2, news coverage of the Republican convention will presumably be diluted, and the impact of that situation (coming some three years after Hurricane Katrina) is impossible to predict.

Hillary Clinton's Speech Well Received

Fifty-two percent of Americans—and 83% of those who tuned in—give Hillary Clinton's August 26 speech at the Democratic convention a positive review. These results are based on a USA Today/Gallup Poll conducted August 27, the day after Clinton's prime-time speech. The speech was one of many attempts by the Clinton and Obama campaigns to unite the Democratic Party behind Obama's presidential candidacy after the long and sometimes acrimonious nomination campaign between the two senators. Hillary Clinton's speech scored better than the speech Bill Clinton gave at the 2000 Democratic National Convention several months before he would complete his second

presidential term: Forty-four percent of Americans rated that speech either excellent or good.

As would be expected, Democrats were especially positive about Hillary Clinton's address, with 69% rating it positively. But close to half of Republicans, 45%, also rated it positively. The high 83% positive rating of the speech among those who watched it was in part due to the partisan nature of the audience. The poll estimates that 49% of those who watched the Clinton speech were Democrats, while 22% were Republicans and the remaining 28% were independents. Ninety-four percent of Democrats who watched the speech rated it positively, as did solid majorities of the Republicans and independents who tuned in.

AUGUST 29

Obama Regains Support of Conservative Democrats

Barack Obama's gain in support among registered voters from August 25 to August 27 was in part the result of gains among conservative Democrats—the group among whom the Democratic nominee had lost ground last week as he slipped into an overall tie with John McCain. Obama and McCain were tied 45% to 45% among voters in interviewing conducted between August 18 and August 24. This represented a small decline for Obama, and analysis of the trend line of support for the two candidates among subgroups showed that it was due to a slippage among the relatively small group of Democrats with a conservative ideology. Now, with Obama holding a six-point lead over McCain, he has gained back that support and then some, moving from 63% support among conservative Democrats to 77%. Obama has the support of 92% of liberal Democrats and 79% of moderate Democrats, basically unchanged from last week's percentages.

It is likely that conservative Democrats consist disproportionately of Hillary Clinton supporters, although this cannot be documented from the tracking data because no question about prior support of candidates was included. Analysis of Gallup Poll daily tracking data from May, however, shows that conservative Democrats disproportionately supported Clinton over Obama for the Democratic nomination by a 48% to 43% margin; she had less support from moderate and, especially, liberal Democrats. (Overall, Democrats in May tilted toward Obama by a 49% to 43% margin.) This suggests that last week's drop in support for Obama may have resulted from defections by conservative Democrats whose loyalty to Clinton was brought to the forefront as the Democratic convention approached, but whose disappointment Clinton assuaged with her strong support for Obama as the convention unfolded. At the same time, despite this hypothesis about the movement of Clinton supporters and despite the high-profile campaign speeches from women—including Michelle Obama as well as Hillary Clinton—Obama's gains in the early days of this week did not come disproportionately from women. He gained three points among women and three points among men.

Can Sarah Palin Appeal to White, Female Independents?

John McCain's surprise selection of Alaska governor Sarah Palin as his vice presidential running mate raises again the issue of gender in presidential politics. McCain, typically for Republican presidential candidates, does significantly less well among women than among men, and an analysis of more than 25,000 Gallup Poll daily tracking interviews in August shows that the biggest gender gap is among whites who are independents.

Here are the key points relating to gender and presidential politics:

1. Among all registered voters Gallup has interviewed in August (through August 28), McCain wins among men by a 6-point, 48% to 42% margin, while Obama wins among women by a 10-point,

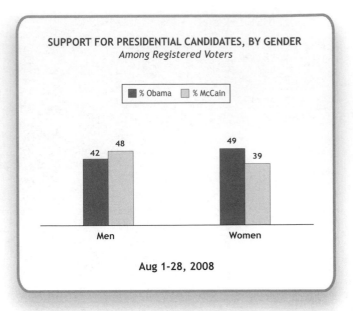

SUPPORT FOR PRESIDENTIAL CANDIDATES, BY GENDER
Among Registered Voters

[Legend: ■ % Obama   □ % McCain]

Men: 42 / 48
Women: 49 / 39

Aug 1-28, 2008

49% to 39% margin. The swing in the margin of support for the two candidates between genders is thus 16 points.

2. Most of this gender gap is evident among whites; there is little difference by gender in candidate support among blacks or Hispanics. Black registered voters very strongly support Obama over McCain regardless of gender. Hispanics also support Obama, though at a lower level—but there is also little meaningful difference by gender. Among non-Hispanic whites, however, it's a different story: White men favor McCain by 21 points, while white women support McCain by a much smaller 4 points. In other words, there is a 17-point swing by gender in candidate support among whites.

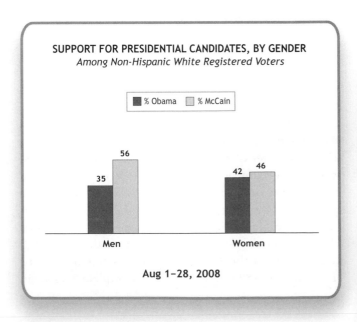

SUPPORT FOR PRESIDENTIAL CANDIDATES, BY GENDER
Among Non-Hispanic White Registered Voters

[Legend: ■ % Obama   □ % McCain]

Men: 35 / 56
Women: 42 / 46

Aug 1-28, 2008

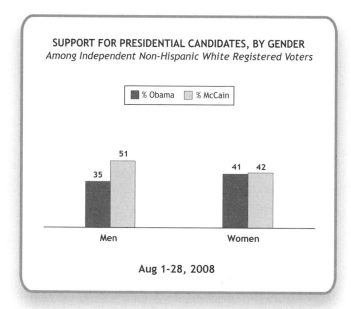

SUPPORT FOR PRESIDENTIAL CANDIDATES, BY GENDER
Among Independent Non-Hispanic White Registered Voters

■ % Obama   ▦ % McCain

Aug 1-28, 2008

3. Among whites, most of the gender difference can be narrowed down to differences among independents. White Republicans overwhelmingly support McCain over Obama, and that doesn't differ meaningfully by gender. White Democrats overwhelmingly support Obama, and that, too, doesn't vary by gender. But there is a big swing in support by gender among independents—individuals who in response to an initial party identification question say they do not identify with either party. White male independents go strongly for McCain, by a 16-point margin, while white female independents are evenly divided, 41% for Obama and 42% for McCain. This represents a 15-point swing by gender in candidate support.

Implications for the Election

There is a significant gender gap in American presidential politics today, but it is confined for the most part to white voters who are politically independent. There is very little difference in presidential vote choice by gender among blacks and Hispanics, or among whites who are Republican or Democratic in their political identification. Many assume that McCain's choice of a female running mate could increase his chances among female voters. If that is the case, it would appear that white independent women—who are currently split almost evenly in terms of their candidate support—would be most susceptible to changing sides, given the strongly skewed (and gender-neutral) existing vote choice among blacks, Hispanics, and loyal partisans. Additionally, of course, McCain's selection may have been designed as much to help reinforce loyalty

Flanked by his wife Michelle and daughters Malia (left) and Sasha (right), Barack Obama waves to the crowd following his acceptance speech at the Democratic National Convention. *(Scott Andrews and Chuck Kennedy/AP Images)*

among his conservative Republican base as to change voters' minds. If that was the case, it would be Governor Palin's conservative positions on issues—including abortion, same-sex marriage, gun control, and taxes—more than her gender that would be the operative factor.

AUGUST 30

Obama Acceptance Speech Gets High Marks from Public

Fifty-eight percent of Americans give Barack Obama's speech a positive review, including 35% who describe it as "excellent." Both marks surpass those given to the 2000 and 2004 presidential candidates, with the excellent ratings for Obama's speech 10 percentage points higher than any other recent candidate has received. These results are based on a one-night USA Today/Gallup Poll conducted on August 29, the night following Obama's acceptance speech. Obama is widely praised for his rhetorical skills, so his positive reviews are perhaps not surprising. His speech was rated even more positively than Hillary Clinton's convention speech, which was also highly regarded by the public. Democrats gave Obama's speech rave reviews, with 62% saying it was an excellent speech and another 21% describing it as good. A majority of independents rated Obama's speech as either excellent (27%) or good (25%), but Republicans were less impressed (12% excellent and 25% good).

In addition to measuring reaction to Obama's speech, the poll attempted to assess the broader impact of the convention on the public. Forty-three percent of Americans say they are more likely to vote for Obama as a result of what they saw, or what they read about the convention; 29% say they are less likely. Those ratings are typical of what Gallup has measured for most conventions since 1984—though the 1992 Democratic convention stands out, with 60% saying that the convention made them more likely to vote for Bill Clinton. The 1988 Democratic convention that nominated Michael Dukakis also got above-average ratings. Obama's speech also produced record television ratings. More generally, 6 in 10 Americans say they watched a "great deal" or "some" of the convention. That is similar to reports from the 2004 conventions but higher than what Gallup found for prior conventions.

Palin Unknown to Most Americans

The initial reaction of the American public to John McCain's surprise selection of Alaska governor Sarah Palin as his running mate is muted, similar to the reaction to Joe Biden's being named Barack Obama's running mate. Perhaps the most significant finding about Palin in the August 29 USA Today/Gallup Poll is that she is largely unknown to most Americans. A substantial majority of Americans don't know enough about her yet to have an opinion, and her name identification is lower than that of any other recent vice presidential candidate when measured immediately after their selection. Among those who do know her, her image is significantly more positive than negative, and her

three-to-one positive-to-negative ratio is better than the two-to-one ratio measured for Biden a week ago. A large majority say that at this point her selection will not have an impact on their presidential vote either way. However, almost as many Americans say that she is not qualified to serve as president as say she is qualified, giving her a more negative reading on this measure than most other recent vice presidential candidates, with the exception of Dan Quayle.

The key findings from the data measured in USA Today/Gallup interviewing conducted on August 29 are outlined below.

1. Overall Reaction to Palin Selection Similar to that of Biden Selection

Americans' overall reaction to the McCain selection of Palin as his vice presidential running mate is very similar to last week's reaction to Obama's selection of Biden. A little less than half of Americans rate the selection of Palin as excellent or pretty good, while 37% rate it as only fair or poor. (The rest have no opinion.) The reaction to Biden's selection on August 23 was only slightly different, even though many more Americans were familiar with the Delaware senator when he was named. The reaction to both the Palin and the Biden selections are well below the positive reaction the public had to John Kerry's choice of John Edwards in 2004, and slightly less positive than Al Gore's selection of Joe Lieberman and George W. Bush's selection of Dick Cheney in 2000. All recent vice presidential selections received more positive reaction than George H. W. Bush's choice of Dan Quayle in 1988, the only vice presidential nominee to be reviewed more negatively than positively by the public.

Does having Sarah Palin as his running mate make you more likely to vote for John McCain in November, less likely, or will it not have much effect on your vote?
Based on Registered Voters

More likely 18% — Less likely 11% — Not much effect 67% — No opinion 3%

Aug 29, 2008

How would you rate each candidate's choice for vice president?
Based on Registered Voters

	Interview dates	Excellent/ Pretty good	Only fair/ Poor	No opinion
2008				
Obama-Biden	Aug 23, 2008	47%	33%	20%
McCain-Palin	Aug 29, 2008	46%	37%	17%
2004				
Kerry-Edwards	Jul 6, 2004	64%	28%	8%
2000				
Bush-Cheney	Jul 24, 2000	55%	34%	11%
Gore-Lieberman	Aug 7, 2000	53%	28%	19%
1988				
Bush-Quayle	Aug 19–21, 1988*	44%	52%	4%

* Poll of likely voters by Louis Harris and Associates

As was the case with respect to Biden a week ago and all vice presidential selections of the last two decades, a substantial majority of Americans say that the selection of Palin will not have much impact on their vote for president this year. Of those who say it will have an impact, the effect is more positive than negative for both Palin and Biden, though the reaction to Palin's selection is the more positive of the two, by a modest margin. These reactions to the 2008 vice presidential running mates are similar to those that greeted both 2000 vice presidential selections but slightly less positive than the reaction to other recent selections, such as Edwards in 2004, Jack Kemp in 1996, Gore in 1992, and Lloyd Bentsen in 1988.

Even among Republicans, the reaction to Palin is muted. Thirty percent of Republicans say that Palin's selection makes them more likely to vote for McCain, while just 5% say they are less likely to vote for him, leaving the rest saying that her selection, at least so far, has had no impact on their vote. Still, this is a slightly stronger partisan reaction than Democrats had to Biden, as just 21% of Democrats said they were more likely to vote for Obama because Biden was his running mate. Among the crucial bloc of independents, the impact of Palin's selection is mixed, with the majority saying "no impact" and about as many of the rest saying that it made them less likely to vote for McCain as more likely to vote for him. Importantly, there is no sign yet of a vehemently negative reaction from Democrats. Just 14% say they are less likely to vote for McCain as a result of the Palin selection, while 6% say they are more likely to vote for him.

2. Palin a Mystery to Most Americans

One reason for the lack of a substantial self-reported impact of Palin's selection may be the fact that she is a mystery to many Americans at this early point. More than 7 out of 10 Americans interviewed said they had never heard of Palin or did not know enough about her to have an opinion. This is a much higher "don't know" than was measured by Gallup immediately after the initial vice presidential announcement of Biden a week ago, or after the selections of Edwards, Lieberman, Cheney, Kemp, or Gore in previous years' elections. This finding is not surprising. The other vice presidential picks in recent years had actively sought their party's presidential nomination in the year they were selected or in previous years, or had well-established careers in Congress or the federal government—whereas Palin has been governor of a small state for less than two years and has no national political experience.

Of interest is the fact that almost 6 out of 10 Republicans say they have never heard of Palin or do not know enough to have an opinion about her. These data underscore that the degree to which Palin is showcased at the Republican

FAVORABLE RATINGS OF VICE PRESIDENTIAL CANDIDATES
Based on Registered Voters

	Interview dates	Favorable	Unfavorable	No opinion
Sarah Palin	Aug 29, 2008	22%	7%	71%
Joe Biden	Aug 23, 2008	34%	15%	51%
John Edwards	Jul 6, 2004	54%	16%	30%
Joe Lieberman	Aug 7, 2000	37%	10%	53%
Dick Cheney	Jul 24, 2000	51%	11%	38%
Jack Kemp	Aug 11, 1996	56%	14%	30%
Al Gore	Jul 23-24, 1992	59%	13%	28%

National Convention next week will be critical in the establishment of her overall image in the minds of many members of her own party, as well as among independents and other potential swing voters. Even at this point, however, Palin has a positive image among those who know enough to have an opinion of her, with more than a three-to-one ratio of favorable to unfavorable ratings—more positive than Biden's ratio as measured last weekend. By comparison, Edwards, Lieberman, Cheney, Kemp, and Gore all had much more positive favorable-to-unfavorable ratios than either of this year's vice presidential selections. All in all, Gallup's initial reads of the recognition and image of both Biden and Palin after their selections this year are more muted than has been the case for other recent vice presidential selections.

3. Potential Problem for Palin: Perceived Qualifications to Serve as President

Palin rates substantially below other recent vice presidential candidates in terms of the perception that she is qualified to serve as president. Asked if, from what they know about Sarah Palin, they believe she is "qualified to serve as president it if becomes necessary," only 39% of Americans say yes, while almost as many, 33%, say no.

These results are highly partisan in nature: Sixty-three percent of Republicans say she is qualified, but 53% of Democrats say she is not. Independents are more likely to say she is qualified (41%) than not (31%). Taken as a whole, the reaction of Americans to Palin's qualifications is much more negative than was accorded Joe Biden a week ago after his selection by Obama, when 57% said Biden was qualified to serve and only 18% said he was not. In terms of the ratio of "yes" to "no" responses, the perception of Palin's qualifications is more negative than the "qualification" rating given to any other recent selection with the exception of Dan Quayle in 1992. The assessment of Quayle's qualifications, however, came when he had already served for four years as vice president, and was thus not directly comparable to these initial reactions to other candidates.

Implications

The initial reaction of the American public to McCain's surprise selection of Sarah Palin as his vice presidential running mate is muted. A substantial majority of Americans don't know enough about her yet to have an opinion, and a large majority say that at this point her selection will not have an impact on their presidential vote either way. The good news for McCain and Palin is that among those who do know her, her image is significantly more positive than negative, and in fact more positive on a ratio basis than the image of Biden when his was measured a week ago. On the negative side of the ledger for the Republicans is that almost as many Americans say Palin is not qualified to serve as president as say she is qualified, giving her a more negative reading on this measure than any other recent vice presidential selection with the exception of Dan Quayle in 1992. Given the fact that so many Americans profess at this point to know nothing about Palin, the next several weeks may be critical to her success as a vice presidential nominee as her image is shaped and formed in the harsh spotlight of national media attention. The data suggest that one major task of the Republican convention in particular will be to convince a skeptical public that she would be able to serve as president if needed.

SEPTEMBER 2008

Over half of Americans say they are worse off financially now than they were a year ago, tied for the most negative reading in Gallup's 32-year history of asking this question. Still, close to 6 in 10 say they hope to be better off at this time next year. And despite the recent financial crisis, these results are no worse than those of four months ago, at the beginning of the summer. Americans are as likely to say they are worse off financially compared with a year ago as they have been at any time since 1976, when Gallup first asked the question. About a quarter of Americans are holding on to a more positive mental attitude and say they are better off than a year ago.

Of interest is that Americans were identical in their negativity in late May/early June 2008 (matching the current reading as the most negative in Gallup's history), well before the current Wall Street and financial crisis that began in mid-September. This is an important reminder that Americans' gloomy financial outlook did not begin just over the last several weeks but has been in place for a while now amid rising gasoline prices, inflation worries, and rising joblessness. On the other hand, in terms of predicting their financial future, Americans are, typically, relatively optimistic. The 58% who say they will be better off in a year is certainly more positive than many previous readings on this measure over the years, including in the late 1970s and early 1980s, when well under half of Americans thought they would be better off financially in a year. The highest reading for "better off in a year" came in March 1998, when 71% gave this positive response. The current "better off in a year" reading is up slightly from late May/early June 2008. This suggests, but of course does not prove, that there may have been some slight perceived benefit from last week's attempts to pass legislation designed to improve the country's financial future. Or it could reflect the relative stabilization of gasoline prices. (The current data were collected through Saturday, September 27, and do not reflect the events of Monday, September 29,

relating to possible congressional legislation and the drop in the stock market.)

The September 25–27 USA Today/Gallup Poll also asked Americans how worried they were about a list of five financial concerns. Based on a rank ordering of those who are "very" and "moderately" worried, Americans are most concerned about not having enough money for retirement and not being able to maintain the standard of living they enjoy. On a relative basis, Americans are least worried that they will not be able to make the minimum payments on their credit cards. The trend data on these measures suggests that worry had increased as of April 2008 but has not increased since then. Just days before the historic 778-point plunge in the Dow Jones Industrial Average on September 29, 20% of Americans had seriously considered taking their money out of the stock market, and 8% already had. But a majority (51%) were not very worried, or not worried at all, about the money they had in banks.

SEPTEMBER 2

Obama Gains Among Former Clinton Supporters

The Democratic National Convention, held on August 25–28, appears to have helped solidify support for Barack Obama among former Hillary Clinton supporters, with the percentage saying they will vote for Obama in November moving from 70% pre-convention to 81% after the convention, and the percentage saying they were certain to vote for Obama jumping from 47% to 65%. Other pre- and post-convention comparisons show that Obama gained modestly in his positioning against John McCain on several dimensions, including on the perception that he is better able to handle terrorism and the situation in Iraq, and that he is a strong and decisive leader.

CHRONOLOGY

SEPTEMBER 2008

September 1–4 The Republican National Convention is held in St. Paul, Minnesota. The first day of the proceedings is abbreviated because of Hurricane Gustav.

September 1 Alaska governor Sarah Palin and her husband issue a statement saying that their 17-year-old unmarried daughter is pregnant and that she intends to have the baby and marry the father.

September 3 Accepting the Republican nomination for vice president, Governor Palin introduces herself to America at the Republican convention as "just your average mom," who is as qualified as Barack Obama to be the president of the United States.

September 4 John McCain accepts the Republican nomination for president. He pledges to move the nation beyond "partisan rancor."

September 7 The Bush administration seizes control of Fannie Mae and Freddie Mac, the nation's two largest mortgage finance companies. This begins a multi-week-long series of major reverberations throughout the world's financial markets.

September 10 Wall Street is gripped by fear that another major

financial institution, the investment bank Lehman Brothers, might founder—and that the government might not come to its rescue.

September 14 Senator Obama's campaign announces that it collected a record $66 million during August, attracting 500,000 first-time donors.

September 14 Merrill Lynch, the brokerage firm, which had suffered staggering losses of more than $45 billion in its mortgage investments, agrees to sell itself to Bank of America. Lehman Brothers announces it will seek bankruptcy protection as the bank hurtles toward liquidation.

September 15 Wall Street suffers its worst loss since the 2001 terrorist attacks. The Dow Jones industrial average drops 4.4%.

September 16 The Federal Reserve agrees to an $85 billion bailout that would give the government control of the troubled insurance giant American International Group (AIG).

September 20 The Bush administration proposes an unprecedented bailout of American financial institutions. The secretary of the treasury would be granted unfettered authority to buy up to $700 billion in distressed mortgages from private firms.

September 23–24 CBS anchor Katie Couric conducts an exclusive interview with Governor Palin, whose answers often seem rambling and incoherent. Supporters argue that Couric's questions were unfair and revealed media bias.

September 24 North Korea announces that it is resuming its nuclear program.

September 24 John McCain announces that he is temporarily suspending his campaign to return to Washington. The Republican candidate says that he plans to forge an agreement on the proposed $700 bailout of financial institutions pending before Congress. Obama rejects McCain's proposal to delay the first presidential debate.

September 25 Obama and McCain meet with President Bush and congressional leaders at the White House to discuss the financial crisis.

September 26 Obama and McCain participate in the first of three presidential debates at the University of Mississippi.

September 29 Defying both President Bush and congressional leaders of both parties, the House of Representatives rejects a $700 billion economic rescue plan for the nation's financial institutions.

The main point of the comparisons is to provide an initial measurement of the impact of the convention on the images of the two candidates (and the two parties). This year's timeline provides a challenge of interpretation. In addition to the Democratic convention, the time period between the two surveys being compared here also encompassed McCain's surprise announcement of Alaska governor Sarah Palin as his vice presidential running mate on August 29 and the intensifying news coverage of the approach of Hurricane Gustav throughout the rest of the

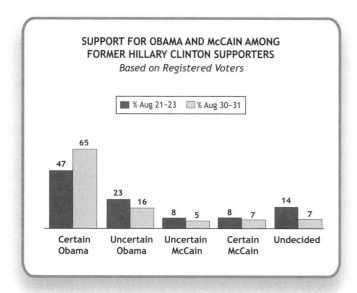

SUPPORT FOR OBAMA AND McCAIN AMONG FORMER HILLARY CLINTON SUPPORTERS
Based on Registered Voters

weekend. Nevertheless, the comparisons provide a basic indication of the overall impact of the convention.

Tracking Clinton Voters

The Democratic convention appears to have increased the amount of certain support for Obama among Democratic voters, including in particular among the critical group of Democrats who earlier this year supported Clinton in the Democratic primaries. Much attention was given to the fact that only 47% of former Clinton supporters said in the pre-convention USA Today/Gallup Poll that they were certain to vote for Obama and that 16% of her supporters said they were going to vote for McCain, with another 14% undecided. The new polling shows that many of these disaffected Clinton voters have now returned to the Democratic fold. The percentage of former Clinton voters who say they are certain to vote for Obama has now jumped to 65%. Although 12% of former Clinton voters persist in saying that they are going to vote for McCain, that's down from 16%, and the percentage who are undecided has dropped in half. Overall, support for Obama among this group has moved from 70% pre-convention to 81% post-convention.

To be sure, former Clinton supporters are still less enthusiastic about the election than former Obama supporters in the post-convention poll. And the fact that 12% still say they are going to vote for McCain is no doubt troubling to the Obama camp. But it appears that, overall, the concentrated effort by Obama's campaign managers to feature both Hillary and Bill Clinton in prominent roles at the convention, along with efforts by Hillary Clinton to emphasize her support for Obama going into the November election, may have paid off. Finally, certainty to vote for Obama also moved up from 80% to 87% among voters who previously

supported Obama in the Democratic primaries, further suggesting that the Democratic convention had the effect of solidifying party support for the Obama candidacy.

Favorable Ratings of the Two Candidates

There was only a slight change in the basic images of the two major party candidates in the time period between these two polls. The expectation would ordinarily be that Obama's image would become more positive while McCain's would become more negative as a result of the Democratic convention. But the data show that Obama's favorable rating actually dropped very slightly, by two percentage points, while McCain's favorable rating dropped by a larger five-point margin, the latter finding more in line with expectations. Obama now has a seven-point-higher favorable percentage than McCain, only slightly more positive for Obama than the four-point margin he held over McCain pre-convention.

More Detailed Images of the Two Candidates

The August 30 and 31 interviewing asked Americans to assess whether McCain or Obama would better handle three key issues: the economy, terrorism, and the situation in Iraq. The surveys also included measures of the positioning of the candidates as best fitting three descriptive phrases: "is a strong and decisive leader," "shares your values," and "is honest and trustworthy." A comparison of the pre-convention and post-convention data shows that Obama gained at least slightly on all six of the dimensions, although for one dimension—best able to handle the economy—the change was not statistically significant.

Obama is now rated about even with McCain with respect to handling the situation in Iraq and has cut into McCain's lead on terrorism. Obama maintains a big advantage on the economy. Importantly, Obama is now even with McCain on the leadership dimension, which was a strong point for McCain prior to the Democratic convention, and he has gained the advantage on honesty, on which the two

PERCENTAGE SELECTING BARACK OBAMA ON ISSUES AND CHARACTERISTICS
Based on Registered Voters

	Aug 21–23	Aug 30–31
Better handle the economy	54	55
Better handle terrorism	35	41
Better handle Iraq	42	47
Strong and decisive leader	40	46
Shares your values	47	52
Honest and trustworthy	39	45

How concerned are you that McCain will pursue policies
too similar to those of George W. Bush?
Based on Registered Voters

	Aug 21–23	Aug 30–31
Very concerned	41	47
Somewhat concerned	25	17
Not too concerned	18	17
Not at all concerned	15	17

were formerly tied. The sorts of gains seen for Obama are generally what would be expected from a convention—which is, after all, a period of time in which the media focus is fairly exclusively on positive messages put out by one party and its presidential candidate. In this case, this positive flow of information about Obama appears to have moved the needle in Obama's direction on five out of six dimensions polled. McCain will have a chance to reverse some of these shifts at the Republican National Convention this week.

MCCAIN AND BUSH; OBAMA'S EXPERIENCE

The percentage of Americans who profess to be "very" concerned that John McCain would pursue policies too similar to those of George W. Bush moved up slightly between the two surveys, from 41% to 47%. At the same time, the percentage "somewhat" concerned dropped slightly, so that the total percentage of Americans concerned about the McCain-Bush connection stayed fairly stable. There was also a slight shift in Obama's favor in perceptions of his experience. There has been a seven-point drop since the Democratic convention in the percentage of Americans who say they are very or somewhat concerned that Obama lacks the experience necessary to be president.

There was almost no change in the images of the Republican and Democratic parties over the time period encompassed by these two polls. The Democratic Party continues to have a significantly higher favorable image than the Republican Party, as it has all year, and the convention and

other events of the previous week seem to have had little impact on these images.

Implications for the Obama Campaign

The Democratic convention appears to have accomplished, at least to a modest degree, some of the objectives Democratic leaders were probably hoping for. A healthy percentage of former supporters of Hillary Clinton, many of whom were public in their disaffection for Obama before the convention, appear to have returned to the fold and now say they are certain to vote for the Democratic nominee. This no doubt reflects the fact that Hillary (and Bill) Clinton were accorded an extraordinary amount of attention during the convention—and that Hillary Clinton was vocal in declaring her loyalty and support for Obama. Still, 19% of former Clinton supporters continue to say they are either going to vote for McCain or are currently undecided, indicating that there may be some residual anger that has not yet been dissipated by Obama's efforts, and that there is still work to do for the Democrats in bringing the remaining Clinton supporters into the Obama camp. The convention also appears to have improved Obama's image on several dimensions, including several that have heretofore been McCain strengths: in particular, handling terrorism and being perceived as a strong leader.

Gallup's Quick Read on the Election

Democrats have a "structural" election advantage. Fewer Americans identify as Republicans than four years ago, and the Republican Party is seen less favorably than the Democratic Party. There is low approval for the incumbent Republican president, and voters want a change in leadership. Not surprisingly, Democrats win on generic ballots for both president and Congress. Still, Barack Obama led John McCain by only an average of three percentage points among registered voters for most of this summer. The two candidates were in a statistical tie just as the Democratic convention began, though Obama then received a predictable convention "bounce" during the convention and was eight points ahead of McCain by September 2. The extent to which McCain may receive his own convention bounce this week remains to be seen.

Broadly speaking, the structure of this race has been similar to the very close elections of 2000 and 2004. Both candidates this year have a high percentage of their party's vote, though McCain has a slightly higher "partisan loyalty" factor. The two candidates are splitting the independent vote. To win by a large margin, a candidate needs a significant advantage among independents and needs to perform

How concerned are you that Obama lacks
the experience to be president?
Based on Registered Voters

	Aug 21–23	Aug 30–31
Very concerned	35	31
Somewhat concerned	22	19
Not too concerned	19	18
Not at all concerned	23	29

at least marginally better among his own party identifiers than the opponent does among his partisans.

Turnout will be a key factor. Obama would benefit if there is unusual (or unprecedented) enthusiasm among young voters and minority voters. McCain would benefit if there is a higher turnout among Republicans, especially highly religious white voters. Results of likely-voter modeling this summer so far have been mixed. Overall enthusiasm about voting, which was higher earlier this year, has dropped off and has remained low even after the Democratic convention. Democrats did not gain enthusiasm as a result of their convention but remain more enthusiastic than Republicans, suggesting a possible Democratic edge in turnout.

The current position of the candidates in the polls predicts little. In the previous two elections, the candidates who led in polls in the summer, before their respective conventions—Bush in 2000 and Kerry in 2004—ended up losing the popular vote. Over the last week, Gallup's polling showed a decline in the number of "swing voters"—those who said they either had not made up their mind or could change their mind about their candidate support. Both Obama's and McCain's supporters became a little more certain in their vote choice. In Obama's case, many of the voters who had previously supported Hillary Clinton—about a third of whom had said before the Democratic convention that they were undecided or voting for McCain—shifted to supporting Obama. Strength of support, like enthusiasm, is slightly higher for Obama than for McCain.

So far Gallup analysis shows no bounce for Obama based on his selection of Delaware senator Joe Biden as his vice presidential running mate, a modest four-point bounce for Obama as a result of his convention, and a two-point bounce for McCain on the day of his selection of Alaska governor Sarah Palin as his vice presidential running mate. History predicts McCain may receive an additional bounce as a result of the Republican convention, although news coverage of Hurricane Gustav may have an as yet unknown impact. Candidate standings after the conventions will be critical.

Early Gallup analysis does not find a disproportionate change in support among highly religious white voters as a result of McCain's choice of Palin. However, all of McCain's short-term gain of two points as a result of the Palin pick appears to have come among women.

The top voter issue this year is the economy. Gasoline prices, Iraq, healthcare, and terrorism remain important. Obama's perceived strengths include domestic issues, compassion, empathy, and bringing about change, while McCain's perceived strengths include experience, international issues, terrorism, and being viewed as a capable commander in chief, although in the days after the Democratic convention Obama gained ground against McCain on several of these. A continuing uptick in consumer confidence, a downward drift in gas prices, and an increase in perceived success in Iraq could benefit McCain.

Republicans Still Face Enthusiasm Gap

The latest USA Today/Gallup Poll finds a slight uptick in voter enthusiasm compared with a week ago, prior to the Democrats' holding their convention and John McCain's choosing his vice presidential running mate. Both Democrats and Republicans show slight increases in their enthusiasm about this year's election, though Democrats continue to hold a significant advantage over Republicans, 61% to 42%. There has been an unmistakable decline in voter enthusiasm over the course of the year, and the recent events have not fully restored enthusiasm to where it was during the intense primary season in January and February, when more than 6 in 10 voters said they were more enthusiastic than usual about voting. The lessened enthusiasm is more apparent among Democrats than among Republicans, though both groups show some decline. The current poll suggests that the decline in Democratic enthusiasm could be the result of a letdown among Hillary Clinton supporters. Among Democrats who say they supported Clinton in the primaries, just 46% now say they are more enthusiastic than usual about voting, compared with 77% of Obama primary supporters. In January and February, 78% of Clinton supporters and 84% of Obama supporters reported being more enthused than usual about voting.

Despite the high levels measured earlier this year, voter enthusiasm has declined to the point that it does not match what it was in 2004. Just after the Democratic

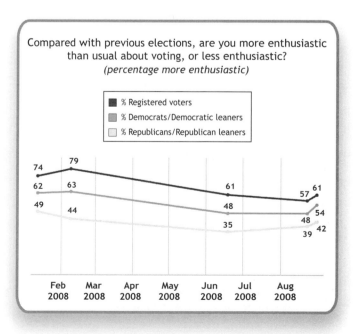

Compared with previous elections, are you more enthusiastic than usual about voting, or less enthusiastic?
(percentage more enthusiastic)

■ % Registered voters
■ % Democrats/Democratic leaners
□ % Republicans/Republican leaners

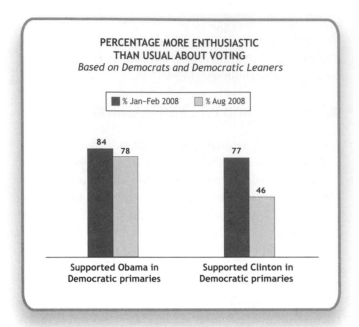

PERCENTAGE MORE ENTHUSIASTIC
THAN USUAL ABOUT VOTING
Based on Democrats and Democratic Leaners

■ % Jan-Feb 2008   ☐ % Aug 2008

84 78   77 46

Supported Obama in
Democratic primaries

Supported Clinton in
Democratic primaries

convention in late July/early August of that year, 69% of voters said they were more enthusiastic than usual about voting, including 73% of Democrats and 62% of Republicans. Enthusiasm remained at high levels throughout that campaign and presaged the highest voter turnout in more than three decades. It is unclear at this point whether voter enthusiasm will return to the levels of earlier this year. McCain and the Republicans have a chance to boost Republicans' excitement at the Republican National Convention in St. Paul, Minnesota, this week. Also, as the campaign kicks into high gear over the next two months, with three presidential debates and more intense campaigning, voters may show renewed enthusiasm about the election.

Gallup does not have enough of a track record of measuring enthusiasm in presidential elections to say what the typical pattern is over the course of an election year, or what the current Democratic advantage in enthusiasm might mean for the election outcome in November. In 2004, in contrast to this year, enthusiasm was lower during the primaries but higher in the general election phase of the campaign. And in the last pre-election measure in 2004 the two parties were even on expressed enthusiasm: Sixty-eight percent of Republicans and 67% of Democrats were more enthusiastic than usual about voting. The only measures from 2000 were taken during the primary season. Gallup has measured voter enthusiasm more regularly in midterm election years, and a prior analysis suggests that when one party had an advantage on enthusiasm in a midterm election year, it tended to fare better in the election. This relationship appears to have more to do with party allegiances shifting in that party's direction than with higher turnout for the party.

Gallup Daily: Obama Hits 50% for the First Time

Gallup Poll daily tracking from August 30 through September 1 finds Barack Obama leading in the race for president with his highest share of support to date. Fully half of national registered voters now favor Obama for president, while 42% back John McCain. Previously, no more than 49% of registered voters supported Obama for president in Gallup Poll daily tracking. Still, Obama's eight-percentage-point lead over McCain in the new poll falls one point shy of the lead he attained in late July 2008 after returning from a well-publicized trip to Europe and the Middle East. At that time, Obama led by nine points, 49% to 40%. McCain's 42% support is well below his top support level of 48%, recorded in late April/early May. It is just slightly better than the 40% he received at several points in July, and than the 41% favoring him just last week, while the Democratic convention was under way. At 8%, the percentage of undecided voters is slightly lower than the 9%-to-11% figures seen for most of August, and this is the lowest this figure has been since early June. This, in part, reflects movement of voters toward Obama over the course of the Democratic convention, a trend that has been sustained in subsequent days.

SEPTEMBER 3
Will the Abortion Issue Help or Hurt McCain?

By choosing Alaska governor Sarah Palin to be his running mate, John McCain is in part gambling that putting a female reform-minded governor (who happens to be staunchly pro-life) on the Republican ticket will help to cut into Obama's substantial lead among female voters. Obama is now countering that strategy by running ads in swing electoral states highlighting McCain's and Palin's opposition to abortion.

Who stands to gain? To start with, female voters as a whole tilt pro-choice over pro-life in how they describe their abortion stances, 50% to 43%. Among the independent and Democratic women who are the primary focus of this battle, the balance of opinion is a bit more strongly pro-choice. However, as Gallup polling in 2008 and all recent past elections shows, only a small fraction of Americans are highly activated on the abortion issue. Most Americans downgrade the importance of abortion to their vote, saying either that it's not a major issue for them (37%) or that it is just one of many important issues they consider (49%). Only 13% of Americans told Gallup in May 2008 that they vote only for candidates for major offices who share their views on abortion. That may largely explain why 32% of

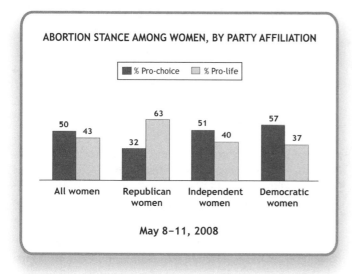

ABORTION STANCE AMONG WOMEN, BY PARTY AFFILIATION

■ % Pro-choice   □ % Pro-life

	% Pro-choice	% Pro-life
All women	50	43
Republican women	32	63
Independent women	51	40
Democratic women	57	37

May 8–11, 2008

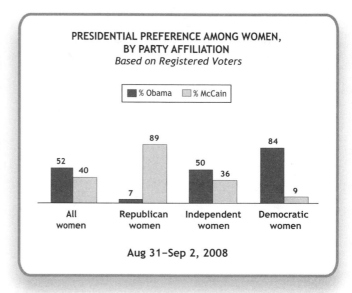

PRESIDENTIAL PREFERENCE AMONG WOMEN, BY PARTY AFFILIATION
Based on Registered Voters

■ % Obama   □ % McCain

	% Obama	% McCain
All women	52	40
Republican women	7	89
Independent women	50	36
Democratic women	84	9

Aug 31–Sep 2, 2008

Republican women call themselves pro-choice, yet only 7% of Republican women are voting for Obama. Similarly, in contrast to the 37% of Democratic women who say they are pro-life, only 9% are voting for McCain. Abortion is simply not a pivotal issue for these voters.

Although a third of Republican women are pro-choice, McCain's selection of Palin already appears to have helped him with his female Republican base. Republican women were more likely to support McCain, not less likely, in polling from August 30 to September 1. There is something closer to a one-to-one correspondence between abortion views and presidential preferences among independent women, at least numerically. Independent women split 51% vs. 40% pro-choice over pro-life in May; today they are voting for Obama over McCain by 50% to 36%. But the abortion issue appears to be even less of a factor for independent women than it is for their partisan counterparts. According to Gallup's May 2008 Values and Beliefs survey, 20% of Republican women said they

vote only for candidates who share their views on abortion, as did 14% of Democratic women—but only 8% of independent women considered a candidate's views on abortion decisive.

Roe v. Wade Versus Partial-Birth Abortion

To the extent that abortion politics makes a difference in the 2008 election, it could come down to how the candidates exploit the public's strong feelings on two specific issues: overturning the landmark 1973 Supreme Court *Roe v. Wade* decision legalizing abortion on the one hand, and the legality of late-term abortions, including the so-called partial-birth abortion procedure, on the other. Americans

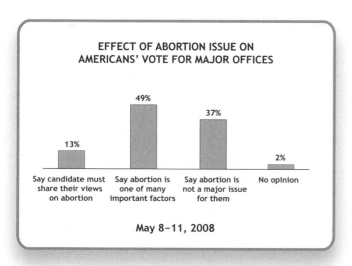

EFFECT OF ABORTION ISSUE ON AMERICANS' VOTE FOR MAJOR OFFICES

	%
Say candidate must share their views on abortion	13%
Say abortion is one of many important factors	49%
Say abortion is not a major issue for them	37%
No opinion	2%

May 8–11, 2008

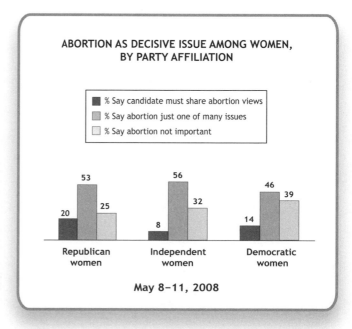

ABORTION AS DECISIVE ISSUE AMONG WOMEN, BY PARTY AFFILIATION

■ % Say candidate must share abortion views
▨ % Say abortion just one of many issues
□ % Say abortion not important

	Must share	One of many	Not important
Republican women	20	53	25
Independent women	8	56	32
Democratic women	14	46	39

May 8–11, 2008

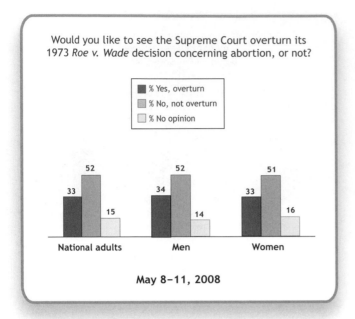

Would you like to see the Supreme Court overturn its 1973 *Roe v. Wade* decision concerning abortion, or not?

- ■ % Yes, overturn
- ■ % No, not overturn
- □ % No opinion

	National adults	Men	Women
% Yes, overturn	33	34	33
% No, not overturn	52	52	51
% No opinion	15	14	16

May 8–11, 2008

(men and women alike) broadly support keeping abortion legal, at least in the first trimester, and the majority oppose overturning *Roe v. Wade*. Thus, highlighting the risk that McCain would appoint judges who might overturn *Roe v. Wade* could be a potent pro-choice selling point for Obama.

From McCain's perspective, the strongest potential pro-life message he can use could be Obama's positions against a ban on partial-birth abortion and against a law that would give a child who survives an abortion the full rights of a human being. Gallup polling has consistently shown a high percentage of Americans in favor of making partial-birth abortion illegal, and widely opposed to late-term abortions

Do you think that the specific abortion procedure known as "late term" abortion or "partial-birth" abortion, which is sometimes performed on women during the last few months of pregnancy, should be legal or illegal?

- ■ % Legal
- □ % Illegal

	National adults	Men	Women
% Legal	22	24	21
% Illegal	72	69	75

May 8–11, 2008

in general. The 2008 Republican and Democratic presidential candidates present a sharp contrast on abortion policy, and that contrast is now bursting into the open with the emerging battle for female voters.

Whether the selection of Palin as his running mate helps or hurts McCain with independent and Democratic women going forward will only partially depend on how Obama and McCain play the abortion issue. Relatively few Democratic women and even fewer independent women say abortion is the most important issue they consider in deciding on their presidential vote. Palin's story as a working mother may prove more compelling to women attracted to the idea of breaking the presidential glass ceiling. If, however, Obama and McCain both take the gloves off and seek to paint each other, respectively, as a dangerous opponent of a woman's choice and a radical proponent of late-term abortions, the issue could resonate with more than the few female voters who typically care. Many women are cross-pressured in their political views (pro-choice Republicans and pro-life Democrats), so there may be significant room for changing voter preferences on the issue on both sides. And if the arguments cut deeply enough, they could also be influential with independents.

SEPTEMBER 4

Intense Political Week Brings Decline in Swing Voters

The percentage of voters who are "up for grabs" has declined sharply in the past week, from 30% to 21%, according to the latest USA Today/Gallup Poll. The decline in the proportion of voters classified as swing voters coincides with two major political events that took place over the past seven days: the Democratic convention and John McCain's announcement of Sarah Palin as his vice presidential running mate. Each event certainly had the potential to ease particular voter concerns, such as Obama's readiness to be president and McCain's commitment to core Republican principles. At this point, 42% of registered voters say they are certain to vote for Obama, up from 36% immediately before the convention. Thirty-seven percent are now committed to McCain, up slightly from 34%. Thus, with 79% of voters committed to one candidate or the other, 21% are "swing voters" who could vote for either candidate or for a third party candidate.

Historically, the proportion of swing voters tends to decline as Election Day approaches. However, there have been examples of temporary increases in the number of uncommitted voters in response to high-profile campaign events such as debates. So it is unclear what impact the Republican convention will have on the electorate in the coming days.

Forced by Hurricane Gustav to remain in Washington, President George W. Bush addresses the Republican National Convention by video on September 2, 2008. *(Susan Walsh/AP Images)*

Who Are the Swing Voters?

Gallup's research on swing voters has shown that, not surprisingly, political independents and moderates are usually among the most likely voters to lack a firm commitment

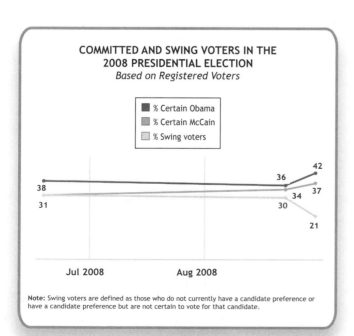

COMMITTED AND SWING VOTERS IN THE 2008 PRESIDENTIAL ELECTION
Based on Registered Voters

■ % Certain Obama
■ % Certain McCain
☐ % Swing voters

Jul 2008   Aug 2008

Note: Swing voters are defined as those who do not currently have a candidate preference or have a candidate preference but are not certain to vote for that candidate.

to either candidate in a presidential election. In the latest poll, 34% of independents and 33% of moderates can be considered swing voters; both percentages are well above the national average of 21%. Beyond those groups, the types of voters more likely to be swing voters have varied across elections. This year, older voters tend to be more in the "swing" category, as 28% of those 65 and older are not committed to a candidate at this point, compared with 16% of 18- to 29-year-olds, 20% of 30- to 49-year-olds, and 19% of those age 50 to 64. Another key voting bloc this year is Democrats who supported Hillary Clinton in the presidential primaries. Since the Democratic Convention, a substantial percentage of her supporters have come back into the Democratic fold, saying they will vote for Obama, but 28% remain uncommitted to him or currently support another candidate. There are no meaningful differences in the proportion of swing voters by gender, education, religiosity, or marital status.

Swing Voters' Political Attitudes

Swing voters' opinions about the candidates may shed some light on why they have yet to commit to a candidate, and possibly on whom they might eventually support. At a basic level, swing voters view both McCain and Obama

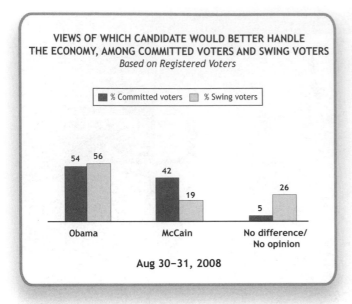

VIEWS OF WHICH CANDIDATE WOULD BETTER HANDLE
THE ECONOMY, AMONG COMMITTED VOTERS AND SWING VOTERS
Based on Registered Voters

Aug 30–31, 2008

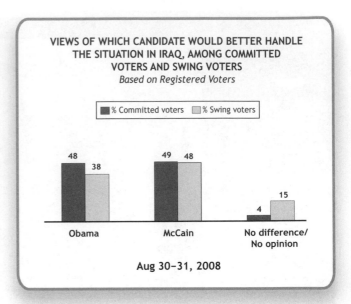

VIEWS OF WHICH CANDIDATE WOULD BETTER HANDLE
THE SITUATION IN IRAQ, AMONG COMMITTED
VOTERS AND SWING VOTERS
Based on Registered Voters

Aug 30–31, 2008

positively: 62% have a favorable opinion of the Republican candidate and 68% of the Democratic nominee. Both figures are higher than the favorable ratings among the broader electorate (57% and 62%, respectively). This suggests that swing voters are essentially deciding between two attractive options. One reason swing voters have yet to commit to a candidate is that they still appear to harbor some doubts about how the candidates would perform on issues that are not obvious areas of strength. For example, only 19% of swing voters say McCain would do a better job than Obama on the economy, much lower than the 42% of committed voters who view McCain as better on economic matters. But that does not mean Obama has convinced swing voters he is the superior candidate on the economy, because roughly as many swing voters (56%)

as committed voters (54%) view Obama as better on this issue.

The same pattern is evident with respect to which candidate would do a better job on terrorism, but on this issue Obama is the candidate whom swing voters are unsure about. McCain does not do any better among swing voters than among committed voters on this issue. On Iraq, Obama again underperforms among swing voters compared with committed voters, but McCain gets similar scores from both groups.

The latest poll did not include any measure of the relative importance of the various issues, so it is not clear which issue might be most fruitfully exploited to attract swing voter support. However, the Aug. 21–23 USA Today/Gallup Poll, conducted before the conventions began, did provide some evidence that swing voters appeared to assign greater importance to the economy as a campaign issue than did committed voters. It is unclear whether that has changed at all since the conventions got under way. The percentage of voters who have yet to commit to a candidate has declined sharply in the past week, and is now similar to what Gallup measured between conventions in 2004. Earlier this year, there was a higher proportion of uncommitted voters than at a comparable time in 2004. And while the Republican Convention and the upcoming debates could help voters make up their minds, these events also have the potential to make voters less certain about their choice, at least in the short run. To some degree, it appears as if swing voters are uncommitted this year because they still have doubts about Obama's and McCain's ability to handle issues that are not their known areas of strength—namely, the economy for McCain and foreign affairs (especially terrorism) for

VIEWS OF WHICH CANDIDATE WOULD BETTER
HANDLE TERRORISM, AMONG COMMITTED
VOTERS AND SWING VOTERS
Based on Registered Voters

Aug 30–31, 2008

Obama. Thus, both candidates stand to gain support if they can address voters' concerns in these areas between now and Election Day.

Gallup Daily: No Dent in Obama Lead So Far

Barack Obama continues to hold a lead over John McCain, 49% to 42%, in the latest Gallup Poll daily tracking update. The results are based on interviewing conducted between September 1 and September 3. The vast majority of interviews on September 3 were conducted before Sarah Palin gave her much-anticipated convention speech. However, the data do indicate that the initial first two nights of the convention—the slimmed-down program in deference to Hurricane Gustav on September 1 and speeches headlined by former senator Fred Thompson on September 2—have, so far, done little to change voter preferences.

SEPTEMBER 5

Religion Remains Major Dividing Factor Among White Voters

John McCain has led Barack Obama all summer among highly religious white voters and continues to do so in the first three days of September, with no sign of change subsequent to his selection of Palin. About 33% of non-Hispanic white registered voters are weekly church attenders, and the data make it clear that this group forms one of Republican McCain's key constituencies. The more than two-to-one support levels for McCain among this group have been remarkably consistent all summer. Much attention was paid to the possibility that the choice of Palin would help boost McCain's support even further among this group. That may happen in the days to come, but interviewing conducted during the first three days of the Republican convention suggests little change in the support patterns among highly religious white voters compared with previous weeks. These religious voters remain about as supportive of McCain as they have been.

McCain also has the support, but by a somewhat smaller margin, of the smaller group of about 19% of white registered voters who attend church nearly weekly or monthly. There has been a little more variation in support levels among this group as the summer has progressed, including a slight shift toward Obama in the September 1–3 data. Finally, there is a distinctly different pattern of candidate support evident among white voters who report seldom or never attending church. This large group—about 47%

of the white registered voter population—skewed toward Obama by a 12-point margin in the last week of August and in the first three days of September. Again, there has been little substantive change in this voter-support pattern all summer.

Religiosity and Voter Preference: Comparison of 2008 with 2004

Indeed, this same pattern of candidate support by religiosity among whites has not only remained fairly constant in 2008, but also is very close to where things stood four years ago, just before the 2004 election. President George W. Bush led John Kerry on the eve of the 2004 election by 66% to 27% among white registered voters who attended church weekly, almost identical to where McCain and Obama stand today. Bush did somewhat better than McCain is doing now among white voters who attend almost weekly or monthly, but the Kerry margin over Bush among infrequent church attenders and nonattenders in 2004 was very close to Obama's margin over McCain among this same group now.

Overall, in the first three days of September, McCain is leading Obama among all non-Hispanic white registered voters by a 49% to 41% margin. This lead is based on his margin among the slightly more than half of all whites who attend church at least monthly being more than enough to compensate for his deficit among those who seldom or never attend church. From a larger perspective, Obama has an overall lead of 7 points over McCain for the period September 1–3. The Democratic nominee's support among non-whites (including blacks, Hispanics, and Asian Americans) is so strong that it more than compensates for McCain's lead among non-Hispanic whites.

McCain has seen no immediate increase in support among highly religious white voters after his selection of Palin. McCain has been ahead of Obama by better than a two-to-one margin among this group all summer, and that

POLLING RESULTS BY CHURCH ATTENDANCE, 2004 AND 2008
Among Non-Hispanic White Registered Voters

Oct 29-31, 2004	John Kerry	George W. Bush
Attend church weekly	27%	66%
Attend almost weekly/monthly	36%	62%
Attend seldom/never	53%	40%

Sep 1-3, 2008	Barack Obama	John McCain
Attend church weekly	26%	65%
Attend almost weekly/monthly	41%	50%
Attend seldom/never	51%	39%

margin continues more or less unchanged in the first three days of September. Meanwhile, Obama continues to dominate McCain among white voters who seldom or never attend church.

SEPTEMBER 8

Republicans' Enthusiasm Jumps After Convention

As the remarkable two-week stretch of back-to-back presidential nomination conventions ends, a weekend USA Today/Gallup Poll finds that the John McCain–Sarah Palin ticket has more than matched the Barack Obama–Joe Biden ticket's convention bounce of last week with a "rebound" bounce, and in the immediate aftermath of the Republican convention McCain and Palin now have a slight edge over their opponents.

The presidential race was dead even at 45% to 45% among registered voters in Gallup tracking conducted prior to the Democratic convention. Then, by the USA Today/Gallup Poll conducted in the first few days after the Democratic convention (which was also after McCain had made his announcement of Sarah Palin as his running mate), Obama had moved ahead by a 47% to 43% margin. (In Gallup Poll daily tracking extending into the beginning of last week, Obama reached a point where he had 50% of the vote and an eight-percentage-point lead.) Obama's lead has now disappeared totally, and McCain sits on a four-point advantage among registered voters in the September 5–7 poll. That's the largest advantage for McCain in either USA Today/Gallup Polls or Gallup Poll daily tracking since May.

The convention and McCain's selection of Sarah Palin as his vice presidential running mate not only had the effect of moving the horserace needle in McCain's direction, but also increased several measures of enthusiasm among the Republicans. There has been a very substantial jump in the

Vice-presidential candidate Sarah Palin addresses the Republican National Convention in St. Paul, Minnesota, on September 3, 2008. *(Ron Edmunds/AP Images)*

percentage of Republicans saying they are more enthusiastic than usual about voting in this election, from 42% a week ago (after the Democratic convention but before the Republican convention) to 60% today. Democrats still retain a slight lead on this measure, having increased their enthusiasm slightly this past week as well. But the enthusiasm gap, which has been so much a part of the story of the presidential election so far this year, has dwindled from 19 points in the Democrats' favor a week ago to only 7 points today.

Likely Versus Registered Voters

The gap between registered voters and likely voters has grown once again in the McCain-Palin ticket's favor in this poll. While the Republican ticket leads by 50% to 46% among registered voters, that lead stretches to a 54% to 44% lead among those Gallup sees as most likely to actually turn out and vote. This difference between likely voters

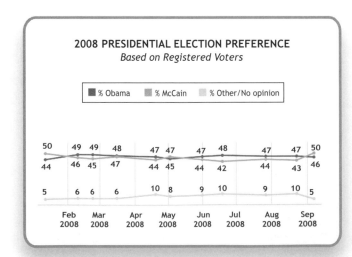

2008 PRESIDENTIAL ELECTION PREFERENCE
Based on Registered Voters

■ % Obama   ■ % McCain   ■ % Other/No opinion

	Feb 2008	Mar 2008	Apr 2008	May 2008	Jun 2008	Jul 2008	Aug 2008	Sep 2008
Obama	50	49	49	48	47	47	47	48	47	47	50
McCain	44	46	45	47	44	45	44	42	44	43	46
Other	5	6	6	6	10	8	9	10	9	10	5

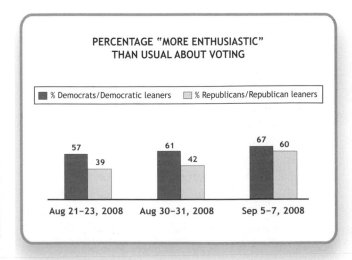

PERCENTAGE "MORE ENTHUSIASTIC" THAN USUAL ABOUT VOTING

■ % Democrats/Democratic leaners   □ % Republicans/Republican leaners

	Aug 21–23, 2008	Aug 30–31, 2008	Sep 5–7, 2008
Democrats	57	61	67
Republicans	39	42	60

and registered voters indicates that *if the election were held today*, McCain would benefit from an advantage over the Democrats in terms of those voters actually likely to turn out and vote—as has often been the case in recent presidential elections.

McCain also had a similar likely voter advantage in the USA Today/Gallup Poll conducted between July 25 and July 27, in the immediate aftermath of Obama's foreign tour, which was interpreted at the time as a significant partisan reaction to the visibility afforded Obama by that tour. That advantage for the Republicans did not appear in the USA Today/Gallup Poll conducted about a month later as the conventions began, but it has appeared again in this poll. The Republican ticket, then, has the *potential* for a significant turnout advantage on Election Day, but that appears to be very dependent on the election environment and is by no means certain.

The Palin Factor

Candidates typically receive a bounce in their standing in the polls after their party's convention, so McCain's moving into a lead over Obama by a slim margin is not unexpected. Obama received a bounce from his convention, and now McCain has received a bounce from his own.

One of the most remarkable things that occurred during the last week, of course, was McCain's highly unexpected selection of Sarah Palin as his vice presidential running mate. That selection, along with Palin's speech at the convention and (coupled with her appearance on a number of different national magazine covers in the days that followed), certainly could be hypothesized as having added a little extra energy to the Republicans' standard convention bounce. The weekend poll on September 5–7 included a number of questions addressing the Palin factor. Palin certainly appears to have made a strong impression with her convention speech, but other indications

in the data show that her selection has engendered an overall polarizing effect—with both high positives and high negatives.

Here are some of the key points:

1. Palin's speech was clearly a success: Her speech was very positively received, and reaction to it overwhelmed the tepid response to McCain's speech on Thursday night. Obama's speech before 80,000 people in a Denver football stadium at the Democratic convention a week and a half ago was not rated in this most recent weekend poll, but was rated in a one-night poll conducted on the evening of August 29, the day after his speech. Obama's speech received very positive ratings, but they were slightly lower than Palin received in this weekend's poll.

2. Other measures included in the weekend poll show a positive rating with respect to some aspects of Palin's selection, alongside a pattern of responses that reinforces the conclusion that McCain's choice may have been risky in other respects. The 36% of voters who said McCain's selection of Palin was "excellent" was higher than was measured in reaction to Obama's selection of Biden. But—and this is a big caveat—the percentage of voters who rated McCain's selection of Palin as "poor"—24%—is also high. Compared with a one-night poll conducted on August 29, the percentage of Americans rating the selection of Palin as excellent has risen—but so has, to a lesser degree, the percentage rating it poor.

3. The important question whether McCain's selection of Palin has influenced voters in either direction showed a similarly polarizing pattern of responses, with relatively high positives but also high negatives. Gallup asked Americans about the selection of Palin in a one-day poll on August 29, and since that time voters have become both more positive about the impact of the selection on their vote and more negative. The net difference between the two reactions has remained almost exactly the same over the last week.

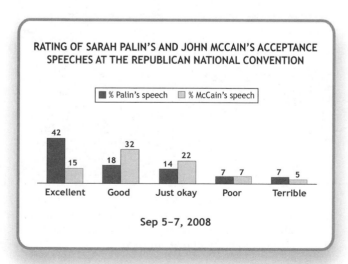

RATING OF SARAH PALIN'S AND JOHN MCCAIN'S ACCEPTANCE SPEECHES AT THE REPUBLICAN NATIONAL CONVENTION

■ % Palin's speech   ☐ % McCain's speech

	Excellent	Good	Just okay	Poor	Terrible
% Palin's speech	42	18	14	7	7
% McCain's speech	15	32	22	7	5

Sep 5–7, 2008

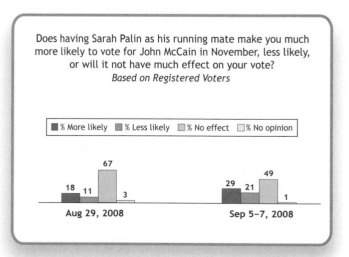

Does having Sarah Palin as his running mate make you much more likely to vote for John McCain in November, less likely, or will it not have much effect on your vote?
Based on Registered Voters

■ % More likely   ■ % Less likely   ☐ % No effect   ☐ % No opinion

	Aug 29, 2008	Sep 5–7, 2008
% More likely	18	29
% Less likely	11	21
% No effect	67	49
% No opinion	3	1

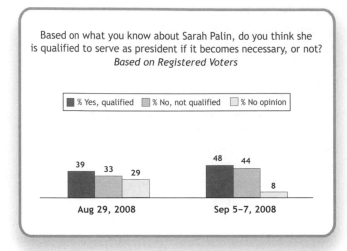

Based on what you know about Sarah Palin, do you think she is qualified to serve as president if it becomes necessary, or not?
Based on Registered Voters

■ % Yes, qualified   ■ % No, not qualified   □ % No opinion

Aug 29, 2008: 39, 33, 29
Sep 5-7, 2008: 48, 44, 8

Does what you saw or read of this week's national convention make you more likely or less likely to vote for the party's candidate?

	More likely	Less likely	No difference	No opinion
	%	%	%	%
Post-Rep. Convention 2008	43	38	13	6
Post-Dem. Convention 2008	43	29	19	8
Post-Rep. Convention 2004	41	38	15	8
Post-Dem. Convention 2004	44	30	18	8
Post-Dem. Convention 2000	43	28	19	10
Post-Rep. Convention 2000	44	27	15	14
Post-Dem. Convention 1996	44	29	19	8
Post-Rep. Convention 1996	45	34	13	8
Post-Dem. Convention 1992	60	15	17	8
Post-Rep. Convention 1988	43	27	16	14
Post-Dem. Convention 1988	56	21	9	14
Post-Dem. Convention 1984	45	29	12	14

4. Voters have also, on balance, not changed their views of Palin's qualifications to be president—and these views remain decidedly mixed. In Gallup's August 29 poll, the spread between those saying that Palin was qualified and those saying she was not qualified was six points. Now, in the weekend poll, although both percentages have risen, the spread is an almost identical four points.

5. A question asking about what the choice of Palin says about McCain's ability to make important presidential decisions shows that while 55% of voters say it reflects favorably on his ability to make important decisions, 40% say it reflects unfavorably.

Republican Convention Highly Watched, but Americans' Reactions Not Unusual

Despite the bounce McCain has received from the convention, a direct question asking voters if the convention affected their vote for McCain in either direction elicited responses roughly on a par with other recent conventions, and somewhat more negative than the responses to the Democratic convention this year—this despite the fact that more respondents reported watching the Republican convention in the weekend poll than reported watching the Democratic convention. (In fact, the self-reported viewership for the Republican convention was higher than for any other recent convention Gallup surveyed.)

Summary: Implications for the Campaign

At least in the short term, McCain appears, as a result of the Republican convention, to have neutralized the bounce Obama received following the Democratic convention, to the point where McCain now has a slight advantage over Obama among registered voters and a larger advantage among likely voters. It remains to be seen whether or not

McCain can hold on to his advantage in the days ahead as news coverage continues to shift from the conventions to the race itself.

The Republican convention certainly seems to have energized the Republican voting base—apparent not only in the data showing a major 18-point jump in enthusiasm among Republicans, but also from the fact that McCain's advantage over Obama increases in this poll when only likely voters are taken into consideration. Again, the issue is whether or not this advantage can be sustained. Republican vice presidential nominee Palin's speech at the Republican convention on Wednesday night received a highly

After delivering his speech accepting the Republican nomination for president, John McCain and his running mate, Sarah Palin, wave to the crowd. Palin's husband, Todd, claps in back (left). *(Kyodo/AP Images)*

positive response, significantly more so than her running mate McCain received for his speech. Other indicators suggest that the selection of Palin was a polarizing move by McCain, generating significant negatives as well as positives. Thus, it is reasonable to expect that the long-term impact of the Palin selection may not be fully understood until her visibility increases, including at the debate with Joe Biden in October.

SEPTEMBER 9

McCain Now Winning a Majority of Independents

John McCain's 6-percentage-point bounce in voter support in the course of the Republican convention is largely explained by political independents shifting to him in fairly big numbers, from 40% pre-convention to 52% post-convention in Gallup Poll daily tracking. Democrats' support for McCain rose 5 percentage points over the Republican convention period, from 9% to 14%, while Republicans' already high support stayed about the same. The surge in the number of political independents favoring McCain for president marks the first time since Gallup began tracking voters' general election preferences in March that a majority of independents have sided with either of the two major party candidates. Prior to now, McCain had received no better than 48% of the independent vote and Obama no better than 46%, making the race for the political middle highly competitive.

Layering voters' political ideology over their party identification provides the additional finding that the slim group of "pure independents"—those with no political leaning toward either major party—grew more favorable to McCain by an even larger amount over the past week or so. McCain was preferred over Obama by 20% of pure

SUPPORT FOR JOHN McCAIN BY PARTY/IDEOLOGY: PRE- AND POST-REPUBLICAN CONVENTION Based on Registered Voters		
	Pre-convention Aug 29–31, 2008	Post-convention Sep 5–7, 2008
	%	%
Liberal Democrats	2	4
Moderate Democrats	11	16
Conservative Democrats	15	25
Independents	20	39
Moderate/Liberal Republicans	81	80
Conservative Republicans	95	95

independents in Gallup Poll daily tracking from August 29 to August 31. In the latest three-day rolling average, from September 5 to September 7, he is favored by 39% of nonleaning independents, a 19-point increase. (Nearly 40% of pure independents remain undecided.) The more modest increase in McCain's support among Democrats has come mainly from the right wing of that party, with 25% of conservative Democrats now favoring him over Obama, compared with 15% just before the Republican gathering. Moderate and liberal Democrats show only slightly more support for McCain than they did prior to the Republican convention. There has been no change in the presidential preferences of either conservative Republicans or moderate-to-liberal Republicans.

In contrast to the differential shifts in support for McCain by party and ideology, Gallup Poll daily tracking finds a uniform increase in support for McCain since late August among men and women. The percentage of men supporting McCain over Obama pre- and post-Republican convention rose from 46% to 52%, while the percentage of women rose from 41% to 46%. Voters 30 and older are more likely to be supporting McCain than

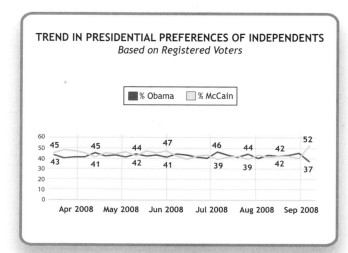

TREND IN PRESIDENTIAL PREFERENCES OF INDEPENDENTS
Based on Registered Voters

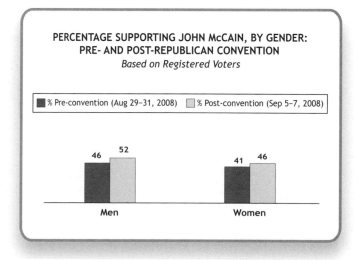

PERCENTAGE SUPPORTING JOHN McCAIN, BY GENDER: PRE- AND POST-REPUBLICAN CONVENTION
Based on Registered Voters

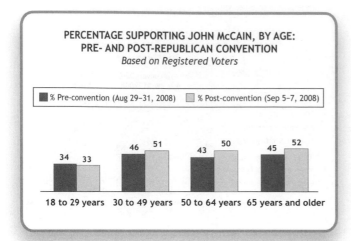

**PERCENTAGE SUPPORTING JOHN McCAIN, BY AGE:
PRE- AND POST-REPUBLICAN CONVENTION**
Based on Registered Voters

■ % Pre-convention (Aug 29–31, 2008)   □ % Post-convention (Sep 5–7, 2008)

	18 to 29 years	30 to 49 years	50 to 64 years	65 years and older
Pre	34	46	43	45
Post	33	51	50	52

they were just prior to the Republican convention, but not young voters. In contrast to the 7-point increases in support seen among those age 50 to 64 and those 65 and older, there has been a 1-point decline in support among 18- to 29-year-olds. Regionally, Gallup finds solid gains for McCain in all areas of the country except the West, where his already fairly high support has held steady. However, the 9-point increase for McCain in the South on top of his previous 49% level of support in that region makes the South now overwhelmingly pro-McCain, 58% to 36%.

The events on the Republican stage in St. Paul, Minnesota, from September 2 to September 4 appear to have provided two important boosts to the McCain-Palin ticket. First, McCain has energized his Republican base and, as a result, has potentially strengthened his position on Election Day among "likely voters." Second, as the Gallup Poll daily trends show, voter movement toward McCain since the Republican convention occurred mainly among independents, thus broadening McCain's appeal beyond the Republican Party. Republicans had already lined up for McCain

before the convention started; now they are excited, and are joined by more independents than at any other time in the campaign. Those gains may not last—"bounces" rarely do—but they enable McCain to launch the next phase of the campaign with knowledge of what his winning coalition might look like.

McCain Regains Upper Hand on Leadership Dimension

After a Republican convention that saw him take the lead over Barack Obama in national trial heat polls, John McCain is once again perceived as superior to Obama in terms of being a strong and decisive leader. Obama had erased McCain's former advantage on this dimension after the Democratic convention, but now McCain has regained the advantage. McCain has a larger advantage over Obama on leadership than on any of the other eight character dimensions tested in the September 5–7 USA Today/Gallup Poll. He also leads Obama in terms of being honest and trustworthy, putting the country's interests ahead of his own political interests, being able to manage the government effectively, and being able to work with both parties to get things done in Washington.

Obama's strengths compared with McCain's this year have been on matters dealing with empathy: The public gives the Democratic nominee the edge when asked which presidential candidate "cares about the needs of people like you" and "shares your values." The public is evenly divided as to which candidate is more "independent in his thoughts and actions," something McCain tried to emphasize during his acceptance speech. Obama has led McCain throughout the campaign on the two empathy dimensions, but his margin on both was reduced after

**PERCENTAGE SUPPORTING JOHN McCAIN, BY REGION:
PRE- AND POST-REPUBLICAN CONVENTION**
Based on Registered Voters

■ % Pre-convention (Aug 29–31, 2008)   □ % Post-convention (Sep 5–7, 2008)

	East	Midwest	South	West
Pre	34	39	49	43
Post	44	46	58	44

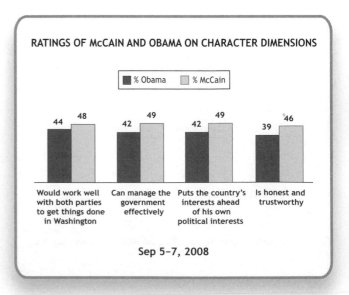

RATINGS OF McCAIN AND OBAMA ON CHARACTER DIMENSIONS

■ % Obama   □ % McCain

	Would work well with both parties to get things done in Washington	Can manage the government effectively	Puts the country's interests ahead of his own political interests	Is honest and trustworthy
Obama	44	42	42	39
McCain	48	49	49	46

Sep 5–7, 2008

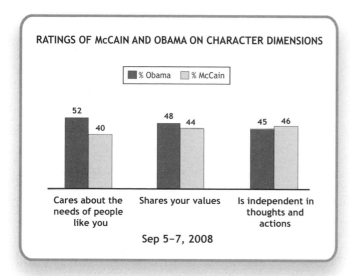

RATINGS OF McCAIN AND OBAMA ON CHARACTER DIMENSIONS

☐ % Obama   ☐ % McCain

	Cares about the needs of people like you	Shares your values	Is independent in thoughts and actions
Obama	52	48	45
McCain	40	44	46

Sep 5–7, 2008

the Republican convention, from a 20-point advantage on "cares about the needs of people like you" to 12 points, and from a 13-point advantage on "shares your values" to 4 points.

It is not unusual for the public's perceptions of the candidates to shift after each is cast in a warm glow at his party's nominating convention. John Kerry gained on George W. Bush on each of eight comparative character ratings asked before and after the 2004 Democratic convention, while Bush gained on five of six dimensions asked before and after the 2004 Republican convention. Bush also saw gains an all nine character ratings asked after the 2000 Republican convention, while Al Gore's ratings improved on the same nine ratings after the 2000 Democratic convention. In fact, in that year, the public rated Bush as better than Gore on all nine dimensions after the Republican convention, but then shifted to rating Gore as better than Bush on eight of the nine dimensions after the Democratic convention. Usually, the public's assessments return to more typical levels once the campaign moves forward after the conventions. Thus, McCain's stronger positioning on these dimensions in the current poll is likely to recede in the coming weeks.

Notwithstanding any short-term movement tied to the party conventions, there seem to be well-established party stereotypes influencing how voters rate the candidates on these comparative character items. The most common are to rate the Democratic candidate as better on caring about people's needs, and the Republican candidate as superior on leadership. Democrats Bill Clinton (1996), Gore (2000), Kerry (2004), and Obama have all been viewed as better than their respective Republican opponents on caring about people for most of their presidential campaigns, while Republicans George W. Bush (2000 and 2004) and McCain have usually been perceived

as stronger leaders than their Democratic rivals. Thus, Obama's advantage on empathy and McCain's on leadership may reflect party stereotypes in addition to an assessment of each individual's relative merits on each dimension.

SEPTEMBER 10
On Economy, McCain Gains Ground on Obama

In the September 5–7 USA Today/Gallup Poll, 48% of Americans say Barack Obama can better handle the economy, while 45% choose John McCain. This marks a significant gain by McCain; just before the Democratic convention in late August, Obama had a 16-point margin over McCain on the economy. It is fair to say that both candidates will continue to focus heavily on the economy between now and the election. That, coupled with the possibility that some of McCain's convention-related gains will dissipate, suggests there could be further change in this measure in the weeks ahead.

The economy is a critically important issue. In this poll, voters overwhelmingly choose it as the most important issue they will take into account in their vote for president. Obama has significant strength on two domestic issues: education and healthcare policy. McCain, on the other hand, has significant strength on five issues, mostly dealing with international matters: terrorism, gun policy, foreign trade, the situation in Iraq, and illegal immigration. These strengths are generally representative of Obama's and McCain's relative positions throughout the campaign, and to a degree are similar to broad Democratic versus Republican strengths in previous elections. Democrats typically have the advantage

Regardless of which presidential candidate you support, please tell me if you think Barack Obama or John McCain would better handle each of the following issues.

	Obama	McCain
Education	53%	36%
Healthcare policy	52%	40%
Abortion	47%	42%
The economy	48%	45%
Energy	46%	46%
Taxes	43%	49%
Illegal immigration	38%	47%
The situation in Iraq	42%	52%
Foreign trade	38%	51%
Gun policy	37%	51%
Terrorism	38%	55%

Sep 5–7, 2008

on domestic issues, while Republicans do better on international issues, and in particular since 9/11 on the issue of terrorism.

Gallup has not previously asked Americans to choose between the two candidates on gun policy. In this poll, McCain wins big on this issue. As has become widely known, Sarah Palin, McCain's vice presidential nominee, is a hunter and a member of the National Rifle Association. Whether this has affected the public's views of the candidates on this issue is unknown.

Similarly, this is the first time respondents have been asked to choose between the two candidates on abortion; Obama has a slight edge on the issue. Palin's strong pro-life position has become widely known since her selection by McCain, particularly because she recently gave birth to a Down syndrome baby (whose condition Palin knew during her pregnancy) and because her daughter is pregnant and electing to have the baby. Americans at this point in time tilt pro-choice in their orientation, so Obama's slight advantage on abortion is perhaps not surprising. But again, it is not possible to determine what impact, if any, McCain's selection of Palin as his running mate may have had on these perceptions.

Majority of Americans Not Fearful of Terrorist Attack

While a new bipartisan report concludes that the United States remains "dangerously vulnerable" to terrorist attacks, most Americans do not fear being directly affected. Only 38% are very or somewhat worried that they or a family member will become a victim of terrorism. This is down from 47% last July, and from a high of 59% in October 2001, but is still short of a post-9/11 low of 28% in January 2004. The report, from the Partnership for a Secure America,

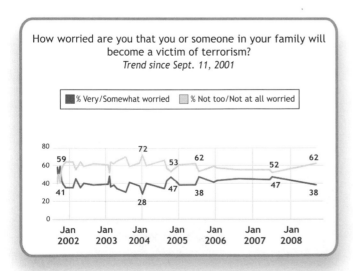

How worried are you that you or someone in your family will become a victim of terrorism?
Trend since Sept. 11, 2001

comes on the eve of the seventh anniversary of the terrorist attacks of September 11, 2001, and less than eight weeks before Americans elect a new leader who will continue the nation's fight against terrorism. The report gives the U.S. government a "C" grade on how it has managed the terrorist threat, and urges the country's next president to improve counterterrorist efforts.

Americans are roughly split on how things are going for the United States in the war on terrorism, with 52% saying they are very or somewhat satisfied and 47% saying they are not very or not at all satisfied. Satisfaction on this measure peaked at 75% during the first year of the war in Afghanistan, subsequently dipping below 60% in 2004 and leveling off in the current range since then. Currently, terrorism does not appear to figure high in Americans' decision-making regarding the presidential election, as only 12% consider terrorism the most important factor in their vote. Earlier this year, when given a choice, a majority of Americans said they would prefer a presidential candidate whose greatest strength is fixing the economy rather than one whose greatest strength is protecting the country from terrorism. This may reflect the huge volume of negative economic news on the airwaves, compared to the more muted discussion of the ongoing global terrorist threat. Any increased attention to the issue of terrorism is most likely to benefit Republican presidential nominee John McCain, as he has consistently outperformed Democratic rival Barack Obama on this issue throughout this election year, most recently by 17 percentage points.

Seven years after the terrorist attacks of 9/11, Americans appear to have mixed feelings about the progress the government has made in protecting them from future attacks. While a majority of Americans express little worry about

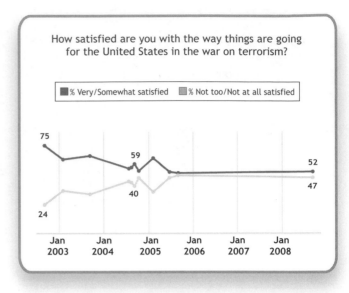

How satisfied are you with the way things are going for the United States in the war on terrorism?

being directly affected by a terrorist attack, only a slim majority are satisfied with how the United States is handling the war on terrorism overall. Although a new report concludes that the next president will have much work to do on the counterterrorism front, up to now, Americans have not been making the terrorism issue a top priority in the ongoing presidential campaign. It is of course possible that the bipartisan report or a terrorism-related news event could change attitudes or bring this issue back to the forefront.

SEPTEMBER 11

Republican Increase in Party Identification After Convention Not Unusual

The percentage of Americans identifying themselves as Republicans has increased from 26% immediately before last week's Republican convention to 30% immediately after it. That increase, combined with a slight 2-point drop in Democratic identification from 37% to 35%, has reduced the Democrats' formidable advantage in national party identification from 11 points to 5.

Democrats have held a large advantage in party identification for much of 2007 and 2008. But the Republican convention—and the exposure it gave to McCain and Palin as the Republican ticket—has encouraged a greater number of Americans to identify as Republicans, thus narrowing the Democratic advantage for the moment. Republicans saw an even larger increase in "leaned" party identification, which is computed by adding to the percentage who initially identify with a party the percentage of Americans who initially identify themselves as independents but then say they "lean" to that party. Before the Republican convention, 39% of Americans said they identified with or leaned to the Republican Party, but that

number has increased to 47%. Forty-eight percent now identify with or lean to the Democratic Party, down from 53% prior to the Republican convention. These results are based on the September 5–7 USA Today/Gallup Poll, but Gallup observed similar trends in its daily tracking survey. Such short-term shifts in party affiliation are a regular occurrence after a party's convention; Gallup has measured an increase averaging 4 percentage points in the percentage of Americans identifying with a party after its convention since 1992. The increases have been slightly larger, averaging five points, when one includes changes in leaned party identification. This year's eight-point surge in Republican identification and leaning matches the Democrats' high from 2000. Each party has enjoyed an increase in leaned party identification after its convention, with the exception of this year's Democratic convention. That may reflect the already high percentage of Americans identifying with or leaning to the Democratic Party this year before its convention began.

Republican Party's Image Improves

Another common measure of a party's standing is the public's favorable rating of that party. Currently, 47% of Americans say they have a favorable view of the Republican Party, an increase from 39% before their convention and the best rating for the Republicans since early 2005. Even in the afterglow of the Republican convention, the Democratic Party is still rated more positively than the Republican Party, with 51% of Americans saying they have a favorable view of the Democrats. That is down slightly from before the Republican convention (54%). A majority of Americans have had a favorable view of the Democratic Party since the summer of 2006.

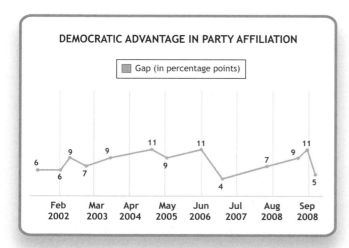

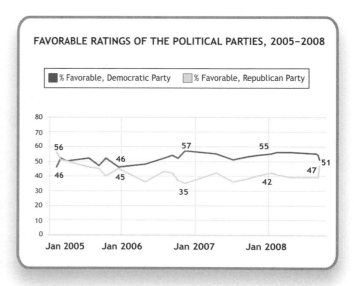

As is the case with respect to party identification, favorable ratings of a party usually increase after that party's convention. The average increase in favorable ratings since 1996 has been four points, with the Republicans' eight-point surge this year the largest (perhaps because the image of the party was so poor going into the convention). Again, the Democratic Party's highly positive image did not improve after its convention this year. The conventions present the parties with an important opportunity to speak directly to their supporters and to the nation at large, and to convey their messages in a positive light. Thus, it is not surprising to see each party's public image improving after its convention.

But are those increases temporary, or do they have some staying power? In general, it appears that the increases are short-lived and fade as the enthusiasm generated by the convention subsides. Since 1996, the percentage of Americans who identify with or lean to a party has dropped in the poll after that year's post-convention poll for each party. So to the extent that history is a guide, Gallup's next survey would likely show a slight drop in the percentage of Americans identifying with or leaning to the Republican Party. And while Gallup does not ask the party-favorable question as regularly as it does party affiliation, the post-convention poll for a party has often marked the high point in favorable ratings for that party each presidential election year. Thus, while the Republicans have cut into the Democratic advantage in party identification, it is likely that this year's election will still take place in a political environment that is more favorable to the Democratic Party than the Republican Party.

No Disproportionate Shift in White Women's Preferences

An analysis of Gallup Poll daily tracking interviewing conducted before and after the two party conventions shows that the impact of the conventions was not materially different for white women than it was for white men, and neither group's shifts were substantially different than the changes among the overall electorate. These conclusions are based on comparisons of very large samples of Gallup Poll daily tracking interviews conducted at intervals before, during, and after the two conventions. In general, the comparison shows only a modest change in vote patterns, with white women shifting in the same broad ways as the overall sample average.

Just before the Democratic convention (in Gallup Poll daily tracking interviewing from August 20 to August 22), white women broke 47% to 40% in favor of McCain over Obama. In interviewing from September 5 to September 8, after both conventions were completed, white women's

margin of support for McCain over Obama edged up modestly to 51% to 40%. This represents a gain of four percentage points for McCain among white women and no change in their support for Obama. Among white men, the change in preference for McCain was very similar to the change among white women, coupled with a slight loss of support for Obama. White men went from 56% to 36% support for McCain over Obama to a 59% to 34% split now. More generally, the data show that McCain gained four points among all white voters (both men and women), and Obama lost one point. For all voters, regardless of race or gender, the race shifted from a 46% to 44% advantage for Obama in August 20–22 polling to a 49% to 44% advantage for McCain after the conventions—a gain of five points for McCain and a loss of two for Obama. In short, it appears that the impact of the two conventions was not materially different for white women than it was for white men, and neither group's shifts were substantially different from the changes among the overall electorate. Among all groups, McCain gained during the time period encompassing the two conventions, while Obama's support was roughly stable. Despite the intense focus on the potential impact on white women of McCain's selection of Sarah Palin as his vice presidential running mate, Gallup's data do not show that to this point white women have been significantly different in their response to the convention period than has the average voter.

SEPTEMBER 12

Both Candidates Share a "Change Washington" Reputation

One reason John McCain has taken a modest lead over Barack Obama among registered voters nationally may be his ability to share the mantle of "change" agent. More than half of Americans now see each candidate as potentially effective

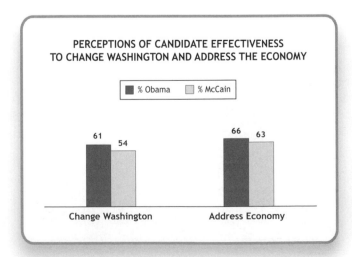

PERCEPTIONS OF CANDIDATE EFFECTIVENESS
TO CHANGE WASHINGTON AND ADDRESS THE ECONOMY

■ % Obama   □ % McCain

Change Washington: 61, 54
Address Economy: 66, 63

in changing the way the government works in Washington. At the same time, about two in three see each as potentially effective in addressing problems in the economy.

One of the disadvantages of incumbency is that the challenger can wear the mantle of change agent. Of course, there is no incumbent in the current election, but McCain is the candidate of the incumbent party, and the Obama campaign has been attempting to link McCain to President Bush. At this point, it appears that one successful outcome of the Republican convention and the selection of Palin as McCain's running mate has been to allow McCain to become surprisingly competitive with Obama in Americans' perceptions of not only his ability to change the way government works in Washington, but also his capacity to address economic problems.

McCain emphasized his independence in his acceptance speech, and his choice of the anti-establishment Palin helps to reinforce that image. The Obama campaign has attempted to corner the market on change based on Obama's status as a relative newcomer to Washington and his policy differences with the Bush administration. Partisans largely buy their candidate's argument, with Democrats dubious about McCain's ability to deliver change and Republicans likewise doubtful Obama could. But 59% of independents say Obama would be effective in bringing about change, and 52% say the same for McCain. And more than two in three independents think either Obama or McCain would be effective at addressing today's domestic economic problems. Republicans and Democrats, not surprisingly, have much more faith in their own party's candidate.

Americans of All Incomes See Both Candidates as Change Agents

With respect to how effective each candidate would be at changing the way Washington works, Obama ties McCain among upper-income Americans, but leads him by 10 to 14 points among those with middle and lower incomes. McCain has a slight edge over Obama among upper-income Americans when asked who would be effective in addressing today's domestic economic problems, while Obama edges McCain among middle- and lower-income Americans. Although McCain wears the incumbent party label, he also shares to a large degree the change-agent mantle, at least in the immediate aftermath of his party's convention. Whether he can maintain this important perception over the next eight weeks remains to be seen.

In this regard, the recent bailout of financial institutions may reveal the kind of change agents the candidates will be, because they clearly will face this as a major issue shortly after they take office—much as the first President Bush did with regard to the savings and loan crisis back in 1989.

By creating a conservatorship for Fannie Mae and Freddie Mac, the Treasury Department has delayed decisions on their ultimate structure so that the next administration and Congress can deal with them. Both Obama and McCain have publicly supported the takeover and conservatorship of these two government-sponsored enterprises. Both have also stated that the pre-conservatorship quasi-governmental status of these entities did not make sense.

What happens to Fannie Mae and Freddie Mac has profound implications for the future of housing finance and the ending of the current financial crisis—and, more broadly, for the recovery of the economy in 2009 and beyond. Their special status before their conservatorship as quasi-governmental agencies raises a wide range of issues concerning how the economy functions and how gains and losses are shared between the public and private sectors. McCain's idea for change in addressing this major economic problem is to break up these two companies into several smaller entities, as suggested by former Federal Reserve Board chairman Alan Greenspan. The idea would be to remove the federal government to a greater degree from the housing finance system. It should be noted that the economy had a well-functioning housing finance system before the rapid expansion of loans and guarantees that were readily available from Fannie Mae and Freddie Mac.

On the other hand, Obama has suggested a more lasting involvement on the part of the federal government. He is concerned that the entities serve an important role in making housing affordable that is not served by any other federal agencies. He argues that the complexity of the issue deserves study and that the public versus private status of these companies must be clarified. In sum, both candidates support change to address this important economic problem. What kind of change Americans want—as exemplified by the potential future structure of housing finance in America—may well play a significant role in determining who is elected in November.

Battle for Congress Suddenly Looks Competitive

A potential shift in fortunes for the Republicans in Congress is seen in the latest USA Today/Gallup survey, with the Democrats now leading the Republicans by just three percentage points, 48% to 45%, in voters' "generic ballot" preferences for Congress. This is down from consistent double-digit Democratic leads seen on this measure over the past year. As is true for the current structure of voting preferences for president, Democratic voters are nearly uniform in their support for the Democratic candidate in their congressional districts (92%), Republican voters are nearly uniform in their support for the Republican candidate (94%), and independents are

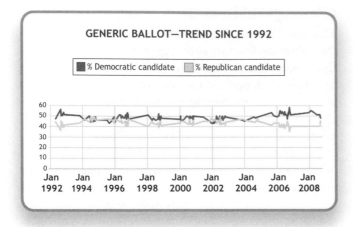

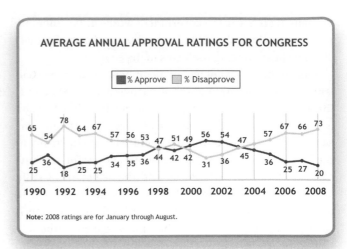

closely split, with 44% backing the Democrat and 40% the Republican.

The new results come from a September 5–7 survey conducted immediately after the Republican convention and mirror the enhanced position of the Republican Party seen in several other indicators—ranging from McCain's improved standing against Obama in the presidential race to improved favorability ratings for the Republicans and Republican gains in party identification. The sustainability of all of these findings is an open question that polling will answer over the next few weeks. The positive impact of the Republican convention on polling indicators of Republican strength is further seen in the operation of Gallup's "likely voter" model in this survey. Republicans, who are now much more enthusiasitc about the 2008 election than they were prior to the convention, show heightened interest in voting and thus outscore Democrats in apparent likelihood to vote in November. As a result, Republican candidates now lead Democratic candidates among likely voters by five percentage points, 50% to 45%. If these numbers are sustained through Election Day—and that is a big if—Republicans could be expected to regain control of the House of Representatives.

As Gallup's long-term "generic ballot" trend shows, the Democrats held a sizable lead on this measure from the time they won back control of Congress in the fall of 2006 through last month. If the current closer positioning of the parties holds, the pattern of congressional voter preferences will be similar to most of the period from 1994 through 2005, when Republicans won and maintained control of Congress.

Congressional Approval Also Troubling for Democrats

With only 18% of Americans in August saying they approve of the job Congress is doing, similar to the average 20% approval rating for Congress all year, the Democrats in Congress have additional cause for concern. This scant level of approval could signal that voters are in the mood for change, and that could disproportionately hurt Democratic incumbents. The last time the yearly average approval rating of Congress approached this low a level was in 2006, when the Republicans lost majority control of Congress after 12 years in power. The previous occasion was in 1994, when the Republicans wrested control from the Democrats. In both of these midterm election years, the average congressional approval score was 25%. However, with an 18% approval rating for Congress in 1992, the Democrats succeeded in holding their majority in Congress. That was a presidential year in which the Democratic candidate, Bill Clinton, won.

The issues raised by today's low approval rating for Congress are reinforced by recent Gallup Poll findings that relatively few voters generally believe that "most members" of Congress deserve re-election. That figure was only 36% in July, much lower than the 51% or better reading found in recent election years when the party of the sitting majority in Congress maintained power. Indeed, the new USA Today/Gallup measurement of generic ballot preferences for Congress casts some doubt on the previously assumed inevitability of the Democrats' maintaining control of Congress. Until now, the dark shadow cast by President Bush's widespread unpopularity has suppressed Republican Party identification nationwide, along with voters' willingness to support the Republican candidate running for Congress in their district. But now that the symbolic leadership of the party is shifting away from Bush and toward the suddenly popular Republican presidential ticket of McCain and Palin, things may be changing. As Bush casts less of a shadow over the Republicans, the Democrats' own vulnerability, stemming from the low approval rating for Congress, is revealed. The key question is how much of this is temporary because of the tremendous bounce in support for the Republicans on many dimensions since their convention. The degree to which the Republican bounce is sustained, rather than dissipated, in the weeks ahead will determine whether the 2008 race for Congress could in fact be highly competitive, rather than a Democratic sweep.

Gallup Daily: McCain 48%, Obama 45%

The latest Gallup Poll daily tracking results for September 9–11 show a slight, but not statistically significant, three percentage point advantage for John McCain over Barack Obama among registered voters, 48% to 45%. These results, based on interviewing conducted between September 9 and September 11, mark the first time since the September 4–6 report that McCain does not have a statistically significant lead over Obama, and also reflect interviewing on September 11 that showed a very close race. It is unknown whether or not the September 11 results may have reflected any possible impact of Republican vice presidential candidate Sarah Palin's widely publicized television interviews with Charles Gibson of ABC News, which began to be broadcast that evening.

The story of the presidential race this year since early June has been a tendency for candidate support levels to return to near parity after one or the other candidate moves into a brief lead, so the days ahead will show whether or not this contest will once again settle back into a "too close to call" structure. Obama and McCain were together on September 11 at memorial services in New York at the site of the 9/11 terrorist attack, but both campaigns have now returned to hot and heavy campaigning, including ads directly attacking each other's positions on issues.

SEPTEMBER 15
Tracking the "Real" Impact of the Historic Financial Crisis

Prior to the recent unraveling of Wall Street and the re-emergence of the financial crisis, consumers had been turning less pessimistic about the economy. As gasoline prices declined, the percentage of consumers with negative views of the current economy had declined as well, from 83% in mid-July to 70% this past weekend. The financial crisis has now reached historic proportions, with Lehman Brothers

Impersonating Sarah Palin on NBC's *Saturday Night Live* on September 27, 2008, Tina Fey stumbles in answering a question posed by Amy Poehler, who is impersonating CBS news anchor Katie Couric. Fey's impersonations were a huge hit, prompting Palin herself to appear on the show in October. *(Dana Edelson/NBC Universal, Inc.)*

going into bankruptcy and Bank of America acquiring Merrill Lynch. Other major financial firms also appear to be under serious financial pressure, so additional fallout on Wall Street is possible in the days and weeks ahead. This follows the Bear Stearns bailout earlier this year and the Fannie Mae/Freddie Mac bailout of a week ago. The Federal Reserve and the Treasury are actively working to maintain orderly financial markets. Even as they undertake these efforts, the key question for the future of the economy involves how Main Street is going to respond to the virtual elimination of what has been known as the independent investment banking business.

Republicans Cry Foul over Media Coverage of Palin

The pundit-fueled firestorm around media coverage of John McCain's running mate, Sarah Palin, is evident in Americans' highly mixed views on the subject. About the same proportion of Americans say media coverage of Palin has been unfairly negative (33%) as say it has been about right (36%). An additional 21% say coverage of her has been unfairly positive. These views—taken from a September 8–11 Gallup Poll conducted mostly before the airing of Palin's September 11 interview with ABC News's Charlie Gibson—are sharply partisan. A majority of Republicans (54%), compared with only 29% of independents and 18% of Democrats, think Palin is getting a raw deal from the press. Three times as many Democrats as Republicans (34% vs. 11%) think coverage of her has been too positive.

By contrast, a majority of Americans say media treatment of McCain has been about right (53%). However, among the remainder, the balance tilts more than two to one toward saying coverage of him has been unfairly negative: 30% vs. 13%. Republicans are closely divided on this, with a slight majority (51%) saying coverage of McCain has been too negative and close to half (43%) saying it has been about right. These perceptions haven't changed much since they were previously measured, in late July. The view that coverage of McCain is about right has increased slightly (from 46% to 53%) as the percentage with no opinion on the issue has declined. But there has been no meaningful change in perceptions that he is getting either unfair positive treatment or unfair negative treatment.

Close to half of Americans—including most Democrats—believe media treatment of Obama is about right. This is a slight increase from late July, when only 39% took this view. At the same time, the perception that media treatment of Obama is unfairly positive has fallen, from 39% to 32%. However, twice as many Americans still hold this view as say coverage of him is unfairly negative. Six in 10 Republicans think Obama has received overly favorable

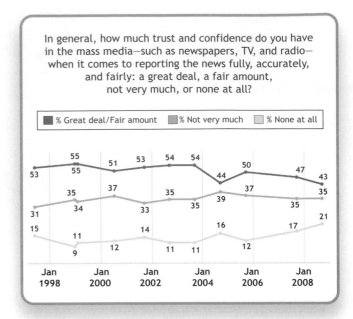

press coverage. Americans broadly view the media's treatment thus far of Joe Biden as fair. Nearly 6 in 10 (59%) say coverage of Obama's running mate has been about right, while much smaller proportions believe it has been either unfairly positive (15%) or unfairly negative (11%). Men and women have nearly identical views of how Palin, Biden, and McCain are being treated in the media. However, men are slightly more likely than women (36% vs. 29%) to say the media's coverage of Obama has been unfairly positive.

Ratings of Media Turn More Negative

Republicans' criticism of how the media are treating their party's presidential and vice presidential candidates may be taking a toll on broader public confidence in the mass

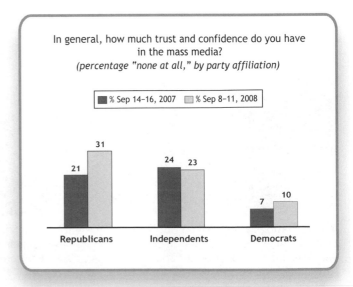

media. The percentage of Americans saying they have a great deal or fair amount of confidence in the media when it comes to fairness and accuracy is now just 43%, the lowest level seen over the past decade. (In 2004, it was a similar 44%.) At 21%, the percentage of Americans saying they have no confidence at all in the media is a record high. The increase since 2007, from 17% to 21%, in those saying they have no confidence in the media is mostly because of worsening attitudes among Republicans.

During the Democratic primary season, Hillary Clinton's campaign representatives issued steady complaints that their candidate wasn't getting the same favorable treatment that Obama was receiving from the media. That charge seemed to filter into public opinion in July, when Gallup found as many Americans saying media coverage of Obama was too positive as said it was about right. (This included 60% of Republicans and 22% of Democrats.) That sentiment has simmered down somewhat, although there is a persistent tilt toward believing Obama is getting a break from the media. Today, there is much more controversy among Americans about the media's coverage of Palin. More than half are dissatisfied with the nature of the coverage of her, saying it is either too positive or too negative. This seems to reflect the raging debate among political pundits over whether the media's commentary on Palin's governmental qualifications and personal life has gone too far. Whether valid or merely a political tactic, the election-year shots at the media for biased coverage seem to be eroding public confidence in the news media as a reputable institution.

SEPTEMBER 16

For Obama's Supporters, It's Change; for McCain's, Experience

Despite John McCain's recent efforts to adopt the "change" positioning that has been central to Barack Obama's campaign strategy for much of the year, new Gallup Poll data show only 3% of McCain supporters volunteering that they are voting for the Republican nominee because of his ability to bring about change. Thirty-seven percent of Obama's supporters, on the other hand, give that as the reason for their support. McCain supporters are most likely to explain their vote by invoking McCain's experience and qualifications. In a September 8–11 poll, Gallup asked voters to cite the main reasons they support their preferred presidential candidate. The open-ended question, asked as a follow-up to the basic ballot question, reads: "What would you say are the one or two most important reasons why you would vote for (John McCain/Barack Obama)?"

It is clear that the "change" mantra has resonated with Obama supporters: The desire for change is by far the most common reason offered by Obama voters for their support. Other reasons given by those supporting Obama include his economic plan or ability to handle the economy, general agreement with his values or positions, the respondent's propensity to vote Democratic, Obama's support for the working and middle classes, his plan for the Iraq War, and his honesty. These themes appear to reflect the dominant thrusts of the Obama campaign: change, fixing the economy, helping the working and middle classes, and Iraq.

There is little indication, however, that McCain's supporters have adopted the change theme as their stated reason for supporting him—notwithstanding McCain's acceptance speech statement that "We need to change the way government does almost everything." (The current data were collected between September 8 and September 11, well after the Republican convention, at which McCain emphasized change as a campaign theme.) Instead, the dominant reason given by McCain's supporters is his experience, named by 27%, followed by 18% who mention McCain's ability to handle terrorism and national security. Ten percent of McCain's supporters say they are planning to vote for McCain because of his selection of Palin as his running mate, suggesting that events occurring in and around the convention are reflected in voters' views in the current poll; another 4% mention that McCain is a maverick and goes against his own party. Other reasons for supporting McCain include his honesty, the fact that the respondent always votes Republican, and McCain's military background and service to his country.

Presidential Contest Remains a Dead Heat

The September 13–15 Gallup Poll daily tracking update shows John McCain (47%) and Barack Obama (46%) locked in a close contest when registered voters are asked whom they would vote for if the election were held today. The race has been in a statistical dead heat for the last five days, after McCain's lead grew to as large as five percentage points following the Republican convention. In essence, the race is back to where it was before the flurry of political activity that began on August 25 with the Democratic convention and continued through the Republican convention, which concluded on September 4. The candidates were dead even at 45% in August 22–24 tracking, the last report of interviews conducted entirely before the beginning of the Democratic convention.

It is unclear to what extent this week's headline news about the collapse of Wall Street financial institutions and the severe downturn in the stock market will affect the race. Obama has generally held the advantage when Americans are asked which candidate would better deal with the economy, though McCain was able to close the gap after the Republican convention. Interviewing on September 15 did show Obama doing better than he has been in recent updates, but it will take several days to see if he can sustain an improved position.

SEPTEMBER 17
Happiness Hits 2008 Low amid Wall Street Woes

The percentage of Americans experiencing a lot of happiness/enjoyment without a lot of stress/worry hit a new low for the year on September 15 at 39%. This depressed mood coincides with the beginning of the turmoil on Wall Street and in the financial markets that began to unfold in the major news media on September 14–15. Gallup asks Americans 18 and older to reflect on the level of happiness and stress they experienced the day before each survey. Each Gallup survey has shown consistent upswings in mood on weekends and holidays for most Americans. Reflecting on the typical Saturday or Sunday, 58% of Americans report a lot of happiness and enjoyment without a lot of stress or worry. This drops to 46% on a typical Monday. Over this past weekend, Saturday, September 13, was like most Saturdays (58%), but Sunday, September 14, was an uncharacteristic (53%), reflecting the news of imminent troubles for Lehman Brothers and Merrill Lynch. Still, the drop from Sunday, September 14, to Monday, September 15, was abnormal at 14 percentage points, and the drop in mood from Saturday to Monday was a full 19 points (compared with a typical 12-point drop in mood over an average weekend-to-weekday transition).

The record-low mood experienced on September 15 came with the news of Lehman Brothers filing for bankruptcy, Merrill Lynch being sold to Bank of America, and the Dow Jones Industrial Average registering a record decline. The lowest previously registered measure of happiness was 41%, with two of the four occasions when the measure dipped to that number also coinciding with economic woes—specifically on March 18, when the Federal Reserve announced a rate cut in response to a weakening economic outlook, and on June 9, when gasoline prices rose to record highs.

Shifts in Last Two Months of Election Not Uncommon

A question of keen interest to election observers is the following: To what degree do presidential elections change between the end of the political conventions and Election Day? There have been 18 presidential elections since Gallup's election polling began in 1936. In each instance, both parties' conventions had concluded by Labor Day, making it possible to look at the difference in the margin between the Gallup Poll that immediately followed Labor Day and the final popular vote outcome. (In 2004, the Labor Day poll was conducted during the Labor Day weekend, just after the Republican convention had ended.)

The *gap change* between Labor Day and Election Day—meaning the difference in the candidates' vote percentages shown in polling around Labor Day compared with the difference in their final Election Day popular vote percentages—has ranged from 1 point (1940, 1960, 1988, and 2004) to 20 points (1936) over these 18 elections. The median in the distribution is 6 points. Based solely on history, that would put the predicted gap change for this year's election (comparing the post–Labor Day poll results with the actual popular vote percentages on Election Day) in the 6- to 7-point range. In theory, a gap change, if it does occur, could be in either direction. But historical analysis suggests that the change is more frequently in the direction of closing a gap, rather than expanding it, between Labor Day and Election Day. In the 18 elections studied, the gap expanded in 6 and shrank in 12. Thus, if there was a change in the gap in past years' elections, the odds were higher that the leader's lead diminished than that the leader moved farther ahead.

Three of the elections in which the gap expanded involved Franklin D. Roosevelt (1936, 1940, 1944). Beginning with the 1948 election, the Labor Day gap between the two major party candidates shrank in all but 3 out of 14 elections. The three post–World War II elections in which the gap expanded were 1956 (Dwight Eisenhower gained steam on Adlai Stevenson as the fall campaign progressed), 1984 (Ronald Reagan expanded his lead over Walter Mondale by Election Day), and 2004 (George W. Bush won over John Kerry by about 2.5 points, just slightly more than the 2-point gap by which he led Kerry in the Labor Day poll).

It is of some interest to look at the relationship between the Gallup Poll numbers for the leader immediately after Labor Day and the winner on Election Day. Across the 18 elections between 1936 and 2004, a candidate who was behind in the post–Labor Day poll went on to win the popular vote on Election Day in only three:

- In 1948, Gallup's post–Labor Day poll had Thomas Dewey up by 8 points; Harry Truman won by 5.
- In 1960, Gallup's post–Labor Day poll had Richard Nixon up by 1 point; John F. Kennedy won by less than 1 percentage point.
- In 1980, Gallup's post–Labor Day poll had Jimmy Carter up by 4 points; Reagan won by 10.

Still, in these previous 18 elections, the candidate who was ahead just after Labor Day has more often than not gone on to win the election, regardless of changes in the margins over the last two months of the campaign.

There were two other recent examples—2000 and 2004—in which the lead changed hands between Labor Day and Election Day, but the candidate who lost the lead regained it to win the popular vote. Both of these elections were close. Al Gore was ahead in Gallup polling conducted after Labor Day in 2000 and went on to win the popular vote, but of course lost the election after the Supreme Court's decision that put Florida's electoral votes in George W. Bush's column. In 2004, Bush was ahead in Gallup polling conducted after Labor Day and went on to win the popular vote, by about 2.5 points.

The results from the previous elections reviewed here were all based on Gallup's first poll conducted after Labor Day. In all of these instances, both political party conventions were completed before Labor Day—in some instances weeks before Labor Day. For example, the last of the two conventions in 2000 was over on August 17, more than two weeks before Labor Day that year; in 1948, the last of the two conventions ended in mid-July.

Labor Day this year was September 1, with the Democratic convention taking place immediately before then (August 25–28) and the Republican convention actually taking place on Labor Day and the three days that followed. Thus, it is obviously not appropriate to use immediate post–Labor Day polling this year to compare with these historical examples. Gallup Poll daily tracking in fact has shown much movement in the race in the days since Labor Day, with Obama having as much as an 8-point lead in a three-day period that included Labor Day, and McCain as much as a 5-point lead after his convention. As of September 13–15, the race is a statistical tie: McCain 47%, Obama 46%.

The historical record reviewed here certifies that a change in the gap of up to 6 or 7 points would not be unusual between Labor Day and Election Day. This year, the data have already shown a change in the gap of 13 points from the high-water Obama gap to the high-water McCain gap since Labor Day. The unusual timing of the conventions, both of which fell close to Labor Day, makes it difficult to project probabilities of victory for one candidate or the other based on historical references to the calendar. More generally, it may be useful to refer back to Gallup's previous analysis showing that, historically, competitive campaigns in which one candidate did not pull to a clear post-conventions lead remained close (with the lead switching back and forth) right through to the election.

SEPTEMBER 18
Gallup Daily: Obama 48%, McCain 44%

The September 15–17 Gallup Poll daily tracking update shows Barack Obama with a 48% to 44% lead over John McCain among registered voters, marking the first time that Obama has held a statistically significant lead in two weeks. The presidential race has essentially devolved back to a pattern very similar to what pertained throughout the months of June and July, during which time Obama consistently averaged a three-percentage-point lead over McCain. There have been fairly significant shifts over the last several weeks, including periods of time in and around the conventions during which both Obama and McCain established leads, and times when the race was essentially tied. But beginning this week, it appears that the voters have settled, for the moment, back into a familiar pattern, in which the race remains close with a slight tilt toward Obama.

Separate Gallup tracking shows that consumer confidence has become significantly more negative as this week progressed, signifying that Americans are clearly paying attention to the major problems facing Wall Street and the big drops in the stock market on September 15 and 17. It is not possible to determine precisely how much of Obama's gain this week was directly caused by Americans' reactions to the economic stories dominating news coverage in newspapers and television and on the Internet, although this is a plausible explanation.

Obama's Voters More Negative on Economy Than McCain's

Supporters of Barack Obama for president have views about the nation's economy that differ strongly from those of John McCain supporters, with Obama's supporters describing it in much more grave terms. According to a September 15–16 USA Today/Gallup Poll, most Obama voters (73%), contrasted with less than half of McCain voters (45%), believe the economy is in either a "recession" or a "depression." In sync with McCain's often-stated view

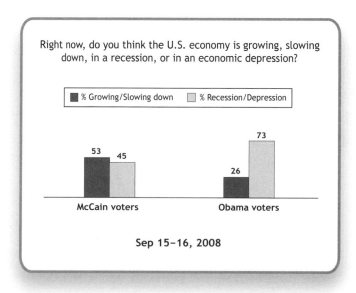

Right now, do you think the U.S. economy is growing, slowing down, in a recession, or in an economic depression?

% Growing/Slowing down   % Recession/Depression

McCain voters: 53, 45
Obama voters: 26, 73

Sep 15–16, 2008

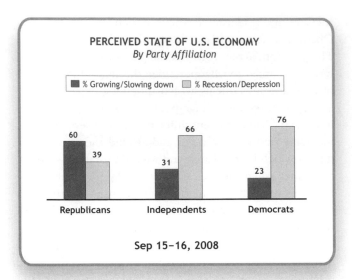

PERCEIVED STATE OF U.S. ECONOMY
By Party Affiliation

Sep 15–16, 2008

Although the United States is technically not in a depression, the current problems on Wall Street are being widely described as the worst crisis since the Great Depression of the 1930s. This could be contributing to the near doubling since January 2008 (from 12% to 23%) of public perceptions that the economy is in a depression. Slightly more Americans today also believe that the economy is in recession—something many economists have already pronounced is under way. This is up five percentage points since January, from 33% to 38%. The increase since January in perceptions that the economy is in a recession or depression coincides with the decline in Americans' more basic consumer confidence over the same period. Gallup Poll daily tracking from January 30 to February 1 found 66% of Americans negative in their economic views and 11% positive. Today, those figures are 78% negative and 7% positive.

that the fundamentals of the economy are strong, voters who plan to back McCain in November are more likely to think the economy is at worst slowing down. A combined 53% of McCain supporters say the economy is either slowing down or, in fact, growing. Only a quarter of Obama's voters (26%) agree.

These voter differences in economic perceptions are similar to those seen, more broadly, between Republicans and Democrats. Importantly, political independents (who represent the swing voting group potentially most influenced by the candidates' stances on this issue) are much closer to Democrats than to Republicans on this question. As a result, a majority of Americans overall—61%—now believe the economy is experiencing either a recession or a depression, up from 45% holding one of those views in January. Few Americans surveyed at either point have said the economy is growing, but in January a slight majority (53%) said it was either growing or slowing down. Today, only 37% hold either of those more positive views.

Better Days to Come

The consumer confidence picture is not entirely bleak, however. In contrast to Americans' grave views of current economic conditions, they are markedly upbeat about where the economy will be a year from now. Nearly half believe the economy will be growing at that point. Only 28% believe it will be in a recession or depression. This outlook is not much different from that measured in January, when Americans' underlying perceptions of current economic conditions were much more positive than they are today.

Still, Americans as a whole have grown substantially more negative in their characterizations of the economy than they were at the outset of 2008. While Republicans (and McCain supporters) view the current situation in less dire terms than do Democrats (and Obama supporters), most political independents share most Democrats' view that the economy is in either a recession or a depression.

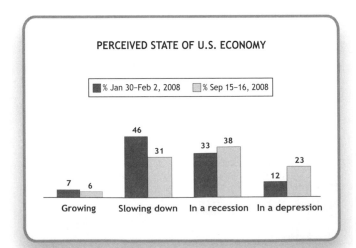

PERCEIVED STATE OF U.S. ECONOMY

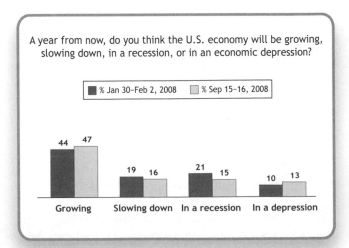

A year from now, do you think the U.S. economy will be growing, slowing down, in a recession, or in an economic depression?

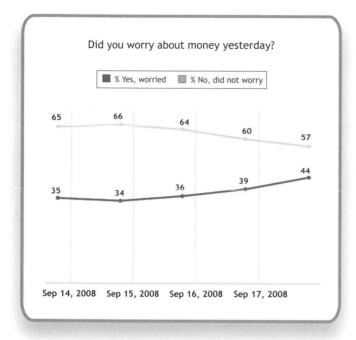

Did you worry about money yesterday?

■ % Yes, worried   ■ % No, did not worry

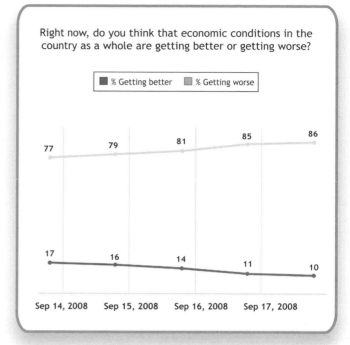

Right now, do you think that economic conditions in the country as a whole are getting better or getting worse?

■ % Getting better   ■ % Getting worse

SEPTEMBER 19

Consumers Increasingly Worried About Money

The September 19 Gallup Poll daily tracking update shows consumer confidence continuing to erode and 44% of Americans saying they worried about money yesterday—the highest percentage this year, and up 10 percentage points in just a matter of days. These results are based on interviews conducted between September 16 and September 18, in a week that has seen a drumbeat of mostly bad financial and economic news, albeit tempered with a

rise in the Dow Jones stock market average of more than 400 points on September 18. The jump in personal worry about money is potentially significant if it translates into restrained consumer spending, which in turn could deliver still another blow to the struggling economy.

Meanwhile, Americans have also grown increasingly negative in a more general sense about the state of the economy as this week has progressed, with 50% rating economic conditions as "poor"—up 10 points from just four days ago, and the highest such rating since mid-July (when gasoline prices had reached new high points). The percentage of Americans who say the economy is getting worse is now at 86%, up 9 points from just four days ago. Ten percent say the economy is getting better. The "getting worse" percentage is, like the rating of the current economy, as negative as it has been since July. But both of these measures have been even more negative at earlier points this year. The "getting worse" percentage was consistently in the high 80s for periods of time in the spring and summer, reaching a yearlong high of 90% in mid-July. Similarly, the "poor" percentage has been as high as 52% earlier this summer.

Gallup summarizes the responses to these two questions in a measure that classifies Americans as positive, mixed, or negative about the economy. In the September 19 update, 81% are classified as negative, with 13% mixed and 5% positive. These numbers are approaching, but have not yet exceeded, the most negative percentages recorded so far this year. In mid-July, 83% of Americans were negative about the economy, and the percentage positive has been at 4% at several points throughout the year.

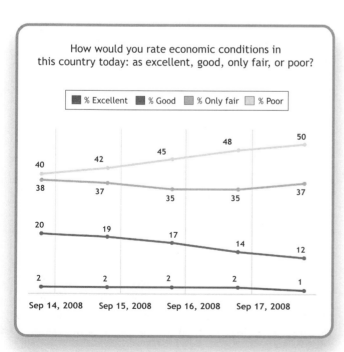

How would you rate economic conditions in this country today: as excellent, good, only fair, or poor?

■ % Excellent   ■ % Good   ■ % Only fair   ■ % Poor

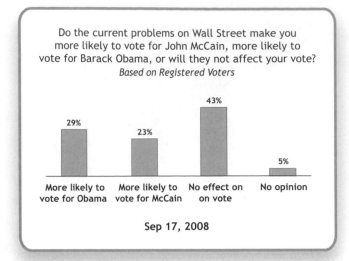

Do the current problems on Wall Street make you
more likely to vote for John McCain, more likely to
vote for Barack Obama, or will they not affect your vote?
Based on Registered Voters

Sep 17, 2008

Wall Street Crisis May Give Obama a Slight Political Benefit

When asked how the Wall Street crisis might affect their presidential vote, slightly more registered voters say it increases their chances of voting for Barack Obama (29%) than say this with respect to John McCain (23%), with roughly 4 in 10 saying it will have no impact on their decision. This is based on a one-night September 17 USA Today/Gallup Poll measuring public reaction to the Wall Street crisis generally, and to the government bailout of AIG, the giant insurance company, in particular. In general, it appears that the crisis may just be reinforcing existing preferences. Most Obama voters say the Wall Street crisis makes them more likely to vote for him, and about half of McCain voters say the crisis increases their chances of supporting him. However, there has been a definite shift toward Obama in Gallup Poll daily

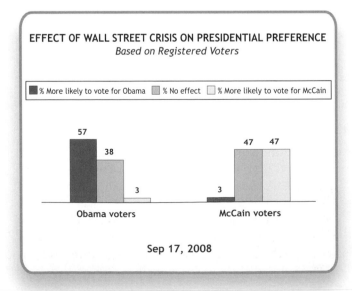

EFFECT OF WALL STREET CRISIS ON PRESIDENTIAL PREFERENCE
Based on Registered Voters

■ % More likely to vote for Obama   ■ % No effect   □ % More likely to vote for McCain

Sep 17, 2008

tracking since September 15, when the crisis began to dominate the headlines. McCain, who had held an advantage ever since the Republican convention, now finds himself trailing Obama by five percentage points in the latest Gallup Poll daily tracking update.

The candidates have spent much of their time on the campaign trail this week discussing the financial crisis, which has in large part overshadowed the presidential election in the news. And while McCain in particular has struggled to reconcile his anti-regulation philosophy with the government's actions to bolster AIG, Fannie Mae, and Freddie Mac, at least as of September 17 the public did not give either candidate an edge in terms of his ability to deal with this issue. This is the case even though Obama has more consistently supported increased government regulation of Wall Street, which 59% of Americans say they favor. Americans' assessments of which candidate would better handle the economic crisis are strongly aligned with their party affiliation, with Republicans overwhelmingly giving McCain the advantage, Democrats doing the same for Obama, and independents roughly equally divided between the two.

SEPTEMBER 20
Gallup Daily: Obama 50%, McCain 44%

Gallup Poll daily tracking from September 17 to September 19 finds Barack Obama maintaining his lead over John McCain among registered voters, by a 50% to 44% margin. Obama has held at least a small margin over McCain in each of the last four daily reports, generally coinciding with the start of the Wall Street financial meltdown that began to dominate the news on September 15. Separate Gallup consumer confidence tracking has shown that Americans' views of the economy deteriorated as the week progressed, and that Americans also began to express increased personal worry about their own finances. There is thus a reasonable inference that Obama's gains may, in part, be related to the way in which the public viewed his and McCain's responses to the financial crisis. September 19's economic news was a bit more positive, with the announcement of a pending major U.S. government bailout for the country's economy; it was also the second day of significant increases in the Dow Jones Industrial Average and other stock market indices. It remains to be seen if this will affect Obama's lead in the days ahead.

Obama's current 50% rating matches his 50% record high reached just after the Democratic convention in late August. However, his current six-percentage-point advantage is not as large as the eight-point lead he had then, or the nine-point lead he held in late July. It is important to note that McCain recovered and moved ahead after each of these Obama high points, suggesting that it is certainly possible that he could recover in this situation as well.

SEPTEMBER 22

Americans More Tuned In Than Ever to Political News

A record-high 43% of Americans say they follow news about national politics very closely, up from 30% at this time last year and 36% during the last presidential election. In the September 8–11 Gallup Poll, an additional 44% say they follow political news "somewhat closely," meaning nearly 9 in 10 Americans (87%) are tuned in to the national political dialogue. This significantly exceeds anything Gallup has measured since it began asking this question in 1995. While it is common for attention to political news to increase in presidential election years, this month's 43% easily surpasses the 36% who in September 2004 said they were very closely following news about national politics.

The unprecedented upswing in interest in political news comes during a presidential election that, still more than six weeks from Election Day, is already historic many times over. Not only did the primaries and caucuses start earlier than ever, triggering a record early interest in the election, but the Democratic nomination battle stayed competitive longer than it ever has, because of the extended primary battle between Hillary Clinton and Barack Obama. Add in the back-and-forth nature of the race between Obama and Republican nominee John McCain, the historical firsts for Obama (as an African American) and vice presidential nominee Sarah Palin (as a Republican woman) and the promise that one of them will make history by being elected, and Americans have more than enough reasons to pay attention.

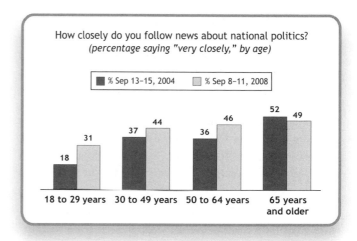

How closely do you follow news about national politics?
(percentage saying "very closely," by age)

■ % Sep 13-15, 2004   ☐ % Sep 8-11, 2008

18 to 29 years	30 to 49 years	50 to 64 years	65 years and older
18 / 31	37 / 44	36 / 46	52 / 49

Americans' hypervigilance also comes at a time when they have more news sources than ever to choose from. In particular, the Internet and blogs have become major sources of election news—so much so that a study released earlier this month by Northwestern University's Media Management Center found young adults to be "overwhelmed" by the amount of election news available online. Nonetheless, voters age 18 to 29 are more interested in the campaign than they have been in the past, with 31% saying they are following national political news very closely, up from 18% at this time during the last presidential election. Yet, because other age groups are paying about the same or more attention, younger voters remain the least engaged overall.

A Skeptical Audience

In an interesting paradox, Americans' record-high interest in political news coincides with their continued distrust of the news media—specifically newspapers, television, and radio. A record-low 43% of Americans say they place

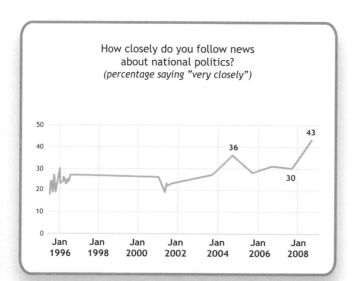

How closely do you follow news about national politics?
(percentage saying "very closely")

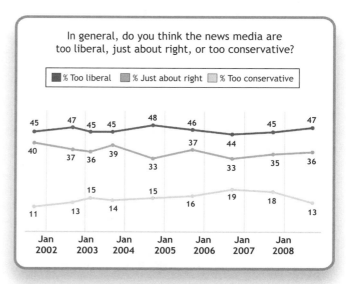

In general, do you think the news media are too liberal, just about right, or too conservative?

■ % Too liberal   ■ % Just about right   ☐ % Too conservative a great deal or fair amount of trust in such media outlets to report the news "fully, accurately, and fairly," down from 47% last year and similar to the 44% who said this during the last presidential election. The distrust expressed in the 2004 and 2008 election seasons likely reflects a perception that the media have become increasingly partisan. This year, 47% perceive the news media to be too liberal and 13% perceive them to be too conservative, with only 36% seeing media coverage as "about right." But interestingly, concern about media bias has been fairly constant over the years.

Word of Bailout Stalls Worsening Consumer Confidence

Mirroring the reaction on Wall Street, Gallup Poll daily tracking found that consumer confidence began deteriorating on September 15, following the announcements of the bankruptcy of Lehman Brothers, the sale of Merrill Lynch, and the government takeover of AIG. This deterioration accelerated over the next several days but leveled off by the end of the week and has remained stable over the September 20–21 weekend, as the announcement of the unprecedented bailout was proposed and was positively received by Congress.

Consumer confidence measured in Gallup's broader economic tracking quickly began to deteriorate early last week—unlike the week before, when consumers showed little reaction to the government's takeover of the mortgage finance giants Fannie Mae and Freddie Mac. The percentage of Americans saying current economic conditions are getting worse increased from 77% on September 14, in Gallup's three-day rolling average of daily polls, to 86% in the interviews conducted through September 18. In all likelihood, this sharp deterioration in consumer expectations was transmitted from Wall Street to Main Street by the plunging Dow Jones Industrial Average, the demise of two major investment banks, the chaos following the bailout of AIG, and real concerns about money market funds.

The percentage of Americans saying the economy is getting worse stabilized in Gallup's reports—including interviewing conducted on September 19 and September 20—coinciding with the announcement of the U.S. Treasury Department's proposed plan to bail out mortgage security holders, the government's decision to federally insure money market mutual funds, and the generally positive congressional reaction to the need for all of these emergency actions. While Main Street's response to this was not nearly as positive as the surge in the Dow Jones average, consumer perceptions did stop deteriorating. It appears that consumer confidence, like the financial markets, remains fragile, even as the government takes historic steps to rebuild confidence in the financial system.

Consumers Worry About Money Surges

Probably the most troubling aspect of last week's reactions on the part of American consumers involves the impact of the economic crisis on their thinking as far as their personal finances are concerned. Gallup's economic tracking measure of personal worry about money ("Did you worry about money yesterday?") jumped 10 percentage points in just three days, from 34% in the interviews conducted between September 13 and September 15 to 44% in those conducted through September 16–18. This change is somewhat remarkable because the money-worry measure has, for the most part, been essentially stable—in the 30% range—all year. The only time it dropped below 30% was over the Fourth of July—when, presumably, Americans' minds were elsewhere. It has been as high as 40% just a few times this year—primarily in July, when gasoline prices spiked to an all-time high. The point is that the panic on Wall Street and the government's response to it clearly had a pronounced impact on the way individual American families thought about their own finances early last week—and they were thinking in very negative terms. As has been the case with consumers' economic moods, these worries appear to have stabilized as last week came to an end. The percentage of Americans saying they worried about money was 43% in the September 20 report and dropped slightly to 41% in the September 21 report. While the newly proposed government bailout proposal has stalled the deterioration in consumer confidence, however, that immediate success may only be temporary. How Congress deals with the Treasury proposals is likely to affect consumer perceptions. So is discussion on the campaign trail of the proposed bailout—not to mention its probable impact on the real economy.

SEPTEMBER 23

Democrats Re-establish Double-Digit Lead in Party Affiliation

Democrats have re-established a double-digit advantage over Republicans in party affiliation, with 49% of Americans identifying themselves as Democrats or leaning to the Democratic Party and 39% identifying as Republicans or leaning to the Republican Party. This is a shift from immediately after the Republican convention, when Democrats enjoyed their smallest advantage of the year, leading only 47% to 42%.

In more than 250,000 Gallup Poll daily tracking interviews conducted in 2008, an average of 50% of Americans have identified themselves as Democrats or have initially identified as independents but said they leaned to the Democratic Party, while 37% have aligned themselves in one or the other manner with the Republican Party, a 13-point average advantage for the Democrats. So with roughly half the country supporting it, 2008 has clearly been a favorable political year for the Democratic Party. Republicans cut into that advantage in the wake of their party's convention, reducing their partisan deficit to single digits from September 3–5 polling through September 12–14 polling, when the averages for party identification were 47% Democratic and 40% Republican (according to the more than 9,000 interviews conducted during that time period). But in the last week, with the Wall Street financial crisis dominating the news, Democrats have regained a double-digit advantage. It is unclear whether the recent movement in partisanship reflects public reaction to the crisis or just a return to a more normal state as the effects of the Republican convention fade.

The Democratic advantage in party affiliation is slightly smaller when the partisan leaners from each party group are excluded. In the September 20–22 tracking data, 35% of Americans identify as Democrats, 26% as Republicans, and 33% as independents, resulting in a nine-point Democratic advantage. For the year, an average of 34% of Americans have identified as Democrats and 26% as Republicans, for an eight-point average Democratic lead. Any momentum the Republican Party had coming out of its convention has been halted in the past week, and the Democrats have essentially re-established their dominant political positioning.

During this past week, Obama has also re-established an advantage over McCain in Gallup's presidential election trial heat. Obama had led by a slight margin most of the summer after clinching the Democratic nomination, but McCain emerged from the Republican convention with the lead and continued to have at least a slim advantage as recently as Sept. 13–15 polling. Even so, the presidential election remains close, in part because McCain has been able to command greater party loyalty than Obama. In the past week, 89% of Republican supporters said they would vote for McCain, compared with 86% of Democratic supporters favoring Obama.

While the Democratic Party is certainly in a more advantageous position than the Republican Party to win the election, the Democrats' ability to do so will depend on their maintaining an advantage in party support over Republicans between now and Election Day, and on ensuring that their supporters remain mostly loyal to Obama and turn out to vote on November 4. So far, the lesser Democratic voting loyalty to their nominee has not hurt the party because of the significant Democratic advantage in partisanship. To the extent the partisan-

ship gap narrows (as it did the week after the Republican convention), Democratic loyalty and turnout will become more critical.

Before Recent Crisis, Public Was Wary of Active Federal Government

An early September Gallup Poll showed that Americans continue to believe the government is doing "too many things that should be left to individuals and businesses," rather than preferring an expanded government role to deal with the country's problems. These results are based on Gallup's annual Governance Poll, conducted between September 8 and September 11 this year, and show 53% believing the government is doing too many things that individuals and businesses should be doing, a slight increase from prior years. These data are helpful in understanding the public opinion environment in which the federal government's massive financial bailout plan is being played out. It is too early yet to measure the public's reaction to that plan, the details of which the Bush administration and Congress are still working out. However, a USA Today/Gallup Poll last week found a majority of Americans in favor of increased regulation of Wall Street but divided on the specific proposal to loan up to $85 billion to AIG. These two findings suggest that it is unclear whether the public will end up supporting the broader government intervention being considered this week.

Since 1992, Gallup has frequently asked Americans about their preferences with respect to government's role in solving the nation's problems. Only twice during that time have more Americans expressed a preference for more government action rather than less—in March 1993, during the early months of the Clinton presidency, and

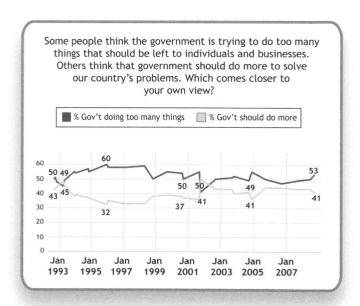

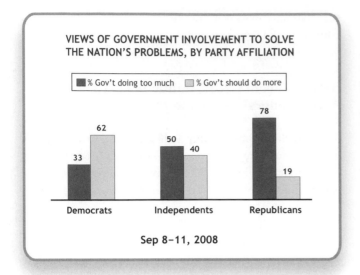

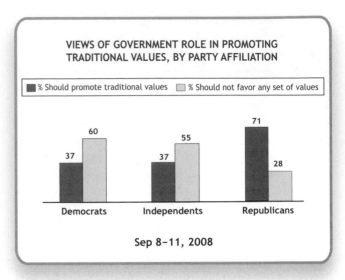

shortly after the September 11, 2001, terrorist attacks. In this year's poll, as is typical, voters' preferences on this question reflect the dominant political philosophies in the United States, with Republicans favoring a lesser role for the government in solving economic problems and Democrats a more active one. Independents also tend to favor a less active government role.

In addition to asking about the government's role in solving economic problems, the poll also measures public preferences for what the government should do in regard to moral values. For the first time since 1993, Americans are evenly divided about what government's role should be, with 48% saying it should promote traditional values and 48% saying it should not favor any set of values. A majority had favored a government role in promoting traditional values from 1993 to 2006; even in 2007, more Americans (though now less than a majority) still favored government's promoting traditional values than favored government's keeping hands off.

Consistent with their respective party platforms, Republicans tend to favor a more active role for government in this area, while Democrats tend to believe the government should not be heavily involved. Independents' preferences are similar to those of Democrats. At least as of early September, it seemed like Americans' preferences more closely aligned with those of the Republican Party and John McCain in terms of what the government's role should be in solving the country's problems. However, since that time, the Republican presidential administration has intervened to develop a government program to help keep major financial institutions from collapsing under the weight of bad loans they have made in recent years. Initial public reaction to the events from early last week gives no strong indication as to whether the public will support or oppose this more comprehensive role.

It is possible that the developments on Wall Street have shifted Americans' preferences on government intervention in the economy, though the direction of that shift is unclear. Both candidates have publicly endorsed the government's approach with some reservations, though McCain's position changed from a more anti-regulation stance taken earlier in the week. In some ways, the public's preferred government role in addressing economic problems in the wake of the Wall Street crisis may hold the key to the election outcome, since Americans are evenly divided as to what role the government should take with regard to morality.

SEPTEMBER 24
Did Palin Help McCain Among White Women?

Did John McCain's selection of Sarah Palin as his vice presidential running mate lead to significant gains for McCain among white women? While this hypothesis fits easily into the media's coverage and the excitement around Palin's historic status as the first female Republican vice presidential candidate, continuing analysis of large Gallup Poll daily tracking samples from recent weeks does not provide evidence to support it. Gallup daily tracking has shown some variation in support levels for the two candidates—McCain and Barack Obama—across the last month and a half, but the shifts in the candidate preferences of white women do not appear to have been much different from those of all voters.

When Obama gained among all voters, he gained among white women. And when McCain gained among all voters—in the week of September 8–14 in particular—he gained among white women as well. By the week of September 15–21, a rising tide for Obama had lifted his strength among white women as much as it did among everyone

PREFERENCE FOR THE PRESIDENTIAL ELECTION
Weekly Aggregate of Registered Voters

	Obama, among white women	McCain, among white women	Obama, among all registered voters	McCain, among all registered voters
Aug 18–24, 2008	39%	48%	45%	45%
Aug 25–31, 2008	43%	47%	48%	42%
Sep 1–7, 2008	42%	49%	47%	45%
Sep 8–14, 2008	40%	51%	45%	47%
Sep 15–21, 2008	45%	47%	49%	44%

PREFERENCE FOR THE PRESIDENTIAL ELECTION, AMONG WOMEN
Aggregate of Registered Voters, Aug 1–Sep 21, 2008

	Barack Obama	John McCain
Non-Hispanic white women	42%	47%
Non-Hispanic black women	91%	3%
Hispanic white women	53%	35%
Asian-American women	60%	28%

else. Obama ended last week in a slightly stronger position among white women than was the case as the political conventions began—in fact, coming within 2 points of McCain. From a more general perspective, Obama continues to do less well among white women than he does among women of other racial or ethnic backgrounds.

An aggregate of more than 23,000 interviews Gallup conducted with female registered voters between August 1 and September 21 shows McCain leading Obama by 47% to 42% among all white women, while McCain loses significantly among black, Hispanic, and Asian-American women. So Obama has a problem among white women (as he does, in terms of losing to McCain, among all white voters), regardless of whether or not it was exacerbated by McCain's selection of Palin as his vice presidential running mate. But from a different perspective, and reflecting the fairly normal gender-gap pattern of recent years, Obama's position among white women is much better than his position among white men, among whom he trails McCain by a large 56% to 35% margin. And, of course, white women are not a monolithic voting group; there are large differences in the level of support given the two candidates within subgroups of the white female population. For example, data show that Obama has significant problems among white women who are not college graduates—among whom he has been losing to McCain by a 50% to 37% margin over the last month and a half—and among married white women, among whom McCain has been winning by a 17-point margin, 54% to 37%.

It has been well established that Obama does not do as well among white women as he does among Hispanic, black, and Asian women. This fact, however, predates McCain's selection of Palin as his running mate. The data reviewed here suggest that Palin's presence on the Republican ticket does not appear to have shifted white women disproportionately toward McCain, nor does it appear to have engendered more loyalty to McCain among white women over the past week, when the general trend was toward Obama. As is true with respect to the entire electorate, McCain is now doing slightly less well among this group than he was doing before the two conventions began.

SEPTEMBER 25
Presidential Debates Rarely Game-Changers

Gallup election polling trends since the advent of televised presidential debates nearly a half-century ago reveal few instances in which the debates may have had a substantive impact on election outcomes. The two exceptions (discussed below) are 1960 and 2000, both very close elections in which even small changes could have determined who won.

In two others—1976 and 2004—public preferences moved quite a bit around the debates, but the debates did not appear to have altered the likely outcome: The candidate leading before the debates eventually won the elections. The debates in those years seem to have made those races more competitive, but they did not change the fundamentals of the races.

In 1976, the debates may have made the race between Jimmy Carter and Gerald Ford more competitive, but they did not change the fact that Carter was ahead of Ford in Gallup polling throughout the debate period (and, of course, Carter won the election). Carter held a substantial lead over Ford among registered voters prior to the first presidential debate; Gallup polling found more Americans saying Ford won that debate than Carter, 38% to 25%, and perhaps as a result, Carter's lead shrank to only 2 points just prior to the second debate. After Ford's statement in the second debate about the lack of Soviet domination of Eastern Europe—widely perceived as a gaffe—Carter's lead expanded slightly to 6 points, and it remained at about that level after the third and final debate. The closer nature of the final outcome (a 2-point margin of victory for Carter) was most likely due to the difference between the preferences of all registered voters and those of actual voters.

In 2004, Bush went from holding an 11-point lead over John Kerry among registered voters just prior to the first debate on September 30 to a 2-point lead right after it—a 9-point loss for Bush. (A post-debate Gallup Poll found Kerry the perceived winner by a wide margin, 53% to 37%.) The race remained close thereafter: It was tied at 48% after the second debate, and Bush was up by 3 points after the third debate. Bush won the election by a 3-point margin, but it might have been larger had he performed better in the debates. (It is notable that Gallup's 2004 debate-reaction polls showed Americans believing that Kerry won each debate; nevertheless, he still lost the election.)

Debates and Third-Party Candidates

In 1980, then president Jimmy Carter consented to only one debate with Ronald Reagan; it was held on October 29, less than a week before Election Day. In an October 24–26 Gallup Poll, Carter led Reagan by 3 percentage points, 45% to 42%, among national registered voters. A post-debate registered voter trial heat figure is not available in Gallup's published records, but in Gallup's final pre-election poll of "likely voters," conducted from October 30 to November 2, Reagan led Carter by 3 points, 46% to 43%. Without comparable pre- and post-debate registered voter figures on presidential preferences, it is unclear what impact the 1980 debate may have had on the election. However, given that Reagan won the election by nearly 10 percentage points, it is not likely to have been a determining factor.

The debates in both 1980 and 1992, however, may have influenced voter support for the third party candidates running in those elections, even if they do not appear to have altered the contours of those races among the two major party candidates. In 1980, third party candidate John Anderson fell from 15% support prior to his only debate (with Ronald Reagan) in late September to only 8% support by mid-October. However, given the long span between polls during this period, and the downward trend in Anderson's support prior to the debates, it is unclear whether his debate with Reagan was a factor. In 1992, Ross Perot's generally well-reviewed debate performances (close to half of Americans thought he won the first debate, and a plurality thought he won the third debate) were no doubt part of the reason he catapulted from a 10% level of support prior to the first debate to 17% support after the last debate.

The presidential debates had little to no impact on voter preferences in the elections of 1984, 1988, and 1996. And in 1964, 1968, and 1972, incumbent president Lyndon Johnson and Republican nominee (and later president) Richard Nixon refused to debate their opponents, so no presidential debates were held in those years.

Game-Changers?: The Debates of 1960 and 2000

By contrast, the debates of 1960 and 2000 seem to have been associated with meaningful shifts in the horse races for those elections, whereby the ultimate winner moved from a deficit position to front-runner.

THE ELECTION OF 1960

Perhaps the most fabled televised presidential debate was the very first one: the September 26, 1960, debate between Richard Nixon and John F. Kennedy, in which a thin, pale, and stiff-looking Nixon sweated under the hot lights of the television studio, while Kennedy proved himself to be a highly telegenic master of the new medium. Gallup trends show that Kennedy and Nixon were about tied among registered voters in August and September polls leading up to that debate. Immediately after it, Kennedy was ahead by three percentage points, and he was ahead by four points by the time the fourth debate was held in late October. Given Kennedy's ultimate margin of victory in the popular vote of only two-tenths of a percentage point, it is clear that the debates didn't produce a major shift in the contours of the election, but this debate-period boost in his support could very well have accounted for the outcome.

THE ELECTION OF 2000

In 2000, Al Gore led George W. Bush by eight percentage points among registered voters right before the first debate (held on October 3). Although a Gallup debate-reaction survey that night found debate watchers closely divided in their views of who won (48% said Gore and 41% Bush), the post-debate media reporting may have been more favorable to Bush. Gallup polling in the first three days after that debate showed the race tied at 43%. Gore recovered somewhat before the second debate on October 11—he was leading by five points in a pre-debate poll—but Bush was again leading right after it, by two points. Gallup's debate-reaction survey on October 11 showed 49% of debate watchers saying Bush had won the debate, compared with only 36% picking Gore.

GALLUP POLL 1960 TRIAL HEATS DURING DEBATE PERIOD
Based on Registered Voters

	Kennedy	Nixon	Net for election winner
	%	%	pct. pts.
Sep 9–14	46	47	−1
Sep 26 — first debate			
Sep 28–Oct 2	49	46	+3
Oct 7 — second debate			
Oct 13 — third debate			
Oct 18–23	49	45	+4
Oct 21 — fourth debate*			

* No poll conducted entirely after the fourth debate, based on registered voters, is available.

GALLUP POLL 2000 TRIAL HEATS DURING DEBATE PERIOD
Based on Registered Voters

	G. W. Bush	Gore	Net for election winner
	%	%	pct. pts.
Sep 30–Oct 2	39	47	–8
Oct 3 – first debate			
Oct 4–6	43	43	0
Oct 8–10	40	45	–5
Oct 11 – second debate			
Oct 12–14	45	43	+2
Oct 14–16	44	44	0
Oct 17 – third debate			
Oct 18–20	46	42	+4

There was another shift toward Bush around the third debate (held on October 17), from a tie at 44% right before it to a four-point lead for Bush, 46% to 42%, immediately after it. Gallup's debate-reaction survey on this night showed the candidates again about tied in perceptions of who won: 46% for Gore and 44% for Bush. Debate watchers mostly credited Gore with expressing himself more clearly (57% for Gore vs. 33% for Bush), while Bush was seen as the more likable candidate, 60% to 31%.

Thus, across the entire 2000 debate period, the race shifted from an eight-point lead for Gore to a four-point lead for Bush. Other factors may have come into play to account for the shift, but Gallup analysts at the time assigned at least some of the cause to the debates themselves. Gore had been consistently ahead in the race (among registered voters) for most of September and October prior to the first debate, whereas Bush generally remained in the lead in most Gallup polling after the third and final debate. (The race tightened up in the last few days before Election Day, with Gore moving into a one- to two-point lead among registered voters.) Gore won the popular vote, but he might also have won the Electoral College vote had his eight-point pre-debate-period lead not slipped away in the last few weeks of the campaign.

Implications for the 2008 Election

In at least two election years, the presidential debates may have had a meaningful impact on the contours of the presidential race; in most others, they probably have not. The debates were less likely to be catalyst events in years when one candidate was a strong front-runner—including 1984, 1988, and 1996. However, in highly competitive election years, any movement in voter preferences can be race-altering, and the debates seem to have the potential to produce

such movement. Probably the most prominent examples of this are the elections of 1960 and 2000. Given this history, and the close nature of the race in recent Gallup Poll daily tracking, the 2008 debates could be an important factor in shifting voter preferences decisively toward one candidate or the other. With so much economic uncertainty and so much political activity of interest going on, however, it may be impossible to disentangle the effect of the debates from the effect of other news events on voter preferences at this critical time.

SEPTEMBER 26
Public Divided on Need for a Third Party

Americans divide evenly in a recent Gallup Poll on whether the two major political parties are adequately representing the public, or whether a third party is needed. That represents a shift from 2007, when a majority said the Democrats and Republicans were doing "such a poor job that a third major party is needed." Gallup has asked this question since 2003, and over that time the public's views on this matter have not been consistent. The first time the question was asked, in October 2003, a majority opposed the idea of a third major party. Two separate polls from last year showed most Americans in favor of another party. This year's results are similar to what Gallup found in September 2006. Not surprisingly, political independents are most likely to favor the emergence of a third major party, with 63% holding this view. In contrast, a majority of Democrats (56%) and Republicans (55%) think the two major parties are doing an adequate job and thus there is no need for another party that would compete with them.

The change in the balance of opinion since 2007 from a majority favoring a third major party to an even division

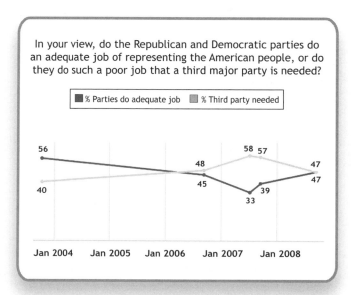

In your view, do the Republican and Democratic parties do an adequate job of representing the American people, or do they do such a poor job that a third major party is needed?

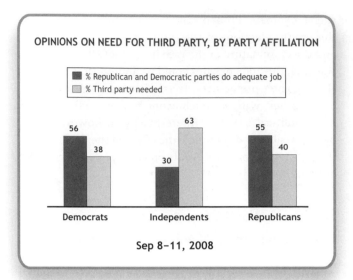

OPINIONS ON NEED FOR THIRD PARTY, BY PARTY AFFILIATION

- % Republican and Democratic parties do adequate job
- % Third party needed

Democrats: 56 / 38
Independents: 30 / 63
Republicans: 55 / 40

Sep 8–11, 2008

tionate percentage of whom also are independent in their partisan orientation, have generally preferred that there be a third party. Conservatives, who in general tend to favor the status quo, have usually expressed satisfaction with the two-party system.

Americans' views on the need for a third political party have varied in recent years, and in this presidential election year the public is divided down the middle. This could reflect general satisfaction with the major parties' presidential candidates, both of whom enjoy favorable ratings near 60%. This question was not asked in 1992, when independent candidate Ross Perot had the best showing for a third party candidate in recent memory.

Americans Favor Congressional Action on Economic Crisis

Americans overwhelmingly favor Congress's passing a plan that would help fix the current Wall Street economic crisis, but a September 24 evening USA Today/Gallup Poll (conducted before the September 25 high-level negotiations between President Bush and congressional leaders on a new plan) shows that by more than a two-to-one ratio, Americans would like to see Congress pass a different plan than the $700 billion bailout plan proposed by the Bush administration. This key question was asked of more than 1,000 Americans on the evening of September 24; it described the Bush administration's plan as allowing "the Treasury Department to buy and resell up to $700 billion of distressed assets from financial companies." With this description, and given three choices of congressional action (pass a plan similar to the Bush proposal, pass a plan different from the Bush proposal, or not take any action at

on this question came about largely because of a shift in Democrats' attitudes. Last September, Democrats favored a third party by 53% to 43%—nearly the mirror image of this year's result, which finds just 38% in favor and 56% opposed. It is not clear why this shift has occurred, but throughout this presidential election year, Gallup polling has found Democrats highly engaged in the election and expressing heightened enthusiasm about voting. Republicans' attitudes are virtually unchanged from September 2007, when 57% supported the current party structure and 40% wanted a third option. Independents are slightly less likely to favor a third party this year (63%) than they were last year (72%). But beyond the differences by party affiliation in attitudes toward a third party, there are fairly consistent differences by political ideology that help reveal what sort of third party Americans would most like to see.

Gallup has typically found self-identified liberals to be the most likely ideological group to say a third party is needed. Even in 2003, when close to 6 in 10 Americans thought the Democratic and Republican parties were doing an adequate job of representing Americans, a majority of liberals disagreed. Liberal support for a third party climbed to 66% in 2007—ironically, shortly after the Democrats had assumed control of Congress for the first time since 1994. This year, with Obama heading the Democratic ticket, marks the low point in liberal support for a third party, at 51% (though that still represents majority support among this subgroup). The lower level of support may suggest that liberals' penchant for favoring a third major party reflects a desire for a party that more closely reflects their political views—and perhaps they see Obama as doing that better than Democratic leaders who have come before him. Those who identify as political moderates, a dispropor-

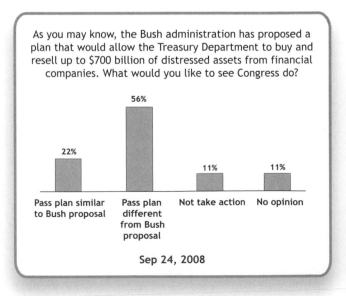

As you may know, the Bush administration has proposed a plan that would allow the Treasury Department to buy and resell up to $700 billion of distressed assets from financial companies. What would you like to see Congress do?

Pass plan similar to Bush proposal: 22%
Pass plan different from Bush proposal: 56%
Not take action: 11%
No opinion: 11%

Sep 24, 2008

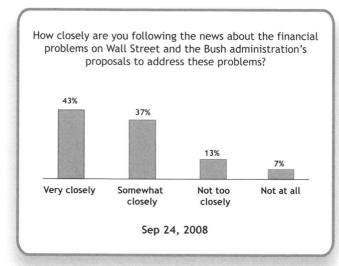

How closely are you following the news about the financial problems on Wall Street and the Bush administration's proposals to address these problems?

Very closely 43% | Somewhat closely 37% | Not too closely 13% | Not at all 7%

Sep 24, 2008

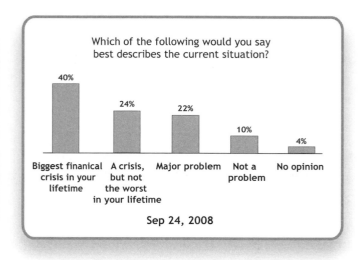

Which of the following would you say best describes the current situation?

Biggest financial crisis in your lifetime 40% | A crisis, but not the worst in your lifetime 24% | Major problem 22% | Not a problem 10% | No opinion 4%

Sep 24, 2008

all), the majority of Americans opted for the middle alternative, with smaller percentages opting for either passing the Bush plan or not taking any action.

These data suggest that Americans should in broad terms favor the type of plan Congress was considering on September 25 but may have some disagreements as the precise details become known, particularly if the plan is viewed as being similar to the original Bush administration proposal. Eight out of 10 Americans say they are following news of the financial problems on Wall Street and the Bush administration's proposals to deal with the crisis very or somewhat closely, with 43% saying "very" closely. This ranks in the upper tier of what Gallup has measured historically for topics in the news.

All discussions of the current financial crisis and proposals to resolve it are highly complex, even for professionals in the financial field. One can assume that Americans who are following the news very closely are more knowl-

edgeable than others, but the views of the closely attentive group on the Bush plan are little different from those of the total sample: 24% of the attentive group favors the Bush proposal, 58% a plan different from the Bush proposal, and 12% taking no action at all. One reason a high percentage of Americans feel some type of rescue plan should be passed is evident from the fact that 74% of Americans believe the economy would get worse if Congress does not act at this time. Moreover, 4 out of 10 Americans describe the current situation as the "biggest financial crisis" in their lifetimes. The biggest variation in responses to this question by age is among those who are 18 to 34. This group—despite having had fewer years to be exposed to other financial crises in their lifetimes—is actually less likely than those who are older to say this is the biggest financial crisis they have experienced. Americans 55 and older, some of whom lived through the Great Depression of the 1930s, are little different from the overall sample average in their views that this is the biggest financial crisis

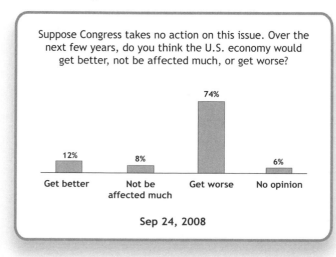

Suppose Congress takes no action on this issue. Over the next few years, do you think the U.S. economy would get better, not be affected much, or get worse?

Get better 12% | Not be affected much 8% | Get worse 74% | No opinion 6%

Sep 24, 2008

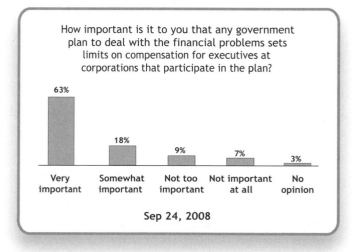

How important is it to you that any government plan to deal with the financial problems sets limits on compensation for executives at corporations that participate in the plan?

Very important 63% | Somewhat important 18% | Not too important 9% | Not important at all 7% | No opinion 3%

Sep 24, 2008

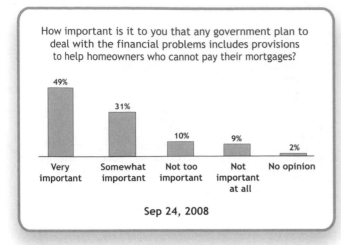

How important is it to you that any government plan to deal with the financial problems includes provisions to help homeowners who cannot pay their mortgages?

Sep 24, 2008

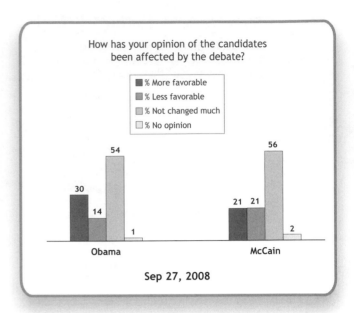

How has your opinion of the candidates been affected by the debate?

Sep 27, 2008

they have witnessed. The bailout plan is still being worked out, but almost two-thirds of Americans say it would be very important to include in any government plan limits on compensation for executives at corporations that participate in the plan. About half say it is very important to include provisions to help homeowners who cannot pay their mortgages.

SEPTEMBER 28

Debate Watchers Give Obama Edge over McCain

Americans who watched the first presidential debate on September 26 gave Barack Obama the edge over John McCain as having done the better job in the debate, by a 46% to 34% margin. These results are based on a special USA Today/Gallup Poll conducted on Saturday, September 27, the first day after the debate. Questions about the debate were asked of a random sample of 1,005 national adults as part of the Gallup Poll daily tracking program on September 27. Of the total sample of adults, 63% said they had watched the debate; another 12% said that they had seen, heard, or read news coverage of the debate; and the rest said they had neither seen the debate nor followed news coverage of it.

The data show a predictably partisan pattern of response from Republicans and Democrats. Seventy-two percent of the former and 74% of the latter said that their party's candidate did the better job in the debate. This reinforces the conventional wisdom that many viewers watch a debate through a preexisting perceptual framework and end up merely reinforcing what they believed before the debate began. But among the crucial group of independents who watched the debate—those most likely to actually be swayed by what transpired—Obama won by 10 points, 43% to 33%.

Not only did Obama win the debate among debate watchers, but they report that their attitudes toward the Democratic candidate also improved as a result. Thirty percent of debate watchers said they came away with a more favorable image of Obama, while just 14% said they had a less favorable image. On the other hand, McCain did not fare as well. Just as many watchers—21%—said that they had a less favorable opinion of McCain as a result of the debate as said they now had a more favorable opinion of him.

Although the debate was supposed to deal with foreign policy, the first questions asked focused on the economy and the financial bailout plan being negotiated by Congress. This economic focus appears to have been a posi-

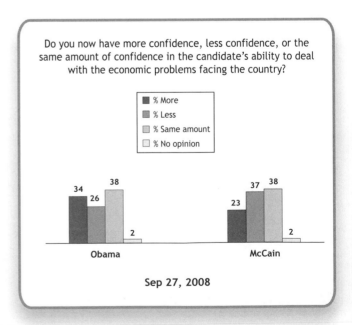

Do you now have more confidence, less confidence, or the same amount of confidence in the candidate's ability to deal with the economic problems facing the country?

Sep 27, 2008

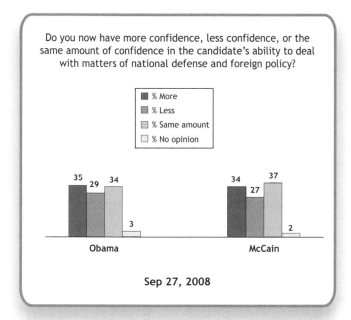

Do you now have more confidence, less confidence, or the same amount of confidence in the candidate's ability to deal with matters of national defense and foreign policy?

■ % More
■ % Less
■ % Same amount
□ % No opinion

Sep 27, 2008

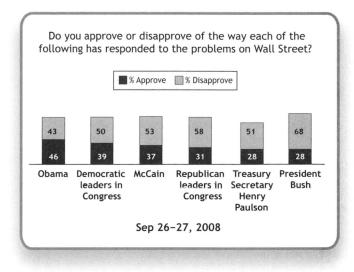

Do you approve or disapprove of the way each of the following has responded to the problems on Wall Street?

■ % Approve   ■ % Disapprove

Sep 26–27, 2008

important indicator of the impact of the first debate may be trends in overall candidate support—on which measure, at the moment, Obama leads McCain.

tive one for Obama; debate watchers ended up with more confidence in Obama's ability to deal with the economic problems facing the country as a result of the debate. By contrast, 37% of debate watchers said that the debate gave them less confidence in McCain on economic matters. Debate watchers saw little difference between the two candidates on national defense and foreign policy as a result of the debate; both Obama and McCain appeared to have come away with slightly improved images on foreign policy. Finally, by a fairly substantial margin, debate watchers said that Obama was the candidate who offered the best proposals for change in the debate, by a 17-percentage-point margin over McCain.

History shows that "winning" the first presidential debate does not necessarily translate into winning the election. Ross Perot, Al Gore, and John Kerry are among those who were seen by debate watchers in quick-reaction polls as having done the better job in the first debate of their campaign year, and all eventually lost their elections. There are two presidential debates (and one vice presidential one) yet to come, and much can still change. The most

SEPTEMBER 29

Leaders Not Getting High Marks on Handling Wall Street Crisis

A USA Today/Gallup Poll conducted on September 26 and September 27 finds more Americans disapproving than approving of how most of the major national political players have handled the recent problems on Wall Street. Only Barack Obama squeaks by, 46% to 43%, with more Americans approving than disapproving of his performance on the issue. The September 26–27 poll was conducted before the September 28 morning announcement that congressional leaders and the Bush administration had reached agreement on a $700 billion bailout plan. It reflects interviews conducted before, during, and after the first presidential debate between Obama and McCain on September 26.

Both Obama and McCain are rated more favorably with respect to their responses to the Wall Street mess than are their respective parties in Congress. Obama wins the approval of 46% of Americans, compared with 39% approving of the Democratic leaders in Congress. Similarly, 37% of Americans approve of how McCain has responded, compared with 31% approving of the response by Republican leaders in Congress.

The higher scores of Obama and the Democrats in Congress relative to McCain and the Republicans in Congress are mainly due to differences in intraparty support for each side. Nearly 8 in 10 Democrats approve of the way Obama has responded to the Wall Street crisis, compared with only 7 in 10 Republicans approving of McCain's response.

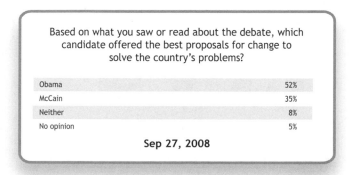

Based on what you saw or read about the debate, which candidate offered the best proposals for change to solve the country's problems?

Obama	52%
McCain	35%
Neither	8%
No opinion	5%

Sep 27, 2008

Similarly, 65% of Democrats approve of the Democratic leaders in Congress, as opposed to 55% of Republicans approving of their party's leaders. Importantly, Obama and McCain receive similar ratings on the Wall Street issue from political independents, with only about a third of this group approving of each.

The worst-rated political players on the Wall Street issue both come from the Bush administration: Treasury Secretary Henry Paulson, one of the chief authors of the original bailout plan, and President George W. Bush himself. Only 28% of Americans approve of how each has responded to the recent financial problems. Of the two, however, Bush has a net score that is significantly worse, as 68% disapprove of his performance, compared with 51% disapproving of Paulson's.

Implications

Though Obama and McCain have offered prescriptions for the Wall Street crisis, and McCain attempted to demonstrate his commitment to solving it by dramatically suspending his campaign last week and returning to Washington, neither candidate has won majority public approval on the issue. Obama outscores McCain in approval on the issue, 46% to 37%, mostly because his fellow Democrats rate his response more highly than Republicans rate McCain's. In terms of winning over the political center, where most swing voters reside, the jury still seems to be out. Obama and McCain receive nearly identical ratings from political independents for their handling of the Wall Street crisis, and they're not positive. Only about a third of independents approve of the way each candidate has responded.

Obama Maintains Eight-Point Lead

The latest Gallup Poll daily tracking update, based on September 26–28 polling, shows Barack Obama with a 50% to 42% lead over John McCain, unchanged from the prior report. Obama's 50% level of support matches his high for the campaign, and his eight-point lead is just one percentage point below his largest, achieved after his international trip in late July.

The trend showed Obama building momentum heading into the debate on September 26, moving from a tie earlier in the week to a five-percentage-point advantage. The debate apparently did nothing to halt or reverse that momentum. Today's report includes two full days of interviewing following the debate, both of which show Obama with a healthy advantage over McCain. A USA Today/Gallup Poll conducted on September 29 showed that Ameri-

cans who saw the debate were more likely to say that Obama did a better job than McCain. The September 30 Gallup report will provide the first fully post-debate three-day rolling average of voter preferences in the presidential election.

SEPTEMBER 30
Late-September Ratings Drag Down Consumer Confidence

Americans' confidence in the economy was better in the first half of September than in August, but that's ancient history now. Consumer attitudes took a sharp turn for the worse after September 15, when Wall Street fell into a worrisome tailspin over the collapse of Lehman Brothers and the bailout of AIG, and they remain highly negative at month's end. Gallup Poll daily tracking underscores the degree to which economic attitudes can change quickly, making it essential to monitor consumer confidence on an ongoing basis rather than taking periodic measurements or reporting monthly averages. The percentage of Americans whom Gallup classifies as "negative" about the economy, now 81% according to Gallup's daily tracking from September 27 to September 29, nearly ties the record high of 83% seen at three points in July. The minuscule 4% currently classified as "positive" ties the lowest scores seen all year. Attitudes had improved to as much as 12% of Americans feeling positive about the economy and 70% feeling negative in Gallup tracking conducted between September 12 and September 14.

The weekly averages of consumer confidence in September underscore the degree to which consumer confidence changed in the middle of the month. Whereas a slightly improved 11% of Americans felt positively about the economy in each of the first two weeks of September, up from 9% in August, this measure fell to 6% in the third

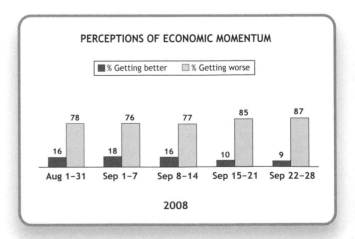

PERCEPTIONS OF ECONOMIC MOMENTUM

■ % Getting better   □ % Getting worse

	Aug 1–31	Sep 1–7	Sep 8–14	Sep 15–21	Sep 22–28
% Getting worse	78	76	77	85	87
% Getting better	16	18	16	10	9

2008

week (September 15–21) and to 4% from in the last full week (September 22–28) as President Bush and congressional leaders began negotiations over a $700 billion financial rescue package. Gallup's consumer mood summary is a composite of Americans' answers to two questions about the economy: one asking for their ratings of current economic conditions, and the other asking about their perceptions of whether conditions are getting better or worse. Since mid-September 2008, attitudes have grown more negative on the latter dimension as well.

Gallup Daily: Obama Holds Six-Point Lead

Barack Obama continues to hold a significant lead over John McCain in Gallup Poll daily tracking, 49% to 43%. This is based on interviewing conducted between September 27 and September 29, spanning an intense period of negotiations over a historic financial recovery package in Congress on September 26 and September 27 and news of a tentative agreement on the package on September 28, followed by collapse of the bill when it came to the House floor on September 29. It also represents the first report, reflecting three full days of tracking, following the September 26 presidential debate.

Today's results mark the fourth straight day on which Obama has held a five-percentage-point or better lead over McCain in Gallup Poll daily tracking, and two full weeks since McCain last had any advantage over Obama in national voter preferences. McCain held a slim lead over Obama for several days following the Republican convention in early September, but that quickly evaporated with the Wall Street financial crisis that began with the bankruptcy of Lehman Brothers on September 15.

Upper Limit for Obama?

Although support for Obama among national registered voters hit the 50% mark in the past two days of Gallup Poll daily tracking (September 28–29)—Obama initially attained 50% in early September—he has yet to cross that symbolic threshold. The importance of that, however, is unclear. Gallup's historical trial heat trends show that the winners in 1988 and 2000—both years with minimal third-party candidate support suppressing the vote for the major-party candidates—rarely attained 50% or greater support from registered voters prior to Gallup's final pre-election poll. Voter support for George W. Bush only once exceeded 50% in his 2004 campaign against John Kerry, that being 53% in mid-September. In 1988, George H. W. Bush reached or surpassed the 50% mark once at the very beginning and then not again until the last two weeks of the campaign.

OCTOBER 2008

Gallup Polls conducted in 73 countries from May to October 2008 reveal widespread international support for Democratic candidate Barack Obama over Republican candidate John McCain in the U.S. presidential election. Among these nations, representing nearly three-quarters of the world's population, 24% say they would rather see Obama elected president, compared with just 7% who favor McCain. At the same time, 69% of world citizens surveyed did not have an opinion. World citizens are more divided over whether the outcome of the U.S. election makes a difference to their country, with 26% saying it does and 22% saying it does not. Again, 52% of those surveyed did not have an opinion.

Overall, it is citizens in Europe who are the most likely to state a preference for the next president of the United States and to think that the election makes a difference to their country; citizens in Asia are the least likely to state a preference and to think the election makes a difference to their country. Among individual countries, only Georgia and the Philippines prefer McCain to Obama by statisti-

Who would you personally rather see elected president of the United States? Do you think who is elected makes a difference to your country or not?
Results for Africa

	Obama	McCain	Don't know/ Refused to answer	Makes a difference	Does not make a difference	Don't know/ Refused to answer
	%	%	%	%	%	%
Benin	20	2	77	7	9	84
Botswana	62	6	33	40	24	35
Burkina Faso	50	7	43	32	30	38
Burundi	61	8	31	31	49	20
Cameroon	44	7	49	29	24	48
Ethiopia	76	6	19	49	40	11
Ghana	31	13	56	39	31	29
Kenya	89	3	8	59	32	18
Liberia	45	27	28	50	32	18
Madagascar	47	28	24	53	37	10
Mali	70	16	15	41	39	21
Mauritania	68	3	29	30	22	48
Niger	59	7	35	34	21	46
Nigeria	23	11	66	36	26	38
Rwanda	57	12	31	46	19	35
Senegal	54	15	31	40	28	32
Sierra Leone	68	18	14	69	20	11
Tanzania	76	9	15	41	34	26
Togo	38	6	55	20	16	64
Uganda	85	8	7	51	43	7
Zambia	47	12	40	40	39	21
Zimbabwe	41	15	44	40	45	14

Who would you personally rather see elected president of the United States? Do you think who is elected makes a difference to your country or not?
Results for the Americas

	Obama	McCain	Don't know/ Refused to answer	Makes a difference	Does not make a difference	Don't know/ Refused to answer
	%	%	%	%	%	%
Argentina	31	6	62	25	28	47
Canada	67	22	11	75	22	3
Chile	43	9	47	29	45	26
Colombia	38	16	46	49	29	22
Costa Rica	44	9	47	36	42	22
Ecuador	30	9	62	29	17	54
El Salvador	24	14	63	43	23	34
Guatemala	27	11	63	32	37	31
Honduras	27	9	64	37	28	35
Mexico	27	9	65	35	36	30
Nicaragua	23	7	70	35	25	41
Panama	35	10	55	38	28	33
Paraguay	26	11	62	22	25	53
Peru	31	11	58	27	37	36
Uruguay	39	7	55	27	34	39

cally significant margins. Not surprisingly, 89% of Kenyans would like to see Obama—whose father was Kenyan—elected president.

Who would you personally rather see elected president of the United States? Do you think who is elected makes a difference to your country or not? *Results for Asia and Australia*						
	Obama	McCain	Don't know/ Refused to answer	Makes a difference	Does not make a difference	Don't know/ Refused to answer
	%	%	%	%	%	%
Australia	64	14	22	76	21	3
Bangladesh	19	8	73	33	16	50
Cambodia	4	9	86	22	15	63
India	7	2	91	6	8	87
Japan	66	15	18	42	46	12
Kuwait	32	12	56	28	46	22
Laos	24	25	52	36	28	36
Lebanon	45	18	38	42	52	6
Pakistan	5	5	91	10	18	72
Palestine	33	11	56	16	72	12
Philippines	20	28	52	49	27	24
Saudi Arabia	50	19	31	27	40	34
Singapore	21	11	68	29	24	47
South Korea	50	24	25	79	12	9

Who would you personally rather see elected president of the United States? Do you think who is elected makes a difference to your country or not? *Results for Europe*						
	Obama	McCain	Don't know/ Refused to Answer	Makes a difference	Does not make a difference	Don't know/ Refused to answer
	%	%	%	%	%	%
Austria	58	10	32	40	50	10
Belgium	64	6	30	56	30	14
Denmark	69	8	23	69	27	4
Estonia	22	17	62	27	61	12
Finland	54	14	32	57	40	3
France	64	4	32	71	15	14
Georgia	15	23	62	27	61	12
Germany	62	10	27	62	32	5
Ireland	67	19	14	77	21	2
Italy	56	6	38	41	33	26
Latvia	23	15	62	34	39	27
Lithuania	13	13	74	39	34	26
Netherlands	74	10	16	69	27	4
Norway	71	13	16	73	20	7
Poland	43	24	33	68	23	9
Spain	49	6	45	51	27	21
Sweden	64	6	29	56	38	6
Turkey	22	8	70	32	33	34
United Kingdom	60	15	25	80	17	3

OCTOBER 1
Obama 48%, McCain 44%

The latest Gallup Poll daily tracking update of registered voters finds Barack Obama at 48% and John McCain at 44%, marking a slight narrowing of the race from the eight-percentage-point margin Obama held earlier this week. The latest results are based on interviewing conducted between September 28 and September 30, a time period in which the American public watched the Dow Jones Industrial Average seesaw between a more than 700-point loss and a more than 400-point gain on September 29 and September 30 while attempts by Congress to pass some type of legislation dealing with the financial crisis continued. Obama has moved to an eight-point or higher lead several times since June, including after his foreign trip in July; after the Democratic National Convention; and, more recently, late last week. In each instance, Obama was unable to sustain his lead, and McCain was able to narrow the gap, as is happening now, at least to a modest degree.

Americans to Congress: Start from Scratch

A majority of Americans—57%—want Congress to start from scratch in devising a plan to deal with the Wall Street financial crisis, rather than pass a bill akin to the $700 billion plan that was defeated on September 29. More broadly, the latest USA Today/Gallup Poll, conducted September 30, finds most Americans in favor of Congress's taking some sort of legislative action to deal with the financial crisis. Only 14% think it should not pass any bill. The poll finds little difference in attitudes on this question between Republicans and Democrats. Political independents are a bit more likely than either partisan

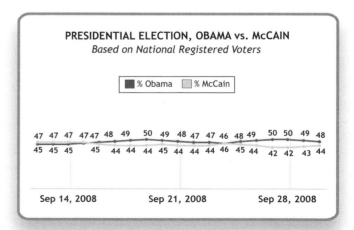

PRESIDENTIAL ELECTION, OBAMA vs. McCAIN
Based on National Registered Voters

■ % Obama   ▢ % McCain

47 47 47 47 47 48 49 50 49 48 47 47 46 48 49 50 50 49 48
45 45 45 45 44 44 44 45 44 44 44 46 45 44 42 42 43 44

Sep 14, 2008   Sep 21, 2008   Sep 28, 2008

CHRONOLOGY

OCTOBER 2008

October 2 Democrat Joe Biden and Republican Sarah Palin meet in St. Louis for their only vice presidential debate of the campaign.

October 3 The House of Representatives, following the Senate, approves a $700 billion rescue package for the struggling financial sector. President Bush quickly signs the measure.

October 4 Governor Sarah Palin seizes on a report about Senator Obama's relationship with a former 1960s radical to accuse him of "palling around with terrorists."

October 7 Barack Obama and John McCain meet at Belmont University in Tennessee for their second presidential debate. Each candidate argues that he has a better plan to lead the country through what both say is a dire financial situation.

October 9 The Dow Jones Industrial Average falls below 9,000 for the first time in five years as panicky investors dump stocks en masse on the busiest day in New York Stock Exchange history.

October 11 International leaders meet in Washington to grapple with the global financial crisis.

October 15 At Hofstra University in New York, Obama and McCain meet for their final debate. During the debate, McCain brings up "Joe the Plumber," referring to Samuel J. Wurzelbacher, an Ohio plumber who had questioned Obama about his tax plans at a recent campaign stop. References to "Joe the Plumber" will be used by the McCain campaign from now until Election Day to suggest that an Obama presidency will be bad for small businesses.

October 15 The Dow plunges 733 points, almost 8%, to 8,577. Federal Reserve chairman Ben Bernanke cautions that the federal bailout will not swiftly lift the economy and that financial weakness will continue.

October 16 In a lighthearted moment, Obama and McCain appear at the annual Alfred E. Smith dinner in New York City. The white-tie affair is a charity benefit where candidates traditionally poke fun at themselves and their opponents.

October 17 The United States and Iraq conclude a security agreement that calls for U.S. troop withdrawal by 2011.

October 18 Sarah Palin appears as a guest on the comedy show *Saturday Night Live*. She briefly meets Tina Fey, the actress who has portrayed her in numerous skits.

October 19 Former secretary of state Colin Powell endorses Obama for president.

October 22 Sarah Palin's wardrobe becomes a campaign issue when it is revealed that the Republican National Committee spent more than $150,000 for her clothes at high-end stores.

October 23 Obama takes a brief leave from his campaign to visit his ailing grandmother in Hawaii.

October 29 Obama purchases 30 minutes of prime television time to broadcast his closing arguments to an estimated 30 million viewers.

---

group to say Congress should not pass any bill. But the majority of all three groups want to see Congress start over and come up with a new plan.

The perceived outlook for the economy if Congress fails to act is generally bleak. Roughly a third of Americans—34%—believe the country would suffer a severe and lengthy recession in the absence of a financial rescue plan, while another 22% believe there would be a "depression." Thirty-one percent believe the country would suffer major problems but not a severe recession, while 5% expect no major problems would result. Democrats are more pessimistic about the economic future if no plan is passed than are either independents or Republicans; Republicans tend to be the most optimistic.

The members of Congress who voted against the original $700 billion rescue bill may enjoy some political benefit from their constituents come November. More Americans say they approve of those members than say they disapprove, by a 10-point margin (47% to 37%). That's better than the mixed ratings accorded the Democratic leaders in Congress and the net negative ratings for the Republican leaders, both of whom pushed for passage

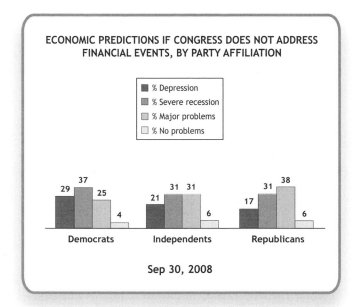

ECONOMIC PREDICTIONS IF CONGRESS DOES NOT ADDRESS FINANCIAL EVENTS, BY PARTY AFFILIATION

- % Depression
- % Severe recession
- % Major problems
- % No problems

Democrats: 29, 37, 25, 4
Independents: 21, 31, 31, 6
Republicans: 17, 31, 38, 6

Sep 30, 2008

OCTOBER 2
Shrinking Job Market: The Next Crisis?

Gallup's Net New Hiring Activity measure shows that workers' perceptions of the job market at their places of employment—already down significantly in August—became much worse in September. With the presidential election just weeks away, the financial crisis and the Treasury bailout are dominating headlines. Still, once Congress acts to shore up the banking system, the focus of most Americans may immediately turn to the Main Street economy and the accelerating pace of job losses taking place across the nation—something the financial crisis has only made worse during recent weeks.

Gallup's Net New Hiring Activity measure, based on interviews with more than 9,000 employees in September, suggests that the jobs situation that worsened significantly during August deteriorated even more significantly during September. The percentage of employees saying their companies are hiring fell to 34.8%, the lowest level of the year, while the percentage saying their companies are letting people go increased to 19.2%—the highest level of the year. In turn, this suggests that the number of jobs not only declined again in September (for the ninth consecutive month), but probably did so by substantially more than the 100,000-jobs decline generally expected. More importantly, the unemployment rate may actually surge past last month's 6.1%. A number of variables make it hard to predict exactly what job numbers the Bureau of Labor Statistics will report on October 3. Regardless, these Gallup jobs findings suggest that the next crisis facing the American people—and just possibly the key issue in the last few weeks before the election—may be jobs.

of the plan. At the same time, the most positive reviews go to Barack Obama, with 51% of Americans saying they approve of his handling of the financial rescue bill process—nine points better than the 42% approving of John McCain. President George W. Bush receives the worst ratings of all the major political players involved for his handling of the issue.

Congress is representing the public's wishes this week by intervening legislatively in the Wall Street financial crisis. The vast majority of Americans want some sort of bill passed addressing it. However, by only tinkering around the edges of the original $700 billion plan that failed in the House of Representatives on September 29, the Senate—now taking the lead on the bill—may not be going far enough in satisfying Americans' desire for a completely different approach.

As the Main Street economy continues to deteriorate rapidly, Gallup's consumer confidence measures show a sharp decline beginning in mid-September. Add in the accelerating decline in job market conditions and the further tightening of consumer credit, together with the fear created by debate surrounding the Treasury's "rescue" plan, and consumer perceptions are likely to continue plummeting in the weeks ahead. The coming elections are not likely to help. Each political party is likely to try to escape blame for the economic policies of the past and to blame the other party instead. But the decline in the jobs market and the deepening recession on Main Street may have many Americans looking for solutions to the deepening economic downturn—not just a villain to blame. Providing those solutions and turning around the increasing pessimism among consumers may be the key to winning the presidential election.

Do you strongly approve, approve, disapprove, or strongly disapprove of the way each of the following handled their role in the efforts to pass the financial rescue bill?

	Total approve	Total disapprove	No opinion
Barack Obama	51%	32%	17%
Members of Congress who voted against bill	47%	37%	16%
John McCain	42%	41%	16%
Democratic leaders in Congress	40%	43%	16%
Republican leaders in Congress	38%	45%	18%
President Bush	31%	57%	12%

Sep 30, 2008

Majority of Americans Angry About Financial Crisis

A USA Today/Gallup Poll finds 53% of Americans describing themselves as "angry" about the financial crisis that has gripped the nation during the past two weeks. Fewer Americans, but still a substantial 41%, say recent events have made them feel "afraid." These results are based on a USA Today/Gallup Poll conducted on September 30, the night after the House rejected the proposed $700 billion plan to deal with the growing financial crisis.

Feelings of anger are more prevalent among Americans of higher socioeconomic status: 63% of college graduates say they have felt anger over the recent events in the financial world, compared with 50% of nongraduates (and only 43% of those who have not attended college). Similarly, 62% of respondents in upper-income households (with annual incomes of $60,000 or more) have been angry, compared with 50% of those in lower-income households.

Fear has not been as common an emotion as anger in response to the financial crisis, and subgroup differences in expressed fear tend to be rather modest. For example, 46% of college graduates say they have felt afraid because of the recent economic problems, compared with 39% of nongraduates. The poll does find that women (49%) are significantly more likely than men (32%) to say they have felt afraid as a result of the economic problems, but it is unclear whether this reflects a real difference in response to these events or a typical pattern in poll results according to which men appear more reluctant than women to express fear. Neither anger nor fear are surprising reactions, given that most Americans already report some harm to their own finances, and an even higher number expect their

finances to be affected in the long term. According to the poll, 56% of Americans say their finances have already been harmed "a great deal" (20%) or "a moderate amount" (36%) by the events of the last two weeks. Only 16% say their own financial situations have not been harmed at all. Upper-income Americans (56%) are only slightly more likely than lower-income Americans (52%) to say their finances have already been harmed by the recent events on Wall Street. An even higher 69% of Americans expect their finances to be harmed in the long term by the recent events, as well as by any future problems resulting from them. Only 7% expect to totally avoid any repercussions. And while both upper-income and lower-income Americans are more likely to expect harm to their financial situations in the long run than in the short term, they are about equally likely to expect this (70% of upper-income Americans and 69% of lower-income). Thus far, 63% of college graduates say their finances have been harmed by the events of the last two weeks, compared with 52% of nongraduates. But both groups are about equally likely to expect harm in the long run (71% and 67%, respectively).

OCTOBER 3

Women Who Are Politically Independent: Up for Grabs?

Independent women who are Catholic, middle-aged, not college graduates, of average religiosity, and of mid-range incomes are most evenly split in their presidential candidate choices, and thus may be most "up for grabs" in the remaining weeks of the campaign. The importance of the female vote has been underscored by John McCain's selection of Sarah Palin as his vice-presidential running mate. The reaction of women to the debate between Palin and Joe Biden on October 2—which will not be fully evident until the days to come—will thus be carefully watched.

Taken as a whole, women who are registered voters—and over half of all voters in the United States are women—tilt in their candidate preferences toward the Democrat Barack Obama, reflecting the usual gender gap that affects national politics today. About two-thirds of women today identify themselves as either Democrats or Republicans, and they are highly likely to be voting for their party's candidate. A Gallup analysis of more than 26,000 interviews conducted in September confirms that Democratic women overwhelmingly support Obama, while Republican women overwhelmingly prefer McCain. This leaves independent women, who are much more evenly divided in their candidate choice.

It is reasonable to assume that changing minds among partisan Democratic and Republican women will be dif-

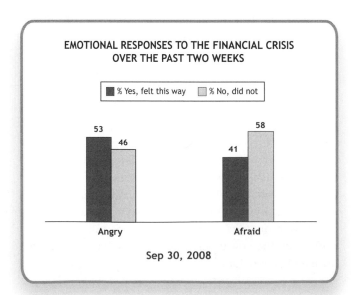

EMOTIONAL RESPONSES TO THE FINANCIAL CRISIS OVER THE PAST TWO WEEKS

■ % Yes, felt this way   ☐ % No, did not

Angry: 53, 46
Afraid: 41, 58

Sep 30, 2008

ficult, but turnout among these groups is of great importance. Indeed, motivating the "base" is a key requirement in modern-day politics. It has been argued that one motivation behind McCain's choice of Palin may have been to increase enthusiasm among Republican women. But it is independent women who—based on the fact that they are currently about evenly divided between the two candidates—were perhaps the most important viewers of the vice presidential debate, at least in terms of the possibility that their voting preferences will change. Assuming that independent female registered voters are indeed a key "swing" group in the campaign, it is useful to delve further into the ways in which they subdivide in terms of candidate preferences. Gallup's large sample of September interviews allows for a careful analysis of the vote patterns of demographic subgroups *within* the larger group of independent women.

Most of these patterns are microcosms of the divisions evident in the overall voting population this year: For example, younger Americans, regardless of their other characteristics, are more likely to support Obama than are those who are older. The segments of independent women who are strongest in their support for Obama—and who were presumably most sympathetic to Biden in the debate—include

those with no religious identification, those age 18 to 34, those with college educations, and those who seldom or never attend church. The segments of independent women who are most likely to support McCain, and who thus may have been sympathetic to Palin in the debate, include those who attend church weekly, those who are married, and those age 55 or older. The groups of independent women most closely divided in their candidate preferences—and who were presumably the most likely to be swayed one way or the other by the debate (and, indeed, by the events of the final few weeks of the campaign generally)—were Catholics, those who do not have a college education, those with no children under 18, those age 35 to 54, those making $24,000 to $60,000 a year in household income, and those mid-range in religiosity, who attend church almost every week or monthly.

Implications for the Remainder of the Campaign

In theory, because of their lack of strong partisan attachment, independent women are more susceptible to changing their voter preference than are women who identify as Republicans or Democrats. Within the group of independent women, subgroups that are currently most evenly divided in their existing preferences between the two major-party candidates may be the most amenable to changing their presidential choice as a result of the campaign. For example, the finding that independent women who are Catholic were exactly split between Obama and McCain (in September interviewing) suggests that there is no strong tendency among this group to go for one candidate or the other. Thus, if the McCain-Palin ticket is to pick up steam either as a result of the debate or based on forthcoming campaigning, one logical place to look for that process to occur is among independent women who are Catholic, middle-aged, not college graduates, of average religiosity, and of mid-range incomes.

Public Gives Supreme Court a Passing Grade

As the Supreme Court begins a new term on October 6, 50% of Americans say they approve of the job the Supreme Court is doing, similar to the ratings from last year. Thirty-nine percent disapprove. Americans had rated the Supreme Court higher earlier this decade, with close to 6 in 10 approving from 2000 to 2002. Approval dropped in subsequent years following controversial decisions on gay rights and the government's ability to seize private property. After a brief recovery in 2006, the ratings have declined again. The recent lower ratings for the Supreme Court may simply reflect greater frustration with government in general, as

PREFERENCE FOR THE GENERAL ELECTION AMONG INDEPENDENT FEMALE VOTERS
Aggregate Registered Voters, Sep 1–29, 2008

	% Obama	% McCain
Married	40	48
Not married	50	34
Have children under 18	48	40
No children under 18	43	42
Attend church weekly	35	50
Attend church almost weekly/monthly	47	41
Attend church seldom/never	52	33
18 to 34 years old	57	30
35 to 54 years old	45	43
55+ years old	38	44
College education	54	37
No college education	41	43
Protestant	40	44
Catholic	43	43
No religion	66	24
Less than $24,000 annual income	46	36
$24,000 to $60,000 annual income	45	43
$60,000 to $90,000 annual income	50	44
More than $90,000 annual income	49	42

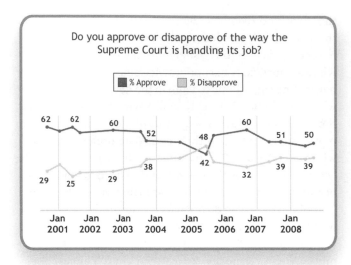

Do you approve or disapprove of the way the Supreme Court is handling its job?

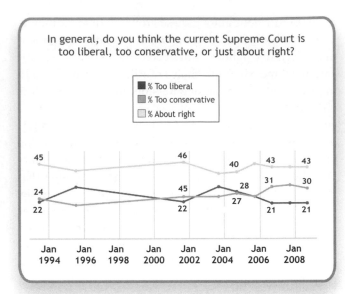

In general, do you think the current Supreme Court is too liberal, too conservative, or just about right?

evidenced by President Bush's job approval ratings near 30% and Congress's near 20%.

Republicans (65%) are more likely than Democrats (38%) and independents (47%) to approve of the Supreme Court, according to the September 8–11 Gallup Poll. This has typically been the case since 2000, when Gallup first began tracking Supreme Court approval. However, the gap between Republicans and Democrats has widened in recent years since President Bush appointed two conservative-leaning jurists (John Roberts and Samuel Alito) to the court. Since 1993, a plurality of Americans has expressed satisfaction with the Supreme Court's ideological orientation. In the poll, 43% of Americans say the Supreme Court is "about right," with slightly more saying it is too conservative (30%) than too liberal (21%). Americans have been more likely to say that the Supreme Court is too conservative than too liberal since Roberts and Alito joined the court. Prior to that, Americans were either more likely to see the court as too liberal than as

too conservative, or about equally divided between the two opinions. Currently, a majority of Republicans and a plurality of independents say the Supreme Court's ideology is about right. Half of Democrats, however, believe it is too conservative. Republicans are much more likely to believe the Supreme Court is too liberal (35%) than too conservative (8%).

OCTOBER 5

Obama Leads for Ninth Straight Day, 50%–43%

Registered voters across the country continue to favor Barack Obama over John McCain, now by 50% to 43% in Gallup Poll daily tracking October 2–4. This is the ninth consecutive Gallup Poll daily report showing Obama leading by a significant margin, tying Obama's record front-runner streak of nine days around the time of the Democratic National Convention in late August and early September.

Today's result includes two full days of interviewing after the October 2 vice-presidential debate between Sarah Palin and Joe Biden, as well as after the news on October 3 that Congress had passed a revised economic rescue plan to help alleviate the Wall Street financial crisis. The race has been slightly closer on both of these two individual days (October 3–4) than over the previous two days (October 1–2). Obama held particularly large leads over McCain in the earlier period, possibly as a result of Americans' focus on the Wall Street financial crisis and the congressional rescue plan dominating the news at that time. Since then, support for Obama has remained about the same, at the 49% to 50% level, while support for McCain has increased slightly, with an associated decline in the percentage of undecided voters.

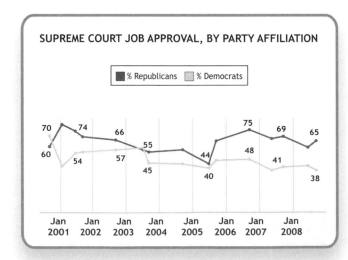

SUPREME COURT JOB APPROVAL, BY PARTY AFFILIATION

OCTOBER 6

Young Voters '08: Pro-Obama and Mindful of the Outcome

America's youngest voters are mindful of history and of the potential impact of this election on their own lives as they prepare to cast ballots. Among 18- to 29-year-old registered voters surveyed for a USA Today/MTV/Gallup Poll, 61% support Obama, versus 32% who prefer McCain, with Obama's voters being far more likely to be certain about their vote than McCain's. Obama's strong appeal to younger voters is apparent in that he outperforms McCain by double digits on every single character dimension tested in the poll of more than 900 18- to 29-year-olds, conducted by Gallup for USA Today and MTV between September 18 and September 28, 2008. The 47-year-old Obama swamps the 72-year-old McCain, 71% to 12%, on understanding the "problems of people your age" and even wins on what is a McCain strength among the broader electorate, being a "strong and decisive leader," by 46% to 36%.

While only a minority (37%) of young adults have qualms about McCain's age, a majority (55%) do have concerns about his running mate Sarah Palin's qualifications to step in as president if necessary. In contrast, a majority are satisfied with both Obama's experience and running mate Joe Biden's qualifications. Obama also beats McCain on several lighter dimensions tested in the poll. A majority of 18- to 29-year-olds would choose Obama over McCain as a teacher, boss, drinking buddy, or adviser. McCain's only appeal on this level with young adults appears to be his personal life story, as young adults are more likely to be interested in reading McCain's private diary than Obama's. While such items may seem trivial, basic likability can be a key indicator of a candidate's ability to win votes. When asked in an open-ended fashion

EXPERIENCE, AGE, AND THE PRESIDENCY *Among 18- to 29-Year-Olds*		
	Yes	No
Does Obama have enough experience to be president?	57%	36%
Is McCain too old to be president?	37%	59%
Is Joe Biden qualified to serve as president if necessary?	59%	19%
Is Sarah Palin qualified to serve as president if necessary?	32%	55%

to name the single most important issue affecting their vote for president this year, 18- to 29-year-old registered voters most often cite the economy (30%), followed by the war in Iraq (13%), healthcare (5%), energy and gas prices (4%), and international issues (4%). These issues are, in a broad sense, little different from those listed by all voters, regardless of age. Asked which candidate they think would do a better job on their top-priority issue, 58% say Obama, versus 27% who say McCain, echoing their basic candidate choice.

The poll results make it clear that young Americans perceive that the outcome of the election really does matter, both to the country and to their own lives. Nearly two-thirds (64%) of 18- to 29-year-olds surveyed say they have already given the election a lot of thought. Nearly half (44%) consider this election to be the most important of the last 50 years, and another 37% consider it more important than other elections. When asked about the consequences of the two possible election outcomes, 84% say an Obama victory would have a great deal (47%) or moderate amount (37%) of impact on their lives, and 72% say the same about McCain (36% great deal, 36% moderate amount). Going a step further, the survey asked those who said an Obama or McCain victory would affect them "a great deal" or "not at all" to explain in their own words why they feel that way. In Obama's case, nearly one in four (24%) volunteered that good or positive changes would take place, while in McCain's case, the most common responses were negative or pertained to the war in Iraq.

Asked in a separate question how a McCain administration might compare to the Bush administration, 55% said they would view a McCain victory as "four more years of the Bush administration," versus 37% who said they would view it as "real change from the Bush administration." The two tickets this year also bear the distinction of the first major-party black presidential nominee, and only the second major-party female vice-presidential nominee. In the eyes of young voters, an Obama-Biden victory would be much more of a historic event than a McCain-Palin victory. A majority (53%) agree that if Obama is elected president, it would be one of the most important advances in racial equality over the past 100 years. By contrast, only one-third (32%) agree that if Palin

Which of the following characteristics and qualities applies more to Barack Obama or more to John McCain? *Among 18- to 29-Year-Olds*		
	Obama	McCain
Understands the problems of people your age	71%	12%
Is inspiring	67%	18%
Has a sense of humor	58%	17%
Is optimistic about the country's future	55%	23%
Is independent in his thoughts and actions	55%	28%
Will unite the country and not divide it	55%	25%
Shows good judgment	54%	29%
Puts the country's interests ahead of his own political interests	53%	29%
Is a strong and decisive leader	46%	36%

becomes vice president, it would be one of the most important advances in gender equality in the past 100 years.

Implications for the Election

A majority of 18- to 29-year-olds are registered to vote in this election and have given it much thought. They prefer Obama, both as an alternative to McCain and as the candidate who is most likely to understand their problems and to bring positive change to their own lives. Casting a ballot for Obama also carries the excitement of making history: Nearly 8 in 10 consider this election to be more important than other elections, if not the most important in the past 50 years. What remains to be seen is how many of this highly sought-after demographic will turn out on Election Day and thus help determine the winner.

U.S. Financial Rescue Plan Wins Slim Public Support

More Americans consider it a "good thing" that Congress passed a financial rescue package for financial institutions last week than call it a "bad thing," but only by a narrow nine-percentage-point margin, 50% to 41%. According to the October 3–5 Gallup Poll, Republicans are nearly as supportive of the financial rescue plan as are Democrats: 54% of Democrats and 50% of Republicans say it's a good thing the plan passed. Both Barack Obama and John McCain voted for the plan, and the new poll shows that about equal levels of Obama and McCain supporters are positive about the plan. However, McCain supporters are slightly more likely than those backing Obama to say it's a bad thing the plan passed. More Obama voters than McCain voters are unsure.

The $700 billion Wall Street bailout bill easily passed in the House of Representatives on a 263–171 vote on October 3, but not without the continued opposition of a majority of House Republicans, who had helped to kill an earlier version of the bill. Their resistance drew on traditional conservative free-market themes. Along the same lines, the highest level of opposition Gallup finds to the bill among political subgroups is from political "conservatives." Half of self-described conservatives say it's a bad thing the plan passed. This contrasts with only 36% of "moderates" and a third of "liberals." Some variation in support for the financial package is also seen by household income. A solid majority of upper-income Americans (57%) are glad the bill passed, compared with only 44% of those making less than $30,000. However, an equal number of both groups—about 40%—say it's a bad thing. Many more lower-income households have no opinion about the bill.

As Congress was debating the details of a financial rescue package after the first deal fell short of the necessary votes in the House of Representatives, Americans expressed greater support for Congress's starting over with a new plan than for merely revising the one that failed. Now that Congress has done just that—passed a retooled version of the original failed bill—Americans seem more likely than not to accept it, albeit by a slim margin. There is, however, relatively little partisan division in the support.

Bush Job Approval at 25%, His Lowest Yet

President Bush's job approval rating is at 25% in the latest October 3–5 Gallup Poll, the lowest of the Bush administration and only three percentage points above the lowest presidential approval rating in Gallup Poll history. The current poll recording Bush's low job approval rating was conducted after Congress passed the economic rescue bill on Octo-

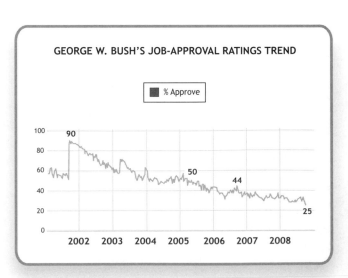

REACTION TO FINANCIAL RESCUE PLAN, BY POLITICAL IDEOLOGY
Based on National Adults

■ % Good thing ▨ % Bad thing ☐ % No opinion

Conservatives: 43, 50, 8
Moderates: 55, 36, 8
Liberals: 59, 33, 8

Oct 3–5, 2008

GEORGE W. BUSH'S JOB-APPROVAL RATINGS TREND

■ % Approve

90 ... 50 ... 44 ... 25

2002 2003 2004 2005 2006 2007 2008

ber 3. Americans recognize the economy as the nation's top problem, but apparently the passage of this bill—which the Bush administration had heavily advocated—did nothing to improve Bush's approval ratings. Indeed, only 55% of members of Bush's own party approve of him in the poll, perhaps a reflection of some pushback from conservatives who do not strongly support the economic bill. Nineteen percent of independents and 5% of Democrats approve of the way Bush is handling his job as president.

OCTOBER 7
Americans' Satisfaction at All-Time Low

Presidential candidates Barack Obama and John McCain are set to meet for the second presidential debate in Nashville on October 7 at a time when only 9% of Americans are satisfied with the way things are going in the United States—the lowest such reading in Gallup Poll history. The previous low point for Gallup's measure of satisfaction had been 12%, recorded back in 1979 in the midst of rising prices and gasoline shortages when Jimmy Carter was president. Gallup has also recorded a 14% satisfaction level at several points—once in George H. W. Bush's administration in 1992 and several times earlier this year. The reason for Americans' extraordinarily low level of satisfaction is straightforward: the economy. Asked in the October 3–5 Gallup Poll to name the most important problem facing the country today, almost 7 in 10 Americans mentioned some aspect of the economy, far ahead of any other problem mentioned.

Images of the Candidates

Despite the fact that Obama has led McCain by a significant margin in Gallup's tracking of presidential preferences

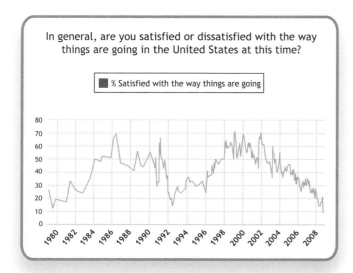

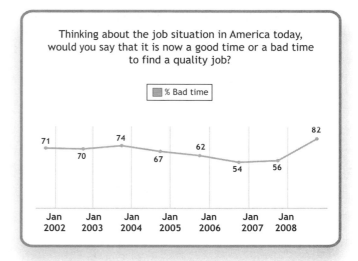

for 10 days now, the two presidential candidates continue to have positive images, with McCain's a little less positive than Obama's. McCain's 40% unfavorable rating is slightly higher than he has recorded so far this year, but his 55% favorable rating is no worse than it was in late August (after the Democratic convention) and earlier in the year. Similarly, Obama's favorable and unfavorable ratings are neither better nor worse than they have been at previous points over the last several months.

Nine-Point Obama Lead Ties Campaign High

The latest Gallup Poll daily tracking poll shows registered voters preferring Barack Obama to John McCain for president by 51% to 42%. The nine-percentage-point lead in October 4–6 tracking matches Obama's highest to date for the campaign, and the highest for either candidate. Obama led McCain by 49% to 40% near the end of his international trip in late July. Obama has now held a statistically significant lead since September 24–26 polling and has not trailed McCain since September 13–15, roughly coinciding with the intensification of the financial crisis.

Record-High Number Call This a Bad Time to Find a Job

Over the first nine months of 2008, the economy lost more than three-quarters of a million jobs—some two-thirds of the 1.1 million jobs created in 2007. And the percentage of Americans saying now is a "bad time" to find a quality job is up 26 percentage points from a year ago and stands at 82%—the highest level since Gallup began asking this question in October 2001. Today's 82% of Americans rating now as a bad time to find a quality job far exceeds the 56% and 54% who felt this way in October 2007 and October

2006, respectively. And this degree of pessimism is shared broadly across demographic groups, with 80% of men and 85% of women holding this view of the job market and 80% or more of Americans in each region of the country having a similar perspective.

Huge Increase in Republican Pessimism About Jobs

In May 2008, the largest differences in job market perceptions were by political affiliation: Republicans were least pessimistic about current labor market conditions, with a relatively low 57% saying it was a bad time to find a quality job. (By contrast, 86% of Democrats felt this way, along with 72% of independents.) Now, in October, the party differences remain, but the percentage of Republicans pessimistic about the jobs outlook has surged 17 points, to 74%; the percentage of Democrats increased 5 points, to 91%; and the percentage of independents increased 8 points, to 80%.

OCTOBER 8

Voters See Economic Plans, Most Other Factors as Net Plus for Obama

Forty-three percent of voters say Barack Obama's economic and tax plans make them more likely to vote for him, compared with 30% who say this about John McCain and his plans. In fact, more voters say McCain's plans for the economy and taxes make them less likely to vote for him. In its October 3–5 poll, Gallup asked a random sample of registered voters nationwide whether each of eight factors—spanning many of the candidates' impor-

FACTORS AFFECTING VOTE FOR PRESIDENT
Based on Registered Voters

	More likely to vote for	No difference	Less likely to vote for	More likely minus less likely
	%	%	%	Pct. pts.
Barack Obama				
His economic and tax plans	43	20	33	10
That he opposed the war in Iraq in 2003	43	26	31	12
His pro-choice position on abortion	39	28	32	7
His choice of Joe Biden as his vice-presidential running mate	37	43	19	18
That he opposed the surge of U.S. troops in Iraq in 2007	32	29	38	–6
That he is a Democrat	29	50	20	9
His age	24	67	9	15
His race	9	85	6	3
John McCain				
That he supported the surge of U.S. troops in Iraq in 2007	38	30	30	8
His pro-life position on abortion	35	27	36	–1
His choice of Sarah Palin as his vice-presidential running mate	33	26	41	–8
That he supported the war in Iraq in 2003	32	27	40	–8
His economic and tax plans	30	21	44	–14
That he is a Republican	23	49	29	–6
His age	7	55	38	–31
His race	7	87	6	1

Oct 3–5, 2008

tant policy differences and background characteristics—made them more likely or less likely to vote for Obama, or made no difference to their vote. The same eight factors were asked separately in regard to McCain.

Most voters say the candidates' past positions on the Iraq War will influence their vote. In general, voters tend to view Obama's past Iraq War opposition as a plus: 43% say it makes them more likely to vote for him, tying his economic plan as the voting factor responsible for the biggest positive contribution to the Obama candidacy. Given this positive endorsement of Obama's opposition to the war, it is not surprising that McCain's support for the decision to go to war in 2003 is viewed as more of a drawback than an asset in voters' minds. However, the candidates' differing positions on the U.S. troop surge in Iraq work to McCain's benefit. Thirty-eight percent say McCain's support of the 2007 troop surge makes them more likely to vote for him, while only 32% cite Obama's opposition to the surge as something that increases their likelihood of voting for him. In fact, this is the only one of the eight items tested in the poll that appears to be a disadvantage for Obama. On the seven others, more voters say it makes them more likely to vote for the Democratic

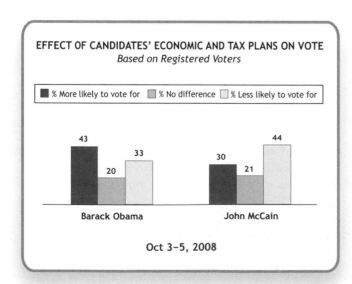

EFFECT OF CANDIDATES' ECONOMIC AND TAX PLANS ON VOTE
Based on Registered Voters

■ % More likely to vote for ■ % No difference □ % Less likely to vote for

Barack Obama: 43, 20, 33
John McCain: 30, 21, 44

Oct 3–5, 2008

A self-proclaimed "hockey mom," Republican vice-presidential candidate Sarah Palin drops the first puck at the National Hockey League season's opening night game between the New York Rangers and Philadelphia Flyers on October 11, 2008. *(Laurence Kesterson/Philadelphia Inquirer/Rapport Press)*

nominee than say it makes them less likely to do so. This could largely reflect Obama's leading position in the polls at this stage of the campaign.

The Running Mates

The October 3-5 poll suggests that, overall, Joe Biden does more to help the Democratic ticket than Sarah Palin does the Republican ticket. Thirty-seven percent of voters say Obama's selection of Biden as his vice-presidential running mate makes them more likely to vote for the Democratic candidate, compared with 19% who say it makes them less likely to do so. By 41% to 33%, voters say McCain's choice of Palin makes them *less* likely to vote for the Republicans in November. Even so, Palin appears to be doing more to fire up her party's natural supporters than Biden is doing to motivate the Democratic base. Sixty-five percent of Republicans say Palin's presence on the ticket makes them more likely to vote for McCain, compared with 57% of Democrats who say Obama's choice of Biden makes them more likely to vote for Obama.

OCTOBER 9
Obama's Race May Be as Much a Plus as a Minus

While 6% of voters say they are less likely to vote for Barack Obama because of his race, 9% say they are more likely to vote for him, making the impact of his race a neutral to slightly positive factor when all voters' self-reported attitudes are taken into account. At the same time, 6% of voters say John McCain's race will make them less likely to vote for him while 7% say it makes them more likely to, leading to the same basic conclusion: McCain's race, like Obama's, is on balance neither a plus nor a minus.

These conclusions are based on eight dimensions potentially affecting the vote for both candidates—included in Gallup's October 3–5 poll and analyzed in the October 8 Gallup study as previously reported. Eighty-five percent of voters say Obama's race makes no difference, and 87% say McCain's race makes no difference. This makes race the single dimension out of the eight tested that is the least likely to have an impact on the vote. Though the potential impact of Obama's race on the election has been highly

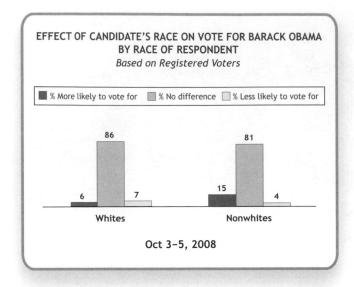

EFFECT OF CANDIDATE'S RACE ON VOTE FOR BARACK OBAMA
BY RACE OF RESPONDENT
Based on Registered Voters

■ % More likely to vote for   ■ % No difference   □ % Less likely to vote for

Oct 3–5, 2008

The data analyzed here show that the impact of Obama's and McCain's race, based on voters' self-reports, appears to cut both ways. Enough voters, particularly nonwhites, say they are more likely to vote for Obama because of his race to offset the small percentage who say they are less likely to vote for him on that account. And the same is true in reverse for McCain: The impact of nonwhites' saying his race is a negative is offset by those who say it is a positive.

The most important finding in these data may be that while 7% of white voters say that Obama's race makes them less likely to vote for him, 6% say it makes them *more* likely to vote for him. And among nonwhite voters, Obama's race is a significant net plus. It is important to note that these data are based on self-reports of survey respondents and may not reflect the unconscious impact of race or the willingness or unwillingness of respondents to admit that the race of a candidate affects their voting behavior. But the racial data discussed here were collected in a grid of eight different dimensions, which may have had the impact of downplaying any particular significance being assigned to race as a concept for respondents to focus on.

Ultimately, it may be impossible to tell exactly what impact the fact that Obama is black and McCain white will have on the outcome of the election. These results indicate that a large majority of American voters at this point say that neither man's race will be a factor in their voting decision. A small percentage of white voters say Obama's race will be a negative for them, and a small percentage of nonwhite voters say McCain's race will be a negative for them—but these results are offset by the fact that each man's race is a plus to other voters. Perhaps more importantly, in the context of other candidate dimensions tested in the recent research, race is actually the least important factor tested.

scrutinized this year, these data, if taken at face value, show that if anything his race could be a net plus. There is, as would be expected, a difference in answers to this question by race of the respondent. Among nonwhites in the sample, there is a net difference of 11 percentage points in Obama's favor in terms of the likelihood of voting for him because of his race. Among non-Hispanic whites in the sample, there is a slight net negative for Obama of –1 point. The impact of McCain's race among nonwhites, on the other hand, is –8 points. Among whites it is +4.

Summary: Race in the Campaign

Much has been written about the impact of race in this year's election—not surprisingly, given that Obama is the first black major-party candidate in presidential history.

Obama Rated as Winner of Second Presidential Debate

A USA Today/Gallup Poll finds a random sample of debate watchers saying Obama (56%) did a better job than McCain (23%) in the October 7 debate. The poll was conducted on October 8, the night after the debate at Belmont University in Nashville, in which Obama and McCain answered questions posed by a group of uncommitted voters. Sixty-six percent of Americans reported watching the debate, up from 63% for the first presidential debate on September 26. Obama also was rated as the winner of the first debate, though by a lesser margin (46% to 34%) than for the second debate.

Gallup has measured public reaction to most presidential debates since 1960—either on the same night, immediately after the debate, or (as is true of the current poll) in the first day(s) after the debate. More often than not, those who have watched the debate have rated the Democratic candi-

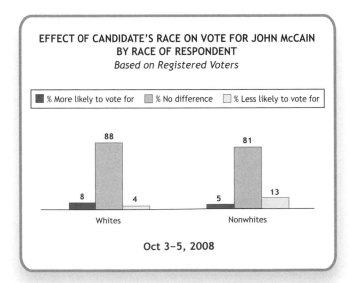

EFFECT OF CANDIDATE'S RACE ON VOTE FOR JOHN McCAIN
BY RACE OF RESPONDENT
Based on Registered Voters

■ % More likely to vote for   ■ % No difference   □ % Less likely to vote for

Oct 3–5, 2008

In the second presidential debate, held in a town-hall format at Belmont University in Nashville, Tennessee, on October 7, 2008, Barack Obama (left) makes a point to the audience. *(Paul J. Richards/AFP Photo)*

date as the winner, so Obama's perceived victories are not unusual from a historical perspective. However, his 56% to 23% victory in the most recent debate is one of the most decisive Gallup has measured, similar to Bill Clinton's wins in the 1992 town hall debate against George H. W. Bush and Ross Perot, and in both 1996 debates against Bob Dole.

While most who watched the debate say their opinions of Obama and McCain have not changed much as a result,

the movement that did occur tended to be in a positive direction for Obama and a negative direction for McCain. The results for Obama are similar to what Gallup measured for him after the first presidential debate (30% more favorable, 14% less favorable, 54% no change). But opinions of McCain seem to have been more unfavorable for him after the second debate (21% more favorable, 21% less favorable, 56% no change) than after the first.

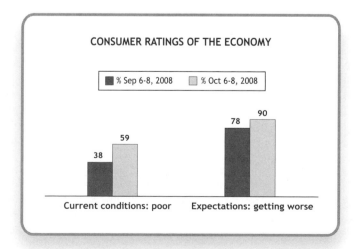

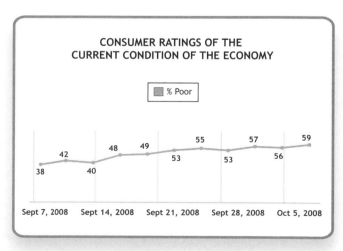

OCTOBER 10

Record Crisis of Confidence on Main Street

Consumer pessimism hit a record high in October 6–8 polling, with the percentage of Americans rating the economy as "poor" (59%) increasing by 21 points from a month ago and the percentage saying the economy is "getting worse" (90%) increasing by 12 points.

Third-Party Candidates Receiving Only Minimal Support

A recent Gallup Poll in which four third-party candidates were explicitly listed for voters along with the two major party candidates found only minimal support for any candidate other than John McCain or Barack Obama. Ralph Nader (independent candidate) received 2% of voter choices; Bob Barr (Libertarian Party) and Cynthia McKinney (Green Party) 1%; and Chuck Baldwin (Constitution Party) received less than 1%. The two major party candidates, Obama and McCain, combined to receive 90% of registered voters' choices.

The percentage of voters choosing Nader has declined from 4% in a similar poll a month ago. Gallup's usual presidential ballot, in which third-party candidates are not read but respondents are given the choice of naming any candidate they choose, finds about 1% who mention candidates other than McCain and Obama. Gallup also monitors interest in third-party candidates by asking an open-ended question in which no candidate names are read to respondents. In an August 7–10 poll, the results showed that only 1% volunteered the name of Nader and 1% Barr, with no other candidates getting enough supporters to round to 1%. Again, Obama and McCain received almost all mentions of candidates in this open-ended format.

McCain's Values/Views a Growing Factor for His Voters

More of McCain's voters cite his "values" or "views" as one of the main reasons they are supporting him for president today than did so a month ago: 20%, up from 7% in early September. McCain's values and views now compete with his experience and qualifications (26%) as the top draw for his voters. According to the new Gallup Poll, conducted between October 3 and October 5, fewer McCain voters today than a month ago mention either national security concerns or Sarah Palin's presence on the ticket as the main reason they are supporting McCain.

Gallup's initial measure of voters' reasons for choosing their candidate was conducted between September 8

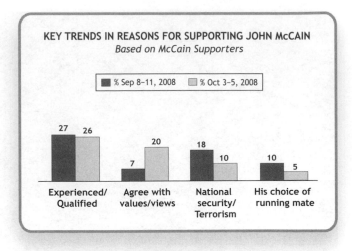

KEY TRENDS IN REASONS FOR SUPPORTING JOHN McCAIN
Based on McCain Supporters

■ % Sep 8–11, 2008   ▨ % Oct 3–5, 2008

	Experienced/Qualified	Agree with values/views	National security/Terrorism	His choice of running mate
Sep 8–11	27	7	18	10
Oct 3–5	26	20	10	5

and September 11, shortly after the Republican National Convention, when McCain was slightly ahead in the race; Gallup Poll daily tracking for September 8–10 showed him leading Obama, 48% to 44%. The new October 3–5 poll is contemporaneous with Gallup Poll daily tracking showing Obama with an eight-point lead, 50% to 42%. In the period between these surveys, the nation became embroiled in a major economic crisis and also had the chance to see the candidates face off in a presidential debate. Both of these factors could explain the shifts in what McCain voters say compels them to back him for president, particularly in terms of the increase in those citing his values and views. However, there has been no real change in the small number specifically mentioning the economy or McCain's economic views (now 4%, versus 6% in September).

Despite the significant increase in voter support for Obama since September 8–11, Gallup finds little change in the voting mindset of his supporters. The dominant rationale they give for favoring Obama—mentioned by 40% of his supporters in Gallup's October 3–5 survey—is that he represents change or a "fresh approach." Lower-ranked fac-

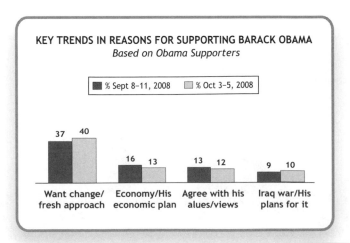

KEY TRENDS IN REASONS FOR SUPPORTING BARACK OBAMA
Based on Obama Supporters

■ % Sept 8–11, 2008   ▨ % Oct 3–5, 2008

	Want change/fresh approach	Economy/His economic plan	Agree with his alues/views	Iraq war/His plans for it
Sept 8–11	37	16	13	9
Oct 3–5	40	13	12	10

tors, mentioned by at least 10% of his supporters, include his economic proposals (13%), his plans for handling the Iraq War (10%), and his values/views more generally (12%). As with McCain's backers, Obama's are no more likely to mention the economy today than they were in September.

Aside from the factors already mentioned, supporters of both major party candidates mention a variety of other positions and traits. Small percentages of Obama's supporters (fewer than 10%) cite his intelligence (8%), his support for the working/middle class (7%), his honesty (5%), and his position on healthcare reform (4%). Fewer than 10% of McCain's supporters cite his honesty (8%), military background (6%), or conservative views (5%). In early September, McCain's supporters were 10 times more likely than Obama's to cite their candidate's running mate as the primary reason they were backing their chosen candidate, 10% vs. 1%. Today, McCain's voters are only about twice as likely to do this, 5% vs. 2%.

Summary: What's Driving Candidates' Supporters

Obama's supporters see him primarily as an agent of change. Relatively few of them mention other specific issues associated with him, including the economy. This has not changed over the past month, despite the enormous changes in the economic landscape, which have largely benefited Obama's candidacy in Gallup's pre-election polling. McCain's image has sharpened somewhat over the past month. In early September, five different factors emerged as important to at least 10% of his supporters: his experience, national security, his honesty and integrity, his being a Republican, and his choice of a running mate. Today, there are only three: his experience, his values and views, and national security. There is little overlap in the top factors identified by each set of voters: In sharp contrast to the 40% of Obama's supporters citing change, only 1% of McCain's mention this reason. Similarly, whereas 26% of McCain's backers mention McCain's experience and qualifications, only 3% of Obama's say the same about Obama.

OCTOBER 12
Obama-McCain Gap Narrows

The latest Gallup Poll daily tracking report finds registered voters preferring Obama (50%) to McCain (43%) when asked who they would vote for if the presidential election were held today. These results, based on October 9–11 polling, represent a narrowing of Obama's lead over McCain. Obama led by double digits for three consecutive days last week, but now his advantage is down to seven percentage points. Obama has led in each of the last three individual days' polling but by

less than double digits each day, suggesting that the race is, in fact, tightening. Obama has generally held an advantage over McCain since mid-September, when the imminent failure of several large financial institutions made the economy an even bigger concern than it had previously been.

Likely-Voter Estimates

Obama's current advantage is slightly less when estimating the preferences of likely voters. Gallup is providing two likely-voter estimates to take into account different turnout scenarios. The first likely-voter model is based on Gallup's traditional assumptions with respect to likely voters, which determine respondents' likelihood to vote based on how they answer questions about their current voting intention and past voting behavior. According to this model, Obama's advantage over McCain is 50% to 46% in October 9–11 tracking data. The second estimate is a variation on the traditional model, based only on respondents' current voting intention. This model would take into account increased voter registration this year and possibly higher turnout among groups that are traditionally less likely to vote, such as young adults and racial minorities. According to this second model, Obama has a 51% to 45% lead over McCain.

OCTOBER 13
Americans' Financial Worries Becoming More Wide-Ranging

A Gallup Poll on Americans' personal financial problems shows that the public has shifted away from a focus on gasoline and energy prices and has started to voice increasing concerns about a wider range of money issues, including personal debt. In July, Americans' worries about three day-to-day pocketbook issues—energy costs, an overall lack of money, and the high cost of living—easily trumped anything else they could think of when asked to name the most important financial problem facing their families. But a Gallup Poll conducted between October 3 and October 5 reflects a more broad-ranging picture today. The percentage of Americans who single out energy costs in this open-ended question has decreased considerably, from 29% to 12%, coinciding with a drop in gasoline prices. Now it is only one of several issues mentioned by about 1 in 10 Americans as their most pressing financial concern, along with lack of money, inflation, healthcare costs, and too much debt. There has been a modest increase since July in the percentage of Americans citing retirement savings, from 4% to 7%. However, the October poll was conducted before this past week's series of stock market losses, so it is possible that concerns about retirement have since increased.

Despite considerable demographic differences generally between Americans who support Obama and those who support McCain, there is not a great deal of difference in the financial concerns voiced by these two groups. Americans' financial concerns do, however, vary across income groups. Those with lower incomes are most likely to be worried about not having enough money, while those with higher incomes are most likely to mention retirement. Gallup Polls are indicating record levels of concern on the part of Americans about the economy and increasing signs of worry about their personal financial situations—and the data show that this economic anxiety is not driven by any one paramount financial issue, but rather by a host of concerns. This echoes the financial crisis itself, which each day seems to touch more industries and companies as well as countries and individuals.

Democrats' Election Enthusiasm Far Outweighs Republicans'

Only 51% of Republicans say they are more enthusiastic about voting than in previous years, compared with 71% of Democrats—marking a shift from October 2004, when enthusiasm was about the same for both partisan groups. This disproportionate enthusiasm, measured in a USA Today/Gallup Poll conducted between October 10 and October 12, is not a new phenomenon this year. Democrats have reported a higher "more enthusiastic" reading each of the seven times Gallup has asked the question in 2008. The smallest gap was a seven-point Democratic advantage in the September 5–7 USA Today/Gallup Poll, conducted just after the Republican National Convention; the largest came in February, in the middle of the heated Democratic primaries, when 79% of

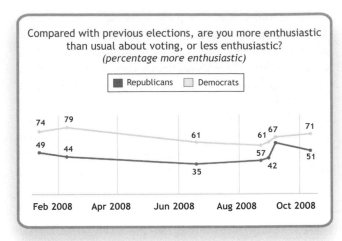

Compared with previous elections, are you more enthusiastic than usual about voting, or less enthusiastic? *(percentage more enthusiastic)*

Democrats said they were more enthusiastic about voting this year, compared with just 44% of Republicans.

Enthusiasm was much more equal between Republicans and Democrats prior to the 2004 election. In Gallup's October 14–16 poll that year, 68% of Republicans and 67% of Democrats said they were more enthusiastic about voting, and in a September 3–5, 2004, poll conducted shortly after the conclusion of the Republican convention, Republicans held a seven-point advantage over Democrats. As a result of the relatively low enthusiasm levels evinced by Republicans this year, the overall percentage of voters who say they are more enthusiastic about voting is slightly lower than it was in 2004 at about this time.

Obama Supporters vs. McCain Supporters

As would be expected given the significant partisan enthusiasm gap, there is a major difference in enthusiasm between Obama supporters and McCain supporters. Seventy-four percent of Obama supporters say they are more enthusiastic about voting as compared with previous elections, with just 15% saying they are less enthusiastic. That yields an extraordinarily high 59-point "more enthusiastic" margin for Obama supporters. Among McCain supporters, it's a substantially different picture: The net "more enthusiastic" margin is just 8 points, with 48% saying they are more enthusiastic than in previous years and 40% less enthusiastic about voting this year.

OCTOBER 14

Obama Wins on the Economy, McCain on Terrorism

Barack Obama enjoys a solid advantage over John McCain—53% to 39%—in public perceptions of which of the two candidates would better handle the economy

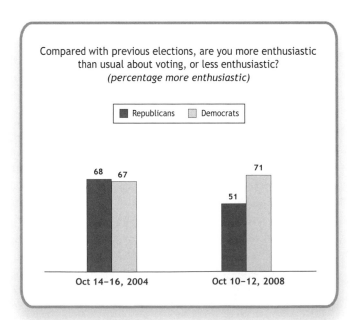

Compared with previous elections, are you more enthusiastic than usual about voting, or less enthusiastic? *(percentage more enthusiastic)*

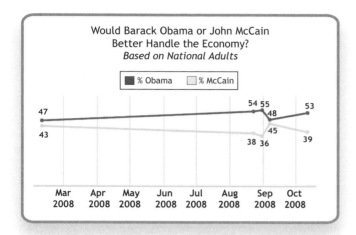

Would Barack Obama or John McCain
Better Handle the Economy?
Based on National Adults

as president. Obama's current 14-point lead on the economy is better than the 3-point edge he held right after the Republican National Convention in early September (48% to 45%), but not quite as great as his 19-point margin after the Democratic convention in late August. At that time, 55% preferred him on the issue, compared with 36% choosing McCain.

According to the new USA Today/Gallup Poll, conducted between October 10 and October 12, most Republicans and Democrats consider their own party's candidate to be more capable of handling the economy than his opponent. The main problem, electorally, for McCain is that a majority of political independents favor Obama on the issue, while only 32% name McCain. The October 10–12 poll shows, additionally, that Obama is preferred over McCain by 12-point margins on the issues of taxes and energy. Obama's lead on these issues is particularly notable because McCain and his running mate, Sarah Palin, have tried to capture the political upper hand on both issues. The Democratic nominee has an even bigger advantage on healthcare, on

which 61% of Americans say Obama would do the better job and just 32% name McCain.

On the other hand, McCain is not entirely without his own perceived strengths on the issues, but they are ones unlikely to surface as major issues in the upcoming debate on October 15. McCain has a strong advantage over Obama—55% to 39%—on the issue of terrorism, and also leads by 50% to 38% on gun policy. He has a slight advantage on the situation in Iraq, although his 4-point edge, 50% to 46%, is not statistically significant. (Earlier this year, McCain led Obama by larger margins on the Iraq issue.)

Implications: Timing Is Everything?

Americans recognize important strengths in both of the major party nominees for president, but the potential impact on the election of their respective strengths could partly be a matter of timing. Seven years ago, nothing was more important to Americans than terrorism. Just a year ago, the Iraq War was a paramount public concern. McCain might have been better positioned to run for president at either of those times than he is today, given Americans' relative confidence in him on those issues. Instead, with the ailing economy swamping all other national concerns and Obama beating McCain by double digits in public confidence on that issue, McCain is running uphill against steady headwinds in trying to convince a majority of voters—and particularly independents—that he's the right man for the times.

Race Steady, with Obama Leading by Nine

With exactly three weeks remaining before Election Day, Obama leads McCain in the presidential preferences of registered voters by nine percentage points, 51% to 42%. Gallup is also looking at the race according to two likely voter scenarios. One, the traditional Gallup approach, takes into

Regardless of which presidential candidate you support, who do you think would better handle each of the following issues, Barack Obama or John McCain?
Based on National Adults

	Obama	McCain	Advantage
Healthcare policy	61%	32%	O, +29
Economy	53%	39%	O, +14
Energy, including gasoline prices	52%	40%	O, +12
Taxes	52%	40%	O, +12
Situation in Iraq	46%	50%	M, +4
Gun policy	38%	50%	M, +12
Terrorism	39%	55%	M, +16

Oct 10–12, 2008

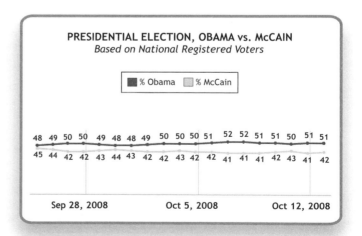

PRESIDENTIAL ELECTION, OBAMA vs. McCAIN
Based on National Registered Voters

account voters' intentions to vote in the current election as well as their self-reported voting history. Among this group, Obama leads McCain by 6 points, 51% to 45%. The other approach counts only voters' self-professed likelihood to vote in 2008 and does not factor in whether respondents have voted in past elections. Among this expanded group, Obama leads by 10 points, 53% to 43%.

Between 50% and 52% of registered voters have favored Obama in each Gallup Poll daily tracking report since October 4. Support for McCain has been a steady 41% to 43% across the same time period. Thus, although the gap between the two candidates has varied from 7 to 11 points in recent days, the preferences of registered voters have, in fact, been quite stable, with Obama averaging a 9-point lead. Today's three-day rolling average, based on interviews conducted between October 11 and October 13, includes two days of interviewing following last week's steep drop in the stock market, along with interviewing on October 13 after the Dow Jones Industrial Average surged a record 936 points. It is unclear from the individual days' tracking results whether these contrasting events have had any immediate impact on voter preferences.

Seven in 10 Say Obama Understands Americans' Problems

Americans are much more likely to believe that Obama understands the problems Americans face in their daily lives than to believe McCain does. These results, based on an October 10–12 USA Today/Gallup Poll, suggest Obama has a significant advantage in a presidential election campaign in which Americans overwhelmingly name the economy as the most important problem facing the country.

Throughout the campaign, Obama has been viewed as a candidate who understands the public's problems, but the

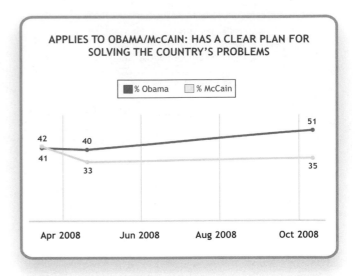

73% who say this about him in the current poll is his high for the year. Meanwhile, Americans are somewhat less convinced today than they were in March that McCain understands their problems. The public not only gives Obama credit for understanding its problems, but also for having a plan to solve them. While neither candidate scores particularly well when the public is asked whether the candidates have "a clear plan for solving the country's problems," Americans are much more likely to say Obama does (51%) than to say this about McCain (35%). And Americans have become increasingly likely to think Obama has a plan to solve the country's problems since this was last measured in the spring. Much of this increase is because of changes in the views of Democrats, who were divided into Hillary Clinton and Obama camps in the spring but are now mostly united behind Obama. In March, just 59% of Democrats thought Obama had a clear plan for solving the nation's problems, while 82% do now.

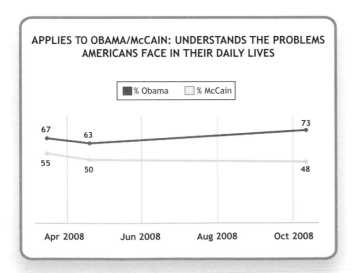

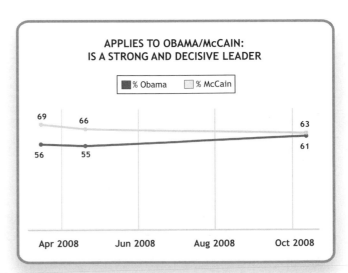

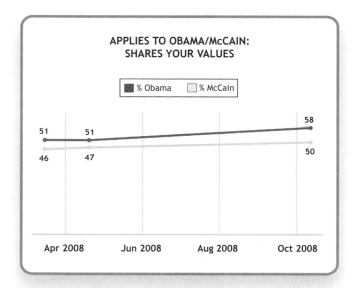

**APPLIES TO OBAMA/McCAIN:
SHARES YOUR VALUES**

■ % Obama   □ % McCain

51   51   58
46   47   50

Apr 2008   Jun 2008   Aug 2008   Oct 2008

McCain is more competitive with Obama on the other three character dimensions tested in the poll. McCain and Obama are viewed similarly in terms of their leadership skills and ability to manage the government. Sixty-three percent say McCain is a strong and decisive leader, while 61% say this about Obama. The two are now essentially tied on this measure, which had been an advantage for McCain earlier this year. Exactly 55% of Americans say each candidate can manage the government effectively, which is an improvement for Obama since the spring (when 48% said he could). Views of McCain's management ability have not changed since April, when the question was last asked, but his rating on this measure is down slightly from a 60% reading in March. At least half of Americans say each candidate shares their values, although more say this about Obama (58%) than McCain (50%). Both candidates now score slightly higher on this dimension than they did in the spring.

Summary and Implications

In an election in which the economy is the top issue on voters' minds, Obama is seen as the candidate who can better handle the issue. During the campaign, Obama has been able to convince a growing number of Americans that he understands their problems and has a clear plan for solving them, and now many more believe that he exhibits these qualities than does McCain—a major plus for Obama's electoral prospects given voter anxiety about the economy. Obama has also been able to largely erase the advantage McCain had over him on perceptions of their leadership ability. That doesn't leave many important dimensions on which Americans believe that McCain is superior to Obama on character

or issues, aside from McCain's continued advantage on handling matters of international policy. Thus, in order for McCain to prevail, in the remaining weeks he will either have to convince voters that he is as good as or better than Obama on the economy, or try to shift the agenda so that international matters carry greater weight in voters' minds.

OCTOBER 15
Previewing the Final Presidential Debate

Despite the fact that McCain trails Obama overall, his image is not substantially different from Obama's, with both candidates viewed favorably by a majority of Americans. McCain has a 56% to 41% favorable to unfavorable ratio, while Obama's is 62% to 35%. These data suggest that in the final debate on October 15, each man will start off with an overall positive image. Despite some discussion that McCain's image may have suffered as a result of his recent negative attacks on his opponent, his unfavorables are only slightly higher now than in previous measures this year. McCain's image now is no worse than it was at the close of the Democratic convention (although it is not as positive as it was after the Republican convention). It is possible that McCain will attempt to tarnish Obama's positive image in the debate by continuing to refer to the latter's association with Bill Ayers, the former member of the Weather Underground whom McCain and others have called a domestic terrorist. There is no clear indication from the data as to whether this could turn out to be an effective line of attack for McCain.

THE POLITICAL PARTIES

Everything else being equal, McCain's Republican Party affiliation would appear to be a relative liability this year. Americans at this point view the Republican Party in a significantly more unfavorable than favorable light, while the opposite is true with respect to the Democratic Party. Both McCain and Obama have higher personal favorable ratings than the parties they represent. Still, each candidate would obviously prefer to be representing a party in good standing with the voters. And that's not the case for McCain this year. McCain also has a distinct liability based on his political association with President George W. Bush, whose job approval rating remains at just 25%. Further, the latest USA Today/Gallup Poll (conducted between October 10 and October 12) shows that almost half of Americans are "very concerned" that as president, McCain would pursue policies that are too similar to those Bush has pursued. Although McCain has attempted to distance himself from Bush in his campaigning this year, the public's concern

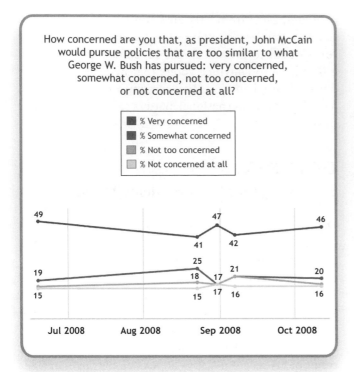

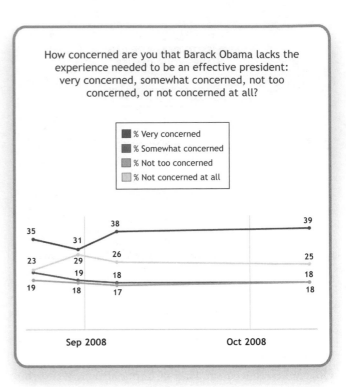

that McCain is too close to Bush is no different now than it was when Gallup asked about it back in June. McCain may thus attempt to present himself as more of an independent ("maverick") candidate in the debate, and he will certainly try to downplay his associations with his party and with President Bush.

THE ISSUES

There is good news and bad news for McCain in terms of Americans' views of his strengths compared with Obama's on the issues of the day. McCain has a significant disadvantage compared with Obama on the economy. This is the bad news for McCain, since the October 10–12 poll shows two-thirds of Americans saying that stabilizing the economy should be the top priority for the new president when he takes office. And the recent poll also shows that while 44% of Americans say Obama can fix the economy, only 31% say this about McCain. These numbers are not rousing public endorsements of either candidate's ability to quickly remedy today's financial morass; but on a relative basis, Obama scores higher than McCain. Thus, a challenge for McCain is to somehow neutralize Obama's perceived strength on economic concerns, perhaps by introducing new economic plans or criticizing Obama's economic proposals. The challenge for Obama is to avoid doing anything that would cause deterioration in his existing strong positioning on this critical issue. McCain does retain strength over Obama in terms of his ability to handle terrorism (and, to a slight degree, Iraq). If McCain is some-

how able to bring national security into the debate, he may be able to score points.

PERSONAL QUALITIES

Obama leads McCain on three out of five personal qualities tested in the October 10–12 poll. In particular, Obama is more likely than McCain to be seen as understanding the problems Americans face in their daily lives, and as having a clear plan for solving the country's problems. (The fact that only about half of Americans believe McCain understands the average American's problems would appear to be a particular liability.) But McCain rates equally with Obama on two other dimensions: being able to manage the government effectively and being a strong and decisive leader. Thus, the final presidential debate could in theory provide an opportunity for McCain to position himself against Obama as the better leader or manager. McCain's potential on this dimension relates to the finding in the poll that about 4 out of 10 Americans are very concerned that Obama is not experienced enough to be an effective president, something that has not changed materially over the past several months.

Implications for the October 15 Debate

Obama is clearly in the driver's seat going into the October 15 debate, leading in the overall preferences of voters, besting McCain on important issues relating to the economy, and dominating public perceptions of who most understands the concerns of the public and is ready with a plan to fix them. McCain, on the other hand, is associated with an unpopular president and represents a political party that is seen significantly less favorably in this election than his opponent's party. Nevertheless, McCain does have some strengths he could play up in an attempt to shake up the race and reduce Obama's lead. McCain retains a strong position against Obama on terrorism and, to a lesser degree, Iraq, and he is just as likely as Obama to be seen as a strong and decisive leader and a good manager. McCain's overall image is also positive—and just slightly less so than Obama's. The focus of the debate is supposed to be on domestic issues. Obama will no doubt attempt to avoid gaffes and focus on his empathetic understanding of Americans' economic woes and his plans to fix them. McCain can attempt to turn the focus to international concerns and to play up his leadership qualities, but the data would suggest that to really "win" the debate, McCain needs to show concern for average Americans and come up with some way of convincing them that he has a plan to fix the economy.

Gallup Daily: Before Final Debate, Obama Leads by Seven

The latest Gallup Poll daily tracking report shows Barack Obama continuing to lead John McCain—now by 7 percentage points among registered voters, 50% to 43%. These results, based on October 12–14 polling, represent a slightly better showing for McCain than has been the case in recent weeks. His 43% share of the vote matches his high over the past two weeks—roughly covering the month of October to date—owing, in part, to a stronger showing in the October 14 evening polling. Obama's 50% support level matches his average for October to date. Obama has held a statistically significant lead over McCain among registered voters, as large as 11 points at times, since just before the first presidential debate in late September.

Likely-Voter Estimates

Gallup is now working with two likely voter estimates in an attempt to allow for either of two different turnout scenarios. In the "expanded" model that anticipates higher turnout among groups of voters traditionally less likely to vote, Obama leads McCain by eight points, 52% to 44%. The "traditional" likely-voter model, which factors in prior voting behavior as well as current voting intention, shows Obama leading 49% to 46%. That is slightly closer than the average five-point advantage for Obama among traditional likely voters since Gallup began measuring them last week.

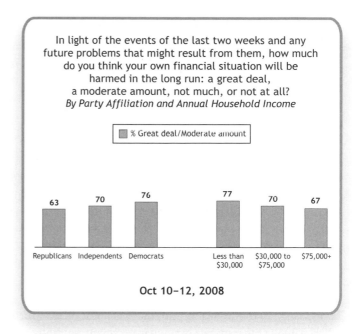

In light of the events of the last two weeks and any future problems that might result from them, how much do you think your own financial situation will be harmed in the long run: a great deal, a moderate amount, not much, or not at all?
By Party Affiliation and Annual Household Income

■ % Great deal/Moderate amount

| Republicans | Independents | Democrats | | Less than $30,000 | $30,000 to $75,000 | $75,000+ |
| 63 | 70 | 76 | | 77 | 70 | 67 |

Oct 10–12, 2008

Most Americans Say They Will Be Hurt in Long Run

Americans of all incomes and party affiliations report that the banking crisis of the past month has harmed their personal financial situations. Given the banking crisis, the credit freeze, the various taxpayer bailouts, and the historic decline in the equity markets last week, it is not surprising that so many Americans believe the economic events over the past month have harmed their personal financial situations. Nor is it unexpected that the percentage saying they have been harmed "a great deal" or "a moderate amount" has increased from 56% at the end of September to 66% two weeks later.

On the other hand, one might think that the impact of the financial crisis would be disproportionately high on upper-income Americans, since the latter tend to have more investable assets and therefore potentially greater losses. However, the sharp reduction in credit availability tends to have a disproportionately negative impact on *middle*-income Americans. And job losses will affect everyone. Probably of even greater economic concern is the generally held perception that the financial damage done by the economic chaos of the past two weeks will do long-term harm. The percentage of Americans holding this view ranges from 63% to 77% across income groups and party affiliations.

Implications: How Americans View the Financial Crisis

There is no doubt that the current financial crisis and the related credit freeze have done real damage not only in terms of Americans' assets and investments, but also to overall economic activity. For example, retail sales fell 1.2% in September—the largest drop in three years—and those data do not reflect economic events of the past few weeks. While the plunge in retail sales may be only the "tip of the iceberg" in terms of the immediate-term fallout from the financial crisis, of even greater concern is the potential longer-term impact. If all of the recent efforts to get the banking system working are successful and credit markets are freed up the in the near term, some might hope that the long-term fallout from the recent financial chaos would be sharply negative but brief—something like the post-9/11 economy of 2001 and 2002. When asked in the current poll to estimate the effects of the recent problems on the overall health of the economy, 47% said they expect it will involve only a temporary downturn, from which the economy will soon recover.

On the other hand, 49% of Americans believe that the recent financial crisis reflects something of a more permanent change in the economy and that it will not recover for a long time. This may be somewhat prescient on the part of many Americans, because no matter what is done, it is unlikely that either Wall Street or Main Street will soon return to the easy-credit and high-risk excesses of the past several years. The Great Depression of the 1930s had a profound psychological effect on the way everyone from financial advisers, bankers, and business executives to average Americans viewed credit, savings, risk, and home ownership, among many other things. It appears that about half of all Americans already perceive that the current financial debacle—regarded as the worst financial crisis since the Great Depression—may have a similarly profound impact on their financial perspectives for years to come.

OCTOBER 16

Recent Obama Surge Evident Among Men and the Less Educated

In the week after the Republican National Convention, John McCain led Barack Obama 47% to 45% among registered voters nationwide. Then the financial crisis emerged as a major issue, and Obama quickly took the lead. In the most recent full week of Gallup Poll daily tracking data (October 6–12), that lead has expanded to 10 percentage points. With only a few exceptions, most voter subgroups have shifted in Obama's direction since mid-September, about the time that the economic crisis came to dominate the news headlines. Some of the more notable shifts among voter subgroups are discussed in what follows.

GENDER

Women, who had been strong supporters of Obama for much of the campaign, quickly returned to the Democratic fold

**PRESIDENTIAL VOTE PREFERENCE,
(OBAMA vs. McCAIN), BY AGE**
Based on Registered Voters

	18 to 29 years	Obama adv.	30 to 49 years	Obama adv.
Sep 8–14, 2008	55% – 40%	+15	44% – 49%	–5
Sep 15–21, 2008	57% – 37%	+20	49% – 45%	+4
Sep 22–28, 2008	59% – 33%	+26	48% – 46%	+2
Sep 29–Oct 5, 2008	60% – 34%	+26	50% – 44%	+6
Oct 6–12, 2008	65% – 31%	+34	49% – 44%	+5

	50 to 64 years	Obama adv.	65 years +	Obama adv.
Sep 8–14, 2008	45% – 48%	–3	40% – 49%	–9
Sep 15–21, 2008	50% – 44%	+6	41% – 48%	–7
Sep 22–28, 2008	48% – 45%	+3	43% – 47%	–4
Sep 29–Oct 5, 2008	47% – 45%	+2	45% – 44%	+1
Oct 6–12, 2008	51% – 42%	+9	45% – 44%	+1

after they had moved more toward McCain after the Republican convention in early September. Women have supported Obama by an average of 53% to 39% over the last four weeks. As recently as the week of September 29–October 5, men continued to show a preference for McCain, but in the last week, Obama has gained the lead among men, 49% to 44%. Even with that recent movement among men, the data continue to reflect a gender gap, with women significantly more likely than men to support the Democratic nominee.

AGE

For much of the campaign, it looked like the election would be decided by middle-aged voters—those between the ages of 30 and 64—given younger voters' strong attraction to Obama and older voters' preference for McCain. The two middle-aged groups (age 30–49 and 50–64) have both swung from a pro-McCain position after the Republican convention to favoring Obama by a significant margin. During this time, McCain's lead among senior citizens has also evaporated. While Obama has made gains among all age groups, the candidates' relative appeal by age group remains in place.

EDUCATION

Obama now holds a lead among voters whose support he struggled to attract during the primaries: namely, those with less formal education. He now leads McCain 51% to 40% among those with a high school education or less, after having trailed McCain by 48% to 41% among this group after the Republican convention. It is possible that the economic crisis has made financial concerns more important to these voters than possible concerns about Obama's experience. Obama maintains the high support among postgraduates that has been evident all year, and he has erased McCain's advantage among college graduates.

PRESIDENTIAL VOTE PREFERENCE,
(OBAMA vs. McCAIN), BY EDUCATIONAL ATTAINMENT
Based on Registered Voters

	High school or less	Obama adv.	Some college	Obama adv.
Sep 8-14, 2008	41% – 48%	-7	42% – 51%	-9
Sep 15-21, 2008	46% – 44%	+2	48% – 45%	+3
Sep 22-28, 2008	46% – 43%	+3	47% – 46%	+1
Sep 29-Oct 5, 2008	47% – 43%	+4	48% – 44%	+4
Oct 6-12, 2008	51% – 40%	+11	49% – 44%	+5

	50 to 64 years	Obama adv.	65 years +	Obama adv.
Sep 8-14, 2008	44% – 51%	-7	58% – 37%	+21
Sep 15-21, 2008	48% – 48%	Even	58% – 37%	+21
Sep 22-28, 2008	49% – 46%	+3	56% – 40%	+16
Sep 29-Oct 5, 2008	49% – 47%	+2	59% – 38%	+21
Oct 6-12, 2008	50% – 44%	+6	59% – 36%	+23

RACE

While white voters still prefer McCain to Obama, the gap has shrunk from 18 points to 4. Black voters continue to show overwhelming support for Obama, as they have for other Democratic candidates in the past.

POLITICAL AFFILIATION

For much of the campaign, the election was close despite a significant advantage in Democratic Party identification because Obama failed to command the same level of party loyalty as McCain. Now, Obama receives the same share of the vote from self-identified Democrats (87%) as McCain does from Republicans. Independents, who have been pretty evenly divided between McCain and Obama most of this election year, have swung from a pro-McCain position after the Republican convention (47% to 40%) to a solidly pro-Obama stance (49% to 39%) at the current time. Within party groups, there have been some recent shifts according to voters' ideology. Since mid-September, Obama's support among conservative Democrats has risen from 66% to 78%, while McCain's

PRESIDENTIAL VOTE PREFERENCE,
(OBAMA vs. McCAIN), BY RACE
Based on Registered Voters

	White	Obama adv.	Black	Obama adv.
Sep 8-14, 2008	37% – 55%	-18	93% – 4%	+89
Sep 15-21, 2008	42% – 51%	-9	93% – 3%	+90
Sep 22-28, 2008	41% – 52%	-11	89% – 5%	+84
Sep 29-Oct 5, 2008	42% – 50%	-8	89% – 2%	+87
Oct 6-12, 2008	44% – 48%	-4	91% – 3%	+88

share of the moderate and liberal Republican vote has fallen from 85% to 77%.

RELIGIOSITY

Regular churchgoers are one group that has maintained a solid level of support for McCain over the past several weeks. Obama has made significant gains among those who attend religious services "nearly every week" or "monthly," and he now leads among this group by 52% to 42% compared with a 51% to 43% McCain lead a month ago.

The 2004 Vote

Perhaps one of the more troubling signs in the data with respect to McCain's electoral prospects is the fact that he is running only even with Obama in states George W. Bush won in 2004—whereas Obama has a commanding 58% to 35% advantage in states John Kerry won. The most competitive states—those in which the winning candidate won by 6 points or less in 2004—have strongly tilted in Obama's direction in recent weeks. In the October 6–12 data, Obama leads McCain by 55% to 38% among registered voters in these states, compared with just a 4-point Obama lead after the Republican convention (48% to 44%). McCain's advantage over Obama in "red states" (those Bush won by more than 6 points in 2004) is down to just 48% to 44%, compared with a 56% to 37% McCain lead after the Republican convention. Meanwhile, Obama enjoys a 21-point edge over McCain, 57% to 36%, among residents of "blue" states—those Kerry won by more than 6 points in 2004.

Summary and Implications

Obama's surge in the polls in recent weeks has been fairly broad-based across demographic and political subgroups of the electorate, but he has made particularly notable gains among men, those with less formal education, and middle-aged voters. These groups have tended to lean in McCain's direction or divide their vote about evenly, so it is clear that their movement toward Obama is a bad sign for the McCain campaign. The data reviewed here are based on weekly aggregates of very large samples, the latest of which is based on October 6–12 interviewing. In the last few days of Gallup Poll daily tracking, including October 13–14 interviewing, Obama has maintained a lead, though not quite as large a one as it had been for much of the prior week. So McCain may be winning back some of the voters who have moved into the Obama camp in recent weeks, but the Republican nominee still has a lot more work to do in order to mount the big comeback he needs in order to prevail on Election Day.

Obama 49%, McCain 43%

The latest Gallup Poll daily tracking report from October 13–15 shows Barack Obama with a 49% to 43% lead over John McCain among registered voters. Almost all of the interviews in this three-day rolling average were conducted before the third and final presidential debate on October 15. Meanwhile, the current rolling average shows that McCain was doing slightly better in the days leading up to the debate. McCain's 43% share of the vote matches his best showing in the last two weeks. Today's average also represents the first time since the September 30–October 2 average that Obama has received less than 50% support from registered voters, although Obama continues to maintain a significant lead among this group. In the "expanded" Gallup model estimate of likely voters, Obama leads McCain by six percentage points today, 51% to 45%. In the "traditional" Gallup model of likely voters, Obama leads McCain by two percentage points, 49% to 47%, which is within the poll's margin of error.

Americans See Serious Challenges Ahead for New President

An overwhelming majority of Americans (84%) believe that the next president will face challenges that are more serious than what other new presidents have faced, though Obama supporters are slightly more likely to say this than are McCain supporters. When a follow-up question is asked of those who say the challenges will be "more serious," the combined results of the two questions show nearly half of Americans (44%) going so far as to see the next president's challenges as the most serious in half a century—though far more Obama supporters (52%) than McCain supporters (34%) believe this.

While one might presume that different challenges come to mind for Obama supporters and McCain supporters, the USA Today/Gallup Poll conducted between October 10 and October 12 finds the two camps in agreement as to what the new president's top priority should be when he takes office on January 20, 2009. Two out of three in each group believe the new president should focus first on stabilizing the economy, outnumbering by a margin of roughly six to one those who would like the new president to prioritize managing the nation's ongoing wars or developing new sources of energy.

OCTOBER 17

Democrats Lead in Congressional Races

A mid-October USA Today/Gallup Poll finds the Democrats leading the race to control the House of Representatives. Gallup's generic congressional ballot finds likely voters preferring the Democratic candidate in their district to the Republican by 51% to 45%, regardless of the likely-voter model used. These results represent an improved positioning for the Democratic Party compared with Gallup's previous reading on congressional voting intention, taken right after the Republican convention. At that time, Republicans led 50% to 45% among likely voters using Gallup's traditional likely-voter model, which assesses likelihood to vote based on current voting intention *and* past voting behavior. But that represented a temporary boost for the Republicans, and it was inconsistent with earlier polls that showed Democrats leading.

A second, "expanded" likely-voter model, which assesses likelihood to vote based only on current voting intention and anticipates increased turnout by groups that have not voted in past elections, also indicates a stronger showing for the Democrats compared with just after the Republican convention. Using this model, Democrats currently lead 51% to 45% in congressional voting, compared with a 48% to 47% Republican advantage in early September. Democrats led in an August 21–23 poll conducted before both parties' conventions took place.

The generic congressional ballot has proven to be an accurate predictor of the overall vote for the House of Representatives and is correlated with the number of seats a party can expect to win. These results indicate that if the election were held today, the Democratic Party would probably retain control of the House. However, it is unclear whether the Democrats would be able to increase their majority much, since the current likely-voter results are similar to Gallup's 2006 House vote estimate of 51% to 44% and to the actual vote for the House that year, 53% to 45%. Party loyalty figures prominently in congressional voting, with 95% of Republicans saying they will vote for the Republican candidate in their district and 93% of Democrats intending to vote for the Democrat. Independents help swing the pendulum in the Democrats' direction, preferring the Democratic candidate to the Republican by 49% to 40%.

Little Impact from Debate So Far

The latest Gallup Poll daily tracking report from October 14 through October 16 shows Barack Obama with a 50% to 43% lead over John McCain among registered voters. This three-day rolling average includes one full night of interviewing after the October 15 final presidential debate and shows little significant change as a result of the debate at this point. Obama has now returned to 50% of the vote among registered voters, while McCain has been stable at 43% of the vote over three consecutive reports. Gallup's two likely-voter scenarios show differing patterns. If turnout in this year's election follows traditional patterns by which the voting electorate skews toward those who usually vote along with those who are especially interested in this year's election, the race is a close one, with Obama holding on to a two-percentage-point margin, 49% to 47%. If a much higher than usual proportion of new voters turn out, Obama has a six-point lead, 51% to 45%.

Obama Viewed as Winner of Third Debate

Roughly two-thirds of Americans reported tuning in to each of the three presidential debates: 63% for the September 26 debate, 66% for the October 7 debate, and 65% for the most recent debate, which, according to a one-night USA Today/Gallup Poll of debate watchers conducted on October 16, went to Obama—completing a sweep of the three debates for Obama. Seventy-three percent of self-identified Democrats, 68% of Republicans, and 55% of independents reported watching the October 15 debate.

Debate watchers were more likely to say McCain did a better job than Obama in the third debate than in the second debate (30% to 23%), but McCain's best showing in the eyes of the viewing public was actually the first debate, when 34% said he did the better job. Still, Obama won all three debates by convincing margins. Obama's debate wins are generally in accordance with what Gallup has found historically. Gallup Polls on reaction to past presidential debates as early as 1960—conducted either immediately after each debate concluded or in the succeeding days—have most often shown that the Democratic candidate has been viewed as the winner over the Republican candidate. Gallup has also found that, despite all the attention paid to the debates, they generally do little to transform the presidential race. For example, John Kerry was viewed as the winner of all three presidential debates in 2004 but still lost the election to George W. Bush.

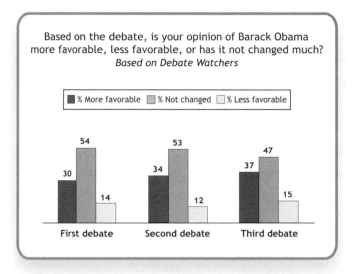

Based on the debate, is your opinion of Barack Obama more favorable, less favorable, or has it not changed much?
Based on Debate Watchers

Opinions of the Candidates

In each of the three debate reaction polls USA Today and Gallup conducted this year, roughly half of the viewers said their opinions of the two candidates were not affected by the debate. But the debates apparently did more to enhance Obama's image than McCain's. After each of the three debates, more debate watchers said their opinion of Obama was more favorable than said it was less favorable. In contrast, those whose opinion of McCain was influenced by the debates, if their opinion changed at all, tended to come away with a less positive view of the Republican nominee.

Surprising Decline in Economic Pessimism This Week

Consumer pessimism, though still overwhelmingly high, has declined somewhat in the past several days, particularly in terms of future economic expectations—with 83%

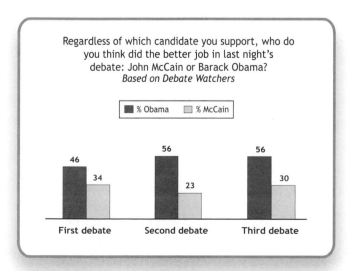

Regardless of which candidate you support, who do you think did the better job in last night's debate: John McCain or Barack Obama?
Based on Debate Watchers

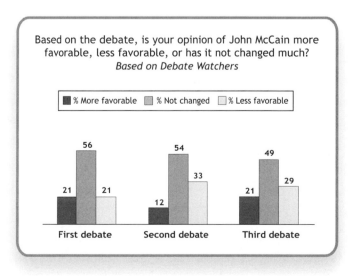

Based on the debate, is your opinion of John McCain more favorable, less favorable, or has it not changed much?
Based on Debate Watchers

of Americans saying economic conditions are "getting worse," down 7 points from last week and only 2 points worse than a month ago. On October 8, 90% of consumers said economic conditions were "getting worse" rather than better—up 12 points from a month earlier. However, the percentage of consumers holding this view has declined 7 points and stands at 83% as of October 16—essentially the same as the 81% of a month ago.

On October 11, Gallup's daily tracking showed the percentage of consumers rating the economy "poor" reaching a new peak of 61%—up 19 points from a month earlier. Since that high point, however, consumer ratings of the current economy have improved on the margin, declining 4 points to 57% as of October 16—still well above the 45% who provided this rating a month ago, but better than the October 11 high.

OCTOBER 20

A Bleak First Look at Holiday Spending

A record-high 35% of Americans say they will spend less on Christmas holiday gifts this year than they spent in 2007. Only 9% plan to spend more. This is based on a Gallup Poll conducted between October 3 and October 5. That survey started on the day the House of Representatives passed, and President Bush signed into law, a $700 billion plan to rescue distressed financial institutions and before much of the slide in the U.S. stock market seen this month, but at a time when general consumer confidence was similar to what it is today.

Gallup trends on this question since 1990 show that Americans are typically conservative in their spending plans, with more saying they will spend less money than the year before on holiday gifts. (The majority tend to say they will spend the same amount, as do 54% this year.) However, this year's more-spending-to-less-spending ratio is by far the most inauspicious Gallup has seen for the nation's retailers. Until now, the worst holiday spending outlook in Gallup records was in late November/early December 1991 (the first holiday season after the 1990–91 recession), when 33% of Americans said they would spend less on gifts than the year before and only 16% said they would spend more.

More recently, a November 2002 Gallup Poll found 27% of Americans saying they would spend less on gifts and only 12% saying they would spend more. That year, December consumer retail spending rose by a mere 1.4% over December of the previous year—one of the worst holiday retail seasons on record in the past 15 years. (According to the Census Bureau, an annual increase of 5% in spending is about the norm.) All of this suggests that the disappoint-

ingly weak holiday retail sales seen in 2007 could be even worse in 2008.

Obama's Lead Edges Higher

Gallup Poll daily tracking from October 17 through October 19 gives Obama an 11-percentage-point lead over McCain in the presidential vote preferences of all registered voters, 52% to 41%. Although the absolute percentages supporting Obama and McCain have varied within a narrow range for nearly the past three weeks, Obama's lead shrank to 6 points late last week, only to expand again in recent days. Gallup's latest three-day rolling average, from October 17 to October 19, spans a weekend when Sarah Palin drew a huge television audience and much post-show media coverage for her cameo appearance on NBC's *Saturday Night Live*. Also, on October 19 former secretary of state and chairman of the Joint Chiefs of Staff General Colin Powell delivered a strong endorsement of Obama for president—calling his candidate "a transformational figure" who is capable of being "an exceptional president."

Gallup Poll daily tracking poll shows no shift in support for the candidates between October 18 and October 19, suggesting that neither of these events had any immediate impact on voter preferences. Gallup's traditional modeling of likely voters indicates the race is somewhat tighter if we assume that voter turnout patterns will be similar to those seen in most presidential elections from 1952 through 2004. Using this traditional definition of likely voters, Obama leads McCain by 5 points, 50% to 45%—which is slightly better than the 2- to 3-point leads he held among this group late last week. Using the expanded likely-voter model, Obama leads by 9 points, 52% to 43%.

Bush Approval Rating Doldrums Continue

President Bush averaged just 29.4% job approval for his 31st quarter in office, spanning the period July 20–October 19. Despite the generally downward trend in Bush's ratings over the last eight years, his rating for the current quarter is slightly better than his 29.0% average rating in the prior quarter. The most recent quarter included two Bush approval ratings of 25%—the worst of his presidency to date, and just three percentage points higher than the all-time low 22% approval rating Harry Truman received in February 1952. Bush had actually been doing slightly better earlier in the quarter, averaging above 30%, until the financial crisis dragged his ratings down beginning in mid-September. As a result, his 31st-quarter average was slightly better than his 30th quarter average of 29.0%, because his ratings in the prior quarter consistently fell below 30%.

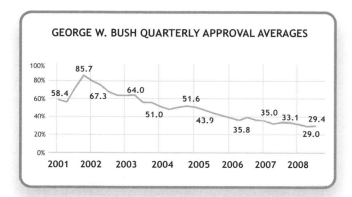

GEORGE W. BUSH QUARTERLY APPROVAL AVERAGES

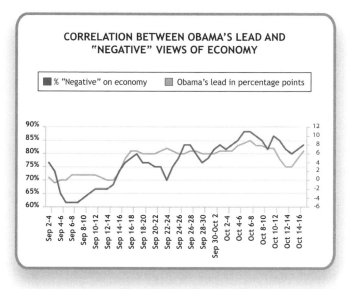

CORRELATION BETWEEN OBAMA'S LEAD AND "NEGATIVE" VIEWS OF ECONOMY

In any case, Bush's latest quarterly average is among the worst Gallup has measured for any president since 1945. (For the 252 presidential quarters for which Gallup has data, only 9 are worse than Bush's most recent.) It looks like Bush will exit office in a manner similar to that of Harry Truman—each suffering from a long string of low approval ratings after registering some of the highest approval ratings early in his presidency. Truman averaged 32% approval in his 31st quarter in office—and, like Bush, was below 50% for most of his second term as president. Three other two-term presidents—Dwight Eisenhower, Ronald Reagan, and Bill Clinton—were rated much more positively at this point in their presidencies. After a stellar 62% average for his first term in office, Bush has averaged just 37% so far in his second term. As a result, his average for his entire presidency now stands at 50%.

OCTOBER 21

As the Economy Goes, So Goes the Vote

A new Gallup analysis of more than 40,000 interviews conducted over the last month and a half shows a strong correlation between trends in voters' candidate preferences in the election and consumer views of the economy. Barack Obama's margin of support over John McCain has

PRESIDENTS' 31ST-QUARTER APPROVAL AVERAGES, GALLUP POLLS, 1945–2008

President	Dates of 31st quarter	Average approval rating	# of polls
Truman	Oct 20, 1952–Jan 19, 1953	32.0%	1
Eisenhower	Jul 20–Oct 19, 1960	61.3%	6
Reagan	Jul 20–Oct 19, 1988	53.5%	2
Clinton	Jul 20–Oct 19, 2000	59.1%	7
G. W. Bush	Jul 20–Oct 19, 2008	29.4%	9

risen proportionately when the percentage of Americans who are negative about the economy increases. Obama's front-runner margin has fallen when economic negativity decreases. The relative rise or fall in the Obama-McCain margin generally tracks the ups and downs in Americans' views of the economy. In particular, as Americans became more negative about the economy coincident with the onset of the Wall Street crisis in mid-September, Obama gained against McCain. Then, beginning around October 13, Americans became somewhat less negative about the economy, and McCain gained back some lost ground. By the end of that week, as the stock market lost much of what it had gained earlier in the week, economic negativity began to rise again, and McCain's relative support dropped. In general, Americans who see the economy as negative are much more likely to say they would vote for Obama than are those who see it as either mixed or positive.

In the Gallup Poll tracking survey, the voter choice questions are asked first; it is only later in the survey that respondents are asked for their views about the economy. Thus, respondents are not "primed" to think about the economy when indicating their candidate choice. The data suggest that one of McCain's best hopes of improving his positioning against Obama in the remaining two weeks of the presidential campaign would be for a sharp drop to take place in the percentage of Americans holding negative views of the economy. Although McCain has been roundly castigated by his opponent for his September comment that the "fundamentals" of the economy are strong, these data suggest that that statement was not necessarily an illogical effort on McCain's part, for it appears that if Americans come to believe things are not as bleak as they may seem, he gains.

Hispanic Voters Divided by Religion

Taken as a group, Hispanic voters solidly support Barack Obama over John McCain for president, but there is a significant difference in the Hispanic vote by religion: Catholic Hispanics support Obama by a 39-point margin, while Hispanics who are Protestant or who identify with some other non-Catholic Christian faith support Obama by a much smaller 10-point margin. An examination of interviews with registered voters conducted between October 1 and October 19 shows Obama leading among all Hispanic registered voters by a 62% to 30% margin. (For purposes of this analysis, Hispanics are those who say "yes" when asked "Are you, yourself, of Hispanic origin or descent, such as Mexican, Puerto Rican, Cuban, or some other Spanish background?")

Catholic Hispanics, who make up 50% of all Hispanic registered voters in this October sample, support Obama by a substantial 65% to 26% margin. But the one-third of Hispanics who identify their religion as Protestant or some other non-Catholic Christian denomination support Obama by only 51% to 41%.

There is also a significant difference in presidential candidate choice among Hispanics by religiosity. Hispanic voters who attend church weekly support Obama by a 51% to 40% margin, compared with a greater 57% to 33% margin among those who attend nearly every week or monthly and an overwhelming 72% to 21% margin among those who seldom or never attend church. These patterns of candidate support by religious identity and religious service attendance reflect the same patterns evident in the general population. Among all voters, Protestants and non-Catholic Christians are more likely than Catholics to support McCain over Obama, as are voters who attend church most frequently.

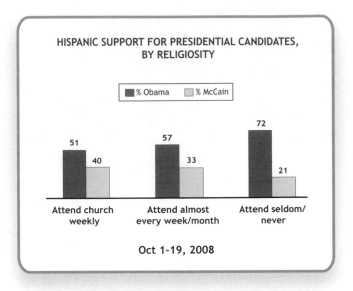

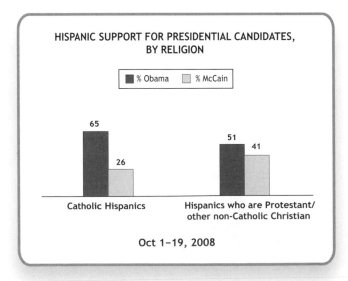

Summary: The Hispanic Vote

Hispanic voters in the United States today represent a diverse group of individuals who share a common, although in some instances distant, Spanish heritage. Not only are there geographic differences and distinctions within the Hispanic electorate based on country of origin, but there are differences based on religion as well. Among Hispanic registered voters Gallup has interviewed in October, about half are Catholic, with a third being of some other non-Catholic Christian faith and the rest either having no religious identity or identifying with a non-Christian religion. This differences in religious identity make a difference in voting preferences. Catholic Hispanics are more supportive of Obama, while non-Catholic Christians are much more even in their support patterns, although still tilting toward Obama. Additionally, as is true in the general population, Hispanics who are most religious are most supportive of McCain, while

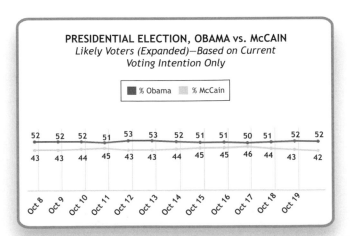

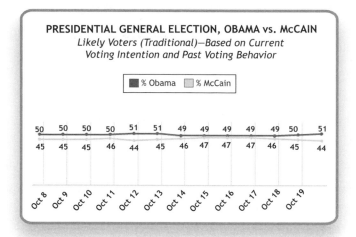

PRESIDENTIAL GENERAL ELECTION, OBAMA vs. McCAIN
Likely Voters (Traditional)—Based on Current
Voting Intention and Past Voting Behavior

Obama garners his greatest support among Hispanics who attend church services least often.

Obama Holds Lead in Various Scenarios

Barack Obama maintains a lead over John McCain in the latest Gallup Poll daily tracking update from October 18–20; the size of the lead varies between 7 and 10 percentage points among likely voters, depending on turnout assumptions. Among all registered voters, there has been fairly little variation in recent days, with Obama receiving between 50% and 52% of the vote over the last five reports and McCain in a range between 41% and 43%. In the current three-day rolling average of registered voters, Obama remains ahead by 52% to 41%. Using the "traditional" definition of likely voters, Obama leads McCain by seven points, 51% to 44%—which ties Obama's largest lead among this group since Gallup began reporting likely voters in Gallup Poll daily tracking. Using the "expanded" likely voter model, Obama leads by 10 points, 52% to 42%.

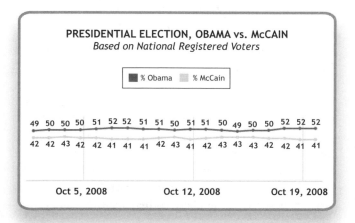

PRESIDENTIAL ELECTION, OBAMA vs. McCAIN
Based on National Registered Voters

OCTOBER 22

Young Voters Favor Obama, but How Many Will Vote?

Although Barack Obama leads John McCain by almost 30 percentage points among 18- to 29-year-old registered voters, these younger voters are still less likely than older voters to report being registered to vote, paying attention to the election, or planning to vote this year. Still, Obama is clearly the favored candidate among young voters, while Obama and McCain are much more competitive among older age groups. Obama leads McCain by 62% to 34% among registered voters 18 to 29 years of age, based on Gallup Poll daily tracking interviewing conducted between October 1 and October 20. That's a much larger margin than in any other age group. Among those age 30 to 49, Obama maintains a 6-point margin; his lead is similar (7 points) among voters between the ages of 50 and 64. The two candidates are essentially tied among senior citizens. (Over this same period, Obama is leading McCain among all registered voters by 9 points, 51% to 42%.)

This strength of support for a Democratic presidential nominee among young voters is not a new phenomenon. In Gallup's final poll before the 2004 election, the Democratic nominee, John Kerry, received 59% of the support of 18- to 29-year-old registered voters, while the Republican, George W. Bush, received 36% support. That compared to the overall sample of registered voters, among whom Kerry was leading Bush by 2 points, 48% to 46%. (Bush led Kerry among likely voters by 49% to 47%.) Despite the skew among 18- to 29-year-old voters toward Obama, it is important to note that their vote is not monolithically for the Democratic nominee: A general increase in voting among younger

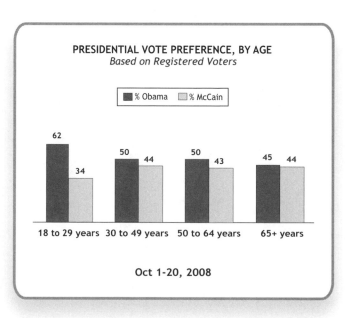

PRESIDENTIAL VOTE PREFERENCE, BY AGE
Based on Registered Voters

Oct 1-20, 2008

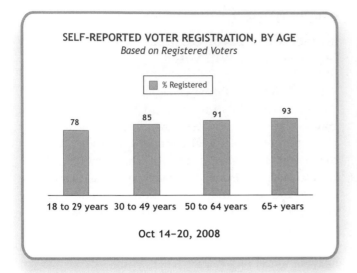

SELF-REPORTED VOTER REGISTRATION, BY AGE
Based on Registered Voters

% Registered

78   85   91   93

18 to 29 years   30 to 49 years   50 to 64 years   65+ years

Oct 14–20, 2008

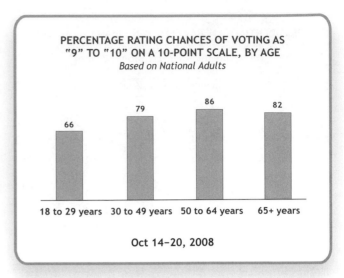

PERCENTAGE RATING CHANCES OF VOTING AS
"9" TO "10" ON A 10-POINT SCALE, BY AGE
Based on National Adults

66   79   86   82

18 to 29 years   30 to 49 years   50 to 64 years   65+ years

Oct 14–20, 2008

voters will bring one McCain voter to the polls for every two Obama voters. Thus, a general increased turnout among the under-30 voting group will increase Obama's overall percentage of the vote, but most likely not as dramatically as would, for example, increased turnout among black voters, of whom 9 out of 10 prefer Obama.

There is evidence of an increase in new-voter registration and of potentially higher participation among young voters, given Obama's appeal. But to what extent can Gallup's large daily tracking samples provide insight into whether younger voters will in fact vote at high rates? Based on October 14–20 tracking data, which include interviews with more than 6,500 registered voters, 18- to 29-year-olds still lag well behind older voters on key predictors of turnout. At the most basic level, younger voters are significantly less likely than those who are older to report that they are registered to vote. This is not a surprising finding. Young people are more mobile, less likely to have a permanent

residence, and in general less plugged in to the political system. This year there has been discussion about efforts to register young people, but these data suggest that those in the under-30 group have a way to go before they are registered at the same rates as those who are older, particularly those age 50 and above.

The data also show that younger voters, despite the impression that they are deeply involved in the political process this year, are less likely than those who are older to say they have given quite a lot of thought to the election. Perhaps most importantly, younger voters are much less likely to self-report that they are likely to vote. One of Gallup's series of likely-voter questions asks respondents to place themselves on a 1 to 10 scale, where 10 means they will definitely vote and 1 means they will definitely *not* vote. The results show that those under 30 are significantly less likely to rate themselves as 9 or 10 than is the case among their elders.

Gallup has found similar patterns by age in past elections, and the current data suggest that younger voters are still far from matching older Americans' levels of registration, interest, and intention to vote. That is not to rule out the possibility that young voters' propensity to vote could increase in the final two weeks of the campaign, or that massive Democratic "get out the vote" efforts on Election Day could motivate many latent Obama supporters to officially register that preference in the voting booth. Gallup has used these measures—in addition to measures of past voting behavior—to identify likely voters in past elections, and these have proven successful in estimating the overall popular vote for president. Because younger voters are less likely to answer these turnout indicator questions in a way that would lead Gallup to identify them as likely voters this year, their share of the likely voting electorate as of mid-

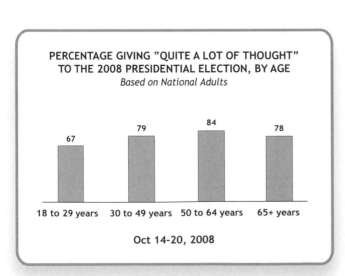

PERCENTAGE GIVING "QUITE A LOT OF THOUGHT"
TO THE 2008 PRESIDENTIAL ELECTION, BY AGE
Based on National Adults

67   79   84   78

18 to 29 years   30 to 49 years   50 to 64 years   65+ years

Oct 14-20, 2008

October appears as if it will be similar to what it has been in past elections.

Estimating Turnout

Obama maintains a significant lead among 18- to 29-year-olds using *both* likely-voter models: 60% to 37% using the expanded model, and a more narrow 54% to 42% using the traditional model, according to October 14–20 tracking data. Among all likely voters over this period, Obama averaged a 51% to 44% lead in the expanded model and a 49% to 46% lead in the traditional model. (Obama's lead has increased slightly in recent days in both models.)

But what would happen if younger voters do make up a greater share of the electorate this year than what the Gallup likely-voter models currently suggest—as, for example, would happen if there is a surge of younger voters responding to massive "get out the vote" efforts? We compared the Obama-McCain results among all likely voters (1) as estimated by Gallup; (2) assuming 18- to 29-year-olds will make up 18% of the electorate; and (3) assuming a surge of young voter turnout that increases their share of the electorate to a record 21% (with the three other age groups' shares dropping by a point each). The results suggest that Obama's share of the vote would increase only if young voter turnout is much higher than it has been in the past—and even so, he would gain only one percentage point. That is the case in both the expanded and traditional likely-voter models, even though the expanded model gives young Americans and infrequent voters the same chance of being reckoned likely voters as it gives Americans with a reliable voting history. McCain's share of the vote could decline by two points if turnout is higher among young voters, but only if the assumptions of the expanded model hold—that is, that new and infrequent

voters with strong voting intentions are just as likely to vote as are seasoned voters with the same intentions.

Summary: Young Voters and the Election

Gallup Poll daily tracking suggests that 18- to 29-year-olds are not nearly as likely as older voters to be registered to vote, to say they are thinking about the election, or to express a strong intention to vote. Thus, as of mid-October, there is not convincing evidence in the Gallup data that young voters will in fact vote at higher rates than in past elections. But even if things change over the next two weeks and many more young adults do become motivated to vote, turnout alone would do little to change the candidates' overall support, according to Gallup's likely-voter models.

Eight Out of 10 Voters Aware of Powell Endorsement

While 80% of registered voters are aware of Colin Powell's endorsement of Obama for president, only 12% of this attentive group say the endorsement makes them more likely to vote for Obama, while 4% say it makes them less likely to vote for the Democratic nominee. Powell's endorsement of Obama received a considerable amount of media coverage. This may help account for the fact that 80% of registered voters interviewed on October 21 were able to correctly identify not only that Powell had made an endorsement, but also that the recipient of that endorsement was Obama. (Eighteen percent of registered voters were unaware of the endorsement, and another 2% either misidentified or were unable to identify the person Powell endorsed.) But only a relatively small 12% of those aware of the Powell endorsement indicated in the survey that Powell's gesture makes them more likely to vote for Obama—which means that only 10% of the entire registered voter population is both aware of the endorsement and report that it makes them more likely to vote for Obama. An even smaller group of 4% of those aware of the endorsement (or 3% of all voters) say it makes them *less* likely to vote for Obama.

The Obama campaign may have hoped that the endorsement would move McCain supporters into the Obama camp. However, its exact impact is difficult to pinpoint, because some voters who are currently for Obama, for example, may have been McCain supporters before the endorsement. Having said that, the October 21 data show that 20% of current Obama supporters (a group that in theory could include voters who are recent converts to Obama as well as longtime Obama voters) say the endorsement makes them more likely to vote for Obama. And only 9% of current McCain supporters (a group that could

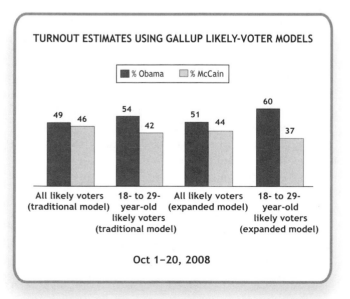

TURNOUT ESTIMATES USING GALLUP LIKELY-VOTER MODELS

■ % Obama   □ % McCain

All likely voters (traditional model): 49, 46
18- to 29-year-old likely voters (traditional model): 54, 42
All likely voters (expanded model): 51, 44
18- to 29-year-old likely voters (expanded model): 60, 37

Oct 1–20, 2008

include defectors from Obama since the endorsement) say it makes them *less* likely to vote for him. It might be expected that Obama supporters would be more aware of Powell's endorsement of their candidate, but the results show no difference in awareness between current supporters of Obama and current supporters of McCain.

Will the Powell Endorsement Matter?

These data suggest that the high-profile Powell endorsement of Obama has had fairly minimal direct impact. A high percentage of voters are aware of the endorsement, but only 12% of those aware and 8% of the total population of registered voters say it makes them more likely to vote for Obama. The endorsement produced a small backlash *against* Obama—all from current McCain voters, many of whom were not going to vote for Obama anyway. There has been little major change in the contours of the presidential race coincident with the October 19 endorsement: Obama was ahead before the endorsement and remains ahead in the latest Gallup Poll daily tracking results. A significant majority of both candidates' current supporters say the endorsement did not affect their candidate choice. So it is difficult to establish that the endorsement has had a major impact on the status of the two candidates in the presidential race—which has in recent weeks been moving in Obama's favor.

Given that most of the "more likely to vote for Obama" sentiment comes from current Obama supporters, one effect of Powell's endorsement may have been to shore up support among the Democratic base and thus to increase Democrats' motivation—and, potentially, their turnout on Election Day. It is also possible that the endorsement had a more subtle effect on voters' perceptions of Obama—one that has not yet translated into a change in voter choice, but that might have that effect before voters cast their ballots.

Obama's Likely-Voter Lead Is Five to Eight Points

Regardless of the predictors used to identify likely voters, the conclusion is the same: Obama maintains a significant lead over McCain in the latest Gallup Poll daily tracking presidential election trial heat. Today's results, based on October 19–21 interviewing, show Obama with a 50% to 45% lead over McCain when likely voters are defined using Gallup's traditional likely-voter model, and a 52% to 44% lead using an expanded model. The estimates for both candidates have generally been stable since Gallup began measuring them about two weeks ago. Obama's support has ranged between 49% and 51% using the tra-

ditional model and a slightly higher 50% to 53% using the expanded model. McCain's support has ranged between 44% and 47% in the traditional model and 42% to 46% in the expanded model. Among all Americans who are registered to vote, Obama currently holds a 51% to 42% lead, which matches his average for October to date. Obama has been ahead among registered voters throughout much of the campaign, except for a brief period in March after McCain clinched the Republican nomination and a second, brief period in early September following the Republican National Convention—and which ended around the time the financial crisis intensified.

OCTOBER 23
No Increase in Proportion of First-Time Voters

Gallup finds 13% of registered voters saying they will vote for president for the first time in 2008. That matches the figure Gallup found in its final 2004 pre-election poll. The current data are based on interviews with more than 2,700 registered voters as part of October 17–19 Gallup Poll daily tracking. Gallup asked these voters a question it had asked in its 2004 election polling: whether this would be the first time they had voted in a presidential election or whether they had voted for president before. Despite much discussion of the possibility of large numbers of new voters in 2008, the percentage of "first time" voters in Gallup polling this election cycle is no higher than it was at approximately the same time in 2004.

The estimate of first-time voters is slightly *lower*, at 11%, using Gallup's expanded likely-voter model. Under this model, Americans who are registered to vote, who say they plan to vote, who indicate they have given "quite a lot" of thought to the election, and who rate their chances of voting as "9" or "10" on a 10-point scale are deemed likely to vote. Gallup's traditional likely-voter model estimates that 8% of likely voters will be voting for the first time.

Who Are First-Time Voters?

Perhaps not surprisingly, the signature characteristic of first-time voters is their youth. Among registered voters, 62% of those who say they will be voting for the first time are below age 30, including one in five who are the minimum voting age of 18. First-time voters age 30 or older are predominantly between the ages of 30 and 49. Given this decidedly young age distribution, it is not surprising that first-time voters exhibit many other characteristics of young adults. Forty-eight percent of first-time voters, for example, report that they are full-time students.

Nearly half of first-time voters (47%) come from a racial or ethnic minority group. That is higher than the proportion of first-time voters who were minorities in 2004 (33%) and could reflect the historic nature of Barack Obama's candidacy. Forty percent of first-time voters identify themselves as Democrats, 37% as independents, and only 23% as Republicans. Thirty-two percent describe their political views as conservative, 34% as moderate, and 28% as liberal. That is a much closer conservative-liberal split than is true of the general public, among whom conservatives outnumber liberals by about a two-to-one margin. Finally, first-time voters show solid support for Obama, 65% to 31%. That is a better showing for the Democratic candidate than in 2004, when first-time voters favored John Kerry over George W. Bush by 55% to 41%.

Summary: First-Time Voters and the Election

Every presidential election brings a new wave of voters into the electoral process. And although there is speculation that Obama's candidacy, given his appeal to young and minority voters, could bring an unusually large number of first-time voters to the polls this year, the proportion of registered voters who say they will be voting for the first time is no higher than it was in 2004. This may to some degree reflect the high turnout in 2004, which was about 10 points higher than it had been in recent elections—which in turn would have significantly diminished the available pool of potential first-time voters for the 2008 election. Thus, the fact that the 2008 estimate of first-time voters is no *lower* than the 2004 estimate may still reflect an impressive influx of new voters this year, even though the proportion of first-time voters may not be higher than in the last election.

Obama Winning Over the Jewish Vote

Jewish voters nationwide have grown increasingly comfortable with voting for Barack Obama for president since the Illinois senator secured the Democratic nomination in June. They now favor Obama over McCain by more than three to one, 74% to 22%. This is based on monthly averages of Gallup Poll daily tracking results, including interviews with more than 500 Jewish registered voters each month. Support for Obama among all registered voters was fairly stable from June through September but then rose sharply in October, in apparent reaction to the economic crisis. Support for Obama among Jewish voters has expanded more gradually, from the low 60% range in June and July to 66% in August, 69% in September, and 74% now, in October.

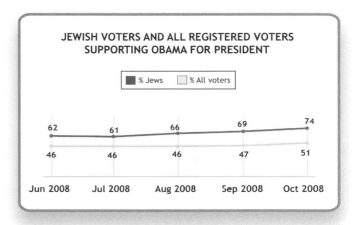

The current proportion of Jews backing Obama is identical to the level of support the Democratic ticket of John Kerry and John Edwards received in the 2004 presidential election (74%). It is only slightly lower than what Al Gore and Joe Lieberman received in 2000 (80%)—when the first Jewish American appeared on the presidential ticket of a major party. Recent support for Obama is a bit higher among older Jews than among Jews younger than 55. According to combined Gallup Poll daily tracking data from September 1 through October 21, an average of 74% of Jews age 55 and older supported Obama for president across this period, compared with about two-thirds of younger Jews.

The slightly more pro-McCain orientation of the youngest category of Jewish voters (those 18 to 34) could be related to the fact that they are more apt than older Jewish voters to consider themselves political conservatives (29%, versus 16% for those 55 and older). However, ideology does not appear to explain the gap between middle-aged and older Jewish voters. Whereas those 35 to 54 are more likely to support McCain than are Jewish voters 55 and older, they are no more likely than older Jewish voters to describe

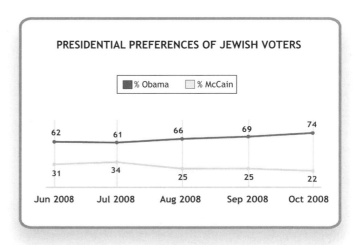

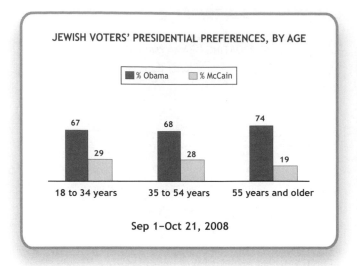

JEWISH VOTERS' PRESIDENTIAL PREFERENCES, BY AGE

% Obama % McCain

Sep 1–Oct 21, 2008

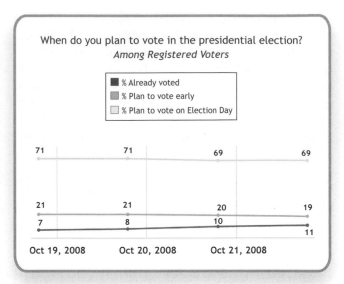

When do you plan to vote in the presidential election?
Among Registered Voters

% Already voted
% Plan to vote early
% Plan to vote on Election Day

their political views as conservative. There is little difference among Jewish voters by age in their basic party identification. Between 55% and 57% of all three age groups are Democratic, 28% to 30% are independent, and only 13% to 17% are Republican.

OCTOBER 24

Early Read on Early Voting: Could Reach 30%

Gallup Poll daily tracking data indicate that about 11% of registered voters who plan to vote had already voted by October 22, with another 19% saying they planned to vote before Election Day. Roughly equal percentages of Barack Obama supporters and John McCain supporters have taken advantage of the early voting opportunity—so far. That leaves just about 7 out of 10 voters who intend to go to the polls on November 4 itself. The percentage

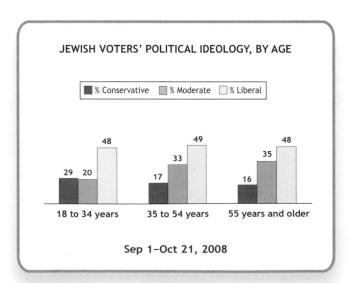

JEWISH VOTERS' POLITICAL IDEOLOGY, BY AGE

% Conservative % Moderate % Liberal

Sep 1–Oct 21, 2008

of early voters has increased from 7% in Gallup's October 17–19 average, when Gallup first began measuring this variable, to the current 11% in the October 19–22 average.

The pace of early voting so far appears to be roughly on par with that in 2004. At about this time before that year's election—October 22–24—9% of registered voters said they had already voted. However, in that 2004 poll, only an additional 13% said they *intended* to vote early, lower than the 19% who say so in the current October 20–22, 2008, average. Thus, early voting this election year may end up being higher than it was in 2004. (In Gallup's final poll before the 2004 presidential election, conducted between October 29 and October 31, 17% said they had voted early, and another 4% claimed they were still going to vote before Election Day.) Projections from this year's data are that as many as 30% of voters could end up voting early.

The impact of early voting on the election outcome, however, is difficult to determine. Having the results for early voters "locked in" means that a last-minute surge in support toward either candidate would not be reflected in the final election totals for those early voters. At this point, there is little significant difference in the propensity to vote early between the Obama supporters and the McCain supporters interviewed in the aggregated sample of all interviews conducted from October 17 to October 22. Obama has been ahead in Gallup Poll daily tracking conducted while these data were being gathered. Thus, while equal percentages of Obama and McCain voters have voted early, there are more of the former than of the latter, meaning that early voting generally reflects the same Obama lead evident in the overall sample. Thus, if McCain gains rapidly in the days left, Obama benefits, since Obama can't lose votes he has already received. If McCain loses support rapidly, Obama will not have the chance to pick up even more support from those who have already voted.

There is a slight tendency for early voting to skew older. Early voting ranges from 14% of voters 55 and older to 5% of those under age 35. In addition, another 22% of voters age 55 and up say they *plan* to vote early, meaning that by Election Day, over a third of voters in this older age group may already have cast their ballots. There is also a significant difference in early voting by region. Voters in the West are the most likely to say they have voted already (16%) and to say that they plan to vote early, before Election Day (34%). Voters in the East are least likely to be early voters, with 3% saying they have voted already and 6% planning to vote before Election Day.

Obama, McCain Two of the Best-Liked Candidates

In the most recent USA Today/Gallup Poll among likely voters, Obama (61%) and McCain (57%) each received favorable ratings near 60%. Both presidential candidates have been near that mark throughout 2008. Gallup has measured presidential candidate favorability in its current format for the last five election cycles, beginning with the 1992 election. Usually, by this late stage of the campaign, presidential candidates' ratings have settled in the 50% range. George W. Bush, just before the 2000 election, had the highest favorable rating at the end of the campaign for any president since 1992, at 58%. Thus, if Obama and McCain can maintain their most recent favorable ratings, they would finish the 2008 campaign as the top three most positively rated presidential candidates in recent history—and either could become the first with a rating of 60% or higher. Obama may be the

better bet to achieve this, as his favorable rating has been 60% or higher since he clinched the Democratic nomination in June, apart from a slight dip to 57% immediately after the Republican National Convention in early September.

Whether McCain and Obama can maintain their lofty scores between now and November 4 is unclear. Historically, candidates' ratings have not varied much from their October average to the final poll before the election, and any variation that has occurred in the final weeks of the campaign has been inconsistent: Some have shown a decline, and others an increase. For example, Bush's high 58% rating at the end of the 2000 campaign represented a drop from what he had been averaging in October 2000 (62%). Bob Dole's favorable rating also declined slightly in the final weeks of the 1996 campaign. But some candidates, such as Bill Clinton and Ross Perot in 1992 and Al Gore in 2000, finished the campaign with a higher favorable rating than they had been getting in October.

FAVORABLE RATINGS FOR PRESIDENTIAL CANDIDATES IN GALLUP'S FINAL PRE-ELECTION POLL, 1992–2004
Based on Likely Voters

Candidate	Year	Favorable rating
George W. Bush	2000	58%
Bill Clinton	1996	56%
Al Gore	2000	55%
George W. Bush	2004	53%
Bill Clinton	1992	51%
Bob Dole	1996	51%
John Kerry	2004	51%
George H. W. Bush	1992	46%
Ross Perot	1992	46%

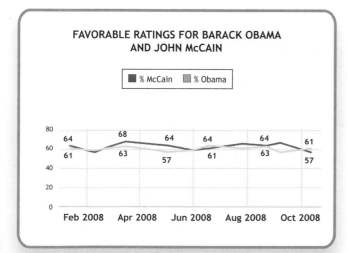

FAVORABLE RATINGS FOR BARACK OBAMA AND JOHN McCAIN

% McCain   % Obama

Feb 2008	Apr 2008	Jun 2008	Aug 2008	Oct 2008
64	68	64	64	64 → 61
61	63	57	61	63 → 57

CHANGE IN FAVORABLE RATINGS FOR PRESIDENTIAL CANDIDATES IN FINAL WEEKS OF CAMPAIGN, 1992–2004
Based on Likely Voters

Candidate	Year	Avg. favorable rating, October	Final rating	Change
George W. Bush	2004	54%	53%	−1
John Kerry	2004	52%	51%	−1
George W. Bush	2000	62%	58%	−4
Al Gore	2000	53%	55%	+2
Bill Clinton	1996	59%	56%	−3
Bob Dole	1996	53%	51%	−2
Bill Clinton	1992	49%	51%	+2
George H.W. Bush	1992	46%	46%	0
Ross Perot	1992	44%	46%	+2

Favorable Ratings as Predictors of the Election Outcome

A positive sign for Obama's prospects of becoming the 44th president is that the candidate who has had the higher favorable rating among likely voters at the end of the election has been elected president in every election since 1992. Given the positive public evaluations that both Obama and McCain have received throughout 2008, it could be argued that Americans will be comfortable with either as the next president. While only one can candidate win, the loser of this year's election is poised to supplant Al Gore as the best-liked presidential candidate not to get elected.

OCTOBER 27

Late Upsets Are Rare, but Have Happened

There have been only two instances in the past 14 elections, from 1952 to 2004, when the presidential candidate ahead in Gallup polling a week or so before the election did not win the national popular vote: in 1980 (Jimmy Carter) and 2000 (George W. Bush). And in only one of these, in 1980, did the candidate who was behind (Ronald Reagan) pull ahead in both the popular vote and the Electoral College and win the election.

The 1980 example is not necessarily one that John McCain can hope to duplicate this year. Reagan's late-breaking surge that year is generally attributed to the only presidential debate between Carter and Reagan—held one week before the election, on October 28—which seemed to move voter preferences in Reagan's direction, as well as to the ongoing Iran hostage crisis, which reached its one-year anniversary on Election Day. After trailing Carter by 8 points among registered voters (and by 3 points among likely voters) right before their debate, Reagan moved into a 3-point lead among likely voters immediately afterward, and he won the November 4 election by 10 points.

The 2000 example may have greater similarities to the kind of upset McCain hopes to achieve. Despite Bush's generally leading position for much of the last month prior to the 2000 election, the race narrowed in the final few days, and Gore squeaked out a popular-vote victory, 48.4% to 47.9%. Of course, Gore failed to win the Electoral College vote and, thus, the election.

Races have tightened toward the end of the campaign in other years, although not to the point where the second-place candidate was able to win either the popular or the Electoral College vote. In 1968, the race between Richard Nixon and Hubert Humphrey narrowed over the last month of the campaign, from double-digit leads for Nixon in late September to only an 8-point lead for him among registered voters in polling conducted between October 17 and October 22. By Gallup's final pre-election survey, conducted between October 29 and November 2, Nixon held only a 1-point edge among likely voters, and he ultimately won the election on November 5 by less than 1 percentage point, 43.4% to 42.7%.

The 1960 presidential election between Nixon and John F. Kennedy was extremely close, with the lead switching back and forth between the two candidates throughout the campaign. And although Kennedy won, it was by the narrowest of margins, rather than by the 4-point lead he held in a Gallup Poll just days before the election. The late campaign polling trends in every other election year since 1952 were fairly stable, and the candidate leading in the Gallup Poll in the week or so prior to the election ultimately won, either by a solid margin or by a very similar one to what the pre-election polls suggested. This was the case in 1952, 1956, 1964, 1972, 1976, 1984, 1988, 1992, 1996, and 2004 (all but two of which involved an incumbent president seeking re-election).

Race Stable, with Obama Leading

Gallup Poll daily tracking from October 24 through October 26 finds Obama with a five-percentage-point lead over McCain, 50% to 45%, in the presidential preferences of likely voters using Gallup's traditional model. He enjoys a more ample 10-point lead, 53% to 43%, using Gallup's expanded model. Obama's 10-point lead in the expanded sample of likely voters matches his largest leads on this basis. It also ties his standing among all registered voters, who now favor Obama over McCain, 52% to 42%.

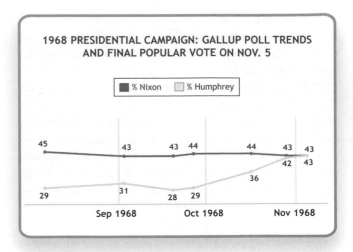

1968 PRESIDENTIAL CAMPAIGN: GALLUP POLL TRENDS AND FINAL POPULAR VOTE ON NOV. 5

McCain Retains Support of Highly Religious White Voters

A Gallup update based on more than 21,000 interviews conducted as part of Gallup Poll daily tracking in October shows that registered voters' religious intensity continues to be a powerful predictor of their presidential vote choice. McCain wins overwhelmingly among non-Hispanic whites who attend church weekly (65% to 28%), while Obama dominates among whites who seldom or never attend church (56% to 37%). The relationship between church attendance and voting has been well established in previous presidential elections, and the analysis of Gallup data collected between October 1 and October 26 suggests that this year is likely to be no different. The swing in candidate choice between groups of non-Hispanic white voters differentiated by their religious intensity is dramatic, ranging from a 37-point McCain advantage among whites who attend church weekly (about 32% of all non-Hispanic white registered voters) to a 19-point Obama advantage among those who seldom or never attend worship services (about 47% of white voters). The middle group of non-Hispanic whites who attend church nearly every week or monthly (20%) support McCain by a 12-point margin.

McCain's selection of Sarah Palin as his running mate just before the Republican National Convention might have been expected to bolster his standing among highly religious whites, given her credentials as a staunch conservative on moral or values issues. However, a comparison of Gallup's October data with data collected in August—for the most part before McCain's selection of Palin as his running mate—shows that McCain's strength among highly religious white voters has not changed substantially over that time period. In August, McCain was beating Obama among weekly church-attending white voters by a 64% to 25% margin, or 39 points, compared to a similar 37 points today. Importantly, McCain was doing better in August among whites than he has been doing in October, winning in August by a 51% to 39% margin compared with a narrower margin of 49% to 44% in the October 1–26 data. The fact that support for McCain did not slip among highly religious whites while slipping overall among whites could in part be attributable to Palin's presence on the Republican ticket, although the precise impact of her selection is not clear. (Among those who seldom or never attend church, McCain was losing by 11 points in August and is losing by 19 points today.)

Black voters overwhelmingly support Obama regardless of their relative level of religiosity. But highly religious blacks who attend church weekly (39% of non-Hispanic black voters) give Obama an 84-point margin, slightly lower than the 92- and 88-point margins for Obama, respectively,

among blacks who attend almost every week or monthly (33%) and those who seldom or never attend (26%).

Among Hispanics, the biggest difference in candidate choice by religion is between those who attend monthly or more frequently and those who seldom or never attend church. Hispanics who attend church weekly (36% of non-white Hispanic registered voters) favor McCain by a very narrow 3-point margin, and those who attend almost every week or monthly (23%) favor Obama by a similarly narrow 6-point margin. But among Hispanics who seldom or never attend church (40%), the margin for Obama swings to a highly significant 33 points.

Summary: McCain and the Religious Right

A positive correlation between religious intensity and voting for the Republican candidate for president has been a part of the American political landscape for a number of years. Early in this election cycle, there was speculation that McCain was perhaps not the favorite candidate of highly religious whites—and, indeed, former Arkansas governor Mike Huckabee (a former Southern Baptist seminarian and preacher) did well among religious whites in some Republican primaries. But McCain appears to have had few problems in gaining the vote of religious whites. The data reviewed here show that McCain was doing very well among highly religious whites in August and continues to do so in October, even though his overall standing has slipped some among whites.

OCTOBER 28

Poll: Seven in 10 Americans Say Obama Will Win

By a 71% to 23% margin, Americans expect that Barack Obama will be elected president on November 4, including a 49% to 46% ratio of John McCain's own supporters who say Obama, rather than their own candidate, will win. On the other hand, perhaps not surprisingly, Obama voters overwhelmingly believe, by a 94% to 2% margin, that their candidate will win. Belief that Obama will win has increased significantly from last June, when Americans viewed his victory as probable by a narrower 52% to 41% margin.

The implications of this belief pattern on the actual vote on Election Day are unclear, as are the implications for the vote of those who have already voted by absentee ballot or early voting. Some may argue that Obama might be hurt if his supporters become complacent and end up not voting (something Obama himself has warned against on the campaign trail). Others may argue that McCain supporters might "give up" and not vote if they feel their candidate does not have a chance of winning. But the October 23–26 poll shows that Republicans (the vast majority of whom say they will vote for McCain) have actually gained significant enthusiasm about voting since Gallup's October 10–12 poll, despite their pessimism about their candidate's chances of winning. In mid-October, 51% of Republicans were more enthusiastic about voting this year than in previous elections; now that number is 65%. (Republicans still lag behind Democrats on this measure, however; 76% of Democrats are more enthusiastic than usual about voting.) Whatever the implications, the data certainly indicate that Obama is winning the expectations game at this point, with a substantial majority of Americans believing that he will be their next president.

Presidential Race Narrows Slightly

The gap between Obama and McCain in Gallup Poll daily tracking from October 25 through October 27 has narrowed slightly, and Obama is now at 49% of the vote to 47% for McCain among likely voters using Gallup's traditional model, and at 51% to 44% using Gallup's expanded model. Both candidates continued vigorous campaigning on October 27. One forthcoming event with the potential to affect voter sentiments is a 30-minute Barack Obama television advertisement, for which his campaign has purchased time on October 29 on several national broadcast and cable networks. The two-percentage-point margin for Obama over McCain in today's traditional likely-voters model, based on Gallup Poll daily tracking from October 25 to October 27, does not mark the first time the race has been this close; it matches the Obama margin that held for three straight reporting periods spanning October 13–17. Obama's seven-point lead among an expanded pool of likely voters is fairly typical of what has been measured over the last two weeks, although it is slightly narrowed in the October 26–27 reports. Obama is also now at a seven-point margin over McCain among registered voters, 50% to 43%.

Voters Not Eager for One-Party Control of Government

Registered voters appear cautious about giving one party control of the federal government in this election. Most would prefer that the Democrats control Congress if McCain is elected, but they divide evenly as to which party should control Congress if Obama becomes the next president. These results are based on an October 23–26 Gallup Poll. They come as McCain has tried to remind voters that electing Obama as president to go along with a Democratically controlled Congress would give the Democratic Party control of two branches of the federal government. That

argument appears to resonate with voters, who seem reluctant to want to give one party such control regardless of who is elected president. Gallup has found a similar pattern of results in prior elections. In 2004, registered voters said they preferred to have the Democrats control Congress if George W. Bush was re-elected, and they were divided as to which party should control Congress if John Kerry were to win. Bush won a second term and Republicans retained control of Congress in that election, before voters returned party control of both houses of Congress back to the Democrats in 2006 for the first time in over a decade.

In the 1996 campaign, when Bill Clinton was strongly favored to win a second term in office, voters were again divided in their views of which party should control Congress. Some credit the expectation of a Clinton win with swaying voters to elect Republicans to Congress, and Republicans were able to maintain control of both houses in that election. This September, Gallup asked Americans directly whether they thought it was better to have Congress and the president controlled by the same political party, or whether it would be better to have different parties controlling the two branches of government. Consistent with the results reported here, the public was evenly divided, with 40% favoring one-party control and 41% split control.

RELATION OF VOTER CHOICE TO DIVIDED-GOVERNMENT PREFERENCE

It is unclear to what extent voters who prefer divided government will split their own votes for president and Congress in a deliberate attempt to achieve divided party control of the two branches. In fact, this sort of ticket-splitting is fairly rare among voters, at least in terms of their votes for president and Congress. In the last two Gallup Polls that asked about both presidential and congressional vote choices, only 9% of voters indicated they would vote for a president of one party and member of Congress of the other. Moreover, a preference for divided control may be only one of many factors influencing their congressional vote, including their opinions of their local incumbent member of Congress. Indeed, despite record-low approval ratings for Congress this year, most voters (59%) continue to say that their own member of Congress deserves to be re-elected. And with Democrats currently in control of Congress, high incumbent re-election rates would help Democrats maintain control.

Early Voting Now Up to 18%

Gallup Poll daily tracking data collected through October 27 indicate that 18% of registered voters who plan to vote have already voted, and another 15% say they will vote before November 4. In Gallup's first report on early voting, based on October 17–19 interviewing, 7% of registered voters who planned to vote said they had already voted, while another 21% said that they were going to vote early. These results continue to suggest that about a third of voters will have already cast their ballot before November 4.

So far the voter preferences of this early voting group are somewhat more tilted toward Obama than the preferences of those who say they will wait to vote until Election Day. The voter preferences of the 1,430 individuals who have already voted and who were interviewed by Gallup between October 17 and October 27 show a 53% to 43% Obama over McCain tilt; among those who say they have not yet voted but will before Election Day, the skew toward Obama is more pronounced, at 54% to 40%. By comparison, those who are going to wait to vote until November 4 manifest a narrower 50% to 44% preference for Obama over McCain. (Among all registered voters over this time period, Obama leads McCain by a 51% to 43% margin.) These results indicate that, with each passing day, Obama appears to be freezing in place a higher and higher percentage of votes in his favor, making that portion of the electorate impervious to any last-minute campaign trends. At the least, the results suggest that the returns on Election Night will be incomplete, and perhaps misleading, if absentee and early voting results are not included.

OCTOBER 29

Economy Reigns Supreme for Voters

As John McCain and Barack Obama begin the final stretch of the 2008 presidential race, a new Gallup Poll identifies the economy as the runaway top election issue for Americans. The 55% of Americans now naming the economy as "extremely important" to their vote for president outranks the situation in Iraq—which received the highest score in February—and energy, which topped the list in June. This finding is from an October 23–26 Gallup Poll in which Americans were asked to rate the importance of 12 policy issues to their vote for president.

Six issues cluster in second place behind the economy, all considered extremely important by between 40% and 44% of Americans: the federal budget deficit (44%), terrorism (42%), energy/gasoline prices (41%), the situation in Iraq (41%), healthcare (41%), and taxes (40%). Education (39%), moral values (39%), and the situation in Afghanistan (37%) fall right below these six in the October ranking. The environment (26%) and illegal immigration (25%) are ranked least important among the 12 issues.

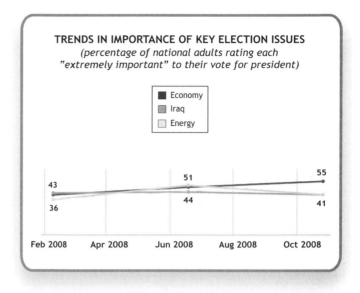

TRENDS IN IMPORTANCE OF KEY ELECTION ISSUES
(percentage of national adults rating each "extremely important" to their vote for president)

In fact, not only is the economy perceived to be the most important issue in this election, but the 55% who rate it as extremely important to their vote is the highest Gallup has found for *any* issue in the last four presidential election years (since 1996). Republicans and Democrats have, predictably, somewhat different outlooks about which issues are most important to their vote. While the economy is the top-rated issue for both groups (as well as for political independents), it is rated extremely important by a higher proportion of Democrats than Republicans (63% vs. 52%). And whereas the economy is clearly the top-rated issue for Democrats, among Republicans the economy is roughly tied with terrorism and moral values in perceived importance.

Healthcare ranks second among Democrats but doesn't appear in the top *five* issues of Republicans or independents. The corresponding issues for Republicans are moral values and taxes: These issues rank tied for second and fourth, respectively, for Republicans, but don't register in the top five for independents or Democrats. Energy is the only election issue aside from the economy that ranks among the top five for all three political groups.

Voters Focusing on the Economy, Taxes, Energy, the Budget Deficit, and Moral Values

Americans have had ample opportunity to consider the issues in this election. The candidates have engaged in numerous political debates during both the primary season and the general election, and both candidates have made certain issues focal points for their campaigns. Perhaps as a result, none of the 12 issues tested is rated significantly less important in October than at the start of 2008. Several have grown in perceived relevance, however. The economy, taxes, energy,

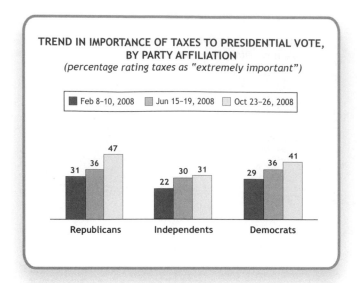

TREND IN IMPORTANCE OF TAXES TO PRESIDENTIAL VOTE,
BY PARTY AFFILIATION
(percentage rating taxes as "extremely important")

the federal budget deficit, and moral values have all seen increases of 5 points or more in the percentage of Americans rating each as "extremely important" to their vote.

The 14-point increase in those rating the economy extremely important is about even among Republicans and Democrats. The widespread problems with the economy have caused a bipartisan decline in consumer confidence throughout 2008, and that is reflected in an increasing likelihood among both groups to call the issue extremely important to their vote. The tax issue has intensified recently, with McCain pouncing on Obama's recent and past statements about redistributing wealth as evidence of a sharp philosophical distinction between the two candidates on tax policy. Despite this, Gallup trends show that both Republicans and Democrats have grown more likely to say the tax issue will be extremely important to their vote this year.

Summary: It's the Economy

In February 2008, it appeared that the situation in Iraq would be on par with the economy with respect to its importance to voters in choosing the next president. By June, the energy issue had emerged as at least as important as the economy, and had displaced Iraq at the top of the rankings. Today, the economy has no peer among the issues Americans say they will consider in when casting their vote. It is the undisputed top concern of independents and Democrats and ties for first among Republicans.

Obama Maintains Edge over McCain

Barack Obama begins the final week of the campaign with an advantage over John McCain in both Gallup likely-voter models, ahead by 49% to 46% using the traditional model

and leading 51% to 44% using an expanded model. These results, based on Gallup Poll daily tracking from October 26 to October 28, are essentially the same as the October 25–27 results, and show a slightly closer race than Gallup tracking had reported prior to that. Gallup has only found about 4% of likely voters to be truly undecided at this late stage of the campaign, in that they do not express a preference or leaning for Obama or McCain or for some other candidate. Obama has a slightly larger lead among the pool of all registered voters, currently at 51% to 42%. These percentages for registered voters have been stable throughout October, and the current figures precisely match the average for the month to date.

Obama Beating McCain on Voter Outreach

More voters say the Obama campaign has contacted them at some point in the last few weeks than say the McCain campaign has done so, 38% vs. 30%. Both campaigns appear to be focusing their voter outreach efforts on those who already support their own candidate—suggesting that "get out the vote" activity is the primary game being played at this late stage of the campaign. Many more Obama voters say they have been contacted by the Obama campaign than by the McCain campaign: 46% and 30%, respectively. Likewise, more McCain voters have heard from the McCain campaign (39%) than from the Obama campaign (24%). Obama has also made greater inroads into the undecided bloc: A third of this group nationwide say they have been contacted by Obama's campaign, compared with 21% who have been contacted by McCain's.

The intensity of the campaign in battleground states such as Florida, Ohio, Pennsylvania, Colorado, and New Hampshire is clear from a regional breakdown of the voter contact question. More than half of voters living in "purple

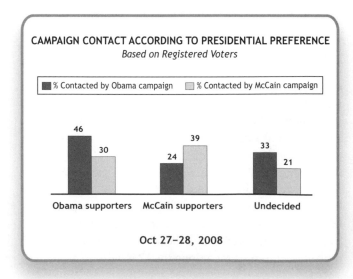

CAMPAIGN CONTACT ACCORDING TO PRESIDENTIAL PREFERENCE
Based on Registered Voters

Oct 27–28, 2008

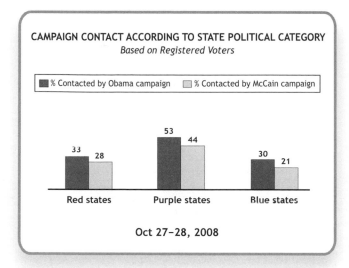

CAMPAIGN CONTACT ACCORDING TO STATE POLITICAL CATEGORY
Based on Registered Voters

Oct 27–28, 2008

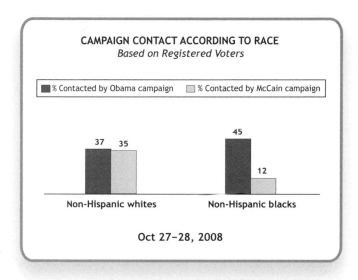

CAMPAIGN CONTACT ACCORDING TO RACE
Based on Registered Voters

Oct 27–28, 2008

states" (53%)—those where the margin of victory for either George W. Bush or John Kerry in 2004 was less than 6 points—say they have been contacted by Obama's campaign. Somewhat fewer, but still close to half (44%), have been contacted by McCain's. Both campaigns appear to be putting far less effort into reaching voters in red and blue states, although whereas about equal proportions of voters in each of these regions say Obama's campaign has contacted them, more red-state than blue-state voters say McCain's campaign has contacted them.*

---

*Red states: Alabama, Alaska, Arizona, Arkansas, Georgia, Idaho, Indiana, Kansas, Kentucky, Louisiana, Mississippi, Missouri, Montana, Nebraska, North Carolina, North Dakota, Oklahoma, South Carolina, South Dakota, Tennessee, Texas, Utah, Virginia, West Virginia, Wyoming.
Blue states: California, Connecticut, Delaware, District of Columbia, Hawaii, Illinois, Maine, Maryland, Massachusetts, New Jersey, New York, Rhode Island, Vermont, Washington.
Purple states: Colorado, Florida, Iowa, Michigan, Minnesota, Nevada, New Hampshire, New Mexico, Ohio, Oregon, Pennsylvania, Wisconsin.

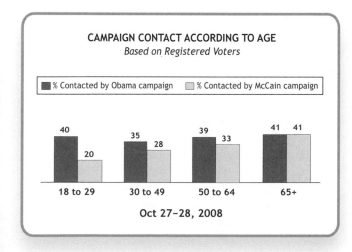

CAMPAIGN CONTACT ACCORDING TO AGE
Based on Registered Voters

Oct 27–28, 2008

YOUNG VOTERS GETTING THE CALL FROM THE OBAMA CAMPAIGN

Adults under 30 years of age are twice as likely to have been contacted by the Obama campaign as by the McCain campaign: 40% vs. 20%. While this in part reflects the higher rate of Obama supporters among young voters, it may also indicate the special emphasis that Obama's team is reportedly putting on getting out new voters to support him on Election Day. Obama has a slight edge in voter outreach among those in the 30 to 49 and 50 to 64 age ranges, while he and McCain are tied among those 65 and older.

BLACK VOTERS ALSO HEARING FROM OBAMA

Given blacks voters' overwhelming support for Obama's candidacy (88%), it is not surprising that the Obama campaign would heavily target blacks in its "get out the vote" campaign. Close to half of all non-Hispanic black registered voters (45%) say the Obama campaign has contacted them in recent weeks. That compares with 37% of all non-Hispanic white voters. Very few black voters have heard from the McCain campaign (12%), compared with 35% of whites.

OCTOBER 30

Campaign Financing Appears to Be Non-Issue for Voters

Most Americans are unsure of whether Barack Obama and John McCain are relying on the public financing system to fund their presidential campaigns. But the minority of Americans who say they do know are generally correct in saying McCain has agreed to take public financing while

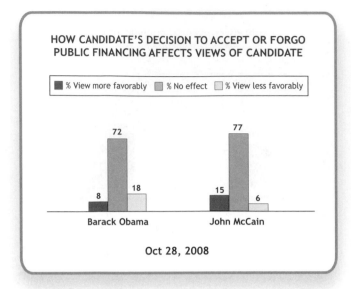

HOW CANDIDATE'S DECISION TO ACCEPT OR FORGO PUBLIC FINANCING AFFECTS VIEWS OF CANDIDATE

Oct 28, 2008

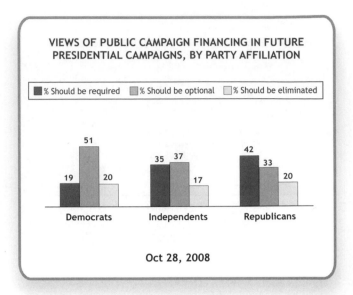

VIEWS OF PUBLIC CAMPAIGN FINANCING IN FUTURE PRESIDENTIAL CAMPAIGNS, BY PARTY AFFILIATION

Oct 28, 2008

Obama has decided not to. When informed of the candidates' decisions on public financing, the vast majority say this does not affect their opinion of the candidates. To the extent Americans see the decisions as consequential, they take a more positive view of McCain's decision (15% say it makes them feel more favorably toward him versus 6% who say less favorably) than of Obama's (8% say it makes them feel more favorably toward him and 18% less favorably).

The October 28 poll was conducted in the midst of a presidential campaign in which the candidates have spent more money than in any previous campaign, and in which Obama has set new standards for fund-raising. He decided to opt out of the public financing system largely because of his ability to raise money well beyond the federal spending limit of $84 million. McCain—one of the leading Senate voices on campaign finance reform—agreed to the spending limit, though it is unclear whether he would have made the same decision had he been able to raise the same large sums of money as Obama. Americans generally agree that spending on the presidential campaigns has exceeded their sense of what is appropriate, as 70% say too much money has been spent on this year's election. That includes 84% of McCain supporters but also a majority (58%) of Obama supporters.

Americans' Views of Spending Limits

Generally speaking, Americans support campaign spending limits. The poll finds 57% saying there should be limits on what presidential candidates can spend, while 38% say candidates should be able to spend whatever money they can raise. Americans also seem to back the current

public financing system, which includes spending limits; only 19% believe the current system should be eliminated. Americans stop short, however, of saying candidates should be required to take public financing—only 32% hold this view. A plurality of 40% think the system should be optional, as it is now. When this group is asked whether the rules should be changed so that candidates would be more likely to take public financing, most said the rules should be kept the same as they are now.

Partisan views on the desirability of campaign limits may be influenced more by the current election campaign situation than by what their respective parties' positions on campaign finance have been historically. Democrats—whose party has generally supported spending limits—oppose them by 54% to 42% in the current poll. Republicans—whose party has generally opposed spending limits—favor them by 64% to 33%. Forty-two percent of Republicans say all candidates should be required to participate in the public financing system—more than say it should be optional (33%). A slim majority of Democrats say the system should be optional, with equal percentages saying it should be required or should not exist at all.

Obama Leads Among Likely Voters by Five to Seven Points

Obama holds a statistically significant lead over McCain in both Gallup likely-voter models, according to October 27–29 Gallup Poll daily tracking Gallup Poll daily tracking. In the traditional model, which defines likely voters based on past voting behavior as well as current voting intention, Obama holds a 50% to 45% lead. In the expanded model, in which only current voting intention is considered, his

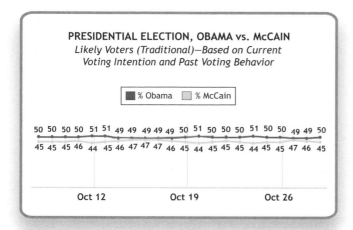

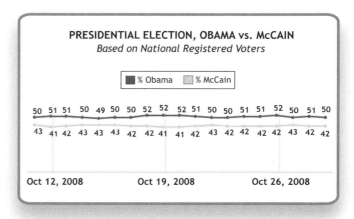

lead is 51% to 44%. As in any election, the final outcome, in large part, hinges on who turns out to vote and who does not. If all registered voters vote on November 4, Obama would probably win comfortably: He leads McCain by 50% to 42% in the latest estimate of registered-voter preferences and has averaged a nine-percentage-point lead since October 1.

Both likely-voter models currently show a slightly closer race than is evident in the registered-voter estimate. Obama has never trailed in either likely-voter model since Gallup began tracking likely-voter preferences in early October, averaging a four-point lead using the traditional model and an eight-point lead using the expanded model. Just five days remain until Election Day, and McCain and the Republicans are campaigning hard in key states to try to change Obama's lead. Late comebacks are rare, but they have occurred—including Harry Truman in 1948 and Ronald Reagan in 1980.

Americans Split on Redistributing Wealth by Taxing the Rich

A majority of Americans (58%) say money and wealth should be more evenly distributed among a larger per-

centage of the people, although slightly less than half (46%) go so far as to say that the government should redistribute wealth by "heavy taxes on the rich." Gallup has been periodically asking Americans for over 20 years whether the distribution of money and wealth in this country is "fair," or whether money and wealth should be "more evenly distributed among a larger percentage of the people." (The question does suggest exactly how money and wealth would be more evenly distributed and does not make any reference to the government.)

Across the nine times the question has been asked, a majority of Americans have agreed that money and wealth should be more evenly distributed. The current 58% who agree is one of the two lowest percentages Gallup has measured (along with a 56% reading in September 2000); 68% agreed in April 2008 and 66% in April 2007. The responses to this question are extraordinarily differentiated by partisan orientation, reflecting a fundamental fissure in Americans' views on the concept of redistributing money and wealth. Just 30% of Republicans say there should be a more even distribution of money and wealth, compared with

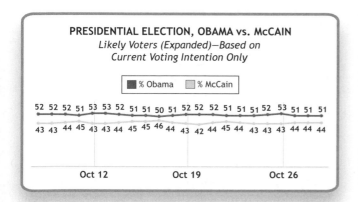

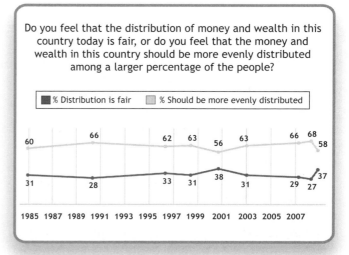

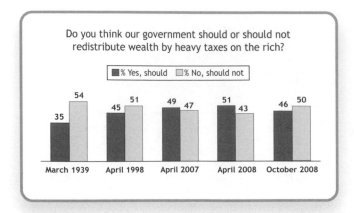

Do you think our government should or should not redistribute wealth by heavy taxes on the rich?

■ % Yes, should   □ % No, should not

| March 1939 | April 1998 | April 2007 | April 2008 | October 2008 |

60% of independents and an overwhelming majority of 84% of Democrats. The sentiment that money and wealth should be more evenly distributed, however, does not address the issue of exactly how this objective should be achieved. One of the more contentious points on the presidential campaign trail in recent weeks has been McCain's continuing assertion that Obama's tax plan, which would involve higher taxes for high-income families, is "redistributionist," with some McCain supporters going so far as to argue that Obama's tax plans would be "socialist." These disputes focus on the longtime argument in economic and political philosophy over government's ideal role, if any, in attempting to redistribute money and wealth through the use of taxes.

Gallup has from time to time asked a question that addresses this issue in part—a question that Elmo Roper first asked in a *Fortune* magazine survey conducted in March 1939, near the end of the Depression. The question is phrased as follows: "People feel differently about how far a government should go. Here is a phrase which some people believe in and some don't. Do you think our government should or should not redistribute wealth by heavy taxes on the rich?" This question is notable because it directly addresses the idea that government should intervene to redistribute wealth through taxes on the rich. The question's phrase "heavy taxes on the rich" is certainly not one the Obama campaign would choose to describe its plan, which Obama repeatedly says would only restore high-income tax rates back to what they were under President Clinton in the 1990s, before the Bush administration tax cuts. Still, the question generally addresses the basic issue of taxing high-income individuals so as to transfer wealth in a society.

Gallup has asked this question only four times over the last decade, and the responses have been closely divided every time. In 1998, there was a slight tilt toward a negative response; in 2007, sentiment was split almost equally; in April 2008, there was a slight tilt toward a positive response;

and in the current poll, sentiment is more evenly divided, with a slight tilt back toward the negative. Still, each of the four times Gallup has asked this question in recent years, between 45% and 51% of Americans have gone so far as to agree with the policy of "redistribut[ing] wealth by heavy taxes on the rich." Although the survey methods used now differ from those for surveys conducted in 1939, the trend lines at least suggest that Americans are currently as willing as, if not more willing than, they were during the Depression to sanction the use of taxes on the rich as a mechanism for redistributing wealth.

Summary: Redistributing Wealth— A Partisan Issue

Perhaps the most important implication of these data is the extraordinary partisan differences found in responses to both questions dealing with money and wealth distribution in this country. Democrats believe that wealth should be more evenly distributed, and that this redistribution should be accomplished by means of heavy taxes on the rich. Although Obama has not advocated what he would call "heavy" taxes on the rich, the general sentiment that taxes on high-income families should be increased in order to help provide tax relief for those making less money is a part of his campaign platform.

Republicans fairly strongly reject both the concept that the current distribution of money and wealth is unfair and the idea of imposing heavy taxes on the rich. In this, they certainly reflect the campaign statements and platform of John McCain. Independents, the most crucial group in a close election, are more ambivalent—as one would expect. Independents swing to the Democratic side in their majority (60%) belief that the distribution of money and wealth is not fair and should be more even, but split almost exactly evenly on accomplishing that via heavy taxes on the rich.

OCTOBER 31
Interest High: One in Five Have Already Voted

A Gallup Poll conducted between October 23 and October 26 found 92% of registered voters saying they had given quite a lot of thought or some thought to the election. This is a classic measure of interest in an election that Gallup has been tracking for decades, and the current reading is one of the highest such percentages found prior to an election in recent Gallup history. There were similarly high attention levels in 1992 and 2004, which turned out to be higher-turnout elections. The campaigns of 1996 and 2000 captured significantly lower levels of voter attention, and were also lower-turnout elections. The unsurprisingly high

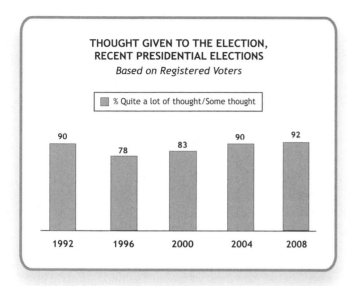

THOUGHT GIVEN TO THE ELECTION, RECENT PRESIDENTIAL ELECTIONS
Based on Registered Voters

■ % Quite a lot of thought/Some thought

1992	1996	2000	2004	2008
90	78	83	90	92

reading on this measure in 2008 suggests a high-turnout election again this year.

EARLY VOTING

Gallup's latest update—based on interviewing conducted through October 29—shows that 21% of registered voters say they have already voted early or by absentee ballot. This percentage has been increasing steadily over the last two weeks. Another 12% of registered voters say they still plan on voting early, leaving about two-thirds of those who plan on voting who indicate they will vote on Election Day. These early voters are more likely to say they have voted for Barack Obama than for John McCain, by a 55% to 40% margin. Among those who plan to vote on Election Day, the spread is much closer—only a 48% to 45% Obama advantage. Despite some perceptions that there may be disproportionate early voting among blacks, Gallup's data show

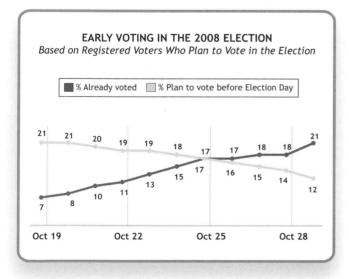

EARLY VOTING IN THE 2008 ELECTION
Based on Registered Voters Who Plan to Vote in the Election

■ % Already voted ☐ % Plan to vote before Election Day

that black voters and white voters are roughly proportionate in their reports of already having voted early. There does continue to be a significant age skew in the early voting patterns: Older voters are significantly more likely than those who are younger to report having already voted.

First-Time Voters

Eleven percent of registered voters interviewed by Gallup between October 27 and October 29 claim to be first-time voters, which is similar to the 13% recorded in 2004. Most of these voters are under age 30, and as is the case for this demographic group in general, they tend to self-report as strongly oriented toward voting for Obama. But an important question is: How many of these first-time voters will actually end up voting? Gallup's traditional likely-voter model estimates that 8% of the electorate will be first-time voters. (Even though this model is based partly on past voting behavior, first-time voters are not penalized if they were too young to vote in past elections.) In an expanded model, which does not rely on past voting behavior to predict turnout in the coming election, they represent a slightly higher 10% of the electorate.

Voter Mobilization Efforts

Gallup has been asking Americans whether they have been contacted by the Obama campaign and by the McCain campaign. Thus far, the Obama campaign appears to have a modest edge in terms of voter contact and get-out-the-vote efforts. Gallup's updated estimate is that about 37% of registered voters say the Obama campaign has contacted them, while 30% say the McCain campaign has done so. Both numbers are likely to grow in the coming few days, as much of the mobilization effort is likely to occur in the final weekend and final days before the election. The contact rates have tended to be higher for those residing in battleground states.

Obama's Lead Widens by All Measures

The political landscape could be improving for Obama in the waning days of the campaign. Gallup Poll daily tracking from October 28 to October 30 shows him with an 8-percentage-point lead over John McCain among traditional likely voters, 51% to 43%—his largest margin to date using this historical Gallup Poll voter model. Since October 28, McCain's support among traditional likely voters has dropped by 4 points (from 47% to 43%), Obama's has risen by 2 points (from 49% to 51%), and the percentage of undecided voters has increased from 4% to 6%. The October 30 interviews were the first conducted entirely after

Obama's widely viewed 30-minute campaign ad, which ran on numerous television networks on October 29. Obama held a substantial lead over McCain in the October 30 polling, but it was no greater than what Gallup found on October 29.

Obama's lead among expanded likely voters is only slightly greater than that seen among traditional likely voters. He now leads McCain by nine points, 52% to 43%, using this looser definition, which does not factor in whether respondents have voted in past elections but instead relies only on their reported level of interest and their intention to vote. Obama's current 11-point lead over McCain among all registered voters—52% to 41%—is up from an 8-point lead yesterday and ties his highest advantage on this basis, last recorded 10 days ago.

Obama's favorable position among traditional likely voters in the latest polling is partially reflective of his strong position among all registered voters. However, at other times when Obama has led McCain by 11 points among registered voters, his likely-voter advantage has been lower (in the 5- to 7-point range) than it is now. Thus, Obama's improved likely-voter standing also reflects a higher propensity for his supporters to turn out and vote than what Gallup has seen at earlier times this month. This could stem from the superiority his well-funded campaign appears to have over the McCain campaign in contacting his supporters to get out and vote.

Obama Retains Slight Edge over McCain on Taxes

A Gallup Poll conducted between October 23 and October 26 finds Americans still favoring Obama over McCain as the candidate better able to handle taxes, 50% to 44%, but to a slightly lesser extent than earlier in October. The positioning of the two candidates on the tax issue has taken on increased importance in the last several weeks as McCain in particular has been focusing heavily on the differences between his approach and Obama's approach to taxes.

The most recent poll continues to reflect a somewhat higher percentage of Americans believing that Obama would raise taxes compared with the percentage who believe this about McCain. The results come at a time when Obama has been emphasizing his pledge to cut taxes for "95% of working families," while McCain says he (McCain) wants to make permanent the Bush tax cuts, which include cuts for higher-income Americans. Thirty-six percent now say McCain will *increase* taxes, compared with 32% in early September. In the same period, the percentage of Americans who think Obama

will increase their taxes has gone down by five points (54% to 49%).

McCain has been emphasizing his proposal to make the Bush tax cuts permanent for all Americans while Obama wants to roll back the Bush tax cuts for those making over $250,000, raising the question of how Americans have reacted to the Bush tax cuts over the years since they were enacted. A review of past Gallup Polls shows that support for the tax cuts ushered in by President George W. Bush after he took office in 2001 was initially fairly high, but support for making the tax cuts permanent eroded somewhat during his first term. In a CNN/USA Today/Gallup Poll conducted between January 5 and January 7, 2001, before Bush took office and before Congress began debating his proposed $1.3 trillion tax cut, over half (52%) of Americans favored Bush's tax cuts. When it came to making the Bush tax cuts permanent, support dropped from 64% in November 2002 to 52% in December 2004, with opposition rising from 29% to 40% during that period. Separate Gallup polling conducted in October 2004 showed that 35% of Americans said the Bush tax cuts had mostly hurt the economy and just 39% said they had mostly helped. Around the same time, a December 2004 poll found Americans generally favoring significant reforms to the federal income tax system, with a majority (59%) saying it either needed to be completely overhauled or needed major changes.

Taxes: Who Benefits?

At the root of the tax issue is the subject of who benefits most from specific tax policies. Both candidates claim that their tax policies will benefit middle-class Americans. These appeals to middle-class sentiment may be resonating with a public that increasingly sees the United States as a nation divided into "haves" and "have-nots." In July of this year, almost half of Americans, 49%, said the United States is divided into two groups: the "haves" and the "have-nots." This was up from 45% two years ago, and from 37% in June 2004. Additionally, in Gallup's annual Economy and Personal Finance poll conducted between April 6 and April 9, 2008, a large majority of Americans (63%—though that was one of the lowest readings in the last two decades) said that upper-income people pay too little in taxes, while just 4% said the same about middle-income people. A large percentage of Americans (73%) also said corporations pay too little in taxes. And in an August 21–23 USA Today/Gallup Poll, more than half of Americans (55%) said they believed that if Obama becomes president, his policies would benefit the middle class (33%) and the poor (22%) the most. However, if McCain were to be elected, 53% believed his policies would benefit the wealthy the most.

Implications for the Election

Outside of the context of the current presidential election, Americans have voiced frustration with tax policies that benefit the wealthy. Currently, Americans are more likely to see Obama rather than McCain as the candidate whose policies would benefit the middle class and the poor the most. This could be a benefit to Obama at a time when about half of the public sees American society as divided into "haves" and "have-nots." Both candidates have used the Bush tax cuts as a reference point, with McCain vowing to continue them while Obama says he will rescind them for upper-income Americans. Although Gallup has not measured attitudes toward the Bush tax cuts in recent years, by 2004 they had become less favorably received. The fact that Obama has an edge over McCain on taxes at this time, albeit a small one, may point to an American public that is ready for a change from the fiscal policy of the Bush years.

Update: Little Evidence of Surge in Youth Vote

Gallup polling in October finds little evidence of a surge in young voter turnout beyond what it was in 2004. While young voter registration may be up slightly over 2004 (86% to 83%), both the reported level of interest in the election and the intention to vote among those under 30 are no higher than they were that year (79% to 78%). What's more, 18- to 29-year-olds continue to lag behind Americans age 30 and older on important turnout indicators. As a result, 18- to 29-year-olds now constitute 12% of Gallup's traditional likely-voter sample, basically the same as the estimate in the final 2004 pre-election poll (13%). Gallup's expanded likely-voter model estimates a slightly higher proportion of young voters in the electorate (14%). However, even if the proportion of young voters is adjusted upward, doing so has little or no impact on the overall Obama-McCain horse race numbers using either likely-voter model.

It is possible that the 18- to 29-year-old share of the likely-voter electorate will grow in the final days of the election. Although interest in the election and voting intentions usually increase as Election Day grows nearer, Gallup did not observe much of an increase from mid- to late October in 2004, because interest was already at high levels (as it is this year). A second possibility for achieving heightened youth turnout would be voter mobilization efforts. Such efforts can convince people with little motivation or interest in the campaign to actually vote on Election Day. Gallup has been measuring voter contact in its daily tracking poll

this week in an effort to gain a better understanding of this important component in the final days of the campaign.

As of October 27–29 polling, 39% of 18- to 29-year-olds had been contacted by either the Obama or McCain campaigns. That is the same contact rate seen among 30- to 49-year-olds, but is well below that for Americans 50 and older (51%). So thus far, mobilization efforts have not reached the young voters to the same extent that they have older voters. The overall contact rates by age hide a significant disparity in contact by the two campaigns. Americans under 30 are about twice as likely to report having been contacted by the Obama campaign as by the McCain campaign: 31% of 18- to 29-year-olds have been contacted by the Obama campaign, compared with just 16% who say the McCain campaign has contacted them. The higher contact rates for Obama among young voters reflect his greater level of support among this group than among the general population, a fact that has been well documented. These contact levels for younger voters no doubt reflect the fact that each candidate's campaign this year appears to be targeting its mobilization efforts toward its known supporters—reflecting the strategic decision that voter contact best serves to reinforce the base and get out the vote rather than to attempt to change voters' minds. And given the historical fact that younger voters are less likely to turn out at the polls and vote, it may be that the Obama campaign sees a fertile opportunity among this group to increase its candidate's votes. It is also clear that the Obama campaign has been more successful in reaching voters generally, regardless of age.

Implications for the Election

While Gallup data do suggest that voter turnout among young people will be high this year—as it was in 2004—compared with historical turnout rates, the data do not suggest that it will be appreciably higher than in 2004. Even if more young voters are registered this year, they do not appear to be any more interested in the campaign or in voting in the election than they were in 2004. Unless turnout rates among older age groups drop substantially from what they were in 2004, young voters should represent about the same share of the electorate as in the last presidential election. And Gallup's data suggest that interest in the campaign and in voting are the same or higher among older voters compared with what they were in 2004.

Blacks Appear Poised for High Turnout

Black voters are scoring highly this election season on several election and voting interest measures, and thus constitute a higher percentage of Gallup's projected likely-voter pool than in previous elections. Additionally, blacks report having received election-related contact from the Obama campaign at a higher rate than do whites, although many fewer blacks have been contacted by the McCain campaign.

As is the case among 18- to 29-year-old voters, blacks report having been contacted in disproportionately higher numbers by the Obama campaign than by the McCain campaign. While rates of contact by the Obama and McCain campaigns are similar among whites (34% to 31%, respectively), blacks are almost four times as likely to report having been contacted by the Obama campaign (41%) as by the McCain campaign (11%). This high level of contact almost certainly reflects an effort by the Obama campaign to help encourage a record-high turnout of black voters—more than 9 out of 10 of whom, based on Gallup data, will pull the lever for Obama if they vote.

Gallup analysis shows that blacks this year are just as likely as whites to report being registered to vote, and match the high levels of interest in the campaign and self-reported intention to vote seen among whites. The increase since 2004 among blacks on the latter two measures most likely reflects black voters' reaction to the candidacy of the first major-party African-American presidential nominee in U.S. history.

Blacks now make up a greater share of Gallup's likely-voter pool than they did in 2004. In Gallup's most recent update on likely voters, blacks constitute 11% of both the expanded and traditional likely-voter groups, higher than the 8% representation in Gallup's final estimate of voters from 2004. If these trends continue through the November 4 election, black turnout rates this year may approach or match turnout rates among whites.

NOVEMBER 2008

NOVEMBER 1

Obama 52%, McCain 42% Among Likely Voters

Barack Obama leads John McCain in Gallup Poll daily tracking interviewing conducted between October 29 and October 31 by an identical 52% to 42% margin among both traditional likely voters and expanded likely voters. Obama leads by a similar 52% to 41% margin among all registered voters. This is the first time since Gallup began estimating likely voters in early October that there is no difference between Gallup's two likely-voter models. Obama's lead of 52% to 42% using Gallup's traditional estimate of likely-voting criteria takes into account past voting as well as current intention; the expanded model takes into account only current voting intention. Both of these likely-voter estimates in turn are almost identical to Gallup's 52% to 41% registered voter estimate.

The candidate preferences of the broad group of all registered voters have been remarkably steady for over two weeks now, showing little fluctuation despite both candidates' intense campaigning, the huge amount of news coverage, and high levels of voter attention to the election. Obama's percentage of the vote among registered voters has varied only between 50 and 52% for the last 16 days, and McCain's has varied only between 41 and 43%. Gallup's estimates of candidate preference among likely voters show more variation; these calculations take into account respondents' interest in the election and their self-reports of intention to vote. The average Obama lead over McCain among traditional likely voters since October 6 has been five points, but that lead has expanded over the last several days' reports, and Obama's current 52–42% lead among this group is the largest to date. Gallup has increased its estimate of turnout in the election slightly to 64% (from the previous 60%), based on internal calculations, which point toward the higher turnout number, and this 64% estimate is reflected in current voter calculations.

CHRONOLOGY

NOVEMBER 2008

November 1–3   Obama uses the last days of the campaign to make incursions into traditional Republican areas. McCain campaigns extensively in Pennsylvania and New Hampshire.

November 4   Barack Obama is elected 44th president of the United States as the nation chooses him as its first African-American chief executive.

Gallup's interviewing conducted between October 29 and October 31 shows that 27% of registered voters have already voted. The incidence of early voting has trended consistently upward on a day-to-day basis, moving from 7% of registered voters who had already voted during the period of October 17–19 to the current estimate of 27%. Another 8% of registered voters still indicate that they plan to vote before Election Day itself. These early voters—all of whom are included in the likely-voter pool since they are definite voters—skew more toward Obama than the sample average. Thus, more and more of these Obama-oriented voters' choices are being "locked in" through early voting, benefiting Obama.

Life Satisfaction Predicts Voter Preferences

Gallup Polls conducted between March 7 and October 22, 2008, show how Americans' current life satisfaction relates to their voting preferences. The connection between current life satisfaction and voting preferences comes into

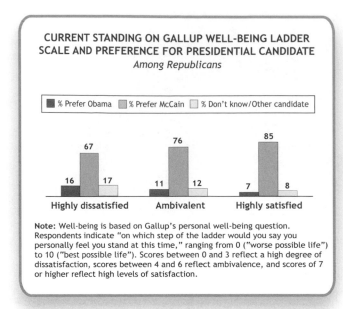

CURRENT STANDING ON GALLUP WELL-BEING LADDER SCALE AND PREFERENCE FOR PRESIDENTIAL CANDIDATE
Among Republicans

■ % Prefer Obama   ■ % Prefer McCain   □ % Don't know/Other candidate

	Highly dissatisfied	Ambivalent	Highly satisfied
% Prefer Obama	16	11	7
% Prefer McCain	67	76	85
% Don't know/Other	17	12	8

Note: Well-being is based on Gallup's personal well-being question. Respondents indicate "on which step of the ladder would you say you personally feel you stand at this time," ranging from 0 ("worse possible life") to 10 ("best possible life"). Scores between 0 and 3 reflect a high degree of dissatisfaction, scores between 4 and 6 reflect ambivalence, and scores of 7 or higher reflect high levels of satisfaction.

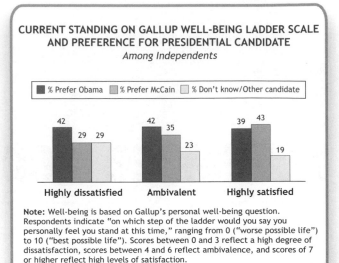

CURRENT STANDING ON GALLUP WELL-BEING LADDER SCALE AND PREFERENCE FOR PRESIDENTIAL CANDIDATE
Among Independents

■ % Prefer Obama   ■ % Prefer McCain   □ % Don't know/Other candidate

	Highly dissatisfied	Ambivalent	Highly satisfied
% Prefer Obama	42	42	39
% Prefer McCain	29	35	43
% Don't know/Other	29	23	19

Note: Well-being is based on Gallup's personal well-being question. Respondents indicate "on which step of the ladder would you say you personally feel you stand at this time," ranging from 0 ("worse possible life") to 10 ("best possible life"). Scores between 0 and 3 reflect a high degree of dissatisfaction, scores between 4 and 6 reflect ambivalence, and scores of 7 or higher reflect high levels of satisfaction.

sharp focus when examining the voting preferences of members of different political parties. The group for whom current life satisfaction is most tightly linked to candidate preference seems to be Republicans.

Republicans who are more highly satisfied with their current lives more strongly prefer Republican John McCain. The gap between the highly dissatisfied and the highly satisfied is 18 percentage points. Furthermore, Republican crossover votes for Democrat Barack Obama, while low overall, are more than twice as high among Republicans who are highly dissatisfied with their current lives. Of note is that Republicans who are dissatisfied with their lives are just as likely to be undecided or to vote for a third party candidate as to support Obama. In contrast to Republicans,

Democrats who are highly satisfied with their lives express only a modest increase in their preference for their party's candidate. The 18-point preference gap among Republicans dwindles to only a 6-point gap among Democrats. Moreover, crossover support for McCain is flat among Democrats across the three levels of current well-being. Being highly dissatisfied with their lives steers Democrats slightly away from Obama but moves them into the ranks of the undecided rather than steering them toward McCain.

In terms of the relationship between current life satisfaction and voting preferences, independent voters resemble Republicans. The more satisfied independent voters are with their lives, the more likely they are to prefer McCain. The 14-point preference gap among independents parallels the 18-point gap among Republicans in the same direction. Independents who are highly satisfied with their current lives are less likely to be undecided or to prefer a third party candidate. Put differently, independents who are highly satisfied with their lives slightly prefer McCain; independents who are highly dissatisfied with their lives strongly prefer Obama.

Future Expectations of Well-Being

There is an entirely different set of relationships regarding voter preferences and Americans' expectations of their *future* rather than their evaluation of their *present* life satisfaction. Americans' expectations of future life satisfaction seem to be more strongly connected to how they feel about Obama than to how they feel about McCain. Republicans with more positive views of their future prefer their own party's candidate. However, the 18-point gap that exists with respect to *current* well-being among Republicans is

CURRENT STANDING ON GALLUP WELL-BEING LADDER SCALE AND PREFERENCE FOR PRESIDENTIAL CANDIDATE
Among Democrats

■ % Prefer Obama   ■ % Prefer McCain   □ % Don't know/Other candidate

	Highly dissatisfied	Ambivalent	Highly satisfied
% Prefer Obama	72	74	78
% Prefer McCain	12	11	11
% Don't know/Other	17	14	11

Note: Well-being is based on Gallup's personal well-being question. Respondents indicate "on which step of the ladder would you say you personally feel you stand at this time," ranging from 0 ("worse possible life") to 10 ("best possible life"). Scores between 0 and 3 reflect a high degree of dissatisfaction, scores between 4 and 6 reflect ambivalence, and scores of 7 or higher reflect high levels of satisfaction.

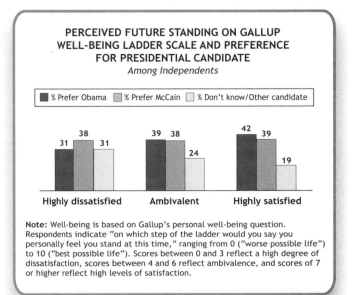

PERCEIVED FUTURE STANDING ON GALLUP
WELL-BEING LADDER SCALE AND PREFERENCE
FOR PRESIDENTIAL CANDIDATE
Among Republicans

■ % Prefer Obama   ▨ % Prefer McCain   ☐ % Don't know/Other candidate

	Highly dissatisfied	Ambivalent	Highly satisfied
% Prefer Obama	10	10	8
% Prefer McCain	72	77	83
% Don't know/Other	17	13	8

Note: Well-being is based on Gallup's personal well-being question. Respondents indicate "on which step of the ladder would you say you personally feel you stand at this time," ranging from 0 ("worse possible life") to 10 ("best possible life"). Scores between 0 and 3 reflect a high degree of dissatisfaction, scores between 4 and 6 reflect ambivalence, and scores of 7 or higher reflect high levels of satisfaction.

PERCEIVED FUTURE STANDING ON GALLUP
WELL-BEING LADDER SCALE AND PREFERENCE
FOR PRESIDENTIAL CANDIDATE
Among Independents

■ % Prefer Obama   ▨ % Prefer McCain   ☐ % Don't know/Other candidate

	Highly dissatisfied	Ambivalent	Highly satisfied
% Prefer Obama	31	39	42
% Prefer McCain	38	38	39
% Don't know/Other	31	24	19

Note: Well-being is based on Gallup's personal well-being question. Respondents indicate "on which step of the ladder would you say you personally feel you stand at this time," ranging from 0 ("worse possible life") to 10 ("best possible life"). Scores between 0 and 3 reflect a high degree of dissatisfaction, scores between 4 and 6 reflect ambivalence, and scores of 7 or higher reflect high levels of satisfaction.

reduced to an 11-point gap based on perceptions of future life satisfaction. Furthermore, perceived future life satisfaction among Republicans is essentially unrelated to their crossover votes for Obama. Republicans who are dissatisfied with their future prospects in life either gravitate toward a third party candidate or remain undecided.

Democrats' views of their future lives play an even stronger role in their preferences for a presidential candidate. Democrats who expect their futures to be brightest are the most likely to prefer Obama—and are less likely to prefer McCain and less likely to be undecided or to prefer a third party candidate. In short, whereas *current* life satisfaction is more strongly related to Republicans' preferences, perceived *future* life satisfaction is more strongly related to Democrats' preferences.

Independent voters who expect to be more satisfied with their lives in the future are substantially more likely to prefer Obama. Preferences for McCain are unrelated to independents' perceived future life satisfaction. However, as is the case for Democrats, independents who expect their futures to be brighter are also substantially less likely to be undecided or to prefer a third-party candidate. In short, the same independent voters who strongly resemble Republicans when it comes to *current* well-being strongly resemble Democrats when it comes to *future* well-being.

Depending on political party affiliation and whether respondents focus on their present or future lives, then, these poll results show that current and future life satisfaction relate to voter preferences in different ways. Whereas Republicans' preferences for a presidential candidate are linked to their current feelings of well-being, the preferences of Democrats seem to have more to do with their expectations of *future* well-being. Perhaps the most important insight provided by these findings is that independent voters tend to be of two different minds. Like Republicans, they tend to prefer McCain when they are more satisfied with where they are today. Like Democrats, they tend to prefer Obama when they expect to be more satisfied in the future.

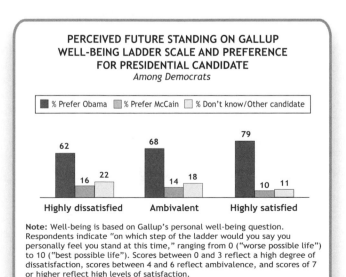

PERCEIVED FUTURE STANDING ON GALLUP
WELL-BEING LADDER SCALE AND PREFERENCE
FOR PRESIDENTIAL CANDIDATE
Among Democrats

■ % Prefer Obama   ▨ % Prefer McCain   ☐ % Don't know/Other candidate

	Highly dissatisfied	Ambivalent	Highly satisfied
% Prefer Obama	62	68	79
% Prefer McCain	16	14	10
% Don't know/Other	22	18	11

Note: Well-being is based on Gallup's personal well-being question. Respondents indicate "on which step of the ladder would you say you personally feel you stand at this time," ranging from 0 ("worse possible life") to 10 ("best possible life"). Scores between 0 and 3 reflect a high degree of dissatisfaction, scores between 4 and 6 reflect ambivalence, and scores of 7 or higher reflect high levels of satisfaction.

NOVEMBER 2

Obama Continues to Outpace McCain

Voters' presidential preferences remain favorable to Barack Obama, with 51% of traditional likely voters supporting the Democratic nominee for president and 43% backing John McCain. An additional 1% say they support some other candidate, leaving 5% undecided. Today's Gallup Poll daily tracking results are from interviews conducted nationwide from October 30 to November 1. The traditional likely-voter model producing an eight-percentage-point lead for Obama takes into account voters' participation in previous presidential elections as well as their interest in, and intention to vote in, the 2008 election. An expanded likely-voter model uses only voters' interest in, and intention to vote in, the current election. On this basis, Obama leads by nine points—52% to 43%—also with 1% supporting some other candidate and 5% undecided. The expanded model assumes that voter turnout may follow different patterns this year than in the past—with greater participation, for example, on the part of new or infrequent voters. The expanded likely-voter results are not much different from those based on all registered voters. Among the entire sample of eligible voters, Obama leads by 11 points, 52% to 41%. Another 1% name a different candidate, while 7% are undecided.

Obama's lead over McCain among all registered voters has been stable, at or above eight points for each of the past five days. Over the same time period, his lead among traditional likely voters has experienced some variation, highlighting the importance of turnout at this stage of the race in determining whether the election ends up being close, or whether Obama could win by a comfortable margin.

NOVEMBER 3

Sharp Increase in Concern About Ineligible Voters This Year

As Americans cast their ballots in this year's historic presidential election, just 18% are very confident that votes across

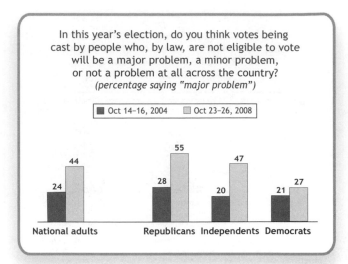

the country will be accurately cast and counted, down sharply from 29% who said so just prior to the 2004 election. In 2000, the Florida recount debacle focused the nation on basic problems in getting all votes counted. This year, concerns about voter irregularities have focused primarily on efforts to register new voters en masse. In particular, the community organizing group ACORN, which has helped to register nearly half a million low-income, minority, and young voters nationwide, has been linked to voter registrations that have been determined to be fraudulent or duplicates. McCain has since alleged that ACORN is "on the verge of maybe perpetrating one of the greatest frauds in voter history in this country," and Republican lawyers have challenged new voter registrations in several states. Possibly reflecting the coverage of the ACORN controversy, nearly half of Americans (44%) say they expect votes cast by people who are ineligible to be a "major problem" in this year's election. This is nearly double the percentage (24%) from four years ago, with the heightened concern driven largely by Republicans and independents.

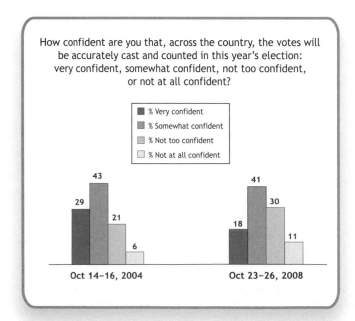

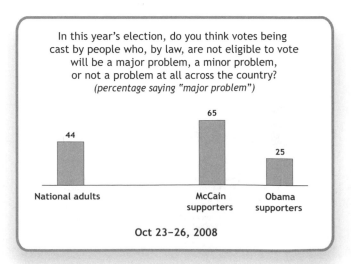

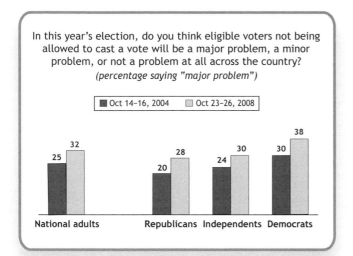

In this year's election, do you think eligible voters not being allowed to cast a vote will be a major problem, a minor problem, or not a problem at all across the country?
(percentage saying "major problem")

■ Oct 14–16, 2004   ☐ Oct 23–26, 2008

National adults	Republicans	Independents	Democrats
25 / 32	20 / 28	24 / 30	30 / 38

McCain supporters are far more likely than Obama supporters to be concerned about ineligible votes being cast. Two out of three McCain supporters (65%) say they think ineligible votes will be a major problem, compared to just one out of four Obama supporters (25%). Concern about eligible voters' not being allowed to vote has also increased since 2004, but not to the same extent. Overall, 32% of Americans say they think it will be a major problem, up from 25% four years ago. Republicans and Democrats each show an eight-point increase in their level of concern about this— larger than the increase among independents.

While Obama supporters are more likely than McCain supporters to be worried about the possibility that eligible voters will be denied the opportunity to vote, 36% to 26%, this 10-percentage-point gap pales in comparison to the 40-percentage-point divide shown when supporters of the two candidates are asked about ineligible voters. These results indicate that concern about eligible voters' being

denied the chance to vote has not struck as much of a chord among Americans as the possibility of ineligible voters' being allowed to cast ballots.

Obama's Support Built on Change, McCain's on Experience

As voters prepare to go to the polls, a new Gallup Poll shows that Obama supporters say they are motivated to vote for their candidate because he would bring about change and provide a fresh approach to governing, while McCain supporters favor their candidate both because of his experience and because they agree with his views on issues. Previous polls asking a similar question found that Obama voters are consistently likely to mention their desire for change as the rationale for their vote choice, a finding that either precedes or echoes the major theme of the Obama campaign. Over a third of his supporters spontaneously mentioned change in this survey. Other key points derived

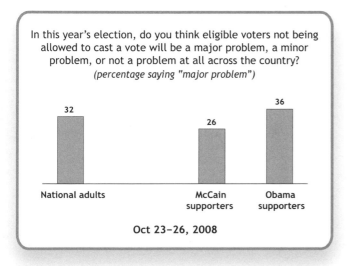

In this year's election, do you think eligible voters not being allowed to cast a vote will be a major problem, a minor problem, or not a problem at all across the country?
(percentage saying "major problem")

National adults	McCain supporters	Obama supporters
32	26	36

Oct 23–26, 2008

Please tell me in your own words why you are supporting Barack Obama or John McCain.

	% National adults	% Obama supporters	% McCain supporters
Want change/Fresh approach	20	35	2
Agree with his values/views (non-specific)	17	17	18
Best man for the job	14	16	11
Experienced/Qualified	10	2	20
Dislike opponent	8	6	10
Economy/His economic plan	7	8	6
Always support that party	7	7	7
Honest/Has integrity/Good character	5	4	6
Taxes/His tax plan	5	4	7
Conservative/More conservative candidate	4	1	8
Like his choice of running mate	3	3	3
For the working/middle class	3	5	1
Healthcare reform	3	4	1
Smart/Intelligent/Knowledgeable	3	4	1
Abortion issue	3	1	5
Lesser of two evils	2	1	4
Opponent too liberal/a socialist	2	*	5
Trustworthy/Trust him	2	1	4
Iraq War/Plans for handling it	2	3	1
Military background/Service to country	2	*	4
International affairs/Foreign policy	2	2	2
National security/Terrorism issue	1	*	2
Education/His education plan	1	2	*
Favors smaller government	1	*	1
Liberal/The more liberal candidate	1	*	1
Independent/Goes against party/A maverick	*	*	1
Energy/His energy plan	*	*	*
Environment/Global warming	*	*	*
Other	2	2	1
No opinion	1	1	2

Based on adults with a candidate preference or leaning, Oct 27–30, 2008
* Less than 1%

from an examination of the volunteered reasons given by Obama voters for supporting their candidate include the following:

- Aside from the change dimension, Obama voters are most likely to give generic reasons for their support: They agree with his views or have the perception that he is the best man for the job.
- Obama voters also mention a number of specific dimensions as reasons why they support him, including his plans for dealing with the economy, the fact that he would work for the working/middle class, and his approach to healthcare.
- Six percent of Obama voters say they are supporting him because they dislike his opponent.

McCain's supporters don't coalesce around any one rationale for their support the way Obama supporters do. As noted, the most frequently given responses by McCain supporters are that he is experienced (which has often been a response by McCain supporters in previous research) and that they agree with his views. Other key points include the following:

- McCain supporters are more likely than Obama supporters to say they are voting for McCain because they dislike his opponent. An additional 5% specifically mention that they are voting for McCain because they believe his opponent is too liberal or a socialist. These responses almost certainly reflect the McCain campaign's focus in recent weeks on reinforcing negative perceptions of Obama.
- Other specifics given by McCain supporters include the fact that he is conservative, his approach to taxes, and his honesty and integrity.

- McCain's pro-life stance on abortion is, apparently, a significant asset to his candidacy, as 5% of his supporters say they are voting for him because of the abortion issue.

Voters Have High Personal Investment in Election Outcome

A recent Gallup Poll finds 74% of Americans saying the outcome of this year's presidential election matters more to them than in previous years—slightly more than said this about the 2004 election, and well above the figures from the 1996 and 2000 elections. The results suggest that Americans have come to view the outcome of elections as increasingly important. While at least 7 in 10 said the election mattered more to them in both 2004 and 2008, fewer than half said this about the 1996 or 2000 elections. The increased importance attributed to election outcomes helps explain the surge in voter turnout in 2004, which experts predict could be eclipsed in this year's election. Gallup has found an extraordinarily high level of interest in the election throughout this year, and its data also suggest turnout will exceed what it was in 2004.

Democrats (80%) are slightly more likely than Republicans (74%) to attribute greater importance to the 2008 election outcome. That is a similar pattern to what Gallup found for the 2004 election. In 2000, Republicans were slightly more likely to view the outcome as more important than in prior elections, and in 1996, Republicans and Democrats were about equal in their perceptions. Voters' personal investment in the outcome is further underscored by the poll finding that 92% of registered voters agree with the statement that "the stakes in this presidential election are higher than in previous years," including 76% who strongly agree. The percentage strongly agreeing exceeds the percentage who said this about the 2004 election and is more than twice what Gallup measured for the 1996 election.

All party groups overwhelmingly agree that the stakes in the 2008 election are higher than in prior years, but Democrats (84%) are slightly more likely to say they strongly agree than are Republicans (76%) or independents (68%).

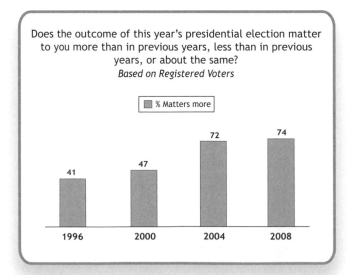

Does the outcome of this year's presidential election matter to you more than in previous years, less than in previous years, or about the same?
Based on Registered Voters

Percentage Saying the Outcome of the Election Matters More Than in Previous Years, by Party Affiliation *Based on Registered Voters*			
	Democrats	Independents	Republicans
1996	45%	34%	47%
2000	45%	43%	52%
2004	77%	73%	69%
2008	80%	68%	74%

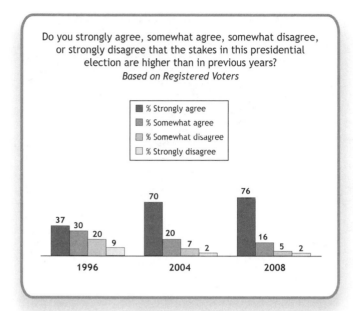

Do you strongly agree, somewhat agree, somewhat disagree, or strongly disagree that the stakes in this presidential election are higher than in previous years?
Based on Registered Voters

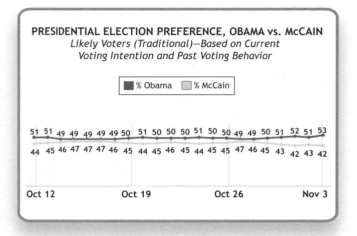

PRESIDENTIAL ELECTION PREFERENCE, OBAMA vs. McCAIN
Likely Voters (Traditional)—Based on Current Voting Intention and Past Voting Behavior

Voters go so far as to express trepidation about the election going against their wishes. Fifty-four percent of voters say they strongly agree that they are "afraid of what will happen if [their] candidate for president does not win." Another 22% agree somewhat. These figures exactly duplicate what Gallup measured in 2004. But voters were far less likely to say they were fearful about how the 1996 election would be decided. Republicans (59%) and Democrats (58%) are about equally likely to say they strongly agree with this statement, while independents (46%) are less likely to.

It would appear that voters as a whole view the outcome of presidential elections as more consequential than they did in the recent past. This fueled a surge in turnout in the

2004 election and is likely to be repeated again this Election Day. It is possible that the contested election outcome in 2000—when Al Gore won the popular vote but lost to George W. Bush in the Electoral College on the basis of the disputed Florida vote—has caused more voters to realize that their vote can make a difference in the outcome and can greatly affect the course of the nation over the subsequent four years.

Final Presidential Estimate: Obama 55%, McCain 44%

The final Gallup 2008 pre-election poll—based on October 31–November 2 Gallup Poll daily tracking—shows Obama with a 53% to 42% advantage over McCain among likely voters. When undecided voters are allocated proportionately to the two candidates to better approximate the likely actual vote, the estimate becomes 55% for Obama to 44% for McCain. The trend data clearly show Obama ending the campaign with an upward movement in support, with 8- to 11-percentage-point leads among likely voters in Gallup's last four reports of data extending back to October 28.

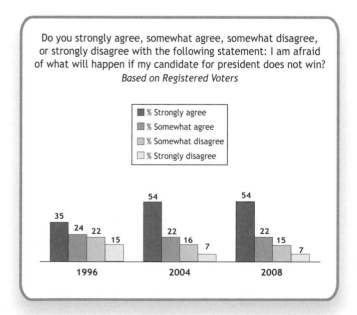

Do you strongly agree, somewhat agree, somewhat disagree, or strongly disagree with the following statement: I am afraid of what will happen if my candidate for president does not win?
Based on Registered Voters

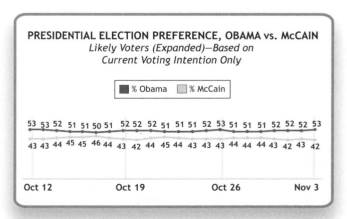

PRESIDENTIAL ELECTION PREFERENCE, OBAMA vs. McCAIN
Likely Voters (Expanded)—Based on Current Voting Intention Only

With his wife, Cindy, standing beside him, John McCain delivers his concession speech in Phoenix, Arizona, on November 4, 2008. *(Brian Baer / Sacramento Bee / MCT)*

Obama's final leads among both registered voters and likely voters are the largest of the campaign.

Gallup's final estimate is based on Gallup's traditional likely-voter model and assumes an estimated turnout of 64% of the voting age population, an increase over 2004. This year's higher turnout estimate is fueled by a surge in early voting—28% of registered voters in the final poll indicated they had already voted—and by higher turnout among blacks than in any of the last four presidential elections. The gap in voter support for Obama versus McCain is slightly wider (53% to 40%) when the preferences of all registered voters are taken into account. The likely-voter model typically shows a reduction in the Democratic candidate's advantage, as has been the case with Obama this year. Nevertheless, Obama has been able to maintain a significant likely-voter lead over McCain in recent days, culminating in his 11-point lead in Gallup's final poll. It would take an improbable last-minute shift in voter preferences or a huge Republican advantage in Election Day turnout for McCain to improve enough upon his predicted share of the

vote in Gallup's traditional likely-voter model to overcome his deficit to Obama.

Democrats have been more energized than Republicans throughout the year. In the final poll, 73% of Democrats and Democratic-leaning independents say they are enthu-

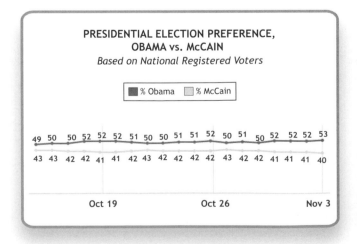

PRESIDENTIAL ELECTION PREFERENCE, OBAMA vs. McCAIN
Based on National Registered Voters

■ % Obama   ☐ % McCain

49 50 50 52 52 52 51 50 50 51 51 52 50 51 50 52 52 52 53
43 43 42 42 41 41 42 43 42 42 42 42 43 42 42 41 41 41 40

Oct 19   Oct 26   Nov 3

siastic about voting, compared with 59% of Republicans and Republican-leaning independents. Additionally, the Obama campaign appears to have done a slightly better job of reaching voters than the McCain campaign: Thus far, 39% of registered voters say they have been contacted by the Obama campaign, compared with 33% contacted by McCain's camp.

Democratic Advantage in Party Identification Difficult to Overcome

Obama was able to match McCain in maintaining party loyalty toward his candidacy: 91% of Democrats say they will vote for Obama, the same as the 91% of Republicans intending to vote for McCain. But Obama's 90%-plus loyalty has a far greater payoff than McCain's, given the significant Democratic advantage in party identification—evident not only in this final poll, but throughout the year. In the final poll, 38% of adults identified as Democrats, 34% as independents, and 26% as Republicans. Among likely voters, the figures are 39%, 31%, and 29%, respectively. Thus, given the Republican deficit in party identification, McCain would have needed a big boost from independent voters in order to prevail. The two nominees—both of whom owe their primary victories earlier this year to solid support from independents—waged a fierce battle for the independent vote, but in the final poll independents preferred Obama to McCain by 48% to 43%. An Obama victory would also owe a great debt to overwhelming support from racial and ethnic minorities. McCain leads among white voters, 51% to 44%, but Obama more than makes up for that with an 83% to 13% advantage among nonwhites, including a 97% to 1% advantage among blacks and a 73% to 24% lead among Hispanics.

According to Gallup's final pre-election polls, the last time a presidential candidate won without winning the white vote was Bill Clinton in 1992. That year, George H. W. Bush narrowly beat Clinton by two points among white voters, 41% to 39%, with 20% supporting third-party candidate, Ross Perot. Prior to that, Gerald Ford in 1976 received 52% of the white vote to Jimmy Carter's 46%, but Carter won the election with 85% of the non-white vote.

While only 4% of voters remain truly undecided, the final Gallup Poll estimates that a slightly larger 10% of likely voters still have the potential to either change their mind or make up their mind. Even if McCain converts the vast majority of swing voters, however, victory for him would be highly unlikely, since 51% of likely voters say they are certain to vote for Obama, compared with 39% who say they are sure they will vote for McCain.

2008 PRESIDENTIAL PREFERENCES
GROUPS SHOWING SUPERMAJORITY
SUPPORT (60% OR MORE) FOR BARACK OBAMA
Based on Likely Voters

	Obama	McCain
Blacks	99%	1%
Postgraduates	64%	36%
18- to 29-year-olds	61%	39%
Seldom/never attend church	61%	39%

Oct 31–Nov 2, 2008

Obama's Road to the White House: A Gallup Review

The final pre-election Gallup Poll daily tracking survey of likely voters shows that Barack Obama won the 2008 presidential election with practically total support from black Americans and heavy backing from those with postgraduate educations, young adults (male and female alike), and non-churchgoers. At least 6 in 10 voters in all of these categories cast their votes for Obama. Additionally, across Gallup's October 31–November 2 final pre-election tracking, Obama won majority support nationwide from women, middle-aged adults (30 to 49 and 50 to 64 years of age), and Catholics. These findings are aside from the typical political support patterns whereby Democrats and liberals are reliably strong supporters of the Democratic presidential candidate, and Republicans and conservatives are strong supporters of the Republican.

Among likely voters, 93% of each partisan group supported their own party's candidate for president, and 7% of each supported the opposing party's candidate. Political independents were evenly divided at 50%. The advantage for Obama came from the fact that many more voters who participated in the 2008 election were Democratic than were Republican (38% vs. 26%). Certain other groups historically aligned with each party showed predictably high support for that party's candidate. Most voters living in households

2008 PRESIDENTIAL PREFERENCES
GROUPS SHOWING MODEST MAJORITY FOR BARACK OBAMA
Based on Likely Voters

	Obama	McCain
Women	56%	44%
50- to 64-year-olds	54%	46%
30- to 49-year-olds	53%	47%
Catholics	53%	47%

Oct 31–Nov 2, 2008

Shortly after John McCain conceded defeat, President-elect Barack Obama addresses an enormous outdoor rally in Grant Park in Chicago. *(Brian Kersey/UPI Photo)*

with at least one union member backed Obama, while veterans and gun owners were solidly behind McCain.

McCain's Hobbled Coalition

McCain's principal electoral strengths were with frequent churchgoers, whites, seniors, Protestants, and men. However, except in the case of Protestants, the extent of support he received from these groups was not as great as Obama's support from their counterparts (non-churchgoers, blacks, young voters, Catholics, and women).

What Changed Since 2004?

Gallup's preliminary analysis of the trends in voting among various subgroups suggests that Obama outper-

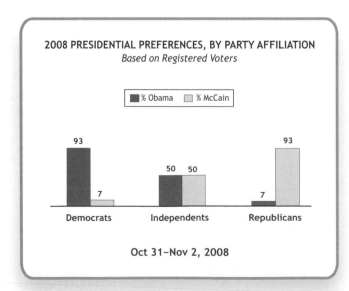

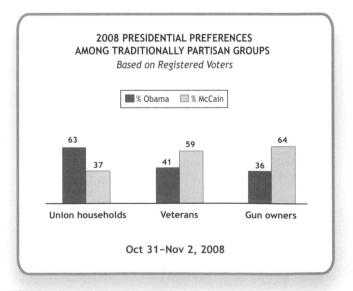

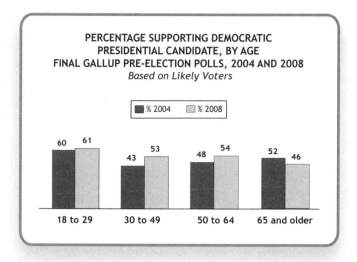

2008 PRESIDENTIAL PREFERENCES
GROUPS SHOWING MODEST MAJORITY FOR JOHN McCAIN
Based on Likely Voters

	Obama	McCain
Attend church weekly	44%	56%
Non-Hispanic whites	44%	56%
65 years and older	46%	54%
Protestants	47%	53%
Men	49%	51%

Oct 31–Nov 2, 2008

PERCENTAGE SUPPORTING DEMOCRATIC
PRESIDENTIAL CANDIDATE, BY AGE
FINAL GALLUP PRE-ELECTION POLLS, 2004 AND 2008
Based on Likely Voters

formed other recent Democratic nominees in attracting the near-universal support of blacks. Black support for the Democratic candidate is always high, but their 99% support for Obama exceeded the 93% received by John Kerry in 2004 and the 88% support for Bill Clinton in 1992 and for Mike Dukakis in 1988. Clinton approached universal support from blacks with his 96% backing in 1996, as did Gore in 2000, with 95%. There has been virtually no change in the percentage of white voters supporting the Democratic candidate in each of the last four presidential elections; it has ranged from 43% to 46%, with Obama's 45% about average.

Gallup's 2004 final pre-election polling showed young voters heavily favoring the Democratic nominee (Kerry), as they did in the 2008 election. What changed is that middle-aged voters moved from the Republican column into the Democratic column. This more than offset a modest shift of seniors from the Democratic to the Republican side.

Another striking change between the 2004 and 2008 elections is the preferences of the most highly educated Americans. Obama attracted the highest level of sup-

port from postgraduate-educated Americans (64%) of any recent Democratic candidate. Four years ago, 53% of this group backed Kerry, which was fairly typical of the historical pattern. Obama also made gains among college graduates and those with only some college. The only group to show a decline in support for the Democratic nominee in 2008 was those with no college education.

Where Did All the Republicans Go?

Obama and McCain both fought hard during the campaign for the independent vote, and in the end it was a draw, with each getting 50% of the independent vote. However, that parity masks a more fundamental shift of voters away from the Republican Party over the past four years. In 2004, Republicans and Democrats were about equally represented in Gallup's final pre-election pool of likely voters: 39% were Republican, 37% Democratic, and 24% independent. This year, only 29% of likely

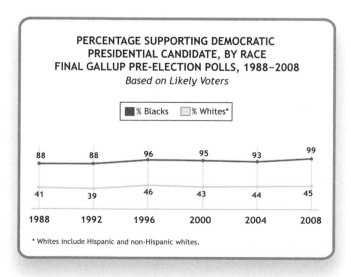

PERCENTAGE SUPPORTING DEMOCRATIC
PRESIDENTIAL CANDIDATE, BY RACE
FINAL GALLUP PRE-ELECTION POLLS, 1988–2008
Based on Likely Voters

* Whites include Hispanic and non-Hispanic whites.

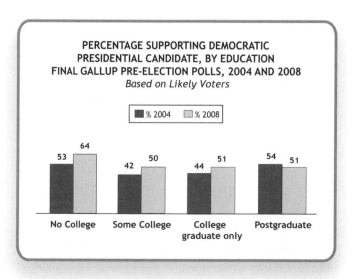

PERCENTAGE SUPPORTING DEMOCRATIC
PRESIDENTIAL CANDIDATE, BY EDUCATION
FINAL GALLUP PRE-ELECTION POLLS, 2004 AND 2008
Based on Likely Voters

GALLUP FINAL PRE-ELECTION ESTIMATE OF VOTE BY GROUPS, 2004 AND 2008
Based on Likely Voters*

	2004	2004	2008	2008
	Kerry	Bush	Obama	McCain
Allocated Final Election Result	48.5%	51.5%	52.9%	47.1%
Sex				
Men	44	56	49	51
Women	52	48	56	44
Race				
White (incl. Hispanics)	44	56	45	55
Nonwhite	83	17	90	10
Non-Hispanic white	43	57	44	56
Nonwhite (incl. Hispanics)	78	22	85	-5
Black	93	7	99	1
Age				
Under 30 years old	60	40	61	39
30 to 49 years old	43	57	53	47
50 to 64 years old	48	52	54	46
65 years and older	52	48	46	54
Education				
Grade school	69	31	67	33
High school	54	46	46	54
College	48	52	54	46
Postgraduate	53	47	64	36
Region				
East	58	42	56	44
Midwest	48	52	53	47
South	43	57	50	50
West	48	52	55	45
Party Affiliation				
Republicans	5	95	7	93
Democrats	93	7	93	7
Independents	52	48	50	50
Ideology				
Conservative	20	80	23	77
Moderate	63	37	62	38
Liberal	88	12	94	6
Religion				
Protestants	38	62	47	53
Catholics	52	48	53	47
Attend church weekly	37	63	44	56
Attend church monthly	45	55	50	50
Seldom/never attend church	60	40	61	39
Marital Status				
Married	40	60	44	56
Not married	60	40	65	35
Married men	39	61	42	58
Married women	42	58	47	53
Unmarried men	55	45	63	37
Unmarried women	64	36	66	34
Labor Union				
Union families	67	33	63	37
Military				
Veteran	40	60	41	59
Military Household	43	57	47	53
Gun Ownership				
Owner	35	65	36	64
Non-owner	56	44	63	37

* Gallup's final figures for each subgroup adjusted by a constant factor to match Gallup's final allocated estimate of the vote to the actual result.

Summary: Why Obama Won

Obama's victory is owed in part to extraordinarily high support from blacks. Not only did nearly all blacks who participated in the election vote for Obama, but blacks came out in record numbers—constituting 13% of Gallup's final likely-voter pool, up from 8% in 2004. Obama won greater support than his Democratic predecessors from highly educated voters, and he attracted significant new support from middle-aged voters. In addition, far fewer voters considered themselves Republican in this election than did so in 2004. Gallup polling has documented this decline over the past four years, coinciding with a steep deterioration in President George W. Bush's approval rating. The resulting more pro-Democratic political climate in the country may be the ultimate reason Obama won.

Obama's victory over McCain concludes a race that was highly competitive throughout the year. The two were essentially tied during the primary election season, from March through May 2008. Obama moved slightly ahead of McCain once he clinched the Democratic nomination in early June; McCain then succeeded in overtaking Obama after the Republican National Convention in September. But the economic crisis that followed helped shift voters back into Obama's column, and it appears to have been a turning point in the campaign. The presidential debates during the fall may have further strengthened Obama's position, buoying him to double-digit leads among registered voters nationwide in the last few weeks of the campaign.

WINNING THE WHITE HOUSE: A COMPETITIVE START

Obama's road to winning the White House was far from ensured during the 2008 primary season when he ran nip and tuck with McCain in early Gallup polling for the general election. In the 85 Gallup Poll daily tracking reports between March 12 and June 7, McCain led Obama by one or more percentage points in 39, Obama led McCain by one or more points in 31, and they were tied exactly in the remaining 15. The only candidate to achieve a statistically significant lead during this phase of the campaign was McCain, who advanced to five- and six-point leads for a brief period in late April/early May. At that point, the Obama campaign was fighting off a hornet's nest of adverse publicity surrounding Obama's former pastor, the Reverend Jeremiah Wright, as well as Obama's comments about "bitter" voters in Pennsylvania and his recent primary loss to Clinton in that state.

The closeness of the race in the primary campaign phase of the election year can likely be credited to the ongoing Democratic nomination fight, which helped depress Obama's support among Democrats who favored

voters were Republican and 39% Democratic, with 31% independent—a political balance much more favorable to Obama than what Kerry faced in 2004.

Barack Obama, elected 44th president of the United States, salutes the crowd on Election Night, November 4, 2008. *(Tom Lynn/Milwaukee Journal-Sentinel/Rapport Press)*

Hillary Clinton for the nomination. Obama's support among Democrats averaged just 75% from March through May, compared with 90% in the final week of the general election campaign in October/November. By comparison, McCain averaged 86% Republican support from March through May and finished the campaign at 87% among Republican registered voters.

WINNING THE WHITE HOUSE: SUMMER WINNING STREAK

After Obama secured the Democratic nomination in early June, support for him immediately expanded, resulting in a 75-day stretch through late August when he continuously led or tied McCain. Obama's average lead over McCain during this period was only three percentage points, but it rose to as much as nine points in late July after his widely covered trip to Europe and the Middle East.

WINNING THE WHITE HOUSE: THE CONVENTION PERIOD

Obama's fortunes turned temporarily on August 26, when Gallup reported him to be trailing McCain by two percentage points. The August 23–25 interviews on which that report were based represented the first three days of tracking after Obama's announcement of Joe Biden as his running mate. The immediate implication was that his vice presidential pick at best delivered no bounce in support for Obama and at worst possibly hurt the ticket. The subsequent Democratic National Convention enabled Obama to turn things back around in his favor. He took the lead again and attained an eight-point advantage over McCain toward the end of the convention in late August.

With the two parties' conventions held back-to-back spanning the Labor Day weekend, public preferences see-sawed, and McCain quickly reversed the Obama tide in early September. McCain moved into the lead immediately after the end of the Republican National Convention, after McCain's, and his vice-presidential running mate Sarah Palin's, highly acclaimed acceptance speeches. At this point, McCain experienced his longest front-runner stretch of the general election phase of the campaign: the 10 days from September 7 to September 16.

WINNING THE WHITE HOUSE: THE ECONOMIC GAME-CHANGER

That trend came to an abrupt halt with the onset of the Wall Street crisis in mid-September. By September 17, the Republican nominee again trailed Obama by a few percentage points, and while the race briefly closed to a tie later in the month, McCain never regained the lead. McCain attempted a bold move by suspending his official campaign in late September in order to return to Washington to focus on legislation to address the financial crisis, but he resumed his campaign in time to debate Obama on September 26 even though Congress had not yet formulated a legislative plan.

The debates were perhaps McCain's best opportunity to reverse Obama's growing momentum, but he was unable to do so. USA Today/Gallup polls found that Americans rated Obama the winner of all three debates, and these may have helped him solidify his gains. October proved to be Obama's best month of the campaign, as he averaged a nine-point lead among registered voters over McCain in Gallup Poll daily tracking.

WINNING THE WHITE HOUSE: THE CONCLUSION

Obama and McCain ran essentially neck and neck for much of the presidential campaign—from March through early September. Obama enjoyed a slight upper hand once he secured the nomination in early June. But as many observers commented, for a long time he failed to "close the sale" with voters, unable to stretch his lead over McCain to 10 or more points or to surpass the 50% threshold in support. He finally reached both of these targets in October.

Still, as close as the race was, Obama technically held the advantage for much of the year. In 230 Gallup Poll daily tracking reports from March through November 2, Obama led McCain in 155 of these (67%), including by a significant margin in 66 (29%). McCain had an advantage in only 50 of these reports (22%), and a statistically significant lead in only 6 (3%). McCain pulled ahead briefly

after the Republican convention. But the economic crisis struck, and he failed to win any of the three presidential debates in the eyes of Americans. Obama—who had struck the right chord with voters on the economy and who met or exceeded expectations in the debates—thus ended the campaign running at his strongest level of the entire race.

Reactions to the Election

Over two-thirds of Americans say Obama's election as president is either the most important advance for blacks in the past 100 years or among the two or three most important such advances. There are some differences in responses to this question between those who said they voted for Obama and those who voted for McCain, but even well over half of McCain voters say the 2008 presidential election marked one of the most important advances of the last 100 years for blacks.

Americans have also become more strongly optimistic about the state of race relations in the United States. After Obama's victory on November 4, 67% of Americans say a solution to relations between blacks and whites will eventually be worked out, the highest value Gallup has measured on this question. These results are based on questions included in Gallup Poll daily tracking on November 5. It is to be expected that such positivity might be at a high ebb the day after the election, when all news is positive and there have yet to be major or controversial, reaction-generating decisions on the part of the new president-elect.

Having said that, the data show an increased positivity on the basic trend question about the future of race relations, a question Gallup has been asking off and on for over four decades. Only 30% of Americans now say race relations will "always be a problem for the United States," while two-thirds say "a solution will eventually be worked out." The previously most positive point on this measure, it should be noted, came this summer, continuing a more upbeat trend over the last two years. Furthermore, 7 out of 10 Americans believe that race relations in this country will get at least a little better as a result of Obama's election, including 28% who say they will get a lot better. More broadly, the survey shows very positive emotional reactions to Obama's election. Two-thirds of Americans report feeling proud and optimistic after Obama's election, and about 6 in 10 say they are excited. Less than a third report feeling pessimistic or afraid.

There are, predictably, significant differences in reactions to Obama's election between those who voted for Obama and those who voted for McCain. Over half of McCain's voters say they are afraid and over half say they are pessimistic after Obama's election, and less than half of these McCain voters say they are excited, proud, or optimistic. Obama voters, on the other hand, are overwhelmingly likely to say they are proud, excited, and optimistic because of the election results.

Obama is clearly enjoying a "honeymoon" period at this point in the immediate afterglow of the election and with generally laudatory, upbeat press coverage. Thus, as these data collected the day after the election show, Americans are perhaps predictably quite positive toward Obama and his coming presidency. The data reviewed also show that Americans believe Obama's election represents a highly significant milestone in the history of race relations in this country. Obama will have to make hard (and almost certainly controversial) decisions as he begins to face the challenge of running the executive branch in earnest—and a key test will be to see if these positive emotions on the part of average Americans continue.

APPENDIX

GALLUP POLL SAMPLING PROCEDURES

Gallup Poll surveys conducted from 1935 through 1984 were based on in-home, face-to-face interviews. From 1985 through 1988, although a few surveys were based on telephone interviews, the majority were based on face-to-face interviews. From 1989 to the present, virtually all Gallup Poll surveys are based on telephone interviews. Gallup began including cell phones in its sample in 2008.

Telephone numbers are selected at random from the pool of total eligible residential numbers in the United States by means of random-digit dialing. Each initial sample includes telephone numbers proportionate by region according to the latest census estimates. The random selection of individual digits in telephone numbers by computer ensures the inclusion in the sample of unlisted or unpublished numbers. This procedure thus avoids "listing bias," or the unrepresentativeness of samples that can occur when those households whose telephone numbers are unlisted or unpublished are excluded from the sample.

GALLUP REGIONS

EAST	MIDWEST	SOUTH	WEST
NEW ENGLAND	**EAST CENTRAL**	**SOUTHEAST**	**MOUNTAIN**
Connecticut	Illinois	Alabama	Arizona
Maine	Indiana	Florida	Colorado
Massachusetts	Michigan	Georgia	Idaho
New Hampshire	Ohio	Kentucky	Montana
Rhode Island		Mississippi	Nevada
Vermont	**WEST CENTRAL**	North Carolina	New Mexico
	Iowa	South Carolina	Utah
	Kansas	Tennessee	Wyoming
MID-ATLANTIC	Minnesota	Virginia	
Delaware	Missouri		**PACIFIC**
District of Columbia	Nebraska	**SOUTHWEST**	Alaska
Maryland	North Dakota	Arkansas	California
New Jersey	South Dakota	Louisiana	Hawaii
New York	Wisconsin	Oklahoma	Oregon
Pennsylvania		Texas	Washington
West Virginia			

When contact with a randomly sampled household is made, Gallup interviewers randomly select a respondent within the household to interview and will only conduct the interview with that chosen respondent, further ensuring a representative sample. The final obtained sample is then weighed by demographic information to conform to the latest U.S. Census Bureau estimates of the characteristics of the national adult population so as to ensure that each Gallup sample is representative of the U.S. adult population and that any one Gallup sample is similar to all other Gallup samples. Gallup weighs its obtained samples by five demographic characteristics—gender, age, race, education, and religion—as well as by the number of telephone lines in the household (to correct for the fact that those with multiple telephone phone lines have a greater chance of being in the sample than persons with just one telephone line).

In interpreting survey results, it should be borne in mind that all sample surveys are subject to sampling error—that is, the extent to which the results may differ from what would be obtained if the whole population were interviewed. The size of such sampling error depends largely on the number of interviews. In addition to sampling error, question wording and practical difficulties in conducting surveys can introduce error or bias into the findings of public opinion polls.

Polling, or survey research, incorporates many facets. A detailed description of survey research is described in the essay "How Polls Are Conducted" in Michael Golay, ed., *Where America Stands 1997* (New York: John Wiley and Sons, 1997). In this essay, Gallup Poll editors address sampling probability, sample selection, sample size, survey interviews, survey questions, and interpreting the results.

INDEX

JK 526 2008 .W56 2009

Winning the White House 2008

GAYLORD